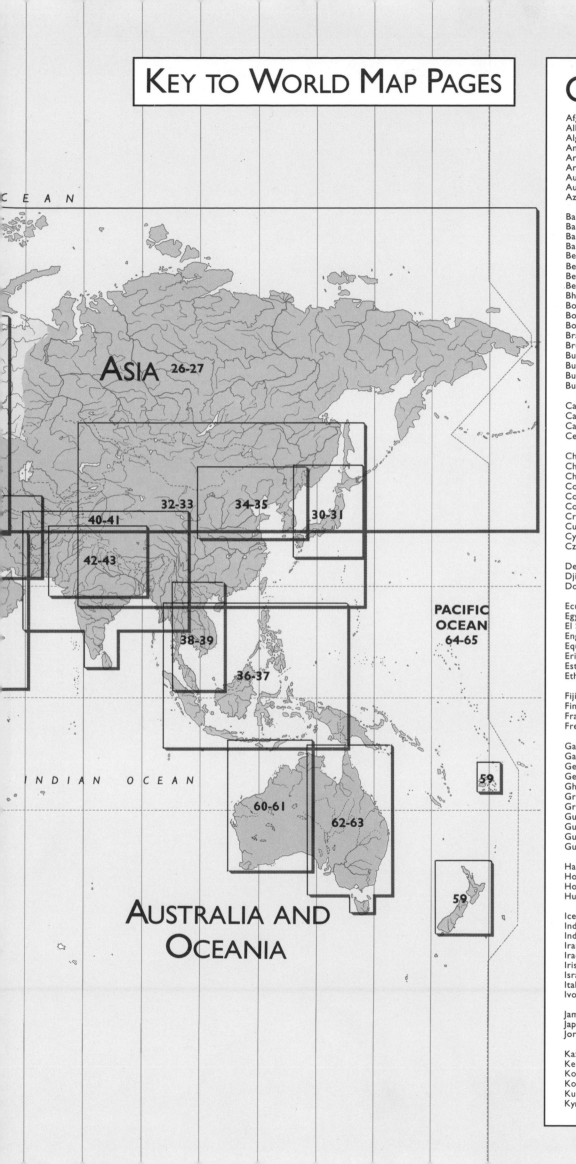

KEY TO WORLD MAP PAGES

OCEAN

ASIA 26-27

32-33

40-41

34-35

30-31

42-43

38-39

36-37

PACIFIC
OCEAN
64-65

INDIAN OCEAN

60-61

62-63

59

59

AUSTRALIA AND
OCEANIA

COUNTRY INDEX

PHILIP'S
WORLD
ATLAS
REFERENCE EDITION

This 1996 edition published by Chancellor Press,
an imprint of Reed Consumer Books,
Michelin House, 81 Fulham Road, London SW3 6RB

Copyright © 1996 Reed International Books Limited

Cartography by Philip's

ISBN 1–85152–986–1

A CIP catalogue record for this book is available
from the British Library

Printed in Hong Kong

PHILIP'S

WORLD ATLAS

REFERENCE EDITION

CHANCELLOR
PRESS

CONTENTS

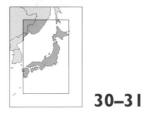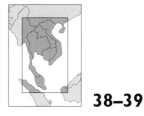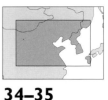

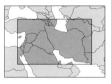

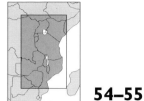

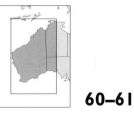

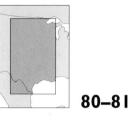

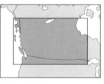

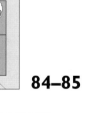

INDEX TO WORLD MAPS
97–176

World Statistics: Countries

This alphabetical list includes all the countries and territories of the world. If a territory is not completely independent, then the country it is associated with is named. The area figures give the total area of land, inland water and ice. The population figures are 1995 estimates. The annual income is the Gross National Product per capita in US dollars. The figures are the latest available, usually 1994.

Country/Territory	Area km^2 *Thousands*	Area $miles^2$ *Thousands*	Population *Thousands*	Capital	Annual Income US $
Adélie Land (Fr.)	432	167	0.03	–	–
Afghanistan	652	252	19,509	Kabul	220
Albania	28.8	11.1	3,458	Tirana	340
Algeria	2,382	920	25,012	Algiers	1,650
American Samoa (US)	0.20	0.08	58	Pago Pago	2,600
Andorra	0.45	0.17	65	Andorra La Vella	14,000
Angola	1,247	481	10,020	Luanda	600
Anguilla (UK)	0.1	0.04	8	The Valley	6,800
Antigua & Barbuda	0.44	0.17	67	St John's	6,390
Argentina	2,767	1,068	34,663	Buenos Aires	7,290
Armenia	29.8	11.5	3,603	Yerevan	660
Aruba (Neths)	0.19	0.07	71	Oranjestad	17,500
Ascension Is. (UK)	0.09	0.03	1.5	Georgetown	–
Australia	7,687	2,968	18,107	Canberra	17,510
Austria	83.9	32.4	8,004	Vienna	23,120
Azerbaijan	86.6	33.4	7,559	Baku	730
Azores (Port.)	2.2	0.87	238	Ponta Delgada	–
Bahamas	13.9	5.4	277	Nassau	11,500
Bahrain	0.68	0.26	558	Manama	7,870
Bangladesh	144	56	118,342	Dhaka	220
Barbados	0.43	0.17	263	Bridgetown	6,240
Belarus	207.6	80.1	10,500	Minsk	2,930
Belgium	30.5	11.8	10,140	Brussels	21,210
Belize	23	8.9	216	Belmopan	2,440
Benin	113	43	5,381	Porto-Novo	420
Bermuda (UK)	0.05	0.02	64	Hamilton	27,000
Bhutan	47	18.1	1,639	Thimphu	170
Bolivia	1,099	424	7,900	La Paz/Sucre	770
Bosnia-Herzegovina	51	20	3,800	Sarajevo	2,500
Botswana	582	225	1,481	Gaborone	2,590
Brazil	8,512	3,286	161,416	Brasília	3,020
British Indian Ocean Terr. (UK)	0.08	0.03	0	–	–
Brunei	5.8	2.2	284	Bandar Seri Begawan	9,000
Bulgaria	111	43	8,771	Sofia	1,160
Burkina Faso	274	106	10,326	Ouagadougou	300
Burma (Myanmar)	677	261	46,580	Rangoon	950
Burundi	27.8	10.7	6,412	Bujumbura	180
Cambodia	181	70	10,452	Phnom Penh	600
Cameroon	475	184	13,232	Yaoundé	770
Canada	9,976	3,852	29,972	Ottawa	20,670
Canary Is. (Spain)	7.3	2.8	1,494	Las Palmas/Santa Cruz	–
Cape Verde Is.	4	1.6	386	Praia	870
Cayman Is. (UK)	0.26	0.10	31	George Town	20,000
Central African Republic	623	241	3,294	Bangui	390
Chad	1,284	496	6,314	Ndjaména	200
Chatham Is. (NZ)	0.96	0.37	0.05	Waitangi	–
Chile	757	292	14,271	Santiago	3,070
China	9,597	3,705	1,226,944	Beijing	490
Christmas Is. (Aus.)	0.14	0.05	2	The Settlement	–
Cocos (Keeling) Is. (Aus.)	0.01	0.005	0.6	West Island	–
Colombia	1,139	440	34,948	Bogotá	1,400
Comoros	2.2	0.86	654	Moroni	520
Congo	342	132	2,593	Brazzaville	920
Cook Is. (NZ)	0.24	0.09	19	Avarua	900
Costa Rica	51.1	19.7	3,436	San José	2,160
Croatia	56.5	21.8	4,900	Zagreb	4,500
Cuba	111	43	11,050	Havana	1,250
Cyprus	9.3	3.6	742	Nicosia	10,380
Czech Republic	78.9	30.4	10,500	Prague	2,730
Denmark	43.1	16.6	5,229	Copenhagen	26,510
Djibouti	23.2	9	603	Djibouti	780
Dominica	0.75	0.29	89	Roseau	2,680
Dominican Republic	48.7	18.8	7,818	Santo Domingo	1,080
Ecuador	284	109	11,384	Quito	1,170
Egypt	1,001	387	64,100	Cairo	660
El Salvador	21	8.1	5,743	San Salvador	1,320
Equatorial Guinea	28.1	10.8	400	Malabo	360
Eritrea	94	36	3,850	Asmara	500
Estonia	44.7	17.3	1,531	Tallinn	3,040
Ethiopia	1,128	436	51,600	Addis Ababa	100
Falkland Is. (UK)	12.2	4.7	2	Stanley	–
Faroe Is. (Den.)	1.4	0.54	47	Tórshavn	23,660
Fiji	18.3	7.1	773	Suva	2,140
Finland	338	131	5,125	Helsinki	18,970
France	552	213	58,286	Paris	22,360
French Guiana (Fr.)	90	34.7	154	Cayenne	5,000
French Polynesia (Fr.)	4	1.5	217	Papeete	7,000
Gabon	268	103	1,316	Libreville	4,050
Gambia, The	11.3	4.4	1,144	Banjul	360
Georgia	69.7	26.9	5,448	Tbilisi	560
Germany	357	138	82,000	Berlin/Bonn	23,560
Ghana	239	92	17,462	Accra	430
Gibraltar (UK)	0.007	0.003	28	Gibraltar Town	5,000
Greece	132	51	10,510	Athens	7,390
Greenland (Den.)	2,176	840	59	Godthåb (Nuuk)	9,000
Grenada	0.34	0.13	94	St George's	2,410
Guadeloupe (Fr.)	1.7	0.66	443	Basse-Terre	9,000
Guam (US)	0.55	0.21	155	Agana	6,000
Guatemala	109	42	10,624	Guatemala City	1,110
Guinea	246	95	6,702	Conakry	510
Guinea-Bissau	36.1	13.9	1,073	Bissau	220
Guyana	215	83	832	Georgetown	350
Haiti	27.8	10.7	7,180	Port-au-Prince	800
Honduras	112	43	5,940	Tegucigalpa	580
Hong Kong (UK)	1.1	0.40	6,000	–	17,860
Hungary	93	35.9	10,500	Budapest	3,330
Iceland	103	40	269	Reykjavik	23,620
India	3,288	1,269	942,989	New Delhi	290
Indonesia	1,905	735	198,644	Jakarta	730
Iran	1,648	636	68,885	Tehran	4,750
Iraq	438	169	20,184	Baghdad	2,000
Ireland	70.3	27.1	3,589	Dublin	12,580
Israel	27	10.3	5,696	Jerusalem	13,760
Italy	301	116	57,181	Rome	19,620
Ivory Coast	322	125	14,271	Yamoussoukro	630
Jamaica	11	4.2	2,700	Kingston	1,390
Jan Mayen Is. (Nor.)	0.38	0.15	0.06	–	–
Japan	378	146	125,156	Tokyo	31,450
Johnston Is. (US)	0.002	0.0009	1	–	–
Jordan	89.2	34.4	5,547	Amman	1,190
Kazakstan	2,717	1,049	17,099	Alma-Ata	1,540
Kenya	580	224	28,240	Nairobi	270
Kerguelen Is. (Fr.)	7.2	2.8	0.7	–	–
Kermadec Is. (NZ)	0.03	0.01	0.1	–	–
Kiribati	0.72	0.28	80	Tarawa	710
Korea, North	121	47	23,931	Pyŏngyang	1,100
Korea, South	99	38.2	45,088	Seoul	7,670
Kuwait	17.8	6.9	1,668	Kuwait City	23,350
Kyrgyzstan	198.5	76.6	4,738	Bishkek	830
Laos	237	91	4,906	Vientiane	290
Latvia	65	25	2,558	Riga	2,030
Lebanon	10.4	4	2,971	Beirut	1,750
Lesotho	30.4	11.7	2,064	Maseru	660
Liberia	111	43	3,092	Monrovia	800
Libya	1,760	679	5,410	Tripoli	6,500
Liechtenstein	0.16	0.06	31	Vaduz	33,510
Lithuania	65.2	25.2	3,735	Vilnius	1,310
Luxembourg	2.6	1	408	Luxembourg	35,850
Macau (Port.)	0.02	0.006	490	Macau	7,500
Macedonia	25.7	9.9	2,173	Skopje	730
Madagascar	587	227	15,206	Antananarivo	240
Madeira (Port.)	0.81	0.31	253	Funchal	–
Malawi	118	46	9,800	Lilongwe	220
Malaysia	330	127	20,174	Kuala Lumpur	3,160
Maldives	0.30	0.12	254	Malé	820
Mali	1,240	479	10,700	Bamako	300
Malta	0.32	0.12	367	Valletta	6,800
Marshall Is.	0.18	0.07	55	Dalap-Uliga-Darrit	1,500
Martinique (Fr.)	1.1	0.42	384	Fort-de-France	3,500
Mauritania	1,025	396	2,268	Nouakchott	510
Mauritius	2.0	0.72	1,112	Port Louis	2,980
Mayotte (Fr.)	0.37	0.14	101	Mamoundzou	1,430
Mexico	1,958	756	93,342	Mexico City	3,750
Micronesia, Fed. States of	0.70	0.27	125	Palikir	1,560
Midway Is. (US)	0.005	0.002	2	–	–
Moldova	33.7	13	4,434	Chişinău	1,180
Monaco	0.002	0.0001	32	Monaco	16,000
Mongolia	1,567	605	2,408	Ulan Bator	400
Montserrat (UK)	0.10	0.04	11	Plymouth	4,500
Morocco	447	172	26,857	Rabat	1,030
Mozambique	802	309	17,800	Maputo	80
Namibia	825	318	1,610	Windhoek	1,660
Nauru	0.02	0.008	12	Yaren District	10,000
Nepal	141	54	21,953	Katmandu	160
Netherlands	41.5	16	15,495	Amsterdam/The Hague	20,710
Neths Antilles (Neths)	0.99	0.38	199	Willemstad	9,700
New Caledonia (Fr.)	19	7.3	181	Nouméa	6,000
New Zealand	269	104	3,567	Wellington	12,900
Nicaragua	130	50	4,544	Managua	360
Niger	1,267	489	9,149	Niamey	270
Nigeria	924	357	88,515	Abuja	310
Niue (NZ)	0.26	0.10	2	Alofi	–
Norfolk Is. (Aus.)	0.03	0.01	2	Kingston	–
Northern Mariana Is. (US)	0.48	0.18	47	Saipan	11,500
Norway	324	125	4,361	Oslo	26,340
Oman	212	82	2,252	Muscat	5,600
Pakistan	796	307	143,595	Islamabad	430
Palau	0.46	0.18	17	Koror	2,260
Panama	77.1	29.8	2,629	Panama City	2,580
Papua New Guinea	463	179	4,292	Port Moresby	1,120
Paraguay	407	157	4,979	Asunción	1,500
Peru	1,285	496	23,588	Lima	1,490
Philippines	300	116	67,167	Manila	830
Pitcairn Is. (UK)	0.03	0.01	0.06	Adamstown	–
Poland	313	121	38,587	Warsaw	2,270
Portugal	92.4	35.7	10,600	Lisbon	7,890
Puerto Rico (US)	9	3.5	3,689	San Juan	7,020
Qatar	11	4.2	594	Doha	15,140
Queen Maud Land (Nor.)	2,800	1,081	0	–	–
Réunion (Fr.)	2.5	0.97	655	Saint-Denis	3,900
Romania	238	92	22,863	Bucharest	1,120
Russia	17,075	6,592	148,385	Moscow	2,350
Rwanda	26.3	10.2	7,899	Kigali	200
St Helena (UK)	0.12	0.05	6	Jamestown	–
St Kitts & Nevis	0.36	0.14	45	Basseterre	4,470
St Lucia	0.62	0.24	147	Castries	3,040
St Pierre & Miquelon (Fr.)	0.24	0.09	6	Saint Pierre	–
St Vincent & Grenadines	0.39	0.15	111	Kingstown	1,730
San Marino	0.06	0.02	26	San Marino	20,000
São Tomé & Príncipe	0.96	0.37	133	São Tomé	330
Saudi Arabia	2,150	830	18,395	Riyadh	8,000
Senegal	197	76	8,308	Dakar	730
Seychelles	0.46	0.18	75	Victoria	6,370
Sierra Leone	71.7	27.7	4,467	Freetown	140
Singapore	0.62	0.24	2,990	Singapore	19,310
Slovak Republic	49	18.9	5,400	Bratislava	1,900
Slovenia	20.3	7.8	2,000	Ljubljana	6,310
Solomon Is.	28.9	11.2	378	Honiara	750
Somalia	638	246	9,180	Mogadishu	500
South Africa	1,220	471	44,000	C. Town/Pretoria/Bloem.	2,900
South Georgia (UK)	3.8	1.4	0.05	–	–
Spain	505	195	39,664	Madrid	13,650
Sri Lanka	65.6	25.3	18,359	Colombo	600
Sudan	2,506	967	29,980	Khartoum	750
Surinam	163	63	421	Paramaribo	1,210
Svalbard (Nor.)	62.9	24.3	4	Longyearbyen	–
Swaziland	17.4	6.7	849	Mbabane	1,050
Sweden	450	174	8,893	Stockholm	24,830
Switzerland	41.3	15.9	7,268	Bern	36,410
Syria	185	71	14,614	Damascus	5,700
Taiwan	36	13.9	21,100	Taipei	11,000
Tajikistan	143.1	55.2	6,102	Dushanbe	470
Tanzania	945	365	29,710	Dodoma	100
Thailand	513	198	58,432	Bangkok	2,040
Togo	56.8	21.9	4,140	Lomé	330
Tokelau (NZ)	0.01	0.005	2	Nukunonu	–
Tonga	0.75	0.29	107	Nuku'alofa	1,610
Trinidad & Tobago	5.1	2	1,295	Port of Spain	3,730
Tristan da Cunha (UK)	0.11	0.04	0.33	Edinburgh	–
Tunisia	164	63	8,906	Tunis	1,780
Turkey	779	301	61,303	Ankara	2,120
Turkmenistan	488.1	188.5	4,100	Ashkhabad	1,400
Turks & Caicos Is. (UK)	0.43	0.17	15	Cockburn Town	5,000
Tuvalu	0.03	0.01	10	Fongafale	600
Uganda	236	91	21,466	Kampala	190
Ukraine	603.7	233.1	52,027	Kiev	1,910
United Arab Emirates	83.6	32.3	2,800	Abu Dhabi	22,470
United Kingdom	243.3	94	58,306	London	17,970
United States of America	9,373	3,619	263,563	Washington, DC	24,750
Uruguay	177	68	3,186	Montevideo	3,910
Uzbekistan	447.4	172.7	22,833	Tashkent	960
Vanuatu	12.2	4.7	167	Port-Vila	1,230
Vatican City	0.0004	0.0002	1	–	–
Venezuela	912	352	21,800	Caracas	2,840
Vietnam	332	127	74,580	Hanoi	170
Virgin Is. (UK)	0.15	0.06	20	Road Town	–
Virgin Is. (US)	0.34	0.13	105	Charlotte Amalie	12,000
Wake Is.	0.008	0.003	0.30	–	–
Wallis & Futuna Is. (Fr.)	0.20	0.08	13	Mata-Utu	–
Western Sahara	266	103	220	El Aaiún	300
Western Samoa	2.8	1.1	169	Apia	980
Yemen	528	204	14,609	Sana	800
Yugoslavia	102.3	39.5	10,881	Belgrade	1,000
Zaïre	2,345	905	44,504	Kinshasa	500
Zambia	753	291	9,500	Lusaka	370
Zimbabwe	391	151	11,453	Harare	540

WORLD STATISTICS: PHYSICAL DIMENSIONS

Each topic list is divided into continents and within a continent the items are listed in order of size. The bottom part of many of the lists is selective in order to give examples from as many different countries as possible. The order of the continents is the same as in the atlas, beginning with Europe and ending with South America. The figures are rounded as appropriate.

WORLD, CONTINENTS, OCEANS

	km²	miles²	%
The World	509,450,000	196,672,000	–
Land	149,450,000	57,688,000	29.3
Water	360,000,000	138,984,000	70.7
Asia	44,500,000	17,177,000	29.8
Africa	30,302,000	11,697,000	20.3
North America	24,241,000	9,357,000	16.2
South America	17,793,000	6,868,000	11.9
Antarctica	14,100,000	5,443,000	9.4
Europe	9,957,000	3,843,000	6.7
Australia & Oceania	8,557,000	3,303,000	5.7
Pacific Ocean	179,679,000	69,356,000	49.9
Atlantic Ocean	92,373,000	35,657,000	25.7
Indian Ocean	73,917,000	28,532,000	20.5
Arctic Ocean	14,090,000	5,439,000	3.9

OCEAN DEPTHS

Atlantic Ocean

	m	ft
Puerto Rico (Milwaukee) Deep	9,220	30,249
Cayman Trench	7,680	25,197
Gulf of Mexico	5,203	17,070
Mediterranean Sea	5,121	16,801
Black Sea	2,211	7,254
North Sea	660	2,165

Indian Ocean

	m	ft
Java Trench	7,450	24,442
Red Sea	2,635	8,454

Pacific Ocean

	m	ft
Mariana Trench	11,022	36,161
Tonga Trench	10,882	35,702
Japan Trench	10,554	34,626
Kuril Trench	10,542	34,587

Arctic Ocean

	m	ft
Molloy Deep	5,608	18,399

MOUNTAINS

Europe

		m	ft
Mont Blanc	France/Italy	4,807	15,771
Monte Rosa	Italy/Switzerland	4,634	15,203
Dom	Switzerland	4,545	14,911
Liskamm	Switzerland	4,527	14,852
Weisshorn	Switzerland	4,505	14,780
Taschorn	Switzerland	4,490	14,730
Matterhorn/Cervino	Italy/Switzerland	4,478	14,691
Mont Maudit	France/Italy	4,465	14,649
Dent Blanche	Switzerland	4,356	14,291
Nadelhorn	Switzerland	4,327	14,196
Grandes Jorasses	France/Italy	4,208	13,806
Jungfrau	Switzerland	4,158	13,642
Grossglockner	Austria	3,797	12,457
Mulhacén	Spain	3,478	11,411
Zugspitze	Germany	2,962	9,718
Olympus	Greece	2,917	9,570
Triglav	Slovenia	2,863	9,393
Gerlachovka	Slovak Republic	2,655	8,711
Galdhöpiggen	Norway	2,468	8,100
Kebnekaise	Sweden	2,117	6,946
Ben Nevis	UK	1,343	4,406

Asia

		m	ft
Everest	China/Nepal	8,848	29,029
K2 (Godwin Austen)	China/Kashmir	8,611	28,251
Kanchenjunga	India/Nepal	8,598	28,208
Lhotse	China/Nepal	8,516	27,939
Makalu	China/Nepal	8,481	27,824
Cho Oyu	China/Nepal	8,201	26,906
Dhaulagiri	Nepal	8,172	26,811
Manaslu	Nepal	8,156	26,758
Nanga Parbat	Kashmir	8,126	26,660
Annapurna	Nepal	8,078	26,502
Gasherbrum	China/Kashmir	8,068	26,469
Broad Peak	China/Kashmir	8,051	26,414
Xixabangma	China	8,012	26,286
Kangbachen	India/Nepal	7,902	25,925
Trivor	Pakistan	7,720	25,328
Pik Kommunizma	Tajikistan	7,495	24,590
Elbrus	Russia	5,642	18,510
Demavend	Iran	5,604	18,386
Ararat	Turkey	5,165	16,945
Gunong Kinabalu	Malaysia (Borneo)	4,101	13,455
Fuji-San	Japan	3,776	12,388

Africa

		m	ft
Kilimanjaro	Tanzania	5,895	19,340
Mt Kenya	Kenya	5,199	17,057
Ruwenzori (Margherita)	Uganda/Zaïre	5,109	16,762
Ras Dashan	Ethiopia	4,620	15,157
Meru	Tanzania	4,565	14,977
Karisimbi	Rwanda/Zaïre	4,507	14,787
Mt Elgon	Kenya/Uganda	4,321	14,176
Batu	Ethiopia	4,307	14,130
Toubkal	Morocco	4,165	13,665
Mt Cameroon	Cameroon	4,070	13,353

Oceania

		m	ft
Puncak Jaya	Indonesia	5,029	16,499
Puncak Trikora	Indonesia	4,750	15,584
Puncak Mandala	Indonesia	4,702	15,427
Mt Wilhelm	Papua New Guinea	4,508	14,790
Mauna Kea	USA (Hawaii)	4,205	13,796
Mauna Loa	USA (Hawaii)	4,170	13,681
Mt Cook	New Zealand	3,753	12,313
Mt Kosciusko	Australia	2,237	7,339

North America

		m	ft
Mt McKinley (Denali)	USA (Alaska)	6,194	20,321
Mt Logan	Canada	5,959	19,551
Citlaltepetl	Mexico	5,700	18,701
Mt St Elias	USA/Canada	5,489	18,008
Popocatepetl	Mexico	5,452	17,887
Mt Foraker	USA (Alaska)	5,304	17,401
Ixtaccihuatl	Mexico	5,286	17,342
Lucania	Canada	5,227	17,149
Mt Steele	Canada	5,073	16,644
Mt Bona	USA (Alaska)	5,005	16,420
Mt Whitney	USA	4,418	14,495
Tajumulco	Guatemala	4,220	13,845
Chirripó Grande	Costa Rica	3,837	12,589
Pico Duarte	Dominican Rep.	3,175	10,417

South America

		m	ft
Aconcagua	Argentina	6,960	22,834
Bonete	Argentina	6,872	22,546
Ojos del Salado	Argentina/Chile	6,863	22,516
Pissis	Argentina	6,779	22,241
Mercedario	Argentina/Chile	6,770	22,211
Huascaran	Peru	6,768	22,204
Llullaillaco	Argentina/Chile	6,723	22,057
Nudo de Cachi	Argentina	6,720	22,047
Yerupaja	Peru	6,632	21,758
Sajama	Bolivia	6,542	21,463
Chimborazo	Ecuador	6,267	20,561
Pico Colon	Colombia	5,800	19,029
Pico Bolivar	Venezuela	5,007	16,427

Antarctica

		m	ft
Vinson Massif		4,897	16,066
Mt Kirkpatrick		4,528	14,855

RIVERS

Europe

		km	miles
Volga	Caspian Sea	3,700	2,300
Danube	Black Sea	2,850	1,770
Ural	Caspian Sea	2,535	1,575
Dnepr (Dnipro)	Volga	2,285	1,420
Kama	Volga	2,030	1,260
Don	Volga	1,990	1,240
Petchora	Arctic Ocean	1,790	1,110
Oka	Volga	1,480	920
Dnister (Dniester)	Black Sea	1,400	870
Vyatka	Kama	1,370	850
Rhine	North Sea	1,320	820
N. Dvina	Arctic Ocean	1,290	800
Elbe	North Sea	1,145	710

Asia

		km	miles
Yangtze	Pacific Ocean	6,380	3,960
Yenisey–Angara	Arctic Ocean	5,550	3,445
Huang He	Pacific Ocean	5,464	3,395
Ob–Irtysh	Arctic Ocean	5,410	3,360
Mekong	Pacific Ocean	4,500	2,795
Amur	Pacific Ocean	4,400	2,730
Lena	Arctic Ocean	4,400	2,730
Irtysh	Ob	4,250	2,640
Yenisey	Arctic Ocean	4,090	2,540
Ob	Arctic Ocean	3,680	2,285
Indus	Indian Ocean	3,100	1,925
Brahmaputra	Indian Ocean	2,900	1,800
Syrdarya	Aral Sea	2,860	1,775
Salween	Indian Ocean	2,800	1,740
Euphrates	Indian Ocean	2,700	1,675
Amudarya	Aral Sea	2,540	1,575

Africa

		km	miles
Nile	Mediterranean	6,670	4,140
Zaïre/Congo	Atlantic Ocean	4,670	2,900
Niger	Atlantic Ocean	4,180	2,595
Zambezi	Indian Ocean	3,540	2,200
Oubangi/Uele	Zaïre	2,250	1,400
Kasai	Zaïre	1,950	1,210
Shaballe	Indian Ocean	1,930	1,200
Orange	Atlantic Ocean	1,860	1,155
Cubango	Okavango Swamps	1,800	1,120
Limpopo	Indian Ocean	1,600	995
Senegal	Atlantic Ocean	1,600	995

Australia

		km	miles
Murray–Darling	Indian Ocean	3,750	2,330
Darling	Murray	3,070	1,905
Murray	Indian Ocean	2,575	1,600
Murrumbidgee	Murray	1,690	1,050

North America

		km	miles
Mississippi–Missouri	Gulf of Mexico	6,020	3,740
Mackenzie	Arctic Ocean	4,240	2,630
Mississippi	Gulf of Mexico	3,780	2,350
Missouri	Mississippi	3,780	2,350
Yukon	Pacific Ocean	3,185	1,980
Rio Grande	Gulf of Mexico	3,030	1,880
Arkansas	Mississippi	2,340	1,450
Colorado	Pacific Ocean	2,330	1,445
Red	Mississippi	2,040	1,270
Columbia	Pacific Ocean	1,950	1,210
Saskatchewan	Lake Winnipeg	1,940	1,205

South America

		km	miles
Amazon	Atlantic Ocean	6,450	4,010
Paraná–Plate	Atlantic Ocean	4,500	2,800
Purus	Amazon	3,350	2,080
Madeira	Amazon	3,200	1,990
São Francisco	Atlantic Ocean	2,900	1,800
Paraná	Plate	2,800	1,740
Tocantins	Atlantic Ocean	2,750	1,710
Paraguay	Paraná	2,550	1,580
Orinoco	Atlantic Ocean	2,500	1,550
Pilcomayo	Paraná	2,500	1,550
Araguaia	Tocantins	2,250	1,400

LAKES

Europe

		km²	miles²
Lake Ladoga	Russia	17,700	6,800
Lake Onega	Russia	9,700	3,700
Saimaa system	Finland	8,000	3,100
Vänern	Sweden	5,500	2,100

Asia

		km²	miles²
Caspian Sea	Asia	371,800	143,550
Aral Sea	Kazakstan/Uzbekistan	33,640	13,000
Lake Baykal	Russia	30,500	11,780
Tonlé Sap	Cambodia	20,000	7,700
Lake Balqash	Kazakstan	18,500	7,100

Africa

		km²	miles²
Lake Victoria	East Africa	68,000	26,000
Lake Tanganyika	Central Africa	33,000	13,000
Lake Malawi/Nyasa	East Africa	29,600	11,430
Lake Chad	Central Africa	25,000	9,700
Lake Turkana	Ethiopia/Kenya	8,500	3,300
Lake Volta	Ghana	8,500	3,300

Australia

		km²	miles²
Lake Eyre	Australia	8,900	3,400
Lake Torrens	Australia	5,800	2,200
Lake Gairdner	Australia	4,800	1,900

North America

		km²	miles²
Lake Superior	Canada/USA	82,350	31,800
Lake Huron	Canada/USA	59,600	23,010
Lake Michigan	USA	58,000	22,400
Great Bear Lake	Canada	31,800	12,280
Great Slave Lake	Canada	28,500	11,000
Lake Erie	Canada/USA	25,700	9,900
Lake Winnipeg	Canada	24,400	9,400
Lake Ontario	Canada/USA	19,500	7,500
Lake Nicaragua	Nicaragua	8,200	3,200

South America

		km²	miles²
Lake Titicaca	Bolivia/Peru	8,300	3,200
Lake Poopo	Peru	2,800	1,100

ISLANDS

Europe

		km²	miles²
Great Britain	UK	229,880	88,700
Iceland	Atlantic Ocean	103,000	39,800
Ireland	Ireland/UK	84,400	32,600
Novaya Zemlya (N.)	Russia	48,200	18,600
Sicily	Italy	25,500	9,800
Corsica	France	8,700	3,400

Asia

		km²	miles²
Borneo	South-east Asia	744,360	287,400
Sumatra	Indonesia	473,600	182,860
Honshu	Japan	230,500	88,980
Celebes	Indonesia	189,000	73,000
Java	Indonesia	126,700	48,900
Luzon	Philippines	104,700	40,400
Hokkaido	Japan	78,400	30,300

Africa

		km²	miles²
Madagascar	Indian Ocean	587,040	226,660
Socotra	Indian Ocean	3,600	1,400
Réunion	Indian Ocean	2,500	965

Oceania

		km²	miles²
New Guinea	Indonesia/Papua NG	821,030	317,000
New Zealand (S.)	Pacific Ocean	150,500	58,100
New Zealand (N.)	Pacific Ocean	114,700	44,300
Tasmania	Australia	67,800	26,200
Hawaii	Pacific Ocean	10,450	4,000

North America

		km²	miles²
Greenland	Atlantic Ocean	2,175,600	839,800
Baffin Is.	Canada	508,000	196,100
Victoria Is.	Canada	212,200	81,900
Ellesmere Is.	Canada	212,000	81,800
Cuba	Caribbean Sea	110,860	42,800
Hispaniola	Dominican Rep./Haiti	76,200	29,400
Jamaica	Caribbean Sea	11,400	4,400
Puerto Rico	Atlantic Ocean	8,900	3,400

South America

		km²	miles²
Tierra del Fuego	Argentina/Chile	47,000	18,100
Falkland Is. (E.)	Atlantic Ocean	6,800	2,600

PHILIP'S WORLD MAPS

The reference maps which form the main body of this atlas have been prepared in accordance with the highest standards of international cartography to provide an accurate and detailed representation of the Earth. The scales and projections used have been carefully chosen to give balanced coverage of the world, while emphasizing the most densely populated and economically significant regions. A hallmark of Philip's mapping is the use of hill shading and relief colouring to create a graphic impression of landforms: this makes the maps exceptionally easy to read. However, knowledge of the key features employed in the construction and presentation of the maps will enable the reader to derive the fullest benefit from the atlas.

Map sequence

The atlas covers the Earth continent by continent: first Europe; then its land neighbour Asia (mapped north before south, in a clockwise sequence), then Africa, Australia and Oceania, North America and South America. This is the classic arrangement adopted by most cartographers since the 16th century. For each continent, there are maps at a variety of scales. First, physical relief and political maps of the whole continent; then a series of larger-scale maps of the regions within the continent, each followed, where required, by still larger-scale maps of the most important or densely populated areas. The governing principle is that by turning the pages of the atlas, the reader moves steadily from north to south through each continent, with each map overlapping its neighbours. A key map showing this sequence, and the area covered by each map, can be found on the endpapers of the atlas.

Map presentation

With very few exceptions (e.g. for the Arctic and Antarctic), the maps are drawn with north at the top, regardless of whether they are presented upright or sideways on the page. In the borders will be found the map title; a locator diagram showing the area covered and the page numbers for maps of adjacent areas; the scale; the projection used; the degrees of latitude and longitude; and the letters and figures used in the index for locating place names and geographical features. Physical relief maps also have a height reference panel identifying the colours used for each layer of contouring.

Map symbols

Each map contains a vast amount of detail which can only be conveyed clearly and accurately by the use of symbols. Points and circles of varying sizes locate and identify the relative importance of towns and cities; different styles of type are employed for administrative, geographical and

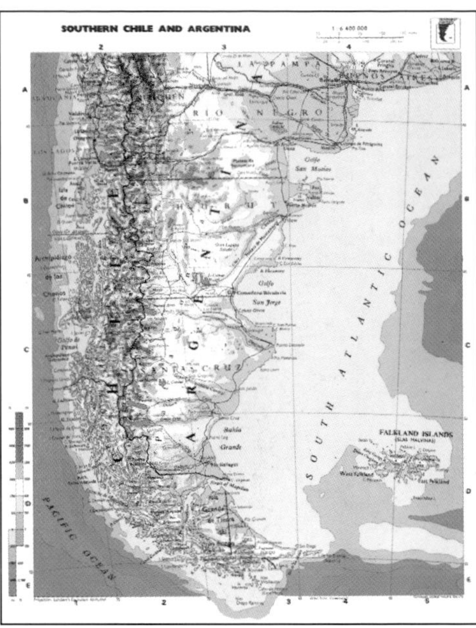

regional place names. A variety of pictorial symbols denote landscape features such as glaciers, marshes and reefs, and man-made structures including roads, railways, airports, canals and dams. International borders are shown by red lines. Where neighbouring countries are in dispute, for example in the Middle East, the maps show the *de facto* boundary between nations, regardless of the legal or historical situation. The symbols are explained on the first page of the World Maps section of the atlas.

Map scales

The scale of each map is given in the numerical form known as the 'representative fraction'. The first figure is always one, signifying one unit of distance on the map; the second figure, usually in millions, is the number by which the map unit must be multiplied to give the equivalent distance on the Earth's surface. Calculations can easily be made in centimetres and kilometres, by dividing the Earth units figure by 100 000 (i.e. deleting the last five 0s). Thus 1:1 000 000 means 1 cm = 10 km. The calculation for inches and miles is more laborious, but 1 000 000 divided by 63 360 (the number of inches in a mile) shows that 1:1 000 000 means approximately 1 inch = 16 miles. The table below provides distance equivalents for scales down to 1:50 000 000.

LARGE SCALE		
1:1 000 000	1 cm = 10 km	1 inch = 16 miles
1:2 500 000	1 cm = 25 km	1 inch = 39.5 miles
1:5 000 000	1 cm = 50 km	1 inch = 79 miles
1:6 000 000	1 cm = 60 km	1 inch = 95 miles
1:8 000 000	1 cm = 80 km	1 inch = 126 miles
1:10 000 000	1 cm = 100 km	1 inch = 158 miles
1:12 000 000	1 cm = 120 km	1 inch = 189 miles
1:15 000 000	1 cm = 150 km	1 inch = 237 miles
1:20 000 000	1 cm = 200 km	1 inch = 316 miles
1:50 000 000	1 cm = 500 km	1 inch = 790 miles
SMALL SCALE		

Measuring distances

Although each map is accompanied by a scale bar, distances cannot always be measured with confidence because of the distortions involved in portraying the curved surface of the Earth on a flat page. As a general rule, the larger the map scale (i.e. the lower the number of Earth units in the representative fraction), the more accurate and reliable will be the distance measured. On small-scale maps such as those of the world and of entire continents, measurement may only be accurate along the 'standard parallels', or central axes, and should not be attempted without first considering the map projection used.

Latitude and longitude

Accurate positioning of individual points on the Earth's surface is made possible by reference to the geometrical system of latitude and longitude. Latitude *parallels* are drawn west–east around the Earth and numbered by degrees north and south of the Equator, which is designated 0° of latitude. Longitude *meridians* are drawn north–south and numbered by degrees east and west of the *prime meridian*, 0° of longitude, which passes through Greenwich in England. By referring to these co-ordinates and their subdivisions of minutes (⅟₆₀th of a degree) and seconds (⅟₆₀th of a minute), any place on Earth can be located to within a few hundred yards. Latitude and longitude are indicated by blue lines on the maps; they are straight or curved according to the projection employed. Reference to these lines is the easiest way of determining the relative positions of places on different large-scale maps, and for plotting compass directions.

Name forms

For ease of reference, both English and local name forms appear in the atlas. Oceans, seas and countries are shown in English throughout the atlas; country names may be abbreviated to their commonly accepted form (e.g. Germany, not The Federal Republic of Germany). Conventional English forms are also used for place names on the smaller-scale maps of the continents. However, local name forms are used on all large-scale and regional maps, with the English form given in brackets only for important cities – the large-scale map of Eastern Europe and Turkey thus shows Moskva (Moscow). For countries which do not use a Roman script, place names have been transcribed according to the systems adopted by the British and US Geographic Names Authorities. For China, the Pin Yin system has been used, with some more widely known forms appearing in brackets, as with Beijing (Peking). Both English and local names appear in the index to the world maps.

THE
WORLD
OF
NATIONS

An A – Z Gazetteer of Countries 1–47
Index and Notes 48

AFGHANISTAN

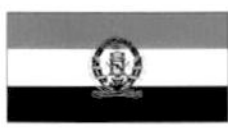

After many changes since the late 1970s, a new flag was introduced in December 1992 based on the colours used by the Mujaheddin during the civil war. The flag bears the new national arms which show wheatsheaves and the shahada, the Muslim statement of faith, above a mosque.

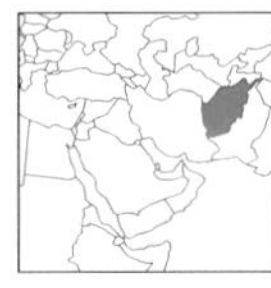

GEOGRAPHY Nearly 75% of Afghanistan is mountainous, comprising most of the Hindu Kush and its foothills. The remainder of the country is desert or semi-desert.

HISTORY AND POLITICS Afghanistan has always been in a critical position in Asia: the Khyber Pass being the gateway to India and the back door to Russia. Numerous historical invasions culminated in the 1979 Soviet invasion, resulting in civil war. The Soviet troops withdrew in 1988–9, but the civil war continued. Finally, Mujaheddin forces set up an Islamic government in 1992, but conflict between rival groups continued into 1994.

ECONOMY Up to 70% of the workforce are peasant farmers. Natural gas is the country's biggest export.

AREA 652,090 sq km [251,772 sq mls]
POPULATION 19,509,000
CAPITAL (POPULATION) Kabul (1,424,000)
GOVERNMENT Islamic republic
ETHNIC GROUPS Pashtun ('Pathan') 52%, Tajik 20%, Uzbek 9%, Hazara 9%
LANGUAGES Pashto 50%, Dari (Persian)
RELIGIONS Sunni Muslim 84%, Shiite Muslim 15%
CURRENCY Afghani = 100 puls
MAIN EXPORTS Natural gas 42%, dried fruit 26%, fresh fruit 9%, carpets and rugs 7%

ALBANIA

The name of the country means 'land of the eagle'. Following the formation of a non-Communist government in March 1992, the star that had been placed above the eagle's head in 1946 was removed and the flag has reverted to its original form.

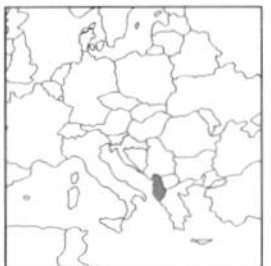

GEOGRAPHY Bordering the Adriatic Sea, Albania has a mountainous interior, with ranges rising to almost 2,000 m [6,500 ft]. The coastal lowlands have a Mediterranean-type climate with hot, dry summers and temperatures that rarely drop below freezing.

HISTORY AND POLITICS As Europe's poorest country, Albania has always been one of the most isolated and backward. Under Enver Hoxha it was run as a rigid Communist state virtually cut off from the outside world. Changes in Eastern Europe in the early 1990s spread to Albania and reforms have started; after elections in 1992, a non-Communist government took over.

ECONOMY Two-thirds of the population live in villages and most people live by farming, with maize, wheat, barley and fruits being the predominant crops. There are large reserves of petroleum, brown coal and iron, but there is still limited industrialization and a poor transport system.

AREA 28,750 sq km [11,100 sq mls]
POPULATION 3,458,000
CAPITAL (POPULATION) Tirana (251,000)
GOVERNMENT Multiparty republic with a unicameral legislature
ETHNIC GROUPS Albanian 96%, Greek 2%, Romanian, Macedonian, Montenegrin, Gypsy
LANGUAGES Albanian (official)
RELIGIONS Sunni Muslim 65%, Christian 33%
CURRENCY Lek = 100 qindars
MAIN EXPORTS Chrome, crude oil, nickel, iron ore, coal

ALGERIA

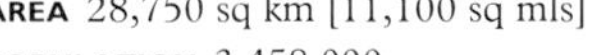

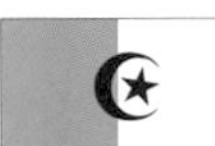

Algeria's flag features traditional Islamic symbols and colours, and the design dates back to the early 19th century. Used by the liberation movement that fought against French rule after 1954, it was adopted on independence in 1962.

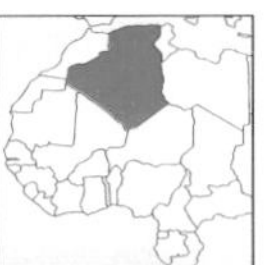

GEOGRAPHY Algeria is the world's 11th largest nation, with 85% (2 million sq km [772,200 sq mls]) of its land area covered by the Sahara Desert. Over 90% of the population live in the Mediterranean coastlands, where the climate is milder.

HISTORY AND POLITICS Algeria was the first Maghreb country to be conquered by France and the last to gain independence after a bitter war between nationalist guerillas and the French.

ECONOMY Revenues from oil (discovered in 1956 in the desert) and natural gas provide 65% of all revenue and account for over 90% of exports. This has enabled rapid industrialization and economic development with industries such as food processing, car manufacturing and oil refining.

AREA 2,381,740 sq km [919,590 sq mls]
POPULATION 27,936,000
CAPITAL (POPULATION) Algiers (1,722,000)
GOVERNMENT Socialist multiparty republic with a unicameral legislature
ETHNIC GROUPS Arab 83%, Berber 16%
LANGUAGES Arabic (official), Berber
RELIGIONS Sunni Muslim 99%
CURRENCY Algerian dinar = 100 centimes
MAIN EXPORTS Crude oil, petroleum products, natural gas
URBAN POPULATION 53% of population

AMERICAN SAMOA

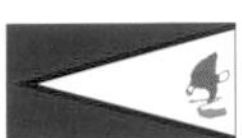

A flag was introduced in 1960 for this American dependency. It shows the American eagle holding two typically Samoan objects: a war-club and a fly-whisk, both symbols of a chief's authority. The colours used on the flag are those of the American flag.

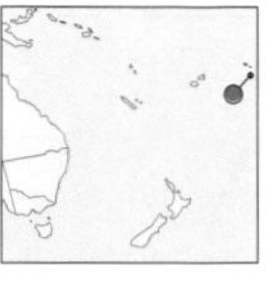

American Samoa is a group of five volcanic islands and two atolls in the South Pacific, with Tutuila the largest. The Samoan Islands were divided between Germany and the USA in 1899, and although the US naval base closed in 1951, there remains a strong American influence, with substantial grants from the USA and with 90% of Samoan exports going to the USA.

AREA 200 sq km [77 sq mls]
POPULATION 58,000
CAPITAL (POPULATION) Pago Pago (3,519)
GOVERNMENT Self-governing 'unincorporated territory of the USA'
ETHNIC GROUPS Samoan 90%, Caucasian 2%, Tongan 2%
LANGUAGES Samoan, English
RELIGIONS Christian

ANDORRA

Andorra is traditionally said to have been granted independence by Charlemagne in the 9th century, after the Moorish Wars. The flag, adopted in 1866, sometimes features the state coat of arms on the obverse in the central yellow band.

Andorra consists mainly of six valleys (the Valls) that drain to the River Valira at the eastern end of the high central Pyrenees. There are deep glaciated valleys lying at altitudes of around 1,000 to 2,900 m [3,280 to 9,500 ft]. The climate is severe in winter and cool in summer. Andorra's economy is very dependent on tourism (skiing) and duty-free sales (every year 10 million visitors come to shop); other sources of income include stock-rearing and agriculture, especially tobacco.

AREA 453 sq km [175 sq mls]
POPULATION 65,000
CAPITAL (POPULATION) Andorra La Vella (22,000)
GOVERNMENT Co-principality of Spain and France
ETHNIC GROUPS Spanish 46%, Andorran 28%, Portuguese 11%, French 8%
LANGUAGES Catalan (official), French
RELIGIONS Roman Catholic

ANGOLA

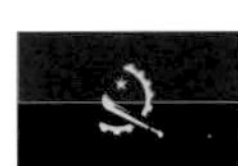

The flag is based on that of the Popular Movement for the Liberation of Angola during the struggle for independence from Portugal (1975). The emblem, incorporating a half gearwheel and a machete, symbolizes Angola's socialist ideology.

GEOGRAPHY Angola extends through 13° of latitude, with climate and vegetation varying from desert on the south coast to equatorial and montane conditions in the centre and north.
HISTORY AND POLITICS As a Portuguese colony, Angola was a centre of the slave trade (with some 3 million captives going to the Americas). Development has been slow, hampered by a civil war between the MPLA government and UNITA rebels, which finally ended when a peace accord was signed in 1994.
ECONOMY Potentially, Angola could be very rich, since there are oil reserves, diamonds, copper, manganese and phosphates.

AREA 1,246,700 sq km [481,351 sq mls]
POPULATION 10,844,000
CAPITAL (POPULATION) Luanda (1,544,000)
GOVERNMENT Multiparty republic
ETHNIC GROUPS Ovimbundu 37%, Mbundu 23%, Kongo, Luimbe, Humbe
LANGUAGES Portuguese (official), Umbundu 38%, Kimbundu 27%
RELIGIONS Roman Catholic 69%, Protestant 20%, traditional beliefs 10%
CURRENCY New kwanza = 100 lwei

ANGUILLA

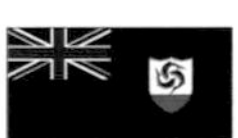

This flag came into use in 1993 and, since Anguilla is a British dependency, the British Blue Ensign is flown. The three dolphins depicted on the shield represent strength, unity and endurance, while the white stands for peace and the blue for the sea.

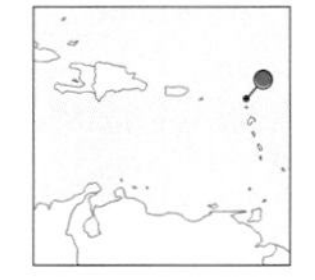

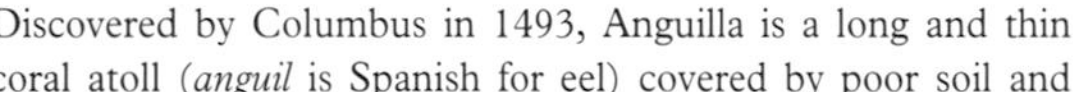

Discovered by Columbus in 1493, Anguilla is a long and thin coral atoll (*anguil* is Spanish for eel) covered by poor soil and scrub. It has been a British colony since 1650 and its main source of revenue is now tourism.

AREA 96 sq km [37 sq mls]
POPULATION 8,000
CAPITAL (POPULATION) The Valley (2,000)
GOVERNMENT British Dependent Territory
ETHNIC GROUPS Mainly of African descent
LANGUAGES English and Creole
RELIGIONS Christian
CURRENCY East Caribbean $ = 100 cents

ANTIGUA AND BARBUDA

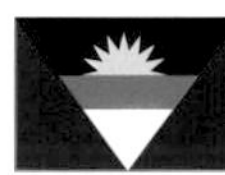

The design of the flag was decided in a competition in 1967. The V depicted in the design denotes victory and the golden sun symbolizes the dawning of a new era. The black represents African heritage and the soil, blue is for hope and red for the dynamism of the people.

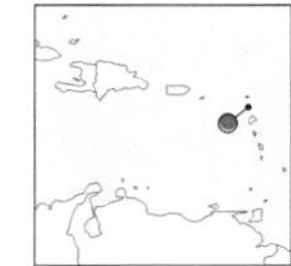

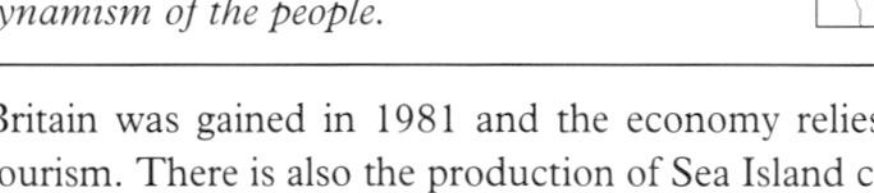

Antigua and Barbuda are part of the Leeward Islands; Barbuda is a wooded low coral atoll, while Antigua is higher with no rivers or forests, but over 365 sandy beaches. Independence from Britain was gained in 1981 and the economy relies heavily on tourism. There is also the production of Sea Island cotton, sugar cane crops and lobster fishing.

AREA 440 sq km [170 sq mls]
POPULATION 67,000
CAPITAL (POPULATION) St John's (38,000)
GOVERNMENT Multiparty constitutional monarchy with a bicameral legislature
ETHNIC GROUPS Of African descent
LANGUAGES English and local dialects
RELIGIONS Christian
CURRENCY East Caribbean $ = 100 cents

ARGENTINA

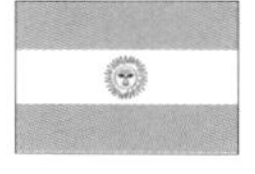

The 'celeste' and white stripes, symbol of independence since 1810 around Buenos Aires, became the national flag in 1816 and influenced other Latin American countries. A yellow May Sun, only used on the state flag, was added two years later.

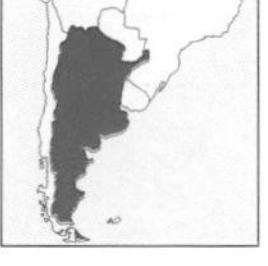

GEOGRAPHY Argentina is the world's eighth largest country and stretches from the Tropic of Capricorn almost into Antarctica. The Andes mountains are to the west, with Mt Aconcagua, at 6,960 m [22,834 ft], the tallest mountain in the western hemisphere. The pampas grasslands cover much of central Argentina and most of the population lives on this fertile land; in the far south are the plateaux of Patagonia.
HISTORY AND POLITICS The 'land of silver' emerged as a national entity in 1816 and there was great economic prosperity between 1850 and 1930, with the development of a good transport system and a strong cereals and meat economy. Military intervention after 1930 culminated in the 'dirty war' of 1976–82, when up to 15,000 people were killed or tortured. After an unsuccessful invasion of the Falkland Islands in 1982, there was a return to constitutional rule.
ECONOMY Economic problems have included a large foreign debt and inflation rates of 3,084%. There are rich natural resources, with agriculture making up 70% of export earnings.

AREA 2,766,890 sq km [1,068,296 sq mls]
POPULATION 34,663,000
CAPITAL (POPULATION) Buenos Aires (11,256,000)
GOVERNMENT Republic
ETHNIC GROUPS European 85%, Mestizo, Amerindian
LANGUAGES Spanish (official) 95%, Italian, Guarani
RELIGIONS Roman Catholic 93%, Protestant 2%
CURRENCY Peso = 10,000 australs
MAIN EXPORTS Vegetable products 43%, textiles and manufactures 4%
MAIN IMPORTS Machinery 23%

ARMENIA

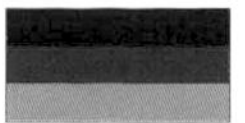

The flag used in the period 1918–22 was readopted on 24 August 1990. The colours represent the blood shed in the past (red), the land of Armenia (blue), and the unity and courage of the people (orange).

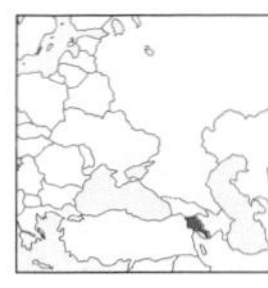

Armenia is a mountainous country, landlocked between hostile neighbours. The economy is weak, with few natural resources and limited industry; agricultural products include wine and tobacco. Historically its peoples have been subject to war and occupation and the western regions are still recovering from an earthquake in 1988, which killed 55,000.

AREA 29,800 sq km [11,506 sq mls]
POPULATION 3,603,000
CAPITAL (POPULATION) Yerevan (1,254,000)
GOVERNMENT Multiparty republic
ETHNIC GROUPS Armenian 93%, Azerbaijani 3%, Russian 2%, Kurd 2%
LANGUAGES Armenian 89%, Azerbaijani, Russian
CURRENCY Dram = 100 couma

ARUBA

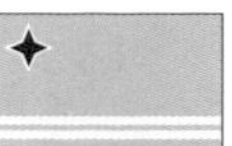

The flag of this Dutch overseas territory was introduced in 1976. The four points of the star represent the four main language groups of the area.

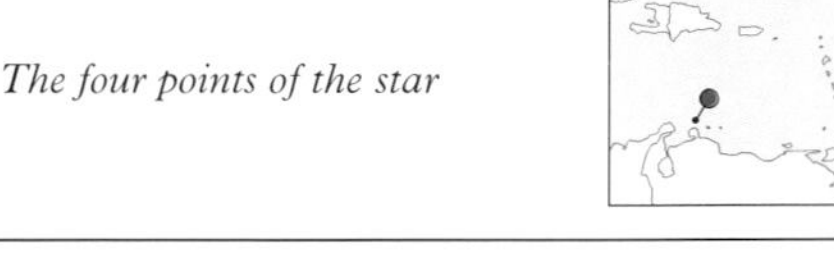

Aruba is the most western of the Lesser Antilles and is a dry, flat limestone island. A Dutch territory, it was part of the Netherlands Antilles until 1986. About half of export earnings come from beverages and tobacco; tourism is also important.

AREA 193 sq km [75 sq mls]
POPULATION 71,000
CAPITAL (POPULATION) Oranjestad (20,000)
GOVERNMENT Self-governing Dutch Territory
ETHNIC GROUPS Mixed European/ Caribbean Indian 80%
LANGUAGES Dutch, Papiamento, English

ASCENSION

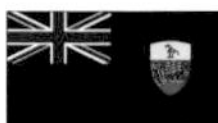

As a dependency of St Helena, Ascension uses her flag, which shows the shield from her coat of arms in the fly of the British Blue Ensign. The main part of the shield shows a ship sailing towards the island, and the chief is yellow and shows a local wirebird.

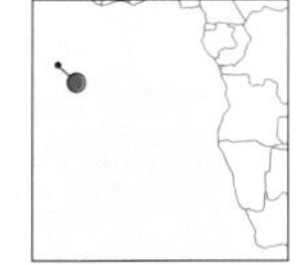

Ascension is a triangular volcanic island standing on the Mid-Atlantic Ridge, with a single high peak and a cool, damp climate. Most of the inhabitants (English, St Helenian or American) work in telecommunications or on the mid-ocean airstrip.

AREA 88 sq km [34 sq mls]
POPULATION 1,500
CAPITAL (POPULATION) Georgetown (1,500)
GOVERNMENT British Dependent Territory
ETHNIC GROUPS No native ones
LANGUAGES English
POPULATION DENSITY 17 people per sq km [44 per sq ml]

AUSTRALIA

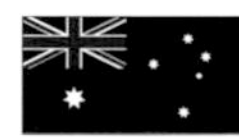

Showing its historical link with Britain, Australia's flag, adopted in 1901, features the British Blue Ensign. The five stars represent the Southern Cross constellation and, together with the larger star, symbolize the six states. Since 1995, the Aboriginal flag has had equal status.

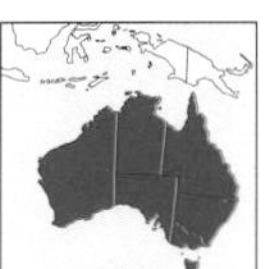

GEOGRAPHY The landscape is largely made up of low to medium plateaux of desert and semi-desert stretching for hundreds of kilometres. At the edges of these plateaux, there are more diverse landscapes: for example, the gorges in the Hamersley Range and Kimberley area of the north and the forests of eucalyptus hardwoods in the extreme south-west of Western Australia. The Great Artesian Basin in the central lowlands is the world's largest underground natural reservoir, discharging some 1,500 million litres [330 million gallons] of water a day. Along the east coast of Queensland lies the Great Barrier Reef, a coral reef stretching about 2,000 km [1,250 mls] with the 2,500 reefs exposed only at low tide.

HISTORY AND POLITICS Aborigines arrived in Australia from Asia over 40,000 years ago, while European settlement did not begin until 1788 when the British established a penal colony first in New South Wales and then in Queensland and Tasmania. During the 19th century the continent was divided into colonies and in 1901 these came together to create the Commonwealth of Australia. Immigration since 1960 has changed the ethnic character of Australia, with Greek, Italian, Turkish and Lebanese communities now living alongside the longer-established Aboriginal, British, Dutch and Chinese communities. Some 60% of the total Australian population live in Sydney, Melbourne, Adelaide, Brisbane, Perth and Hobart. A good transport system and good communications, particularly radio, help the many remote and isolated settlements. Since 1991, with a worsening economic situation and Britain's closer links with the European Union, Australia has increasingly turned to the Pacific countries, especially Japan, for trade. The former prime minister, Paul Keating, was a keen republican but the new prime minister, John Howard, is keen to maintain Australia's ties with the UK.

ECONOMY Much of Australia's early development was based on its mineral resources, such as copper, lead, zinc and silver. In 1993, it produced over a third of the world's diamonds and bauxite, 11% of iron ore, 7% of uranium and over 5% of zinc and lead. On the agricultural side, there is extensive sheep and cattle production, with 140 million sheep producing 25% of the world's wool. Metals, minerals and farm products account for the bulk of Australia's exports. Wine production around Perth, Adelaide and in Victoria has expanded in recent years.

AREA 7,686,850 sq km [2,967,893 sq mls]
POPULATION 18,107,000
CAPITAL (POPULATION) Canberra (310,000)
GOVERNMENT Federal constitutional monarchy with a bicameral legislature
ETHNIC GROUPS White 94%, Aboriginal 1.5%, Asian 1.3%
LANGUAGES English (official)
RELIGIONS Roman Catholic 26%, Anglican 24%, other Christian 22%
CURRENCY Australian dollar = 100 cents
MAIN EXPORTS Food and live animals 22%, coal, oil and gas 19%, metallic ores 14%

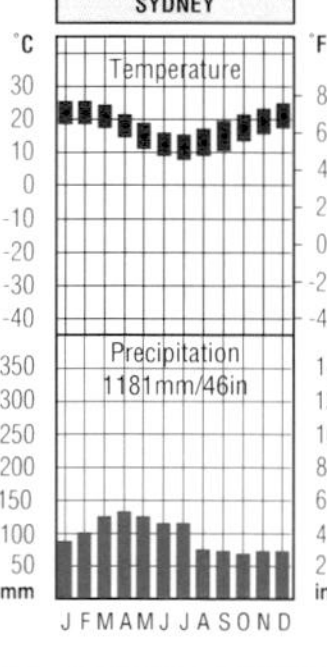

In the south-east, the annual rainfall total is fairly high, with maxima between April and June. Rain falls on 12–13 days each month. The valleys inland of the Great Divide, in the lee of rain-bearing winds, are drier. Temperatures are moderate, with winter night frosts in the south and interior, but the lowest temperatures in Sydney are 2–4°C [36–39°F].

AUSTRIA

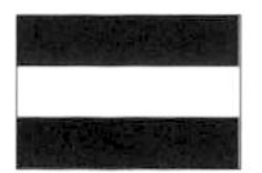

According to legend, the colours of the Austrian flag date from the battle of Ptolemais in 1191, when the only part of the Duke of Bebenberg's tunic not bloodstained was under his swordbelt. The design was officially adopted in 1918.

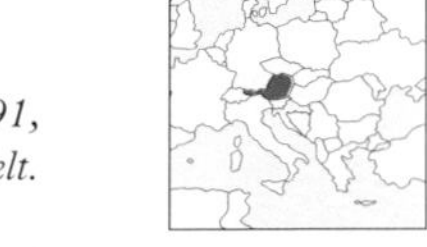

GEOGRAPHY Austria is a mountainous country, with two-thirds of its territory and slightly less than a third of its population within the eastern Alps. Forests cover 37% of the country.

HISTORY AND POLITICS Austria's boundaries derive from the Versailles Treaty of 1919, which dissolved the Austro-Hungarian Empire. It regained its full independence in 1955 after occupation by the Germans in 1938 and the Allies in 1945. A member of EFTA since 1960, in 1994 two-thirds of the population voted in favour of joining the European Union, and on 1 January 1995 Austria became a member (at the same time as Finland and Sweden).

ECONOMY There are important heavy industries based mainly on indigenous resources; oil and gas are found in the Vienna Basin and the mountains are a source of hydroelectric power.

AREA 83,850 sq km [32,374 sq mls]
POPULATION 8,004,000
CAPITAL (POPULATION) Vienna (1,560,000)
GOVERNMENT Federal multiparty republic
ETHNIC GROUPS Austrian 94%, Slovene 2%, Turkish, German
LANGUAGES German 94% (official), Slovene, Croat, Turkish, Slovak, Magyar
RELIGIONS Roman Catholic 78%, Protestant 6%, Muslim 2%
CURRENCY Schilling = 100 Groschen
MAIN EXPORTS Machinery and transport equipment 34%, iron and steel 7%

AZERBAIJAN

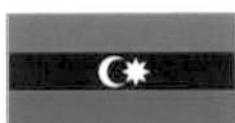

This flag was instituted on 5 February 1991. The blue stands for the sky, the red for freedom and the green for land and the Islamic religion; the crescent and star symbolize Islam, and the points of the star represent the eight races of Azerbaijan.

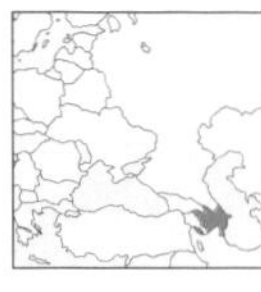

GEOGRAPHY Azerbaijan is mostly semi-arid, with the Caspian Sea to the east and the Caucasus Mountains to the north.

HISTORY AND POLITICS Independence was declared in 1991 but fighting broke out with Armenia over the predominantly Armenian enclave of Nagorno-Karabakh in the south-west. A cease-fire was agreed in 1994, however, with about 20% of Azerbaijan territory under Armenian control. Azerbaijan has its own enclave, Nakhichevan, between Armenia and Turkey.

ECONOMY Oil and natural gas, together with carpet, timber and cement industries, make up a viable economy.

AREA 86,600 sq km [33,436 sq mls]
POPULATION 7,559,000
CAPITAL (POPULATION) Baku (1,149,000)
GOVERNMENT Transitional government
ETHNIC GROUPS Azerbaijani 83%, Russian 6%, Armenian 6%, Daghestani 3%
LANGUAGES Azerbaijani 82%, Russian, Armenian
RELIGIONS Muslim 87%, Christian
CURRENCY Manat = 100 gopik
URBAN POPULATION 55% of population

AZORES

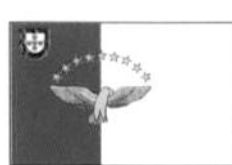

The flag dates from 1979 and shows the hawk (or açor) after which the islands are named, below an arc of nine stars (one for each island). The colours recall the fact that the old Portuguese flag was first adopted in the Azores.

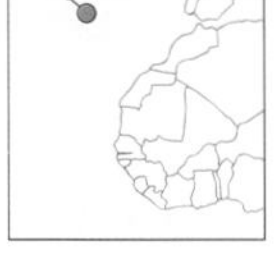

Part of the Mid-Atlantic Ridge, the Azores comprise nine large and several smaller islands; of recent volcanic origin, they have high cliffs and narrow beaches. Occupations include small-scale farming and fishing, with the export of fruit and canned fish.

AREA 2,247 sq km [868 sq mls]
POPULATION 280,000
CAPITAL (POPULATION) Ponta Delgada (21,000)
GOVERNMENT Portuguese Autonomous Region
ETHNIC GROUPS Portuguese
CURRENCY Portuguese escudo

BAHAMAS

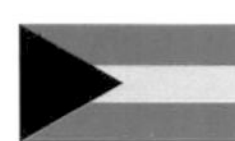

The black hoist triangle symbolizes the unity of the Bahamian people and their resolve to develop the island's natural resources. The golden sand and blue sea of the islands are depicted by the yellow and aquamarine stripes.

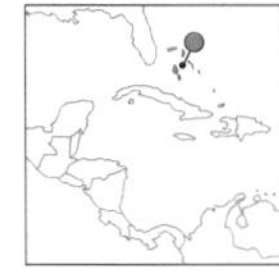

The Bahamas are made up of a coral-limestone archipelago of 29 inhabited low-lying islands and over 3,000 uninhabited cays, reefs and rocks; tourism now accounts for more than half the country's revenues (over 90% of its visitors are American) and involves 40% of the workforce. Other activities include offshore banking and some traditional fishing and agriculture.

AREA 13,880 sq km [5,359 sq mls]
POPULATION 277,000
CAPITAL (POPULATION) Nassau (190,000)
GOVERNMENT Constitutional monarchy with a bicameral legislature
ETHNIC GROUPS Black 80%, Mixed 10%, White 10%
LANGUAGES English, English Creole 80%
RELIGIONS Christian 95%

BAHRAIN

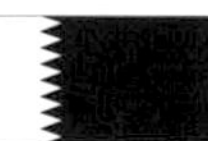

The flag dates from about 1932, with the white section a result of the British request that it be included in the flags of all friendly Arab states around the Arabian Gulf. Red is the traditional colour of Kharijite Muslims. The serrated edge was added to distinguish between the colours.

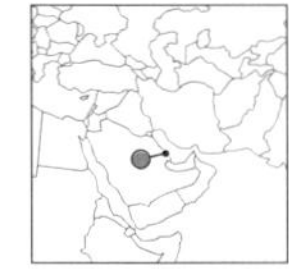

GEOGRAPHY Bahrain comprises 35 small islands in the southern Gulf, the largest of which is called Bahrain. Most of the land is barren, but soil imports have created fertile areas.

HISTORY, POLITICS AND ECONOMY Bahrain led the region into oil production after discovery in 1932, and there are also banking and aluminium-smelting activities. Tensions between the Sunni and majority Shiite population (the latter favouring an Islamic republic) have always been a problem.

AREA 678 sq km [262 sq mls]
POPULATION 558,000
CAPITAL (POPULATION) Manama (143,000)
GOVERNMENT Monarchy (emirate) with a cabinet appointed by the Emir
ETHNIC GROUPS Bahraini Arab 68%, Persian, Indian and Pakistani 25%, other Arab 4%, European 3%
LANGUAGES Arabic (official)
RELIGIONS Muslim 85%, Christian 7%

BANGLADESH

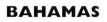

Bangladesh adopted this flag in 1971 following the break from Pakistan. The green is said to represent the fertility of the land, while the red disc, as the sun of independence, commemorates the blood shed in the struggle for freedom.

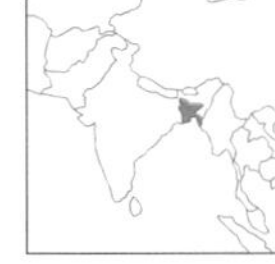

GEOGRAPHY Apart from hills covered in bamboo forest in the south-east, Bangladesh consists of lowlands made up mostly from the (greater) eastern part of the huge delta formed jointly by the Ganges and Brahmaputra. Known as the 'active delta', it frequently floods, making it hazardous to life, health and property, but also creating fertile alluvial silts.

HISTORY AND POLITICS Once known as Golden Bengal, Bangladesh was East Pakistan until 1971 when the state of 'Free Bengal' was set up. It is now one of Asia's poorest countries, with the world's ninth biggest population. In 1991 Bangladesh held its first free elections since independence.

ECONOMY Up to three rice crops a year and the world's best jute are grown on the fertile delta areas, but political problems, flooding and sheer population numbers hinder development.

AREA 144,000 sq km [55,598 sq mls]
POPULATION 118,342,000
CAPITAL (POPULATION) Dhaka (6,105,000)
GOVERNMENT Multiparty republic
ETHNIC GROUPS Bengali 98%, Bihari, tribal groups
LANGUAGES Bengali (official), English, nearly 100 tribal dialects
RELIGIONS Sunni Muslim 87%, Hindu 12%, Buddhist, Christian
CURRENCY Taka = 100 paisas
MAIN EXPORTS Jute goods and raw jute 33%, fish and fish preparations 12%

BARBADOS

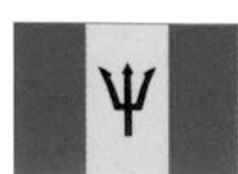

The flag was adopted on independence in 1960. The trident had been part of the colonial badge of Barbados and was retained as the centre to its flag, maintaining the link between old and new. The gold stripe represents the beaches and the two blue stripes the sea and the sky.

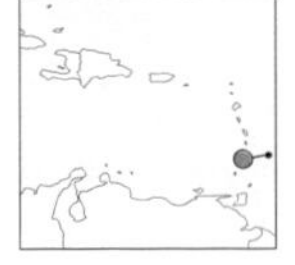

GEOGRAPHY Barbados is the easternmost of the West Indies, and its landscape is underlain with limestone and capped with coral. The coral structure acts as a natural filter and makes the water very pure. Soils are fertile and deep. It has a mild climate, but its location makes it susceptible to hurricanes.

HISTORY, POLITICS AND ECONOMY Barbados became British in 1627 and sugar (one of the principal exports) production, using African slave labour, began then. Tourism is now the leading industry; the island itself is densely populated and emigration is high, particularly to the USA and the UK.

AREA 430 sq km [166 sq mls]
POPULATION 263,000
CAPITAL (POPULATION) Bridgetown (8,000)
GOVERNMENT Constitutional monarchy with a bicameral legislature
ETHNIC GROUPS Black 80%, Mixed 16%, White 4%
LANGUAGES English (official), Creole 90%
RELIGIONS Protestant 65%, Roman Catholic 4%
CURRENCY Barbados dollar = 100 cents

BELARUS

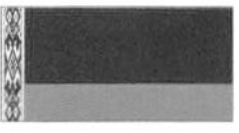

In September 1991, Belarus adopted a red and white flag to replace the one used in the Soviet era. But, in June 1995, after a referendum in which Belarussians voted to improve relations with Russia, this was replaced with a design similar to that of 1958 minus the hammer and sickle.

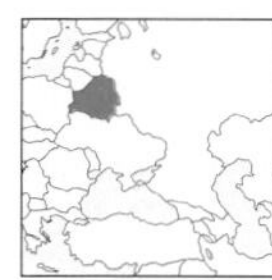

GEOGRAPHY The Republic of Belarus ('White Russia') is a landlocked country in Eastern Europe, formerly part of the Soviet Union. The land is low-lying and mostly flat. In the south, much of the land is marshy. This area contains Europe's largest marsh and peat bog, the Pripet Marshes. A hilly region extends from north-east to south-west through the centre of the country. Forests cover about a third of the country, but farmland and pasture have replaced most of the original forest.

HISTORY AND POLITICS In 1918, Belarus became an independent republic, but Russia invaded the country and, in 1919, a Communist state was set up. In 1922, Belarus became a founder republic of the Soviet Union. Most observers were surprised when this most conservative and Communist-dominated of parliaments declared independence on 25 August 1991, forcing the Party president to stand down. The quiet state of the European Soviet Union, it played a big supporting role in its deconstruction and the creation of the CIS; the latter's first meeting was in Minsk – subsequently chosen as its capital. Like the Ukraine, Belarus has been a separate UN member since 1945, the end of World War II, during which it bore much of the force of the German invasion; one in four of its population died.

ECONOMY The World Bank classifies Belarus as an 'upper-middle-income' economy. It faces many problems in working to turn a government-run economy into a free-market one. Though mainly agricultural – 46% of the land is used efficiently for flax, potatoes, cereals, dairying, pigs and peat digging – it also has the largest petrochemical complex in Europe and the giant Belaz heavy-truck plants; these, however, like its many light industries, are heavily reliant on Russia for electricity and raw materials, including steel.

AREA 207,600 sq km [80,154 sq mls]
POPULATION 10,500,000
CAPITAL (Population) Minsk (1,613,000)
ETHNIC GROUPS Belarussian 78%, Russian 14%, Polish 4%, Ukrainian 3%, Jewish 1%
LANGUAGES Belarussian 70%, Russian 25%
RELIGIONS Belarussian Orthodox, Roman Catholic, Evangelical

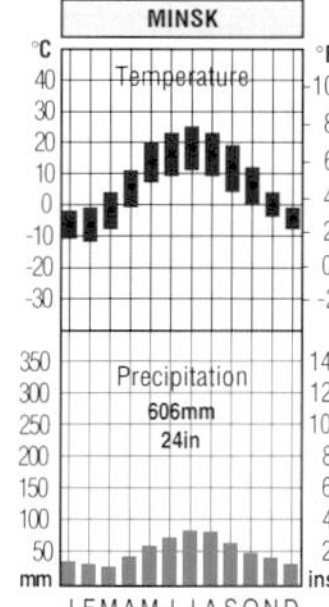

The climate of Belarus is affected by both the moderating influence of the Baltic Sea to the extreme north of the country and the continental conditions to the east. The winter months are cold and the summers warm. The average annual rainfall is between about 550 mm and 700 mm [22 in to 28 in], falling mainly in the summer months.

BELGIUM

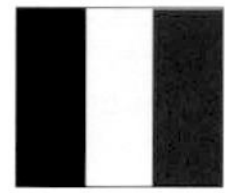

The colours of Belgium's flag derive from the arms of the province of Brabant which rebelled against Austrian rule in 1787. It was adopted as the national flag in 1830 when Belgium gained independence from the Netherlands.

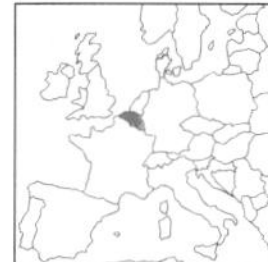

GEOGRAPHY Physically Belgium may be divided into the uplands of the Ardennes in the south-east and the lowland plains which are drained by the rivers Meuse and Schelde. The Ardennes, rising in Belgium to about 700 m [2,296 ft] at the highest point, is largely moorland, peat bogs and woodland. There is a cool temperate maritime climate and temperatures may reach 30°C [86°F] between May and September.

HISTORY AND POLITICS After the Napoleonic Wars, from 1815, Belgium and the Netherlands were united as the 'Low Countries', but Belgium regained independence in 1830, although it was occupied by Germany in both world wars. Since the end of World War II economic progress has been fast, since its geographical position gives it a significant position in Europe, especially in the European Union (it was a founder member of the European Community). There are tensions between its peoples, however – with the Flemings of Flanders in the north and the Walloons of Wallonia in the south.

ECONOMY Belgium has a very high urban population (97%), and most of its people work in industry. Coal is the only significant mineral resource and the other raw materials that are needed are imported. The textile industry, in existence since medieval times, is important, based around Ghent.

AREA 30,510 sq km [11,780 sq mls]
POPULATION 10,140,000
CAPITAL (Population) Brussels (952,000)
GOVERNMENT Constitutional monarchy with a bicameral legislature
ETHNIC GROUPS Fleming 55%, Walloon 34%, Italian 3%, German, French, Dutch, Turkish, Moroccan
LANGUAGES Flemish (Dutch) 57%, Walloon (French) 32%, German 1% – all official languages; 10% of population is officially bilingual
RELIGIONS Roman Catholic 72%, Protestant, Muslim
CURRENCY Belgian franc = 100 centimes
MAIN EXPORTS Vehicles 15%, chemicals 13%, foodstuffs 9%, iron and steel 7%

BELIZE

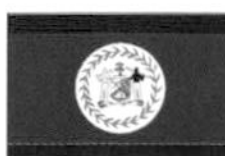

The badge shows loggers bearing axes and oars, tools employed in the industry responsible for developing Belize. The motto underneath reads 'Sub Umbra Floreo' ('Flourish in the Shade') and the tree is a mahogany, the national tree.

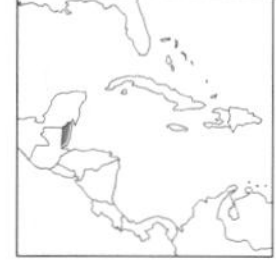

GEOGRAPHY Belize is a sparsely populated enclave on the Caribbean coast of Central America. The northern half is low-lying swamp, the south a high plateau, while offshore is the world's second biggest coral reef. The climate is hot and wet.

HISTORY AND POLITICS Formerly known as British Honduras, Belize became independent in 1981. There has been a long border dispute with Guatemala, but British troops, stationed here since the 1970s, were finally withdrawn at the end of 1993.

ECONOMY After independence there was an economic boom, with the processing of citrus fruits and tourism helping to allay the dependency on timber, bananas and sugar. Sugar still accounts for 30% of export earnings.

AREA 22,960 sq km [8,865 sq mls]
POPULATION 216,000
CAPITAL (Population) Belmopan (4,000)
GOVERNMENT Constitutional monarchy with a bicameral National Assembly
ETHNIC GROUPS Mestizo (Spanish Maya) 44%, Creole 30%, Mayan Indian 11%, Garifuna (Black Carib Indian) 7%, White 4%, East Indian 3%
LANGUAGES English, Creole, Spanish, Indian, Carib
RELIGIONS Roman Catholic 58%

BENIN

This flag, showing the red, yellow and green Pan-African colours, was first used after independence from France in 1960 and has now been readopted. While Benin was a Communist state after 1975, another flag, showing a red Communist star, was used.

GEOGRAPHY Benin is one of Africa's smallest countries, with a coastline that is only 100 km [62 mls] long. The equatorial and more fertile south is the most populated area and has a hot and humid climate. There is a central rainforest belt and savanna in the far north.

HISTORY AND POLITICS Known as Dahomey until 1975, Benin was inhabited by the Portuguese in the 16th century. They were expelled by the Dutch in 1642 and Dahomey became the base of a flourishing slave trade, mainly going to Brazil. Until 1850, when the French began to establish control, many rival tribal kingdoms flourished. In 1904 Dahomey became part of French West Africa. After independence in 1960 a series of coups and power struggles followed, until a multiparty democracy was established in 1991.

ECONOMY During the 18th and 19th centuries Benin was a major trading point for pepper and ivory. Now Benin has little to sell abroad, with its main exports being palm-oil produce, cotton and groundnuts. There is some offshore oil production, but this has been hampered by low prices. There are hopes for increased tourism in the future, based on the wildlife parks in the north.

AREA 112,620 sq km [43,483 sq mls]
POPULATION 5,381,000
CAPITAL (Population) Porto-Novo (179,000)
GOVERNMENT Multiparty republic with a unicameral legislature
ETHNIC GROUPS Fon 66%, Bariba 10%, Yoruba 9%, Somba 5%
LANGUAGES French (official), Fon 47%
RELIGIONS Traditional beliefs 61%, Christian 23%, Sunni Muslim 15%
CURRENCY CFA franc = 100 centimes
MAIN EXPORTS Fuels, raw cotton, palm products
MAIN IMPORTS Manufactured goods, textiles
URBAN POPULATION 30% of population

BERMUDA

BERMUDA

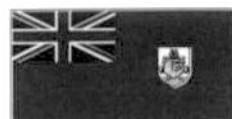

 Instead of the customary British Blue Ensign, the Red Ensign with the shield from Bermuda's badge is on the fly. The shield depicts a red lion holding another shield in which the shipwreck of the Sea Venture in 1609 is shown.

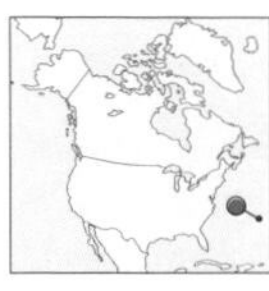

Comprising about 150 small islands, the coral caps of ancient submarine volcanoes rising over 4,000 m [13,000 ft] from the ocean floor, Bermuda has a mild climate. Twenty of the islands are inhabited, particularly the biggest island of Great Bermuda.

It is Britain's oldest dependency, but has strong ties with the USA. Tourism is vital to the economy, with over 500,000 visitors a year, and the islands are also a tax haven for companies and individuals; foodstuffs and energy dominate imports.

AREA 53 sq km [20 sq mls]
POPULATION 64,000
CAPITAL (POPULATION) Hamilton (6,000)
GOVERNMENT British Dependent Territory
ETHNIC GROUPS Black 61%, White 37%
LANGUAGES English
RELIGIONS Anglican 37%, Roman Catholic 14%, other Christian 25%
CURRENCY Bermuda dollar = 100 cents
MAIN EXPORTS Drugs (legal), medicines

BHUTAN

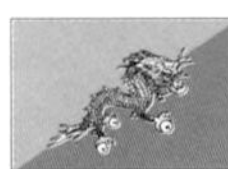

 The striking image on Bhutan's flag is explained by the name of this Himalayan kingdom in the local language, Druk Yil, which means 'land of the dragon'. The saffron colour stands for royal power and the orange-red for Buddhist spiritual power.

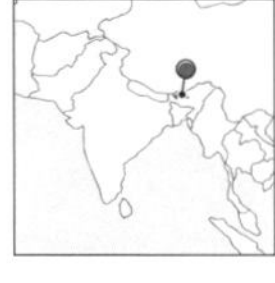

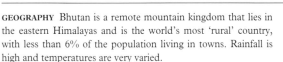

GEOGRAPHY Bhutan is a remote mountain kingdom that lies in the eastern Himalayas and is the world's most 'rural' country, with less than 6% of the population living in towns. Rainfall is high and temperatures are very varied.

HISTORY AND POLITICS Although Bhutan is ruled by a king, its foreign affairs are under Indian guidance following a treaty of 1949. There were small-scale pro-democracy demonstrations in 1990, but there has been little political progress since then.

ECONOMY Over 90% of the population are dependent on agriculture, producing mainly rice and maize as staple crops and fruit and cardamom as cash crops. Cement and talcum exports earn much-needed foreign exchange.

AREA 47,000 sq km [18,147 sq mls]
POPULATION 1,639,000
CAPITAL (POPULATION) Thimphu (30,000)
GOVERNMENT Constitutional monarchy
ETHNIC GROUPS Bhote 60%, Nepalese 25%
LANGUAGES Dzongkha (official, a Tibetan dialect), Sharchop, Bumthap, Nepali and English
RELIGIONS Buddhist 75%, Hindu 25%
CURRENCY Ngultrum = 100 chetrum
MAIN EXPORTS Cement, talcum, timber
URBAN POPULATION 6% of the population

BOLIVIA

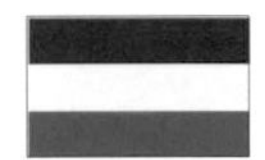

 Dating from liberation in 1825, the tricolour has been used as both national and merchant flag since 1888. The red stands for Bolivia's animals and the army's courage, the yellow for mineral resources and the green for its agricultural wealth.

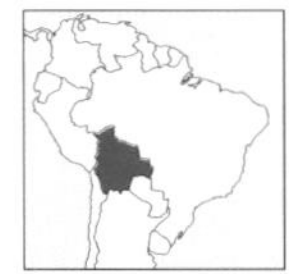

GEOGRAPHY Bolivia is landlocked and made up of a wide stretch of the Andes and a long, broad Oriente – part of the south-western fringe of the Amazon Basin. To the east lies the Altiplano, a high grassland plateau, which in prehistoric times was a great lake; Lake Titicaca, the highest navigable body of water in the world, lies at its northern end.

HISTORY AND POLITICS In pre-Conquest days Bolivia was the homeland of the Tiahuanaco culture (7th to 11th centuries AD) and was later absorbed into the Inca empire. The silver mines of the high Andean plain area were exploited by Spanish *conquistadores*. The local population seized independence in 1824. Today Bolivia is one of the poorest South American republics and is renowned for its political volatility.

ECONOMY Bolivia does have abundant natural resources, especially petroleum and natural gas but there is a lack of investment. The trade in cocaine may well account for two-thirds of the country's exports and employs 5% of the population; there are attempts to stifle this, with US help.

AREA 1,098,580 sq km [424,162 sq mls]
POPULATION 7,900,000
CAPITAL (POPULATION) La Paz (1,126,000)/ Sucre (131,000)
GOVERNMENT Unitary multiparty republic with a bicameral legislature
ETHNIC GROUPS Mestizo 31%, Quechua 25%, Aymara 17%, White 15%
LANGUAGES Spanish, Aymara, Quechua
RELIGIONS Roman Catholic 94%
CURRENCY Boliviano = 100 centavos
MAIN EXPORTS Tin, zinc, natural gas
POPULATION DENSITY 7 per sq km [19 per sq ml]

BOSNIA-HERZEGOVINA

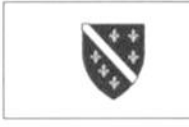

 The flag was adopted when independence was declared in April 1992 and has a shield recalling the ancient Bosnian monarchy of pre-Turkish times. The fleur-de-lis is thought to be derived from the lily specific to Bosnia, Lilium bosniacum.

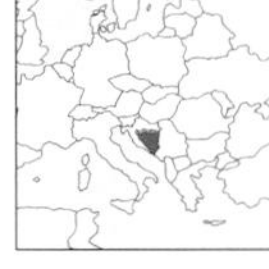

Bosnia-Herzegovina has been in a state of chaos since declaring independence in April 1992. The latest figures put its population at 49% Muslim, 31% Serb and 17% Croat – a mixture that has proved unworkable. At first the Muslim-dominated government allied itself uneasily with the Croat minority, but was at once under attack from the local Serbs, supported by their co-nationals from beyond Bosnia's borders. By early 1993, the Muslims controlled less than a third of the former federal republic and the capital, Sarajevo, became disputed territory. In 1995, warring parties agreed to a solution. This involved dividing the country into two self-governing provinces: a Bosnian-Serb one and a Muslim-Croat one, under a central, multi-ethnic government.

AREA 51,129 sq km [19,745 sq mls]
POPULATION 4,400,000
CAPITAL (POPULATION) Sarajevo (526,000)
ETHNIC GROUPS Muslim, Serb, Croat
LANGUAGES Serbo-Croat 99%
RELIGIONS Muslim 40%, Orthodox 31%, Roman Catholic 15%
CURRENCY Dinar = 100 paras
POPULATION DENSITY 86 per sq km [223 per sq ml]
LAND USE Arable 16%, grass 31%, forest 48%

BOTSWANA

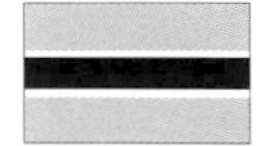

 Botswana's flag dates from independence from Britain in 1966. The white-black-white zebra stripe represents the racial harmony of the people and the coat of the zebra, the national animal. The blue symbolizes the country's most vital need – rainwater.

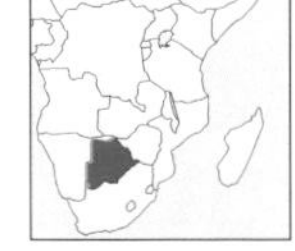

GEOGRAPHY More than half of Botswana's land area is covered by the Kalahari Desert, which stretches into Namibia and South Africa in the south-west. The desert is not uniform; occasional rainfall allows the growth of grasses and thorny scrub, on which cattle can graze. Much of the rest of the country is taken up by salt pans and the Okavango Swamp in the north-west.

HISTORY AND POLITICS Botswana was the British protectorate of Bechuanaland from 1885 to 1966, when it became independent after a peaceful six-year transition period. Political stability has been achieved since then, first under Seretse Khama and then under Quett Masire.

ECONOMY Large numbers of cattle are kept by the Bantu-speaking herdsmen, and provide the main export. Diamonds (Botswana is the world's third largest producer) and copper are mined in the east. Recently, tourism has become important: 17% of the land (Africa's highest figure) is set aside for wildlife conservation and game reserves and attracts some half a million visitors a year, particularly from South Africa.

AREA 581,730 sq km [224,606 sq mls]
POPULATION 1,481,000
CAPITAL (POPULATION) Gaborone (133,000)
GOVERNMENT Multiparty republic
ETHNIC GROUPS Tswana 76%, Shona 12%, San (Bushmen) 3%
LANGUAGES English (official), Setswana (Siswana, Tswana – national language)
RELIGIONS Traditional beliefs 50%, Christian (mainly Anglican) 30%
CURRENCY Pula = 100 thebe
MAIN EXPORTS Diamonds, copper-nickel matte, meat and meat products
MAIN IMPORTS Food, beverages, tobacco, machinery, electrical goods

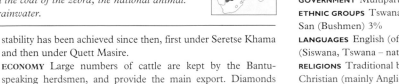

BRAZIL

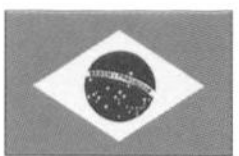

The sphere bears the motto 'Order and Progress' and its 27 stars, arranged in the pattern of the night sky over Rio de Janeiro, represent the states and federal district. Green symbolizes the nation's rainforests, and the yellow diamond represents its mineral wealth.

AREA 8,511,970 sq km [3,286,472 sq mls]
POPULATION 161,416,000
CAPITAL (POPULATION) Brasília (1,596,000)
GOVERNMENT Federal republic with a bicameral legislature
ETHNIC GROUPS White 53%, Mulatto 22%, Mestizo 12%, Black 11%, Amerindian
LANGUAGES Portuguese, Spanish, English, French, native dialects

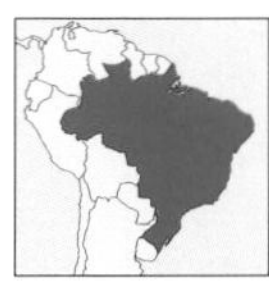

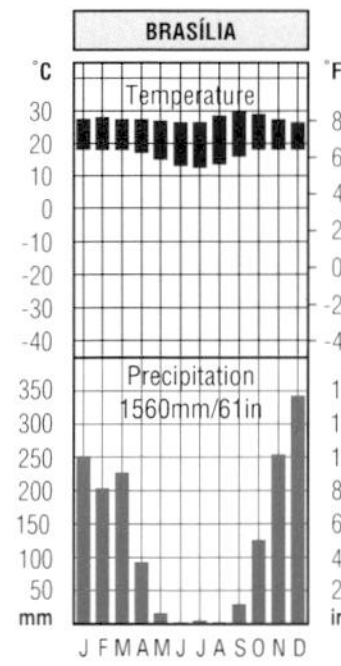

Brazil lies almost entirely within the tropics. The monthly temperatures are high – over 25°C [77°F] – and there is little annual variation. Brasília has only a 4°C [7°F] difference between July and October; Rio has twice this range. The hottest part of the country is in the northeast. Frosts do occur in the eastern highlands and in the far south.

GEOGRAPHY Brazil covers nearly 48% of South America and is the world's fifth largest country. In the north, the huge Amazon Basin covers the landscape, once an inland sea and now drained by a river system that carries one-fifth of the Earth's running water. The rainforest here is the world's largest, although it is being destroyed at an alarming rate, and the rest of the area is covered by an upland plateau of thorny scrub forest. In the centre and south of Brazil lies the Brazilian Highlands, a huge extent of hard crystalline rock deeply dissected into rolling uplands. Here the vegetation of wooded savanna (*campo cerrado*) covers 2 million sq km [770,000 sq mls]. The narrow coastal plain is fertile and swampy in places, with high rainfall all year. Over 60% of the population live in four southern and south-eastern states that make up only 17% of the total land area.

HISTORY AND POLITICS Brazil was 'discovered' by Pedro Alvarez Cabral in 1500 and gradually penetrated by Portuguese settlers and explorers during the 17th and 18th centuries. In 1822 Brazil declared itself independent from Portugal and established an empire, first under Pedro I and then ruled by his son, Pedro II, whose liberal policies included the abolition of slavery in 1888. In 1889 Brazil became a republic. Since then there have been dictatorships and military rule: between 1964 and 1985 there were five military presidents. A new constitution came into force in 1988, with a return to democracy in 1990.

ECONOMY Brazil is one of the world's largest farming countries, with agriculture employing a quarter of the population and providing 40% of exports. The main agricultural exports are coffee, sugar, soya beans, orange juice concentrates, beef, cocoa, poultry, sisal, tobacco, maize and cotton. There are also huge mineral resources, particularly in Minas Gerais and the Amazon area, including bauxite, tin, iron ore, chrome, nickel, uranium, industrial diamonds, platinum and manganese.

BRUNEI

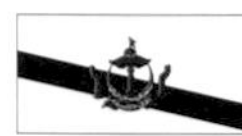

The yellow background represents the flag of the Sultan, with the black and white stripes standing for his two main advisers (wazirs). The arms contain the inscription in Arabic 'Brunei, Gate of Peace' and a crescent, the symbol of Islam.

AREA 5,770 sq km [2,228 sq mls]
POPULATION 284,000
CAPITAL (POPULATION) Bandar Seri Begawan (55,000)
GOVERNMENT Constitutional monarchy with an advisory council
ETHNIC GROUPS Malay 69%, Chinese 18%, Indian
LANGUAGES Malay and English (both official), Chinese
RELIGIONS Muslim 63%, Buddhist 14%, Christian 10%
CURRENCY Brunei dollar = 100 cents

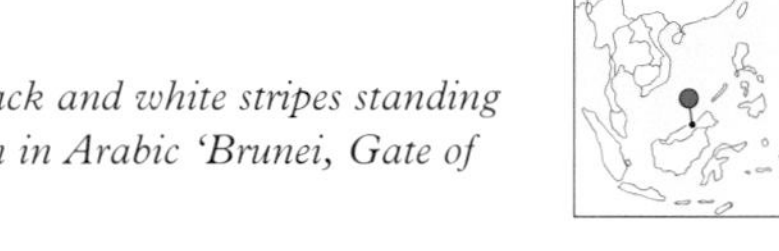

GEOGRAPHY Brunei comprises two enclaves on the north-east coast of Borneo. The landscape rises from humid plains to forested mountains over 1,800 m [6,000 ft] high along the Malaysian border. The climate is tropical with high rainfall and temperatures varying between 24°C [75°F] and 30°C [86°F].

HISTORY AND POLITICS Brunei was a British protectorate from 1888 to 1971 and still retains very close ties with the UK. The Sultan and his family now rule Brunei by ancient hereditary rights and the Sultan himself, through the oil and gas revenues, is thought to be one of the world's richest men.

ECONOMY The oil and gas fields lie offshore and account for 70% of GDP and even more of exports earnings (oil 41%, gas 53%). Machinery, manufactures and foodstuffs are imported. There is no income tax, and free health services and education.

BULGARIA

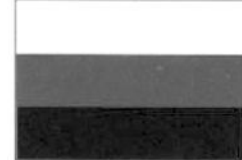

The Slav colours of white, green and red were used in the Bulgarian flag from 1878. The national emblem, incorporating a lion (a symbol of Bulgaria since the 14th century), was first added to the flag in 1947, but the crest is now only added for official government occasions.

AREA 110,910 sq km [42,822 sq mls]
POPULATION 9,020,000
CAPITAL (POPULATION) Sofia (1,221,000)
GOVERNMENT Multiparty republic
ETHNIC GROUPS Bulgarian 85%, Turkish 9%, Gypsy 3%, Macedonian 3%, Armenian, Romanian, Greek
LANGUAGES Bulgarian (official), Turkish, Romany
RELIGIONS Eastern Orthodox 80%, Sunni Muslim
CURRENCY Lev = 100 stotinki
MAIN EXPORTS Machinery and equipment 57%, foodstuffs, wine and tobacco 14%
MAIN IMPORTS Machinery and equipment 43%, fuels, mineral raw materials

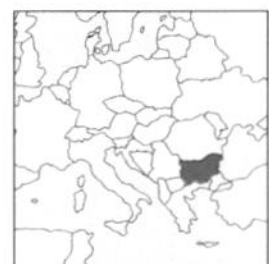

GEOGRAPHY Bulgaria lies in south-eastern Europe, with a coastline on the Black Sea. The Balkan Mountains (Stara Planina), in central Bulgaria, rise to heights of over 2,000 m [6,500 ft]. These are separated from the Rhodopi Mountains in the south by the central valley of the River Maritsa, which is the main farming region. The climate is varied, with the south generally warmer and drier than the north.

HISTORY AND POLITICS From 1396 Bulgaria was ruled by Islamic Turks as part of the Ottoman Empire; in 1878 Russian forces helped liberate the country and it became an independent country. After World War II, Bulgaria was heavily dependent on the USSR and was one of the last Communist governments to fall in the early 1990s. It has now moved towards establishing a free-market economy.

ECONOMY Fertile soils means that agriculture is important, with the most productive land found on the lowland plains. Crops include maize, wheat and fruits. Attar of roses is exported worldwide to the cosmetics industry. However, Bulgaria's economy suffers many problems such as inflation, rising unemployment, strikes and a large foreign debt.

BURKINA FASO

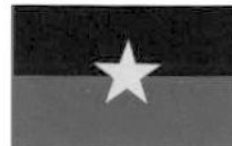

Formerly Upper Volta, this country adopted a new name and flag in 1984, replacing those used since independence from France in 1960. The colours are the Pan-African shades of Burkina Faso's neighbours, representing the desire for unity.

AREA 274,200 sq km [105,869 sq mls]
POPULATION 10,326,000
CAPITAL (POPULATION) Ouagadougou (634,000)
GOVERNMENT Multiparty republic
ETHNIC GROUPS Mossi 48%, Mande 8%, Fulani 8%
LANGUAGES French (official)
RELIGIONS Traditional beliefs 45%, Sunni Muslim 43%, Christian 12%
CURRENCY CFA franc = 100 centimes
MAIN EXPORTS Ginned cotton, livestock
MAIN IMPORTS Transport equipment, non-electrical machinery, petroleum products and cereals

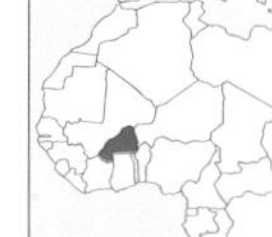

GEOGRAPHY Landlocked Burkina Faso ('land of upright people') is a West African country made up mostly of low plateaux. The valleys, drained by the Black, Red and White Volta rivers, have the most fertile and best watered lands. Among these is the 'W' national park, shared with Niger and Benin.

HISTORY AND POLITICS Burkina Faso is the successor to Mossi, an early West African state dating from 1100. In 1919 Upper Volta was created as a French colony; it became independent in 1960 before changing its name to Burkina Faso in 1984. Since then there has been a long period of military rule, broken in 1991, when the first elections for a decade were held and a new constitution was drawn up.

ECONOMY With low and erratic rainfall, thin, eroded soils and a lack of natural resources, the country remains very poor and heavily reliant on aid. Cotton, millet, guinea corn and groundnuts are grown for food; migrants working in other countries send money back and provide most of the foreign income. Manganese and gold mining could be developed.

BURMA (MYANMAR)

BURMA (MYANMAR)

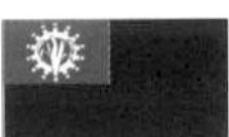

The colours were adopted following independence from Britain in 1948. The Socialist symbol, added in 1974, includes a ring of 14 stars for the country's states. The gearwheel represents industry and the rice plant symbolizes agriculture.

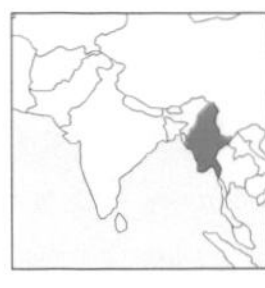

GEOGRAPHY Burma's core area is a great structural depression, largely drained by the Chindwin and Irrawaddy rivers. Within this, the region between Prome and Mandalay is a 'dry zone', sheltered from the monsoon and receiving less than 1,000 mm [40 in] of rain a year. To the west are the fold mountains of the Arakan Yoma, and to the east rises the Shan Plateau. In the south-east, along the isthmus that leads on to the Malay Peninsula, are the Tenasserim uplands, with hundreds of islands along the coast. More than 60% of the country is forested, with teak as the indigenous species.

HISTORY AND POLITICS Burma was annexed by Britain in 1895 and separated from India as a crown colony in 1937. In 1948 it became an independent republic and left the Commonwealth. A military dictatorship was replaced by a one-party state in 1974 and 'The Burmese Way to Socialism' has seen rigid state control, Buddhism and international isolation. Prosperity has turned to poverty. The results of a multiparty election in 1990 were disallowed by the ruling junta and much of the country remains closed to foreigners.

ECONOMY More than 60% of the working population are farmers and the largest crop is rice (until 1964 Burma was the world's leading exporter). There are also reserves of oil and natural gas. However, more than 35% of the budget is spent on the suppression of political opposition and of human rights.

AREA 676,577 sq km [261,228 sq mls]
POPULATION 46,580,000
CAPITAL (POPULATION) Rangoon (2,513,000)
GOVERNMENT Transitional government
ETHNIC GROUPS Burman 69%, Shan 9%, Karen 6%, Rakhine 5%, Mon 2%, Chin 2%, Kachin 1%
LANGUAGES Burmese (official), English
RELIGIONS Buddhist 85%, Christian 5%, Muslim 4%, Hindu, animist
CURRENCY Kyat = 100 pyas
MAIN EXPORTS Rice 41%, teak 24%, metals and ores 9%
MAIN IMPORTS Machinery 18%, base metals 10%, transport equipment 8%
POPULATION DENSITY 69 per sq km [178 per sq ml]
URBAN POPULATION 25% of population

BURUNDI

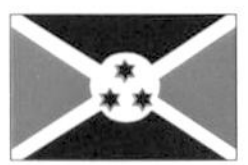

Burundi adopted this unusual design when it became a republic in 1966. The three stars symbolize the nation's motto 'Unity, Work, Progress'. Green represents hope for the future, red the struggle for independence, and white the desire for peace.

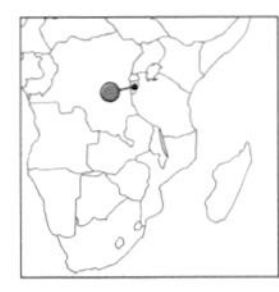

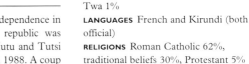

GEOGRAPHY From the captial of Bujumbura on Lake Tanganyika a great escarpment rises in the west to the rift highlands (reaching 2,670 m [8,769 ft]) and makes up most of Burundi. In the east there are plateaux with steep slopes and swamps. The climate is cool, with two wet seasons. This small country must support a dense population and employment is often sought in neighbouring countries.

HISTORY AND POLITICS In 1897 the region became part of the German East African colony and from 1919 it formed part of Ruanda-Urundi, a Belgian trust territory. After independence in 1962 a monarchy existed until 1966 when a republic was established. Ancient rivalries exist between the Hutu and Tutsi tribes and there was a massacre of 20,000 Hutu in 1988. A coup in October 1993 by the army and Tutsi tribe saw the murder of the first democratically elected president.

ECONOMY Coffee is widely grown for export throughout the highlands (80% of total earnings). Cotton and tea are also exported, and goats make up the largest numbers of livestock.

AREA 27,830 sq km [10,745 sq mls]
POPULATION 6,412,000
CAPITAL (POPULATION) Bujumbura (235,000)
GOVERNMENT Transitional government
ETHNIC GROUPS Hutu 85%, Tutsi 14%, Twa 1%
LANGUAGES French and Kirundi (both official)
RELIGIONS Roman Catholic 62%, traditional beliefs 30%, Protestant 5%
CURRENCY Burundi franc = 100 centimes
MAIN EXPORTS Coffee, tea, cotton
POPULATION DENSITY 230 per sq km [597 per sq ml]
URBAN POPULATION 7% of population

CAMBODIA

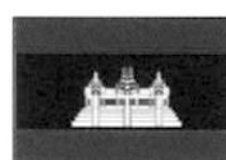

As well as being associated with Communism and revolution, red is the traditional colour of Cambodia. The silhouette is the historic temple of Angkor Wat. The blue symbolizes the water resources which are so vital to the people of Cambodia.

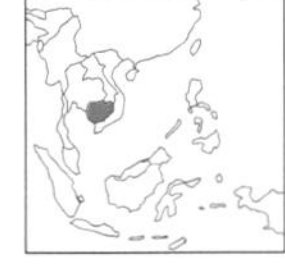

GEOGRAPHY At the heart of Cambodia is a wide basin drained by the Mekong River, at the centre of which lies the Tonlé Sap ('Great Lake'), a former arm of the sea surrounded by a broad plain. During the rainy season and period of high river water between June and October the lake more than doubles its size to become the largest freshwater lake in Asia. Up to 90% of the population live on these fertile plains, while in the north the Phanom Dangrek uplands bound the country with a prominent sandstone escarpment. Three-quarters of Cambodia is forested and there is a tropical monsoon climate.

HISTORY AND POLITICS The Tonlé Sap lowlands were the cradle of the Khmer Empire, which lasted from 802 to 1432, during which time the great temple of Angkor Wat was built (together with Angkor Thom, these 600 Hindu temples form the world's largest group of religious buildings). Cambodia was under French rule from 1863 to 1954, when it became independent. The ruthless dictatorship of the Khmer Rouge and several civil wars in the 1970s and 1980s left Cambodia devastated and up to 2.5 million people dead. Following UN-supervised elections in 1993 a government of national unity has been formed with Prince Sihanouk becoming monarch.

ECONOMY The economy is based largely on agriculture (rice and maize) and rubber plantations, but these have been widely destroyed in the civil wars. There are few mineral resources.

AREA 181,040 sq km [69,900 sq mls]
POPULATION 10,452,000
CAPITAL (POPULATION) Phnom Penh (900,000)
GOVERNMENT Constitutional monarchy with a unicameral legislature
ETHNIC GROUPS Khmer 93%, Vietnamese, Chinese, Cham, Thai, Lao, Kola
LANGUAGES Khmer (official), French
RELIGIONS Buddhist 88%, Muslim 2%
CURRENCY Riel = 100 sen
MAIN EXPORTS Iron and steel, rubber manufactures
MAIN IMPORTS Machinery and transport equipment
POPULATION DENSITY 58 per sq km [150 per sq ml]
URBAN POPULATION 12% of population

CAMEROON

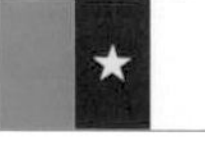

Cameroon's flag employs the Pan-African colours, as used by many former African colonies. The design, with the yellow liberty star, dates from 1975 and is based on the tricolour adopted in 1957 before independence from France in 1960.

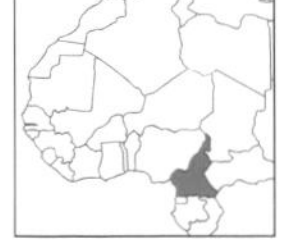

GEOGRAPHY Located in west-central Africa on the Gulf of Guinea, Cameroon has a mixture of vegetation, with desert to the north, dense tropical rainforest in the south and dry savanna in the middle. The mountains on the border with Nigeria are mostly volcanic in origin, including Mt Cameroon (4,070 m [13,353 ft]), which is sometimes active.

HISTORY AND POLITICS The word Cameroon comes from the Portuguese *camarões* – prawns fished by Portuguese explorers in the coastal estuaries in the 1400s. It was ruled as a German protectorate from 1884, but divided between France (mainly) and Britain. French Cameroon became independent in 1960 and southern British Cameroon in 1961; a republic was created in 1984. Since 1987 President Paul Biya has led a repressive regime, but elections were held in 1992. Cameroon joined the Commonwealth in November 1995.

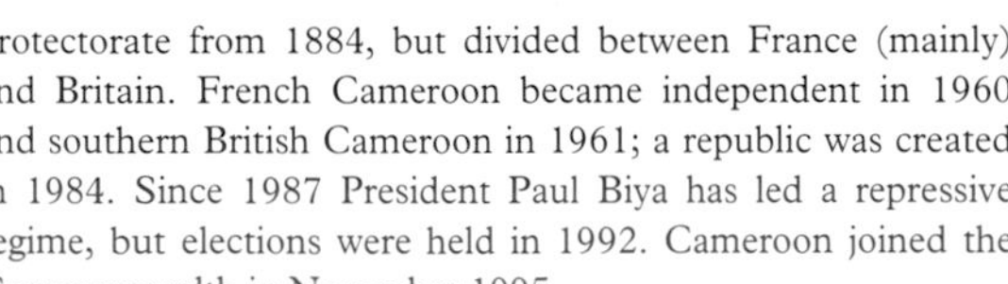

ECONOMY Cameroon is one of tropical Africa's richer nations, with self-sufficiency in food. There is diverse agriculture; coffee, cocoa and aluminium products are the chief exports.

AREA 475,440 sq km [183,567 sq mls]
POPULATION 13,232,000
CAPITAL (POPULATION) Yaoundé (750,000)
GOVERNMENT Multiparty republic with a unicameral legislature
ETHNIC GROUPS Fang 20%, Bamileke and Mamum 19%, Duala, Luanda and Basa 15%, Fulani 10%
LANGUAGES French and English (both official), Sudanic, Bantu
RELIGIONS Animist 25%, Sunni Muslim 22%, Roman Catholic 21%, Protestant 18%
CURRENCY CFA franc = 100 centimes
URBAN POPULATION 42% of population

CANADA

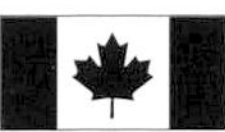

The British Red Ensign was used from 1892 but became unpopular with Canada's French community. After many attempts to find a more acceptable design, the present flag – featuring the simple maple leaf emblem – was finally adopted in 1965.

AREA 9,976,140 sq km [3,851,788 sq mls]
POPULATION 29,972,000
CAPITAL (POPULATION) Ottawa (921,000)
GOVERNMENT Federal multiparty republic with a bicameral legislature
ETHNIC GROUPS British 40%, French 27%, other European 20%, Asiatic 2%, Amerindian/Inuit (Eskimo) 2%
LANGUAGES English 63% and French 25% (both official)
RELIGIONS Roman Catholic 47%, Protestant 41%, Eastern Orthodox, Jewish, Muslim, Hindu
CURRENCY Canadian dollar = 100 cents
MAIN EXPORTS Passenger vehicles, trucks and parts 26%, food, feed, beverages and tobacco 6%, timber 5%, newspaper print 5%, wood pulp 4%, petroleum 4%, natural gas 3%, industrial machinery 3%

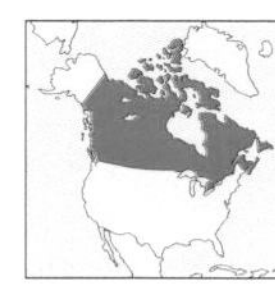

GEOGRAPHY Canada is the world's second largest country (after Russia) and has an even longer coastline (250,00 km [155,000 mls]). Some 80% of the land is uninhabited and there are huge areas of virtually unoccupied mountains, forests, tundra and polar desert in the north and west. To the east lie the Maritime provinces of Newfoundland, Nova Scotia, New Brunswick, Prince Edward Islands and Québec; they are clustered about the Gulf of St Lawrence and based on ancient worn-down mountains – the northern extension of the Appalachians – and the eastern uptilted edge of the even older Canadian Shield. The central province of Ontario borders the Great Lakes and further to the west are the prairie provinces of Manitoba, Saskatchewan and Alberta. Most of the population is to be found on the fertile farmland in the south of these provinces and in Québec and Ontario. A large part of the Rocky Mountains are found in south-west Alberta, with peaks rising to over 4,000 m [13,120 ft]. In the huge northern area tundra replaces boreal forest; here, glaciation has scoured the rocks and although the surface of the soil thaws in summer, the subsoil remains frozen.

HISTORY AND POLITICS John Cabot's discovery of North America in 1497 began the annex of lands and wealth, with France and Britain the main contenders. The French established themselves first by discovering the St Lawrence River in 1534 and then the Great Lakes. British settlers based themselves on the Atlantic coast and in the 1780s moved north from the USA into Nova Scotia, New Brunswick and Lower Canada.

Eventually, the bulk of Canada east and west became predominantly British, while the fertile lowlands of the St Lawrence Basin and on the Shield remained French. The union of British Upper Canada and French Lower Canada was sealed by the Confederation of 1867 and Canada became largely self-governing, although it remained technically subject to the British Imperial parliament until 1931. The creation of the British Commonwealth made the country a sovereign nation under the crown. The proximity of the USA and its economic dominance has caused problems, as has the persistence of French culture in Québec province. In 1995, Québeckers voted against a move to make Québec a sovereign state, but the majority was less than 1% and this issue seems unlikely to disappear.

ECONOMY Agriculture plays an important role with 50% of produce being exported. Industry has transformed some of the more remote areas: cheap hydroelectric power in Québec and Ontario, coupled with improved transmission technology, has encouraged the further development of wood pulp and paper industries, even in distant parts of the northern forests, and stimulated industry and commerce in the south. Tourism is important (35.7 million people visited Canada in 1992), while 90% of the country's oil output comes from Alberta. Trade with the USA represents the world's largest single bilateral trade route. There is still potential for development in the north, with abundant mineral resources under the frozen subsoil, but the cost of their extraction and transportation would be very high.

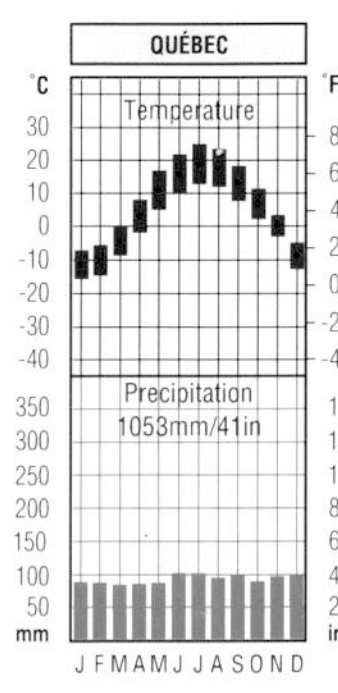

The effect of the Great Lakes is felt in the Ontario Peninsula with slighly warmer winters than in Québec. The temperatures in northern Canada are violent; along the Arctic Circle the mean monthly temperatures for over seven months are below freezing. In Québec rainfall is moderate throughout the year, with some snow.

CANARY ISLANDS

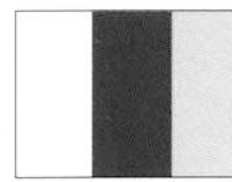

As a Spanish Autonomous Region, the Canary Islands have their own arms and flag. This flag was adopted in 1982 on the basis of colours used by the dominant political movement. The arms can be added in the centre.

AREA 7,273 sq km [2,807 sq mls]
POPULATION 1,700,000
CAPITAL (POPULATION) Las Palmas (342,000)/Santa Cruz (223,000)
GOVERNMENT Spanish Autonomous Region
LANGUAGES Spanish
RELIGIONS Roman Catholic
POPULATION DENSITY 234 per sq km [606 per sq ml]

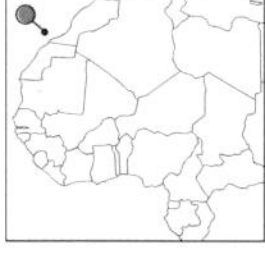

Ceded to Spain from Portugal in 1479, the Canary Islands comprise seven large islands and numerous small volcanic islands situated off southern Morocco, the nearest within 100 km [60 mls] of the mainland. The islands have a subtropical climate, dry at sea level but damp on higher ground. Soils are fertile and there is large-scale irrigation. Industries include food and fish processing, boat-building and crafts; the islands are also a year-round major tourist destination.

CAPE VERDE

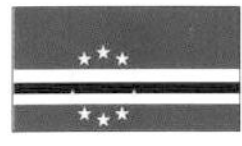

This new flag was adopted in September 1992 to replace the red-yellow-green one adopted in 1975. The flag was adopted to symbolize the end of the rule of the 'Partido Africano da Independencia de Cabo Verde' and the election of the Movement for Democracy.

AREA 4,030 sq km [1,556 sq mls]
POPULATION 386,000
CAPITAL (POPULATION) Praia (69,000)
GOVERNMENT Multiparty republic
ETHNIC GROUPS Mixed 71%, Black 28%, White 1%
LANGUAGES Portuguese (official), Crioulo
RELIGIONS Roman Catholic 97%, Protestant 2%
CURRENCY Cape Verde escudo = 100 centavos
POPULATION DENSITY 96 per sq km [248 per sq ml]

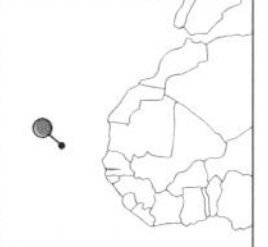

GEOGRAPHY Cape Verde is an archipelago of ten large and five small islands off the coast of Senegal. They are volcanic and mainly mountainous, with steep cliffs and rocky headlands; the highest, Fogo, rises to 2,829 m [9,281 ft] and is active. The islands are tropical, hot for most of the year and mainly dry at sea level. Endemic droughts have killed 75,000 since 1900.

HISTORY, POLITICS AND ECONOMY Portuguese since the 15th century, the colony became an overseas territory in 1951 and independent in 1975. In the first multiparty elections in 1991, the ruling socialist PAICV was beaten by a newly legalized opposition. Poor soils and the lack of surface water have hindered development and much food is imported. Exports comprise mainly bananas (36%) and tuna (30%); there is a dependency on foreign aid and much emigration.

CAYMAN ISLANDS

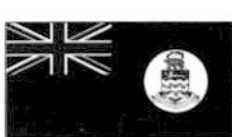

As a British Dependency, the Cayman Islands fly the Blue Ensign with a white roundel, depicting the islands' coat of arms in the fly. The coat of arms shows an English heraldic lion, with the blue and white wavy lines representing the sea.

AREA 259 sq km [100 sq mls]
POPULATION 31,000
CAPITAL (POPULATION) George Town (13,000)
ETHNIC GROUPS Mixed 40%, White 20%, Black 20%
LANGUAGES English (official)
RELIGIONS Christian
CURRENCY Caymanian dollar = 100 cents
POPULATION DENSITY 120 per sq km [310 per sq ml]

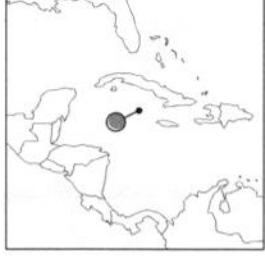

The Cayman Islands comprise three low-lying islands south of Cuba, with the capital George Town on the biggest, Grand Cayman. A dependent territory of Britain (Crown Colony since 1959), they were occupied mainly with farming and fishing until the 1960s, when an economic revolution turned them into the world's biggest offshore financial centre, offering a tax haven to 18,000 companies and 450 banks. The luxury tourist industry accounts for more than 70% of the official GDP and foreign earnings. An immigrant labour force, chiefly Jamaican, makes up about a fifth of the population.

CENTRAL AFRICAN REPUBLIC

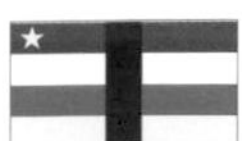

 The national flag of the Central African Republic, adopted in 1958, combines the green, yellow and red of Pan-African unity with the blue, white and red of the flag of the country's former colonial ruler, France.

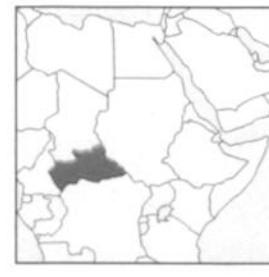

GEOGRAPHY Central African Republic is landlocked, lying on an undulating plateau between the Chad and Zaïre (Congo) basins. The vegetation is mostly savanna and the climate is tropical, with day temperatures rarely falling below 30°C [86°F].

HISTORY AND POLITICS The country became an independent republic in 1960, having been part of the colony of French Equatorial Africa since 1910. The repressive regime of Jean-Bedel Bokassa lasted from 1976 to 1979, when the army took over. Multiparty elections took place in 1993.

ECONOMY Only 5% of the land is cultivated, yet 90% of the population are involved in agriculture, mainly for subsistence. Coffee, cotton, groundnuts and diamonds are exported.

AREA 622,980 sq km [240,533 sq mls]
POPULATION 3,294,000
CAPITAL (POPULATION) Bangui (597,000)
GOVERNMENT Multiparty republic
ETHNIC GROUPS Banda 29%, Baya 25%, Ngbandi 11%, Azande 10%, Sara, Mbaka
LANGUAGES French (official), Sango (linguafranca)
RELIGIONS Traditional beliefs 57%, Christian 35%, Sunni Muslim 8%
CURRENCY CFA franc = 100 centimes
URBAN POPULATION 38% of population

CHAD

 Adopted in 1959, Chad's colours are a compromise between the French and Pan-African flags. Blue represents the sky, the streams of the south and hope, yellow represents the sun and the Sahara Desert in the north, and red represents national sacrifice.

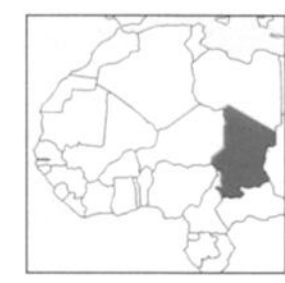

GEOGRAPHY Chad is Africa's largest landlocked country, with part of the Sahara Desert in the north (containing the volcanic Tibesti Mountains). In the south there is wooded savanna, while Lake Chad, in the west, is the focal point of much of Chad's drainage, affecting two-thirds of the country.

HISTORY AND POLITICS After independence from France in 1960 Chad has been plagued by almost continuous civil wars, primarily between the Muslim Arab north and the Christian and animist black south. In 1973 Libya, supporters of the Arabs, occupied the mineral-rich Aozou Strip in the north and tried further incursions in 1983 and 1987. In 1994 the International Court of Justice ruled in favour of Chad, but Libyan troops remained within the strip.

ECONOMY Over 90% of the population work in crop cultivation or herding and there is little industry. A large foreign debt and frequent droughts have caused much poverty.

AREA 1,284,000 sq km [495,752 sq mls]
POPULATION 6,314,000
CAPITAL (POPULATION) Ndjamena (530,000)
GOVERNMENT Transitional government
ETHNIC GROUPS Bagirmi, Sara and Kreish 31%, Sudanic Arab 26%, Teda, Mbum
LANGUAGES French and Arabic (official), but more than 100 languages and dialects are spoken
RELIGIONS Sunni Muslim 44%, animist 38%, various Christian 17%
CURRENCY CFA franc = 100 centimes
MAIN EXPORTS Cotton, live cattle, animal products

CHILE

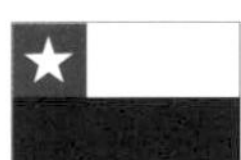

 Inspired by the US Stars and Stripes, the flag was designed by an American serving with the Chilean Army in 1817 and adopted that year. White represents the snow-capped Andes, blue the sky and red the blood of the nation's patriots.

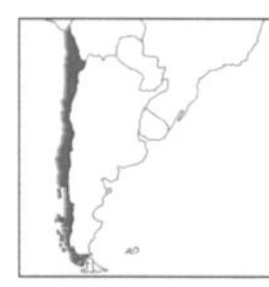

GEOGRAPHY Chile runs down the west coast of South America, extending from latitude 17°30'S (inside the Tropics) to 55°50'S at Cape Horn, and is the world's thinnest country. There are three parallel zones: from the Bolivian border runs an extension of the high plateau of Bolivia, with several volcanic peaks of more than 6,000 m [19,680 ft]; there is then a sheltered and fertile central valley, with 60% of the population living in an 800 km [500 ml] stretch of land south of Santiago. Finally, the parallel coastal ranges create a rolling, hilly belt, rising no more than 3,000 m [10,000 ft].

HISTORY AND POLITICS A Spanish colony from the 16th century, Chile developed as a mining enterprise in the north and a series of vast ranches, or haciendas, in the fertile central region. Chile became independent in 1818. In 1970 Chile had the world's first democratically elected Marxist government under President Allende; this was overthrown in a CIA-backed military coup in 1973 and General Pinochet took control, establishing a repressive regime. Free elections finally took place in 1989 and there has been a gradual return to democracy.

ECONOMY Chile's economy continues to depend on agriculture (crops include wheat, barley and rice), fishing (anchovetas, mackerel and sardines) and, particularly, mining: the country is the world's leading producer of copper ore (22% of the world total) and it accounts for nearly half of all export earnings.

AREA 756,950 sq km [292,258 sq mls]
POPULATION 14,271,000
CAPITAL (POPULATION) Santiago (5,343,000)
GOVERNMENT Multiparty republic with a bicameral legislature
ETHNIC GROUPS Mestizo 92%, Amerindian 7%
LANGUAGES Spanish (official)
RELIGIONS Roman Catholic 80%, Protestant 6%
CURRENCY Peso = 100 centavos
MAIN EXPORTS Copper, iron, molybdenum, nitrate, pulp and paper, fishmeal, fruit
POPULATION DENSITY 19 per sq km [49 per sq ml]
URBAN POPULATION 86% of population
ADULT LITERACY 93%

CHINA

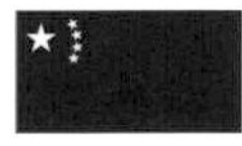

 Red, the traditional colour of both China and Communism, was chosen for the People's Republic flag in 1949. The large star represents the Communist Party programme; the small stars represent the four principal social classes.

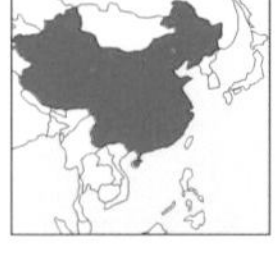

GEOGRAPHY China is the world's most populous country, with its population making up 20% of the world's total, and its land area is the world's third largest. It also has the greatest number of international frontiers in the world (15), but its huge size and complex landscape have meant that one of the main determining influences on the evolution of Chinese civilization has been its geographical isolation from the rest of the world. Landscapes include two intersecting mountain chains, one stretching from the north-east to the south-west, the other from east to west; in the south the Yangtze delta is made up of large lakes; and in the south-west, the Red Basin of Sichuan (Szechwan) is protected by high mountains and, with its mild climate and fertile soils, is one of the most densely populated and productive regions of China.

HISTORY AND POLITICS The earliest Chinese civilization began on the North China Plain over 4,000 years ago, but it was not until the 3rd century BC that China was unified into a centrally administered empire. The Great Wall of China, the world's longest fortification at 6,400 km [4,000 mls] long, was completed under the Ch'in dynasty (221–206 BC). Over the centuries the population has gradually moved from the north to the warmer and more productive south, often accelerated by northern invasions. China became a republic in 1912, from when followed a long period of anarchy until the Communists declared a People's Republic of China in October 1949. Under the centrally planned economy and despite many problems, order was brought to China and living standards raised.

ECONOMY Although only 10% of the land is suitable for agriculture, farmers and their families make up 73% of the population and China is the world's leading producer of rice. Since 1976 industrialization has become important, with sufficient resources in oil, coal and iron ore to support an independent economy.

AREA 9,596,960 sq km [3,705,386 sq mls]
POPULATION 1,226,944,000
CAPITAL (POPULATION) Beijing (6,690,000)
GOVERNMENT Single-party Communist State
ETHNIC GROUPS Han (Chinese) 93%, 55 others
LANGUAGES Mandarin Chinese; local dialects spoken in the south and west

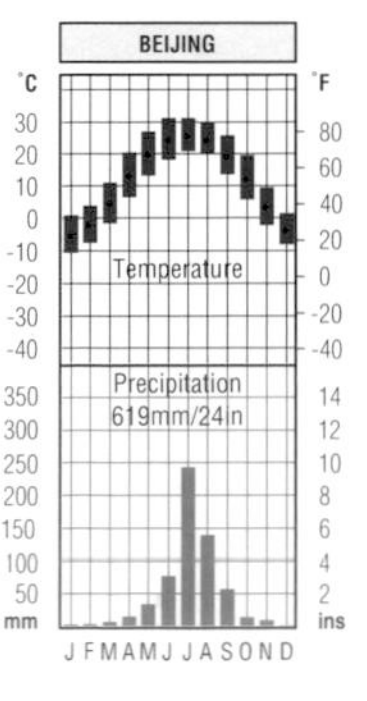

China's climate is controlled by the air masses of Asia and the Pacific, and the mountains in the west. In winter the cold, dry Siberian air blows southwards. In summer the tropical Pacific air dominates, bringing rain and high temperatures. Annual rain decreases from over 2,000 mm [80 in] in the south to the desert conditions of the north-west.

CROATIA

COLOMBIA

Colombia's colours – showing the (yellow) land of the nation separated by the (blue) sea from the tyranny of Spain, whose rule the people fought with their (red) blood – are shared by Ecuador and Venezuela. It was first used in 1806.

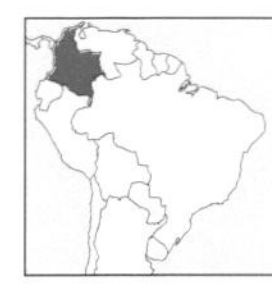

GEOGRAPHY The Andes cross Colombia from south to north, fanning out into three ranges with two intervening fertile valleys, in which some three-quarters of the population live. North-west of the mountains lies the broad Atlantic plain crossed by many rivers. The Andean foothills to the east, falling away into the Orinoco and Amazon basins and densely covered with rainforest, occupy about two-thirds of the total land area. The tropical climate is affected by the altitude of the Andes, causing lower temperatures and increased rainfall.

HISTORY AND POLITICS Christopher Columbus sighted what was to become Colombia in 1499, and the Spanish conquest of the territory began ten years later. Independence was gained in 1819, and since the 19th century the two political parties (Conservatives and Liberals) have alternated in power. There have been two civil wars (1899–1902 and 1949–57), in which some 400,000 people have been killed. A coalition in 1957 was unsuccessful and led to the election of a Liberal president in 1986, but there is still political instability.

ECONOMY The variety of climates and conditions result in many crops, including coffee, bananas and cotton. There are huge coal reserves, as well as gold, silver and emeralds. Drugs, however, may be the country's biggest industry.

AREA 1,138,910 sq km [439,733 sq mls]
POPULATION 34,948,000
CAPITAL (POPULATION) Bogotá (5,132,000)
GOVERNMENT Multiparty republic
ETHNIC GROUPS Mestizo 68%, White 20%, Amerindian 7%, Black 5%
LANGUAGES Spanish (official), over 100 Indian languages and dialects
RELIGIONS Roman Catholic 95%
CURRENCY Peso = 100 centavos
MAIN EXPORTS Coffee 43%, crude petroleum 8%, bananas 6%, cotton 3%
MAIN IMPORTS Machinery 28%, chemicals 18%, vehicles 13%
POPULATION DENSITY 31 per sq km [79 per sq ml]
URBAN POPULATION 71% of population

COMOROS

Since independence in 1975 a flag depicting a crescent and four stars has been flown. This latest design, adopted in 1978, shows the crescent representing the Muslim faith, and the stars representing the four islands, on a plain green background, representing Islam.

The Comoros are three large mountainous islands and several smaller coral islands lying between Madagascar and the East African coast. Formerly a French overseas territory, the Comoros became independent following a referendum in 1974.

Fertile soils, originally forested, are now mostly under subsistence agriculture and produce coconuts, coffee, cocoa and spices, with vanilla accounting for 78% of exports. The islands remain one of the world's poorest countries.

AREA 2,230 sq km [861 sq mls]
POPULATION 654,000
CAPITAL (POPULATION) Moroni (22,000)
GOVERNMENT Islamic republic
ETHNIC GROUPS Mainly mixture of Arab, Bantu and Malagasy peoples
LANGUAGES Shaafi (Swahili dialect), Malagasy, French
RELIGIONS Sunni Muslim 86%, Roman Catholic 14%

CONGO

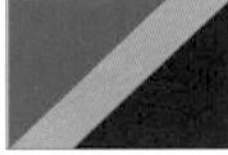

The People's Republic of the Congo was created in 1970, ten years after it achieved independence from France, becoming Africa's first Communist state. Marxism was officially abandoned in 1990 and this new flag was adopted.

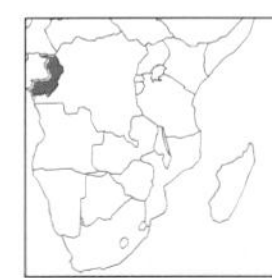

GEOGRAPHY Congo lies across the Equator, but only the near-coastal Mayombe ridges and the east-central and northern parts of the Congo basin have a truly equatorial climate and vegetation, with swamps and rainforests. The climate is hot all year round and there is heavy rainfall.

HISTORY AND POLITICS Part of French Equatorial Africa until 1960 when it gained independence, Congo became Africa's first declared Communist state in 1970. Marxism was officially abandoned in 1990 and elections were held in 1992 to create a multiparty republic, with further elections in 1993.

ECONOMY The vast deposits of offshore oil have become the main source of revenue; there are also reserves of diamonds, lead and copper. About a third of the workforce work in subsistence agriculture, mainly for cassava, but also bananas and maize. The timber industry is potentially important, but is hampered by a lack of transport.

AREA 342,000 sq km [132,046 sq mls]
POPULATION 2,593,000
CAPITAL (POPULATION) Brazzaville (938,000)
GOVERNMENT Multiparty republic
ETHNIC GROUPS Kongo 52%, Teke 17%, Mboshi 12%, Mbete 5%
LANGUAGES French (official), Kongo, Teke, Ubangi
RELIGIONS Roman Catholic 54%, Protestant 24%
CURRENCY CFA franc = 100 centimes
MAIN EXPORTS Petroleum, timber, diamonds
MAIN IMPORTS Machinery, iron, steel

COSTA RICA

Dating from 1848, Costa Rica's ('rich coast') national flag is based on the blue/white/blue sequence of the flag of the Central American Federation (see Guatemala), which is itself based on the Argentinian flag, but with an additional red stripe in the centre.

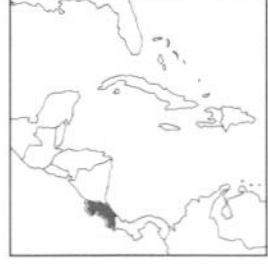

GEOGRAPHY Three mountain ranges running the length of the country make up the skeleton landscape and provide fertile uplands for growing crops. There are coastlines with both the Pacific Ocean and Caribbean Sea, where the climate is hot and humid and there are thick forests.

HISTORY, POLITICS AND ECONOMY With the first free elections in Central America in 1890, Costa Rica established a record of democratic and stable government and is exceptional among the other Central American republics. Coffee is the most important crop; together with bananas, they supply about half of the country's overseas earnings. Cattle are raised in the far north-west and there are reserves of gold and silver.

AREA 51,100 sq km [19,730 sq mls]
POPULATION 3,436,000
CAPITAL (POPULATION) San José (303,000)
GOVERNMENT Multiparty republic
ETHNIC GROUPS White 87%, Mestizo 7%
LANGUAGES Spanish (official), Creole, Indian
RELIGIONS Roman Catholic 92%
CURRENCY Colón = 100 céntimos
POPULATION DENSITY 67 per sq km [174 per sq ml]
URBAN POPULATION 50% of population

CROATIA

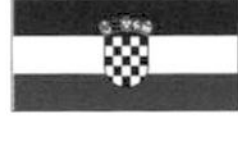

The red, white and blue flag was originally adopted in 1848. During the Communist period a red star appeared in the centre, but this was replaced by the present arms, which symbolize the various parts of the country.

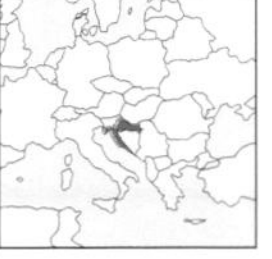

Croatia has a narrow strip of land running along the Adriatic Sea and then curves inland in the north. The coast is fairly mountainous and barren, with a climate of warm winters and hot, dry summers. Formerly Yugoslavia's second largest and second most populous republic, Croatia suffered some of the worst damage in the war following the break-up of Yugoslavia. The tourist industry has been devastated, especially the medieval city of Dubrovnik on the Dalmatian coast and a massive reconstruction programme is needed. In 1994 Croatia helped to end Croat-Muslim conflict in Bosnia-Herzegovina.

AREA 56,538 sq km [21,824 sq mls]
POPULATION 4,900,000
CAPITAL (POPULATION) Zagreb (931,000)
GOVERNMENT Multiparty republic
ETHNIC GROUPS Croat 78%, Serb 12%, Muslim 1%
LANGUAGES Serbo-Croat 96%
RELIGIONS Roman Catholic 77%, Orthodox 11%
POPULATION DENSITY 87 per sq km [225 per sq ml]

CUBA

CUBA

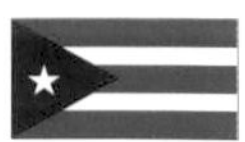

First designed in 1849, Cuba's flag, the 'Lone Star' banner, was not officially adopted until the island finally gained its independence from Spain in 1901. The red triangle represents the Cuban people's bloody struggle for independence.

GEOGRAPHY Cuba is only 193 km [120 mls] across at its widest, but stretches for over 1,200 km [750 mls] from the Gulf of Mexico to the Windward Passage. There is a varied landscape, including mountains and fertile plains. The climate is tropical, with high temperatures and some hurricanes.

HISTORY AND POLITICS A colony until 1898, Cuba took on many Spanish immigrants in the early years of independence.

The revolution in 1959 deposed the right-wing dictator Fulgencio Batista and brought Fidel Castro to power, and saw 600,000 people flee the island. A close ally of the former USSR, the rapid changes in Eastern Europe and the USSR have left Cuba isolated as a hardline Marxist state.

ECONOMY Sugar cane is the most important cash crop, taking up a third of the cultivated land and making up 75% of exports.

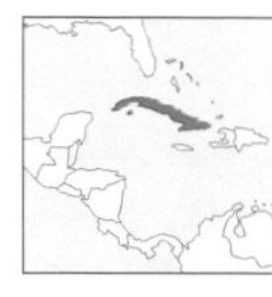

AREA 110,860 sq km [42,803 sq mls]
POPULATION 11,050,000
CAPITAL (POPULATION) Havana (2,119,000)
GOVERNMENT Socialist republic
ETHNIC GROUPS White 66%, Mulatto 22%, Black 12%
LANGUAGES Spanish (official)
RELIGIONS Roman Catholic 40%, Protestant 3%
CURRENCY Cuban peso = 100 centavos
MAIN EXPORTS Sugar, tobacco
POPULATION DENSITY 97 per sq km [258 sq ml]

CYPRUS

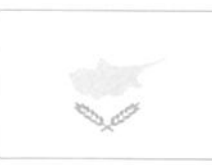

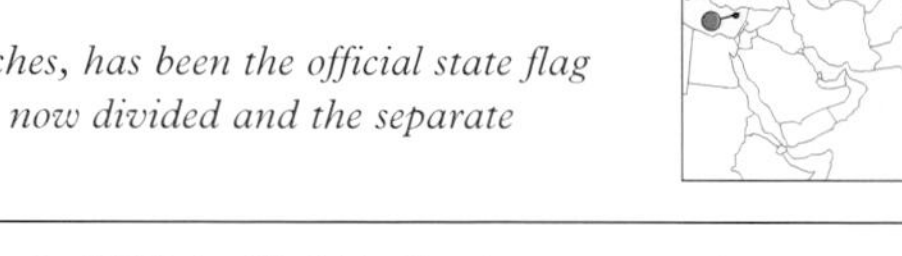

The design, featuring a map of the island with two olive branches, has been the official state flag since independence from Britain in 1960. However, Cyprus is now divided and the separate communities fly the Greek and Turkish flags.

Cyprus is a small but strategically situated Mediterranean island, comprising a detached fragment of the mainland mountains to the east. The northern coast is backed by the long limestone range of Kyrenia and in the south is the broad massif of Troodos. The fertile central plain grows fruits, flowers and early

vegetables. In 1968 the Turkish Cypriots set up an 'autonomous administration' in the north, but in 1974 Turkey invaded the mainland and took control of the northern 40% of the country, displacing 200,000 Greek Cypriots. The UN has since supervised an uneasy partition of the country.

AREA 9,250 sq km [3,571 sq mls]
POPULATION 742,000
CAPITAL (POPULATION) Nicosia (177,000)
GOVERNMENT Multiparty republic
ETHNIC GROUPS Greek Cypriot 81%, Turkish Cypriot 19%
LANGUAGES Greek, Turkish
RELIGIONS Greek Orthodox, Muslim
CURRENCY Cyprus pound = 100 cents
MAIN EXPORTS Wine, vegetables, fruit, clothing, shoes

CZECH REPUBLIC

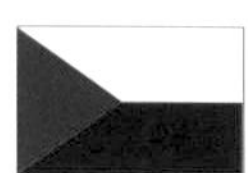

On independence in January 1993, the Czech Republic adopted the flag of the former Czechoslovakia. It features the red and white of Bohemia with the blue of Moravia and Slovakia, the colours of Pan-Slavic liberation.

The Czech Republic has 61% of the land area of the former Czechoslovakia; it is split into two units, Bohemia in the west, with Prague at its centre, and Moravia, divided from Bohemia by plateau land known as the Moravian Heights. There are rich mineral resources in the mountains and reserves of hard coal and lignite. Agriculture is also well developed. The 'velvet revolution'

of 1989 was one of the easiest transitions in Eastern Europe, replacing Communism with a multiparty system. The move to democracy was not as easy and resurgent Slovak nationalism in 1992 ended the old federation and split the country into two. Czechs and Slovaks have maintained some economic ties and the break-up has been amicable.

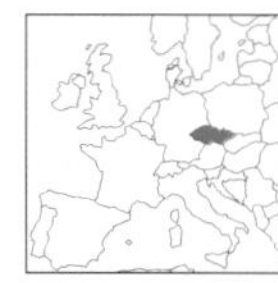

AREA 78,864 sq km [30,449 sq mls]
POPULATION 10,500,000
CAPITAL (POPULATION) Prague (1,216,000)
GOVERNMENT Multiparty republic with a bicameral legislature
ETHNIC GROUPS Czech 81%, Moravian 13%, Slovak 3%
LANGUAGES Czech
RELIGIONS Roman Catholic, Protestant
CURRENCY Koruna = 100 haler
MAIN EXPORTS Machinery, vehicles
URBAN POPULATION 65% of population

DENMARK

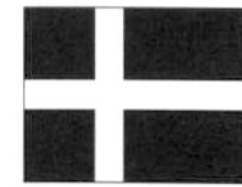

The Dannebrog ('the spirit of Denmark') flag is said to represent King Waldemar II's vision of a white cross against a red sky before the Battle of Lyndanisse in 1219, and is possibly the oldest national flag in continuous use.

GEOGRAPHY Denmark consists of the Jutland (Jylland) peninsula, which is an extension of the North German Plain, and an archipelago of 406 islands, of which 89 are inhabited. The largest and most densely populated of the islands is Zealand (Sjaelland), which lies close to the coast of Sweden. The climate reflects Denmark's position at the meeting of the Arctic, continental and maritime influences, giving it warm summers and average rainfall. Structurally the land is made up of low-lying sedimentary rocks, nowhere higher than 171 m [561 ft].

HISTORY AND POLITICS Control of the entrances to the Baltic Sea contributed to the power of Denmark in the Middle Ages,

when the kingdom dominated its neighbours and expanded its territories to include Norway, Iceland, Greenland and the Faroe Islands. Greenland and the Faroes still retain connections. Denmark has good relations with its neighbours and partners, as a member of the EU and as part of the Nordic Council (with the other Scandinavian countries).

ECONOMY There are few mineral resources and no coal, but there is some oil and natural gas from the North Sea. Denmark is, however, one of Europe's wealthiest industrial nations, with a strong agricultural base and advanced methods of processing and distributing farm produce.

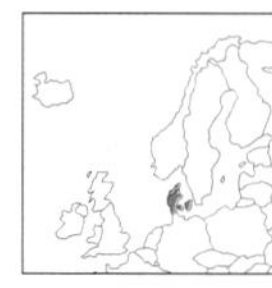

AREA 43,070 sq km [16,629 sq mls]
POPULATION 5,229,000
CAPITAL (POPULATION) Copenhagen (1,337,000)
GOVERNMENT Constitutional monarchy with a unicameral legislature
ETHNIC GROUPS Danish 97%
LANGUAGES Danish (official)
RELIGIONS Lutheran 91%, Roman Catholic 1%
CURRENCY Krone = 100 øre
MAIN EXPORTS Meat, dairy produce, fish 27%, machinery and electronic equipment 24%, chemicals
MAIN IMPORTS Machinery and transport equipment 31%, chemicals 10%
URBAN POPULATION 86% of population

DJIBOUTI

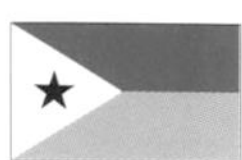

Djibouti's flag was adopted on independence from France in 1977, though its use by the independence movement had begun five years earlier. The colours represent the two principal peoples in the country: the Issas (blue) and the Afars (green).

Djibouti was previously the French territory of the Afars and the Issas and lies in the Afro-Asian rift valley system at the mouth of the Red Sea. Part of the country lies below sea level; much of this is hot, arid and unproductive basalt plain. Mt Goudah, the principal mountain, rises to 1,783 m [5,850 ft], and is covered

with juniper and box forest. Djibouti is important because of the railway link with Addis Ababa and is Ethiopia's main artery for overseas trade. The capital city grew from 1862 around a French naval base and the French still maintain a garrison there and offer support to the government.

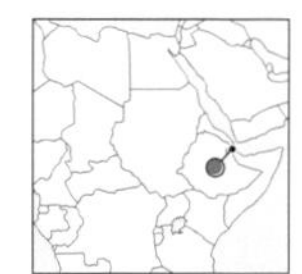

AREA 23,200 sq km [8,958 sq mls]
POPULATION 603,000
CAPITAL (POPULATION) Djibouti (310,000)
GOVERNMENT Multiparty republic
ETHNIC GROUPS Issa 47%, Afar 38%, Arab 6%
LANGUAGES Arabic and French (official), Cushitic
RELIGIONS Sunni Muslim 94%, Roman Catholic 4%
CURRENCY Djibouti franc = 100 centimes

DOMINICA

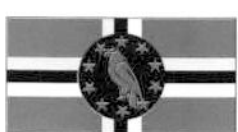

The Caribbean island of Dominica adopted its flag on independence from Britain in 1978 and slightly amended it in 1981. The parrot, from the coat of arms, is the national bird, the sisserou, and the stars represent the ten island parishes.

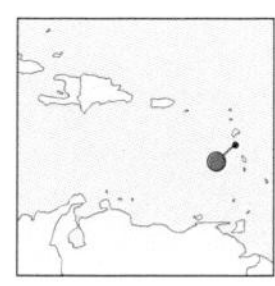

Dominica has been an independent republic since 1978, after 11 years as a self-governing UK colony. A mountainous ridge forms the island's spine, and it is from this central region that the main rivers flow to the indented coast. Rich soils support dense vegetation, but less than 10% is cultivated. Bananas account for 48% of exports, coconut-based soaps for 25%. Much food is imported and future prospects depend greatly on the development of luxury tourism.

AREA 751 sq km [290 sq mls]
POPULATION 89,000
CAPITAL (Population) Roseau (21,000)
GOVERNMENT Multiparty republic with a unicameral legislature
ETHNIC GROUPS Of African descent
LANGUAGES English (official), French patois
RELIGIONS Roman Catholic 75%, Protestant 15%

DOMINICAN REPUBLIC

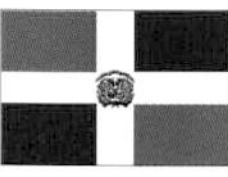

The Dominican Republic's flag dates from 1844, when the country finally gained its independence from both Spain and Haiti. The design developed from Haiti's flag, adding a white cross and rearranging the position of the colours.

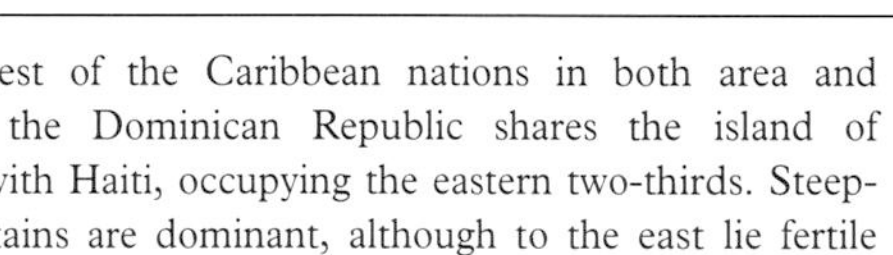

Second largest of the Caribbean nations in both area and population, the Dominican Republic shares the island of Hispaniola with Haiti, occupying the eastern two-thirds. Steep-sided mountains are dominant, although to the east lie fertile valleys and lowlands, including the coastal plains where most of the sugar plantations are found. Hispaniola was a Spanish colony before it won independence in 1821. Haiti then held the territory until 1844, when sovereignty was restored. Recently a fragile democracy has been established. Industry, mining and tourism help the traditional agricultural economy.

AREA 48,730 sq km [18,815 sq mls]
POPULATION 7,818,000
CAPITAL (Population) Santo Domingo (2,200,000)
GOVERNMENT Multiparty republic
ETHNIC GROUPS Mulatto 73%, White 16%, Black 11%
LANGUAGES Spanish (official)
RELIGIONS Roman Catholic 93%
CURRENCY Peso = 100 centavos
URBAN POPULATION 62% of population

ECUADOR

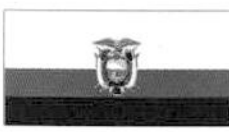

Shared in different proportions by Colombia and Venezuela, Ecuador's colours were used in the flag created by the patriot Francisco de Miranda in 1806 and flown by Simón Bolivar, whose armies also liberated Peru and Bolivia.

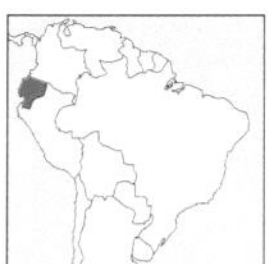

GEOGRAPHY Ecuador's name comes from the Equator, which divides the country unequally. There are three distinct regions – the coastal plain (Costa), the Andes, and the eastern alluvial plains of the Oriente. The coastal plain, averaging 100 km [60 mls] wide, is a hot, fertile area of variable rainfall that has now been cleared to create good farmland. The Galápagos Islands lie 970 km [610 mls] west of Ecuador and consist of six main islands and over 50 smaller ones: they contain many unique species of flora and fauna.

HISTORY AND POLITICS The Incas of Peru conquered Ecuador in the 15th century, but in 1532 a colony was founded by the Spaniards in the territory, then called Quito. Independence from Spain was achieved in 1822, when it became part of Gran Colombia, and full independence was gained in 1830. Since then it has remained a democratic republic.

ECONOMY Originally the economy was based on the export of bananas (and they are still the biggest export), but in 1972 oil was first exploited and petroleum and derivatives now account for about 40% of export earnings. There have been recent problems with foreign debt repayment.

AREA 283,560 sq km [109,483 sq mls]
POPULATION 11,384,000
CAPITAL (Population) Quito (1,101,000)
GOVERNMENT Unitary multiparty republic with a unicameral legislature
ETHNIC GROUPS Mestizo 40%, Amerindian 40%, White 5%, Black 5%
LANGUAGES Spanish 93% (official), Quechua
RELIGIONS Roman Catholic 93%, Protestant 6%
CURRENCY Sucre = 100 centavos
MAIN EXPORTS Petroleum and derivatives, seafood, bananas, coffee
POPULATION DENSITY 40 per sq km [104 per sq ml]

EGYPT

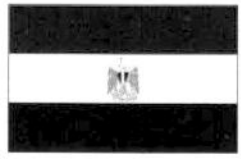

Egypt has flown a flag of red, white and black (the Pan-Arab colours) since 1958 but with various emblems in the centre. The present design, with the gold eagle emblem symbolizing the Arab hero Saladin, was introduced in 1984.

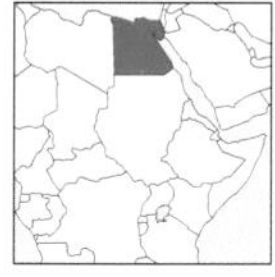

GEOGRAPHY The vast majority of Egypt is made up of desert and semi-desert, both with varied landscapes. For example, the Western Desert includes almost three-quarters of Egypt and consists of low vales and scarps, while the Sinai peninsula in the south is mountainous and rugged. The Nile Valley and its delta supports 96% of the population and was one of the cradles of civilization; now the control and storage of the water is essential.

HISTORY AND POLITICS Egypt was part of the Ottoman Empire from 1517, though British influence was important after 1882 and the country was a British protectorate from 1914 to 1922, when it acquired limited independence. In 1952 the corrupt regime of King Farouk, the last ruler of a dynasty dating back to 1841, was toppled by the army. Arab nationalism was then prominent until 1970.

ECONOMY Industrial development has become important since World War II, with textiles forming the largest industry. Other manufactures derive from local agricultural and mineral raw materials (for example, sugar refining and milling).

AREA 1,001,450 sq km [386,660 sq mls]
POPULATION 64,100,000
CAPITAL (Population) Cairo (6,800,000)
GOVERNMENT Multiparty republic with a bicameral legislature
ETHNIC GROUPS Egyptian 99%
LANGUAGES Arabic (official), French, English
RELIGIONS Sunni Muslim 90%
CURRENCY Egyptian pound = 100 piastres or 1,000 millièmes
MAIN EXPORTS Mineral products including crude petroleum 65%, textiles
POPULATION DENSITY 64 per sq km [166 per sq ml]

EL SALVADOR

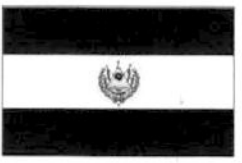

The original flag, the 'Stars and Stripes', was replaced in 1912 by the current one. The blue and white stripes are a common feature of the flags of Central American countries that gained their independence from Spain at the same time in 1821.

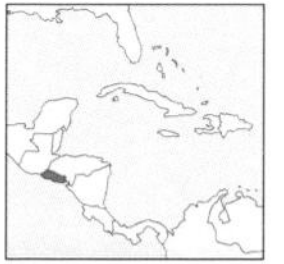

El Salvador is the only Central American country without a Caribbean coastline, and is also the smallest and most densely populated. The Pacific coastal plain is narrow and backed by a volcanic range averaging about 1,200 m [4,000 ft] in altitude. The country has over 20 volcanoes, some still active, and crater lakes occupying a central fertile plain 400 to 800 m [1,300 to 2,600 ft] above sea level. Coffee, tobacco, maize and sugar make up the bulk of the agricultural economy, with coffee accounting for over half the total value of exports. El Salvador has had a full-blown civil war since 1980, with more than 75,000 people dead and many homeless. A cease-fire took effect in February 1992 but the country remains in chaos.

AREA 21,040 sq km [8,124 sq mls]
POPULATION 5,743,000
CAPITAL (Population) San Salvador (1,522,000)
GOVERNMENT Republic with a unicameral legislature
ETHNIC GROUPS Mestizo 90%, Indian 5%, White 5%
LANGUAGES Spanish (official)
RELIGIONS Roman Catholic 75%
CURRENCY Colón = 100 céntavos
URBAN POPULATION 44% of population

EQUATORIAL GUINEA

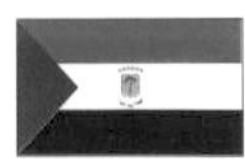

Equatorial Guinea's flag dates from independence from Spain in 1968. Green represents the country's natural resources, blue the sea, red the nation's struggle for independence and the white stands for peace.

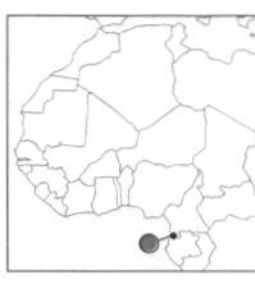

AREA 28,050 sq km [10,830 sq mls]
POPULATION 400,000
CAPITAL (Population) Malabo (35,000)
GOVERNMENT Multiparty republic (transitional)
ETHNIC GROUPS Fang 83%, Bubi 10%, Ndowe 4%
LANGUAGES Spanish (official), Fang, Bubi
RELIGIONS Christian (mainly Roman Catholic) 89%
CURRENCY CFA franc = 100 centimes
POPULATION DENSITY 14 per sq km [36 per sq ml]

GEOGRAPHY Equatorial Guinea comprises the low-lying mainland area of Mbini in West Africa and five volcanic and mountainous offshore islands, the largest of which is Fernando Poó (now known as Bioko) which lies in the Gulf of Guinea and contains the capital city.

HISTORY AND POLITICS Guinea, a name which derives from an ancient African kingdom, was once used to describe the whole coastal region of West Africa. Equatorial Guinea was granted partial autonomy from Spain in 1963, and gained full independence in 1968. The ensuing 11-year dictatorship of President Macías Nguema left the economy in ruins and some 100,000 Equatorial Guineans now live outside the country.

ECONOMY Plantations of cocoa and coffee are found on the islands, with cocoa beans as the chief cash crop.

ERITREA

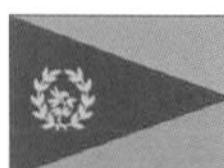

The new flag was hoisted on 24 May 1993 to celebrate independence from Ethiopia. It is a variation on the flag of the Eritrean People's Liberation Front, and shows an olive wreath which featured on the flag of the region between 1952 and 1959.

AREA 94,000 sq km [36,293 sq mls]
POPULATION 3,850,000
CAPITAL (Population) Asmara (358,000)
GOVERNMENT Transitional government
ETHNIC GROUPS Tigre, Afar, Beja, Saho, Agau
LANGUAGES Arabic, English, Tigrinya, Tigre, Saho, Agail, Afar
RELIGIONS Coptic Christian 50%, Muslim 50%

Until May 1993 Eritrea was the far northern and third largest province of Ethiopia. It was an Italian colony until 1941, when it passed to British military administration. In 1952 it became an autonomous region within the Federation of Ethiopia and Eritrea; in 1962 the region was annexed by Emperor Haile Selassie. The Eritrean People's Liberation Front (EPLF) then pushed for independence, with a guerilla campaign, until it was granted after the fall of the Mengistu regime in 1991.

ESTONIA

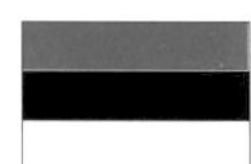

Used for the independent republic of 1918–40, the Estonian flag was readopted in June 1988. The colours are said to symbolize the country's blue skies, its black earth and the snows of its long winter.

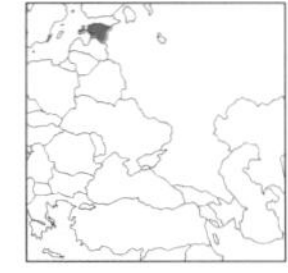

AREA 44,700 sq km [17,300 sq mls]
POPULATION 1,531,000
CAPITAL (Population) Tallinn (435,000)
ETHNIC GROUPS Estonian 62%, Russian 30%, Ukrainian 3%, Belarussian 2%
LANGUAGES Estonian 64% (official), Russian 31%
RELIGIONS Christian (Lutheran and Orthodox)
CURRENCY Kroon = 100 sents
POPULATION DENSITY 34 per sq km [88 per sq ml]

GEOGRAPHY Estonia is the smallest of the three Baltic States, bounded on the north by the Gulf of Finland and on the west by the Baltic Sea. The country mainly comprises flat, rock-strewn, glaciated lowlands and has over 1,500 lakes.

HISTORY, POLITICS AND ECONOMY Estonia and the other Baltic States became part of the Russian Empire in the 18th century, and after a period of independence in the early 20th century, became part of the USSR in 1940. All three states became independent in 1990. The timber industry is one of the country's most important industries, together with metal-working, shipbuilding and food processing. Oats, barley and potatoes are grown and fishing is a major occupation.

ETHIOPIA

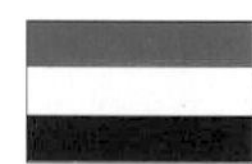

Ethiopia's tricolour was first flown as three separate pennants, one above the other. The combination of red, yellow and green dates from the late 19th century and appeared in flag form in 1897. The present sequence was adopted in 1941.

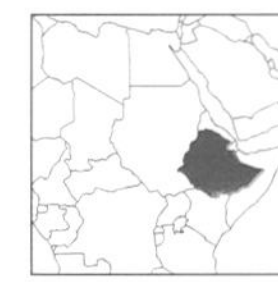

AREA 1,128,000 sq km [435,521 sq mls]
POPULATION 51,600,000
CAPITAL (Population) Addis Ababa (2,213,000)
GOVERNMENT Transitional federal republic with a unicameral legislature
ETHNIC GROUPS Amharic 38%, Galla 35%, Tigre 9%, Gurage 3%, Ometo 3%
LANGUAGES Amharic, Galla, Tigre
RELIGIONS Ethiopian Orthodox 53%, Muslim 31%, traditional beliefs 11%
CURRENCY Ethiopian Birr = 100 cents
MAIN EXPORTS Coffee 56%, hides and skins 11%
MAIN IMPORTS Machinery and transport equipment 39%, petroleum 17%
POPULATION DENSITY 46 per sq km [118 per sq ml]

GEOGRAPHY The main geographical feature is a massive block of volcanic mountains, rising to 4,620 m [15,150 ft] and divided into the Western and Eastern Highlands by the Great Rift Valley. The Western Highlands, generally higher and far more extensive and deeply trenched, are the sources of the Blue Nile and its tributaries. Off their north-eastern flank lies the Danakil Depression, an extensive desert that falls to 116 m [380 ft] below sea level. Ethiopia suffers periodically from severe droughts, which cause widespread famine.

HISTORY AND POLITICS Ethiopia (then known as Abyssinia) was a colonial power between 1897 and 1908, taking Somali and other peoples into its feudal empire. Invaded by Italy in 1935, Ethiopia became independent again in 1941 when British troops forced the Italians out. Emperor Haile Selassie ('the lion of Judah') was deposed after his 44-year rule by a revolutionary military government in 1974. Ethiopia became a socialist state and President Mengistu took control in 1977, with his period of 'Red Terror' causing the deaths of many thousands of people. In 1991 the military regime collapsed and in 1995 Ethiopia was divided into nine provinces, each with its own regional assembly.

ECONOMY Most people make a living from agriculture, with such crops as maize, barley, sugar cane and coffee. Coffee is the main cash crop and the main industry is textiles. The droughts and civil wars have caused serious economic problems, however.

FALKLAND ISLANDS

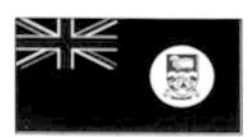

The white roundel in the flag contains the islands' badge which shows the ship Desire, *which discovered the islands in 1592, and a sheep, representing the main farming activity.*

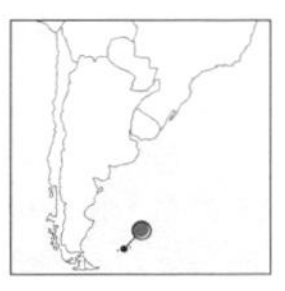

AREA 12,170 sq km [4,699 sq mls]
POPULATION 2,000
CAPITAL (Population) Stanley (2,120)
GOVERNMENT British Dependent Territory
ETHNIC GROUPS British
LANGUAGES English
RELIGIONS Christian
CURRENCY Falkland pound = 100 pence
POPULATION DENSITY 0.2 per sq km [0.5 per sq ml]
LAND USE Grass 98%

Comprising two main islands and over 200 small islands, the Falkland Islands lie 480 km [300 mls] from South America. The landscape is covered with peat moorland and tussock grass. Sheep farming is the main activity. Discovered in 1592, the Falklands were first occupied by the French and the British. Argentina, on independence in 1806, assumed the French interest and the British, who had withdrawn in 1774, returned to dispossess the Argentinians in 1832 and create a Crown Colony. Argentina invaded in 1982 only to be thrown out by the British, who refuse to discuss the issue of sovereignty.

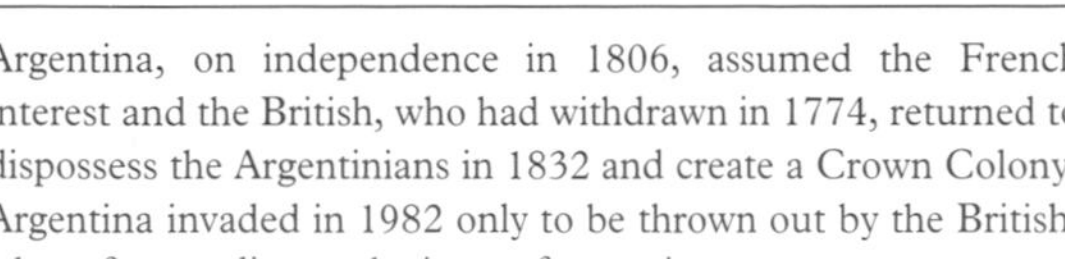

FAROE ISLANDS

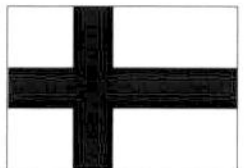

In 1948 the Faroe Islands, which are part of Denmark, adopted a flag combining the local arms with the Danish arms. The cross, like that on other Scandinavian flags, is slightly off-centre. Red and blue are ancient Faroese colours and the white represents the foam of the sea.

AREA 1,400 sq km [541 sq mls]
POPULATION 47,000
CAPITAL (POPULATION) Tórshavn (14,601)
GOVERNMENT Danish self-governing region
ETHNIC GROUPS Of Scandinavian descent
LANGUAGES Faroese (official), Danish
CURRENCY Faroese króna
MAIN EXPORTS Fish products
POPULATION DENSITY 34 per sq km [13 per sq ml]

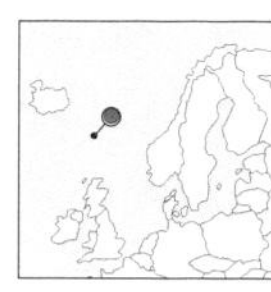

The Faroes are a group of rocky islands situated in the North Atlantic 450 km [280 mls] south-east of Iceland. They are mostly composed of volcanic material, which has been dramatically moulded by glacial action. Sheep farming is the main occupation, but salted, dried, processed and frozen fish, fishmeal and oil comprise the chief exports. The islands have been part of the Danish kingdom since 1386, although they secured a large degree of self-government in 1948.

FIJI

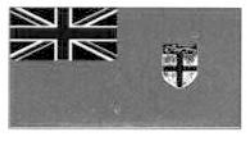

The Fijian flag, based on the British Blue Ensign, was adopted in 1970 after independence from Britain. The state coat of arms shows a British lion, sugar cane (the most important crop), a coconut palm, bananas and a dove of peace.

AREA 18,270 sq km [7,054 sq mls]
POPULATION 773,000
CAPITAL (POPULATION) Suva (75,000)
GOVERNMENT Republic with a non-elected senate
ETHNIC GROUPS Indian 49%, Fijian 46%
LANGUAGES English, Bauan, Hindustani
RELIGIONS Christian 53%, Hindu 38%, Muslim 8%
CURRENCY Fiji dollar = 100 cents
MAIN EXPORTS Sugar, gold, food products
POPULATION DENSITY 42 per sq km [110 per sq ml]

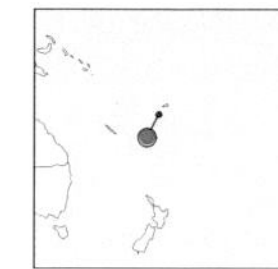

GEOGRAPHY Fiji comprises more than 800 Melanesian islands, the larger one volcanic, mountainous and surrounded by coral reefs, the rest being low coral atolls. The biggest are Viti and Vanua Levu. The south-east trade winds blow all year round and rain usually falls on 200 days per year.

HISTORY AND POLITICS Fiji became a British Crown Colony in 1874 and the British brought in Indians to work on the sugar plantations, which has caused many racial problems as the Indians now outnumber the native Fijians. Two military coups in 1987 overthrew the first Indian-majority government and suspended the constitution. Full civilian rule returned in 1990.

ECONOMY The economy is largely agricultural, with sugar cane making up 45% of exports. Ginger, copra, fish and timber are also important, as well as the sale of gold abroad.

FINLAND

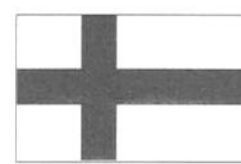

Finland became an independent republic only in 1917 after separation from Russia, then in the throes of the Revolution, and the present flag was adopted soon after. The colours symbolize Finland's blue lakes and white snow.

AREA 338,130 sq km [130,552 sq mls]
POPULATION 5,125,000
CAPITAL (POPULATION) Helsinki (516,000)
GOVERNMENT Multiparty republic
ETHNIC GROUPS Finnish 93%, Swedish 6%
LANGUAGES Finnish and Swedish (both official)
RELIGIONS Lutheran 87%, Greek Orthodox 1%
CURRENCY Markka = 100 penniä
MAIN EXPORTS Machinery 27%, paper and paperboard 26%, wood, lumber, cork and wastepaper 10%
MAIN IMPORTS Machinery and transport equipment 44%, basic manufactures, textiles and metals 16%, petroleum and petroleum products 10%, chemicals 10%

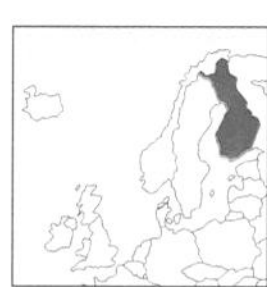

GEOGRAPHY Located almost entirely between latitudes 60°N and 70°N, Finland is the most northerly state on the mainland of Europe; a third of its total area lies within the Arctic Circle. Geologically, Finland is made up of a central plateau of ancient crystalline rocks surrounded by lowlands composed of recent glacial deposits. More than two-thirds of the country is covered by lakes (which are long, narrow and shallow) and forests (mainly of pine, spruce and birch). Winters are long and cold and in severe cases the sea freezes over for several miles offshore. Summers are short but can be warm: July temperatures at Helsinki have an average of 17°C [63°F].

HISTORY AND POLITICS Between 1150 and 1809 Finland was under Swedish rule and, as a legacy of this period, there is a Swedish-speaking minority in the country. In 1809 Finland was annexed by Russia and did not become independent until 1917. Formerly a member of EFTA, Finland joined the EU on 1 January 1995, following a referendum in 1994.

ECONOMY With forests occupying 60% of the land surface, forest-based products form the majority of Finland's exports. Since World War II engineering, shipbuilding and metallurgical industries have greatly expanded. Acid rain and pollution from wood processing and fertilizers are continuing problems.

FRANCE

The colours of the French flag originated during the Revolution of 1789. The red and blue are said to represent Paris and the white the monarchy. The present design, adopted in 1794, is meant to symbolize republican principles.

AREA 551,500 sq km [212,934 sq mls]
POPULATION 58,286,000
CAPITAL (POPULATION) Paris (9,319,000)
GOVERNMENT Multiparty republic with a bicameral legislature
ETHNIC GROUPS French 93%, Arab 3%, German 2%, Breton 1%, Catalan 1%
LANGUAGES French (official), Arabic, Breton, Catalan, Basque
RELIGIONS Roman Catholic 76%, other Christian 4%, Muslim 3%
CURRENCY Franc = 100 centimes
URBAN POPULATION 73% of population

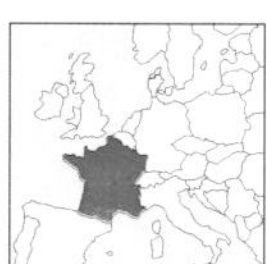

GEOGRAPHY France is Europe's third largest country after Russia and the Ukraine. Some 60% of the country lies less than 250 m [800 ft] above sea level. Rivers, including the Rhône, Garonne, Loire and Seine, along with their tributaries, drain large lowland basins. There are also several distinctive upland areas, particularly the Alps and the Pyrenees, and also the ancient massifs of Brittany and the Central Plateau. The Alps are formed of complex folded rocks of intricate structure, with relief made even more complicated by the successive glaciations of the Ice Age. Areas of permanent snow exist on Mont Blanc and many other high peaks. Almost half of France's frontiers (which total 5,500 km [3,440 mls]) consist of sea coast and another 1,000 km [620 mls] winds through the Pyrenees and the Alps. The Paris basin is a vast area floored by sedimentary rocks, while Paris lies on the Île de la Cité, where the River Seine was easily crossed.

HISTORY AND POLITICS France has a long history dating back to the 50s BC when it was conquered by the Romans; in the south there are famous Roman remains – for example, at Arle and Carcassonne. It became an independent kingdom in AD 486, although the monarchy was overthrown by the Revolution in 1789. Local government was reorganized, with the country divided into *départements* – areas in which everyone could reach the central town within one day. There followed many changes, with the country becoming first a republic, then an empire, a monarchy, a republic, and another empire before finally being established as a republic in 1875. France was invaded by Germany in both world wars, but Germany has since become one of France's closest allies, while France itself was one of the founder members of the European Community. There remains a disparity between the richer (east) and poorer (west) areas.

ECONOMY Agriculture is a very important part of the economy, making up 17% of export earnings, with about 5% of the world's barley and wheat produced in France. Other crops include maize, a wide range of vegetables, olives and grapes. In terms of minerals, France is a declining but still significant producer of iron ore (mostly from Lorraine), and also bauxite, potash, salt and sulphur. New sources of energy are used, including experiments with solar power in the Pyrenees and the world's first major tidal power station on the Rance estuary in Brittany.

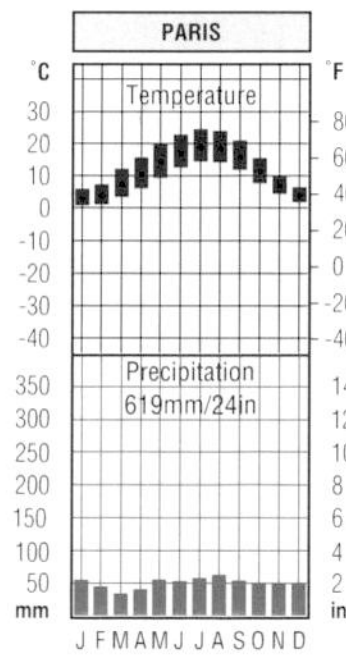

The climate of France is formed from three influences: the Atlantic, the Mediterranean and the continent. With no mountain barriers to affect it the Atlantic regime extends far inland, giving mild weather with wind and rain, but little snow. To the east the climate gets warmer, but with colder winters. At Paris low rainfall is evenly distributed all year.

FRENCH GUIANA

FRENCH GUIANA

The official flag flown over 'Guyane' is the French tricolour. A French possession since 1676 (apart from 1809–17), the territory is treated as part of mainland France and its citizens send representatives to the Paris parliament.

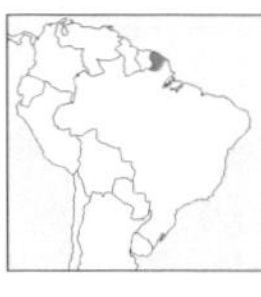

French Guiana is the smallest country in South America and has a narrow coastal plain covered with mangrove swamps and marshes, and a drier, forested interior. A French settlement was established in 1604 by a group of merchant adventurers, but it did not become permanently French until 1817. From 1852 to 1939 it was used as a French penal colony, (the notorious Devil's Island was located here, but this was closed in 1945). The economy is very dependent on France for food and manufactured goods. Timber is the most important natural resource; fishing (for shrimps) and tourism are also important.

AREA 90,000 sq km [34,749 sq mls]
POPULATION 154,000
CAPITAL (POPULATION) Cayenne (42,000)
GOVERNMENT Overseas Department of France
ETHNIC GROUPS Creole 42%, Chinese 14%, French 10%, Haitian 7%
LANGUAGES French (official), Creole patois
RELIGIONS Roman Catholic 80%, Protestant 4%

FRENCH POLYNESIA

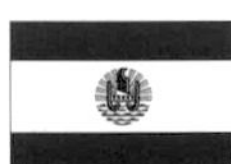

The flag was adopted in 1984 and is in the traditional colours of Tahiti, but can only be flown in conjunction with the French tricolour since it is still a French territory. The emblem in the centre is a native canoe (pirogue) against the background of a rising sun over the sea.

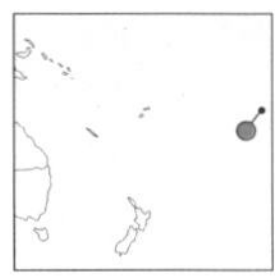

French Polynesia consists of 130 islands, scattered over 4 million sq km [1.5 million sq mls] of ocean halfway between Australia and South America. Tahiti is the largest island and the climate is warm and humid. The tribal chiefs eventually agreed to a French protectorate in 1843, and by the end of the century France controlled all the present islands. They formed an overseas territory from 1958 and in 1984 gained increased autonomy with a territorial assembly; there are calls for independence, but the high standard of living comes largely from the links with France, including a military presence. The main earners are petroleum re-exports, cultured pearls, vanilla and citrus fruits. Tourism is vital to the economy – there were 148,000 tourists in 1993.

AREA 3,941 sq km [1,520 sq mls]
POPULATION 217,000
CAPITAL (POPULATION) Papeete (26,000)
GOVERNMENT Overseas Territory of France
ETHNIC GROUPS Polynesian 78%, Chinese 12%, French
LANGUAGES French (official), Tahitian
RELIGIONS Protestant 54%, Roman Catholic 30%
CURRENCY CFP franc = 100 centimes
URBAN POPULATION 67% of population

GABON

Gabon's tricolour was adopted on independence from France in 1960. The yellow, now representing the sun, used to be thinner to symbolize the Equator on which the country lies. The green stands for Gabon's forests and blue for the sea.

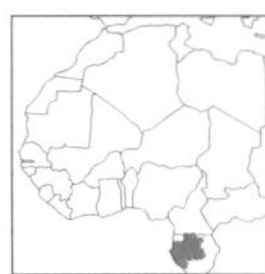

Gabon lies in south-west Africa and derives its name from that given by a 16th-century Portuguese explorer. Most of the country is densely forested (covering 75% of the land) and the climate is mainly equatorial with uniform heat and humidity throughout the year and very high rainfall. The capital city of Libreville was founded in 1849 by the French as a home for slaves rescued from illegal slaving ships. Timber was the main export until 1962, when minerals began to be developed, but largely by foreign companies whose profits leave the country. Oil now provides 65% of export earnings and Gabon has about a quarter of the world's known reserves of manganese; there are also reserves of natural gas and uranium.

AREA 267,670 sq km [103,347 sq mls]
POPULATION 1,316,000
CAPITAL (POPULATION) Libreville (418,000)
GOVERNMENT Multiparty republic
ETHNIC GROUPS Fang 36%, Mpongwe 15%, Mbete 14%, Punu 12%
LANGUAGES French (official), Bantu languages
RELIGIONS Christian 96% (Roman Catholic 65%)
CURRENCY CFA franc = 100 centimes
URBAN POPULATION 48% of population

GAMBIA, THE

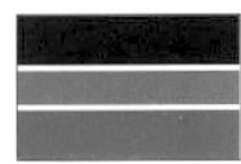

The blue stripe in the Republic of The Gambia's flag represents the Gambia River that flows through the country, while the red stands for the sun overhead and the green for the land. The design was adopted on independence from Britain in 1965.

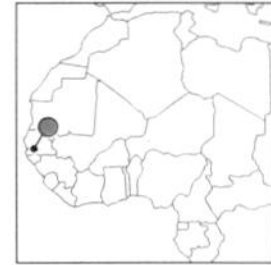

GEOGRAPHY The smallest and most westerly country in mainland Africa, The Gambia is low-lying and forms a narrow strip on either side of the River Gambia, making it almost an enclave of Senegal. The capital, Banjul, is the main port and is by far the largest town. All the large settlements are on the river, which provides the main source of communication.
HISTORY AND POLITICS The Gambia was a British colony (the first one) from 1888 and became independent in 1965 (the last to gain independence). A republic was created in 1970. There are close links with Senegal, but The Gambia, as the poorer nation, rejects any suggestions of unification.
ECONOMY Rice is grown in swamps and on the floodplains of the river, with millet, sorghum and cassava on the higher ground. Groundnuts provide nine-tenths of export earnings but tourism is the country's biggest foreign exchange earner; in 1990–91, 101,500 tourists visited the country.

AREA 11,300 sq km [4,363 sq mls]
POPULATION 1,144,000
CAPITAL (POPULATION) Banjul (150,000)
GOVERNMENT Military government
ETHNIC GROUPS Madinka 40%, Fulani 19%, Wolof 15%, Jola 10%, Soninke 8%
LANGUAGES English (official), Madinka, Fula, Wolof
RELIGIONS Sunni Muslim 95%, Christian 4%
CURRENCY Dalasi = 100 butut
POPULATION DENSITY 101 per sq km [262 per sq ml]

GEORGIA

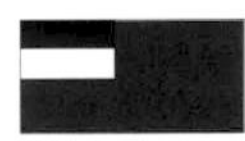

The flag was first adopted in 1917 and lasted until 1921. The colours represent the good times of the past and the future (wine-red), the period of Russian rule (black) and the hope for peace (white). It was readopted on independence in 1990.

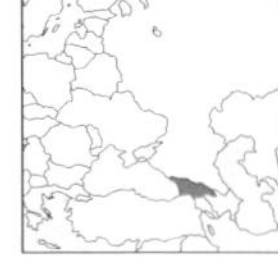

GEOGRAPHY Positioned between Russia and Turkey, Georgia comprises four main areas: the Caucasus Mountains in the north; the Black Sea coastal plain in the west; the eastern end of the mountains of Asia Minor to the south; and a low plateau in the east, protruding into Azerbaijan. Separating the two mountain sections is the crucial Kura Valley.
HISTORY AND POLITICS Georgia has a strong national culture. Land of the legendary Golden Fleece of Greek mythology, the area was conquered by the Romans, Persians and Arabs before establishing autonomy in the 10th century. It came under Russian rule in 1800 and was the first Soviet republic to declare independence after the Baltic states and the only one not to join the CIS at its inception (it later joined in 1994). The former Soviet foreign minister, Eduard Shevardnadze, became head of state in 1992, but there have been recent political problems.
ECONOMY Important crops include citrus fruits, wine, tea, tobacco, wheat, barley and vegetables. Perfume is made from flowers and herbs and there is a silk industry in Imeretiya.

AREA 69,700 sq km [26,910 sq mls]
POPULATION 5,448,000
CAPITAL (POPULATION) Tbilisi (1,279,000)
GOVERNMENT Multiparty republic
ETHNIC GROUPS Georgian 70%, Armenian 8%, Russian 6%
LANGUAGES Georgian 69%, Armenian 8%, Russian 6%, Azerbaijani 5%, Ossetian 3%
RELIGIONS Orthodox (Georgian 65%, Russian 10%, Armenian 8%), Muslim 11%
CURRENCY Lari
POPULATION DENSITY 78 per sq km [202 per sq ml]
URBAN POPULATION 57% of population
LAND USE Arable 3%, grass 30%

GERMANY

The red, black and gold, dating back to the Holy Roman Empire, are associated with the struggle for a united Germany from the 1830s. The horizontal design was officially adopted for the FRG in 1949, and accepted by 'East Germany' on reunification.

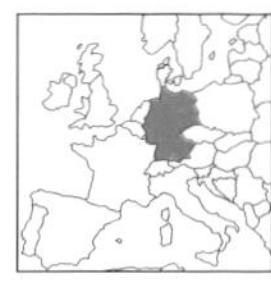

GEOGRAPHY Germany extends from the North Sea and Baltic coasts in the north to the flanks of the central Alps in the south and has the most international borders of any European country. Although there is only a narrow fringe of Alpine mountains, there is a wide section of the associated Alpine foreland bordering Switzerland and Austria that is largely covered by moraines and outwash plains as relics of the last Ice Age. Much of the rest of the country is covered by the central uplands of Europe, including block mountains, which are remnants of pre-Alpine fold mountains and down-faulted basins filled with softer deposits of more recent age (for example, the Upper Rhine plain between Basle and Mainz). The northern lowlands and coast owe much of their topography to glaciation and the retreat of the ice-sheets, with the leached older moraines leaving poor soils.

HISTORY AND POLITICS The German Empire was created under Prussian dominance in 1871 and comprised four kingdoms, six grand duchies, five duchies and seven principalities, and centred on the great imperial capital of Berlin. Following the fall of Hitler in 1945, a defeated Germany was obliged to transfer to Poland and the Soviet Union nearly a quarter of the country's pre-war area. The German-speaking inhabitants were expelled and the remainder of Germany was occupied by the four victorious Allied powers. The dividing line between the zones occupied by the three Western Allies (USA, UK and France) and that occupied by the USSR rapidly became a political boundary dividing the country. In 1948 West Germany was proclaimed as the independent Federal Republic of Germany and East Germany became the German Democratic Republic. In 1990 West and East Germany reunited and the former East Germany was absorbed into the European Union. Problems have arisen from the huge cost of reconstruction and the length of time it was taking to achieve.

ECONOMY Germany has impressive agriculture and industry. In agricultural production it is the world's third largest producer of rye (11% of the total), sugar beet and cheese, and fourth in barley, butter and milk. There are important coal reserves; oil and gas are extracted from beneath the northern lowland; and potash is mined south of the Harz.

AREA 356,910 sq km [137,803 sq mls]
POPULATION 82,000,000
CAPITAL (POPULATION) Berlin (3,475,000)/ Bonn (297,000)
GOVERNMENT Federal multiparty republic with a bicameral legislature
ETHNIC GROUPS German 93%, Turkish, Yugoslav, Italian, Greek, Polish, Spanish
LANGUAGES German (official)
RELIGIONS Protestant 45%, Roman Catholic 37%, Muslim 2%
CURRENCY Deutsche Mark = 100 Pfennig

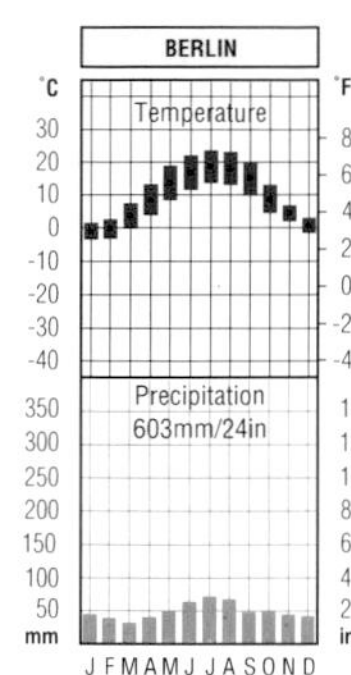

The climate of northern Germany is due mainly to the weather coming in from the the Atlantic. January and February are the only months with mean temperatures just below 0°C [32°F], and the summers are warm. Humidity is always high, with fog in the autumn. In the south the climate is a little warmer in summer and a little colder in winter. It is also wetter.

GHANA

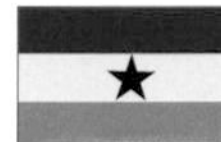

Adopted on independence from Britain in 1957, Ghana's flag features the colours first used by Ethiopia, Africa's oldest independent nation. Following Ghana's lead, other ex-colonies adopted them as a symbol of black Pan-African unity.

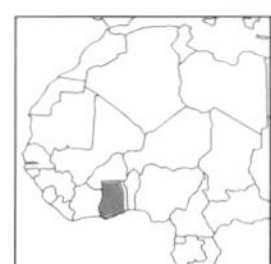

GEOGRAPHY Ghana is located in West Africa, with a southern coast on the Atlantic Ocean. It is mostly low-lying and has a climate with uniformly high temperatures and humidity. Lake Volta, one of the world's largest artificial lakes, is located here.

HISTORY AND POLITICS Ghana was known as the Gold Coast from the 8th to the 13th centuries. In 1957 it became the first tropical African country to become independent of colonial rule, and was led by Dr Kwame Nkrumah, a prominent Third World spokesman and pioneer of Pan-African socialism. He was overthrown in 1966 and replaced in 1981 by a hardline regime led by Flight Lieutenant Jerry Rawlings. In 1992, multiparty elections were won by Rawlings.

ECONOMY Cocoa has been the leading export since 1924 with a recent expansion of fishing, tourism and agriculture.

AREA 238,540 sq km [92,100 sq mls]
POPULATION 17,462,000
CAPITAL (POPULATION) Accra (965,000)
GOVERNMENT Multiparty republic with a unicameral legislature
ETHNIC GROUPS Akan, Mossi, Ewe, Ga-Adangme, Gurma
LANGUAGES English (official), Akan 54%, Mossi 16%, Ewe 12%, Ga-Adangme 8%, Gurma 3%, Yoruba 1%, Hausa
RELIGIONS Protestant 28%, traditional beliefs 21%, Roman Catholic 19%, Muslim
CURRENCY Cedi = 100 pesewas

GIBRALTAR

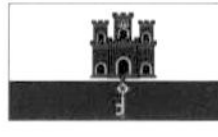

The official flag is the Union Jack but this flag has been in use unofficially (on land only) since about 1966. It is a banner of the city arms granted to Gibraltar in 1502 by Spain; the key symbolizes Gibraltar's strategic importance as the gateway to the Mediterranean.

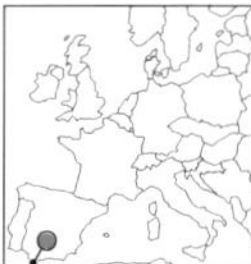

The Rock, as it is popularly known, stands at the north-eastern end of the Strait of Gibraltar, largely consisting of a narrow ridge thrusting south along the eastern side of Algeciras Bay. The topography prohibits cultivation, so the Gibraltarians rely on the port, the ship-repairing yards, the military and air bases, and on tourism for their livelihood. It was formally recognized as a British possession at the Treaty of Utrecht in 1713 and has remained so ever since.

AREA 6.5 sq km [2.5 sq mls]
POPULATION 28,000
CAPITAL Gibraltar Town
GOVERNMENT British Dependent Territory
ETHNIC GROUPS British, Spanish, Maltese, Portuguese
LANGUAGES English, Spanish
RELIGIONS Roman Catholic 74%, Protestant 11%, Muslim 8%
CURRENCY Gibraltar pound = 100 pence

GREECE

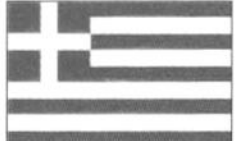

Blue and white became Greece's national colours during the war of independence. Finally adopted in 1970, the stripes represent the battle cry 'Eleutheria i thanatos' ('Freedom or Death') used during the struggle against Ottoman (Turkish) domination in the war of 1821–9.

GEOGRAPHY Mainland Greece consists of a mountainous peninsula which projects 500 km [312 mls] into the Mediterranean and an 80 km [50 ml] coastal belt along the northern shore of the Aegean Sea. Nearly a fifth of the total land area of Greece is made up of its 2,000 or so islands, mainly in the Aegean Sea, of which only 154 are inhabited. The Pindos Mountains are the main structural feature, extending south-eastwards from the Albanian border to cover most of the peninsula. Nowhere in Greece is more than 80 km [50 mls] from the sea, and most of the towns are on the coast.

HISTORY AND POLITICS In the days of classical Greece, during the thousand years before Christ, Greek colonies were established all round the shores of the Mediterranean, and for a short period in the 4th century BC Alexander the Great built a huge empire extending from the Danube to northern India. Greece was ruled by the Romans in 146 BC and then by Turkey from AD 365; in 1830 it became independent as a monarchy. Greece joined the European Union in 1981, but a vast economic difference has always existed between it and the other members.

ECONOMY Only a third of the land area is suitable for cultivation, yet 40% of the population depend on agriculture for their living, the major crops being wheat, olives, vines and citrus fruits. The tourist industry is vital to the economy. There are few industrial raw materials and most energy is imported.

AREA 131,990 sq km [50,961 sq mls]
POPULATION 10,510,000
CAPITAL (POPULATION) Athens (3,097,000)
GOVERNMENT Multiparty republic
ETHNIC GROUPS Greek 96%, Macedonian 2%, Turkish 1%, Albanian, Slav
LANGUAGES Greek (official)
RELIGIONS Greek Orthodox 97%, Muslim 2%
CURRENCY Drachma = 100 lepta
MAIN EXPORTS Foodstuffs, olive oil and tobacco 28%, textiles 23%, petroleum products 8%
MAIN IMPORTS Machinery and transport equipment 23%, foodstuffs 17%
POPULATION DENSITY 80 per sq km [206 per sq ml]
URBAN POPULATION 64% of population

GREENLAND

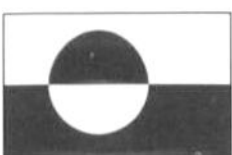

The flag was introduced in 1985 after a competition to decide a design and can be used on land and at sea. The design is in the Danish colours, with the red depicting the midsummer sun rising over the (white) polar ice.

AREA 2,175,600 sq km [839,999 sq mls]
POPULATION 59,000
CAPITAL (POPULATION) Godthåb (12,650)
GOVERNMENT Self-governing overseas region of Denmark
ETHNIC GROUPS Greenlander 86%, Danish 14%
LANGUAGES Eskimo dialects, Danish
RELIGIONS Lutheran
CURRENCY Danish krone
MAIN EXPORTS Shrimps, prawns and molluscs, fish, lead, zinc

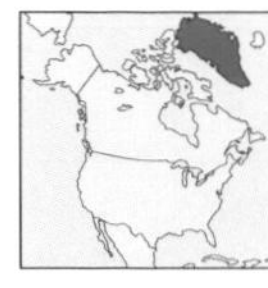

Recognized by geographers as the world's largest island, Greenland is almost three times the size of the second largest, New Guinea. More than 85% of the land is covered in continuous permafrost, an ice-cap with an average depth of about 1,500 m [5,000 ft], and though there are a few sandy and clay plains in the ice-free areas, settlement is confined to the rocky coasts. Greenland became a Danish possession in 1380 and part of the Danish kingdom in 1953; full internal self-government was granted in 1981. The economy still depends greatly on Danish subsidies and Denmark remains its chief trading partner. The main rural occupations are sheep rearing and fishing and the main manufacturing is fish canning.

GRENADA

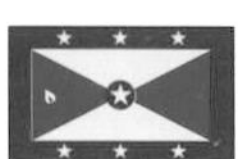

Each star represents one of Grenada's seven parishes. The country's traditional cash crop, nutmeg, is depicted in the hoist triangle. The people are represented by the colours red (for unity) and yellow (for friendliness and the sunshine), the island by the colour green.

AREA 344 sq km [133 sq mls]
POPULATION 94,000
CAPITAL (POPULATION) St George's (7,000)
GOVERNMENT Constitutional monarchy with a bicameral legislature
ETHNIC GROUPS Black 84%, Mixed 12%, East Indian 3%, White 1%
LANGUAGES English, French patois
RELIGIONS Roman Catholic 64%, Protestant 34%
CURRENCY East Caribbean $ = 100 cents
MAIN EXPORTS Nutmeg, bananas
POPULATION DENSITY 273 per sq km [707 per sq ml]

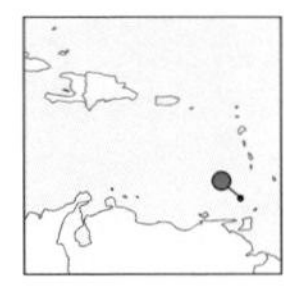

GEOGRAPHY Grenada is the most southern of the Windward Islands and the territory also includes the Southern Grenadines, principally Carriacou. The landscape is mountainous, consisting of the remains of extinct volcanoes; the only flat land is along the rivers' lower courses and part of the coastline. A hurricane in 1955 virtually destroyed the capital of St George's.
HISTORY AND POLITICS British since 1783, Grenada became a self-governing colony in 1967 and independent in 1974. It went Communist after a coup in 1979 when links with Cuba were established by Maurice Bishop. Bishop was executed in 1983 and the USA sent in troops to restore democracy; since then there has been a heavy reliance on American aid.
ECONOMY Grenada is known as 'the spice island of the Caribbean' and is the world's leading producer of nutmeg, its main crop. Cocoa, bananas and mace are also produced. The tourist industry has gradually recovered since the 1983 invasion.

GUADELOUPE

As an overseas department of France, Guadeloupe uses the French tricolour for its flag.

AREA 1,710 sq km [660 sq mls]
POPULATION 443,000
CAPITAL (POPULATION) Basse-Terre (14,000)
GOVERNMENT Overseas Department of France
ETHNIC GROUPS Mixed (Black and White) 90%
LANGUAGES French
RELIGIONS Roman Catholic 88%
CURRENCY French franc

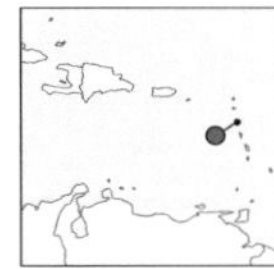

Slightly the larger of France's two Caribbean overseas departments, Guadeloupe comprises seven islands including Saint-Martin and Saint-Barthélemy to the north-west. Over 90% of the area, however, is taken up by Basse-Terre, which is volcanic, and the smaller Grande-Terre, made of low limestone. Food is the main import (mostly from France) and bananas are the biggest export. French aid has helped create a reasonable standard of living, although unemployment is high.

GUAM

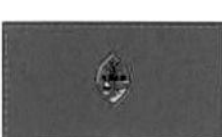

The flag was adopted in 1917. The badge in the centre is based on the island seal and depicts the mouth of the Agana River and a prao sailing off Point Ritidian. Guam has been a dependency of the USA since 1898 and flies its flag only with the American 'Stars and Stripes'.

AREA 541 sq km [209 sq mls]
POPULATION 155,000
CAPITAL (POPULATION) Agana (4,000)
GOVERNMENT US Territory
ETHNIC GROUPS Chamorro 47%, Filipino 25%, American
LANGUAGES English, Chamorro, Japanese
RELIGIONS Roman Catholic 98%
MAIN EXPORTS Textiles, beverages, tobacco, copra

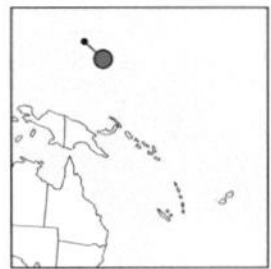

Largest of the Mariana Islands, Guam is composed mainly of a coralline limestone plateau, with mountains in the south, hills in the centre and narrow coastal lowlands in the north. Populated for over 3,000 years, colonized by Spain from 1668, but ceded to the USA after the 1896–8 war and occupied by the Japanese 1941–4, it is today of huge strategic importance to the USA and a third of its usable land is taken up by American naval and airforce establishments.

GUATEMALA

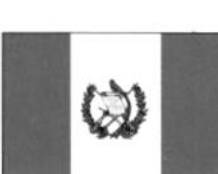

The simple design of Guatemala's flag was adopted in 1871, but its origins date back to the Central American Federation (1823–39) formed with Honduras, El Salvador, Nicaragua and Costa Rica after the break from Spanish rule in 1821.

AREA 108,890 sq km [42,042 sq mls]
POPULATION 10,624,000
CAPITAL (POPULATION) Guatemala City (2,000,000)
GOVERNMENT Republic with a unicameral legislature
ETHNIC GROUPS Mayaquiche Indian 55%, Ladino (Mestizo) 42%
LANGUAGES Spanish (official) 40%, 20 Indian dialects
RELIGIONS Roman Catholic 75%, Protestant 23%
CURRENCY Guatemalan quetzal = 100 centavos
MAIN EXPORTS Coffee, bananas, sugar, cardamom
POPULATION DENSITY 98 per sq km [253 per sq ml]

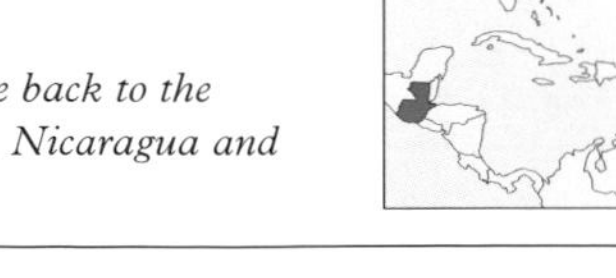

GEOGRAPHY Most populous of the Central American countries, Guatemala's Pacific coastline, two and a half times longer than its Caribbean coast, is backed by broad alluvial plains, formed from material washed down from the 27 volcanoes that front the ocean. These include extinct Tajumulco (4,217 m [13,830 ft]), the highest peak in central America. Its position between the seas and its mountainous interior gives Guatemala a variety of climates. On the Caribbean coast, with the trade winds always blowing onshore, rainfall is high in all months, whereas inland there is a dry, almost arid, season in January and February.
HISTORY AND POLITICS The remains of the largest of the pre-Colombian Maya Indian cities at Tikal indicates the importance of this civilization in the 3rd to 10th centuries. In the 1520s the Spanish conquered the region and independence was not granted until 1821. The Indians are still in the majority, but society and government is run on often repressive lines by the mestizos of mixed Indian and European stock; a 'low-intensity' civil war between the army and the left-wing guerillas (often Indians) carried on in the 1980s, with defence spending at 15% of the budget. In March 1994 a human rights agreement was reached, allowing for the establishment of a UN observer mission.
ECONOMY Coffee production dominates the economy, with the lower mountain slopes providing ideal conditions for growth. Bananas, cotton and cattle are also important.

GUINEA

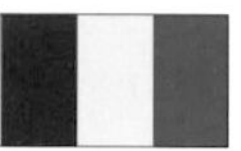

Guinea's Pan-African colours, adopted on independence from France in 1958, represent the three words of the national motto 'Travail, Justice, Solidarité': Work (red), Justice (yellow) and Solidarity (green). The design is based on the French tricolour.

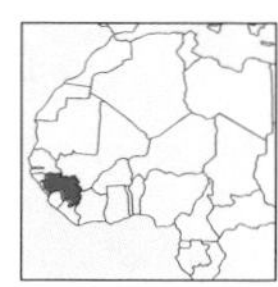

GEOGRAPHY Guinea is a country of varied landscapes, ranging from the grasslands and scattered woodland of the interior highlands and Upper Niger plains, to the swampy mangrove-fringed plains of the Atlantic coast. Dense forests occupy the western foothills of the Fouta Djalon plateau.

HISTORY AND POLITICS In the 1400s the Portuguese developed a slave trade from Guinea, before the French took over after 1849. Independence was granted in 1958 after a referendum (it became the first independent state of French-speaking Africa) and until 1984 Guinea was ruled by the repressive regime of President Ahmed Sékou Touré, who isolated Guinea from the West. It was not until after his death that economic reforms began to work and relations with France were restored.

ECONOMY Two-thirds of the population are involved in agriculture and there are also considerable natural resources: huge reserves of bauxite account for 80% of export earnings.

AREA 245,860 sq km [94,927 sq mls]
POPULATION 6,702,000
CAPITAL (POPULATION) Conakry (810,000)
GOVERNMENT Multiparty republic
ETHNIC GROUPS Fulani 40%, Malinké 26%, Susu 11%
LANGUAGES French (official), Susu, Malinké
RELIGIONS Muslim 85%, traditional beliefs 5%
CURRENCY Guinean franc = 100 cauris
POPULATION DENSITY 27 per sq km [71 per sq ml]
URBAN POPULATION 28% of population

GUINEA-BISSAU

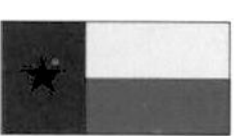

This flag, using the Pan-African colours, was adopted on gaining independence from Portugal in 1973. It is based on the one used by the PAIGC political party that led the struggle from 1962, who in turn based it on the flag of Ghana, the first of the African colonies to gain independence.

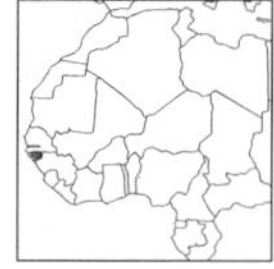

GEOGRAPHY Guinea-Bissau lies between Guinea and Senegal in West Africa. Thick forest and mangrove swamps cover the area nearest to the Atlantic Ocean, with savanna covering the inland area. The climate is tropical.

HISTORY AND POLITICS Formerly known as Portuguese Guinea, Portugal ruled for 500 years before independence was granted in 1973 after a guerilla war. In 1991 the Supreme Court ended 17 years of Socialist one-party rule by legalizing the opposition Democratic Front; multiparty elections were held in 1994.

ECONOMY About 85% of the active population are subsistence farmers. A fishing industry and cash crops such as tropical fruits, cotton and tobacco are being developed.

AREA 36,120 sq km [13,946 sq mls]
POPULATION 1,073,000
CAPITAL (POPULATION) Bissau (125,000)
GOVERNMENT Multiparty republic
ETHNIC GROUPS Balante 27%, Fulani 23%, Malinké 12%, Mandyako 11%, Pepel 10%
LANGUAGES Portuguese (official), Crioulo
RELIGIONS Traditional beliefs 54%, Muslim 38%
CURRENCY Peso = 100 centavos
POPULATION DENSITY 30 per sq km [77 per sq ml]

GUYANA

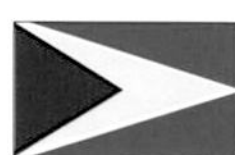

This striking design, adopted by Guyana on independence from Britain in 1966, has colours representing the people's energy building a new nation (red), their perseverance (black), minerals (yellow), rivers (white), and agriculture and forests (green).

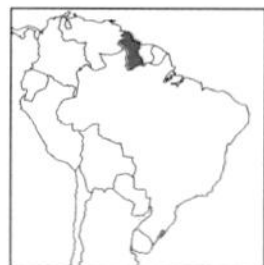

GEOGRAPHY With its name meaning 'land of many waters', Guyana has a vast interior with low forest-covered plateaux, the wooded Rapunumi savannas, river valleys and the Roraima Massif on the Venezuela-Brazil border. The coastal plain is mainly artificial, reclaimed from the marshes and swamps.

HISTORY, POLITICS AND ECONOMY Guyana was settled by the Dutch between 1616 and 1621. The territory was ceded to Britain in 1814 and became British Guiana. Independent since 1966, Guyana became a republic in 1970. It is largely uninhabited, with 95% of the population living within a few kilometres of the coast. Sugar production, bauxite mining and alumina production provide 80% of the overseas earnings.

AREA 214,970 sq km [83,000 sq mls]
POPULATION 832,000
CAPITAL (POPULATION) Georgetown (200,000)
GOVERNMENT Multiparty republic with a unicameral legislature
ETHNIC GROUPS Asian Indian 49%, Black 36%, Amerindian 7%, Mixed 7%
LANGUAGES English (official), Hindi, Urdu, Amerindian dialects
RELIGIONS Hindu 34%, Protestant 34%, Roman Catholic 18%, Sunni Muslim 9%

HAITI

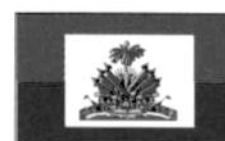

Although the colours, first used in 1803, are said to represent the country's two communities (the blacks [blue] and the mulattos [red]), the design of Haiti's flag derives from that of France, to which it once belonged. The present version was first used in 1843 and restored in 1986.

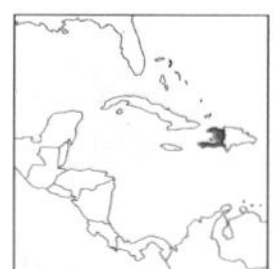

GEOGRAPHY Occupying the western third of Hispaniola, the Caribbean's second largest island, Haiti is mainly mountainous with a long, indented coast. Most of the country is centred around the Massif du Nord, with the narrow Massif de la Hotte forming the southern peninsula.

HISTORY AND POLITICS Ceded to France in 1697, Haiti developed as a sugar-producing colony. Once the richest part of the Caribbean, it is now one of the world's poorest nations. Since a slave revolt in 1804, it has been plagued by continuous instability and violence, particularly during the regimes of François Duvalier ('Papa Doc') and his son Jean-Claude ('Baby Doc') from 1957. The first multiparty elections were held in 1990, but the military took over in 1991. In 1994, the USA sent in troops to restore democracy and Father Aristide was reinstated as president.

ECONOMY With few natural resources, coffee is the main cash crop; 60% of the population live at or below the poverty line.

AREA 27,750 sq km [10,714 sq mls]
POPULATION 7,180,000
CAPITAL (POPULATION) Port-au-Prince (1,402,000)
GOVERNMENT Multiparty republic
ETHNIC GROUPS Black 95%, Mulatto 5%
LANGUAGES French (official) 10%, Haitian Creole 88%
RELIGIONS Christian (Roman Catholic 80%), Voodoo
CURRENCY Gourde = 100 centimes
POPULATION DENSITY 259 per sq km [670 per sq ml]

HONDURAS

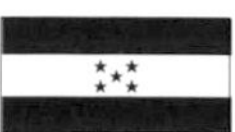

Officially adopted in 1949, the flag of Honduras is based on that of the Central American Federation (see Guatemala). Honduras left the organization in 1838, but in 1866 added the five stars to the flag to express a hope for a future federation.

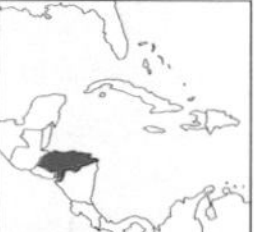

GEOGRAPHY Some 80% of Honduras is mountainous, with peaks of more than 2,500 m [8,000 ft] in the west. The mountain ranges are metalliferous: gold and silver deposits were, and still are, very important to the economy.

HISTORY AND POLITICS The first Spanish *conquistadores* came to Honduras to search for gold and founded the capital city in 1524. It became an independent republic in 1838, and after a civil war in the 1920s a series of military regimes ruled until 1980, when civilians took over. Since then there have been democratic governments but the military retains an interest.

ECONOMY Bananas and coffee are the chief cash crops and there is little industrialization. Lead, silver and zinc are mined.

AREA 112,090 sq km [43,278 sq mls]
POPULATION 5,940,000
CAPITAL (POPULATION) Tegucigalpa (679,000)
GOVERNMENT Multiparty republic with a unicameral legislature
ETHNIC GROUPS Mestizo 90%, Amerindian 7%, Black (including Black Carib) 2%, White 1%
LANGUAGES Spanish (official), Black Carib (Garifuna), English Creole, Miskito
RELIGIONS Roman Catholic 85%

HONG KONG

HONG KONG

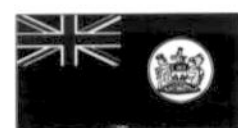

Hong Kong has flown the Blue Ensign since 1841 when it became a British dependent territory. The coat of arms dates from 1959, and includes the British lion and the Chinese dragon. In 1997 Hong Kong will revert to Chinese government control and a new flag will be adopted.

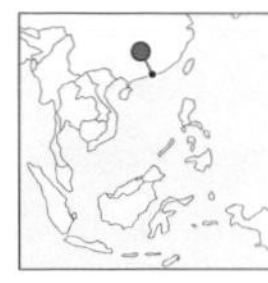

GEOGRAPHY The British Dependency of Hong Kong is made up of Hong Kong Island (which is 13 km [8 mls] long), about 235 smaller islands, the Kowloon peninsula in the Chinese province of Guangdong and the 'New Territories' adjoining it. Summers are hot and humid with heavy rain, while winters are mild and dry. Hong Kong is very densely populated, but has few natural resources of its own and most of its water, food and raw materials comes from China.

HISTORY AND POLITICS Hong Kong was acquired by Britain in three stages between 1842 and 1898. In 1898 Britain signed a 99-year lease with the Chinese government, and in 1997 the country will revert to Chinese rule. Under a 1984 accord, China agreed to allow Hong Kong full economic autonomy and the ability to pursue its capitalist path for at least another 50 years, by operating it as a special administrative region.

ECONOMY Hong Kong's successful economy is based on manufacturing (including textiles and plastics), banking and commerce. It has the world's biggest container port, is the biggest exporter of clothes and the tenth biggest trader. China will increase its export earnings by over 25% on changeover.

AREA 1,071 sq km [413 sq mls]
POPULATION 6,000,000
CAPITAL –
GOVERNMENT British Dependent territory with a unicameral legislature
ETHNIC GROUPS Chinese 97%, others 2% (including European)
LANGUAGES English and Chinese (official)
RELIGIONS Buddhist majority, Confucian, Taoist, Christian, Muslim, Hindu, Sikh, Jewish
CURRENCY Hong Kong dollar = 100 cents
MAIN EXPORTS Textiles, clothing, plastic and light metal products
POPULATION DENSITY 5,602 per sq km [14,527 per sq ml]

HUNGARY

The tricolour became popular in the European revolutions of 1848, though the colours had been in the Hungarian arms since the 15th century. Adopted in 1919, the design was amended in 1957 to remove the state emblem, which had been added in 1949.

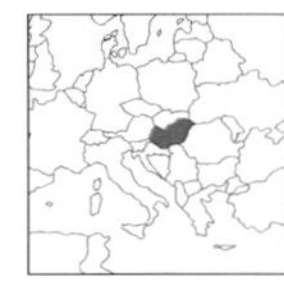

GEOGRAPHY Hungary has two large lowland areas – the Great Plain (Nagyalföld) in the south-east, which is dissected by the country's two main rivers, the Danube and the Tisza, and the Little Plain (Kisalföld) in the north-west. These plains make extremely fertile agricultural land. Europe's second longest river, the Danube, flows through Hungary on its way to the Black Sea.

HISTORY AND POLITICS As a large part of the Austro-Hungarian Empire, Hungary enjoyed an autonomous position within the Dual Monarchy from 1867, but defeat in World War I saw nearly 70% of its territory apportioned to Czechoslovakia, Yugoslavia and Romania. A Communist state was established in 1949 after occupation by the Soviet Red Army. The Uprising of 1956 was put down by Soviet troops, but successive governments have been fairly progressive. In 1989 a new constitution was adopted, making Hungary a multiparty state.

ECONOMY There are reserves of gas and bauxite, but other natural resources are scarce. Many raw materials are imported and the main industrial centres are in the north.

AREA 93,030 sq km [35,919 sq mls]
POPULATION 10,500,000
CAPITAL (POPULATION) Budapest (2,009,000)
GOVERNMENT Multiparty republic
ETHNIC GROUPS Magyar 97%, Gypsy, German, Slovak
LANGUAGES Hungarian (official), German, Slovak
RELIGIONS Roman Catholic 68%, Protestant 25%
CURRENCY Forint = 100 fillér
MAIN EXPORTS Machinery, vehicles, iron and steel
POPULATION DENSITY 113 per sq km [292 per sq ml]

ICELAND

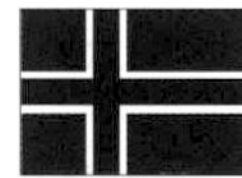

Dating from 1915, the flag became official on independence from Denmark in 1944. It uses the traditional Icelandic colours of blue and white and is in fact the same as the Norwegian flag, but with the blue and red colours reversed.

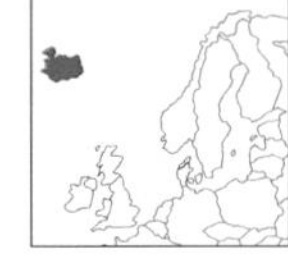

GEOGRAPHY Iceland is situated far out in the North Atlantic Ocean and arises geologically from the boundary between Europe and America – the Mid-Atlantic Ridge. A central zone of recently active volcanoes and fissures crosses Iceland from north to south: in the thousand years of settlement, between 150 and 200 eruptions have occurred in the active zones. Four large ice-caps cover 11% of the land surface.

HISTORY AND POLITICS Colonized by Viking farmers in the 9th century, Iceland became a dependency of first Norway, and then Denmark, although it was mainly self-governing after what is thought to be one of the world's earliest parliaments was set up in AD 930. In 1944 it became a republic after sharing a sovereign with Denmark after 1918.

ECONOMY The economy is based on deep-sea fishing; fish and fish products make up 70% of exports. About a fifth of the land is used for agriculture, mostly to graze cattle and sheep.

AREA 103,000 sq km [39,768 sq mls]
POPULATION 269,000
CAPITAL (POPULATION) Reykjavik (103,000)
GOVERNMENT Multiparty republic with a unicameral parliament
ETHNIC GROUPS Icelandic 97%
LANGUAGES Icelandic (official)
RELIGIONS Lutheran 92%, Roman Catholic 1%
CURRENCY Króna = 100 aurar
MAIN EXPORTS Fish products, unwrought aluminium
POPULATION DENSITY 3 per sq km [8 per sq ml]

INDIA

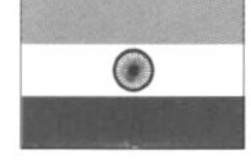

India's flag evolved during the struggle for freedom from British rule. The orange represents the Hindu majority, green the country's many Muslims and white peace. The Buddhist wheel symbol, the blue charka, was added on independence in 1947.

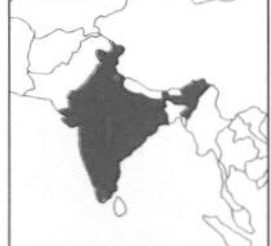

GEOGRAPHY India is the world's seventh largest country and extends from high in the Himalayas through the Tropic of Cancer to the warm waters of the Indian Ocean at 8°N. There are a wide variety of landscapes. These include: the Himalayan foothills in the north, where there are harsh, dry highlands and fertile valleys with rice-terraces; the lowlands of Uttar Pradesh, criss-crossed by the Ganges and Jumna rivers and their many tributaries and densely populated; the Thar or Great Indian Desert which lies mostly in Rajasthan; and the coastline of peninsular India lined with coconut groves, rising to the mountain chain of the Western Ghats.

HISTORY AND POLITICS India's earliest settlers were widely scattered across the subcontinent in Stone Age times. The first of its civilizations developed in the Indus Valley about 2600 BC and by the 3rd and 4th centuries BC Pataliputra (modern Patna) formed the centre of a loosely held empire that extended across the peninsula and beyond into Afghanistan. By 1805 the British East India Company was virtually in control after many battles fought by Britain in both Europe and India to gain superiority over local factions and other European rivals (such as Denmark and France). In 1947 the Indian subcontinent became independent from Britain, but divided into India (Hindu) and Pakistan (Muslim). The sheer size and population of India has caused many problems of organization and development, leaving a complex society.

ECONOMY Some 70% of the population works in agriculture, mostly on small farms and growing crops such as rice, wheat, tea, barley, jute, sorghum and millet. India is the world's third largest coal producer and industrialization has progressed rapidly since independence, with a series of five-year plans.

AREA 3,287,590 sq km [1,269,338 sq mls]
POPULATION 942,989,000
CAPITAL (POPULATION) New Delhi (301,000)
GOVERNMENT Multiparty federal republic with a bicameral legislature
ETHNIC GROUPS Indo-Aryan (Caucasoid) 72%, Dravidian (Aboriginal) 25%, other (mainly Mongoloid) 3%

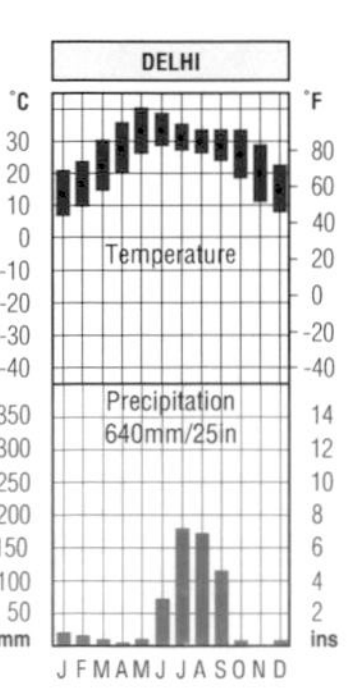

The summer rains, typical of the Indian monsoon, arrive later and are less intense at Delhi than in the lower parts of the Ganges Valley. Between November and May, the dry season, there is abundant sunshine and temperatures increase rapidly until the arrival of the rains in June. During the rainy season the temperature is uniformly hot.

INDONESIA

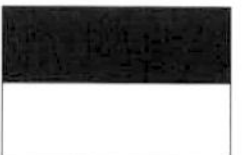

While the colours date back to the Middle Ages, they were adopted by political groups in the struggle against the Netherlands in the 1920s and became the national flag in 1945, when Indonesia finally proclaimed its independence.

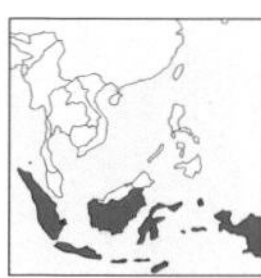

GEOGRAPHY Indonesia is the world's largest island chain with about 13,000 islands, of which less than half are inhabited. There are over 100 active volcanoes – the eruption of Krakatoa in 1883 killed 30,000 people. All the islands are mountainous. The natural vegetation of the tropical lowlands is rainforest, much of which has now been cleared for cultivation. Rainfall is heaviest in summer, most of it falling in thunderstorms. Temperatures are high throughout the year.

HISTORY AND POLITICS From the 16th century onwards the influences of European powers grew, dominated by the Dutch

East India Company. Freedom movements in the early 20th century found expression under Japanese occupation in World War II, and Indonesia declared independence in 1945. After four years of fighting, the Dutch finally recognized the country as a sovereign state in 1949.

ECONOMY Indonesia is a mainly agricultural nation with about a tenth of the land area under permanent cultivation, mostly producing rice, maize, cassava and sweet potato. There are also large plantations of rubber (second in the world), sugar cane, coffee and tea. The tourist industry is growing rapidly.

AREA 1,904,570 sq km [735,354 sq mls]
POPULATION 198,644,000
CAPITAL (POPULATION) Jakarta (8,259,000)
GOVERNMENT Multiparty republic
ETHNIC GROUPS Javanese 39%, Sundanese 16%, Bahasa Indonesian 12%, Madurese 5%, over 300 others
LANGUAGES Bahasa Indonesia (official), Javanese, Sundanese, Dutch, over 20 others
RELIGIONS Sunni Muslim 87%, Christian 10% (Roman Catholic 4%), Hindu 2%, Buddhist 1%
CURRENCY Rupiah = 100 sen
POPULATION DENSITY 104 per sq km [270 per sq ml]

IRAN

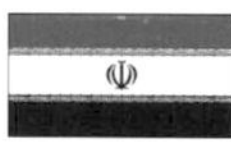

Iran's flag has been in use since July 1980 after the fall of the Shah and the rise of the Islamic Republic. Along the edges of the stripes is the legend 'Allah Akbar' (God is Great) repeated 22 times; in the centre is the new national emblem, symbolizing Allah (God).

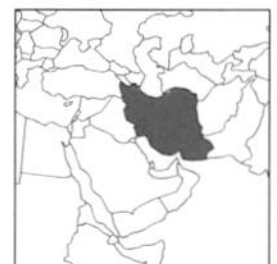

GEOGRAPHY The deserts of Kavir and Lut lie in the middle of Iran, surrounded by mountain ranges, which broaden in the west into the high plateaux of the Zagros. Fertile land is found near the Caspian Sea in the north, an area which is subject to earthquakes. The cities of the interior depend on complex arrangements of tunnels and channels for tapping underground water, and these have been supplemented by high dams, notably at Dezful. Most of the population live in the mountainous north and west of the country.

HISTORY AND POLITICS Before 1935 Iran was called Persia and retained its Shah until 1979 when a revolution toppled the

regime and replaced it with a radical fundamentalist Islamic republic, led by the exiled Ayatollah Khomeini. The Iran-Iraq war of 1980–8 saw Iranian casualties of between 150,000 and 630,000 and left its vital oil production at less than half the 1979 level (although still seventh in the world); consequently, Iran began to look to Western powers and recent years have seen closer links with them.

ECONOMY Oil and natural gas deposits are Iran's most important sources of wealth (oil was first discovered in 1908). About 20% of the population work on the land, while Iran is also known for its caviar and its carpets and rugs.

AREA 1,648,000 sq km [636,293 sq mls]
POPULATION 68,885,000
CAPITAL (POPULATION) Tehran (6,476,000)
GOVERNMENT Unitary Islamic republic, religious leader (elected by Council of Experts) exercises supreme authority
ETHNIC GROUPS Persian 46%, Azerbaijani 17%, Kurdish 9%, Gilaki 5%, Luri, Mazandarani, Baluchi, Arab
LANGUAGES Farsi (Persian) 48% (official), Kurdish, Baluchi, Turkic, Arabic, French
RELIGIONS Shiite Muslim 91%, Sunni Muslim 8%
CURRENCY Rial = 100 dinars
POPULATION DENSITY 42 per sq km [108 per sq ml]
URBAN POPULATION 57% of population

IRAQ

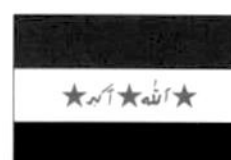

Using the four Pan-Arab colours, Iraq's flag was adopted in 1963 at the time of the proposed federation with Egypt and Syria. Iraq retained the three green stars, symbolizing the three countries, even though the union failed to materialize.

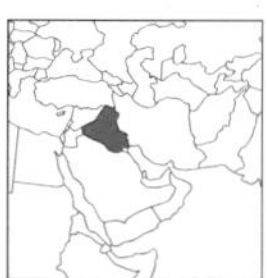

GEOGRAPHY Iraq essentially comprises the lower valleys and combined deltas of the Tigris and Euphrates rivers, which provide fertile land when supplied with water. In the north-east there is a hilly region, including part of the Zagros Mountains, and in the west is a large part of the Hamad or Syrian Desert. The country is landlocked except for its outlet to the Gulf at Shatt Al Arab Waterway, which is shared with Iran.

HISTORY AND POLITICS Absorbed into the Ottoman Empire in the 16th century, Iraq was captured by British forces in 1916 and run as a virtual colony. The Hashemite dynasty ruled an independent kingdom from 1932, but in 1958 a republic was set up after a military coup. In 1968 the Pan-Arab Baathists seized

control and Saddam Hussein became president in 1979. The Iran-Iraq war of 1980–8 left over a million Iraqi men killed or wounded and nearly crippled the economy; this was worsened by the Second Gulf War when Iraq invaded Kuwait in August 1990 and annexed it as an Iraqi province. The international community first imposed sanctions and then sent in a multinational force to drive back the Iraqis, leaving Iraq with a crumbling infrastructure and a severe shortage of food.

ECONOMY The chief mineral resource is oil, with some sulphur and gypsum deposits and some crops (such as dates) and livestock. However, sanctions and war damage have caused economic chaos and much personal hardship.

AREA 438,320 sq km [169,235 sq mls]
POPULATION 20,184,000
CAPITAL (POPULATION) Baghdad (3,841,000)
GOVERNMENT Unitary republic
ETHNIC GROUPS Arab 77%, Kurd 19%, Turkmen 2%, Persian 2%, Assyrian
LANGUAGES Arabic (official), Kurdish, Turkish
RELIGIONS Shiite Muslim 62%, Sunni Muslim 34%
CURRENCY Dinar = 20 dirhams = 1,000 fils
MAIN EXPORTS Fuels and other energy 98%
MAIN IMPORTS Machinery and transport equipment, manufactured goods
POPULATION DENSITY 46 per sq km [119 per sq ml]
URBAN POPULATION 73% of population

IRELAND

The Irish flag was first used by nationalists in 1848 in the struggle for freedom from Britain and adopted in 1922 after independence. Green represents the Roman Catholics and orange the Protestants, with white in the middle representing the desire for peace between the two.

GEOGRAPHY The word 'Ireland' is today used as shorthand for the Republic of Ireland, which occupies some 80% of the whole island of Ireland, with the rest as Northern Ireland, which remains part of the United Kingdom. The landscape is made up of a central lowland and a series of different mountain chains, including the Wicklow Mountains in the south-east. The climate is mild and damp with high humidity and frequent fog.

HISTORY AND POLITICS The Anglo-Irish Treaty of 1921 established southern Ireland – Eire – as an independent state,

after it had been part of the United Kingdom since 1801. It became a republic in 1949 and joined the EU in 1973.

ECONOMY Agriculture is the traditional occupation of the Irish, together with fishing, home crafts and local labouring as extra sources of income. The eastern and south-eastern areas tend to be richer than the western areas, with large farms supporting cattle, sheep and racehorses. European Union grants have helped greatly and increased prosperity. Tourism and high-tech industries are important in the north-east.

AREA 70,280 sq km [27,135 sq mls]
POPULATION 3,589,000
CAPITAL (POPULATION) Dublin (1,024,000)
GOVERNMENT Unitary multiparty republic with a bicameral legislature
ETHNIC GROUPS Irish 94%
LANGUAGES Irish and English (both official)
RELIGIONS Roman Catholic 93%, Protestant 3%
CURRENCY Punt = 100 pence
MAIN EXPORTS Machinery and transport equipment 32%
POPULATION DENSITY 51 per sq km [132 per sq ml]

ISRAEL

ISRAEL

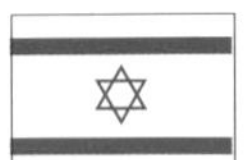

The blue and white stripes on Israel's flag are based on the tallit, *a Hebrew prayer shawl. In the centre is the ancient six-pointed Star of David. The flag was designed in America in 1891 and officially adopted by the new Jewish state in 1948.*

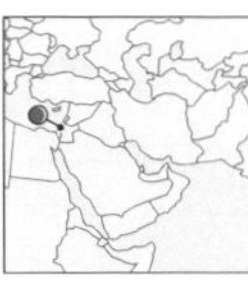

GEOGRAPHY About half of the total territory of Israel is covered by the desert plateau of the Negev in the south of the country. Its bedrock is covered with blown sand and loess, which, if irrigated, will grow grapes and tomatoes. The Dead Sea to the east is the world's lowest point (396 m [1,279 ft] below sea level), while in the north the Sea of Galilee is Israel's main reservoir of fresh water. The north has the most fertile land; the excellent farmland in the Upper Jordan Valley is reclaimed from Lake Huleh.

HISTORY AND POLITICS The state of Israel was created in 1948 and the return of the Jewish people to their homeland marked the end of 18 centuries of exile. After the Six Day War in 1967 Israel took over the administration of the 'West Bank' (from Jordan), the Gaza Strip (from Egypt) and the Golan Heights (from Syria). There have been five wars since 1948 in which Arab nations and Palestinians have fought against Israel. A peace accord was signed in September 1993 between Israel and the Palestinian Liberation Organization (PLO) and Palestinian self-rule has been established in the Gaza Strip and part of the West Bank. On 4 November 1995, Prime Minister Yitzhak Rabin was assassinated and Shimon Peres took over.

ECONOMY Although Israel is the world's top recipient of aid, mainly from the USA, it has become the most industrialized country in the Near East. Important industries include textiles and ceramics, plus iron smelting and chemical manufacturing at Haifa. Some 14% of the population work on the land, with crops such as oranges and olives, helped by extensive irrigation.

AREA 26,650 sq km [10,290 sq mls]
POPULATION 5,696,000
CAPITAL (POPULATION) Jerusalem (544,000)
GOVERNMENT Multiparty republic
ETHNIC GROUPS Jewish 82%, Arab 18%
LANGUAGES Hebrew and Arabic (official)
RELIGIONS Jewish 82%, Muslim 14%, Christian 2%
CURRENCY New Israeli shekel = 100 agorat
MAIN EXPORTS Machinery 29%, diamonds 29%, chemicals 22%, textiles 8%, foodstuffs 5%
MAIN IMPORTS Diamonds 20%, capital goods 15%, consumer goods 11%, fuels and lubricants 8%
POPULATION DENSITY 214 per sq km [554 per sq ml]
URBAN POPULATION 91% of population
LAND USE Arable 21%, grass 7%

ITALY

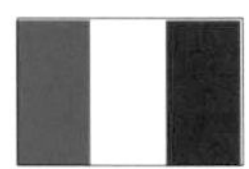

When Napoleon invaded Italy in 1796, the French Republican National Guard carried a military standard of vertical green, white and red stripes. After many changes, it was finally adopted as the national flag after the unification of Italy in 1861.

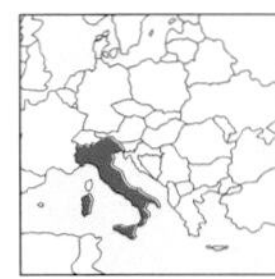

GEOGRAPHY The Alpine period of mountain building, when the main ranges of the Alps and the Apennines were uplifted together, determined much of Italy's topographical structure. The Apennines, in central Italy, reach their highest peaks – almost 3,000 m [9,800 ft] – in the Gran Sasso range overlooking the central Adriatic Sea near Pescara. Between the mountains are long, narrow basins, some of which contain lakes. In the north lies the large Lombardy plain, drained by the River Po, and the most productive industrial and agricultural area in Italy. The islands of Sicily and Sardinia are also Italian; Sardinia lies 480 km [300 mls] from the Italian coast and has a rugged, windswept terrain.

HISTORY AND POLITICS In 1800 present-day Italy was made up of several political units, including the Papal States, and a substantial part of the north-east was occupied by Austria. Unification – the *Risorgimento* – began early in the 19th century, but little progress was made until an alliance between France and Piedmont drove Austria from Lombardy in 1859. The other states were soon brought into the alliance and by 1861 King Victor Emmanuel was proclaimed ruler of a united Italy, with Venetia acquired from Austria in 1866 and Rome annexed in 1871. A republic was set up in 1946 and Italy was a founder member of the EC. Northern and southern Italy still have very different characteristics, mostly due to the distance between them and their very disparate social and historical backgrounds.

ECONOMY With few natural resources, Italy has managed to make great economic progress. Textiles, metal-working, engineering and food processing industries all flourish in the north and crops include grapes, olives, tomatoes and wheat. The black economy may boost official GNP by as much as 10%.

AREA 301,270 sq km [116,320 sq mls]
POPULATION 58,181,000
CAPITAL (POPULATION) Rome (2,723,000)
GOVERNMENT Multiparty republic with a bicameral legislature
ETHNIC GROUPS Italian 94%, German
LANGUAGES Italian 94%, Sardinian 3%
RELIGIONS Roman Catholic 83%

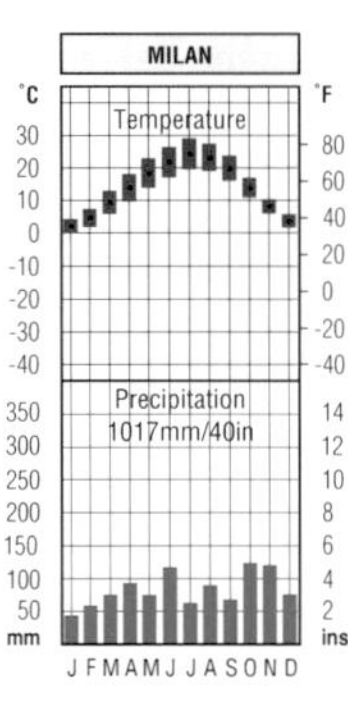

Although the plains of Lombardy lie within the Mediterranean basin they have a climate more like that of central Europe, though with hotter summers and warmer winters. Sunshine averages under 5 hours a day, whereas in southern Italy it can average 8 to 10 hours between May and September. Winter is relatively dry and cold with some snow.

IVORY COAST (CÔTE D'IVOIRE)

On independence from France in 1960 this former colony adopted a compromise between the French tricolour and the colours of the Pan-African movement. Orange represents the northern savannas, white is for peace and unity, and green for the forests and agriculture.

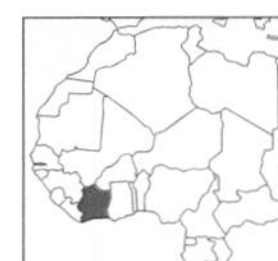

GEOGRAPHY Known as the Côte d'Ivoire since 1986, it is located in West Africa with a coastline on the Gulf of Guinea. There are substantial rainforests in the south, although their rate of depletion is rapid. The climate has uniformly high temperatures and humidity.

HISTORY AND POLITICS France came to the region in the 1500s, when traders started buying slaves and ivory. It became a colony in 1893 and part of French West Africa in 1904. In 1960 independence was gained and in 1990 the first multiparty elections were held, returning to power (until his death in 1993) Felix Houphouët-Boigny, Africa's longest-ruling head of state.

ECONOMY The Ivory Coast is the world's largest producer and exporter of cocoa and Africa's biggest producer of coffee. Its free-market economy has attracted many foreign investors.

AREA 322,460 sq km [124,502 sq mls]
POPULATION 14,271,000
CAPITAL (POPULATION) Yamoussoukro (126,000)
GOVERNMENT Multiparty republic
ETHNIC GROUPS Akan 41%, Kru 18%, Voltaic 16%, Malinké 15%, Southern Mande 10%
LANGUAGES French (official), African languages
RELIGIONS Muslim 38%, Christian 38%, traditional beliefs 17%
CURRENCY CFA franc = 100 centimes

JAMAICA

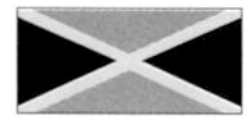

Jamaica's distinctive flag dates from independence from Britain in 1962. The gold stands for the country's natural resources and sunshine, the green for its agriculture and hope for the future, and black for the nation's hardships.

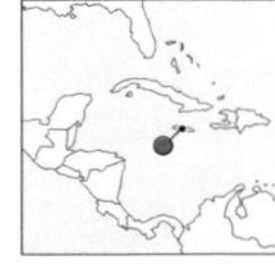

GEOGRAPHY Third largest of the Caribbean islands, Jamaica has a central range culminating in Blue Mountain Peak (2,256 m [7,402 ft]). Called Xaymaca ('land of wood and water') by the Arawak Indians, half the country lies above 300 m [1,000 ft] and moist south-east trade winds bring rain to the mountains. There is a rich variety of tropical and subtropical vegetation.

HISTORY AND POLITICS Britain took Jamaica from the Spaniards in the 17th century and it became a centre of slavery before emancipation in 1838. After independence Michael Manley led a democratic socialist government, which led to some economic growth in the 1980s, but migration, unemployment and underemployment levels are high.

ECONOMY Tourism and bauxite production are the most important industries, having replaced the traditional sugar trade.

AREA 10,990 sq km [4,243 sq mls]
POPULATION 2,700,000
CAPITAL (POPULATION) Kingston (644,000)
GOVERNMENT Constitutional monarchy
ETHNIC GROUPS Black 76%, Afro-European 15%, East Indian and Afro-East Indian 3%, White 3%
LANGUAGES English (official), English Creole, Hindi, Chinese, Spanish
RELIGIONS Protestant 70%, Roman Catholic 8%
POPULATION DENSITY 246 per sq km [636 per sq ml]

JAPAN

The geographical position of Japan in the East is expressed in the name of the country, Nihon-Koku *(Land of the Rising Sun), and in the flag. Officially adopted in 1870, the simple design had been used by Japanese emperors for many centuries.*

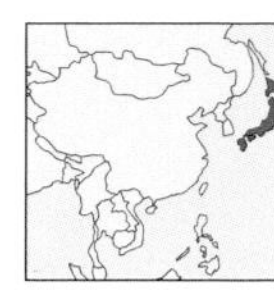

AREA 377,800 sq km [145,869 sq mls]
POPULATION 125,156,000
CAPITAL (POPULATION) Tokyo (11,927,000)
GOVERNMENT Constitutional monarchy with a bicameral legislature

GEOGRAPHY The Japanese archipelago lies off the Asian mainland and 98% of the territory is on four large and closely grouped islands (Hokkaido, Honshu, Shikoku and Kyushu), the remainder being made up of some 4,000 smaller islands. Japan is predominantly mountainous and only 16% of the land is cultivable; this small area of land must support the eighth largest population in the world. The islands are located in one of the Earth's zones of geological instability, meaning volcanic eruptions and earthquakes are frequent. The folding and faulting has produced a wide variety of landforms.

HISTORY AND POLITICS Early Japanese development saw the arrival of many immigrants from Korea and elsewhere in Asia, so that by the 5th century BC the country was divided into numerous clans. The Japanese imperial dynasty emerged from about AD 200 and government was conducted in the name of the emperor by warrior leaders (*shoguns*). Modern Japan has seen the power of the emperor reduced, with rapid industrialization and the growth of overseas colonies in the early 20th century; after World War II there was a period of US administration, during which many reforms were enacted, until 1952.

ECONOMY The Japanese boom of the late 20th century gave Japan the world's second most powerful economy, leading world markets in high-technology and electronic equipment. Its huge trade surpluses have caused some resentment worldwide.

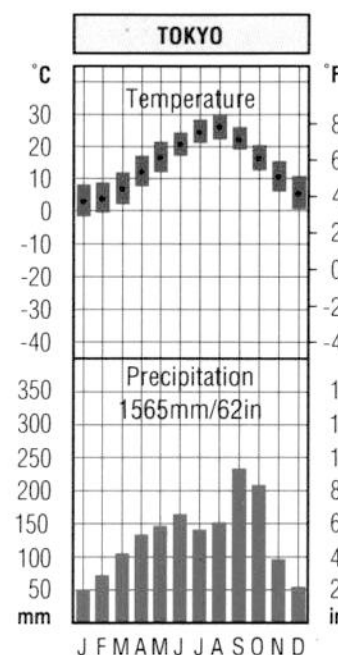

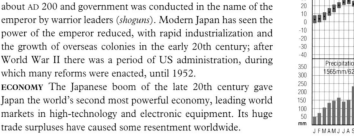

Despite its maritime location, Tokyo has a large annual range of temperature (23°C [41°F]) due to the seasonal reversal of wind, blowing from the cold heart of Asia in winter and from the warm Pacific in the summer. Winter weather is usually fine and sunny with some frost, while summer in Tokyo is hot and humid with abundant rainfall.

JORDAN

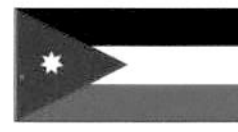

Green, white and black are the colours of the three tribes that led the Arab Revolt against the Turks in 1917, while red is the colour of the Hussein dynasty. The star was added in 1928 with its seven points representing the first seven verses of the Koran.

AREA 89,210 sq km [34,444 sq mls]
POPULATION 5,547,000
CAPITAL (POPULATION) Amman (1,272,000)
GOVERNMENT Constitutional monarchy with a bicameral legislature
ETHNIC GROUPS Arab 99%, (Palestinian 60%)
LANGUAGES Arabic (official)
RELIGIONS Sunni Muslim 93%, Christian 5%
CURRENCY Jordan dinar = 1,000 fils
MAIN EXPORTS Potash, phosphates, citrus fruits, vegetables
POPULATION DENSITY 62 per sq km [161 per sq ml]
URBAN POPULATION 70% of population

GEOGRAPHY Jordan lies to the east of Israel and some 87% of the land is desert. There is a small stretch of Red Sea coast centred on the important port of Aqaba, and fertile uplands are found along the rift valley that contains the River Jordan and the Dead Sea along the border with Israel.

HISTORY AND POLITICS After World War I the Arab territories of the Ottoman Empire were divided up and Jordan (known as Transjordan until 1949) passed from Turkish to British control. In 1946 it became independent and in 1948 acquired the crucial Palestinian West Bank area, but lost it to Israel in the 1967 Arab-Israeli war. In 1988 King Hussein renounced all responsibility for the West Bank, but ten UN refugee camps for Palestinians are located within Jordan and 60% of the population is Palestinian. There have been signs of political progress with martial law lifted in 1991 after 21 years.

ECONOMY Only 5% of the land is cultivable and the 1967 war deprived Jordan of 80% of its fruit-growing area (the West Bank). The limited agricultural base (including tomatoes, olives, barley and wheat) and few natural resources are supported by the mining of phosphates and potash, the main exports.

KAZAKSTAN

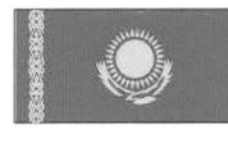

The flag of Kazakstan was adopted on 4 June 1992. The soaring eagle and the golden sun represent the love of freedom and the blue represents the cloudless skies. There is also a hoist-based vertical strip of golden ornamentation.

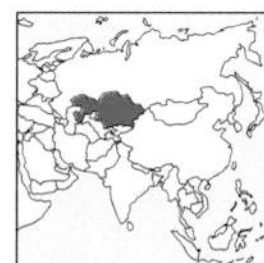

AREA 2,717,300 sq km [1,049,150 sq mls]
POPULATION 17,099,000
CAPITAL (POPULATION) Alma-Ata (1,147,000)
GOVERNMENT Multiparty republic
ETHNIC GROUPS Kazak 41%, Russian 37%, German 5%, Ukrainian 5%, Uzbek, Tatar
LANGUAGES Kazak, Russian
RELIGIONS Sunni Muslim, Christian
CURRENCY Tenge = 500 rubles
MAIN INDUSTRIES Oil refining (notably for aviation fuel), metallurgy, engineering, chemicals, footwear
POPULATION DENSITY 6 per sq km [16 per sq ml]
URBAN POPULATION 58% of population

GEOGRAPHY Kazakstan is a huge country, ninth largest in the world, and comprises mainly vast plains with a (mineral-rich) central plateau. North to south the steppe gradually gives way to desert. The climate is continental with hot summers and very cold winters.

HISTORY AND POLITICS Successive Soviet regimes have used Kazakstan as a dumping-ground and test-bed (for nuclear weapons) and the Aral Sea has shrunk by 70% after Soviet irrigation projects dried up its two feeder rivers. However, in 1991 it led the Central Asian states into the new Commonwealth of States (CIS) as an independent republic and has now emerged as a powerful country, wealthier and more diversified than the other Asian republics.

ECONOMY There are rich deposits of oil and gas, as well as coal, iron ore, bauxite and gold, and rapid industrialization (for example, chemical and footwear industries) has taken place in recent years. Agriculture is mostly concentrated on livestock rearing, although there is quite substantial grain production.

KENYA

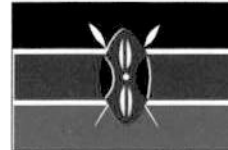

The Kenyan flag, which dates from independence from Britain in 1963, is based on the flag of the Kenya African National Union, which led the colonial struggle. The Masai warrior's shield and crossed spears represent the defence of freedom.

AREA 580,370 sq km [224,081 sq mls]
POPULATION 28,240,000
CAPITAL (POPULATION) Nairobi (1,429,000)
GOVERNMENT Multiparty republic with a unicameral legislature
ETHNIC GROUPS Kikuyu 18%, Luhya 12%, Luo 11%, Kamba 10%, Kalenjin 10%
LANGUAGES Swahili and English (both official), Kikuyu, over 200 tribal languages
RELIGIONS Christian 73% (Roman Catholic 27%, Protestant 19%, others 27%), African indigenous 19%, Muslim 6%
CURRENCY Kenyan shilling = 100 cents
POPULATION DENSITY 49 per sq km [126 per sq ml]
URBAN POPULATION 25% of population
LAND USE Arable 4%, grass 67%

GEOGRAPHY Lying on the Equator, most of Kenya comprises plains cut across old crystalline rocks. The Kenya Highlands were formed by volcanoes and lava flows, with Mt Kenya at 5,199 m [17,000 ft], and are bisected by the Great Rift Valley. Some 80% of the population live on about 15% of the plains in the south-west, where average rainfalls of over 750 mm [30 in] a year support the dense farming populations. The climate is tropical, but greatly affected by altitude; for example, in summer, Nairobi is 10°C [18°F] cooler than Mombasa on the coast.

HISTORY AND POLITICS Kenya has been known as the 'cradle of mankind' since the discovery of the earliest human bones on the shores of Lake Turkana. It had one of the world's highest birth rates (47 per 1,000) but has made substantial efforts to reduce this in recent years. The first multiparty elections for 26 years were held in 1992, although Daniel arap Moi was re-elected amid allegations of vote-rigging.

ECONOMY By some African standards and even being such a large aid recipient, Kenya has a fairly stable economy. About 80% of the population work in agriculture, producing crops such as maize, coffee, tea (Kenya is the world's fourth largest producer) and sisal. Tourism is now a very important source of foreign exchange, with many game parks and beach resorts.

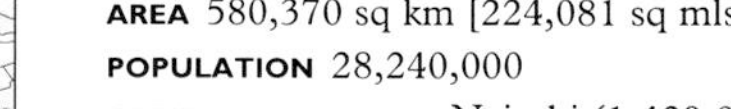

KIRIBATI

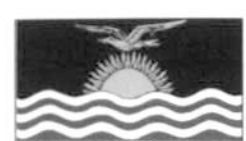

The flag is a banner of the arms granted to the Gilbert and Ellice Islands in 1937 and was adopted on independence in 1979. Kiribati is the sole Commonwealth country to use an armorial banner, that is, a flag whose design corresponds exactly to the shield of its arms.

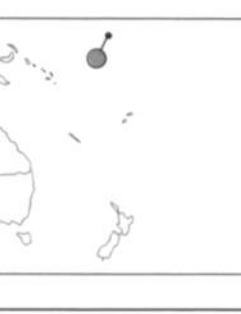

Known as the Gilbert Islands until independence from Britain in 1979, Kiribati comprises three groups of coral atolls scattered over 5 million sq km [2 million sq mls] of the Pacific Ocean. Very little of the islands rises over 4 m [13 ft] and temperatures are always high. The main crops are coconuts, bananas, papayas and taro (*babai* – the staple vegetable), and the main export is copra. There is a heavy dependency on foreign aid and a real problem of overcrowding.

AREA 728 sq km [281 sq mls]
POPULATION 80,000
CAPITAL (POPULATION) Tarawa (20,000)
GOVERNMENT Multiparty republic
ETHNIC GROUPS Micronesian
LANGUAGES English (official), Gilbertese
RELIGIONS Roman Catholic 53%, Protestant 51%
CURRENCY Australian dollar
URBAN POPULATION 39% of population

KOREA, NORTH

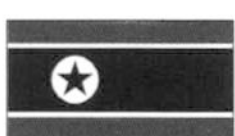

The Korean Democratic People's Republic has flown this flag since the country was split into two separate states in 1948. The colours are those of the traditional Korean standard, but in a new Communist design with a red star.

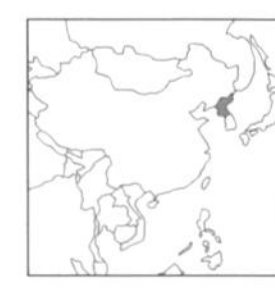

GEOGRAPHY North Korea covers the northern half of the Korean peninsula (with 55% of the land area) and has a largely mountainous landscape. Only 20% of the surface area is suitable for cultivation and the climate can be harsh, with long and severe winters. Coniferous and broadleaf forests cover some two-thirds of the country.
HISTORY AND POLITICS After World War II Korea split into North and South and the Soviet Union installed a Stalinist regime in the North. In the Korean War of 1950–3 North Korea was supported by China and a demilitarized zone was established between North and South. Despite the death of the dictator Kim Il Sung in July 1994, the country remains isolated.
ECONOMY 90% of cultivated land is under the control of co-operative farms and four out of every ten North Koreans work on the land. There are rich deposits of minerals, including coal, which supplies 70% of energy needs.

AREA 120,540 sq km [46,540 sq mls]
POPULATION 23,931,000
CAPITAL (POPULATION) Pyongyang (2,639,000)
GOVERNMENT Single-party socialist republic
ETHNIC GROUPS Korean 99%
LANGUAGES Korean (official), Chinese
RELIGIONS Traditional beliefs 16%, Chondogyo 14%, Buddhist 2%, Christian 1%
CURRENCY North Korean won = 100 chon
POPULATION DENSITY 199 per sq km [514 per sq ml]

KOREA, SOUTH

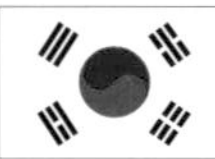

Adopted in 1950, South Korea's flag is the traditional white of peace. The central emblem signifies nature's opposing forces: the black symbols stand for the four seasons, the points of the compass, and the Sun, Moon, Earth and Heaven.

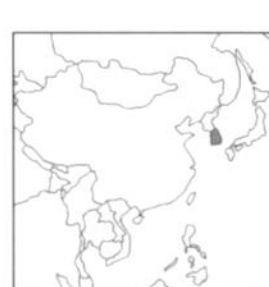

GEOGRAPHY South Korea has a smaller land area than North Korea but about twice as many people. The landscape is mostly made up of highlands (the Taebaek Mountains), with an eastern coastline that is steep and largely uninhabited and a western coastline that is indented, with many islands and natural harbours. Summers are hot and wet, and winters are cold and dry with strong north-westerly winds blowing from central Asia.
HISTORY AND POLITICS Before partition Korea was known as the 'Land of the Morning Calm' and was very much a united kingdom. After the civil war at the beginning of the 1950s, South Korea had a very different development to North Korea. An economic miracle based on slender natural resources and cheap and plentiful labour transformed the economy and made South Korea into one of the strongest countries in Asia (the economy grew at nearly 9% a year between 1960 and 1990).
ECONOMY South Korea is now a world leader in the manufacture of footwear and consumer electronics and in shipbuilding. The manufacturing base of textiles remains important, as does agriculture; rice is the main crop and South Korea's fishing fleet is ninth in the world, with, for example, catches of oysters.

AREA 99,020 sq km [38,232 sq mls]
POPULATION 45,088,000
CAPITAL (POPULATION) Seoul (10,628,000)
GOVERNMENT Unitary multiparty republic
ETHNIC GROUPS Korean 99%
LANGUAGES Korean (official)
RELIGIONS Buddhist 28%, Protestant 19%, Roman Catholic 6%, Confucian 1%
CURRENCY South Korean won = 100 chon
MAIN EXPORTS Transport equipment 11%, electrical machinery 9%, footwear 6%, textile fabrics 5%
MAIN IMPORTS Petroleum and petroleum products 11%, electronic components 6%
POPULATION DENSITY 455 per sq km [1,179 per sq ml]

KUWAIT

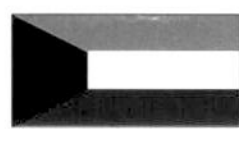

Kuwait's national flag dates from 1961, when the country ceased to be a British protectorate and gained its independence. The flag features the four Pan-Arab colours, the black portion having an unusual trapezium shape.

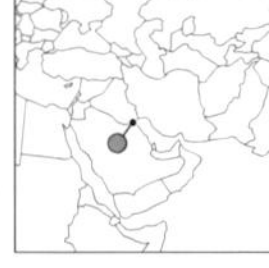

GEOGRAPHY Kuwait lies at the northern end of the Arabian Gulf, and is largely made up of desert, with a climate of high summer temperatures and little rainfall.
HISTORY, POLITICS AND ECONOMY A former British protectorate, Kuwait became fully independent in 1961. Its oil reserves are the third largest in the world and have made it very prosperous. However, in 1990 Iraq invaded Kuwait and claimed it as its own. A multinational force liberated Kuwait in January 1991, but not before almost all industrial and commercial installations had been destroyed and the Iraqis had set fire to more than 500 oil-wells. In spite of the devastation, oil and gas production remains the mainstay of the Kuwaiti economy.

AREA 17,820 sq km [6,880 sq mls]
POPULATION 1,668,000
CAPITAL (POPULATION) Kuwait City (189,000)
GOVERNMENT Constitutional monarchy
ETHNIC GROUPS Kuwaiti Arab 44%, non-Kuwaiti Arab 36%, various Asian 20%
LANGUAGES Arabic 78%, Kurdish 10%, Farsi 4%
RELIGIONS Muslim 90% (Sunni 63%), Christian 8%, Hindu 2%
CURRENCY Kuwaiti dinar = 1,000 fils

KYRGYZSTAN

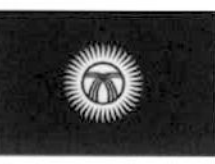

The flag was adopted in March 1992 and depicts a bird's-eye view of a yurt within a radiant sun. The yurt stands for the ancient nomadic way of life and the rays of the sun for the 40 traditional tribes.

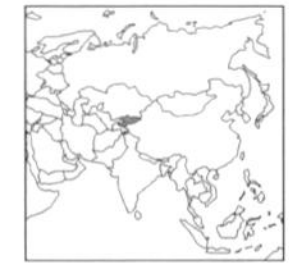

GEOGRAPHY Kyrgyzstan is geographically isolated and mainly mountainous, dominated by the western end of the Tian Shan, with peaks rising to the 7,439 m [24,405 ft] of Pik Pobedy.
HISTORY AND POLITICS 'European'-style policies towards a capitalist democracy have been pursued since independence in 1991. The president, Askar Akayev (re-elected in 1996), has encouraged rapid privatization and foreign trade and has established important links with China.
ECONOMY Kyrgyzstan has a strong agricultural economy producing such crops as cotton, tobacco, mulberry trees and sugar beet. The main manufacturing industry is textiles and there are large reserves of uranium, mercury and gold.

AREA 198,500 sq km [76,640 sq mls]
POPULATION 4,738,000
CAPITAL (POPULATION) Bishkek (628,000)
GOVERNMENT Multiparty republic
ETHNIC GROUPS Kyrgyz 53%, Russian 22%, Uzbek 13%, Ukrainian 3%, Tatar 2%, German 2%
LANGUAGES Kyrgyz, Russian
RELIGIONS Sunni Muslim, Christian
CURRENCY Som = 100 tyiyn
POPULATION DENSITY 24 per sq km [62 per sq ml]

LAOS

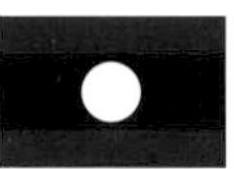

Since 1975 Laos has flown the flag of the Pathet Lao, the Communist movement which won the long struggle for control of the country. The blue stands for the Mekong River, the white disc for the moon, the red for the unity and purpose of the people.

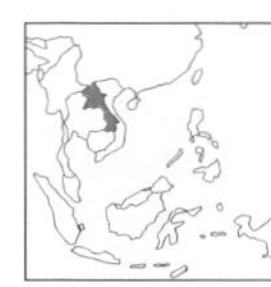

GEOGRAPHY Laos is a narrow, landlocked, largely mountainous country in South-east Asia, with no railways – the Mekong River is the main artery. The hilly terrain broadens in the north to a wide plateau, 2,000 m [6,500 ft] above sea level. The climate is affected by the seasonal reversal of winds associated with the monsoon, with a wet season between April and October.
HISTORY AND POLITICS Laos became a French protectorate in 1893 and was ruled as part of Indochina. Independence was granted in 1954, after which followed two decades of civil war. The Communists took power in 1975 and some reforms began in 1986, but Laos remains one of Asia's poorest countries and there is little chance of a multiparty democracy very soon.
ECONOMY Some 85% of the sparse population work on collective farms at subsistence level, growing mainly rice.

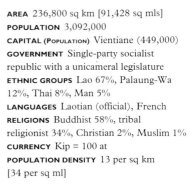

AREA 236,800 sq km [91,428 sq mls]
POPULATION 3,092,000
CAPITAL (POPULATION) Vientiane (449,000)
GOVERNMENT Single-party socialist republic with a unicameral legislature
ETHNIC GROUPS Lao 67%, Palaung-Wa 12%, Thai 8%, Man 5%
LANGUAGES Laotian (official), French
RELIGIONS Buddhist 58%, tribal religionist 34%, Christian 2%, Muslim 1%
CURRENCY Kip = 100 at
POPULATION DENSITY 13 per sq km [34 per sq ml]

LATVIA

The burgundy and white Latvian flag, revived after independence from the USSR in 1991, dates back to at least 1280. According to one legend, it was first made from a white sheet stained with the blood of a Latvian hero who was wrapped in it.

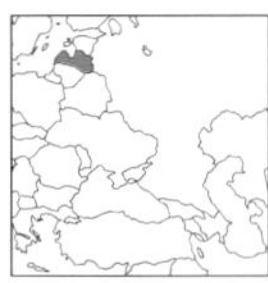

GEOGRAPHY Its Baltic coast heavily indented by the Gulf of Riga, Latvia is a small country of flat glaciated lowland. The land is covered by coniferous forests and lakes. The climate has long, cold winters and short summers, the warmest months being June to August, when temperatures may rise over 15°C [59°F].
HISTORY AND POLITICS The native Latvians (Letts) have a long history and highly developed culture, with nationalist movements dating to the late 19th century. Over 100 years later, Latvia became independent from the Soviet Union in 1991 and had joined the UN by the end of the year, together with the two other Baltic states (Estonia and Lithuania). Strong ties with Russia and the Ukraine remain, especially for energy supplies.
ECONOMY Latvia contains many of the less traditional former Soviet industries, such as electronics and consumer goods.

AREA 64,589 sq km [24,938 sq mls]
POPULATION 2,558,000
CAPITAL (POPULATION) Riga (840,000)
GOVERNMENT Multiparty republic
ETHNIC GROUPS Latvian 54%, Russian 33%, Belarussian 4%, Ukrainian 3%, Polish 2%
LANGUAGES Latvian (official) 54%, Russian 40%
RELIGIONS Christian (Lutheran, Catholic, Orthodox)
POPULATION DENSITY 40 per sq km [103 per sq ml]

LEBANON

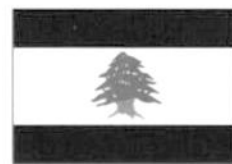

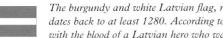

Adopted on independence in 1943, Lebanon's colours are those of the Lebanese Legion in World War I. The cedar tree, many of which grow in the country's mountains, has been a Lebanese symbol since biblical times.

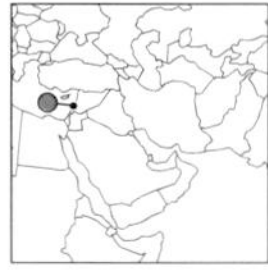

GEOGRAPHY Lebanon is located on the eastern shores of the Mediterranean, with the Lebanon Mountains rising behind a narrow coastal plain, and the fertile land of the Beqaa Valley covering much of central Lebanon.
HISTORY AND POLITICS Lebanon was originally part of the Ottoman Empire, before coming under French rule in 1918. Independence was granted in 1944 and there followed three decades of relative peace and prosperity. Beirut, the capital, was a centre of international commerce and a playground for the wealthy. However, in 1975 civil war broke out between the Christians, Muslims and Druses and plunged Lebanon into chaos, with frequent bombings, assassinations and kidnappings, made more complicated by the involvement of Israeli troops, Palestinians, the Syrian army and the UN. Israel still occupies the south of the country from where it launched a military offensive, with heavy civilian casualties, against Hezbollah in April 1996 in retaliation for rocket attacks by this group on northern Israel.
ECONOMY The economy has been severely damaged by the war.

AREA 10,400 sq km [4,015 sq mls]
POPULATION 2,971,000
CAPITAL (POPULATION) Beirut (1,500,000)
GOVERNMENT Multiparty republic
ETHNIC GROUPS Arab 93% (Lebanese 83%, Palestinian 10%), Armenian 5%
LANGUAGES Arabic and French (official), English, Armenian
RELIGIONS Muslim 57%, Christian 40%, Druse 3%
CURRENCY Lebanese pound = 100 piastres
POPULATION DENSITY 286 per sq km [740 per sq ml]
MAIN EXPORTS Clothing, jewellery, aluminium and pharmaceutical products

LESOTHO

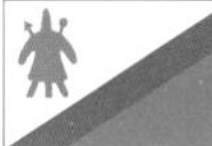

In 1987 this succeeded the flag adopted on independence from Britain in 1966. The white, blue and green represent peace, rain and prosperity – the words of the national motto. The emblem comprises a shield, knobkerrie and ostrich feather sceptre.

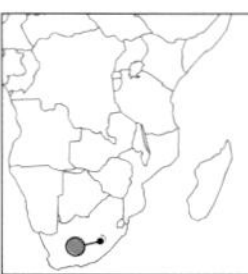

Consisting mainly of a high mountainous plateau deeply fretted by the headwaters of the Orange (Oranje) River, Lesotho declines altitudinally from east to west. The higher ridges are treeless and the steep valleys suffer from an excess of water, making the land boggy in summer and frozen in winter. This physical environment and the presence on all sides of South Africa causes major political and economic problems for Lesotho. Most of the population survive on subsistence farming and there is migration to the small towns or to the mines in South Africa to look for work. Tourism is developing.

AREA 30,350 sq km [11,718 sq mls]
POPULATION 2,064,000
CAPITAL (POPULATION) Maseru (130,000)
GOVERNMENT Constitutional monarchy
ETHNIC GROUPS Sotho 85%, Zulu 15%
LANGUAGES Sesotho and English (both official)
RELIGIONS Christian 93% (Roman Catholic 44%)
POPULATION DENSITY 68 per sq km [176 per sq ml]

LIBERIA

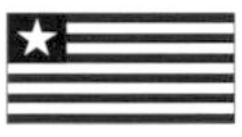

Liberia was founded in the early 19th century as an American colony for freed black slaves. The flag, based on the American flag, was adopted on independence in 1847, with its 11 red and white stripes representing the 11 men who signed the Liberian declaration of independence.

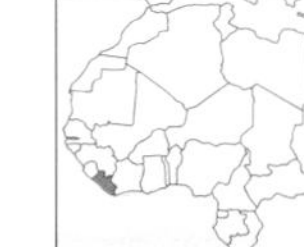

GEOGRAPHY Liberia is West Africa's oldest independent state. Sparsely populated, it has large tracts of inaccessible tropical rainforest, with a coastal plain made up of swamps and savanna.
HISTORY, POLITICS AND ECONOMY Liberia became an independent republic in 1847, thus lacking a legacy of colonial administration. In 1989 civil war broke out when a force invaded from the Ivory Coast. The president was assassinated and conflicts broke out between the rebel forces, with peacekeeping forces from five West African countries unable to stop the fighting. In 1995 a cease-fire was finally agreed and a council of state was set up, but the fighting flared up again in early 1996. The largely agricultural economy has been devastated by the civil war.

AREA 111,370 sq km [43,000 sq mls]
POPULATION 3,092,000
CAPITAL (POPULATION) Monrovia (490,000)
GOVERNMENT Multiparty republic
ETHNIC GROUPS Kpelle 19%, Bassa 14%, Grebo 9%, Gio 8%, Kru 7%, Mano 7%
LANGUAGES English (official), Mande, West Atlantic, Kwa
RELIGIONS Christian 68%, traditional beliefs 18%, Muslim 14%
POPULATION DENSITY 28 per sq km [72 per sq ml]

LIBYA

LIBYA

The simplest of all world flags, Libya's flag represents the nation's quest for a green revolution in agriculture. Libya flew the flag of the Federation of Arab Republics until 1977, when it left the organization.

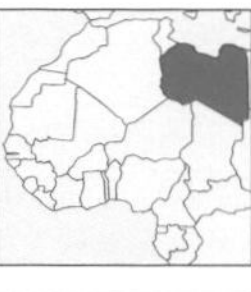

GEOGRAPHY Located in North Africa with a coastline on the Mediterranean, Libya has a mainly desert environment with a largely nomadic population. The climate on the coast has less extreme temperatures and higher rainfall than inland.

HISTORY AND POLITICS Italy controlled Libya from 1912 until it was defeated in World War II and lost the colony. In 1951 it became an independent monarchy under King Idris. In 1969 a group of 12 army officers overthrew the king in a coup and control passed to the Revolutionary Command Council under Colonel Gaddafi, with pro-Palestinian and anti-Western policies and continual disputes with Libya's neighbours.

ECONOMY Until 1959, when vast reserves of oil and natural gas were discovered, Libya was very poor and backward. Since then standards of living have risen dramatically.

AREA 1,759,540 sq km [679,358 sq mls]
POPULATION 5,410,000
CAPITAL (POPULATION) Tripoli (990,000)
GOVERNMENT Single-party socialist state
ETHNIC GROUPS Arab-Berber 89%
LANGUAGES Arabic, Berber
RELIGIONS Sunni Muslim 97%
CURRENCY Libyan dinar = 1,000 dirhams
POPULATION DENSITY 3 per sq km [8 per sq ml]
MAIN EXPORTS Oil, natural gas
URBAN POPULATION 84% of population
LAND USE Arable 1%, grass 8%

LIECHTENSTEIN

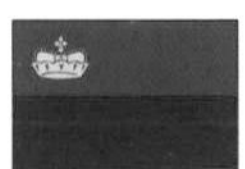

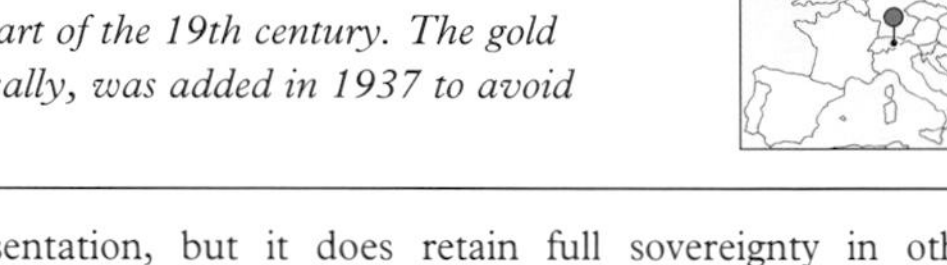

The colours of Liechtenstein's flag originated in the early part of the 19th century. The gold crown, often rotated 90° so that the flag can be hung vertically, was added in 1937 to avoid confusion with the flag then used by Haiti.

Standing at the end of the eastern Alps between Austria and Switzerland, the tiny state of Liechtenstein became an independent principality within the Holy Roman Empire in 1719. Since 1923 Liechtenstein has been in customs and currency union with Switzerland, which also provides overseas representation, but it does retain full sovereignty in other spheres. It is particularly known abroad for its postage stamps and as a haven for international companies, with low taxation and strict, secretive banking codes. Tourism has been increasing over recent years as has a growth in specialized manufacturing.

AREA 157 sq km [61 sq mls]
POPULATION 31,000
CAPITAL (POPULATION) Vaduz (4,919)
GOVERNMENT Principality
ETHNIC GROUPS Alemannic 95%
LANGUAGES German, Alemannic dialects
RELIGIONS Roman Catholic 81%, Protestant 7%
CURRENCY Swiss franc
POPULATION DENSITY 197 per sq km [508 per sq ml]

LITHUANIA

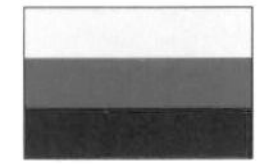

The flag was created in 1918, at the birth of the independent republic; it was suppressed after the Soviet annexation in 1940, and restored in November 1988. The colours are reputed to represent Lithuania's rich forests and agricultural wealth.

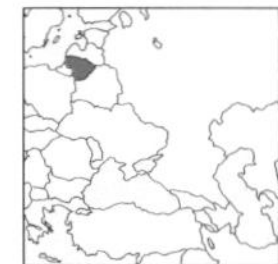

Lithuania is the largest and most populous of the Baltic States, with a landscape consisting mostly of a low, glaciated but fairly fertile central plain. In the east of the country is an area of forested sandy ridges, dotted with lakes. Lithuania was the first of the former Soviet republics to declare itself an independent, non-Communist country in March 1990. This resulted in the occupation of much of Vilnius by Soviet troops and a crippling economic blockade. Since then the situation has improved, helped by the president, Vytautas Landsbergis, though his party was defeated in elections in 1992. There are a range of industries, many of them the most advanced in the former Soviet Union, including timber, fertilizers and plastics.

AREA 65,200 sq km [25,200 sq mls]
POPULATION 3,735,000
CAPITAL (POPULATION) Vilnius (576,000)
GOVERNMENT Multiparty republic
ETHNIC GROUPS Lithuanian 81%, Russian 9%, Polish 7%, Belarussian 2%
LANGUAGES Lithuanian 70%, Russian 30%
RELIGIONS Christian
CURRENCY Litas = 100 centai
POPULATION DENSITY 57 per sq km [148 per sq ml]
URBAN POPULATION 57% population

LUXEMBOURG

Luxembourg's colours are taken from the Grand Duke's 14th-century coat of arms. The Grand Duchy's flag is almost identical to that of the Netherlands, but the blue stripe is a lighter shade and the flag itself is longer.

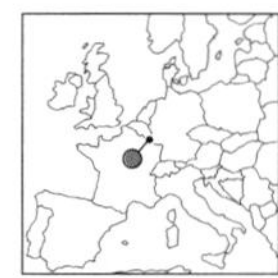

GEOGRAPHY Located in central Europe and bordered by France, Germany and Belgium, Luxembourg consists partly of the picturesque Ardennes region in the north, well wooded and famed for its deer and wild boar. Further south the land is flatter and more fertile. The climate is fairly mild with some rain, making it ideal for farming.

HISTORY AND POLITICS Declaring itself a Grand Duchy in 1354, Luxembourg was ruled by Spain and then Austria until 1795. It was then annexed by France before becoming part of the Netherlands in 1815. Part of the Grand Duchy was taken by Belgium in 1831 and the rest became independent in 1839. It is now the only one out of hundreds of independent duchies, which once comprised much of continental Europe, still surviving. In 1922 Luxembourg formed an economic union with Belgium, which was extended in 1944 to include the Netherlands under the composite name of Benelux. Luxembourg was a founder member of NATO in 1949 and of the EEC in 1957 and therefore plays an important part in Western European affairs.

ECONOMY Stock-rearing, especially of dairy cattle, is important, and crops include grains, potatoes, roots and fruit, and vines in the Moselle Valley. There is also a prosperous iron and steel industry based on rich iron-ore deposits.

AREA 2,590 sq km [1,000 sq mls]
POPULATION 408,000
CAPITAL (POPULATION) Luxembourg (76,000)
GOVERNMENT Constitutional monarchy with a bicameral legislature
ETHNIC GROUPS Luxembourger 70%, Portuguese 11%, Italian 5%, French 4%, German 2%, Belgian 1%
LANGUAGES Letzeburgish (Luxembourgian – official), French, German
RELIGIONS Roman Catholic 94%
CURRENCY Luxembourg franc = 100 centimes
POPULATION DENSITY 158 per sq km [408 per sq ml]
MAIN EXPORTS Base metals, plastic and rubber manufactures

MACAU

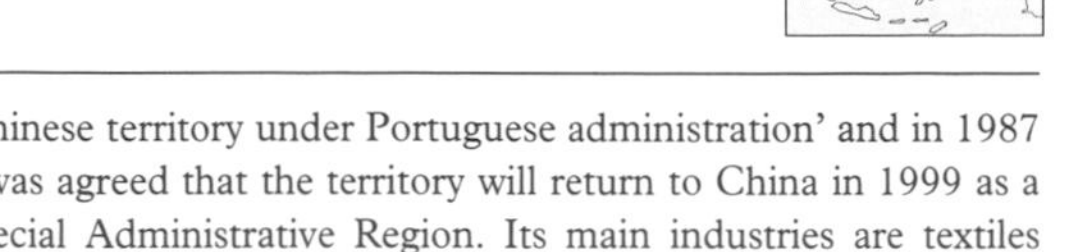

Portugal declared Macau independent from China in 1849, and a century later proclaimed it an Overseas Province. This new flag for Macau replaces that of Portugal in the run-up to retrocession to China, on 20 December 1999.

Macau is a peninsula at the head of the Zhu Jiang (Pearl) River, 64 km [40 mls] west of Hong Kong and connected to China by a narrow isthmus. As a Portuguese colony from 1557, Macau was for 200 years one of the great trading centres for silk, gold, spices and opium. In 1979 the status of Macau was redefined as a 'Chinese territory under Portuguese administration' and in 1987 it was agreed that the territory will return to China in 1999 as a Special Administrative Region. Its main industries are textiles and tourism but Macau is heavily reliant on China for water, food and raw materials. A new $1 billion airport opened in 1995.

AREA 16 sq km [6 sq mls]
POPULATION 490,000
GOVERNMENT Overseas Territory of Portugal
ETHNIC GROUPS Chinese 95%, Portuguese 3%
LANGUAGES Cantonese, Portuguese
RELIGIONS Buddhist 45%, Roman Catholic 7%
POPULATION DENSITY 30,625 per sq km [81,667 per sq ml]

MACEDONIA

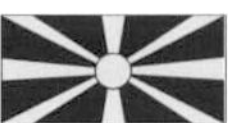

Macedonia's flag was first introduced in August 1992 but was altered by parliamentary decree on 5 October 1995. The effect was to replace the 'Star of Vergina' on the previous flag with a modified form of sunburst. This follows a treaty with Greece, who had objected to the star.

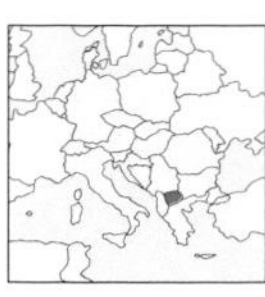

With a northern frontier dangerously contiguous with Serbia's troubled Kosovo region, Macedonia has so far avoided the long-running and devastating civil war that has marked the disintegration of the former Yugoslavia. It is a landlocked and mountainous country surrounded by Greece, Bulgaria and

Albania. To begin with, international recognition proved difficult to obtain, since Greece, with its own Macedonian region, vetoed any acknowledgement of an independent Macedonia. Formal diplomatic relations with Greece were assumed in 1995 when Greece recognized Macedonia as an independent country.

AREA 25,710 sq km [9,927 sq mls]
POPULATION 2,173,000
CAPITAL (POPULATION) Skopje (563,000)
ETHNIC GROUPS Macedonian 65%, Albanian 21%
LANGUAGES Macedonian 70%, Albanian 21%, Turkish, Serbo-Croat
RELIGIONS Eastern Orthodox, Muslim
CURRENCY Dinar = 100 paras
POPULATION DENSITY 87 per sq km [226 per sq ml]

MADAGASCAR

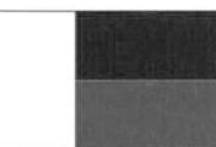

Madagascar's colours are those of historical flags of South-east Asia, from where the island's first inhabitants came before AD 1000. The present flag was adopted in 1958 when the country first became a republic after French rule.

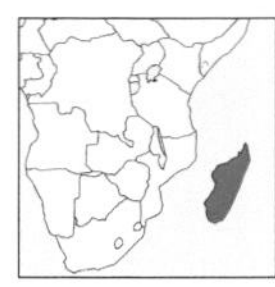

GEOGRAPHY The world's fourth largest island, Madagascar has a huge variety of physical, ecological and cultural features. Most geological eras are represented, and made more vivid by steep faulting and deeply-trenched valleys. The coasts are hostile, with little natural shelter, and the climate is varied, from hot and wet in the north and east to arid in the south and south-west.

HISTORY AND POLITICS Separated from the African mainland for more than 50 million years, Madagascar contains a distinct flora and fauna and mixture of peoples. A monarchy existed

before French occupation in 1895, and after independence in 1958 the government continued the links with France until 1975 when Didier Ratsiraka seized power and established a dictatorial socialist one-party state. He was defeated in elections in 1993, but not before plunging Madagascar into poverty.

ECONOMY Two-thirds of the world's vanilla is produced here, along with other crops of coffee, sugar, spices and essential oils. With 90% of its forest gone (it once covered most of the island), Madagascar is today one of the most eroded places in the world.

AREA 587,040 sq km [226,656 sq mls]
POPULATION 15,206,000
CAPITAL (POPULATION) Antananarivo (1,053,000)
GOVERNMENT Unitary republic with a bicameral legislature
ETHNIC GROUPS Merina 26%, Betsimisaraka 15%, Betsileo 12%
LANGUAGES Malagasy, French, English
RELIGIONS Christian 51% (Roman Catholic 28%), traditional beliefs 47%, Muslim 2%
CURRENCY Malagasy franc = 100 centimes
POPULATION DENSITY 26 per sq km [67 per sq ml]

MADEIRA

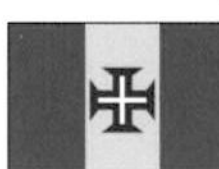

The emblem in the flag is the cross of the Order of Christ, which inspired the colonization of the islands in the 15th century. The flag was adopted in 1978.

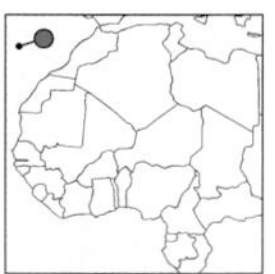

Madeira is the largest of the group of picturesque volcanic islands of that name lying 550 km [350 mls] from the Moroccan coast in the Atlantic Ocean and 900 km [560 mls] south-west of the national Portuguese capital, Lisbon. Porto Santo and the

uninhabited Ilhas Selvagens and Sesertas complete the group. With a warm temperate climate and good soils, Madeira was originally forested, but early settlers cleared the uplands for plantations. Tourism is now very important to the economy.

AREA 813 sq km [314 sq mls]
POPULATION 300,000
CAPITAL (POPULATION) Funchal (45,000)
GOVERNMENT Portuguese Autonomous Region
LANGUAGES Portuguese
RELIGIONS Roman Catholic
CURRENCY Portuguese escudo
POPULATION DENSITY 369 per sq km [955 per sq ml]

MALAWI

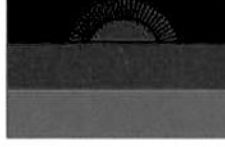

The colours in Malawi's flag come from the flag adopted by the Malawi Congress Party in 1953. The rising sun symbol, representing the beginning of a new era for Malawi and Africa, was added when the country gained independence from Britain in 1964.

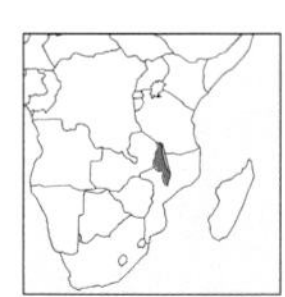

GEOGRAPHY A small and hilly country, Malawi is nowhere more than 160 km [100 mls] wide and was derived from a 19th-century missionaries' and traders' route up the Zambezi, Shire and Lake Nyasa (Malawi). The climate around the lake is very hot and humid, with cooler conditions in the south.

HISTORY AND POLITICS Malawi's recent history has been dominated by one man, Dr Hastings Kamuzu Banda, who led

the country to independence in 1964 and then declared a one-party republic, with himself as president for life, in 1971. At first successful in helping the economy, his austere regime saw a return to poverty and a high incidence of AIDS in the late 1980s. In 1993 there was a return to a multiparty system, and in the 1994 presidential elections Banda was defeated by Bakili Muluzi.

ECONOMY Agriculture is the mainstay of the economy.

AREA 118,480 sq km [45,745 sq mls]
POPULATION 9,800,000
CAPITAL (POPULATION) Lilongwe (268,000)
GOVERNMENT Multiparty republic
ETHNIC GROUPS Maravi 58%, Lomwe 18%, Yao 13%, Ngoni 7%
LANGUAGES Chichewa, English
RELIGIONS Christian 64%, Muslim 16%, Animist
CURRENCY Kwacha = 100 tambala
POPULATION DENSITY 83 per sq km [214 per sq ml]
MAIN EXPORTS Tobacco, tea and sugar

MALAYSIA

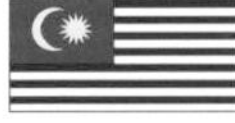

The red and white bands date back to a revolt in the 13th century. The star and crescent are symbols of Islam; the blue represents Malaysia's role in the Commonwealth. This version of the flag was first flown after federation in 1963.

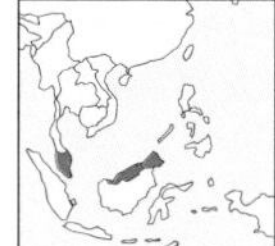

GEOGRAPHY The present federation of Malaysia comprises 11 states and a federal territory (Kuala Lumpur) on the Malay Peninsula, and two states and a federal territory (Labuan) in northern Borneo. The Peninsula is dominated by fold mountains with a north-south axis. There are seven or eight ranges, with frequently exposed granite cores. The natural vegetation of most of Malaysia is lowland rainforest and its montane variants.

HISTORY AND POLITICS In the 15th century Malay political power was at its peak with the rise of the kingdom of Malacca,

which controlled the important sea routes and trade of the region. In 1414 the ruler of Malacca accepted the Islamic faith, which remains the official religion today. There is, however, a great diversity of ethnic and religious groups, and tensions have arisen between the politically dominant Muslim Malays and the economically dominant Buddhists, mostly Chinese.

ECONOMY Economic growth has been rapid with rice, plus exports of rubber, palm oil and tin, as the traditional mainstays of the economy, together with a growing tourist industry.

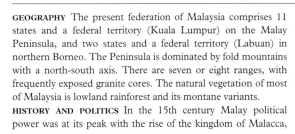

AREA 329,750 sq km [127,316 sq mls]
POPULATION 20,174,000
CAPITAL (POPULATION) Kuala Lumpur (1,145,000)
GOVERNMENT Federal constitutional monarchy with a bicameral legislature
ETHNIC GROUPS Malay 62%, Chinese 30%, Indian 8%
LANGUAGES Malay, Chinese, Tamil, Iban, Dusan, English
RELIGIONS Sunni Muslim 53%, Buddhist 17%, Chinese folk religionist 12%, Hindu 7%, Christian 6%
POPULATION DENSITY 61 per sq km [158 per sq ml]

MALDIVES

MALDIVES

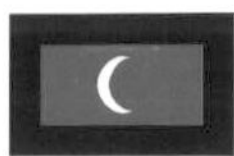

The Maldives used to fly a plain red flag until the Islamic green panel with white crescent was added early this century. The present design was officially adopted in 1965, after the British left the islands.

AREA 298 sq km [115 sq mls]
POPULATION 254,000
CAPITAL (POPULATION) Malé (55,000)
GOVERNMENT Republic with a unicameral legislature
ETHNIC GROUPS Mixture of Sinhalese, Indian and Arab
LANGUAGES Divehi (Sinhala dialect)
RELIGIONS Sunni Muslim
CURRENCY Rufiyaa = 100 laaris

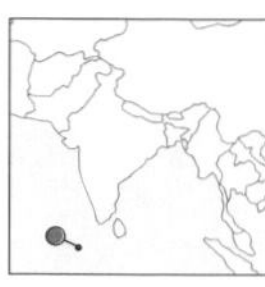

The archipelago of the Maldives comprises over 1,190 small low-lying islands and atolls (202 of them inhabited), scattered along a broad north-south line in the Indian Ocean. The islands were settled from Sri Lanka about 500 BC. They became a British protectorate in 1887, administered from Ceylon (now Sri Lanka) but retaining local sultanates. Independence was achieved in 1965 and the last sultan deposed in 1968. Fishing (for bonito and tuna) and tourism are the main activities.

MALI

Adopted on independence from France in 1960, Mali's flag uses the Pan-African colours, employed by the African Democratic Rally, and symbolizing the desire for African unity. Its design is based on the French tricolour.

AREA 1,240,190 sq km [478,837 sq mls]
POPULATION 10,700,000
CAPITAL (POPULATION) Bamako (746,000)
GOVERNMENT Multiparty republic with a unicameral legislature
ETHNIC GROUPS Bambara 32%, Fulani 14%, Senufo 12%, Soninké 9%
LANGUAGES French, languages of the Mande group 60%
RELIGIONS Muslim 90%, traditional Animist beliefs 9%, Christian 1%

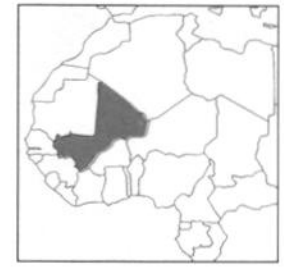

In the 14th century the centre of a huge West African Malinka empire based on the legendary city of Timbuktu, Mali is today a poor, landlocked country consisting mainly of empty Saharan desert plains. Lack of water is a real problem and most of the country's population lives along the Senegal and Niger rivers, which provide water for stock and irrigation and act as communication routes. Millet, cotton and groundnuts are grown on unirrigated land, while rice is grown intensively with irrigation. Industry is very limited. The 23-year repressive regime of Moussa Traoré ended in 1991 after student-led protests.

MALTA

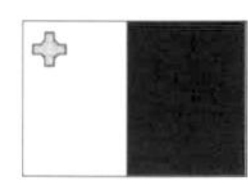

The colours of Malta's flag, adopted on independence in 1964, are those of the Knights of Malta, who ruled the islands from 1530 to 1798. The George Cross was added in 1943 to commemorate the heroism of the Maltese people during World War II.

AREA 316 sq km [122 sq mls]
POPULATION 367,000
CAPITAL (POPULATION) Valletta (102,000)
GOVERNMENT Multiparty republic
ETHNIC GROUPS Maltese 96%, English 2%
LANGUAGES Maltese, English
RELIGIONS Roman Catholic 96%
CURRENCY Maltese lira = 100 cents
POPULATION DENSITY 1,161 per sq km [3,008 per sq ml]

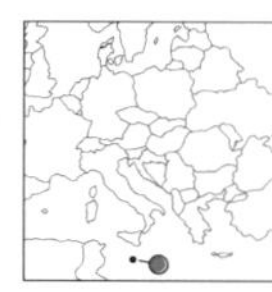

Malta lies in the centre of the Mediterranean, roughly halfway between Gibraltar and Suez and 290 km [180 mls] from North Africa. Its strategic importance arises from its position, and from its possession of good natural harbours. The three islands of Malta, Comino and Gozo have few natural resources (apart from building stone) and with no rivers and little rainfall, agricultural possibilities are limited. Year-round tourism is important and a new port, wharf and storage facilities are being developed.

MARSHALL ISLANDS

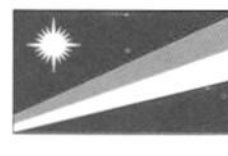

The flag dates from 1 May 1979 and has two rays which represent the two chains of islands: Ratik (Sunrise) is in orange and Ralik (Sunset) is in white. The 24 points on the star represent the municipalities of the area, all set against the blue of the Pacific Ocean.

AREA 181 sq km [70 sq mls]
POPULATION 55,000
CAPITAL Dalap-Uliga-Darrit
GOVERNMENT Republic with a unicameral legislature
ETHNIC GROUPS Micronesian
LANGUAGES English, Marshallese dialects, Japanese
RELIGIONS Christian (mainly Protestant)
CURRENCY US dollar

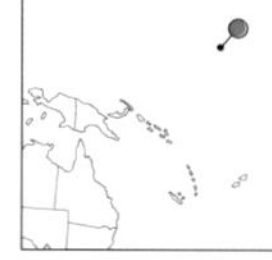

The Marshall Islands comprise over 1,250 islands and atolls – including the former US nuclear testing sites of Bikini and Enewetak – located in the Pacific Ocean. The islands became a republic 'in free association with the USA' in 1986, moving from Trust Territory status to a sovereign state responsible for its own foreign policy but not (until 2001) for its defence and security. The economy, based on agriculture and tourism, is very heavily supported by aid from the USA.

MARTINIQUE

The appearance of the French tricolour here is a reminder that there are three overseas departments of France in this region: Martinique, Guadeloupe and French Guiana.

AREA 1,100 sq km [425 sq mls]
POPULATION 384,000
CAPITAL (POPULATION) Fort-de-France (102,000)
GOVERNMENT Overseas Department of France
ETHNIC GROUPS Of African descent, Mixed, White
LANGUAGES French, Creole patois
RELIGIONS Roman Catholic 85%

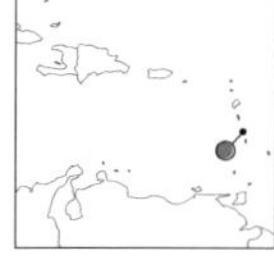

Martinique comprises three groups of volcanic hills and the intervening lowlands in the Caribbean Sea. It was 'discovered' by Columbus in 1493, colonized by France from 1635 and, apart from brief British interludes, has been French ever since. It became an overseas department in 1946 and was made an administrative region in 1974. Bananas (40%), rum and pineapples are the main agricultural exports, but tourism is the biggest earner. Oil products account for another 14% of exports.

MAURITANIA

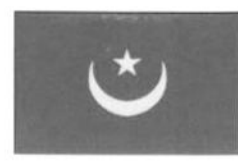

The Mauritanian Islamic Republic's flag features the star and the crescent, traditional symbols of the Islamic religion, as is the colour green. It was adopted in 1959, the year before the country gained its independence from France.

AREA 1,025,220 sq km [395,593 sq mls]
POPULATION 2,268,000
CAPITAL (POPULATION) Nouakchott (600,000)
GOVERNMENT Multiparty Islamic republic
ETHNIC GROUPS Moor (Arab-Berber) 70%, Wolof 7%, Tukulor 5%, Soninké, Fulani
LANGUAGES Arabic, Soninké, Wolof, French
RELIGIONS Sunni Muslim 99%
CURRENCY Ouguiya = 5 khoums

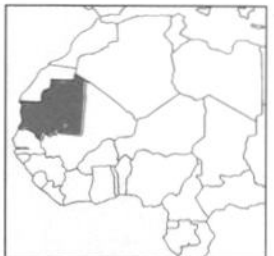

Over two-thirds of Mauritania consists of desert wastes, much of it in the Sahara. Apart from the main north-south highway and routes associated with mineral developments, land communications consist of rough tracks. The only permanent arable agriculture is in the south, concentrated in a narrow strip along the Senegal River. Crops of millet, sorghum, beans, peanuts and rice are grown. The fishing industry, based off the Atlantic coast, is still growing and a new port and capital city have been constructed at Nouakchott. Democratization did not reach Mauritania until the early 1990s when elections were held.

MAURITIUS

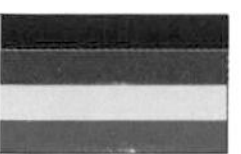

The flag of this small island state was adopted on independence from Britain in 1968. Red stands for the struggle for independence, blue for the Indian Ocean, yellow for the bright future, and green for the lush vegetation.

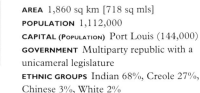

AREA 1,860 sq km [718 sq mls]
POPULATION 1,112,000
CAPITAL (POPULATION) Port Louis (144,000)
GOVERNMENT Multiparty republic with a unicameral legislature
ETHNIC GROUPS Indian 68%, Creole 27%, Chinese 3%, White 2%
LANGUAGES English, Creole, French
RELIGIONS Hindu 51%, Roman Catholic

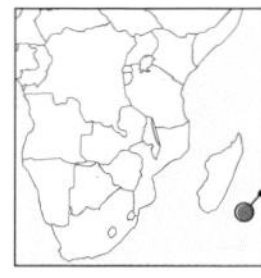

Mauritius consists of the main island, which is fringed with coral reefs, Rodrigues, 20 nearby islets and the dependencies of the Agalega Islands and the tiny Cargados Carajas shoals (St Brandon). French from 1715 and British from 1810, the colony gained independence in 1968. Sugar cane accounts for over 40% of exports and tourism and textiles have become very important.

MEXICO

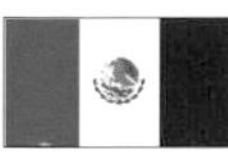

The stripes on the Mexican flag were inspired by the French tricolour and date from 1821. The emblem of the eagle, snake and cactus is based on an ancient Aztec legend about the founding of Mexico City. The design was adopted for the Olympic year, 1968.

AREA 1,958,200 sq km [756,061 sq mls]
POPULATION 93,342,000
CAPITAL (POPULATION) Mexico City (15,048,000)
GOVERNMENT Federal multiparty republic
ETHNIC GROUPS Mestizo 60%, Amerindian 30%, European 9%
LANGUAGES Spanish 92%, 59 native dialects
RELIGIONS Roman Catholic 90%, Protestant 5%
POPULATION DENSITY 48 per sq km [123 per sq ml]

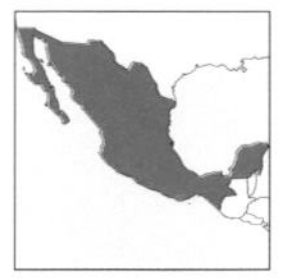

GEOGRAPHY Mexico is the world's largest and most populous Spanish-speaking nation and is a land of great physical variety. The northern, emptier, half is open basin-and-range country of the Mesa Central; mountains dominate southern Mexico, broken only by the low, narrow isthmus of Tehuantepec. In the south-east is the flat, low-lying Yucatán peninsula.

HISTORY AND POLITICS After independence in 1821 there was a century of political chaos, climaxing in the violent revolution of 1920–21. The PRI was then in power for more than six decades after 1929 and instituted crucial land reforms in the 1930s. There is now high unemployment and rural-urban migration.

ECONOMY Mexico is the world's fifth biggest producer of oil, much of it exported to the USA, but the economy is very diverse with important silver production and also textiles and tourism.

MICRONESIA, FEDERATED STATES OF

The flag was adopted in 1978 when the country broke away from the United States Trust Territory of Micronesia and became the Federated States of Micronesia. The four stars stand for the four states (Kosrai, Pohnpei, Truk and Yap) that remained in the federation.

AREA 705 sq km [272 sq mls]
POPULATION 125,000
CAPITAL Palikir
GOVERNMENT Federal multiparty republic with a unicameral legislature
ETHNIC GROUPS Micronesian, Polynesian
LANGUAGES English, local languages
RELIGIONS Christian
CURRENCY US currency

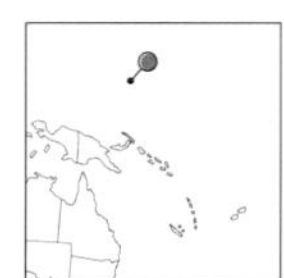

Comprising the bulk of the Caroline Islands, the Federation stretches across more than 2,300 km [2,000 mls] of the Pacific Ocean, with the Equator as the southern boundary. The 607 islands divide into four groups and range from mountains to low atolls. Traditional subsistence farming and fishing are still important, with copra as the main crop and tuna the main export.

MOLDOVA

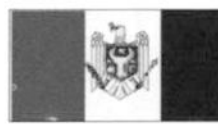

The flag and eagle are based on those of pre-Communist Romania, and the bull's head is the distinctive emblem of Moldova. The flag was adopted in November 1990. According to the official description, the tricolour represents 'the past, present and future' of Moldova.

AREA 33,700 sq km [13,010 sq mls]
POPULATION 4,434,000
CAPITAL (POPULATION) Chişinău (667,000)
GOVERNMENT Multiparty republic
ETHNIC GROUPS Moldovan 65%, Ukrainian 14%, Russian 13%, Gagauz 4%, Jewish 2%, Bulgarian
LANGUAGES Moldovan 61%, Russian
RELIGIONS Russian Orthodox, Evangelical
CURRENCY Leu = 100 bani

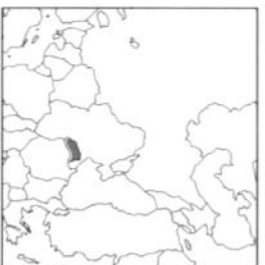

Moldova is the most densely populated of the former Soviet republics and has an ethnically complex society. The majority 'Moldovan' population is Romanian, while there are Gagauz (the Christian Orthodox Turks) in the south and Russians and Ukrainians. Independence from Moscow was declared in August 1991 and multiparty elections were held in February 1994. The economy is fairly prosperous; fertile lands and a tolerant climate provide vines, tobacco and honey. Light industry is expanding.

MONACO

An independent state since AD 980, Monaco has been ruled by the Grimaldi family since 1297. The colours of the flag, which was officially adopted in 1881, come from the Prince of Monaco's coat of arms, which dates to medieval times.

AREA 1.5 sq km [0.6 sq mls]
POPULATION 32,000
CAPITAL Monaco
GOVERNMENT Constitutional monarchy with a unicameral legislature
ETHNIC GROUPS French 47%, Monégasque 16%, Italian 16%
LANGUAGES French, Monégasque
RELIGIONS Roman Catholic 95%
CURRENCY French franc

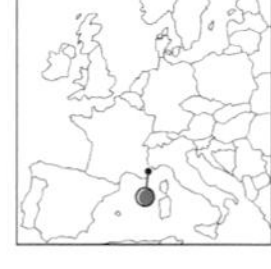

The tiny principality of Monaco comprises a rocky peninsula and a narrow stretch of coast, but has increased in size by 20% since its land reclamation programme began in 1958. The greater part of it was annexed by France in 1848 and the remainder came under its protection in 1861 – a situation that essentially survives today within a customs union. Its considerable income is mostly derived from services: banking, finance and, especially, tourism; this is based not only on its climate but also on its famous casino.

MONGOLIA

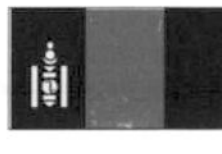

On Mongolia's flag the blue represents the country's national colour. In the hoist is the Golden Soyonbo, a Buddhist symbol, representing freedom. Within this, the flame is seen as a promise of prosperity and progress.

AREA 1,566,500 sq km [604,826 sq mls]
POPULATION 2,408,000
CAPITAL (POPULATION) Ulan Bator (601,000)
GOVERNMENT Multiparty republic
ETHNIC GROUPS Khalkha Mongol 79%, Kazak 6%
LANGUAGES Khalkha Mongolian, Chinese, Russian
RELIGIONS Buddhist, Shamanist, Muslim
CURRENCY Tugrik = 100 möngös
URBAN POPULATION 59% of population

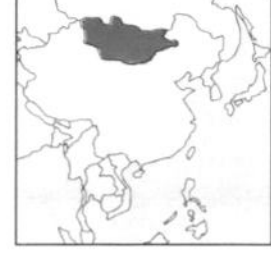

Mongolia is the world's most sparsely populated country. There are high mountains in the north and west and the arid Gobi Desert forms 25% of the country. Outer Mongolia broke away from China following the collapse of the Ch'ing dynasty in 1911, but full independence was not achieved until 1921. The country then fell increasingly under Soviet influence. In 1990 the first multiparty elections were held. Early in 1992 a new constitution was adopted, shunning Communism and enshrining democracy. The traditional mainstay of the economy is herding (of sheep, goats, yaks, camels and horses).

MONTSERRAT

MONTSERRAT

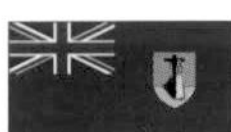

The flag is the British Blue Ensign with the arms in a white roundel in the fly. The shield dates from 1909 and shows a black Passion cross rising from the (brown) ground, grasped in the right arm of a female figure in a green robe, representing the Irish origin of the island's immigrants.

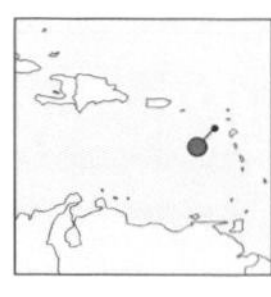

Located in the middle of the Caribbean Sea with a warm, tropical climate, Montserrat was colonized by Britain from 1632, which brought in Irish settlers. Although it is still a dependent territory of the UK, it became self-governing in 1960. Cotton was once the main industry, but with generous tax concessions new ones moved in. Tourism is now the mainstay of the economy (25% of GDP in 1993), supported by exports of electronic equipment, Sea Island cotton, fruit and vegetables.

AREA 102 sq km [39 sq mls]
POPULATION 11,000
CAPITAL Plymouth
GOVERNMENT British Dependent Territory
ETHNIC GROUPS Black, European
LANGUAGES English
RELIGIONS Christian
POPULATION DENSITY 108 per sq km [282 per sq ml]
CURRENCY East Caribbean $ = 100 cents

MOROCCO

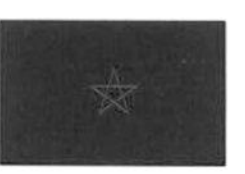

A red flag had been flown in Morocco since the 16th century and the star-shaped green pentagram, the Seal of Solomon, was added in 1915. This design was retained when Morocco gained independence from French and Spanish rule in 1956.

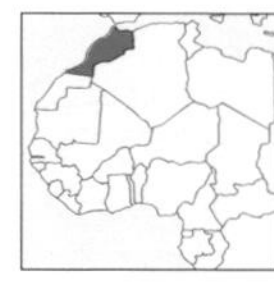

GEOGRAPHY The name Morocco is derived from the Arabic *Maghreb-el-Aksa* ('the Farthest West'), due to its position in the far north-western corner of Africa. More than a third of the country is mountainous, with the main uplands being 'arms' of the Atlas Mountains in the west and north.

HISTORY AND POLITICS Morocco was the last North African country to succumb to European colonialism; not until 1912 did the Sultan of Morocco accept the French protectorate, with Spain controlling certain areas. In 1956 Morocco became independent (with Tangier incorporated into a unified Morocco in 1958). Since 1961 it has been ruled by the authoritarian regime of King Hassan II. The state of Western Sahara lies between Mauritania and the Atlantic coast and is occupied by Morocco in a long-running dispute. Morocco claims that the northern two-thirds are historically part of 'Greater Morocco'.

ECONOMY Peasant cultivation and nomadic pastoralism exist in the mountains, while modern economic development is found in the Atlantic plains and plateaux. Tourism is now very important.

AREA 446,550 sq km [172,413 sq mls]
POPULATION 26,857,000
CAPITAL (POPULATION) Rabat (1,344,000)
GOVERNMENT Constitutional monarchy
ETHNIC GROUPS Arab 70%, Berber 30%
LANGUAGES Arabic, Berber
RELIGIONS Muslim 99%, Christian 1%
POPULATION DENSITY 60 per sq km [156 per sq ml]
MAIN EXPORTS Food and beverages 27%, phosphoric acid 15%, phosphates 13%, clothing 10%
MAIN IMPORTS Capital goods 21%, crude oil 15%, consumer goods 12%
CURRENCY Dirham = 100 centimes

MOZAMBIQUE

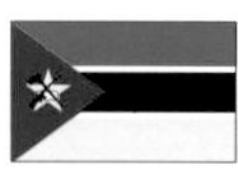

The green stripe represents the fertile land, the black stripe Africa and the yellow stripe mineral wealth. The badge on the red triangle contains a rifle, hoe, cogwheel and book, which are all Marxist symbols of the struggle against colonialism.

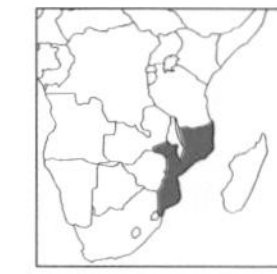

GEOGRAPHY With the warm Mozambique (Agulhas) Current running offshore in the Indian Ocean, all the country is tropical. Coral reefs lie just offshore, and the only real natural harbour is Maputo (Lourenço Marques). The coastal plain is wide and the only high area is found around the inner borderlands.

HISTORY AND POLITICS Mozambique developed (like many other ex-Portuguese colonies) from the search for a route round Africa to the riches of Asia. Independence from Portugal was granted in 1975, with civil wars both before and after, and a series of droughts and floods, leaving it as one of the world's poorest countries. The civil war officially ended in 1992 and multiparty elections were held in 1994.

ECONOMY Coconut, sisal and sugar are grown on the plains, and maize, groundnuts and cotton are produced on the higher ground. Large deposits of coal, copper and bauxite have yet to be exploited.

AREA 801,590 sq km [309,494 sq mls]
POPULATION 17,800,000
CAPITAL (POPULATION) Maputo (1,070,000)
GOVERNMENT Multiparty republic
ETHNIC GROUPS Makua/Lomwe 47%, Tsonga 23%, Malawi 12%, Shona 11%, Yao 4%, Swahili 1%, Makonde 1%
LANGUAGES Portuguese, Bantu
RELIGIONS Traditional beliefs 48%, Roman Catholic 31%, Muslim 13%
POPULATION DENSITY 22 per sq km [56 per sq ml]
CURRENCY Metical = 100 centavos
URBAN POPULATION 30% of population

NAMIBIA

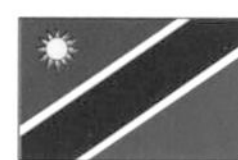

Namibia adopted its flag after independence from South Africa in 1990. The red and white colours symbolize the country's human resources, while the green, blue and the gold sun represent the natural resources, mostly minerals.

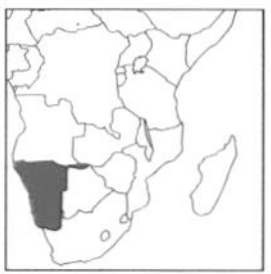

GEOGRAPHY Namibia has a diverse physical landscape, with the arid Namib Desert fringing the southern Atlantic coastline. A major escarpment separates this from a north-south spine of mountains which culminate in the Khomas Highlands near Windhoek. To the east the country occupies the fringes of the Kalahari Desert. The climate is very dry, with much sunshine.

HISTORY AND POLITICS Apart from the British enclave of Walvis Bay, Namibia was (as South West Africa) a German protectorate from 1884 before being occupied by the Union of South Africa at the request of the Allied powers in 1915. South Africa began a long period of exploitation of Namibia and in 1971 the International Court of Justice ruled that its occupation was illegal; but it was not until 1990 that independence was gained.

ECONOMY Some 90% of Namibia's income comes from exports of minerals, particularly uranium and diamonds. There are rich fishing grounds offshore and good prospects for oil and gas.

AREA 825,414 sq km [318,434 sq mls]
POPULATION 1,610,000
CAPITAL (POPULATION) Windhoek (126,000)
GOVERNMENT Multiparty republic
ETHNIC GROUPS Ovambo 47%, Kavango 9%, Herero 7%, Damara 7%, White 6%, Nama 5%
LANGUAGES English, Afrikaans
RELIGIONS Christian 90% (Lutheran 51%), animist
POPULATION DENSITY 2 per sq km [5 per sq ml]
CURRENCY Namibian dollar = 100 cents
URBAN POPULATION 34% of population

NAURU

The flag represents the geographical location of Nauru, south of the Equator in the middle of the Pacific Ocean. The 12 points of the star stand for the traditional tribes, and the flag was adopted on independence in 1968.

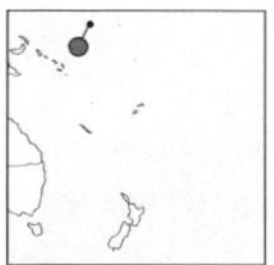

A low-lying coral atoll located halfway between Australia and Hawaii, 40 km [25 mls] south of the Equator, Nauru is the world's smallest republic. The climate is hot and wet, though the rains can fail. Discovered by Britain in 1798, the island was under the control of Germany (1888), Australia (1914), Japan (1942) and Australia again (with a UN trusteeship from 1946) before it gained independence in 1968. There are rich deposits of high-grade phosphate rock (providing 98% of exports), exported to the Pacific Rim countries for fertilizers, although supplies may be exhausted by the end of the century.

AREA 21 sq km [8 sq mls]
POPULATION 12,000
CAPITAL Yaren District
GOVERNMENT Democratic republic
ETHNIC GROUPS Nauruan 58%, other Pacific groups 26%
LANGUAGES Nauruan, English
RELIGIONS Christian
POPULATION DENSITY 571 per sq km [1,500 per sq ml]
CURRENCY Australian dollar

NEPAL

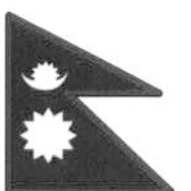

This Himalayan kingdom's uniquely shaped flag was adopted in 1962. It came from the joining together in the 19th century of two triangular pennants – the royal family's crescent moon emblem and the powerful Rana family's sun symbol.

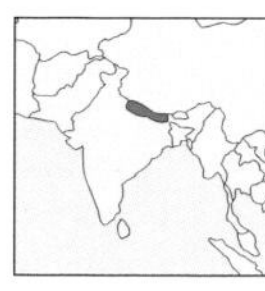

GEOGRAPHY Over three-quarters of Nepal lies in a mountain heartland located between the Himalayas, the subject of an inconclusive boundary negotiation with China in 1961, and the far lower Siwalik Range overlooking the Ganges plain. The high altitude gives sub-zero temperatures in some parts.

HISTORY AND POLITICS Before 1951 (when it was first opened up to foreigners) Nepal had been a patchwork of feudal valley kingdoms until they were conquered by the Gurkhas in the 18th century to form the present country. Local leaders remained loyal to their clans and reduced the power of the central king, although in 1951 the monarchy was re-established. A new constitution incorporating basic human rights was drawn up and the first democratic elections for 32 years were held in 1991.

ECONOMY Nepal remains an under-developed rural country.

AREA 140,800 sq km [54,363 sq mls]
POPULATION 21,953,000
CAPITAL (POPULATION) Katmandu (419,000)
GOVERNMENT Constitutional monarchy
ETHNIC GROUPS Nepalese 53%, Bihari 18%, Tharu 5%, Tamang 5%, Newar 3%
LANGUAGES Nepali 58%
RELIGIONS Hindu 86%, Buddhist 8%, Muslim 4%
POPULATION DENSITY 156 per sq km [404 per sq ml]
CURRENCY Nepalese rupee = 100 paisa

NETHERLANDS

The Dutch national flag dates from 1630, during the long war of independence from Spain that began in 1568. The tricolour became a symbol of liberty and inspired many other revolutionary flags around the world.

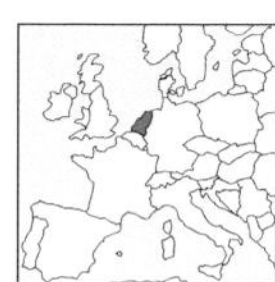

GEOGRAPHY The Netherlands (the 'Low Countries') is a low-lying country of which more than two-fifths would be flooded without the protection of dykes and sand dunes along the coast. Reclamation since 1900 has added almost 3,000 sq km [1,160 sq mls] to the land area, but the danger of flooding remains. The countryside is mostly made up of richly cultivated fields, mainly rectangular, with water-filled ditches between them. It is a very crowded country, with the greatest concentration of population in the towns and cities of Randstad Holland.

HISTORY AND POLITICS The Dutch gained independence after 1648, following periods of rule under the dukes of Burgundy, the German empire and then Spain. In 1948 the Netherlands formed a customs union with Belgium and Luxembourg called Benelux and in 1957 it became a member of the EEC.

ECONOMY Industry and commerce are important, with good mineral resources including china clay, natural gas and oil. There is widespread production of flowers and vegetables and the port and industrial area at Europoort is very successful.

AREA 41,526 sq km [16,033 sq mls]
POPULATION 15,495,000
CAPITAL (POPULATION) Amsterdam (1,091,000); Seat of government: The Hague (694,000)
GOVERNMENT Constitutional monarchy with a bicameral legislature
ETHNIC GROUPS Dutch 95%, Indonesian, Turkish, Moroccan, Surinamese, German
LANGUAGES Dutch
RELIGIONS Roman Catholic 33%, Dutch Reformed Church 15%, Reformed Churches 8%, Muslim 3%
CURRENCY Guilder (florin) = 100 cents
URBAN POPULATION 89% of population

NETHERLANDS ANTILLES

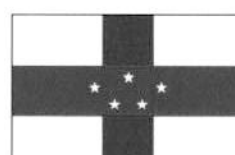

The flag was originally introduced in 1959 with six white stars in the centre, but these were reduced to five in 1986 when Aruba became a separate territory. Each star represents one of the five islands that make up the territory.

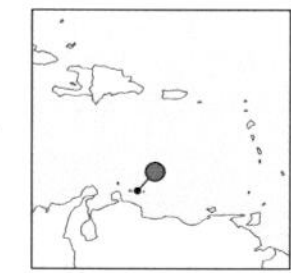

The Netherlands Antilles consists of two very different island groups – Curaçao and Bonaire, off the coast of Venezuela, and Saba, St Eustatius and the southern part of St Maarten, at the northern end of the Leeward Islands, some 800 km [500 mls] away. With Aruba, they formed part of the Dutch West Indies before attaining internal self-government in 1954. Curaçao is dominant, with 45% of the land area and 80% of the population. Tourism, offshore banking and oil refining buoy the economy.

AREA 993 sq km [383 sq mls]
POPULATION 199,000
CAPITAL (POPULATION) Willemstad (125,000)
GOVERNMENT Self-governing Dutch Territory
ETHNIC GROUPS African descent 85%, European
LANGUAGES Dutch, Papiamento (Span., Port., Dutch and Eng. dialect), English
RELIGIONS Christian

NEW CALEDONIA

New Caledonia has been a French possession since 1853. It became a French Overseas Territory in 1958 and therefore uses the French tricolour as its flag.

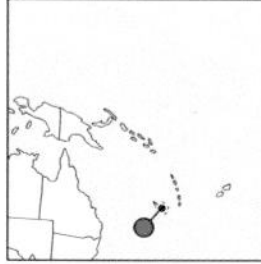

Most southerly of the Melanesian countries in the Pacific Ocean, New Caledonia comprises the main island of Grande Terre and the dependencies of the Loyalty Islands. The remaining islands are all small and uninhabited. A French possession since 1853 and Overseas Territory since 1958, there is today a fundamental split over the question of independence between the indigenous Melanesians and the French settlers. The economy is dominated by nickel, which provides over 56% of export earnings.

AREA 18,580 sq km [7,174 sq mls]
POPULATION 181,000
CAPITAL (POPULATION) Nouméa (98,000)
GOVERNMENT French Overseas Territory
ETHNIC GROUPS Melanesian 43%, European 37%
LANGUAGES French, Melanesian and Polynesian dialects
RELIGIONS Roman Catholic 60%, Protestant 30%

NEW ZEALAND

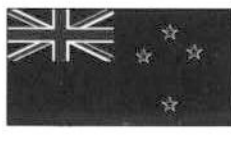

Like Australia, New Zealand flies a flag based on the design of the British Blue Ensign. Designed in 1869 and adopted in 1907 on acquiring Dominion status, it displays four of the five stars of the Southern Cross constellation.

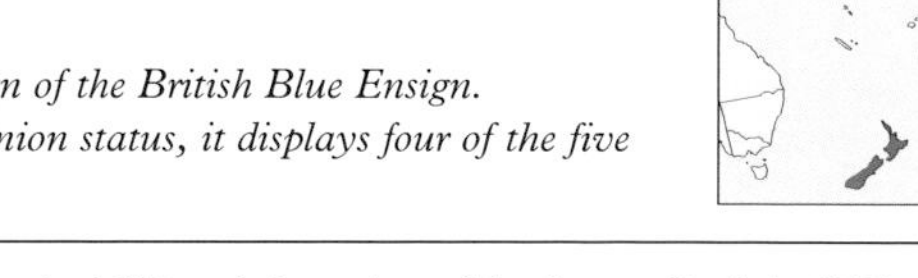

GEOGRAPHY Geologically part of the Circum-Pacific Mobile belt of tectonic activity, New Zealand is mountainous and partly volcanic with about 75% of the total land area rising above the 200 m [650 ft] contour. Much of the North Island was formed by volcanic action, mainly in the last 1 to 4 million years. Minor earthquakes are common and there are several areas of volcanic and geothermal activity. The location of New Zealand in the huge Pacific Ocean moderates temperatures and there is a well-distributed rainfall throughout the year.

HISTORY AND POLITICS New Zealand was discovered by Abel Tasman in 1642 and then charted by James Cook in 1769–70. Already settled there were Maoris-Polynesians, who were joined by about 2,000 Europeans by the early 1830s. In 1840 Britain took possession and thousands of new settlers began to arrive, leading to problems of land ownership with the Maoris (these still exist). Recently, New Zealand has begun to look towards Asia for new markets, as its links with Britain begin to decline.

ECONOMY The economy is prosperous and agricultural products are the main exports. New Zealand is the world's third largest producer of lamb, with wheat and other cereals also grown.

AREA 268,680 sq km [103,737 sq mls]
POPULATION 3,567,000
CAPITAL (POPULATION) Wellington (326,000)
GOVERNMENT Constitutional monarchy with a unicameral legislature
ETHNIC GROUPS White 74%, Maori 10%, Polynesian 4%
LANGUAGES English, Maori
RELIGIONS Anglican 21%, Presbyterian 16%, Roman Catholic 15%, Methodist 4%
POPULATION DENSITY 13 per sq km [34 per sq ml]
MAIN EXPORTS Meat and meat preparations 20%, wool 14%, fruit and vegetables 7%, forestry products 7%

NICARAGUA

NICARAGUA

Nicaragua's flag, adopted in 1908, is identical to that of the Central American Federation (see Guatemala) to which it once belonged. Except for a difference in the shading of the blue and the motif, it is also the same as the flag of El Salvador.

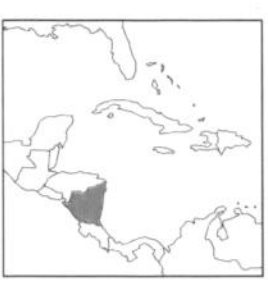

GEOGRAPHY The largest and least densely populated country in South America, Nicaragua has an almost empty eastern half. The Caribbean plain is extensive, and the coast contains lagoons and sandy beaches. Inland mountain ranges are broken by fertile valleys and contain some 40 volcanoes, many still active.

HISTORY AND POLITICS Independence was granted in 1821 from Spain. Between 1832 and 1838 the country was part of the Central American Federation, and between 1937 and 1979 it was ruled by the corrupt Samoza family. Civil war was virtually continuous from the 1960s until a cease-fire in 1989. An uprising by the Sandanistas saw the end of the Samozas' rule, but elections in 1991 brought the UNO party to power.

ECONOMY Cotton and coffee provide the main exports, but the economy is in a chaotic state as a result of the fighting.

AREA 130,000 sq km [50,193 sq mls]
POPULATION 4,544,000
CAPITAL (POPULATION) Managua (974,000)
GOVERNMENT Multiparty republic
ETHNIC GROUPS Mestizo 69%, White 17%, Black 9%
LANGUAGES Spanish, Indian, Creole
RELIGIONS Christian (Roman Catholic 89%)
POPULATION DENSITY 35 per sq km [91 per sq ml]
CURRENCY Córdoba = 100 centavos
URBAN POPULATION 62% of population

NIGER

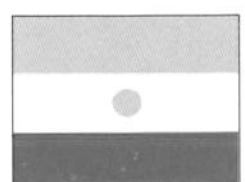

Niger's flag was adopted shortly before independence from France in 1960. The circle represents the sun, the orange stripe the Sahara Desert in the north, the green stripe the grasslands of the south, divided by the (white) River Niger.

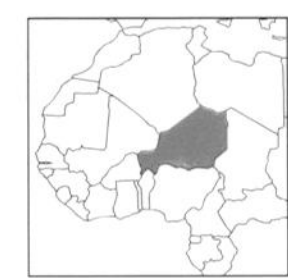

GEOGRAPHY Although Niger's name comes from the Tuareg word meaning 'flowing water', the country (apart from its fertile southern area where the River Niger flows) is arid and hot, with sandy and stony basins. The Aïr Mountains rise to 1,900 m [6,230 ft] above the desert in the north. Droughts are common.

HISTORY AND POLITICS Niger came under French colonial rule between 1922 and 1960. The post-independence government was overthrown in 1974 by the military. Civilian control was reinstated in 1989 and in 1992 a multiparty constitution was adopted. In January 1996 the military once again took control.

ECONOMY Drought and desertification have caused widespread poverty and migration to the already crowded cities.

AREA 1,267,000 sq km [489,189 sq mls]
POPULATION 9,149,000
CAPITAL (POPULATION) Niamey (398,000)
GOVERNMENT Multiparty republic suspended by a military regime
ETHNIC GROUPS Hausa 53%, Djerma-Songhai 21%, Tuareg 11%, Fulani 10%
LANGUAGES French, Hausa
RELIGIONS Sunni Muslim 99%
POPULATION DENSITY 7 per sq km [19 per sq ml]
CURRENCY CFA franc = 100 centimes

NIGERIA

The design of Nigeria's flag was selected after a competition to find a new national flag in time for independence from Britain in 1960. The green represents the country's forests and the white is for peace.

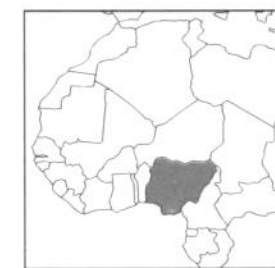

GEOGRAPHY Nigeria is Africa's most populous country. The landscape is varied: savanna in the north gives way to mountains and tropical rainforests and then to mangrove swamps and sandy beaches on the Gulf of Guinea. Much of the coast is formed by the Niger delta and its many creeks.

HISTORY AND POLITICS Nigeria was a British colony between 1914 and 1960 and became a full republic in 1963. A tripartite federal structure first introduced in 1954 was unable to contain rivalries between the 250 ethnic and linguistic groups that make up Nigeria. A military coup in 1966 saw the start of a vicious civil war, in which the Eastern Region (Biafra) attempted to split from the rest of the country; this ended in 1971. Between 1960 and 1995, Nigeria has enjoyed only nine years of civilian rule.

ECONOMY Oil accounts for over 90% of exports, although 50% of the population rely on farming. Falling oil prices and a large foreign debt have caused serious economic problems recently.

AREA 923,770 sq km [356,668 sq mls]
POPULATION 88,515,000
CAPITAL Abuja (306,000)
GOVERNMENT Transitional government
ETHNIC GROUPS Hausa 21%, Yoruba 21%, Ibo 18%, Fulani 11%, Ibibio 6%
LANGUAGES English, Hausa, Yoruba, Ibo
RELIGIONS Sunni Muslim 45%, Protestant 26%, Roman Catholic 12%, African indigenous 11%
POPULATION DENSITY 96 per sq km [248 per sq ml]
CURRENCY Naira = 100 kobo
URBAN POPULATION 37% of population

NORTHERN MARIANA ISLANDS

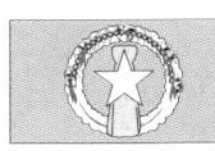

The sea-blue flag of this island group shows a grey latte stone, a Polynesian taga, surrounded by a wreath of flowers and shells. The flag was originally adopted in 1972 and the wreath was added in 1989. The latte stone represents the old traditions of the Chamorro people.

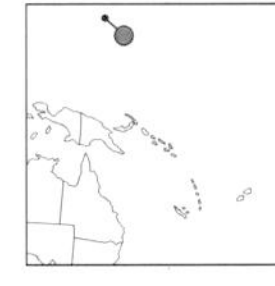

The Northern Marianas in the Pacific Ocean comprise all 17 Mariana Islands except Guam. Part of the US Trust Territory of the Pacific from 1947, its people voted in a 1975 plebiscite for Commonwealth status in union with the USA. US citizenship was granted in 1976 and internal self-government followed in 1978. The tourist industry is growing rapidly.

AREA 477 sq km [184 sq mls]
POPULATION 50,000
CAPITAL (POPULATION) Saipan (39,000)
GOVERNMENT Commonwealth in union with USA
ETHNIC GROUPS Chamorro, Micronesian, Spanish
LANGUAGES English, Chamorro
RELIGIONS Christian

NORWAY

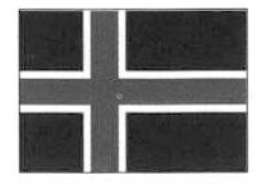

Norway's flag has been used since 1898, though its use as a merchant flag dates back to 1821. The design is based on the Dannebrog flag of Denmark, which ruled Norway from the 14th century to the early 19th century.

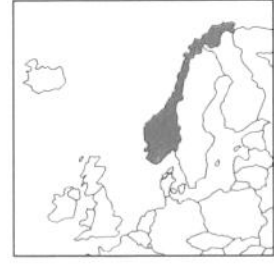

GEOGRAPHY A distinctly shaped country, Norway occupies the western part of the Scandinavian peninsula. The relatively small population lives mainly in the southern half of the country. The landscape is mountainous, dominated by rolling plateaux, the *vidda*, generally 300 to 900 m [1,000 to 3,000 ft] high; these are broken by deep river valleys. The highest areas retain permanent ice fields. The coastline is the longest in Europe, with long, narrow, steep-sided fjords. Hundreds of islands offshore protect the inner coast from the Atlantic waves.

HISTORY AND POLITICS The sea has been very important throughout Norway's history. A thousand years ago Viking sailors from Norway travelled around the northern seas, founding colonies around the coasts of Britain, Iceland and North America. Today fishing, shipbuilding and the merchant fleets are of vital importance to the economy. Norway is a member of NATO and EFTA (but not the EU), and co-operates closely with its Scandinavian neighbours on many issues.

ECONOMY Rapid industrial development since World War II has given Norway a prosperous economy. There are many mineral resources, particularly oil and natural gas from the North Sea.

AREA 323,900 sq km [125,050 sq mls]
POPULATION 4,361,000
CAPITAL (POPULATION) Oslo (714,000)

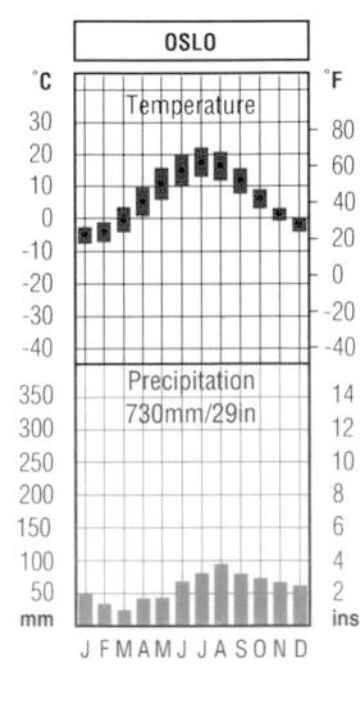

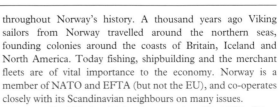

The warm waters and cyclones of the North Atlantic Ocean give the western coastlands of Norway a warm maritime climate of mild winters and cool summers, although wet. The rainfall is heavy on the coast but less inland and northwards. Inland the winters are more severe and the summers warmer. At Oslo the snows may last from November to March.

OMAN

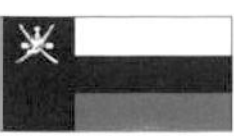

Formerly Muscat and Oman, the state's flag was plain red – the traditional colour of the people who lived in the area. When Oman was established in 1970, the state arms of sword and dagger were added with stripes of white and green. The proportions of the stripes were changed in 1995.

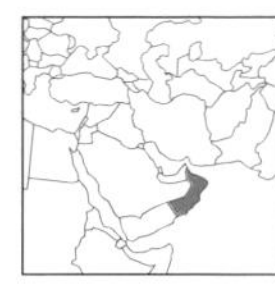

GEOGRAPHY Located on the south-eastern coast of the Persian Gulf, Oman has an arid and inhospitable landscape, where temperatures are high all year round.

HISTORY AND POLITICS Oman was backward compared to the other Gulf countries before 1970, with Sultan Said in power, and a civil war against Yemen-backed separatist guerillas in the southern province of Dhofar (Zufar). Sultan Said was deposed by his son Qaboos in 1970 and growth has since been rapid.

ECONOMY Petroleum accounts for 90% of government revenues and huge reserves of natural gas were discovered in 1991.

AREA 212,460 sq km [82,031 sq mls]
POPULATION 2,252,000
CAPITAL (POPULATION) Muscat (350,000)
GOVERNMENT Monarchy with a unicameral consultative council
ETHNIC GROUPS Omani Arab 74%, other Asian 25%
LANGUAGES Arabic, Baluchi, English
RELIGIONS Muslim 86%, Hindu 13%
POPULATION DENSITY 11 per sq km [27 per sq ml]

PAKISTAN

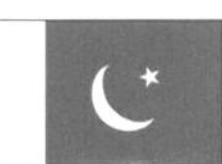

Pakistan's flag was adopted when the country gained independence from Britain in 1947. The green, the crescent moon and five-pointed star are traditionally associated with Islam. The white stripe represents Pakistan's other religions.

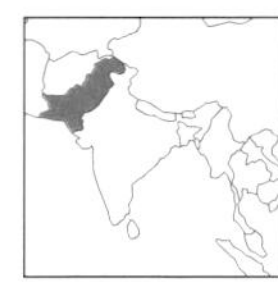

GEOGRAPHY The Indus delta and its tributaries on the coast of Pakistan have been vital for development, supplying irrigation for farming. West of the delta the arid coastal plain of Makran rises first to the Coast Range, then in successive ridges to the north. In the North-West Frontier province is the world's second highest mountain, K2, on the border with China.

HISTORY AND POLITICS Pakistan was part of the British Indian Empire until 1947, when Pakistan was granted independence as a separate Muslim state. East Pakistan (Bangladesh) broke away from the west in 1971, following a bitter civil war and Indian military intervention. Pakistan has been subject to military rule and martial law for most of its life, interspersed with periods of fragile democracy resting on army consent. In one of these periods, in 1988, Benazir Bhutto became prime minister, the Muslim world's first female premier. She was re-elected in 1993.

ECONOMY Reserves of some minerals have yet to be exploited (such as copper and bauxite). However, the economy faces many problems, including a chronic trade deficit and debt burden.

AREA 796,100 sq km [307,374 sq mls]
POPULATION 143,595,000
CAPITAL (POPULATION) Islamabad (204,000)
GOVERNMENT Federal republic
ETHNIC GROUPS Punjabi 60%, Pushtun 13%, Sindhi 12%, Baluchi, Muhajir
LANGUAGES Punjabi 60%, Pashto 13%, Sindhi 12%, Urdu 8%, Baluchi, Brahvi, English
RELIGIONS Muslim 96%, Hindu, Christian, Buddhist
POPULATION DENSITY 180 per sq km [467 per sq ml]
CURRENCY Rupee = 100 paisa

PALAU

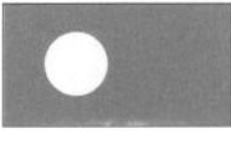

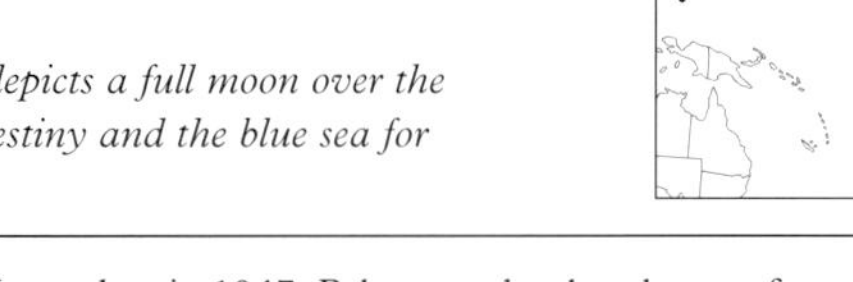

The flag dates from 1980 when Palau became a republic and depicts a full moon over the blue Pacific Ocean. The moon stands for national unity and destiny and the blue sea for the achievement of independence.

The Republic of Palau comprises an archipelago of six Caroline groups, totalling 26 islands and over 300 islets varying in terrain from mountain to reef. Eight of the islands are permanently inhabited. Agriculture is still largely at subsistence level, with copra the main export crop, but luxury tourism is growing, based strongly on scuba-diving and sea fishing. The country relies heavily on US aid. The last remaining member of the four states that comprised the US Trust Territory of the Pacific, established under UN mandate in 1947, Palau voted to break away from the Federated States of Micronesia in 1978. The territory then entered into 'free association with the USA', but in 1983 the people voted to reject the association, since the USA refused to accede to a 1979 referendum that declared the nation a nuclear-free zone. The result was stalemate until 1 October 1994 when the republic became independent. Palau joined the UN, as the 185th member, in December of the same year.

AREA 458 sq km [177 sq mls]
POPULATION 18,000
CAPITAL (POPULATION) Koror (9,000)
GOVERNMENT Republic
ETHNIC GROUPS Palauan (mixture of Polynesian, Melanesian and Malay)
LANGUAGES Palauan (official), English
RELIGIONS Christian (mainly Roman Catholic)
POPULATION DENSITY 39 per sq km [102 per sq ml]
CURRENCY US dollar
MAIN EXPORTS Copra

PANAMA

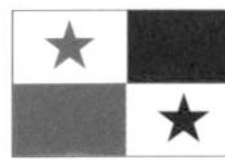

The Panamanian flag dates from the break with Colombia in 1903. Blue stands for the Conservative Party, red for the Liberal Party and white for the hope of peace. The red star represents law and order and the blue star represents 'public honesty'.

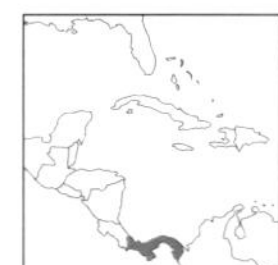

GEOGRAPHY Less than 60 km [37 mls] wide at its narrowest point, the Isthmus of Panama not only links Central and South America but also, via its canal, the Atlantic and Pacific Oceans. Most of the country, including some 750 offshore islands, lies below 700 m [2,300 ft], with a hot and humid climate.

HISTORY, POLITICS AND ECONOMY A French company began cutting the canal in 1880, but various problems stopped work after ten years. In 1903 the province of Panama declared independence from Colombia and granted the USA rights in perpetuity over a 16 km [10 ml] wide Canal Zone (this reverted to Panama in 1979). The canal opened for shipping in 1914. In 1994, 12,337 commercial vessels passed through the canal.

AREA 77,080 sq km [29,761 sq mls]
POPULATION 2,629,000
CAPITAL (POPULATION) Panama City (584,000)
GOVERNMENT Multiparty republic
ETHNIC GROUPS Mestizo 64%, Black and Mulatto 14%, White 10%, Amerindian 8%
LANGUAGES Spanish
RELIGIONS Roman Catholic 80%, Protestant 10%, Muslim 5%
CURRENCY Balboa = 100 centésimos

PAPUA NEW GUINEA

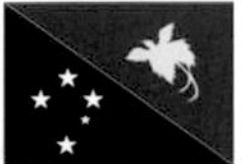

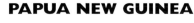

When Papua New Guinea became independent from Australia in 1975, it adopted a flag which had been used for the country since 1971. The design includes a local bird of paradise, the kumul, *in flight and the stars of the Southern Cross constellation.*

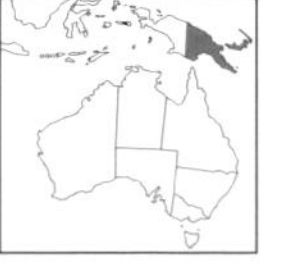

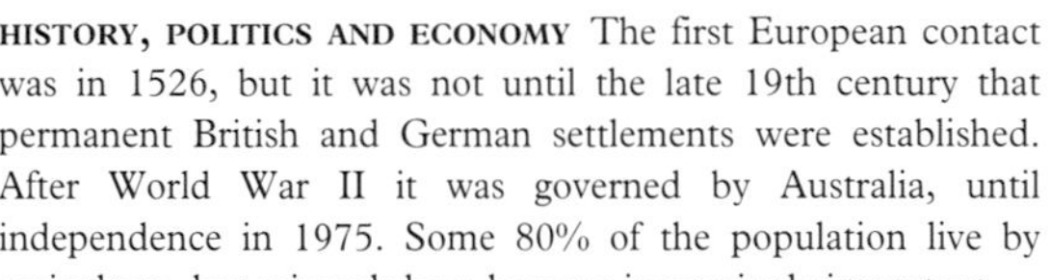

GEOGRAPHY Forming part of Melanesia, Papua New Guinea is the eastern section of the island of New Guinea, plus the Bismarck Archipelago and the island of Bougainville. The main island has a high cordillera of rugged fold mountains covered with montane 'cloud' forest. With few roads, communication is dependent on the country's 400 airports and strips.

HISTORY, POLITICS AND ECONOMY The first European contact was in 1526, but it was not until the late 19th century that permanent British and German settlements were established. After World War II it was governed by Australia, until independence in 1975. Some 80% of the population live by agriculture, but minerals have become increasingly important.

AREA 462,840 sq km [178,703 sq mls]
POPULATION 4,292,000
CAPITAL (POPULATION) Port Moresby (174,000)
GOVERNMENT Constitutional monarchy with a unicameral legislature
ETHNIC GROUPS Papuan 84%, Melanesian 15%
LANGUAGES Motu, English
RELIGIONS Christian, traditional beliefs
POPULATION DENSITY 9 per sq km [24 per sq ml]

PARAGUAY

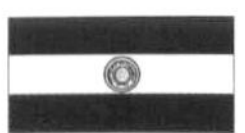

Paraguay's tricolour is a national flag with different sides. On the obverse the state emblem, illustrated here, displays the May Star to commemorate liberation from Spain (1811); the reverse shows the treasury seal – a lion and staff, with the words 'Peace and Justice'.

AREA 406,750 sq km [157,046 sq mls]
POPULATION 4,979,000
CAPITAL (POPULATION) Asunción (945,000)
GOVERNMENT Multiparty republic
ETHNIC GROUPS Mestizo 90%, Amerindian 3%
LANGUAGES Spanish 60%, Guarani 40%
RELIGIONS Roman Catholic 93%
POPULATION DENSITY 12 per sq km [32 per sq ml]
CURRENCY Guaraní = 100 céntimos
URBAN POPULATION 51% of population
MAIN EXPORTS Cotton, soya, oil seeds, timber

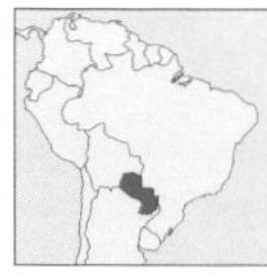

GEOGRAPHY A landlocked nation in the heart of South America, Paraguay is bounded mainly by rivers; for example, the Paraná (South America's second longest) in the south and east. The eastern area is an extension of the Brazilian plateau and is densely forested. In the west is the Northern Chaco, a flat, alluvial plain that rises gently from the Paraguay river valley.

HISTORY AND POLITICS Paraguay was settled in 1537 by the Spanish, and from 1766 formed part of the Rio de la Plata Viceroyalty. It broke free in 1811 and achieved independence in 1813. A long period of internal conflict then followed, including the dictatorship of General Stroessner which lasted from 1954 to 1989. General Rodriguez took over and a new constitution was drawn up but he was replaced in 1993 by Juan Carlos Wasmosy, Paraguay's first civilian president since 1954.

ECONOMY There was considerable economic growth in the 1970s, but debt and inflation problems have now arisen.

PERU

Flown since 1825, the flag's colours are said to have come about when the Argentine patriot General José de San Martin, arriving to liberate Peru from Spain in 1820, saw a flock of red and white flamingos flying over his marching army.

AREA 1,285,220 sq km [496,223 sq mls]
POPULATION 23,588,000
CAPITAL (POPULATION) Lima (6,601,000)
GOVERNMENT Unitary republic
ETHNIC GROUPS Quechua 47%, Mestizo 32%, White 12%
LANGUAGES Spanish, Quechua, Aymara
RELIGIONS Roman Catholic 93%
CURRENCY New sol = 100 centavos
MAIN EXPORTS Copper 19%, petroleum and derivatives 10%, lead 9%, zinc 8%, fishmeal 8%, coffee 5%
MAIN IMPORTS Fuels, machinery, chemicals, food

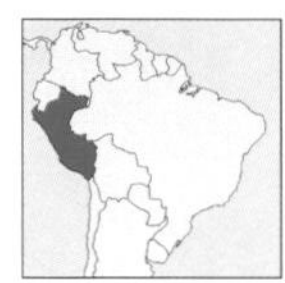

GEOGRAPHY Peru is spread over coastal plain, mountains and forested Amazon lowlands in the interior, with a coastline on the Pacific Ocean. The Amazon lowlands themselves are hot and wet with dense tropical rainforest.

HISTORY AND POLITICS Peru was the homeland of Inca and other ancient civilizations, and has a history of human settlement stretching back over 10,500 years. The last Inca empire ended in the 16th century with the arrival of the Spaniards, who made Peru the most important of their viceroyalties in South America. Independence was gained in 1824, but development has been hampered by problems of communication, political strife, an unbalanced economy and earthquakes.

ECONOMY Agricultural production has failed to keep up with population, so many foods are imported. Peru is the leading producer of coca, used in the production of cocaine. Fishing is also important, and copper, silver and zinc are exported.

PHILIPPINES

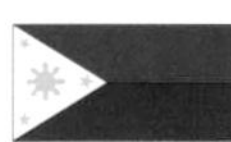

The eight rays of the large sun represent the eight provinces that led the revolt against Spanish rule in 1898 and the three smaller stars stand for the three main island groups. The flag was adopted on independence from the USA in 1946.

AREA 300,000 sq km [115,300 sq mls]
POPULATION 67,167,000
CAPITAL (POPULATION) Manila (6,720,000)
GOVERNMENT Unitary republic with a bicameral legislature
ETHNIC GROUPS Tagalog 30%, Cebuano 24%, Ilocano 10%, Hiligayon Ilongo 9%, Bicol 6%, Samar-Leyte 4%
LANGUAGES Pilipino (Tagalog) and English (both official), Spanish, Cebuano, Ilocano, over 80 others
RELIGIONS Roman Catholic 84%, Agilpayan
CURRENCY Peso = 100 centavos

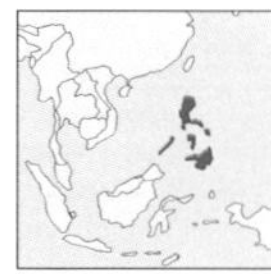

GEOGRAPHY The Republic of the Philippines consists of 7,107 islands stretching for 1,800 km [1,120 mls]. About 1,000 of the islands are inhabited. There are over 20 active volcanoes in the islands, including Mt Apo and Mt Pinatubo, which erupted violently in 1991.

HISTORY AND POLITICS After 300 years of Spanish rule, the islands were ceded to the USA in 1898. Ties with the USA have remained strong even through the corrupt regime of President Ferdinand Marcos from 1965–86. Marcos was overthrown by the 'people power' revolution that brought to office Corazon Aquino, but the political situation has remained extremely volatile. Fidel V. Ramos became president in the 1992 elections.

ECONOMY There are few natural resources and the economy is weak, with high levels of unemployment and emigration.

PITCAIRN ISLANDS

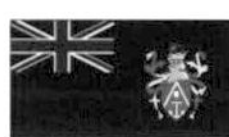

A flag for local use was granted to Pitcairn in 1984. The flag is the British Blue Ensign with the whole arms in the fly. The arms were first used in 1969.

AREA 48 sq km [19 sq mls]
POPULATION 60
CAPITAL (POPULATION) Adamstown (50)
GOVERNMENT British Dependent Territory
ETHNIC GROUPS English, Tahitian
POPULATION DENSITY 1.3 per sq km [3.2 per sq ml]
CURRENCY New Zealand dollar

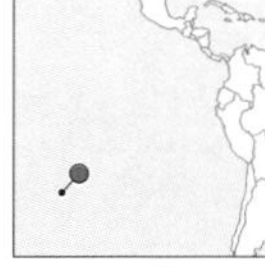

Pitcairn is a British dependent territory of four islands situated halfway between New Zealand and Panama. Uninhabited until 1790, Pitcairn was occupied by nine mutineers from HMS *Bounty* and some people from Tahiti. The islands were annexed by Britain in 1902. The present population all live in the capital, administered by the British High Commission in New Zealand.

POLAND

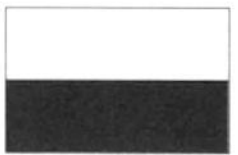

The colours of Poland's flag were derived from the 13th-century coat of arms of a white eagle on a red field, which still appears on the Polish merchant flag. The flag's simple design was adopted when Poland became a republic in 1919.

AREA 312,680 sq km [120,726 sq mls]
POPULATION 38,587,000
CAPITAL (POPULATION) Warsaw (1,655,000)
GOVERNMENT Multiparty republic
ETHNIC GROUPS Polish 99%, Ukrainian
LANGUAGES Polish (official)
RELIGIONS Roman Catholic 91%, Orthodox 2%
POPULATION DENSITY 123 per sq km [320 per sq ml]
CURRENCY Zloty = 100 groszy
MAIN EXPORTS Machinery and transport equipment 39%, chemicals 11%, fuel and power 10%, metals 10%, textiles 7%

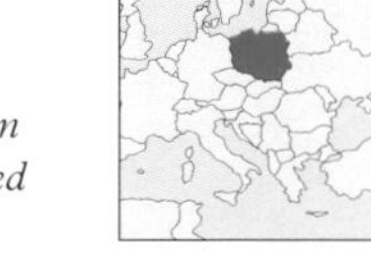

GEOGRAPHY Poland's geographical location has had a strong influence on the country's complex history. Invasions by neighbouring countries have changed the frontiers on several occasions, most recently after the end of World War II, when 17% of the population was lost and territory was given up to the USSR in return for land from Germany. Part of these gains was a length of Baltic coastline, giving Poland a chance to develop its maritime interests; as a result, it is now a leading fishing nation.

HISTORY AND POLITICS Under the banner of the independent trade union Solidarity, based originally in the Gdansk shipyards and led by Lech Walesa, Poland was the first of the Soviet satellites to challenge and bring down its Communist regime.

ECONOMY Two-thirds of the land surface is farmed, with such crops as rye, potatoes, oats and sugar beet. Industrial growth was rapid after World War II – there are reserves of coal, lignite and lead – but restructuring and diversification is now needed.

PORTUGAL

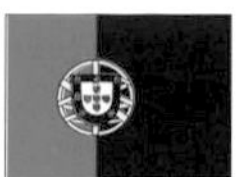

Portugal's colours, adopted in 1910 when it became a republic, represent Henry the Navigator (green) and the monarchy (red). The armillary sphere – an early navigational instrument – reflects Portugal's leading role in world exploration.

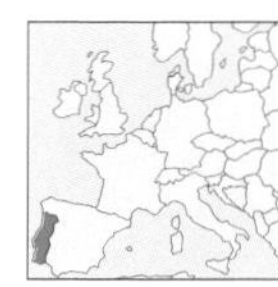

GEOGRAPHY Portugal occupies an oblong coastland in the south-west of the Iberian peninsula, facing the Atlantic Ocean. Here the Meseta edge has splintered and in part foundered to leave upstanding mountain ranges, particularly in the Serra da Estrêla. Over a quarter of the country is forested, with tree growth helped by the mild, moist airflow from the Atlantic. Pines are the most common species, especially on the sandy 'littorals' near the coast. The climate is drier and warmer in the south.

HISTORY AND POLITICS Portugal had an important historical role in maritime exploration and established colonies in Africa and Asia. The country became a republic in 1910 and joined the European Union in 1986, but it is its poorest member.

ECONOMY The Portuguese economy relies heavily on agriculture and fishing, which together employ over a quarter of the national workforce. These industries are still fairly primitive, but produce a wide range of crops including maize, rye, olives and grapes. Fish include oysters, sardines and cod. The manufacture of textiles and ceramics is also important, as is the tourist industry.

AREA 92,390 sq km [35,670 sq mls]
POPULATION 10,600,000
CAPITAL (POPULATION) Lisbon (2,561,000)
GOVERNMENT Multiparty republic with a unicameral legislature
ETHNIC GROUPS Portuguese 99%, Cape Verdean, Brazilian, Spanish, British
LANGUAGES Portuguese
RELIGIONS Roman Catholic 95%
POPULATION DENSITY 115 per sq km [297 per sq ml]
CURRENCY Escudo = 100 centavos
MAIN EXPORTS Clothing 26%, machinery and transport equipment 20%, paper and paper products 8%, footwear 8%

PUERTO RICO

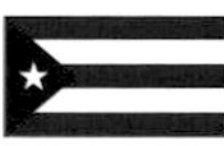

Puerto Rico fought with Cuba for independence from Spain and their flags are almost identical (the red and blue colours are transposed). The island is a dependent territory of the United States and the flag, adopted in 1952, is flown only with the American 'Stars and Stripes'.

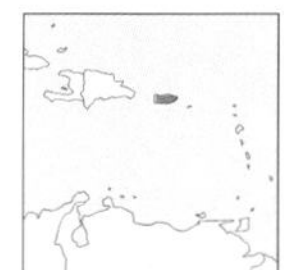

GEOGRAPHY Puerto Rico is the easternmost of the major Greater Antilles and is mainly mountainous, with a narrow coastal plain. Cerro de Punta (1,338 m [4,389 ft]) is the highest peak. The climate is hot and wet, but there are no great extremes of temperature; the winds from the north-east or east, blowing over a warm sea, cause rain which falls on over 200 days a year.

HISTORY AND POLITICS Ceded by Spain to the USA in 1898, Puerto Rico became a 'self-governing Commonwealth in free association with the USA' after a referendum in 1952. Even with this degree of autonomy, there is a strong US influence; as full US citizens Puerto Ricans pay no federal taxes, but neither do they vote in US elections. Migration to the USA is common.

ECONOMY The island is the most industrialized in the Caribbean with chemicals constituting 36% of exports and metal products (based on copper deposits) a further 17%. Manufacturing and tourism are growing and crops include sugar, coffee and spices.

AREA 8,900 sq km [3,436 sq mls]
POPULATION 3,689,000
CAPITAL (POPULATION) San Juan (1,816,000)
GOVERNMENT Self-governing Commonwealth in association with the USA
ETHNIC GROUPS Spanish 99%, African American, Indian
LANGUAGES Spanish, English
RELIGIONS Christian (mainly Roman Catholic)
POPULATION DENSITY 414 per sq km [1,074 per sq ml]
CURRENCY US dollar
URBAN POPULATION 77% of population

QATAR

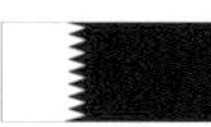

The flag was adopted in 1971. The maroon colour is said to result from the natural effect of the sun on the traditional red banner, while the white was added after a British request in 1820 that white should be included in the flags of friendly states in the Arabian Gulf.

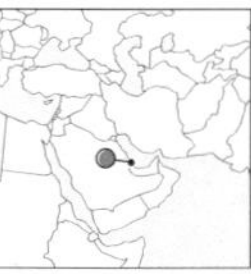

Qatar occupies a low, barren peninsula that extends northwards into the Arabian Gulf. The climate is hot and dry all year round and much of the landscape is made up of desert. A British protectorate between 1916 and 1971, there is a high standard of living for its inhabitants, which is mainly derived from oil and gas. These two account for over 80% of exports. There has been some recent diversification into cement, steel and fertilizers. Much of the workforce is made up of immigrant labour.

AREA 11,000 sq km [4,247 sq mls]
POPULATION 594,000
CAPITAL (POPULATION) Doha (243,000)
GOVERNMENT Constitutional absolute monarchy
ETHNIC GROUPS Southern Asian 34%, Qatari 20%
LANGUAGES Arabic
RELIGIONS Sunni Muslim 92%, Christian, Hindu

RÉUNION

As a French Overseas Department, Réunion uses the French tricolour as its flag.

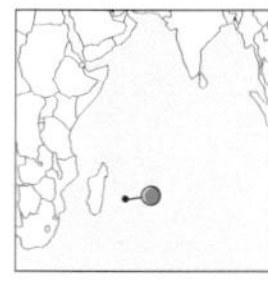

Réunion is the largest of the Mascarene Islands, lying in the Indian Ocean east of Madagascar and south-west of Mauritius. The island is made up of a rugged, mountainous forested centre surrounded by a fertile coastal plain. The volcanic mountains rise to the peak of Piton des Neiges (3,070 m [10,076 ft]). It became an overseas department of France in 1946 and the French still subsidize Réunion heavily in return for the use of the island as its main military base in the area. Intensive cultivation takes place on the lowlands, with sugar cane providing 75% of exports. Vanilla, perfume and tea are also produced.

AREA 2,510 sq km [969 sq mls]
POPULATION 655,000
CAPITAL (POPULATION) St-Denis (123,000)
GOVERNMENT Overseas Department of France
ETHNIC GROUPS Mixed 64%, East Indian 28%, Chinese 2%, White 2%
LANGUAGES French, Creole
RELIGIONS Roman Catholic 90%, Muslim 1%
CURRENCY French franc

ROMANIA

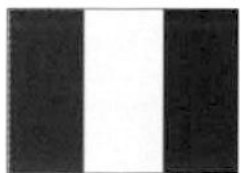

Romania's colours come from the arms of the provinces that united to form the country in 1861, and the design was adopted in 1948. The central state coat of arms, added in 1965, was deleted in 1990 after the fall of the Communist Ceausescu regime.

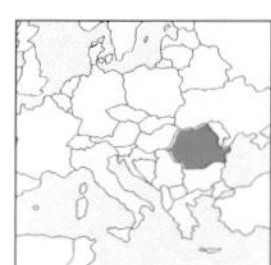

GEOGRAPHY Romania has clearly defined natural borders on three sides: the Danube in the south, the Black Sea coast in the east and the River Prut in the north-east. The landscape is dominated by an arc of high fold mountains, the Carpathians; south and east of these lie the plains of the lower Danube.

HISTORY AND POLITICS Romania was formed in 1861 when the provinces of Moldavia and Wallachia united. It became a Communist republic in 1946 and the dictator Nicolae Ceausescu took control in 1965. His corrupt regime lasted for 24 years, until he and his wife were executed following an army-backed revolt in 1989. In the 1970s his programmes of industrialization and urbanization caused severe food shortages. In 1990, Romania held its first free elections since the end of the World War II. Further elections held in 1992 were won by Ion Illiescu.

ECONOMY Despite the industrialization programmes, Romania is an agricultural nation, with crops of cereals, timber and fruit.

AREA 237,500 sq km [91,699 sq mls]
POPULATION 22,863,000
CAPITAL (POPULATION) Bucharest (2,067,000)
GOVERNMENT Multiparty republic
ETHNIC GROUPS Romanian 89%, Hungarian 8%
LANGUAGES Romanian, Hungarian, German
RELIGIONS Romanian Orthodox 87%, Roman Catholic 5%, Greek Orthodox 4%
POPULATION DENSITY 96 per sq km [249 per sq ml]
CURRENCY Leu = 100 bani

RUSSIA

RUSSIA

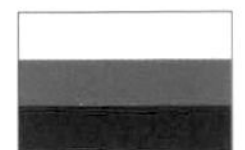

Distinctive Russian flags were first instituted by Peter the Great, based on those of the Netherlands. This flag became the official national flag in 1799 but was suppressed in the Bolshevik Revolution. It was restored on 22 August 1991.

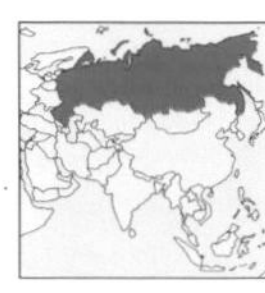

GEOGRAPHY Even with the break-up of the Soviet Union in 1991, the Russian Federation remains the largest country in the world. The landscape and climates are very diverse, ranging from tundra in the north, to the coniferous forests of the taiga, to the steppe regions of the south, once grassland but now largely under cultivation. There are several mountain ranges, including the Ural Mountains, and many long rivers, including the Volga, which flows for 3,700 km [2,300 mls] to the Caspian Sea.

HISTORY AND POLITICS The present size of Russia is the product of a long period of evolution dating to early medieval times. It has always been a centralized state. The 1917 Revolution, when the Tsarist Order was overthrown and a Communist government established under Lenin, was a landmark in Russian history. The next fundamental changes began when Gorbachev took charge after 1985. Russia's huge size and numbers of different peoples have always posed potential problems and continue to do so.

ECONOMY The Soviet economy was transformed after 1917 into one of the most industrialized in the world, based initially on the iron and steel industry. Although strong, the Russian economy is now in chaos, with food shortages and unemployment.

AREA 17,075,000 sq km [6,592,800 sq mls]
POPULATION 148,385,000
CAPITAL (POPULATION) Moscow (8,957,000)
GOVERNMENT Federal republic
ETHNIC GROUPS Russian 82%, Tatar 4%, Ukrainian 3%, Chuvash 2%
LANGUAGES Russian
RELIGIONS Christian, Muslim, Buddhist
POPULATION DENSITY 9 per sq km [22 per sq ml]
CURRENCY Rouble = 100 kopeks
URBAN POPULATION 75% of population
LAND USE Arable 8%, grass 6%, forest 45%
ANNUAL INCOME $2,350 per person

RWANDA

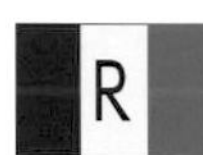

Adopted in 1961, Rwanda's tricolour in the Pan-African colours features the letter 'R' to distinguish it from Guinea's flag. Red represents the blood shed in the 1959 revolution, yellow for victory over tyranny, and green for hope.

GEOGRAPHY Rwanda is a small, landlocked and poor rural country and Africa's most densely populated. Geological uplift of the western arm of the Great Rift Valley has raised most of the country to well over 2,000 m [6,000 ft].

HISTORY, POLITICS AND ECONOMY Rwanda was merged with Burundi by Germany in 1899, making Ruanda-Urundi part of German East Africa. Belgium occupied it during World War I and then administered it afterwards. It was divided into two in 1959, with Rwanda achieving full independence in 1962. Civil war erupted in 1994, with appalling loss of life.

AREA 26,340 sq km [10,170 sq mls]
POPULATION 7,899,000
CAPITAL (POPULATION) Kigali (233,000)
GOVERNMENT Transitional government
ETHNIC GROUPS Hutu 90%, Tutsi 9%, Twa 1%
LANGUAGES English, French, Kinyarwanda
RELIGIONS Roman Catholic 65%, Protestant 12%, traditional beliefs 17%, Muslim 9%
CURRENCY Rwandan franc = 100 centimes

ST HELENA

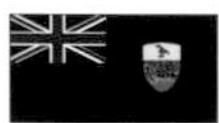

Since 1984 the British dependent territory of St Helena, with its dependencies of Ascension Island and the Tristan da Cunha group, has used the shield from its new coat of arms in the fly of the British Blue Ensign. The main part of the shield shows a ship sailing towards the island.

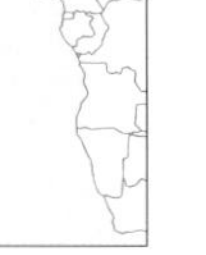

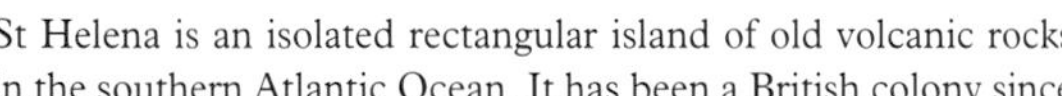

St Helena is an isolated rectangular island of old volcanic rocks in the southern Atlantic Ocean. It has been a British colony since 1834 and the administrative centre for six of the UK's South Atlantic islands and is very dependent on subsidies.

AREA 360 sq km [139 sq mls]
POPULATION 45,000
CAPITAL (POPULATION) Basseterre (15,000)
GOVERNMENT Constitutional monarchy
ETHNIC GROUPS Of African descent
LANGUAGES English
RELIGIONS Christian
CURRENCY East Caribbean $ = 100 cents

ST KITTS AND NEVIS

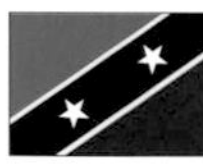

The colours represent fertility (green), sunshine (yellow), the independence struggle (red) and the African heritage (black); the two stars stand for hope and liberty. The flag was adopted on independence from Britain in 1983.

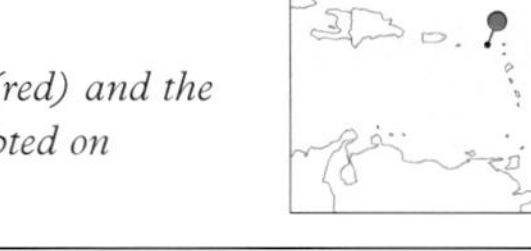

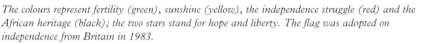

St Kitts (formerly St Christopher) and Nevis are two well-watered volcanic islands, about 20% forested. They were the first West Indian islands to be colonized by Britain – in 1623 and 1628. Tourism has now replaced sugar as the main earner.

AREA 122 sq km [47 sq mls]
POPULATION 6,000
CAPITAL (POPULATION) Jamestown (1,500)
GOVERNMENT British Dependent Territory
ETHNIC GROUPS Mixed European (British), Asian and African
LANGUAGES English
CURRENCY St Helena pound = 100 pence

ST LUCIA

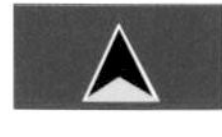

This Caribbean island became an Associated State of Great Britain in 1967 and adopted this modern-looking flag. It is a symbolic representation of St Lucia itself: the black volcanic hills of the island rising from the blue ocean.

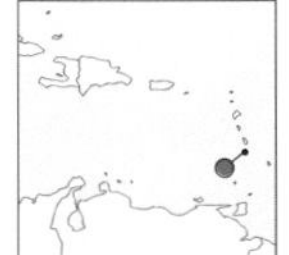

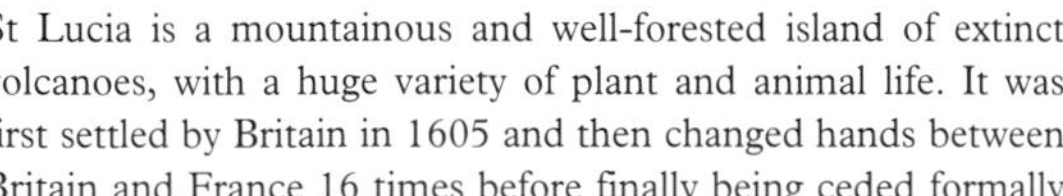

St Lucia is a mountainous and well-forested island of extinct volcanoes, with a huge variety of plant and animal life. It was first settled by Britain in 1605 and then changed hands between Britain and France 16 times before finally being ceded formally in 1814. It gained full independence in 1979. St Lucia is still overdependent on bananas, which provide 71% of exports but are easily destroyed by hurricane and disease. Other crops include cocoa and coconuts. Clothing is the second main export.

AREA 610 sq km [236 sq mls]
POPULATION 147,000
CAPITAL (POPULATION) Castries (53,000)
GOVERNMENT Constitutional monarchy
ETHNIC GROUPS African descent 90%, Mixed 6%, East Indian 3%
LANGUAGES English, French patois
RELIGIONS Roman Catholic 79%, Protestant 16%, Anglican
CURRENCY East Caribbean $ = 100 cents

ST VINCENT AND THE GRENADINES

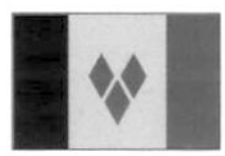

On independence from Britain in 1979, St Vincent adopted this tricolour, but with the islands' coat of arms in the centre. In 1985 this was replaced by the present three green diamonds representing the islands as the 'gems of the Antilles'.

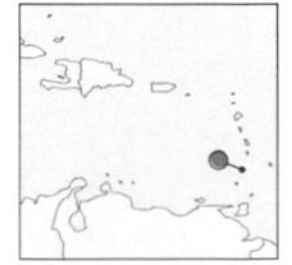

St Vincent and the Grenadines comprise the main island (with 89% of the land area and 95% of the population) and the Northern Grenadines. St Vincent was settled in the 16th century and became a British colony in 1783. The colony became self-governing in 1969 and independent in 1979. Less prosperous than some of its neighbours, the tourist industry is growing.

AREA 388 sq km [150 sq mls]
POPULATION 111,000
CAPITAL (POPULATION) Kingstown (27,000)
GOVERNMENT Constitutional monarchy
ETHNIC GROUPS Of African descent
LANGUAGES English, French patois
RELIGIONS Christian
POPULATION DENSITY 286 per sq km [740 per sq ml]

SAN MARINO

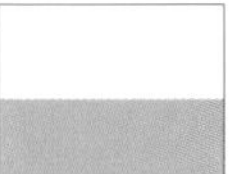

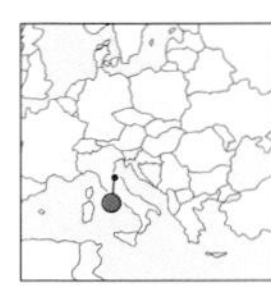

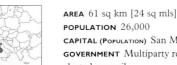

The tiny republic of San Marino, enclosed completely within the territory of Italy, has been an independent state since AD 885. The flag's colours – white for the snowy mountains and blue for the sky – derive from the state coat of arms.

San Marino is the world's smallest republic and lies 20 km [12 mls] south-west of Rimini. The territory consists mainly of the limestone mass of Monte Titano. Most of the population live in the medieval fortified city of San Marino. There is a friendship and co-operation treaty with Italy dating back to 1862 and tourism and limestone quarrying are the chief occupations.

AREA 61 sq km [24 sq mls]
POPULATION 26,000
CAPITAL (POPULATION) San Marino (2,395)
GOVERNMENT Multiparty republic with an elected council
ETHNIC GROUPS San Marinese, Italian
LANGUAGES Italian
RELIGIONS Roman Catholic
CURRENCY Italian lira and San Marino lira

SÃO TOMÉ AND PRÍNCIPE

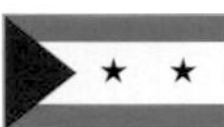

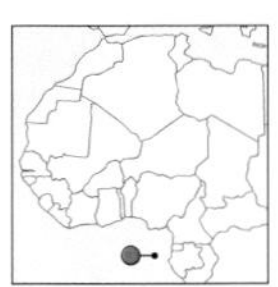

Adopted on independence from Portugal in 1975, this variation of the familiar Pan-African colours had previously been the emblem of the national liberation movement. The two black stars represent the two islands that comprise the country.

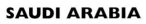

São Tomé and Principe are two mountainous, volcanic and heavily forested Atlantic islands some 145 km [90 mls] apart. A Portuguese colony since 1522, the islands were suddenly granted independence in 1975 and a one-party Socialist state was set up. Marxism was abandoned in 1990 and São Tomé held multiparty elections in 1991. Cocoa is the most important crop.

AREA 964 sq km [372 sq mls]
POPULATION 133,000
CAPITAL (POPULATION) São Tomé (36,000)
GOVERNMENT Multiparty republic
ETHNIC GROUPS Mainly descendants of slaves
LANGUAGES Portuguese
RELIGIONS Christian (mainly Roman Catholic)

SAUDI ARABIA

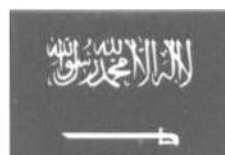

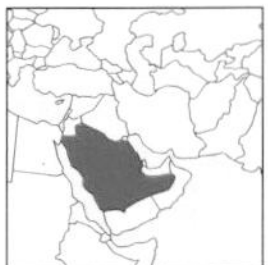

The inscription on the Saudi flag above the sword means 'There is no God but Allah, and Muhammad is the Prophet of Allah'. The only national flag with an inscription as its main feature, the design was adopted in 1938.

GEOGRAPHY Saudi Arabia is the largest state in the Middle East but is more than 95% desert. At its heart is the province of Najd, containing three main groups of oases. To the south lies the Rub 'al Khali ('empty quarter'), the world's largest expanse of sand.
HISTORY, POLITICS AND ECONOMY During and shortly after World War I, the Saudis of Najd (central Arabia) extended their territory and took control over the greater part of the Arabian peninsula, including the holy city of Mecca. Its vast reserves of oil (the world's largest) were discovered after World War II and the strictly Muslim society soon had some of the world's most advanced facilities. Saudi Arabia has always been an ally of the West, but this has conflicted with its Islamic role.

AREA 2,149,690 sq km [829,995 sq mls]
POPULATION 18,395,000
CAPITAL (POPULATION) Riyadh (2,000,000)
GOVERNMENT Absolute monarchy with a consultative assembly
ETHNIC GROUPS Arab 92% (Saudi 82%, Yemeni 10%)
LANGUAGES Arabic
RELIGIONS Muslim 99%, Christian 1%
CURRENCY Saudi riyal = 100 halalas
POPULATION DENSITY 9 per sq km [22 per sq ml]

SENEGAL

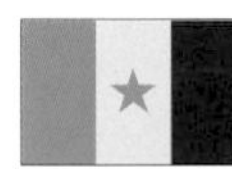

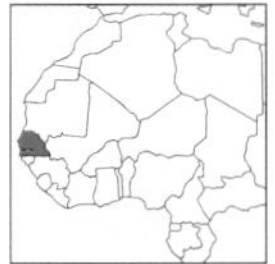

Apart from the green five-pointed star, which symbolizes the Muslim faith of the majority of the population, Senegal's flag is identical to that of Mali. It was adopted in 1960 when the country gained its independence from France.

GEOGRAPHY One-fifth of Senegal's population lives in Dakar and the area around volcanic Cape Verde, the most westerly point on mainland Africa. In the north-east there is scrub and semi-desert, while the south is wetter and more fertile.
HISTORY, POLITICS AND ECONOMY Senegal's name derives from the Zenega Berbers, who invaded from Mauritania in the 14th century. The country became the administrative centre for French West Africa, benefitting from this with a good road network and a well-planned capital. Groundnuts dominate the economy and exports, with phosphates as the other main export.

AREA 196,720 sq km [75,954 sq mls]
POPULATION 8,308,000
CAPITAL (POPULATION) Dakar (1,730,000)
GOVERNMENT Multiparty republic with a unicameral legislature
ETHNIC GROUPS Wolof 44%, Fulani 23%, Serer 14%, Tukulor 8%, Dyola 8%
LANGUAGES French, African languages
RELIGIONS Sunni Muslim 94%, Christian 5%, animist
CURRENCY CFA franc = 100 centimes

SEYCHELLES

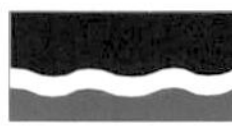

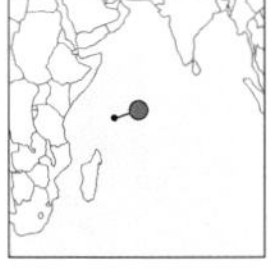

The flag dates from 1977 following a coup d'état *by the People's Progressive Front, and diagrammatically shows the Indian Ocean (in white) surrounding the islands of the group and the resources contained in it. Green represents agriculture and red is for revolution and progress.*

The Seychelles are a compact group of four large and 36 small granitic islands, plus a wide scattering of coralline islands lying mainly to the south and west. Some 98% of the population live on the four main islands, particularly on the biggest, Mahé. French from 1756 and British from 1814, the islands gained independence in 1976. A one-party Socialist state was set up in 1977; multiparty democracy was restored after elections in 1992. Fishing and luxury tourism are the two main industries.

AREA 455 sq km [176 sq mls]
POPULATION 75,000
CAPITAL (POPULATION) Victoria (30,000)
GOVERNMENT Multiparty republic
ETHNIC GROUPS Mixture of African, Asian and European
LANGUAGES English, French, Creole
RELIGIONS Roman Catholic 89%, Anglican 9%
CURRENCY Seychelles rupee = 100 cents

SIERRA LEONE

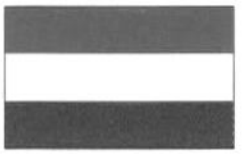

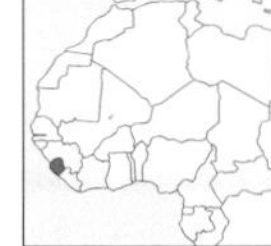

The colours of Sierra Leone's flag, adopted on independence from Britain in 1961, come from the coat of arms. Green represents the country's agriculture, white stands for peace and blue for the Atlantic Ocean.

GEOGRAPHY Sierra Leone ('lion mountain') is located in West Africa and has a coastline on the Atlantic Ocean. The interior of the country is made up of plateaux and mountains, while the coastal plain is more swampy. The climate is tropical.
HISTORY, POLITICS AND ECONOMY The capital was established as a settlement for freed slaves in the 18th century and the country became a British colony in 1808. Independence was gained in 1961 and from 1968 Sierra Leone was ruled by the military as a one-party state. In 1994-5, civil war caused a collapse of law and order. Diamonds and iron-ore mining provide revenue.

AREA 71,740 sq km [27,699 sq mls]
POPULATION 4,467,000
CAPITAL (POPULATION) Freetown (505,000)
GOVERNMENT Transitional government
ETHNIC GROUPS Mende 34%, Temne 31%, Limba 8%, Kono 5%
LANGUAGES English, Creole, Mende, Limba, Temne
RELIGIONS Traditional beliefs 51%, Sunni Muslim 39%, Christian 9%
CURRENCY Leone = 100 cents

SINGAPORE

Adopted in 1959, this flag was retained when Singapore broke away from the Federation of Malaysia in 1963. The crescent stands for the nation's ascent and the stars for its aims of democracy, peace, progress, justice and equality.

GEOGRAPHY Singapore comprises the main island itself and an additional 54 much smaller islands lying within its territorial waters. The highest point on the main island is Bukit Tiamah (177 m [581 ft]). The uplands were originally forested, while the lowlands were swampy with mangrove forests along the inlets. Much of the forest has been cleared for farming and building, creating problems of soil erosion. Temperatures are uniformly high throughout the year, with high humidity and heavy rain.

HISTORY AND POLITICS Its position at the southernmost point of the Malay Peninsula has been of great strategic importance to Singapore. A British colony from 1867, it became self-governing in 1959. Part of the Federation of Malaysia from 1963, it became fully independent in 1965. Singapore's success owes much to Lee Kuan Yew, prime minister from 1959 to 1990, who brought in an ambitious, but rigid, policy of industrialization. His successor, Goh Chok Tong, seems set to continue his work.

ECONOMY The successful economy is based on its vast port, and its manufacturing, commercial and financial services.

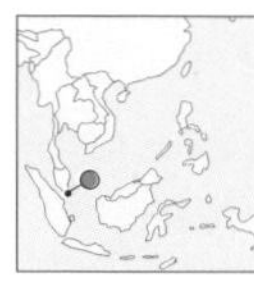

AREA 618 sq km [239 sq mls]
POPULATION 2,990,000
CAPITAL (POPULATION) Singapore (2,874,000)
GOVERNMENT Unitary multiparty republic with a unicameral legislature
ETHNIC GROUPS Chinese 76%, Malay 14%, Indian 7%
LANGUAGES Chinese, Malay, Tamil, English
RELIGIONS Buddhist 28%, Muslim 15%, Christian 13%, Taoist 13%, Hindu 4%
CURRENCY Singapore dollar = 100 cents
POPULATION DENSITY 4,838 per sq km [12,510 per sq ml]

SLOVAK REPUBLIC

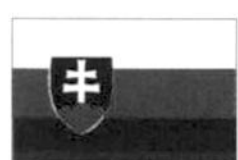

The horizontal tricolour which the Slovak Republic adopted in September 1992 dates from 1848. The red, white and blue colours are typical of Slavonic flags. The three blue mounds in the shield represent the traditional mountains of Slovakia: Tatra, Matra and Fatra.

GEOGRAPHY One part of the former Czechoslovakia, the Slovak Republic consists of a mountainous region in the north, part of the Carpathian system that divides Slovakia from Poland, and a southern lowland area drained by the River Danube.

HISTORY AND POLITICS As part of the Austro-Hungarian Empire the Slovaks were subject to enforced 'Magyarization' and their development was stifled. They gained independence from it in 1918 and joined the Czechs to form Czechoslovakia. This was formally broken up in January 1993, but the split was amicable and the two new states maintain close links with each other.

ECONOMY There are reserves of coal, copper, lead and zinc. Agriculture is important, with crops of potatoes and sugar beet.

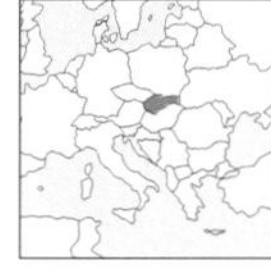

AREA 49,035 sq km [18,932 sq mls]
POPULATION 5,400,000
CAPITAL (POPULATION) Bratislava (441,000)
GOVERNMENT Multiparty republic with a unicameral legislature
ETHNIC GROUPS Slovak, Hungarian, Czech
LANGUAGES Slovak, Hungarian, Czech
RELIGIONS Roman Catholic 60%, Protestant 8%, Orthodox 3%
CURRENCY Slovak koruna = 100 haler
POPULATION DENSITY 110 per sq km [285 per sq ml]

SLOVENIA

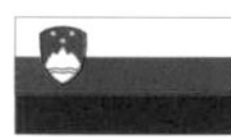

The Slovene flag, based on the flag of Russia, was originally adopted in 1848. During the Communist period a red star appeared in the centre. This was replaced in June 1991 after independence, with the new emblem showing an outline of Mount Triglav.

GEOGRAPHY Slovenia is a mountainous state at the northern end of the former Yugoslavia. It has access to the Adriatic Sea through the port of Koper, near the Italian border, giving it a flourishing trade from landlocked central Europe.

HISTORY AND POLITICS Part of the Austro-Hungarian Empire until 1918, Slovenia's Roman Catholic population found support from neighbours Italy and Austria as well as Germany during its fight for independence in 1991. The most ethnically homogeneous of Yugoslavia's component republics, it made the transition to independence fairly peacefully.

ECONOMY There are strong agricultural sectors (wheat, maize) and industry (textiles, timber) and some mineral resources.

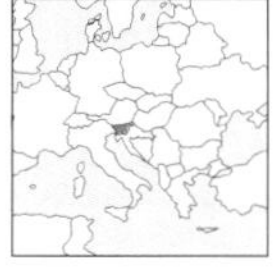

AREA 20,251 sq km [7,817 sq mls]
POPULATION 2,000,000
CAPITAL (POPULATION) Ljubljana (323,000)
GOVERNMENT Multiparty republic
ETHNIC GROUPS Slovene 88%, Croat 3%, Serb 2%, Muslim 1%
LANGUAGES Slovene 90%, Serbo-Croat 7%
RELIGIONS Roman Catholic 98%, Orthodox 2%, Muslim 1%
POPULATION DENSITY 99 per sq km [256 per sq ml]

SOLOMON ISLANDS

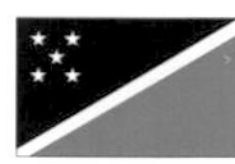

In 1978 the Solomon Islands became independent from Britain and adopted a new flag. The five white-pointed stars represent the five main islands, whilst the colours stand for the forests (green) and waters (blue) lighted by the sun (yellow).

The double chain of islands forming the Solomons and Vanuatu extends for some 2,250 km [1,400 mls] in the Pacific Ocean. It represents the drowned outermost crustal fold on the borders of the ancient Australian continent. Occupied by the Japanese during World War II, the islands were the scene of fierce fighting, notably the battle for the island of Guadalcanal, on which the capital stands. Known as the British Solomons, the islands won full independence in 1978. Subsistence farming occupies about 90% of the population. Coconuts and cocoa are the most important exports, while tuna fish is the main earner.

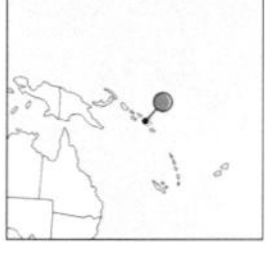

AREA 28,900 sq km [11,158 sq mls]
POPULATION 378,000
CAPITAL (POPULATION) Honiara (37,000)
GOVERNMENT Constitutional monarchy with a unicameral legislature
ETHNIC GROUPS Melanesian 94%, Polynesian 4%
LANGUAGES Many Melanesian languages, English
RELIGIONS Christian
CURRENCY Solomon Is. $ = 100 cents

SOMALIA

In 1960 British Somaliland united with Italian Somaliland to form present-day Somalia and the flag of the southern region was adopted. It is based on the colours of the UN flag with the points of the star representing the five regions of East Africa where Somalis live.

With a coastline on the Gulf of Aden in the north and one on the Indian Ocean in the east, Somalia occupies the literal 'Horn of Africa'. The northern area is the highest and most arid, with mountains rising to 2,408 m [7,900 ft] and wooded with box and cedar. In the south there is low plain or plateau, covered in grass and thorn bush; bananas are a major export from this area. Northern Somalia was ruled as British Somaliland from the 1880s and the south was ruled as Italian Somaliland after 1905.

The two parts joined and became independent in 1960. The repressive Socialist government of Siyad Barre took over in 1969, leading to the start of problems with secessionist guerillas in the north. The situation deteriorated in 1991, with worsening violence and a growing number of refugees. The UN and the USA sent in troops in 1993 but they had to withdraw in 1994. By 1995, Somalia was divided into three main regions: the north, the north-east and the south, and had no national government.

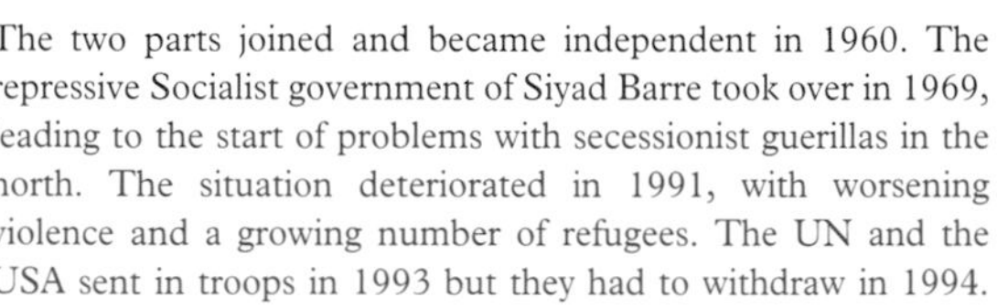

AREA 637,660 sq km [246,201 sq mls]
POPULATION 9,180,000
CAPITAL (POPULATION) Mogadishu (1,000,000)
GOVERNMENT Single-party republic, suspended due to civil war
ETHNIC GROUPS Somali 98%, Arab 1%
LANGUAGES Somali, Arabic, English, Italian
RELIGIONS Sunni Muslim 99%
CURRENCY Shilling = 100 cents
POPULATION DENSITY 14 per sq km [37 per sq ml]
URBAN POPULATION 25% of population

SOUTH AFRICA

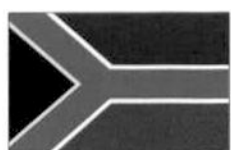

This new flag was adopted in May 1994, after the country's first multiracial elections were held in April and a new constitution was drawn up. The colours are a combination of the ANC colours (black, yellow and green) and the traditional Afrikaner ones (red, white and blue).

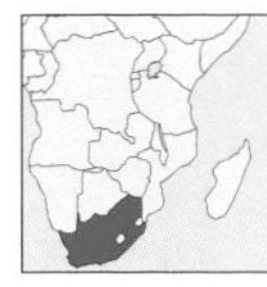

GEOGRAPHY South Africa is divisible into two major natural zones – the interior and the coastal fringe, with the interior itself divisible into two major parts. Most of Northern Cape Province and Free State are drained by the Orange River and its tributaries. The Northern Transvaal is occupied by the Bushveld, an area of granites and igneous intrusions. The coastal fringe is divided from the interior by the Fringing Escarpment; in the east this is shown by the huge rock wall of the Drakensberg, which rises to over 3,000 m [over 10,000 ft].

HISTORY AND POLITICS The country was first peopled by negroids from the north, who moved southwards into land occupied by Bushmanoid peoples and reached the south-east by the 18th century. At the same time Europeans were establishing a site for the Dutch East India Company on what is now Cape Town; they then spread out throughout the south of the country. Eventually black and white met near the Kei River and the black-dominated and white-dominated areas first arose. The policy of apartheid was instituted by the ruling National Party in 1948, with racial segregation and discrimination against the blacks rigidly enforced. It was not until President F.W. de Klerk was elected in 1989 that reforms slowly began. The first multiracial elections were held in April 1994, with Nelson Mandela elected president, after which all the internal boundaries were changed.

ECONOMY Despite apartheid, South Africa's economy has been very successful (for the white population). There are valuable mineral resources, such as gold, chrome, uranium and nickel.

AREA 1,219,916 sq km [470,566 sq mls]
POPULATION 44,000,000
CAPITAL (POPULATION) Pretoria (1,080,000)/ Cape Town (1,912,000)/ Bloemfontein (300,000)
GOVERNMENT Multiparty republic

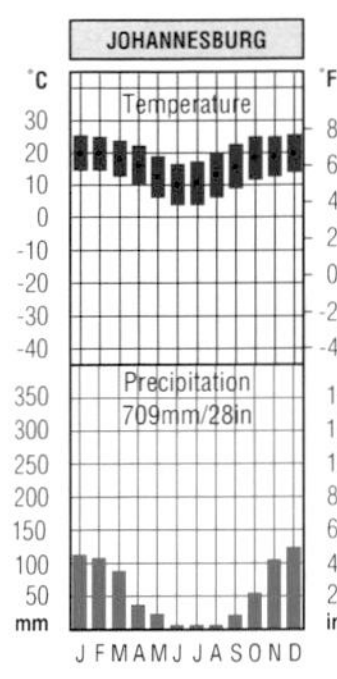

In winter the air is very dry and the sky almost cloudless on the High Veld. The large diurnal range of temperature resembles that of other places on the high plateaux of southern Africa; it often exceeds 15°C [27°F]. Summer is the rainy season, when north-easterly winds bring moist air from the Indian Ocean. In winter it rains on 1–3 days per month.

SPAIN

The colours of the Spanish flag date back to the old kingdom of Aragon in the 12th century. The present design, in which the central yellow stripe is twice as wide as each of the red stripes, was adopted during the Civil War in 1938.

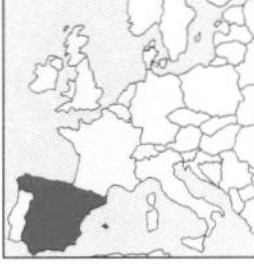

GEOGRAPHY Spain occupies an important geographical position between Europe and Africa, with the narrow Strait of Gibraltar encouraging African contact. The chief physical feature of Spain is the vast central plateau, the Meseta, which tilts gently towards Portugal. This is crossed by the mountain range of the Central Sierras. In the north-east and south of the country are lowlands, while in Andalusia (in the south) a mountain chain rises to the peak of the Sierra Nevada (3,478 m [11,400 ft]). Spain has three main categories of vegetation: forests (about 10% of the land surface) in the north and north-west, *matorral* (which is scrub and covers a fifth of the land), and steppe.

HISTORY AND POLITICS Spain became united in 1479 when the different independent kingdoms that existed joined together after the marriage of Isabella of Castille and Ferdinand of Aragon. The country remained neutral in both world wars, but suffered a civil war between 1936 and 1939, which was won by the Nationalists under Franco. He then ruled as a dictator until 1975 when democracy was restored under King Juan Carlos.

ECONOMY Agriculture occupies nearly one-third of the work-force, even though the soils are poor and there is little rain. Crops include wheat, maize, barley, olives and vines, with vegetables and fruit grown where there is irrigation. Spain is one of the world's largest producers of olive oil. Manufacturing industries include textiles and food processing. Tourism is very important.

AREA 504,780 sq km [194,896 sq mls]
POPULATION 39,664,000
CAPITAL (POPULATION) Madrid (3,041,000)
GOVERNMENT Constitutional monarchy
CURRENCY Peseta = 100 céntimos

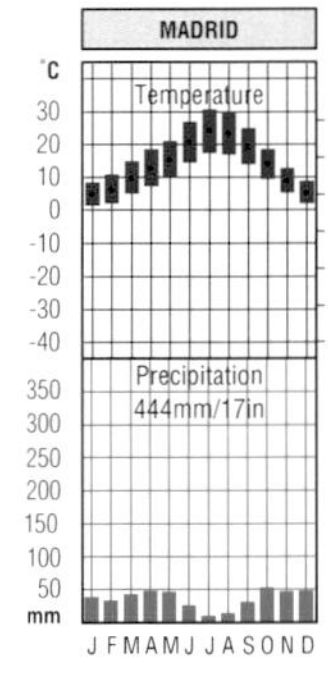

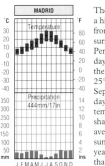

The interior of Spain is a high plateau, isolated from the seas which surround the Iberian Peninsula. Summer days are very hot despite the altitude, above 25°C [77°F] June to September during the day, but at night temperatures fall sharply. Madrid has an average of eight hours of sunshine a day over the year. Winters are colder than in coastal districts.

SRI LANKA

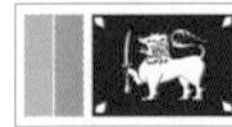

This unusual flag was adopted in 1951, three years after 'Ceylon' gained independence from Britain. The lion banner represents the ancient Buddhist kingdom and the stripes the island's minorities – Muslims (green) and Hindus (orange).

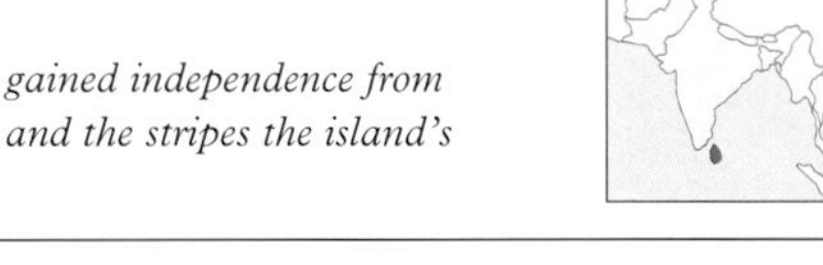

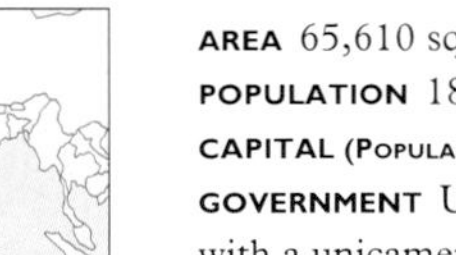

GEOGRAPHY The island of Sri Lanka (known as Ceylon until 1972) lies in the Indian Ocean and has a mountainous core. The 'wet zone' of the south-west supports rainforests and tea gardens near Kandy and evergreen forests and palm-fringed beaches in between Colombo and Galle. The north and east are drier.

HISTORY AND POLITICS The island was first inhabited by forest-dwelling Veddas and then by Aryans from India. Portuguese, Dutch and then British (who ruled from 1796 to 1948) traders and colonists came to Sri Lanka, as well as immigrant Tamils. Civil war and violence have been common since independence, with the main conflict between the Sinhalese Buddhist majority and the Tamil Hindu minority. The conflict has been almost continuous since 1983 as the Tamils fight for independence in the north, despite Indian attempts to manage a cease-fire.

ECONOMY Tea, rubber and coconuts are the main products, with some light industry, but the violence has slowed progress.

AREA 65,610 sq km [25,332 sq mls]
POPULATION 18,359,000
CAPITAL (POPULATION) Colombo (1,863,000)
GOVERNMENT Unitary multiparty republic with a unicameral legislature
ETHNIC GROUPS Sinhalese 74%, Tamil 18%, Sri Lankan Moor 7%
LANGUAGES Sinhala, Tamil, English
RELIGIONS Buddhist 69%, Hindu 16%, Muslim 8%, Christian 7%
CURRENCY Rupee = 100 cents
POPULATION DENSITY 280 per sq km [725 per sq ml]
URBAN POPULATION 22% of population

SUDAN

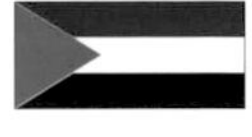

The design of Sudan's flag is based on the flag of the Arab revolt used in Syria, Iraq and Jordan after 1918. Adopted in 1969, it features the Pan-Arab colours and an Islamic green triangle symbolizing material prosperity and spiritual wealth.

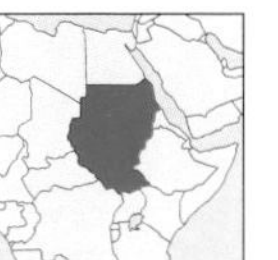

GEOGRAPHY The Sudan is the largest African state and consists mainly of huge clay plains and sandy areas, part of the Nile basin and the Sahara Desert. The extreme north is virtually uninhabited and most of the population is concentrated in a belt across the centre of the country, especially near the Blue and White Niles. The climate changes from desert to equatorial as the influence of the inter-tropical rainbelt increases southwards.

HISTORY AND POLITICS Sudan was ruled as an Anglo-Egyptian Condominium from 1889 and gained independence in 1956. Civil war then raged until 1975 and was again rekindled in 1983 by the (largely effective) pressure from extremists for the reinstatement of fundamental Sharic law. The renewed rivalries of the Arab north and the non-Muslim south have led to many hundreds of thousands of deaths and a severe deterioration in living standards. A return to democracy seems unlikely.

ECONOMY Cotton and oilseed are grown for export, but civil war, repression, a huge foreign debt, prolonged drought and food shortages have caused economic chaos.

AREA 2,505,810 sq km [967,493 sq mls]
POPULATION 29,980,000
CAPITAL (POPULATION) Khartoum (561,000)
GOVERNMENT Military regime
ETHNIC GROUPS Sudanese Arab 49%, Dinka 12%, Nuba 8%, Beja 6%, Nuer 5%, Azande 3%
LANGUAGES Arabic, Nubian, local languages, English
RELIGIONS Sunni Muslim 75%, traditional beliefs 17%, Roman Catholic 4%, Protestant 2%
CURRENCY Dinar = 10 Sudanese pounds
POPULATION DENSITY 12 per sq km [31 per sq ml]

SURINAM

SURINAM

Adopted on independence from the Dutch in 1975, Surinam's flag features the colours of the main political parties, the yellow star symbolizing unity and a golden future. The red is twice the width of the green, and four times that of the white.

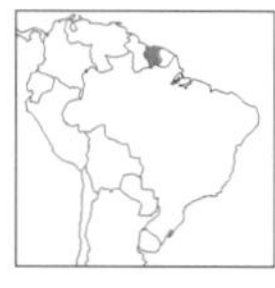

Surinam has a coastline of 350 km [218 mls] of Amazonian mud and silt, fringed by extensive mangrove swamps. Behind lies an old coastal plain of sands and clays, bordering a stretch of savanna. Forest covers 92% of the land surface. The country was first settled by British colonists in 1651. It was ceded to Holland in 1667 and became Dutch Guiana in 1816. Independence was won in 1975. Since 1992 there has been some instability. Bauxite and its derivatives, bananas and shrimps are the main exports.

AREA 163,270 sq km [63,039 sq mls]
POPULATION 421,000
CAPITAL (POPULATION) Paramaribo (201,000)
GOVERNMENT Multiparty republic with a unicameral legislature
ETHNIC GROUPS Creole 35%, Asian Indian 33%, Indonesian 16%, Black 10%, Amerindian 3%
LANGUAGES Dutch, English
RELIGIONS Hindu, Roman Catholic

SWAZILAND

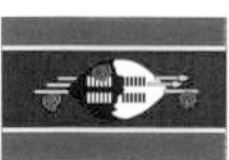

The kingdom has flown this distinctive flag, whose background is based on that of the Swazi Pioneer Corps of World War II, since independence from Britain in 1968. The emblem has the weapons of a warrior – ox-hide shield, two assegai (spears) and a fighting stick.

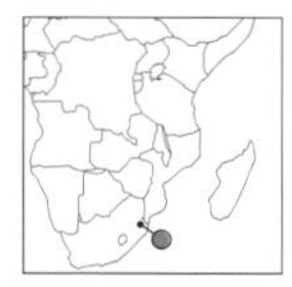

Swaziland is the smallest state in sub-Saharan Africa, but has a wide variety of landscapes. From west to east the land descends in three altitudinal steps: the High Veld (1,200 m [4,000 ft]), the Middle Veld and the Low Veld (270 m [900 ft]). In the east are the Lebombo Mountains. Europeans settled Swaziland in the late 19th century. Independence was won from Britain in 1968 and Swaziland is part of a customs union which includes South Africa. Swaziland has some mineral reserves (such as iron ore, coal, gold and diamonds) and tourism is increasing in importance. Sugar, citrus fruits and wood pulp are exported.

AREA 17,360 sq km [6,703 sq mls]
POPULATION 849,000
CAPITAL (POPULATION) Mbabane (42,000)
GOVERNMENT Monarchy with a bicameral legislature
ETHNIC GROUPS African 97%, European 3%
LANGUAGES English, Swazi
RELIGIONS Christian 77%, traditional beliefs 21%
CURRENCY Lilangeni = 100 cents

SWEDEN

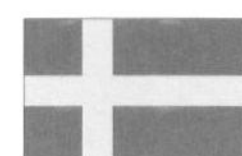

While Sweden's national flag has been flown since the reign of King Gustavus Vasa in the early 16th century, it was not officially adopted until 1906. The colours were derived from the ancient state coat of arms dating from 1364.

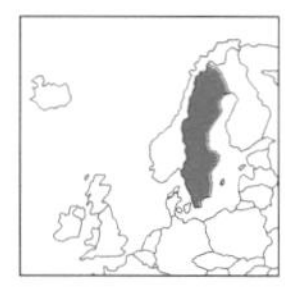

GEOGRAPHY Sweden occupies the eastern half of the Scandinavian peninsula, with a much smaller Arctic area than Finland or Norway. The northern part of the country forms part of the Baltic or Fenno-Scandian Shield, and is an area of low plateaux. In the south there is a belt of lowlands, which contain several large lakes (including Vänern). The topography has been greatly affected by the Ice Age, which has shaped the lakes and left fertile soils. Half of Sweden's land area is covered by forests.
HISTORY AND POLITICS Between 1397 and 1523 Sweden was united with Norway and Denmark, and after it broke away it was for a period the leading Baltic nation. More recent history has seen the end of the Social Democrat government in 1991, which had been in power for all but six years since 1932. Sweden applied for entry to the EU in 1991 and finally joined on 1 January 1995, following a referendum.
ECONOMY Sweden is famous for high-quality engineering products such as ball-bearings, agricultural machines, cars and ships. It is also the world's largest exporter of wood pulp.

AREA 449,960 sq km [173,730 sq mls]
POPULATION 8,893,000
CAPITAL (POPULATION) Stockholm (1,539,000)
GOVERNMENT Constitutional monarchy and a parliamentary state with a unicameral legislature
ETHNIC GROUPS Swedish 90%, Finnish 2%
LANGUAGES Swedish, Finnish
RELIGIONS Lutheran 88%, Roman Catholic 2%
CURRENCY Swedish krona = 100 öre
POPULATION DENSITY 20 per sq km [51 per sq ml]

SWITZERLAND

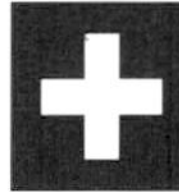

Switzerland's square flag was officially adopted in 1848, though the white cross on a red shield has been the Swiss emblem since the 14th century. The flag of the International Red Cross, based in Geneva, derives from this Swiss flag.

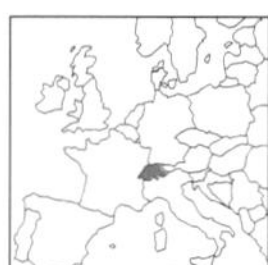

GEOGRAPHY Nearly 60% of Swiss territory is in the Alps, with two notable peaks on the Italian border: the Matterhorn (4,478 m [14,700 ft]) and the Monte Rosa (4,634 m [15,200 ft]). The Alps are drained by the upper Rhine tributaries and by the Rhône Valley via Lac Léman (Lake Geneva). Within the mountains are many lakes and much permanent snow.
HISTORY AND POLITICS Switzerland is made up of 26 multi-lingual cantons, each of which has control over housing and economic policy. Six of the cantons are French-speaking, one Italian-speaking, one with a significant Romansch-speaking community and the rest German-speaking. It is a strongly united country and is politically stable. It remained neutral in both world wars and has a high standard of living, helped by its central European location and good organizational ability. It is now the location of many headquarters of international bodies, including the Red Cross and 10 UN agencies in Geneva.
ECONOMY Agriculture is efficient, with a wide range of produce including maize and other cereals, fruits and vegetables. Industry is progressive, particularly engineering. There are strong banking and insurance industries and the Alps attract many tourists.

AREA 41,290 sq km [15,942 sq mls]
POPULATION 7,268,000
CAPITAL (POPULATION) Bern (299,000)
GOVERNMENT Federal state with a bicameral legislature
ETHNIC GROUPS Swiss German 65%, Swiss French 18%, Swiss Italian 10%, Spanish 2%, Yugoslav 2%, Romansch 1%
LANGUAGES French, German, Italian, Romansch
RELIGIONS Roman Catholic 46%, Protestant 40%, Muslim 2%
CURRENCY Swiss franc = 100 centimes
POPULATION DENSITY 176 per sq km [456 per sq ml]
URBAN POPULATION 60% of population

SYRIA

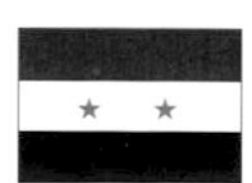

The flag of Syria is the one adopted in 1958 by the former United Arab Republic and is in the colours of the Pan-Arab movement. At various times in their history Egypt and Syria have shared the same flag, but since 1980 Syria has used this design.

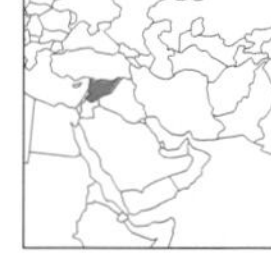

GEOGRAPHY Syria stretches from the Mediterranean to the Tigris and has most of the Hamad or stony desert in the south. There is one large harbour, at Latakia, and the Lebanon and Anti-Lebanon Mountains are found in the west and south-west.
HISTORY AND POLITICS Syria now occupies what was the northern part of the Ottoman province of Syria. It became an independent country in 1946 but was then part of the United Arab Republic, with Egypt and Yemen, between 1958 and 1961. Syria has always played a key role in Middle East affairs, usually with a pro-Arab stance (except during the 1991 Gulf War).
ECONOMY Crops include cotton and cereals and there are good irrigation schemes. Oil has been struck in the far north-east.

AREA 185,180 sq km [71,498 sq mls]
POPULATION 14,614,000
CAPITAL (POPULATION) Damascus (1,451,000)
GOVERNMENT Unitary multiparty republic with a unicameral legislature
ETHNIC GROUPS Arab 89%, Kurdish 6%
LANGUAGES Arabic, Kurdish, Armenian
RELIGIONS Muslim 90%, Christian 9%
CURRENCY Syrian pound = 100 piastres
POPULATION DENSITY 79 per sq km [204 per sq ml]

TAIWAN

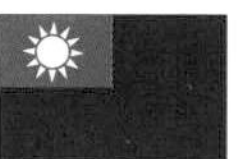

In 1928 the Nationalists adopted this design as China's national flag and used it in the long struggle against Mao Tse-tung's Communist army. When they were forced to retreat to Taiwan (then Formosa) in 1949, the flag went with them.

AREA 36,000 sq km [13,900 sq mls]
POPULATION 21,100,000
CAPITAL (POPULATION) Taipei (2,653,000)
GOVERNMENT Unitary multiparty republic with a unicameral legislature
ETHNIC GROUPS Taiwanese (Han Chinese) 84%, mainland Chinese 14%
LANGUAGES Mandarin Chinese
RELIGIONS Buddhist 43%, Taoist & Confucian 49%, Christian 7%
CURRENCY New Taiwan dollar = 100 cents
POPULATION DENSITY 586 per sq km [1,518 per sq ml]
URBAN POPULATION 75% of population

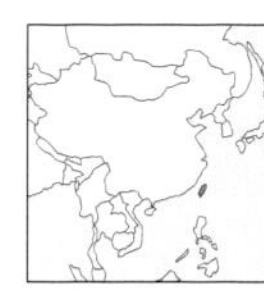

GEOGRAPHY Taiwan was formerly known by the Portuguese as Isla Formosa, meaning 'beautiful island'. High mountain ranges, extending the length of the island, occupy the central and eastern areas and carry dense forests. The climate is warm and moist, thereby producing a good environment for agriculture.

HISTORY AND POLITICS Chinese settlers occupied Taiwan from the 7th century onwards, before the Portuguese discovered it in 1590. In 1895 the province was seized by Japan and developed as a colony. Returned to China after World War II, Taiwan became the final refuge of the Nationalists that had been driven from China by Mao Tse-tung's forces in 1949. With US help, Taiwan set about ambitious land reforms and industrial expansion. The first full general election was held in 1991.

ECONOMY A wide range of manufactured goods are produced, including colour television sets, electronic calculators, footwear and clothing, and Taiwan is the world's leading shipbreaker.

TAJIKISTAN

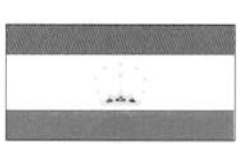

The new flag was adopted early in 1993 and denotes a gold crown of unusual design under an arc of seven stars. The proportions of the flag are 1:2.

AREA 143,100 sq km [55,250 sq mls]
POPULATION 6,102,000
CAPITAL (POPULATION) Dushanbe (602,000)
GOVERNMENT Transitional democracy
ETHNIC GROUPS Tajik 64%, Uzbek 24%, Russian 7%
LANGUAGES Tajik
RELIGIONS Sunni Muslim, some Christian
CURRENCY Tajik rouble = 100 kopeks
URBAN POPULATION 32% of population

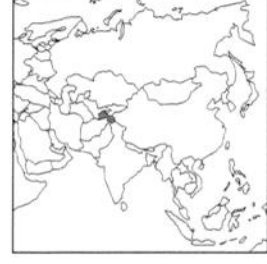

Tajikistan lies on the borders of Afghanistan and China and only 7% of the land area lies below 1,000 m [3,280 ft]. The eastern half is almost all above 3,000 m [9,840 ft]. The country is the poorest of the former Soviet republics and independence (in 1991) brought huge economic problems. As a Persian people the Tajiks are more likely to follow Islamic influences rather than Western ones. In 1992, civil war broke out between the government and an alliance of democrats and Islamic forces.

TANZANIA

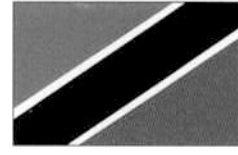

In 1964 Tanganyika united with the island of Zanzibar to form the United Republic of Tanzania and a new flag was adopted. The colours represent agriculture (green), minerals (yellow), the people (black), water and Zanzibar (blue).

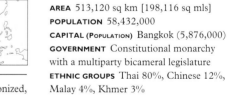

AREA 945,090 sq km [364,899 sq mls]
POPULATION 29,710,000
CAPITAL (POPULATION) Dodoma (204,000)
GOVERNMENT Multiparty republic
ETHNIC GROUPS Nyamwezi and Sukuma 21%, Swahili 9%, Hehet and Bena 7%, Makonde 6%, Haya 6%
LANGUAGES English and Swahili (both official)
RELIGIONS Christian 34%, Sunni Muslim 33%, traditional beliefs
CURRENCY Shilling = 100 cents
URBAN POPULATION 22% of population

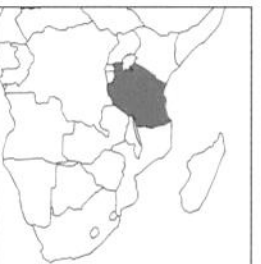

GEOGRAPHY Tanzania extends across the high plateau of eastern Africa, mostly above 1,000 m [3,000 ft], to the rift valleys filled by Lakes Tanganyika and Nyasa (Malawi). The Northern Highlands are part of the eastern rift valley and are dominated by the ice-capped extinct volcano of Kilimanjaro, the highest mountain in Africa. Temperatures are uniformly high all year.

HISTORY AND POLITICS Tanzania was formed in 1964 when mainland Tanganyika (which had become independent from Britain in 1961) was joined by the island state of Zanzibar. For 20 years President Julius Nyerere ruled with policies of self-help (*ujamaa*) and egalitarian socialism. Progress was slowed and Nyerere's successor is now attempting to liberalize the economy.

ECONOMY Export crops include coffee, tea, cotton, sisal and tobacco. There are hopes for a rise in tourism.

THAILAND

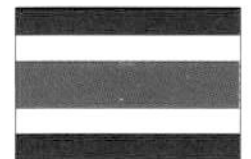

The two red and white stripes are all that remains of Thailand's traditional red-on-white elephant emblem, removed from the flag in 1916. The blue stripe was added in 1917 to show solidarity with the Allies in World War I.

AREA 513,120 sq km [198,116 sq mls]
POPULATION 58,432,000
CAPITAL (POPULATION) Bangkok (5,876,000)
GOVERNMENT Constitutional monarchy with a multiparty bicameral legislature
ETHNIC GROUPS Thai 80%, Chinese 12%, Malay 4%, Khmer 3%
LANGUAGES Thai, Chinese, Malay
RELIGIONS Buddhist 95%, Muslim 4%, Christian 1%
CURRENCY Baht = 100 satang
POPULATION DENSITY 114 per sq km [295 per sq ml]
URBAN POPULATION 19% of population
LAND USE Arable 33%, forest 26%

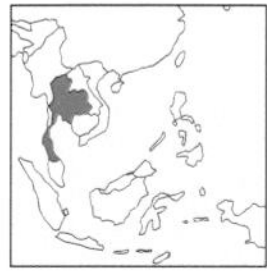

GEOGRAPHY Thailand is centred on the valley of the Chao Phraya River that flows across the central plain extending from the Gulf of Siam to the foothills of the northern fold mountains. In the east, separated from the central plain by low hills, is the Khorat Plateau, which is covered by savanna woodlands. The long southern part of Thailand, linked to the Malay Peninsula by the Isthmus of Kra, is a forested region. The climate is tropical, with fairly high rainfall and temperatures all year round.

HISTORY AND POLITICS Known as Siam until 1939, Thailand is the only South-east Asian country that has not been colonized, or occupied by foreign powers, except in war. It was an absolute monarchy until 1932, when the king surrendered. Military rulers dominated the next 40 years; after being forced into alliance with Japan in World War II, the Thais then aligned themselves to the USA after 1945. It now has a system of constitutional rule that has helped Thailand to prosper.

ECONOMY Rice is the most important crop, with others such as rubber and sugar. Manufacturing is increasing rapidly.

TOGO

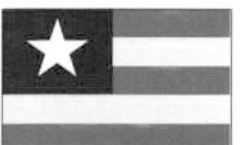

Togo's Pan-African colours stand for agriculture and the future (green), mineral wealth and the value of hard work (yellow), and the blood shed in the struggle for independence from France in 1960 (red), with the white star for national purity.

AREA 56,790 sq km [21,927 sq mls]
POPULATION 4,140,000
CAPITAL (POPULATION) Lomé (590,000)
GOVERNMENT Multiparty republic
ETHNIC GROUPS Ewe-Adja 43%, Tem-Kabre 26%, Gurma 16%
LANGUAGES French, Ewe, Kabre
RELIGIONS Traditional beliefs 59%, Christian 28%, Sunni Muslim 12%
CURRENCY CFA franc = 100 centimes
POPULATION DENSITY 73 per sq km [189 per sq ml]

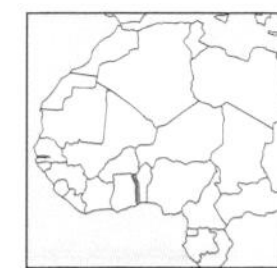

GEOGRAPHY A small country in West Africa nowhere more than 120 km [75 mls] wide, Togo stretches inland from the Gulf of Guinea. The Togo-Atacora Mountains cross the country from south-west to north-east and there are forests in the south-west.

HISTORY, POLITICS AND ECONOMY As Togoland, the country was colonized by Germany in 1884 and then occupied by Franco-British troops during World War I. It was partitioned between the two powers in 1922, with British Togoland later becoming part of Ghana and the larger eastern French section gaining independence as Togo in 1960. In 1991 multiparty elections ended the military regime, but there has since been fighting. Phosphates, coffee and cocoa are the main exports.

TONGA

TONGA

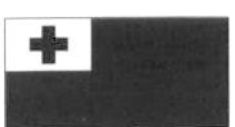

The flag was introduced in 1862 by Taufa'ahau Tupou, the first king of all Tonga, and represents the Christian faith of the islanders. The red cross, similar to the methodist badge and the Red Cross flag, illustrates the Tongans' adherence to the Christian religion.

The Tongan archipelago comprises more than 170 islands in the southern Pacific Ocean, 36 of which are inhabited. The landscape is a mixture of low coralline and higher volcanic outcrops covered with dense vegetation. Nearly two-thirds of the population live on the largest island of Tongatapu. Tonga has been ruled by Taufa'ahau Tupou IV since 1965, who presided over the transition of the islands to an independent state in 1970. Coconut oil products and bananas are the main exports.

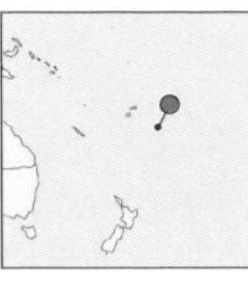

AREA 750 sq km [290 sq mls]
POPULATION 107,000
CAPITAL (POPULATION) Nuku'alofa (29,000)
GOVERNMENT Constitutional monarchy
ETHNIC GROUPS Tongan 96%
LANGUAGES Tongan, English
RELIGIONS Christian
CURRENCY Pa'anga = 100 seniti
POPULATION DENSITY 143 per sq km [369 per sq ml]

TRINIDAD AND TOBAGO

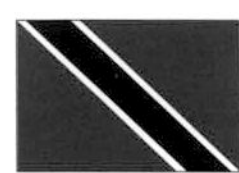

The islands of Trinidad and Tobago have flown this flag since independence from Britain in 1962. Red stands for the people's warmth and vitality, black for their strength, and white for their hopes and the surf of the sea.

GEOGRAPHY Furthest south of the West Indies, Trinidad is an island situated just 16 km [10 mls] off Venezuela. Tobago is a detached extension of its Northern Range of hills, lying 34 km [21 mls] to the north-east. The landscape is forested and hilly.
HISTORY, POLITICS AND ECONOMY Trinidad was 'discovered' by Columbus in 1498 and then settled by Spanish and French. It became British in 1797. Tobago came under British control in 1814, with the two islands joining to form a united colony in 1899. Independence came in 1962 and a republic was formed in 1976, although Tobago is keen for internal self-government. Oil was very important in economic development, but falling prices have caused problems. There are also reserves of asphalt and gas.

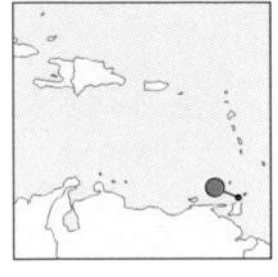

AREA 5,130 sq km [1,981 sq mls]
POPULATION 1,295,000
CAPITAL (POPULATION) Port of Spain (60,000)
GOVERNMENT Republic with a bicameral legislature
ETHNIC GROUPS Black 40%, East Indian 40%, Mixed 18%, White 1%, Chinese 1%
LANGUAGES English
RELIGIONS Christian 40%, Hindu 24%, Muslim 6%

TRISTAN DA CUNHA

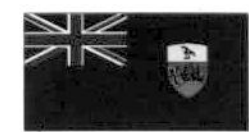

The flag is the British Blue Ensign with the shield from the arms in the fly. A new coat of arms was introduced in 1984.

Tristan da Cunha is located towards the southern end of the Mid-Atlantic Ridge and has a volcanic cone ringed by a lava plain that drops steeply to the sea. The small population live on a flat coastal strip. It is administered as a dependency of St Helena.

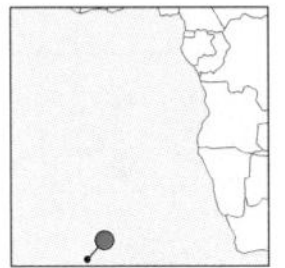

AREA 104 sq km [40 sq mls]
POPULATION 330
CAPITAL Edinburgh
GOVERNMENT Dependent Territory of the UK
LANGUAGES English
POPULATION DENSITY 3.2 per sq km [8 per sq ml]

TUNISIA

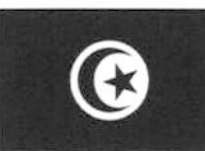

The Tunisian flag features the crescent moon and five-pointed star, traditional symbols of Islam. It originated in about 1835 when the country was still officially under Turkish rule and was adopted after independence from France in 1956.

GEOGRAPHY Tunisia is the smallest of the three Maghreb countries that comprise north-west Africa. The country is made up of the eastern end of the Atlas Mountains together with the central steppelands to the south, which are separated from the country's Saharan sector by the huge low-lying saltpans of the Chott Djerid. In the north the lower Medjerda Valley and low-lying plains of Bizerte and Tunis were densely colonized.
HISTORY AND POLITICS Tunisia has a long and varied history. It was the first part of the region to be conquered by the Phoenicians, Romans (Carthage is now a suburb of Tunis) and later the Arabs and Turks (as part of the Ottoman Empire after 1537). Each successive civilization has left a marked impression on the country, giving Tunisia a distinct national identity. France established a protectorate in 1881 and Tunisia became independent in 1956. Today it is effectively ruled by one party, the RCD, with some elements of democracy slowly introduced.
ECONOMY Major irrigarion schemes in the northern lowlands have turned it into an important agricultural area, producing cereals, vines, citrus fruits, olives and vegetables. New industries and some tourism have been important along the coast.

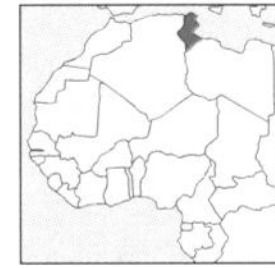

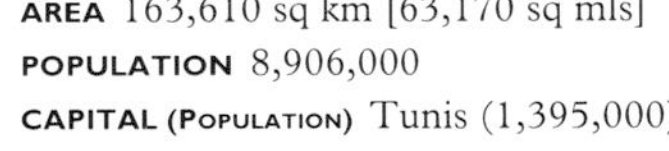

AREA 163,610 sq km [63,170 sq mls]
POPULATION 8,906,000
CAPITAL (POPULATION) Tunis (1,395,000)

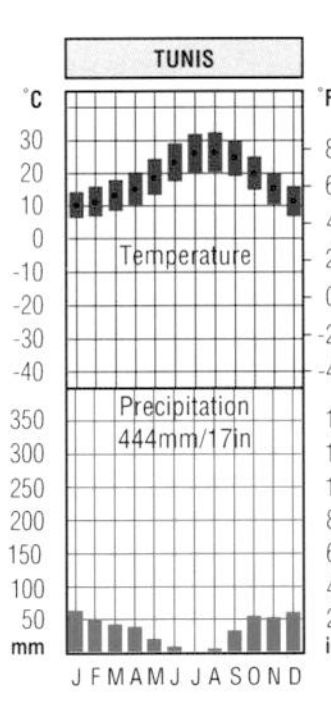

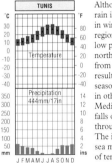

Although most of the rain in Tunisia falls in winter when the region is affected by low pressure, prevailing north-easterly winds from the sea in summer result in a shorter dry season than is found in other parts of the Mediterranean. Rain falls on only a few days throughout the summer. The influence of the sea moderates extremes of temperatures.

TURKEY

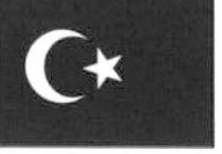

Although the crescent moon and the five-pointed star are symbols of Islam, their presence on Turkey's flag dates from long before the country became a Muslim state. The flag was officially adopted when the republic was founded in 1923.

GEOGRAPHY The most populous country in south-west Asia, Turkey comprises the broad peninsula of Asia Minor and in Europe that part of Thrace (Thraki) which lies to the east of the lower Maritsa River. The Straits separating the European (5%) and Asiatic parts of Turkey have been of strategic importance for thousands of years. The heart of the country is the high karst plateau of Anatolia with semi-desert around the central salt lake. The northern Pontic ranges are wooded, with fertile plains. Istanbul controls the straits between the Black Sea and the Mediterranean and is Turkey's chief port and commercial city.
HISTORY AND POLITICS The huge Ottoman Empire of Constantinople (modern Istanbul) extended through the Balkans to south-west Asia and north Africa for many hundreds of years. After alliance with Germany in World War I, all non-Turkish areas were lost. Nationalists led by Mustafa Kemal rejected peace proposals favouring Greece and after a civil war set up a republic. Turkey's present frontiers were established in 1923, when Atatürk became president, and until 1938 he ruled as a virtual dictator, secularizing and modernizing the traditional Islamic state. Democracy has been relatively stable since 1983 with the return of civilian rule, but there is a poor human rights record and a low standard of living.
ECONOMY Manufacturing is important, particularly textiles and clothing. Export crops include tobacco, figs and cotton.

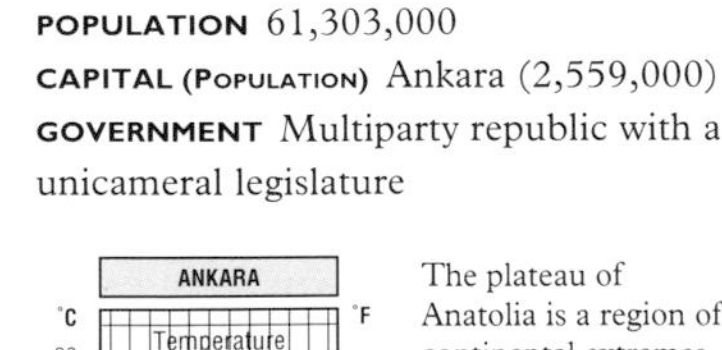

AREA 779,450 sq km [300,946 sq mls]
POPULATION 61,303,000
CAPITAL (POPULATION) Ankara (2,559,000)
GOVERNMENT Multiparty republic with a unicameral legislature

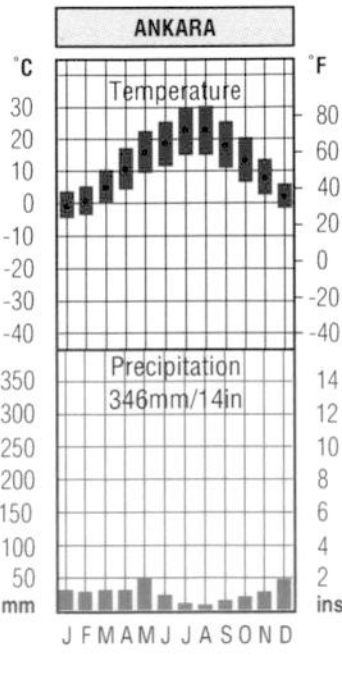

The plateau of Anatolia is a region of continental extremes and little precipitation. Ankara lies just to the north of the driest part of the plateau which is situated around the large saltwater Lake Tuz. Summer days are hot and sunny and nights pleasantly cool; over 11 hours of sunshine and 15–30°C [59–86°F]. Annual rainfall is low.

TURKMENISTAN

The flag dates from February 1992 and depicts a typical Turkmen carpet design and a crescent and five stars. The stars and the five elements of the carpet represent the traditional tribes of Turkmenistan.

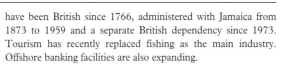

AREA 488,100 sq km [188,450 sq mls]
POPULATION 4,100,000
CAPITAL (POPULATION) Ashkhabad (407,000)
GOVERNMENT Single-party republic
ETHNIC GROUPS Turkmen 73%, Russian 10%, Uzbek 9%, Kazak 2%
LANGUAGES Turkmen 72%, Russian 12%
RELIGIONS Sunni Muslim 85%, Christian
CURRENCY Manat
POPULATION DENSITY 8 per sq km [22 per sq ml]

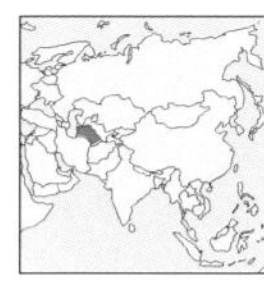

More than 90% of Turkmenistan is arid, with over half the country covered by the Karakum, Asia's largest sand desert. It declared independence from the former Soviet Union in October 1991 and has since looked south to the Muslim countries more than the CIS for support. Like its Turkic associates, Azerbaijan and Uzbekistan, it has joined the Economic Co-operation Organization formed by Turkey, Iran and Pakistan in 1985. Crops include cereals, cotton and fruit. Apart from astrakhan rugs and food processing, industry is confined to mining sulphur and salt and the production of natural gas, its biggest export.

TURKS AND CAICOS ISLANDS

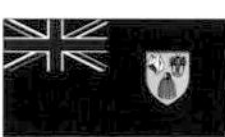

Since this group of islands is a British dependent territory, the flag has the same basic design of the British Blue Ensign. The gold roundel in the fly contains the islands' badge which shows a conch shell, a spiny lobster and a turk's head cactus, all of which are found on the islands.

AREA 430 sq km [166 sq mls]
POPULATION 15,000
CAPITAL (POPULATION) Cockburn Town (4,000)
GOVERNMENT British Dependent Territory
ETHNIC GROUPS Of African descent
LANGUAGES English
RELIGIONS Christian
CURRENCY US dollar
URBAN POPULATION 55% of population

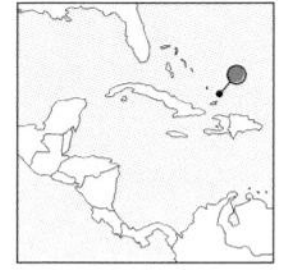

A group of 30 islands (eight of them inhabited), lying at the eastern end of the Grand Bahama Bank, north of Haiti, the Turks and Caicos are composed of low, flat limestone terrain with scrub, marsh and swamp providing little agriculture. They have been British since 1766, administered with Jamaica from 1873 to 1959 and a separate British dependency since 1973. Tourism has recently replaced fishing as the main industry. Offshore banking facilities are also expanding.

TUVALU

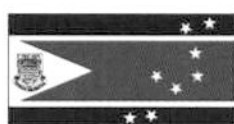

This new flag for Tuvalu was adopted on Independence Day, 1 October 1995, to replace a flag based on the British Blue Ensign. The design of the flag incorporates the national arms and eight stars signifying the islands' name, which means 'Eight Together'.

AREA 24 sq km [9 sq mls]
POPULATION 10,000
CAPITAL (POPULATION) Fongafale (2,810)
GOVERNMENT Constitutional monarchy
ETHNIC GROUPS Polynesian
LANGUAGES Tuvaluan, English
RELIGIONS Christian
CURRENCY Tuvaluan dollar = 100 cents
POPULATION DENSITY 417 per sq km [1,111 per sq ml]

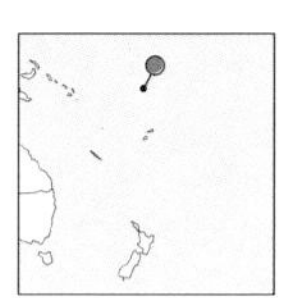

Tuvalu comprises nine coral atolls in the southern Pacific Ocean, none of which rise more than 4.6 m [15 ft] out of the sea. Poor soils have restricted vegetation to coconut palms, breadfruit trees and bush. The islands became an independent constitutional monarchy within the Commonwealth in 1978, three years after separation from the Gilbert Islands. The population survive by subsistence farming and by fishing. Copra and the sale of elaborate postage stamps are the main foreign exchange earners.

UGANDA

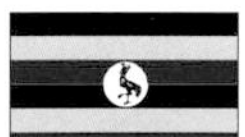

Adopted on independence from Britain in 1962, Uganda's flag is that of the party which won the first national election. The colours represent the people (black), the sun (yellow), and brotherhood (red); the country's emblem is a crested crane.

AREA 235,880 sq km [91,073 sq mls]
POPULATION 21,466,000
CAPITAL (POPULATION) Kampala (773,000)
GOVERNMENT Transitional republic
ETHNIC GROUPS Baganda 18%, Banyoro 14%, Teso 9%, Banyan 8%, Basoga 8%, Bagisu 7%, Bachiga 7%, Lango 6%, Acholi 5%
LANGUAGES English, Swahili
RELIGIONS Roman Catholic 40%, Protestant 29%, animist 18%, Sunni Muslim 7%
CURRENCY Shilling = 100 cents
POPULATION DENSITY 91 per sq km [236 per sq ml]
URBAN POPULATION 12% of population

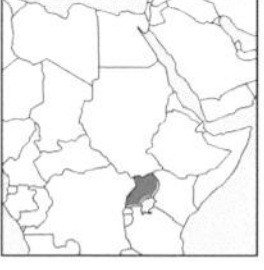

GEOGRAPHY Extending from Lake Victoria to the western arm of the Great Rift Valley, landlocked Uganda has many lakes originating from the tilting and faulting associated with the rift valley system. On the western side of the country the Ruwenzori block has been uplifted to 5,109 m [16,762 ft], while the eastern frontier bisects the large extinct volcano of Mt Elgon. In the south rainfall is abundant in two seasons, and patches of the original rainforest (25% of the land area) remain. To the north, one rainy season supports a savanna of trees and grassland.
HISTORY AND POLITICS Uganda was a British protectorate from 1894 to 1962. After independence the country suffered a succession of linked civil wars, violent coups, armed invasions and tribal massacres. The worst period was during the regime of Idi Amin, who in 1971 replaced the first Prime Minister Milton Obote. His eight-year reign saw up to 300,000 deaths and the suspension of all political and human rights. Obote returned to power briefly after Amin was removed, but he was ousted again in 1985. Museveni took over in 1986 and began some reforms.
ECONOMY Uganda is the world's seventh largest coffee producer. Other crops include tea and sugar. Rising inflation is a problem.

UKRAINE

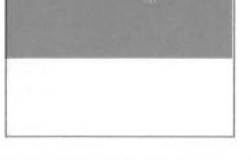

The colours of the Ukrainian flag were first adopted in 1848 and were heraldic in origin, first used on the coat of arms of one of the medieval Ukrainian kingdoms. The flag was first used in the period 1918–20 and was readopted on 4 September 1991.

AREA 603,700 sq km [233,100 sq mls]
POPULATION 52,027,000
CAPITAL (POPULATION) Kiev (2,643,000)
GOVERNMENT Multiparty republic

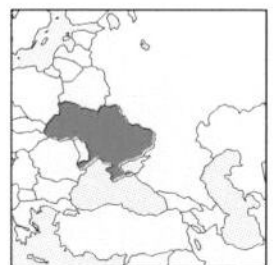

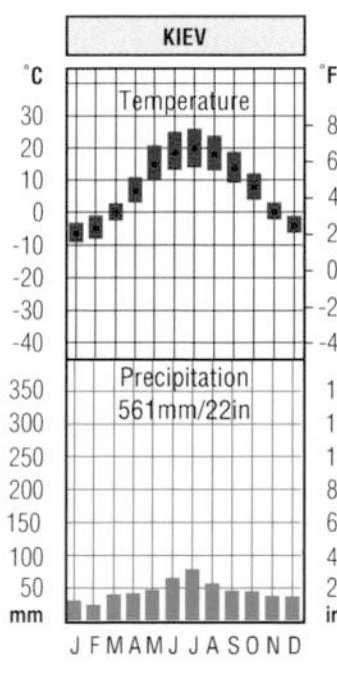

Although on the same latitude as many European cities, Kiev is distant from maritime effects. Rainfall is low and evenly distributed throughout the year with a slight summer peak. Snow may lie for over 80 days, and there is precipitation on over 160 days in the year. Winter temperatures are not too severe and only four months of the year are sub-zero.

GEOGRAPHY The Ukraine became the largest nation wholly within Europe following its declaration of independence on 24 August 1991 and the subsequent disintegration of the Soviet Union. The western Ukraine comprises the fertile uplands of Volhynia, with the Carpathians in the far western corner of the country. The north is mainly lowlands, with the Dnepr River at its heart; this was the area that suffered most from the Chernobyl nuclear disaster of 1986, with huge areas of land contaminated by radioactivity. In the south are dry lowlands bordering the Black Sea and the Sea of Azov, with Odesa the main port.
HISTORY AND POLITICS The Ukraine was invaded in 1941 by the Germans who stayed until 1944 and were responsible for the deportation and deaths of more than 5 million Ukrainians and Ukrainian Jews. After Soviet control was reinstated in 1945, the Ukraine was given a seat on the UN as some sort of compensation. The Ukraine's declaration of independence was ratified by referendum in December 1991 and Leonid Kravchuk was voted president. In 1992 Russia and the Ukraine reached a number of agreements, particularly over military issues.
ECONOMY The main industries are coalmining, iron and steel, agricultural machinery, petrochemicals and plastics. Chronic food shortages and hyperinflation have caused problems.

UNITED ARAB EMIRATES

UNITED ARAB EMIRATES

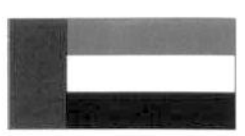

When seven small states around the Gulf combined to form the United Arab Emirates in 1971, this flag was agreed for the new nation. It features the Pan-Arab colours, first used in the Arab revolt against the Turks from 1916.

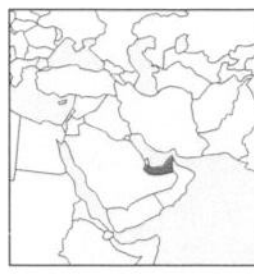

The United Arab Emirates (UAE) were formed in 1971, when six of the British-run Trucial States of the Gulf – Abu Dhabi, Ajman, Dubai, Fujairah, Sharjah and Umm al-Qaiwain – opted to join together and form their own independent country. The state of Ras-al-Khaimah joined in 1972. The country has a coastline on the Gulf and comprises mainly low-lying desert, with little fertile land. The climate is very hot and arid. The oil and gas reserves have provided the highest GNP per capita figure in Asia after Japan. However, only 20% of the population are citizens; the rest are expatriate workers. There is some agriculture, but only where there are oases or the land is irrigated. Crops grown include dates, fruits and vegetables.

AREA 83,600 sq km [32,278 sq mls]
POPULATION 2,800,000
CAPITAL (POPULATION) Abu Dhabi (243,000)
GOVERNMENT Federation of seven emirates, each with its own government
ETHNIC GROUPS Arab 87%, Indo-Pakistani 9%, Iranian 2%
LANGUAGES Arabic, English
RELIGIONS Muslim 95%, Christian 4%
CURRENCY Dirham = 100 fils
POPULATION DENSITY 33 per sq km [87 per sq ml]

UNITED KINGDOM

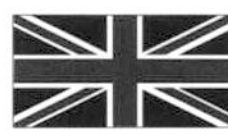

The first Union flag, combining England's cross of St George and Scotland's cross of St Andrew, dates from 1603 when James VI became James I of England. The Irish emblem, the cross of St Patrick, was added in 1801 to form the present flag.

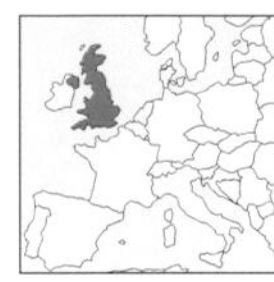

GEOGRAPHY The British Isles stand on the westernmost edge of the continental shelf – two large and several hundred small islands. The United Kingdom of Great Britain and Northern Ireland is made up of England, Scotland and Wales (Great Britain), Northern Ireland and the many off-lying islands from the Scillies to the Shetlands. The Isle of Man and the Channel Islands are separate dependencies of the Crown, with a degree of political autonomy and their own taxation systems. There are a variety of physical landscapes. The present English landscape has been marked by events in the past, including complex folding, laval outpourings, volcanic upheavals and eruptions, glacial planing, and changes of sea level. Upland areas include the Pennines, the Lake District and Exmoor, while lowland areas largely consist of chalk downlands – examples are the North Downs and the Hampshire Downs. Wales is predominantly hilly and mountainous, although two-thirds of the rural area is farmland and one-third is moorland. Scotland is also hilly, with a landscape of many deep, glaciated valleys dominated by mountains. Despite its subarctic position Britain is favoured climatically; this is due to the North Atlantic Drift, a current of warm surface water from the southern Atlantic Ocean.

HISTORY AND POLITICS While Britain is physically close to the rest of Europe (32 km [20 mls] at the nearest point), it has a long history of political independence from its neighbours. Its peoples are of mixed stock, after invasions by several groups and immigrants arriving from all over the world. The most important invasions were those of the Romans in AD 43, the Anglo-Saxons after AD 500 and the Normans in 1066. The United Kingdom itself was formed by the unions of the different kingdoms. England became the most powerful kingdom in the Middle Ages and annexed Wales in 1535. The Union of 1707 joined Scotland, with Ireland joining in 1800. Southern Ireland broke away in 1921 to form what is now the Republic of Ireland.

ECONOMY Historically the growth of the British economy was due to an agricultural revolution and the Industrial Revolution in the 18th and 19th centuries. Today only 2% of the working population is employed in agriculture, but there is a wide range of produce, particularly wheat, dairy products, vegetables and wool. The Industrial Revolution was based on coal and iron ore reserves, found largely in northern areas, and there was a huge growth in towns and communications at this time. The discovery of North Sea oil and gas in the 1960s gave a vital boost to the economy as mineral reserves diminished. Important industries today include textiles and high-skilled engineering.

AREA 243,368 sq km [94,202 sq mls]
POPULATION 58,306,000
CAPITAL (POPULATION) London (6,967,000)
GOVERNMENT Constitutional monarchy with a bicameral legislature
ETHNIC GROUPS White 94%, Asian Indian 1%, West Indian 1%, Pakistani 1%
LANGUAGES English, Welsh, Scots-Gaelic
RELIGIONS Anglican 57%, Roman Catholic 13%, Presbyterian 7%, Methodist 4%, other Christian 6%, Muslim 2%, Jewish 1%, Hindu 1%, Sikh 1%
CURRENCY Pound sterling = 100 pence
POPULATION DENSITY 240 per sq km [619 per sq ml]

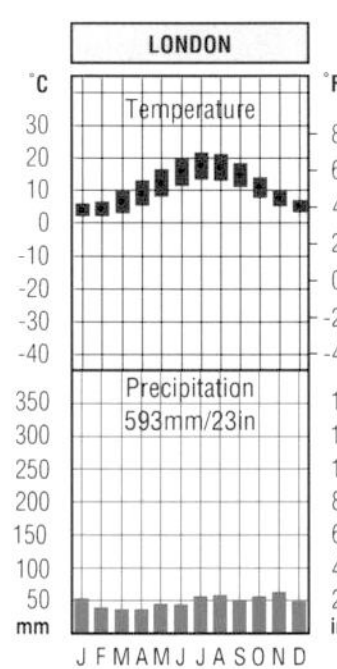

South-eastern England, sheltered from the ocean to the west, is one of the driest parts of the British Isles. Although rainfall varies little throughout the year, greater evaporation creates a deficit between May and August. Like other parts of north-west Europe, London has a small temperature range. The metropolis creates its own local climate.

UNITED STATES OF AMERICA

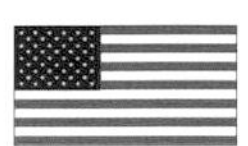

The 'Stars and Stripes' has had the same basic design since 1777, during the War of Independence. The 13 stripes represent the original colonies that rebelled against British rule, and the 50 stars are for the present states of the Union.

GEOGRAPHY The United States of America is the world's fourth largest country and the third most populous. It fills the North American continent between Canada and Mexico and also includes Alaska and Hawaii. Geographically, the bulk of the USA falls into three main sections: eastern, central and western. Eastern North America is crossed by a band of low, folded mountains which nowhere rise more than 2,000 m [6,500 ft] and include the Appalachians. The coastal plain includes the six New England states with their fertile, wooded landscape. The central section is very different in character. Within the 1,400 km [875 mls] from the Mississippi River to the foothills of the Rockies, the land rises 3,000 m [9,580 ft] almost imperceptibly. The plains are crossed by a series of rivers that drain off the Rockies. This area suffers great seasonal contrasts of climate with hot, moist air from the Gulf of Mexico in the summer and cold, dry Arctic air in winter. The western USA is a complex mountain and plateau system bordered by a rugged coast that starts in the semi-desert of the south and ends in the coniferous forests of the north. The Rocky Mountains are the highest in the area, rising in Colorado to over 3,000 m [10,000 ft].

HISTORY AND POLITICS The USA was established in 1776 after 13 colonies declared their independence from Britain and set up a federal republic. This spread westwards and southwards, especially after the Civil War (1861–5) when slaves were freed from the southern states. The eastern USA is the heartland of many of America's rural and urban traditions. In the 19th century many European immigrants arrived in Boston, New York, Philadelphia and Baltimore, with some then moving into the interior. As resources were discovered here new cities began to develop, such as Chicago. The patterns established then still exist, with the highest concentrations of industry and population in the north-east. The central and western states were first inhabited by over 30 major tribes of Native Americans. Their ways of life were transformed (and often ruined) by the arrival of the Europeans. Americans began to arrive in the west in the 1840s and the south-west became part of the USA. Today the USA has one of the most diverse populations in the world.

ECONOMY The USA became the world's leading industrial society after the Civil War and still maintains very high standards of living and levels of production. Agriculture is now a highly mechanized industry and the USA is a leading producer of many crops, including corn and cotton, as well as meat and dairy foods. It is also one of the leading oil producers. Other industries include iron and steel, uranium and many manufacturing industries.

AREA 9,372,610 sq km [3,618,765 sq mls]
POPULATION 263,563,000
CAPITAL (POPULATION) Washington, DC (4,360,000)
GOVERNMENT Federal republic with a bicameral legislature
ETHNIC GROUPS White 85%, African American 12%, other races 8%
LANGUAGES English, Spanish
RELIGIONS Protestant 53%, Roman Catholic 26%, Jewish 2%, Eastern Orthodox 2%, Muslim 2%
CURRENCY United States $ = 100 cents
POPULATION DENSITY 28 per sq km [73 per sq ml]

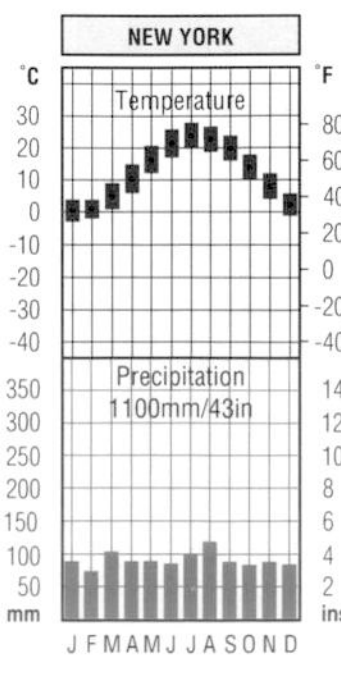

New York is 40°N, but its average temperature December to February is only just above freezing. Temperatures below –20°C [–4°F] have been recorded between December and February, while the daily high from May to August is above 20°C [68°F]. Rain and snow are evenly distributed throughout the year, with rainfall on about a third of the days.

URUGUAY

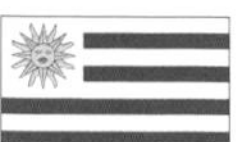

Displayed since 1830, the stripes represent the nine provinces of Uruguay on independence from Spain two years earlier. The blue and white and the May Sun derive from the flag originally employed by Argentina in the colonial struggle.

GEOGRAPHY After Surinam, Uruguay is the smallest South American state. It is a low-lying country of tall prairie grasses and woodlands with the highest land less than 600 m [2,000 ft] above sea level. The Atlantic coast and River Plate estuary are fringed with lagoons and sand dunes; the centre of the country is a low plateau, rising in the north towards the Brazilian border. The Uruguay River forms the western border with Argentina.

HISTORY AND POLITICS Uruguay was once simply a hinterland to the Spanish base at Montevideo, forming a buffer area between northern Portuguese and western Spanish territories.

Spain gained control of Uruguay in 1777 but the country became independent in 1828. Since this time Uruguay has been dominated by two political parties – Colorados (Liberals) and Blancos (Conservatives). From 1973 to 1985, there was a strict military regime, with an appalling human rights record. A civilian (Blanco) government is now back in office.

ECONOMY Historically, the economy was based on a meat-and-hide export industry and today it still depends largely on exports of animal products (especially meat, wool and dairy products) for revenue. The country is moderately prosperous.

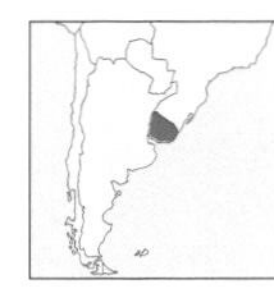

AREA 177,410 sq km [68,498 sq mls]
POPULATION 3,186,000
CAPITAL (POPULATION) Montevideo (1,384,000)
GOVERNMENT Unitary multiparty republic with a bicameral legislature
ETHNIC GROUPS White 86%, Mestizo 8%, Black 6%
LANGUAGES Spanish
RELIGIONS Roman Catholic 66%, Protestant 2%, Jewish 1%
CURRENCY Peso = 100 centésimos
POPULATION DENSITY 18 per sq km [47 per sq ml]
URBAN POPULATION 90% of population
LAND USE Grass 77%, arable 7%

UZBEKISTAN

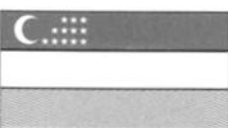

This flag replaced the Soviet-style flag on 18 November 1991. The blue recalls the blue flag of Timur (a former ruler), the white peace, the green nature and the red vitality. The crescent moon is for Islam and the 12 stars represent the months of the Islamic calendar.

Uzbekistan stretches from the shores of the Aral Sea in the north, through desert and increasingly fertile semi-arid lands, to the peaks of the Western Pamirs and the mountainous border with Afghanistan, with a populous eastern spur jutting into Kyrgyzstan. There is little rainfall and very high summer temperatures.

The Uzbeks were the ruling race in southern central Asia before the Russians took over in the 19th century. The country declared its independence from the former Soviet Union in 1990 and joined the CIS in 1991. Cotton production is important to the economy, and there are also oil, gas, coal and copper reserves.

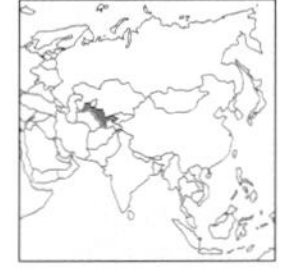

AREA 447,400 sq km [172,740 sq mls]
POPULATION 22,833,000
CAPITAL (POPULATION) Tashkent (2,094,000)
GOVERNMENT Socialist republic
ETHNIC GROUPS Uzbek 73%, Russian 8%, Tajik 5%, Kazak 4%, Tatar 2%, Kara-Kalpak 2%
LANGUAGES Uzbek 85%, Russian 5%
RELIGIONS Sunni Muslim 75%
CURRENCY Som = 100 tiyin
URBAN POPULATION 41% of population

VANUATU

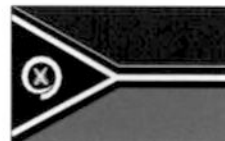

The device in the triangle is a boar's tusk surrounding two crossed fern leaves, the emblems of war and peace. The flag is in the colours of the Vanuaaku Pati, the dominant political party at the time of independence in 1980.

Vanuatu is an archipelago of 13 large islands and 70 islets in the southern Pacific Ocean. The majority of them are mountainous and volcanic in origin, with coral beaches, reefs and forest.

Formerly the New Hebrides and governed jointly by France and Britain from 1906, the islands became independent in 1980. Copra (45% of total), beef and veal are the main exports.

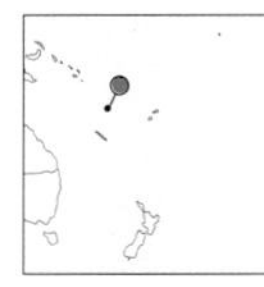

AREA 12,190 sq km [4,707 sq mls]
POPULATION 167,000
CAPITAL (POPULATION) Port-Vila (20,000)
GOVERNMENT Multiparty republic
ETHNIC GROUPS Melanesian 98%, French 1%
LANGUAGES English, French, Pidgin
RELIGIONS Christian
CURRENCY Vatu = 100 centimes

VATICAN CITY

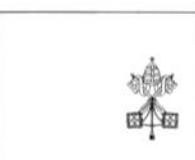

Since the 13th century the emblem on the flag has represented the Vatican's role as the headquarters of the Roman Catholic Church. Consisting of the triple tiara of the Popes above the keys of heaven given to St Peter, it was adopted in 1929.

The Vatican City State is a walled enclave on the west bank of the River Tiber in Rome and is the world's smallest nation. It exists to provide an independent base for the Holy See, governing body of the Roman Catholic Church. It is all that

remains of the Papal States, which until 1870, occupied most of central Italy. The Popes have lived here since the 5th century. The Vatican City has its own newspaper and radio station, police and railway station, and issues its own stamps and coins.

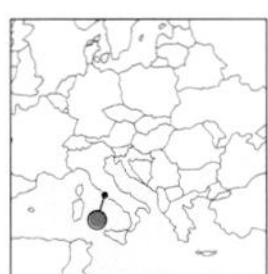

AREA 0.44 sq km [0.17 sq mls]
POPULATION 1,000
CAPITAL –
GOVERNMENT Papal Commission
ETHNIC GROUPS Italian, Swiss
LANGUAGES Latin, Italian
RELIGIONS Roman Catholic
CURRENCY Vatican lira = 100 centesimi
POPULATION DENSITY 2,273 per sq km [5,882 per sq ml]

VENEZUELA

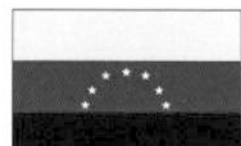

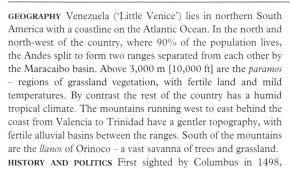

The seven stars on the tricolour represent the provinces forming the Venezuelan Federation in 1811 (see Colombia and Ecuador). The proportions of the stripes are equal to distinguish it from the flags of Colombia and Ecuador.

GEOGRAPHY Venezuela ('Little Venice') lies in northern South America with a coastline on the Atlantic Ocean. In the north and north-west of the country, where 90% of the population lives, the Andes split to form two ranges separated from each other by the Maracaibo basin. Above 3,000 m [10,000 ft] are the *paramos* – regions of grassland vegetation, with fertile land and mild temperatures. By contrast the rest of the country has a humid tropical climate. The mountains running west to east behind the coast from Valencia to Trinidad have a gentler topography, with fertile alluvial basins between the ranges. South of the mountains are the *llanos* of Orinoco – a vast savanna of trees and grassland.

HISTORY AND POLITICS First sighted by Columbus in 1498,

Venezuela became part of the Spanish colony of New Granada. In 1821 it became independent, first in federation with Colombia and Ecuador and then, from 1830, as a separate independent republic under Simón Bolivar. Between 1830 and 1945 the country was governed mainly by dictators; after frequent changes of president a new constitution came into force in 1961. Since then a fragile democracy has existed but it has rested on a system of widespread repression and corruption.

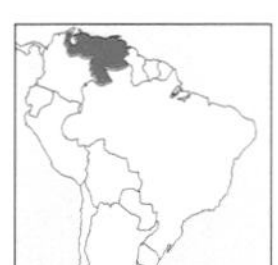

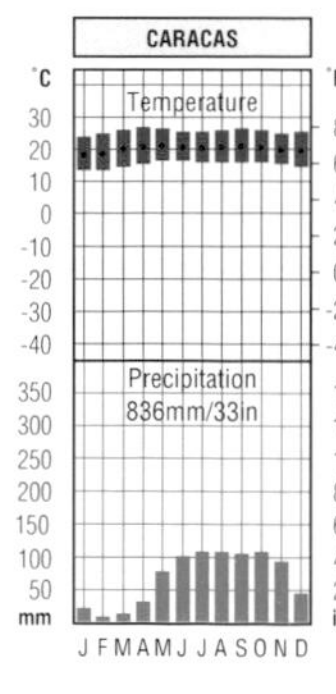

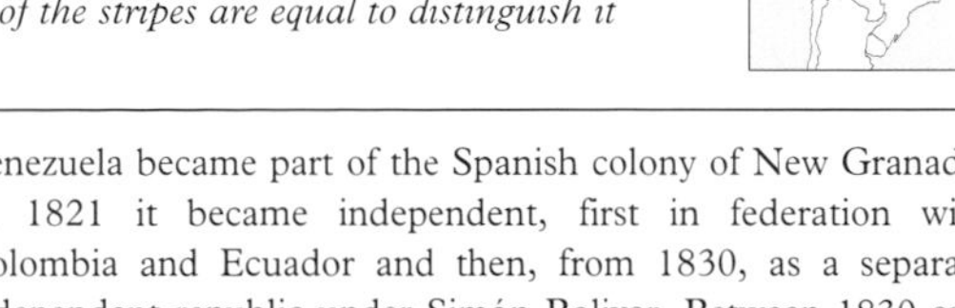

ECONOMY Oil has made Venezuela prosperous, but the wealth is unevenly distributed. It provides 86% of export earnings and there are signs of overdependence on this single commodity. Principal crops include coffee, sugar cane and bananas.

AREA 912,050 sq km [352,143 sq mls]
POPULATION 21,810,000
CAPITAL (POPULATION) Caracas (2,784,000)
GOVERNMENT Federal republic with a bicameral legislature

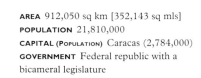

The country has a tropical climate. There is little variation in the temperature from month to month, but there are marked wet and dry seasons, the rain falling from May to November. The north-east trade winds leave little rain in the coastal lowlands, but the total increases when they hit the mountains. Some of the Andean peaks have permanent snow.

VIETNAM

VIETNAM

First used by the forces of Ho Chi Minh in the liberation struggle against Japan in World War II, the design was adopted as the national flag of North Vietnam in 1945. It was retained when the two parts of the country were reunited in 1975.

AREA 331,689 sq km [128,065 sq mls]
POPULATION 74,580,000
CAPITAL (POPULATION) Hanoi (3,056,000)
GOVERNMENT Unitary single-party socialist republic
ETHNIC GROUPS Vietnamese 87%, Tho (Tay) 2%, Chinese (Hoa) 2%, Meo 2%, Thai 2%, Khmer, Muong, Nung
LANGUAGES Vietnamese, Chinese, Tho, Khmer, Muong, Thai, Nung, Miao, Jarai, Rhadé, Hre, Bahnar
RELIGIONS Buddhist 67%, Roman Catholic 8%
CURRENCY Dong = 10 hao or 100 xu

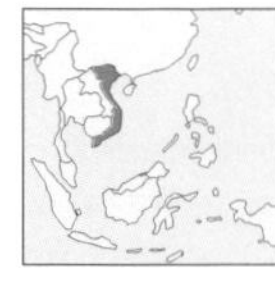

GEOGRAPHY Vietnam is one of Asia's most strangely shaped countries. In the north coastal lands widen into the valley and delta of the Hongha (Red) River and the valley of the Da. These lowlands are backed in the west by mountains of the Anamite chain. To the north are the plateaux of Laos and Tongking.
HISTORY, POLITICS AND ECONOMY Vietnam became a French protectorate in 1883 and was later joined by Laos and Cambodia in the French Indo-Chinese Union. Communist-led guerillas under Ho Chi Minh declared Vietnam free after Japanese occupation in World War II, before embarking on a war with the French between 1946 and 1954. This produced a Communist North Vietnam and a non-Communist South Vietnam and saw the start of the war against the USA between 1964 and 1976, when Vietnam was reunited as a Communist state. The war left economic chaos, from which it is only now beginning to emerge. Much of the population subsists on agriculture.

VIRGIN ISLANDS, BRITISH

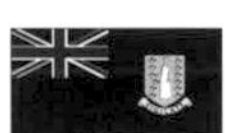

In the British Blue Ensign is the green badge of the islands, which shows a vestal virgin dressed in white and carrying a lamp. On either side of her are rows of lamps, five on the left and six on the right. Below the shield is a gold scroll bearing the motto Vigilate *('Be Alert').*

AREA 153 sq km [59 sq mls]
POPULATION 20,000
CAPITAL (POPULATION) Road Town (6,330)
GOVERNMENT British Dependent Territory
ETHNIC GROUPS African American 90%
LANGUAGES English
RELIGIONS Protestant 86%
CURRENCY US dollar
POPULATION DENSITY 131 per sq km [339 per sq ml]

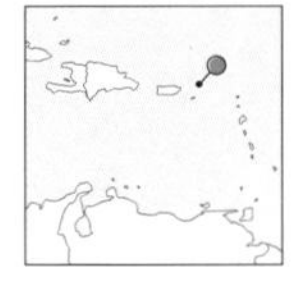

Most northerly of the Lesser Antilles, the British Virgin Islands comprise four low-lying islands and 36 islets and cays. Three-quarters of the population live on the largest island, Tortola. Dutch from 1648 but British since 1666, they are now a British dependency enjoying (since 1977) a strong measure of self-government. The main source of income is tourism. Offshore banking has been important since 1985 and the facilities are increasingly a rival to the Caymans and the Turks and Caicos.

VIRGIN ISLANDS, US

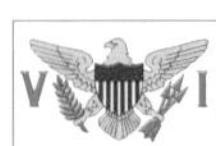

The flag was adopted in 1921 and is based on the seal of the USA. The three arrows grasped by the eagle stand for the three main islands. The emblem appears between the initial letters of the islands' name, 'V' and 'I', in blue.

AREA 340 sq km [130 sq mls]
POPULATION 105,000
CAPITAL (POPULATION) Charlotte Amalie (12,330)
GOVERNMENT Self-governing US Territory
ETHNIC GROUPS Black 80%, White 15%
LANGUAGES English, Spanish, Creole
RELIGIONS Baptist 42%, Roman Catholic 34%

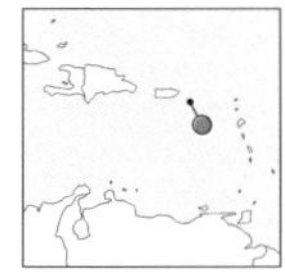

St Thomas, St Croix and St John are the largest of the 68 islands of the US Virgin Islands. The islands were Spanish from 1553, Danish from 1672 and, for a sum of US$25 million, American in 1917 – so they could protect the approaches to the newly-built Panama Canal. From 1973 they have had an elected delegate in the House of Representatives. Tourism is the main industry.

WALLIS AND FUTUNA ISLANDS

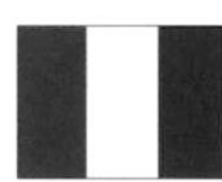

As a French Overseas Territory, the Wallis and Futuna Islands use the French tricolour as their flag.

AREA 200 sq km [77 sq mls]
POPULATION 13,000
CAPITAL (POPULATION) Mata-Utu (850)
GOVERNMENT French Overseas Territory
ETHNIC GROUPS Polynesian
LANGUAGES French, Wallisian
RELIGIONS Roman Catholic
POPULATION DENSITY 65 per sq km [169 per sq ml]

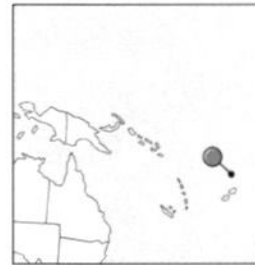

The smallest, least populous and poorest of France's three Pacific Overseas Territories, the Wallis and Futuna Islands comprise three main islands and numerous islets. Futuna and uninhabited Alofi are mountainous; the much larger Uvea is hilly with coral reefs and contains 60% of the population. The economy is based mainly on tropical subsistence agriculture.

WESTERN SAMOA

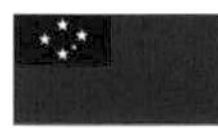

The red and white are traditional colours used in Samoan flags of the 19th century. The design of the flag, in use since 1948 (14 years before independence), links Samoa with other nations of the southern hemisphere by its inclusion of the Southern Cross constellation.

AREA 2,840 sq km [1,097 sq mls]
POPULATION 169,000
CAPITAL (POPULATION) Apia (37,000)
GOVERNMENT Constitutional monarchy
ETHNIC GROUPS Samoan, mixed European and Polynesian
LANGUAGES Samoan, English
RELIGIONS Christian
CURRENCY Tala = 100 sene

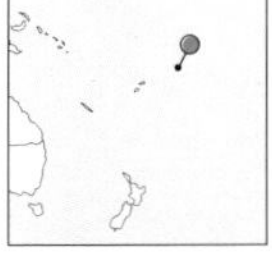

Western Samoa comprises two large islands, seven small islands and a number of islets, all lying in the Pacific Ocean. The cradle of Polynesian civilization, the islands were first independent in 1889, but became a German protectorate in 1899. They were administered by New Zealand from 1920 until independence in 1962. Coconut oil, taro and cocoa are the main exports.

YEMEN

The new straightforward design of Yemen's flag, incorporating the Pan-Arab colours, dates from 1990 when the Yemen Arab Republic (in the north and west) united with the People's Democratic Republic of Yemen (in the south and east).

AREA 527,970 sq km [203,849 sq mls]
POPULATION 14,609,000
CAPITAL (POPULATION) Sana (427,000)
GOVERNMENT Multiparty republic
ETHNIC GROUPS Arab 96%, Somali 1%
LANGUAGES Arabic
RELIGIONS Sunni Muslim, Shiite Muslim
CURRENCY N. Yemeni riyal = 100 fils, S. Yemeni dinar = 1,000 fils
POPULATION DENSITY 28 per sq km [72 per sq ml]

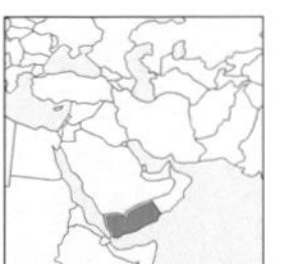

Located at the southern end of the Arabian peninsula, Yemen has a coastline on the Gulf of Aden. There is a narrow coastal plain behind which rise mountains and plateaux. There is little annual rainfall. Aden in South Yemen was a British colony from 1839 to 1967 and an important British staging post on the journey to India. The two states of North Yemen (an independent kingdom since 1918) and South Yemen (under Marxist control) united in 1990 to form the Yemeni Republic. Clashes between the north and south in 1994 escalated into a full civil war until June when government troops captured Aden.

YUGOSLAVIA (SERBIA AND MONTENEGRO)

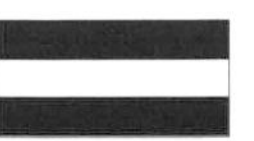

Only the republics of Serbia and Montenegro now remain in Yugoslavia. The same flag is still used with its colours identifying it as a Slavic state which was once part of the Austro-Hungarian Empire. It used to have a red star in the centre, but this was dropped in 1992.

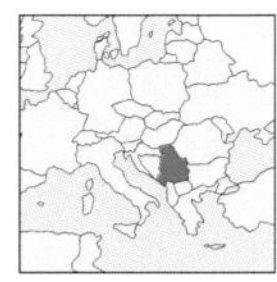

'Yugoslavia' today only contains the federal republics of Serbia and Montenegro and further changes are likely. Known from 1918 as the Kingdom of the Serbs, Croats and Slovenes, and from 1929 as Yugoslavia ('land of the South Slavs'), the unity of the country has always been fragile, with a long history of nationalist and ethnic tensions. In the interwar period the country was virtually a 'Greater Serbia', and after Hitler invaded in 1941 Yugoslavs fought both the Germans and each other. The Communist-led partisans of 'Tito' (a Croat) were the victors in 1945 and reformed Yugoslavia as a republic based on the Soviet model. The region was fairly peaceful until Tito died in 1990. In the first free elections since the war there were nationalist victories in four out of the six federal republics. Slovenia and Croatia became independent in 1991 with Bosnia-Herzegovina following in 1992. Bosnia was at once the centre of a vicious civil war until a fragile peace was negotiated at the end of 1995. The Yugoslavia that now exists is therefore much reduced, with many problems of its own, including severe international sanctions.

AREA 102,170 sq km [39,449 sq mls]
POPULATION 10,881,000
CAPITAL (POPULATION) Belgrade (1,137,000)
GOVERNMENT Federal republic
ETHNIC GROUPS Serb 62%, Albanian 17%, Montenegrin 5%, Hungarian 4%
LANGUAGES Serbo-Croatian
RELIGIONS Orthodox 65%, Muslim 19%
CURRENCY New Yugoslav dinar = 100 paras
POPULATION DENSITY 106 per sq km [276 per sq ml]
URBAN POPULATION 52% of population
LAND USE Arable 36%, grass 21%, forest 30%

ZAÏRE

The Pan-African colours of red, yellow and green were adopted for Zaïre's flag in 1971. The central emblem symbolizes the revolutionary spirit of the nation and was used by the Popular Movement of the Revolution, formed in 1967.

GEOGRAPHY Zaïre is Africa's third biggest country and the world's 12th biggest, and is 77 times the size of its former colonial ruler, Belgium. Much of the northern part of the country lies in the equatorial Congo Basin, the world's second largest river drainage system, where the landscape is mostly tropical rainforest. The Congo (Zaïre) River was developed as a major artery, its rapids and falls bypassed by railways. In the south and east is part of the Great Rift Valley and there are highlands and plateaux. Despite its huge size, it has a coastline on the Atlantic Ocean of only 27 km [17 mls].

HISTORY AND POLITICS Zaïre was made up of several African kingdoms before becoming the Congo Free State between 1884 and 1908, owned by Belgium's King Léopold II. The country then became the Belgian Congo colony until independence in 1960. Soon after independence a violent civil war began which lasted until General Mobutu seized power in 1965, declaring a one-party state in 1967 and renaming the country Zaïre as part of a wide-ranging Africanization policy. His long dictatorship was characterized by repression and inefficiency and by 1990 increasing protests forced him to agree to multiparty elections. Since then there has been chaos, with Mobutu still in power.

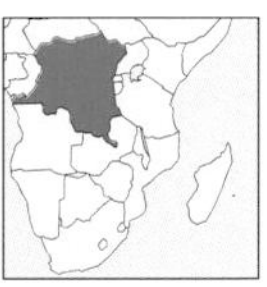

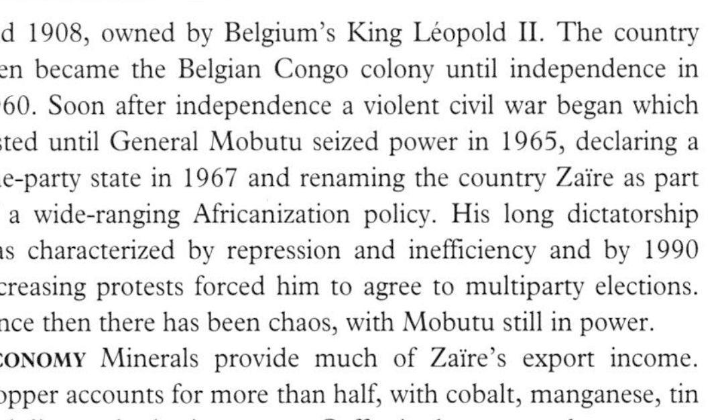

ECONOMY Minerals provide much of Zaïre's export income. Copper accounts for more than half, with cobalt, manganese, tin and diamonds also important. Coffee is also exported.

AREA 2,344,885 sq km [905,365 sq mls]
POPULATION 44,504,000
CAPITAL (POPULATION) Kinshasa (3,804,000)
GOVERNMENT Transitional government
URBAN POPULATION 29% of population

LUBUMBASHI

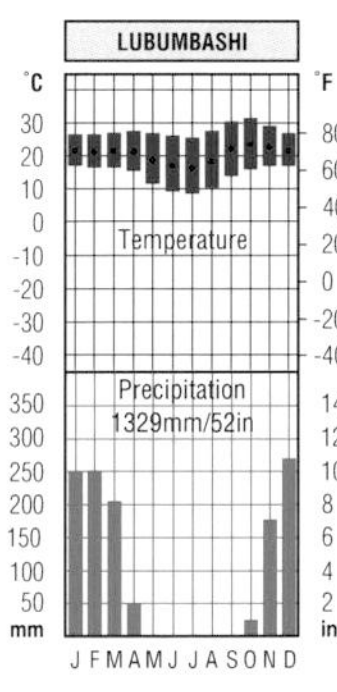

The Equator passes through the northern half of Zaïre, and here the rainfall and temperature are high throughout the year. To the north and south is a subtropical zone with lower temperatures and a marked wet and dry season. The climate near the coast, because of a cold ocean current, is cooler and drier. In the east there is a mountain climate.

ZAMBIA

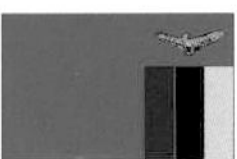

The colours of Zambia's distinctive national flag are those of the United Nationalist Independence Party, which led the struggle against Britain. The flying eagle represents freedom. The design was adopted on independence in 1964.

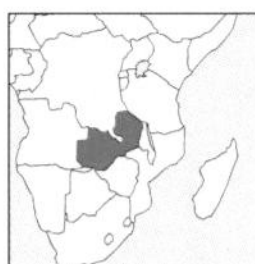

GEOGRAPHY A vast expanse of high plateaux (about 1,200 m [3,900 ft] above sea level) in the interior of south-central Africa, most of Zambia is drained by the Zambezi and two of its major tributaries, the Kafue and the Luangwa. In the south the latter and the central section of the Zambezi occupy a low-lying rift valley bounded by rugged escarpments. The Victoria Falls lie on the border with Zimbabwe. In the north are the swamps of the Bangweulu Depression and the Muchinga Mountains.

HISTORY AND POLITICS In the 1890s Britain took control over Zambia and named it Northern Rhodesia. Between 1953 and 1963 it was part of a federation with Southern Rhodesia (now Zimbabwe) and Nyasaland. It became independent in 1964 and Kenneth Kaunda became president. His 27-year, single-party rule (he declared his party, the UNIP, the only legal party in 1972) ended in 1991 when he conceded to multiparty elections and union leader Frederick Chiluba became president.

ECONOMY Zambia is the world's fifth biggest producer of copper ore and the economy is heavily dependent on the income gained from this, despite attempts to diversify. There are high levels of rural-urban migration, mostly in search of scarce employment.

AREA 752,614 sq km [290,586 sq mls]
POPULATION 9,500,000
CAPITAL (POPULATION) Lusaka (982,000)
GOVERNMENT Multiparty republic with a unicameral legislature
ETHNIC GROUPS Bemba 36%, Nyanja 18%, Malawi 14%, Lozi 9%, Tonga 5%
LANGUAGES English, Bemba, Tonga, Nyanja, Lozi, Lunda, Luvale, Kaonde
RELIGIONS Christian 72%, animist
CURRENCY Kwacha = 100 ngwee
POPULATION DENSITY 13 per sq km [33 per sq ml]
URBAN POPULATION 42% of population
LAND USE Arable 7%, grass 40%, forest 39%

ZIMBABWE

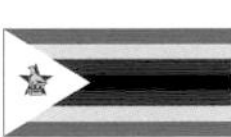

Adopted when legal independence was secured in 1980, Zimbabwe's flag is based on the colours of the ruling Patriotic Front. Within the white triangle is the soapstone bird national emblem and a red star, symbolizing the party's socialist policy.

GEOGRAPHY Zimbabwe is a landlocked country lying astride the high plateaux between the Zambezi (in the north) and Limpopo (in the south) rivers. Almost all the country is over 300 m [1,000 ft] above sea level. In the north-west it shares Lake Kariba, Africa's second largest artificial lake, with Zambia. The vegetation on the plateaux is that of the High Veld, which is mostly grassland.

HISTORY AND POLITICS Britain controlled Zimbabwe from 1894, naming it Southern Rhodesia after the politician Cecil Rhodes and nurturing it as a 'white man's country'. From 1923 it became a self-governing colony and in 1965 Ian Smith's white government declared itself independent as Rhodesia. The ensuing guerrilla action against Smith led to a full-scale civil war and eventually forced a move to black majority rule in 1980. The rift that followed independence, between Robert Mugabe's ruling ZANU and Joshua Nkomo's ZAPU, was resolved in 1989 when they merged and Mugabe renounced his Marxist ideology. In 1990 Mugabe was elected president and the state of emergency that had lasted since 1965 was ended.

ECONOMY The economy is relatively strong, founded on gold and tobacco but now more diverse. There are varied mineral resources, including copper, nickel and iron ore.

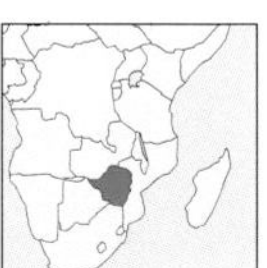

AREA 390,579 sq km [150,873 sq mls]
POPULATION 11,453,000
CAPITAL (POPULATION) Harare (1,189,000)
GOVERNMENT Multiparty republic

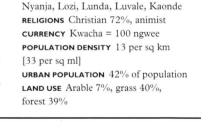

HARARE

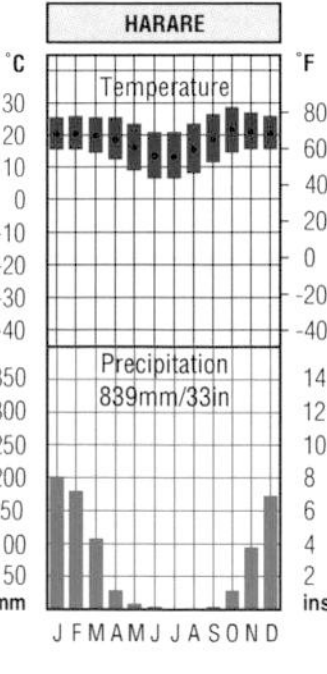

Like other places on the high interior plateau of southern Africa, Harare has a large diurnal range of temperature, particularly in the dry, sunny winter, and is much cooler than lowlands at the same latitude. Frosts have been recorded between June and August. The main rains of summer are brought by south-easterly winds from the Indian Ocean.

WORLD OF NATIONS: INDEX TO COUNTRIES

NOTES

The countries are arranged alphabetically, with Afghanistan as the first entry and Zimbabwe as the last. Information is given for all countries and territories, except for some of the smallest and near uninhabited islands.

The form of names for the many new countries that now exist follows the conventions used in all Philip's world atlases. The region that is generally called Serbia is listed under Yugoslavia (Serbia and Montenegro) and for two countries the traditional English conventional name has been used: Burma (Myanmar) and Ivory Coast (Côte d'Ivoire).

The statistical data is the latest available, usually for 1995, or within the period 1994–5. In the statistics' boxes:

Country area includes inland water and land areas covered in ice, as in Greenland and Canada, for example.

City populations are usually those of the 'urban agglomerations' rather than within the legal city boundaries.

WORLD MAPS

SETTLEMENTS

◫ **PARIS**   ▣ **Berne**   ◉ **Livorno**   ◎ **Brugge**   ⊚ *Algeciras*   ⊙ *Fréjus*   ○ *Oberammergau*   ○ *Thira*

Settlement symbols and type styles vary according to the scale of each map and indicate the importance
of towns on the map rather than specific population figures

∴ Ruins or Archæological Sites   ˘ Wells in Desert

ADMINISTRATION

—————— International Boundaries

– – – International Boundaries
(Undefined or Disputed)

·········· Internal Boundaries

National Parks

Country Names

NICARAGUA

Administrative
Area Names

K E N T

C A L A B R I A

International boundaries show the *de facto* situation where there are rival claims to territory

COMMUNICATIONS

—————— Principal Roads

~~~~~ Other Roads

·–·–·– Trails and Seasonal Roads

⋈ Passes

✿ Airfields

⌢ Principal Railroads

·–·–· Railroads
Under Construction

⌢ Other Railroads

⊣–––⊢ Railroad Tunnels

wwwww Principal Canals

PHYSICAL FEATURES

~~~ Perennial Streams

·····– Intermittent Streams

⬭ Perennial Lakes

⬭ Intermittent Lakes

Swamps and Marshes

Permanent Ice
and Glaciers

▲ 8848 Elevations (m)

▼ 8050 Sea Depths (m)

1134 Height of Lake Surface
Above Sea Level (m)

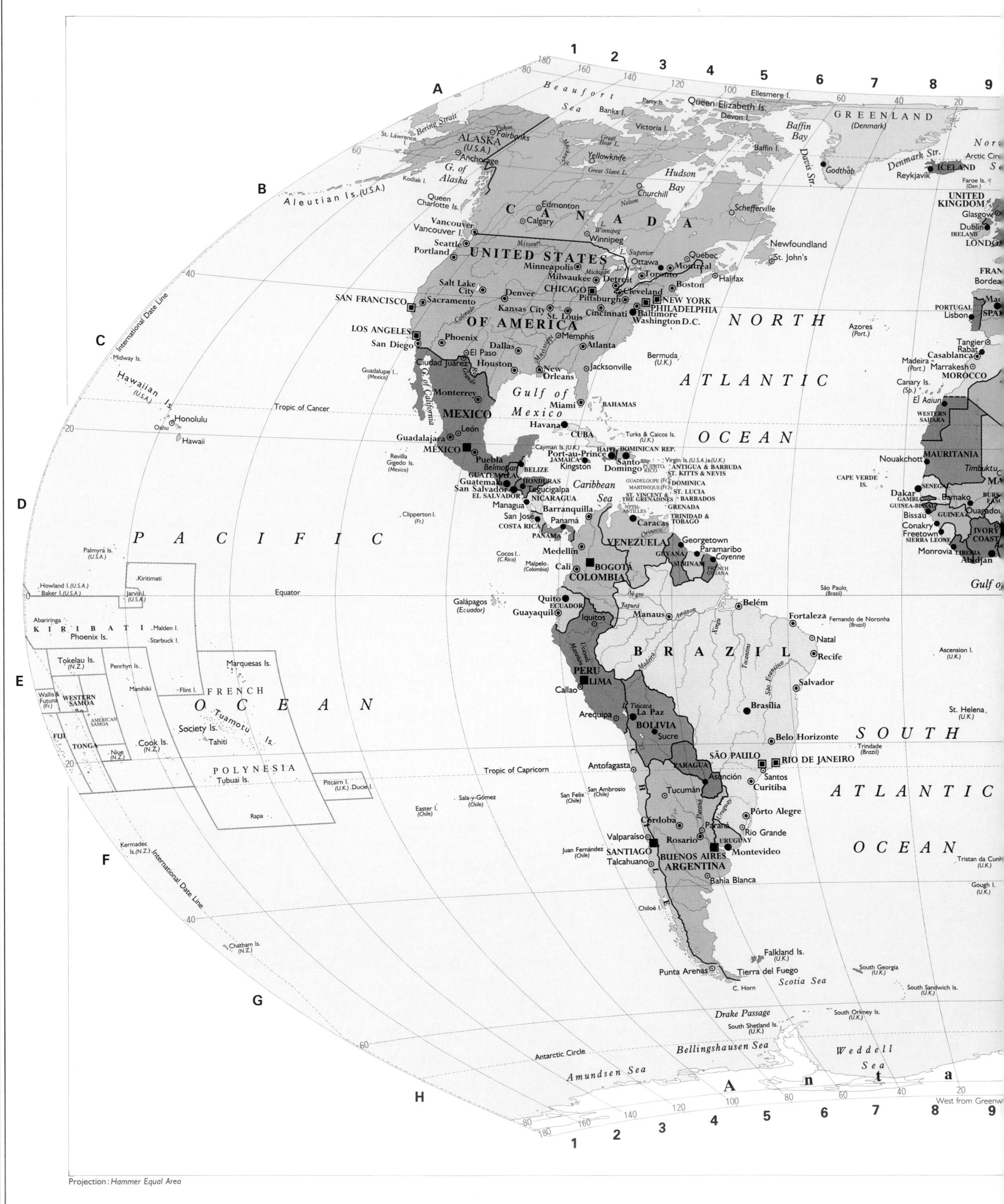

Projection: *Hammer Equal Area*

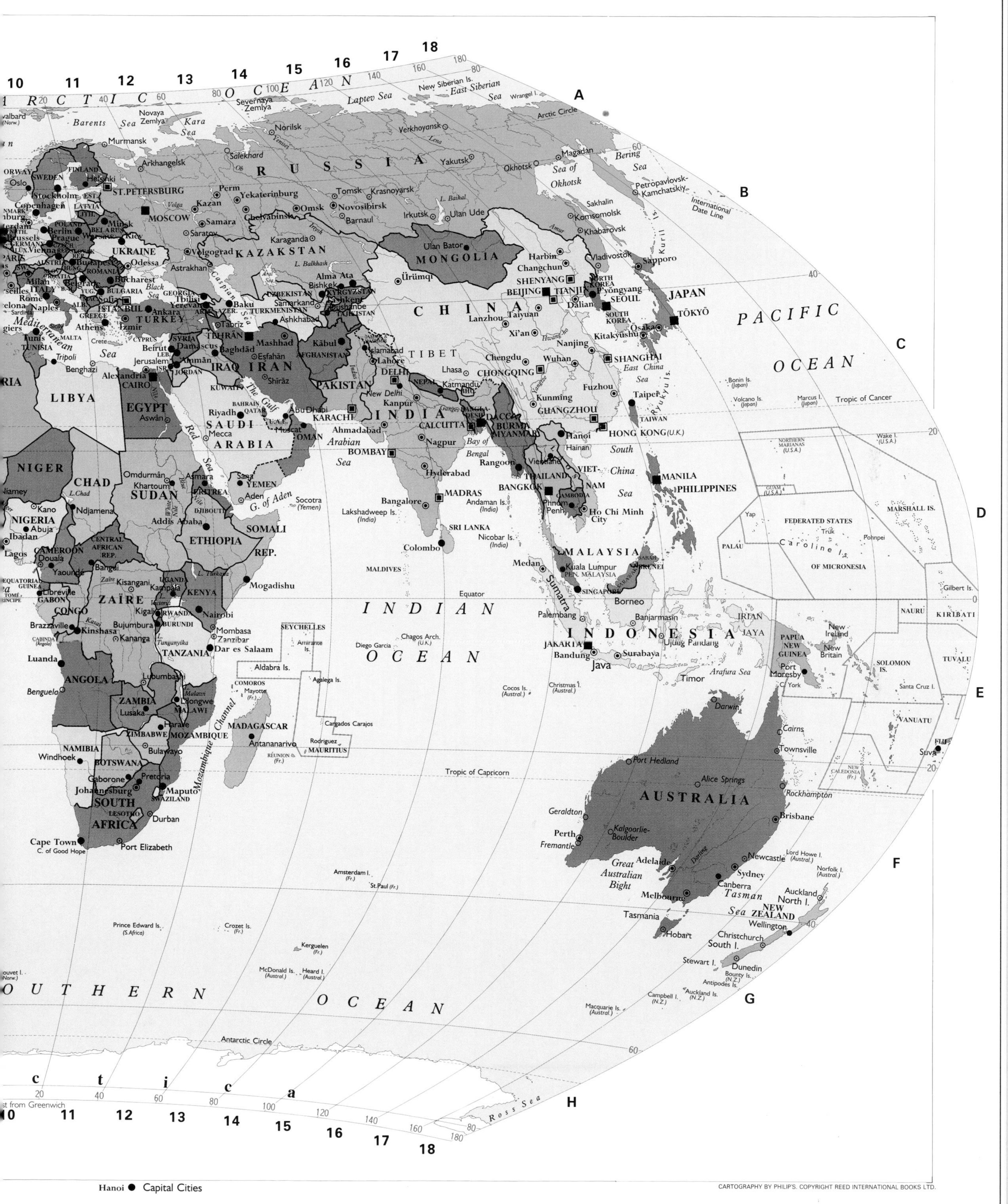
10 11 12 13 14 15 16 17 18
A
B
C
D
E
F
G
H
ARCTIC OCEAN
Barents Sea
Kara Sea
Laptev Sea
East Siberian Sea
New Siberian Is.
Wrangel I.
Arctic Circle
Novaya Zemlya
Severnaya Zemlya
Norilsk
Verkhoyansk
Murmansk
Arkhangelsk
Salekhard
RUSSIA
Yakutsk
Magadan
Okhotsk
Sea of Okhotsk
Bering Sea
Petropavlovsk-Kamchatskiy
International Date Line
Sakhalin
Komsomolsk
Khabarovsk
Kuril Is.
FINLAND
SWEDEN
Helsinki
Oslo
Stockholm
ST. PETERSBURG
Copenhagen
MOSCOW
Perm
Yekaterinburg
Tomsk
Krasnoyarsk
L. Baikal
Kazan
Omsk
Novosibirsk
Irkutsk
Ulan Ude
Samara
Chelyabinsk
Barnaul
Saratov
Minsk
BELARUS
POLAND
Berlin
Brussels
Prague
Warsaw
Kiev
UKRAINE
Volgograd
KAZAKSTAN
Karaganda
Astrakhan
Odessa
Budapest
Vienna
ROMANIA
Bucharest
L. Balkhash
Alma Ata
Bishkek
Tashkent
Ulan Bator
MONGOLIA
Ürümqi
Harbin
Changchun
SHENYANG
Vladivostok
Sapporo
BEIJING
TIANJIN
Dalian
Pyongyang
NORTH KOREA
SEOUL
SOUTH KOREA
JAPAN
TŌKYŌ
Ōsaka
Kitakyushu
PACIFIC OCEAN
Milan
Rome
Naples
ITALY
Black Sea
Sofia
BULGARIA
GREECE
Athens
Istanbul
Ankara
TURKEY
Izmir
Tbilisi
Yerevan
Baku
Caspian Sea
Tabriz
Samarkand
TURKMENISTAN
Ashkhabad
Dushanbe
TAJIKISTAN
CHINA
Lanzhou
Taiyuan
Xi'an
Nanjing
SHANGHAI
East China Sea
Mediterranean Sea
Tunis
TUNISIA
MALTA
Crete
CYPRUS
Tripoli
Benghazi
LIBYA
Beirut
SYRIA
Damascus
Jerusalem
Amman
JORDAN
Baghdad
IRAQ
TEHRAN
Mashhad
IRAN
Esfahān
Shīrāz
Kābul
AFGHANISTAN
Islamabad
Lahore
TIBET
Chengdu
Wuhan
CHONGQING
Lhasa
Alexandria
CAIRO
EGYPT
Aswân
KUWAIT
The Gulf
BAHRAIN
QATAR
Abu Dhabi
U.A.E.
Muscat
OMAN
Riyadh
SAUDI ARABIA
Mecca
Red Sea
PAKISTAN
KARACHI
New Delhi
DELHI
NEPAL
Katmandu
BHUTAN
Kanpur
INDIA
Ahmadabad
CALCUTTA
BANGLADESH
DACCA
BURMA MYANMAR
Kunming
Fuzhou
Taipei
TAIWAN
Ryukyu Is.
GUANGZHOU
HONG KONG (U.K.)
Hanoi
Hainan
Arabian Sea
BOMBAY
Nagpur
Bay of Bengal
Rangoon
Hyderabad
Bangalore
MADRAS
Vientiane
THAILAND
BANGKOK
VIETNAM
South China Sea
MANILA
PHILIPPINES
CAMBODIA
Phnom Penh
Ho Chi Minh City
Andaman Is. (India)
Lakshadweep Is. (India)
SRI LANKA
Colombo
Nicobar Is. (India)
MALDIVES
Medan
MALAYSIA
Kuala Lumpur
BRUNEI
SINGAPORE
Sumatra
Borneo
NIGER
CHAD
L. Chad
SUDAN
Omdurmân
Khartoum
Asmara
ERITREA
Sana
YEMEN
Aden
G. of Aden
Socotra (Yemen)
DJIBOUTI
Addis Ababa
ETHIOPIA
SOMALI REP.
Niamey
Kano
NIGERIA
Abuja
Ibadan
Ndjamena
CENTRAL AFRICAN REP.
Lagos
CAMEROON
Douala
Yaoundé
Bangui
EQUATORIAL GUINEA
Libreville
GABON
CONGO
Kisangani
ZAÏRE
UGANDA
Kampala
KENYA
Nairobi
Mogadishu
Brazzaville
Kinshasa
Kigali
RWANDA
Bujumbura
BURUNDI
Kananga
Mombasa
Zanzibar
Dar es Salaam
TANZANIA
CABINDA (Angola)
Luanda
ANGOLA
Benguela
Lubumbashi
ZAMBIA
Lusaka
Lilongwe
MALAWI
Harare
ZIMBABWE
MOZAMBIQUE
Mozambique Channel
COMOROS
Mayotte (Fr.)
MADAGASCAR
Antananarivo
Aldabra Is.
SEYCHELLES
Amirante Is.
Agalega Is.
Cargados Carajos
Rodriguez
MAURITIUS
RÉUNION (Fr.)
NAMIBIA
Windhoek
BOTSWANA
Bulawayo
Gaborone
Pretoria
Johannesburg
Maputo
SWAZILAND
SOUTH AFRICA
LESOTHO
Durban
Cape Town
C. of Good Hope
Port Elizabeth
Equator
INDIAN OCEAN
Diego Garcia
Chagos Arch. (U.K.)
Palembang
Banjarmasin
INDONESIA
JAKARTA
Bandung
Java
Surabaya
Ujung Pandang
IRIAN JAYA
Timor
Arafura Sea
PAPUA NEW GUINEA
Port Moresby
New Ireland
New Britain
C. York
Cocos Is. (Austral.)
Christmas I. (Austral.)
Tropic of Capricorn
Tropic of Cancer
Darwin
Cairns
Townsville
Port Hedland
Alice Springs
AUSTRALIA
Rockhampton
Brisbane
Geraldton
Kalgoorlie-Boulder
Perth
Fremantle
Great Australian Bight
Adelaide
Darling
Newcastle
Sydney
Canberra
Melbourne
Tasmania
Hobart
Tasman Sea
Lord Howe I. (Austral.)
Norfolk I. (Austral.)
Auckland
North I.
NEW ZEALAND
Wellington
Christchurch
South I.
Stewart I.
Dunedin
Bounty Is. (N.Z.)
Antipodes Is.
Auckland Is. (N.Z.)
Campbell I. (N.Z.)
Macquarie Is. (Austral.)
Bonin Is. (Japan)
Volcano Is. (Japan)
Marcus I. (Japan)
Wake I. (U.S.A.)
NORTHERN MARIANAS (U.S.A.)
GUAM (U.S.A.)
Yap
PALAU
FEDERATED STATES OF MICRONESIA
Truk
Pohnpei
Caroline Is.
MARSHALL IS.
Gilbert Is.
NAURU
KIRIBATI
SOLOMON IS.
Santa Cruz I.
TUVALU
VANUATU
NEW CALEDONIA (Fr.)
FIJI
Suva
Amsterdam I. (Fr.)
St. Paul (Fr.)
Prince Edward Is. (S. Africa)
Crozet Is. (Fr.)
Kerguelen (Fr.)
McDonald Is. (Austral.)
Heard I. (Austral.)
SOUTHERN OCEAN
Antarctic Circle
Antarctica
Ross Sea
East from Greenwich
Hanoi ● Capital Cities

1:35 000 000

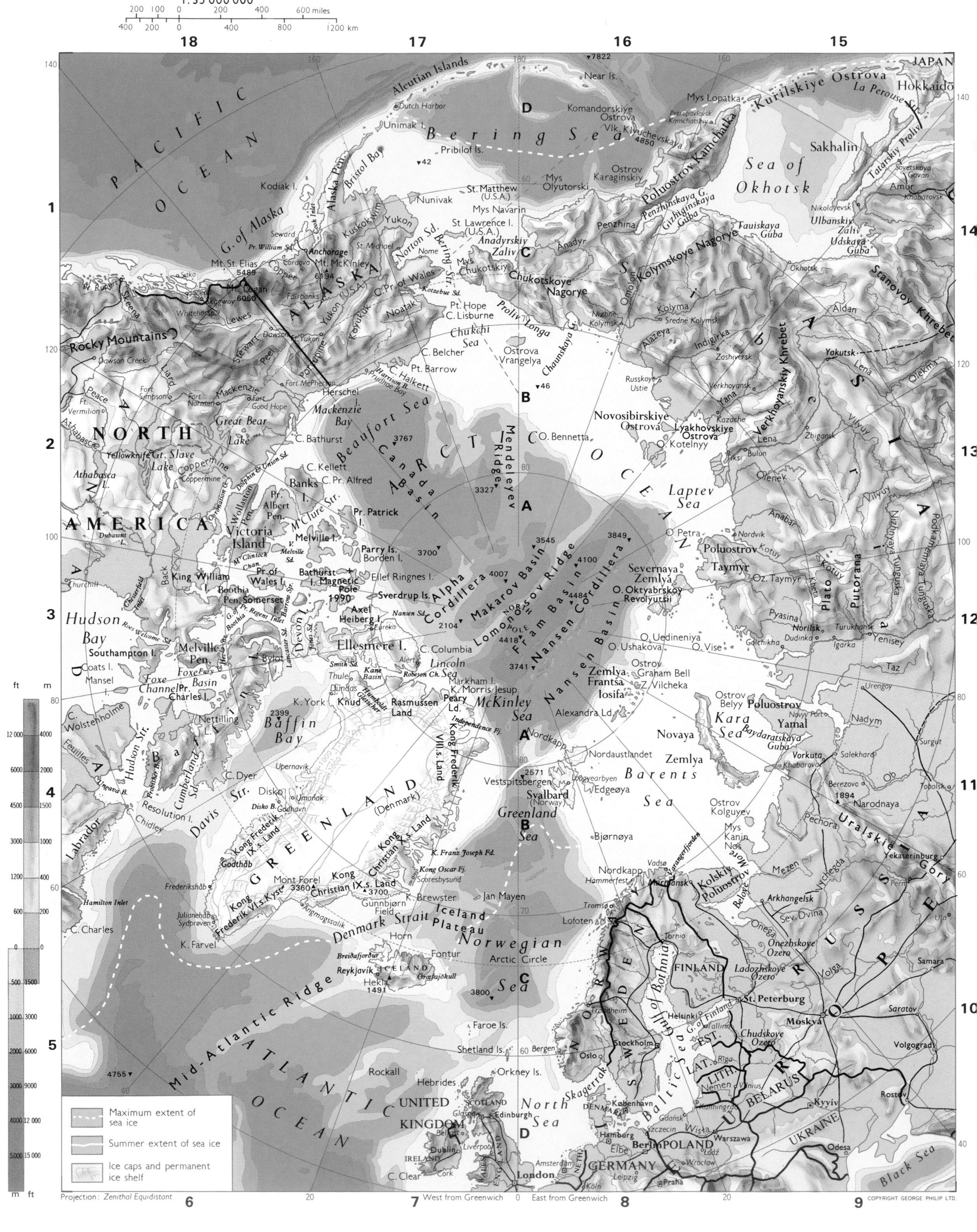

Maximum extent of sea ice

Summer extent of sea ice

Ice caps and permanent ice shelf

Projection: Zenithal Equidistant   West from Greenwich   East from Greenwich   COPYRIGHT GEORGE PHILIP LTD.

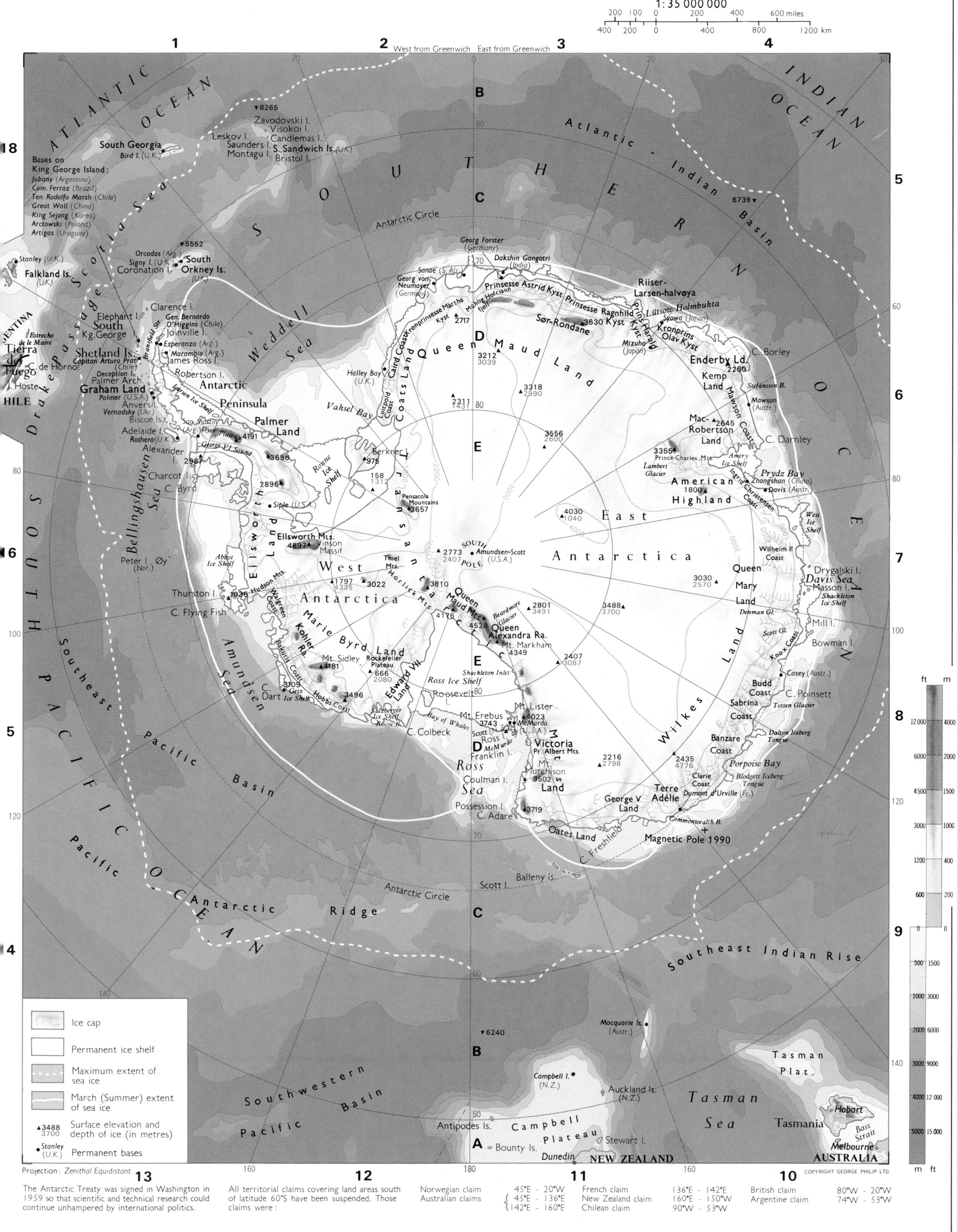

Projection: Zenithal Equidistant

The Antarctic Treaty was signed in Washington in 1959 so that scientific and technical research could continue unhampered by international politics.

All territorial claims covering land areas south of latitude 60°S have been suspended. Those claims were:

Claim	Longitudes
Norwegian claim	45°E - 20°W
Australian claims	45°E - 136°E; 142°E - 160°E
French claim	136°E - 142°E
New Zealand claim	160°E - 150°W
Chilean claim	90°W - 53°W
British claim	80°W - 20°W
Argentine claim	74°W - 53°W

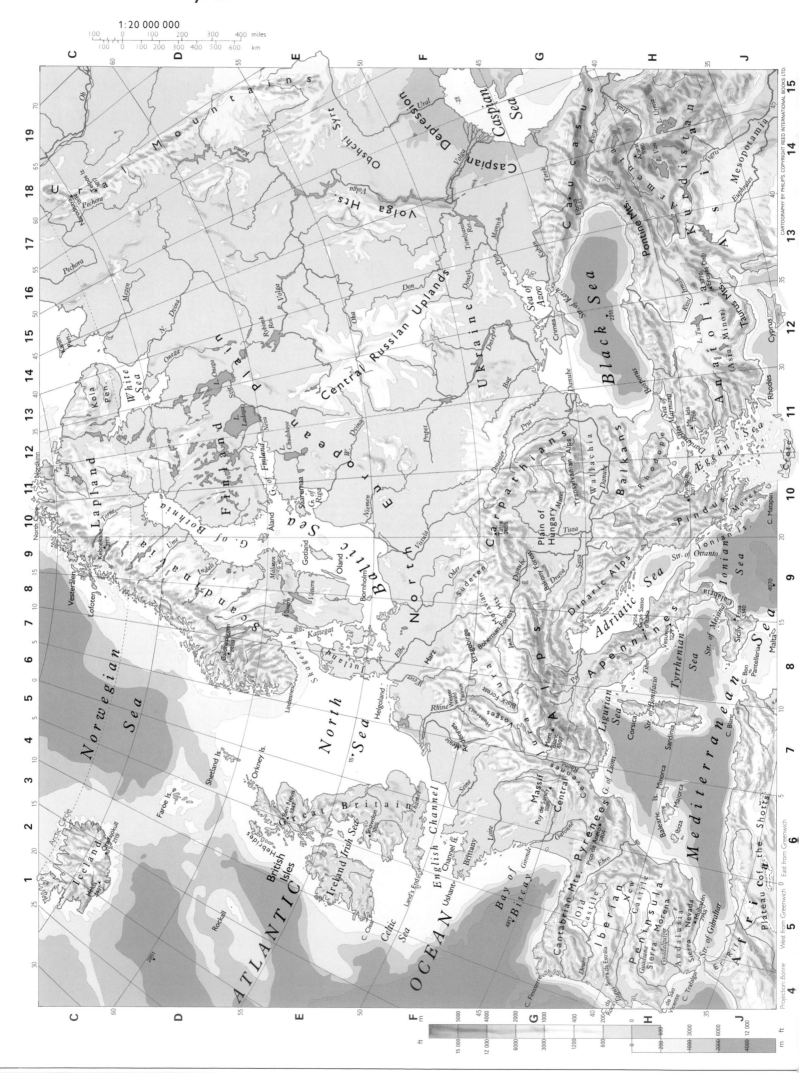

1 : 20 000 000

CARTOGRAPHY BY PHILIP'S COPYRIGHT REED INTERNATIONAL BOOKS LTD.

Projection: Bonne

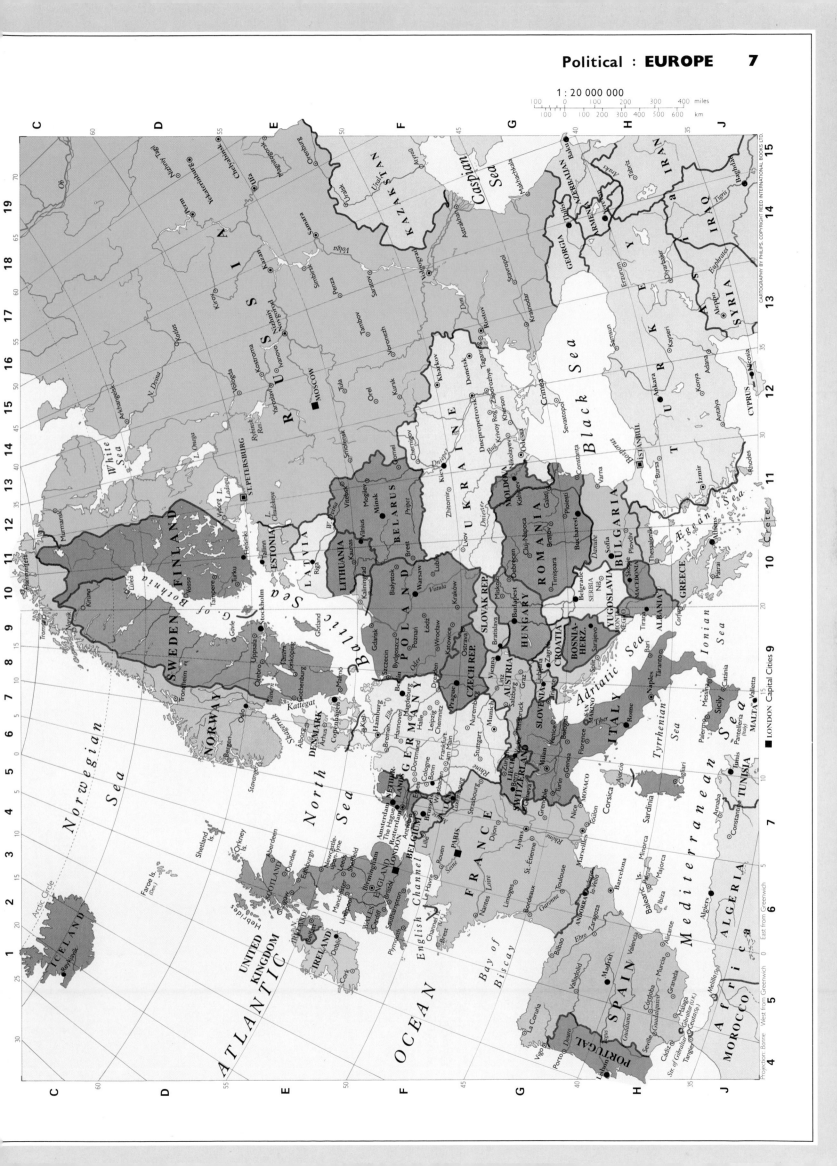

1 : 20 000 000

100   0   100   200   300   400 miles
100 0 100 200 300 400 500 600 km

ICELAND
Reykjavik

ATLANTIC

OCEAN

Faroe Is.
(Den.)

Shetland Is.

Orkney Is.

Hebrides

UNITED
KINGDOM

SCOTLAND
Aberdeen
Dundee
Edinburgh
Glasgow

Newcastle-upon-Tyne
ENGLAND
Leeds
Manchester
Liverpool
Sheffield
Birmingham
WALES
Cardiff
Bristol
Southampton
LONDON
Plymouth

IRELAND
Belfast
Dublin
Cork

Norwegian

Sea

Tromsø

NORWAY

Narvik

Trondheim

Bergen
Stavanger
Oslo

Kristiansand

Skagerrak

DENMARK
Århus
Copenhagen
Odense

Kattegat

Kiel
Hamburg
Bremen
Hannover
NETHER-
LANDS
Amsterdam
The Hague
Rotterdam
BELGIUM
Antwerp
Brussels

Kiruna

Luleå

SWEDEN

Umeå

Sundsvall

Örebro
Uppsala
Stockholm

Göteborg
Jönköping
Malmö

Gotland

Baltic
Sea

Gulf of Bothnia

FINLAND

Vaasa

Tampere
Turku
Helsinki

ESTONIA
Tallinn

LATVIA
Riga

LITHUANIA
Kaunas
Vilnius

Kaliningrad

Gdansk
Szczecin
Bydgoszcz
POLAND
Poznań
Warsaw
Lodz
Wroclaw
Katowice
Kraków

Vistula

Białystok

RUSSIA

Murmansk
Arkhangelsk

White
Sea

N. Dvina

L. Onega

L. Ladoga

S.PETERSBURG

Vyborg

Helsinki

Novgorod
Rybinsk Res.
Yaroslavl
Vologda
Kostroma
Ivanovo
Nizhniy Novgorod
MOSCOW
Tula
Ryazan
Smolensk
Orel
Kursk

Minsk
BELARUS
Mogilev
Vitebsk
Gomel
Pripet
Brest

W. Dvina

UKRAINE

Lvov
Chernigov
Kiev
Zhitomir
Dnieper

Dniester

English Channel

FRANCE

Brest
Le Havre
Rouen
PARIS
Seine
Nantes
Loire
Dijon
Lyons
Limoges
St.-Étienne
Bordeaux
Garonne
Toulouse
Marseilles
Rhône

Bay of
Biscay

Strasbourg
Lille

GERMANY
Dortmund
Essen
Cologne
Bonn
Wiesbaden
Frankfurt
am Main
Mannheim
Stuttgart
Nuremberg
Munich
Elbe
Magdeburg
Leipzig
Halle
Dresden
Chemnitz
Rhine

LUX.
Luxembourg

SWITZERLAND
Basle
Bern
Zürich
Geneva

LIECH.

AUSTRIA
Salzburg
Innsbruck
Vienna
Linz
Graz

CZECH REP.
Prague

Bratislava
SLOVAK REP.

HUNGARY
Budapest

Debrecen

SLOVENIA
Ljubljana

CROATIA
Zagreb

BOSNIA-
HERZ.
Sarajevo

SAN
MARINO

ITALY
Milan
Turin
Genoa
Venice
Trieste
Bologna
Florence
Tiber
Rome
Naples
Bari
Taranto

MONACO
Nice

Corsica

Grenoble

SPAIN
Valladolid
Madrid
La Coruña
Vigo
Porto
Douro
PORTUGAL
Lisbon
Seville
Córdoba
Granada
Málaga
Guadalquivir
Cádiz
Str. of Gibraltar
Gibraltar (U.K.)
Tangier

Ebro
Zaragoza
Barcelona
Valencia
Alicante
Murcia
Majorca
Minorca
Ibiza
Balearic Is.

MOROCCO

ALGERIA
Oran
Algiers

Mediterranean

Melilla (Sp.)
Ceuta (Sp.)

Sardinia
Cagliari

Tyrrhenian
Sea

Palermo
Sicily
Catánia
Messina

MALTA
Valletta

Pantelleria
(Italy)

TUNISIA
Tunis
Annaba
Constantine

Sea

Africa

North
Sea

Germany

Odense

Belgrade
SERBIA
YUGOSLAVIA
Niš
MONTE-
NEGRO
MACEDONIA
Skopje

ALBANIA
Tiranë

Adriatic Sea
Split
Dubrovnik

Ionian
Sea

GREECE
Corfu
Patrai
Athens

Ægean
Sea

Crete

ROMANIA
Cluj-Napoca
Timisoara
Brasov
Bucharest
Ploiesti
Galati

MOLDOVA
Kishinev

BULGARIA
Sofia
Plovdiv
Danube
Varna

Black

Sea

Constanta

Bosporus

ISTANBUL
Bursa
TURKEY
Ankara
Konya
Izmir
Antalya
Adana
Kayseri

Rhodes

CYPRUS
Nicosia

SYRIA
Aleppo

IRAQ
Baghdad
Tigris
Euphrates

IRAN
Tabriz

AZERBAIJAN
Baku
ARMENIA
Yerevan
GEORGIA
Tbilisi

Erzurum
Diyarbakir

Kharkov
Donetsk
Dnepropetrovsk
Krivoy Rog
Zaporozhye
Taganrog
Nikolayev
Kherson
Odessa
Sevastopol
Crimea

Caspian
Sea

Volga
Saratov
Penza
Tambov
Voronezh
Rostov
Don
Volgograd
Astrakhan
Stavropol
Krasnodar
Makhachkala

Samara
Ulyanovsk
Penza
Kazan
Kirov

Vyatka
Perm

Ufa
Chelyabinsk
Magnitogorsk

Ural

KAZAKHSTAN
Uralsk

Ob

Nizhniy Tagil

Yekaterinburg

Arctic Circle

■ LONDON Capital Cities

■ LONDON Capital Cities

Projection: Bonne   West from Greenwich   0   East from Greenwich

CARTOGRAPHY BY PHILIP'S. COPYRIGHT REED INTERNATIONAL BOOKS LTD.

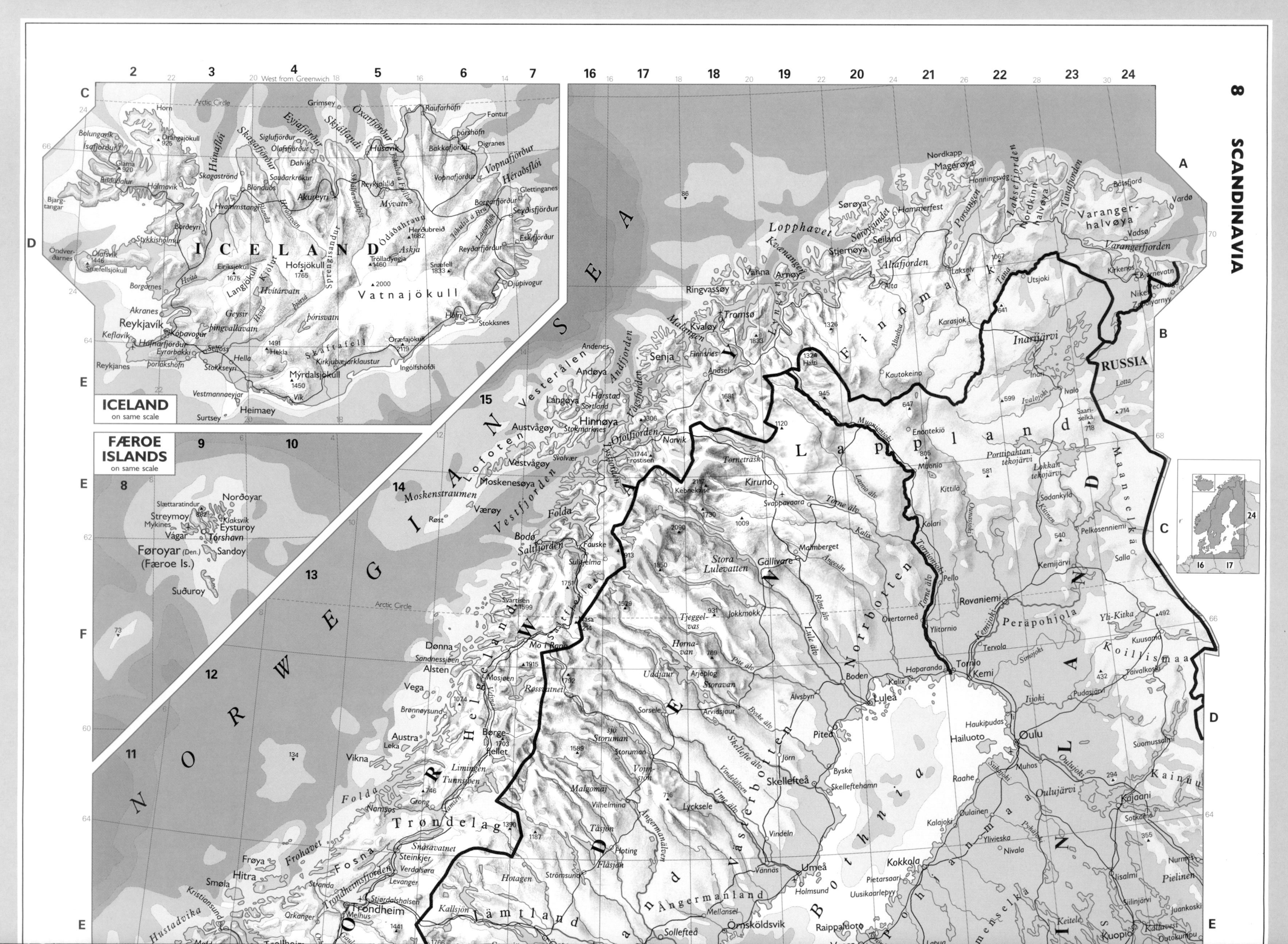
ICELAND
on same scale
FÆROE ISLANDS
on same scale
NORWEGIAN SEA
RUSSIA
ICELAND
Vatnajökull
Reykjavík
Akureyri
Heimaey
Føroyar (Den.)
(Færoe Is.)
Tórshavn
Lofoten
Vesterålen
Finnmark
Lappland
Norrbotten
Trøndelag
Gulf of Bothnia
Tromsø
Hammerfest
Nordkapp
Narvik
Bodø
Trondheim
Kiruna
Gällivare
Luleå
Umeå
Skellefteå
Oulu
Kemi
Tornio
Haparanda
Rovaniemi
Arctic Circle
20 West from Greenwich 18

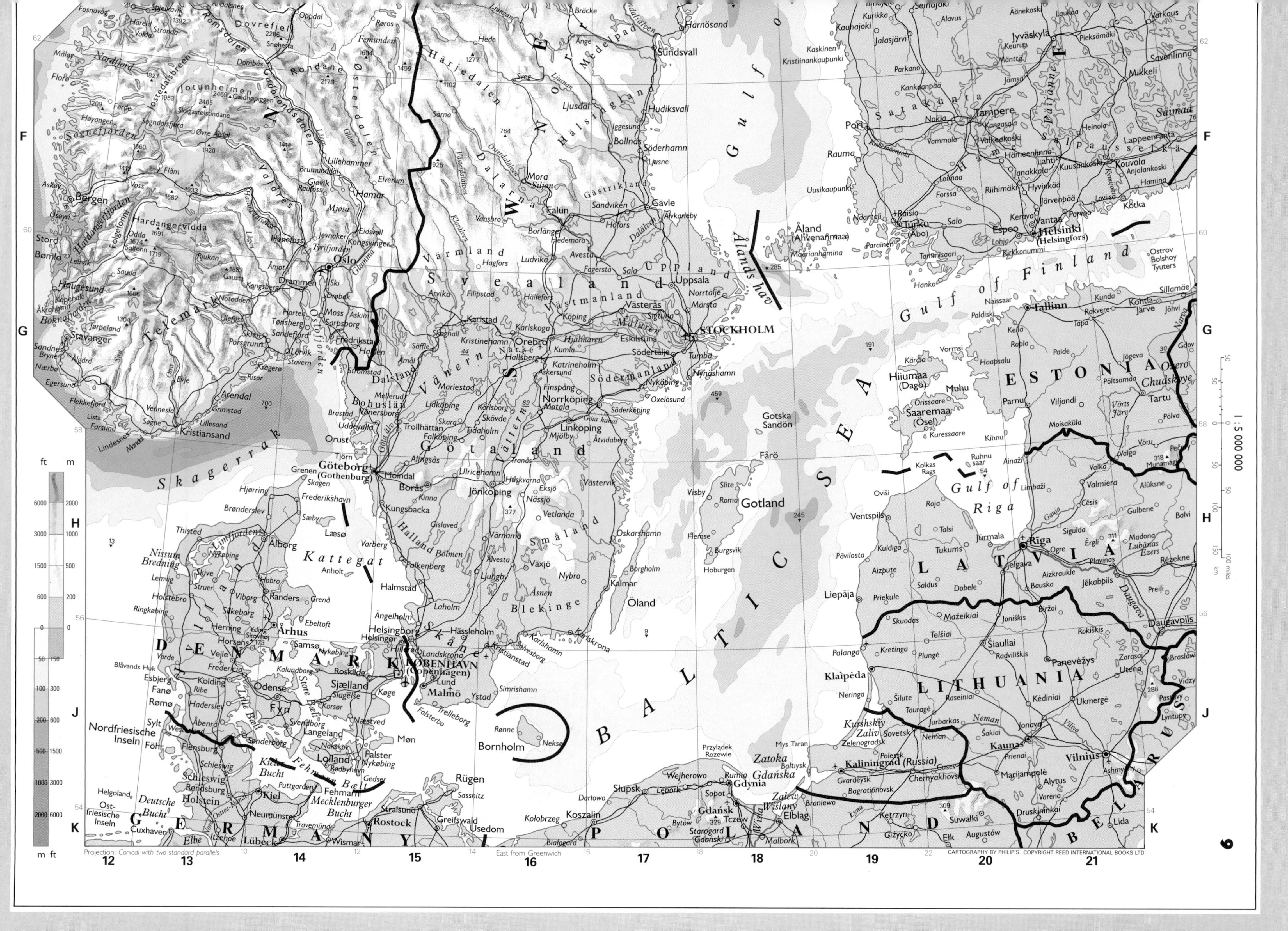

1 : 5 000 000

Projection: Conical with two standard parallels

CARTOGRAPHY BY PHILIP'S. COPYRIGHT REED INTERNATIONAL BOOKS LTD

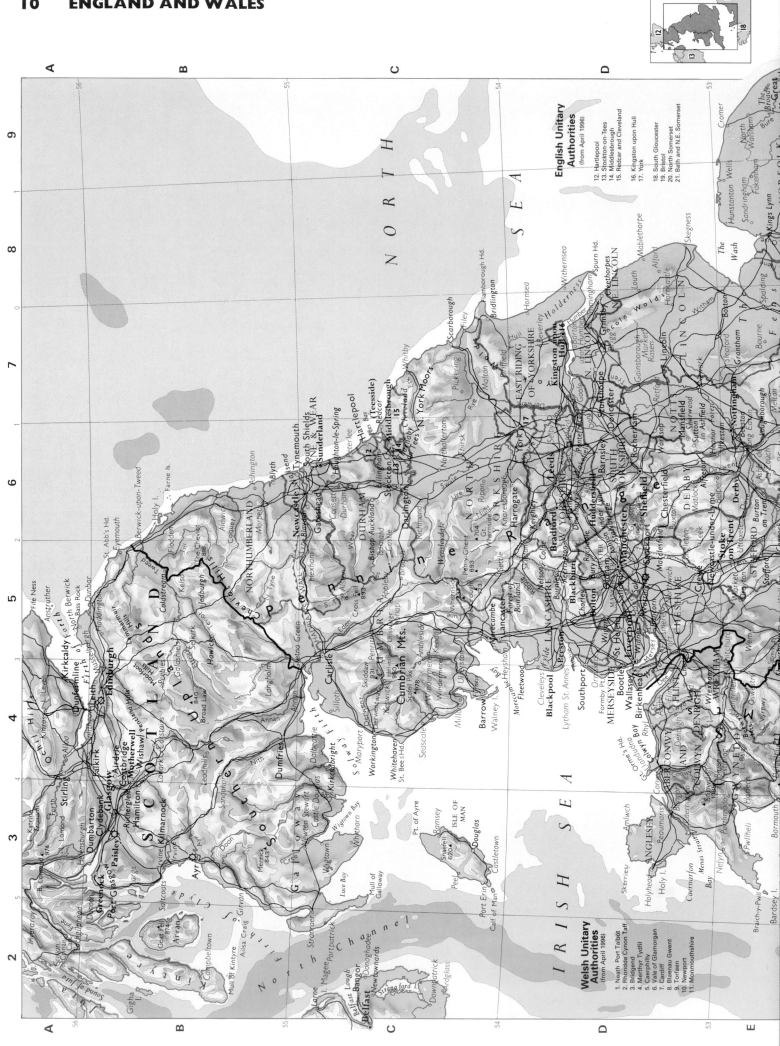

English Unitary Authorities
(from April 1996)

12. Hartlepool
13. Stockton-on-Tees
14. Middlesbrough
15. Redcar and Cleveland
16. Kingston upon Hull
17. York
18. South Gloucester
19. Bristol
20. North Somerset
21. Bath and N.E. Somerset

Welsh Unitary Authorities
(from April 1996)

1. Neath Port Talbot
2. Rhondda Cynon Taff
3. Bridgend
4. Merthyr Tydfil
5. Vale of Glamorgan
6. Caerphilly
7. Cardiff
8. Blaenau Gwent
9. Torfaen
10. Newport
11. Monmouthshire

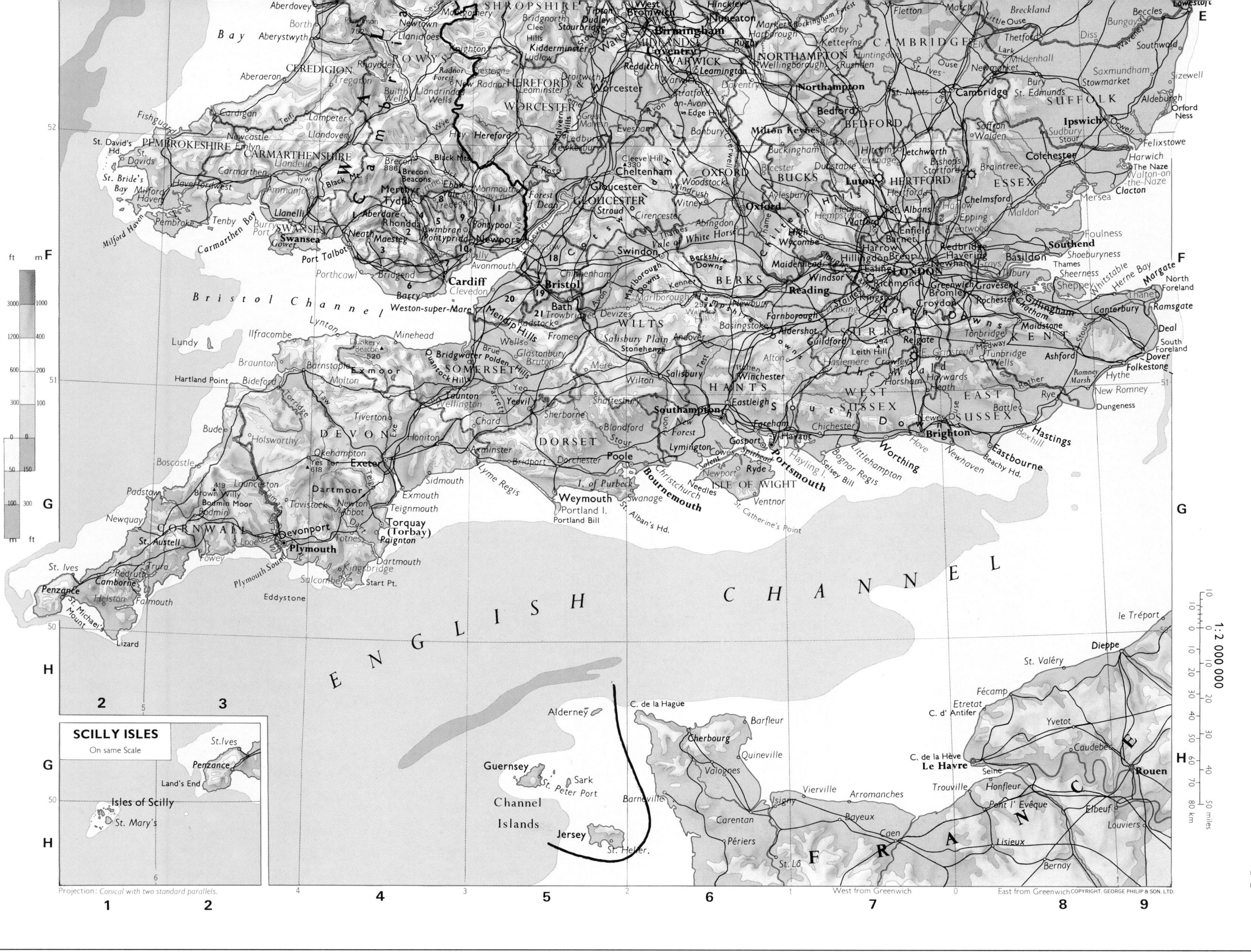

1 : 2 000 000

Projection: Conical with two standard parallels.

East from Greenwich   COPYRIGHT. GEORGE PHILIP & SON, Ltd.

ENGLISH CHANNEL

F R A N C E

Rouen
Dieppe
le Tréport
St. Valéry
Fécamp
Étretat
C. d'Antifer
C. de la Hève
Le Havre
Trouville
Honfleur
Pont l'Évêque
Lisieux
Bernay
Louviers
Elbeuf
Caudebec
Yvetot
Seine
Caen
Bayeux
Vierville
Arromanches
St. Lô
Périers
Carentan
Isigny
Valognes
Quineville
Barfleur
Cherbourg
C. de la Hague
Barneville
St. Helier
Jersey
Sark
St. Peter Port
Guernsey
Alderney
Channel Islands

Christchurch
Bournemouth
Poole
Swanage
St. Alban's Hd.
I. of Purbeck
Weymouth
Portland I.
Portland Bill

Ventnor
St. Catherine's Point
ISLE OF WIGHT
Ryde
Needles
Cowes
Gosport
Portsmouth
Havant
Hayling I.
Selsey Bill
Bognor Regis
Littlehampton
Worthing
Hove
Brighton
Newhaven
Beachy Hd.
Eastbourne
Bexhill
Hastings
Rye
Dungeness
New Romney
Romney Marsh
Hythe
Folkestone
Dover
South Foreland
Deal
Ramsgate
North Foreland
Margate
Whitstable Bay
Herne Bay
Reculver

SCILLY ISLES
On same Scale

St. Ives
Penzance
Land's End
Isles of Scilly
St. Mary's

ft   m
3000   1000
1200   400
600   200
300   100
150   50
0   0

West from Greenwich

1 : 2 000 000

Scale bar:
10 0 10 20 30 40 50 miles
10 0 10 20 30 40 50 60 70 80 km

Scottish Local Authorities
(From April 1996)
1. City of Aberdeen
2. Dundee City
3. West Dunbartonshire
4. East Dunbartonshire
5. City of Glasgow
6. Inverclyde
7. Renfrewshire
8. East Renfrewshire
9. North Lanarkshire
10. Falkirk
11. Clackmannan
12. West Lothian
13. City of Edinburgh
14. Midlothian

ORKNEY IS.
On same scale

North Ronaldsay
Westray
Rousay
Sanday
Eday
Stronsay
Stromness
Shapinsay
ORKNEY
Kirkwall
Scapa Flow
Hoy
South Ronaldsay
Pentland Firth
Dunnet Hd.
John o'Groats

SHETLAND IS.
On same scale

Unst
Fetlar
Yell
Yell Sound
SHETLAND
Whalsay
Mainland
Bressay
Scalloway
Lerwick
Foula
Sumburgh Hd.

Projection: Conical with two standard parallels.

COPYRIGHT. GEORGE PHILIP & SON, LTD.

ATLANTIC OCEAN

NORTH SEA

WESTERN ISLES

HIGHLAND

GRAMPIAN HIGHLANDS

ABERDEENSHIRE

ANGUS

PERTH

FIFE

STIRLING

ARGYLL & BUTE

NORTH AYRSHIRE

EAST AYRSHIRE

SOUTH AYRSHIRE

SOUTH LANARKSHIRE

DUMFRIES AND GALLOWAY

BORDERS

Southern Uplands

Cheviot Hills

ENGLAND

NORTHERN IRELAND

West from Greenwich

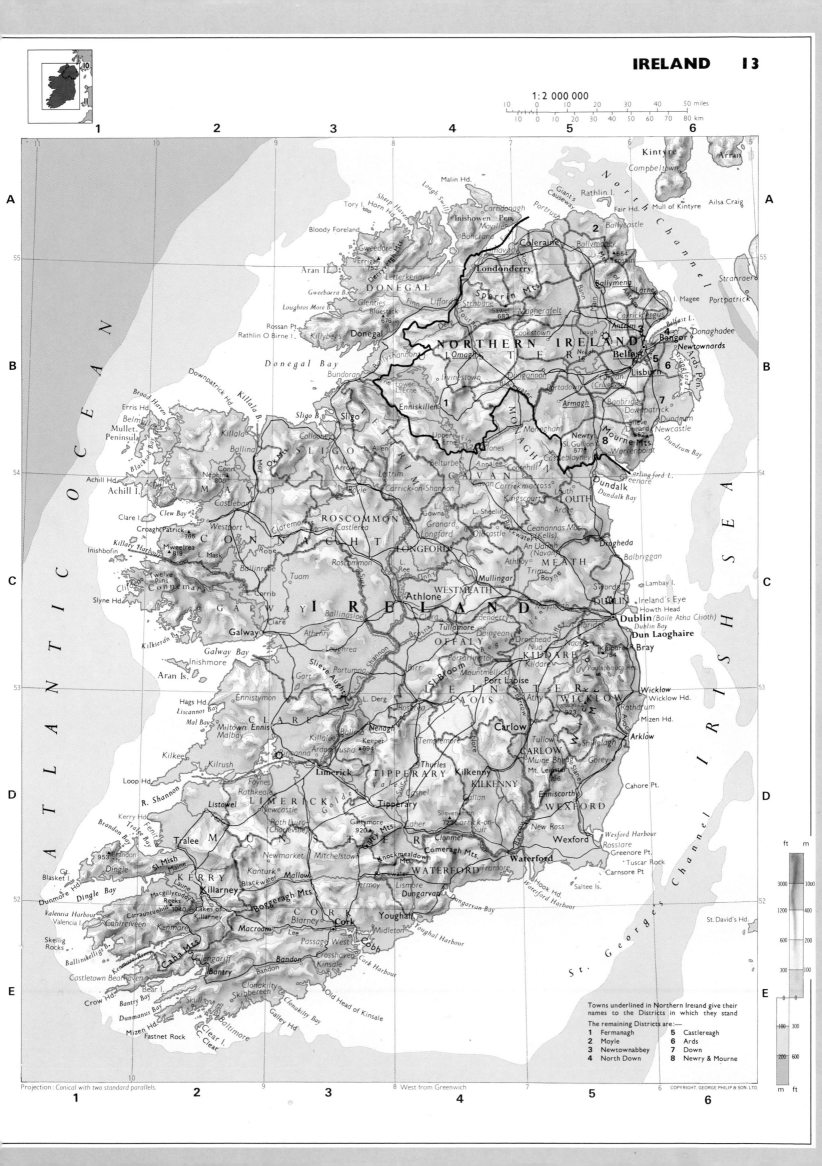

1:2 000 000

Towns underlined in Northern Ireland give their names to the Districts in which they stand

The remaining Districts are:—

1 Fermanagh	5 Castlereagh
2 Moyle	6 Ards
3 Newtownabbey	7 Down
4 North Down	8 Newry & Mourne

Projection: Conical with two standard parallels.

COPYRIGHT. GEORGE PHILIP & SON. LTD.

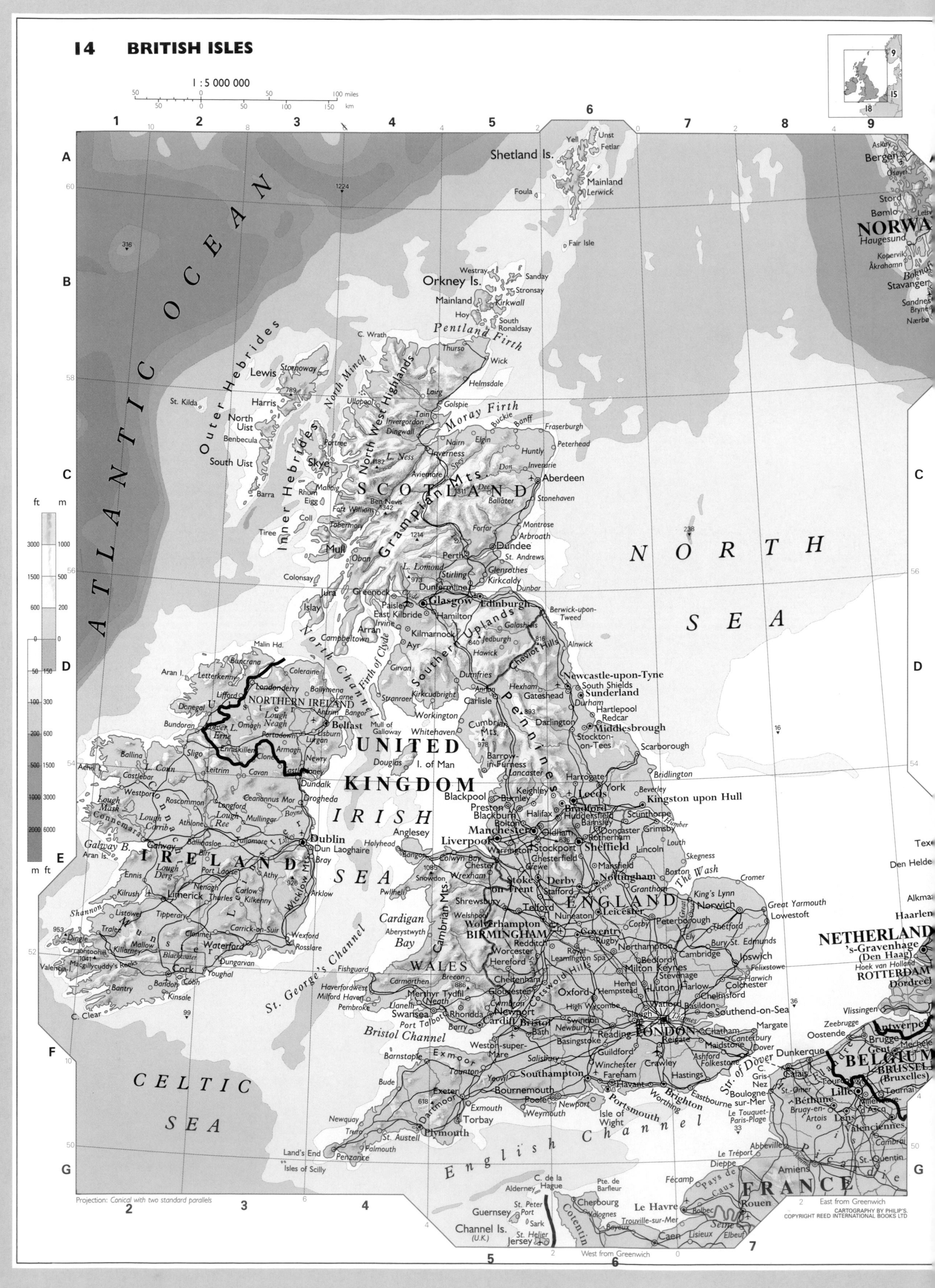

1 : 5 000 000

Projection: Conical with two standard parallels

CARTOGRAPHY BY PHILIP'S.
COPYRIGHT REED INTERNATIONAL BOOKS LTD

ATLANTIC OCEAN

NORTH SEA

NORTH CHANNEL

IRISH SEA

CELTIC SEA

ENGLISH CHANNEL

ST. GEORGE'S CHANNEL

BRISTOL CHANNEL

UNITED KINGDOM

SCOTLAND

IRELAND

NORTHERN IRELAND

WALES

ENGLAND

NORWAY

NETHERLANDS

BELGIUM

FRANCE

Shetland Is.
Orkney Is.
Outer Hebrides
Inner Hebrides
Grampian Mts.
North West Highlands
Southern Uplands
Cheviot Hills
Pennines
Cumbrian Mts.
Cambrian Mts.
Cotswold Hills
Dartmoor
Exmoor
Wicklow Mts.
Connemara

LONDON
Glasgow
Edinburgh
BIRMINGHAM
Dublin
Belfast
Cardiff
ROTTERDAM
's-Gravenhage (Den Haag)
BRUSSELS (Bruxelles)
Channel Is. (U.K.)

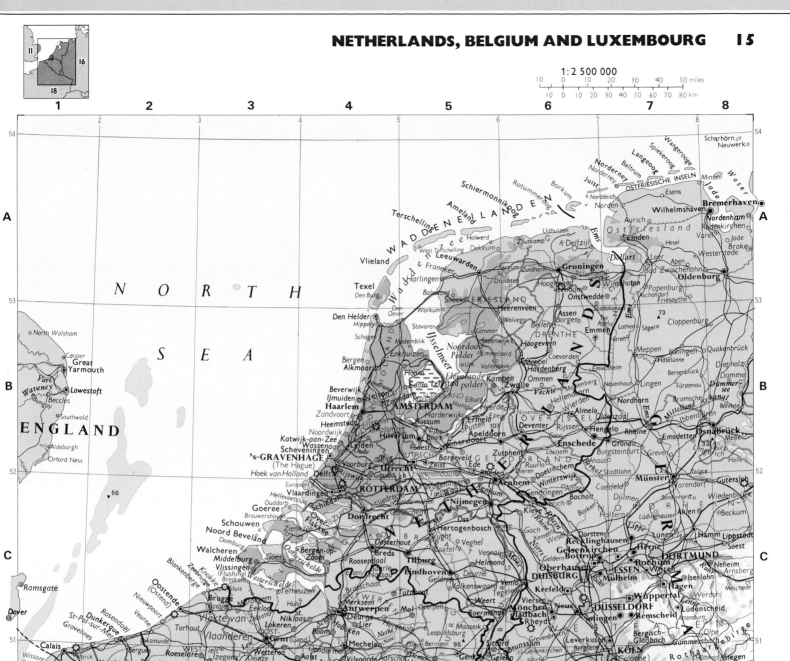

1 : 2 500 000

10 0 10 20 30 40 50 miles

10 0 10 20 30 40 50 60 70 80 km

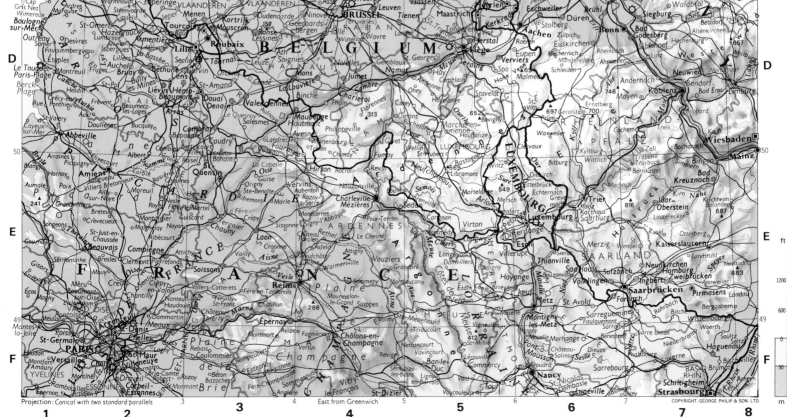

Projection: Conical with two standard parallels

East from Greenwich

COPYRIGHT. GEORGE PHILIP & SON. LTD.

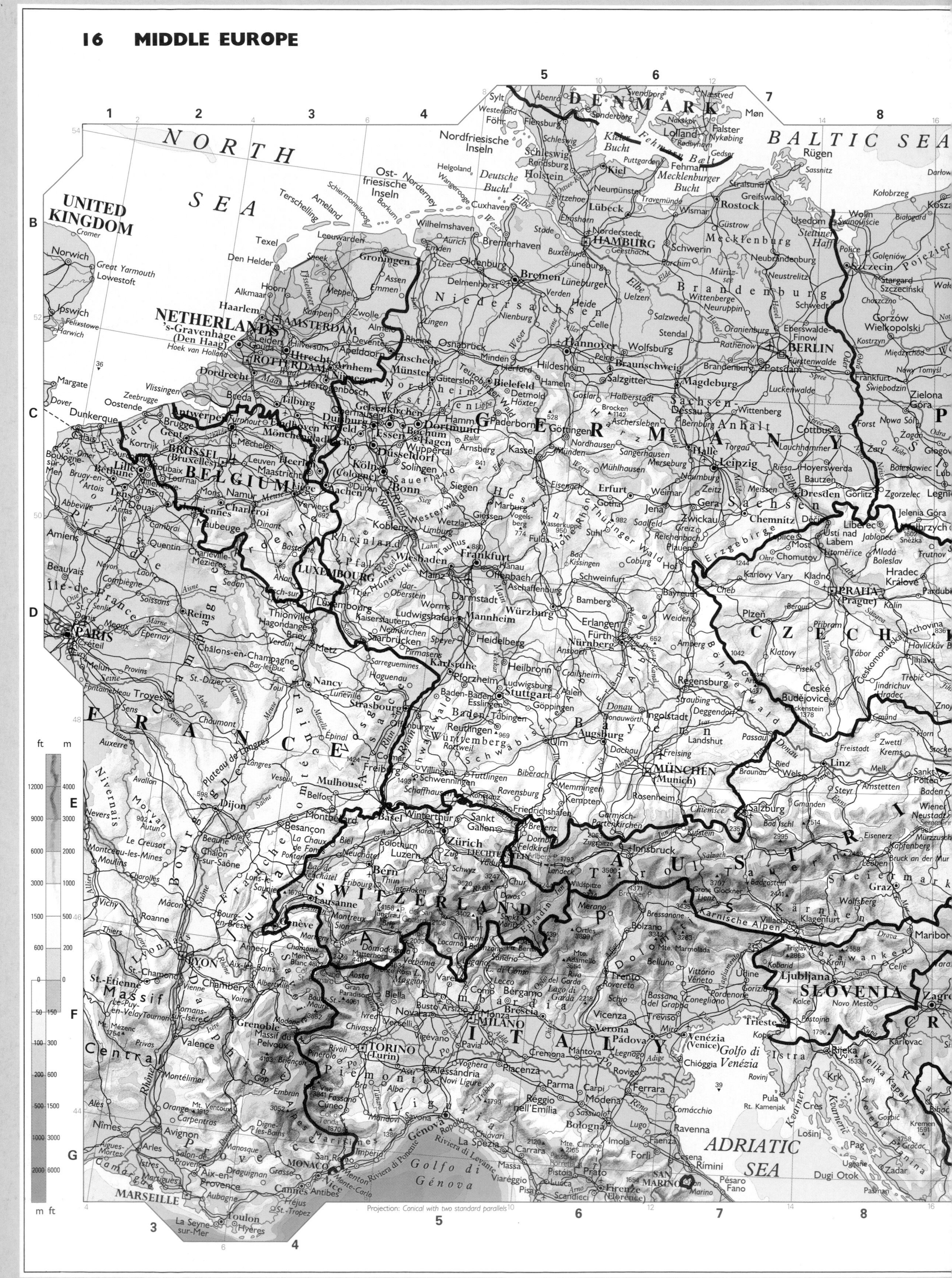
NORTH SEA
BALTIC SEA
UNITED KINGDOM
NETHERLANDS
BELGIUM
LUXEMBOURG
GERMANY
DENMARK
FRANCE
SWITZERLAND
LIECHTENSTEIN
AUSTRIA
CZECH
SLOVENIA
ITALY
MONACO
SAN MARINO
ADRIATIC SEA
Golfo di Génova
Golfo di Venézia
AMSTERDAM
's-Gravenhage (Den Haag)
ROTTERDAM
BRUSSEL (Bruxelles)
PARIS
BERLIN
HAMBURG
MÜNCHEN (Munich)
PRAHA (Prague)
MILANO
TORINO (Turin)
LYON
MARSEILLE
Frankfurt
Köln (Cologne)
Stuttgart
Zürich
Bern
Ljubljana
Projection: Conical with two standard parallels

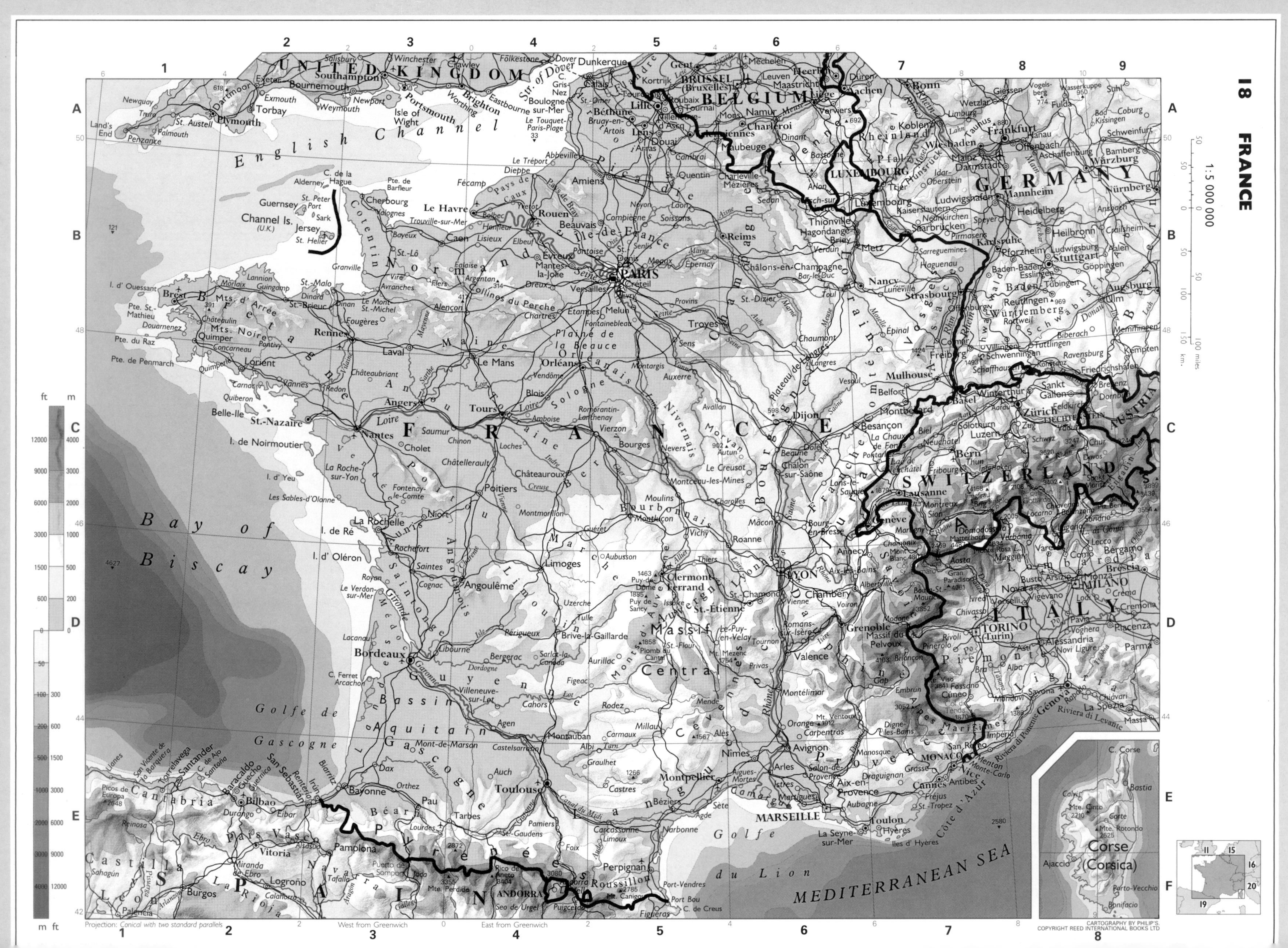
1:5 000 000
50 0 50 100 miles
50 0 50 100 150 km.
English Channel
Bay of Biscay
Golfe de Gascogne
Golfe du Lion
MEDITERRANEAN SEA
FRANCE
UNITED KINGDOM
BELGIUM
LUXEMBOURG
GERMANY
SWITZERLAND
ITALY
SPAIN
ANDORRA
MONACO
AUSTRIA
Normandie
Bretagne
Massif Central
Pyrénées
PARIS
MARSEILLE
LYON
Bordeaux
Toulouse
Nantes
Corse (Corsica)
Projection: Conical with two standard parallels
West from Greenwich
East from Greenwich
CARTOGRAPHY BY PHILIP'S.
COPYRIGHT REED INTERNATIONAL BOOKS LTD

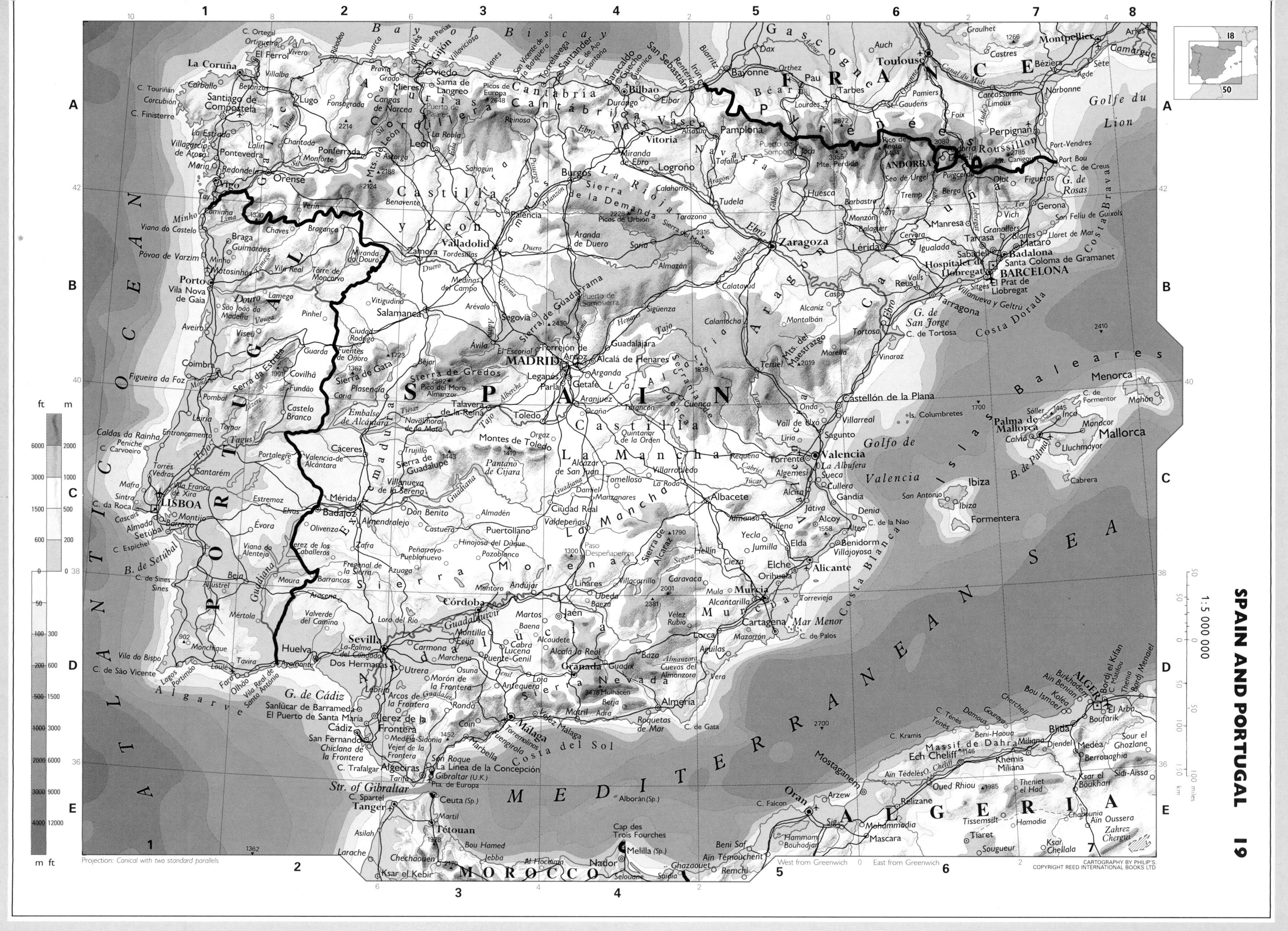
1:5 000 000
50 0 50 100 miles
50 0 50 100 150 km
SPAIN
PORTUGAL
FRANCE
ALGERIA
MOROCCO
ANDORRA
MADRID
LISBOA
BARCELONA
Valencia
Sevilla
Zaragoza
Málaga
Bilbao
Porto
Palma de Mallorca
Mallorca
Menorca
Ibiza
Formentera
Golfe du Lion
Golfo de Valencia
G. de Cádiz
Str. of Gibraltar
Projection: Conical with two standard parallels
West from Greenwich
East from Greenwich
CARTOGRAPHY BY PHILIP'S. COPYRIGHT REED INTERNATIONAL BOOKS LTD
m ft
ft m

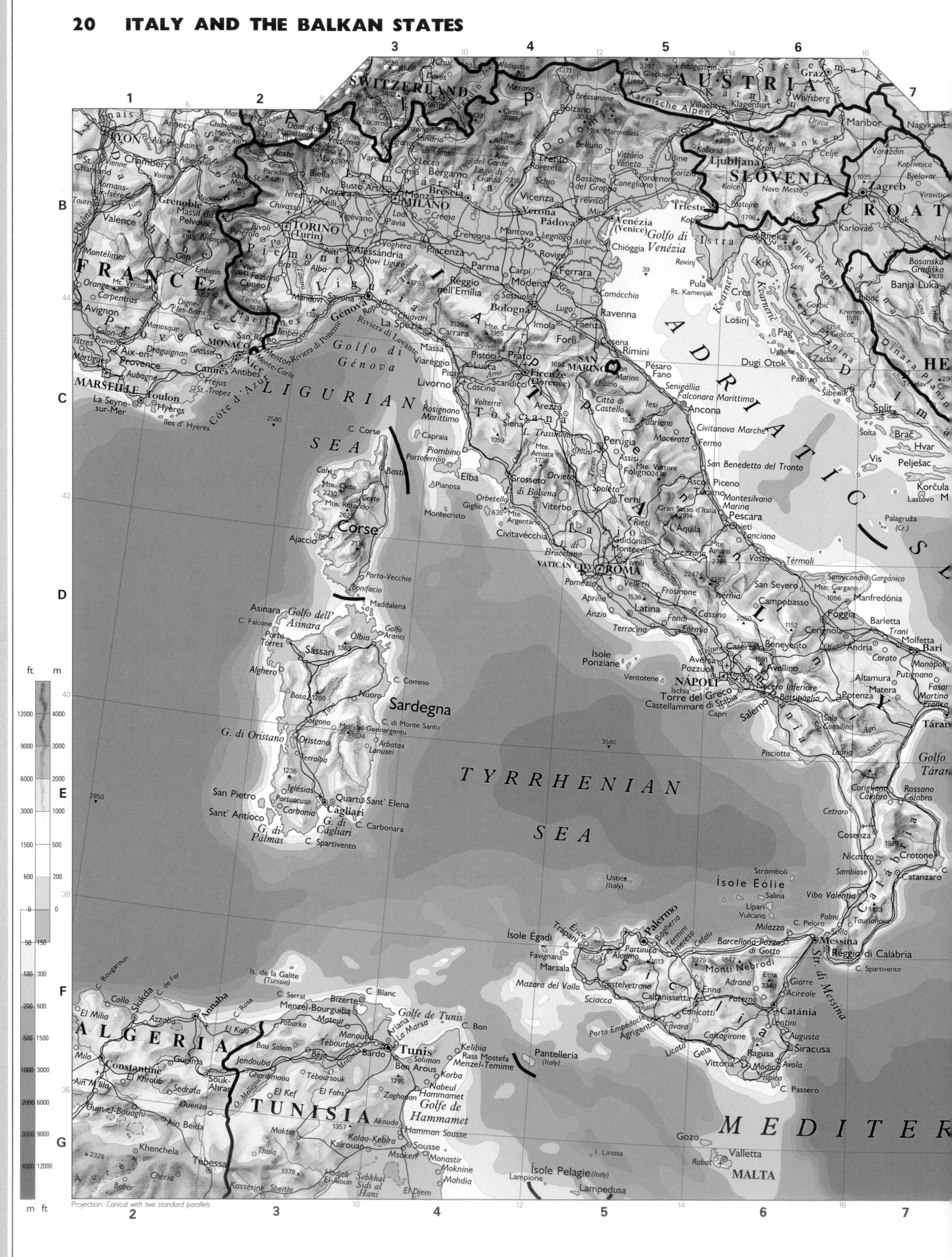
SWITZERLAND
AUSTRIA
SLOVENIA
CROATIA
FRANCE
MONACO
SAN MARINO
VATICAN CITY
ITALY
ALGERIA
TUNISIA
MALTA
LIGURIAN SEA
TYRRHENIAN SEA
ADRIATIC SEA
MEDITER
Golfo di Génova
Golfo di Venézia
Golfo di Táranto
Golfe de Tunis
Golfe de Hammamet
Golfo dell' Asinara
G. di Oristano
G. di Cágliari
G. di Pálmas
Sir. di Messina
Corse
Sardegna
Elba
Sicilia
Ísole Eólie
Ísole Égadi
Ísole Ponziane
Ísole Pelagie (Italy)
Ustica (Italy)
Pantelleria (Italy)
Lampedusa
Linosa
Gozo
Valletta
Capri
Ischia
Montecristo
Giglio
Capraia
Pianosa
San Pietro
Sant' Antioco
Asinara
Maddalena
Strómboli
Salina
Lípari
Vulcano
Favignana
Marsala
Lampione
Is. de la Galite (Tunisia)
MILANO
TORINO (Turin)
ROMA
NÁPOLI
Venézia (Venice)
Génova
Firenze (Florence)
Bologna
Palermo
Catánia
Messina
Réggio di Calábria
Bari
Táranto
Cágliari
Sassari
Ancona
Pescara
Perúgia
Verona
Pádova
Trieste
Ljubljana
Zagreb
Rijeka
Split
Zadar
Graz
Klagenfurt
Villach
Maribor
Bolzano
Trento
Brescia
Bérgamo
Parma
Modena
Ferrara
Ravenna
Rímini
Livorno
Pisa
La Spezia
Siena
Arezzo
Grosseto
Viterbo
Terni
Foggia
Salerno
Caserta
Avellino
Benevento
Potenza
Cosenza
Catanzaro
Crotone
Siracusa
Ragusa
Trápani
Agrigento
Caltanissetta
Enna
Tunis
Bizerte
Sousse
Kairouan
Monastir
Annaba
Constantine
Skikda
Tébessa
Marseille
Toulon
Nice
Cannes
Aix-en-Provence
Avignon
Grenoble
Lyon
Chambéry
Valence
Ajaccio
Bastia
Bonifacio
Porto-Vecchio
Calvi
Corte
C. Corse
C. Bon
C. Passero
C. Spartivento
C. Carbonara
C. Peloro
C. Blanc
C. Serrat
C. Bougaroun
C. de Fer
C. Rosa
C. Falcone
C. Comino
C. di Monte Santu
Mte. Cinto 2710
Mte. Rotondo 2625
Etna 3340
Mtes. Gran Sasso d'Italia 2914
Mte. Amaro 2795
Mte. Vettore 2478
Mte. Cimone 2165
Monti Nebrodi
Mti. del Gennargentu 1834
Gran Paradiso 4061
Mont Blanc 4807
Matterhorn 4478
Gross Glockner 3797
Karnische Alpen
Dolomiti
Alpes Maritimes
Côte d'Azur
Riviera di Ponente
Riviera di Levante
Lombardia
Piemonte
Liguria
Toscana
Lazio
Calabria
L. di Bolsena
L. Trasimeno
L. di Bracciano
Lago di Garda
1 2 3 4 5 6 7
B C D E F G
ft m
12000 4000
9000 3000
6000 2000
3000 1000
1500 500
600 200
0 0
50 150
100 300
200 600
500 1500
1000 3000
2000 6000
3000 9000
4000 12000
m ft
Projection: Conical with two standard parallels

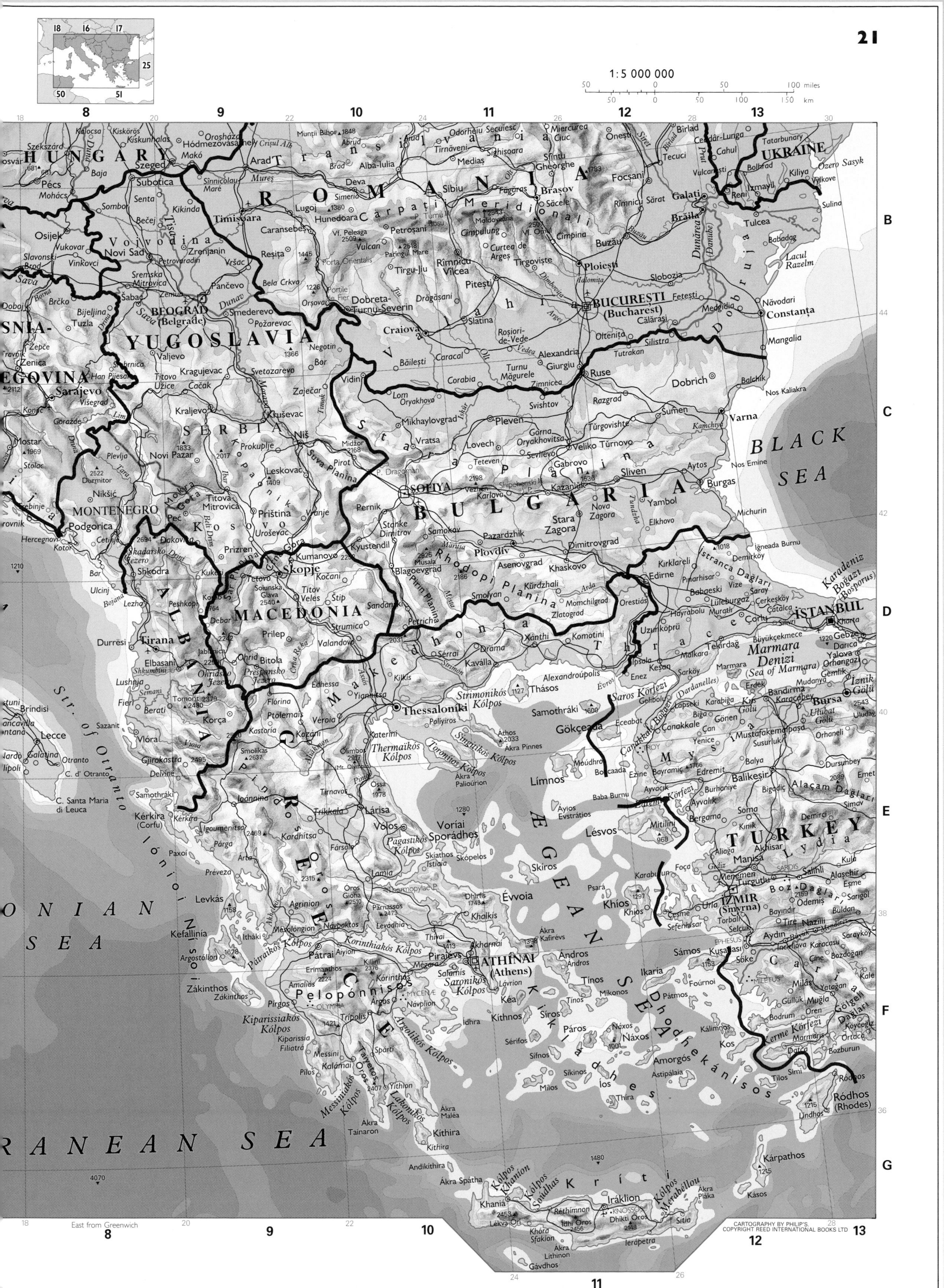
1:5 000 000
miles
km
HUNGARY
ROMANIA
YUGOSLAVIA
BULGARIA
MACEDONIA
ALBANIA
GREECE
TURKEY
UKRAINE
MONTENEGRO
SERBIA
BLACK SEA
AEGEAN SEA
IONIAN SEA
MEDITERRANEAN SEA
BEOGRAD (Belgrade)
BUCUREŞTI (Bucharest)
SOFIYA
ATHINAI (Athens)
İSTANBUL
Thessaloníki
Skopje
Tirana
Sarajevo
Marmara Denizi (Sea of Marmara)
East from Greenwich
CARTOGRAPHY BY PHILIP'S. COPYRIGHT REED INTERNATIONAL BOOKS LTD

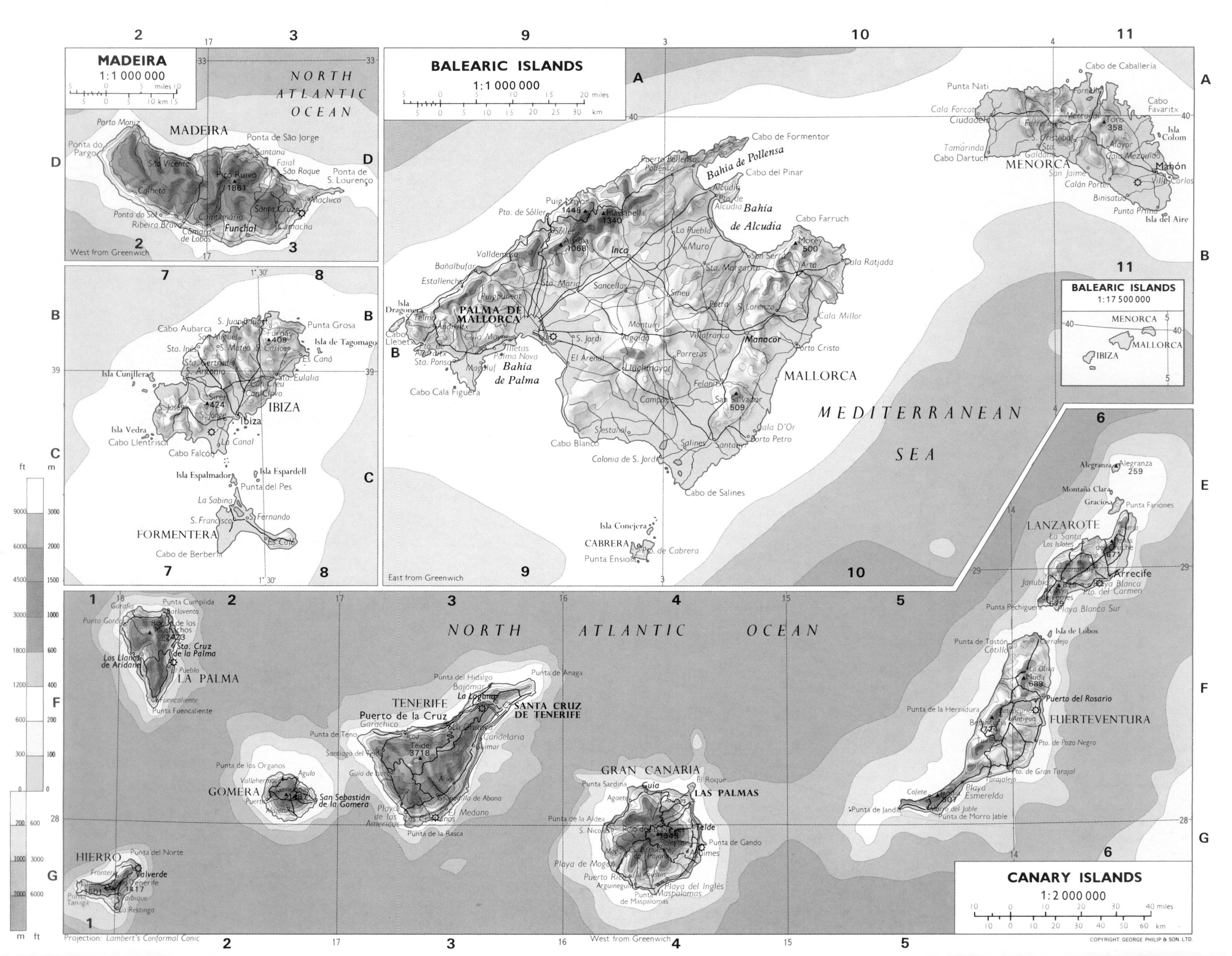

BALEARIC ISLANDS
1:17 500 000

MENORCA
MALLORCA
IBIZA

MENORCA

BALEARIC ISLANDS
1:1 000 000

MALLORCA

MEDITERRANEAN SEA

MADEIRA
1:1 000 000

NORTH ATLANTIC OCEAN

MADEIRA

IBIZA

FORMENTERA

NORTH ATLANTIC OCEAN

CANARY ISLANDS
1:2 000 000

LANZAROTE

FUERTEVENTURA

GRAN CANARIA
LAS PALMAS

TENERIFE
SANTA CRUZ DE TENERIFE

GOMERA

LA PALMA

HIERRO

Projection Lambert's Conformal Conic

COPYRIGHT GEORGE PHILIP & SON LTD

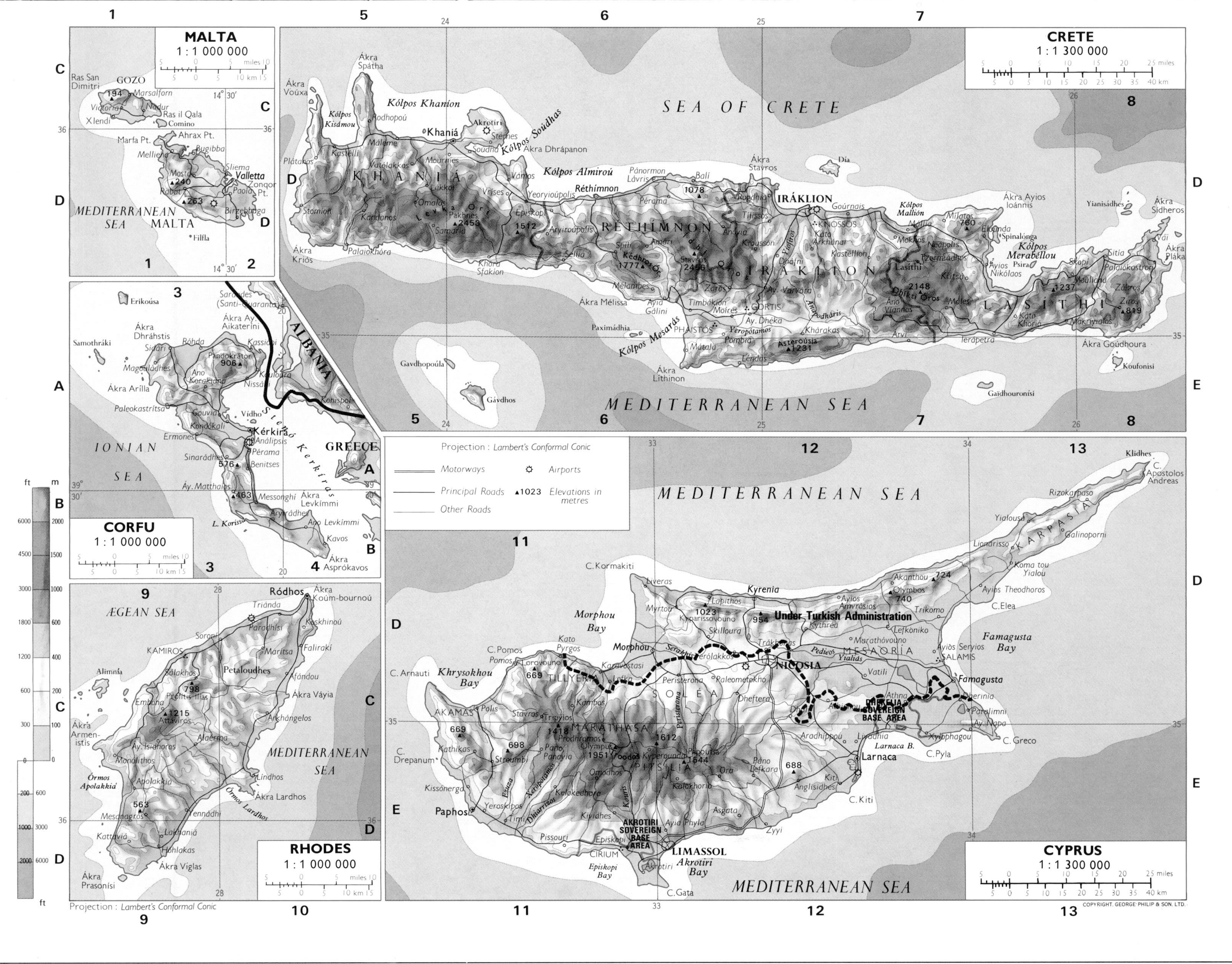
MALTA
1 : 1 000 000
GOZO
Victoria
Marsalforn
Ras il Qala
Comino
MALTA
Valletta
Filfla
MEDITERRANEAN SEA
CRETE
1 : 1 300 000
SEA OF CRETE
MEDITERRANEAN SEA
Kólpos Khaníon
Khaniá
Kólpos Soúdhas
Kólpos Almiroú
Réthimnon
IRÁKLION
Kólpos Maliíon
Kólpos Merabéllou
Kólpos Mesarás
KHANIÁ
RÉTHIMNON
IRÁKLION
LASÍTHI
Dia
Gávdhos
Gavdhopoúla
CORFU
1 : 1 000 000
Kérkira
ALBANIA
GREECE
IONIAN SEA
Stenó Kerkíras
RHODES
1 : 1 000 000
Ródhos
ÆGEAN SEA
MEDITERRANEAN SEA
Projection : Lambert's Conformal Conic
Motorways
Principal Roads
Other Roads
Airports
▲1023 Elevations in metres
CYPRUS
1 : 1 300 000
MEDITERRANEAN SEA
Kyrenia
Under Turkish Administration
NICOSIA
Famagusta
Famagusta Bay
Morphou
Morphou Bay
Khrysokhou Bay
Larnaca
Larnaca B.
LIMASSOL
Akrotiri Bay
Episkopi Bay
Paphos
AKROTIRI SOVEREIGN BASE AREA
DHEKELIA SOVEREIGN BASE AREA
KARPASIA
MESAORIA
TROÖDOS
COPYRIGHT, GEORGE PHILIP & SON, LTD.

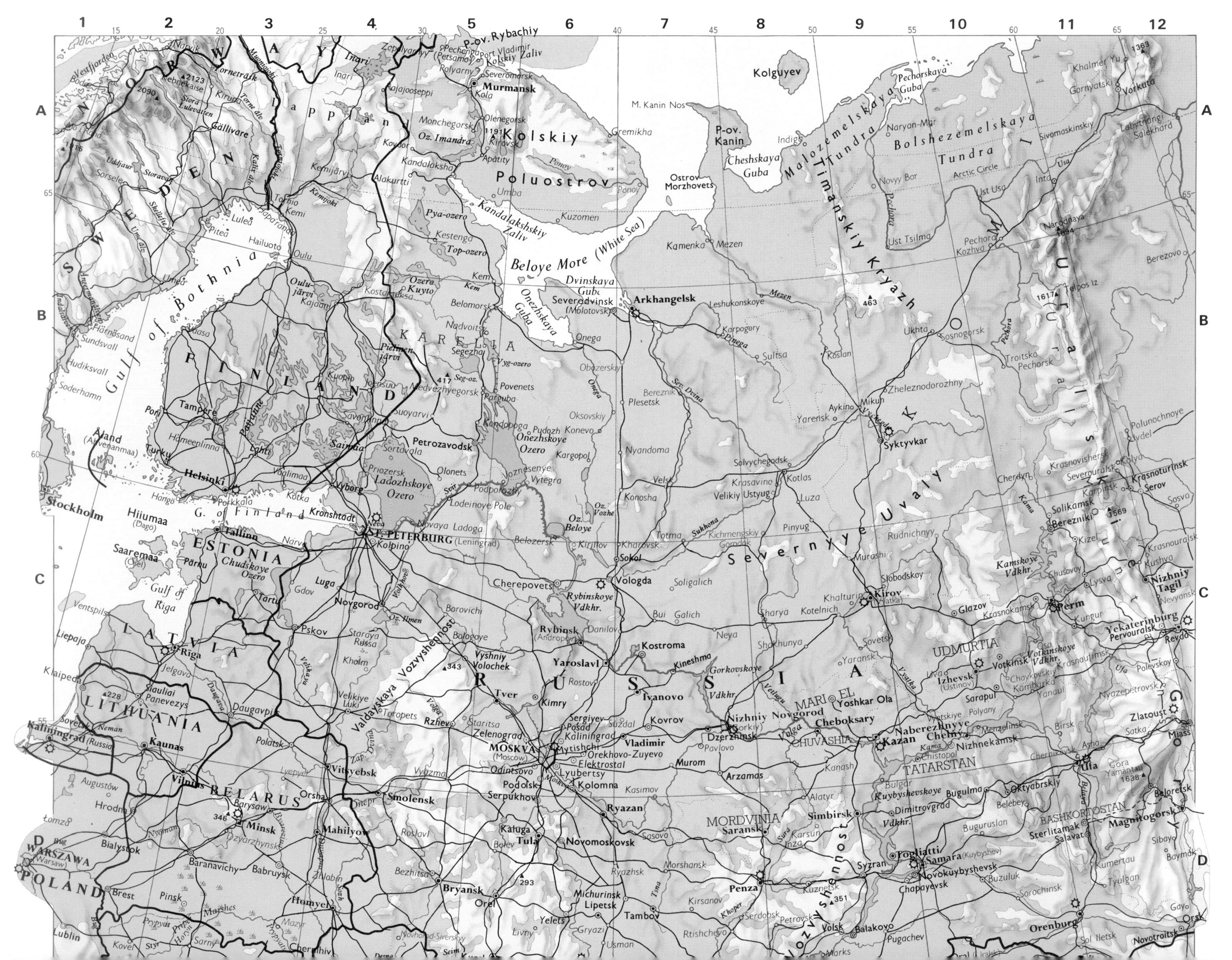
Kolguyev
Timanskiy Kryazh
Bolshezemelskaya Tundra
Kolskiy Poluostrov
Beloye More (White Sea)
Onezhskaya Guba
Dvinskaya Guba
Murmansk
Arkhangelsk
Syktyvkar
Kirov
Perm
Yekaterinburg
Ufa
Orenburg
Samara (Kuybyshev)
Kazan
Nizhniy Novgorod
Yaroslavl
Vologda
Kostroma
Ivanovo
Vladimir
MOSKVA (Moscow)
Tula
Ryazan
Penza
Tambov
Bryansk
Smolensk
Tver
Novgorod
ST. PETERSBURG
Petrozavodsk
Ladozhskoye Ozero
Helsinki
Tallinn
Riga
Vilnius
Kaunas
Minsk
Kaliningrad
WARSZAWA (Warsaw)
Stockholm
FINLAND
ESTONIA
LATVIA
LITHUANIA
BELARUS
POLAND
TATARSTAN
UDMURTIA
MORDVINIA
CHUVASHIA
MARI EL
BASHKORTOSTAN
Gulf of Bothnia
G. of Finland
Gulf of Riga

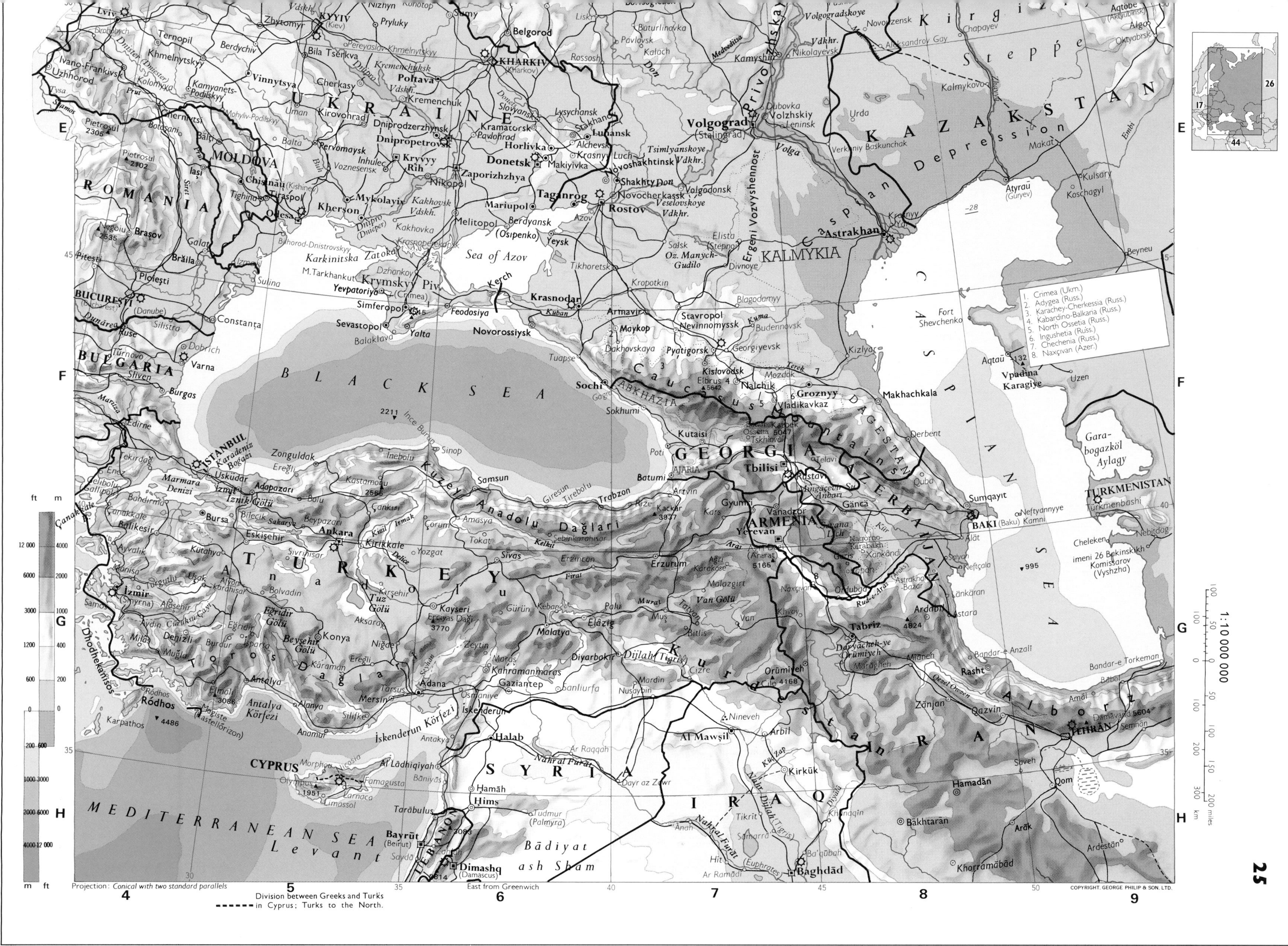
1:10 000 000
100 50 0 50 100 150 200 miles
100 0 100 200 300 km
1. Crimea (Ukr.)
2. Adygea (Russ.)
3. Karachey-Cherkessia (Russ.)
4. Kabardino-Balkana (Russ.)
5. North Ossetia (Russ.)
6. Ingushetia (Russ.)
7. Chechenia (Russ.)
8. Naxçivan (Azer.)
UKRAINE
MOLDOVA
ROMANIA
BULGARIA
TURKEY
GEORGIA
ARMENIA
AZERBAIJAN
KAZAKSTAN
KALMYKIA
DAGESTAN
ABKHAZIA
AJARIA
TURKMENISTAN
SYRIA
IRAQ
IRAN
LEBANON
CYPRUS
BLACK SEA
CASPIAN SEA
Sea of Azov
MEDITERRANEAN SEA
Levant
Caspian Depression
Caucasus Mountains
Anadolu Dağlari
Toros Dağlari
Kurdistan
Alborz
Bādiyat ash Sham
Garabogazköl Aylagy
KYYIV (Kiev)
KHARKIV (Kharkov)
Volgograd (Stalingrad)
Astrakhan
Rostov
Donetsk
Dnipropetrovsk
Odesa
Chişinău
BUCUREŞTI (Bucharest)
Varna
Burgas
Constanţa
Sevastopol
Simferopol
Yalta
Kerch
Krasnodar
Novorossiysk
Sochi
Stavropol
Groznyy
Makhachkala
Tbilisi
Yerevan
BAKI (Baku)
İSTANBUL
Ankara
İzmir (Smyrna)
Bursa
Konya
Adana
Kayseri
Trabzon
Samsun
Erzurum
Tabriz
TEHRĀN
Rasht
Hamadān
Halab
Hamāh
Hims
Dimashq (Damascus)
Bayrūt (Beirut)
Al Mawşil
Kirkūk
Baghdād
Elbrus 5642
Kazbek 5047
Ağri Daği (Ararat) 5165
Damāvand 5604
Erciyas Daği 3770
2211
4486
995
-28
Projection: Conical with two standard parallels
Division between Greeks and Turks in Cyprus; Turks to the North.
East from Greenwich
ft m
12 000 4000
6000 2000
3000 1000
1200 400
600 200
0 0
200-600
1000-3000
2000-6000
4000-12 000
m ft

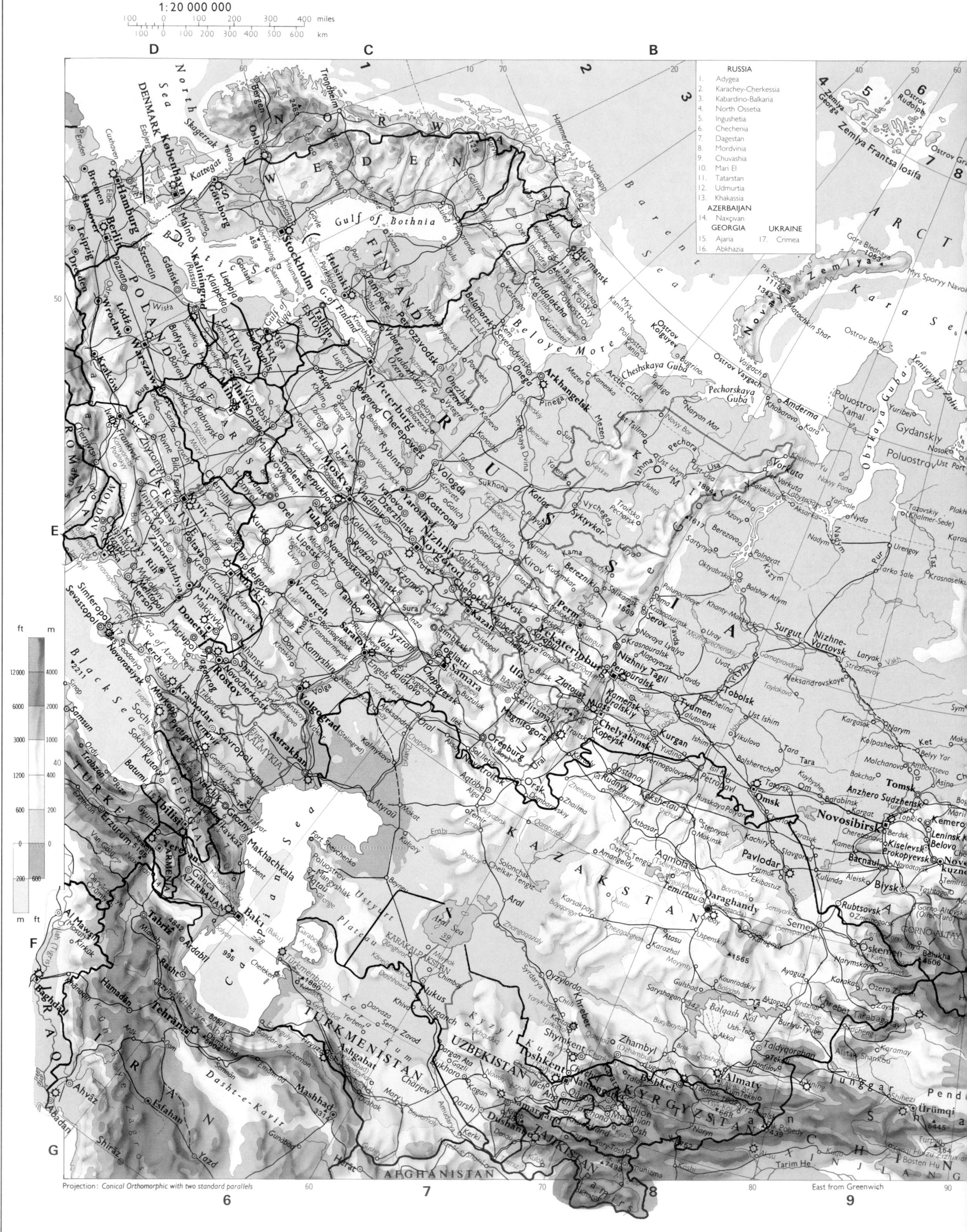

1:20 000 000
100 0 100 200 300 400 miles
100 0 100 200 300 400 500 600 km
D
C
B
E
F
G
6
7
8
9
RUSSIA
1. Adygea
2. Karachey-Cherkessia
3. Kabardino-Balkaria
4. North Ossetia
5. Ingushetia
6. Chechenia
7. Dagestan
8. Mordvinia
9. Chuvashia
10. Mari El
11. Tatarstan
12. Udmurtia
13. Khakassia
AZERBAIJAN
14. Naxçivan
GEORGIA
15. Ajaria
16. Abkhazia
UKRAINE
17. Crimea
North Sea
Skagerrak
Kattegat
Gulf of Bothnia
G. of Finland
Barents Sea
Beloye More
Kara Sea
Zemlya Frantsa Iosifa
Black Sea
Sea of Azov
Caspian Sea
Aral Sea
Balqash Köl
NORWAY
SWEDEN
FINLAND
DENMARK
POLAND
ESTONIA
LATVIA
LITHUANIA
BELARUS
UKRAINE
MOLDOVA
ROMANIA
RUSSIA
GEORGIA
ARMENIA
AZERBAIJAN
TURKEY
IRAN
IRAQ
KAZAKSTAN
UZBEKISTAN
TURKMENISTAN
KYRGYZSTAN
TAJIKISTAN
AFGHANISTAN
ft
m
Projection: Conical Orthomorphic with two standard parallels
East from Greenwich

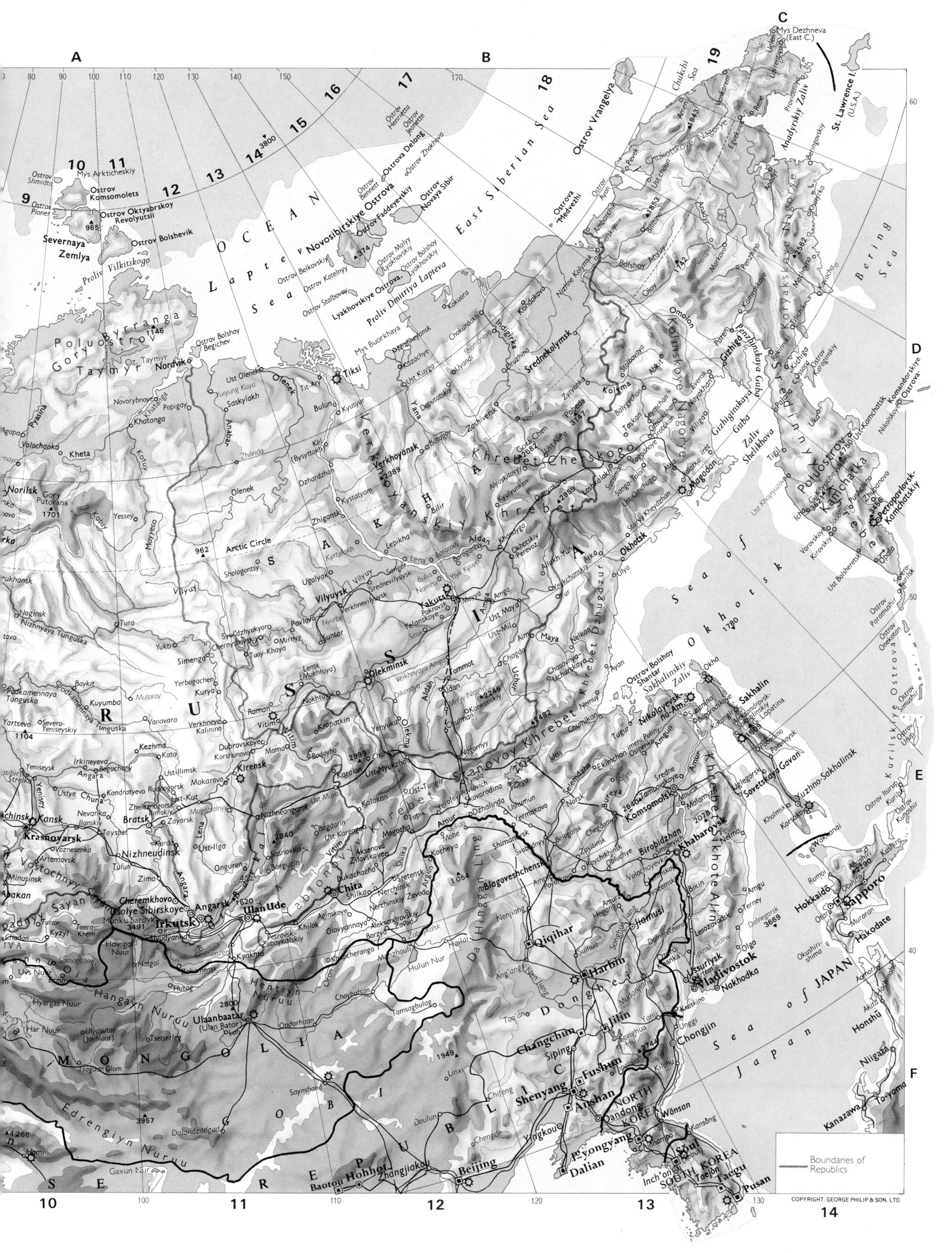

A   B   C

80   90   100   110   120   130   140   150   160   170   180

10   11   12   13   14   15   16   17   18   19

Mys Dezhneva (East C.)

St. Lawrence I. (U.S.A.)

Chukchi Sea

ARCTIC OCEAN

Laptev Sea

East Siberian Sea

Ostrov Vrangelya

Ostrov Shmidta
Mys Arkticheskiy
Ostrov Pioner
Ostrov Komsomolets
Ostrov Oktyabrskoy Revolyutsii
965
Ostrov Bolshevik
Severnaya Zemlya
Proliv Vilkitskogo

Novosibirskiye Ostrava
Ostrova Delong
Ostrov Zhokhova
Ostrov Henrietta
Ostrova Bennetta
Ostrov Faddeyevskiy
Ostrov Novaya Sibir
Ostrova Medvezhi

Poluostrov Taymyr
Gory Byrranga 1146
Oz. Taymyr

Norilsk
Gory Putorana 1701

RUSSIA

Bering Sea

Poluostrov Kamchatka

Sea of Okhotsk

Sakhalin

Vladivostok

Sea of JAPAN

Hokkaidō
Sapporo
Hakodate
Honshū

MONGOLIA
Ulaanbaatar (Ulan Bator)

Beijing
Shenyang
Harbin
Changchun
Jilin

NORTH KOREA
Pyongyang

SOUTH KOREA
Seoul
Taegu
Pusan

GOBI DESERT

Boundaries of Republics

10   11   12   13   14

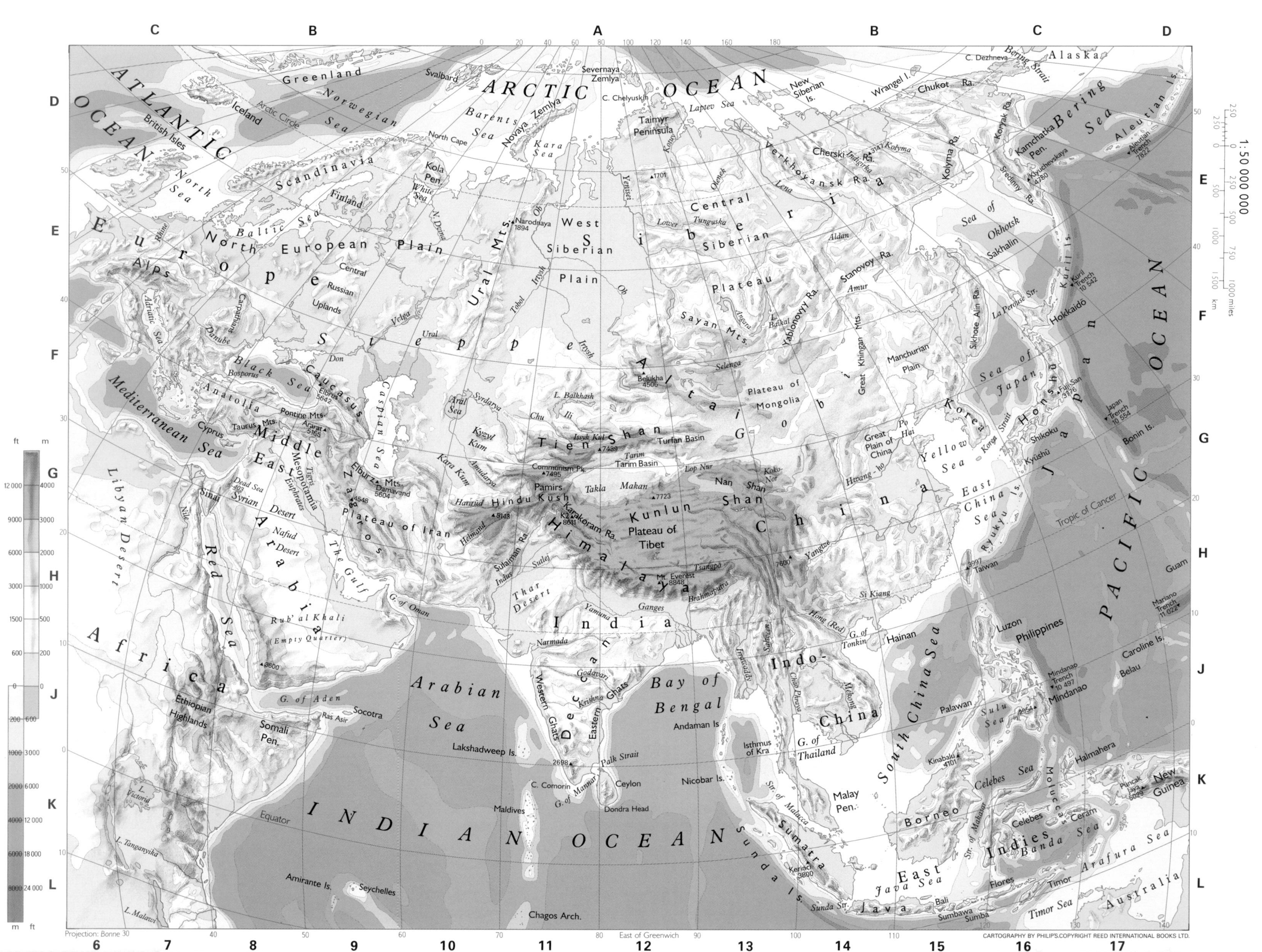
1:50 000 000
250 0 250 500 750 1000 miles
250 0 500 1000 1500 km
ARCTIC OCEAN
PACIFIC OCEAN
INDIAN OCEAN
ATLANTIC OCEAN
Tropic of Cancer
Arctic Circle
Equator
Greenland
Iceland
British Isles
Svalbard
Norwegian Sea
North Sea
Baltic Sea
Barents Sea
Kara Sea
Laptev Sea
Novaya Zemlya
Severnaya Zemlya
C. Chelyuskin
Taimyr Peninsula
New Siberian Is.
Wrangel I.
C. Dezhneva
Bering Strait
Alaska
Bering Sea
Aleutian Is.
Aleutian Trench 7822
Chukot Ra.
Koryak Ra.
Kolyma Ra.
Cherski Ra.
Kamchatka Pen.
Klyuchevskaya 4750
Sredinny Ra.
Kuril Is.
Kuril Trench 10 542
Sea of Okhotsk
Sakhalin
La Perouse Str.
Hokkaido
Honshu
Fuji San 3776
Japan
Japan Trench 10 554
Sea of Japan
Korea
Korea Strait
Shikoku
Kyūshū
Bonin Is.
Yellow Sea
East China Sea
Ryukyu Is.
Taiwan
3997
Guam
Mariana Trench 11 022
Luzon
Philippines
Mindanao
Mindanao Trench 10 497
Caroline Is.
Belau
Hainan
G. of Tonkin
South China Sea
Palawan
Sulu Sea
Kinabalu 4101
Borneo
Celebes
Celebes Sea
Molucca Sea
Halmahera
Ceram
Puncak Jaya 5029
New Guinea
East Indies
Banda Sea
Arafura Sea
Timor
Timor Sea
Australia
Str. of Makasar
Flores
Bali
Sumbawa
Sumba
Java
Java Sea
Sunda Str.
Sunda Is.
Sumatra
Kerinci 3800
Str. of Malacca
Malay Pen.
G. of Thailand
Isthmus of Kra
Indo-China
Mekong
Chao Phraya
Salween
Irrawaddy
Hong (Red)
Si Kiang
Yangtze
Hwang-ho
Great Plain of China
Po Hai
China
Manchurian Plain
Great Khingan Mts.
Sikhote Alin Ra.
Amur
Stanovoy Ra.
Aldan
Yablonovyy Ra.
L. Baikal
Selenga
Angara
Sayan Mts.
Plateau of Mongolia
Gobi
Altai
Belukha 4506
Koko Nor
Nan Shan
Lop Nur
Turfan Basin
Tarim
Tarim Basin
Takla Makan
7723
Kunlun Shan
Plateau of Tibet
Tsangpo
Brahmaputra
7600
Mt. Everest 8848
Himalaya
Karakoram Ra.
K2 8611
Hindu Kush
Pamirs
Communism Pk. 7495
Tien Shan
Issyk Kul
7439
Ili
Chu
L. Balkhash
Syrdarya
Amudarya
Aral Sea
Kyzyl Kum
Kara Kum
Harirud
Helmand
7143
Sulaiman Ra.
Indus
Sutlej
Thar Desert
India
Yamuna
Ganges
Narmada
Godavari
Krishna
Deccan
Western Ghats
Eastern Ghats
2698
Palk Strait
G. of Mannar
C. Comorin
Ceylon
Dondra Head
Bay of Bengal
Andaman Is.
Nicobar Is.
Arabian Sea
Lakshadweep Is.
Maldives
Chagos Arch.
Seychelles
Amirante Is.
Central Siberian Plateau
Lower Tunguska
Olenek
Lena
Verkhoyansk Ra.
Kolyma
Indigirka
3147
1701
Yenisei
Khatanga
West Siberian Plain
Siberia
Ob
Irtysh
Tobol
Narodnaya 1894
Ural Mts.
Ural
Steppe
Volga
Don
Caspian Sea
Caucasus
Elbrus 5642
Black Sea
Bosporus
Anatolia
Pontine Mts.
Ararat 5165
Taurus Mts.
Cyprus
Middle East
Mesopotamia
Tigris
Euphrates
Elburz Mts.
Damavand 5604
4548
Zagros
Plateau of Iran
The Gulf
G. of Oman
Arabia
Syrian Desert
Dead Sea -403
Sinai
Nafud Desert
Rub' al Khali (Empty Quarter)
3600
Red Sea
G. of Aden
Ras Asir
Socotra
Somali Pen.
Ethiopian Highlands
Africa
Nile
Libyan Desert
L. Victoria
L. Tanganyika
L. Malawi
Mediterranean Sea
Adriatic Sea
Alps
Rhine
Danube
Carpathians
Europe
North European Plain
Central Russian Uplands
Scandinavia
Finland
Kola Pen.
White Sea
N. Dvina
North Cape
ft m
12 000 4000
9000 3000
6000 2000
3000 1000
1500 500
600 200
0 0
200 600
1000 3000
2000 6000
4000 12 000
6000 18 000
8000 24 000
m ft
Projection: Bonne 30
East of Greenwich
CARTOGRAPHY BY PHILIPS.COPYRIGHT REED INTERNATIONAL BOOKS LTD.

1:50 000 000

250 0 250 500 750 1000 miles

250 0 500 1000 1500 km

Projection: Bonne 30

East from Greenwich

Hanoi ● Capital Cities

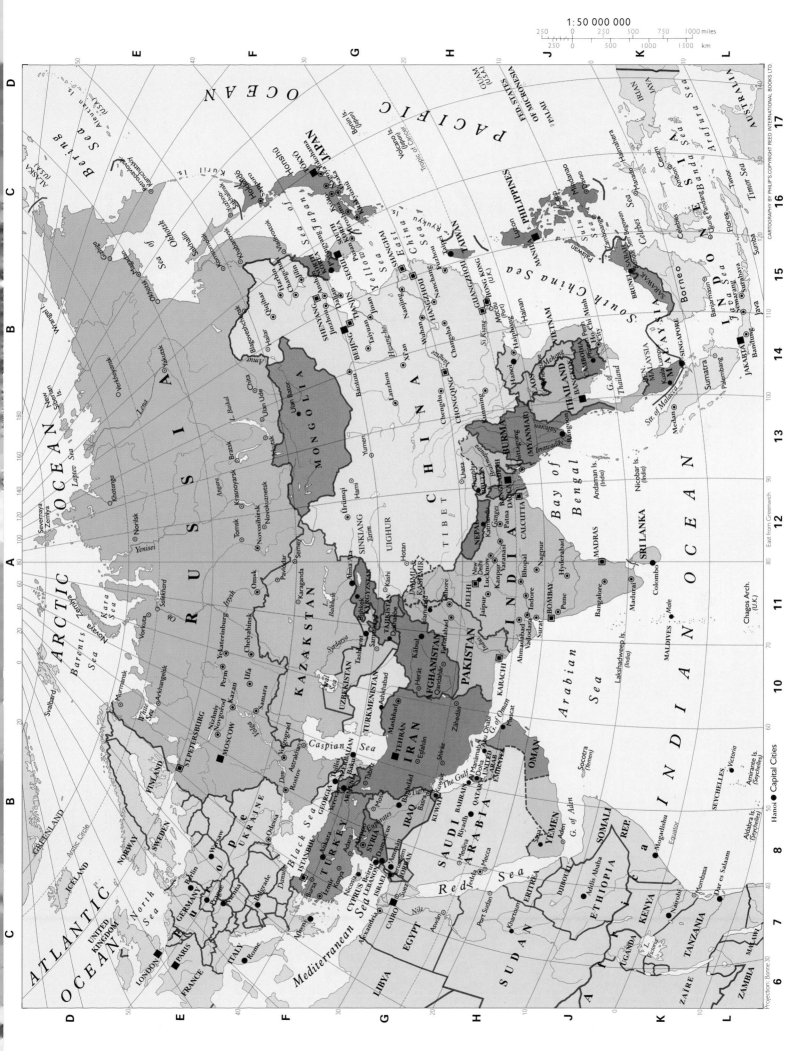

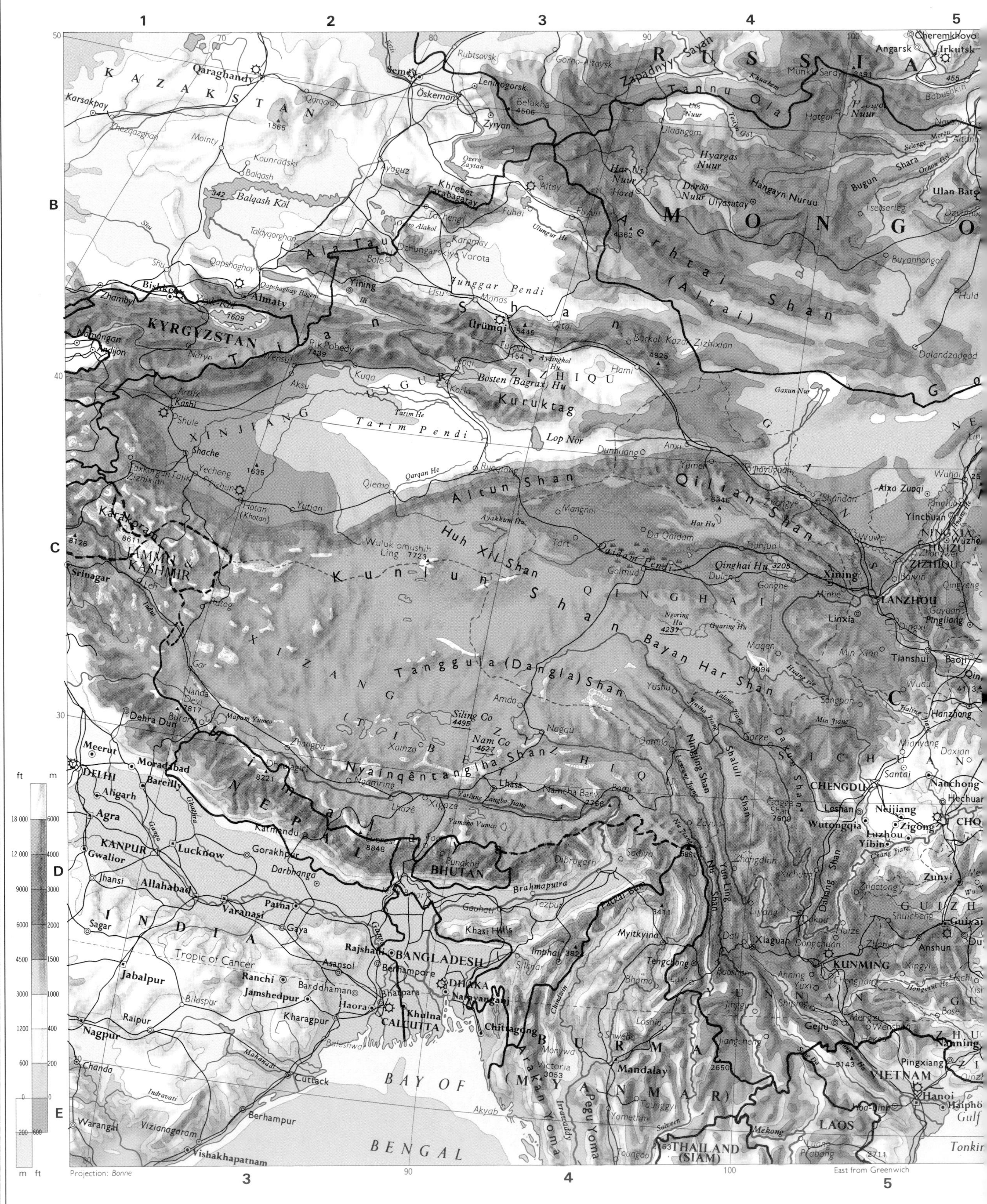

RUSSIA
KAZAKSTAN
KYRGYZSTAN
MONGOLIA
XINJIANG UYGUR ZIZHIQU
XIZANG ZIZHIQU (TIBET)
QINGHAI
SICHUAN
GANSU
NINGXIA HUIZU ZIZHIQU
GUIZHOU
YUNNAN
NEPAL
BHUTAN
BANGLADESH
INDIA
BURMA (MYANMAR)
THAILAND (SIAM)
LAOS
VIETNAM
JAMMU & KASHMIR
Qaraghandy
Semey
Öskemen
Rubtsovsk
Gorno-Altaysk
Leninogorsk
Zyryan
Balqash
Balqash Köl
Almaty
Bishkek
Yining
Ürümqi
Turpan
Hami
Kashi
Shache
Hotan (Khotan)
Tarim Pendi
Junggar Pendi
Tian Shan
Kuruktag
Lop Nor
Altun Shan
Qilian Shan
Kunlun Shan
Tanggula (Dangla) Shan
Bayan Har Shan
Nyainqêntanglha Shan
Himalaya
Qaidam Pendi
Qinghai Hu
Xining
LANZHOU
Yinchuan
CHENGDU
Chongqing
KUNMING
Lhasa
Xigazê
Katmandu
DELHI
Agra
KANPUR
Lucknow
Allahabad
Varanasi
Patna
Jabalpur
Nagpur
Ranchi
Jamshedpur
CALCUTTA
DHAKA
Chittagong
Mandalay
Hanoi
Tropic of Cancer
BAY OF BENGAL
Ulan Bator
Irkutsk
Hangayn Nuruu
Aerhtai (Altai) Shan
Dunhuang
Golmud
Tianshui
Baoji
Hanzhong
Nanchong
Leshan
Neijiang
Zigong
Yibin
Dali
Lijiang
Gejiu
Nanning
Projection: Bonne
East from Greenwich

1:15 000 000

100 0 100 200 300 400 miles
100 0 100 200 300 400 500 600 km

27
40
38 37
6

Map labels (China / Korea / Japan region):

z. Baykal
Ilan Ude
Ikalski
Chita
Sretensk
Nerchinsk
Olovyannaya
Borzya
Bokachacha
Svobodny
Shimanovsk
Blagoveshchensk
Komsomolsk
C. Terpeniya
Poronaysk
Aleksandrovsk
Sakhalin
Dolinsk
Yuzhno-Sakhalinsk
Kholmsk
Khabarovsk
Troitskoye
Birobidzhan
Obluchye
Bikin
Wakkanai
La Perouse Str.
Asahigawa
HOKKAIDO
SAPPORO
Otaru
Muroran
Kushiro
C. Erimo
Hakodate
Tsugaru-kaikyo
Aomori
Hachinohe
Morioka
Akita
Ishinomaki
Sado
Sendai
Niigata
Koriyama
Toyama
Utsunomiya
Kanazawa
TOKYO
Wajima
Kawasaki
NAGOYA
YOKOHAMA
Yokosuka
Shizuoka
Hamamatsu
OSAKA
Sakai
Wakayama
KOBE
Okayama
Hiroshima
Kure
Kochi
SHIKOKU
Matsuyama
KITAKYUSHU
FUKUOKA
Shimonoseki
Sasebo
Kumamoto
Nagasaki
Kyushu
Kagoshima
Tanega-shima

SEA OF JAPAN
YELLOW SEA
EAST CHINA SEA
SOUTH CHINA SEA
PACIFIC OCEAN
Korea Bay
Bo Hai
Hangzhou Wan
Formosa Strait
Ryūkyū-rettō
Tropic of Cancer

Gulian
Mohe
Heilong Jiang
Yilehuli Shan
Da Hinggan Ling
Oroqen Zizhiqi
Nenjiang
Bei'an
Yichun
Hegang
Hamusi
Shuangyashan
Hulin
Mishan
Ozero Khanka
Ussuriysk
Vladivostok
Nakhodka
Partizansk
Artem
Tumen
Hunchun
Najin
Chongjin
NORTH KOREA
Hungnam
Wonsan
Kaesong
SŎUL
Inch'ŏn
SOUTH KOREA
Taejon
Taegu
PUSAN
Masan
Kwangju
Cheju Do
1950
1953
1945

Barnaul
Hailar
Hulun Nur
Buir Nur
Manzhouli
Arxan
Horqin Youyi Qianqi
Ulan Hot
Solon
Baicheng
Tao'an
Qiqihar
Anda
Suihua
HARBIN
Mudanjiang
Shuangcheng
Jixi
Jiamusi
Yanji
CHANGCHUN
Jilin
Shuangliao
Liaoyuan
Siping
Tongliao
FUSHUN
SHENYANG
Benxi
Liaoyang
ANSHAN
Dandong
Yingkou
Jinzhou
Chengde
Zhangjiakou
Zhangbei
Hohhot
Jining
Datong
Xuanhua
Qinhuangdao
Tangshan
BEIJING SHI
Peking
BEIJING
Baoding
TIANJIN SHI
TIANJIN
Shijiazhuang
TAIYUAN
Cangzhou
Dezhou
JINAN
Zibo
Weifang
Yantai
Weihai
Dalian
Liaodong Wan
P'YŎNGYANG
DALIAN

Tamsagbulag
Dzamin Uud
Erenhot
Linxi
Chifeng
Duolun
Baynshand
Abagnar Qi
MONGGOL
Baotou
Yuanping
Taiyue Shan
Yangquan
Fenyang
Taiyuan
Handan
Anyang
Xinxiang
ZHENGZHOU
HENAN
Luoyang
Nanyang
Pingdingshan
Xuzhou
Qingjiang
Yancheng
Lianyungang
Zaozhuang
QINGDAO
SHANDONG
Ye Xian
Huang He
Jining
Kaifeng
Shangqiu
Shangshui
Fuyang
Huainan
Bengbu
NANJING
Yangzhou
Nantong
Changzhou
Wuxi
SHANGHAI SHI
Suzhou
SHANGHAI
Taizhou
Huaibei
HUBEI
ANHUI
Hefei
Ma'anshan
Wuhu
Wuxing
Hangzhou
Jiaxing
Ningbo
Shaoxing
ZHEJIANG
Tunxi
Jingdezhen
Shangrao
Jinhua
Qu Xian
Linhai
Wenzhou
Nanchang
JIANGXI
Yiyang
Changsha
Xiangtan
Pingxiang
Ji'an
Nanping
Fuzhou
Fujian
Sanming
Ruijin
Longyan
Zhangzhou
Xiamen
Chilung
Hsinchu
TAIPEI
T'aichung
Changhua
Chiai
T'ainan
Kaohsiung
Pingtung
T'aitung
TAIWAN (FORMOSA)
GUANGDONG
GUANGZHOU
Foshan
HONG KONG (Br.)
Macau (Port.)
Jiangmen
Zhaoqing
Maoming
Zhanjiang
Haikou
Hainan Dao
HAINAN
Shantou
Mei Xian
Shaoguan
Wuzhou
Guilin
Hengyang
Shaoyang
GUANGXI
HUNAN
Sakishima Gunto
Amami-ō-Shima
Naha
Okinawa
Batan Is.
Babuyan Is.
Pratas

COPYRIGHT GEORGE PHILIP & SON LTD

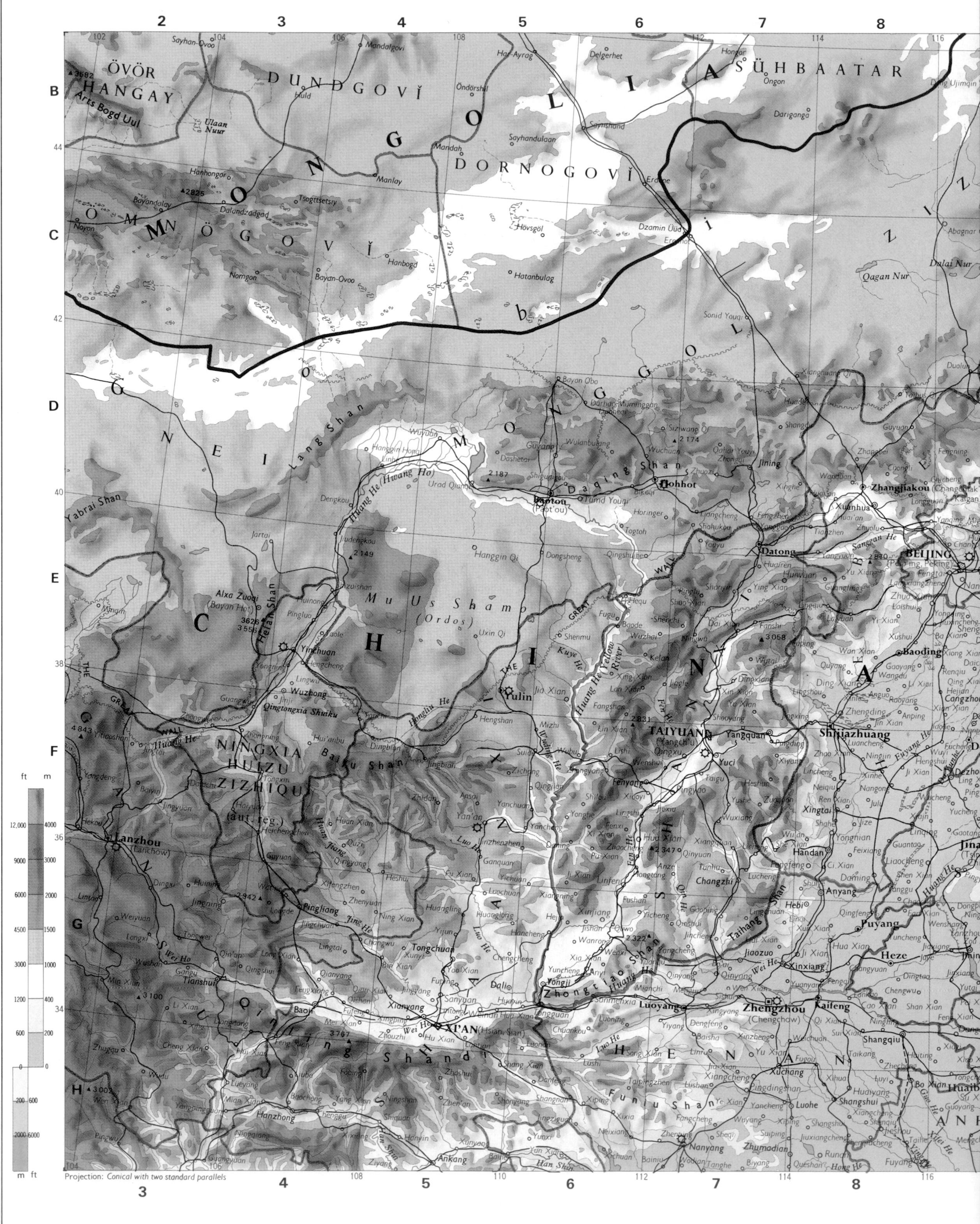
MONGOLIA
DUNDGOVĬ
ÖVÖR HANGAY
SÜHBAATAR
DORNOGOVĬ
ÖMNÖGOVĬ
NEI MONGGOL ZIZHIQU
CHINA
NINGXIA HUIZU ZIZHIQU (aut. reg.)
SHANXI
HENAN
Mu Us Shamo (Ordos)
Huang He (Hwang Ho)
Lang Shan
Daqing Shan
Helan Shan
Qinling Shandi
Taihang Shan
Zhongtiao Shan
Funiu Shan
THE GREAT WALL
BEIJING
Baotou
Hohhot
Datong
Zhangjiakou
Shijiazhuang
TAIYUAN
Yinchuan
Lanzhou
Xi'an
Luoyang
Zhengzhou (Chengchow)
Kaifeng
Baoding
Yan'an
Yulin
Tianshui
Pingliang
Handan
Anyang
Xinxiang
Nanyang
Hanzhong
Ankang
Projection: Conical with two standard parallels

1:6 000 000

50 0 50 100 150 miles

50 0 50 100 150 200 km

9 10 11 12 13 14 15 16

B C D E F G H

NORTH KOREA

SOUTH KOREA

JAPAN

SEA OF JAPAN

HUANG HAI (Yellow Sea)

Bo Hai (Gulf of Chihli)

Korea Bay

Liaodong Wan

Korea Strait

Tsushima-kaikyō

East from Greenwich

9 10 11 12 13 14 15

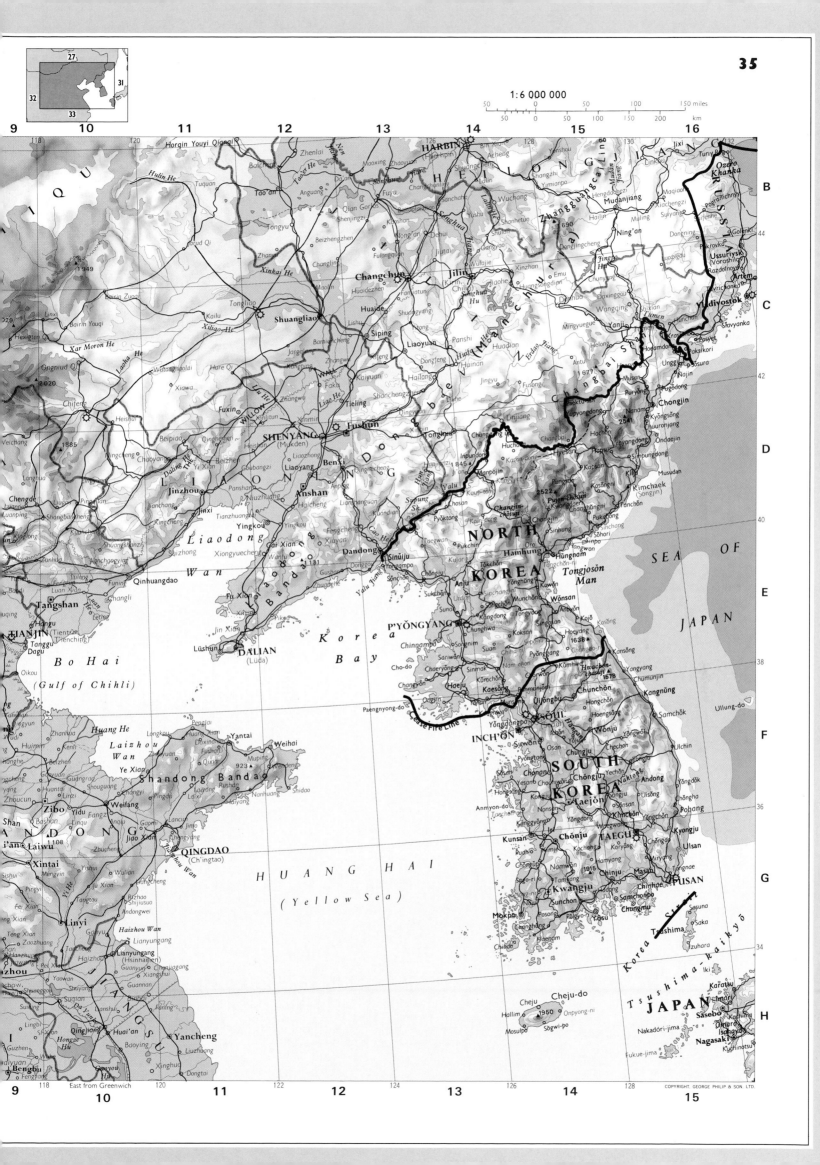

32 33 58 60 62

1 2 3 4 5

A B C D E F

THAILAND
CAMBODIA
LAOS
VIET-NAM
BURMA (MYANMAR)
PENINSULAR MALAYSIA
MALAYSIA
SARAWAK
SABAH
BRUNEI
SINGAPORE
BORNEO
KALIMANTAN
SUMATERA
JAWA
INDONESIA

ANDAMAN SEA
Gulf of Thailand
SOUTH CHINA SEA
Strait of Malacca
INDIAN OCEAN
JAVA SEA
Java Trench
Greater Sunda Islands
Spratly Is.
Paracel I.

BANGKOK
RANGOON
PHANH BHO HO CHI MINH (Saigon)
Phnom Penh
Vientiane
Kuala Lumpur
JAKARTA
Bandar Seri Begawan
Kota Kinabalu
Medan
Palembang
Padang
Pontianak
Banjarmasin
Surabaya
Semarang
Bandung

ft m
12 000 4000
9000 3000
6000 2000
4500 1500
3000 1000
1200 400
600 200
0 0
200 600
2000 6000
4000 12 000
6000 18 000
8000 24 000
m ft

Projection: Mercator

100 105 110 115

East from Greenwich

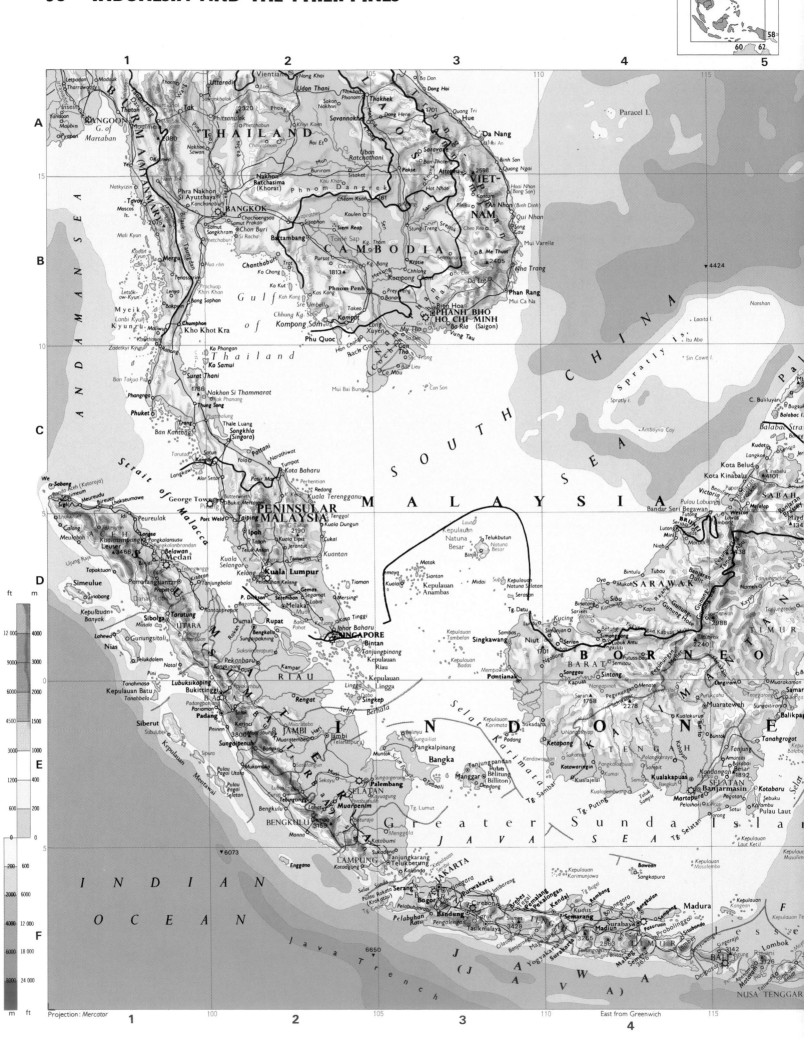

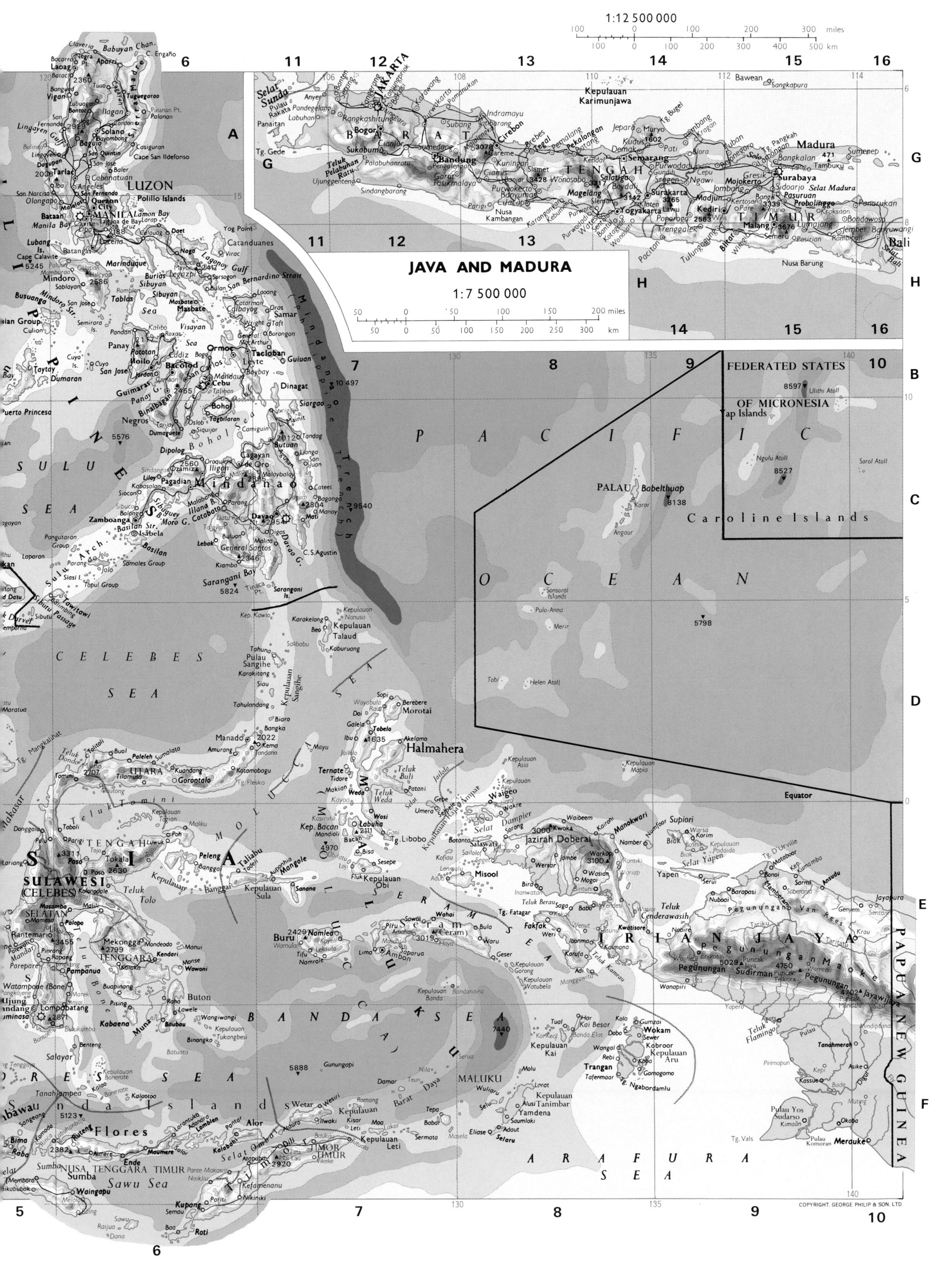

JAVA AND MADURA

1:7 500 000

1:12 500 000

FEDERATED STATES OF MICRONESIA

PACIFIC OCEAN

Caroline Islands

LUZON

PHILIPPINE

SULU SEA

CELEBES SEA

MINDANAO

MOLUCCA SEA

HALMAHERA

ASIA

SULAWESI (CELEBES)

BANDA SEA

CERAM SEA

IRIAN JAYA

PAPUA NEW GUINEA

FLORES SEA

SAWU SEA

TIMOR TIMUR

ARAFURA SEA

MALUKU

NUSA TENGGARA TIMUR

COPYRIGHT. GEORGE PHILIP & SON. LTD.

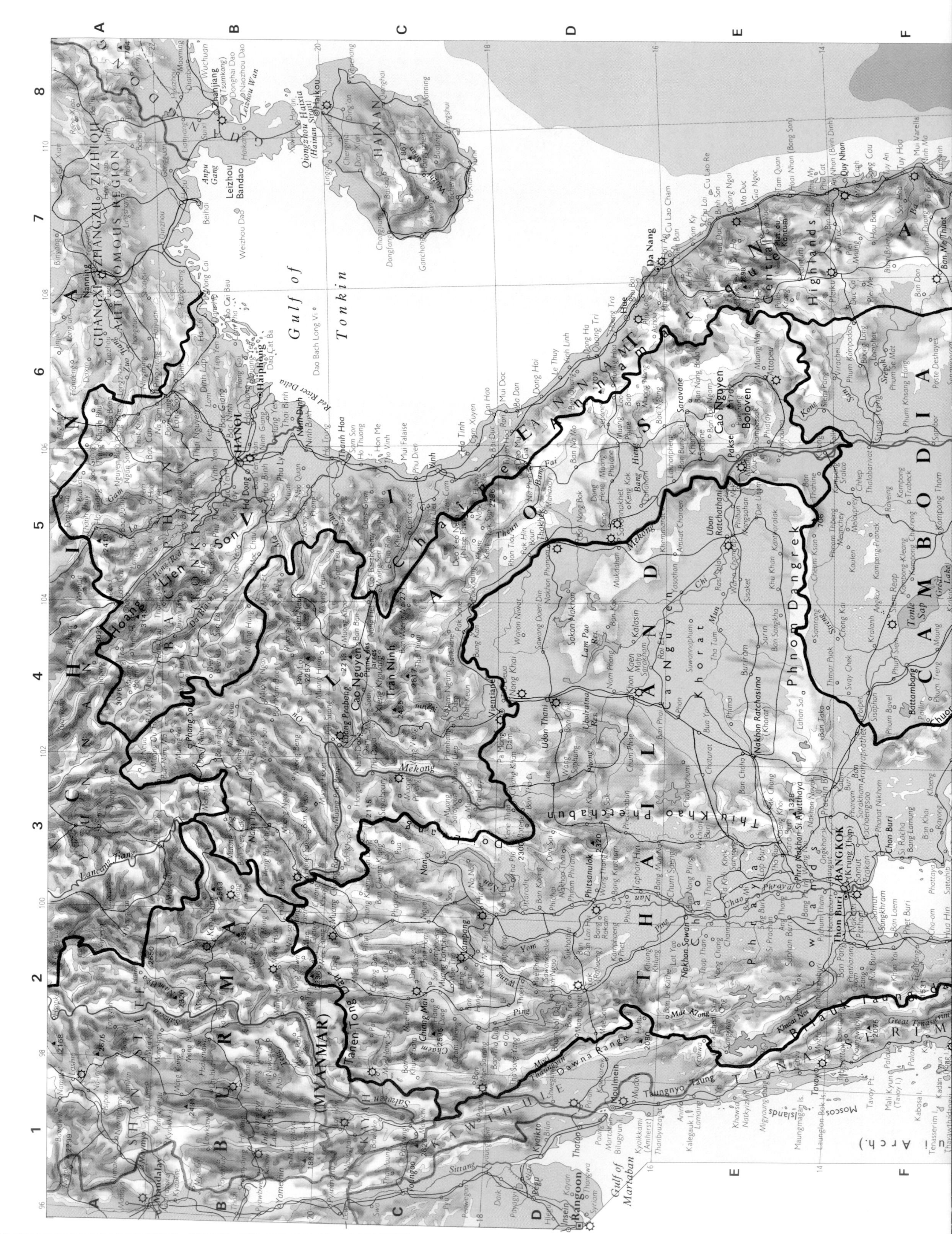
Gulf of Tonkin
HAINAN
Haikou
Zhanjiang
Nanning
HANOI
Haiphong
Red River Delta
Thanh Hoa
Vinh
Hue
Da Nang
Central Highlands
Qui Nhon
Luang Prabang
Vientiane
Mekong
Udon Thani
Khon Kaen
Nakhon Ratchasima (Khorat)
Ubon Ratchathani
Phnom Dangrek
Chiang Mai
Lampang
Phitsanulok
Nakhon Sawan
BANGKOK (Krung Thep)
Thon Buri
Battambang
Tonle Sap
Mandalay
Moulmein
Rangoon
Gulf of Martaban
Dawna Range
BURMA (MYANMAR)
CAMBODIA

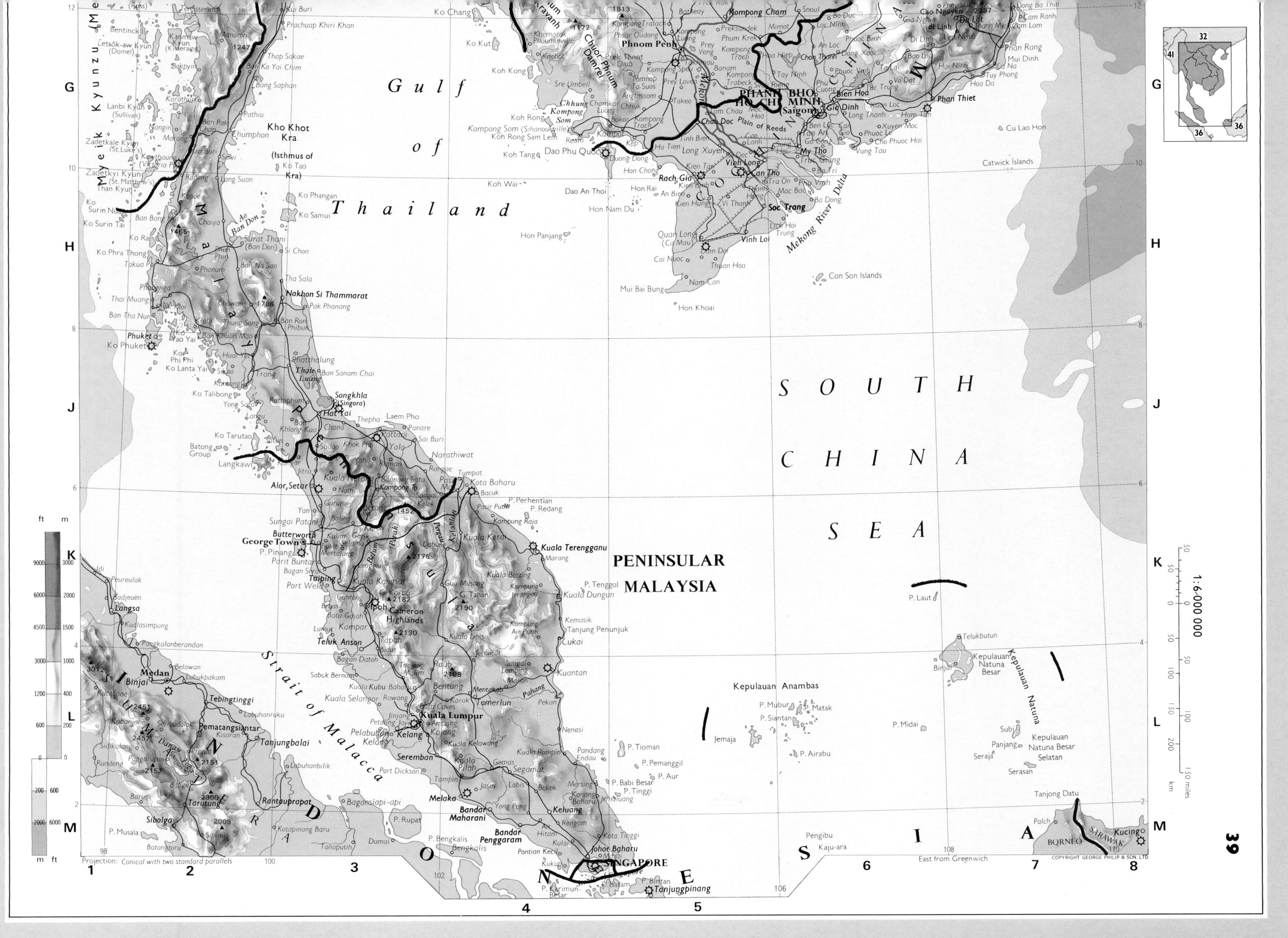
1:6 000 000
50 0 50 100 150 miles
50 0 50 100 150 200 km
SOUTH CHINA SEA
Gulf of Thailand
Strait of Malacca
PENINSULAR MALAYSIA
Phnom Penh
Saigon
Phan Thiet
Mekong River Delta
Plain of Reeds
Vinh Long
Can Tho
Soc Trang
Vinh Loi
Rach Gia
My Tho
Con Son Islands
Catwick Islands
Cu Lao Hon
Dao Phu Quoc
Dao An Thoi
Hon Panjang
Hon Khoai
Mui Bai Bung
Kompong Som
Kompong Cham
Ko Chang
Ko Kut
Koh Kong
Koh Wai
Kho Khot Kra
(Isthmus of Kra)
Ko Phangan
Ko Samui
Surat Thani
Nakhon Si Thammarat
Phuket
Ko Phuket
Ko Lanta Yai
Songkhla
Hat Yai
Pattani
Narathiwat
Langkawi
Alor Setar
Butterworth
George Town
Kota Baharu
P. Perhentian
P. Redang
Kuala Terengganu
Kuala Dungun
Kuantan
Taiping
Ipoh
Cameron Highlands
Teluk Anson
Kuala Lumpur
Kelang
Seremban
Port Dickson
Melaka
Keluang
Johor Baharu
SINGAPORE
Tanjungpinang
P. Tioman
P. Aur
Kepulauan Anambas
Jemaja
P. Airabu
P. Laut
Kepulauan Natuna
Natuna Besar
Kepulauan Natuna Besar Selatan
Serasan
Tanjong Datu
BORNEO
SARAWAK
Kuching
Medan
Binjai
Langsa
Tebingtinggi
Pematangsiantar
Tanjungbalai
Rantauprapat
Tarutung
Sibolga
P. Musala
P. Rupat
Dumai
Bengkalis
Bandar Penggaram
Bandar Maharani
East from Greenwich
Projection: Conical with two standard parallels
COPYRIGHT GEORGE PHILIP & SON LTD.

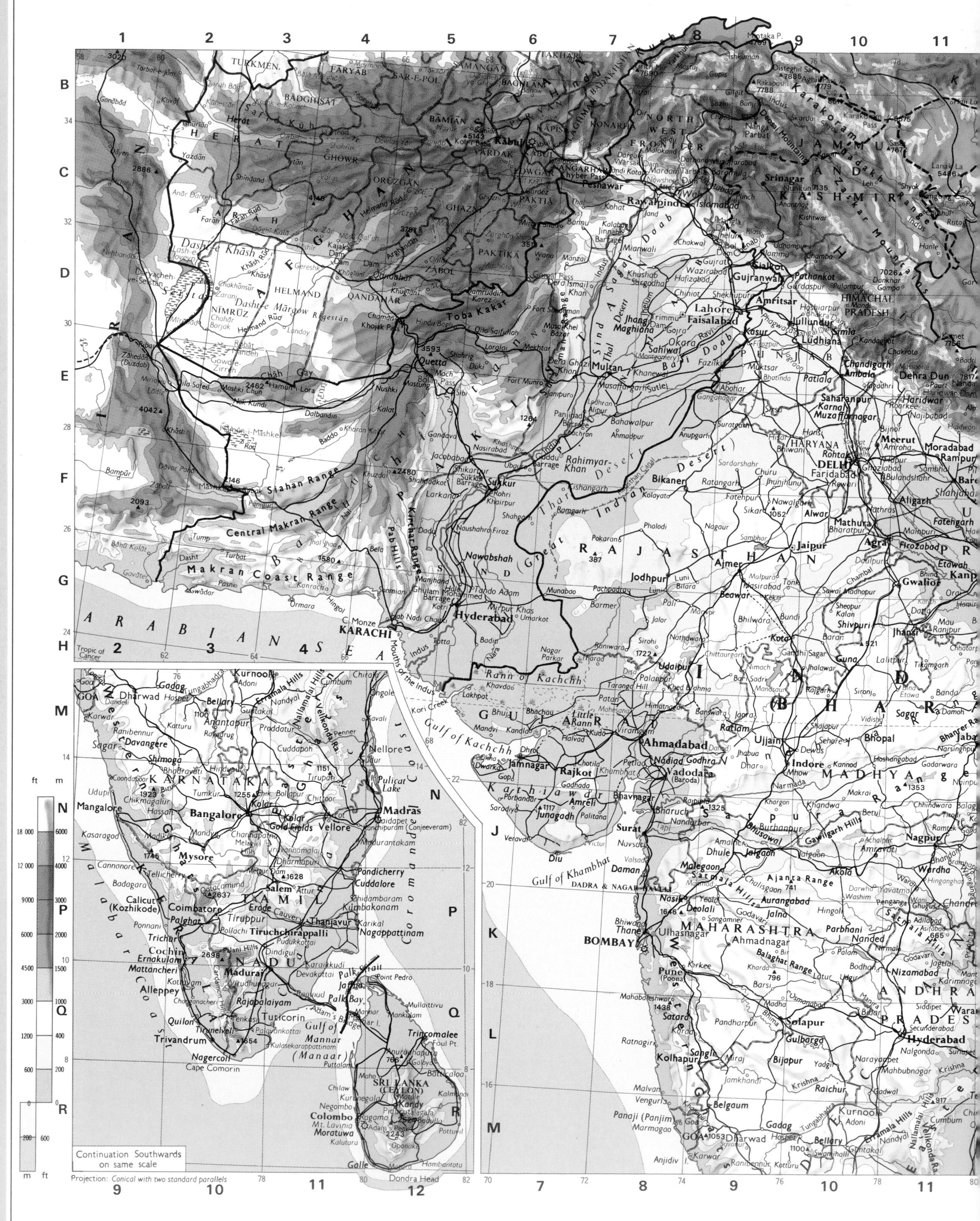

Continuation Southwards on same scale

Projection: Conical with two standard parallels

Dondra Head

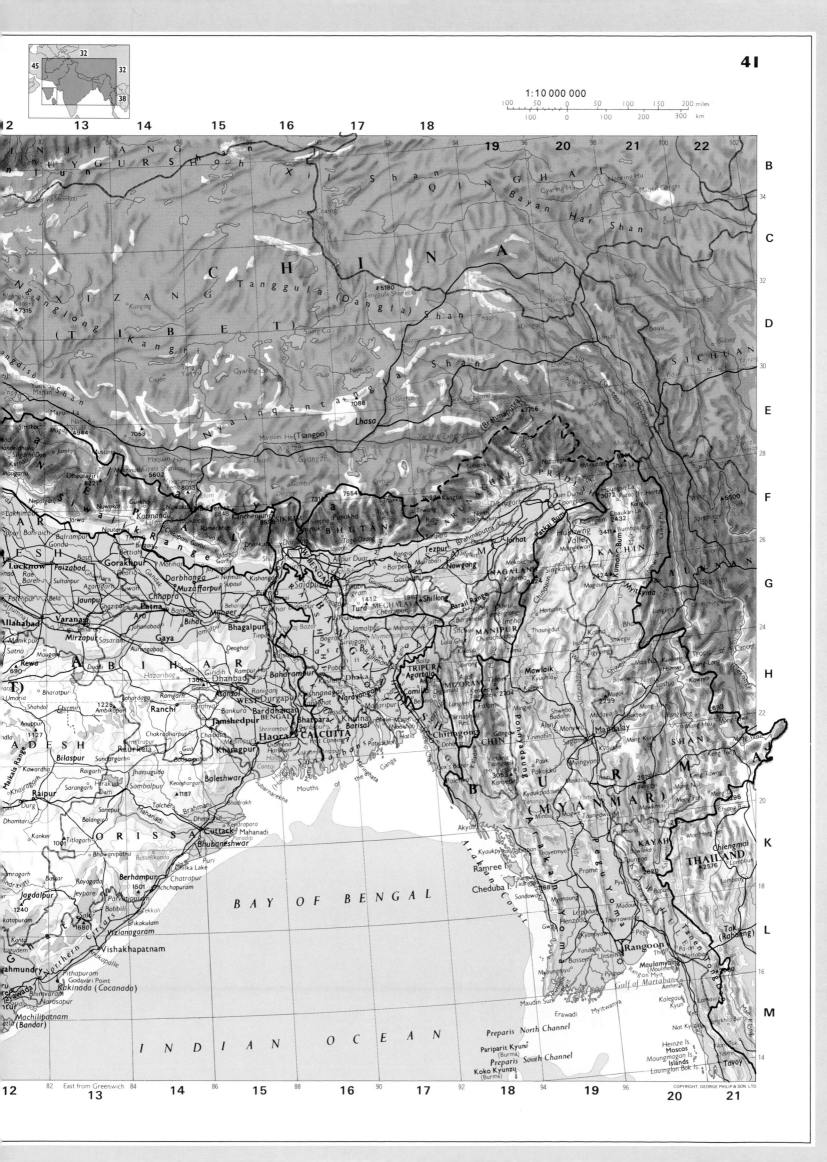

1:10 000 000

100   50   0   50   100   150   200 miles
100   0   100   200   300 km

19   20   21   22

B
34
C
32
D
30
E
28
F
26
G
24
H
22
K
20
L
18
M
16
14

X I N J I A N G   U Y G U R   S H .

X i l   S h a n

Q I N G H A I

Bayan   Har   Shan

C H I N A

Tanggula   (Dangla)   Shan

SICHUAN

X I Z A N G

(T   I   B   E   T   )

Lhasa

Nyainqêntanglha

Maquan He (Tsangpo)

Yarlung Zangbo Jiang

(Brahmaputra)

ARUNACHAL   PRADESH

KACHIN

NAGALAND

MEGHALAYA

MANIPUR

Kohima

Shillong

Cherrapunji

Imphal

BENGAL

BIHAR

ORISSA

WEST   BENGAL

BANGLADESH

TRIPURA

MIZORAM

Dhaka

Agartala

Comilla

Chittagong

CALCUTTA

Haora

Khulna

Barisal

Kharagpur

Jamshedpur

Ranchi

Cuttack

Bhubaneshwar

Puri

Berhampur

Vishakhapatnam

Kakinada (Cocanada)

Machilipatnam
(Bandar)

B U R M A

(M Y A N M A R)

Mandalay

KAYAH

SHAN

CHIN

THAILAND

Chiengmai

Rangoon

Maulamyaing
(Moulmein)

Bassein

Pegu

Prome

Akyab

Ramree I.

Cheduba I.

Arakan   Coast

Gulf of Martaban

Moscos
Islands

Heinze Is.

Maungmagan Is.

Tavoy

B A Y   O F   B E N G A L

I N D I A N   O C E A N

Preparis   North   Channel

Pariparit Kyun
(Burma)

Preparis   South   Channel

Koko Kyunzu
(Burma)

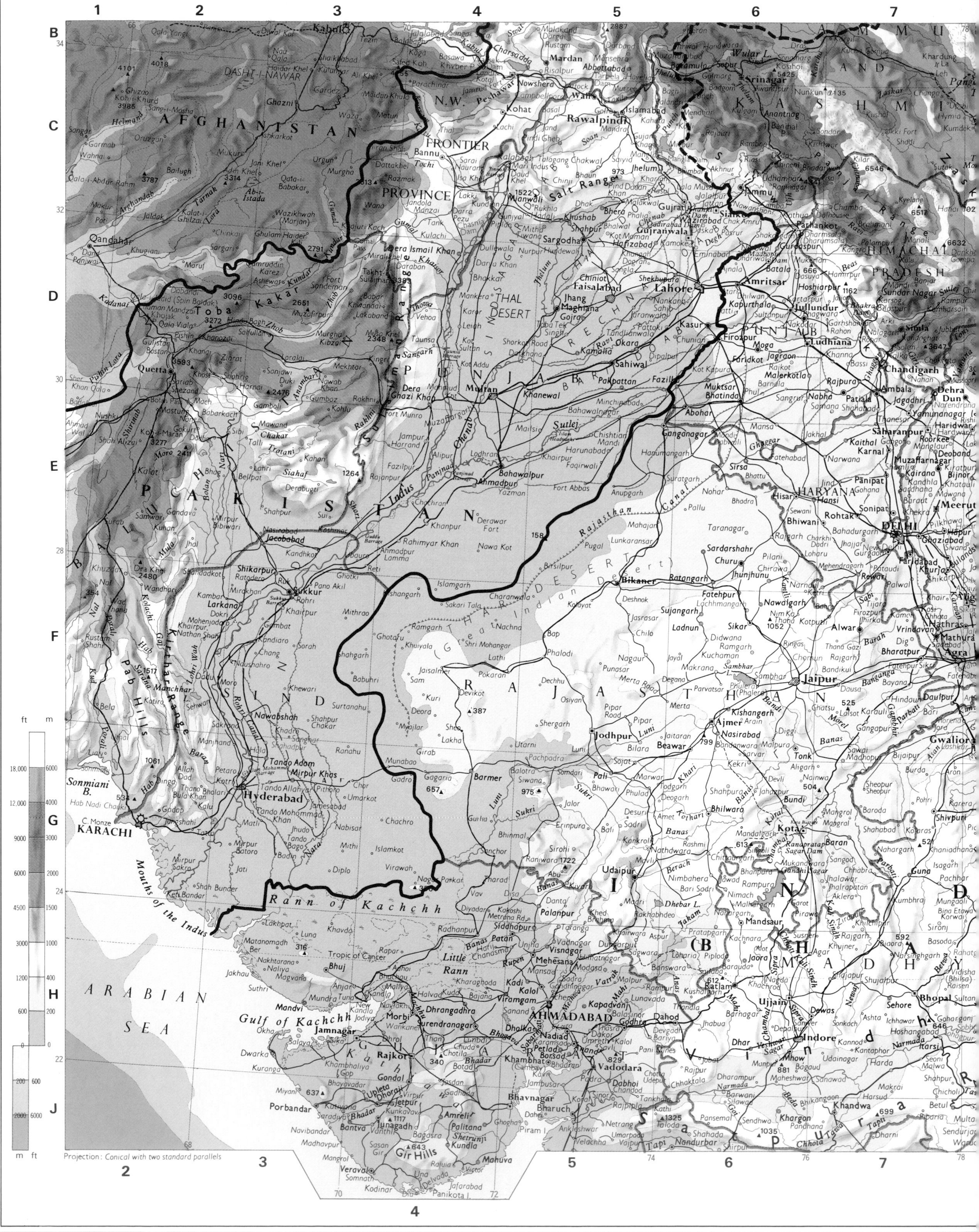

1
2
3
4
5
6
7
B
C
D
E
F
G
H
J
AFGHANISTAN
DASHT-I-NAWAR
Kabul
Ghazni
Qandahar
Helmand
N.W. FRONTIER PROVINCE
Peshawar
Mardan
Kohat
Bannu
Rawalpindi
Islamabad
Salt Range
Srinagar
KASHMIR
JAMMU AND
Jammu
Sialkot
Gujranwala
Gujrat
Sargodha
Faisalabad
Lahore
Amritsar
Jullundur
Ludhiana
Simla
Chandigarh
HIMACHAL PRADESH
PUNJAB
THAL DESERT
Multan
Sahiwal
Bahawalpur
Dera Ghazi Khan
Dera Ismail Khan
Quetta
Toba Kakar
BALUCHISTAN
PAKISTAN
Sulaiman Range
Indus
Chenab
Sutlej
Jhelum
Ravi
Beas
Sukkur
Shikarpur
Jacobabad
Larkana
SIND
Kirthar Range
Pab Hills
Hyderabad
KARACHI
Sonmiani B.
Mouths of the Indus
Rann of Kachchh
Little Rann
ARABIAN SEA
Gulf of Kachchh
Bhuj
Mandvi
Jamnagar
Rajkot
Porbandar
Junagadh
Gir Hills
Veraval
Bhavnagar
Ahmadabad
AHMADABAD
Vadodara
Bharuch
Surendranagar
Dhrangadhra
Morbi
THAR DESERT
(Great Indian Desert)
Bikaner
Jaisalmer
Barmer
Jodhpur
RAJASTHAN
Ajmer
Jaipur
Udaipur
Kota
Bhilwara
HARYANA
Hisar
Rohtak
DELHI
Meerut
Agra
Gwalior
MADHYA PRADESH
Bhopal
Ujjain
Indore
Ratlam
Mandsaur
Sehore
Vindhya
Satpura
Khandwa
Dehra Dun
Saharanpur
Muzaffarnagar
Panipat
Karnal
Ambala
Patiala
Bhatinda
Firozpur
Ganganagar
Rajasthan Canal
Tropic of Cancer
Sabarmati
Mahi
Narmada
Tapi
ft
m
18,000
12,000
9000
6000
4500
3000
1200
600
200
2000
6000
4000
3000
2000
1500
1000
400
200
0
600
6000
Projection: Conical with two standard parallels

1:6 000 000

50   0   50   100 miles
50   0   50   100   150 km

JAMMU AND KASHMIR
On same scale as Main Map

East from Greenwich

COPYRIGHT. GEORGE PHILIP & SON. LTD.

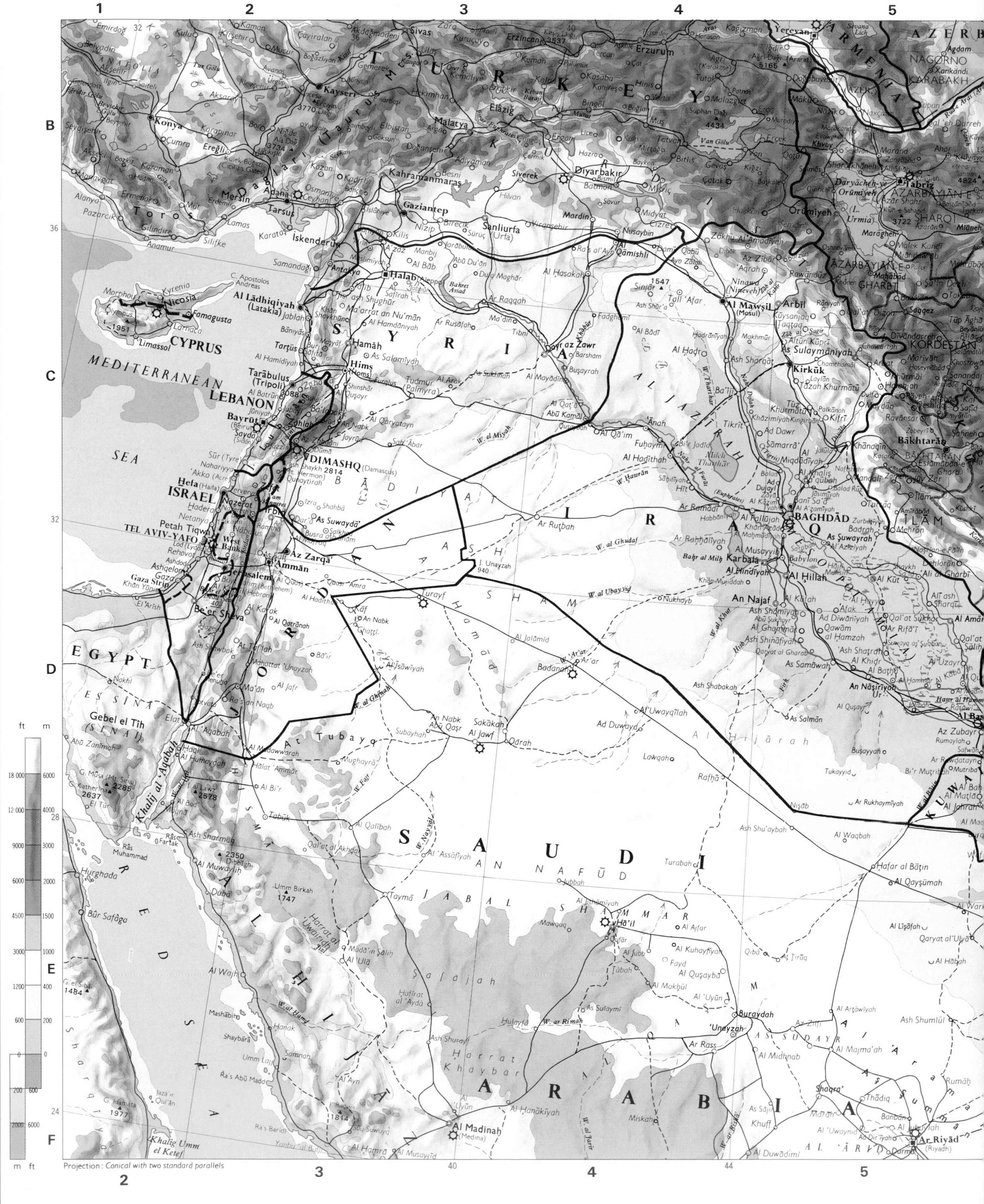
TURKEY
SYRIA
IRAQ
SAUDI ARABIA
JORDAN
LEBANON
ISRAEL
CYPRUS
EGYPT
ARMENIA
KUWAIT
MEDITERRANEAN SEA
RED SEA
Konya
Kayseri
Sivas
Erzurum
Malatya
Elâzig
Diyarbakır
Gaziantep
Adana
Mersin
Tarsus
İskenderun
Sanliurfa
Mardin
Yerevan
Nicosia
Famagusta
Limassol
Larnaca
Halab (Aleppo)
Al Lādhiqiyah (Latakia)
Ḥamāh
Ḥimṣ (Homs)
Tudmur (Palmyra)
Ar Raqqah
Dayr az Zawr
Al Ḥasakah
Al Qāmishlī
Ṭarābulus (Tripoli)
Bayrūt (Beirut)
Ṣaydā (Sidon)
Ṣūr (Tyre)
DIMASHQ (Damascus)
Ḥefa (Haifa)
TEL AVIV-YAFO
Jerusalem
Gaza Strip
West Bank
Be'er Sheva
Elat
Al 'Aqabah
'Ammān
Az Zarqā'
As Suwaydā'
Ma'ān
Al Mawṣil (Mosul)
Arbīl
Kirkūk
As Sulaymānīyah
BAGHDĀD
Karbalā'
An Najaf
Al Ḥillah
Al Kūt
An Nāṣirīyah
Ar Ruṭbah
Tabrīz
Orūmīyeh
Bākhtarān
Ar Riyāḍ (Riyadh)
Al Madīnah (Medina)
Ḥā'il
Buraydah
'Unayzah
Tabūk
Al Jawf
Sakākah
Ḥafar al Bāṭin
AN NAFŪD
Jabal Shammar
Ḥarrat Khaybar
SINAI
Gebel el Tīh
Hurghada
Bûr Safâga
Projection: Conical with two standard parallels

1:7 000 000

50 0 50 100 150 200 miles

50 0 50 100 150 200 250 300 km

6 7 8 9 10

TURKMENISTAN

KARAKUM

CASPIAN SEA

IRAN

AFGHANISTAN

PAKISTAN

OMAN

QATAR

BAHRAIN

UNITED ARAB EMIRATES

THE GULF

Gulf of Oman

DASHT-E-KAVĪR

DASHT-E-LUT

Reshteh-ye Kūhhā-ye Alborz

Kūhhā-ye Zāgros

Kūhhā-ye Bashākerd

Kopet Dag

TEHRĀN

Mashhad (Meshed)

Eşfahān

Shīrāz

Tabrīz

Kermān

Yazd

Qom

Ahvāz

Ashgabat

BAKI (Baku)

Herāt

Kuwayt (Kuwait)

Ad Dammām

Manāmah

Ad Dawḩah (Doha)

Abū Zaby (Abu Dhabi)

Dubayy (Dubai)

Ash Shāriqah (Sharjah)

Ra's al Khaymah

Bandar-e 'Abbās

Zāhedān (Duzdab)

Chah Bahār

Ābādān

Khorramshahr

Shatt al Arab

Mary

Chärjew

Amudarya

MĀZANDARĀN

SEMNĀN

KHORĀSĀN

MARKAZĪ

ESFAHĀN

YAZD

KERMĀN

FĀRS

HORMOZGĀN

SĪSTĀN VA BALŪCHESTĀN

KHŪZESTĀN

BŪSHEHR

GĪLĀN

East from Greenwich

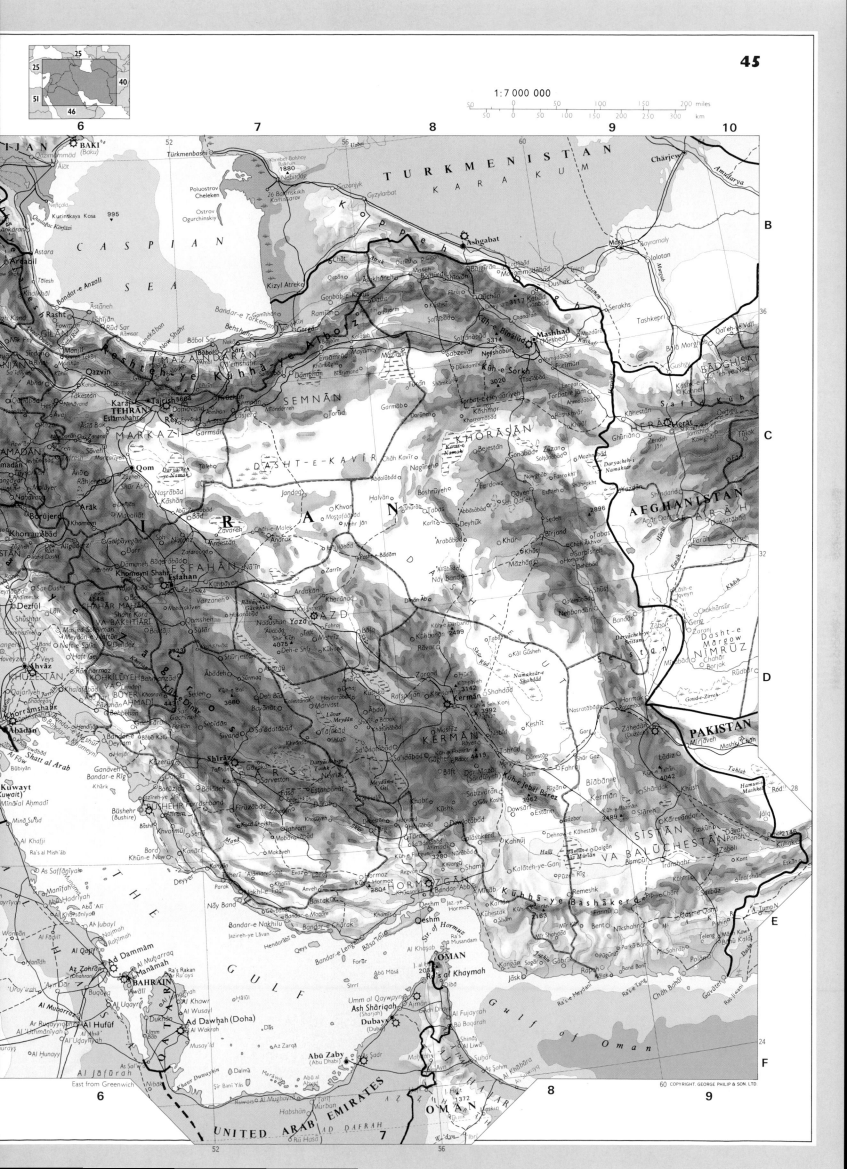

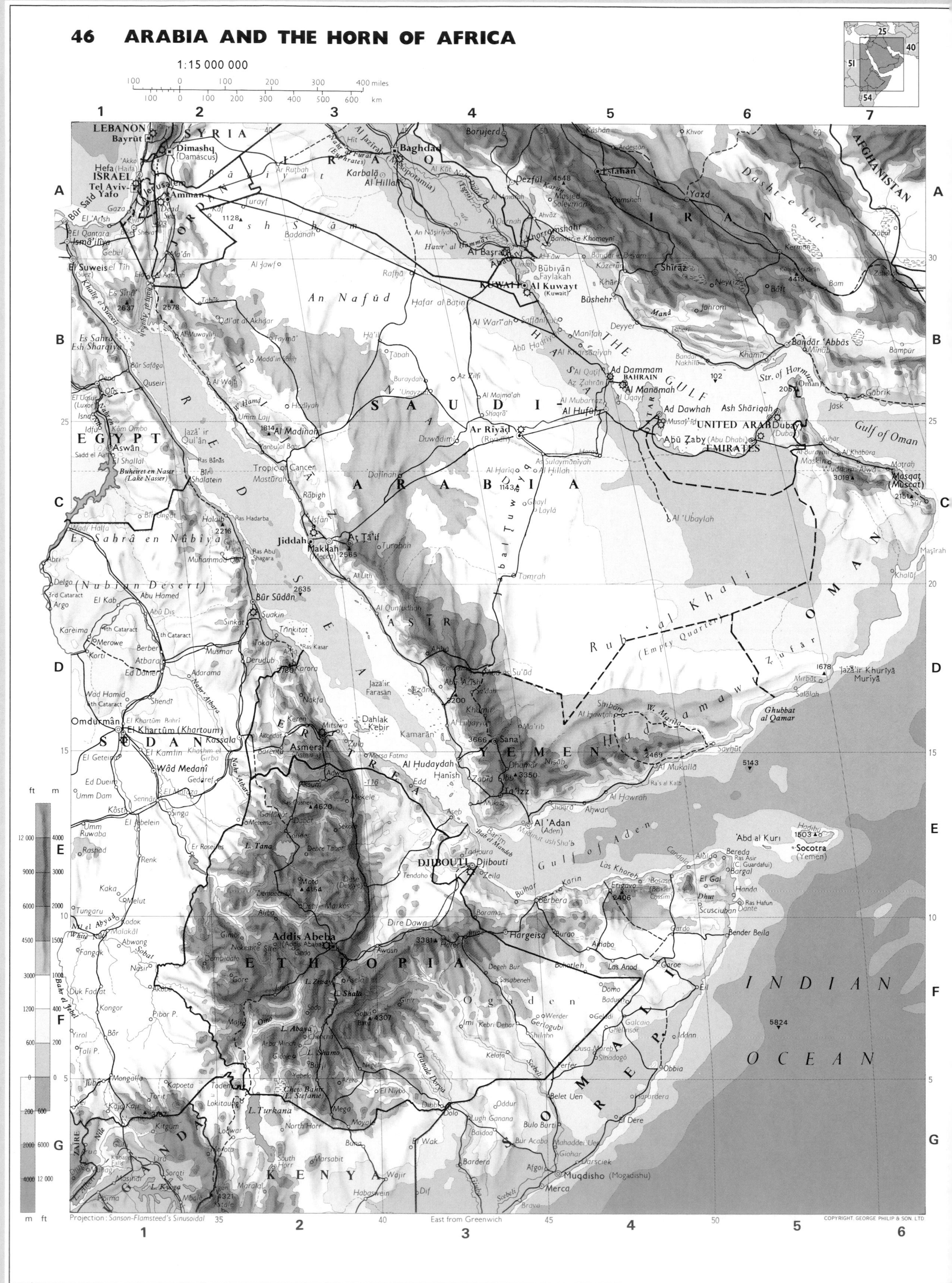
46 ARABIA AND THE HORN OF AFRICA
1:15 000 000
miles
km
Projection: Sanson-Flamsteed's Sinusoidal
East from Greenwich
COPYRIGHT, GEORGE PHILIP & SON, LTD
LEBANON
Bayrūt
SYRIA
Dimashq (Damascus)
ISRAEL
Tel Aviv-Yafo
Jerusalem
Amman
JORDAN
Baghdad
IRAQ
Karbalā
Al Hillah
Al Başrah
KUWAIT
Al Kuwayt (Kuwait)
IRAN
Eşfahān
Yazd
Shīrāz
Kermān
Dasht-e Lūt
AFGHANISTAN
Būshehr
Bandar 'Abbās
Str. of Hormuz
Gulf of Oman
Masqat (Muscat)
OMAN
THE GULF
Ad Dammam
BAHRAIN
Al Manāmah
Al Hufūf
QATAR
Ad Dawhah
Ash Shāriqah
Dubayy (Dubai)
Abū Zaby (Abu Dhabi)
UNITED ARAB EMIRATES
SAUDI ARABIA
Ar Riyāḍ (Riyadh)
An Nafūd
Al Madīnah
Makkah (Mecca)
Jiddah
Aṭ Ṭā'if
Rub' al Khali (Empty Quarter)
Tropic of Cancer
RED SEA
EGYPT
Aswân
El Suweis (Suez)
Buheiret en Naser (Lake Nasser)
Es Sahrâ en Nûbîya (Nubian Desert)
Bûr Sûdân
SUDAN
Omdurmân
El Khartûm (Khartoum)
Kassala
Wâd Medanî
ERITREA
Asmera
YEMEN
Sana
Al Ḥudaydah
Ta'izz
Al 'Adan (Aden)
Al Mukallā
Ḥaḍramawt
Gulf of Aden
Socotra (Yemen)
DJIBOUTI
Djibouti
ETHIOPIA
Addis Abeba
L. Tana
Dire Dawa
Hargeisa
Berbera
Ogaden
SOMALI REP.
Muqdisho (Mogadishu)
Ras Asir (C. Guardafui)
KENYA
L. Turkana
UGANDA
ZAIRE
INDIAN OCEAN
ft
m

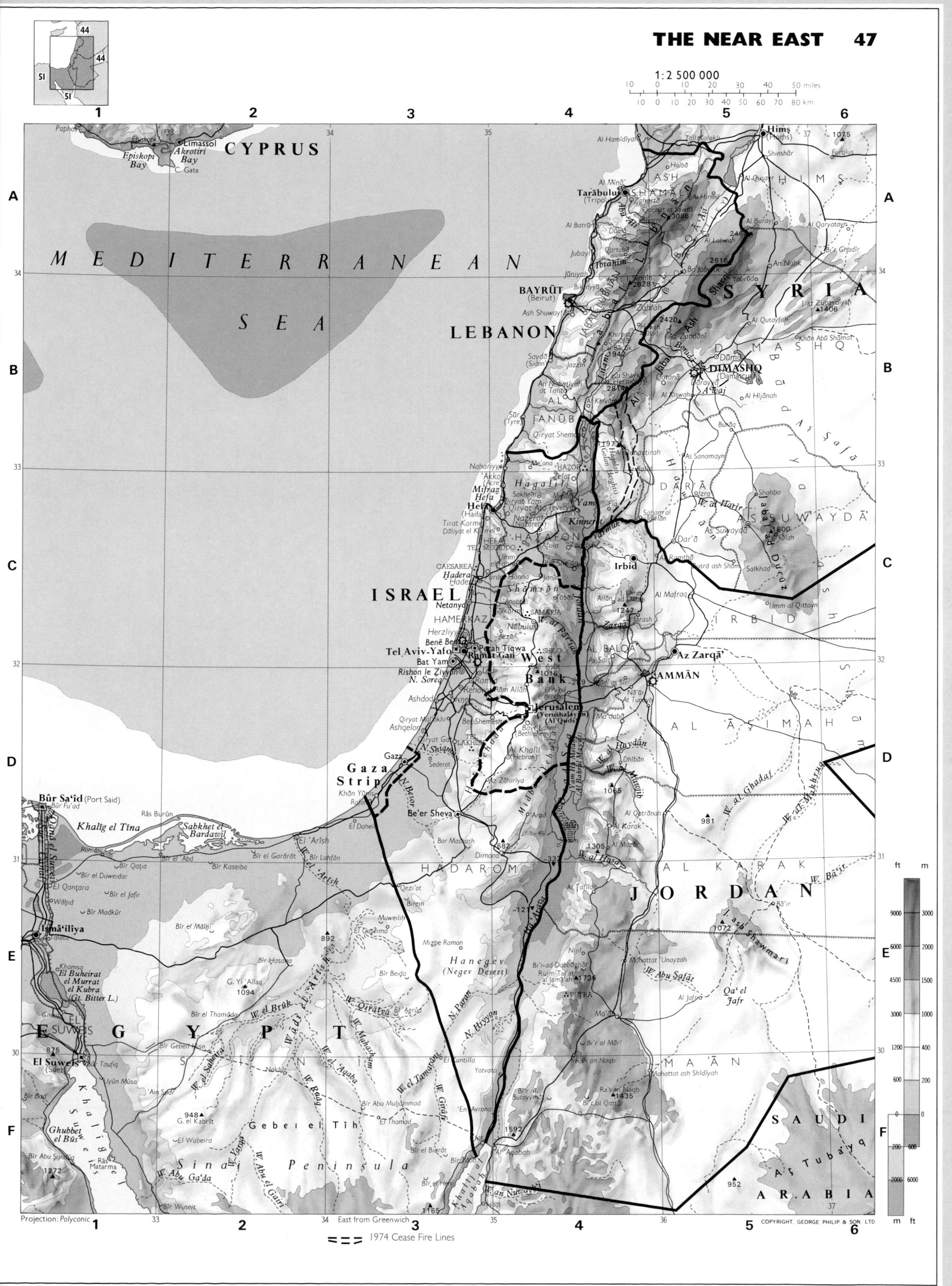

1:2 500 000

CYPRUS
Paphos
Episkopi Bay
Limassol
Akrotiri Bay
C. Gata

M E D I T E R R A N E A N
S E A

BAYRŪT
(Beirut)
LEBANON

Tarābulus
(Tripoli)
ASH SHAMĀL

Al Hamidiyah
Tall Kalakh
Hims
(Homs)
Furglus
1075

DIMASHQ
(Damascus)
SYRIA
DIMASHQ

ISRAEL
HAMERKAZ
Tel Aviv-Yafo
Bat Yam
Ramat Gan
Rishon le Ziyyon
Herzliyya
Benē Beraq
Petah Tiqwa

Netanya
Hadera
CAESAREA
HAIFA

Akko
(Acre)
Hefa
(Haifa)
Nazerat
(Nazareth)

WEST
BANK
Nablus
SAMARIA
SHILO
Jerusalem
(Yerushalayim)
(Al Quds)
Bethlehem

Gaza
Strip
Gaza
Khān Yūnis
Rafah

Be'er Sheva
Ashdod
Ashqelon

Irbid
AMMĀN
Az Zarqā

JORDAN
AL KARAK
MA'ĀN

PETRA

HADAROM
Hanegev
(Negev Desert)
Mizpe Ramon

Bûr Sa'îd (Port Said)
Bûr Fu'ad
Khalîg el Tîna
Sabkhet el Bardawil

El 'Arîsh

Ismâ'ilîya
El Buheirat el Murrat el Kubra
(Gt. Bitter L.)

EL SUWEIS
El Suweis (Suez)

E G Y P T
Sinai Peninsula
Gebel el Tîh
W. el 'Arîsh

SAUDI
ARABIA

Projection: Polyconic

East from Greenwich

COPYRIGHT. GEORGE PHILIP & SON. LTD.

= = = 1974 Cease Fire Lines

ft   m
9000 3000
6000 2000
4500 1500
3000 1000
1200 400
600   200
0   0
200   600
2000 6000
m   ft

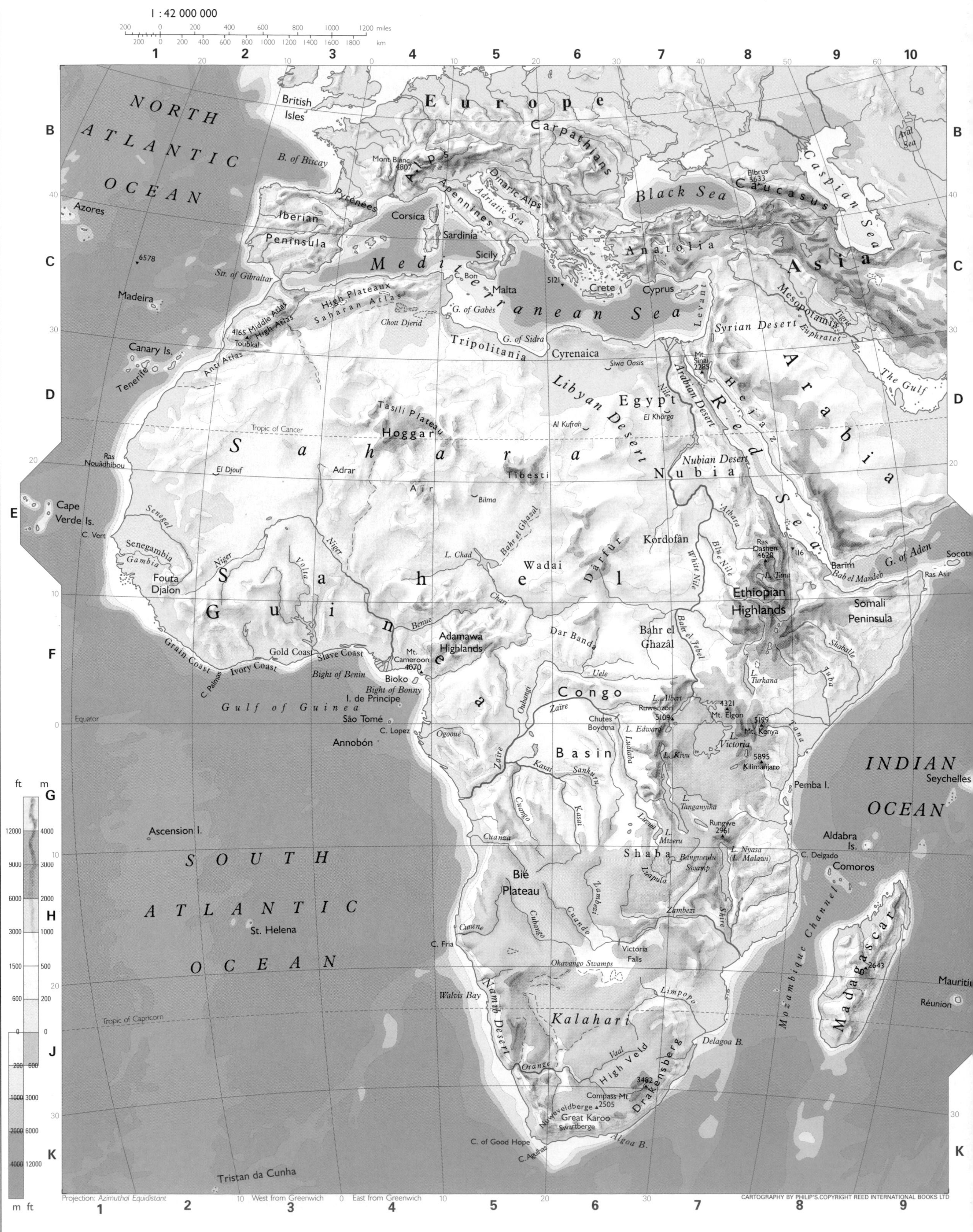

1 : 42 000 000

NORTH
ATLANTIC
OCEAN

E u r o p e

British Isles

Carpathians

Alps
Mont Blanc 4807

B. of Biscay

Pyrénées
Iberian Peninsula
Corsica
Azores
6578
Madeira
Str. of Gibraltar
High Plateaux
Saharan Atlas
Middle Atlas 4165
High Atlas
Toubkal
Antr Atlas
Canary Is.
Tenerife
Ras Nouâdhibou

Dinaric Alps
Adriatic Sea
Apennines
Sardinia
Sicily
Malta
C. Bon
G. of Gabès
Chott Djerid
Tripolitania
G. of Sidra
Cyrenaica

M e d i t e r r a n e a n   S e a

Crete
Cyprus
5121
Levant

Black Sea
Elbrus 5633
Caucasus
Anatolia
A s i a
Caspian Sea
Aral Sea

Mesopotamia
Euphrates
Tigris
Syrian Desert
The Gulf
A r a b i a

Mt. Sinai 2285
Arabian Desert
Hejaz
Red Sea

Siwa Oasis
El Khârga
Libyan Desert
Egypt
Al Kufrah

S a h a r a
Tasili Plateau
Hoggar
Adrar
Aïr
Bilma
Tibesti
El Djouf

Nubian Desert
Nubia
Atbara
Ras Dashen 4620
116
Barim
Bab el Mandeb
G. of Aden
Socotra
Ras Asir

Tropic of Cancer

Cape Verde Is.
C. Vert
Senegal
Senegambia
Gambia
Fouta Djalon
Niger
Volta
Niger

S u d a n
G u i n e a

Benue
Adamawa Highlands
Mt. Cameroon 4070
Bioko
Bight of Bonny
I. de Principe
São Tomé
C. Lopez
Annobón
Ogooué

L. Chad
Bahr el Ghazal
Wadai
Chari
Dar Banda
Uele
Onbangi
Uele

D a r f û r
Kordofân
White Nile
Blue Nile

Ethiopian Highlands
L. Tana
Somali Peninsula
Shaballe
Juba

Bahr el Ghazâl
Bahr el Jebel
C o n g o
Zaïre
Chutes Boyoma
L. Albert
Ruwenzori 5094
4321
Mt. Elgon
5199
Mt. Kenya
L. Edward
L. Victoria
L. Kivu
5895
Kilimanjaro
Basin
Kasai
Sankuru
Lualaba
L. Turkana
Tana

Grain Coast
Gold Coast
Ivory Coast
Slave Coast
Bight of Benin
C. Palmas
Gulf of Guinea

Equator

INDIAN OCEAN
Seychelles

Ascension I.
SOUTH
ATLANTIC
OCEAN
St. Helena

Zaïre
Kasai
Cuango
Cuanza
Shaba
Bié Plateau

Pemba I.
L. Tanganyika
L. Mweru
Rungwe 2961
Bangweulu Swamp
Lualaba
Luapula
L. Nyasa (L. Malawi)
C. Delgado
Aldabra Is.
Comoros

Zambezi
Cubango
Cuando
Okavango Swamps
Victoria Falls
Limpopo
Kalahari
Vaal
Orange
High Veld
Drakensberg
3482
Compass Mt. 2505
Nieuveldberge
Great Karoo
Swartberge
C. of Good Hope
C. Agulhas
Algoa B.

C. Fria
Namib Desert
Walvis Bay
Tropic of Capricorn

Madagascar
2643
Mozambique Channel
Mauritius
Réunion

Delagoa B.

Tristan da Cunha

ft   m
12000 4000
9000   3000
6000   2000
3000   1000
1500   500
600   200
0   0
200   600
1000   3000
2000   6000
4000 12000
m ft

Projection: Azimuthal Equidistant
West from Greenwich   East from Greenwich
CARTOGRAPHY BY PHILIP'S. COPYRIGHT REED INTERNATIONAL BOOKS LTD

1 : 42 000 000

Projection: Azimuthal Equidistant

CARTOGRAPHY BY PHILIP'S. COPYRIGHT REED INTERNATIONAL BOOKS LTD

● Dakar Capital Cities

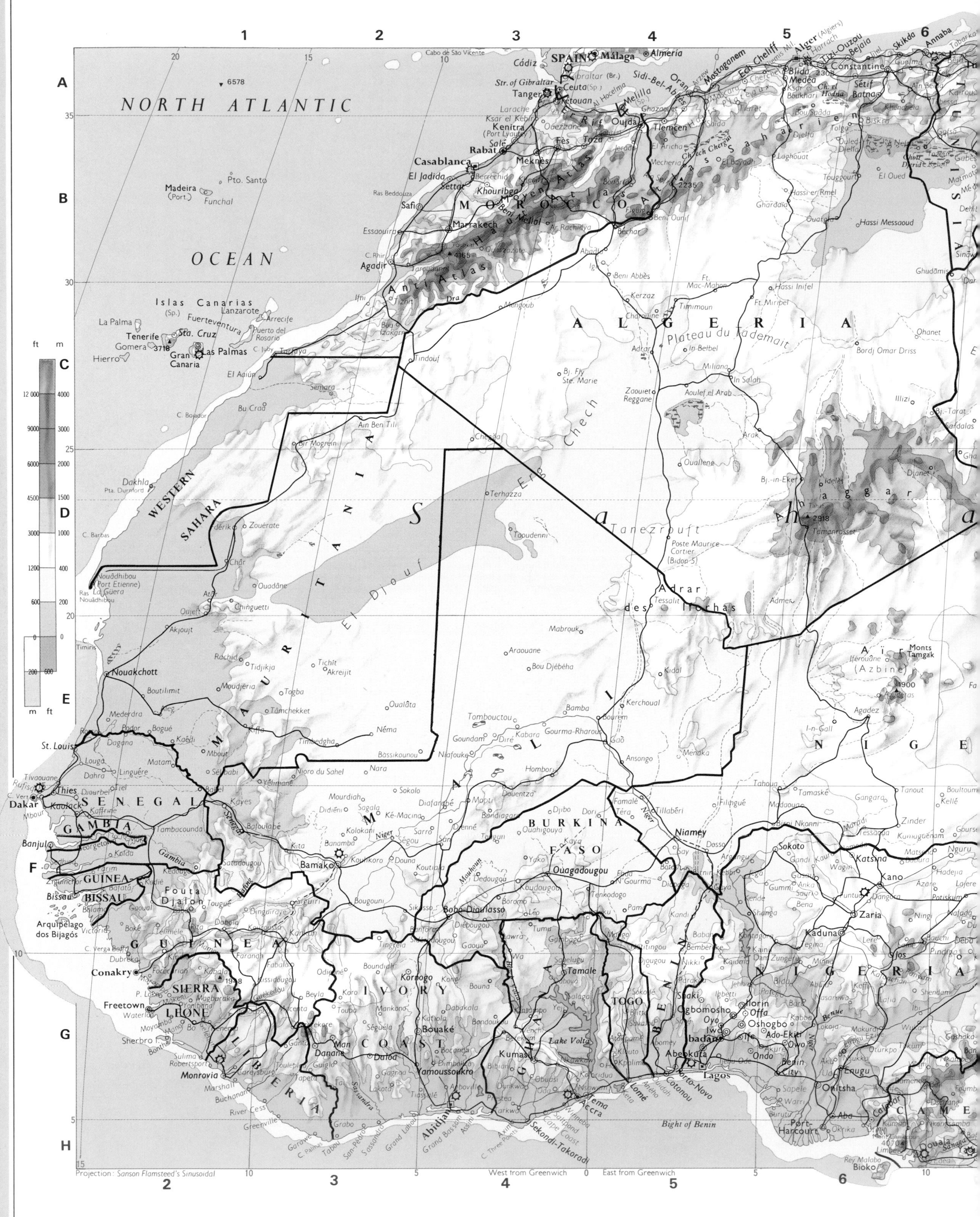
NORTH ATLANTIC
OCEAN
Madeira (Port.)
Pto. Santo
Funchal
Islas Canarias (Sp.)
La Palma
Tenerife
Gomera
Hierro
Gran Canaria
Las Palmas
Sta. Cruz
Fuerteventura
Lanzarote
Arrecife
SPAIN
Málaga
Almería
Cádiz
Str. of Gibraltar
Gibraltar (Br.)
Ceuta (Sp.)
Tanger
Tetouan
Melilla (Sp.)
Oran
Mostaganem
Alger (Algiers)
Tizi-Ouzou
Bejaia
Skikda
Annaba
Constantine
Sétif
Batna
Blida
Médéa
Ech Cheliff
Tlemcen
Oujda
Sidi-Bel-Abbès
Larache
Kenitra (Port Lyautey)
Salé
Rabat
Casablanca
El Jadida
Settat
Khouribga
Meknès
Fès
Taza
Safi
Essaouira
Marrakech
Agadir
MOROCCO
Anti Atlas
Béchar
Laghouat
Ghardaïa
Ouargla
Touggourt
Hassi Messaoud
Biskra
El Oued
Djelfa
ALGERIA
Plateau du Tademaït
In Salah
Adrar
Reggane
Tindouf
Beni Abbès
Timimoun
El Golea
Hassi Inifel
Bordj Omar Driss
Illizi
Djanet
Ahaggar
Tamanrasset
Tanezrouft
Poste Maurice Cortier (Bidon 5)
Adrar des Iforhas
Tessalit
El Aaiún
Semara
Bu Craa
C. Bojador
Dakhla
WESTERN SAHARA
C. Barbas
Nouâdhibou (Port Etienne)
Ras La Güera
Zouérate
Fdérik
Atar
Chinguetti
Akjoujt
Nouakchott
Ouadâne
Tidjikja
Tichît
Kiffa
Néma
Oualâta
Boutilimit
Aleg
Rosso
Kaédi
MAURITANIA
El Djouf
Erg Chech
Taoudenni
Tombouctou
Gao
Kidal
Araouane
Mabrouk
Bourem
Ansongo
Ménaka
Goundam
Niafounké
Hombori
Mopti
Ségou
Bamako
Kayes
Nioro du Sahel
Sikasso
MALI
Aïr (Azbine)
Agadez
Monts Tamgak
Iférouane
Tahoua
Zinder
Maradi
Niamey
Dosso
Tillabéri
NIGER
Sokoto
Katsina
Kano
Zaria
Kaduna
Jos
Ilorin
Oshogbo
Oyo
Ibadan
Ife
Abeokuta
Lagos
Benin City
Onitsha
Enugu
Port Harcourt
Calabar
NIGERIA
Bight of Benin
Cotonou
Porto-Novo
BENIN
Lomé
TOGO
Accra
Tema
Kumasi
Tamale
Lake Volta
Sekondi-Takoradi
GHANA
Ouagadougou
Bobo-Dioulasso
Koudougou
Dori
BURKINA FASO
Abidjan
Bouaké
Yamoussoukro
Korhogo
Man
Daloa
IVORY COAST
Monrovia
LIBERIA
Freetown
SIERRA LEONE
Conakry
GUINEA
Fouta Djalon
Bissau
GUINEA-BISSAU
Arquipélago dos Bijagós
Banjul
GAMBIA
Dakar
Thiès
Kaolack
St. Louis
SENEGAL
Tambacounda
Douala
Bioko
Projection: Sanson Flamsteed's Sinusoidal
West from Greenwich
East from Greenwich

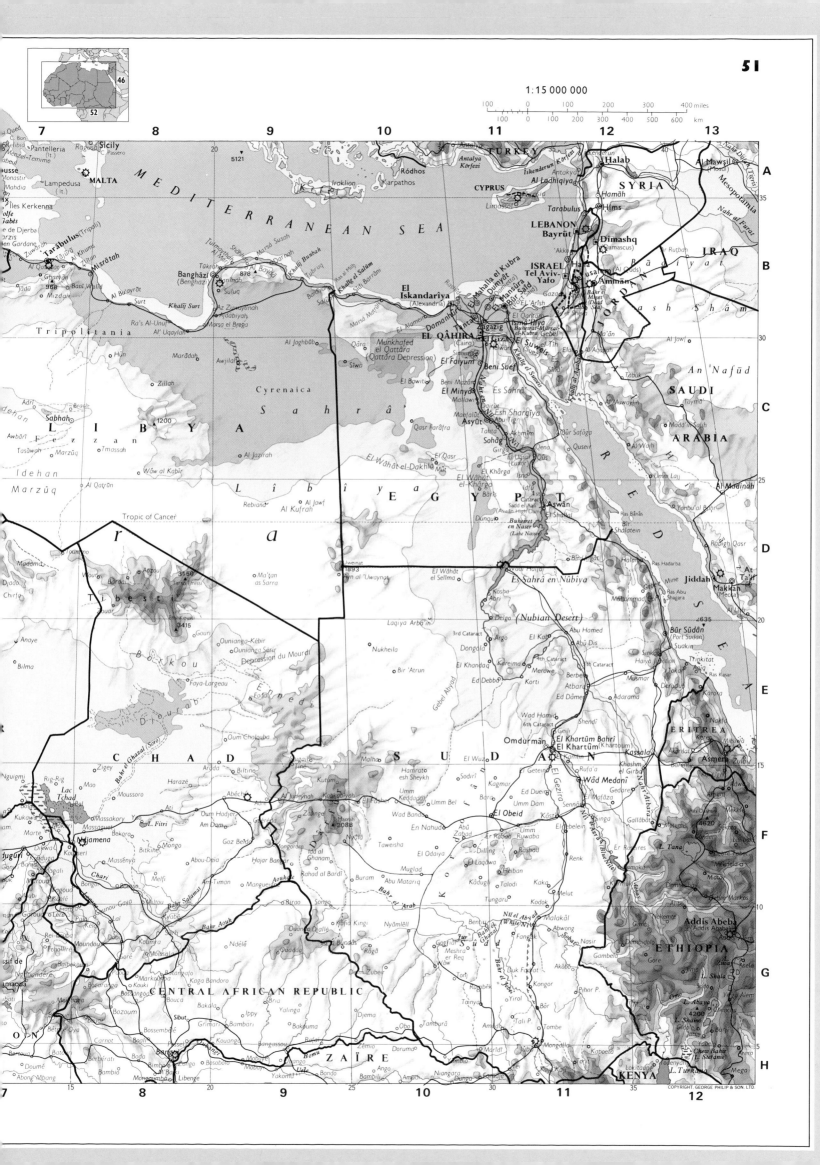

1:15 000 000

MEDITERRANEAN SEA

TURKEY
Antalya
Antalya Körfezi
Iskenderun Körfezi
Al Mawşil (Mosul)
Halab
CYPRUS
Al Ladhiqiya
Antakya
Hamāh
SYRIA
Mesopotamia
Tarabulus
Hims
Ar Rutbah
IRAQ
LEBANON
Bayrūt
Dimashq
Damascus
ISRAEL
Tel Aviv-Yafo
'Ammān
JORDAN
Bādiyat
ash Shām

MALTA
Pantelleria
Sicily
Ragusa
Passero
Ródhos
Iraklion
Karpathos

Tarābulus (Tripoli)
Al Khums
Misrātah
Banghāzi (Benghazi)
El Iskandariya (Alexandria)
El Qāhira (Cairo)
Giza
Es Suweis
El Faiyum
Beni Suef
SAUDI
ARABIA
Al Madīnah
Makkah (Mecca)
Jiddah
At Ta'if

Tropic of Cancer

LIBYA
Sahara
Cyrenaica
EGYPT
Libîyê
Aswān
Buheiret en Naser (Lake Nasser)

Tibesti
CHAD
Borkou
Ennedi
SUDAN
Nubian Desert
El Khartûm (Khartoum)
Omdurmān
ERITREA
Asmera
Kassala

N'djamena
Lac Tchad
Abéché
El Fasher
El Obeid
Wâd Medanî
ETHIOPIA
Addis Abeba (Addis Ababa)
L. Tana

CENTRAL AFRICAN REPUBLIC

ZAÏRE
KENYA
L. Turkana

COPYRIGHT. GEORGE PHILIP & SON. LTD.

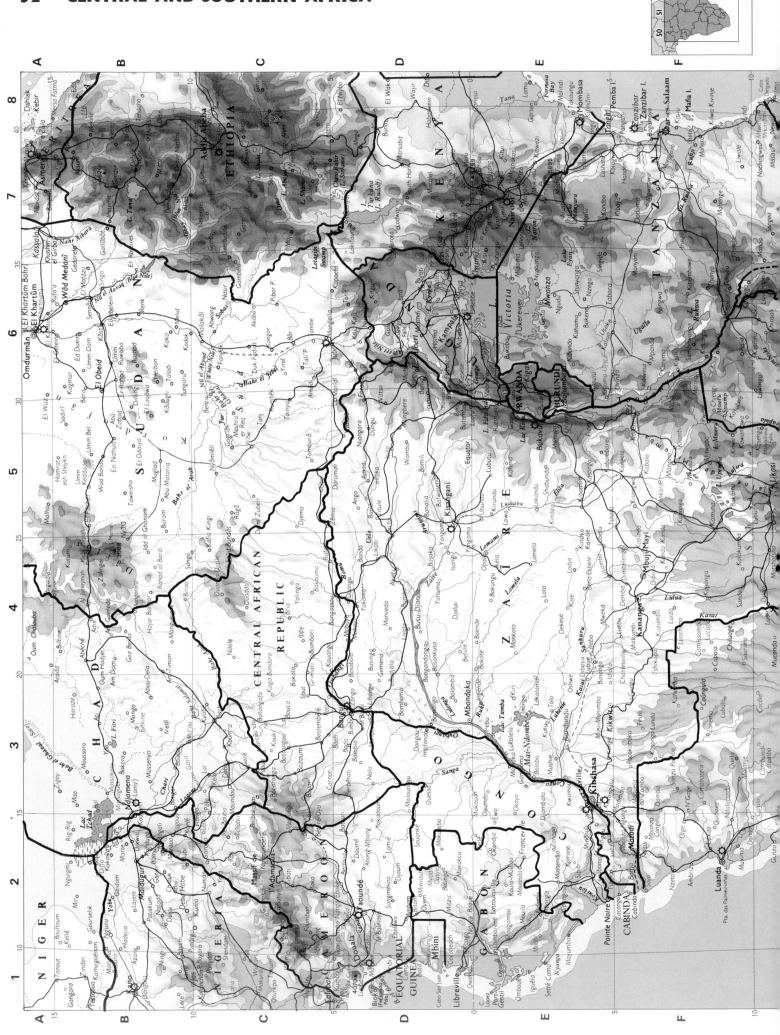

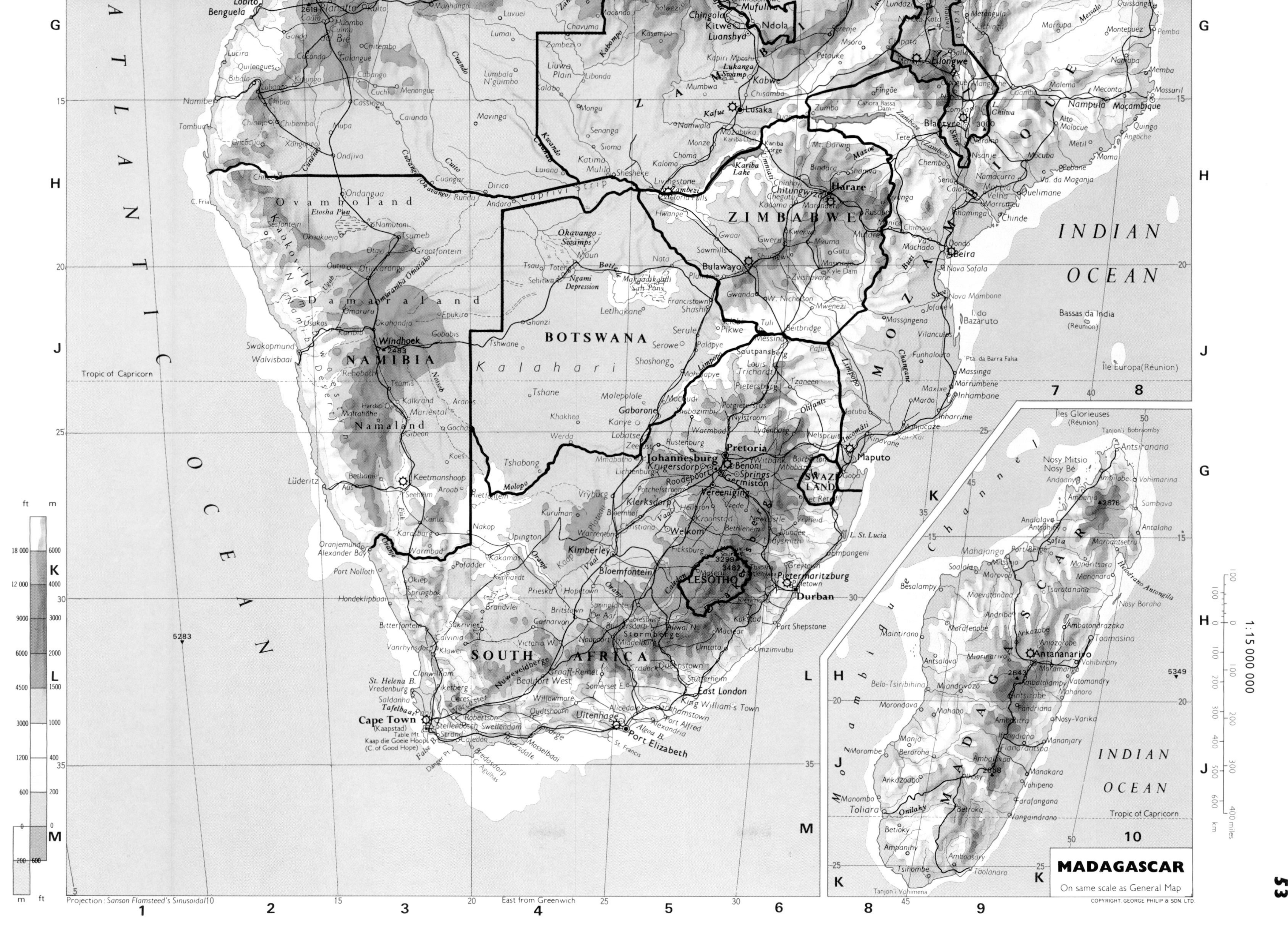

1 : 15 000 000

100   0   100   200   300   400 miles

100   0   100   200   300   400   500   600   km

MADAGASCAR
On same scale as General Map

COPYRIGHT GEORGE PHILIP & SON, LTD

INDIAN

OCEAN

INDIAN

OCEAN

MOZAMBIQUE

ZIMBABWE

Harare

Bulawayo

BOTSWANA

Kalahari

NAMIBIA

Namib Desert

Namaqualand

SOUTH AFRICA

LESOTHO

SWAZILAND

Johannesburg

Pretoria

Durban

Cape Town

Port Elizabeth

East London

Windhoek

Gaborone

Maputo

Beira

Lusaka

Tropic of Capricorn

ATLANTIC   OCEAN

Lobito

Benguela

Projection Sanson Flamsteed's Sinusoidal

East from Greenwich

Tropic of Capricorn

Antananarivo

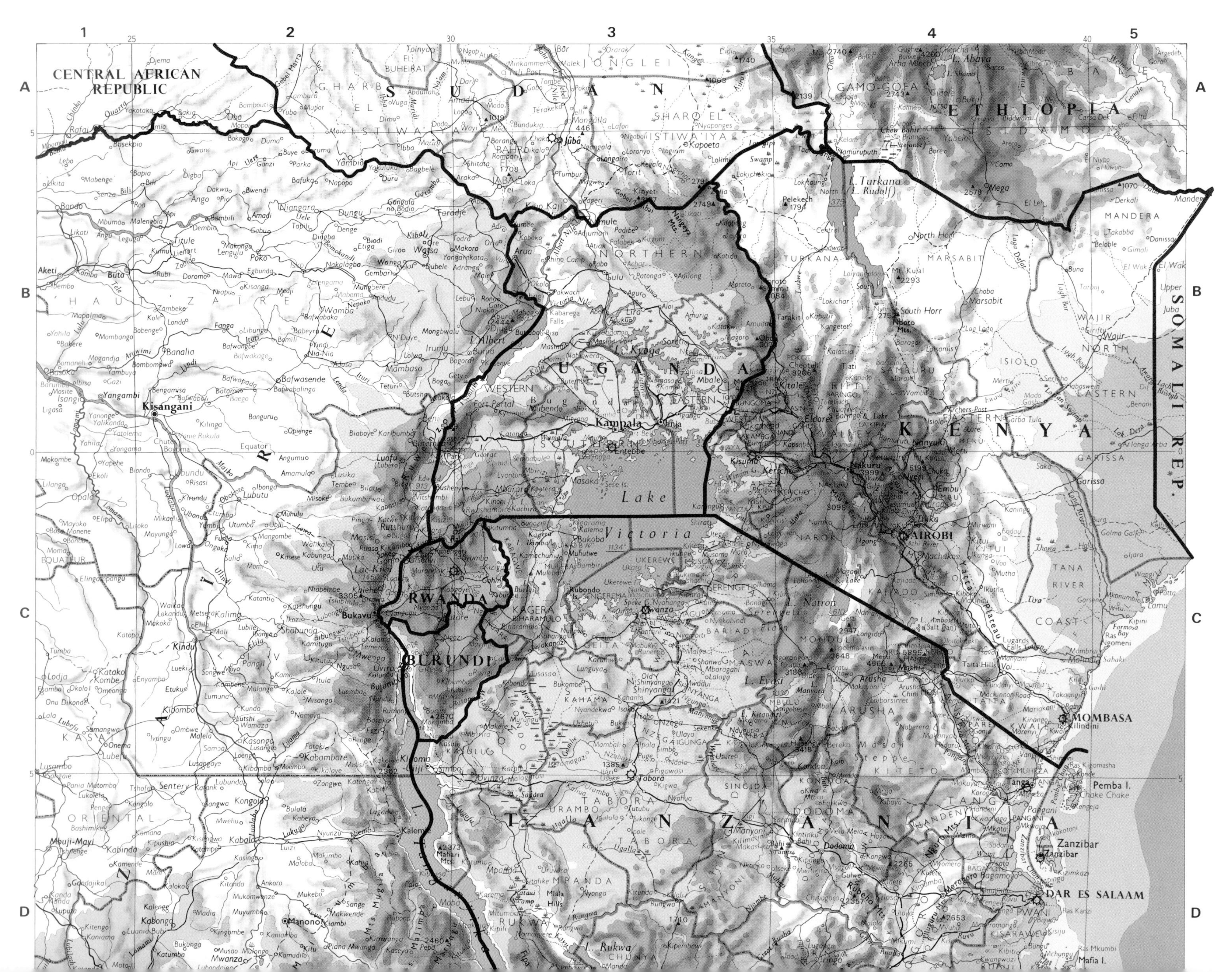

CENTRAL AFRICAN REPUBLIC
SUDAN
ETHIOPIA
SOMALI REP.
KENYA
UGANDA
TANZANIA
RWANDA
BURUNDI
L. Turkana (L. Rudolf)
Lake Victoria
L. Albert
L. Kyoga
L. Natron
L. Eyasi
L. Rukwa
NAIROBI
MOMBASA
DAR ES SALAAM
Zanzibar
Pemba I.
Mafia I.
Kampala
Entebbe
Kisangani
Juba
Tabora
Dodoma
Arusha
Bukavu
Kisumu
Nakuru
Tanga
Marsabit
Garissa
Yattaa Plateau

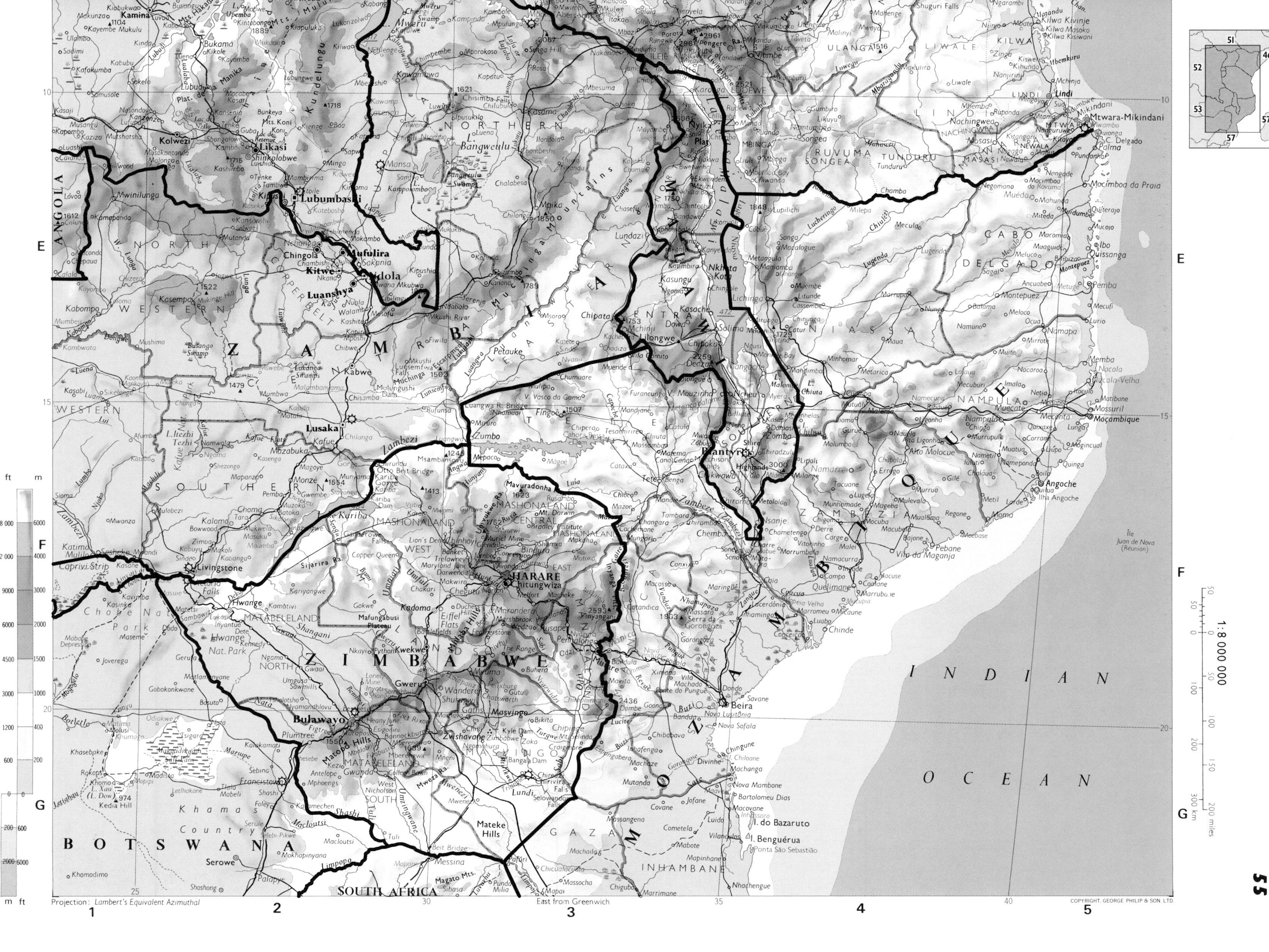

INDIAN
OCEAN
MOZAMBIQUE
MALAWI
ZAMBIA
ZIMBABWE
BOTSWANA
ANGOLA
SOUTH AFRICA
HARARE
Lusaka
Bulawayo
Beira
Blantyre
Lilongwe
Kitwe
Ndola
Mufulira
Luanshya
Chingola
Lubumbashi
Likasi
Kolwezi
Kamina
Livingstone
Lindi
Mtwara-Mikindani
Moçambique
Angoche
Quelimane
Chinde
Masvingo
Gweru
Kwekwe
Kadoma
Chitungwiza
Francistown
Serowe
Kabwe
Kafue
Chipata
Petauke
Zumbo
Hwange
Tete
Nampula
Nacala
Pemba
Lichinga
Mansa
Kasama
Mpika
Messina
NORTHERN
WESTERN
SOUTHERN
CENTRAL
COPPERBELT
EASTERN
NORTH-WESTERN
MASHONALAND CENTRAL
MASHONALAND WEST
MASHONALAND EAST
MATABELELAND NORTH
MATABELELAND SOUTH
CABO DELGADO
NIASSA
NAMPULA
ZAMBEZIA
SOFALA
MANICA
TETE
GAZA
INHAMBANE
Caprivi Strip
Chobe National Park
Khama's Country
Mateke Hills
Zambezi
Limpopo
Île Juan de Nova (Réunion)
I. do Bazaruto
I. Benguérua
1:8 000 000
50 0 50 100 150 200 miles
50 0 100 200 300 km
Projection: Lambert's Equivalent Azimuthal
East from Greenwich
ft m
18 000 6000
12 000 4000
9000 3000
6000 2000
4500 1500
3000 1000
1200 400
600 200
0 0
200 600
2000 6000
m ft

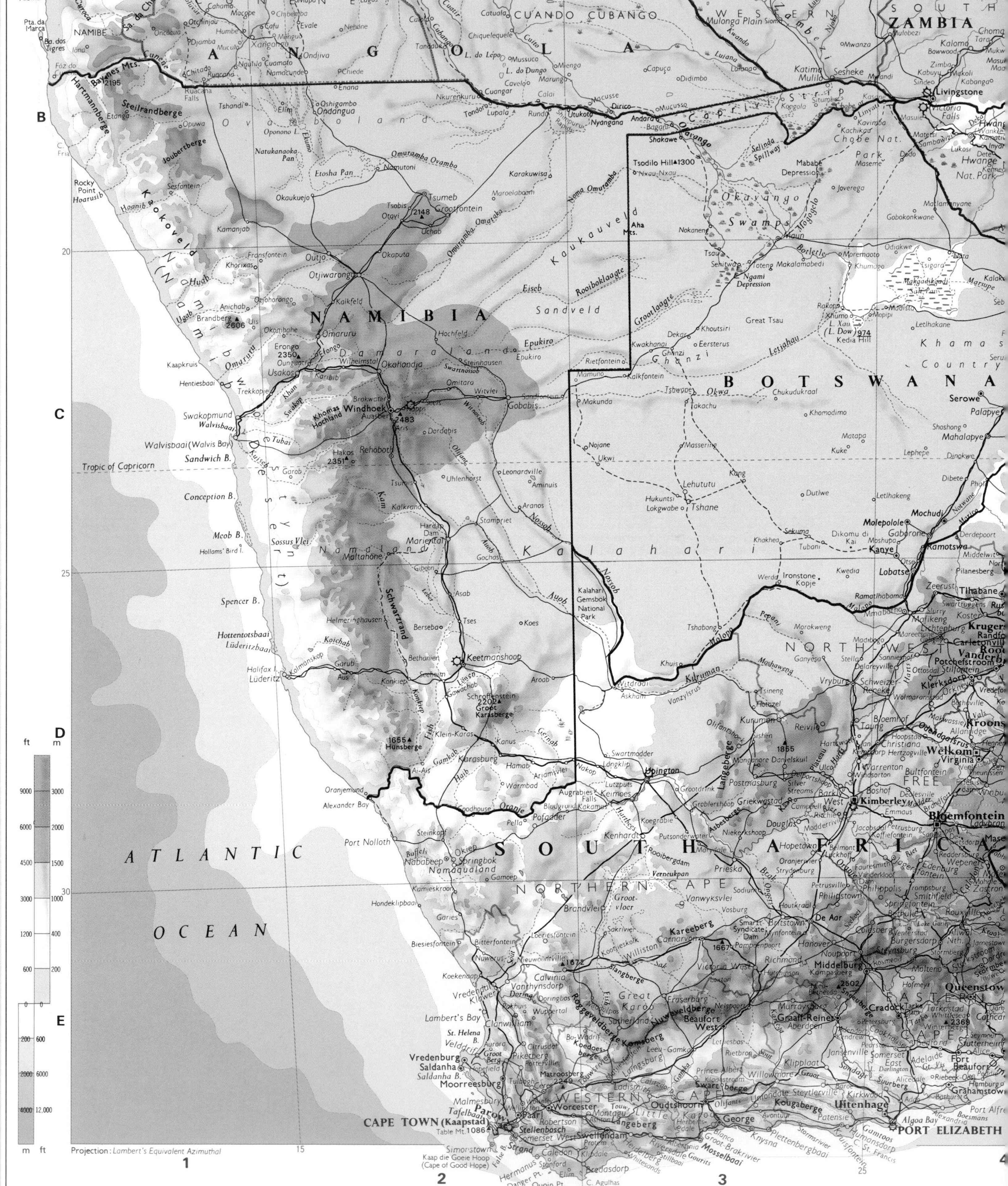
ATLANTIC OCEAN
NAMIBIA
BOTSWANA
SOUTH AFRICA
ZAMBIA
ANGOLA
Tropic of Capricorn
Projection: Lambert's Equivalent Azimuthal

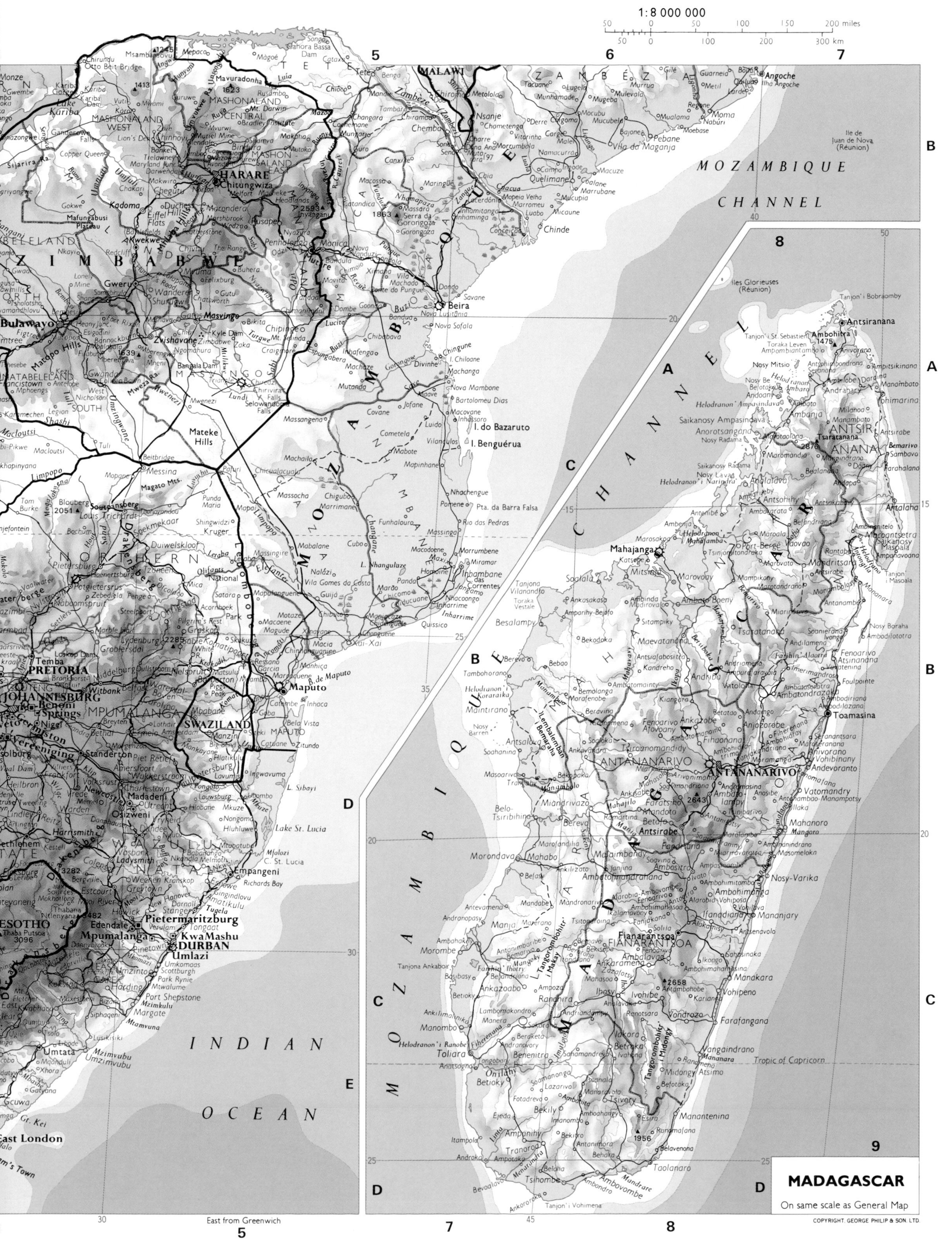

1:8 000 000

50   0   100   150   200 miles

50   0   100   200   300 km

MOZAMBIQUE

CHANNEL

INDIAN

OCEAN

Tropic of Capricorn

East from Greenwich

MADAGASCAR

On same scale as General Map

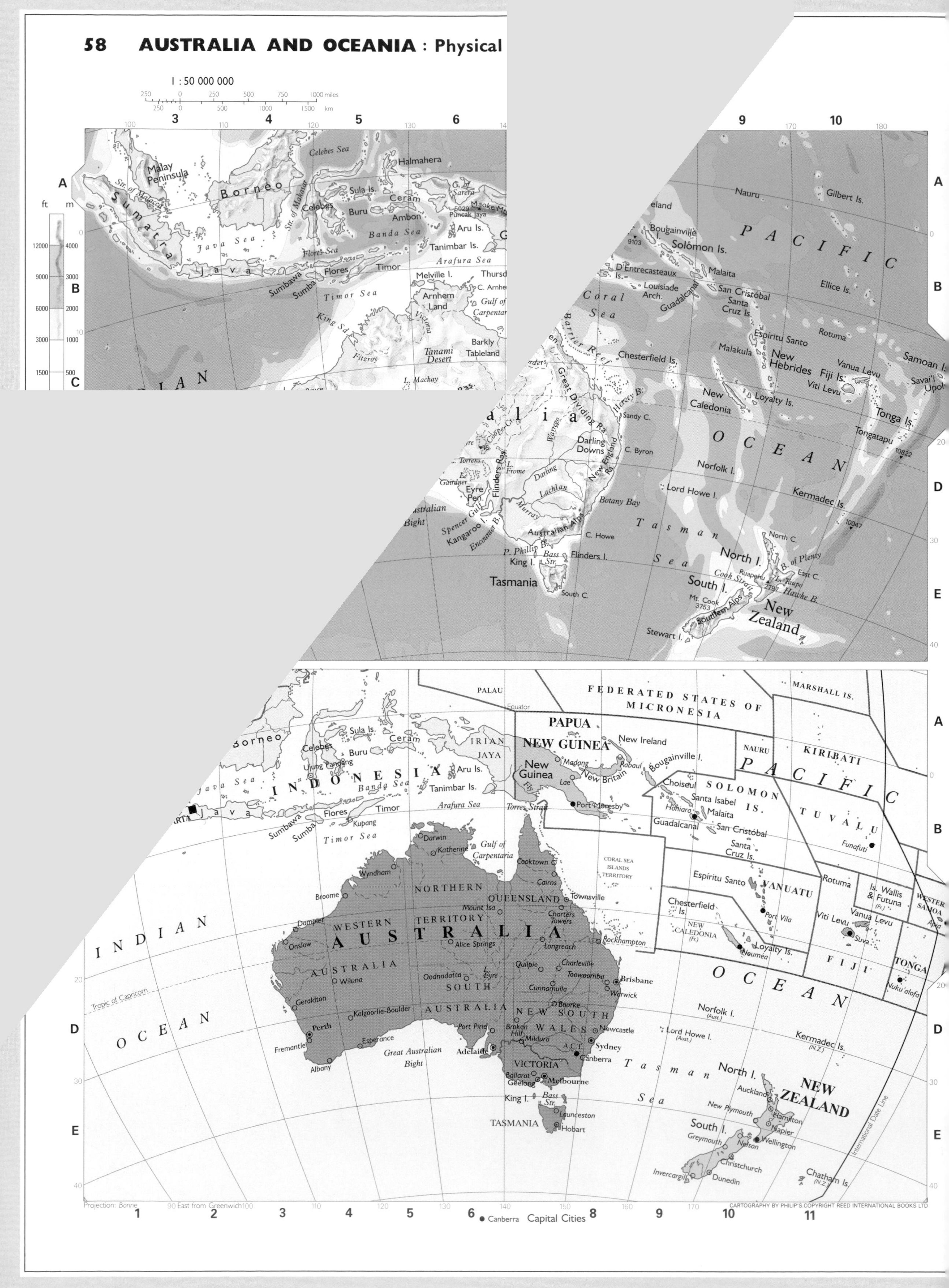

1 : 50 000 000

ft   m

12000   4000
9000   3000
6000   2000
3000   1000
1500   500

Malay Peninsula
Str. of Malacca
Sumatra
Borneo
Celebes Sea
Sula Is.
Celebes
Buru
Ceram
Ambon
6029
Puncak Jaya
Maoke Mts.
Halmahera
G. M.
Sorera
Aru Is.
Java Sea
Java
Flores Sea
Sumbawa
Flores
Sumba
Timor
Banda Sea
Tanimbar Is.
Arafura Sea
Timor Sea
Melville I.
Thursd
C. Arnhe
Arnhem Land
Gulf of Carpentaria
King Sd.
Victoria
Fitzroy
Tanami Desert
Barkly Tableland
L. Mackay

Nauru
Gilbert Is.
PACIFIC
land
Bougainville
9103
Solomon Is.
D'Entrecasteaux
Malaita
Ellice Is.
Coral
Louisiade Arch.
San Cristóbal
Santa Cruz Is.
Guadalcanal
Espíritu Santo
Rotuma
Samoan Is.
Sea
Chesterfield Is.
Malakula
New Hebrides
Vanua Levu
Savai'i
Upol
Barrier Reef
Fiji Is.
Viti Levu
New Caledonia
Loyalty Is.
OCEAN
Tonga Is.
Tongatapu
10822
Great Dividing Ra.
Honey B.
Sandy C.
Darling Downs
New England
C. Byron
Norfolk I.
Lord Howe I.
Kermadec Is.
Torrens
Frome
Darling
Eyre Pen.
Gairdner
Flinders Ra.
Lachlan
Murray
Botany Bay
10047
Australian
Bight
Kangaroo I.
Encounter B.
Spencer Gulf
Australian Alps
C. Howe
Tasman
North C.
Australia
P. Philip B.
Bass Str.
Flinders I.
King I.
Sea
North I.
B. of Plenty
Ruapehu
2797
L. Taupo
East C.
Hawke B.
Tasmania
South C.
South I.
Mt. Cook
3753
Southern Alps
New Zealand
Stewart I.

PALAU
Equator
FEDERATED STATES OF MICRONESIA
MARSHALL IS.
Borneo
Sula Is.
Ceram
IRIAN JAYA
PAPUA NEW GUINEA
New Ireland
NAURU
KIRIBATI
Celebes
Buru
New Guinea
Madang
Rabaul
Bougainville I.
PACIFIC
Ujung Pandang
INDONESIA
Aru Is.
Lae
New Britain
Choiseul
SOLOMON IS.
TUVALU
Java Sea
Banda Sea
Tanimbar Is.
Port Moresby
Santa Isabel
Java
Flores
Timor
Arafura Sea
Torres Strait
Honiara
Malaita
Sumbawa
Sumba
Kupang
Timor Sea
Guadalcanal
San Cristóbal
Funafuti
Darwin
Gulf of Carpentaria
Santa Cruz Is.
Katherine
Cooktown
CORAL SEA ISLANDS TERRITORY
Espíritu Santo
VANUATU
Rotuma
Is. Wallis & Futuna (Fr.)
WESTER SAMOA
Wyndham
NORTHERN
Cairns
Apia
Broome
TERRITORY
QUEENSLAND
Townsville
Chesterfield Is.
NEW CALEDONIA (Fr.)
Port Vila
Viti Levu
Vanua Levu
INDIAN
Dampier
WESTERN
Mount Isa
Charters Towers
Suva
Onslow
AUSTRALIA
Alice Springs
Longreach
Rockhampton
Noumea
Loyalty Is.
FIJI
TONGA
Wiluna
AUSTRALIA
Quilpie
Charleville
Toowoomba
Oodnadatta
SOUTH
Cunnamulla
Warwick
Brisbane
Norfolk I. (Aust.)
Nuku'alofa
Geraldton
Kalgoorlie-Boulder
L. Eyre
AUSTRALIA
Bourke
Perth
OCEAN
Tropic of Capricorn
Broken Hill
NEW SOUTH
Newcastle
Lord Howe I. (Aust.)
Kermadec Is. (N.Z.)
Fremantle
Port Pirie
Mildura
WALES
Esperance
Great Australian Bight
Adelaide
A.C.T.
Sydney
North I.
NEW
Albany
VICTORIA
Canberra
Tasman
Auckland
ZEALAND
Ballarat
Geelong
Melbourne
King I.
Bass Str.
Sea
New Plymouth
Hamilton
TASMANIA
Launceston
South I.
Napier
Hobart
Greymouth
Nelson
Wellington
Invercargill
Dunedin
Christchurch
Chatham Is. (N.Z.)
International Date Line

• Canberra Capital Cities

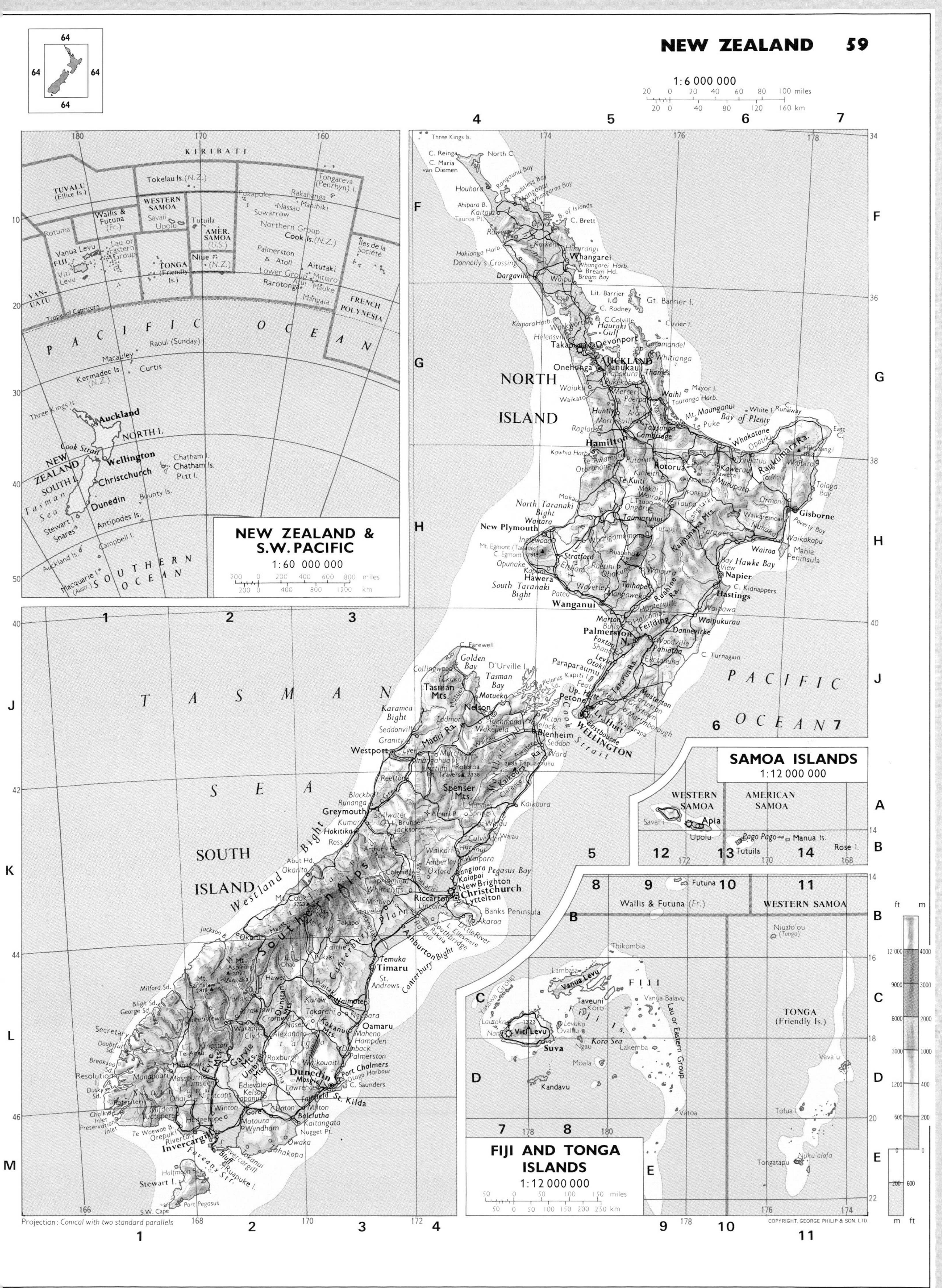

1:6 000 000

20 0   20 40 60 80 100 miles
20 0   40   80 120 160 km

NEW ZEALAND &
S.W. PACIFIC

1:60 000 000

200 0   200 400 600 800 miles
200 0   400   800   1200 km

NORTH
ISLAND

SOUTH
ISLAND

SAMOA ISLANDS
1:12 000 000

WESTERN
SAMOA

AMERICAN
SAMOA

FIJI AND TONGA
ISLANDS
1:12 000 000

50 0   50   100   150 miles
50 0 50 100 150 200 250 km

Projection: Conical with two standard parallels

COPYRIGHT. GEORGE PHILIP & SON. LTD.

INDONESIA
TIMOR SEA
INDIAN OCEAN
Timor
Sumba
Sumbawa
Lombok
Roti
Sawa
Melville I.
Bathurst I.
Darwin
Joseph Bonaparte Gulf
Bonaparte Archipelago
King Leopold Ranges
Great Sandy Desert
Gibson Desert
Tanami Desert
NORTHERN TERRITORY
Hamersley Range
Eighty Mile Beach
Port Hedland
Broome
Karratha
Dampier Archipelago
Lake Mackay
Lake Disappointment
Macdonnell Ranges
Rowley Shoals
Exmouth Gulf

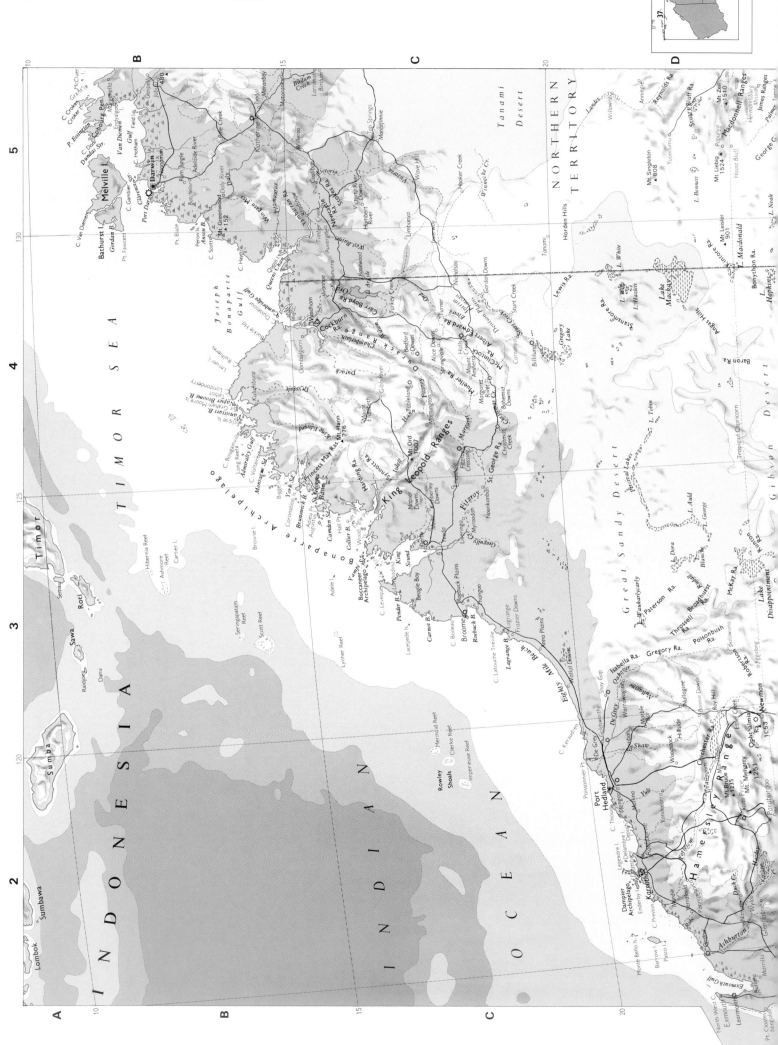

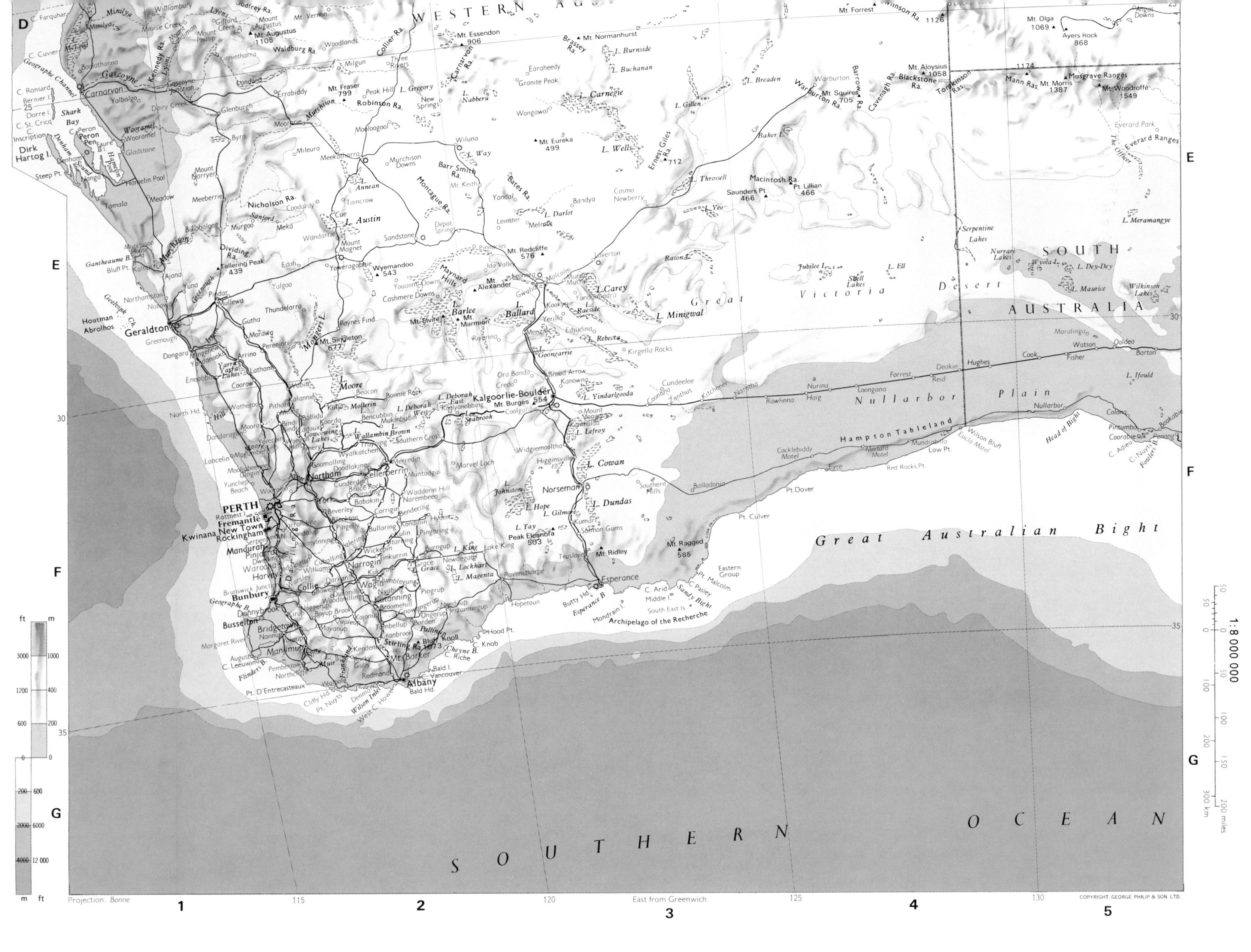

1:8 000 000

50   0   50   100   150   200 miles
50   0   50   100   200   300 km

SOUTH

AUSTRALIA

WESTERN AUST

Great Victoria Desert

Gibson Desert

Nullarbor Plain

Hampton Tableland

Great Australian Bight

SOUTHERN

OCEAN

Mt. Olga 1069
Ayers Rock 868
Musgrave Ranges
Mt. Morris 1387
Mann Ra. 1387
Mt. Woodroffe 1549
The Officer
Everard Park
Everard Ranges

Mt. Forest
Winston Ra. 1126
Mt. Aloysius 1058
Blackstone Ra.
Cavenagh Ra.
Barrow Ra.
Warburton Ra.
Mt. Squires 705
Warburton Ra.
J. Breaden
Baker
Macintosh Ra. 466
Saunders Pt. 466
Throssell
Yeo
Cosmo Newberg
L. Minigwal

L. Disy-Dey
L. Yeo
L. Maurice
Serpentine Lakes
Narrara Lakes
Wilkinson Lakes
Ooldea
Barton

L. Ifould
Cook
Watson
Fisher
Cook

Nurina
Hog
Forrest
Deakin
Red
Loongana
Rawlinna
Naretha
Reid

Cocklebiddy Motel
Madura Motel
Mundrabilla
Eucla Motel
Wilson Bluff
Low Pt.
Eyre
Coorabie
C. Nuyts
Fowlers
Denial

Pt. Culver
Pt. Dover

C. Arid
C. Pasley
Eastern Group
Middle I.
South East Is.

Esperance
Archipelago of the Recherche
Mt. Ragged 585

Mt. Burnside
Mt. Normanhurst
J. Buchanan
Carnegie
L. Carey
L. Wells
Ernest Giles Ra. 712
Raeside L.
Mt. Essendon 906
Bates Ra.
Mt. Eureka 499
Granite Peak
Earaheedy
Carnarvon Ra.
Wongawol
Barr Smith Ra.
Wiluna
Depot Springs
New Springs
Montague Ra.
Sandstone
Murchison Downs
Mt. Keith
Leinster
Yardok
Yarlok
Mt. Redcliffe 576
Melrose
Leonora
Bullard
Mt. Alexander
Leonora
Bandya
Cosmo Newberg
Laverton
Mt. Weld
Murrin Murrin

L. Darlot
Diorite
Bullabulling
L. Deborah
L. Deborah West
Bonnie Rock
Mt. Barlee
Maynard Hills
Barlee
Mt. Marmion
Marvel Loch
Southern Cross
Kalgoorlie-Boulder 554
Coolgardie
Kanowna
Broad Arrow
Ora Banda
Bullfinch
Gnarowna
Widgiemooltha

L. Cowan
L. Dundas
Norseman
Hope
Mt. Gilmore
L. Tay
Peak Eleanora 503
Mt. Ridley
Grass Patch
Scaddan
Salmon Gums
Gibson
Mt. Malcolm
Pt. Malcolm

WESTERN

AUSTRALIA

Mt. Fraser 719
Cue
Austin
Mount Magnet
Mt. Singleton 677
Mt. Morell
Dalwallinu
Wongan Hills
Wyalkatchem
Merredin
Kellerberrin
Quairading
Bruce Rock
Narembeen
Hyden
Lake King
L. King
Ravensthorpe
Hopetoun
C. Knob
C. Riche
Bremer B.
C. Vancouver
Mt. Barker
Albany
Bald Hd.
Stirling Ra.
Gnowangerup
Jerramungup
Ongerup
Cranbrook
Kojonup
Katanning
Wagin
Narrogin
Pingelly
Brookton
Beverley
York
Northam
Toodyay
New Norcia
Gingin
Chittering
Moora
Dongara
Mingenew
Three Springs
Carnamah
Coorow
Moora

Geraldton
Houtman Abrolhos
Greenough
North Hd.
Leeman
Jurien B.
Lancelin
Yanchep

PERTH
Fremantle
Rottnest I.
Kwinana
Rockingham
Mandurah
Pinjarra
Harvey
Waroona
Yarloop
Bunbury
Busselton
Margaret River
C. Naturaliste
C. Leeuwin
Augusta
Pemberton
Manjimup
Bridgetown
Nannup
Collie
Donnybrook
Boyup Brook
Kojonup

Carnarvon
Gascoyne R.
Shark Bay
Denham
Dirk Hartog I.
Hamelin Pool
Geographe Channel
C. Cuvier
C. Ronsard
Bernier I.
Dorre I.
C. St. Cricq
C. Peron

Mt. Augustus 1106
Mt. Vernon
Waldburg Ra.
Nicholson Ra.
Robinson Ra.
Peak Hill
L. Gregory
Meekatharra
Kennedy Ra.
Lyons R.
Williambury
Collier Ra.
Godfrey Ra.

East from Greenwich

COPYRIGHT GEORGE PHILIP & SON LTD.

Projection: Bonne

m   ft
3000
1200
600
0
200
600
2000
4000   12 000

E   F   G

1   2   3   4   5

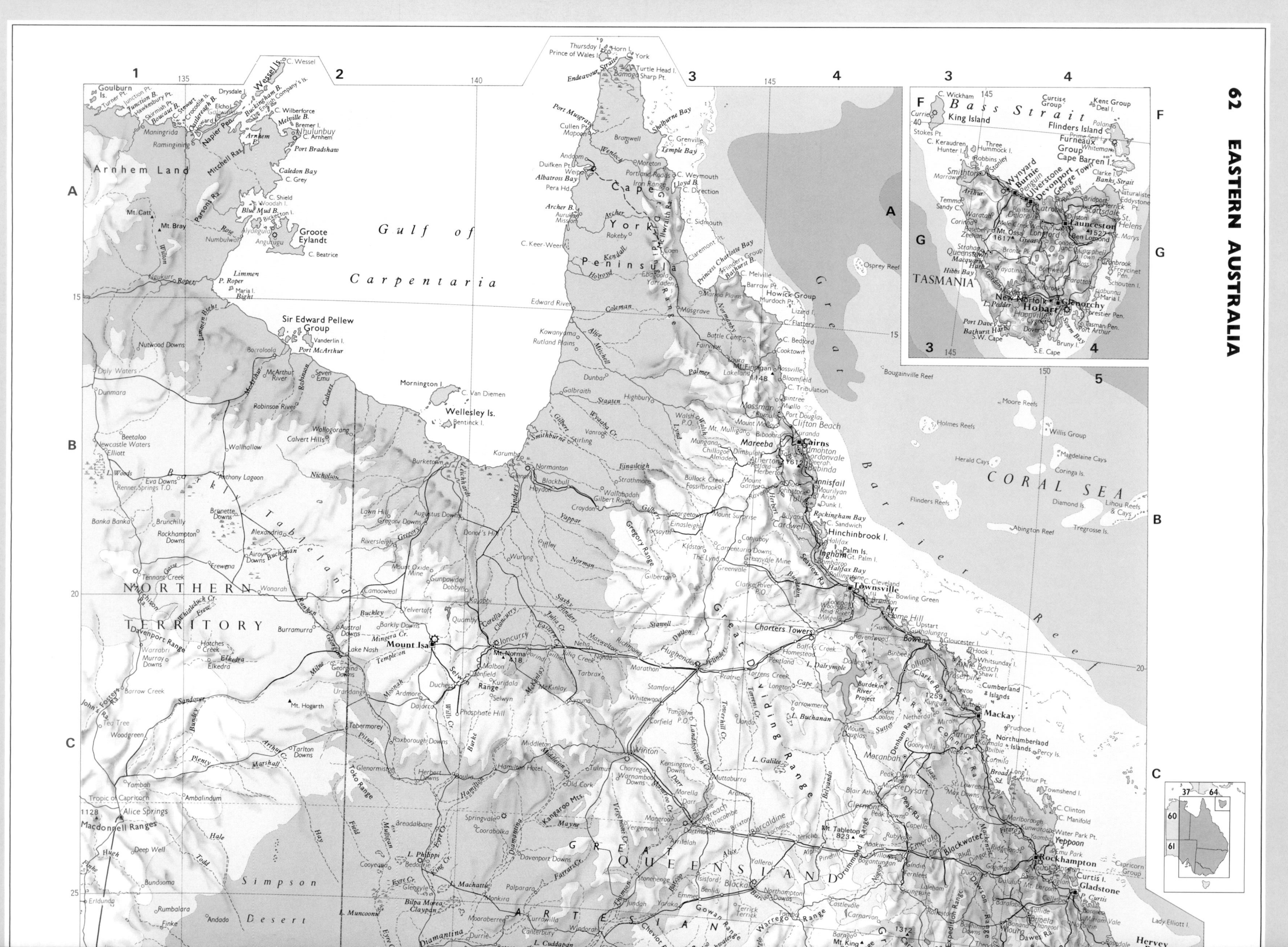

Gulf of Carpentaria
Great Barrier Reef
CORAL SEA
Cape York Peninsula
Arnhem Land
NORTHERN TERRITORY
QUEENSLAND
GREAT ARTESIAN BASIN
Great Dividing Range
Simpson Desert
Barkly Tableland
Groote Eylandt
Wellesley Is.
Sir Edward Pellew Group
Mornington I.
Cairns
Townsville
Mackay
Rockhampton
Gladstone
Mount Isa
Cloncurry
Charters Towers
Hughenden
Winton
Longreach
Barcaldine
Emerald
Alice Springs
Macdonnell Ranges
Normanton
Mareeba
Bowen
Ingham
Innisfail
Hinchinbrook I.
TASMANIA
Bass Strait
King Island
Flinders Island
Launceston
Hobart
Devonport
Burnie

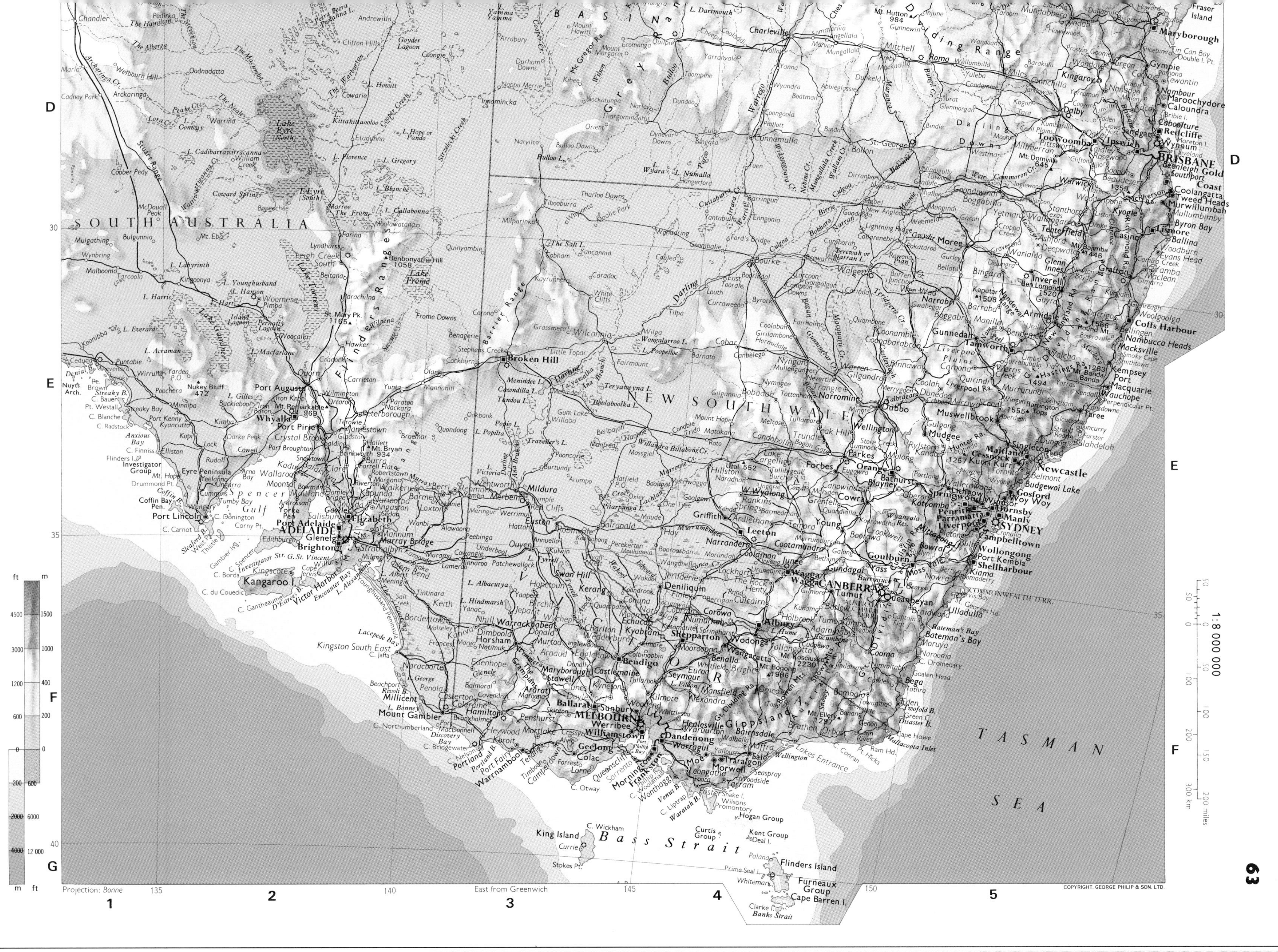

1:8 000 000

50   0   50   100   150   200 miles
50   0   100   200   300 km

TASMAN

SEA

Projection: Bonne

East from Greenwich

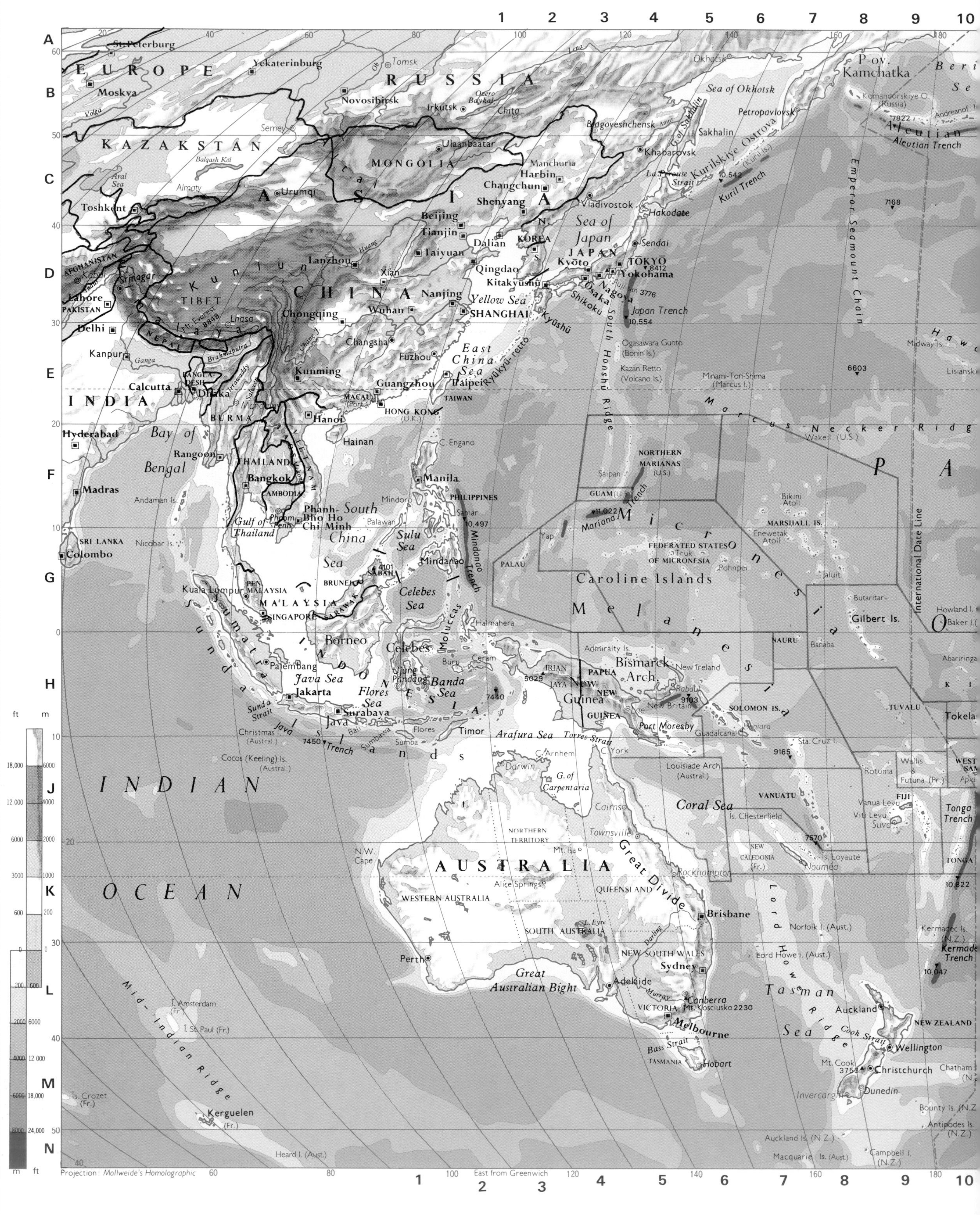

1 2 3 4 5 6 7 8 9 10
A B C D E F G H J K L M N
St. Peterburg
EUROPE
Yekaterinburg
Tomsk
RUSSIA
Moskva
Volga
Novosibirsk
Ozero Baykal
Irkutsk
Chita
Lena
Okhotsk
P-ov. Kamchatka
Sea of Okhotsk
Petropavlovsk
Komandorskiye O. (Russia)
Andreanof Is.
Aleutian
Aleutian Trench
7822
Semey
Blagoveshchensk
Amur
Sakhalin
Ulaanbaatar
KAZAKSTAN
Balqash Köl
MONGOLIA
Manchuria
Harbin
Khabarovsk
La Pérouse Strait
Kurilskiye Ostrova (Kuril Is.)
10,542
Kuril Trench
Emperor Seamount Chain
Aral Sea
Almaty
Urumqi
ASIA
Changchun
Shenyang
Vladivostok
Hakodate
7168
Toshkent
Beijing
Tianjin
Dalian
N. KOREA
S.
Sea of Japan
JAPAN
Sendai
Taiyuan
Lanzhou
Huang
Xian
Qingdao
Kyōto
TŌKYŌ
8412
Yokohama
AFGHANISTAN
Srinagar
Kunlun
TIBET
CHINA
Nanjing
Kitakyushu
Ōsaka
Nagoya
Fujisan 3776
Shikoku
Lahore
PAKISTAN
Mt. Everest 8848
Lhasa
Himalaya
NEPAL
Chongqing
Wuhan
Yellow Sea
SHANGHAI
Kyūshū
Japan Trench
10,554
Delhi
Chang Jiang
Changsha
East China Sea
South Honshu Ridge
Ryukyu-retto
Ogasawara Gunto (Bonin Is.)
Kanpur
Ganga
Brahmaputra
Fuzhou
Kazan Retto (Volcano Is.)
Minami-Tori-Shima (Marcus I.)
6603
Midway Is.
Hawaiian
Lisianski
BANGLADESH
Irrawaddy
Salween
Kunming
Calcutta
Dhaka
Guangzhou
Taipei
TAIWAN
INDIA
Mandalay
MACAU (Port.)
HONG KONG (U.K.)
Marcus Necker Ridge
BURMA
Hanoi
Hyderabad
Bay of Bengal
Hainan
C. Engano
Wake I. (U.S.)
Rangoon
THAILAND
VIETNAM
Bangkok
CAMBODIA
Manila
NORTHERN MARIANAS (U.S.)
Saipan
GUAM (U.S.)
PACIFIC
Madras
Andaman Is.
Mindoro
PHILIPPINES
Bikini Atoll
Phnom Penh
Phanh-Bho Ho Chi Minh
Gulf of Thailand
South China Sea
Palawan
Samar
10,497
11,022
Mariana Trench
Micronesia
Enewetak Atoll
MARSHALL IS.
International Date Line
SRI LANKA
Colombo
Nicobar Is.
Sulu Sea
Mindanao
Mindanao Trench
Yap
PALAU
FEDERATED STATES OF MICRONESIA
Truk
Pohnpei
Jaluit
PEN. MALAYSIA
MALAYSIA
BRUNEI
SABAH
4101
Caroline Islands
Kuala Lumpur
SINGAPORE
SARAWAK
Celebes Sea
Melanesia
Butaritari
Gilbert Is.
Howland I.
Baker I.
Sumatra
Borneo
Halmahera
Moluccas
NAURU
Banaba
Abariringa
Celebes
Buru
Ceram
Admiralty Is.
Bismarck Arch.
New Ireland
Palembang
INDONESIA
Java Sea
Jakarta
Ujung Pandang
Banda Sea
Flores Sea
7440
IRIAN JAYA
5029
PAPUA NEW GUINEA
New Guinea
Rabaul
New Britain
9103
SOLOMON IS.
TUVALU
Tokelau
Sunda Strait
Surabaya
Java
Christmas I. (Austral.)
Java Trench
7450
Sunda Islands
Sumbawa
Bali
Sumba
Flores
Timor
Arafura Sea
Torres Strait
C. York
Port Moresby
Guadalcanal
Honiara
Sta. Cruz I.
9165
Cocos (Keeling) Is. (Austral.)
C. Arnhem
Darwin
G. of Carpentaria
Louisiade Arch. (Austral.)
Rotuma
Wallis & Futuna (Fr.)
WESTERN SAMOA
Apia
INDIAN OCEAN
Cairns
Coral Sea
VANUATU
FIJI
Vanua Levu
Viti Levu
Suva
Tonga Trench
NORTHERN TERRITORY
Townsville
Is. Chesterfield
7570
NEW CALEDONIA (Fr.)
Is. Loyauté
Nouméa
TONGA
N.W. Cape
Mt. Isa
AUSTRALIA
Great Dividing Range
Rockhampton
10,822
Alice Springs
QUEENSLAND
WESTERN AUSTRALIA
L. Eyre
SOUTH AUSTRALIA
Brisbane
Lord Howe Ridge
Norfolk I. (Aust.)
Kermadec Is. (N.Z.)
Kermadec Trench
Darling
NEW SOUTH WALES
Lord Howe I. (Aust.)
Perth
Sydney
10,047
Great Australian Bight
Adelaide
Murray
Canberra
Mt. Kosciusko 2230
Tasman Sea
Auckland
I. Amsterdam (Fr.)
VICTORIA
Melbourne
NEW ZEALAND
I. St. Paul (Fr.)
Bass Strait
Cook Strait
Wellington
Mid-Indian Ridge
TASMANIA
Hobart
Mt. Cook 3753
Christchurch
Chatham Is. (N.Z.)
Is. Crozet (Fr.)
Invercargill
Dunedin
Kerguelen (Fr.)
Bounty Is. (N.Z.)
Antipodes Is. (N.Z.)
Auckland Is. (N.Z.)
Heard I. (Aust.)
Macquarie Is. (Aust.)
Campbell I. (N.Z.)
ft m
18,000 6000
12 000 4000
6000 2000
3000 1000
600 200
0 0
200 600
2000 6000
4000 12 000
6000 18,000
8000 24,000
m ft
Projection: Mollweide's Homolographic
East from Greenwich
20 40 60 80 100 120 140 160 180
60 50 40 30 20 10 0 10 20 30 40 50

1:54 000 000

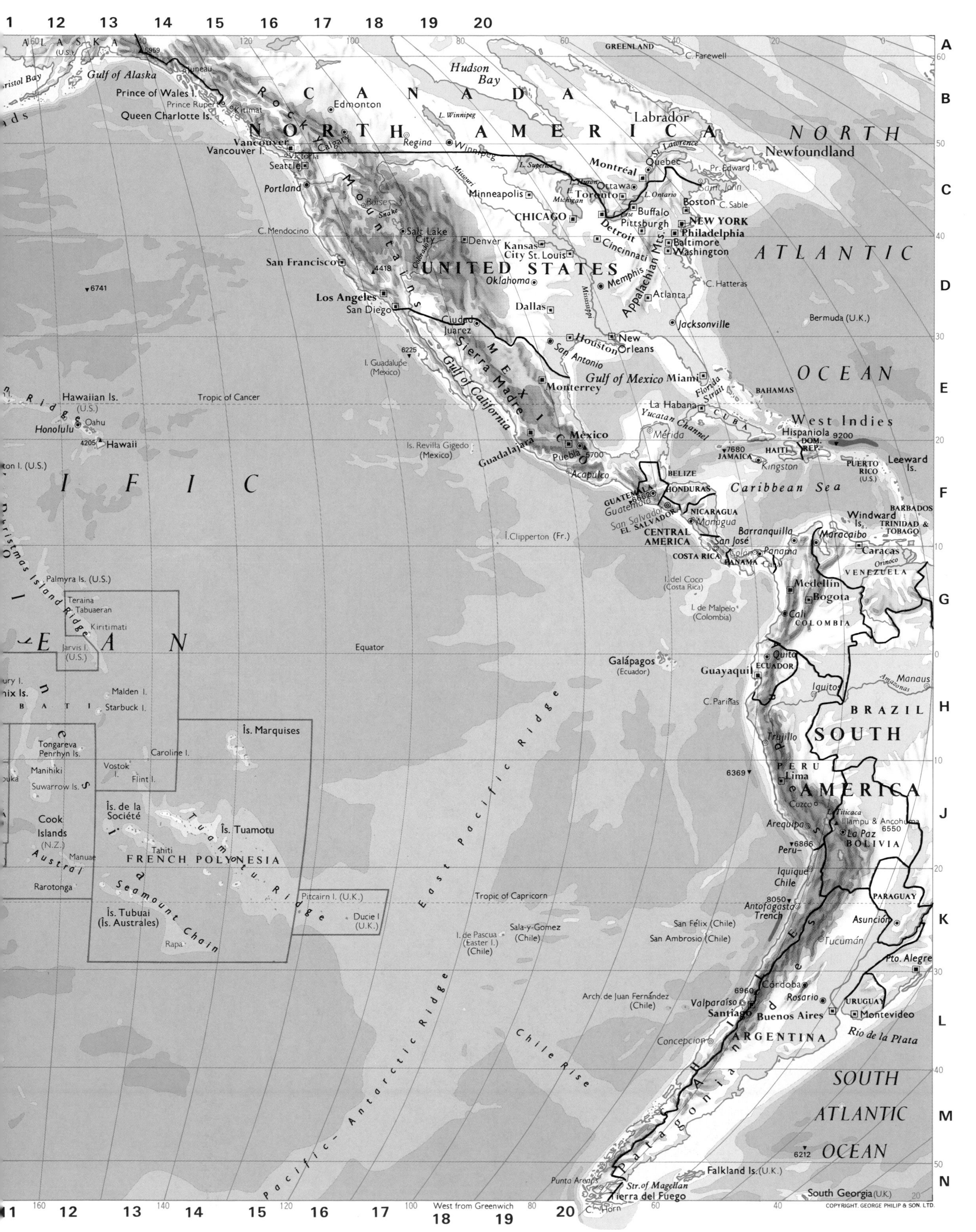

C A N A D A
NORTH AMERICA
UNITED STATES
MEXICO
Hudson Bay
Labrador
Newfoundland
Gulf of Alaska
Prince of Wales I.
Queen Charlotte Is.
Vancouver I.
Edmonton
Calgary
Regina
Winnipeg
Vancouver
Victoria
Seattle
Portland
Minneapolis
CHICAGO
Montréal
Québec
Ottawa
Toronto
Buffalo
Detroit
Pittsburgh
NEW YORK
Philadelphia
Baltimore
Washington
Boston
Cincinnati
Salt Lake City
Denver
Kansas City
St. Louis
San Francisco
Los Angeles
San Diego
Oklahoma
Dallas
Memphis
Atlanta
Jacksonville
Houston
New Orleans
San Antonio
Monterrey
Miami
Rocky Mountains
Appalachian Mts.
Sierra Madre
Gulf of California
Gulf of Mexico
La Habana
CUBA
Yucatan Channel
Florida Strait
BAHAMAS
West Indies
Hispaniola
HAITI
DOM. REP.
JAMAICA
Kingston
PUERTO RICO (U.S.)
Leeward Is.
Windward Is.
BARBADOS
TRINIDAD & TOBAGO
Caribbean Sea
México
Guadalajara
Puebla
Acapulco
BELIZE
HONDURAS
GUATEMALA
EL SALVADOR
NICARAGUA
CENTRAL AMERICA
COSTA RICA
PANAMA
Barranquilla
Maracaibo
Caracas
VENEZUELA
Medellín
Bogota
Cali
COLOMBIA
Quito
ECUADOR
Guayaquil
Iquitos
Manaus
BRAZIL
SOUTH AMERICA
PERU
Trujillo
Lima
Cuzco
Arequipa
BOLIVIA
La Paz
Titicaca
Illampu & Ancohuma 6550
Iquique
Chile
PARAGUAY
Asunción
Tucumán
Antofagasta
Córdoba
Rosario
URUGUAY
Montevideo
Buenos Aires
Valparaíso
Santiago
ARGENTINA
Concepción
Río de la Plata
Patagonia
Andes
Pto. Alegre
Str. of Magellan
Tierra del Fuego
Punta Arenas
C. Horn
Falkland Is. (U.K.)
South Georgia (U.K.)
ATLANTIC OCEAN
SOUTH ATLANTIC OCEAN
GREENLAND
C. Farewell
Bermuda (U.K.)
C. Hatteras
C. Sable
C. Mendocino
Hawaiian Is. (U.S.)
Honolulu
Oahu
Hawaii
Tropic of Cancer
I. Guadalupe (Mexico)
Is. Revilla Gigedo (Mexico)
I. Clipperton (Fr.)
I. del Coco (Costa Rica)
I. de Malpelo (Colombia)
Galápagos (Ecuador)
C. Pariñas
Equator
Palmyra Is. (U.S.)
Christmas Island Ridge
Teraina
Tabuaeran
Kiritimati
Jarvis I. (U.S.)
Malden I.
Starbuck I.
Tongareva
Penrhyn Is.
Manihiki
Suwarrow Is.
Caroline I.
Vostok I.
Flint I.
Is. Marquises
Is. de la Société
Tahiti
Is. Tuamotu
Tuamotu Ridge
FRENCH POLYNESIA
Cook Islands (N.Z.)
Rarotonga
Austral Seamount Chain
Is. Tubuai (Is. Australes)
Rapa
Pitcairn I. (U.K.)
Ducie I (U.K.)
East Pacific Ridge
Pacific-Antarctic Ridge
Chile Rise
Tropic of Capricorn
I. de Pascua (Easter I.) (Chile)
Sala-y-Gomez (Chile)
San Félix (Chile)
San Ambrosio (Chile)
Arch. de Juan Fernández (Chile)
Peru-Chile Trench
West from Greenwich
COPYRIGHT. GEORGE PHILIP & SON. LTD.

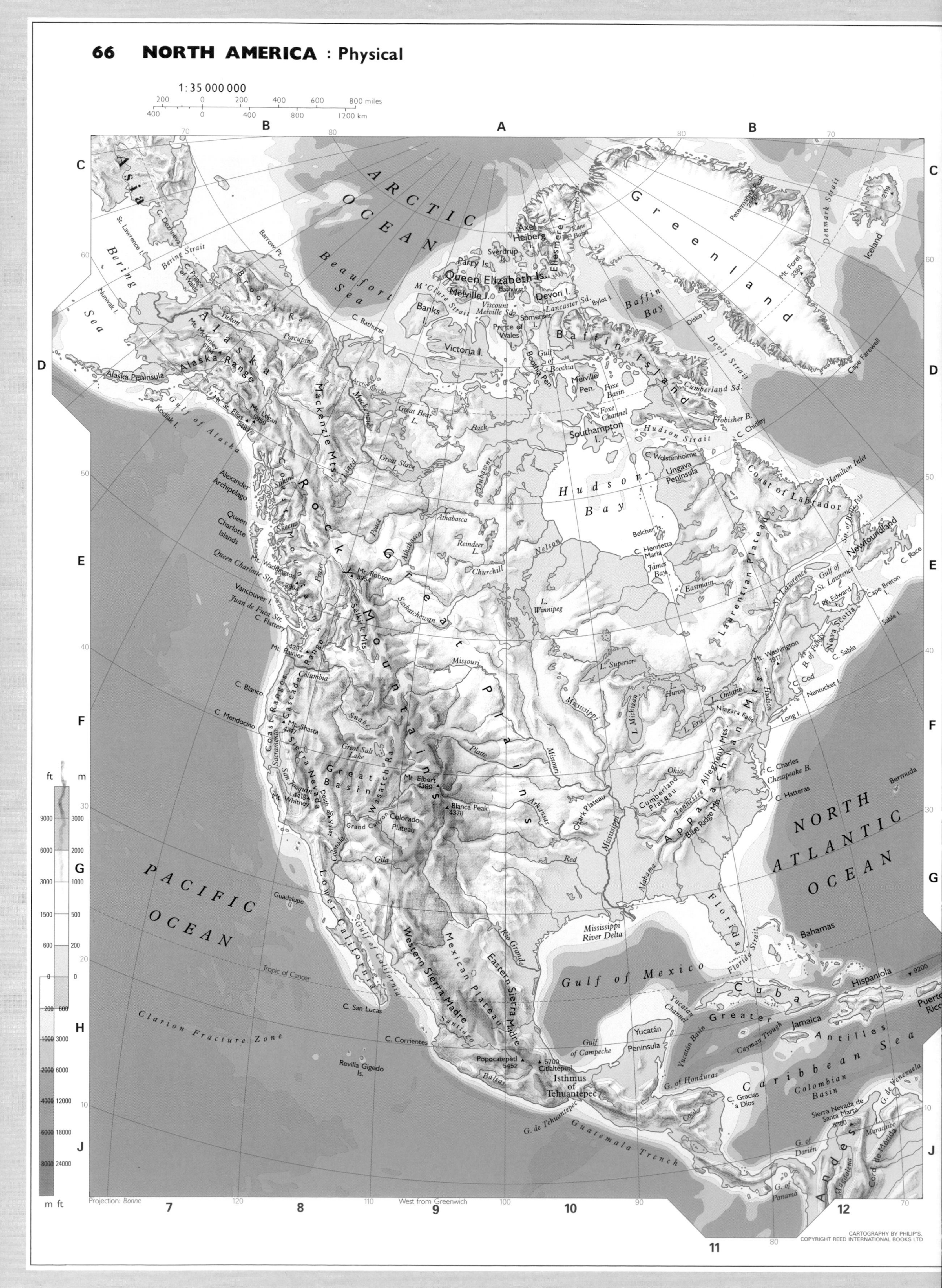

1:35 000 000

C Asia

ARCTIC OCEAN

Greenland

Iceland

Bering Strait
Beaufort Sea
Baffin Bay
Denmark Strait

Queen Elizabeth Is.
Parry Is.
Melville I.
Banks
Victoria I.
Southampton I.
Baffin Island
Davis Strait
Cape Farewell

Brooks Ra.
Alaska Range
Mackenzie Mts.
Great Bear L.
Great Slave L.
Hudson Bay
Ungava Peninsula
Coast of Labrador
Newfoundland

Gulf of Alaska
Kodiak I.
Alexander Archipelago
Queen Charlotte Islands
Vancouver I.

Rocky Mountains

Athabasca
Reindeer L.
Nelson
Churchill
L. Winnipeg
Saskatchewan

L. Superior
L. Huron
L. Michigan
L. Ontario
L. Erie
Niagara Falls

Mt. Robson 3954
Mt. Waddington 3996
Mt. Rainier 4392
Cascade Range
Coast Ranges
Columbia
Snake
Mt. Shasta 4317
Sierra Nevada
Great Salt Lake
Great Basin
Wasatch Ra.
Mt. Whitney 4418
Mt. Elbert 4399
Blanca Peak 4378
Death Valley 86
Grand Canyon
Colorado Plateau
Gila
Lower California
Gulf of California

Missouri
Platte
Arkansas
Red
Ohio
Mississippi

Great Plains

Ozark Plateau
Cumberland Plateau
Tennessee
Allegheny Mts.
Appalachian Mts.
Blue Ridge Mts.
Florida

Mt. Washington 1917
Nova Scotia
Cape Breton I.
C. Cod
Nantucket I.
Long I.
Hudson
Chesapeake B.
C. Charles
C. Hatteras

NORTH ATLANTIC OCEAN

Bermuda

PACIFIC OCEAN

Guadalupe
Tropic of Cancer
C. San Lucas
Clarion Fracture Zone
Revilla Gigedo Is.

Western Sierra Madre
Eastern Sierra Madre
Mexican Plateau
Santiago
Balsas
Popocatepetl 5452
Citlaltepetl 5700
Isthmus of Tehuantepec
G. de Tehuantepec
Guatemala Trench

Rio Grande
Gulf of Mexico
Mississippi River Delta
Bahamas

Gulf of Campeche
Yucatán Peninsula
Yucatán Channel
Cuba
Florida Strait

Hispaniola 9200
Puerto Rico
Jamaica
Greater Antilles
Cayman Trough
Caribbean Sea
Colombian Basin
G. of Honduras
C. Gracias a Dios
Sierra Nevada de Santa Marta 5800
Andes
G. of Darién
G. of Panama
G. of Venezuela
Maracaibo

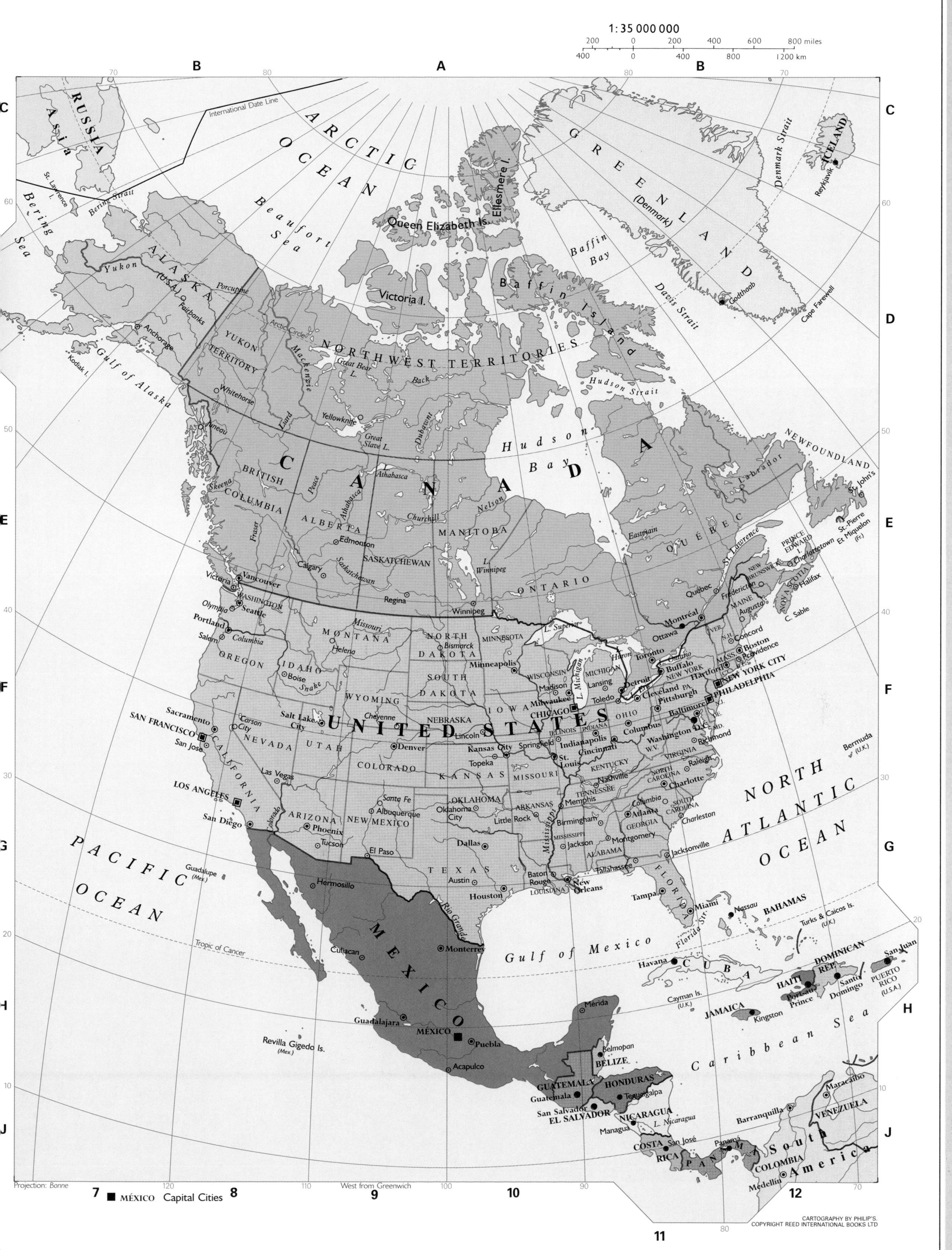

1 : 35 000 000

| 200 | 0 | 200 | 400 | 600 | 800 miles |
| 400 | 0 | 400 | 800 | 1200 km |

B   **A**   **B**

C   RUSSIA   Asia   International Date Line   GREENLAND   ICELAND   C
Reykjavik

Denmark Strait

St. Lawrence   Bering Strait   ARCTIC   Baffin   OCEAN   Bay   (Denmark)   D

Bering Sea   Beaufort Sea   Queen Elizabeth Is.   Ellesmere I.   Godthaab   Davis Strait   Cape Farewell

ALASKA   Yukon   Victoria I.   Baffin   Island
(U.S.A.)   Porcupine
Anchorage   Fairbanks   E

Kodiak I.   Gulf of Alaska   YUKON   Arctic Circle   NORTHWEST TERRITORIES   Hudson Strait   NEWFOUNDLAND   50
TERRITORY   Mackenzie   Great Bear L.   Back   Labrador
Whitehorse   Yellowknife   Hudson   St-Pierre
Juneau   Lard   Great Slave L.   Dubawnt   Bay   Et Miquelon (Fr.)
BRITISH   Peace   Athabasca   Nelson   St. John's
COLUMBIA   Athabasca   CANADA   QUÉBEC   PRINCE   E
Skeena   L.   Churchill   EDWARD
Fraser   ALBERTA   MANITOBA   Eastmain   I.   Charlottetown
Edmonton   SASKATCHEWAN   St. Lawrence   NEW   NOVA
Victoria   Vancouver   Calgary   Saskatchewan   ONTARIO   BRUNSWICK   SCOTIA   Halifax
Olympia   WASHINGTON   Regina   Winnipeg   L. Winnipeg   Québec   Fredericton   C. Sable
Seattle   Winnipeg   Ottawa   MAINE   Augusta   40
Portland   Columbia   Missouri   L. Superior   Montréal   VER.   Concord
Salem   OREGON   MONTANA   Bismarck   MINNESOTA   L. Huron   Toronto   Ontario   MASS.   Boston   F
Helena   NORTH   Minneapolis   WISCONSIN   MICHIGAN   Detroit   Buffalo   Providence
IDAHO   DAKOTA   Madison   Lansing   NEW YORK   Hartford   NEW YORK CITY
Boise   Snake   SOUTH   Milwaukee   L. Michigan   Cleveland   PA   Pittsburgh   PHILADELPHIA
Sacramento   WYOMING   DAKOTA   IOWA   Chicago   Toledo   OHIO   Baltimore   N.J.
Carson   Cheyenne   NEBRASKA   Nashville   Columbus   Washington D.C.   Richmond   Bermuda
City   Salt Lake   Lincoln   ILLINOIS   Indianapolis   Cincinnati   W.V.   VIRGINIA   (U.K.)
SAN FRANCISCO   NEVADA   UTAH   Denver   Kansas City   Springfield   KENTUCKY   NORTH   Raleigh   30
San Jose   CALIFORNIA   Topeka   St.   CAROLINA   Charlotte
LOS ANGELES   Las Vegas   COLORADO   KANSAS   MISSOURI   Louis   TENNESSEE   Columbia   SOUTH   G
Santa Fe   Memphis   Birmingham   Atlanta   CAROLINA   Charleston
San Diego   ARIZONA   NEW MEXICO   OKLAHOMA   ARKANSAS   MISSISSIPPI   GEORGIA
Phoenix   Albuquerque   Oklahoma   Little Rock   ALABAMA   Jacksonville   NORTH
Guadalupe   Tucson   City   Dallas   Jackson   Montgomery   ATLANTIC
(Mex.)   El Paso   TEXAS   Baton   Tallahassee   FLORIDA   OCEAN
PACIFIC   Austin   Rouge   New   Tampa
Hermosillo   Houston   LOUISIANA   Orleans   Miami   Nassau   BAHAMAS   20
OCEAN   Rio Grande   Gulf of Mexico   Florida   Turks & Caicos Is.
Tropic of Cancer   Culiacan   MÉXICO   Monterrey   Havana   CUBA   (U.K.)   H
Guadalupe   Merida   Cayman Is.   HAITI   DOMINICAN   San Juan
Revilla Gigedo Is.   Guadalajara   MÉXICO   Puebla   (U.K.)   Port-au-   REP.   PUERTO
(Mex.)   Acapulco   BELIZE   JAMAICA   Prince   Santo   RICO
Belmopan   Kingston   Domingo   (U.S.A.)
GUATEMALA   HONDURAS   Caribbean   Sea   Maracaibo
Guatemala   Tegucigalpa   Barranquilla   VENEZUELA   J
San Salvador   NICARAGUA
EL SALVADOR   Managua   L. Nicaragua
COSTA   San José   Panama   South   COLOMBIA   America
RICA   PANAMA   Medellín

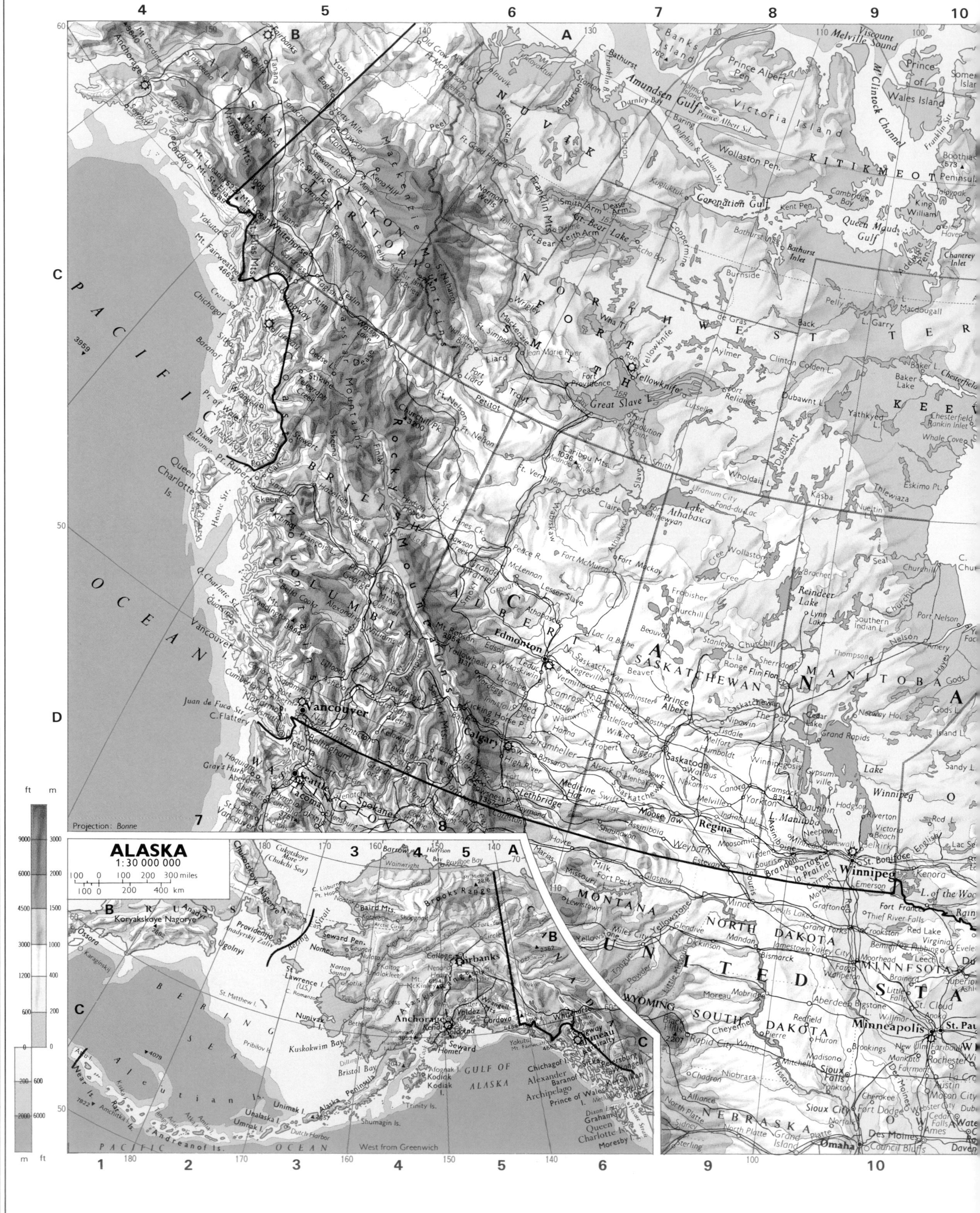

Projection: Bonne

ALASKA
1 : 30 000 000

100 0   100 200 300 miles
100 0 200 400 km

PACIFIC OCEAN   West from Greenwich

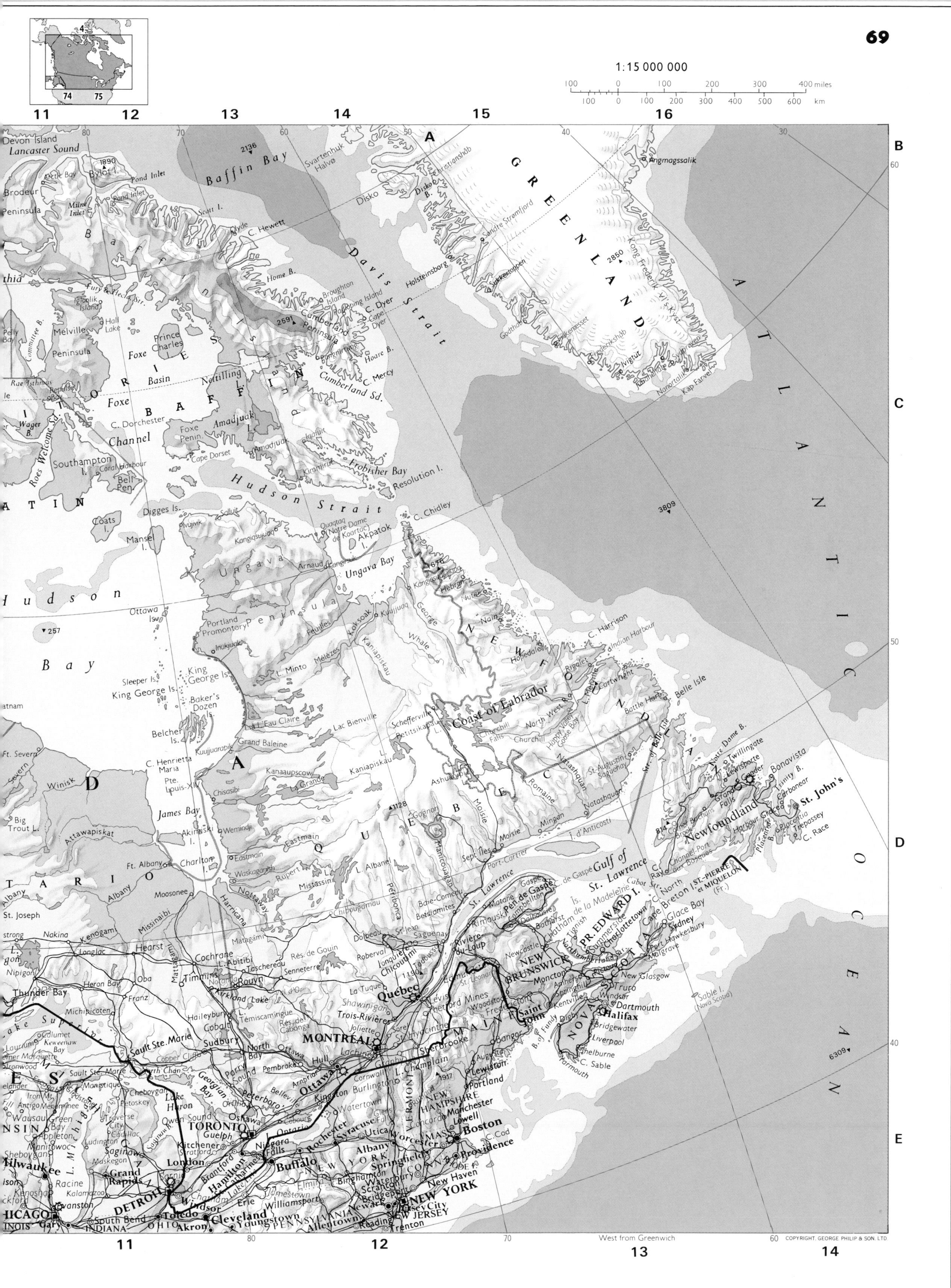

1:15 000 000

100   0   100   200   300   400 miles

100   0   100   200   300   400   500   600 km

West from Greenwich   COPYRIGHT. GEORGE PHILIP & SON. LTD.

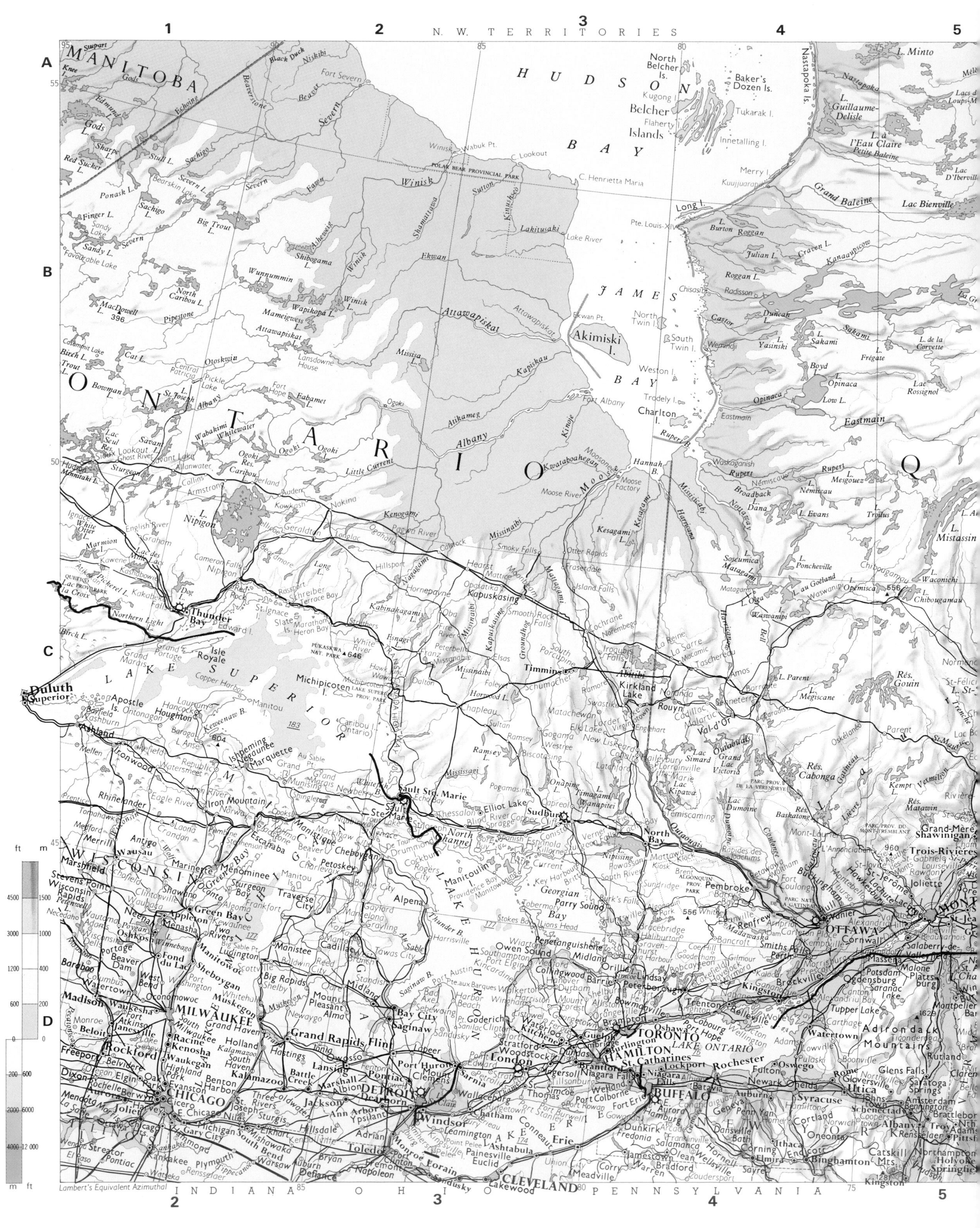
N. W. TERRITORIES
HUDSON BAY
JAMES BAY
MANITOBA
ONTARIO
Q
LAKE SUPERIOR
LAKE HURON
LAKE ONTARIO
LAKE ERIE
MICHIGAN
WISCONSIN
NEW YORK
INDIANA
OHIO
PENNSYLVANIA
ILLINOIS
Belcher Islands
North Belcher Is.
Baker's Dozen Is.
Akimiski I.
Isle Royale
Manitoulin I.
Georgian Bay
Adirondack Mountains
Catskill Mts.
Lac Bienville
Rés. Gouin
Rés. Cabonga
L. Mistassini
L. Nipigon
Thunder Bay
Duluth
Superior
Sault Ste. Marie
Sudbury
Timmins
Kirkland Lake
North Bay
Elliot Lake
Moose Factory
Fort Albany
Fort Severn
Kapuskasing
Hearst
Cochrane
Val-d'Or
Rouyn
Amos
Chibougamau
Trois-Rivières
Grand-Mère
Shawinigan
OTTAWA
Hull
Kingston
Brockville
TORONTO
HAMILTON
St. Catharines
Niagara Falls
BUFFALO
Rochester
Syracuse
Utica
Oswego
Watertown
Binghamton
Elmira
Albany
Schenectady
Erie
CLEVELAND
Toledo
DETROIT
Windsor
London
Kitchener
Guelph
Brantford
Sarnia
Port Huron
Flint
Saginaw
Bay City
Lansing
Grand Rapids
Kalamazoo
Jackson
Ann Arbor
MILWAUKEE
CHICAGO
Rockford
Madison
Green Bay
Appleton
Oshkosh
Sheboygan
Racine
Kenosha
Marquette
Houghton
Ashland
Ironwood
Iron Mountain
Escanaba
Traverse City
Alpena
Cheboygan
Petoskey
Owen Sound
Barrie
Orillia
Peterborough
Belleville
Pembroke
Parry Sound
Lambert's Equivalent Azimuthal
ft
m
4500
3000
1200
600
1500
1000
400
200
200
2000
4000
6000
12 000
1
2
3
4
5
A
B
C
D
95
90
85
80
75
55
50
45

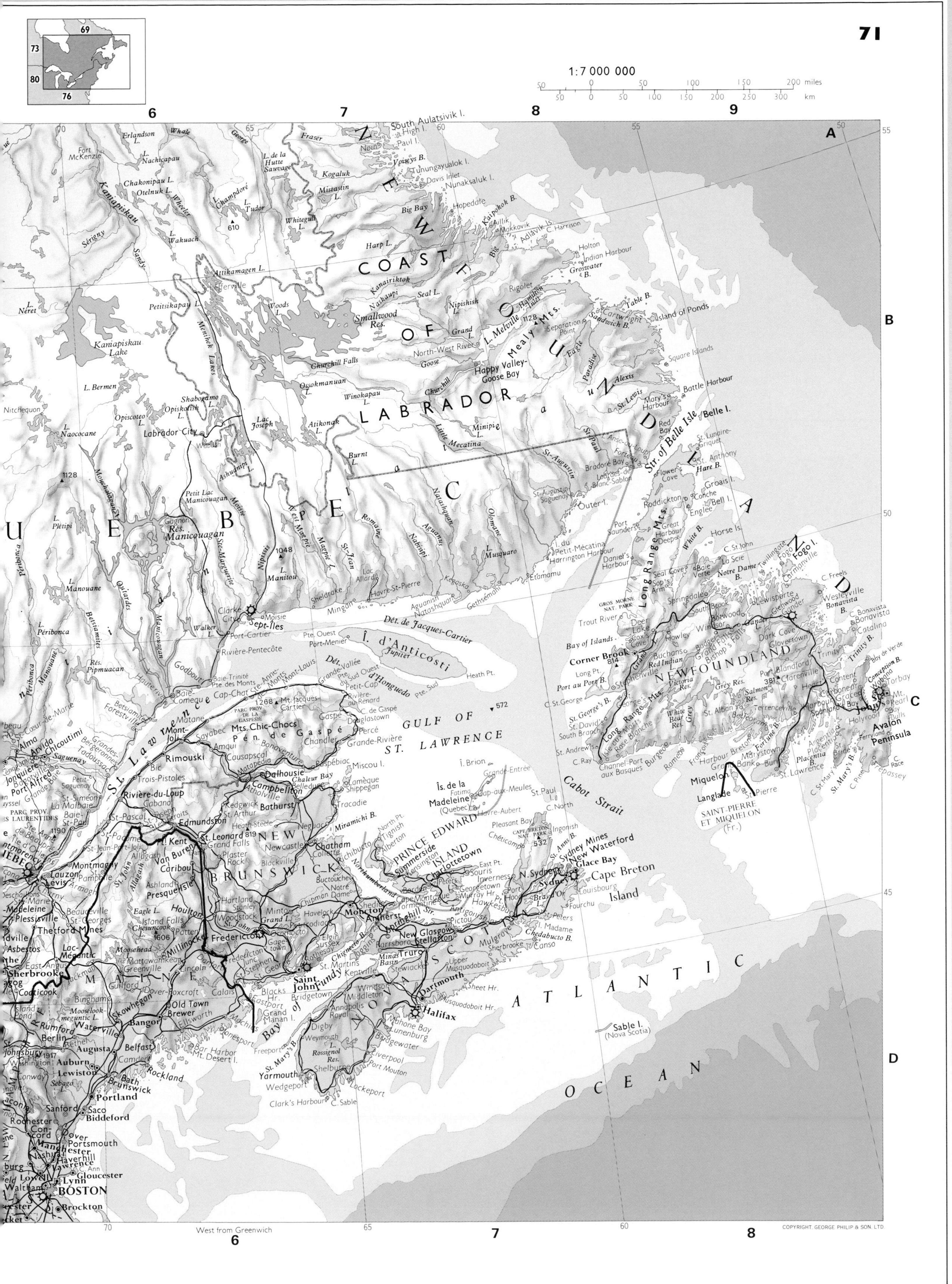

69
73
80
76
1:7 000 000
50 0 50 100 150 200 miles
50 0 50 100 150 200 250 300 km
6
7
8
9
A
B
C
D
55
50
45
70
65
60
South Aulatsivik I.
Nain
Voisey B.
Tunungayualok I.
Davis Inlet
Nunaksaluk I.
Kogaluk
Mistastin L.
Hopedale
Big Bay
Kaipokok B.
Makkovik
Aillik
C. Harrison
Holton
Indian Harbour
Groswater B.
Rigolet
Hamilton Inlet
COAST
OF
LABRADOR
NEWFOUNDLAND
QUEBEC
Smallwood Res.
Seal L.
Nipishish L.
Grand L.
L. Melville
Mealy Mts.
Cartwright
Table B.
Sandwich B.
Island of Ponds
Separation Point
North-West River
Goose
Happy Valley-Goose Bay
Churchill Falls
Eagle
Paradise
Square Islands
Alexis
St. Lewis
Mary's Harbour
Battle Harbour
Red Bay
Belle I.
Str. of Belle Isle
Little Mecatina
Minipi L.
Winokapau L.
Ossokmanuan L.
Atikonak L.
Burnt L.
Labrador City
Wabush
Lac Joseph
Ashuanipi L.
Shabogamo L.
Opiskotish L.
Opiscoteo L.
Nitchequon
L. Naococane
L. Bermen
Kaniapiskau Lake
Kaniapiskau
Schefferville
Attikamagen L.
Petitsikapau L.
Menihek Lakes
Woods L.
Whitegull L.
Harp L.
Kanairiktok
Naskaupi
L. Champdoré
L. Tudor
610
L. Wakuach
Chakonipau L.
Otelnuk L.
L. Nachicapau
Fort McKenzie
Erlandson L.
Whale
George
Fraser
L. de la Hutte Sauvage
Sérigny
Sandy
Wheeler
L. Néret
1128
Petit Lac Manicouagan
Gagnon
Rés. Manicouagan
Ste-Marguerite
Moisie
L. Plétipi
Péribonca
Manouane
L. Manouane
Outardes
Manicouagan
Betsiamites
Rés. Pipmuacan
Sept-Îles
Clarke City
Port-Cartier
Rivière-Pentecôte
Godbout
Walker L.
Baie-Trinité
Pte. des Monts
Baie-Comeau
Forestville
Nipissis
1048
L. Manitou
Romaine
Aguanus
Natashquan
Olomane
Musquaro
Mingan
Havre-St-Pierre
Sheldrake
Lac Allard
Aguanish
Natashquan
Kegaska
Gethsémani
Étamamu
Harrington Harbour
Petit-Mécatina
St-Augustin
St-Augustin Saguenay
Outer I.
Brador Bay
Lourdes-de-Blanc-Sablon
Forteau
Anse-au-Loup
St. Paul
St. Lunaire-Griquet
St. Anthony
Hare B.
Flower's Cove
Roddickton
Conche
Groais I.
Englee
Bell I.
Port Saunders
Great Harbour Deep
White B.
Horse Is.
C. St. John
La Scie
Baie Verte
Fogo I.
Twillingate
Carmanville
Notre Dame B.
Long Range Mts.
Daniel's Harbour
Sop's Arm
GROS MORNE NAT. PARK
Trout River
Deer Lake
Springdale
Lewisporte
Botwood
Gander
Windsor
Grand Falls
Bishop's Falls
Bay of Islands
Corner Brook
814
Red Indian L.
Buchans
NEWFOUNDLAND
Long Pt.
Port au Port B.
Stephenville
C. St. George
St. George's B.
St. David's
South Branch
St. Andrew's
C. Ray
Channel-Port aux Basques
Burgeo
Ramea
Victoria Res.
Grey Res.
Salmon Res.
White Bear Res.
Rose Blanche
Fortune B.
Harbour Breton
Grand Bank
Marystown
Burin
St. Lawrence
Placentia B.
St. Mary's B.
C. St. Mary's
C. Pine
Trepassey
C. Race
Avalon Peninsula
St. John's
Holyrood
Carbonear
Harbour Grace
Conception B.
Trinity B.
Bay de Verde
Torbay
Clarenville
Bonavista B.
Bonavista
C. Bonavista
Catalina
C. Freels
Wesleyville
Gander B.
Terrenceville
St. Alban's
Miquelon
Langlade
St. Pierre
SAINT-PIERRE ET MIQUELON (Fr.)
Cabot Strait
St. Paul I.
C. North
GULF OF ST. LAWRENCE
572
Î. Brion
Îs. de la Madeleine (Quebec)
Grande-Entrée
Cap-aux-Meules
Havre-Aubert
Î. d'Anticosti
Dét. de Jacques-Cartier
Jupiter
Heath Pt.
Pte. Ouest
Port-Menier
Dét. d'Honguedo
Pte. Sud
Mont-Louis
Grande-Vallée
Petit-Cap
Rivière-au-Renard
C. de Gaspé
Gaspé
Douglastown
Percé
Grande-Rivière
Chandler
Pén. de Gaspé
Mts. Chic-Chocs
1268 Mt. Jacques Cartier
PARC PROV. DE LA GASPÉSIE
Cap-Chat
Ste-Anne-des-Monts
Matane
Mont-Joli
Sayabec
Amqui
Causapscal
Matapédia
Bonaventure
Paspébiac
Miscou I.
Lamèque
Shippegan
Tracadie
Chaleur Bay
Dalhousie
Campbellton
Belledune
Bathurst
Miramichi B.
St. Lawrence
Rimouski
Bic
Trois-Pistoles
Rivière-du-Loup
Cabano
Edmundston
St. Leonard
Grand Falls
819
Kedgwick
St. Arthur
Heath Steele
Chatham
Newcastle
NEW BRUNSWICK
Blackville
Richibucto
Buctouche
Moncton
Shediac
Sackville
Amherst
Chipman
Minto
Fredericton
Grand L.
Woodstock
Hartland
Plaster Rock
Perth
St. John
Saint John
Sussex
St. Stephen
St. Martins
Bay of Fundy
Grand Manan I.
Calais
Eastport
PRINCE EDWARD ISLAND
Summerside
Charlottetown
Souris
East Pt.
Georgetown
Montague
Tignish
North Pt.
Alberton
Kensington
Northumberland Str.
Borden
Tormentine
Pictou
New Glasgow
Stellarton
Antigonish
Truro
Minas Basin
Parrsboro
Windsor
Kentville
Middleton
Annapolis Royal
Digby
Weymouth
Yarmouth
Wedgeport
Clark's Harbour
C. Sable
Shelburne
Lockeport
Liverpool
Port Mouton
Bridgewater
Lunenburg
Mahone Bay
Halifax
Dartmouth
Musquodoboit Hr.
Sheet Hr.
Upper Musquodoboit
Sherbrooke
Mulgrave
Canso
Chedabucto B.
I. Madame
St. Peters
Port Hawkesbury
Bras d'Or L.
Inverness
Chéticamp
Pleasant Bay
CAPE BRETON NAT. PARK
532
Ingonish
St. Ann's B.
Sydney Mines
New Waterford
Glace Bay
N. Sydney
Sydney
Louisbourg
Fourchu
Cape Breton Island
NOVA SCOTIA
Sable I. (Nova Scotia)
ATLANTIC OCEAN
MAINE
Houlton
Presque Isle
Caribou
Van Buren
Fort Kent
Allagash
Ashland
Eagle L.
Island Falls
Patten
Millinocket
Chesuncook L.
1606
Moosehead L.
Mattawamkeag
Greenville
Lincoln
Old Town
Brewer
Bangor
Ellsworth
Machias
Bar Harbor
Mt. Desert I.
Belfast
Camden
Rockland
Bath
Brunswick
Augusta
Waterville
Skowhegan
Dover-Foxcroft
Guilford
Bingham
Moosehead
Rumford
Berlin
Lewiston
Auburn
Sebago L.
Portland
Saco
Biddeford
Sanford
Rochester
Concord
Dover
Portsmouth
Manchester
Nashua
Haverhill
Lawrence
Lowell
Lynn
Gloucester
C. Ann
Waltham
BOSTON
Brockton
Worcester
St. Johnsbury
Washington
1917
Conway
Sherbrooke
Coaticook
Lac-Mégantic
East Angus
Thetford Mines
Asbestos
Plessisville
St-Georges
Beauceville
Lévis
Lauzon
Québec
Montmagny
St-Jean-Port-Joli
La Pocatière
La Malbaie
St-Siméon
Baie-St-Paul
1190
PARC PROV. DES LAURENTIDES
Chicoutimi
Jonquière
Arvida
Alma
Port Alfred
Saguenay
Tadoussac
Bergeronnes
Grandes-Bergeronnes
Betsiamites
Forestville
West from Greenwich
COPYRIGHT, GEORGE PHILIP & SON, LTD.

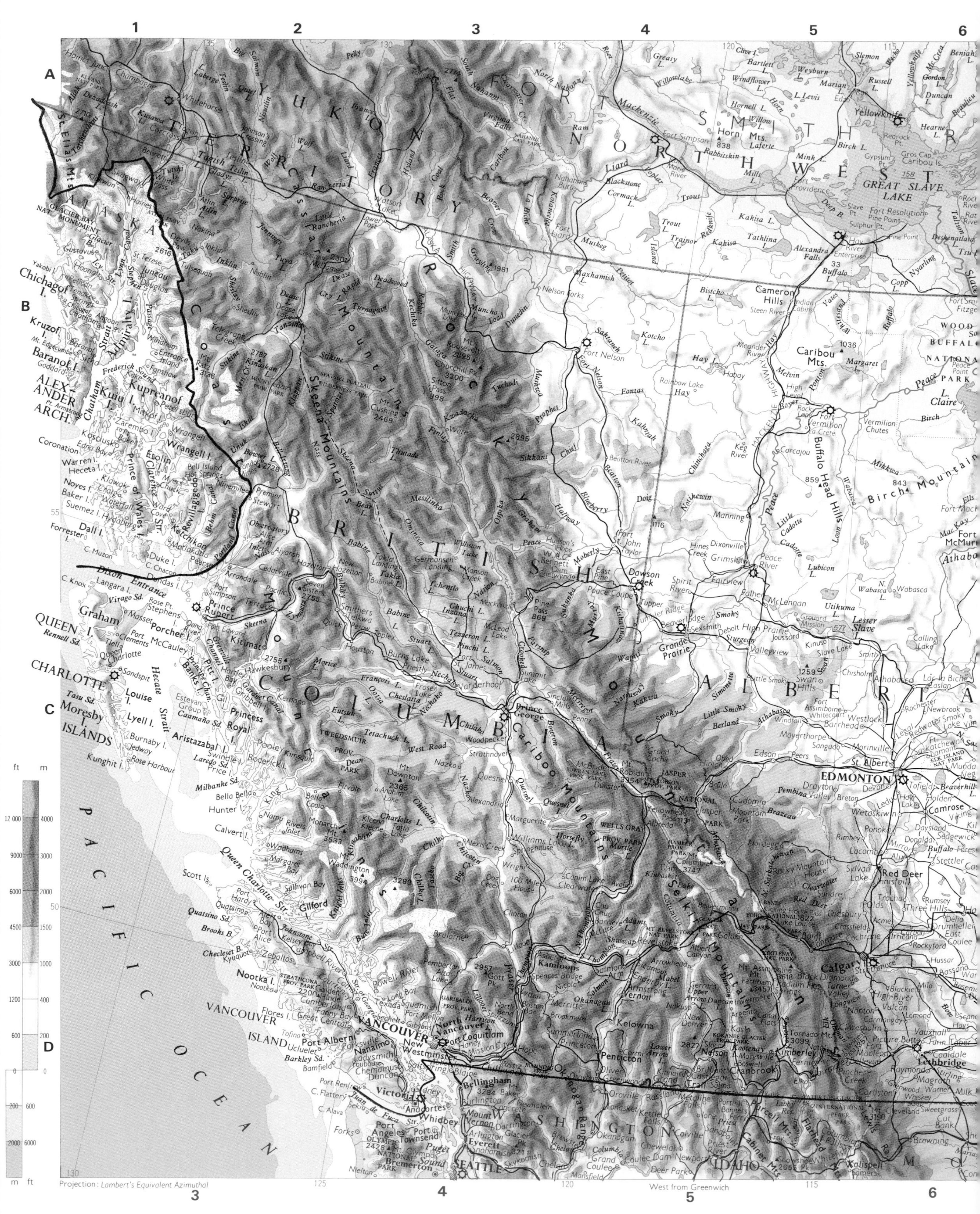

Projection: Lambert's Equivalent Azimuthal

West from Greenwich

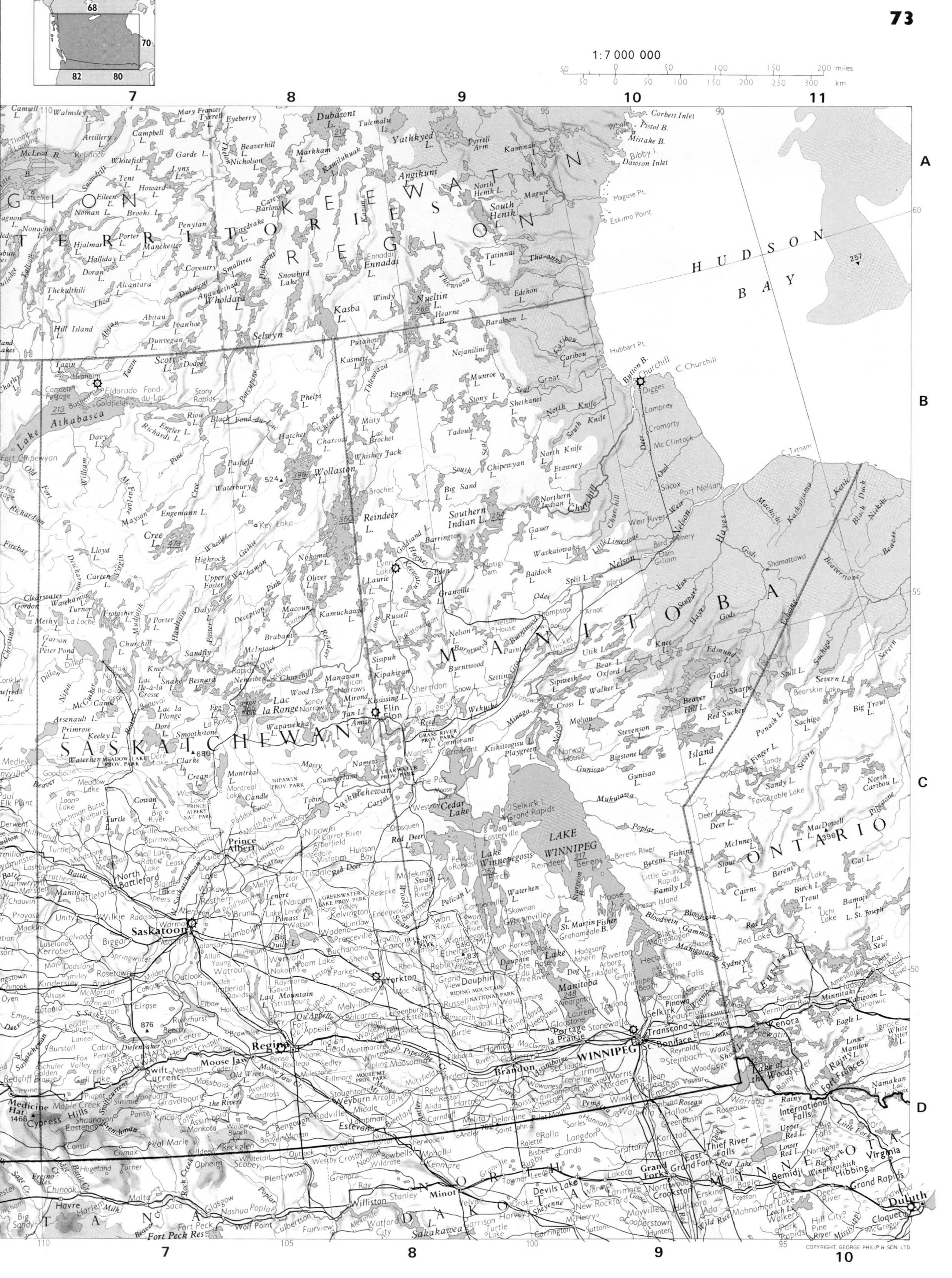

1:7 000 000
miles
km
KEEWATIN
REGION
HUDSON
BAY
MANITOBA
SASKATCHEWAN
ONTARIO
NORTH DAKOTA
MINNESOTA
LAKE WINNIPEG
Lake Winnipegosis
Lake Manitoba
Lake of the Woods
Athabasca
Reindeer L.
Wollaston L.
Southern Indian L.
Cedar Lake
Churchill
Saskatoon
Regina
Winnipeg
Prince Albert
Moose Jaw
Brandon
Yorkton
Flin Flon
The Pas
Thompson
Swift Current
Medicine Hat
North Battleford
Minot
Grand Forks
Kenora
Duluth
COPYRIGHT, GEORGE PHILIP & SON, LTD

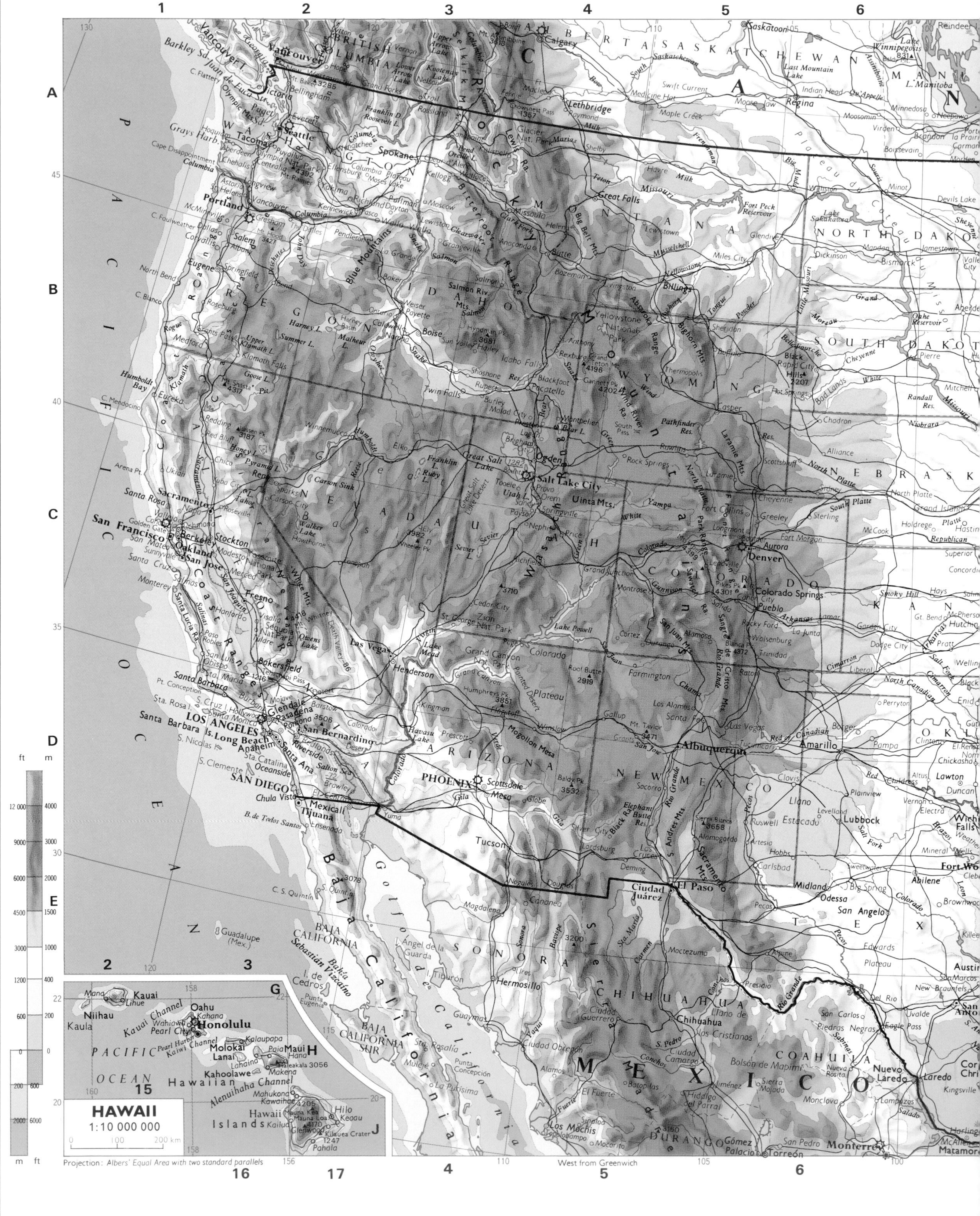

HAWAII
1:10 000 000

Projection : Albers' Equal Area with two standard parallels

West from Greenwich

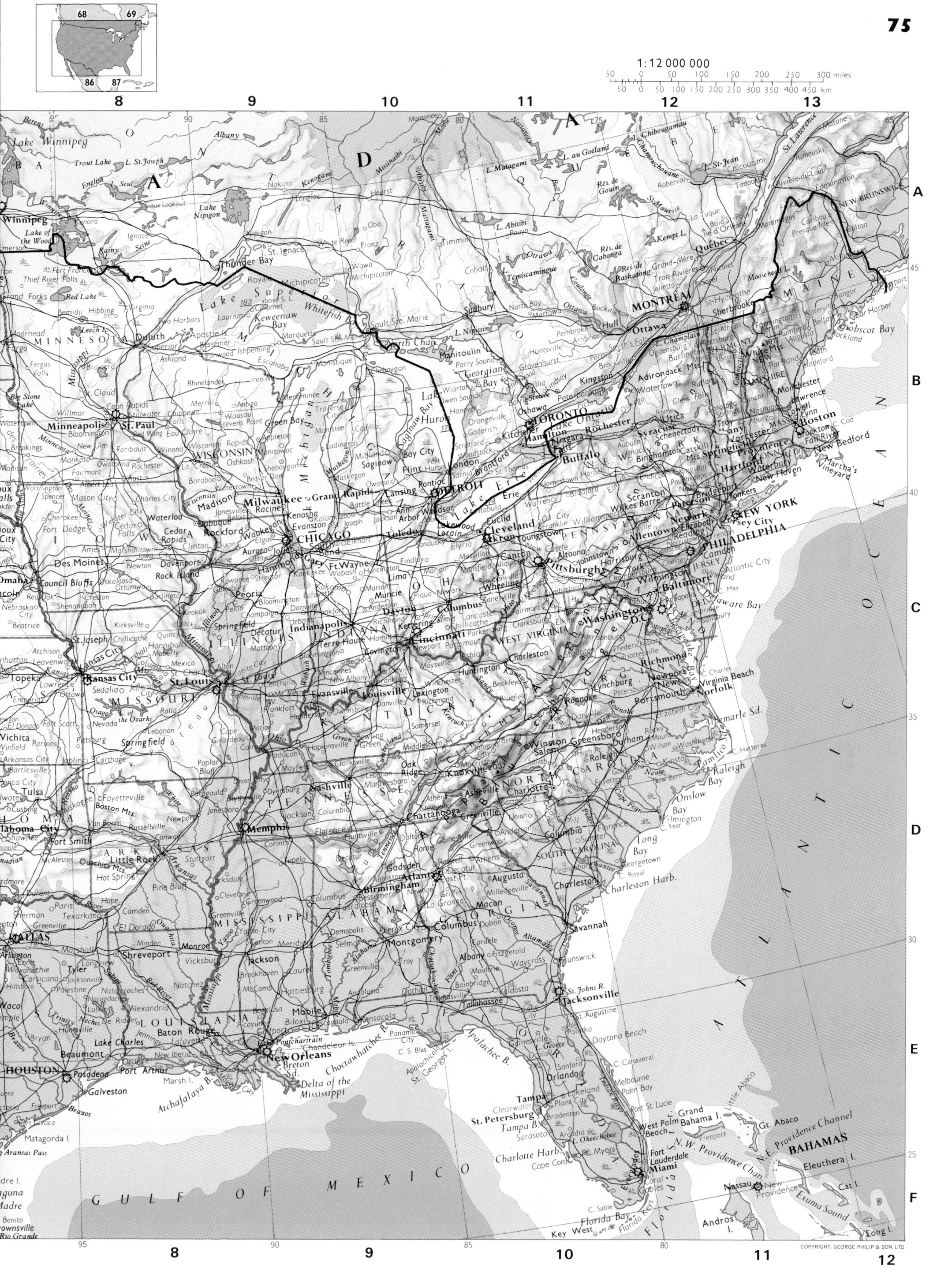
68
69
86
87
1:12 000 000
300 miles
450 km
8
9
10
11
12
13
A
B
C
D
E
F
Lake Winnipeg
Winnipeg
Lake of the Woods
Thunder Bay
Lake Superior
Duluth
MINNESOTA
Minneapolis
St. Paul
WISCONSIN
Milwaukee
CHICAGO
Lake Michigan
Lake Huron
Georgian Bay
DETROIT
Lake Erie
Cleveland
Toledo
Pittsburgh
Buffalo
TORONTO
Lake Ontario
Ottawa
MONTREAL
Québec
Rochester
Syracuse
Albany
Boston
Providence
Hartford
NEW YORK
PHILADELPHIA
Baltimore
Washington D.C.
Richmond
Norfolk
Virginia Beach
Indianapolis
Cincinnati
Columbus
Dayton
Louisville
St. Louis
Kansas City
Des Moines
Omaha
Nashville
Knoxville
Memphis
Little Rock
Charlotte
Atlanta
Birmingham
Montgomery
Jackson
Shreveport
New Orleans
Baton Rouge
Mobile
Jacksonville
Savannah
Charleston
Tampa
St. Petersburg
Orlando
Miami
West Palm Beach
Fort Lauderdale
Key West
DALLAS
HOUSTON
Galveston
Beaumont
MISSOURI
ILLINOIS
INDIANA
OHIO
KENTUCKY
TENNESSEE
MISSISSIPPI
ALABAMA
GEORGIA
FLORIDA
LOUISIANA
WEST VIRGINIA
NEW YORK
MAINE
NEW BRUNSWICK
SOUTH CAROLINA
NORTH CAROLINA
BAHAMAS
Nassau
Andros I.
Grand Bahama I.
Gt. Abaco
Eleuthera I.
Cat I.
GULF OF MEXICO
ATLANTIC OCEAN
Delta of the Mississippi
Florida Bay
Florida Keys
C. Hatteras
C. Canaveral
C. Fear
Chesapeake Bay
Delaware Bay
Cape Cod
Martha's Vineyard
COPYRIGHT. GEORGE PHILIP & SON. LTD

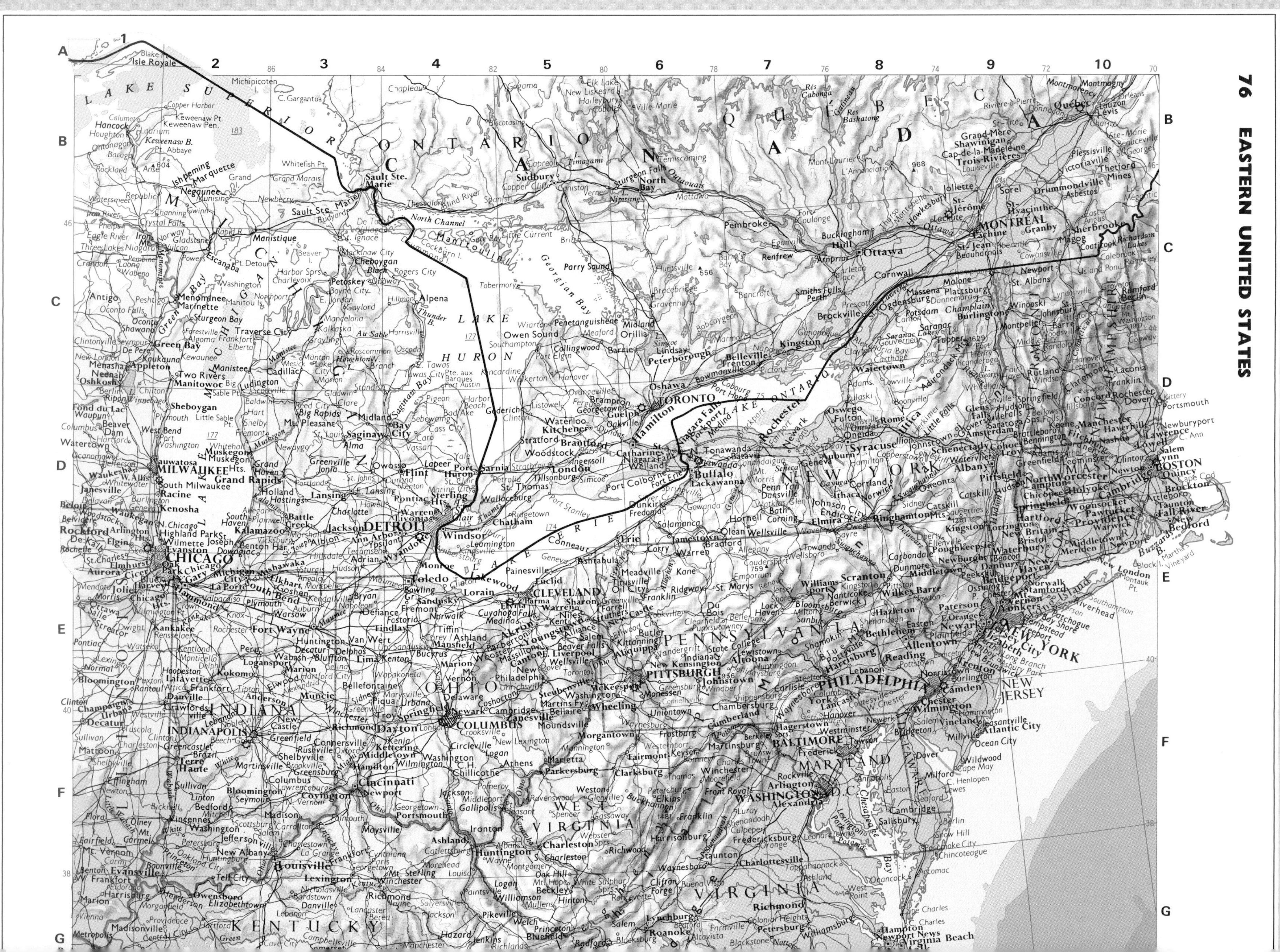

LAKE SUPERIOR
LAKE HURON
Georgian Bay
LAKE ONTARIO
LAKE ERIE
QUÉBEC
ONTARIO
CANADA
MICHIGAN
NEW YORK
PENNSYLVANIA
OHIO
INDIANA
KENTUCKY
WEST VIRGINIA
VIRGINIA
MARYLAND
NEW JERSEY
MONTREAL
Ottawa
TORONTO
BOSTON
NEW YORK
PHILADELPHIA
BALTIMORE
WASHINGTON D.C.
PITTSBURGH
CLEVELAND
DETROIT
CHICAGO
MILWAUKEE
COLUMBUS
INDIANAPOLIS
Cincinnati
Buffalo
Toledo
Québec

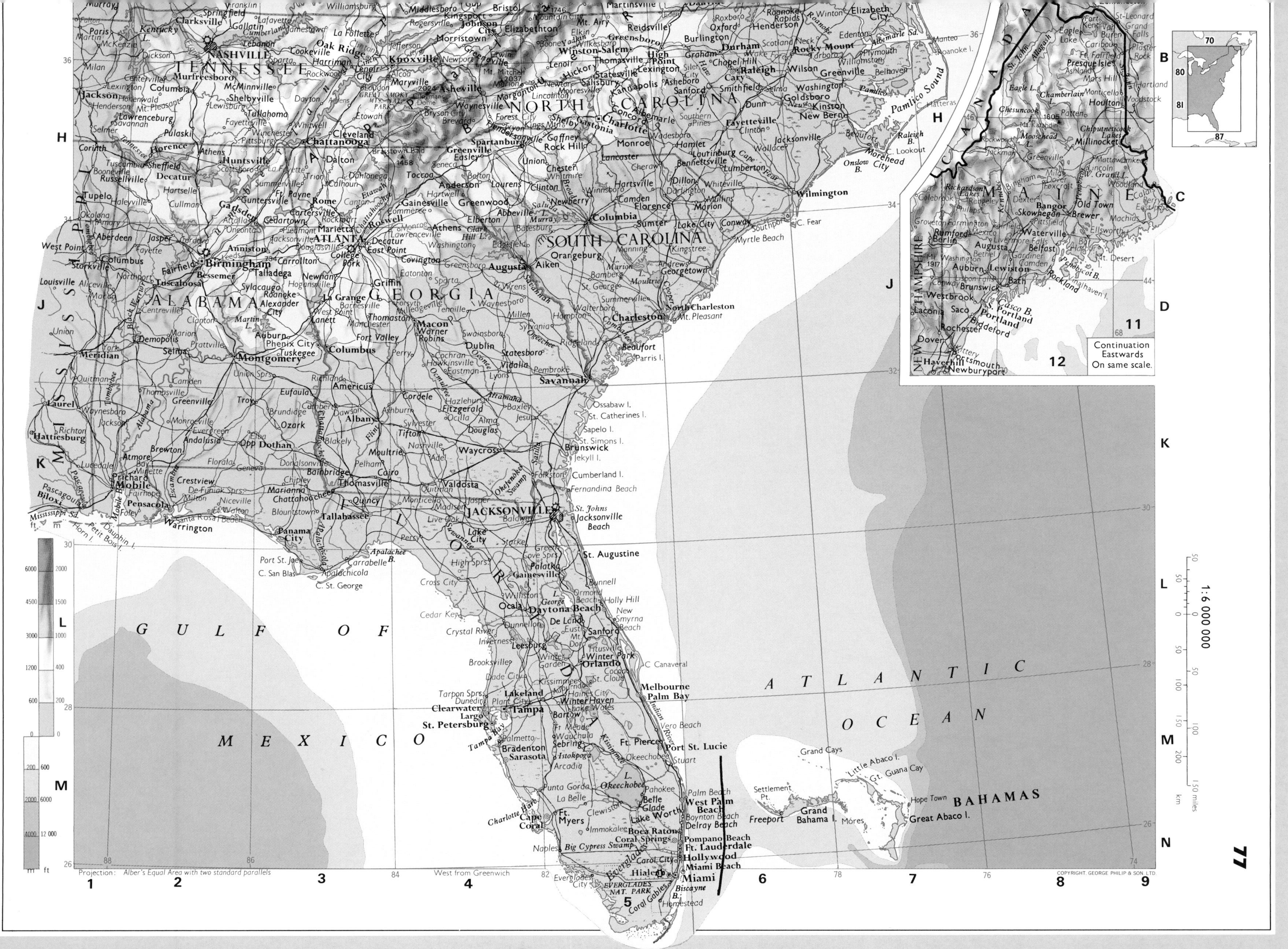

1:6 000 000

50   0   50   100   150 miles
50   0   50   100   150   200   km

Continuation
Eastwards
On same scale.

ATLANTIC OCEAN

GULF OF MEXICO

BAHAMAS

Great Abaco I.

Grand Bahama I.

NORTH CAROLINA
SOUTH CAROLINA
GEORGIA
ALABAMA
FLORIDA
TENNESSEE
MISSISSIPPI

MAINE
NEW HAMPSHIRE

CANADA

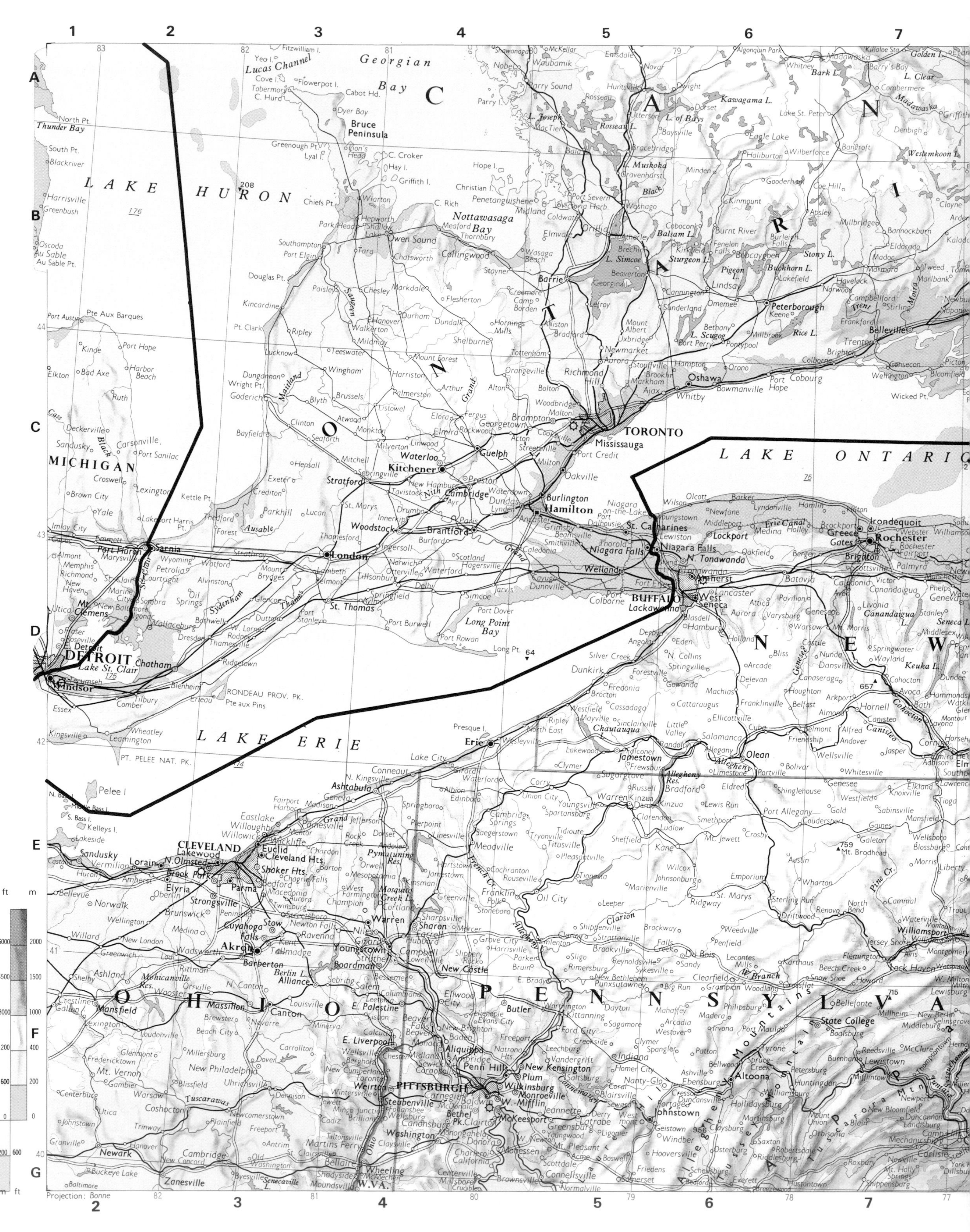
Georgian Bay
LAKE HURON
LAKE ONTARIO
LAKE ERIE
MICHIGAN
ONTARIO
NEW
OHIO
PENNSYLVANIA
Bruce Peninsula
Nottawasaga Bay
Long Point Bay
TORONTO
Mississauga
Hamilton
London
Kitchener
DETROIT
Windsor
BUFFALO
Rochester
Erie
CLEVELAND
Akron
Youngstown
PITTSBURGH
Canton
Lake St. Clair
L. Simcoe
Projection: Bonne

1:2 500 000

10 0 10 20 30 40 50 miles

10 0 10 20 30 40 50 60 70 80 km

8 9 10 11 12 13 14

A B C D E F G

MONTREAL
QUEBEC
VERMONT
NEW HAMPSHIRE
MAINE
MASSACHUSETTS
CONNECTICUT
RHODE ISLAND
NEW JERSEY
NEW YORK
ATLANTIC OCEAN
Long Island
Ottawa
Sherbrooke
Syracuse
Utica
Schenectady
Albany
Troy
Burlington
Springfield
BOSTON
Providence
Hartford
New Haven
Bridgeport
Stamford
Yonkers
Paterson
Newark
Elizabeth
Allentown
Reading
PHILADELPHIA
Camden
Trenton
Binghamton
Scranton
Wilkes-Barre
Worcester
Manchester
Concord
Portsmouth
Lake Champlain
Adirondack Mountains
Green Mountains
White Mountains
Catskill Mts.
Block Island Sound
Long Island Sound

West from Greenwich

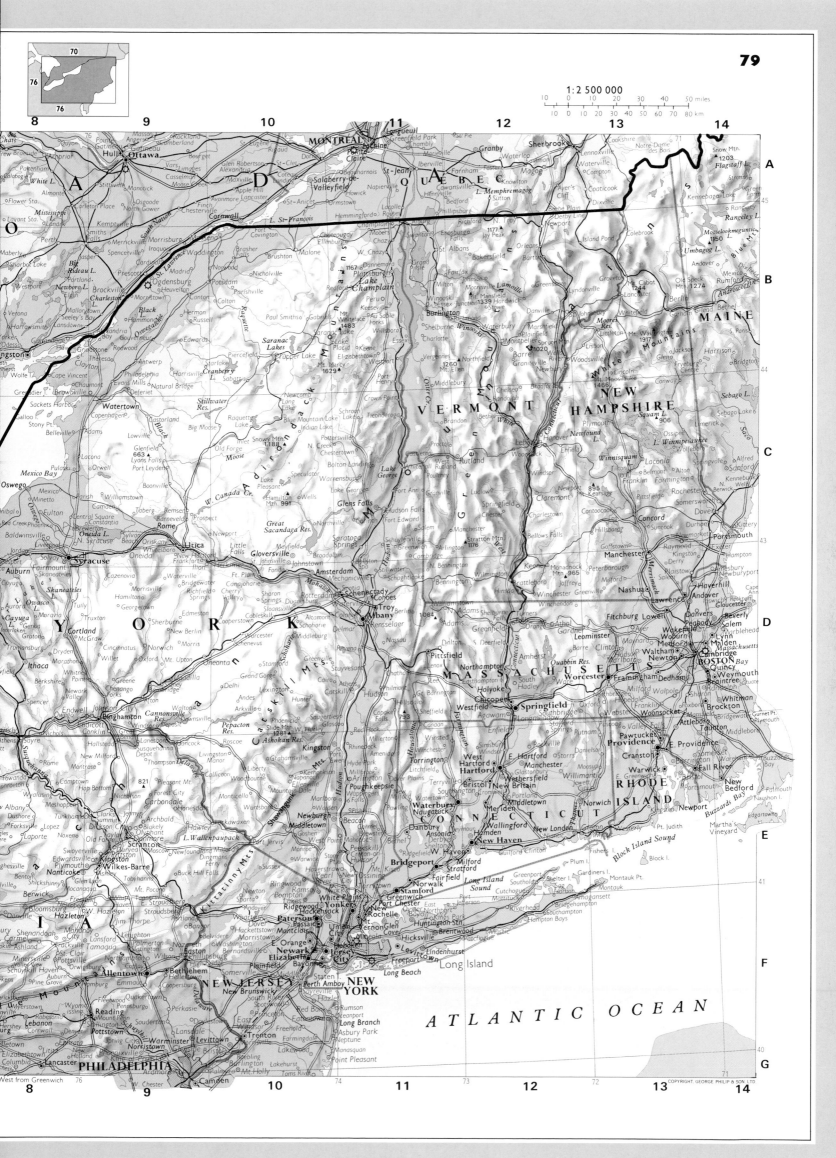

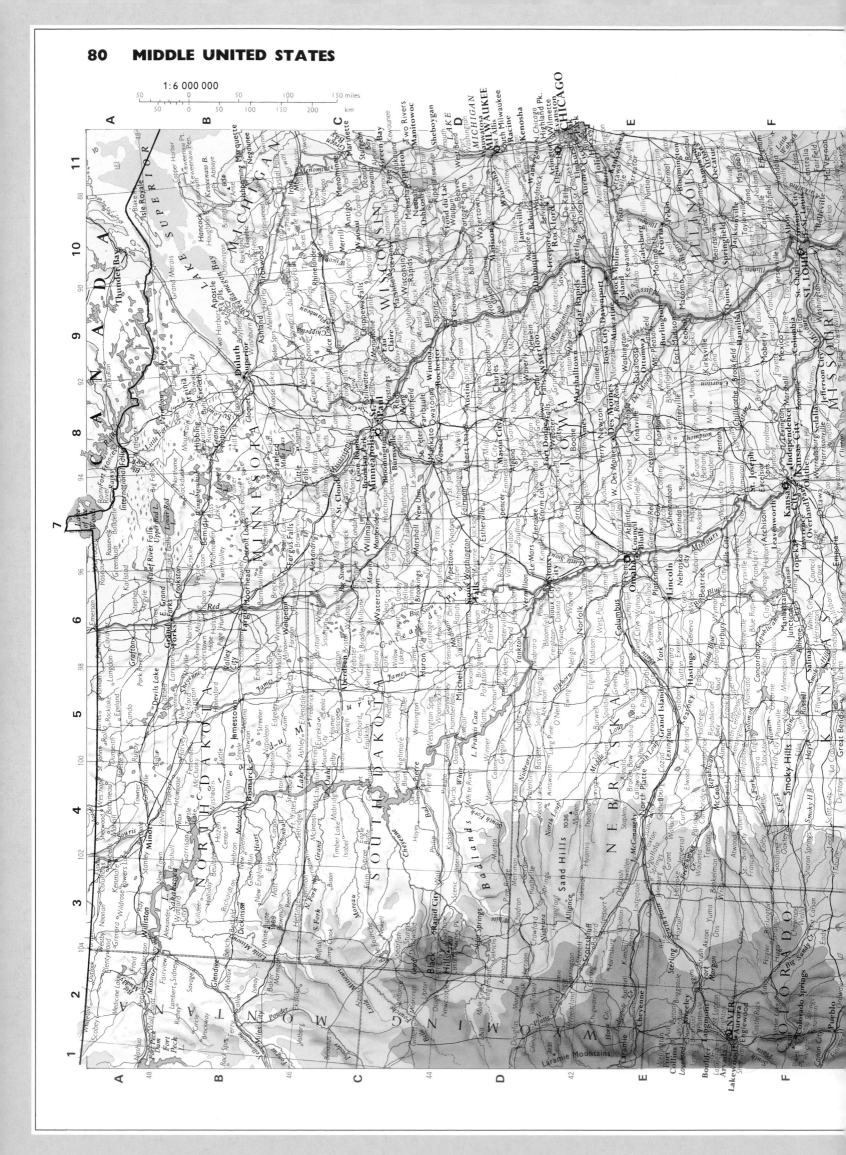

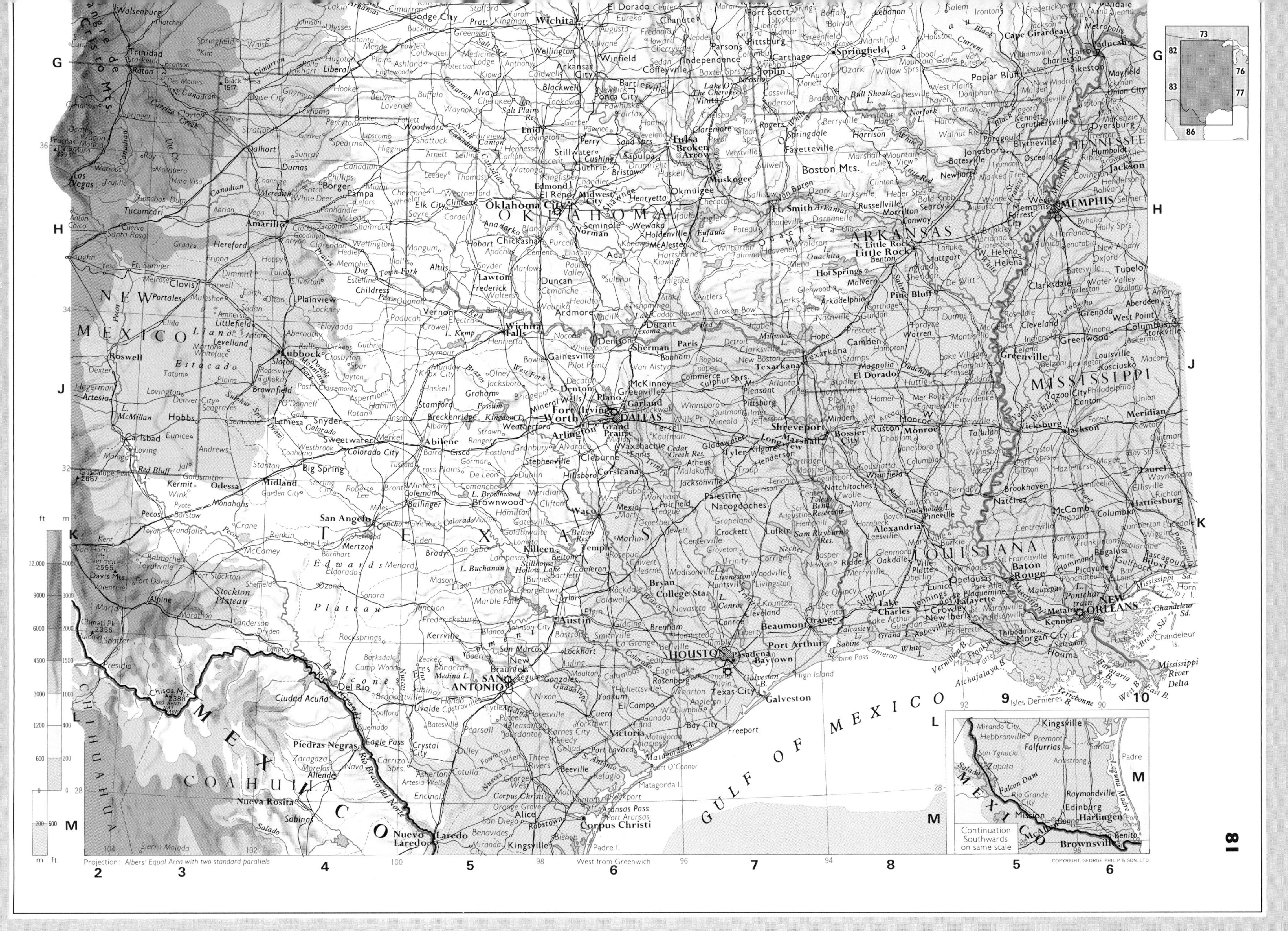
NEW MEXICO
TEXAS
OKLAHOMA
ARKANSAS
LOUISIANA
MISSISSIPPI
TENNESSEE
MEXICO
COAHUILA
CHIHUAHUA
GULF OF MEXICO
Oklahoma City
Tulsa
Wichita
Amarillo
Lubbock
Dallas
Fort Worth
Houston
San Antonio
Austin
Waco
Corpus Christi
Laredo
Nuevo Laredo
Brownsville
El Paso
Shreveport
Little Rock
Memphis
Jackson
New Orleans
Baton Rouge
Galveston
Beaumont
Port Arthur
Abilene
San Angelo
Midland
Odessa
Sangre de Cristo Mts.
Llano Estacado
Edwards Plateau
Stockton Plateau
Boston Mts.
Ouachita Mts.
Chisos Mts.
Rio Grande
Rio Bravo del Norte
Red
Canadian
Pecos
Brazos
Colorado
Mississippi
Mississippi River Delta
Continuation Southwards on same scale
Projection: Albers' Equal Area with two standard parallels
West from Greenwich
ft
m
12,000
9000
6000
4500
3000
1200
600
0
200
600
4000
3000
2000
1500
1000
400
200
0
28
G
H
J
K
L
M
2
3
4
5
6
7
8
9
10
100
98
96
94
92
90
104
102
36
34
32
28
73
76
77
82
83
86

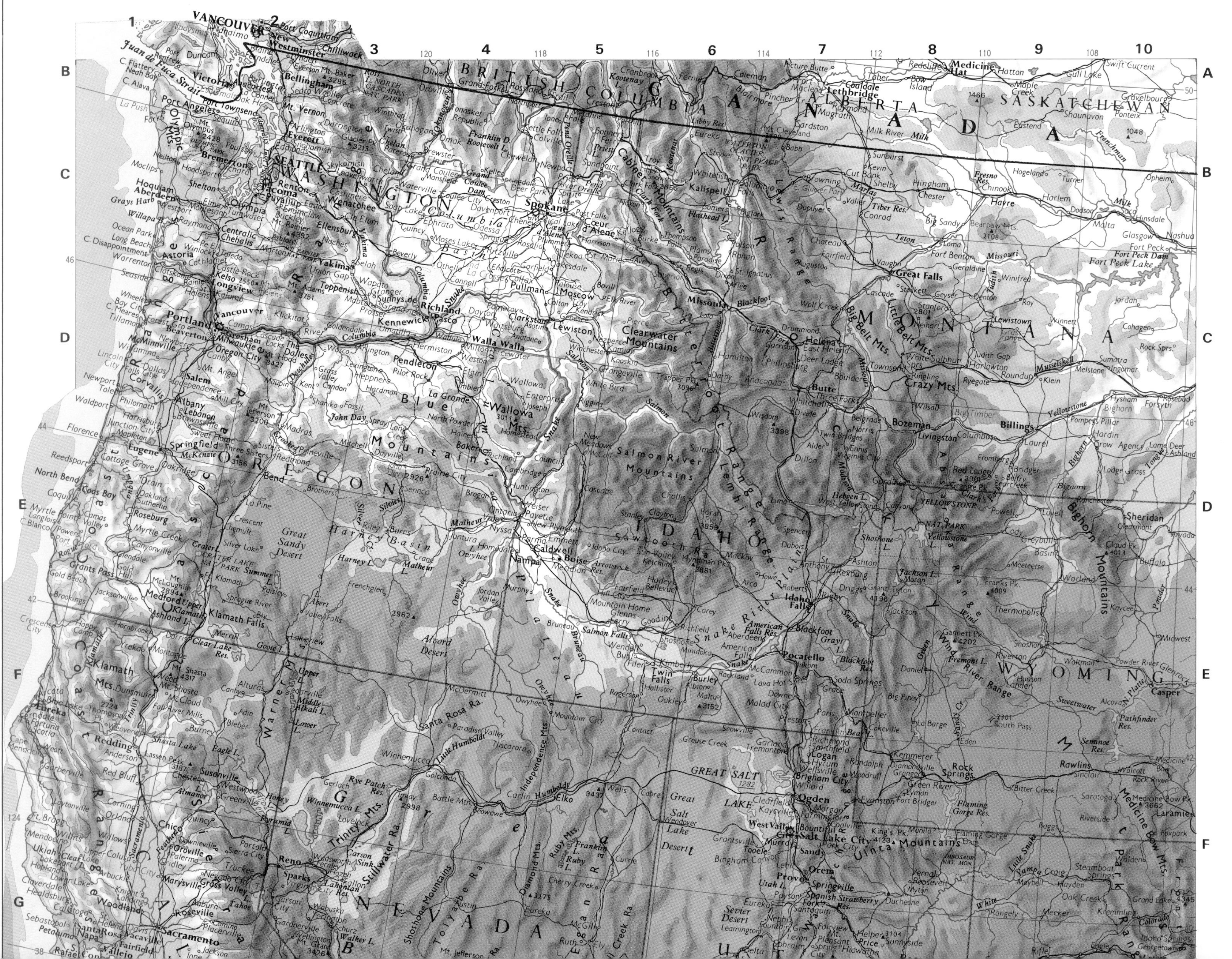
BRITISH COLUMBIA
SASKATCHEWAN
ALBERTA
CANADA
WASHINGTON
MONTANA
IDAHO
WYOMING
OREGON
NEVADA
VANCOUVER
Victoria
SEATTLE
Tacoma
Olympia
Spokane
Yakima
Walla Walla
Portland
Salem
Eugene
Medford
Klamath Falls
Missoula
Helena
Butte
Great Falls
Billings
Bozeman
Boise
Pocatello
Idaho Falls
Twin Falls
Casper
Sheridan
Rock Springs
Ogden
Salt Lake City
Provo
Reno
Sacramento
Elko
Lethbridge
Medicine Hat
Bighorn Mountains
Blue Mountains
Clearwater Mountains
Salmon River Mountains
Wind River Range
Uinta Mountains
Great Salt Lake
Great Sandy Desert
Olympic Mts.
Crazy Mts.
Little Belt Mts.
Big Belt Mts.
Medicine Bow Mts.
Lewis Range
Lemhi Range
Cabinet Mountains
Harney Basin
Columbia
Snake
Juan de Fuca Strait

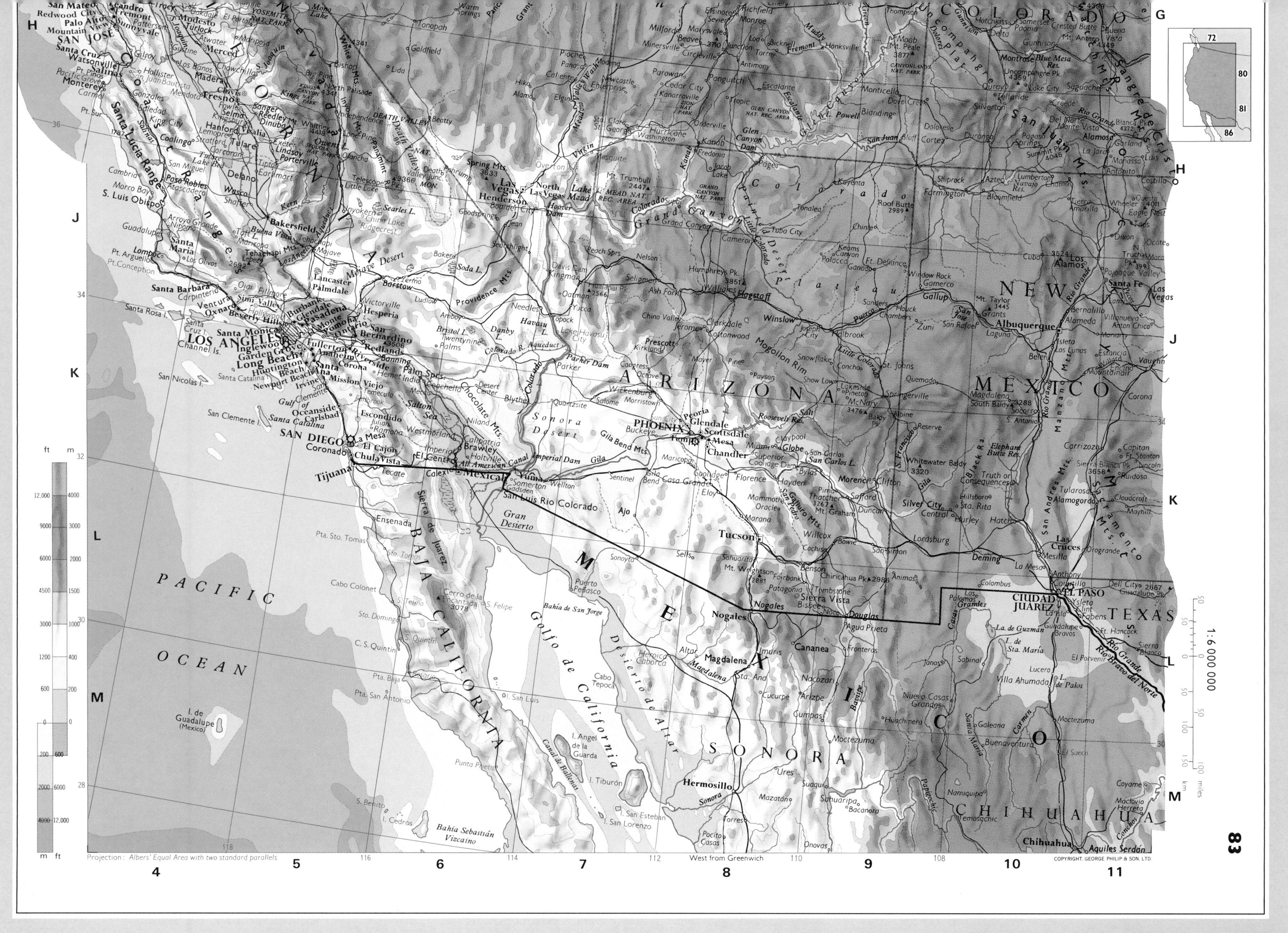
1:6 000 000
miles
km
PACIFIC
OCEAN
ARIZONA
NEW MEXICO
COLORADO
TEXAS
MEXICO
SONORA
CHIHUAHUA
BAJA CALIFORNIA
Golfo de California
Desierto de Altar
Gran Desierto
Sonora Desert
Colorado Plateau
Painted Desert
Grand Canyon
Death Valley
Mojave Desert
Santa Lucia Range
Coast Ranges
San Juan Mts.
Sacramento Mts.
Sierra de Juarez
LOS ANGELES
SAN DIEGO
SAN JOSE
PHOENIX
Tucson
Albuquerque
Santa Fe
Las Vegas
CIUDAD JUAREZ
EL PASO
Hermosillo
Chihuahua
Tijuana
Mexicali
Yuma
Flagstaff
Bakersfield
Fresno
Nogales
Santa Barbara
I. de Guadalupe (Mexico)
Channel Is.
Projection: Albers' Equal Area with two standard parallels
West from Greenwich
COPYRIGHT. GEORGE PHILIP & SON. LTD.

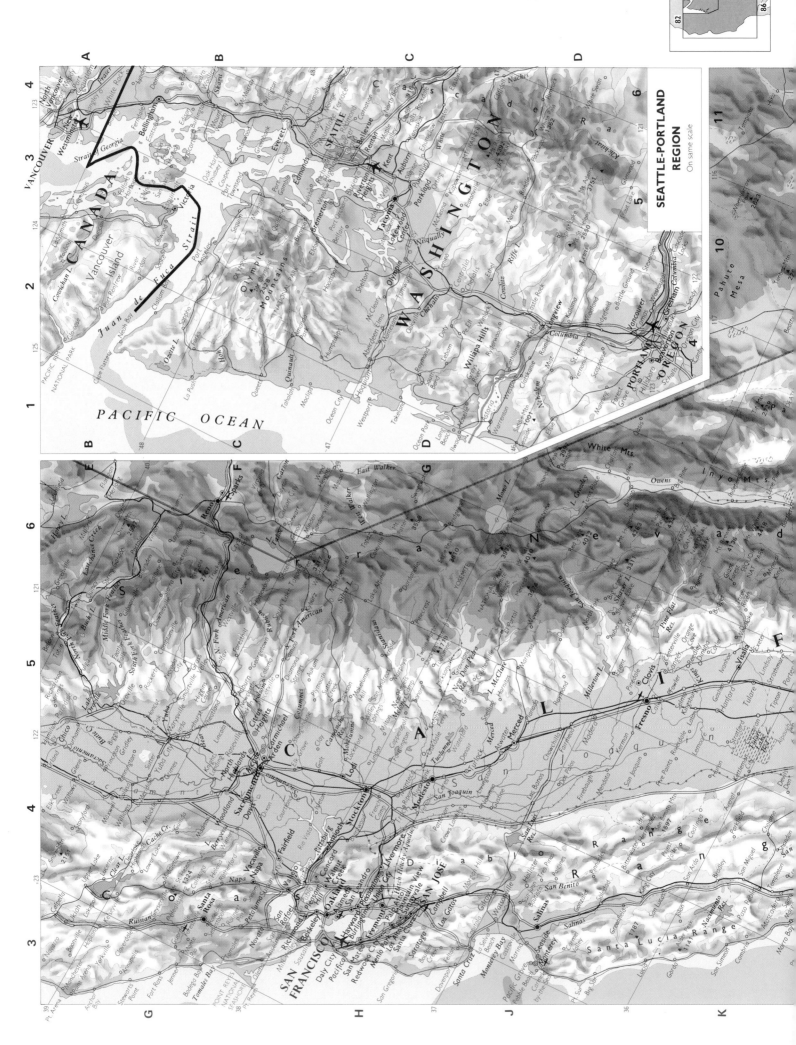

SEATTLE-PORTLAND
REGION
On same scale

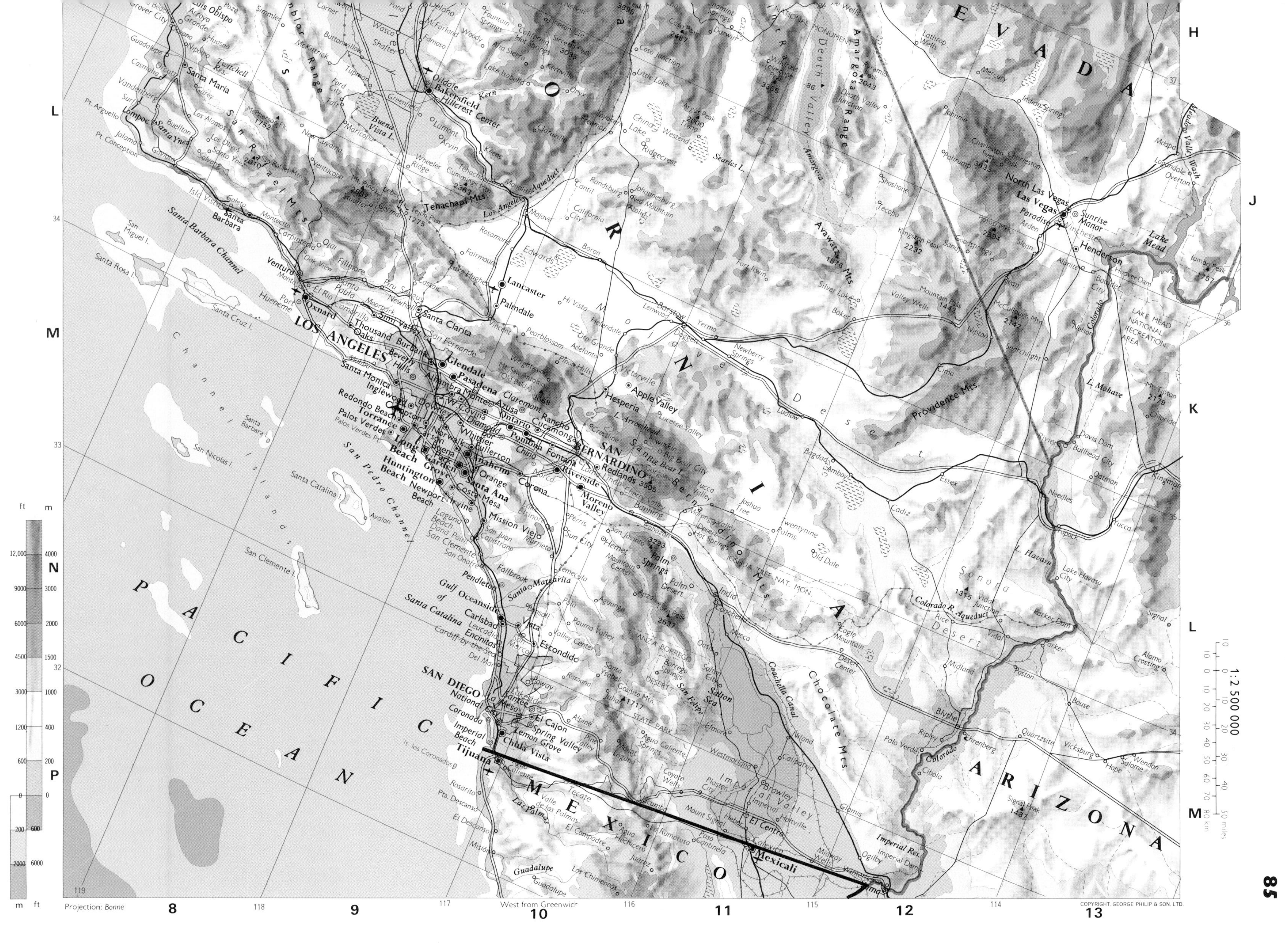

1 : 2 500 000

10   0   10   20   30   40   50 miles
10   0   10   20   30   40   50   60   70   80 km

COPYRIGHT GEORGE PHILIP & SON, LTD.

West from Greenwich

Projection: Bonne

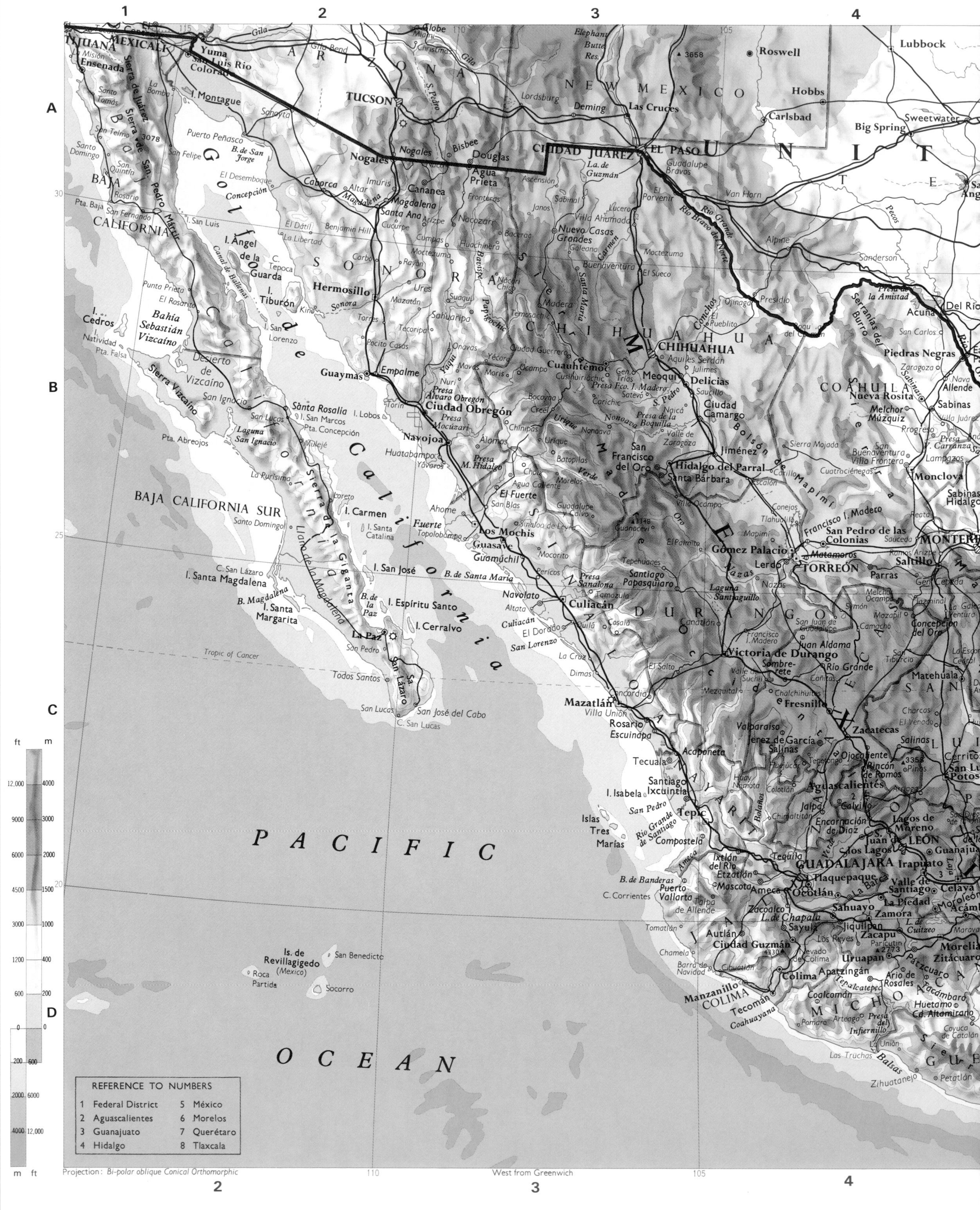

REFERENCE TO NUMBERS

1	Federal District	5	México
2	Aguascalientes	6	Morelos
3	Guanajuato	7	Querétaro
4	Hidalgo	8	Tlaxcala

Projection: Bi-polar oblique Conical Orthomorphic

West from Greenwich

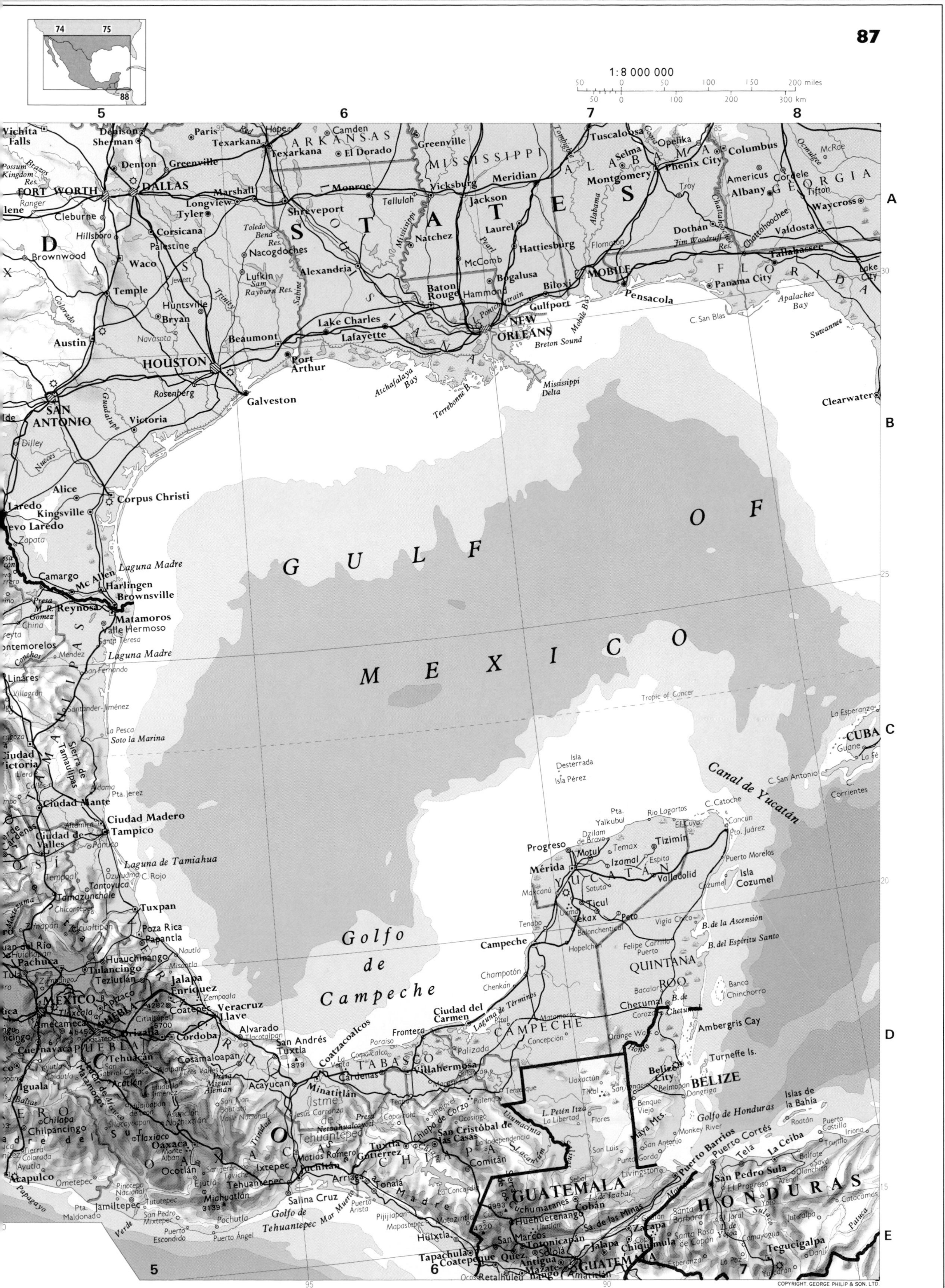
1:8 000 000
GULF OF MEXICO
Golfo de Campeche
Canal de Yucatán
UNITED STATES
TEXAS
LOUISIANA
MISSISSIPPI
ALABAMA
GEORGIA
FLORIDA
ARKANSAS
YUCATÁN
CAMPECHE
QUINTANA ROO
TABASCO
CHIAPAS
GUATEMALA
BELIZE
HONDURAS
CUBA
HOUSTON
DALLAS
FORT WORTH
SAN ANTONIO
NEW ORLEANS
MOBILE
Mérida
Campeche
Veracruz Llave
Tampico
Golfo de Honduras
Tropic of Cancer

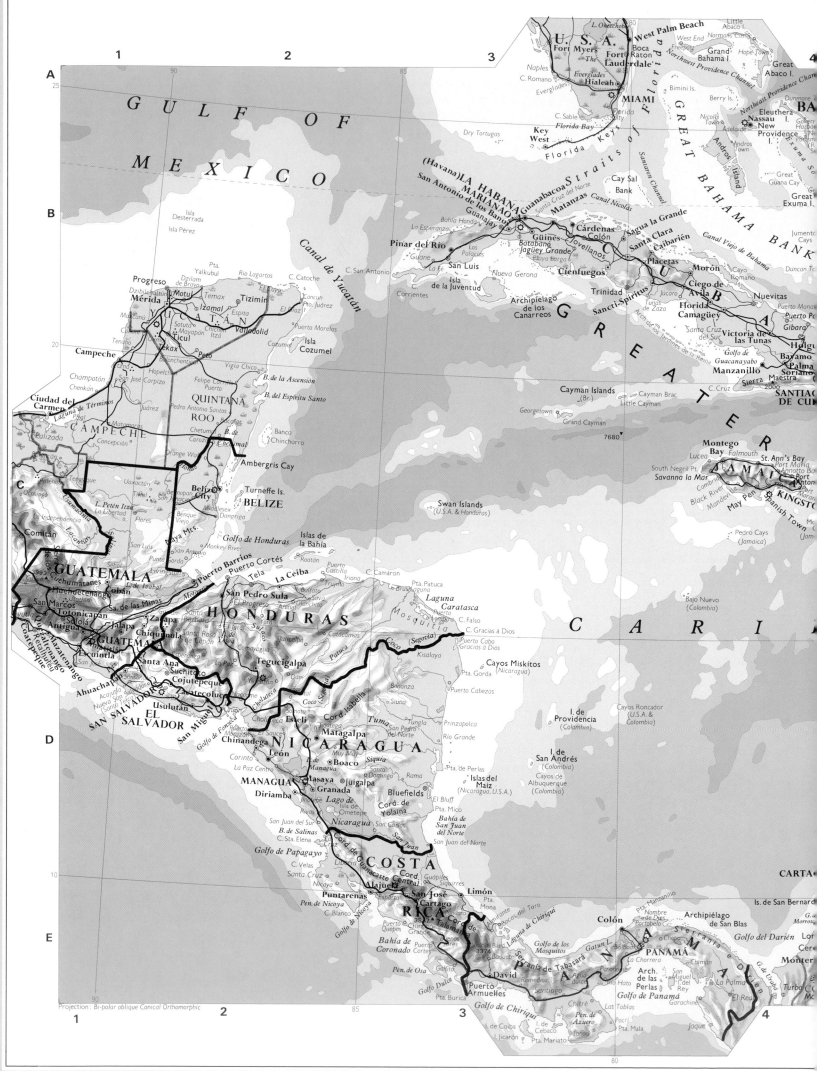

GULF OF MEXICO

U.S.A.

GREATER

CARIB

Projection: Bi-polar oblique Conical Orthomorphic

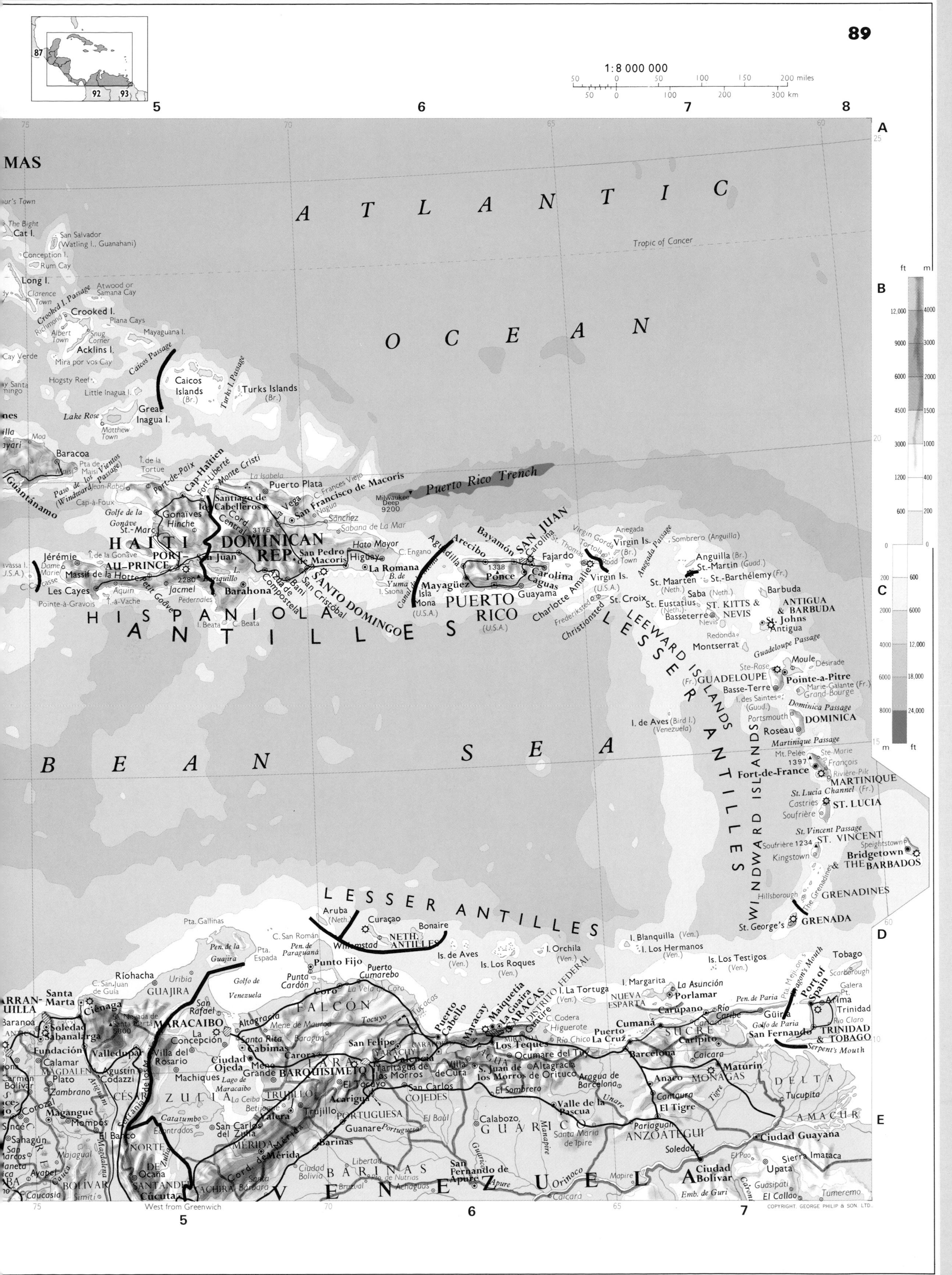
1:8 000 000
ATLANTIC OCEAN
Tropic of Cancer
Puerto Rico Trench
Milwaukee Deep 9200
HAITI
DOMINICAN REP.
HISPANIOLA
ANTILLES
PUERTO RICO (U.S.A.)
SAN JUAN
SANTO DOMINGO
PORT-AU-PRINCE
LEEWARD ISLANDS
LESSER ANTILLES
WINDWARD ISLANDS
CARIBBEAN SEA
GUADELOUPE
DOMINICA
MARTINIQUE
ST. LUCIA
ST. VINCENT
BARBADOS
GRENADA
GRENADINES
ANTIGUA & BARBUDA
ST. KITTS & NEVIS
NETH. ANTILLES
TRINIDAD & TOBAGO
Port of Spain
CARACAS
MARACAIBO
BARQUISIMETO
VENEZUELA
Turks Islands
Caicos Islands
Great Inagua I.
Acklins I.
Crooked I.
Long I.
Cat I.
Virgin Is.
Anguilla
St. Croix
Montserrat
Aruba
Curaçao
Bonaire
West from Greenwich
COPYRIGHT. GEORGE PHILIP & SON. LTD.

1 : 35 000 000

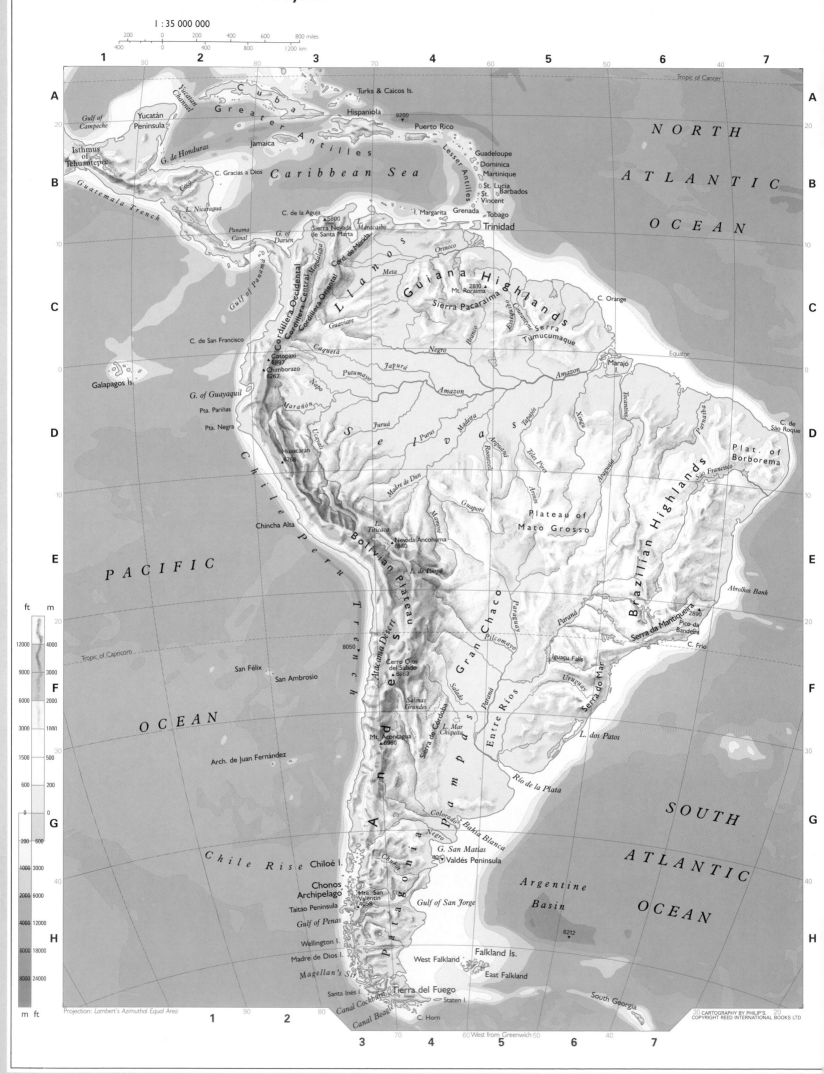

ft m

12000 4000

9000 3000

6000 2000

3000 1000

1500 500

600 200

0 0

200 600

1000 3000

2000 6000

4000 12000

6000 18000

8000 24000

m ft

Projection: *Lambert's Azimuthal Equal Area*

1 : 35 000 000

Havana
BAHAMAS
Turks & Caicos Is.
(U.K.)
CUBA
DOMINICAN
REP.
HAITI
Port-au-
Prince
San Juan
Virgin Is.
(U.K.)
JAMAICA
Kingston
PUERTO
RICO
(U.S.A.)
ST. KITTS-
NEVIS
ANTIGUA &
BARBUDA
Basse-Terre
GUADELOUPE
(Fr.)
DOMINICA
Fort-de-France
MARTINIQUE
(Fr.)
Castries
ST. LUCIA
ST. VINCENT
Kingstown
BARBADOS
Bridgetown
GRENADA
St. George's
TRINIDAD &
TOBAGO

MEXICO
BELIZE
GUATEMALA
HONDURAS
Guatemala
Tegucigalpa
San Salvador
EL SALVADOR
NICARAGUA
Managua
COSTA
RICA
San José
PANAMÁ
Panamá

Caribbean Sea

C. de
la Aguja
Barranquilla
Maracaibo
Aruba
Curaçao
Caracas
Port of
Spain
Cartagena
Barquisimeto
Valencia
G. of
Darién
Cúcuta
San Cristóbal
Orinoco
Ciudad Guayana
Medellín
Bucaramanga
VENEZUELA
Georgetown
GUYANA
Paramaribo
Cali
Bogotá
SURINAM
Cayenne
C. Orange
FRENCH
GUIANA
Gulf of Panama
COLOMBIA
RORAIMA
Branco
Essequibo
AMAPÁ

Galapagos Is.
(Ecuador)
Quito
ECUADOR
Guayaquil
Napo
Putumayo
Japurá
Amazon
*Marajó
I.*
Belém
Equator
G. of Guayaquil
Iquitos
Marañón
Amazon
Manaus
Santarém
São Luís
AMAZONAS
PARÁ
Fortaleza
Ucayali
Juruá
Purus
Madeira
Tapajós
Xingu
MARANHÃO
Teresina
CEARÁ
C. de
São Roque
Chiclayo
Madre de Dios
ACRE
Pôrto Velho
RONDÔNIA
Araguaia
Tocantins
PIAUÍ
Parnaíba
RIO G.
DO NORTE
Natal
Trujillo
PARAÍBA
Campina Grande
Chimbote
PERNAMBUCO
Recife
PERU
Mamoré
BRAZIL
TOCANTINS
ALAGOAS
Maceió
Callao
LIMA
MATO GROSSO
BAHÍA
SERGIPE
Aracaju
Cuzco
São Francisco
Salvador
L.
Titicaca
BOLIVIA
Cuiabá
GOIÁS
DIS. FED.
Brasília
Arequipa
La Paz
Cochabamba
Santa Cruz
Goiânia
Iquique
Sucre
Paraguay
MATO GROSSO
DO SUL
MINAS GERAIS
Belo
Horizonte
ESPÍRITO
SANTO
Antofagasta
PARAGUAY
Pilcomayo
Paraná
Ribeirão
Prêto
Juiz
de Fora
Vitória
San Félix
(Chile)
San Ambrosio
(Chile)
Salta
PARANÁ
SÃO PAULO
Campinas
R. DE J.
Campos
San Miguel
de Tucumán
SÃO
PAULO
RIO DE
JANEIRO
Niterói
Resistencia
Corrientes
Uruguay
SANTA CATARINA
Curitiba
Córdoba
San Juan
Santa Fe
Paraná
RIO GRANDE
DO SUL
Pelotas
Arch. de Juan Fernández
(Chile)
Salado
Rosario
URUGUAY
Pôrto Alegre
Viña del Mar
Valparaíso
SANTIAGO
Mendoza
BUENOS AIRES
Montevideo
Talca
La Plata
Rio de la Plata
Concepción
Bahía
Blanca
Mar del Plata
Colorado
Valdivia
Negro
Viedma
Puerto Montt
Chubut
Comodoro Rivadavia
Gulf of San Jorge
Gulf of Penas
ARGENTINA
CHILE

NORTH
ATLANTIC
OCEAN

PACIFIC
OCEAN

SOUTH
ATLANTIC
OCEAN

West Falkland
FALKLAND IS.
(U.K.)
Stanley
East Falkland
Punta Arenas
Magellan's Str.
Tierra del Fuego
C. Horn
South Georgia
(U.K.)

Tropic of Cancer
Tropic of Capricorn

West from Greenwich

CARTOGRAPHY BY PHILIP'S
COPYRIGHT REED INTERNATIONAL BOOKS LTD

■ LIMA Capital Cities

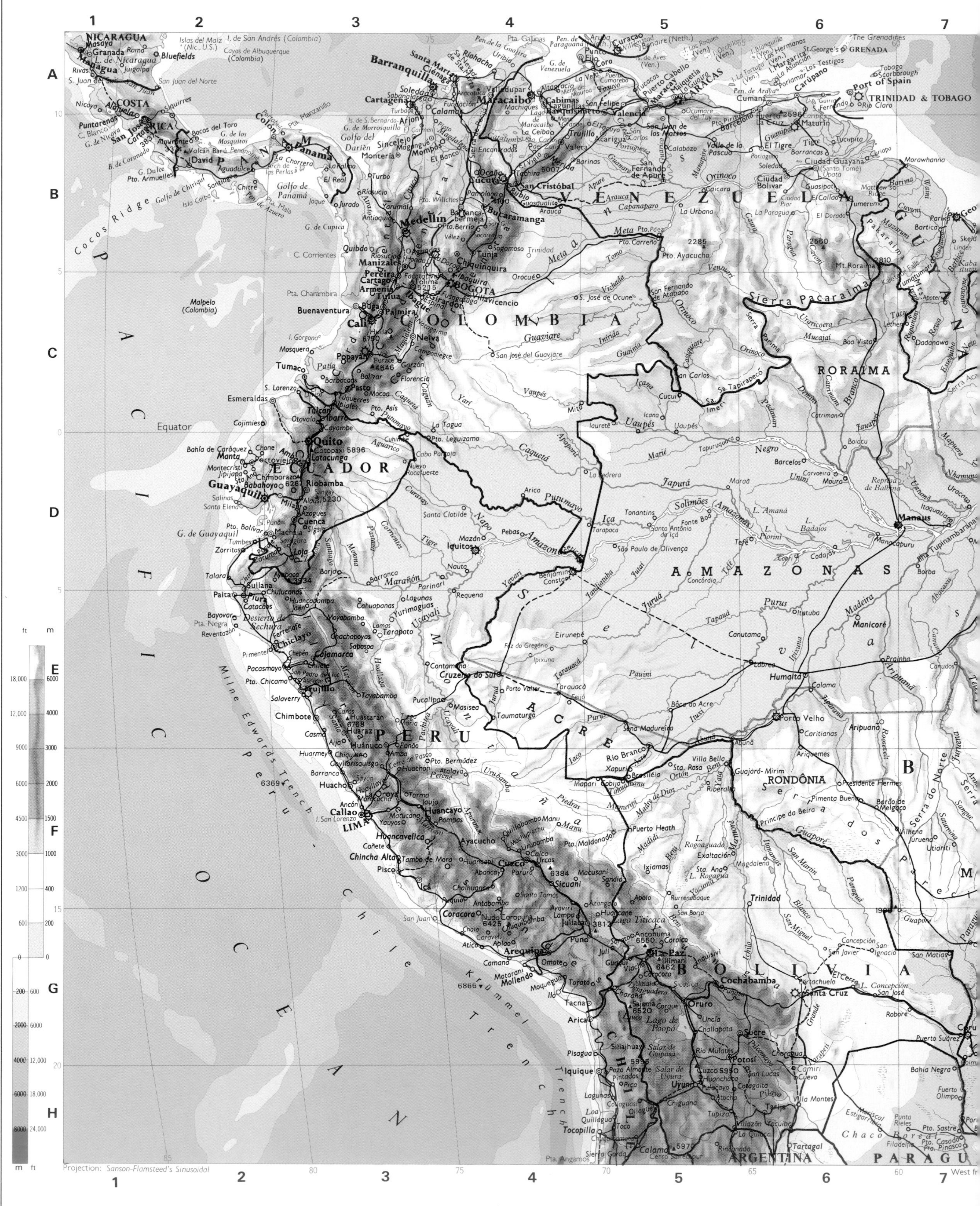

NICARAGUA
Managua
L. de Nicaragua
Bluefields
COSTA RICA
San José
PANAMA
Panamá
Colón
David
Golfo de Panamá
Cocos Ridge
Malpelo (Colombia)
Barranquilla
Cartagena
Santa Marta
Maracaibo
Caracas
Valencia
Barquisimeto
Maracay
Cumaná
Port of Spain
TRINIDAD & TOBAGO
GRENADA
Curaçao
Aruba
Bonaire (Neth.)
Ciudad Bolívar
Ciudad Guayana
Orinoco
Barinas
San Cristóbal
Cúcuta
Mérida
VENEZUELA
Medellín
Bucaramanga
Manizales
Pereira
Armenia
Ibagué
BOGOTÁ
Villavicencio
Buenaventura
Cali
Palmira
Popayán
Neiva
Pasto
Tumaco
COLOMBIA
Guaviare
Meta
Vaupés
Caquetá
Putumayo
Sierra Pacaraima
RORAIMA
Boa Vista
Mt. Roraima
GUYANA
Equator
Esmeraldas
Quito
Cotopaxi 5896
Latacunga
Chimborazo 6267
Riobamba
Guayaquil
Cuenca
Loja
Machala
ECUADOR
Iquitos
Napo
Amazonas
Marañón
Ucayali
Negro
Japurá
Solimões (Amazonas)
Manaus
AMAZONAS
Purus
Juruá
Madeira
Humaitá
Porto Velho
RONDÔNIA
Rio Branco
ACRE
Talara
Sullana
Piura
Paita
Desierto de Sechura
Chiclayo
Cajamarca
Trujillo
Chimbote
Huascarán 6768
Huaraz
Huánuco
Callao
LIMA
Huancayo
Huancavelica
Ayacucho
Cuzco
Ica
Pisco
Arequipa
Mollendo
PERU
Madre de Dios
Puerto Maldonado
Lago Titicaca
Puno
Juliaca
La Paz
Illimani 6462
Oruro
Cochabamba
Santa Cruz
Sucre
Potosí
Trinidad
Lago de Poopó
Salar de Uyuni
BOLIVIA
Arica
Iquique
Tocopilla
Calama
CHILE
ARGENTINA
PARAGUAY
Chaco Boreal
PACIFIC OCEAN
Milne Edwards Trench
Peru - Chile Trench
Krümmel Trench
Projection: Sanson-Flamsteed's Sinusoidal

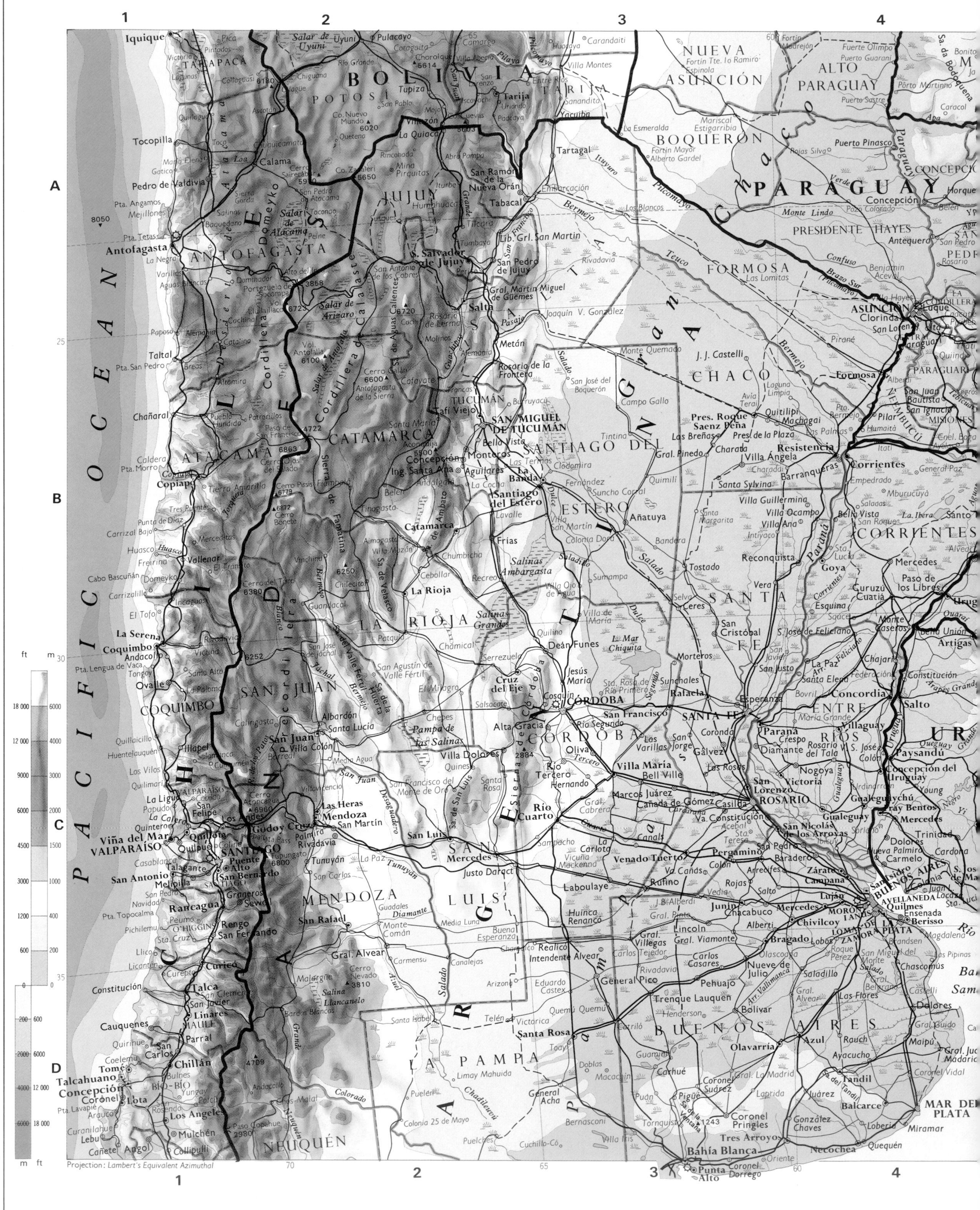
1
2
3
4
A
B
C
D
BOLIVIA
POTOSÍ
TARIJA
NUEVA ASUNCIÓN
ALTO PARAGUAY
BOQUERÓN
PARAGUAY
PRESIDENTE HAYES
Chaco
FORMOSA
CHACO
JUJUY
SALTA
ANTOFAGASTA
ATACAMA
COQUIMBO
CATAMARCA
TUCUMÁN
SANTIAGO DEL ESTERO
LA RIOJA
SAN JUAN
CÓRDOBA
SANTA FE
CORRIENTES
ENTRE RÍOS
MENDOZA
SAN LUIS
LA PAMPA
BUENOS AIRES
NEUQUÉN
CHILE
ARGENTINA
Gran Chaco
ANDES
PACIFIC OCEAN
Iquique
Tocopilla
Calama
Pedro de Valdivia
Antofagasta
Taltal
Chañaral
Copiapó
Vallenar
La Serena
Coquimbo
Ovalle
Illapel
Viña del Mar
VALPARAÍSO
SANTIAGO
San Antonio
Rancagua
Curicó
Talca
Linares
Cauquenes
Chillán
Talcahuano
Concepción
Los Angeles
Uyuni
Tupiza
Tarija
Villazón
La Quiaca
Tartagal
San Ramón de la Nueva Orán
S. Salvador de Jujuy
Salta
Metán
SAN MIGUEL DE TUCUMÁN
Santiago del Estero
Catamarca
La Rioja
San Juan
Mendoza
San Rafael
San Luis
Villa Dolores
CÓRDOBA
Río Cuarto
Villa María
SANTA FE
Paraná
ROSARIO
Resistencia
Corrientes
Formosa
ASUNCIÓN
Concepción
Pres. Roque Saenz Peña
Reconquista
Goya
Concordia
Paysandú
Mercedes
Pergamino
Junín
Campana
Zárate
BUENOS AIRES
AVELLANEDA
Quilmes
LA PLATA
Santa Rosa
General Pico
Trenque Lauquen
Olavarría
Azul
Tandil
Bahía Blanca
Tres Arroyos
Necochea
MAR DEL PLATA
Balcarce
Dolores
Punta Alto
Salar de Uyuni
Salar de Atacama
Salinas Grandes
Pilcomayo
Bermejo
Salado
Paraná
Uruguay
Colorado
Desaguadero
Projection: Lambert's Equivalent Azimuthal
70
65
60
25
30
35
ft
m
18 000
12 000
9000
6000
4500
3000
2000
1200
600
0
6000
4000
3000
2000
1500
1000
400
200
200
2000
4000
6000
600
6000
12 000
18 000

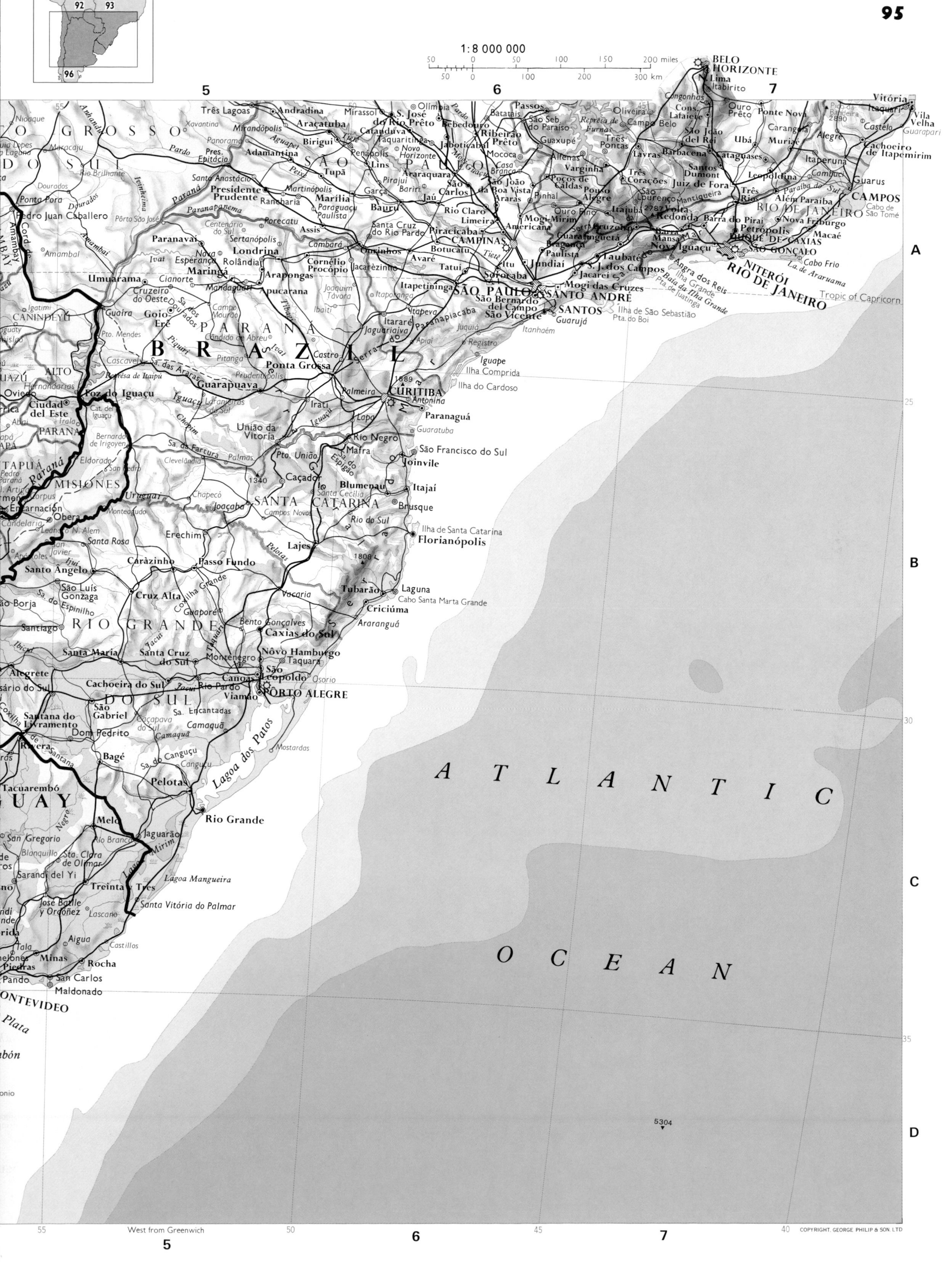

BELO
HORIZONTE

1:8 000 000

50   0   100   150   200 miles
50   0   100   200   300 km

A T L A N T I C

O C E A N

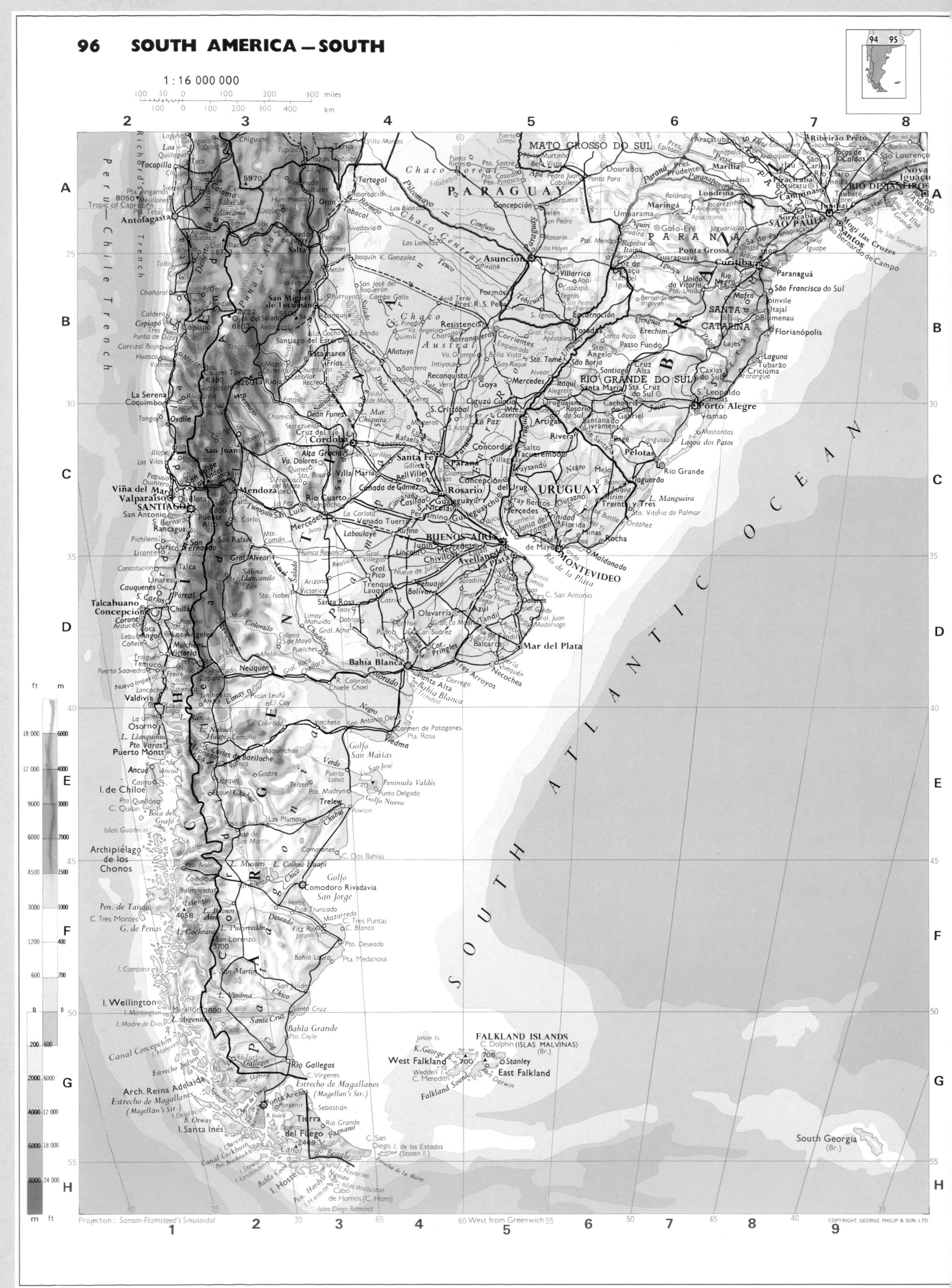

1 : 16 000 000

Projection : Sanson-Flamsteed's Sinusoidal

60 West from Greenwich

COPYRIGHT GEORGE PHILIP & SON. LTD.

INDEX

The index contains the names of all the principal places and features shown on the World Maps. Each name is followed by an additional entry in italics giving the country or region within which it is located. The alphabetical order of names composed of two or more words is governed primarily by the first word and then by the second. This is an example of the rule:

Mīr Kūh, *Iran*	**45 E8**	26 22 N	58 55 E
Mīr Shahdād, *Iran*	**45 E8**	26 15 N	58 29 E
Miraj, *India*	**40 L9**	16 50 N	74 45 E
Miram Shah, *Pakistan*	**42 C4**	33 0 N	70 2 E
Miramar, *Mozam.*	**57 C6**	23 50 S	35 35 E

Physical features composed of a proper name (Erie) and a description (Lake) are positioned alphabetically by the proper name. The description is positioned after the proper name and is usually abbreviated:

Erie, L., *N. Amer.*	**78 D3**	42 15 N	81 0 W

Where a description forms part of a settlement or administrative name, however, it is always written in full and put in its true alphabetic position:

Mount Morris, *U.S.A.*	**78 D7**	42 44 N	77 52 W

Names beginning with M' and Mc are indexed as if they were spelled Mac. Names beginning St. are alphabetized under Saint, but Sankt, Sint, Sant', Santa and San are all spelled in full and are alphabetized accordingly. If the same place name occurs two or more times in the index and all are in the same country, each is followed by the name of the administrative subdivision in which it is located. The names are placed in the alphabetical order of the subdivisions. For example:

Jackson, *Ky., U.S.A.*	**76 G4**	37 33 N	83 23 W
Jackson, *Mich., U.S.A.*	**76 D3**	42 15 N	84 24 W
Jackson, *Minn., U.S.A.*	**80 D7**	43 37 N	95 1 W

The number in bold type which follows each name in the index refers to the number of the map page where that feature or place will be found. This is usually the largest scale at which the place or feature appears.

The letter and figure which are in bold type immediately after the page number give the grid square on the map page, within which the feature is situated. The letter represents the latitude and the figure the longitude.

In some cases the feature itself may fall within the specified square, while the name is outside. This is usually the case only with features which are larger than a grid square.

For a more precise location the geographical coordinates which follow the letter/figure references give the latitude and the longitude of each place. The first set of figures represent the latitude which is the distance north or south of the Equator measured as an angle at the centre of the Earth. The Equator is latitude 0°, the North Pole is 90°N, and the South Pole 90°S.

The second set of figures represent the longitude, which is the distance East or West of the prime meridian, which runs through Greenwich, England. Longitude is also measured as an angle at the centre of the earth and is given East or West of the prime meridian, from 0° to 180° in either direction.

The unit of measurement for latitude and longitude is the degree, which is subdivided into 60 minutes. Each index entry states the position of a place in degrees and minutes, a space being left between the degrees and the minutes.

The latitude is followed by N(orth) or S(outh) and the longitude by E(ast) or W(est).

Rivers are indexed to their mouths or confluences, and carry the symbol → after their names. A solid square ■ follows the name of a country while, an open square □ refers to a first order administrative area.

Abbreviations used in the index

A.C.T. — Australian Capital Territory
Afghan. — Afghanistan
Ala. — Alabama
Alta. — Alberta
Amer. — America(n)
Arch. — Archipelago
Ariz. — Arizona
Ark. — Arkansas
Atl. Oc. — Atlantic Ocean
B. — Baie, Bahía, Bay, Bucht, Bugt
B.C. — British Columbia
Bangla. — Bangladesh
Barr. — Barrage
Bos. & H. — Bosnia and Herzegovina
C. — Cabo, Cap, Cape, Coast
C.A.R. — Central African Republic
C. Prov. — Cape Province
Calif. — California
Cent. — Central
Chan. — Channel
Colo. — Colorado
Conn. — Connecticut
Cord. — Cordillera
Cr. — Creek
Czech. — Czech Republic
D.C. — District of Columbia
Del. — Delaware
Dep. — Dependency
Des. — Desert
Dist. — District
Dj. — Djebel
Domin. — Dominica
Dom. Rep. — Dominican Republic
E. — East

El Salv. — El Salvador
Eq. Guin. — Equatorial Guinea
Fla. — Florida
Falk. Is. — Falkland Is.
G. — Golfe, Golfo, Gulf, Guba, Gebel
Ga. — Georgia
Gt. — Great, Greater
Guinea-Biss. — Guinea-Bissau
H.K. — Hong Kong
H.P. — Himachal Pradesh
Hants. — Hampshire
Harb. — Harbor, Harbour
Hd. — Head
Hts. — Heights
I.(s). — Île, Ilha, Insel, Isla, Island, Isle
Ill. — Illinois
Ind. — Indiana
Ind. Oc. — Indian Ocean
Ivory C. — Ivory Coast
J. — Jabal, Jebel, Jazira
Junc. — Junction
K. — Kap, Kapp
Kans. — Kansas
Kep. — Kepulauan
Ky. — Kentucky
L. — Lac, Lacul, Lago, Lagoa, Lake, Limni, Loch, Lough
La. — Louisiana
Liech. — Liechtenstein
Lux. — Luxembourg
Mad. P. — Madhya Pradesh
Madag. — Madagascar
Man. — Manitoba
Mass. — Massachusetts

Md. — Maryland
Me. — Maine
Medit. S. — Mediterranean Sea
Mich. — Michigan
Minn. — Minnesota
Miss. — Mississippi
Mo. — Missouri
Mont. — Montana
Mozam. — Mozambique
Mt.(e). — Mont, Monte, Monti, Montaña, Mountain
N. — Nord, Norte, North, Northern, Nouveau
N.B. — New Brunswick
N.C. — North Carolina
N. Cal. — New Caledonia
N. Dak. — North Dakota
N.H. — New Hampshire
N.I. — North Island
N.J. — New Jersey
N. Mex. — New Mexico
N.S. — Nova Scotia
N.S.W. — New South Wales
N.W.T. — North West Territory
N.Y. — New York
N.Z. — New Zealand
Nebr. — Nebraska
Neths. — Netherlands
Nev. — Nevada
Nfld. — Newfoundland
Nic. — Nicaragua
O. — Oued, Ouadi
Occ. — Occidentale
Okla. — Oklahoma
Ont. — Ontario
Or. — Orientale

Oreg. — Oregon
Os. — Ostrov
Oz. — Ozero
P. — Pass, Passo, Pasul, Pulau
P.E.I. — Prince Edward Island
Pa. — Pennsylvania
Pac. Oc. — Pacific Ocean
Papua N.G. — Papua New Guinea
Pass. — Passage
Pen. — Peninsula, Péninsule
Phil. — Philippines
Pk. — Park, Peak
Plat. — Plateau
P-ov. — Poluostrov
Prov. — Province, Provincial
Pt. — Point
Pta. — Ponta, Punta
Pte. — Pointe
Qué. — Québec
Queens. — Queensland
R. — Rio, River
R.I. — Rhode Island
Ra.(s). — Range(s)
Raj. — Rajasthan
Reg. — Region
Rep. — Republic
Res. — Reserve, Reservoir
S. — San, South, Sea
Si. Arabia — Saudi Arabia
S.C. — South Carolina
S. Dak. — South Dakota
S.I. — South Island
S. Leone — Sierra Leone
Sa. — Serra, Sierra
Sask. — Saskatchewan
Scot. — Scotland

Sd. — Sound
Sev. — Severnaya
Sib. — Siberia
Sprs. — Springs
St. — Saint, Sankt, Sint
Sta. — Santa, Station
Ste. — Sainte
Sto. — Santo
Str. — Strait, Stretto
Switz. — Switzerland
Tas. — Tasmania
Tenn. — Tennessee
Tex. — Texas
Tg. — Tanjung
Trin. & Tob. — Trinidad & Tobago
U.A.E. — United Arab Emirates
U.K. — United Kingdom
U.S.A. — United States of America
Ut. P. — Uttar Pradesh
Va. — Virginia
Vdkhr. — Vodokhranilishche
Vf. — Vîrful
Vic. — Victoria
Vol. — Volcano
Vt. — Vermont
W. — Wadi, West
W. Va. — West Virginia
Wash. — Washington
Wis. — Wisconsin
Wlkp. — Wielkopolski
Wyo. — Wyoming
Yorks. — Yorkshire

A Coruña

A

A Coruña = La Coruña, Spain 19 A1 43 20N 8 25W
Aachen, Germany 16 C4 50 45N 6 6 E
Aalborg = Ålborg, Denmark 9 H13 57 2N 9 54 E
Aalen, Germany 16 D6 48 51N 10 6 E
Aalsmeer, Neths. 15 B4 52 17N 4 43 E
Aalst, Belgium 15 D4 50 56N 4 2 E
Aalten, Neths. 15 C6 51 56N 6 35 E
Äänekoski, Finland 9 E21 62 36N 25 44 E
Aarau, Switz. 16 E5 47 23N 8 4 E
Aare →, Switz. 16 E5 47 33N 8 14 E
Aarhus = Århus, Denmark 9 H14 56 8N 10 11 E
Aarschot, Belgium 15 D4 50 59N 4 49 E
Aba, Nigeria 50 G6 5 10N 7 19 E
Aba, Zaïre 54 B3 3 58N 30 17 E
Ābādān, Iran 45 D6 30 22N 48 20 E
Ābādeh, Iran 45 D7 31 8N 52 40 E
Abadla, Algeria 50 B4 31 2N 2 45W
Abaetetuba, Brazil 93 D9 1 40S 48 50W
Abagnar Qi, China 34 C9 43 52N 116 2 E
Abai, Paraguay 95 B4 25 58S 55 54W
Abakan, Russia 27 D10 53 40N 91 10 E
Abancay, Peru 92 F4 13 35S 72 55W
Abariringa, Kiribati 64 H10 2 50S 171 40W
Abarqū, Iran 45 D7 31 10N 53 20 E
Abashiri, Japan 30 B12 44 0N 144 15 E
Abashiri-Wan, Japan 30 B12 44 0N 144 30 E
Abay, Kazakstan 26 E8 49 38N 72 53 E
Abaya, L., Ethiopia 51 G12 6 30N 37 50 E
Abaza, Russia 26 D10 52 39N 90 6 E
'Abbāsābād, Iran 45 C8 33 34N 58 23 E
Abbay = Nîl el Azraq →, Sudan 51 E11 15 38N 32 31 E
Abbaye, Pt., U.S.A. 76 B1 46 58N 88 8W
Abbeville, France 18 A4 50 6N 1 49 E
Abbeville, La., U.S.A. 81 K8 29 58N 92 8W
Abbeville, S.C., U.S.A. 77 H4 34 11N 82 23W
Abbieglassie, Australia 63 D4 27 15S 147 28 E
Abbot Ice Shelf, Antarctica 5 D16 73 0S 92 0W
Abbotsford, Canada 72 D4 49 5N 122 20W
Abbotsford, U.S.A. 80 C9 44 57N 90 19W
Abbottabad, Pakistan 42 B5 34 10N 73 15 E
Abd al Kūrī, Ind. Oc. 46 E5 12 5N 52 20 E
Ābdar, Iran 45 D7 30 16N 55 19 E
'Abdolābād, Iran 45 C8 34 12N 56 30 E
Abéché, Chad 51 F9 13 50N 20 35 E
Åbenrå, Denmark 9 J13 55 3N 9 25 E
Abeokuta, Nigeria 50 G5 7 3N 3 19 E
Aber, Uganda 54 B3 2 12N 32 25 E
Aberaeron, U.K. 11 E3 52 15N 4 15W
Aberayron = Aberaeron, U.K. 11 E3 52 15N 4 15W
Aberconwy & Colwyn □, U.K. 10 D4 53 10N 3 44W
Abercorn = Mbala, Zambia 55 D3 8 46S 31 24 E
Abercorn, Australia 63 D5 25 12S 151 5 E
Aberdare, U.K. 11 F4 51 43N 3 27W
Aberdare Ra., Kenya 54 C4 0 15S 36 50 E
Aberdeen, Australia 63 E5 32 9S 150 56 E
Aberdeen, Canada 73 C7 52 20N 106 8W
Aberdeen, S. Africa 56 E3 32 28S 24 2 E
Aberdeen, U.K. 12 D6 57 9N 2 5W
Aberdeen, Ala., U.S.A. 77 J1 33 49N 88 33W
Aberdeen, Idaho, U.S.A. 82 E7 42 57N 112 50W
Aberdeen, S. Dak., U.S.A. 80 C5 45 28N 98 29W
Aberdeen, Wash., U.S.A. 84 D3 46 59N 123 50W
Aberdeenshire □, U.K. 12 D6 57 17N 2 36W
Aberdovey = Aberdyfi, U.K. 11 E3 52 33N 4 3W
Aberdyfi, U.K. 11 E3 52 33N 4 3W
Aberfeldy, U.K. 12 E5 56 37N 3 51W
Abergavenny, U.K. 11 F4 51 49N 3 1W
Abernathy, U.S.A. 81 J4 33 50N 101 51W
Abert, L., U.S.A. 82 E3 42 38N 120 14W
Aberystwyth, U.K. 11 E3 52 25N 4 5W
Abhar, Iran 45 B6 36 9N 49 13 E
Abhayapuri, India 43 F14 26 24N 90 38 E
Abidjan, Ivory C. 50 G4 5 26N 3 58W
Abilene, Kans., U.S.A. 80 F6 38 55N 97 13W
Abilene, Tex., U.S.A. 81 J5 32 28N 99 43W
Abingdon, U.K. 11 F6 51 40N 1 17W
Abingdon, Ill., U.S.A. 80 E9 40 48N 90 24W
Abingdon, Va., U.S.A. 77 G5 36 43N 81 59W
Abington Reef, Australia 62 B4 18 0S 149 35 E
Abitau →, Canada 73 B7 59 53N 109 3W
Abitau L., Canada 73 A7 60 27N 107 15W
Abitibi L., Canada 70 C4 48 40N 79 40W
Abkhaz Republic □ = Abkhazia □, Georgia 25 F7 43 12N 41 5 E
Abkhazia □, Georgia 25 F7 43 12N 41 5 E
Abkit, Russia 27 C16 64 10N 157 10 E
Abminga, Australia 63 D1 26 8S 134 51 E
Åbo = Turku, Finland 9 F20 60 30N 22 19 E
Abohar, India 42 D6 30 10N 74 10 E
Abomey, Benin 50 G5 7 10N 2 5 E
Abong-Mbang, Cameroon 52 D2 4 0N 13 8 E
Abou-Deïa, Chad 51 F8 11 20N 19 20 E
Aboyne, U.K. 12 D6 57 4N 2 47W
Abra Pampa, Argentina 94 A2 22 43S 65 42W
Abreojos, Pta., Mexico 86 B2 26 50N 113 40W
Abri, Sudan 51 D11 20 50N 30 27 E
Abrolhos, Banka, Brazil 93 G11 18 0S 38 0W
Abrud, Romania 17 E12 46 19N 23 5 E
Absaroka Range, U.S.A. 82 D9 44 45N 109 50W
Abū al Khaşīb, Iraq 45 D6 30 25N 48 0 E
Abū 'Alī, Si. Arabia 45 E6 27 20N 49 27 E
Abū 'Alī →, Lebanon 47 A4 34 25N 35 50 E
Abu 'Arīsh, Si. Arabia 46 D3 16 53N 42 48 E
Abu Dhabi = Abū Ẓāby, U.A.E. 45 E7 24 28N 54 22 E
Abū Dis, Sudan 51 E11 19 12N 33 38 E
Abū Du'ān, Syria 44 B3 36 25N 38 15 E
Abu el Gairi, W. →, Egypt 47 F2 29 35N 33 30 E
Abu Ga'da, W. →, Egypt 47 F1 29 15N 32 53 E
Abū Ḩadrīyah, Si. Arabia 45 E6 27 20N 48 58 E
Abu Hamed, Sudan 51 E11 19 32N 33 13 E
Abū Kamāl, Syria 44 C4 34 30N 41 0 E
Abū Madd, Ra's, Si. Arabia 44 E3 24 50N 37 7 E
Abu Matariq, Sudan 51 F10 10 59N 26 9 E
Abu Şafāt, W. →, Jordan 47 E5 30 24N 36 7 E
Abū Şukhayr, Iraq 44 D5 31 54N 44 30 E
Abu Tig, Egypt 51 C11 27 4N 31 15 E
Abū Zabad, Sudan 51 F10 12 25N 29 10 E
Abū Ẓāby, U.A.E. 45 E7 24 28N 54 22 E
Abū Zeydābād, Iran 45 C6 33 54N 51 45 E
Abuja, Nigeria 50 G6 9 16N 7 2 E
Abukuma-Gawa →, Japan 30 E10 38 6N 140 52 E
Abukuma-Sammyaku, Japan 30 F10 37 30N 140 45 E
Abunã, Brazil 92 E5 9 40S 65 20W
Abunã →, Brazil 92 E5 9 41S 65 20W
Aburo, Zaïre 54 B3 2 4N 30 53 E
Abut Hd., N.Z. 59 K3 43 7S 170 15 E
Abwong, Sudan 51 G11 9 2N 32 14 E
Acajutla, El Salv. 88 D2 13 36N 89 50W
Acámbaro, Mexico 86 C4 20 0N 100 40W
Acaponeta, Mexico 86 C3 22 30N 105 20W
Acapulco, Mexico 87 D5 16 51N 99 56W
Acarigua, Venezuela 92 B5 9 33N 69 12W
Acatlán, Mexico 87 D5 18 10N 98 3W
Acayucan, Mexico 87 D6 17 59N 94 58W
Accomac, U.S.A. 76 G8 37 43N 75 40W
Accra, Ghana 50 G4 5 35N 0 6W
Accrington, U.K. 10 D5 53 45N 2 22W
Acebal, Argentina 94 C3 33 20S 60 50W
Aceh □, Indonesia 36 D1 4 15N 97 30 E
Achalpur, India 40 J10 21 22N 77 32 E
Acheng, China 35 B14 45 30N 126 58 E
Acher, India 42 H5 23 10N 72 32 E
Achill, Ireland 13 C2 53 56N 9 55W
Achill Hd., Ireland 13 C1 53 58N 10 15W
Achill I., Ireland 13 C1 53 58N 10 1W
Achill Sd., Ireland 13 C2 53 54N 9 56W
Achinsk, Russia 27 D10 56 20N 90 20 E
Acireale, Italy 20 F6 37 37N 15 10 E
Ackerman, U.S.A. 81 J10 33 19N 89 11W
Acklins I., Bahamas 89 B5 22 30N 74 0W
Acme, Canada 72 C6 51 33N 113 30W
Aconcagua, Cerro, Argentina 94 C2 32 39S 70 0W
Aconquija, Mt., Argentina 94 B2 27 0S 66 0W
Açores, Is. dos = Azores, Atl. Oc. 48 C1 38 44N 29 0W
Acraman, L., Australia 63 E2 32 2S 135 23 E
Acre = 'Akko, Israel 47 C4 32 55N 35 4 E
Acre □, Brazil 92 E4 9 1S 71 0W
Acre →, Brazil 92 E5 8 45S 67 22W
Acton, Canada 78 C4 43 38N 80 3W
Ad Dammām, Si. Arabia 45 E6 26 20N 50 5 E
Ad Dawḩah, Qatar 45 E6 25 15N 51 35 E
Ad Dawr, Iraq 44 C4 34 27N 43 47 E
Ad Dir'īyah, Si. Arabia 44 E5 24 44N 46 35 E
Ad Dīwānīyah, Iraq 44 D5 32 0N 45 0 E
Ad Dujayl, Iraq 44 C5 33 51N 44 14 E
Ad Durūz, J., Jordan 47 C5 32 35N 36 40 E
Ada, Minn., U.S.A. 80 B6 47 18N 96 31W
Ada, Okla., U.S.A. 81 H6 34 46N 96 41W
Adaja →, Spain 19 B3 41 32N 4 52W
Adamaoua, Massif de l', Cameroon 51 G7 7 20N 12 20 E
Adamawa Highlands = Adamaoua, Massif de l', Cameroon 51 G7 7 20N 12 20 E
Adamello, Mte., Italy 20 A4 46 9N 10 30 E
Adaminaby, Australia 63 F4 36 0S 148 45 E
Adams, Mass., U.S.A. 79 D11 42 38N 73 7W
Adams, N.Y., U.S.A. 79 C8 43 49N 76 1W
Adams, Wis., U.S.A. 80 D10 43 57N 89 49W
Adam's Bridge, Sri Lanka 40 Q11 9 15N 79 40 E
Adams L., Canada 72 C5 51 10N 119 40W
Adams Mt., U.S.A. 84 D5 46 12N 121 30W
Adam's Peak, Sri Lanka 40 R12 6 48N 80 30 E
Adana, Turkey 25 G6 37 0N 35 16 E
Adapazan, Turkey 25 F5 40 48N 30 25 E
Adarama, Sudan 51 E11 17 10N 34 52 E
Adare, C., Antarctica 5 D11 71 0S 171 0 E
Adaut, Indonesia 37 F8 8 8S 131 7 E
Adavale, Australia 63 D3 25 52S 144 32 E
Adda →, Italy 20 B3 45 8N 9 53 E
Addis Ababa = Addis Abeba, Ethiopia 51 G12 9 2N 38 42 E
Addis Abeba, Ethiopia 51 G12 9 2N 38 42 E
Addis Alem, Ethiopia 51 G12 9 0N 38 17 E
Addison, U.S.A. 78 D7 42 1N 77 14W
Addo, S. Africa 56 E4 33 32S 25 45 E
Ādeh, Iran 44 B5 37 42N 45 11 E
Adel, U.S.A. 77 K4 31 8N 83 25W
Adelaide, Australia 63 E2 34 52S 138 30 E
Adelaide, Bahamas 88 A4 25 4N 77 31W
Adelaide, S. Africa 56 E4 32 42S 26 20 E
Adelaide I., Antarctica 5 C17 67 15S 68 30W
Adelaide Pen., Canada 68 B10 68 15N 97 30W
Adelaide River, Australia 60 B5 13 15S 131 7 E
Adelanto, U.S.A. 85 L9 34 35N 117 22W
Adele I., Australia 60 C3 15 32S 123 9 E
Adélie, Terre, Antarctica 5 C10 68 0S 140 0 E
Adélie Land = Adélie, Terre, Antarctica 5 C10 68 0S 140 0 E
Aden = Al 'Adan, Yemen 46 E4 12 45N 45 0 E
Aden, G. of, Asia 46 E4 12 30N 47 30 E
Adendorp, S. Africa 56 E3 32 15S 24 30 E
Adh Dhayd, U.A.E. 45 E7 25 17N 55 53 E
Adhoi, India 42 H4 23 26N 70 32 E
Adi, Indonesia 37 E8 4 15S 133 30 E
Adi Ugri, Eritrea 51 F12 14 58N 38 48 E
Adieu, C., Australia 61 F5 32 0S 132 10 E
Adieu Pt., Australia 60 C3 15 14S 124 35 E
Adige →, Italy 20 B5 45 9N 12 20 E
Adilabad, India 40 K11 19 33N 78 20 E
Adin, U.S.A. 82 F3 41 12N 120 57W
Adin Khel, Afghan. 40 C6 32 45N 68 5 E
Adirondack Mts., U.S.A. 79 C10 44 0N 74 0W
Adjumani, Uganda 54 B3 3 20N 31 50 E
Adlavik Is., Canada 71 B8 55 2N 57 45W
Admer, Algeria 50 D6 20 21N 5 27 E
Admiralty G., Australia 60 B4 14 20S 125 55 E
Admiralty I., U.S.A. 68 C6 57 30N 134 30W
Admiralty Inlet, U.S.A. 82 C2 48 8N 122 58W
Admiralty Is., Papua N. G. 64 H6 2 0S 147 0 E
Ado-Ekiti, Nigeria 50 G6 7 38N 5 12 E
Adonara, Indonesia 37 F6 8 15S 123 5 E
Adoni, India 40 M10 15 33N 77 18 E
Adour →, France 18 E3 43 32N 1 32W
Adra, India 43 H12 23 30N 86 42 E
Adra, Spain 19 D4 36 43N 3 3W
Adrano, Italy 20 F6 37 40N 14 50 E
Adrar, Algeria 50 C4 27 51N 0 11W
Adré, Chad 51 F9 13 40N 22 20 E
Adrī, Libya 51 C7 27 32N 13 2 E
Adrian, Mich., U.S.A. 76 E3 41 54N 84 2W
Adrian, Tex., U.S.A. 81 H3 35 16N 102 40W
Adriatic Sea, Medit. S. 20 C6 43 0N 16 0 E
Adua, Indonesia 37 E7 1 45S 129 50 E
Adwa, Ethiopia 51 F12 14 15N 38 52 E
Adzhar Republic □ = Ajaria □, Georgia 25 F7 41 30N 42 0 E
Ægean Sea, Medit. S. 21 E11 38 30N 25 0 E
Aerhtai Shan, Mongolia 32 B4 46 40N 92 45 E
'Afak, Iraq 44 C5 32 4N 45 15 E
Afándou, Greece 23 C10 36 18N 28 12 E
Afghanistan ■, Asia 40 C4 33 0N 65 0 E
Afgoi, Somali Rep. 46 G3 2 7N 44 59 E
Afognak I., U.S.A. 68 C4 58 15N 152 30W
'Afrīn, Syria 44 B3 36 32N 36 50 E
Afton, U.S.A. 79 D9 42 14N 75 32W
Afuá, Brazil 93 D8 0 15S 50 20W
Afula, Israel 47 C4 32 37N 35 17 E
Afyonkarahisar, Turkey 25 G5 38 45N 30 33 E
Agadès = Agadez, Niger 50 E6 16 58N 7 59 E
Agadez, Niger 50 E6 16 58N 7 59 E
Agadir, Morocco 50 B3 30 28N 9 55W
Agaete, Canary Is. 22 F4 28 6N 15 43W
Agapa, Russia 27 B9 71 27N 89 15 E
Agar, India 42 H7 23 40N 76 2 E
Agartala, India 41 H17 23 50N 91 23 E
Agassiz, Canada 72 D4 49 14N 121 46W
Agats, Indonesia 37 F9 5 33S 138 0 E
Agboville, Ivory C. 50 G4 5 55N 4 15W
Agde, France 18 E5 43 19N 3 28 E
Agen, France 18 D4 44 12N 0 38 E
Āgh Kand, Iran 45 B6 37 15N 48 4 E
Aginskoye, Russia 27 D12 51 6N 114 32 E
Agra, India 42 F7 27 17N 77 58 E
Agri →, Italy 20 D7 40 13N 16 44 E
Ağrı Dağı, Turkey 25 G7 39 50N 44 15 E
Ağrı Karakose, Turkey 25 G7 39 44N 43 3 E
Agrigento, Italy 20 F5 37 19N 13 34 E
Agrinion, Greece 21 E9 38 37N 21 27 E
Agua Caliente, Baja Calif., Mexico 85 N10 32 29N 116 59W
Agua Caliente, Sinaloa, Mexico 86 B3 26 30N 108 20W
Agua Caliente Springs, U.S.A. 85 N10 32 56N 116 19W
Água Clara, Brazil 93 H8 20 25S 52 45W
Agua Hechicero, Mexico 85 N10 32 26N 116 14W
Agua Prieta, Mexico 86 A3 31 20N 109 32W
Aguadas, Colombia 92 B3 5 40N 75 38W
Aguadilla, Puerto Rico 89 C6 18 26N 67 10W
Aguadulce, Panama 88 E3 8 15N 80 32W
Aguanga, U.S.A. 85 M10 33 27N 116 51W
Aguanish, Canada 71 B7 50 14N 62 2W
Aguanus →, Canada 71 B7 50 13N 62 5W
Aguapey →, Argentina 94 B4 29 7S 56 36W
Aguaray Guazú →, Paraguay 94 A4 24 47S 57 19W
Aguarico →, Ecuador 92 D3 0 59S 75 11W
Aguas Blancas, Chile 94 A2 24 15S 69 55W
Aguas Calientes, Sierra de, Argentina 94 B2 25 26S 66 40W
Aguascalientes, Mexico 86 C4 21 53N 102 12W
Aguascalientes □, Mexico 86 C4 22 0N 102 20W
Aguilares, Argentina 94 B2 27 26S 65 35W
Aguilas, Spain 19 D5 37 23N 1 35W
Agüimes, Canary Is. 22 G4 27 58N 15 27W
Aguja, C. de la, Colombia 90 B3 11 18N 74 12W
Agulhas, C., S. Africa 56 E3 34 52S 20 0 E
Agulo, Canary Is. 22 F2 28 11N 17 12W
Agung, Indonesia 36 F5 8 20S 115 28 E
Agur, Uganda 54 B3 2 28N 32 55 E
Agusan →, Phil. 37 C7 9 0N 125 30 E
Aha Mts., Botswana 56 B3 19 45S 21 0 E
Ahaggar, Algeria 50 D6 23 0N 6 30 E
Ahar, Iran 44 B5 38 35N 47 0 E
Ahipara B., N.Z. 59 F4 35 5S 173 5 E
Ahiri, India 40 K12 19 30N 80 0 E
Ahmad Wal, Pakistan 42 E1 29 18N 65 58 E
Ahmadabad, India 42 H5 23 0N 72 40 E
Aḩmadābād, Khorāsān, Iran 45 C9 35 3N 60 50 E
Aḩmadābād, Khorāsān, Iran 45 C8 35 49N 59 42 E
Aḩmadī, Iran 45 E8 27 56N 56 42 E
Ahmadnagar, India 40 K9 19 7N 74 46 E
Ahmadpur, Pakistan 42 E4 29 12N 71 10 E
Ahmedabad = Ahmadabad, India 42 H5 23 0N 72 40 E
Ahmednagar = Ahmadnagar, India 40 K9 19 7N 74 46 E
Ahome, Mexico 86 B3 25 55N 109 11W
Ahram, Iran 45 D6 28 52N 51 16 E
Ahrax Pt., Malta 23 D1 35 59N 14 22 E
Āhū, Iran 45 C6 34 33N 50 2 E
Ahuachapán, El Salv. 88 D2 13 54N 89 52W
Ahvāz, Iran 45 D6 31 20N 48 40 E
Ahvenanmaa = Åland, Finland 9 F19 60 15N 20 0 E
Aḩwar, Yemen 46 E4 13 30N 46 40 E
Aichi □, Japan 31 G8 35 0N 137 15 E
Aigua, Uruguay 95 C5 34 13S 54 46W
Aigues-Mortes, France 18 E6 43 35N 4 12 E
Aihui, China 33 A7 50 10N 127 30 E
Aija, Peru 92 E3 9 50S 77 45W
Aikawa, Japan 30 E9 38 2N 138 15 E
Aiken, U.S.A. 77 J5 33 34N 81 43W
Aillik, Canada 71 A8 55 11N 59 18W
Ailsa Craig, U.K. 12 F3 55 15N 5 6W
'Ailūn, Jordan 47 C4 32 18N 35 47 E
Aim, Russia 27 D14 59 0N 133 55 E
Aimere, Indonesia 37 F6 8 45S 121 3 E
Aimogasta, Argentina 94 B2 28 33S 66 50W
Aimorés, Brazil 93 G10 19 30S 41 4W
Aïn Beïda, Algeria 50 A6 35 50N 7 29 E
Aïn Ben Tili, Mauritania 50 C3 25 59N 9 27W
Aïn-Sefra, Algeria 50 B4 32 47N 0 37W
'Ain Sudr, Egypt 47 F2 29 50N 33 6 E
Ainabo, Somali Rep. 46 F4 9 0N 46 25 E
Ainaži, Latvia 9 H21 57 50N 24 24 E
Ainsworth, U.S.A. 80 D5 42 33N 99 52W
Aïr, Niger 50 E6 18 30N 8 0 E
Air Hitam, Malaysia 39 M4 1 55N 103 11 E
Airdrie, U.K. 12 F5 55 52N 3 57W
Aire →, U.K. 10 D7 53 43N 0 55W
Aire, I. del, Spain 22 B11 39 48N 4 16 E
Airlie Beach, Australia 62 C4 20 16S 148 43 E
Aisne →, France 18 B5 49 26N 2 50 E
Aitkin, U.S.A. 80 B8 46 32N 93 42W
Aiud, Romania 17 E12 46 19N 23 44 E
Aix-en-Provence, France 18 E6 43 32N 5 27 E
Aix-la-Chapelle = Aachen, Germany 16 C4 50 45N 6 6 E
Aix-les-Bains, France 18 D6 45 41N 5 53 E
Aiyansh, Canada 72 B3 55 17N 129 2W
Aiyion, Greece 21 E10 38 15N 22 5 E
Aizawl, India 41 H18 23 40N 92 44 E
Aizkraukle, Latvia 9 H21 56 36N 25 11 E
Aizpute, Latvia 9 H19 56 43N 21 40 E
Aizuwakamatsu, Japan 30 F9 37 30N 139 56 E
Ajaccio, France 18 F8 41 55N 8 40 E
Ajalpan, Mexico 87 D5 18 22N 97 15W
Ajanta Ra., India 40 J9 20 28N 75 50 E
Ajari Rep. = Ajaria □, Georgia 25 F7 41 30N 42 0 E
Ajaria □, Georgia 25 F7 41 30N 42 0 E
Ajax, Canada 78 C5 43 50N 79 1W
Ajdābiyah, Libya 51 B9 30 54N 20 4 E
Ajka, Hungary 17 E9 47 4N 17 31 E
'Ajmān, U.A.E. 45 E7 25 25N 55 30 E
Ajmer, India 42 F6 26 28N 74 37 E
Ajo, U.S.A. 83 K7 32 22N 112 52W
Ajo, C. de, Spain 19 A4 43 31N 3 35W
Akabira, Japan 30 C11 43 33N 142 5 E
Akamas □, Cyprus 23 D11 35 3N 32 18 E
Akanthou, Cyprus 23 D12 35 22N 33 45 E
Akaroa, N.Z. 59 K4 43 49S 172 59 E
Akashi, Japan 31 G7 34 45N 134 58 E
Akelamo, Indonesia 37 D7 1 35N 129 40 E
Aketi, Zaïre 52 D4 2 38N 23 47 E
Akharnai, Greece 21 E10 38 5N 23 44 E
Akhelóös →, Greece 21 E9 38 19N 21 7 E
Akhisar, Turkey 21 E12 38 56N 27 48 E
Akhmîm, Egypt 51 C11 26 31N 31 47 E
Akhnur, India 43 C6 32 52N 74 45 E
Aki, Japan 31 H6 33 30N 133 54 E
Akimiski I., Canada 70 B3 52 50N 81 30W
Akita, Japan 30 E10 39 45N 140 7 E
Akita □, Japan 30 E10 39 40N 140 30 E
Akjoujt, Mauritania 50 E2 19 45N 14 15W
Akkeshi, Japan 30 C12 43 2N 144 51 E
'Akko, Israel 47 C4 32 55N 35 4 E
Akkol, Kazakstan 26 E8 45 0N 75 39 E
Aklavik, Canada 68 B6 68 12N 135 0W
Akmolinsk = Aqmola, Kazakstan 26 D8 51 10N 71 30 E
Akō, Japan 31 G7 34 45N 134 24 E
Akobo →, Ethiopia 51 G11 7 48N 33 3 E
Akola, India 40 J10 20 42N 77 2 E
Akordat, Eritrea 51 E12 15 30N 37 40 E
Akpatok I., Canada 69 B13 60 25N 68 8W
Åkrahamn, Norway 9 G11 59 15N 5 10 E
Akranes, Iceland 8 D2 64 19N 22 5W
Akreijit, Mauritania 50 E3 18 19N 9 11W
Akron, Colo., U.S.A. 80 E3 40 10N 103 13W
Akron, Ohio, U.S.A. 78 E3 41 5N 81 31W
Akrotiri, Cyprus 23 E11 34 36N 32 57 E
Akrotiri Bay, Cyprus 23 E12 34 35N 33 10 E
Aksai Chin, India 43 B8 35 15N 79 55 E
Aksarka, Russia 26 C7 66 31N 67 50 E
Aksay, Kazakstan 24 D9 51 11N 53 0 E
Aksenovo Zilovskoye, Russia 27 D12 53 20N 117 40 E
Aksu, China 32 B3 41 5N 80 10 E
Aksum, Ethiopia 51 F12 14 5N 38 40 E
Aktogay, Kazakstan 26 E8 46 57N 79 40 E
Aktsyabrski, Belarus 17 B15 52 38N 28 53 E
Aktyubinsk = Aqtöbe, Kazakstan 25 D10 50 17N 57 10 E
Aku, Nigeria 50 G6 6 40N 7 18 E
Akure, Nigeria 50 G6 7 15N 5 5 E
Akureyri, Iceland 8 D4 65 40N 18 6W
Akuseki-Shima, Japan 31 K4 29 27N 129 37 E
Akyab = Sittwe, Burma 41 J18 20 18N 92 45 E
Al 'Adan, Yemen 46 E4 12 45N 45 0 E
Al Aḩsā, Si. Arabia 45 E6 25 50N 49 0 E
Al Ajfar, Si. Arabia 44 E4 27 26N 43 0 E
Al Amādīyah, Iraq 44 B4 37 5N 43 30 E
Al Amārah, Iraq 44 D5 31 55N 47 15 E
Al 'Aqabah, Jordan 47 F4 29 31N 35 0 E
Al Arak, Syria 44 C3 34 38N 38 35 E
Al 'Aramah, Si. Arabia 44 E5 25 30N 46 0 E
Al Arţāwīyah, Si. Arabia 44 E5 26 31N 45 20 E
Al 'Āşimah □, Jordan 47 D5 31 40N 36 30 E
Al' Assāfīyah, Si. Arabia 44 D3 28 17N 38 59 E
Al 'Ayn, Oman 45 E7 24 15N 55 45 E
Al 'Ayn, Si. Arabia 44 E3 25 4N 38 6 E
Al A'ẓamīyah, Iraq 44 C5 33 22N 44 22 E
Al 'Azīzīyah, Iraq 44 C5 32 54N 45 4 E
Al Bāb, Syria 44 B3 36 23N 37 29 E
Al Bad', Si. Arabia 44 D2 28 28N 35 1 E
Al Bādī, Iraq 44 C4 35 56N 41 32 E
Al Baḩrah, Kuwait 44 D5 29 40N 47 52 E
Al Balqā' □, Jordan 47 C4 32 5N 35 45 E
Al Bārūk, J., Lebanon 47 B4 33 39N 35 40 E
Al Başrah, Iraq 44 D5 30 30N 47 50 E
Al Baţḩā, Iraq 44 D5 31 6N 45 53 E
Al Batrūn, Lebanon 47 A4 34 15N 35 40 E
Al Bayḑā, Libya 51 B9 32 50N 21 44 E
Al Biqā □, Lebanon 47 A5 34 10N 36 10 E
Al Bi'r, Si. Arabia 44 D3 28 51N 36 16 E
Al Bu'ayrāt al Ḩasūn, Libya 51 B8 31 24N 15 44 E
Al Burayj, Syria 47 A5 34 15N 36 46 E
Al Fallūjah, Iraq 44 C4 33 20N 43 55 E
Al Fāw, Iraq 45 D6 30 0N 48 30 E
Al Fujayrah, U.A.E. 45 E8 25 7N 56 18 E
Al Ghadaf, W. →, Jordan 47 D5 31 26N 36 43 E
Al Ghammās, Iraq 44 D5 31 45N 44 37 E

Amadi

Al Hābah, *Si. Arabia* **44 E5** 27 10N 47 0 E
Al Ḥadīthah, *Iraq* **44 C4** 34 0N 41 13 E
Al Ḥadīthah, *Si. Arabia* **44 D3** 31 28N 37 8 E
Al Ḥājānah, *Syria* **47 B5** 33 20N 36 33 E
Al Ḥāmad, *Si. Arabia* **44 D3** 31 30N 39 30 E
Al Hamdānīyah, *Syria* **44 C3** 35 25N 36 50 E
Al Ḥamidīyah, *Syria* **47 A4** 34 42N 35 57 E
Al Ḥammār, *Iraq* **44 D5** 30 57N 46 51 E
Al Harīr, W. →, *Syria* **47 C4** 32 44N 35 59 E
Al Ḥasā, W. →, *Jordan* **47 D4** 31 4N 35 29 E
Al Ḥasakah, *Syria* **44 B4** 36 35N 40 45 E
Al Ḥawrah, *Yemen* **46 E4** 13 50N 47 35 E
Al Ḥaydān, W. →, *Jordan* **47 D4** 31 29N 35 34 E
Al Ḥayy, *Iraq* **44 C5** 32 5N 46 5 E
Al Ḥijāz, *Si. Arabia* **46 B2** 26 0N 37 30 E
Al Ḥillah, *Iraq* **44 C5** 32 30N 44 25 E
Al Ḥillah, *Si. Arabia* **46 C4** 23 35N 46 50 E
Al Hirmil, *Lebanon* **47 A5** 34 26N 36 24 E
Al Hoceïma, *Morocco* **50 A4** 35 8N 3 58W
Al Ḥudaydah, *Yemen* **46 E3** 14 50N 43 0 E
Al Hufūf, *Si. Arabia* **45 E6** 25 25N 49 45 E
Al Ḥumayḍah, *Si. Arabia* **44 D2** 29 14N 34 56 E
Al Ḥunayy, *Si. Arabia* **45 E6** 25 58N 48 45 E
Al ʿĪsāwīyah, *Si. Arabia* **44 D3** 30 43N 37 59 E
Al Ittihad = Madīnat ash Sha'b, *Yemen* **46 E3** 12 50N 45 0 E
Al Jafr, *Jordan* **47 E5** 30 18N 36 14 E
Al Jaghbūb, *Libya* **51 C9** 29 42N 24 38 E
Al Jahrah, *Kuwait* **44 D5** 29 25N 47 40 E
Al Jalāmīd, *Si. Arabia* **44 D3** 31 20N 39 45 E
Al Jamalīyah, *Qatar* **45 E6** 25 37N 51 5 E
Al Janūb □, *Lebanon* **47 B4** 33 20N 35 20 E
Al Jawf, *Libya* **51 D9** 24 10N 23 24 E
Al Jawf, *Si. Arabia* **44 D3** 29 55N 39 40 E
Al Jazirah, *Iraq* **44 C5** 33 30N 44 0 E
Al Jazirah, *Libya* **51 C9** 26 10N 21 20 E
Al Jithāmīyah, *Si. Arabia* **44 E4** 27 41N 41 43 E
Al Jubayl, *Si. Arabia* **45 E6** 27 0N 49 50 E
Al Jubaylah, *Si. Arabia* **44 E5** 24 55N 46 25 E
Al Jubb, *Si. Arabia* **44 E4** 27 11N 42 17 E
Al Junaynah, *Sudan* **51 F9** 13 27N 22 45 E
Al Kabā'ish, *Iraq* **44 D5** 30 58N 47 0 E
Al Karak, *Jordan* **47 D4** 31 11N 35 42 E
Al Karak □, *Jordan* **47 E5** 31 0N 36 0 E
Al Kāzim Tyah, *Iraq* **44 C5** 33 22N 44 12 E
Al Khalīl, *West Bank* **47 D4** 31 32N 35 6 E
Al Khawr, *Qatar* **45 E6** 25 41N 51 30 E
Al Khiḍr, *Iraq* **44 D5** 31 12N 45 33 E
Al Khiyām, *Lebanon* **47 B4** 33 20N 35 36 E
Al Kiswah, *Syria* **47 B5** 33 23N 36 14 E
Al Kufrah, *Libya* **51 D9** 24 17N 23 15 E
Al Kuhayfīyah, *Si. Arabia* **44 E4** 27 12N 43 3 E
Al Kūt, *Iraq* **44 C5** 32 30N 46 0 E
Al Kuwayt, *Kuwait* **44 D5** 29 30N 48 0 E
Al Labwah, *Lebanon* **47 A5** 34 11N 36 20 E
Al Lādhiqīyah, *Syria* **44 C2** 35 30N 35 45 E
Al Liwā', *Oman* **45 E8** 24 31N 56 36 E
Al Luḥayyah, *Yemen* **46 D3** 15 45N 42 40 E
Al Madīnah, *Iraq* **44 D5** 30 57N 47 16 E
Al Madīnah, *Si. Arabia* **46 C2** 24 35N 39 52 E
Al-Mafraq, *Jordan* **47 C5** 32 17N 36 14 E
Al Maḥmūdīyah, *Iraq* **44 C5** 33 3N 44 21 E
Al Majma'ah, *Si. Arabia* **44 E5** 25 57N 45 22 E
Al Makhruq, W. →, *Jordan* **47 D6** 31 28N 37 0 E
Al Makḥūl, *Si. Arabia* **44 E4** 26 37N 42 39 E
Al Manāmah, *Bahrain* **45 E6** 26 10N 50 30 E
Al Maqwa', *Kuwait* **44 D5** 29 10N 47 59 E
Al Marj, *Libya* **51 B9** 32 25N 20 30 E
Al Maṭlā, *Kuwait* **44 D5** 29 24N 47 40 E
Al Mawjib, W. →, *Jordan* **47 D4** 31 28N 35 36 E
Al Mawṣil, *Iraq* **44 B4** 36 15N 43 5 E
Al Mayādin, *Syria* **44 C4** 35 1N 40 27 E
Al Mazār, *Jordan* **47 D4** 31 4N 35 41 E
Al Midhnab, *Si. Arabia* **44 E5** 25 50N 44 18 E
Al Minā', *Lebanon* **47 A4** 34 24N 35 49 E
Al Miqdādīyah, *Iraq* **44 C5** 34 0N 45 0 E
Al Mubarraz, *Si. Arabia* **45 E6** 25 30N 49 40 E
Al Mughayrā', *U.A.E.* **45 E7** 24 5N 53 32 E
Al Muḥarraq, *Bahrain* **45 E6** 26 15N 50 40 E
Al Mukallā, *Yemen* **46 E4** 14 33N 49 2 E
Al Mukhā, *Yemen* **46 E3** 13 18N 43 15 E
Al Musayjīd, *Si. Arabia* **44 E3** 24 5N 39 5 E
Al Musayyib, *Iraq* **44 C5** 32 49N 44 20 E
Al Muwaylīḥ, *Si. Arabia* **44 E2** 27 40N 35 30 E
Al Qā'im, *Iraq* **44 C4** 34 21N 41 7 E
Al Qalībah, *Si. Arabia* **44 D3** 28 24N 37 42 E
Al Qaryatayn, *Syria* **47 A6** 34 12N 37 13 E
Al Qaṣabāt, *Libya* **51 B7** 32 39N 14 1 E
Al Qaṭ'ā, *Syria* **44 C4** 34 40N 40 48 E
Al Qaṭīf, *Si. Arabia* **45 E6** 26 35N 50 0 E
Al Qatrānah, *Jordan* **47 D5** 31 12N 36 6 E
Al Qaṭrūn, *Libya* **51 D8** 24 56N 15 3 E
Al Qayṣūmah, *Si. Arabia* **44 D5** 28 20N 46 7 E
Al Quds = Jerusalem, *Israel* **47 D4** 31 47N 35 10 E
Al Qunaytirah, *Syria* **47 C4** 32 55N 35 45 E
Al Qurnah, *Iraq* **44 D5** 31 1N 47 25 E
Al Quṣayr, *Iraq* **44 D5** 30 39N 45 50 E
Al Quṣayr, *Syria* **47 A5** 34 31N 36 34 E
Al Qutayfah, *Syria* **47 B5** 33 44N 36 36 E
Al' Uḍaylīyah, *Si. Arabia* **45 E6** 25 8N 49 18 E
Al 'Ulā, *Si. Arabia* **44 E3** 26 35N 38 0 E
Al Uqaylah ash Sharqīgah, *Libya* **51 B8** 30 12N 19 10 E
Al Uqayr, *Si. Arabia* **45 E6** 25 40N 50 15 E
Al 'Uwaynid, *Si. Arabia* **44 E5** 24 50N 46 0 E
Al 'Uwayqilah, *Si. Arabia* **44 D4** 30 30N 42 10 E
Al 'Uyūn, *Si. Arabia* **44 E4** 26 30N 43 50 E
Al 'Uyūn, *Si. Arabia* **44 E3** 24 33N 39 35 E
Al Wajh, *Si. Arabia* **44 E3** 26 10N 36 30 E
Al Wakrah, *Qatar* **45 E6** 25 10N 51 40 E
Al Wannān, *Si. Arabia* **45 E6** 26 55N 48 24 E
Al Waqbah, *Si. Arabia* **44 D5** 28 48N 45 33 E
Al Wari'āh, *Si. Arabia* **44 E5** 27 51N 47 25 E
Al Wusayl, *Qatar* **45 E6** 25 29N 51 29 E
Ala Tau Shankou = Dzhungarskiye Vorota, *Kazakstan* **32 B3** 45 0N 82 0 E
Alabama □, *U.S.A.* **77 J2** 33 0N 87 0W
Alabama →, *U.S.A.* **77 K2** 31 8N 87 57W
Alaçam Dağlan, *Turkey* **21 E13** 39 18N 28 49 E
Alaérma, *Greece* **23 C9** 36 9N 27 57 E
Alagoa Grande, *Brazil* **93 E11** 7 3S 35 35W
Alagoas □, *Brazil* **93 E11** 9 0S 36 0W
Alagoinhas, *Brazil* **93 F11** 12 7S 38 20W
Alajero, *Canary Is.* **22 F2** 28 3N 17 13W
Alajuela, *Costa Rica* **88 D3** 10 2N 84 8W
Alakamisy, *Madag.* **57 C8** 21 19S 47 14 E
Alakurtti, *Russia* **24 A5** 67 0N 30 30 E
Alameda, *Calif., U.S.A.* **84 H4** 37 46N 122 15W
Alameda, *N. Mex., U.S.A.* **83 J10** 35 11N 106 37W
Alamo, *U.S.A.* **85 J11** 36 21N 115 10W
Alamo Crossing, *U.S.A.* **85 L13** 34 16N 113 33W
Alamogordo, *U.S.A.* **83 K11** 32 54N 105 57W
Alamos, *Mexico* **86 B3** 27 0N 109 0W
Alamosa, *U.S.A.* **83 H11** 37 28N 105 52W
Åland, *Finland* **9 F19** 60 15N 20 0 E
Ålands hav, *Sweden* **9 F18** 60 0N 19 30 E
Alandur, *India* **40 N12** 13 0N 80 15 E
Alania = North Ossetia □, *Russia* **25 F7** 43 30N 44 30 E
Alanya, *Turkey* **25 G5** 36 38N 32 0 E
Alaotra, Farihin', *Madag.* **57 B8** 17 30S 48 30 E
Alapayevsk, *Russia* **26 D7** 57 52N 61 42 E
Alaşehir, *Turkey* **21 E13** 38 23N 28 30 E
Alaska □, *U.S.A.* **68 B5** 64 0N 154 0W
Alaska, G. of, *Pac. Oc.* **68 C5** 58 0N 145 0W
Alaska Highway, *Canada* **72 B3** 60 0N 130 0W
Alaska Peninsula, *U.S.A.* **68 C4** 56 0N 159 0W
Alaska Range, *U.S.A.* **68 B4** 62 50N 151 0W
Älät, *Azerbaijan* **25 G8** 39 58N 49 25 E
Alatyr, *Russia* **24 D8** 54 55N 46 35 E
Alausi, *Ecuador* **92 D3** 2 0S 78 50W
Alava, C., *U.S.A.* **82 B1** 48 10N 124 44W
Alavus, *Finland* **9 E20** 62 35N 23 36 E
Alawoona, *Australia* **63 E3** 34 45S 140 30 E
'Alayh, *Lebanon* **47 B4** 33 46N 35 33 E
Alayor, *Spain* **22 B11** 39 57N 4 8 E
Alba, *Italy* **20 B3** 44 42N 8 2 E
Alba-Iulia, *Romania* **17 E12** 46 8N 23 39 E
Albacete, *Spain* **19 C5** 39 0N 1 50W
Albacutya, L., *Australia* **63 F3** 35 45S 141 58 E
Albania ■, *Europe* **21 D9** 41 0N 20 0 E
Albany, *Australia* **61 G2** 35 1S 117 58 E
Albany, *Ga., U.S.A.* **77 K3** 31 35N 84 10W
Albany, *Minn., U.S.A.* **80 C7** 45 38N 94 34W
Albany, *N.Y., U.S.A.* **79 D11** 42 39N 73 45W
Albany, *Oreg., U.S.A.* **82 D2** 44 38N 123 6W
Albany, *Tex., U.S.A.* **81 J5** 32 44N 99 18W
Albany →, *Canada* **70 B3** 52 17N 81 31W
Albardón, *Argentina* **94 C2** 31 20S 68 30W
Albatross B., *Australia* **62 A3** 12 45S 141 30 E
Albemarle, *U.S.A.* **77 H5** 35 21N 80 11W
Albemarle Sd., *U.S.A.* **77 H7** 36 5N 76 0W
Alberche →, *Spain* **19 C3** 39 58N 4 46W
Alberdi, *Paraguay* **94 B4** 26 14S 58 20W
Albert, L., *Australia* **63 F2** 35 30S 139 10 E
Albert Canyon, *Canada* **72 C5** 51 8N 117 41W
Albert Edward Ra., *Australia* **60 C4** 18 17S 127 57 E
Albert L., *Africa* **54 B3** 1 30N 31 0 E
Albert Lea, *U.S.A.* **80 D8** 43 39N 93 22W
Albert Nile →, *Uganda* **54 B3** 3 36N 32 2 E
Albert Town, *Bahamas* **89 B5** 22 37N 74 33W
Alberta □, *Canada* **72 C6** 54 40N 115 0W
Alberti, *Argentina* **94 D3** 35 1S 60 16W
Albertinia, *S. Africa* **56 E3** 34 11S 21 34 E
Alberton, *Canada* **71 C7** 46 50N 64 0W
Albertville = Kalemie, *Zaïre* **54 D2** 5 55S 29 9 E
Albertville, *France* **18 D7** 45 40N 6 22 E
Albi, *France* **18 E5** 43 56N 2 9 E
Albia, *U.S.A.* **80 E8** 41 2N 92 48W
Albina, *Surinam* **93 B8** 5 37N 54 15W
Albina, Ponta, *Angola* **56 B1** 15 52S 11 44 E
Albion, *Idaho, U.S.A.* **82 E7** 42 25N 113 35W
Albion, *Mich., U.S.A.* **76 D3** 42 15N 84 45W
Albion, *Nebr., U.S.A.* **80 E5** 41 42N 98 0W
Albion, *Pa., U.S.A.* **78 E4** 41 53N 80 22W
Alborán, *Medit. S.* **19 E4** 35 57N 3 0W
Ålborg, *Denmark* **9 H13** 57 2N 9 54 E
Alborz, Reshteh-ye Kūhhā-ye, *Iran* **45 C7** 36 0N 52 0 E
Albreda, *Canada* **72 C5** 52 35N 119 10W
Albuquerque, *U.S.A.* **83 J10** 35 5N 106 39W
Albuquerque, Cayos de, *Caribbean* **88 D3** 12 10N 81 50W
Alburg, *U.S.A.* **79 B11** 44 59N 73 18W
Albury, *Australia* **63 F4** 36 3S 146 56 E
Alcalá de Henares, *Spain* **19 B4** 40 28N 3 22W
Alcalá la Real, *Spain* **19 D4** 37 27N 3 57W
Álcamo, *Italy* **20 F5** 37 59N 12 55 E
Alcañiz, *Spain* **19 B5** 41 2N 0 8W
Alcântara, *Brazil* **93 D10** 2 20S 44 30W
Alcántara, Embalse de, *Spain* **19 C2** 39 44N 6 50W
Alcantara L., *Canada* **73 A7** 60 57N 108 9W
Alcantarilla, *Spain* **19 D5** 37 59N 1 12W
Alcaraz, Sierra de, *Spain* **19 C4** 38 40N 2 20W
Alcaudete, *Spain* **19 D3** 37 35N 4 5W
Alcázar de San Juan, *Spain* **19 C4** 39 24N 3 12W
Alchevsk, *Ukraine* **25 E6** 48 30N 38 45 E
Alcira, *Spain* **19 C5** 39 9N 0 30W
Alcoa, *U.S.A.* **77 H4** 35 48N 83 59W
Alcova, *U.S.A.* **82 E10** 42 34N 106 43W
Alcoy, *Spain* **19 C5** 38 43N 0 30W
Alcudia, *Spain* **22 B10** 39 51N 3 7 E
Alcudia, B. de, *Spain* **22 B10** 39 47N 3 15 E
Aldabra Is., *Seychelles* **49 G8** 9 22S 46 28 E
Aldama, *Mexico* **87 C5** 23 0N 98 4W
Aldan, *Russia* **27 D13** 58 40N 125 30 E
Aldan →, *Russia* **27 C13** 63 28N 129 35 E
Aldea, Pta. de la, *Canary Is.* **22 G4** 28 0N 15 50W
Aldeburgh, *U.K.* **11 E9** 52 10N 1 37 E
Alder, *U.S.A.* **82 D7** 45 19N 112 6W
Alder Pk., *U.S.A.* **84 K5** 35 53N 121 22W
Alderney, *U.K.* **11 H5** 49 42N 2 11W
Aldershot, *U.K.* **11 F7** 51 15N 0 44W
Aledo, *U.S.A.* **80 E9** 41 12N 90 45W
Aleg, *Mauritania* **50 E2** 17 3N 13 55W
Alegranza, *Canary Is.* **22 E6** 29 23N 13 32W
Alegranza, I., *Canary Is.* **22 E6** 29 23N 13 32W
Alegre, *Brazil* **95 A7** 20 50S 41 30W
Alegrete, *Brazil* **95 B4** 29 40S 56 0W
Aleisk, *Russia* **26 D9** 52 40N 83 0 E
Aleksandriya = Oleksandriya, *Ukraine* **17 C14** 50 37N 26 19 E
Aleksandrovsk-Sakhalinskiy, *Russia* **27 D15** 50 50N 142 20 E
Aleksandrovskiy Zavod, *Russia* **27 D12** 50 40N 117 50 E
Aleksandrovskoye, *Russia* **26 C8** 60 35N 77 50 E
Além Paraíba, *Brazil* **95 A7** 21 52S 42 41W
Alemania, *Argentina* **94 B2** 25 40S 65 30W
Alemania, *Chile* **94 B2** 25 10S 69 55W
Alençon, *France* **18 B4** 48 27N 0 4 E
Alenuihaha Channel, *U.S.A.* **74 H17** 20 30N 156 0W
Aleppo = Ḥalab, *Syria* **44 B3** 36 10N 37 15 E
Alert Bay, *Canada* **72 C3** 50 30N 126 55W
Alès, *France* **18 D6** 44 9N 4 5 E
Alessándria, *Italy* **20 B3** 44 54N 8 37 E
Ålesund, *Norway* **9 E12** 62 28N 6 12 E
Aleutian Is., *Pac. Oc.* **68 C2** 52 0N 175 0W
Aleutian Trench, *Pac. Oc.* **64 B10** 48 0N 180 0 E
Alexander, *U.S.A.* **80 B3** 47 51N 103 39W
Alexander, Mt., *Australia* **61 E3** 28 58S 120 16 E
Alexander Arch., *U.S.A.* **72 B2** 56 0N 136 0W
Alexander Bay, *S. Africa* **56 D2** 28 40S 16 30 E
Alexander City, *U.S.A.* **77 J3** 32 56N 85 58W
Alexander I., *Antarctica* **5 C17** 69 0S 70 0W
Alexandra, *Australia* **63 F4** 37 8S 145 40 E
Alexandra, *N.Z.* **59 L2** 45 14S 169 25 E
Alexandra Falls, *Canada* **72 A5** 60 29N 116 18W
Alexandria = El Iskandarîya, *Egypt* **51 B10** 31 13N 29 58 E
Alexandria, *Australia* **62 B2** 19 5S 136 40 E
Alexandria, *B.C., Canada* **72 C4** 52 35N 122 27W
Alexandria, *Ont., Canada* **70 C5** 45 19N 74 38W
Alexandria, *Romania* **17 G13** 43 57N 25 24 E
Alexandria, *S. Africa* **56 E4** 33 38S 26 28 E
Alexandria, *Ind., U.S.A.* **76 E3** 40 16N 85 41W
Alexandria, *La., U.S.A.* **81 K8** 31 18N 92 27W
Alexandria, *Minn., U.S.A.* **80 C7** 45 53N 95 22W
Alexandria, *S. Dak., U.S.A.* **80 D6** 43 39N 97 47W
Alexandria, *Va., U.S.A.* **76 F7** 38 48N 77 3W
Alexandria Bay, *U.S.A.* **79 B9** 44 20N 75 55W
Alexandrina, L., *Australia* **63 F2** 35 25S 139 10 E
Alexandroúpolis, *Greece* **21 D11** 40 50N 25 54 E
Alexis →, *Canada* **71 B8** 52 33N 56 8W
Alexis Creek, *Canada* **72 C4** 52 10N 123 20W
Alfabia, *Spain* **22 B9** 39 44N 2 44 E
Alfenas, *Brazil* **95 A6** 21 20S 46 10W
Alford, *U.K.* **12 D6** 57 14N 2 41W
Alfred, *Maine, U.S.A.* **79 C14** 43 29N 70 43W
Alfred, *N.Y., U.S.A.* **78 D7** 42 16N 77 48W
Alfreton, *U.K.* **10 D6** 53 6N 1 24W
Alga, *Kazakstan* **25 E10** 49 53N 57 20 E
Algaida, *Spain* **22 B9** 39 33N 2 53 E
Ålgård, *Norway* **9 G11** 58 46N 5 53 E
Algarve, *Portugal* **19 D1** 36 58N 8 20W
Algeciras, *Spain* **19 D3** 36 9N 5 28W
Algemesí, *Spain* **19 C5** 39 11N 0 27W
Alger, *Algeria* **50 A5** 36 42N 3 8 E
Algeria ■, *Africa* **50 C5** 28 30N 2 0 E
Alghero, *Italy* **20 D3** 40 33N 8 19 E
Algiers = Alger, *Algeria* **50 A5** 36 42N 3 8 E
Algoa B., *S. Africa* **56 E4** 33 50S 25 45 E
Algoma, *U.S.A.* **76 C2** 44 36N 87 26W
Algona, *U.S.A.* **80 D7** 43 4N 94 14W
Algonac, *U.S.A.* **78 D2** 42 37N 82 32W
Alhambra, *U.S.A.* **74 D3** 34 8N 118 6W
Alhucemas = Al Hoceïma, *Morocco* **50 A4** 35 8N 3 58W
'Alī al Gharbī, *Iraq* **44 C5** 32 30N 46 45 E
'Alī ash Sharqī, *Iraq* **44 C5** 32 7N 46 44 E
'Alī Khēl, *Afghan.* **42 C3** 33 57N 69 43 E
Alī Shāh, *Iran* **44 B5** 38 9N 45 50 E
'Alīābād, *Khorāsān, Iran* **45 C8** 32 30N 57 30 E
'Alīābād, *Kordestān, Iran* **44 C5** 35 4N 46 58 E
'Alīābād, *Yazd, Iran* **45 D7** 31 41N 53 49 E
Aliağa, *Turkey* **21 E12** 38 47N 26 59 E
Aliákmon →, *Greece* **21 D10** 40 30N 22 36 E
Alibo, *Ethiopia* **51 G12** 9 52N 37 5 E
Alicante, *Spain* **19 C5** 38 23N 0 30W
Alice, *S. Africa* **56 E4** 32 48S 26 55 E
Alice, *U.S.A.* **81 M5** 27 45N 98 5W
Alice →, *Queens., Australia* **62 C3** 24 2S 144 50 E
Alice →, *Queens., Australia* **62 B3** 15 35S 142 20 E
Alice Arm, *Canada* **72 B3** 55 29N 129 31W
Alice Downs, *Australia* **60 C4** 17 45S 127 56 E
Alice Springs, *Australia* **62 C1** 23 40S 133 50 E
Alicedale, *S. Africa* **56 E4** 33 15S 26 4 E
Aliceville, *U.S.A.* **77 J1** 33 8N 88 9W
Alick Cr. →, *Australia* **62 C3** 20 55S 142 20 E
Alida, *Canada* **73 D8** 49 25N 101 55W
Aligarh, *Raj., India* **42 G7** 25 55N 76 15 E
Aligarh, *Ut. P., India* **42 F8** 27 55N 78 10 E
Alīgūdarz, *Iran* **45 C6** 33 25N 49 45 E
Alimnía, *Greece* **23 C9** 36 16N 27 43 E
Alingsås, *Sweden* **9 H15** 57 56N 12 31 E
Alipur, *Pakistan* **42 E4** 29 25N 70 55 E
Alipur Duar, *India* **41 F16** 26 30N 89 35 E
Aliquippa, *U.S.A.* **78 F4** 40 37N 80 15W
Alitus = Alytus, *Lithuania* **9 J21** 54 24N 24 3 E
Aliwal North, *S. Africa* **56 E4** 30 45S 26 45 E
Alix, *Canada* **72 C6** 52 24N 113 11W
Aljustrel, *Portugal* **19 D1** 37 55N 8 10W
Alkmaar, *Neths.* **15 B4** 52 37N 4 45 E
All American Canal, *U.S.A.* **83 K6** 32 45N 115 15W
Allah Dad, *Pakistan* **42 G2** 25 38N 67 34 E
Allahabad, *India* **43 G9** 25 25N 81 58 E
Allakh-Yun, *Russia* **27 C14** 60 50N 137 5 E
Allan, *Canada* **73 C7** 51 53N 106 4W
Allanmyo, *Burma* **41 K19** 19 30N 95 17 E
Allanridge, *S. Africa* **56 D4** 27 45S 26 40 E
Allanwater, *Canada* **70 B1** 50 14N 90 10W
Allegan, *U.S.A.* **76 D3** 42 32N 85 51W
Allegany, *U.S.A.* **78 D6** 42 6N 78 30W
Allegheny →, *U.S.A.* **78 F5** 40 27N 80 1W
Allegheny Mts., *U.S.A.* **66 F11** 38 15N 80 10W
Allegheny Plateau, *U.S.A.* **76 G6** 38 0N 80 0W
Allegheny Reservoir, *U.S.A.* **78 E6** 41 50N 79 0W
Allen, Bog of, *Ireland* **13 C4** 53 15N 7 0W
Allen, L., *Ireland* **13 B3** 54 8N 8 4W
Allende, *Mexico* **86 B4** 28 20N 100 50W
Allentown, *U.S.A.* **79 F9** 40 37N 75 29W
Alleppey, *India* **40 Q10** 9 30N 76 28 E
Aller →, *Germany* **16 B5** 52 56N 9 12 E
Alliance, *Nebr., U.S.A.* **80 D3** 42 6N 102 52W
Alliance, *Ohio, U.S.A.* **78 F3** 40 55N 81 6W
Allier →, *France* **18 C5** 46 57N 3 4 E
Alliston, *Canada* **70 D4** 44 9N 79 52W
Alloa, *U.K.* **12 E5** 56 7N 3 47W
Allora, *Australia* **63 D5** 28 2S 152 0 E
Alluitsup Paa = Sydprøven, *Greenland* **4 C5** 60 30N 45 35W
Alma, *Canada* **71 C5** 48 35N 71 40W
Alma, *Ga., U.S.A.* **77 K4** 31 33N 82 28W
Alma, *Kans., U.S.A.* **80 F6** 39 1N 96 17W
Alma, *Mich., U.S.A.* **76 D3** 43 23N 84 39W
Alma, *Nebr., U.S.A.* **80 E5** 40 6N 99 22W
Alma, *Wis., U.S.A.* **80 C9** 44 20N 91 55W
Alma Ata = Almaty, *Kazakstan* **26 E8** 43 15N 76 57 E
Almada, *Portugal* **19 C1** 38 40N 9 9W
Almaden, *Australia* **62 B3** 17 22S 144 40 E
Almadén, *Spain* **19 C3** 38 49N 4 52W
Almanor, L., *U.S.A.* **82 F3** 40 14N 121 9W
Almansa, *Spain* **19 C5** 38 51N 1 5W
Almanzor, Pico del Moro, *Spain* **19 B3** 40 15N 5 18W
Almanzora →, *Spain* **19 D5** 37 14N 1 46W
Almaty, *Kazakstan* **26 E8** 43 15N 76 57 E
Almazán, *Spain* **19 B4** 41 30N 2 30W
Almeirim, *Brazil* **93 D8** 1 30S 52 34W
Almelo, *Neths.* **15 B6** 52 22N 6 42 E
Almendralejo, *Spain* **19 C2** 38 41N 6 26W
Almería, *Spain* **19 D4** 36 52N 2 27W
Almirante, *Panama* **88 E3** 9 10N 82 30W
Almiroú, Kólpos, *Greece* **23 D6** 35 23N 24 20 E
Almont, *U.S.A.* **78 D1** 42 55N 83 3W
Almonte, *Canada* **79 A8** 45 14N 76 12W
Almora, *India* **43 E8** 29 38N 79 40 E
Alnwick, *U.K.* **10 B6** 55 24N 1 42W
Aloi, *Uganda* **54 B3** 2 16N 33 10 E
Alon, *Burma* **41 H19** 22 12N 95 5 E
Alor, *Indonesia* **37 F6** 8 15S 124 30 E
Alor Setar, *Malaysia* **39 J3** 6 7N 100 22 E
Aloysius, Mt., *Australia* **61 E4** 26 0S 128 38 E
Alpaugh, *U.S.A.* **84 K7** 35 53N 119 29W
Alpena, *U.S.A.* **76 C4** 45 4N 83 27W
Alpha, *Australia* **62 C4** 23 39S 146 37 E
Alpine, *Ariz., U.S.A.* **83 K9** 33 51N 109 9W
Alpine, *Calif., U.S.A.* **85 N10** 32 50N 116 46W
Alpine, *Tex., U.S.A.* **81 K3** 30 22N 103 40W
Alps, *Europe* **16 E5** 46 30N 9 30 E
Alroy Downs, *Australia* **62 B2** 19 20S 136 5 E
Alsace, *France* **18 B7** 48 15N 7 25 E
Alsask, *Canada* **73 C7** 51 21N 109 59W
Alsásua, *Spain* **19 A4** 42 54N 2 10W
Alsten, *Norway* **8 D15** 65 58N 12 40 E
Alta, *Norway* **8 B20** 69 57N 23 10 E
Alta Gracia, *Argentina* **94 C3** 31 40S 64 30W
Alta Lake, *Canada* **72 C4** 50 10N 123 0W
Alta Sierra, *U.S.A.* **85 K8** 35 42N 118 33W
Altaelva →, *Norway* **8 B20** 69 54N 23 17 E
Altafjorden, *Norway* **8 A20** 70 5N 23 5 E
Altagracia, *Venezuela* **92 A4** 10 45N 71 30W
Altai = Aerhtai Shan, *Mongolia* **32 B4** 46 40N 92 45 E
Altamaha →, *U.S.A.* **77 K5** 31 20N 81 20W
Altamira, *Brazil* **93 D8** 3 12S 52 10W
Altamira, *Chile* **94 B2** 25 47S 69 51W
Altamira, *Mexico* **87 C5** 22 24N 97 55W
Altamont, *U.S.A.* **79 D10** 42 43N 74 3W
Altamura, *Italy* **20 D7** 40 49N 16 33 E
Altanbulag, *Mongolia* **32 A5** 50 16N 106 30 E
Altar, *Mexico* **86 A2** 30 40N 111 50W
Altata, *Mexico* **86 C3** 24 30N 108 0W
Altavista, *U.S.A.* **76 G6** 37 6N 79 17W
Altay, *China* **32 B3** 47 48N 88 10 E
Altea, *Spain* **19 C5** 38 38N 0 2W
Alto Araguaia, *Brazil* **93 G8** 17 15S 53 20W
Alto Cuchumatanes = Cuchumatanes, Sierra de los, *Guatemala* **88 C1** 15 35N 91 25W
Alto del Inca, *Chile* **94 A2** 24 10S 68 10W
Alto Ligonha, *Mozam.* **55 F4** 15 30S 38 11 E
Alto Molocue, *Mozam.* **55 F4** 15 50S 37 35 E
Alto Paraguay □, *Paraguay* **94 A4** 21 0S 58 30W
Alto Paraná □, *Paraguay* **95 B5** 25 30S 54 50W
Alton, *Canada* **78 C4** 43 54N 80 5W
Alton, *U.S.A.* **80 F9** 38 53N 90 11W
Alton Downs, *Australia* **63 D2** 26 7S 138 57 E
Altoona, *U.S.A.* **78 F6** 40 31N 78 24W
Altūn Kūprī, *Iraq* **44 C5** 35 45N 44 9 E
Altun Shan, *China* **32 C3** 38 30N 88 0 E
Alturas, *U.S.A.* **82 F3** 41 29N 120 32W
Altus, *U.S.A.* **81 H5** 34 38N 99 20W
Alūksne, *Latvia* **9 H22** 57 24N 27 3 E
Alùla, *Somali Rep.* **46 E5** 11 50N 50 45 E
Alunite, *U.S.A.* **85 K12** 35 59N 114 55W
Alusi, *Indonesia* **37 F8** 7 35S 131 40 E
Al'Uzayr, *Iraq* **44 D5** 31 19N 47 25 E
Alva, *U.S.A.* **81 G5** 36 48N 98 40W
Alvarado, *Mexico* **87 D5** 18 40N 95 50W
Alvarado, *U.S.A.* **81 J6** 32 24N 97 13W
Alvaro Obregón, Presa, *Mexico* **86 B3** 27 55N 109 52W
Alvear, *Argentina* **94 B4** 29 5S 56 30W
Alvesta, *Sweden* **9 H16** 56 54N 14 35 E
Alvie, *Australia* **63 F3** 38 14S 143 30 E
Alvin, *U.S.A.* **81 L7** 29 26N 95 15W
Alvinston, *Canada* **78 D3** 42 49N 81 52W
Älvkarleby, *Sweden* **9 F17** 60 34N 17 26 E
Älvsbyn, *Sweden* **8 D19** 65 40N 21 0 E
Alwar, *India* **42 F7** 27 38N 76 34 E
Alxa Zuoqi, *China* **34 E3** 38 50N 105 40 E
Alyaskitovyy, *Russia* **27 C15** 64 45N 141 30 E
Alyata = Älät, *Azerbaijan* **25 G8** 39 58N 49 25 E
Alyth, *U.K.* **12 E5** 56 38N 3 13W
Alytus, *Lithuania* **9 J21** 54 24N 24 3 E
Alzada, *U.S.A.* **80 C2** 45 2N 104 25W
Am Dam, *Chad* **51 F9** 12 40N 20 35 E
Am-Timan, *Chad* **51 F9** 11 0N 20 10 E
Amadeus, L., *Australia* **61 D5** 24 54S 131 0 E
Amâdi, *Sudan* **51 G11** 5 29N 30 25 E
Amadi, *Zaïre* **54 B2** 3 40N 26 40 E

Asilah

Asilah, *Morocco* 50 A3 35 29N 6 0W
Asinara, *Italy* 20 D3 41 4N 8 16 E
Asinara, G. dell', *Italy* 20 D3 41 0N 8 30 E
Asino, *Russia* 26 D9 57 0N 86 0 E
Asipovichy, *Belarus* 17 B15 53 19N 28 33 E
'Asir □, *Si. Arabia* 46 D3 18 40N 42 30 E
Asir, Ras, *Somali Rep.* 46 E5 11 55N 51 10 E
Askersund, *Sweden* 9 G16 58 53N 14 55 E
Askham, *S. Africa* 56 D3 26 59S 20 47 E
Askim, *Norway* 9 G14 59 35N 11 10 E
Askja, *Iceland* 8 D5 65 3N 16 48W
Askøy, *Norway* 9 F11 60 29N 5 10 E
Asmara = Asmera, *Eritrea* 51 E12 15 19N 38 55 E
Asmera, *Eritrea* 51 E12 15 19N 38 55 E
Åsnen, *Sweden* 9 H16 56 37N 14 45 E
Asotin, *U.S.A.* 82 C5 46 20N 117 3W
Aspen, *U.S.A.* 83 G10 39 11N 106 49W
Aspermont, *U.S.A.* 81 J4 33 8N 100 14W
Aspiring, Mt., *N.Z.* 59 L2 44 23S 168 46 E
Asprókavos, Ákra, *Greece* 23 B4 39 21N 20 6 E
Aspur, *India* 42 H6 23 58N 74 7 E
Asquith, *Canada* 73 C7 52 8N 107 13W
Assad, Bahret, *Syria* 44 C3 36 0N 38 15 E
Assam □, *India* 41 F18 26 0N 93 0 E
Asse, *Belgium* 15 D4 50 24N 4 10 E
Assen, *Neths.* 15 B6 53 0N 6 35 E
Assini, *Ivory C.* 50 G4 5 9N 3 17W
Assiniboia, *Canada* 73 D7 49 40N 105 59W
Assiniboine →, *Canada* 73 D9 49 53N 97 8W
Assis, *Brazil* 95 A5 22 40S 50 20W
Assisi, *Italy* 20 C5 43 4N 12 37 E
Assynt, L., *U.K.* 12 C3 58 10N 5 3W
Astara, *Azerbaijan* 25 G8 38 30N 48 50 E
Asteroúsia, *Greece* 23 E7 34 59N 25 3 E
Asti, *Italy* 20 B3 44 54N 8 12 E
Astipálaia, *Greece* 21 F12 36 32N 26 22 E
Astorga, *Spain* 19 A2 42 29N 6 8W
Astoria, *U.S.A.* 84 D3 46 11N 123 50W
Astrakhan, *Russia* 25 E8 46 25N 48 5 E
Astrakhan-Bazàr, *Azerbaijan* 25 G8 39 14N 48 30 E
Asturias □, *Spain* 19 A3 43 15N 6 0W
Asunción, *Paraguay* 94 B4 25 10S 57 30W
Asunción Nochixtlán, *Mexico* 87 D5 17 28N 97 14W
Aswa →, *Uganda* 54 B3 3 43N 31 55 E
Aswân, *Egypt* 51 D11 24 4N 32 57 E
Aswân High Dam = Sadd el Aali, *Egypt* 51 D11 23 54N 32 54 E
Asyût, *Egypt* 51 C11 27 11N 31 4 E
At Ţafilah, *Jordan* 47 E4 30 45N 35 30 E
At Tā'if, *Si. Arabia* 46 C3 21 5N 40 27 E
Aţ Ţirāq, *Si. Arabia* 44 E5 27 19N 44 33 E
Atacama □, *Chile* 94 B2 27 30S 70 0W
Atacama, Desierto de, *Chile* 94 A2 24 0S 69 20W
Atacama, Salar de, *Chile* 94 A2 23 30S 68 20W
Atakpamé, *Togo* 50 G5 7 31N 1 13 E
Atalaya, *Peru* 92 F4 10 45S 73 50W
Atalaya de Femes, *Canary Is.* 22 F6 28 56N 13 47W
Atami, *Japan* 31 G9 35 5N 139 4 E
Atapupu, *Indonesia* 37 F6 9 0S 124 51 E
Atâr, *Mauritania* 50 D2 20 30N 13 5W
Atascadero, *U.S.A.* 83 J3 35 29N 120 40W
Atasu, *Kazakstan* 26 E8 48 30N 71 0 E
Atauro, *Indonesia* 37 F7 8 10S 125 30 E
Atbara, *Sudan* 51 E11 17 42N 33 59 E
'Atbara →, *Sudan* 51 E11 17 40N 33 56 E
Atbasar, *Kazakstan* 26 D7 51 48N 68 20 E
Atchafalaya B., *U.S.A.* 81 L9 29 25N 91 25W
Atchison, *U.S.A.* 80 F7 39 34N 95 7W
Ath, *Belgium* 15 D3 50 38N 3 47 E
Athabasca, *Canada* 72 C6 54 45N 113 20W
Athabasca →, *Canada* 73 B6 58 40N 110 50W
Athabasca, L., *Canada* 73 B7 59 15N 109 15W
Athboy, *Ireland* 13 C5 53 37N 6 56W
Athenry, *Ireland* 13 C3 53 18N 8 44W
Athens = Athínai, *Greece* 21 F10 37 58N 23 46 E
Athens, *Ala., U.S.A.* 77 H2 34 48N 86 58W
Athens, *Ga., U.S.A.* 77 J4 33 57N 83 23W
Athens, *N.Y., U.S.A.* 79 D11 42 16N 73 49W
Athens, *Ohio, U.S.A.* 76 F4 39 20N 82 6W
Athens, *Pa., U.S.A.* 79 E8 41 57N 76 31W
Athens, *Tenn., U.S.A.* 77 H3 35 27N 84 36W
Athens, *Tex., U.S.A.* 81 J7 32 12N 95 51W
Atherley, *Canada* 78 B5 44 37N 79 20W
Atherton, *Australia* 62 B4 17 17S 145 30 E
Athienou, *Cyprus* 23 D12 35 3N 33 32 E
Athínai, *Greece* 21 F10 37 58N 23 46 E
Athlone, *Ireland* 13 C4 53 25N 7 56W
Athna, *Cyprus* 23 D12 35 3N 33 47 E
Atholl, Forest of, *U.K.* 12 E5 56 51N 3 50W
Atholville, *Canada* 71 C6 47 59N 66 43W
Áthos, *Greece* 21 D11 40 9N 24 22 E
Athy, *Ireland* 13 D5 53 0N 7 0W
Ati, *Chad* 51 F8 13 13N 18 20 E
Atiak, *Uganda* 54 B3 3 12N 32 2 E
Atico, *Peru* 92 G4 16 14S 73 40W
Atikokan, *Canada* 70 C1 48 45N 91 37W
Atikonak L., *Canada* 71 B7 52 40N 64 32W
Atka, *Russia* 27 C16 60 50N 151 48 E
Atkinson, *U.S.A.* 80 D5 42 32N 98 59W
Atlanta, *Ga., U.S.A.* 77 J3 33 45N 84 23W
Atlanta, *Tex., U.S.A.* 81 J7 33 7N 94 10W
Atlantic, *U.S.A.* 80 E7 41 24N 95 1W
Atlantic City, *U.S.A.* 76 F8 39 21N 74 27W
Atlantic Ocean 2 E9 0 0 20 0W
Atlas Mts. = Haut Atlas, *Morocco* 50 B3 32 30N 5 0W
Atlin, *Canada* 72 B2 59 31N 133 41W
Atlin, L., *Canada* 72 B2 59 26N 133 45W
Atmore, *U.S.A.* 77 K2 31 2N 87 29W
Atoka, *U.S.A.* 81 H6 34 23N 96 8W
Atolia, *U.S.A.* 85 K9 35 19N 117 37W
Atoyac →, *Mexico* 87 D5 16 30N 97 31W
Atrak = Atrek →, *Turkmenistan* 45 B8 37 35N 53 58 E
Atrauli, *India* 42 E8 28 2N 78 20 E
Atrek →, *Turkmenistan* 45 B8 37 35N 53 58 E
Atsuta, *Japan* 30 C10 43 24N 141 26 E
Attalla, *U.S.A.* 77 H2 34 1N 86 6W
Attáviros, *Greece* 23 C9 36 12N 27 50 E
Attawapiskat, *Canada* 70 B3 52 56N 82 24W
Attawapiskat →, *Canada* 70 B3 52 57N 82 18W
Attawapiskat, L., *Canada* 70 B2 52 18N 87 54W
Attica, *U.S.A.* 76 E2 40 18N 87 15W
Attikamagen L., *Canada* 71 A6 55 0N 66 30W
Attleboro, *U.S.A.* 79 E13 41 57N 71 17W
Attock, *Pakistan* 42 C5 33 52N 72 20 E
Attopeu, *Laos* 38 E6 14 48N 106 50 E
Attur, *India* 40 P11 11 35N 78 30 E
Atuel →, *Argentina* 94 D2 36 17S 66 50W
Åtvidaberg, *Sweden* 9 G17 58 12N 16 0 E
Atwater, *U.S.A.* 83 H3 37 21N 120 37W
Atwood, *Canada* 78 C3 43 40N 81 1W
Atwood, *U.S.A.* 80 F4 39 48N 101 3W
Atyraū, *Kazakstan* 25 E9 47 5N 52 0 E
Au Sable →, *U.S.A.* 76 C4 44 25N 83 20W
Au Sable Pt., *U.S.A.* 70 C2 46 40N 86 10W
Aubagne, *France* 18 E6 43 17N 5 37 E
Aubarca, C., *Spain* 22 B7 39 4N 1 22 E
Aube →, *France* 18 B5 48 34N 3 43 E
Auberry, *U.S.A.* 84 H7 37 7N 119 29W
Auburn, *Ala., U.S.A.* 77 J3 32 36N 85 29W
Auburn, *Calif., U.S.A.* 84 G5 38 54N 121 4W
Auburn, *Ind., U.S.A.* 76 E3 41 22N 85 4W
Auburn, *N.Y., U.S.A.* 79 D8 42 56N 76 34W
Auburn, *Nebr., U.S.A.* 80 E7 40 23N 95 51W
Auburn, *Wash., U.S.A.* 84 C4 47 18N 122 14W
Auburn Ra., *Australia* 63 D5 25 15S 150 30 E
Auburndale, *U.S.A.* 77 L5 28 4N 81 48W
Aubusson, *France* 18 D5 45 57N 2 11 E
Auch, *France* 18 E4 43 39N 0 36 E
Auckland, *N.Z.* 59 G5 36 52S 174 46 E
Auckland Is., *Pac. Oc.* 64 N8 50 40S 166 5 E
Aude →, *France* 18 E5 43 13N 3 14 E
Auden, *Canada* 70 B2 50 14N 87 53W
Audubon, *U.S.A.* 80 E7 41 43N 94 56W
Augathella, *Australia* 63 D4 25 48S 146 35 E
Augrabies Falls, *S. Africa* 56 D3 28 35S 20 20 E
Augsburg, *Germany* 16 D6 48 25N 10 52 E
Augusta, *Italy* 20 F6 37 13N 15 13 E
Augusta, *Ark., U.S.A.* 81 H9 35 17N 91 22W
Augusta, *Ga., U.S.A.* 77 J5 33 28N 81 58W
Augusta, *Kans., U.S.A.* 81 G6 37 41N 96 59W
Augusta, *Maine, U.S.A.* 71 D6 44 19N 69 47W
Augusta, *Mont., U.S.A.* 82 C7 47 30N 112 24W
Augusta, *Wis., U.S.A.* 80 C9 44 41N 91 7W
Augustów, *Poland* 17 B12 53 51N 23 0 E
Augustus, Mt., *Australia* 60 D2 24 20S 116 50 E
Augustus Downs, *Australia* 62 B2 18 35S 139 55 E
Augustus I., *Australia* 60 C3 15 20S 124 30 E
Aukum, *U.S.A.* 84 G6 38 34N 120 43W
Auld, L., *Australia* 60 D3 22 25S 123 50 E
Ault, *U.S.A.* 80 E2 40 35N 104 44W
Aunis, *France* 18 C3 46 5N 0 50W
Auponhia, *Indonesia* 37 E7 1 58S 125 27 E
Aur, P., *Malaysia* 39 L5 2 35N 104 10 E
Auraiya, *India* 43 F8 26 28N 79 33 E
Aurangabad, *Bihar, India* 43 G11 24 45N 84 18 E
Aurangabad, *Maharashtra, India* 40 K9 19 50N 75 23 E
Aurich, *Germany* 16 B4 53 28N 7 28 E
Aurillac, *France* 18 D5 44 55N 2 26 E
Aurora, *Canada* 78 C5 44 0N 79 28W
Aurora, *S. Africa* 56 E2 32 40S 18 29 E
Aurora, *Colo., U.S.A.* 80 F2 39 44N 104 52W
Aurora, *Ill., U.S.A.* 76 E1 41 45N 88 19W
Aurora, *Mo., U.S.A.* 81 G8 36 58N 93 43W
Aurora, *Nebr., U.S.A.* 80 E6 40 52N 98 0W
Aurora, *Ohio, U.S.A.* 78 E3 41 21N 81 20W
Aurukun Mission, *Australia* 62 A3 13 20S 141 45 E
Aus, *Namibia* 56 D2 26 35S 16 12 E
Auschwitz = Oświęcim, *Poland* 17 C10 50 2N 19 11 E
Austin, *Minn., U.S.A.* 80 D8 43 40N 92 58W
Austin, *Nev., U.S.A.* 82 G5 39 30N 117 4W
Austin, *Pa., U.S.A.* 78 E6 41 38N 78 6W
Austin, *Tex., U.S.A.* 81 K6 30 17N 97 45W
Austin, L., *Australia* 61 E2 27 40S 118 0 E
Austra, *Norway* 8 D14 65 8N 11 55 E
Austral Downs, *Australia* 62 C2 20 30S 137 45 E
Austral Is. = Tubuai Is., *Pac. Oc.* 65 K12 25 0S 150 0W
Austral Seamount Chain, *Pac. Oc.* 65 K13 24 0S 150 0W
Australia ■, *Oceania* 64 K5 23 0S 135 0 E
Australian Alps, *Australia* 63 F4 36 30S 148 30 E
Australian Capital Territory □, *Australia* 63 F4 35 30S 149 0 E
Austria ■, *Europe* 16 E8 47 0N 14 0 E
Austvågøy, *Norway* 8 B16 68 20N 14 40 E
Autlán, *Mexico* 86 D4 19 40N 104 30W
Autun, *France* 18 C6 46 58N 4 17 E
Auvergne, *Australia* 60 C5 15 39S 130 1 E
Auvergne, *France* 18 D5 45 20N 3 15 E
Auvergne, Mts. d', *France* 18 D5 45 20N 2 55 E
Auxerre, *France* 18 C5 47 48N 3 32 E
Avallon, *France* 18 C5 47 30N 3 53 E
Avalon, *U.S.A.* 85 M8 33 21N 118 20W
Avalon Pen., *Canada* 71 C9 47 30N 53 20W
Avaré, *Brazil* 95 A6 23 4S 48 58W
Avawatz Mts., *U.S.A.* 85 K10 35 40N 116 30W
Aveiro, *Brazil* 93 D7 3 10S 55 5W
Aveiro, *Portugal* 19 B1 40 37N 8 38W
Āvej, *Iran* 45 C6 35 40N 49 15 E
Avellaneda, *Argentina* 94 C4 34 50S 58 10W
Avellino, *Italy* 20 D6 40 54N 14 47 E
Avenal, *U.S.A.* 84 K6 36 0N 120 8W
Aversa, *Italy* 20 D6 40 58N 14 12 E
Avery, *U.S.A.* 82 C6 47 15N 115 49W
Aves, I. de, *W. Indies* 89 C7 15 45N 63 55W
Aves, Is. de, *Venezuela* 89 D6 12 0N 67 30W
Avesta, *Sweden* 9 F17 60 9N 16 10 E
Avezzano, *Italy* 20 C5 42 2N 13 25 E
Aviá Terai, *Argentina* 94 B3 26 45S 60 50W
Avignon, *France* 18 E6 43 57N 4 50 E
Ávila, *Spain* 19 B3 40 39N 4 43W
Avila Beach, *U.S.A.* 85 K6 35 11N 120 44W
Avilés, *Spain* 19 A3 43 35N 5 57W
Avoca, *Ireland* 13 D5 52 51N 6 13W
Avoca, *U.S.A.* 78 D7 42 25N 77 25W
Avoca →, *Australia* 63 F3 35 40S 143 43 E
Avola, *Canada* 72 C5 51 45N 119 19W
Avola, *Italy* 20 F6 36 56N 15 7 E
Avon, *N.Y., U.S.A.* 78 D7 42 55N 77 45W
Avon, *S. Dak., U.S.A.* 80 D5 43 0N 98 4W
Avon →, *Australia* 61 F2 31 40S 116 7 E
Avon →, *Bristol, U.K.* 11 F5 51 29N 2 41W
Avon →, *Dorset, U.K.* 11 G6 50 44N 1 46W
Avon →, *Warks., U.K.* 11 F5 52 10N 1 51W
Avondale, *Zimbabwe* 55 F3 17 43S 30 58 E
Avonlea, *Canada* 73 D7 50 0N 105 0W
Avonmore, *Canada* 79 A10 45 10N 74 58W
Avonmouth, *U.K.* 11 F5 51 30N 2 42W
Avranches, *France* 18 B3 48 40N 1 20W
A'waj →, *Syria* 47 B5 33 23N 36 20 E
Awaji-Shima, *Japan* 31 G7 34 30N 134 50 E
'Awālī, *Bahrain* 45 E6 26 0N 50 30 E
Awantipur, *India* 43 C6 33 55N 75 3 E
Awash, *Ethiopia* 46 F3 9 1N 40 10 E
Awatere →, *N.Z.* 59 J5 41 37S 174 10 E
Awbārī, *Libya* 51 C7 26 46N 12 57 E
Awe, L., *U.K.* 12 E3 56 17N 5 16W
Awjilah, *Libya* 51 C9 29 8N 21 7 E
Axel Heiberg I., *Canada* 4 B3 80 0N 90 0W
Axim, *Ghana* 50 H4 4 51N 2 15W
Axiós →, *Greece* 21 D10 40 57N 22 35 E
Axminster, *U.K.* 11 G4 50 46N 3 0W
Ayabaca, *Peru* 92 D3 4 40S 79 53W
Ayabe, *Japan* 31 G7 35 20N 135 20 E
Ayacucho, *Argentina* 94 D4 37 5S 58 20W
Ayacucho, *Peru* 92 F4 13 0S 74 0W
Ayaguz, *Kazakstan* 26 E9 48 10N 80 10 E
Ayamonte, *Spain* 19 D2 37 12N 7 24W
Ayan, *Russia* 27 D14 56 30N 138 16 E
Ayaviri, *Peru* 92 F4 14 50S 70 35W
Aydın, *Turkey* 21 F12 37 51N 27 51 E
Ayer's Cliff, *Canada* 79 A12 45 10N 72 3W
Ayers Rock, *Australia* 61 E5 25 23S 131 5 E
Ayia Aikateríni, Ákra, *Greece* 23 A3 39 50N 19 50 E
Ayia Dhéka, *Greece* 23 D6 35 3N 24 58 E
Ayia Gálini, *Greece* 23 D6 35 6N 24 41 E
Ayia Napa, *Cyprus* 23 E13 34 59N 34 0 E
Ayia Phyla, *Cyprus* 23 E12 34 43N 33 1 E
Ayia Varvára, *Greece* 23 D7 35 8N 25 1 E
Áyios Amvrósios, *Cyprus* 23 D12 35 20N 33 35 E
Áyios Evstrátios, *Greece* 21 E11 39 34N 24 58 E
Áyios Ioánnis, Ákra, *Greece* 23 D7 35 20N 25 40 E
Áyios Isídhoros, *Greece* 23 C9 36 9N 27 51 E
Áyios Matthaíos, *Greece* 23 B3 39 30N 19 47 E
Áyios Nikólaos, *Greece* 23 D7 35 11N 25 41 E
Áyios Seryios, *Cyprus* 23 D12 35 12N 33 53 E
Ayios Theodhoros, *Cyprus* 23 D13 35 22N 34 1 E
Aykino, *Russia* 24 B8 62 15N 49 56 E
Aylesbury, *U.K.* 11 F7 51 49N 0 49W
Aylmer, *Canada* 78 D4 42 46N 80 59W
Aylmer, L., *Canada* 68 B8 64 0N 110 8W
Ayolas, *Paraguay* 94 B4 27 10S 56 59W
Ayon, Ostrov, *Russia* 27 C17 69 50N 169 0 E
Ayr, *Australia* 62 B4 19 35S 147 25 E
Ayr, *U.K.* 12 F4 55 28N 4 38W
Ayr →, *U.K.* 12 F4 55 28N 4 38W
Ayre, Pt. of, *U.K.* 10 C3 54 25N 4 21W
Aytos, *Bulgaria* 21 C12 42 42N 27 16 E
Ayu, Kepulauan, *Indonesia* 37 D8 0 35N 131 5 E
Ayutla, *Guatemala* 88 D1 14 40N 92 10W
Ayutla, *Mexico* 87 D5 16 58N 99 17W
Ayvacık, *Turkey* 21 E12 39 36N 26 24 E
Ayvalık, *Turkey* 21 E12 39 20N 26 46 E
Az Zabdānī, *Syria* 47 B5 33 43N 36 5 E
Az Zāhirīyah, *West Bank* 47 D3 31 25N 34 58 E
Az Zahrān, *Si. Arabia* 45 E6 26 10N 50 7 E
Az Zarqā, *Jordan* 47 C5 32 5N 36 4 E
Az Zibār, *Iraq* 44 B5 36 52N 44 4 E
Az-Zilfī, *Si. Arabia* 44 E5 26 12N 44 52 E
Az Zubayr, *Iraq* 44 D5 30 26N 47 40 E
Az Zuwaytīnah, *Libya* 51 B9 30 58N 20 7 E
Azamgarh, *India* 43 F10 26 5N 83 13 E
Āzār Shahr, *Iran* 44 B5 37 45N 45 59 E
Azärbayjan = Azerbaijan ■, *Asia* 25 F8 40 20N 48 0 E
Āzarbāyjān-e Gharbī □, *Iran* 44 B5 37 0N 44 30 E
Āzarbāyjān-e Sharqī □, *Iran* 44 B5 37 20N 47 0 E
Azare, *Nigeria* 50 F7 11 55N 10 10 E
A'zāz, *Syria* 44 B3 36 36N 37 4 E
Azbine = Aïr, *Niger* 50 E6 18 30N 8 0 E
Azerbaijan ■, *Asia* 25 F8 40 20N 48 0 E
Azerbaijchan = Azerbaijan ■, *Asia* 25 F8 40 20N 48 0 E
Azimganj, *India* 43 G13 24 14N 88 16 E
Azogues, *Ecuador* 92 D3 2 35S 78 0W
Azores, *Atl. Oc.* 48 C1 38 44N 29 0W
Azov, *Russia* 25 E6 47 3N 39 25 E
Azov, Sea of, *Europe* 25 E6 46 0N 36 30 E
Azovskoye More = Azov, Sea of, *Europe* 25 E6 46 0N 36 30 E
Azovy, *Russia* 26 C7 64 55N 65 1 E
Aztec, *U.S.A.* 83 H10 36 49N 107 59W
Azúa, *Dom. Rep.* 89 C5 18 25N 70 44W
Azuaga, *Spain* 19 C3 38 16N 5 39W
Azuero, Pen. de, *Panama* 88 E3 7 30N 80 30W
Azul, *Argentina* 94 D4 36 42S 59 43W
Azusa, *U.S.A.* 85 L9 34 8N 117 52W
'Azzūn, *West Bank* 47 C4 32 10N 35 2 E

B

Ba Don, *Vietnam* 38 D6 17 45N 106 26 E
Ba Dong, *Vietnam* 39 H6 9 40N 106 33 E
Ba Ngoi = Cam Lam, *Vietnam* 39 G7 11 54N 109 10 E
Ba Ria, *Vietnam* 39 G6 10 30N 107 10 E
Ba Tri, *Vietnam* 39 G6 10 2N 106 36 E
Ba Xian, *China* 34 E9 39 8N 116 22 E
Baa, *Indonesia* 37 F6 10 50S 123 0 E
Baarle Nassau, *Belgium* 15 C4 51 27N 4 56 E
Baarn, *Neths.* 15 B5 52 12N 5 17 E
Bab el Mandeb, *Red Sea* 46 E3 12 35N 43 25 E
Baba Burnu, *Turkey* 21 E12 39 29N 26 2 E
Bābā Kalū, *Iran* 45 D6 30 7N 50 49 E
Babadag, *Romania* 17 F15 44 53N 28 44 E
Babadayhan, *Turkmenistan* 26 F7 37 42N 60 23 E
Babaeski, *Turkey* 21 D12 41 26N 27 6 E
Babahoyo, *Ecuador* 92 D3 1 40S 79 30W
Babakin, *Australia* 61 F2 32 7S 118 1 E
Babana, *Nigeria* 50 F5 10 31N 3 46 E
Babar, *Indonesia* 37 F7 8 0S 129 30 E
Babar, *Pakistan* 42 D3 31 7N 69 32 E
Babarkach, *Pakistan* 42 E2 29 45N 68 0 E
Babb, *U.S.A.* 82 B7 48 51N 113 27W
Babi Besar, P., *Malaysia* 39 L4 2 25N 103 59 E
Babinda, *Australia* 62 B4 17 20S 145 56 E
Babine, *Canada* 72 B3 55 22N 126 37W
Babine →, *Canada* 72 B3 55 45N 127 44W
Babine L., *Canada* 72 C3 54 48N 126 0W
Babo, *Indonesia* 37 E8 2 30S 133 30 E
Bābol, *Iran* 45 B7 36 40N 52 50 E
Bābol Sar, *Iran* 45 B7 36 45N 52 45 E
Baboua, *C.A.R.* 52 C2 5 49N 14 58 E
Babruysk, *Belarus* 17 B15 53 10N 29 15 E
Babura, *Nigeria* 50 F6 12 51N 8 59 E
Babusar Pass, *Pakistan* 43 B5 35 12N 73 59 E
Babuyan Chan., *Phil.* 37 A6 18 40N 121 30 E
Babylon, *Iraq* 44 C5 32 34N 44 22 E
Bac Can, *Vietnam* 38 A5 22 8N 105 49 E
Bac Giang, *Vietnam* 38 B6 21 16N 106 11 E
Bac Ninh, *Vietnam* 38 B6 21 13N 106 4 E
Bac Phan, *Vietnam* 38 B5 22 0N 105 0 E
Bac Quang, *Vietnam* 38 A5 22 30N 104 48 E
Bacabal, *Brazil* 93 D10 4 15S 44 45W
Bacalar, *Mexico* 87 D7 18 50N 87 27W
Bacan, Kepulauan, *Indonesia* 37 E7 0 35S 127 30 E
Bacan, Pulau, *Indonesia* 37 E7 0 50S 127 30 E
Bacarra, *Phil.* 37 A6 18 15N 120 37 E
Bacău, *Romania* 17 E14 46 35N 26 55 E
Bacerac, *Mexico* 86 A3 30 18N 108 50W
Bach Long Vi, Dao, *Vietnam* 38 B6 20 10N 107 40 E
Bachelina, *Russia* 26 D7 57 45N 67 20 E
Back →, *Canada* 68 B9 65 10N 104 0W
Backstairs Passage, *Australia* 63 F2 35 40S 138 5 E
Bacolod, *Phil.* 37 B6 10 40N 122 57 E
Bacuk, *Malaysia* 39 J4 6 4N 102 25 E
Bād, *Iran* 45 C7 33 41N 52 1 E
Bad →, *U.S.A.* 80 C4 44 21N 100 22W
Bad Axe, *U.S.A.* 78 C2 43 48N 83 0W
Bad Ischl, *Austria* 16 E7 47 44N 13 38 E
Bad Kissingen, *Germany* 16 C6 50 11N 10 4 E
Bad Lands, *U.S.A.* 80 D3 43 40N 102 10W
Badagara, *India* 40 P9 11 35N 75 40 E
Badajoz, *Spain* 19 C2 38 50N 6 59W
Badalona, *Spain* 19 B7 41 26N 2 15 E
Badalzai, *Afghan.* 42 E1 29 50N 65 35 E
Badampahar, *India* 41 H15 22 10N 86 10 E
Badanah, *Si. Arabia* 44 D4 30 58N 41 30 E
Badarinath, *India* 43 D8 30 45N 79 30 E
Badas, *Brunei* 36 D4 4 33N 114 25 E
Badas, Kepulauan, *Indonesia* 36 D3 0 45N 107 5 E
Baddo →, *Pakistan* 40 F4 28 0N 64 20 E
Bade, *Indonesia* 37 F9 7 10S 139 35 E
Baden, *Austria* 16 D9 48 1N 16 13 E
Baden-Baden, *Germany* 16 D5 48 44N 8 13 E
Baden-Württemberg □, *Germany* 16 D5 48 20N 8 40 E
Badenoch, *U.K.* 12 E4 56 59N 4 15W
Badgastein, *Austria* 16 E7 47 7N 13 9 E
Badger, *Canada* 71 C8 49 0N 56 4W
Badger, *U.S.A.* 84 J7 36 38N 119 1W
Bādghīsāt □, *Afghan.* 40 B3 35 0N 63 0 E
Badgom, *India* 43 B6 34 1N 74 45 E
Badin, *Pakistan* 42 G3 24 38N 68 54 E
Baduen, *Somali Rep.* 46 F4 7 15N 47 40 E
Badulla, *Sri Lanka* 40 R12 7 1N 81 7 E
Baena, *Spain* 19 D3 37 37N 4 20W
Baeza, *Spain* 19 D4 37 57N 3 25W
Bafatá, *Guinea-Biss.* 50 F2 12 8N 14 40W
Baffin B., *Canada* 4 B4 72 0N 64 0W
Baffin I., *Canada* 69 B12 68 0N 75 0W
Bafia, *Cameroon* 50 H7 4 40N 11 10 E
Bafing →, *Mali* 50 F2 13 49N 10 50W
Bafliyūn, *Syria* 44 B3 36 37N 36 59 E
Bafoulabé, *Mali* 50 F2 13 50N 10 55W
Bāfq, *Iran* 45 D7 31 40N 55 25 E
Bāft, *Iran* 45 D8 29 15N 56 38 E
Bafwasende, *Zaïre* 54 B2 1 3N 27 5 E
Bagamoyo, *Tanzania* 54 D4 6 28S 38 55 E
Bagamoyo □, *Tanzania* 54 D4 6 20S 38 30 E
Bagan Datoh, *Malaysia* 39 L3 3 59N 100 47 E
Bagan Serai, *Malaysia* 39 K3 5 1N 100 32 E
Baganga, *Phil.* 37 C7 7 34N 126 33 E
Bagani, *Namibia* 56 B3 18 7S 21 41 E
Bagansiapiapi, *Indonesia* 36 D2 2 12N 100 50 E
Bagasra, *India* 42 J4 21 30N 71 0 E
Bagdad, *U.S.A.* 85 L11 34 35N 115 53W
Bagdarin, *Russia* 27 D12 54 26N 113 36 E
Bagé, *Brazil* 95 C5 31 20S 54 15W
Bagenalstown = Muine Bheag, *Ireland* 13 D5 52 42N 6 58W
Baggs, *U.S.A.* 82 F10 41 2N 107 39W
Bagh, *Pakistan* 43 C5 33 59N 73 45 E
Baghdād, *Iraq* 44 C5 33 20N 44 30 E
Bagheria, *Italy* 20 E5 38 5N 13 30 E
Baghlān, *Afghan.* 40 A6 36 12N 69 0 E
Bagley, *U.S.A.* 80 B7 47 32N 95 24W
Bagotville, *Canada* 71 C5 48 22N 70 54W
Bagrationovsk, *Russia* 9 J19 54 23N 20 39 E
Baguio, *Phil.* 37 A6 16 26N 120 34 E
Bahadurgarh, *India* 42 E7 28 40N 76 57 E
Bahama, Canal Viejo de, *W. Indies* 88 B4 22 10N 77 30W
Bahamas ■, *N. Amer.* 89 B5 24 0N 75 0W
Baharampur, *India* 43 G13 24 2N 88 27 E
Bahau, *Malaysia* 39 L4 2 48N 102 26 E
Bahawalnagar, *Pakistan* 42 D5 30 0N 73 15 E
Bahawalpur, *Pakistan* 42 E4 29 24N 71 40 E
Baheri, *India* 43 E8 28 45N 79 34 E
Bahi, *Tanzania* 54 D4 5 58S 35 21 E
Bahi Swamp, *Tanzania* 54 D4 6 10S 35 0 E
Bahia = Salvador, *Brazil* 93 F11 13 0S 38 30W
Bahia □, *Brazil* 93 F10 12 0S 42 0W
Bahía, Is. de la, *Honduras* 88 C2 16 45N 86 15W

Bareilly

Bahía Blanca, Argentina **94 D3** 38 35S 62 13W
Bahía de Caráquez, Ecuador **92 D2** 0 40S 80 27W
Bahía Honda, Cuba **88 B3** 22 54N 83 10W
Bahía Laura, Argentina **96 F3** 48 10S 66 30W
Bahía Negra, Paraguay **92 H7** 20 5S 58 5W
Bahmanzād, Iran **45 D6** 31 15N 51 47 E
Bahr Aouk →, C.A.R. **52 C3** 8 40N 19 0 E
Bahr el Ghazâl □, Sudan **48 F6** 7 0N 28 0 E
Bahr Salamat →, Chad **51 G8** 9 20N 18 0 E
Bahraich, India **43 F9** 27 38N 81 37 E
Bahrain ■, Asia **45 E6** 26 0N 50 35 E
Bahror, India **42 F7** 27 51N 76 20 E
Bāhū Kalāt, Iran **45 E9** 25 43N 61 25 E
Bai Bung, Mui, Vietnam **39 H5** 8 38N 104 44 E
Bai Duc, Vietnam **38 C5** 18 3N 105 49 E
Bai Thuong, Vietnam **38 C5** 19 54N 105 23 E
Baia Mare, Romania **17 E12** 47 40N 23 35 E
Baïbokoum, Chad **51 G8** 7 46N 15 43 E
Baicheng, China **35 B12** 45 38N 122 42 E
Baidoa, Somali Rep. **46 G3** 3 8N 43 30 E
Baie Comeau, Canada **71 C6** 49 12N 68 10W
Baie-St-Paul, Canada **71 C5** 47 28N 70 32W
Baie Trinité, Canada **71 C6** 49 25N 67 20W
Baie Verte, Canada **71 C8** 49 55N 56 12W
Baihe, China **34 H6** 32 50N 110 5 E
Ba'ījī, Iraq **44 C4** 35 0N 43 30 E
Baikal, L. = Baykal, Oz., Russia **27 D11** 53 0N 108 0 E
Baile Atha Cliath = Dublin, Ireland **13 C5** 53 21N 6 15W
Băileşti, Romania **17 F12** 44 1N 23 20 E
Bailundo, Angola **53 G3** 12 10S 15 50 E
Bainbridge, Ga., U.S.A. **77 K3** 30 55N 84 35W
Bainbridge, N.Y., U.S.A. **79 D9** 42 18N 75 29W
Baing, Indonesia **37 F6** 10 14S 120 34 E
Bainiu, China **34 H7** 32 50N 112 15 E
Bainville, U.S.A. **80 A2** 48 8N 104 13W
Bā'ir, Jordan **47 E5** 30 45N 36 55 E
Baird, U.S.A. **81 J5** 32 24N 99 24W
Baird Mts., U.S.A. **68 B3** 67 0N 160 0W
Bairin Youqi, China **35 C10** 43 30N 118 35 E
Bairin Zuoqi, China **35 C10** 43 58N 119 15 E
Bairnsdale, Australia **63 F4** 37 48S 147 36 E
Baisha, China **34 G7** 34 20N 112 32 E
Baitadi, Nepal **43 E9** 29 35N 80 25 E
Baiyin, China **34 F3** 36 45N 104 14 E
Baiyu Shan, China **34 F4** 37 15N 107 30 E
Baj Baj, India **43 H13** 22 30N 88 5 E
Baja, Hungary **17 E10** 46 12N 18 59 E
Baja, Pta., Mexico **86 B1** 29 50N 116 0W
Baja California, Mexico **86 A1** 31 10N 115 12W
Baja California □, Mexico **86 B2** 30 0N 115 0W
Baja California Sur □, Mexico **86 B2** 25 50N 111 50W
Bajamar, Canary Is. **22 F3** 28 33N 16 20W
Bajana, India **42 H4** 23 7N 71 49 E
Bājgīrān, Iran **45 B8** 37 36N 58 24 E
Bajimba, Mt., Australia **63 D5** 29 17S 152 6 E
Bajo Nuevo, Caribbean **88 C4** 15 40N 78 50W
Bajool, Australia **62 C5** 23 40S 150 35 E
Bakala, C.A.R. **51 G9** 6 15N 20 20 E
Bakchar, Russia **26 D9** 57 1N 82 5 E
Bakel, Senegal **50 F2** 14 56N 12 20W
Baker, Calif., U.S.A. **85 K10** 35 16N 116 4W
Baker, Mont., U.S.A. **80 B2** 46 22N 104 17W
Baker, Oreg., U.S.A. **82 D5** 44 47N 117 50W
Baker, L., Canada **68 B10** 64 0N 96 0W
Baker I., Pac. Oc. **64 G10** 0 10N 176 35W
Baker L., Australia **61 E4** 26 54S 126 5 E
Baker Lake, Canada **68 B10** 64 20N 96 3W
Baker Mt., U.S.A. **82 B3** 48 50N 121 49W
Bakers Creek, Australia **62 C4** 21 13S 149 7 E
Baker's Dozen Is., Canada **70 A4** 56 45N 78 45W
Bakersfield, Calif., U.S.A. **85 K7** 35 23N 119 1W
Bakersfield, Vt., U.S.A. **79 B12** 44 45N 72 48W
Bākhtarān, Iran **44 C5** 34 23N 47 0 E
Bākhtarān □, Iran **44 C5** 34 0N 46 30 E
Bakı, Azerbaijan **25 F8** 40 29N 49 56 E
Bakkafjörður, Iceland **8 C6** 66 2N 14 48W
Bakony Forest = Bakony Hegyseg, Hungary **17 E9** 47 10N 17 30 E
Bakony Hegyseg, Hungary **17 E9** 47 10N 17 30 E
Bakouma, C.A.R. **51 G9** 5 40N 22 56 E
Baku = Bakı, Azerbaijan **25 F8** 40 29N 49 56 E
Bakutis Coast, Antarctica **5 D15** 74 0S 120 0W
Baky = Bakı, Azerbaijan **25 F8** 40 29N 49 56 E
Bala, Canada **78 A5** 45 1N 79 37W
Bala, L., U.K. **10 E4** 52 53N 3 37W
Balabac I., Phil. **36 C5** 8 0N 117 0 E
Balabac Str., E. Indies **36 C5** 7 53N 117 5 E
Balabagh, Afghan. **42 B4** 34 25N 70 12 E
Ba'labakk, Lebanon **47 A5** 34 0N 36 10 E
Balabalangan, Kepulauan, Indonesia **36 E5** 2 20S 117 30 E
Balad, Iraq **44 C5** 34 1N 44 9 E
Balad Rūz, Iraq **44 C5** 33 42N 45 5 E
Bālādeh, Fārs, Iran **45 D6** 29 17N 51 56 E
Bālādeh, Māzandaran, Iran **45 B6** 36 12N 51 48 E
Balaghat, India **40 J12** 21 49N 80 12 E
Balaghat Ra., India **40 K10** 18 50N 76 30 E
Balaguer, Spain **19 B6** 41 50N 0 50 E
Balaklava, Australia **63 E2** 34 7S 138 22 E
Balaklava, Ukraine **25 F5** 44 30N 33 30 E
Balakovo, Russia **24 D8** 52 4N 47 55 E
Balancán, Mexico **87 D6** 17 48N 91 32W
Balashov, Russia **24 D7** 51 30N 43 10 E
Balasinor, India **42 H5** 22 57N 73 23 E
Balasore = Baleshwar, India **41 J15** 21 35N 87 3 E
Balaton, Hungary **17 E9** 46 50N 17 40 E
Balbina, Reprêsa de, Brazil **92 D7** 2 0S 59 30W
Balboa, Panama **88 E4** 8 57N 79 34W
Balbriggan, Ireland **13 C5** 53 37N 6 11W
Balcarce, Argentina **94 D4** 38 0S 58 10W
Balcarres, Canada **73 C8** 50 50N 103 35W
Balchik, Bulgaria **21 C13** 43 28N 28 11 E
Balclutha, N.Z. **59 M2** 46 15S 169 45 E
Bald Hd., Australia **61 G2** 35 6S 118 1 E
Bald I., Australia **61 F2** 34 57S 118 27 E
Bald Knob, U.S.A. **81 H9** 35 19N 91 34W
Baldock L., Canada **73 B9** 56 33N 97 57W
Baldwin, Fla., U.S.A. **77 K4** 30 18N 81 59W
Baldwin, Mich., U.S.A. **76 D3** 43 54N 85 51W
Baldwinsville, U.S.A. **79 C8** 43 10N 76 20W
Baldy Peak, U.S.A. **83 K9** 33 54N 109 34W
Baleares, Is., Spain **22 B10** 39 30N 3 0 E
Balearic Is. = Baleares, Is., Spain **22 B10** 39 30N 3 0 E
Baler, Phil. **37 A6** 15 46N 121 34 E
Baleshwar, India **41 J15** 21 35N 87 3 E
Balfate, Honduras **88 C2** 15 48N 86 25W
Balfe's Creek, Australia **62 C4** 20 12S 145 55 E
Bali, Cameroon **50 G7** 5 54N 10 0 E
Bali, Greece **23 D6** 35 25N 24 47 E
Bali, Indonesia **36 F5** 8 20S 115 0 E
Bali □, Indonesia **36 F5** 8 20S 115 0 E
Bali, Selat, Indonesia **37 H16** 8 18S 114 25 E
Balikeşir, Turkey **21 E12** 39 35N 27 58 E
Balikpapan, Indonesia **36 E5** 1 10S 116 55 E
Balimbing, Phil. **37 C5** 5 5N 119 58 E
Baling, Malaysia **39 K3** 5 41N 100 55 E
Balipara, India **41 F18** 26 50N 92 45 E
Baliza, Brazil **93 G8** 16 0S 52 20W
Balkan Mts. = Stara Planina, Bulgaria **21 C10** 43 15N 23 0 E
Balkhash = Balqash, Kazakstan **26 E8** 46 50N 74 50 E
Balkhash, Ozero = Balqash Köl, Kazakstan **26 E8** 46 0N 74 50 E
Balla, Bangla. **41 G17** 24 10N 91 35 E
Ballachulish, U.K. **12 E3** 56 41N 5 8W
Balladonia, Australia **61 F3** 32 27S 123 51 E
Ballarat, Australia **63 F3** 37 33S 143 50 E
Ballard, L., Australia **61 E3** 29 20S 120 40 E
Ballater, U.K. **12 D5** 57 3N 3 3W
Ballenas, Canal de, Mexico **86 B2** 29 10N 113 45W
Balleny Is., Antarctica **5 C11** 66 30S 163 0 E
Ballia, India **43 G11** 25 46N 84 12 E
Ballidu, Australia **61 F2** 30 35S 116 45 E
Ballina, Australia **63 D5** 28 50S 153 31 E
Ballina, Mayo, Ireland **13 B2** 54 7N 9 9W
Ballina, Tipp., Ireland **13 D3** 52 49N 8 26W
Ballinasloe, Ireland **13 C3** 53 20N 8 13W
Ballinger, U.S.A. **81 K5** 31 45N 99 57W
Ballinrobe, Ireland **13 C2** 53 38N 9 13W
Ballinskelligs B., Ireland **13 E1** 51 48N 10 13W
Ballycastle, U.K. **13 A5** 55 12N 6 15W
Ballymena, U.K. **13 B5** 54 52N 6 17W
Ballymena □, U.K. **13 B5** 54 53N 6 18W
Ballymoney, U.K. **13 A5** 55 5N 6 31W
Ballymoney □, U.K. **13 A5** 55 5N 6 23W
Ballyshannon, Ireland **13 B3** 54 30N 8 11W
Balmaceda, Chile **96 F2** 46 0S 71 50W
Balmoral, Australia **63 F3** 37 15S 141 48 E
Balmoral, U.K. **12 D5** 57 3N 3 13W
Balmorhea, U.S.A. **81 K3** 30 59N 103 45W
Balonne →, Australia **63 D4** 28 47S 147 56 E
Balqash, Kazakstan **26 E8** 46 50N 74 50 E
Balqash Köl, Kazakstan **26 E8** 46 0N 74 50 E
Balrampur, India **43 F10** 27 30N 82 20 E
Balranald, Australia **63 E3** 34 38S 143 33 E
Balsas, Mexico **87 D5** 18 0N 99 40W
Balsas →, Mexico **86 D4** 17 55N 102 10W
Balston Spa, U.S.A. **79 D11** 43 0N 73 52W
Balta, Ukraine **17 D15** 48 2N 29 45 E
Balta, U.S.A. **80 A4** 48 10N 100 2W
Bălţi, Moldova **17 E14** 47 48N 28 0 E
Baltic Sea, Europe **9 H18** 57 0N 19 0 E
Baltimore, Ireland **13 E2** 51 29N 9 22W
Baltimore, U.S.A. **76 F7** 39 17N 76 37W
Baltit, Pakistan **43 A6** 36 15N 74 40 E
Baltiysk, Russia **9 J18** 54 41N 19 58 E
Baluchistan □, Pakistan **40 F4** 27 30N 65 0 E
Balurghat, India **43 G13** 25 15N 88 44 E
Balvi, Latvia **9 H22** 57 8N 27 15 E
Balya, Turkey **21 E12** 39 44N 27 35 E
Balygychan, Russia **27 C16** 63 56N 154 12 E
Bam, Iran **45 D8** 29 7N 58 14 E
Bama, Nigeria **51 F7** 11 33N 13 41 E
Bamako, Mali **50 F3** 12 34N 7 55W
Bamba, Mali **50 E4** 17 5N 1 24W
Bambari, C.A.R. **51 G9** 5 40N 20 35 E
Bambaroo, Australia **62 B4** 18 50S 146 10 E
Bamberg, Germany **16 D6** 49 54N 10 54 E
Bamberg, U.S.A. **77 J5** 33 18N 81 2W
Bambili, Zaïre **54 B2** 3 40N 26 0 E
Bamenda, Cameroon **50 G7** 5 57N 10 11 E
Bamfield, Canada **72 D3** 48 45N 125 10W
Bāmīān □, Afghan. **40 B5** 35 0N 67 0 E
Bamiancheng, China **35 C13** 43 15N 124 2 E
Bampūr, Iran **45 E9** 27 15N 60 21 E
Ban Aranyaprathet, Thailand **38 F4** 13 41N 102 30 E
Ban Ban, Laos **38 C4** 19 31N 103 30 E
Ban Bang Hin, Thailand **39 H2** 9 32N 98 35 E
Ban Chiang Klang, Thailand **38 C3** 19 25N 100 55 E
Ban Chik, Laos **38 D4** 17 15N 102 22 E
Ban Choho, Thailand **38 E4** 15 2N 102 9 E
Ban Dan Lan Hoi, Thailand **38 D2** 17 0N 99 35 E
Ban Don = Surat Thani, Thailand **39 H2** 9 6N 99 20 E
Ban Don, Vietnam **38 F6** 12 53N 107 48 E
Ban Don, Ao, Thailand **39 H2** 9 20N 99 25 E
Ban Dong, Thailand **38 C3** 19 30N 100 59 E
Ban Hong, Thailand **38 C2** 18 18N 98 50 E
Ban Kaeng, Thailand **38 D3** 17 29N 100 7 E
Ban Keun, Laos **38 C4** 18 22N 102 35 E
Ban Khai, Thailand **38 F3** 12 46N 101 18 E
Ban Kheun, Laos **38 B3** 20 13N 101 7 E
Ban Khlong Kua, Thailand **39 J3** 6 57N 100 8 E
Ban Khuan Mao, Thailand **39 J2** 7 50N 99 37 E
Ban Khun Yuam, Thailand **38 C1** 18 49N 97 57 E
Ban Ko Yai Chim, Thailand **39 G2** 11 17N 99 26 E
Ban Kok, Thailand **38 D4** 16 40N 103 40 E
Ban Laem, Thailand **38 F2** 13 13N 99 59 E
Ban Lao Ngam, Laos **38 E6** 15 28N 106 10 E
Ban Le Kathe, Thailand **38 E2** 15 49N 98 53 E
Ban Mae Chedi, Thailand **38 C2** 19 11N 99 31 E
Ban Mae Laeng, Thailand **38 B2** 20 1N 99 17 E
Ban Mae Sariang, Thailand **38 C1** 18 10N 97 56 E
Ban Mê Thuôt = Buon Me Thuot, Vietnam **38 F7** 12 40N 108 3 E
Ban Mi, Thailand **38 E3** 15 3N 100 32 E
Ban Muong Mo, Laos **38 C4** 19 4N 103 58 E
Ban Na Mo, Laos **38 D5** 17 7N 105 40 E
Ban Na San, Thailand **39 H2** 8 53N 99 52 E
Ban Na Tong, Laos **38 B3** 20 56N 101 47 E
Ban Nam Bac, Laos **38 B4** 20 38N 102 20 E
Ban Nam Ma, Laos **38 A3** 22 2N 101 37 E
Ban Ngang, Laos **38 E6** 15 59N 106 11 E
Ban Nong Bok, Laos **38 D5** 17 5N 104 48 E
Ban Nong Boua, Laos **38 E6** 15 40N 106 33 E
Ban Nong Pling, Thailand **38 E3** 15 40N 100 10 E
Ban Pak Chan, Thailand **39 G2** 10 32N 98 51 E
Ban Phai, Thailand **38 D4** 16 4N 102 44 E
Ban Pong, Thailand **38 F2** 13 50N 99 55 E
Ban Ron Phibun, Thailand **39 H2** 8 9N 99 51 E
Ban Sanam Chai, Thailand **39 J3** 7 33N 100 25 E
Ban Sangkha, Thailand **38 E4** 14 37N 103 52 E
Ban Tak, Thailand **38 D2** 17 2N 99 4 E
Ban Tako, Thailand **38 E4** 14 5N 102 40 E
Ban Tha Dua, Thailand **38 D2** 17 59N 98 39 E
Ban Tha Li, Thailand **38 D3** 17 37N 101 25 E
Ban Tha Nun, Thailand **39 H2** 8 12N 98 18 E
Ban Thahine, Laos **38 E5** 14 12N 105 33 E
Ban Xien Kok, Laos **38 B3** 20 54N 100 39 E
Ban Yen Nhan, Vietnam **38 B6** 20 57N 106 2 E
Banaba, Kiribati **64 H8** 0 45S 169 50 E
Bañalbufar, Spain **22 B9** 39 42N 2 31 E
Banalia, Zaïre **54 B2** 1 32N 25 5 E
Banam, Cambodia **39 G5** 11 20N 105 17 E
Banamba, Mali **50 F3** 13 29N 7 22W
Banana, Australia **62 C5** 24 28S 150 8 E
Bananal, I. do, Brazil **93 F8** 11 30S 50 30W
Banaras = Varanasi, India **43 G10** 25 22N 83 0 E
Banas →, Gujarat, India **42 H4** 23 45N 71 25 E
Banas →, Mad. P., India **43 G9** 24 15N 81 30 E
Banbān, Si. Arabia **44 E5** 25 1N 46 35 E
Banbridge, U.K. **13 B5** 54 22N 6 16W
Banbridge □, U.K. **13 B5** 54 21N 6 16W
Banbury, U.K. **11 E6** 52 4N 1 20W
Banchory, U.K. **12 D6** 57 3N 2 29W
Bancroft, Canada **70 C4** 45 3N 77 51W
Band Bonī, Iran **45 E8** 25 30N 59 33 E
Band Qīr, Iran **45 D6** 31 39N 48 53 E
Banda, India **43 G9** 25 30N 80 26 E
Banda, Kepulauan, Indonesia **37 E7** 4 37S 129 50 E
Banda Aceh, Indonesia **36 C1** 5 35N 95 20 E
Banda Banda, Mt., Australia **63 E5** 31 10S 152 28 E
Banda Elat, Indonesia **37 F8** 5 40S 133 5 E
Banda Is. = Banda, Kepulauan, Indonesia **37 E7** 4 37S 129 50 E
Banda Sea, Indonesia **37 F7** 6 0S 130 0 E
Bandai-San, Japan **30 F10** 37 36N 140 4 E
Bandān, Iran **45 D9** 31 23N 60 44 E
Bandanaira, Indonesia **37 E7** 4 32S 129 54 E
Bandanwara, India **42 F6** 26 9N 74 38 E
Bandar = Machilipatnam, India **41 L12** 16 12N 81 8 E
Bandār 'Abbās, Iran **45 E8** 27 15N 56 15 E
Bandar-e Anzalī, Iran **45 B6** 37 30N 49 30 E
Bandar-e Bushehr = Būshehr, Iran **45 D6** 28 55N 50 55 E
Bandar-e Chārak, Iran **45 E7** 26 45N 54 20 E
Bandar-e Deylam, Iran **45 D6** 30 5N 50 10 E
Bandar-e Khomeynı, Iran **45 D6** 30 30N 49 5 E
Bandar-e Lengeh, Iran **45 E7** 26 35N 54 58 E
Bandar-e Maqām, Iran **45 E7** 26 56N 53 29 E
Bandar-e Ma'shur, Iran **45 D6** 30 35N 49 10 E
Bandar-e Nakhīlū, Iran **45 E7** 26 58N 53 30 E
Bandar-e Rīg, Iran **45 D6** 29 29N 50 38 E
Bandar-e Torkeman, Iran **45 B7** 37 0N 54 10 E
Bandar Maharani = Muar, Malaysia **39 L4** 2 3N 102 34 E
Bandar Penggaram = Batu Pahat, Malaysia **39 M4** 1 50N 102 56 E
Bandar Seri Begawan, Brunei **36 C4** 4 52N 115 0 E
Bandawe, Malawi **55 E3** 11 58S 34 5 E
Bandeira, Pico da, Brazil **95 A7** 20 26S 41 47W
Bandera, Argentina **94 B3** 28 55S 62 20W
Bandera, U.S.A. **81 L5** 29 44N 99 5W
Banderas, B. de, Mexico **86 C3** 20 40N 105 30W
Bandiagara, Mali **50 F4** 14 12N 3 29W
Bandırma, Turkey **21 D13** 40 20N 28 0 E
Bandon, Ireland **13 E3** 51 44N 8 44W
Bandon →, Ireland **13 E3** 51 43N 8 37W
Bandula, Mozam. **55 F3** 19 0S 33 7 E
Bandundu, Zaïre **52 E3** 3 15S 17 22 E
Bandung, Indonesia **37 G12** 6 54S 107 36 E
Bandya, Australia **61 E3** 27 40S 122 5 E
Bāneh, Iran **44 C5** 35 59N 45 53 E
Banes, Cuba **89 B4** 21 0N 75 42W
Banff, Canada **72 C5** 51 10N 115 34W
Banff, U.K. **12 D6** 57 40N 2 33W
Banff Nat. Park, Canada **72 C5** 51 30N 116 15W
Banfora, Burkina Faso **50 F4** 10 40N 4 40W
Bang Fai →, Laos **38 D5** 16 57N 104 45 E
Bang Hieng →, Laos **38 D5** 16 10N 105 10 E
Bang Krathum, Thailand **38 D3** 16 34N 100 18 E
Bang Lamung, Thailand **38 F3** 13 3N 100 56 E
Bang Mun Nak, Thailand **38 D3** 16 2N 100 23 E
Bang Pa In, Thailand **38 E3** 14 14N 100 35 E
Bang Rakam, Thailand **38 D3** 16 45N 100 7 E
Bang Saphan, Thailand **39 G2** 11 14N 99 28 E
Bangala Dam, Zimbabwe **55 G3** 21 7S 31 25 E
Bangalore, India **40 N10** 12 59N 77 40 E
Bangaon, India **43 H13** 23 0N 88 47 E
Bangassou, C.A.R. **52 D4** 4 55N 23 7 E
Banggai, Kepulauan, Indonesia **37 E6** 1 40S 123 30 E
Banggi, P., Malaysia **36 C5** 7 17N 117 12 E
Banghāzī, Libya **51 B9** 32 11N 20 3 E
Bangil, Indonesia **37 G15** 7 36S 112 50 E
Bangka, P., Sulawesi, Indonesia **37 D7** 1 50N 125 5 E
Bangka, P., Sumatera, Indonesia **36 E3** 2 0S 105 50 E
Bangka, Selat, Indonesia **36 E3** 2 30S 105 30 E
Bangkalan, Indonesia **37 G15** 7 2S 112 46 E
Bangkinang, Indonesia **36 D2** 0 18N 101 5 E
Bangko, Indonesia **36 E2** 2 5S 102 9 E
Bangkok, Thailand **38 F3** 13 45N 100 35 E
Bangladesh ■, Asia **41 H17** 24 0N 90 0 E
Bangong Co, India **43 B8** 35 50N 79 20 E
Bangor, Down, U.K. **13 B6** 54 40N 5 40W
Bangor, Gwynedd, U.K. **10 D3** 53 14N 4 8W
Bangor, Maine, U.S.A. **71 D6** 44 48N 68 46W
Bangor, Pa., U.S.A. **79 F9** 40 52N 75 13W
Bangued, Phil. **37 A6** 17 40N 120 37 E
Bangui, C.A.R. **52 D3** 4 23N 18 35 E
Banguru, Zaïre **54 B2** 0 30N 27 10 E
Bangweulu, L., Zambia **55 E3** 11 0S 30 0 E
Bangweulu Swamp, Zambia **55 E3** 11 20S 30 15 E
Bani, Dom. Rep. **89 C5** 18 16N 70 22W
Banī Sa'd, Iraq **44 C5** 33 34N 44 32 E
Banī Walīd, Libya **51 B7** 31 36N 13 53 E
Banihal Pass, India **43 C6** 33 30N 75 12 E
Banīnah, Libya **51 B9** 32 0N 20 12 E
Bāniyās, Syria **44 C3** 35 10N 36 0 E
Banja Luka, Bos.-H. **20 B7** 44 49N 17 11 E
Banjar, Indonesia **37 G13** 7 24S 108 30 E
Banjarmasin, Indonesia **36 E4** 3 20S 114 35 E
Banjarnegara, Indonesia **37 G13** 7 24S 109 42 E
Banjul, Gambia **50 F1** 13 28N 16 40W
Banka Banka, Australia **62 B1** 18 50S 134 0 E
Banket, Zimbabwe **55 F3** 17 27S 30 19 E
Bankipore, India **43 G11** 25 35N 85 10 E
Banks I., B.C., Canada **72 C3** 53 20N 130 0W
Banks I., N.W.T., Canada **68 A7** 73 15N 121 30W
Banks Pen., N.Z. **59 K4** 43 45S 173 15 E
Banks Str., Australia **62 G4** 40 40S 148 10 E
Bankura, India **43 H12** 23 11N 87 18 E
Bann →, Arm., U.K. **13 B5** 54 30N 6 31W
Bann →, L'derry., U.K. **13 A5** 55 8N 6 41W
Bannang Sata, Thailand **39 J3** 6 16N 101 16 E
Banning, U.S.A. **85 M10** 33 56N 116 53W
Banningville = Bandundu, Zaïre **52 E3** 3 15S 17 22 E
Bannockburn, Canada **78 B7** 44 39N 77 33W
Bannockburn, U.K. **12 E5** 56 5N 3 55W
Bannockburn, Zimbabwe **55 G2** 20 17S 29 48 E
Bannu, Pakistan **40 C7** 33 0N 70 18 E
Banská Bystrica, Slovak Rep. **17 D10** 48 46N 19 14 E
Banswara, India **42 H6** 23 32N 74 24 E
Banten, Indonesia **37 G12** 6 5S 106 8 E
Bantry, Ireland **13 E2** 51 41N 9 27W
Bantry B., Ireland **13 E2** 51 37N 9 44W
Bantul, Indonesia **37 G14** 7 55S 110 19 E
Bantva, India **42 J4** 21 29N 70 12 E
Banu, Afghan. **40 B6** 35 35N 69 5 E
Banyak, Kepulauan, Indonesia **36 D1** 2 10N 97 10 E
Banyo, Cameroon **50 G7** 6 52N 11 45 E
Banyumas, Indonesia **37 G13** 7 32S 109 18 E
Banyuwangi, Indonesia **37 H16** 8 13S 114 21 E
Banzare Coast, Antarctica **5 C9** 68 0S 125 0 E
Banzyville = Mobayi, Zaïre **52 D4** 4 15N 21 8 E
Bao Ha, Vietnam **38 A5** 22 11N 104 21 E
Bao Lac, Vietnam **38 A5** 22 57N 105 40 E
Bao Loc, Vietnam **39 G6** 11 32N 107 48 E
Baocheng, China **34 H4** 33 12N 106 56 E
Baode, China **34 E6** 39 1N 111 5 E
Baodi, China **35 E9** 39 38N 117 20 E
Baoding, China **34 E8** 38 50N 115 28 E
Baoji, China **34 G4** 34 20N 107 5 E
Baoshan, China **32 D4** 25 10N 99 5 E
Baotou, China **34 D6** 40 32N 110 2 E
Baoying, China **35 H10** 33 17N 119 20 E
Bap, India **42 F5** 27 23N 72 18 E
Bapatla, India **41 M12** 15 55N 80 30 E
Bāqerābād, Iran **45 C6** 33 2N 51 58 E
Ba'qūbah, Iraq **44 C5** 33 45N 44 50 E
Baquedano, Chile **94 A2** 23 20S 69 52W
Bar, Montenegro, Yug. **21 C8** 42 8N 19 8 E
Bar, Ukraine **17 D14** 49 4N 27 40 E
Bar Bigha, India **43 G11** 25 21N 85 47 E
Bar Harbor, U.S.A. **71 D6** 44 23N 68 13W
Bar-le-Duc, France **18 B6** 48 47N 5 10 E
Barabai, Indonesia **36 E5** 2 32S 115 34 E
Barabinsk, Russia **26 D8** 55 20N 78 20 E
Baraboo, U.S.A. **80 D10** 43 28N 89 45W
Baracaldo, Spain **19 A4** 43 18N 2 59W
Baracoa, Cuba **89 B5** 20 20N 74 30W
Baradero, Argentina **94 C4** 33 52S 59 29W
Baraga, U.S.A. **80 B10** 46 47N 88 30W
Barahona, Dom. Rep. **89 C5** 18 13N 71 7W
Barail Range, India **41 G18** 25 15N 93 20 E
Barakhola, India **41 G18** 25 0N 92 45 E
Barakot, India **43 J11** 21 33N 84 59 E
Barakpur, India **43 H13** 22 44N 88 30 E
Barakula, Australia **63 D5** 26 30S 150 33 E
Baralaba, Australia **62 C4** 24 13S 149 50 E
Baralzon L., Canada **73 B9** 60 0N 98 3W
Baramula, India **43 B6** 34 15N 74 20 E
Baran, India **42 G7** 25 9N 76 40 E
Baranavichy, Belarus **17 B14** 53 10N 26 0 E
Baranof I., U.S.A. **72 B1** 57 0N 135 0W
Barão de Melgaço, Brazil **92 F6** 11 50S 60 45W
Barapasi, Indonesia **37 E9** 2 15S 137 5 E
Barasat, India **43 H13** 22 46N 88 31 E
Barat Daya, Kepulauan, Indonesia **37 F7** 7 30S 128 0 E
Barataria B., U.S.A. **81 L10** 29 20N 89 55W
Baraut, India **42 E7** 29 13N 77 7 E
Barbacena, Brazil **95 A7** 21 15S 43 56W
Barbacoas, Colombia **92 C3** 1 45N 78 0W
Barbados ■, W. Indies **89 D8** 13 10N 59 30W
Barbastro, Spain **19 A6** 42 2N 0 5 E
Barberton, S. Africa **57 D5** 25 42S 31 2 E
Barberton, U.S.A. **78 E3** 41 0N 81 39W
Barbourville, U.S.A. **77 G4** 36 52N 83 53W
Barbuda, W. Indies **89 C7** 17 30N 61 40W
Barcaldine, Australia **62 C4** 23 43S 145 6 E
Barcellona Pozzo di Gotto, Italy **20 E6** 38 9N 15 13 E
Barcelona, Spain **19 B7** 41 21N 2 10 E
Barcelona, Venezuela **92 A6** 10 10N 64 40W
Barcelos, Brazil **92 D6** 1 0S 63 0W
Barcoo →, Australia **62 D3** 25 30S 142 50 E
Bardai, Chad **51 D8** 21 25N 17 0 E
Bardas Blancas, Argentina **94 D2** 35 49S 69 45W
Barddhaman, India **43 H12** 23 14N 87 39 E
Bardejov, Slovak Rep. **17 D11** 49 18N 21 15 E
Bardera, Somali Rep. **46 G3** 2 20N 42 27 E
Bardīyah, Libya **51 B9** 31 45N 25 5 E
Bardsey I., U.K. **10 E3** 52 45N 4 47W
Bardstown, U.S.A. **76 G3** 37 49N 85 28W
Bareilly, India **43 E8** 28 22N 79 27 E

Barents Sea

Barents Sea, *Arctic* ..... **4 B9** 73 0N 39 0 E
Barentu, *Eritrea* .... **51 E12** 15 2N 37 35 E
Barfleur, Pte. de, *France* . **18 B3** 49 42N 1 16W
Bargal, *Somali Rep.* ..... **46 E5** 11 25N 51 0 E
Bargara, *Australia* ..... **62 C5** 24 50S 152 25 E
Barguzin, *Russia* .... **27 D11** 53 37N 109 37 E
Barh, *India* .... **43 G11** 25 29N 85 46 E
Barhaj, *India* .... **43 F10** 26 18N 83 44 E
Barhi, *India* .... **43 G11** 24 15N 85 25 E
Bari, *India* .... **42 F7** 26 39N 77 39 E
Bari, *Italy* .... **20 D7** 41 8N 16 51 E
Bari Doab, *Pakistan* ..... **42 D5** 30 20N 73 0 E
Bariadi □, *Tanzania* ..... **54 C3** 2 45S 34 40 E
Barīm, *Yemen* .... **46 E3** 12 39N 43 25 E
Barinas, *Venezuela* **92 B4** 8 36N 70 15W
Baring, C., *Canada* **68 B8** 70 0N 117 30W
Baringo, *Kenya* .... **54 B4** 0 47N 36 16 E
Baringo □, *Kenya* ...... **54 B4** 0 55N 36 0 E
Baringo, L., *Kenya* ...... **54 B4** 0 47N 36 16 E
Bârîs, *Egypt* .... **51 D11** 24 42N 30 31 E
Barisal, *Bangla.* .... **41 H17** 22 45N 90 20 E
Barisan, Bukit, *Indonesia* **36 E2** 3 30S 102 15 E
Barito ~▸, *Indonesia* .... **36 E4** 4 0S 114 50 E
Bark L., *Canada* **78 A7** 45 27N 77 51W
Barker, *U.S.A.* **78 C6** 43 20N 78 33W
Barkley Sound, *Canada* .. **72 D3** 48 50N 125 10W
Barkly Downs, *Australia* . **62 C2** 20 30S 138 30 E
Barkly East, *S. Africa* .... **56 E4** 30 58S 27 33 E
Barkly Tableland, *Australia* **62 B2** 17 50S 136 40 E
Barkly West, *S. Africa* .... **56 D3** 28 5S 24 31 E
Barkol, *China* .... **32 B4** 43 37N 93 2 E
Barksdale, *U.S.A.* **81 L4** 29 44N 100 2W
Barlee, L., *Australia* ..... **61 E2** 29 15S 119 30 E
Barlee, Mt., *Australia* .... **61 D4** 24 38S 128 13 E
Barletta, *Italy* .... **20 D7** 41 19N 16 17 E
Barlovento, *Canary Is.* ... **22 F2** 28 48N 17 48W
Barlow L., *Canada* **73 A8** 62 0N 103 0W
Barmedman, *Australia* ... **63 E4** 34 9S 147 21 E
Barmer, *India* .... **42 G4** 25 45N 71 20 E
Barmera, *Australia* ...... **63 E3** 34 15S 140 28 E
Barmouth, *U.K.* **10 E3** 52 44N 4 4W
Barnagar, *India* .... **42 H6** 23 7N 75 19 E
Barnard Castle, *U.K.* **10 C6** 54 33N 1 55W
Barnato, *Australia* ...... **63 E3** 31 38S 145 0 E
Barnaul, *Russia* .... **26 D9** 53 20N 83 40 E
Barnesville, *U.S.A.* **77 J3** 33 3N 84 9W
Barnet, *U.K.* **11 F7** 51 38N 0 9W
Barneveld, *Neths.* .... **15 B5** 52 7N 5 36 E
Barneveld, *U.S.A.* **79 C9** 43 16N 75 14W
Barngo, *Australia* .... **62 D4** 25 3S 147 20 E
Barnhart, *U.S.A.* **81 K4** 31 8N 101 10W
Barnsley, *U.K.* **10 D6** 53 34N 1 27W
Barnstaple, *U.K.* **11 F3** 51 5N 4 4W
Barnsville, *U.S.A.* **80 B6** 46 43N 96 28W
Baro, *Nigeria* .... **50 G6** 8 35N 6 18 E
Baroda = Vadodara, *India* **42 H5** 22 20N 73 10 E
Baroda, *India* .... **42 G7** 25 29N 76 35 E
Baroe, *S. Africa* .... **56 E3** 33 13S 24 33 E
Baron Ra., *Australia* ..... **60 D4** 23 30S 127 45 E
Barpeta, *India* .... **41 F17** 26 20N 91 10 E
Barques, Pt. Aux, *U.S.A.* . **76 C4** 44 4N 82 58W
Barquísimeto, *Venezuela* . **92 A5** 10 4N 69 19W
Barra, *Brazil* **93 F10** 11 5S 43 10W
Barra, *U.K.* **12 E1** 57 0N 7 29W
Barra, Sd. of, *U.K.* **12 D1** 57 4N 7 25W
Barra de Navidad, *Mexico* **86 D4** 19 12N 104 41W
Barra do Corda, *Brazil* ... **93 E9** 5 30S 45 10W
Barra do Piraí, *Brazil* **95 A7** 22 30S 43 50W
Barra Falsa, Pta. da,
Mozam. .... **57 C6** 22 58S 35 37 E
Barra Hd., *U.K.* **12 E1** 56 47N 7 40W
Barra Mansa, *Brazil* **95 A7** 22 35S 44 12W
Barraba, *Australia* ...... **63 E5** 30 21S 150 35 E
Barrackpur = Barakpur,
India .... **43 H13** 22 44N 88 30 E
Barraigh = Barra, *U.K.* ... **12 E1** 57 0N 7 29W
Barranca, *Lima, Peru* **92 F3** 10 45S 77 50W
Barranca, *Loreto, Peru* .. **92 D3** 4 50S 76 50W
Barrancabermeja,
Colombia **92 B4** 7 0N 73 50W
Barrancas, *Venezuela* **92 B6** 8 55N 62 5W
Barrancos, *Portugal* **19 C2** 38 10N 6 58W
Barranqueras, *Argentina* . **94 B4** 27 30S 59 0W
Barranquilla, *Colombia* .. **92 A4** 11 0N 74 50W
Barras, *Brazil* **93 D10** 4 15S 42 18W
Barraute, *Canada* **70 C4** 48 26N 77 38W
Barre, *Mass., U.S.A.* **79 D12** 42 25N 72 6W
Barre, *Vt., U.S.A.* **79 B12** 44 12N 72 30W
Barreal, *Argentina* **94 C2** 31 33S 69 28W
Barreiras, *Brazil* **93 F10** 12 8S 45 0W
Barreirinhas, *Brazil* **93 D10** 2 30S 42 50W
Barreiro, *Portugal* **19 C1** 38 40N 9 6W
Barreiros, *Brazil* **93 E11** 8 49S 35 12W
Barren, Nosy, *Madag.* ... **57 B7** 18 25S 43 40 E
Barretos, *Brazil* **93 H9** 20 30S 48 35W
Barrhead, *Canada* **72 C6** 54 10N 114 24W
Barrie, *Canada* **70 D4** 44 24N 79 40W
Barrier Ra., *Australia* .... **63 E3** 31 0S 141 30 E
Barrière, *Canada* **72 C4** 51 12N 120 7W
Barrington, *U.S.A.* **79 E13** 41 44N 71 18W
Barrington L., *Canada* ... **73 B8** 56 55N 100 15W
Barrington Tops, *Australia* **63 E5** 32 6S 151 28 E
Barringun, *Australia* ..... **63 D4** 29 1S 145 41 E
Barrow, *U.S.A.* **68 A4** 71 18N 156 47W
Barrow ~▸, *Ireland* **13 D4** 52 25N 6 58W
Barrow Creek, *Australia* . **62 C1** 21 30S 133 55 E
Barrow I., *Australia* ..... **60 D2** 20 45S 115 20 E
Barrow-in-Furness, *U.K.* . **10 C4** 54 7N 3 14W
Barrow Pt., *Australia* .... **62 A3** 14 20S 144 40 E
Barrow Pt., *U.S.A.* **66 B4** 71 24N 156 29W
Barrow Ra., *Australia* .... **61 E4** 26 0S 127 40 E
Barrow Str., *Canada* **4 B3** 74 20N 95 0W
Barry, *U.K.* **11 F4** 51 24N 3 16W
Barry's Bay, *Canada* **70 C4** 45 29N 77 41W
Barsat, *Pakistan* .... **43 A5** 36 10N 72 45 E
Barsham, *Syria* .... **44 C4** 35 21N 40 33 E
Barsi, *India* .... **40 K9** 18 10N 75 50 E
Barsoi, *India* .... **41 G15** 25 48N 87 57 E
Barstow, *Calif., U.S.A.* ... **85 L9** 34 54N 117 1W
Barstow, *Tex., U.S.A.* **81 K3** 31 28N 103 24W
Barthélemy, Col, *Vietnam* **38 C5** 19 26N 104 6 E
Bartica, *Guyana* **92 B7** 6 25N 58 40W
Bartlesville, *U.S.A.* **81 G7** 36 45N 95 59W
Bartlett, *Calif., U.S.A.* **84 J8** 36 29N 118 2W
Bartlett, *Tex., U.S.A.* **81 K6** 30 48N 97 26W
Bartlett, L., *Canada* **72 A5** 63 5N 118 20W
Bartolomeu Dias, *Mozam.* **55 G4** 21 10S 35 8 E
Barton, *Australia* .... **61 F5** 30 31S 132 39 E
Barton upon Humber, *U.K.* **10 D7** 53 41N 0 25W
Bartow, *U.S.A.* **77 M5** 27 54N 81 50W
Barú, Volcan, *Panama* ... **88 E3** 8 55N 82 35W
Barumba, *Zaïre* .... **54 B1** 1 3N 23 37 E
Barwani, *India* .... **42 H6** 22 2N 74 57 E
Barysaw, *Belarus* .... **17 A15** 54 17N 28 28 E
Barzān, *Iraq* .... **44 B5** 36 55N 44 3 E
Bāsa'idū, *Iran* .... **45 E7** 26 35N 55 20 E
Basal, *Pakistan* .... **42 C5** 33 33N 72 13 E
Basankusa, *Zaïre* .... **52 D3** 1 5N 19 50 E
Basarabeasca, *Moldova* . **17 E15** 46 21N 28 58 E
Basawa, *Afghan.* .... **42 B4** 34 15N 70 50 E
Bascuñán, C., *Chile* **94 B1** 28 52S 71 35W
Basel, *Switz.* .... **16 E4** 47 35N 7 35 E
Bāshī, *Iran* .... **45 D6** 28 41N 51 4 E
Bashkir Republic =
Bashkortostan □, *Russia* **24 D10** 54 0N 57 0 E
Bashkortostan □, *Russia* . **24 D10** 54 0N 57 0 E
Basilan, *Phil.* .... **37 C6** 6 35N 122 0 E
Basilan Str., *Phil.* .... **37 C6** 6 50N 122 0 E
Basildon, *U.K.* .... **11 F8** 51 34N 0 28 E
Basim = Washim, *India* . **40 J10** 20 3N 77 0 E
Basin, *U.S.A.* **82 D9** 44 23N 108 2W
Basingstoke, *U.K.* **11 F6** 51 15N 1 5W
Baskatong, Rés., *Canada* . **70 C4** 46 46N 75 50W
Basle = Basel, *Switz.* .... **16 E4** 47 35N 7 35 E
Basoda, *India* .... **42 H7** 23 52N 77 54 E
Basoka, *Zaïre* .... **54 B1** 1 16N 23 40 E
Basongo, *Zaïre* .... **52 E4** 4 15S 20 20 E
Basque Provinces = País
Vasco □, *Spain* **19 A4** 42 50N 2 45W
Basra = Al Başrah, *Iraq* . **44 D5** 30 30N 47 50 E
Bass Rock, *U.K.* **12 E6** 56 5N 2 38W
Bass Str., *Australia* ..... **62 F4** 39 15S 146 30 E
Bassano, *Canada* **72 C6** 50 48N 112 20W
Bassano del Grappa, *Italy* **20 B4** 45 46N 11 44 E
Bassas da India, *Ind. Oc.* . **53 J7** 22 0S 39 0 E
Basse-Terre, *Guadeloupe* **89 C7** 16 0N 61 44W
Bassein, *Burma* .... **41 L19** 16 45N 94 30 E
Basseterre,
St. Kitts & Nevis **89 C7** 17 17N 62 43W
Bassett, *Nebr., U.S.A.* ... **80 D5** 42 35N 99 32W
Bassett, *Va., U.S.A.* **77 G6** 36 46N 79 59W
Bassi, *India* .... **42 D7** 30 44N 76 21 E
Bassikounou, *Mauritania* **50 E3** 15 55N 6 1W
Bastak, *Iran* .... **45 E7** 27 15N 54 25 E
Baştām, *Iran* .... **45 B7** 36 29N 55 4 E
Bastar, *India* .... **41 K12** 19 15N 81 40 E
Basti, *India* .... **43 F10** 26 52N 82 55 E
Bastia, *France* .... **18 E8** 42 40N 9 30 E
Bastogne, *Belgium* ..... **15 D5** 50 1N 5 43 E
Bastrop, *U.S.A.* **81 K6** 30 7N 97 19W
Bat Yam, *Israel* .... **47 C3** 32 2N 34 44 E
Bata, *Eq. Guin.* .... **52 D1** 1 57N 9 50 E
Bataan, *Phil.* .... **37 B6** 14 40N 120 25 E
Batabanó, *Cuba* **88 B3** 22 40N 82 20W
Batabanó, G. de, *Cuba* .. **88 B3** 22 30N 82 30W
Batac, *Phil.* .... **37 A6** 18 3N 120 34 E
Batagoy, *Russia* .... **27 C14** 67 38N 134 38 E
Batama, *Zaïre* .... **54 B2** 0 58N 26 33 E
Batamay, *Russia* .... **27 C13** 63 30N 129 15 E
Batang, *Indonesia* ...... **37 G13** 6 55S 109 45 E
Batangafo, *C.A.R.* ...... **51 G8** 7 25N 18 20 E
Batangas, *Phil.* .... **37 B6** 13 35N 121 10 E
Batanta, *Indonesia* ..... **37 E8** 0 55S 130 40 E
Batatais, *Brazil* **95 A6** 20 54S 47 37W
Batavia, *U.S.A.* **78 D6** 43 0N 78 11W
Batchelor, *Australia* ..... **60 B5** 13 4S 131 1 E
Bateman's B., *Australia* .. **63 F5** 35 40S 150 12 E
Batemans Bay, *Australia* . **63 F5** 35 44S 150 11 E
Bates Ra., *Australia* ..... **61 E3** 27 27S 121 5 E
Batesburg, *U.S.A.* **77 J5** 33 54N 81 33W
Batesville, *Ark., U.S.A.* .. **81 H9** 35 46N 91 39W
Batesville, *Miss., U.S.A.* . **81 H10** 34 19N 89 57W
Batesville, *Tex., U.S.A.* .. **81 L5** 28 58N 99 37W
Bath, *U.K.* **11 F5** 51 23N 2 22W
Bath, *Maine, U.S.A.* **71 D6** 43 55N 69 49W
Bath, *N.Y., U.S.A.* **78 D7** 42 20N 77 19W
Bath & North East
Somerset □, *U.K.* **11 F5** 51 21N 2 27W
Batheay, *Cambodia* ..... **39 G5** 11 59N 104 57 E
Bathgate, *U.K.* **12 F5** 55 54N 3 39W
Bathurst = Banjul, *Gambia* **50 F1** 13 28N 16 40W
Bathurst, *Australia* ...... **63 E4** 33 25S 149 31 E
Bathurst, *Canada* **71 C6** 47 37N 65 43W
Bathurst, *S. Africa* ...... **56 E4** 33 30S 26 50 E
Bathurst, C., *Canada* **68 A7** 70 34N 128 0W
Bathurst B., *Australia* ... **62 A3** 14 16S 144 25 E
Bathurst Harb., *Australia* . **62 G4** 43 15S 146 10 E
Bathurst I., *Australia* .... **60 B5** 11 30S 130 10 E
Bathurst I., *Canada* **4 B2** 76 0N 100 30W
Bathurst Inlet, *Canada* ... **68 B9** 66 50N 108 1W
Batlow, *Australia* .... **63 F4** 35 31S 148 9 E
Batna, *Algeria* .... **50 A6** 35 34N 6 15 E
Batoka, *Zambia* .... **55 F2** 16 45S 27 15 E
Baton Rouge, *U.S.A.* **81 K9** 30 27N 91 11W
Batong, Ko, *Thailand* .... **39 J2** 6 32N 99 12 E
Batopilas, *Mexico* **86 B3** 27 0N 107 45W
Batouri, *Cameroon* ..... **52 D2** 4 30N 14 25 E
Båtsfjord, *Norway* ...... **8 A23** 70 38N 29 39 E
Battambang, *Cambodia* .. **38 F4** 13 7N 103 12 E
Batticaloa, *Sri Lanka* .... **40 R12** 7 43N 81 45 E
Battipáglia, *Italy* .... **20 D6** 40 37N 14 58 E
Battle, *U.K.* .... **11 G8** 50 55N 0 30 E
Battle ~▸, *Canada* **73 C7** 52 43N 108 15W
Battle Camp, *Australia* .. **62 B3** 15 20S 144 40 E
Battle Creek, *U.S.A.* **76 D3** 42 19N 85 11W
Battle Ground, *U.S.A.* ... **84 E4** 45 47N 122 32W
Battle Harbour, *Canada* .. **71 B8** 52 16N 55 35W
Battle Lake, *U.S.A.* **80 B7** 46 17N 95 43W
Battle Mountain, *U.S.A.* . **82 F5** 40 38N 116 56W
Battlefields, *Zimbabwe* .. **55 F2** 18 37S 29 47 E
Battleford, *Canada* **73 C7** 52 45N 108 15W
Batu, *Ethiopia* .... **46 F2** 6 55N 39 45 E
Batu, Kepulauan,
Indonesia .... **36 E1** 0 30S 98 25 E
Batu Caves, *Malaysia* ... **39 L3** 3 15N 101 40 E
Batu Gajah, *Malaysia* ... **39 K3** 4 28N 101 3 E
Batu Is. = Batu,
Kepulauan, *Indonesia* . **36 E1** 0 30S 98 25 E
Batu Pahat, *Malaysia* .... **39 M4** 1 50N 102 56 E
Batuata, *Indonesia* ...... **37 F6** 6 12S 122 42 E
Batumi, *Georgia* .... **25 F7** 41 39N 41 44 E
Baturaja, *Indonesia* ..... **36 E2** 4 11S 104 15 E
Baturité, *Brazil* **93 D11** 4 28S 38 45W
Bau, *Malaysia* .... **36 D4** 1 25N 110 9 E
Baubau, *Indonesia* ...... **37 F6** 5 25S 122 38 E
Bauchi, *Nigeria* .... **50 F6** 10 22N 9 48 E
Baudette, *U.S.A.* **80 A7** 48 43N 94 36W
Bauer, C., *Australia* ..... **63 E1** 32 44S 134 4 E
Bauhinia Downs, *Australia* **62 C4** 24 35S 149 18 E
Baukau, *Indonesia* ...... **37 F7** 8 27S 126 27 E
Bauru, *Brazil* **95 A6** 22 10S 49 0W
Baús, *Brazil* **93 G8** 18 22S 52 47W
Bauska, *Latvia* .... **9 H21** 56 24N 24 15 E
Bautzen, *Germany* ...... **16 C8** 51 10N 14 26 E
Bavānāt, *Iran* .... **45 D7** 30 28N 53 27 E
Bavaria = Bayern □,
Germany .... **16 D6** 48 50N 12 0 E
Bavi Sadri, *India* .... **42 G6** 24 28N 74 30 E
Bavispe ~▸, *Mexico* **86 B3** 29 30N 109 11W
Bawdwin, *Burma* .... **41 H20** 23 5N 97 20 E
Bawean, *Indonesia* ..... **36 F4** 5 46S 112 35 E
Bawku, *Ghana* **50 F4** 11 3N 0 19W
Bawlake, *Burma* .... **41 K20** 19 11N 97 21 E
Baxley, *U.S.A.* **77 K4** 31 47N 82 21W
Baxter Springs, *U.S.A.* ... **81 G7** 37 2N 94 44W
Bay, L. de, *Phil.* .... **37 B6** 14 20N 121 11 E
Bay Bulls, *Canada* **71 C9** 47 19N 52 50W
Bay City, *Mich., U.S.A.* .. **76 D4** 43 36N 83 54W
Bay City, *Oreg., U.S.A.* .. **82 D2** 45 31N 123 53W
Bay City, *Tex., U.S.A.* ... **81 L7** 28 59N 95 58W
Bay de Verde, *Canada* ... **71 C9** 48 5N 52 54W
Bay Minette, *U.S.A.* **77 K2** 30 53N 87 46W
Bay St. Louis, *U.S.A.* **81 K10** 30 19N 89 20W
Bay Springs, *U.S.A.* **81 K10** 31 59N 89 17W
Bay View, *N.Z.* .... **59 H6** 39 25S 176 50 E
Baya, *Zaïre* .... **55 E2** 11 53S 27 25 E
Bayamo, *Cuba* **88 B4** 20 20N 76 40W
Bayamón, *Puerto Rico* ... **89 C6** 18 24N 66 10W
Bayan Har Shan, *China* .. **32 C4** 34 0N 98 0 E
Bayan Hot = Alxa Zuoqi,
China .... **34 E3** 38 50N 105 40 E
Bayan Obo, *China* ...... **34 D5** 41 52N 109 59 E
Bayan-Ovoo, *Mongolia* .. **34 C4** 42 55N 106 5 E
Bayana, *India* .... **42 F7** 26 55N 77 18 E
Bayanaūyl, *Kazakstan* ... **26 D8** 50 45N 75 45 E
Bayandalay, *Mongolia* ... **34 C2** 43 30N 103 29 E
Bayanhongor, *Mongolia* . **32 B5** 46 8N 102 43 E
Bayard, *U.S.A.* **80 E3** 41 45N 103 20W
Baybay, *Phil.* .... **37 B6** 10 40N 124 55 E
Bayern □, *Germany* ..... **16 D6** 48 50N 12 0 E
Bayeux, *France* **18 B3** 49 17N 0 42W
Bayfield, *Canada* **78 C3** 43 34N 81 42W
Bayfield, *U.S.A.* **80 B9** 46 49N 90 49W
Bayındır, *Turkey* .... **21 E12** 38 13N 27 39 E
Baykal, Oz., *Russia* ..... **27 D11** 53 0N 108 0 E
Baykit, *Russia* .... **27 C10** 61 50N 95 50 E
Baykonur = Bayqongyr,
Kazakstan .... **26 E7** 47 48N 65 50 E
Baymak, *Russia* .... **24 D10** 52 36N 58 19 E
Baynes Mts., *Namibia* ... **56 B1** 17 15S 13 0 E
Bayombong, *Phil.* .... **37 A6** 16 30N 121 10 E
Bayonne, *France* **18 E3** 43 30N 1 28W
Bayonne, *U.S.A.* **79 F10** 40 40N 74 7W
Bayovar, *Peru* **92 E2** 5 50S 81 0W
Bayqongyr, *Kazakstan* ... **26 E7** 47 48N 65 50 E
Bayram-Ali = Bayramaly,
Turkmenistan .... **26 F7** 37 37N 62 10 E
Bayramaly, *Turkmenistan* **26 F7** 37 37N 62 10 E
Bayramiç, *Turkey* .... **21 E12** 39 48N 26 36 E
Bayreuth, *Germany* ..... **16 D6** 49 56N 11 35 E
Bayrūt, *Lebanon* .... **47 B4** 33 53N 35 31 E
Bayt Lahm, *West Bank* ... **47 D4** 31 43N 35 12 E
Baytown, *U.S.A.* **81 L7** 29 43N 94 59W
Baza, *Spain* **19 D4** 37 30N 2 47W
Bazaruto, I. do, *Mozam.* . **57 C6** 21 40S 35 28 E
Bazmān, Kūh-e, *Iran* .... **45 D9** 28 4N 60 1 E
Beach, *U.S.A.* **80 B3** 46 58N 104 0W
Beach City, *U.S.A.* **78 F3** 40 39N 81 35W
Beachport, *Australia* .... **63 F2** 37 29S 140 0 E
Beachy Hd., *U.K.* .... **11 G8** 50 44N 0 15 E
Beacon, *Australia* ...... **61 F2** 30 26S 117 52 E
Beacon, *U.S.A.* **79 E11** 41 30N 73 58W
Beaconia, *Canada* **73 C9** 50 25N 96 31W
Beagle, Canal, *S. Amer.* . **96 G3** 55 0S 68 30W
Beagle Bay, *Australia* ... **60 C3** 16 58S 122 40 E
Bealanana, *Madag.* ..... **57 A8** 14 33S 48 44 E
Beamsville, *Canada* **78 C5** 43 12N 79 28W
Bear ~▸, *U.S.A.* **84 G5** 38 56N 121 36W
Bear I., *Ireland* **13 E2** 51 38N 9 50W
Bear L., *B.C., Canada* **72 B3** 56 10N 126 52W
Bear L., *Man., Canada* ... **73 B9** 55 8N 96 0W
Bear L., *U.S.A.* **82 E8** 41 59N 111 21W
Bearcreek, *U.S.A.* **82 D9** 45 11N 109 6W
Beardmore, *Canada* **70 C2** 49 36N 87 57W
Beardmore Glacier,
Antarctica .... **5 E11** 84 30S 170 0 E
Beardstown, *U.S.A.* **80 F9** 40 1N 90 26W
Béarn, *France* **18 E3** 43 20N 0 30W
Bearpaw Mts., *U.S.A.* **82 B9** 48 12N 109 30W
Bearskin Lake, *Canada* .. **70 B1** 53 58N 91 2W
Beata, C., *Dom. Rep.* **89 C5** 17 40N 71 30W
Beata, I., *Dom. Rep.* **89 C5** 17 34N 71 31W
Beatrice, *U.S.A.* **80 E6** 40 16N 96 45W
Beatrice, *Zimbabwe* ..... **55 F3** 18 15S 30 55 E
Beatrice, C., *Australia* ... **62 A2** 14 20S 136 55 E
Beatton ~▸, *Canada* **72 B4** 56 15N 120 45W
Beatton River, *Canada* ... **72 B4** 57 26N 121 20W
Beatty, *U.S.A.* **83 H5** 36 54N 116 46W
Beauce, Plaine de la,
France .... **18 B4** 48 10N 1 45 E
Beauceville, *Canada* **71 C5** 46 13N 70 46W
Beaudesert, *Australia* ... **63 D5** 27 59S 153 0 E
Beaufort, *Malaysia* ...... **36 C5** 5 30N 115 40 E
Beaufort, *N.C., U.S.A.* ... **77 H7** 34 43N 76 40W
Beaufort, *S.C., U.S.A.* ... **77 J5** 32 26N 80 40W
Beaufort Sea, *Arctic* **4 B1** 72 0N 140 0W
Beaufort West, *S. Africa* . **56 E3** 32 18S 22 36 E
Beauharnois, *Canada* **70 C5** 45 20N 73 52W
Beaulieu ~▸, *Canada* **72 A6** 62 3N 113 11W
Beauly, *U.K.* **12 D4** 57 30N 4 28W
Beauly ~▸, *U.K.* **12 D4** 57 29N 4 27W
Beaumaris, *U.K.* **10 D3** 53 16N 4 6W
Beaumont, *U.S.A.* **81 K7** 30 5N 94 6W
Beaune, *France* .... **18 C6** 47 2N 4 50 E
Beauséjour, *Canada* **73 C9** 50 5N 96 35W
Beauvais, *France* .... **18 B5** 49 25N 2 8 E
Beauval, *Canada* **73 B7** 55 9N 107 37W
Beaver, *Alaska, U.S.A.* ... **68 B5** 66 22N 147 24W
Beaver, *Okla., U.S.A.* **81 G4** 36 49N 100 31W
Beaver, *Pa., U.S.A.* **78 F4** 40 42N 80 19W
Beaver, *Utah, U.S.A.* **83 G7** 38 17N 112 38W
Beaver ~▸, *B.C., Canada* **72 B4** 59 52N 124 20W
Beaver ~▸, *Ont., Canada* **70 A2** 55 55N 87 48W
Beaver ~▸, *Sask., Canada* **73 B7** 55 26N 107 45W
Beaver City, *U.S.A.* **80 E5** 40 8N 99 50W
Beaver Dam, *U.S.A.* **80 D10** 43 28N 88 50W
Beaver Falls, *U.S.A.* **78 F4** 40 46N 80 20W
Beaver Hill L., *Canada* ... **73 C10** 54 5N 94 50W
Beaver I., *U.S.A.* **76 C3** 45 40N 85 33W
Beaverhill L., *Alta., Canada* **72 C6** 53 27N 112 32W
Beaverhill L., *N.W.T.*,
Canada **73 A8** 63 2N 104 22W
Beaverlodge, *Canada* ... **72 B5** 55 11N 119 29W
Beavermouth, *Canada* ... **72 C5** 51 32N 117 23W
Beaverstone ~▸, *Canada* **70 B2** 54 59N 89 25W
Beaverton, *Canada* **78 B5** 44 26N 79 9W
Beaverton, *U.S.A.* **84 E4** 45 29N 122 48W
Beawar, *India* .... **42 F6** 26 3N 74 18 E
Bebedouro, *Brazil* **95 A6** 21 0S 48 25W
Beboa, *Madag.* .... **57 B7** 17 22S 44 33 E
Beccles, *U.K.* .... **11 E9** 52 27N 1 35 E
Bečej, *Serbia, Yug.* ..... **21 B9** 45 36N 20 3 E
Béchar, *Algeria* **50 B4** 31 38N 2 18W
Beckley, *U.S.A.* **76 G5** 37 47N 81 11W
Bedford, *Canada* **70 C5** 45 7N 72 59W
Bedford, *S. Africa* ...... **56 E4** 32 40S 26 10 E
Bedford, *U.K.* **11 E7** 52 8N 0 28W
Bedford, *Ind., U.S.A.* ... **76 F2** 38 52N 86 29W
Bedford, *Iowa, U.S.A.* ... **80 E7** 40 40N 94 44W
Bedford, *Ohio, U.S.A.* ... **78 E3** 41 23N 81 32W
Bedford, *Pa., U.S.A.* **78 F6** 40 1N 78 30W
Bedford, *Va., U.S.A.* **76 G6** 37 20N 79 31W
Bedford, C., *Australia* ... **62 B4** 15 14S 145 21 E
Bedford Downs, *Australia* **60 C4** 17 19S 127 20 E
Bedfordshire □, *U.K.* **11 E7** 52 4N 0 28W
Bedourie, *Australia* ..... **62 C2** 24 30S 139 30 E
Beech Grove, *U.S.A.* **76 F2** 39 44N 86 3W
Beechy, *Canada* **73 C7** 50 53N 107 24W
Beenleigh, *Australia* ..... **63 D5** 27 43S 153 10 E
Be'er Menuḥa, *Israel* .... **44 D2** 30 19N 35 8 E
Be'er Sheva, *Israel* ..... **47 D3** 31 15N 34 48 E
Beersheba = Be'er Sheva,
Israel .... **47 D3** 31 15N 34 48 E
Beeston, *U.K.* **10 E6** 52 56N 1 14W
Beetaloo, *Australia* ..... **62 B1** 17 15S 133 50 E
Beeville, *U.S.A.* **81 L6** 28 24N 97 45W
Befale, *Zaïre* .... **52 D4** 0 25N 20 45 E
Befandriana, *Madag.* .... **57 C7** 21 55S 44 0 E
Befotaka, *Madag.* .... **57 C8** 23 49S 47 0 E
Bega, *Australia* .... **63 F4** 36 41S 149 51 E
Begusarai, *India* .... **43 G12** 25 24N 86 9 E
Behābād, *Iran* .... **45 C8** 32 24N 59 47 E
Behara, *Madag.* .... **57 C8** 24 55S 46 20 E
Behbehān, *Iran* .... **45 D6** 30 30N 50 15 E
Behshahr, *Iran* .... **45 B7** 36 45N 53 35 E
Bei Jiang ~▸, *China* ..... **33 D6** 23 2N 112 58 E
Bei'an, *China* .... **33 B7** 48 10N 126 20 E
Beihai, *China* .... **33 D5** 21 28N 109 6 E
Beijing, *China* .... **34 E9** 39 55N 116 20 E
Beijing □, *China* .... **34 E9** 39 55N 116 20 E
Beilen, *Neths.* .... **15 B6** 52 52N 6 27 E
Beilpajah, *Australia* .... **63 E3** 32 54S 143 52 E
Beinn na Faoghla =
Benbecula, *U.K.* **12 D1** 57 26N 7 21W
Beipiao, *China* .... **35 D11** 41 52N 120 32 E
Beira, *Mozam.* .... **55 F3** 19 50S 34 52 E
Beirut = Bayrūt, *Lebanon* **47 B4** 33 53N 35 31 E
Beitaolaizhao, *China* .... **35 B13** 44 58N 125 58 E
Beitbridge, *Zimbabwe* ... **55 G3** 22 12S 30 0 E
Beizhen, *Liaoning, China* **35 D11** 41 38N 121 54 E
Beizhen, *Shandong, China* **35 F10** 37 20N 118 2 E
Beizhengzhen, *China* .... **35 B12** 44 31N 123 30 E
Beja, *Portugal* **19 C2** 38 2N 7 53W
Béja, *Tunisia* .... **50 A6** 36 43N 9 12 E
Bejaia, *Algeria* .... **50 A6** 36 42N 5 2 E
Béjar, *Spain* **19 B3** 40 23N 5 46W
Bejestān, *Iran* .... **45 C8** 34 30N 58 5 E
Bekaa Valley = Al Biqā □,
Lebanon .... **47 A5** 34 10N 36 10 E
Bekasi, *Indonesia* ...... **37 G12** 6 14S 106 59 E
Békéscsaba, *Hungary* ... **17 E11** 46 40N 21 5 E
Bekily, *Madag.* .... **57 C8** 24 13S 45 19 E
Bekok, *Malaysia* .... **39 L4** 2 20N 103 7 E
Bela, *India* .... **43 G9** 25 50N 82 0 E
Bela, *Pakistan* .... **42 F2** 26 12N 66 20 E
Bela Crkva, *Serbia, Yug.* . **21 B9** 44 55N 21 27 E
Bela Vista, *Brazil* **94 A4** 22 12S 56 20W
Bela Vista, *Mozam.* ..... **57 D5** 26 10S 32 44 E
Belarus ■, *Europe* ...... **17 B14** 53 30N 27 0 E
Belau = Palau ■, *Pac. Oc.* **28 J17** 7 30N 134 30 E
Belavenona, *Madag.* .... **57 C8** 24 50S 47 4 E
Belawan, *Indonesia* ..... **36 D1** 3 33N 98 32 E
Belaya ~▸, *Russia* ...... **24 C9** 54 40N 56 0 E
Belaya Tserkov = Bila
Tserkva, *Ukraine* ..... **17 D16** 49 45N 30 10 E
Belcher Is., *Canada* **69 C12** 56 15N 78 45W
Belden, *U.S.A.* **84 E5** 40 2N 121 17W
Belebey, *Russia* .... **24 D9** 54 7N 54 7 E
Belém, *Brazil* **93 D9** 1 20S 48 30W
Belén, *Argentina* **94 B2** 27 40S 67 5W
Belén, *Paraguay* **94 A4** 23 30S 57 6W
Belen, *U.S.A.* **83 J10** 34 40N 106 46W
Belet Uen, *Somali Rep.* .. **46 G4** 4 30N 45 5 E
Belev, *Russia* .... **24 D6** 53 50N 36 5 E
Belfair, *U.S.A.* **84 C4** 47 27N 122 50W
Belfast, *S. Africa* .... **57 D5** 25 42S 30 2 E
Belfast, *U.K.* **13 B6** 54 35N 5 56W
Belfast, *Maine, U.S.A.* ... **71 D6** 44 26N 69 1W
Belfast, *N.Y., U.S.A.* **78 D6** 42 21N 78 7W
Belfast □, *U.K.* **13 B6** 54 35N 5 56W
Belfast L., *U.K.* **13 B6** 54 40N 5 50W
Belfield, *U.S.A.* **80 B3** 46 53N 103 12W
Belfort, *France* .... **18 C7** 47 38N 6 50 E
Belfry, *U.S.A.* **82 D9** 45 9N 109 1W
Belgaum, *India* .... **40 M9** 15 55N 74 35 E
Belgium ■, *Europe* ..... **15 D5** 50 30N 5 0 E

Bihar

Belgorod, Russia 25 D6 50 35N 36 35 E
Belgorod-Dnestrovskiy = Bilhorod-Dnistrovskyy, Ukraine 25 E6 46 11N 30 23 E
Belgrade = Beograd, Serbia, Yug. 21 B9 44 50N 20 37 E
Belgrade, U.S.A. 82 D8 45 47N 111 11W
Belhaven, U.S.A. 77 H7 35 33N 76 37W
Beli Drim →, Europe 21 C9 42 6N 20 25 E
Belinga, Gabon 52 D2 1 10N 13 2 E
Belinyu, Indonesia 36 E3 1 35S 105 50 E
Beliton Is. = Belitung, Indonesia 36 E3 3 10S 107 50 E
Belitung, Indonesia 36 E3 3 10S 107 50 E
Belize ■, Cent. Amer. 87 D7 17 0N 88 30W
Belize City, Belize 87 D7 17 25N 88 0W
Belkovskiy, Ostrov, Russia 27 B14 75 32N 135 44 E
Bell →, Canada 70 C4 49 48N 77 38W
Bell Bay, Australia 62 G4 41 6S 146 53 E
Bell I., Canada 71 B8 50 46N 55 35W
Bell-Irving →, Canada 72 B3 56 12N 129 5W
Bell Peninsula, Canada 69 B11 63 50N 82 0W
Bell Ville, Argentina 94 C3 32 40S 62 40W
Bella Bella, Canada 72 C3 52 10N 128 10W
Bella Coola, Canada 72 C3 52 25N 126 40W
Bella Unión, Uruguay 94 C4 30 15S 57 40W
Bella Vista, Corrientes, Argentina 94 B4 28 33S 59 0W
Bella Vista, Tucuman, Argentina 94 B2 27 10S 65 25W
Bellaire, U.S.A. 78 F4 40 1N 80 45W
Bellary, India 40 M10 15 10N 76 56 E
Bellata, Australia 63 D4 29 53S 149 46 E
Belle Fourche, U.S.A. 80 C3 44 40N 103 51W
Belle Fourche →, U.S.A. 80 C3 44 26N 102 18W
Belle Glade, U.S.A. 77 M5 26 41N 80 40W
Belle-Ile, France 18 C2 47 20N 3 10W
Belle Isle, Canada 71 B8 51 57N 55 25W
Belle Isle, Str. of, Canada 71 B8 51 30N 56 30W
Belle Plaine, Iowa, U.S.A. 80 E8 41 54N 92 17W
Belle Plaine, Minn., U.S.A. 80 C8 44 37N 93 46W
Belledune, Canada 71 C6 47 55N 65 50W
Bellefontaine, U.S.A. 76 E4 40 22N 83 46W
Bellefonte, U.S.A. 78 F7 40 55N 77 47W
Belleoram, Canada 71 C8 47 31N 55 25W
Belleville, Canada 70 D4 44 10N 77 23W
Belleville, Ill., U.S.A. 80 F10 38 31N 89 59W
Belleville, Kans., U.S.A. 80 F6 39 50N 97 38W
Belleville, N.Y., U.S.A. 79 C8 43 46N 76 10W
Bellevue, Canada 72 D6 49 35N 114 22W
Bellevue, Idaho, U.S.A. 82 E6 43 28N 114 16W
Bellevue, Ohio, U.S.A. 78 E2 41 17N 82 51W
Bellevue, Wash., U.S.A. 84 C4 47 37N 122 12W
Bellin = Kangirsuk, Canada 69 B13 60 0N 70 0W
Bellingen, Australia 63 E5 30 25S 152 50 E
Bellingham, U.S.A. 84 B4 48 46N 122 29W
Bellingshausen Sea, Antarctica 5 C17 66 0S 80 0W
Bellinzona, Switz. 16 E5 46 11N 9 1 E
Bellows Falls, U.S.A. 79 C12 43 8N 72 27W
Bellpat, Pakistan 42 E3 29 0N 68 5 E
Belluno, Italy 20 A5 46 9N 12 13 E
Bellville, U.S.A. 81 L6 29 57N 96 15W
Bellwood, U.S.A. 78 F6 40 36N 78 20W
Belmont, Australia 63 E5 33 4S 151 42 E
Belmont, Canada 78 D3 42 53N 81 5W
Belmont, S. Africa 56 D3 29 28S 24 22 E
Belmont, U.S.A. 78 D6 42 14N 78 2W
Belmonte, Brazil 93 G11 16 0S 39 0W
Belmopan, Belize 87 D7 17 18N 88 30W
Belmullet, Ireland 13 B2 54 14N 9 58W
Belo Horizonte, Brazil 93 G10 19 55S 43 56W
Belo-sur-Mer, Madag. 57 C7 20 42S 44 0 E
Belo-Tsiribihina, Madag. 57 B7 19 40S 44 30 E
Belogorsk, Russia 27 D13 51 0N 128 20 E
Beloha, Madag. 57 D8 25 10S 45 3 E
Beloit, Kans., U.S.A. 80 F5 39 28N 98 6W
Beloit, Wis., U.S.A. 80 D10 42 31N 89 2W
Belokorovichi, Ukraine 17 C15 51 7N 28 2 E
Belomorsk, Russia 24 B5 64 35N 34 54 E
Belonia, India 41 H17 23 15N 91 30 E
Beloretsk, Russia 24 D10 53 58N 58 24 E
Belorussia ■ = Belarus ■, Europe 17 B14 53 30N 27 0 E
Belovo, Russia 26 D9 54 30N 86 0 E
Beloye, Ozero, Russia 24 B6 60 10N 37 35 E
Beloye More, Russia 24 A6 66 30N 38 0 E
Belozersk, Russia 24 B6 60 1N 37 45 E
Beltana, Australia 63 E2 30 48S 138 25 E
Belterra, Brazil 93 D8 2 45S 55 0W
Belton, S.C., U.S.A. 77 H4 34 31N 82 30W
Belton, Tex., U.S.A. 81 K6 31 3N 97 28W
Belton Res., U.S.A. 81 K6 31 8N 97 32W
Beltsy = Bălţi, Moldova 17 E14 47 48N 28 0 E
Belturbet, Ireland 13 B4 54 6N 7 26W
Belukha, Russia 26 E9 49 50N 86 50 E
Beluran, Malaysia 36 C5 5 48N 117 35 E
Belvidere, Ill., U.S.A. 80 D10 42 15N 88 50W
Belvidere, N.J., U.S.A. 79 F9 40 50N 75 5W
Belyando →, Australia 62 C4 21 38S 146 50 E
Belyy, Ostrov, Russia 26 B8 73 30N 71 0 E
Belyy Yar, Russia 26 D9 58 26N 84 39 E
Belzoni, U.S.A. 81 J9 33 11N 90 29W
Bemaraha, Lembalemban' i, Madag. 57 B7 18 40S 44 45 E
Bemarivo, Madag. 57 C7 21 45S 44 45 E
Bemarivo →, Madag. 57 B8 15 27S 47 40 E
Bemavo, Madag. 57 C8 21 33S 45 25 E
Bembéréke, Benin 50 F5 10 11N 2 43 E
Bembesi, Zimbabwe 55 F2 20 0S 28 58 E
Bembesi →, Zimbabwe 55 F2 18 57S 27 47 E
Bemidji, U.S.A. 80 B7 47 28N 94 53W
Ben, Iran 45 C6 32 32N 50 45 E
Ben Cruachan, U.K. 12 E3 56 26N 5 8W
Ben Dearg, U.K. 12 D4 57 47N 4 56W
Ben Gardane, Tunisia 51 B7 33 11N 11 11 E
Ben Hope, U.K. 12 C4 58 25N 4 36W
Ben Lawers, U.K. 12 E4 56 32N 4 14W
Ben Lomond, N.S.W., Australia 63 E5 30 1S 151 43 E
Ben Lomond, Tas., Australia 62 G4 41 38S 147 42 E
Ben Lomond, U.K. 12 E4 56 11N 4 38W
Ben Luc, Vietnam 39 G6 10 39N 106 29 E
Ben Macdhui, U.K. 12 D5 57 4N 3 40W
Ben Mhor, U.K. 12 D1 57 15N 7 18W
Ben More, Arg. & Bute, U.K. 12 E2 56 26N 6 1W
Ben More, Stirl., U.K. 12 E4 56 23N 4 32W
Ben More Assynt, U.K. 12 C4 58 8N 4 52W
Ben Nevis, U.K. 12 E4 56 48N 5 1W
Ben Quang, Vietnam 38 D6 17 3N 106 55 E
Ben Tre, Vietnam 39 G6 10 3N 106 36 E
Ben Vorlich, U.K. 12 E4 56 21N 4 14W
Ben Wyvis, U.K. 12 D4 57 40N 4 35W
Bena, Nigeria 50 F6 11 20N 5 50 E
Bena Dibele, Zaïre 52 E4 4 4S 22 50 E
Benagerie, Australia 63 E3 31 25S 140 22 E
Benalla, Australia 63 F4 36 30S 146 0 E
Benambra, Mt., Australia 63 F4 36 31S 147 34 E
Benares = Varanasi, India 43 G10 25 22N 83 0 E
Benavente, Spain 19 A3 42 2N 5 43W
Benavides, U.S.A. 81 M5 27 36N 98 25W
Benbecula, U.K. 12 D1 57 26N 7 21W
Benbonyathe, Australia 63 E2 30 25S 139 11 E
Bencubbin, Australia 61 F2 30 48S 117 52 E
Bend, U.S.A. 82 D3 44 4N 121 19W
Bender Beila, Somali Rep. 46 F5 9 30N 50 48 E
Bendering, Australia 61 F2 32 23S 118 18 E
Bendery = Tighina, Moldova 17 E15 46 50N 29 30 E
Bendigo, Australia 63 F3 36 40S 144 15 E
Benē Beraq, Israel 47 C3 32 6N 34 51 E
Benenitra, Madag. 57 C8 23 27S 45 5 E
Benevento, Italy 20 D6 41 8N 14 45 E
Benga, Mozam. 55 F3 16 11S 33 40 E
Bengal, Bay of, Ind. Oc. 41 K16 15 0N 90 0 E
Bengbu, China 35 H9 32 58N 117 20 E
Benghazi = Banghāzī, Libya 51 B9 32 11N 20 3 E
Bengkalis, Indonesia 36 D2 1 30N 102 10 E
Bengkulu, Indonesia 36 E2 3 50S 102 12 E
Bengkulu □, Indonesia 36 E2 3 48S 102 16 E
Bengough, Canada 73 D7 49 25N 105 10W
Benguela, Angola 53 G2 12 37S 13 25 E
Benguérua, I., Mozam. 57 C6 21 58S 35 28 E
Beni, Zaïre 54 B2 0 30N 29 27 E
Beni →, Bolivia 92 F5 10 23S 65 24W
Beni Abbès, Algeria 50 B4 30 5N 2 5W
Beni Mazâr, Egypt 51 C11 28 32N 30 44 E
Beni Mellal, Morocco 50 B3 32 21N 6 21W
Beni Ounif, Algeria 50 B4 32 0N 1 10W
Beni Suef, Egypt 51 C11 29 5N 31 6 E
Beniah L., Canada 72 A6 63 23N 112 17W
Benicia, U.S.A. 84 G4 38 3N 122 9W
Benidorm, Spain 19 C5 38 33N 0 9W
Benin ■, Africa 50 G5 10 0N 2 0 E
Benin, Bight of, W. Afr. 50 H5 5 0N 3 0 E
Benin City, Nigeria 50 G6 6 20N 5 31 E
Benitses, Greece 23 A3 39 32N 19 55 E
Benjamin Aceval, Paraguay 94 A4 24 58S 57 34W
Benjamin Constant, Brazil 92 D4 4 40S 70 15W
Benjamin Hill, Mexico 86 A2 30 10N 111 10W
Benkelman, U.S.A. 80 E4 40 3N 101 32W
Benlidi, Australia 62 C3 24 35S 144 50 E
Bennett, Canada 72 B2 59 56N 134 53W
Bennett, L., Australia 60 D5 22 50S 131 2 E
Bennett, Ostrov, Russia 27 B15 76 21N 148 56 E
Bennettsville, U.S.A. 77 H6 34 37N 79 41W
Bennington, U.S.A. 79 D11 43 0N 71 55W
Benoni, S. Africa 57 D4 26 11S 28 18 E
Benque Viejo, Belize 87 D7 17 5N 89 8W
Benson, U.S.A. 83 L8 31 58N 110 18W
Bent, Iran 45 E8 26 20N 59 31 E
Benteng, Indonesia 37 F6 6 10S 120 30 E
Bentinck I., Australia 62 B2 17 3S 139 35 E
Bento Gonçalves, Brazil 95 B5 29 10S 51 31W
Benton, Ark., U.S.A. 81 H8 34 34N 92 35W
Benton, Calif., U.S.A. 84 H8 37 48N 118 32W
Benton, Ill., U.S.A. 80 F10 38 0N 88 55W
Benton Harbor, U.S.A. 76 D2 42 6N 86 27W
Bentung, Malaysia 39 L3 3 31N 101 55 E
Benue →, Nigeria 50 G6 7 48N 6 46 E
Benxi, China 35 D12 41 20N 123 48 E
Beo, Indonesia 37 D7 4 25N 126 50 E
Beograd, Serbia, Yug. 21 B9 44 50N 20 37 E
Beowawe, U.S.A. 82 F5 40 35N 116 29W
Beppu, Japan 31 H5 33 15N 131 30 E
Beqaa Valley = Al Biqā □, Lebanon 47 A5 34 10N 36 10 E
Berati, Albania 21 D8 40 43N 19 59 E
Berau, Teluk, Indonesia 37 E8 2 30S 132 30 E
Berber, Sudan 51 E11 18 0N 34 0 E
Berbera, Somali Rep. 46 E4 10 30N 45 2 E
Berbérati, C.A.R. 52 D3 4 15N 15 40 E
Berberia, C. del, Spain 22 C7 38 39N 1 24 E
Berbice →, Guyana 92 B7 6 20N 57 32W
Berdichev = Berdychiv, Ukraine 17 D15 49 57N 28 30 E
Berdsk, Russia 26 D9 54 47N 83 2 E
Berdyansk, Ukraine 25 E6 46 45N 36 50 E
Berdychiv, Ukraine 17 D15 49 57N 28 30 E
Berea, U.S.A. 76 G3 37 34N 84 17W
Berebere, Indonesia 37 D7 2 25N 128 45 E
Bereda, Somali Rep. 46 E5 11 45N 51 0 E
Berehove, Ukraine 17 D12 48 15N 22 35 E
Berekum, Ghana 50 G4 7 29N 2 34W
Berens →, Canada 73 C9 52 25N 97 2W
Berens I., Canada 73 C9 52 18N 97 18W
Berens River, Canada 73 C9 52 25N 97 0W
Berestechko, Ukraine 17 C13 50 22N 25 5 E
Berevo, Mahajanga, Madag. 57 B7 17 14S 44 17 E
Berevo, Toliara, Madag. 57 B7 19 44S 44 58 E
Bereza, Belarus 17 B13 52 31N 24 51 E
Berezhany, Ukraine 17 D13 49 26N 24 58 E
Berezina = Byarezina →, Belarus 17 B16 52 33N 30 14 E
Berezniki, Russia 26 D6 59 24N 56 46 E
Berezovo, Russia 24 B11 64 0N 65 0 E
Berga, Spain 19 A6 42 6N 1 48 E
Bergama, Turkey 21 E12 39 8N 27 15 E
Bérgamo, Italy 20 B3 45 41N 9 43 E
Bergen, Neths. 15 B4 52 40N 4 43 E
Bergen, Norway 9 F11 60 20N 5 20 E
Bergen, U.S.A. 78 C7 43 5N 77 57W
Bergen-op-Zoom, Neths. 15 C4 51 28N 4 18 E
Bergerac, France 18 D4 44 51N 0 30 E
Bergum, Neths. 15 A5 53 13N 5 59 E
Bergville, S. Africa 57 D4 28 52S 29 18 E
Berhala, Selat, Indonesia 36 E2 1 0S 104 15 E
Berhampore = Baharampur, India 43 G13 24 2N 88 27 E
Berhampur, India 41 K14 19 15N 84 54 E
Bering Sea, Pac. Oc. 68 C1 58 0N 171 0 E
Bering Strait, U.S.A. 68 B3 65 30N 169 0W
Beringen, Belgium 15 C5 51 3N 5 14 E
Beringovskiy, Russia 27 C18 63 3N 179 19 E
Berisso, Argentina 94 C4 34 56S 57 50W
Berja, Spain 19 D4 36 50N 2 56W
Berkeley, U.K. 11 F5 51 41N 2 27W
Berkeley, U.S.A. 84 H4 37 52N 122 16W
Berkeley Springs, U.S.A. 76 F6 39 38N 78 14W
Berkner I., Antarctica 5 D18 79 30S 50 0W
Berkshire □, U.K. 11 F6 51 25N 1 17W
Berland →, Canada 72 C5 54 0N 116 50W
Berlin, Germany 16 B7 52 30N 13 25 E
Berlin, Md., U.S.A. 76 F8 38 20N 75 13W
Berlin, N.H., U.S.A. 79 B13 44 28N 71 11W
Berlin, Wis., U.S.A. 76 D1 43 58N 88 57W
Bermejo →, Formosa, Argentina 94 B4 26 51S 58 23W
Bermejo →, San Juan, Argentina 94 C2 32 30S 67 30W
Bermuda ■, Atl. Oc. 66 F13 32 45N 65 0W
Bern, Switz. 16 E4 46 57N 7 28 E
Bernado, U.S.A. 83 J10 34 30N 106 53W
Bernalillo, U.S.A. 83 J10 35 18N 106 33W
Bernardo de Irigoyen, Argentina 95 B5 26 15S 53 40W
Bernardo O'Higgins □, Chile 94 C1 34 15S 70 45W
Bernasconi, Argentina 94 D3 37 55S 63 44W
Bernburg, Germany 16 C6 51 47N 11 44 E
Berne = Bern, Switz. 16 E4 46 57N 7 28 E
Bernier I., Australia 61 D1 24 50S 113 12 E
Bernina, Piz, Switz. 16 E5 46 20N 9 54 E
Beroroha, Madag. 57 C8 21 40S 45 10 E
Beroun, Czech. 16 D8 49 57N 14 5 E
Berrechid, Morocco 50 B3 33 18N 7 36W
Berri, Australia 63 E3 34 14S 140 35 E
Berry, Australia 63 E5 34 46S 150 43 E
Berry, France 18 C5 46 50N 2 0 E
Berry Is., Bahamas 88 A4 25 40N 77 50W
Berryessa L., U.S.A. 84 G4 38 31N 122 6W
Berryville, U.S.A. 81 G8 36 22N 93 34W
Bershad, Ukraine 17 D15 48 22N 29 31 E
Berthold, U.S.A. 80 A4 48 19N 101 44W
Berthoud, U.S.A. 80 E2 40 19N 105 5W
Bertoua, Cameroon 52 D2 4 30N 13 45 E
Bertrand, U.S.A. 80 E5 40 32N 99 38W
Berwick, U.S.A. 79 E8 41 3N 76 14W
Berwick-upon-Tweed, U.K. 10 B5 55 46N 2 0W
Berwyn Mts., U.K. 10 E4 52 54N 3 26W
Besal, Pakistan 43 B5 35 4N 73 56 E
Besalampy, Madag. 57 B7 16 43S 44 29 E
Besançon, France 18 C7 47 15N 6 2 E
Besar, Indonesia 36 E5 2 40S 116 0 E
Besnard L., Canada 73 B7 55 25N 106 0W
Besor, N. →, Egypt 47 D3 31 28N 34 22 E
Bessarabiya, Moldova 17 E15 47 0N 28 10 E
Bessarabka = Basarabeasca, Moldova 17 E15 46 21N 28 58 E
Bessemer, Ala., U.S.A. 77 J2 33 24N 86 58W
Bessemer, Mich., U.S.A. 80 B9 46 29N 90 3W
Bet She'an, Israel 47 C4 32 30N 35 30 E
Bet Shemesh, Israel 47 D3 31 44N 35 0 E
Betafo, Madag. 57 B8 19 50S 46 51 E
Betancuria, Canary Is. 22 F5 28 25N 14 3W
Betanzos, Spain 19 A1 43 15N 8 12W
Bétaré Oya, Cameroon 52 C2 5 40N 14 5 E
Bethal, S. Africa 57 D4 26 27S 29 28 E
Bethanien, Namibia 56 D2 26 31S 17 8 E
Bethany, U.S.A. 80 E7 40 16N 94 2W
Bethel, Alaska, U.S.A. 68 B3 60 48N 161 45W
Bethel, Vt., U.S.A. 79 C12 43 50N 72 38W
Bethel Park, U.S.A. 78 F4 40 20N 80 1W
Bethlehem = Bayt Lahm, West Bank 47 D4 31 43N 35 12 E
Bethlehem, S. Africa 57 D4 28 14S 28 18 E
Bethlehem, U.S.A. 79 F9 40 37N 75 23W
Bethulie, S. Africa 56 E4 30 30S 25 59 E
Béthune, France 18 A5 50 30N 2 38 E
Bethungra, Australia 63 E4 34 45S 147 51 E
Betioky, Madag. 57 C7 23 48S 44 20 E
Betong, Thailand 39 K3 5 45N 101 5 E
Betoota, Australia 62 D3 25 45S 140 42 E
Betroka, Madag. 57 C8 23 16S 46 0 E
Betsiamites, Canada 71 C6 48 56N 68 40W
Betsiamites →, Canada 71 C6 48 56N 68 38W
Betsiboka →, Madag. 57 B8 16 3S 46 36 E
Bettiah, India 43 F11 26 48N 84 33 E
Betul, India 40 J10 21 58N 77 59 E
Betung, Malaysia 36 D4 1 24N 111 31 E
Beulah, U.S.A. 80 B4 47 16N 101 47W
Beverley, Australia 61 F2 32 9S 116 56 E
Beverley, U.K. 10 D7 53 51N 0 26W
Beverly, Mass., U.S.A. 79 D14 42 33N 70 53W
Beverly, Wash., U.S.A. 82 C4 46 50N 119 56W
Beverly Hills, U.S.A. 85 L8 34 4N 118 25W
Beverwijk, Neths. 15 B4 52 28N 4 38 E
Beya, Russia 27 D10 52 40N 92 30 E
Beyānlū, Iran 44 C5 36 0N 47 51 E
Beyla, Guinea 50 G3 8 30N 8 38W
Beyneu, Kazakstan 25 E10 45 18N 55 9 E
Beypazan, Turkey 25 F5 40 10N 31 56 E
Beyşehir Gölü, Turkey 25 G5 37 41N 31 33 E
Bezhitsa, Russia 24 D5 53 19N 34 17 E
Béziers, France 18 E5 43 20N 3 12 E
Bezwada = Vijayawada, India 41 L12 16 31N 80 39 E
Bhachau, India 40 H7 23 20N 70 16 E
Bhadarwah, India 43 C6 32 58N 75 46 E
Bhadrakh, India 41 J15 21 10N 86 30 E
Bhadravati, India 40 N9 13 49N 75 40 E
Bhagalpur, India 43 G12 25 10N 87 0 E
Bhakkar, Pakistan 42 D4 31 40N 71 5 E
Bhakra Dam, India 42 D7 31 30N 76 45 E
Bhamo, Burma 41 G20 24 15N 97 15 E
Bhandara, India 40 J11 21 5N 79 42 E
Bhanrer Ra., India 42 H8 23 40N 79 45 E
Bharat = India ■, Asia 40 K11 20 0N 78 0 E
Bharatpur, India 42 F7 27 15N 77 30 E
Bhatinda, India 42 D6 30 15N 74 57 E
Bhatpara, India 43 H13 22 50N 88 25 E
Bhaun, Pakistan 42 C5 32 55N 72 40 E
Bhaunagar = Bhavnagar, India 42 J5 21 45N 72 10 E
Bhavnagar, India 42 J5 21 45N 72 10 E
Bhawanipatna, India 41 K12 19 55N 80 10 E
Bhera, Pakistan 42 C5 32 29N 72 57 E
Bhilsa = Vidisha, India 42 H7 23 28N 77 53 E
Bhilwara, India 42 G6 25 25N 74 38 E
Bhima →, India 40 L10 16 25N 77 17 E
Bhimavaram, India 41 L12 16 30N 81 30 E
Bhimbar, Pakistan 43 C6 32 59N 74 3 E
Bhind, India 43 F8 26 30N 78 46 E
Bhiwandi, India 40 K8 19 20N 73 0 E
Bhiwani, India 42 E7 28 50N 76 9 E
Bhola, Bangla. 41 H17 22 45N 90 35 E
Bhopal, India 42 H7 23 20N 77 30 E
Bhubaneshwar, India 41 J14 20 15N 85 50 E
Bhuj, India 42 H3 23 15N 69 49 E
Bhumiphol Dam = Phumiphon, Khuan, Thailand 38 D2 17 15N 98 58 E
Bhusaval, India 40 J9 21 3N 75 46 E
Bhutan ■, Asia 41 F17 27 25N 90 30 E
Biafra, B. of = Bonny, Bight of, Africa 52 D1 3 30N 9 20 E
Biak, Indonesia 37 E9 1 10S 136 6 E
Biała Podlaska, Poland 17 B12 52 4N 23 6 E
Białogard, Poland 16 A8 54 2N 15 58 E
Białystok, Poland 17 B12 53 10N 23 10 E
Bīārjmand, Iran 45 B7 36 6N 55 53 E
Biaro, Indonesia 37 D7 2 5N 125 26 E
Biarritz, France 18 E3 43 29N 1 33W
Bibai, Japan 30 C10 43 19N 141 52 E
Bibala, Angola 53 G2 14 44S 13 24 E
Bibby I., Canada 73 A10 61 55N 93 0W
Biberach, Germany 16 D5 48 5N 9 47 E
Bibiani, Ghana 50 G4 6 30N 2 8W
Biboohra, Australia 62 B4 16 56S 145 25 E
Bibungwa, Zaïre 54 C2 2 40S 28 15 E
Bic, Canada 71 C6 48 20N 68 41W
Bickerton I., Australia 62 A2 13 45S 136 10 E
Bicknell, Ind., U.S.A. 76 F2 38 47N 87 19W
Bicknell, Utah, U.S.A. 83 G8 38 20N 111 33W
Bida, Nigeria 50 G6 9 3N 5 58 E
Bidar, India 40 L10 17 55N 77 35 E
Biddeford, U.S.A. 71 D5 43 30N 70 28W
Bideford, U.K. 11 F3 51 1N 4 13W
Bidon 5 = Poste Maurice Cortier, Algeria 50 D5 22 14N 1 2 E
Bidor, Malaysia 39 K3 4 6N 101 15 E
Bié, Planalto de, Angola 53 G3 12 0S 16 0 E
Bieber, U.S.A. 82 F3 41 7N 121 8W
Biel, Switz. 16 E4 47 8N 7 14 E
Bielé Karpaty, Europe 17 D9 49 5N 18 0 E
Bielefeld, Germany 16 B5 52 1N 8 33 E
Biella, Italy 20 B3 45 34N 8 3 E
Bielsk Podlaski, Poland 17 B12 52 47N 23 12 E
Bielsko-Biała, Poland 17 D10 49 50N 19 2 E
Bien Hoa, Vietnam 39 G6 10 57N 106 49 E
Bienfait, Canada 73 D8 49 10N 102 50W
Bienne = Biel, Switz. 16 E4 47 8N 7 14 E
Bienville, L., Canada 70 A5 55 5N 72 40W
Biesiesfontein, S. Africa 56 E2 30 57S 17 58 E
Big →, Canada 71 B8 54 50N 58 55W
Big B., Canada 71 A7 55 43N 60 35W
Big Bear City, U.S.A. 85 L10 34 16N 116 51W
Big Bear Lake, U.S.A. 85 L10 34 15N 116 56W
Big Beaver, Canada 73 D7 49 10N 105 10W
Big Belt Mts., U.S.A. 82 C8 46 30N 111 25W
Big Bend, Swaziland 57 D5 26 50S 31 58 E
Big Bend National Park, U.S.A. 81 L3 29 20N 103 5W
Big Black →, U.S.A. 81 J9 32 3N 91 4W
Big Blue →, U.S.A. 80 F6 39 35N 96 34W
Big Cr. →, Canada 72 C4 51 42N 122 41W
Big Creek, U.S.A. 84 H7 37 11N 119 14W
Big Cypress Swamp, U.S.A. 77 M5 26 12N 81 10W
Big Falls, U.S.A. 80 A8 48 12N 93 48W
Big Fork →, U.S.A. 80 A8 48 31N 93 43W
Big Horn Mts. = Bighorn Mts., U.S.A. 82 D10 44 30N 107 30W
Big Lake, U.S.A. 81 K4 31 12N 101 28W
Big Moose, U.S.A. 79 C10 43 49N 74 58W
Big Muddy Cr. →, U.S.A. 80 A2 48 8N 104 36W
Big Pine, U.S.A. 83 H4 37 10N 118 17W
Big Piney, U.S.A. 82 E8 42 32N 110 7W
Big Quill L., Canada 73 C8 51 55N 104 50W
Big Rapids, U.S.A. 76 D3 43 42N 85 29W
Big River, Canada 73 C7 53 50N 107 0W
Big Run, U.S.A. 78 F6 40 57N 78 55W
Big Sable Pt., U.S.A. 76 C2 44 3N 86 1W
Big Sand L., Canada 73 B9 57 45N 99 45W
Big Sandy, U.S.A. 82 B8 48 11N 110 7W
Big Sandy Cr. →, U.S.A. 80 F3 38 7N 102 29W
Big Sioux →, U.S.A. 80 D6 42 29N 96 27W
Big Spring, U.S.A. 81 J4 32 15N 101 28W
Big Springs, U.S.A. 80 E3 41 4N 102 5W
Big Stone City, U.S.A. 80 C6 45 18N 96 28W
Big Stone Gap, U.S.A. 77 G4 36 52N 82 47W
Big Stone L., U.S.A. 80 C6 45 30N 96 35W
Big Sur, U.S.A. 84 J5 36 15N 121 48W
Big Timber, U.S.A. 82 D9 45 50N 109 57W
Big Trout L., Canada 70 B1 53 40N 90 0W
Biğa, Turkey 21 D12 40 13N 27 14 E
Bigadiç, Turkey 21 E13 39 22N 28 7 E
Bigfork, U.S.A. 82 B6 48 4N 114 4W
Biggar, Canada 73 C7 52 4N 108 0W
Biggar, U.K. 12 F5 55 38N 3 32W
Bigge I., Australia 60 B4 14 35S 125 10 E
Biggenden, Australia 63 D5 25 31S 152 4 E
Biggs, U.S.A. 84 F5 39 25N 121 43W
Bighorn, U.S.A. 82 C10 46 10N 107 27W
Bighorn →, U.S.A. 82 C10 46 10N 107 28W
Bighorn Mts., U.S.A. 82 D10 44 30N 107 30W
Bigstone L., Canada 73 C9 53 42N 95 44W
Bigwa, Tanzania 54 D4 7 10S 39 10 E
Bihać, Bos.-H. 16 F8 44 49N 15 57 E
Bihar, India 43 G11 25 5N 85 40 E

Bihar

106

107

Bristow

Bristow, *U.S.A.* **81 H6** 35 50N 96 23W
British Columbia □, *Canada* **72 C3** 55 0N 125 15W
British Isles, *Europe* **6 E5** 54 0N 4 0W
Brits, *S. Africa* **57 D4** 25 37S 27 48 E
Britstown, *S. Africa* **56 E3** 30 37S 23 30 E
Britt, *Canada* **70 C3** 45 46N 80 34W
Brittany = Bretagne, *France* **18 B2** 48 10N 3 0W
Britton, *U.S.A.* **80 C6** 45 48N 97 45W
Brive-la-Gaillarde, *France* **18 D4** 45 10N 1 32 E
Brixen = Bressanone, *Italy* **20 A4** 46 43N 11 39 E
Brixton, *Australia* **62 C3** 23 32S 144 57 E
Brlik, *Kazakstan* **26 E8** 43 40N 73 49 E
Brno, *Czech.* **17 D9** 49 10N 16 35 E
Broad →, *U.S.A.* **77 J5** 34 1N 81 4W
Broad Arrow, *Australia* **61 F3** 30 23S 121 15 E
Broad B., *U.K.* **12 C2** 58 14N 6 18W
Broad Haven, *Ireland* **13 B2** 54 20N 9 55W
Broad Law, *U.K.* **12 F5** 55 30N 3 21W
Broad Sd., *Australia* **62 C4** 22 0S 149 45 E
Broadhurst Ra., *Australia* **60 D3** 22 30S 122 30 E
Broads, The, *U.K.* **10 E9** 52 45N 1 30 E
Broadus, *U.S.A.* **80 C2** 45 27N 105 25W
Broadview, *Canada* **73 C8** 50 22N 102 35W
Brochet, *Canada* **73 B8** 57 53N 101 40W
Brochet, L., *Canada* **73 B8** 58 36N 101 35W
Brock, *Canada* **73 C7** 51 26N 108 43W
Brocken, *Germany* **16 C6** 51 47N 10 37 E
Brockport, *U.S.A.* **78 C7** 43 13N 77 56W
Brockton, *U.S.A.* **79 D13** 42 5N 71 1W
Brockville, *Canada* **70 D4** 44 35N 75 41W
Brockway, *Mont., U.S.A.* **80 B2** 47 18N 105 45W
Brockway, *Pa., U.S.A.* **78 E6** 41 15N 78 47W
Brocton, *U.S.A.* **78 D5** 42 23N 79 26W
Brodeur Pen., *Canada* **69 A11** 72 30N 88 10W
Brodick, *U.K.* **12 F3** 55 35N 5 9W
Brodnica, *Poland* **17 B10** 53 15N 19 25 E
Brody, *Ukraine* **17 C13** 50 5N 25 10 E
Brogan, *U.S.A.* **82 D5** 44 15N 117 31W
Broken Arrow, *U.S.A.* **81 G7** 36 3N 95 48W
Broken Bow, *Nebr., U.S.A.* **80 E5** 41 24N 99 38W
Broken Bow, *Okla., U.S.A.* **81 H7** 34 2N 94 44W
Broken Hill = Kabwe, *Zambia* **55 E2** 14 30S 28 29 E
Broken Hill, *Australia* **63 E3** 31 58S 141 29 E
Bromfield, *U.K.* **11 E5** 52 24N 2 45W
Bromley, *U.K.* **11 F8** 51 24N 0 2 E
Brønderslev, *Denmark* **9 H13** 57 16N 9 57 E
Bronkhorstspruit, *S. Africa* **57 D4** 25 46S 28 45 E
Brønnøysund, *Norway* **8 D15** 65 28N 12 14 E
Bronte, *U.S.A.* **81 K4** 31 53N 100 18W
Bronte Park, *Australia* **62 G4** 42 8S 146 30 E
Brook Park, *U.S.A.* **78 E4** 41 24N 80 51W
Brookfield, *U.S.A.* **80 F8** 39 47N 93 4W
Brookhaven, *U.S.A.* **81 K9** 31 35N 90 26W
Brookings, *Oreg., U.S.A.* **82 E1** 42 3N 124 17W
Brookings, *S. Dak., U.S.A.* **80 C6** 44 19N 96 48W
Brooklin, *Canada* **78 C6** 43 55N 78 55W
Brooklyn Park, *U.S.A.* **80 C8** 45 6N 93 23W
Brookmere, *Canada* **72 D4** 49 52N 120 53W
Brooks, *Canada* **72 C6** 50 35N 111 55W
Brooks B., *Canada* **72 C3** 50 15N 127 55W
Brooks L., *Canada* **73 A7** 61 55N 106 35W
Brooks Ra., *U.S.A.* **68 B5** 68 40N 147 0W
Brooksville, *U.S.A.* **77 L4** 28 33N 82 23W
Brookville, *U.S.A.* **76 F3** 39 25N 85 1W
Brooloo, *Australia* **63 D5** 26 30S 152 43 E
Broom, L., *U.K.* **12 D3** 57 55N 5 15W
Broome, *Australia* **60 C3** 18 0S 122 15 E
Broomehill, *Australia* **61 F2** 33 51S 117 39 E
Brora, *U.K.* **12 C5** 58 0N 3 52W
Brora →, *U.K.* **12 C5** 58 0N 3 51W
Brosna →, *Ireland* **13 C4** 53 14N 7 58W
Brothers, *U.S.A.* **82 E3** 43 49N 120 36W
Brough, *U.K.* **10 C5** 54 32N 2 18W
Broughton Island, *Canada* **69 B13** 67 33N 63 0W
Broughty Ferry, *U.K.* **12 E6** 56 29N 2 51W
Brouwershaven, *Neths.* **15 C3** 51 45N 3 55 E
Browerville, *U.S.A.* **80 B7** 46 5N 94 52W
Brown, Pt., *Australia* **63 E1** 32 32S 133 50 E
Brown Willy, *U.K.* **11 G3** 50 35N 4 37W
Brownfield, *U.S.A.* **81 J3** 33 11N 102 17W
Browning, *U.S.A.* **82 B7** 48 34N 113 1W
Brownlee, *Canada* **73 C7** 50 43N 106 1W
Brownsville, *Oreg., U.S.A.* **82 D2** 44 24N 122 59W
Brownsville, *Tenn., U.S.A.* **81 H10** 35 36N 89 16W
Brownsville, *Tex., U.S.A.* **81 N6** 25 54N 97 30W
Brownwood, *U.S.A.* **81 K5** 31 43N 98 59W
Brownwood, L., *U.S.A.* **81 K5** 31 51N 98 35W
Browse I., *Australia* **60 B3** 14 7S 123 33 E
Bruas, *Malaysia* **39 K3** 4 30N 100 47 E
Bruay-en-Artois, *France* **18 A5** 50 29N 2 33 E
Bruce, Mt., *Australia* **60 D2** 22 37S 118 8 E
Bruce Pen., *Canada* **78 A3** 45 0N 81 30W
Bruce Rock, *Australia* **61 F2** 31 52S 118 8 E
Bruck an der Leitha, *Austria* **17 D9** 48 1N 16 47 E
Bruck an der Mur, *Austria* **16 E8** 47 24N 15 16 E
Brue →, *U.K.* **11 F5** 51 13N 2 59W
Bruges = Brugge, *Belgium* **15 C3** 51 13N 3 13 E
Brugge, *Belgium* **15 C3** 51 13N 3 13 E
Brûlé, *Canada* **72 C5** 53 15N 117 58W
Brumado, *Brazil* **93 F10** 14 14S 41 40W
Brumunddal, *Norway* **9 F14** 60 53N 10 56 E
Brunchilly, *Australia* **62 B1** 18 50S 134 30 E
Brundidge, *U.S.A.* **77 K3** 31 43N 85 49W
Bruneau, *U.S.A.* **82 E6** 42 53N 115 48W
Bruneau →, *U.S.A.* **82 E6** 42 56N 115 57W
Brunei = Bandar Seri Begawan, *Brunei* **36 C4** 4 52N 115 0 E
Brunei ■, *Asia* **36 D4** 4 50N 115 0 E
Brunette Downs, *Australia* **62 B2** 18 40S 135 55 E
Brunner, L., *N.Z.* **59 K3** 42 37S 171 27 E
Bruno, *Canada* **73 C7** 52 20N 105 30W
Brunswick = Braunschweig, *Germany* **16 B6** 52 15N 10 31 E
Brunswick, *Ga., U.S.A.* **77 K5** 31 10N 81 30W
Brunswick, *Maine, U.S.A.* **71 D6** 43 55N 69 58W
Brunswick, *Md., U.S.A.* **76 F7** 39 19N 77 38W
Brunswick, *Mo., U.S.A.* **80 F8** 39 26N 93 8W
Brunswick, *Ohio, U.S.A.* **78 E3** 41 14N 81 51W
Brunswick, Pen. de, *Chile* **96 G2** 53 30S 71 30W
Brunswick B., *Australia* **60 C3** 15 15S 124 50 E
Brunswick Junction, *Australia* **61 F2** 33 15S 115 50 E
Bruny I., *Australia* **62 G4** 43 20S 147 15 E
Brus Laguna, *Honduras* **88 C3** 15 47N 84 35W
Brush, *U.S.A.* **80 E3** 40 15N 103 37W
Brushton, *U.S.A.* **79 B10** 44 50N 74 31W
Brusque, *Brazil* **95 B6** 27 5S 49 0W
Brussel, *Belgium* **15 D4** 50 51N 4 21 E
Brussels = Brussel, *Belgium* **15 D4** 50 51N 4 21 E
Brussels, *Canada* **78 C3** 43 44N 81 15W
Bruthen, *Australia* **63 F4** 37 42S 147 50 E
Bruxelles = Brussel, *Belgium* **15 D4** 50 51N 4 21 E
Bryan, *Ohio, U.S.A.* **76 E3** 41 28N 84 33W
Bryan, *Tex., U.S.A.* **81 K6** 30 40N 96 22W
Bryan, Mt., *Australia* **63 E2** 33 30S 139 0 E
Bryansk, *Russia* **24 D5** 53 13N 34 25 E
Bryant, *U.S.A.* **80 C6** 44 35N 97 28W
Bryne, *Norway* **9 G11** 58 44N 5 38 E
Bryson City, *U.S.A.* **77 H4** 35 26N 83 27W
Bsharri, *Lebanon* **47 A5** 34 15N 36 0 E
Bū Baqarah, *U.A.E.* **45 E8** 25 35N 56 25 E
Bu Craa, *W. Sahara* **50 C2** 26 45N 12 50W
Bū Ḩasā, *U.A.E.* **45 F7** 23 30N 53 20 E
Bua Yai, *Thailand* **38 E4** 15 33N 102 26 E
Buapinang, *Indonesia* **37 E6** 4 40S 121 30 E
Buayan, *Phil.* **37 C7** 6 3N 125 6 E
Bubanza, *Burundi* **54 C2** 3 6S 29 23 E
Būbiyān, *Kuwait* **45 D6** 29 45N 48 15 E
Bucaramanga, *Colombia* **92 B4** 7 0N 73 0W
Buccaneer Arch., *Australia* **60 C3** 16 7S 123 20 E
Buchach, *Ukraine* **17 D13** 49 5N 25 25 E
Buchan, *U.K.* **12 D6** 57 32N 2 21W
Buchan Ness, *U.K.* **12 D7** 57 29N 1 46W
Buchanan, *Canada* **73 C8** 51 40N 102 45W
Buchanan, *Liberia* **50 G2** 5 57N 10 2W
Buchanan, L., *Queens., Australia* **62 C4** 21 35S 145 52 E
Buchanan, L., *W. Austral., Australia* **61 E3** 25 33S 123 2 E
Buchanan, L., *U.S.A.* **81 K5** 30 45N 98 25W
Buchanan Cr. →, *Australia* **62 B2** 19 13S 136 33 E
Buchans, *Canada* **71 C8** 48 50N 56 52W
Bucharest = Bucureşti, *Romania* **17 F14** 44 27N 26 10 E
Buchon, Pt., *U.S.A.* **84 K6** 35 15N 120 54W
Buckeye, *U.S.A.* **83 K7** 33 22N 112 35W
Buckhannon, *U.S.A.* **76 F5** 39 0N 80 8W
Buckhaven, *U.K.* **12 E5** 56 11N 3 3W
Buckie, *U.K.* **12 D6** 57 41N 2 58W
Buckingham, *Canada* **70 C4** 45 37N 75 24W
Buckingham, *U.K.* **11 F7** 51 59N 0 57W
Buckingham B., *Australia* **62 A2** 12 10S 135 40 E
Buckinghamshire □, *U.K.* **11 F7** 51 53N 0 55W
Buckle Hd., *Australia* **60 B4** 14 26S 127 52 E
Buckleboo, *Australia* **63 E2** 32 54S 136 12 E
Buckley, *U.S.A.* **82 C2** 47 10N 122 2W
Buckley →, *Australia* **62 C2** 20 10S 138 49 E
Bucklin, *U.S.A.* **81 G5** 37 33N 99 38W
Bucks L., *U.S.A.* **84 F5** 39 54N 121 12W
Buctouche, *Canada* **71 C7** 46 30N 64 45W
Bucureşti, *Romania* **17 F14** 44 27N 26 10 E
Bucyrus, *U.S.A.* **76 E4** 40 48N 82 59W
Budalin, *Burma* **41 H19** 22 20N 95 10 E
Budapest, *Hungary* **17 E10** 47 29N 19 5 E
Budaun, *India* **43 E8** 28 5N 79 10 E
Budd Coast, *Antarctica* **5 C8** 68 0S 112 0 E
Bude, *U.K.* **11 G3** 50 49N 4 34W
Budennovsk, *Russia* **25 F7** 44 50N 44 10 E
Budge Budge = Baj Baj, *India* **43 H13** 22 30N 88 5 E
Budgewoi, *Australia* **63 E5** 33 13S 151 34 E
Budjala, *Zaïre* **52 D3** 2 50N 19 40 E
Buellton, *U.S.A.* **85 L6** 34 37N 120 12W
Buena Park, *U.S.A.* **85 M9** 33 52N 117 59W
Buena Vista, *Colo., U.S.A.* **83 G10** 38 51N 106 8W
Buena Vista, *Va., U.S.A.* **76 G6** 37 44N 79 21W
Buena Vista L., *U.S.A.* **85 K7** 35 12N 119 18W
Buenaventura, *Colombia* **92 C3** 3 53N 77 4W
Buenaventura, *Mexico* **86 B3** 29 50N 107 30W
Buenos Aires, *Argentina* **94 C4** 34 30S 58 20W
Buenos Aires, *Costa Rica* **88 E3** 9 10N 83 20W
Buenos Aires □, *Argentina* **94 D4** 36 30S 60 0W
Buenos Aires, L., *Chile* **96 F2** 46 35S 72 30W
Buffalo, *Mo., U.S.A.* **81 G8** 37 39N 93 6W
Buffalo, *N.Y., U.S.A.* **78 D6** 42 53N 78 53W
Buffalo, *Okla., U.S.A.* **81 G5** 36 50N 99 38W
Buffalo, *S. Dak., U.S.A.* **80 C3** 45 35N 103 33W
Buffalo, *Wyo., U.S.A.* **82 D10** 44 21N 106 42W
Buffalo →, *Canada* **72 A5** 60 5N 115 5W
Buffalo Head Hills, *Canada* **72 B5** 57 25N 115 55W
Buffalo L., *Canada* **72 C6** 52 27N 112 54W
Buffalo Narrows, *Canada* **73 B7** 55 51N 108 29W
Buffels →, *S. Africa* **56 D2** 29 36S 17 3 E
Buford, *U.S.A.* **77 H4** 34 10N 84 0W
Bug → = Buh →, *Ukraine* **25 E5** 46 59N 31 58 E
Bug →, *Poland* **17 B11** 52 31N 21 5 E
Buga, *Colombia* **92 C3** 4 0N 76 15W
Buganda, *Uganda* **54 C3** 0 0 31 30 E
Buganga, *Uganda* **54 C3** 0 3N 32 0 E
Bugel, Tanjung, *Indonesia* **36 F4** 6 26S 111 3 E
Bugibba, *Malta* **23 D1** 35 57N 14 25 E
Bugsuk, *Phil.* **36 C5** 8 15N 117 15 E
Bugulma, *Russia* **24 D9** 54 33N 52 48 E
Bugun Shara, *Mongolia* **32 B5** 49 0N 104 0 E
Buguruslan, *Russia* **24 D9** 53 39N 52 26 E
Buh →, *Ukraine* **25 E5** 46 59N 31 58 E
Buheirat-Murrat-el-Kubra, *Egypt* **51 B11** 30 18N 32 26 E
Buhl, *Idaho, U.S.A.* **82 E6** 42 36N 114 46W
Buhl, *Minn., U.S.A.* **80 B8** 47 30N 92 46W
Buick, *U.S.A.* **81 G9** 37 38N 91 2W
Builth Wells, *U.K.* **11 E4** 52 9N 3 25W
Buir Nur, *Mongolia* **33 B6** 47 50N 117 42 E
Bujumbura, *Burundi* **54 C2** 3 16S 29 18 E
Bukachacha, *Russia* **27 D12** 52 55N 116 50 E
Bukama, *Zaïre* **55 D2** 9 10S 25 50 E
Bukavu, *Zaïre* **54 C2** 2 20S 28 52 E
Bukene, *Tanzania* **54 C3** 4 15S 32 48 E
Bukhara = Bukhoro, *Uzbekistan* **26 F7** 39 48N 64 25 E
Bukhoro, *Uzbekistan* **26 F7** 39 48N 64 25 E
Bukima, *Tanzania* **54 C3** 1 50S 33 25 E
Bukit Mertajam, *Malaysia* **39 K3** 5 22N 100 28 E
Bukittinggi, *Indonesia* **36 E2** 0 20S 100 20 E
Bukoba, *Tanzania* **54 C3** 1 20S 31 49 E
Bukoba □, *Tanzania* **54 C3** 1 30S 32 0 E
Bukuya, *Uganda* **54 B3** 0 40N 31 52 E
Bula, *Indonesia* **37 E8** 3 6S 130 30 E
Bulahdelah, *Australia* **63 E5** 32 23S 152 13 E
Bulan, *Phil.* **37 B6** 12 40N 123 52 E
Bulandshahr, *India* **42 E7** 28 28N 77 51 E
Bulawayo, *Zimbabwe* **55 G2** 20 7S 28 32 E
Buldan, *Turkey* **21 E13** 38 2N 28 50 E
Bulgaria ■, *Europe* **21 C11** 42 35N 25 30 E
Bulgroo, *Australia* **63 D3** 25 47S 143 58 E
Bulgunnia, *Australia* **63 E1** 30 10S 134 53 E
Bulhar, *Somali Rep.* **46 E3** 10 25N 44 30 E
Buli, Teluk, *Indonesia* **37 D7** 1 5N 128 25 E
Buliluyan, C., *Phil.* **36 C5** 8 20N 117 15 E
Bulkley →, *Canada* **72 B3** 55 15N 127 40W
Bull Shoals L., *U.S.A.* **81 G8** 36 22N 92 35W
Bullara, *Australia* **60 D1** 22 40S 114 3 E
Bullaring, *Australia* **61 F2** 32 30S 117 45 E
Bulli, *Australia* **63 E5** 34 15S 150 57 E
Bullock Creek, *Australia* **62 B3** 17 43S 144 31 E
Bulloo →, *Australia* **63 D3** 28 43S 142 30 E
Bulloo Downs, *Queens., Australia* **63 D3** 28 31S 142 57 E
Bulloo Downs, *W. Austral., Australia* **60 D2** 24 0S 119 32 E
Bulloo L., *Australia* **63 D3** 28 43S 142 25 E
Bulls, *N.Z.* **59 J5** 40 10S 175 24 E
Bulnes, *Chile* **94 D1** 36 42S 72 19W
Bulo Burti, *Somali Rep.* **46 G4** 3 50N 45 33 E
Bulsar = Valsad, *India* **40 J8** 20 40N 72 58 E
Bultfontein, *S. Africa* **56 D4** 28 18S 26 10 E
Bulukumba, *Indonesia* **37 F6** 5 33S 120 11 E
Bulun, *Russia* **27 B13** 70 37N 127 30 E
Bulus, *Russia* **27 C13** 63 10N 129 10 E
Bumba, *Zaïre* **52 D4** 2 13N 22 30 E
Bumbiri I., *Tanzania* **54 C3** 1 40S 31 55 E
Bumhpa Bum, *Burma* **41 F20** 26 51N 97 14 E
Bumi →, *Zimbabwe* **55 F2** 17 0S 28 20 E
Buna, *Kenya* **54 B4** 2 58N 39 30 E
Bunazi, *Tanzania* **54 C3** 1 3S 31 23 E
Bunbah, Khalīj, *Libya* **51 B9** 32 20N 23 15 E
Bunbury, *Australia* **61 F2** 33 20S 115 35 E
Buncrana, *Ireland* **13 A4** 55 8N 7 27W
Bundaberg, *Australia* **63 C5** 24 54S 152 22 E
Bundey →, *Australia* **62 C2** 21 46S 135 37 E
Bundi, *India* **42 G6** 25 30N 75 35 E
Bundooma, *Australia* **62 C1** 24 54S 134 16 E
Bundoran, *Ireland* **13 B3** 54 28N 8 16W
Bung Kan, *Thailand* **38 C4** 18 23N 103 37 E
Bungatakada, *Japan* **31 H5** 33 35N 131 25 E
Bungil Cr. →, *Australia* **62 D4** 27 5S 149 5 E
Bungo-Suidō, *Japan* **31 H6** 33 0N 132 15 E
Bungoma, *Kenya* **54 B3** 0 34N 34 34 E
Bungu, *Tanzania* **54 D4** 7 35S 39 0 E
Bunia, *Zaïre* **54 B3** 1 35N 30 20 E
Bunji, *Pakistan* **43 B6** 35 45N 74 40 E
Bunkie, *U.S.A.* **81 K8** 30 57N 92 11W
Bunnell, *U.S.A.* **77 L5** 29 28N 81 16W
Buntok, *Indonesia* **36 E4** 1 40S 114 58 E
Bunyu, *Indonesia* **36 D5** 3 35N 117 50 E
Buol, *Indonesia* **37 D6** 1 15N 121 32 E
Buon Brieng, *Vietnam* **38 F7** 13 9N 108 12 E
Buon Me Thuot, *Vietnam* **38 F7** 12 40N 108 3 E
Buong Long, *Cambodia* **38 F6** 13 44N 106 59 E
Buorkhaya, Mys, *Russia* **27 B14** 71 50N 132 40 E
Buqayq, *Si. Arabia* **45 E6** 26 0N 49 45 E
Bur Acaba, *Somali Rep.* **46 G3** 3 12N 44 20 E
Bûr Safâga, *Egypt* **51 C11** 26 43N 33 57 E
Bûr Sa'îd, *Egypt* **51 B11** 31 16N 32 18 E
Bûr Sûdân, *Sudan* **51 E12** 19 32N 37 9 E
Bura, *Kenya* **54 C4** 1 4S 39 58 E
Burao, *Somali Rep.* **46 F4** 9 32N 45 32 E
Burāq, *Syria* **47 B5** 33 11N 36 29 E
Buras, *U.S.A.* **81 L10** 29 22N 89 32W
Buraydah, *Si. Arabia* **44 E5** 26 20N 44 8 E
Burbank, *U.S.A.* **85 L8** 34 11N 118 19W
Burcher, *Australia* **63 E4** 33 30S 147 16 E
Burdekin →, *Australia* **62 B4** 19 38S 147 25 E
Burdett, *Canada* **72 D6** 49 50N 111 32W
Burdur, *Turkey* **25 G5** 37 45N 30 17 E
Burdwan = Barddhaman, *India* **43 H12** 23 14N 87 39 E
Bure →, *U.K.* **10 E9** 52 38N 1 43 E
Bureya →, *Russia* **27 E13** 49 27N 129 30 E
Burford, *Canada* **78 C4** 43 7N 80 27W
Burgas, *Bulgaria* **21 C12** 42 33N 27 29 E
Burgeo, *Canada* **71 C8** 47 37N 57 38W
Burgersdorp, *S. Africa* **56 E4** 31 0S 26 20 E
Burges, Mt., *Australia* **61 F3** 30 50S 121 5 E
Burgos, *Spain* **19 A4** 42 21N 3 41W
Burgsvik, *Sweden* **9 H18** 57 3N 18 19 E
Burgundy = Bourgogne, *France* **18 C6** 47 0N 4 50 E
Burhaniye, *Turkey* **21 E12** 39 30N 26 58 E
Burhanpur, *India* **40 J10** 21 18N 76 14 E
Burias, *Phil.* **37 B6** 12 55N 123 5 E
Burica, Pta., *Costa Rica* **88 E3** 8 3N 82 51W
Burigi, L., *Tanzania* **54 C3** 2 2S 31 22 E
Burin, *Canada* **71 C8** 47 1N 55 14W
Buriram, *Thailand* **38 E4** 15 0N 103 0 E
Burj Sāfitā, *Syria* **44 C3** 34 48N 36 7 E
Burji, *Ethiopia* **51 G12** 5 29N 37 51 E
Burkburnett, *U.S.A.* **81 H5** 34 6N 98 34W
Burke, *U.S.A.* **82 C6** 47 31N 115 49W
Burke →, *Australia* **62 C2** 23 12S 139 33 E
Burketown, *Australia* **62 B2** 17 45S 139 33 E
Burkina Faso ■, *Africa* **50 F4** 12 0N 1 0W
Burk's Falls, *Canada* **70 C4** 45 37N 79 24W
Burley, *U.S.A.* **82 E7** 42 32N 113 48W
Burlingame, *U.S.A.* **84 H4** 37 35N 122 21W
Burlington, *Canada* **78 C5** 43 18N 79 45W
Burlington, *Colo., U.S.A.* **80 F3** 39 18N 102 16W
Burlington, *Iowa, U.S.A.* **80 E9** 40 49N 91 14W
Burlington, *Kans., U.S.A.* **80 F7** 38 12N 95 45W
Burlington, *N.C., U.S.A.* **77 G6** 36 6N 79 26W
Burlington, *N.J., U.S.A.* **79 F10** 40 4N 74 51W
Burlington, *Vt., U.S.A.* **79 B11** 44 29N 73 12W
Burlington, *Wash., U.S.A.* **84 B4** 48 28N 122 20W
Burlington, *Wis., U.S.A.* **76 D1** 42 41N 88 17W
Burlyu-Tyube, *Kazakstan* **26 E8** 46 30N 79 10 E
Burma ■, *Asia* **41 J20** 21 0N 96 30 E
Burnaby I., *Canada* **72 C2** 52 25N 131 19W
Burnet, *U.S.A.* **81 K5** 30 45N 98 14W
Burney, *U.S.A.* **82 F3** 40 53N 121 40W
Burngup, *Australia* **61 F2** 33 2S 118 42 E
Burnham, *U.S.A.* **78 F7** 40 38N 77 34W
Burnie, *Australia* **62 G4** 41 4S 145 56 E
Burnley, *U.K.* **10 D5** 53 47N 2 14W
Burns, *Oreg., U.S.A.* **82 E4** 43 35N 119 3W
Burns, *Wyo., U.S.A.* **80 E2** 41 12N 104 21W
Burns Lake, *Canada* **72 C3** 54 20N 125 45W
Burnside →, *Canada* **68 B9** 66 51N 108 4W
Burnside, L., *Australia* **61 E3** 25 22S 123 0 E
Burnsville, *U.S.A.* **80 C8** 44 47N 93 17W
Burnt River, *Canada* **78 B6** 44 41N 78 42W
Burntwood →, *Canada* **73 B9** 56 8N 96 34W
Burntwood L., *Canada* **73 B8** 55 22N 100 26W
Burqān, *Kuwait* **44 D5** 29 0N 47 57 E
Burra, *Australia* **63 E2** 33 40S 138 55 E
Burramurra, *Australia* **62 C2** 20 25S 137 15 E
Burren Junction, *Australia* **63 E4** 30 7S 148 59 E
Burrendong Dam, *Australia* **63 E4** 32 39S 149 6 E
Burrinjuck Res., *Australia* **63 F4** 35 0S 148 36 E
Burro, Serranías del, *Mexico* **86 B4** 29 0N 102 0W
Burruyacú, *Argentina* **94 B3** 26 30S 64 40W
Burry Port, *U.K.* **11 F3** 51 41N 4 15W
Bursa, *Turkey* **21 D13** 40 15N 29 5 E
Burstall, *Canada* **73 C7** 50 39N 109 54W
Burton L., *Canada* **70 B4** 54 45N 78 20W
Burton upon Trent, *U.K.* **10 E6** 52 48N 1 38W
Burtundy, *Australia* **63 E3** 33 45S 142 15 E
Buru, *Indonesia* **37 E7** 3 30S 126 30 E
Burûn, Râs, *Egypt* **47 D2** 31 14N 33 7 E
Burundi ■, *Africa* **54 C3** 3 15S 30 0 E
Bururi, *Burundi* **54 C2** 3 57S 29 37 E
Burutu, *Nigeria* **50 G6** 5 20N 5 29 E
Burwell, *U.S.A.* **80 E5** 41 47N 99 8W
Bury, *U.K.* **10 D5** 53 35N 2 17W
Bury St. Edmunds, *U.K.* **11 E8** 52 15N 0 43 E
Buryatia □, *Russia* **27 D11** 53 0N 110 0 E
Busango Swamp, *Zambia* **55 E2** 14 15S 25 45 E
Buşayrah, *Syria* **44 C4** 35 9N 40 26 E
Buşayyah, *Iraq* **44 D5** 30 0N 46 10 E
Būshehr, *Iran* **45 D6** 28 55N 50 55 E
Būshehr □, *Iran* **45 D6** 28 20N 51 45 E
Bushell, *Canada* **73 B7** 59 31N 108 45W
Bushenyi, *Uganda* **54 C3** 0 35S 30 10 E
Bushire = Būshehr, *Iran* **45 D6** 28 55N 50 55 E
Bushnell, *Ill., U.S.A.* **80 E9** 40 33N 90 31W
Bushnell, *Nebr., U.S.A.* **80 E3** 41 14N 103 54W
Busia □, *Kenya* **54 B3** 0 25N 34 6 E
Businga, *Zaïre* **52 D4** 3 16N 20 59 E
Busra ash Shām, *Syria* **47 C5** 32 30N 36 25 E
Busselton, *Australia* **61 F2** 33 42S 115 15 E
Bussum, *Neths.* **15 B5** 52 16N 5 10 E
Busto Arsizio, *Italy* **20 B3** 45 37N 8 51 E
Busu-Djanoa, *Zaïre* **52 D4** 1 43N 21 23 E
Busuanga, *Phil.* **37 B5** 12 10N 120 0 E
Buta, *Zaïre* **54 B1** 2 50N 24 53 E
Butare, *Rwanda* **54 C2** 2 31S 29 52 E
Butaritari, *Kiribati* **64 G9** 3 30N 174 0 E
Bute, *U.K.* **12 F3** 55 48N 5 2W
Bute Inlet, *Canada* **72 C4** 50 40N 124 53W
Butemba, *Uganda* **54 B3** 1 9N 31 37 E
Butembo, *Zaïre* **54 B2** 0 9N 29 18 E
Butha Qi, *China* **33 B7** 48 0N 122 32 E
Butiaba, *Uganda* **54 B3** 1 50N 31 20 E
Butler, *Mo., U.S.A.* **80 F7** 38 16N 94 20W
Butler, *Pa., U.S.A.* **78 F5** 40 52N 79 54W
Buton, *Indonesia* **37 E6** 5 0S 122 45 E
Butte, *Mont., U.S.A.* **82 C7** 46 0N 112 32W
Butte, *Nebr., U.S.A.* **80 D5** 42 58N 98 51W
Butte Creek →, *U.S.A.* **84 F5** 39 12N 121 56W
Butterworth = Gcuwa, *S. Africa* **57 E4** 32 20S 28 11 E
Butterworth, *Malaysia* **39 K3** 5 24N 100 23 E
Buttfield, Mt., *Australia* **61 D4** 24 45S 128 9 E
Button B., *Canada* **73 B10** 58 45N 94 23W
Buttonwillow, *U.S.A.* **85 K7** 35 24N 119 28W
Butty Hd., *Australia* **61 F3** 33 54S 121 39 E
Butuan, *Phil.* **37 C7** 8 57N 125 33 E
Butung = Buton, *Indonesia* **37 E6** 5 0S 122 45 E
Buturlinovka, *Russia* **25 D7** 50 50N 40 35 E
Buxar, *India* **43 G10** 25 34N 83 58 E
Buxtehude, *Germany* **16 B5** 53 28N 9 39 E
Buxton, *U.K.* **10 D6** 53 16N 1 54W
Buy, *Russia* **24 C7** 58 28N 41 28 E
Büyük Menderes →, *Turkey* **21 F12** 37 28N 27 11 E
Büyükçekmece, *Turkey* **21 D13** 41 2N 28 35 E
Buzău, *Romania* **17 F14** 45 10N 26 50 E
Buzău →, *Romania* **17 F14** 45 26N 27 44 E
Buzen, *Japan* **31 H5** 33 35N 131 5 E
Buzi →, *Mozam.* **55 F3** 19 50S 34 43 E
Buzuluk, *Russia* **24 D9** 52 48N 52 12 E
Buzzards Bay, *U.S.A.* **79 E14** 41 45N 70 37W
Bwana Mkubwe, *Zaïre* **55 E2** 13 8S 28 38 E
Byarezina →, *Belarus* **17 B16** 52 33N 30 14 E
Bydgoszcz, *Poland* **17 B9** 53 10N 18 0 E
Byelarus = Belarus ■, *Europe* **17 B14** 53 30N 27 0 E
Byelorussia = Belarus ■, *Europe* **17 B14** 53 30N 27 0 E
Byers, *U.S.A.* **80 F2** 39 43N 104 14W
Byesville, *U.S.A.* **78 G3** 39 58N 81 32W
Byhalia, *U.S.A.* **81 H10** 34 52N 89 41W
Bykhaw, *Belarus* **17 B16** 53 31N 30 14 E
Bykhov = Bykhaw, *Belarus* **17 B16** 53 31N 30 14 E
Bylas, *U.S.A.* **83 K8** 33 8N 110 7W
Bylot I., *Canada* **69 A12** 73 13N 78 34W
Byrd, C., *Antarctica* **5 C17** 69 38S 76 7W
Byro, *Australia* **61 E2** 26 5S 116 11 E
Byrock, *Australia* **63 E4** 30 40S 146 27 E
Byron Bay, *Australia* **63 D5** 28 43S 153 37 E
Byrranga, Gory, *Russia* **27 B11** 75 0N 100 0 E

Cape York Peninsula

Byrranga Mts. = Byrranga, Gory, *Russia* **27 B11** 75 0N 100 0 E
Byske, *Sweden* **8 D19** 64 57N 21 11 E
Byske älv →, *Sweden* **8 D19** 64 57N 21 13 E
Bytom, *Poland* **17 C10** 50 25N 18 54 E
Bytów, *Poland* **17 A9** 54 10N 17 30 E
Byumba, *Rwanda* **54 C3** 1 35S 30 4 E

C

Ca →, *Vietnam* **38 C5** 18 45N 105 45 E
Ca Mau = Quan Long, *Vietnam* **39 H5** 9 7N 105 8 E
Ca Mau, Mui = Bai Bung, Mui, *Vietnam* **39 H5** 8 38N 104 44 E
Ca Na, *Vietnam* **39 G7** 11 20N 108 54 E
Caacupé, *Paraguay* **94 B4** 25 23S 57 5W
Caála, *Angola* **53 G3** 12 46S 15 30 E
Caamano Sd., *Canada* **72 C3** 52 55N 129 25W
Caazapá, *Paraguay* **94 B4** 26 8S 56 19W
Caazapá □, *Paraguay* **95 B4** 26 10S 56 0W
Caballeria, C. de, *Spain* **22 A11** 40 5N 4 5 E
Cabanatuan, *Phil.* **37 A6** 15 30N 120 58 E
Cabano, *Canada* **71 C6** 47 40N 68 56W
Cabazon, *U.S.A.* **85 M10** 33 55N 116 47W
Cabedelo, *Brazil* **93 E12** 7 0S 34 50W
Cabildo, *Chile* **94 C1** 32 30S 71 5W
Cabimas, *Venezuela* **92 A4** 10 23N 71 25W
Cabinda, *Angola* **52 F2** 5 33S 12 11 E
Cabinda □, *Angola* **52 F2** 5 0S 12 30 E
Cabinet Mts., *U.S.A.* **82 C6** 48 0N 115 30W
Cabo Blanco, *Argentina* **96 F3** 47 15S 65 47W
Cabo Frio, *Brazil* **95 A7** 22 51S 42 3W
Cabo Pantoja, *Peru* **92 D3** 1 0S 75 10W
Cabonga, Réservoir, *Canada* **70 C4** 47 20N 76 40W
Cabool, *U.S.A.* **81 G8** 37 7N 92 6W
Caboolture, *Australia* **63 D5** 27 5S 152 58 E
Cabora Bassa Dam = Cahora Bassa Dam, *Mozam.* **55 F3** 15 20S 32 50 E
Caborca, *Mexico* **86 A2** 30 40N 112 10W
Cabot, Mt., *U.S.A.* **79 B13** 44 30N 71 25W
Cabot Str., *Canada* **71 C8** 47 15N 59 40W
Cabra, *Spain* **19 D3** 37 30N 4 28W
Cabrera, *Spain* **22 B9** 39 8N 2 57 E
Cabri, *Canada* **73 C7** 50 35N 108 25W
Cabriel →, *Spain* **19 C5** 39 14N 1 3W
Čačak, *Serbia, Yug.* **21 C9** 43 54N 20 20 E
Cáceres, *Brazil* **92 G7** 16 5S 57 40W
Cáceres, *Spain* **19 C2** 39 26N 6 23W
Cache Bay, *Canada* **70 C4** 46 22N 80 0W
Cache Cr. →, *U.S.A.* **84 G5** 38 42N 121 42W
Cachi, *Argentina* **94 B2** 25 5S 66 10W
Cachimbo, Serra do, *Brazil* **93 E7** 9 30S 55 30W
Cachoeira, *Brazil* **93 F11** 12 30S 39 0W
Cachoeira de Itapemirim, *Brazil* **95 A7** 20 51S 41 7W
Cachoeira do Sul, *Brazil* **95 C5** 30 3S 52 53W
Cacólo, *Angola* **52 G3** 10 9S 19 21 E
Caconda, *Angola* **53 G3** 13 48S 15 8 E
Cacongo, *Angola* **52 F2** 5 11S 12 5 E
Caddo, *U.S.A.* **81 H6** 34 7N 96 16W
Cadell Cr. →, *Australia* **62 C3** 22 35S 141 51 E
Cader Idris, *U.K.* **10 E4** 52 42N 3 53W
Cadibarrawirracanna, L., *Australia* **63 D2** 28 52S 135 27 E
Cadillac, *Canada* **70 C4** 48 14N 78 23W
Cadillac, *U.S.A.* **76 C3** 44 15N 85 24W
Cadiz, *Phil.* **37 B6** 10 57N 123 15 E
Cádiz, *Spain* **19 D2** 36 30N 6 20W
Cadiz, *U.S.A.* **78 F4** 40 22N 81 0W
Cádiz, G. de, *Spain* **19 D2** 36 40N 7 0W
Cadney Park, *Australia* **63 D1** 27 55S 134 3 E
Cadomin, *Canada* **72 C5** 53 2N 117 20W
Cadotte →, *Canada* **72 B5** 56 43N 117 10W
Cadoux, *Australia* **61 F2** 30 46S 117 7 E
Caen, *France* **18 B3** 49 10N 0 22W
Caernarfon, *U.K.* **10 D3** 53 8N 4 16W
Caernarfon B., *U.K.* **10 D3** 53 4N 4 40W
Caernarvon = Caernarfon, *U.K.* **10 D3** 53 8N 4 16W
Caerphilly, *U.K.* **11 F4** 51 35N 3 13W
Caerphilly □, *U.K.* **11 F4** 51 37N 3 12W
Caesarea, *Israel* **47 C3** 32 30N 34 53 E
Caeté, *Brazil* **93 G10** 19 55S 43 40W
Caetité, *Brazil* **93 F10** 13 50S 42 32W
Cafayate, *Argentina* **94 B2** 26 2S 66 0W
Cafu, *Angola* **56 B2** 16 30S 15 8 E
Cagayan →, *Phil.* **37 A6** 18 25N 121 42 E
Cagayan de Oro, *Phil.* **37 C6** 8 30N 124 40 E
Cágliari, *Italy* **20 E3** 39 13N 9 7 E
Cágliari, G. di, *Italy* **20 E3** 39 8N 9 11 E
Caguas, *Puerto Rico* **89 C6** 18 14N 66 2W
Caha Mts., *Ireland* **13 E2** 51 45N 9 40W
Cahama, *Angola* **56 B1** 16 17S 14 19 E
Caher, *Ireland* **13 D4** 52 22N 7 56W
Caherciveen, *Ireland* **13 E1** 51 56N 10 14W
Cahora Bassa Dam, *Mozam.* **55 F3** 15 20S 32 50 E
Cahore Pt., *Ireland* **13 D5** 52 33N 6 12W
Cahors, *France* **18 D4** 44 27N 1 27 E
Cahuapanas, *Peru* **92 E3** 5 15S 77 0W
Cahul, *Moldova* **17 F15** 45 50N 28 15 E
Cai Bau, Dao, *Vietnam* **38 B6** 21 10N 107 27 E
Cai Nuoc, *Vietnam* **39 H5** 8 56N 105 1 E
Caia, *Mozam.* **55 F4** 17 51S 35 24 E
Caianda, *Angola* **55 E1** 11 2S 23 31 E
Caibarién, *Cuba* **88 B4** 22 30N 79 30W
Caicara, *Venezuela* **92 B5** 7 38N 66 10W
Caicó, *Brazil* **93 E11** 6 20S 37 0W
Caicos Is., *W. Indies* **89 B5** 21 40N 71 40W
Caicos Passage, *W. Indies* **89 B5** 22 45N 72 45W
Caird Coast, *Antarctica* **5 D1** 75 0S 25 0W
Cairn Gorm, *U.K.* **12 D5** 57 7N 3 39W
Cairn Toul, *U.K.* **12 D5** 57 3N 3 44W
Cairngorm Mts., *U.K.* **12 D5** 57 6N 3 42W
Cairns, *Australia* **62 B4** 16 57S 145 45 E
Cairo = El Qâhira, *Egypt* **51 B11** 30 1N 31 14 E
Cairo, *Ga., U.S.A.* **77 K3** 30 52N 84 13W
Cairo, *Ill., U.S.A.* **81 G10** 37 0N 89 11W
Caithness, Ord of, *U.K.* **12 C5** 58 8N 3 36W
Caiundo, *Angola* **53 H3** 15 50S 17 28 E
Caiza, *Bolivia* **92 H5** 20 2S 65 40W
Cajamarca, *Peru* **92 E3** 7 5S 78 28W
Cajàzeiras, *Brazil* **93 E11** 6 52S 38 30W
Cala d'Or, *Spain* **22 B10** 39 23N 3 14 E
Cala Figuera, C., *Spain* **22 B9** 39 27N 2 31 E
Cala Forcat, *Spain* **22 A10** 40 0N 3 47 E
Cala Mayor, *Spain* **22 B9** 39 33N 2 37 E
Cala Mezquida, *Spain* **22 B11** 39 55N 4 16 E
Cala Millor, *Spain* **22 B10** 39 35N 3 22 E
Cala Ratjada, *Spain* **22 B10** 39 43N 3 27 E
Calabar, *Nigeria* **50 H6** 4 57N 8 20 E
Calábria □, *Italy* **20 E7** 39 0N 16 30 E
Calafate, *Argentina* **96 G2** 50 19S 72 15W
Calahorra, *Spain* **19 A5** 42 18N 1 59W
Calais, *France* **18 A4** 50 57N 1 56 E
Calais, *U.S.A.* **71 C6** 45 11N 67 17W
Calalaste, Cord. de, *Argentina* **94 B2** 25 0S 67 0W
Calama, *Brazil* **92 E6** 8 0S 62 50W
Calama, *Chile* **94 A2** 22 30S 68 55W
Calamar, *Bolívar, Colombia* **92 A4** 10 15N 74 55W
Calamar, *Vaupés, Colombia* **92 C4** 1 58N 72 32W
Calamian Group, *Phil.* **37 B5** 11 50N 119 55 E
Calamocha, *Spain* **19 B5** 40 50N 1 17W
Calán Porter, *Spain* **22 B11** 39 52N 4 8 E
Calang, *Indonesia* **36 D1** 4 37N 95 37 E
Calapan, *Phil.* **37 B6** 13 25N 121 7 E
Călăraşi, *Romania* **17 F14** 44 12N 27 20 E
Calatayud, *Spain* **19 B5** 41 20N 1 40W
Calauag, *Phil.* **37 B6** 13 55N 122 15 E
Calavite, C., *Phil.* **37 B6** 13 26N 120 20 E
Calbayog, *Phil.* **37 B6** 12 4N 124 38 E
Calca, *Peru* **92 F4** 13 22S 72 0W
Calcasieu L., *U.S.A.* **81 L8** 29 55N 93 18W
Calcutta, *India* **43 H13** 22 36N 88 24 E
Caldas da Rainha, *Portugal* **19 C1** 39 24N 9 8W
Calder →, *U.K.* **10 D6** 53 44N 1 22W
Caldera, *Chile* **94 B1** 27 5S 70 55W
Caldwell, *Idaho, U.S.A.* **82 E5** 43 40N 116 41W
Caldwell, *Kans., U.S.A.* **81 G6** 37 2N 97 37W
Caldwell, *Tex., U.S.A.* **81 K6** 30 32N 96 42W
Caledon, *S. Africa* **56 E2** 34 14S 19 26 E
Caledon →, *S. Africa* **56 E4** 30 31S 26 5 E
Caledon B., *Australia* **62 A2** 12 45S 137 0 E
Caledonia, *Canada* **78 C5** 43 7N 79 58W
Caledonia, *U.S.A.* **78 D7** 42 58N 77 51W
Calemba, *Angola* **56 B2** 16 0S 15 44 E
Calexico, *U.S.A.* **85 N11** 32 40N 115 30W
Calf of Man, *U.K.* **10 C3** 54 3N 4 48W
Calgary, *Canada* **72 C6** 51 0N 114 10W
Calheta, *Madeira* **22 D2** 32 44N 17 11W
Calhoun, *U.S.A.* **77 H3** 34 30N 84 57W
Cali, *Colombia* **92 C3** 3 25N 76 35W
Calicut, *India* **40 P9** 11 15N 75 43 E
Caliente, *U.S.A.* **83 H6** 37 37N 114 31W
California, *Mo., U.S.A.* **80 F8** 38 38N 92 34W
California, *Pa., U.S.A.* **78 F5** 40 4N 79 54W
California □, *U.S.A.* **83 H4** 37 30N 119 30W
California, Baja, *Mexico* **86 A1** 32 10N 115 12W
California, Baja, T.N. □ = Baja California □, *Mexico* **86 B2** 30 0N 115 0W
California, Baja, T.S. □ = Baja California Sur □, *Mexico* **86 B2** 25 50N 111 50W
California, G. de, *Mexico* **86 B2** 27 0N 111 0W
California City, *U.S.A.* **85 K9** 35 10N 117 55W
California Hot Springs, *U.S.A.* **85 K8** 35 51N 118 41W
Calingasta, *Argentina* **94 C2** 31 15S 69 30W
Calipatria, *U.S.A.* **85 M11** 33 8N 115 31W
Calistoga, *U.S.A.* **84 G4** 38 35N 122 35W
Calitzdorp, *S. Africa* **56 E3** 33 33S 21 42 E
Callabonna, L., *Australia* **63 D3** 29 40S 140 5 E
Callan, *Ireland* **13 D4** 52 32N 7 24W
Callander, *U.K.* **12 E4** 56 15N 4 13W
Callao, *Peru* **92 F3** 12 0S 77 0W
Callaway, *U.S.A.* **80 E5** 41 18N 99 56W
Calles, *Mexico* **87 C5** 23 2N 98 42W
Callide, *Australia* **62 C5** 24 18S 150 28 E
Calling Lake, *Canada* **72 B6** 55 15N 113 12W
Calliope, *Australia* **62 C5** 24 0S 151 16 E
Calola, *Angola* **56 B2** 16 25S 17 48 E
Caloundra, *Australia* **63 D5** 26 45S 153 10 E
Calpella, *U.S.A.* **84 F3** 39 14N 123 12W
Calpine, *U.S.A.* **84 F6** 39 40N 120 27W
Calstock, *Canada* **70 C3** 49 47N 84 9W
Caltagirone, *Italy* **20 F6** 37 14N 14 31 E
Caltanissetta, *Italy* **20 F6** 37 29N 14 4 E
Calulo, *Angola* **52 G2** 10 1S 14 56 E
Calumet, *U.S.A.* **76 B1** 47 14N 88 27W
Calunda, *Angola* **53 G4** 12 7S 23 36 E
Calvert, *U.S.A.* **81 K6** 30 59N 96 40W
Calvert →, *Australia* **62 B2** 16 17S 137 44 E
Calvert Hills, *Australia* **62 B2** 17 15S 137 20 E
Calvert I., *Canada* **72 C3** 51 30N 128 0W
Calvert Ra., *Australia* **60 D3** 24 0S 122 30 E
Calvi, *France* **18 E8** 42 34N 8 45 E
Calviá, *Spain* **19 C7** 39 34N 2 31 E
Calvillo, *Mexico* **86 C4** 21 51N 102 43W
Calvinia, *S. Africa* **56 E2** 31 28S 19 45 E
Calwa, *U.S.A.* **84 J7** 36 42N 119 46W
Cam →, *U.K.* **11 E8** 52 21N 0 16 E
Cam Lam, *Vietnam* **39 G7** 11 54N 109 10 E
Cam Pha, *Vietnam* **38 B6** 21 7N 107 18 E
Cam Ranh, *Vietnam* **39 G7** 11 54N 109 12 E
Cam Xuyen, *Vietnam* **38 C6** 18 15N 106 0 E
Camabatela, *Angola* **52 F3** 8 20S 15 26 E
Camacha, *Madeira* **22 D3** 32 41N 16 49W
Camacho, *Mexico* **86 C4** 24 25N 102 18W
Camacupa, *Angola* **53 G3** 11 58S 17 22 E
Camagüey, *Cuba* **88 B4** 21 20N 78 0W
Camaná, *Peru* **92 G4** 16 30S 72 50W
Camanche Reservoir, *U.S.A.* **84 G6** 38 14N 121 1W
Camaquã →, *Brazil* **95 C5** 31 17S 51 47W
Câmara de Lobos, *Madeira* **22 D3** 32 39N 16 59W
Camargo, *Bolivia* **92 H5** 20 38S 65 15W
Camargue, *France* **18 E6** 43 34N 4 34 E
Camarillo, *U.S.A.* **85 L7** 34 13N 119 2W
Camarón, C., *Honduras* **88 C2** 16 0N 85 5W
Camarones, *Argentina* **96 E3** 44 50S 65 40W
Camas, *U.S.A.* **84 E4** 45 35N 122 24W
Camas Valley, *U.S.A.* **82 E2** 43 2N 123 40W
Cambará, *Brazil* **95 A5** 23 2S 50 5W
Cambay = Khambhat, *India* **42 H5** 22 23N 72 33 E
Cambay, G. of = Khambat, G. of, *India* **42 J5** 20 45N 72 30 E
Cambodia ■, *Asia* **38 F5** 12 15N 105 0 E
Camborne, *U.K.* **11 G2** 50 12N 5 19W
Cambrai, *France* **18 A5** 50 11N 3 14 E
Cambria, *U.S.A.* **83 J3** 35 34N 121 5W
Cambrian Mts., *U.K.* **11 E4** 52 3N 3 57W
Cambridge, *Canada* **70 D3** 43 23N 80 15W
Cambridge, *Jamaica* **88 C4** 18 18N 77 54W
Cambridge, *N.Z.* **59 G5** 37 54S 175 29 E
Cambridge, *U.K.* **11 E8** 52 12N 0 8 E
Cambridge, *Idaho, U.S.A.* **82 D5** 44 34N 116 41W
Cambridge, *Mass., U.S.A.* **79 D13** 42 22N 71 6W
Cambridge, *Md., U.S.A.* **76 F7** 38 34N 76 5W
Cambridge, *Minn., U.S.A.* **80 C8** 45 34N 93 13W
Cambridge, *N.Y., U.S.A.* **79 C11** 43 2N 73 22W
Cambridge, *Nebr., U.S.A.* **80 E4** 40 17N 100 10W
Cambridge, *Ohio, U.S.A.* **78 F3** 40 2N 81 35W
Cambridge Bay, *Canada* **68 B9** 69 10N 105 0W
Cambridge G., *Australia* **60 B4** 14 55S 128 15 E
Cambridge Springs, *U.S.A.* **78 E4** 41 48N 80 4W
Cambridgeshire □, *U.K.* **11 E8** 52 25N 0 7W
Cambuci, *Brazil* **95 A7** 21 35S 41 55W
Cambundi-Catembo, *Angola* **52 G3** 10 10S 17 35 E
Camden, *Ala., U.S.A.* **77 K2** 31 59N 87 17W
Camden, *Ark., U.S.A.* **81 J8** 33 35N 92 50W
Camden, *Maine, U.S.A.* **71 D6** 44 13N 69 4W
Camden, *N.J., U.S.A.* **79 G9** 39 56N 75 7W
Camden, *S.C., U.S.A.* **77 H5** 34 16N 80 36W
Camden Sd., *Australia* **60 C3** 15 27S 124 25 E
Camdenton, *U.S.A.* **81 F8** 38 1N 92 45W
Cameron, *Ariz., U.S.A.* **83 J8** 35 53N 111 25W
Cameron, *La., U.S.A.* **81 L8** 29 48N 93 20W
Cameron, *Mo., U.S.A.* **80 F7** 39 44N 94 14W
Cameron, *Tex., U.S.A.* **81 K6** 30 51N 96 59W
Cameron Falls, *Canada* **70 C2** 49 8N 88 19W
Cameron Highlands, *Malaysia* **39 K3** 4 27N 101 22 E
Cameron Hills, *Canada* **72 B5** 59 48N 118 0W
Cameroon ■, *Africa* **51 G7** 6 0N 12 30 E
Cameroun, Mt., *Cameroon* **50 H6** 4 13N 9 10 E
Cametá, *Brazil* **93 D9** 2 12S 49 30W
Caminha, *Portugal* **19 B1** 41 50N 8 50W
Camino, *U.S.A.* **84 G6** 38 44N 120 41W
Camira Creek, *Australia* **63 D5** 29 15S 152 58 E
Camissombo, *Angola* **52 F4** 8 7S 20 38 E
Cammal, *U.S.A.* **78 E7** 41 24N 77 28W
Camocim, *Brazil* **93 D10** 2 55S 40 50W
Camooweal, *Australia* **62 B2** 19 56S 138 7 E
Camopi →, *Fr. Guiana* **93 C8** 3 10N 52 20W
Camp Crook, *U.S.A.* **80 C3** 45 33N 103 59W
Camp Nelson, *U.S.A.* **85 J8** 36 8N 118 39W
Camp Wood, *U.S.A.* **81 L4** 29 40N 100 1W
Campana, *Argentina* **94 C4** 34 10S 58 55W
Campana, I., *Chile* **96 F1** 48 20S 75 20W
Campanário, *Madeira* **22 D2** 32 39N 17 2W
Campánia □, *Italy* **20 D6** 41 0N 14 30 E
Campbell, *S. Africa* **56 D3** 28 48S 23 44 E
Campbell, *Calif., U.S.A.* **84 H5** 37 17N 121 57W
Campbell, *Ohio, U.S.A.* **78 E4** 41 5N 80 37W
Campbell I., *Pac. Oc.* **64 N8** 52 30S 169 0 E
Campbell L., *Canada* **73 A7** 63 14N 106 55W
Campbell River, *Canada* **72 C3** 50 5N 125 20W
Campbell Town, *Australia* **62 G4** 41 52S 147 30 E
Campbellford, *Canada* **78 B7** 44 18N 77 48W
Campbellpur, *Pakistan* **42 C5** 33 46N 72 26 E
Campbellsville, *U.S.A.* **76 G3** 37 21N 85 20W
Campbellton, *Canada* **71 C6** 47 57N 66 43W
Campbelltown, *Australia* **63 E5** 34 4S 150 49 E
Campbeltown, *U.K.* **12 F3** 55 26N 5 36W
Campeche, *Mexico* **87 D6** 19 50N 90 32W
Campeche □, *Mexico* **87 D6** 19 50N 90 32W
Campeche, B. de, *Mexico* **87 D6** 19 30N 93 0W
Camperdown, *Australia* **63 F3** 38 14S 143 9 E
Camperville, *Canada* **73 C8** 51 59N 100 9W
Campina Grande, *Brazil* **93 E11** 7 20S 35 47W
Campinas, *Brazil* **95 A6** 22 50S 47 0W
Campo, *Cameroon* **52 D1** 2 22N 9 50 E
Campo, *U.S.A.* **85 N10** 32 36N 116 28W
Campo Belo, *Brazil* **93 H9** 20 52S 45 16W
Campo Formoso, *Brazil* **93 F10** 10 30S 40 20W
Campo Grande, *Brazil* **93 H8** 20 25S 54 40W
Campo Maíor, *Brazil* **93 D10** 4 50S 42 12W
Campo Mourão, *Brazil* **95 A5** 24 3S 52 22W
Campoalegre, *Colombia* **92 C3** 2 41N 75 20W
Campobasso, *Italy* **20 D6** 41 34N 14 39 E
Campos, *Brazil* **95 A7** 21 50S 41 20W
Campos Belos, *Brazil* **93 F9** 13 10S 47 3W
Campos del Puerto, *Spain* **22 B10** 39 26N 3 1 E
Campos Novos, *Brazil* **95 B5** 27 21S 51 50W
Camptonville, *U.S.A.* **84 F5** 39 27N 121 3W
Campuya →, *Peru* **92 D4** 1 40S 73 30W
Camrose, *Canada* **72 C6** 53 0N 112 50W
Camsell Portage, *Canada* **73 B7** 59 37N 109 15W
Çan, *Turkey* **21 D12** 40 2N 27 3 E
Can Clavo, *Spain* **22 C7** 38 57N 1 27 E
Can Creu, *Spain* **22 C7** 38 58N 1 28 E
Can Gio, *Vietnam* **39 G6** 10 25N 106 58 E
Can Tho, *Vietnam* **39 G5** 10 2N 105 46 E
Canaan, *U.S.A.* **79 D11** 42 2N 73 20W
Canada ■, *N. Amer.* **68 C10** 60 0N 100 0W
Cañada de Gómez, *Argentina* **94 C3** 32 40S 61 30W
Canadian, *U.S.A.* **81 H4** 35 55N 100 23W
Canadian →, *U.S.A.* **81 H7** 35 28N 95 3W
Canadian Shield, *Canada* **69 C10** 53 0N 75 0W
Çanakkale, *Turkey* **21 D12** 40 8N 26 24 E
Çanakkale Boğazı, *Turkey* **21 D12** 40 17N 26 32 E
Canal Flats, *Canada* **72 C5** 50 10N 115 48W
Canalejas, *Argentina* **94 D2** 35 15S 66 34W
Canals, *Argentina* **94 C3** 33 35S 62 53W
Canandaigua, *U.S.A.* **78 D7** 42 54N 77 17W
Cananea, *Mexico* **86 A2** 31 0N 110 20W
Canarias, Is., *Atl. Oc.* **22 F4** 28 30N 16 0W
Canarreos, Arch. de los, *Cuba* **88 B3** 21 35N 81 40W
Canary Is. = Canarias, Is., *Atl. Oc.* **22 F4** 28 30N 16 0W
Canatlán, *Mexico* **86 C4** 24 31N 104 47W
Canaveral, C., *U.S.A.* **77 L5** 28 27N 80 32W
Canavieiras, *Brazil* **93 G11** 15 39S 39 0W
Canbelego, *Australia* **63 E4** 31 32S 146 18 E
Canberra, *Australia* **63 F4** 35 15S 149 8 E
Canby, *Calif., U.S.A.* **82 F3** 41 27N 120 52W
Canby, *Minn., U.S.A.* **80 C6** 44 43N 96 16W
Canby, *Oreg., U.S.A.* **84 E4** 45 16N 122 42W
Cancún, *Mexico* **87 C7** 21 8N 86 44W
Candala, *Somali Rep.* **46 E4** 11 30N 49 58 E
Candelaria, *Argentina* **95 B4** 27 29S 55 44W
Candelaria, *Canary Is.* **22 F3** 28 22N 16 22W
Candelo, *Australia* **63 F4** 36 47S 149 43 E
Candia = Iráklion, *Greece* **23 D7** 35 20N 25 12 E
Candle L., *Canada* **73 C7** 53 50N 105 18W
Candlemas I., *Antarctica* **5 B1** 57 3S 26 40W
Cando, *U.S.A.* **80 A5** 48 32N 99 12W
Canea = Khaniá, *Greece* **23 D6** 35 30N 24 4 E
Canelones, *Uruguay* **95 C4** 34 32S 56 17W
Cañete, *Chile* **94 D1** 37 50S 73 30W
Cañete, *Peru* **92 F3** 13 8S 76 30W
Cangas de Narcea, *Spain* **19 A2** 43 10N 6 32W
Canguaretama, *Brazil* **93 E11** 6 20S 35 5W
Canguçu, *Brazil* **95 C5** 31 22S 52 43W
Cangzhou, *China* **34 E9** 38 19N 116 52 E
Canicattì, *Italy* **20 F5** 37 21N 13 51 E
Canigou, Mt., *France* **18 E5** 42 31N 2 27 E
Canim Lake, *Canada* **72 C4** 51 47N 120 54W
Canindeyu □, *Paraguay* **95 A4** 24 10S 55 0W
Canipaan, *Phil.* **36 C5** 8 33N 117 15 E
Canisteo, *U.S.A.* **78 D7** 42 16N 77 36W
Canisteo →, *U.S.A.* **78 D7** 42 7N 77 8W
Cañitas, *Mexico* **86 C4** 23 36N 102 43W
Çankırı, *Turkey* **25 F5** 40 40N 33 37 E
Cankuzo, *Burundi* **54 C3** 3 10S 30 31 E
Canmore, *Canada* **72 C5** 51 7N 115 18W
Cann River, *Australia* **63 F4** 37 35S 149 7 E
Canna, *U.K.* **12 D2** 57 3N 6 33W
Cannanore, *India* **40 P9** 11 53N 75 27 E
Cannes, *France* **18 E7** 43 32N 7 1 E
Canning Town = Port Canning, *India* **43 H13** 22 23N 88 40 E
Cannington, *Canada* **78 B5** 44 20N 79 2W
Cannock, *U.K.* **10 E5** 52 41N 2 1W
Cannon Ball →, *U.S.A.* **80 B4** 46 20N 100 38W
Cannondale Mt., *Australia* **62 D4** 25 13S 148 57 E
Canoas, *Brazil* **95 B5** 29 56S 51 11W
Canoe L., *Canada* **73 B7** 55 10N 108 15W
Canon City, *U.S.A.* **80 F2** 38 27N 105 14W
Canora, *Canada* **73 C8** 51 40N 102 30W
Canowindra, *Australia* **63 E4** 33 35S 148 38 E
Canso, *Canada* **71 C7** 45 20N 61 0W
Cantabria □, *Spain* **19 A4** 43 10N 4 0W
Cantabrian Mts. = Cantábrica, Cordillera, *Spain* **19 A3** 43 0N 5 10W
Cantábrica, Cordillera, *Spain* **19 A3** 43 0N 5 10W
Cantal, Plomb du, *France* **18 D5** 45 3N 2 45 E
Canterbury, *Australia* **62 D3** 25 23S 141 53 E
Canterbury, *U.K.* **11 F9** 51 16N 1 6 E
Canterbury □, *N.Z.* **59 K3** 43 45S 171 19 E
Canterbury Bight, *N.Z.* **59 L3** 44 16S 171 55 E
Canterbury Plains, *N.Z.* **59 K3** 43 55S 171 22 E
Cantil, *U.S.A.* **85 K9** 35 18N 117 58W
Canton = Guangzhou, *China* **33 D6** 23 5N 113 10 E
Canton, *Ga., U.S.A.* **77 H3** 34 14N 84 29W
Canton, *Ill., U.S.A.* **80 E9** 40 33N 90 2W
Canton, *Miss., U.S.A.* **81 J9** 32 37N 90 2W
Canton, *Mo., U.S.A.* **80 E9** 40 8N 91 32W
Canton, *N.Y., U.S.A.* **79 B9** 44 36N 75 10W
Canton, *Ohio, U.S.A.* **78 F3** 40 48N 81 23W
Canton, *Okla., U.S.A.* **81 G5** 36 3N 98 35W
Canton, *S. Dak., U.S.A.* **80 D6** 43 18N 96 35W
Canton L., *U.S.A.* **81 G5** 36 6N 98 35W
Canudos, *Brazil* **92 E7** 7 13S 58 5W
Canutama, *Brazil* **92 E6** 6 30S 64 20W
Canutillo, *U.S.A.* **83 L10** 31 55N 106 36W
Canyon, *Tex., U.S.A.* **81 H4** 34 59N 101 55W
Canyon, *Wyo., U.S.A.* **82 D8** 44 43N 110 36W
Canyonlands National Park, *U.S.A.* **83 G9** 38 15N 110 0W
Canyonville, *U.S.A.* **82 E2** 42 56N 123 17W
Cao Bang, *Vietnam* **38 A6** 22 40N 106 15 E
Cao He →, *China* **35 D13** 40 10N 124 32 E
Cao Lanh, *Vietnam* **39 G5** 10 27N 105 38 E
Cao Xian, *China* **34 G8** 34 50N 115 35 E
Cap-aux-Meules, *Canada* **71 C7** 47 23N 61 52W
Cap-Chat, *Canada* **71 C6** 49 6N 66 40W
Cap-de-la-Madeleine, *Canada* **70 C5** 46 22N 72 31W
Cap-Haïtien, *Haiti* **89 C5** 19 40N 72 20W
Cap St.-Jacques = Vung Tau, *Vietnam* **39 G6** 10 21N 107 4 E
Capa, *Vietnam* **38 A4** 22 21N 103 50 E
Capaia, *Angola* **52 F4** 8 27S 20 13 E
Capanaparo →, *Venezuela* **92 B5** 7 1N 67 7W
Cape →, *Australia* **62 C4** 20 59S 146 51 E
Cape Barren I., *Australia* **62 G4** 40 25S 148 15 E
Cape Breton Highlands Nat. Park, *Canada* **71 C7** 46 50N 60 40W
Cape Breton I., *Canada* **71 C7** 46 0N 60 30W
Cape Charles, *U.S.A.* **76 G8** 37 16N 76 1W
Cape Coast, *Ghana* **50 G4** 5 5N 1 15W
Cape Coral, *U.S.A.* **77 M5** 26 33N 81 57W
Cape Dorset, *Canada* **69 B12** 64 14N 76 32W
Cape Dyer, *Canada* **69 B13** 66 30N 61 22W
Cape Fear →, *U.S.A.* **77 H6** 33 53N 78 1W
Cape Girardeau, *U.S.A.* **81 G10** 37 19N 89 32W
Cape Jervis, *Australia* **63 F2** 35 40S 138 5 E
Cape May, *U.S.A.* **76 F8** 38 56N 74 56W
Cape May Point, *U.S.A.* **75 C12** 38 56N 74 58W
Cape Tormentine, *Canada* **71 C7** 46 8N 63 47W
Cape Town, *S. Africa* **56 E2** 33 55S 18 22 E
Cape Verde Is. ■, *Atl. Oc.* **49 E1** 17 10N 25 20W
Cape Vincent, *U.S.A.* **79 B8** 44 8N 76 20W
Cape York Peninsula, *Australia* **62 A3** 12 0S 142 30 E

Capela

Capela, Brazil 93 F11 10 30S 37 0W
Capella, Australia 62 C4 23 2S 148 1 E
Capim →, Brazil 93 D9 1 40S 47 47W
Capitan, U.S.A. 83 K11 33 35N 105 35W
Capitola, U.S.A. 84 J5 36 59N 121 57W
Capoche →, Mozam. 55 F3 15 35S 33 0 E
Capraia, Italy 20 C3 43 2N 9 50 E
Capreol, Canada 70 C3 46 43N 80 56W
Capri, Italy 20 D6 40 33N 14 14 E
Capricorn Group, Australia 62 C5 23 30S 151 55 E
Capricorn Ra., Australia 60 D2 23 20S 116 50 E
Caprivi Strip, Namibia 56 B3 18 0S 23 0 E
Captainganj, India 43 F10 26 55N 83 45 E
Captain's Flat, Australia 63 F4 35 35S 149 27 E
Caquetá →, Colombia 92 D5 1 15S 69 15W
Caracal, Romania 17 F13 44 8N 24 22 E
Caracas, Venezuela 92 A5 10 30N 66 55W
Caracol, Brazil 93 E10 9 15S 43 22W
Caradoc, Australia 63 E3 30 35S 143 5 E
Carajás, Serra dos, Brazil 93 E8 6 0S 51 30W
Carangola, Brazil 95 A7 20 44S 42 5W
Carani, Australia 61 F2 30 57S 116 28 E
Caransebeş, Romania 17 F12 45 28N 22 18 E
Caratasca, L., Honduras 88 C3 15 20N 83 40W
Caratinga, Brazil 93 G10 19 50S 42 10W
Caraúbas, Brazil 93 E11 5 43S 37 33W
Caravaca, Spain 19 C5 38 8N 1 52W
Caravelas, Brazil 93 G11 17 45S 39 15W
Caraveli, Peru 92 G4 15 45S 73 25W
Caràzinho, Brazil 95 B5 28 16S 52 46W
Carballo, Spain 19 A1 43 13N 8 41W
Carberry, Canada 73 D9 49 50N 99 25W
Carbó, Mexico 86 B2 29 42N 110 58W
Carbon, Canada 72 C6 51 30N 113 9W
Carbonara, C., Italy 20 E3 39 6N 9 31 E
Carbondale, Colo., U.S.A. 82 G10 39 24N 107 13W
Carbondale, Ill., U.S.A. 81 G10 37 44N 89 13W
Carbondale, Pa., U.S.A. 79 E9 41 35N 75 30W
Carbonear, Canada 71 C9 47 42N 53 13W
Carbonia, Italy 20 E3 39 10N 8 30 E
Carcajou, Canada 72 B5 57 47N 117 6W
Carcasse, C., Haiti 89 C5 18 30N 74 28W
Carcassonne, France 18 E5 43 13N 2 20 E
Carcross, Canada 68 B6 60 13N 134 45W
Cardabia, Australia 60 D1 23 2S 113 48 E
Cardamon Hills, India 40 Q10 9 30N 77 15 E
Cárdenas, Cuba 88 B3 23 0N 81 30W
Cárdenas, San Luis Potosí, Mexico 87 C5 22 0N 99 41W
Cárdenas, Tabasco, Mexico 87 D6 17 59N 93 21W
Cardiff, U.K. 11 F4 51 29N 3 10W
Cardiff □, U.K. 11 F4 51 31N 3 12W
Cardiff-by-the-Sea, U.S.A. 85 M9 33 1N 117 17W
Cardigan, U.K. 11 E3 52 5N 4 40W
Cardigan B., U.K. 11 E3 52 30N 4 30W
Cardinal, Canada 79 B9 44 47N 75 23W
Cardona, Uruguay 94 C4 33 53S 57 18W
Cardross, Canada 73 D7 49 50N 105 40W
Cardston, Canada 72 D6 49 15N 113 20W
Cardwell, Australia 62 B4 18 14S 146 2 E
Careen L., Canada 73 B7 57 0N 108 11W
Carei, Romania 17 E12 47 40N 22 29 E
Careme, Indonesia 37 G13 6 55S 108 27 E
Carey, Idaho, U.S.A. 82 E7 43 19N 113 57W
Carey, Ohio, U.S.A. 76 E4 40 57N 83 23W
Carey, L., Australia 61 E3 29 0S 122 15 E
Carey L., Canada 73 A8 62 12N 102 55W
Careysburg, Liberia 50 G2 6 34N 10 30W
Carhué, Argentina 94 D3 37 10S 62 50W
Caria, Turkey 21 F13 37 20N 28 10 E
Cariacica, Brazil 93 H10 20 16S 40 25W
Caribbean Sea, W. Indies 89 C5 15 0N 75 0W
Cariboo Mts., Canada 72 C4 53 0N 121 0W
Caribou, U.S.A. 71 C6 46 52N 68 1W
Caribou →, Man., Canada 73 B10 59 20N 94 44W
Caribou →, N.W.T., Canada 72 A3 61 27N 125 45W
Caribou I., Canada 70 C2 47 22N 85 49W
Caribou Is., Canada 72 A6 61 55N 113 15W
Caribou L., Man., Canada 73 B9 59 21N 96 10W
Caribou L., Ont., Canada 70 B2 50 25N 89 5W
Caribou Mts., Canada 72 B5 59 12N 115 40W
Carichic, Mexico 86 B3 27 56N 107 3W
Carillo, Mexico 86 B4 26 50N 103 55W
Carinda, Australia 63 E4 30 20S 147 41 E
Carinhanha, Brazil 93 F10 14 15S 44 46W
Carinthia □ = Kärnten □, Austria 16 E8 46 52N 13 30 E
Caripito, Venezuela 92 A6 10 8N 63 6W
Caritianas, Brazil 92 E6 9 20S 63 6W
Carleton Place, Canada 70 C4 45 8N 76 9W
Carletonville, S. Africa 56 D4 26 23S 27 22 E
Carlin, U.S.A. 82 F5 40 43N 116 7W
Carlingford L., U.K. 13 B5 54 3N 6 9W
Carlinville, U.S.A. 80 F10 39 17N 89 53W
Carlisle, U.K. 10 C5 54 54N 2 56W
Carlisle, U.S.A. 78 F7 40 12N 77 12W
Carlos Casares, Argentina 94 D3 35 32S 61 20W
Carlos Tejedor, Argentina 94 D3 35 25S 62 25W
Carlow, Ireland 13 D5 52 50N 6 56W
Carlow □, Ireland 13 D5 52 43N 6 50W
Carlsbad, Calif., U.S.A. 85 M9 33 10N 117 21W
Carlsbad, N. Mex., U.S.A. 81 J2 32 25N 104 14W
Carlyle, Canada 73 D8 49 40N 102 20W
Carlyle, U.S.A. 80 F10 38 37N 89 22W
Carmacks, Canada 68 B6 62 5N 136 16W
Carman, Canada 73 D9 49 30N 98 0W
Carmangay, Canada 72 C6 50 10N 113 10W
Carmanville, Canada 71 C9 49 23N 54 19W
Carmarthen, U.K. 11 F3 51 52N 4 19W
Carmarthen B., U.K. 11 F3 51 40N 4 30W
Carmarthenshire □, U.K. 11 F3 51 55N 4 13W
Carmaux, France 18 D5 44 3N 2 10 E
Carmel, U.S.A. 79 E11 41 26N 73 41W
Carmel-by-the-Sea, U.S.A. 83 H3 36 33N 121 55W
Carmel Valley, U.S.A. 84 J5 36 29N 121 43W
Carmelo, Uruguay 94 C4 34 0S 58 20W
Carmen, Colombia 92 B3 9 43N 75 8W
Carmen, Paraguay 95 B4 27 13S 56 12W
Carmen →, Mexico 86 A3 30 42N 106 29W
Carmen, I., Mexico 86 B2 26 0N 111 20W
Carmen de Patagones, Argentina 96 E4 40 50S 63 0W
Carmensa, Argentina 94 D2 35 15S 67 40W
Carmi, U.S.A. 76 F1 38 5N 88 10W
Carmichael, U.S.A. 84 G5 38 38N 121 19W
Carmila, Australia 62 C4 21 55S 149 24 E
Carmona, Spain 19 D3 37 28N 5 42W
Carnac, France 18 C2 47 45N 3 6W
Carnarvon, Queens., Australia 62 C4 24 48S 147 45 E
Carnarvon, W. Austral., Australia 61 D1 24 51S 113 42 E
Carnarvon, S. Africa 56 E3 30 56S 22 8 E
Carnarvon Ra., Queens., Australia 62 D4 25 15S 148 30 E
Carnarvon Ra., W. Austral., Australia 61 E3 25 20S 120 45 E
Carnation, U.S.A. 84 C5 47 39N 121 55W
Carndonagh, Ireland 13 A4 55 16N 7 15W
Carnduff, Canada 73 D8 49 10N 101 50W
Carnegie, U.S.A. 78 F4 40 24N 80 5W
Carnegie, L., Australia 61 E3 26 5S 122 30 E
Carnic Alps = Karnische Alpen, Europe 16 E7 46 36N 13 0 E
Carniche Alpi = Karnische Alpen, Europe 16 E7 46 36N 13 0 E
Carnot, C.A.R. 52 D3 4 59N 15 56 E
Carnot, C., Australia 63 E2 34 57S 135 38 E
Carnot B., Australia 60 C3 17 20S 122 15 E
Carnsore Pt., Ireland 13 D5 52 10N 6 22W
Caro, U.S.A. 76 D4 43 29N 83 24W
Carol City, U.S.A. 77 N5 25 56N 80 16W
Carolina, Brazil 93 E9 7 10S 47 30W
Carolina, Puerto Rico 89 C6 18 23N 65 58W
Carolina, S. Africa 57 D5 26 5S 30 6 E
Caroline I., Kiribati 65 H12 9 15S 150 3W
Caroline Is., Pac. Oc. 28 J17 8 0N 150 0 E
Caron, Canada 73 C7 50 30N 105 50W
Caroni →, Venezuela 92 B6 8 21N 62 43W
Caronie = Nébrodi, Monti, Italy 20 F6 37 54N 14 35 E
Caroona, Australia 63 E5 31 24S 150 26 E
Carpathians, Europe 17 D11 49 30N 21 0 E
Carpaţii Meridionali, Romania 17 F13 45 30N 25 0 E
Carpentaria, G. of, Australia 62 A2 14 0S 139 0 E
Carpentaria Downs, Australia 62 B3 18 44S 144 20 E
Carpentras, France 18 D6 44 3N 5 2 E
Carpi, Italy 20 B4 44 47N 10 53 E
Carpinteria, U.S.A. 85 L7 34 24N 119 31W
Carpolac = Morea, Australia 63 F3 36 45S 141 18 E
Carr Boyd Ra., Australia 60 C4 16 15S 128 35 E
Carrabelle, U.S.A. 77 L3 29 51N 84 40W
Carranya, Australia 60 C4 19 14S 127 46 E
Carrara, Italy 20 B4 44 5N 10 6 E
Carrauntoohill, Ireland 13 E2 52 0N 9 45W
Carrick-on-Shannon, Ireland 13 C3 53 57N 8 5W
Carrick-on-Suir, Ireland 13 D4 52 21N 7 24W
Carrickfergus, U.K. 13 B6 54 43N 5 49W
Carrickfergus □, U.K. 13 B6 54 43N 5 49W
Carrickmacross, Ireland 13 C5 53 59N 6 43W
Carrieton, Australia 63 E2 32 25S 138 31 E
Carrington, U.S.A. 80 B5 47 27N 99 8W
Carrizal Bajo, Chile 94 B1 28 5S 71 20W
Carrizalillo, Chile 94 B1 29 5S 71 30W
Carrizo Cr. →, U.S.A. 81 G3 36 55N 103 55W
Carrizo Springs, U.S.A. 81 L5 28 31N 99 52W
Carrizozo, U.S.A. 83 K11 33 38N 105 53W
Carroll, U.S.A. 80 D7 42 4N 94 52W
Carrollton, Ga., U.S.A. 77 J3 33 35N 85 5W
Carrollton, Ill., U.S.A. 80 F9 39 18N 90 24W
Carrollton, Ky., U.S.A. 76 F3 38 41N 85 11W
Carrollton, Mo., U.S.A. 80 F8 39 22N 93 30W
Carrollton, Ohio, U.S.A. 78 F3 40 34N 81 5W
Carron →, U.K. 12 D3 57 19N 5 26W
Carron, L., U.K. 12 D3 57 22N 5 35W
Carrot →, Canada 73 C8 53 50N 101 17W
Carrot River, Canada 73 C8 53 17N 103 35W
Carruthers, Canada 73 C7 52 52N 109 16W
Carse of Gowrie, U.K. 12 E5 56 30N 3 10W
Carson, Calif., U.S.A. 85 M8 33 48N 118 17W
Carson, N. Dak., U.S.A. 80 B4 46 25N 101 34W
Carson →, U.S.A. 84 F8 39 45N 118 40W
Carson City, U.S.A. 84 F7 39 10N 119 46W
Carson Sink, U.S.A. 82 G4 39 50N 118 25W
Carstairs, U.K. 12 F5 55 42N 3 41W
Cartagena, Colombia 92 A3 10 25N 75 33W
Cartagena, Spain 19 D5 37 38N 0 59W
Cartago, Colombia 92 C3 4 45N 75 55W
Cartago, Costa Rica 88 E3 9 50N 83 55W
Cartersville, U.S.A. 77 H3 34 10N 84 48W
Carterton, N.Z. 59 J5 41 2S 175 31 E
Carthage, Ark., U.S.A. 81 H8 34 4N 92 33W
Carthage, Ill., U.S.A. 80 E9 40 25N 91 8W
Carthage, Mo., U.S.A. 81 G7 37 11N 94 19W
Carthage, S. Dak., U.S.A. 80 C6 44 10N 97 43W
Carthage, Tex., U.S.A. 81 J7 32 9N 94 20W
Cartier I., Australia 60 B3 12 31S 123 29 E
Cartwright, Canada 71 B8 53 41N 56 58W
Caruaru, Brazil 93 E11 8 15S 35 55W
Carúpano, Venezuela 92 A6 10 39N 63 15W
Caruthersville, U.S.A. 81 G10 36 11N 89 39W
Carvoeiro, Brazil 92 D6 1 30S 61 59W
Carvoeiro, C., Portugal 19 C1 39 21N 9 24W
Cary, U.S.A. 77 H6 35 47N 78 46W
Casa Grande, U.S.A. 83 K8 32 53N 111 45W
Casablanca, Chile 94 C1 33 20S 71 25W
Casablanca, Morocco 50 B3 33 36N 7 36W
Casas Grandes, Mexico 86 A3 30 22N 108 0W
Cascade, Idaho, U.S.A. 82 D5 44 31N 116 2W
Cascade, Mont., U.S.A. 82 C8 47 16N 111 42W
Cascade Locks, U.S.A. 84 E5 45 40N 121 54W
Cascade Ra., U.S.A. 84 D5 47 0N 121 30W
Cascade Range, U.S.A. 66 E7 45 0N 121 45W
Cascais, Portugal 19 C1 38 41N 9 25W
Cascavel, Brazil 95 A5 24 57S 53 28W
Cáscina, Italy 20 C4 43 41N 10 33 E
Caserta, Italy 20 D6 41 4N 14 20 E
Cashel, Ireland 13 D4 52 30N 7 53W
Cashmere, U.S.A. 82 C3 47 31N 120 28W
Cashmere Downs, Australia 61 E2 28 57S 119 35 E
Casiguran, Phil. 37 A6 16 22N 122 7 E
Casilda, Argentina 94 C3 33 10S 61 10W
Casino, Australia 63 D5 28 52S 153 3 E
Casiquiare →, Venezuela 92 C5 2 1N 67 7W
Caslan, Canada 72 C6 54 38N 112 31W
Casma, Peru 92 E3 9 30S 78 20W
Casmalia, U.S.A. 85 L6 34 50N 120 32W
Caspe, Spain 19 B5 41 14N 0 1W
Casper, U.S.A. 82 E10 42 51N 106 19W
Caspian Depression, Eurasia 25 E8 47 0N 48 0 E
Caspian Sea, Eurasia 25 F9 43 0N 50 0 E
Cass City, U.S.A. 76 D4 43 36N 83 11W
Cass Lake, U.S.A. 80 B7 47 23N 94 37W
Casselman, Canada 79 A9 45 19N 75 5W
Casselton, U.S.A. 80 B6 46 54N 97 13W
Cassiar, Canada 72 B3 59 16N 129 40W
Cassiar Mts., Canada 72 B2 59 30N 130 30W
Cassinga, Angola 53 H3 15 5S 16 4 E
Cassino, Italy 20 D5 41 30N 13 49 E
Cassville, U.S.A. 81 G8 36 41N 93 52W
Castaic, U.S.A. 85 L8 34 30N 118 38W
Castellammare di Stábia, Italy 20 D6 40 42N 14 29 E
Castelli, Argentina 94 D4 36 7S 57 47W
Castellón de la Plana, Spain 19 C5 39 58N 0 3W
Castelo, Brazil 95 A7 20 33S 41 14W
Castelo Branco, Portugal 19 C2 39 50N 7 31W
Castelsarrasin, France 18 E4 44 2N 1 7 E
Castelvetrano, Italy 20 F5 37 41N 12 47 E
Casterton, Australia 63 F3 37 30S 141 30 E
Castilla La Mancha □, Spain 19 C4 39 30N 3 30W
Castilla y Leon □, Spain 19 B3 42 0N 5 0W
Castillos, Uruguay 95 C5 34 12S 53 52W
Castle Dale, U.S.A. 82 G8 39 13N 111 1W
Castle Douglas, U.K. 12 G5 54 56N 3 56W
Castle Rock, Colo., U.S.A. 80 F2 39 22N 104 51W
Castle Rock, Wash., U.S.A. 84 D4 46 17N 122 54W
Castlebar, Ireland 13 C2 53 52N 9 18W
Castleblaney, Ireland 13 B5 54 7N 6 44W
Castlegar, Canada 72 D5 49 20N 117 40W
Castlemaine, Australia 63 F3 37 2S 144 12 E
Castlerea, Ireland 13 C3 53 46N 8 29W
Castlereagh □, U.K. 13 B6 54 33N 5 53W
Castlereagh →, Australia 63 E4 30 12S 147 32 E
Castlereagh B., Australia 62 A2 12 10S 135 10 E
Castletown, U.K. 10 C3 54 5N 4 38W
Castletown Bearhaven, Ireland 13 E2 51 39N 9 55W
Castlevale, Australia 62 C4 24 30S 146 48 E
Castor, Canada 72 C6 52 15N 111 50W
Castres, France 18 E5 43 37N 2 13 E
Castries, St. Lucia 89 D7 14 2N 60 58W
Castro, Brazil 95 A5 24 45S 50 0W
Castro, Chile 96 E2 42 30S 73 50W
Castro Alves, Brazil 93 F11 12 46S 39 33W
Castroville, Calif., U.S.A. 84 J5 36 46N 121 45W
Castroville, Tex., U.S.A. 81 L5 29 21N 98 53W
Castuera, Spain 19 C3 38 43N 5 37W
Casummit Lake, Canada 70 B1 51 29N 92 22W
Cat Ba, Dao, Vietnam 38 B6 20 50N 107 0 E
Cat I., Bahamas 89 B4 24 30N 75 30W
Cat I., U.S.A. 81 K10 30 14N 89 6W
Cat L., Canada 70 B1 51 40N 91 50W
Catacamas, Honduras 88 D2 14 54N 85 56W
Catacáos, Peru 92 E2 5 20S 80 45W
Cataguases, Brazil 95 A7 21 23S 42 39W
Catahoula L., U.S.A. 81 K8 31 31N 92 7W
Catalão, Brazil 93 G9 18 10S 47 57W
Çatalca, Turkey 21 D13 41 8N 28 27 E
Catalina, Canada 71 C9 48 31N 53 4W
Catalonia = Cataluña □, Spain 19 B6 41 40N 1 15 E
Cataluña □, Spain 19 B6 41 40N 1 15 E
Catamarca, Argentina 94 B2 28 30S 65 50W
Catamarca □, Argentina 94 B2 27 0S 65 50W
Catanduanes, Phil. 37 B6 13 50N 124 20 E
Catanduva, Brazil 95 A6 21 5S 48 58W
Catánia, Italy 20 F6 37 30N 15 6 E
Catanzaro, Italy 20 E7 38 54N 16 35 E
Catarman, Phil. 37 B6 12 28N 124 35 E
Cateel, Phil. 37 C7 7 47N 126 24 E
Cathcart, S. Africa 56 E4 32 18S 27 10 E
Cathlamet, U.S.A. 84 D3 46 12N 123 23W
Catlettsburg, U.S.A. 76 F4 38 25N 82 36W
Catoche, C., Mexico 87 C7 21 40N 87 8W
Catrimani, Brazil 92 C6 0 27N 61 41W
Catskill, U.S.A. 79 D11 42 14N 73 52W
Catskill Mts., U.S.A. 79 D10 42 10N 74 25W
Catt, Mt., Australia 62 A1 13 49S 134 23 E
Cattaraugus, U.S.A. 78 D6 42 22N 78 52W
Catuala, Angola 56 B2 16 25S 19 2 E
Catur, Mozam. 55 E4 13 45S 35 30 E
Catwick Is., Vietnam 39 G7 10 0N 109 0 E
Cauca →, Colombia 92 B4 8 54N 74 28W
Caucaia, Brazil 93 D11 3 40S 38 35W
Caucasus Mountains, Eurasia 25 F7 42 50N 44 0 E
Caúngula, Angola 52 F3 8 26S 18 38 E
Cauquenes, Chile 94 D1 36 0S 72 22W
Caura →, Venezuela 92 B6 7 38N 64 53W
Cauresi →, Mozam. 55 F3 17 8S 33 0 E
Causapscal, Canada 71 C6 48 19N 67 12W
Cauvery →, India 40 P11 11 9N 78 52 E
Caux, Pays de, France 18 B4 49 38N 0 35 E
Cavalier, U.S.A. 80 A6 48 48N 97 37W
Cavan, Ireland 13 C4 54 0N 7 22W
Cavan □, Ireland 13 C4 54 1N 7 16W
Cave City, U.S.A. 76 G3 37 8N 85 58W
Cavenagh Ra., Australia 61 E4 26 12S 127 55 E
Cavendish, Australia 63 F3 37 31S 142 2 E
Caviana, I., Brazil 93 C8 0 10N 50 10W
Cavite, Phil. 37 B6 14 29N 120 55 E
Cawndilla L., Australia 63 E3 32 30S 142 15 E
Cawnpore = Kanpur, India 43 F9 26 28N 80 20 E
Caxias, Brazil 93 D10 4 55S 43 20W
Caxias do Sul, Brazil 95 B5 29 10S 51 10W
Caxito, Angola 52 F2 8 30S 13 30 E
Cay Sal Bank, Bahamas 88 B3 23 45N 80 0W
Cayambe, Ecuador 92 C3 0 3N 78 8W
Cayenne, Fr. Guiana 93 B8 5 5N 52 18W
Cayman Brac, Cayman Is. 88 C4 19 43N 79 49W
Cayman Is. ■, W. Indies 88 C3 19 40N 80 30W
Cayo Romano, Cuba 89 B4 22 0N 78 0W
Cayuga, Canada 78 D5 42 59N 79 50W
Cayuga, U.S.A. 79 D8 42 54N 76 44W
Cayuga L., U.S.A. 79 D8 42 41N 76 41W
Cazombo, Angola 53 G4 11 54S 22 56 E
Ceadâr-Lunga, Moldova 17 E15 46 3N 28 51 E
Ceanannus Mor, Ireland 13 C5 53 44N 6 53W
Ceará = Fortaleza, Brazil 93 D11 3 45S 38 35W
Ceará □, Brazil 93 E11 5 0S 40 0W
Ceará Mirim, Brazil 93 E11 5 38S 35 25W
Cebaco, I. de, Panama 88 E3 7 33N 81 9W
Cebollar, Argentina 94 B2 29 10S 66 35W
Cebu, Phil. 37 B6 10 18N 123 54 E
Cecil Plains, Australia 63 D5 27 30S 151 11 E
Cedar →, U.S.A. 80 E9 41 17N 91 21W
Cedar City, U.S.A. 83 H7 37 41N 113 4W
Cedar Creek Reservoir, U.S.A. 81 J6 32 11N 96 4W
Cedar Falls, Iowa, U.S.A. 80 D8 42 32N 92 27W
Cedar Falls, Wash., U.S.A. 84 C5 47 25N 121 45W
Cedar Key, U.S.A. 77 L4 29 8N 83 2W
Cedar L., Canada 73 C8 53 10N 100 0W
Cedar Rapids, U.S.A. 80 E9 41 59N 91 40W
Cedartown, U.S.A. 77 H3 34 1N 85 15W
Cedarvale, Canada 72 B3 55 1N 128 22W
Cedarville, S. Africa 57 E4 30 23S 29 3 E
Cedarville, U.S.A. 82 F3 41 32N 120 10W
Cedral, Mexico 86 C4 23 50N 100 42W
Cedro, Brazil 93 E11 6 34S 39 3W
Cedros, I. de, Mexico 86 B1 28 10N 115 20W
Ceduna, Australia 63 E1 32 7S 133 46 E
Cefalù, Italy 20 E6 38 2N 14 1 E
Cegléd, Hungary 17 E10 47 11N 19 47 E
Celaya, Mexico 86 C4 20 31N 100 37W
Celbridge, Ireland 13 C5 53 20N 6 32W
Celebes = Sulawesi □, Indonesia 37 E6 2 0S 120 0 E
Celebes Sea, Indonesia 37 D6 3 0N 123 0 E
Celina, U.S.A. 76 E3 40 33N 84 35W
Celje, Slovenia 16 E8 46 16N 15 18 E
Celle, Germany 16 B6 52 37N 10 4 E
Cement, U.S.A. 81 H5 34 56N 98 8W
Center, N. Dak., U.S.A. 80 B4 47 7N 101 18W
Center, Tex., U.S.A. 81 K7 31 48N 94 11W
Centerfield, U.S.A. 83 G8 39 8N 111 49W
Centerville, Calif., U.S.A. 84 J7 36 44N 119 30W
Centerville, Iowa, U.S.A. 80 E8 40 44N 92 52W
Centerville, Pa., U.S.A. 78 F5 40 3N 79 59W
Centerville, S. Dak., U.S.A. 80 D6 43 7N 96 58W
Centerville, Tenn., U.S.A. 77 H2 35 47N 87 28W
Centerville, Tex., U.S.A. 81 K7 31 16N 95 59W
Central, U.S.A. 83 K9 32 47N 108 9W
Central □, Kenya 54 C4 0 30S 37 30 E
Central □, Malawi 55 E3 13 30S 33 30 E
Central □, Zambia 55 E2 14 25S 28 50 E
Central, Cordillera, Colombia 92 C4 5 0N 75 0W
Central, Cordillera, Costa Rica 88 D3 10 10N 84 5W
Central, Cordillera, Dom. Rep. 89 C5 19 15N 71 0W
Central African Rep. ■, Africa 51 G9 7 0N 20 0 E
Central City, Ky., U.S.A. 76 G2 37 18N 87 7W
Central City, Nebr., U.S.A. 80 E5 41 7N 98 0W
Central I., Kenya 54 B4 3 30N 36 0 E
Central Makran Range, Pakistan 40 F4 26 30N 64 15 E
Central Patricia, Canada 70 B1 51 30N 90 9W
Central Russian Uplands, Europe 6 E13 54 0N 36 0 E
Central Siberian Plateau, Russia 28 C14 65 0N 105 0 E
Centralia, Ill., U.S.A. 80 F10 38 32N 89 8W
Centralia, Mo., U.S.A. 80 F8 39 13N 92 8W
Centralia, Wash., U.S.A. 84 D4 46 43N 122 58W
Centreville, Ala., U.S.A. 77 J2 32 57N 87 8W
Centreville, Miss., U.S.A. 81 K9 31 5N 91 4W
Cephalonia = Kefallinía, Greece 21 E9 38 20N 20 30 E
Cepu, Indonesia 37 G14 7 9S 111 35 E
Ceram = Seram, Indonesia 37 E7 3 10S 129 0 E
Ceram Sea = Seram Sea, Indonesia 37 E7 2 30S 128 30 E
Ceres, Argentina 94 B3 29 55S 61 55W
Ceres, S. Africa 56 E2 33 21S 19 18 E
Ceres, U.S.A. 84 H6 37 35N 120 57W
Ceridigion □, U.K. 11 E3 52 16N 4 15W
Cerignola, Italy 20 D6 41 17N 15 53 E
Cerigo = Kíthira, Greece 21 F10 36 8N 23 0 E
Çerkeşköy, Turkey 21 D12 41 17N 27 59 E
Cerralvo, I., Mexico 86 C3 24 20N 109 45W
Cerritos, Mexico 86 C4 22 27N 100 20W
Cervera, Spain 19 B6 41 40N 1 16 E
Cesena, Italy 20 B5 44 8N 12 15 E
Cēsis, Latvia 9 H21 57 18N 25 15 E
Česka Republika = Czech Rep. ■, Europe 16 D8 50 0N 15 0 E
České Budějovice, Czech. 16 D8 48 55N 14 25 E
Ceskomoravská Vrchovina, Czech. 16 D8 49 30N 15 40 E
Çeşme, Turkey 21 E12 38 20N 26 23 E
Cessnock, Australia 63 E5 32 50S 151 21 E
Cetinje, Montenegro, Yug. 21 C8 42 23N 18 59 E
Cetraro, Italy 20 E6 39 31N 15 55 E
Ceuta, N. Afr. 19 E3 35 52N 5 18W
Cévennes, France 18 D5 44 10N 3 50 E
Ceyhan →, Turkey 25 G6 36 38N 35 40 E
Ceylon = Sri Lanka ■, Asia 40 R12 7 30N 80 50 E
Cha-am, Thailand 38 F2 12 48N 99 58 E
Chacabuco, Argentina 94 C3 34 40S 60 27W
Chachapoyas, Peru 92 E3 6 15S 77 50W
Chachoengsao, Thailand 38 F3 13 42N 101 5 E
Chachran, Pakistan 40 E7 28 55N 70 30 E
Chachro, Pakistan 42 G4 25 5N 70 15 E
Chaco □, Argentina 94 B3 26 30S 61 0W
Chaco □, Paraguay 94 B3 26 0S 60 0W
Chad ■, Africa 51 E8 15 0N 17 15 E
Chad, L. = Tchad, L., Chad 51 F7 13 30N 14 30 E

Corinth

Cloverdale, U.S.A. **84 G4** 38 48N 123 1W
Clovis, Calif., U.S.A. **83 H4** 36 49N 119 42W
Clovis, N. Mex., U.S.A. **81 H3** 34 24N 103 12W
Cluj-Napoca, Romania **17 E12** 46 47N 23 38 E
Clunes, Australia **63 F3** 37 20S 143 45 E
Clutha →, N.Z. **59 M2** 46 20S 169 49 E
Clwyd →, U.K. **10 D4** 53 19N 3 31W
Clyde, N.Z. **59 L2** 45 12S 169 20 E
Clyde, U.S.A. **78 C8** 43 5N 76 52W
Clyde →, U.K. **12 F4** 55 55N 4 30W
Clyde, Firth of, U.K. **12 F4** 55 22N 5 1W
Clyde River, Canada **69 A13** 70 30N 68 30W
Clydebank, U.K. **12 F4** 55 54N 4 23W
Clymer, U.S.A. **78 D5** 40 40N 79 1W
Coachella, U.S.A. **85 M10** 33 41N 116 10W
Coachella Canal, U.S.A. **85 N12** 32 43N 114 57W
Coahoma, U.S.A. **81 J4** 32 18N 101 18W
Coahuayana →, Mexico **86 D4** 18 41N 103 45W
Coahuayutla, Mexico **86 D4** 18 19N 101 42W
Coahuila □, Mexico **86 B4** 27 0N 103 0W
Coal →, Canada **72 B3** 59 39N 126 57W
Coalane, Mozam. **55 F4** 17 48S 37 2 E
Coalcomán, Mexico **86 D4** 18 40N 103 10W
Coaldale, Canada **72 D6** 49 45N 112 35W
Coalgate, U.S.A. **81 H6** 34 32N 96 13W
Coalinga, U.S.A. **83 H3** 36 9N 120 21W
Coalville, U.K. **10 E6** 52 44N 1 23W
Coalville, U.S.A. **82 F8** 40 55N 111 24W
Coari, Brazil **92 D6** 4 8S 63 7W
Coast □, Kenya **54 C4** 2 40S 39 45 E
Coast Mts., Canada **72 C3** 55 0N 129 20W
Coast Ranges, U.S.A. **84 G4** 39 0N 123 0W
Coatbridge, U.K. **12 F4** 55 52N 4 6W
Coatepec, Mexico **87 D5** 19 27N 96 58W
Coatepeque, Guatemala **88 D1** 14 46N 91 55W
Coatesville, U.S.A. **76 F8** 39 59N 75 50W
Coaticook, Canada **71 C5** 45 10N 71 46W
Coats I., Canada **69 B11** 62 30N 83 0W
Coats Land, Antarctica **5 D1** 77 0S 25 0W
Coatzacoalcos, Mexico **87 D6** 18 7N 94 25W
Cobalt, Canada **70 C4** 47 25N 79 42W
Cobán, Guatemala **88 C1** 15 30N 90 21W
Cobar, Australia **63 E4** 31 27S 145 48 E
Cóbh, Ireland **13 E3** 51 51N 8 17W
Cobham, Australia **63 E3** 30 18S 142 7 E
Cobija, Bolivia **92 F5** 11 0S 68 50W
Cobleskill, U.S.A. **79 D10** 42 41N 74 29W
Coboconk, Canada **78 B6** 44 39N 78 48W
Cobourg, Canada **70 D4** 43 58N 78 10W
Cobourg Pen., Australia **60 B5** 11 20S 132 15 E
Cobram, Australia **63 F4** 35 54S 145 40 E
Cobre, U.S.A. **82 F6** 41 7N 114 24W
Cóbué, Mozam. **55 E3** 12 0S 34 58 E
Coburg, Germany **16 C6** 50 15N 10 58 E
Cocanada = Kakinada, India **41 L13** 16 57N 82 11 E
Cochabamba, Bolivia **92 G5** 17 26S 66 10W
Cochemane, Mozam. **55 F3** 17 0S 32 54 E
Cochin, India **40 Q10** 9 59N 76 22 E
Cochin China = Nam-Phan, Vietnam **39 G6** 10 30N 106 0 E
Cochise, U.S.A. **83 K9** 32 7N 109 55W
Cochran, U.S.A. **77 J4** 32 23N 83 21W
Cochrane, Alta., Canada **72 C6** 51 11N 114 30W
Cochrane, Ont., Canada **70 C3** 49 0N 81 0W
Cochrane →, Canada **73 B8** 59 0N 103 40W
Cochrane, L., Chile **96 F2** 47 10S 72 0W
Cockburn, Australia **63 E3** 32 5S 141 0 E
Cockburn, Canal, Chile **96 G2** 54 30S 72 0W
Cockburn I., Canada **70 C3** 45 55N 83 22W
Cockburn Ra., Australia **60 C4** 15 46S 128 0 E
Cocklebiddy Motel, Australia **61 F4** 32 0S 126 3 E
Coco →, Cent. Amer. **88 D3** 15 0N 83 8W
Cocoa, U.S.A. **77 L5** 28 21N 80 44W
Cocobeach, Gabon **52 D1** 0 59N 9 34 E
Cocos, I. del, Pac. Oc. **65 G19** 5 25N 87 55W
Cocos Is., Ind. Oc. **64 J1** 12 10S 96 55 E
Cod, C., U.S.A. **75 B13** 42 5N 70 10W
Codajás, Brazil **92 D6** 3 55S 62 0W
Coderre, Canada **73 C7** 50 11N 106 31W
Codó, Brazil **93 D10** 4 30S 43 55W
Cody, U.S.A. **82 D9** 44 32N 109 3W
Coe Hill, Canada **70 D4** 44 52N 77 50W
Coelemu, Chile **94 D1** 36 30S 72 48W
Coen, Australia **62 A3** 13 52S 143 12 E
Cœur d'Alene, U.S.A. **82 C5** 47 45N 116 51W
Cœur d'Alene L., U.S.A. **82 C5** 47 32N 116 48W
Coevorden, Neths. **15 B6** 52 40N 6 44 E
Cofete, Canary Is. **22 F5** 28 6N 14 23W
Coffeyville, U.S.A. **81 G7** 37 2N 95 37W
Coffin B., Australia **63 E2** 34 38S 135 28 E
Coffin Bay Peninsula, Australia **63 E2** 34 32S 135 15 E
Coffs Harbour, Australia **63 E5** 30 16S 153 5 E
Cognac, France **18 D3** 45 41N 0 20W
Cohagen, U.S.A. **82 C10** 47 3N 106 37W
Cohoes, U.S.A. **79 D11** 42 46N 73 42W
Cohuna, Australia **63 F3** 35 45S 144 15 E
Coiba, I., Panama **88 E3** 7 30N 81 40W
Coig →, Argentina **96 G3** 51 0S 69 10W
Coihaique, Chile **96 F2** 45 30S 71 45W
Coimbatore, India **40 P10** 11 2N 76 59 E
Coimbra, Brazil **92 G7** 19 55S 57 48W
Coimbra, Portugal **19 B1** 40 15N 8 27W
Coín, Spain **19 D3** 36 40N 4 48W
Cojimies, Ecuador **92 C2** 0 20N 80 0W
Cojutepequé, El Salv. **88 D2** 13 41N 88 54W
Cokeville, U.S.A. **82 E8** 42 5N 110 57W
Colac, Australia **63 F3** 38 21S 143 35 E
Colatina, Brazil **93 G10** 19 32S 40 37W
Colbeck, C., Antarctica **5 D13** 77 6S 157 48W
Colbinabbin, Australia **63 F3** 36 38S 144 48 E
Colborne, Canada **78 B7** 44 0N 77 53W
Colby, U.S.A. **80 F4** 39 24N 101 3W
Colchagua □, Chile **94 C1** 34 30S 71 0W
Colchester, U.K. **11 F8** 51 54N 0 55 E
Coldstream, U.K. **12 F6** 55 39N 2 15W
Coldwater, Canada **78 B5** 44 42N 79 40W
Coldwater, U.S.A. **81 G5** 37 16N 99 20W
Colebrook, Australia **62 G4** 42 31S 147 21 E
Colebrook, U.S.A. **79 B13** 44 54N 71 30W
Coleman, Canada **72 D6** 49 40N 114 30W
Coleman, U.S.A. **81 K5** 31 50N 99 26W
Coleman →, Australia **62 B3** 15 6S 141 38 E
Colenso, S. Africa **57 D4** 28 44S 29 50 E
Coleraine, Australia **63 F3** 37 36S 141 40 E
Coleraine, U.K. **13 A5** 55 8N 6 41W
Coleraine □, U.K. **13 A5** 55 8N 6 40W
Coleridge, L., N.Z. **59 K3** 43 17S 171 30 E
Colesberg, S. Africa **56 E4** 30 45S 25 5 E
Coleville, U.S.A. **84 G7** 38 34N 119 30W
Colfax, Calif., U.S.A. **84 F6** 39 6N 120 57W
Colfax, La., U.S.A. **81 K8** 31 31N 92 42W
Colfax, Wash., U.S.A. **82 C5** 46 53N 117 22W
Colhué Huapi, L., Argentina **96 F3** 45 30S 69 0W
Coligny, S. Africa **57 D4** 26 17S 26 15 E
Colima, Mexico **86 D4** 19 14N 103 43W
Colima □, Mexico **86 D4** 19 10N 103 40W
Colima, Nevado de, Mexico **86 D4** 19 35N 103 45W
Colina, Chile **94 C1** 33 13S 70 45W
Colinas, Brazil **93 E10** 6 0S 44 10W
Coll, U.K. **12 E2** 56 39N 6 34W
Collaguasi, Chile **94 A2** 21 5S 68 45W
Collarenebri, Australia **63 D4** 29 33S 148 34 E
Collbran, U.S.A. **83 G10** 39 14N 107 58W
Colleen Bawn, Zimbabwe **55 G2** 21 0S 29 12 E
College Park, U.S.A. **77 J3** 33 40N 84 27W
College Station, U.S.A. **81 K6** 30 37N 96 21W
Collette, Canada **71 C6** 46 40N 65 30W
Collie, Australia **61 F2** 33 22S 116 8 E
Collier B., Australia **60 C3** 16 10S 124 15 E
Collier Ra., Australia **60 D2** 24 45S 119 10 E
Collingwood, Canada **78 B4** 44 29N 80 13W
Collingwood, N.Z. **59 J4** 40 41S 172 40 E
Collins, Canada **70 B2** 50 17N 89 27W
Collinsville, Australia **62 C4** 20 30S 147 56 E
Collipulli, Chile **94 D1** 37 55S 72 30W
Collooney, Ireland **13 B3** 54 11N 8 29W
Colmar, France **18 B7** 48 5N 7 20 E
Colne, U.K. **10 D5** 53 51N 2 9W
Colo →, Australia **63 E5** 33 25S 150 52 E
Cologne = Köln, Germany **16 C4** 50 56N 6 57 E
Colom, I., Spain **22 B11** 39 58N 4 16 E
Coloma, U.S.A. **84 G6** 38 48N 120 53W
Colomb-Béchar = Béchar, Algeria **50 B4** 31 38N 2 18W
Colômbia, Brazil **93 H9** 20 10S 48 40W
Colombia ■, S. Amer. **92 C4** 3 45N 73 0W
Colombian Basin, S. Amer. **66 H12** 14 0N 76 0W
Colombo, Sri Lanka **40 R11** 6 56N 79 58 E
Colome, U.S.A. **80 D5** 43 16N 99 43W
Colón, Argentina **94 C4** 32 12S 58 10W
Colón, Cuba **88 B3** 22 42N 80 54W
Colón, Panama **88 E4** 9 20N 79 54W
Colona, Australia **61 F5** 31 38S 132 4 E
Colonia, Uruguay **94 C4** 34 25S 57 50W
Colonia de San Jordi, Spain **22 B9** 39 19N 2 59 E
Colonia Dora, Argentina **94 B3** 28 34S 62 59W
Colonial Heights, U.S.A. **76 G7** 37 15N 77 25W
Colonsay, Canada **73 C7** 51 59N 105 52W
Colonsay, U.K. **12 E2** 56 5N 6 12W
Colorado □, U.S.A. **83 G10** 39 30N 105 30W
Colorado →, Argentina **96 D4** 39 50S 62 8W
Colorado →, N. Amer. **83 L6** 31 45N 114 40W
Colorado →, U.S.A. **81 L7** 28 36N 95 59W
Colorado City, U.S.A. **81 J4** 32 24N 100 52W
Colorado Desert, U.S.A. **74 D3** 34 20N 116 0W
Colorado Plateau, U.S.A. **83 H8** 37 0N 111 0W
Colorado River Aqueduct, U.S.A. **85 L12** 34 17N 114 10W
Colorado Springs, U.S.A. **80 F2** 38 50N 104 49W
Colotlán, Mexico **86 C4** 22 6N 103 16W
Colton, N.Y., U.S.A. **79 B10** 44 33N 74 56W
Colton, Wash., U.S.A. **82 C5** 46 34N 117 8W
Columbia, La., U.S.A. **81 J8** 32 6N 92 5W
Columbia, Miss., U.S.A. **81 K10** 31 15N 89 50W
Columbia, Mo., U.S.A. **80 F8** 38 57N 92 20W
Columbia, Pa., U.S.A. **79 F8** 40 2N 76 30W
Columbia, S.C., U.S.A. **77 H5** 34 0N 81 2W
Columbia, Tenn., U.S.A. **77 H2** 35 37N 87 2W
Columbia →, U.S.A. **82 C1** 46 15N 124 5W
Columbia, C., Canada **4 A4** 83 0N 70 0W
Columbia, District of □, U.S.A. **76 F7** 38 55N 77 0W
Columbia, Mt., Canada **72 C5** 52 8N 117 20W
Columbia Basin, U.S.A. **82 C4** 46 45N 119 5W
Columbia Falls, U.S.A. **82 B6** 48 23N 114 11W
Columbia Heights, U.S.A. **80 C8** 45 3N 93 15W
Columbiana, U.S.A. **78 F4** 40 53N 80 42W
Columbretes, Is., Spain **19 C6** 39 50N 0 50 E
Columbus, Ga., U.S.A. **77 J3** 32 28N 84 59W
Columbus, Ind., U.S.A. **76 F3** 39 13N 85 55W
Columbus, Kans., U.S.A. **81 G7** 37 10N 94 50W
Columbus, Miss., U.S.A. **77 J1** 33 30N 88 25W
Columbus, Mont., U.S.A. **82 D9** 45 38N 109 15W
Columbus, N. Dak., U.S.A. **80 A3** 48 54N 102 47W
Columbus, N. Mex., U.S.A. **83 L10** 31 50N 107 38W
Columbus, Nebr., U.S.A. **80 E6** 41 26N 97 22W
Columbus, Ohio, U.S.A. **76 F4** 39 58N 83 0W
Columbus, Tex., U.S.A. **81 L6** 29 42N 96 33W
Columbus, Wis., U.S.A. **80 D10** 43 21N 89 1W
Colusa, U.S.A. **84 F4** 39 13N 122 1W
Colville, U.S.A. **82 B5** 48 33N 117 54W
Colville →, U.S.A. **68 A4** 70 25N 150 30W
Colville, C., N.Z. **59 G5** 36 29S 175 21 E
Colwyn Bay, U.K. **10 D4** 53 18N 3 44W
Comácchio, Italy **20 B5** 44 42N 12 11 E
Comalcalco, Mexico **87 D6** 18 16N 93 13W
Comallo, Argentina **96 E2** 41 0S 70 5W
Comanche, Okla., U.S.A. **81 H6** 34 22N 97 58W
Comanche, Tex., U.S.A. **81 K5** 31 54N 98 36W
Comayagua, Honduras **88 D2** 14 25N 87 37W
Combahee →, U.S.A. **77 J5** 32 30N 80 31W
Comber, Canada **78 D2** 42 14N 82 33W
Comblain-au-Pont, Belgium **15 D5** 50 29N 5 35 E
Comeragh Mts., Ireland **13 D4** 52 18N 7 34W
Comet, Australia **62 C4** 23 36S 148 38 E
Comilla, Bangla. **41 H17** 23 28N 91 10 E
Comino, Malta **23 C1** 36 2N 14 20 E
Comino, C., Italy **20 D3** 40 32N 9 49 E
Comitán, Mexico **87 D6** 16 18N 92 9W
Commerce, Ga., U.S.A. **77 H4** 34 12N 83 28W
Commerce, Tex., U.S.A. **81 J7** 33 15N 95 54W
Committee B., Canada **69 B11** 68 30N 86 30W
Commonwealth B., Antarctica **5 C10** 67 0S 144 0 E
Commoron Cr. →, Australia **63 D5** 28 22S 150 8 E
Communism Pk. = Kommunizma, Pik, Tajikistan **26 F8** 39 0N 72 2 E
Como, Italy **20 B3** 45 47N 9 5 E
Como, L. di, Italy **20 B3** 46 0N 9 11 E
Comodoro Rivadavia, Argentina **96 F3** 45 50S 67 40W
Comorin, C., India **40 Q10** 8 3N 77 40 E
Comoro Is. = Comoros ■, Ind. Oc. **49 H8** 12 10S 44 15 E
Comoros ■, Ind. Oc. **49 H8** 12 10S 44 15 E
Comox, Canada **72 D4** 49 42N 124 55W
Compiègne, France **18 B5** 49 24N 2 50 E
Compostela, Mexico **86 C4** 21 15N 104 53W
Comprida, I., Brazil **95 A6** 24 50S 47 42W
Compton, U.S.A. **85 M8** 33 54N 118 13W
Compton Downs, Australia **63 E4** 30 28S 146 30 E
Comrat, Moldova **17 E15** 46 18N 28 40 E
Con Cuong, Vietnam **38 C5** 19 2N 104 54 E
Con Son, Vietnam **39 H6** 8 41N 106 37 E
Conakry, Guinea **50 G2** 9 29N 13 49W
Conara Junction, Australia **62 G4** 41 50S 147 26 E
Concarneau, France **18 C2** 47 52N 3 56W
Conceição, Mozam. **55 F4** 18 47S 36 7 E
Conceição da Barra, Brazil **93 G11** 18 35S 39 45W
Conceição do Araguaia, Brazil **93 E9** 8 0S 49 2W
Concepción, Argentina **94 B2** 27 20S 65 35W
Concepción, Bolivia **92 G6** 16 15S 62 8W
Concepción, Chile **94 D1** 36 50S 73 0W
Concepción, Mexico **87 D6** 18 15N 90 5W
Concepción, Paraguay **94 A4** 23 22S 57 26W
Concepción □, Chile **94 D1** 37 0S 72 30W
Concepción →, Mexico **86 A2** 30 32N 113 2W
Concepción, L., Bolivia **92 G6** 17 20S 61 20W
Concepción, Punta, Mexico **86 B2** 26 55N 111 59W
Concepción del Oro, Mexico **86 C4** 24 40N 101 30W
Concepción del Uruguay, Argentina **94 C4** 32 35S 58 20W
Conception, Pt., U.S.A. **85 L6** 34 27N 120 28W
Conception B., Namibia **56 C1** 23 55S 14 22 E
Conception I., Bahamas **89 B4** 23 52N 75 9W
Concession, Zimbabwe **55 F3** 17 27S 30 56 E
Conchas Dam, U.S.A. **81 H2** 35 22N 104 11W
Conche, Canada **71 B8** 50 55N 55 58W
Concho, U.S.A. **83 J9** 34 28N 109 36W
Concho →, U.S.A. **81 K5** 31 34N 99 43W
Conchos →, Chihuahua, Mexico **86 B4** 29 32N 105 0W
Conchos →, Tamaulipas, Mexico **87 B5** 25 9N 98 35W
Concord, Calif., U.S.A. **84 H4** 37 59N 122 2W
Concord, N.C., U.S.A. **77 H5** 35 25N 80 35W
Concord, N.H., U.S.A. **79 C13** 43 12N 71 32W
Concordia, Argentina **94 C4** 31 20S 58 2W
Concórdia, Brazil **92 D5** 4 36S 66 36W
Concordia, Mexico **86 C3** 23 18N 106 2W
Concordia, U.S.A. **80 F6** 39 34N 97 40W
Concrete, U.S.A. **82 B3** 48 32N 121 45W
Condamine, Australia **63 D5** 26 56S 150 9 E
Conde, U.S.A. **80 C5** 45 9N 98 6W
Condeúba, Brazil **93 F10** 14 52S 42 0W
Condobolin, Australia **63 E4** 33 4S 147 6 E
Condon, U.S.A. **82 D3** 45 14N 120 11W
Conegliano, Italy **20 B5** 45 53N 12 18 E
Conejera, I., Spain **22 B9** 39 11N 2 58 E
Conejos, Mexico **86 B4** 26 14N 103 53W
Confuso →, Paraguay **94 B4** 25 9S 57 34W
Congleton, U.K. **10 D5** 53 10N 2 13W
Congo = Zaïre →, Africa **52 F2** 6 4S 12 24 E
Congo (Kinshasa) = Zaïre ■, Africa **52 E4** 3 0S 23 0 E
Congo ■, Africa **52 E3** 1 0S 16 0 E
Congo Basin, Africa **48 G6** 0 10S 24 30 E
Congonhas, Brazil **95 A7** 20 30S 43 52W
Congress, U.S.A. **83 J7** 34 9N 112 51W
Coniston, Canada **70 C3** 46 29N 80 51W
Conjeeveram = Kanchipuram, India **40 N11** 12 52N 79 45 E
Conjuboy, Australia **62 B3** 18 35S 144 35 E
Conklin, Canada **73 B6** 55 38N 111 5W
Conlea, Australia **63 E3** 30 7S 144 35 E
Conn, L., Ireland **13 B2** 54 3N 9 15W
Connacht □, Ireland **13 C3** 53 43N 9 12W
Conneaut, U.S.A. **78 E4** 41 57N 80 34W
Connecticut □, U.S.A. **79 E12** 41 30N 72 45W
Connecticut →, U.S.A. **79 E12** 41 16N 72 20W
Connell, U.S.A. **82 C4** 46 40N 118 52W
Connellsville, U.S.A. **78 F5** 40 1N 79 35W
Connemara, Ireland **13 C2** 53 29N 9 45W
Connemaugh →, U.S.A. **78 F5** 40 28N 79 19W
Connersville, U.S.A. **76 F3** 39 39N 85 8W
Connors Ra., Australia **62 C4** 21 40S 149 10 E
Conoble, Australia **63 E3** 32 55S 144 33 E
Cononaco →, Ecuador **92 D3** 1 32S 75 35W
Cononbridge, U.K. **12 D4** 57 34N 4 27W
Conquest, Canada **73 C7** 51 32N 107 14W
Conrad, U.S.A. **82 B8** 48 10N 111 57W
Conran, C., Australia **63 F4** 37 49S 148 44 E
Conroe, U.S.A. **81 K7** 30 19N 95 27W
Conselheiro Lafaiete, Brazil **95 A7** 20 40S 43 48W
Consort, Canada **73 C6** 52 1N 110 46W
Constance = Konstanz, Germany **16 E5** 47 40N 9 10 E
Constance, L. = Bodensee, Europe **16 E5** 47 35N 9 25 E
Constanța, Romania **17 F15** 44 14N 28 38 E
Constantine, Algeria **50 A6** 36 25N 6 42 E
Constitución, Chile **94 D1** 35 20S 72 30W
Constitución, Uruguay **94 C4** 31 0S 57 50W
Consul, Canada **73 D7** 49 20N 109 30W
Contact, U.S.A. **82 F6** 41 46N 114 45W
Contai, India **43 J12** 21 54N 87 46 E
Contamana, Peru **92 E4** 7 19S 74 55W
Contas →, Brazil **93 F11** 14 17S 39 1W
Contoocook, U.S.A. **79 C13** 43 13N 71 45W
Contra Costa, Mozam. **57 D5** 25 9S 33 30 E
Conway = Conwy, U.K. **10 D4** 53 17N 3 50W
Conway = Conwy →, U.K. **10 D4** 53 17N 3 50W
Conway, Ark., U.S.A. **81 H8** 35 5N 92 26W
Conway, N.H., U.S.A. **79 C13** 43 59N 71 7W
Conway, S.C., U.S.A. **77 J6** 33 51N 79 3W
Conway, L., Australia **63 D2** 28 17S 135 35 E
Conwy, U.K. **10 D4** 53 17N 3 50W
Conwy →, U.K. **10 D4** 53 17N 3 50W
Coober Pedy, Australia **63 D1** 29 1S 134 43 E
Cooch Behar = Koch Bihar, India **41 F16** 26 22N 89 29 E
Coodardy, Australia **61 E2** 27 15S 117 39 E
Cook, Australia **61 F5** 30 37S 130 25 E
Cook, U.S.A. **80 B8** 47 49N 92 39W
Cook, B., Chile **96 H3** 55 10S 70 0W
Cook, Mt., N.Z. **59 K3** 43 36S 170 9 E
Cook Inlet, U.S.A. **68 C4** 60 0N 152 0W
Cook Is., Pac. Oc. **65 J11** 17 0S 160 0W
Cook Strait, N.Z. **59 J5** 41 15S 174 29 E
Cookeville, U.S.A. **77 G3** 36 10N 85 30W
Cookhouse, S. Africa **56 E4** 32 44S 25 47 E
Cookshire, Canada **79 A13** 45 25N 71 38W
Cookstown, U.K. **13 B5** 54 39N 6 45W
Cookstown □, U.K. **13 B5** 54 40N 6 43W
Cooksville, Canada **78 C5** 43 36N 79 35W
Cooktown, Australia **62 B4** 15 30S 145 16 E
Coolabah, Australia **63 E4** 31 1S 146 43 E
Cooladdi, Australia **63 D4** 26 37S 145 23 E
Coolah, Australia **63 E4** 31 48S 149 41 E
Coolamon, Australia **63 E4** 34 46S 147 8 E
Coolangatta, Australia **63 D5** 28 11S 153 29 E
Coolgardie, Australia **61 F3** 30 55S 121 8 E
Coolibah, Australia **60 C5** 15 33S 130 56 E
Coolidge, U.S.A. **83 K8** 32 59N 111 31W
Coolidge Dam, U.S.A. **83 K8** 33 0N 110 20W
Cooma, Australia **63 F4** 36 12S 149 8 E
Coon Rapids, U.S.A. **80 C8** 45 9N 93 19W
Coonabarabran, Australia **63 E4** 31 14S 149 18 E
Coonamble, Australia **63 E4** 30 56S 148 27 E
Coonana, Australia **61 F3** 31 0S 123 0 E
Coondapoor, India **40 N9** 13 42N 74 40 E
Coongie, Australia **63 D3** 27 9S 140 8 E
Coongoola, Australia **63 D4** 27 43S 145 51 E
Cooninie, L., Australia **63 D2** 26 4S 139 59 E
Cooper, U.S.A. **81 J7** 33 23N 95 42W
Cooper →, U.S.A. **77 J6** 33 0N 79 56W
Cooper Cr. →, Australia **63 D2** 28 29S 137 46 E
Cooperstown, N. Dak., U.S.A. **80 B5** 47 27N 98 8W
Cooperstown, N.Y., U.S.A. **79 D10** 42 42N 74 56W
Coorabie, Australia **61 F5** 31 54S 132 18 E
Coorabulka, Australia **62 C3** 23 41S 140 20 E
Coorow, Australia **61 E2** 29 53S 116 2 E
Cooroy, Australia **63 D5** 26 22S 152 54 E
Coos Bay, U.S.A. **82 E1** 43 22N 124 13W
Cootamundra, Australia **63 E4** 34 36S 148 1 E
Cootehill, Ireland **13 B4** 54 4N 7 5W
Cooyar, Australia **63 D5** 26 59S 151 51 E
Cooyeana, Australia **62 C2** 24 29S 138 45 E
Copahue Paso, Argentina **94 D1** 37 49S 71 8W
Copainalá, Mexico **87 D6** 17 8N 93 11W
Copán, Honduras **88 D2** 14 50N 89 9W
Cope, U.S.A. **80 F3** 39 40N 102 51W
Copenhagen = København, Denmark **9 J15** 55 41N 12 34 E
Copiapó, Chile **94 B1** 27 30S 70 20W
Copiapó →, Chile **94 B1** 27 19S 70 56W
Copley, Australia **63 E2** 30 36S 138 26 E
Copp L., Canada **72 A6** 60 14N 114 40W
Copper Center, U.S.A. **68 B5** 61 58N 145 18W
Copper Cliff, Canada **70 C3** 46 28N 81 4W
Copper Harbor, U.S.A. **76 B2** 47 28N 87 53W
Copper Queen, Zimbabwe **55 F2** 17 29S 29 18 E
Copperbelt □, Zambia **55 E2** 13 15S 27 30 E
Coppermine = Kuglugtuk, Canada **68 B8** 67 50N 115 5W
Coppermine →, Canada **68 B8** 67 49N 116 4W
Copperopolis, U.S.A. **84 H6** 37 58N 120 38W
Coquet →, U.K. **10 B6** 55 20N 1 32W
Coquilhatville = Mbandaka, Zaïre **52 D3** 0 1N 18 18 E
Coquille, U.S.A. **82 E1** 43 11N 124 11W
Coquimbo, Chile **94 B1** 30 0S 71 20W
Coquimbo □, Chile **94 C1** 31 0S 71 0W
Corabia, Romania **17 G13** 43 48N 24 30 E
Coracora, Peru **92 G4** 15 5S 73 45W
Coral Gables, U.S.A. **77 N5** 25 45N 80 16W
Coral Harbour, Canada **69 B11** 64 8N 83 10W
Coral Sea, Pac. Oc. **64 J7** 15 0S 150 0 E
Coral Springs, U.S.A. **77 M5** 26 16N 80 13W
Coraopolis, U.S.A. **78 F4** 40 31N 80 10W
Corato, Italy **20 D7** 41 9N 16 25 E
Corbin, U.S.A. **76 G3** 36 57N 84 6W
Corby, U.K. **11 E7** 52 30N 0 41W
Corby Glen, U.K. **11 E7** 52 49N 0 30W
Corcaigh = Cork, Ireland **13 E3** 51 54N 8 29W
Corcoran, U.S.A. **83 H4** 36 6N 119 33W
Corcubión, Spain **19 A1** 42 56N 9 12W
Cordele, U.S.A. **77 K4** 31 58N 83 47W
Cordell, U.S.A. **81 H5** 35 17N 98 59W
Córdoba, Argentina **94 C3** 31 20S 64 10W
Córdoba, Mexico **87 D5** 18 50N 97 0W
Córdoba, Spain **19 D3** 37 50N 4 50W
Córdoba □, Argentina **94 C3** 31 22S 64 15W
Córdoba, Sierra de, Argentina **94 C3** 31 10S 64 25W
Cordon, Phil. **37 A6** 16 42N 121 32 E
Cordova, Ala., U.S.A. **77 J2** 33 46N 87 11W
Cordova, Alaska, U.S.A. **68 B5** 60 33N 145 45W
Corella →, Australia **62 B3** 19 34S 140 47 E
Corfield, Australia **62 C3** 21 40S 143 21 E
Corfu = Kérkira, Greece **23 A3** 39 38N 19 50 E
Corfu, Str of, Greece **23 A4** 39 34N 20 0 E
Coria, Spain **19 C2** 39 58N 6 33W
Corigliano Cálabro, Italy **20 E7** 39 36N 16 31 E
Coringa Is., Australia **62 B4** 16 58S 149 58 E
Corinna, Australia **62 G4** 41 35S 145 10 E
Corinth = Kórinthos, Greece **21 F10** 37 56N 22 55 E
Corinth, Miss., U.S.A. **77 H1** 34 56N 88 31W
Corinth, N.Y., U.S.A. **79 C11** 43 15N 73 49W

Dera Ghazi Khan

Dadri = Charkhi Dadri, India 42 E7 28 37N 76 17 E
Dadu, Pakistan 42 F2 26 45N 67 45 E
Daet, Phil. 37 B6 14 2N 122 55 E
Dagana, Senegal 50 E1 16 30N 15 35W
Dagestan □, Russia 25 F8 42 30N 47 0 E
Daggett, U.S.A. 85 L10 34 52N 116 52W
Daghestan Republic = Dagestan □, Russia 25 F8 42 30N 47 0 E
Dagö = Hiiumaa, Estonia 9 G20 58 50N 22 45 E
Dagu, China 35 E9 38 59N 117 40 E
Dagupan, Phil. 37 A6 16 3N 120 20 E
Dahlak Kebir, Eritrea 46 D3 15 50N 40 10 E
Dahlonega, U.S.A. 77 H4 34 32N 83 59W
Dahod, India 42 H6 22 50N 74 15 E
Dahomey = Benin ■, Africa 50 G5 10 0N 2 0 E
Dahra, Senegal 50 E1 15 22N 15 30W
Dai Hao, Vietnam 38 C6 18 1N 106 25 E
Dai-Sen, Japan 31 G6 35 22N 133 32 E
Dai Xian, China 34 E7 39 4N 112 58 E
Daicheng, China 34 E9 38 42N 116 38 E
Daingean, Ireland 13 C4 53 18N 7 17W
Daintree, Australia 62 B4 16 20S 145 20 E
Daiō-Misaki, Japan 31 G8 34 15N 136 45 E
Dairût, Egypt 51 C11 27 34N 30 43 E
Daisetsu-Zan, Japan 30 C11 43 30N 142 57 E
Dajarra, Australia 62 C2 21 42S 139 30 E
Dak Dam, Cambodia 38 F6 12 20N 107 21 E
Dak Nhe, Vietnam 38 E6 15 28N 107 48 E
Dak Pek, Vietnam 38 E6 15 4N 107 44 E
Dak Song, Vietnam 39 F6 12 19N 107 35 E
Dak Sui, Vietnam 38 E6 14 55N 107 43 E
Dakar, Senegal 50 F1 14 34N 17 29W
Dakhla, W. Sahara 50 D1 23 50N 15 53W
Dakhla, El Wâhât el-, Egypt 51 C10 25 30N 28 50 E
Dakhovskaya, Russia 25 F7 44 13N 40 13 E
Dakor, India 42 H5 22 45N 73 11 E
Dakota City, U.S.A. 80 D6 42 25N 96 25W
Đakovica, Serbia, Yug. 21 C9 42 22N 20 26 E
Dalachi, China 34 F3 36 48N 105 0 E
Dalai Nur, China 34 C9 43 20N 116 45 E
Dālakī, Iran 45 D6 29 26N 51 17 E
Dalälven, Sweden 9 F17 60 12N 16 43 E
Dalaman →, Turkey 21 F13 36 41N 28 43 E
Dalandzadgad, Mongolia 34 C3 43 27N 104 30 E
Dalarna, Sweden 9 F16 61 0N 14 0 E
Dālbandīn, Pakistan 40 E4 29 0N 64 23 E
Dalbeattie, U.K. 12 G5 54 56N 3 50W
Dalby, Australia 63 D5 27 10S 151 17 E
Dalgān, Iran 45 E8 27 31N 59 19 E
Dalhart, U.S.A. 81 G3 36 4N 102 31W
Dalhousie, Canada 71 C6 48 5N 66 26W
Dalhousie, India 42 C6 32 38N 75 58 E
Dali, Shaanxi, China 34 G5 34 48N 109 58 E
Dali, Yunnan, China 32 D5 25 40N 100 10 E
Dalian, China 35 E11 38 50N 121 40 E
Daliang Shan, China 32 D5 28 0N 102 45 E
Daling He →, China 35 D11 40 55N 121 40 E
Dāliyat el Karmel, Israel 47 C4 32 43N 35 2 E
Dalkeith, U.K. 12 F5 55 54N 3 4W
Dall I., U.S.A. 72 C2 54 59N 133 25W
Dallarnil, Australia 63 D5 25 19S 152 2 E
Dallas, Oreg., U.S.A. 82 D2 44 55N 123 19W
Dallas, Tex., U.S.A. 81 J6 32 47N 96 49W
Dalmacija, Croatia 20 C7 43 20N 17 0 E
Dalmatia = Dalmacija, Croatia 20 C7 43 20N 17 0 E
Dalmellington, U.K. 12 F4 55 19N 4 23W
Dalnegorsk, Russia 27 E14 44 32N 135 33 E
Dalnerechensk, Russia 27 E14 45 50N 133 40 E
Daloa, Ivory C. 50 G3 7 0N 6 30W
Dalsland, Sweden 9 G14 58 50N 12 15 E
Daltenganj, India 43 G11 24 0N 84 4 E
Dalton, Canada 70 C3 48 11N 84 1W
Dalton, Ga., U.S.A. 77 H3 34 46N 84 58W
Dalton, Mass., U.S.A. 79 D11 42 28N 73 11W
Dalton, Nebr., U.S.A. 80 E3 41 25N 102 58W
Dalton Iceberg Tongue, Antarctica 5 C9 66 15S 121 30 E
Dalvík, Iceland 8 D4 65 58N 18 32W
Daly →, Australia 60 B5 13 35S 130 19 E
Daly City, U.S.A. 84 H4 37 42N 122 28W
Daly L., Canada 73 B7 56 32N 105 39W
Daly Waters, Australia 62 B1 16 15S 133 24 E
Dam Doi, Vietnam 39 H5 8 50N 105 12 E
Dam Ha, Vietnam 38 B6 21 21N 107 36 E
Daman, India 40 J8 20 25N 72 57 E
Dāmaneh, Iran 45 C6 33 1N 50 29 E
Damanhûr, Egypt 51 B11 31 0N 30 30 E
Damanzhuang, China 34 E9 38 5N 116 35 E
Damar, Indonesia 37 F7 7 7S 128 40 E
Damaraland, Namibia 56 C2 21 0S 17 0 E
Damascus = Dimashq, Syria 47 B5 33 30N 36 18 E
Damāvand, Iran 45 C7 35 47N 52 0 E
Damāvand, Qolleh-ye, Iran 45 C7 35 56N 52 10 E
Damba, Angola 52 F3 6 44S 15 20 E
Dame Marie, Haiti 89 C5 18 36N 74 26W
Dāmghān, Iran 45 B7 36 10N 54 17 E
Damiel, Spain 19 C4 39 4N 3 37W
Damietta = Dumyât, Egypt 51 B11 31 24N 31 48 E
Daming, China 34 F8 36 15N 115 6 E
Damīr Qābū, Syria 44 B4 36 58N 41 51 E
Dammam = Ad Dammām, Si. Arabia 45 E6 26 20N 50 5 E
Damodar →, India 43 H12 23 17N 87 35 E
Damoh, India 43 H8 23 50N 79 28 E
Dampier, Australia 60 D2 20 41S 116 42 E
Dampier, Selat, Indonesia 37 E8 0 40S 131 0 E
Dampier Arch., Australia 60 D2 20 38S 116 32 E
Damrei, Chuor Phnum, Cambodia 39 G4 11 30N 103 0 E
Dana, Indonesia 37 F6 11 0S 122 52 E
Dana, L., Canada 70 B4 50 53N 77 20W
Dana, Mt., U.S.A. 84 H7 37 54N 119 12W
Danbury, U.S.A. 79 E11 41 24N 73 28W
Danby L., U.S.A. 83 J6 34 13N 115 5W
Dand, Afghan. 42 D1 31 28N 65 32 E
Dandaragan, Australia 61 F2 30 40S 115 40 E
Dandeldhura, Nepal 43 E9 29 20N 80 35 E
Dandeli, India 40 M9 15 5N 74 30 E
Dandenong, Australia 63 F4 38 0S 145 15 E
Dandong, China 35 D13 40 10N 124 20 E
Danfeng, China 34 H6 33 45N 110 25 E
Danforth, U.S.A. 71 C6 45 40N 67 52W
Danger Is. = Pukapuka, Cook Is. 65 J11 10 53S 165 49W
Danger Pt., S. Africa 56 E2 34 40S 19 17 E
Dangora, Nigeria 50 F6 11 30N 8 7 E
Dangrek, Phnom, Thailand 38 E5 14 15N 105 0 E
Dangriga, Belize 87 D7 17 0N 88 13W
Dangshan, China 34 G9 34 27N 116 22 E
Daniel, U.S.A. 82 E8 42 52N 110 4W
Daniel's Harbour, Canada 71 B8 50 13N 57 35W
Danielskuil, S. Africa 56 D3 28 11S 23 33 E
Danielson, U.S.A. 79 E13 41 48N 71 53W
Danilov, Russia 24 C7 58 16N 40 13 E
Daning, China 34 F6 36 28N 110 45 E
Danissa, Kenya 54 B5 3 15N 40 58 E
Dankhar Gompa, India 40 C11 32 10N 78 10 E
Danlí, Honduras 88 D2 14 4N 86 35W
Dannemora, U.S.A. 79 B11 44 43N 73 44W
Dannevirke, N.Z. 59 J6 40 12S 176 8 E
Dannhauser, S. Africa 57 D5 28 0S 30 3 E
Dansville, U.S.A. 78 D7 42 34N 77 42W
Dantan, India 43 J12 21 57N 87 20 E
Dante, Somali Rep. 46 E5 10 25N 51 16 E
Danube = Dunărea →, Europe 17 F15 45 20N 29 40 E
Danube →, Europe 6 F11 45 20N 29 40 E
Danvers, U.S.A. 79 D14 42 34N 70 56W
Danville, Ill., U.S.A. 76 E2 40 8N 87 37W
Danville, Ky., U.S.A. 76 G3 37 39N 84 46W
Danville, Va., U.S.A. 77 G6 36 36N 79 23W
Danzig = Gdańsk, Poland 17 A10 54 22N 18 40 E
Dao, Phil. 37 B6 10 30N 121 57 E
Daoud = Aïn Beïda, Algeria 50 A6 35 50N 7 29 E
Daqing Shan, China 34 D6 40 40N 111 0 E
Dar Banda, Africa 48 F6 8 0N 23 0 E
Dar el Beida = Casablanca, Morocco 50 B3 33 36N 7 36W
Dar es Salaam, Tanzania 54 D4 6 50S 39 12 E
Dar Mazār, Iran 45 D8 29 14N 57 20 E
Dar'ā, Syria 47 C5 32 36N 36 7 E
Dar'ā □, Syria 47 C5 32 55N 36 10 E
Dārāb, Iran 45 D7 28 50N 54 30 E
Daraj, Libya 50 B7 30 10N 10 28 E
Dārān, Iran 45 C6 32 59N 50 24 E
Dārayyā, Syria 47 B5 33 28N 36 15 E
Darband, Pakistan 42 B5 34 20N 72 50 E
Darband, Kūh-e, Iran 45 D8 31 34N 57 8 E
Darbhanga, India 43 F11 26 15N 85 55 E
Darby, U.S.A. 82 C6 46 1N 114 11W
Dardanelle, Ark., U.S.A. 81 H8 35 13N 93 9W
Dardanelle, Calif., U.S.A. 84 G7 38 20N 119 50W
Dardanelles = Çanakkale Boğazı, Turkey 21 D12 40 17N 26 32 E
Dārestān, Iran 45 D8 29 9N 58 42 E
Dârfûr, Sudan 51 F9 13 40N 24 0 E
Dargai, Pakistan 42 B4 34 25N 71 55 E
Dargan Ata, Uzbekistan 26 E7 40 29N 62 10 E
Dargaville, N.Z. 59 F4 35 57S 173 52 E
Darhan Muminggan Lianheqi, China 34 D6 41 40N 110 28 E
Darica, Turkey 21 D13 40 45N 29 23 E
Darién, G. del, Colombia 92 B3 9 0N 77 0W
Dariganga, Mongolia 34 B7 45 21N 113 45 E
Darjeeling = Darjiling, India 43 F13 27 3N 88 18 E
Darjiling, India 43 F13 27 3N 88 18 E
Dark Cove, Canada 71 C9 48 47N 54 13W
Darkan, Australia 61 F2 33 20S 116 43 E
Darkhazīneh, Iran 45 D6 31 54N 48 39 E
Darkot Pass, Pakistan 43 A5 36 45N 73 26 E
Darling →, Australia 63 E3 34 4S 141 54 E
Darling Downs, Australia 63 D5 27 30S 150 30 E
Darling Ra., Australia 61 F2 32 30S 116 0 E
Darlington, U.K. 10 C6 54 32N 1 33W
Darlington, S.C., U.S.A. 77 H6 34 18N 79 52W
Darlington, Wis., U.S.A. 80 D9 42 41N 90 7W
Darlington, L., S. Africa 56 E4 33 10S 25 9 E
Darlot, L., Australia 61 E3 27 48S 121 35 E
Darłowo, Poland 16 A9 54 25N 16 25 E
Darmstadt, Germany 16 D5 49 51N 8 39 E
Darnah, Libya 51 B9 32 45N 22 45 E
Darnall, S. Africa 57 D5 29 23S 31 18 E
Darnley, C., Antarctica 5 C6 68 0S 69 0 E
Darnley B., Canada 68 B7 69 30N 123 30W
Darr, Australia 62 C3 23 13S 144 7 E
Darr →, Australia 62 C3 23 39S 143 50 E
Darrington, U.S.A. 82 B3 48 15N 121 36W
Dart →, U.K. 11 G4 50 24N 3 39W
Dart, C., Antarctica 5 D14 73 6S 126 20W
Dartmoor, U.K. 11 G4 50 38N 3 57W
Dartmouth, Australia 62 C3 23 31S 144 44 E
Dartmouth, Canada 71 D7 44 40N 63 30W
Dartmouth, U.K. 11 G4 50 21N 3 36W
Dartmouth, L., Australia 63 D4 26 4S 145 18 E
Dartuch, C., Spain 22 B10 39 55N 3 49 E
Darvaza, Turkmenistan 26 E6 40 11N 58 24 E
Darvel, Teluk, Malaysia 37 D5 4 50N 118 20 E
Darwha, India 40 J10 20 15N 77 45 E
Darwin, Australia 60 B5 12 25S 130 51 E
Darwin, U.S.A. 85 J9 36 15N 117 35W
Darwin River, Australia 60 B5 12 50S 130 58 E
Daryoi Amu = Amudarya →, Uzbekistan 26 E6 43 58N 59 34 E
Dās, U.A.E. 45 E7 25 20N 53 30 E
Dashetai, China 34 D5 41 0N 109 5 E
Dashhowuz, Turkmenistan 26 E6 41 49N 59 58 E
Dasht, Iran 45 B8 37 17N 56 7 E
Dasht →, Pakistan 40 G2 25 10N 61 40 E
Dasht-e Mārgow, Afghan. 40 D3 30 40N 62 30 E
Dasht-i-Nawar, Afghan. 42 C3 33 52N 68 0 E
Daska, Pakistan 42 C6 32 20N 74 20 E
Datça, Turkey 21 F12 36 46N 27 40 E
Datia, India 43 G8 25 39N 78 27 E
Datong, China 34 D7 40 6N 113 18 E
Datu, Tanjung, Indonesia 36 D3 2 5N 109 39 E
Datu Piang, Phil. 37 C6 7 2N 124 30 E
Daugava →, Latvia 9 H21 57 4N 24 3 E
Daugavpils, Latvia 9 J22 55 53N 26 32 E
Daulpur, India 42 F7 26 45N 77 59 E
Dauphin, Canada 73 C8 51 9N 100 5W
Dauphin I., U.S.A. 77 K1 30 15N 88 11W
Dauphin L., Canada 73 C9 51 20N 99 45W
Dauphiné, France 18 D6 45 15N 5 25 E
Dausa, India 42 F7 26 52N 76 20 E
Davangere, India 40 M9 14 25N 75 55 E
Davao, Phil. 37 C7 7 0N 125 40 E
Davao, G. of, Phil. 37 C7 6 30N 125 48 E
Dāvar Panāh, Iran 45 E9 27 25N 62 15 E
Davenport, Calif., U.S.A. 84 H4 37 1N 122 12W
Davenport, Iowa, U.S.A. 80 E9 41 32N 90 35W
Davenport, Wash., U.S.A. 82 C4 47 39N 118 9W
Davenport Downs, Australia 62 C3 24 8S 141 7 E
Davenport Ra., Australia 62 C1 20 28S 134 0 E
David, Panama 88 E3 8 30N 82 30W
David City, U.S.A. 80 E6 41 15N 97 8W
David Gorodok = Davyd Haradok, Belarus 17 B14 52 4N 27 8 E
Davidson, Canada 73 C7 51 16N 105 59W
Davis, U.S.A. 84 G5 38 33N 121 44W
Davis Dam, U.S.A. 85 K12 35 11N 114 34W
Davis Inlet, Canada 71 A7 55 50N 60 59W
Davis Mts., U.S.A. 81 K2 30 50N 103 55W
Davis Sea, Antarctica 5 C7 66 0S 92 0 E
Davis Str., N. Amer. 69 B14 65 0N 58 0W
Davos, Switz. 16 E5 46 48N 9 49 E
Davy L., Canada 73 B7 58 53N 108 18W
Davyd Haradok, Belarus 17 B14 52 4N 27 8 E
Dawes Ra., Australia 62 C5 24 40S 150 40 E
Dawson, Canada 68 B6 64 10N 139 30W
Dawson, Ga., U.S.A. 77 K3 31 46N 84 27W
Dawson, N. Dak., U.S.A. 80 B5 46 52N 99 45W
Dawson, I., Chile 96 G2 53 50S 70 50W
Dawson Creek, Canada 72 B4 55 45N 120 15W
Dawson Inlet, Canada 73 A10 61 50N 93 25W
Dawson Ra., Australia 62 C4 24 30S 149 48 E
Dax, France 18 E3 43 44N 1 3W
Daxian, China 32 C5 31 15N 107 23 E
Daxindian, China 35 F11 37 30N 120 50 E
Daxinggou, China 35 C15 43 25N 129 40 E
Daxue Shan, China 32 C5 30 30N 101 30 E
Daylesford, Australia 63 F3 37 21S 144 9 E
Dayr az Zawr, Syria 44 C4 35 20N 40 5 E
Daysland, Canada 72 C6 52 50N 112 20W
Dayton, Nev., U.S.A. 84 F7 39 14N 119 36W
Dayton, Ohio, U.S.A. 76 F3 39 45N 84 12W
Dayton, Pa., U.S.A. 78 F5 40 53N 79 15W
Dayton, Tenn., U.S.A. 77 H3 35 30N 85 1W
Dayton, Wash., U.S.A. 82 C4 46 19N 117 59W
Daytona Beach, U.S.A. 77 L5 29 13N 81 1W
Dayville, U.S.A. 82 D4 44 28N 119 32W
De Aar, S. Africa 56 E3 30 39S 24 0 E
De Funiak Springs, U.S.A. 77 K2 30 43N 86 7W
De Grey, Australia 60 D2 20 12S 119 12 E
De Grey →, Australia 60 D2 20 12S 119 13 E
De Kalb, U.S.A. 80 E10 41 56N 88 46W
De Land, U.S.A. 77 L5 29 2N 81 18W
De Leon, U.S.A. 81 J5 32 7N 98 32W
De Pere, U.S.A. 76 C1 44 27N 88 4W
De Queen, U.S.A. 81 H7 34 2N 94 21W
De Quincy, U.S.A. 81 K8 30 27N 93 26W
De Ridder, U.S.A. 81 K8 30 51N 93 17W
De Smet, U.S.A. 80 C6 44 23N 97 33W
De Soto, U.S.A. 80 F9 38 8N 90 34W
De Tour Village, U.S.A. 76 C4 46 0N 83 56W
De Witt, U.S.A. 81 H9 34 18N 91 20W
Dead Sea, Asia 47 D4 31 30N 35 30 E
Deadwood, U.S.A. 80 C3 44 23N 103 44W
Deadwood L., Canada 72 B3 59 10N 128 30W
Deakin, Australia 61 F4 30 46S 128 58 E
Deal, U.K. 11 F9 51 13N 1 25 E
Deal I., Australia 62 F4 39 30S 147 20 E
Dealesville, S. Africa 56 D4 28 41S 25 44 E
Dean, Forest of, U.K. 11 F5 51 45N 2 33W
Deán Funes, Argentina 94 C3 30 20S 64 20W
Dearborn, U.S.A. 70 D3 42 19N 83 11W
Dease →, Canada 72 B3 59 56N 128 32W
Dease L., Canada 72 B2 58 40N 130 5W
Dease Lake, Canada 72 B2 58 25N 130 6W
Death Valley, U.S.A. 85 J10 36 15N 116 50W
Death Valley Junction, U.S.A. 85 J10 36 20N 116 25W
Death Valley National Monument, U.S.A. 85 J10 36 45N 117 15W
Deba Habe, Nigeria 50 F7 10 14N 11 20 E
Debar, Macedonia 21 D9 41 31N 20 30 E
Debden, Canada 73 C7 53 30N 106 50W
Dębica, Poland 17 C11 50 2N 21 25 E
Debolt, Canada 72 B5 55 12N 118 1W
Deborah East, L., Australia 61 F2 30 45S 119 0 E
Deborah West, L., Australia 61 F2 30 45S 118 50 E
Debre Markos, Ethiopia 51 F12 10 20N 37 40 E
Debre Tabor, Ethiopia 51 F12 11 50N 38 26 E
Debrecen, Hungary 17 E11 47 33N 21 42 E
Decatur, Ala., U.S.A. 77 H2 34 36N 86 59W
Decatur, Ga., U.S.A. 77 J3 33 47N 84 18W
Decatur, Ill., U.S.A. 80 F10 39 51N 88 57W
Decatur, Ind., U.S.A. 76 E3 40 50N 84 56W
Decatur, Tex., U.S.A. 81 J6 33 14N 97 35W
Deccan, India 40 M10 18 0N 79 0 E
Deception L., Canada 73 B8 56 33N 104 13W
Děčín, Czech. 16 C8 50 47N 14 12 E
Deckerville, U.S.A. 78 C2 43 32N 82 44W
Decorah, U.S.A. 80 D9 43 18N 91 48W
Dedéagach = Alexandroúpolis, Greece 21 D11 40 50N 25 54 E
Dedham, U.S.A. 79 D13 42 15N 71 10W
Dédougou, Burkina Faso 50 F4 12 30N 3 25W
Dedza, Malawi 55 E3 14 20S 34 20 E
Dee →, C. of Aberd., U.K. 12 D6 57 9N 2 5W
Dee →, Wales, U.K. 10 D4 53 22N 3 17W
Deep B., Canada 72 A5 61 15N 116 35W
Deep Well, Australia 62 C1 24 20S 134 0 E
Deepwater, Australia 63 D5 29 25S 151 51 E
Deer →, Canada 73 B10 58 23N 94 13W
Deer Lake, Nfld., Canada 71 C8 49 11N 57 27W
Deer Lake, Ont., Canada 73 C10 52 36N 94 20W
Deer Lodge, U.S.A. 82 C7 46 24N 112 44W
Deer Park, U.S.A. 82 C5 47 57N 117 28W
Deer River, U.S.A. 80 B8 47 20N 93 48W
Deeral, Australia 62 B4 17 14S 145 55 E
Deerdepoort, S. Africa 56 C4 24 37S 26 27 E
Deferiet, U.S.A. 79 B9 44 2N 75 41W
Defiance, U.S.A. 76 E3 41 17N 84 22W
Degeh Bur, Ethiopia 46 F3 8 11N 43 31 E
Deggendorf, Germany 16 D7 48 50N 12 57 E
Deh Bīd, Iran 45 D7 30 39N 53 11 E
Deh-e Shīr, Iran 45 D7 31 29N 53 45 E
Dehaj, Iran 45 D7 30 42N 54 53 E
Dehdez, Iran 45 D6 31 43N 50 17 E
Dehestān, Iran 45 D7 28 30N 55 35 E
Dehgolān, Iran 44 C5 35 17N 47 25 E
Dehi Titan, Afghan. 40 C3 33 45N 63 50 E
Dehibat, Tunisia 50 B7 32 0N 10 47 E
Dehlorān, Iran 44 C5 32 41N 47 16 E
Dehnow-e Kūhestān, Iran 45 E8 27 58N 58 32 E
Dehra Dun, India 42 D8 30 20N 78 4 E
Dehri, India 43 G11 24 50N 84 15 E
Dehui, China 35 B13 44 30N 125 40 E
Deinze, Belgium 15 D3 50 59N 3 32 E
Dej, Romania 17 E12 47 10N 23 52 E
Dekese, Zaïre 52 E4 3 24S 21 24 E
Del Mar, U.S.A. 85 N9 32 58N 117 16W
Del Norte, U.S.A. 83 H10 37 41N 106 21W
Del Rio, U.S.A. 81 L4 29 22N 100 54W
Delano, U.S.A. 85 K7 35 46N 119 15W
Delareyville, S. Africa 56 D4 26 41S 25 26 E
Delavan, U.S.A. 80 D10 42 38N 88 39W
Delaware, U.S.A. 76 E4 40 18N 83 4W
Delaware □, U.S.A. 76 F8 39 0N 75 20W
Delaware →, U.S.A. 76 F8 39 15N 75 20W
Delaware B., U.S.A. 75 C12 39 0N 75 10W
Delegate, Australia 63 F4 37 4S 148 56 E
Delft, Neths. 15 B4 52 1N 4 22 E
Delfzijl, Neths. 15 A6 53 20N 6 55 E
Delgado, C., Mozam. 55 E5 10 45S 40 40 E
Delgerhet, Mongolia 34 B6 45 50N 110 30 E
Delgo, Sudan 51 D11 20 6N 30 40 E
Delhi, Canada 78 D4 42 51N 80 30W
Delhi, India 42 E7 28 38N 77 17 E
Delhi, U.S.A. 79 D10 42 17N 74 55W
Delia, Canada 72 C6 51 38N 112 23W
Delice →, Turkey 25 G5 39 45N 34 15 E
Delicias, Mexico 86 B3 28 10N 105 30W
Delījān, Iran 45 C6 33 59N 50 40 E
Déline, Canada 68 B7 65 10N 123 30W
Dell City, U.S.A. 83 L11 31 56N 105 12W
Dell Rapids, U.S.A. 80 D6 43 50N 96 43W
Delmar, U.S.A. 79 D11 42 37N 73 47W
Delmenhorst, Germany 16 B5 53 3N 8 37 E
Delmiro Gouveia, Brazil 93 E11 9 24S 38 6W
Delong, Ostrova, Russia 27 B15 76 40N 149 20 E
Deloraine, Australia 62 G4 41 30S 146 40 E
Deloraine, Canada 73 D8 49 15N 100 29W
Delphi, U.S.A. 76 E2 40 36N 86 41W
Delphos, U.S.A. 76 E3 40 51N 84 21W
Delportshoop, S. Africa 56 D3 28 22S 24 20 E
Delray Beach, U.S.A. 77 M5 26 28N 80 4W
Delta, Colo., U.S.A. 83 G9 38 44N 108 4W
Delta, Utah, U.S.A. 82 G7 39 21N 112 35W
Delungra, Australia 63 D5 29 39S 150 51 E
Delvinë, Albania 21 E9 39 59N 20 4 E
Demanda, Sierra de la, Spain 19 A4 42 15N 3 0W
Demavand = Damāvand, Iran 45 C7 35 47N 52 0 E
Demba, Zaïre 52 F4 5 28S 22 15 E
Dembecha, Ethiopia 51 F12 10 32N 37 30 E
Dembia, Zaïre 54 B2 3 33N 25 48 E
Dembidolo, Ethiopia 51 G11 8 34N 34 50 E
Demer →, Belgium 15 D4 50 57N 4 42 E
Deming, N. Mex., U.S.A. 83 K10 32 16N 107 46W
Deming, Wash., U.S.A. 84 B4 48 50N 122 13W
Demini →, Brazil 92 D6 0 46S 62 56W
Demirci, Turkey 21 E13 39 2N 28 38 E
Demirköy, Turkey 21 D12 41 49N 27 45 E
Demopolis, U.S.A. 77 J2 32 31N 87 50W
Dempo, Indonesia 36 E2 4 2S 103 15 E
Den Burg, Neths. 15 A4 53 3N 4 47 E
Den Chai, Thailand 38 D3 17 59N 100 4 E
Den Haag = 's-Gravenhage, Neths. 15 B4 52 7N 4 17 E
Den Helder, Neths. 15 B4 52 57N 4 45 E
Den Oever, Neths. 15 B5 52 56N 5 2 E
Denain, France 15 D3 50 20N 3 22 E
Denair, U.S.A. 84 H6 37 32N 120 48W
Denau, Uzbekistan 26 F7 38 16N 67 54 E
Denbigh, U.K. 10 D4 53 12N 3 25W
Denbighshire □, U.K. 10 D4 53 8N 3 22W
Dendang, Indonesia 36 E3 3 7S 107 56 E
Dendermonde, Belgium 15 C4 51 2N 4 5 E
Dengfeng, China 34 G7 34 25N 113 2 E
Dengkou, China 34 D4 40 18N 106 55 E
Denham, Australia 61 E1 25 56S 113 31 E
Denham Ra., Australia 62 C4 21 55S 147 46 E
Denham Sd., Australia 61 E1 25 45S 113 15 E
Denia, Spain 19 C6 38 49N 0 8 E
Denial B., Australia 63 E1 32 14S 133 32 E
Deniliquin, Australia 63 F3 35 30S 144 58 E
Denison, Iowa, U.S.A. 80 D7 42 1N 95 21W
Denison, Tex., U.S.A. 81 J6 33 45N 96 33W
Denison Plains, Australia 60 C4 18 35S 128 0 E
Denizli, Turkey 25 G4 37 42N 29 2 E
Denman Glacier, Antarctica 5 C7 66 45S 99 25 E
Denmark, Australia 61 F2 34 59S 117 25 E
Denmark ■, Europe 9 J13 55 30N 9 0 E
Denmark Str., Atl. Oc. 4 C6 66 0N 30 0W
Dennison, U.S.A. 78 F3 40 24N 81 19W
Denpasar, Indonesia 36 F5 8 45S 115 14 E
Denton, Mont., U.S.A. 82 C9 47 19N 109 57W
Denton, Tex., U.S.A. 81 J6 33 13N 97 8W
D'Entrecasteaux, Pt., Australia 61 F2 34 50S 115 57 E
Denver, U.S.A. 80 F2 39 44N 104 59W
Denver City, U.S.A. 81 J3 32 58N 102 50W
Deoband, India 42 E7 29 42N 77 43 E
Deoghar, India 43 G12 24 30N 86 42 E
Deolali, India 40 K8 19 58N 73 50 E
Deoli = Devli, India 42 G6 25 50N 75 20 E
Deoria, India 43 F10 26 31N 83 48 E
Deosai Mts., Pakistan 43 B6 35 40N 75 0 E
Deping, China 35 F9 37 25N 116 58 E
Deposit, U.S.A. 79 D9 42 4N 75 25W
Depot Springs, Australia 61 E3 27 55S 120 3 E
Deputatskiy, Russia 27 C14 69 18N 139 54 E
Dera Ghazi Khan, Pakistan 42 D4 30 5N 70 43 E

Eastport

Dosso, Niger 50 F5 13 0N 3 13 E
Dothan, U.S.A. 77 K3 31 13N 85 24W
Doty, U.S.A. 84 D3 46 38N 123 17W
Douai, France 18 A5 50 21N 3 4 E
Douala, Cameroon 50 H6 4 0N 9 45 E
Douarnenez, France 18 B1 48 6N 4 21W
Double Island Pt., Australia 63 D5 25 56S 153 11 E
Doubs →, France 18 C6 46 53N 5 1 E
Doubtful Sd., N.Z. 59 L1 45 20S 166 49 E
Doubtless B., N.Z. 59 F4 34 55S 173 26 E
Douentza, Mali 50 F4 14 58N 2 48W
Douglas, S. Africa 56 D3 29 4S 23 46 E
Douglas, U.K. 10 C3 54 10N 4 28W
Douglas, Alaska, U.S.A. 72 B2 58 17N 134 24W
Douglas, Ariz., U.S.A. 83 L9 31 21N 109 33W
Douglas, Ga., U.S.A. 77 K4 31 31N 82 51W
Douglas, Wyo., U.S.A. 80 D2 42 45N 105 24W
Douglastown, Canada 71 C7 48 46N 64 24W
Douglasville, U.S.A. 77 J3 33 45N 84 45W
Doumé, Cameroon 52 D2 4 15N 13 25 E
Dounreay, U.K. 12 C5 58 35N 3 44W
Dourados, Brazil 95 A5 22 9S 54 50W
Dourados →, Brazil 95 A5 21 58S 54 18W
Douro →, Europe 19 B1 41 8N 8 40W
Dove →, U.K. 10 E6 52 51N 1 36W
Dove Creek, U.S.A. 83 H9 37 46N 108 54W
Dover, Australia 62 G4 43 18S 147 2 E
Dover, U.K. 11 F9 51 7N 1 19 E
Dover, Del., U.S.A. 76 F8 39 10N 75 32W
Dover, N.H., U.S.A. 79 C14 43 12N 70 56W
Dover, N.J., U.S.A. 79 F10 40 53N 74 34W
Dover, Ohio, U.S.A. 78 F3 40 32N 81 29W
Dover, Pt., Australia 61 F4 32 32S 125 32 E
Dover, Str. of, Europe 18 A4 51 0N 1 30 E
Dover-Foxcroft, U.S.A. 71 C6 45 11N 69 13W
Dover Plains, U.S.A. 79 E11 41 43N 73 35W
Dovey = Dyfi →, U.K. 11 E4 52 32N 4 3W
Dovrefjell, Norway 9 E13 62 15N 9 33 E
Dow Rūd, Iran 45 C6 33 28N 49 4 E
Dowa, Malawi 55 E3 13 38S 33 58 E
Dowagiac, U.S.A. 76 E2 41 59N 86 6W
Dowgha'i, Iran 45 B8 36 54N 58 32 E
Dowlatābād, Iran 45 D8 28 20N 56 40 E
Down □, U.K. 13 B6 54 23N 6 2W
Downey, Calif., U.S.A. 85 M8 33 56N 118 7W
Downey, Idaho, U.S.A. 82 E7 42 26N 112 7W
Downham Market, U.K. 11 E8 52 37N 0 23 E
Downieville, U.S.A. 84 F6 39 34N 120 50W
Downpatrick, U.K. 13 B6 54 20N 5 43W
Downpatrick Hd., Ireland 13 B2 54 20N 9 21W
Dowsārī, Iran 45 D8 28 25N 57 59 E
Doyle, U.S.A. 84 E6 40 2N 120 6W
Doylestown, U.S.A. 79 F9 40 21N 75 10W
Draa, Oued →, Morocco 50 C2 28 40N 11 10W
Drachten, Neths. 15 A6 53 7N 6 5 E
Drăgăşani, Romania 17 F13 44 39N 24 17 E
Dragichyn, Belarus 17 B13 52 15N 25 8 E
Dragoman, Prokhod, Bulgaria 21 C10 42 58N 22 53 E
Dragonera, I., Spain 22 B9 39 35N 2 19 E
Draguignan, France 18 E7 43 32N 6 27 E
Drain, U.S.A. 82 E2 43 40N 123 19W
Drake, Australia 63 D5 28 55S 152 25 E
Drake, U.S.A. 80 B4 47 55N 100 23W
Drake Passage, S. Ocean 5 B17 58 0S 68 0W
Drakensberg, S. Africa 57 E4 31 0S 28 0 E
Dráma, Greece 21 D11 41 9N 24 10 E
Drammen, Norway 9 G14 59 42N 10 12 E
Drangajökull, Iceland 8 C2 66 9N 22 15W
Dras, India 43 B6 34 25N 75 48 E
Drau = Drava →, Croatia 21 B8 45 33N 18 55 E
Drava →, Croatia 21 B8 45 33N 18 55 E
Drayton Valley, Canada 72 C6 53 12N 114 58W
Drenthe □, Neths. 15 B6 52 52N 6 40 E
Drepanum, C., Cyprus 23 E11 34 54N 32 19 E
Dresden, Canada 78 D2 42 35N 82 11W
Dresden, Germany 16 C7 51 3N 13 44 E
Dreux, France 18 B4 48 44N 1 23 E
Driffield, U.K. 10 C7 54 0N 0 26W
Driftwood, U.S.A. 78 E6 41 20N 78 8W
Driggs, U.S.A. 82 E8 43 44N 111 6W
Drina →, Bos.-H. 21 B8 44 53N 19 21 E
Drini →, Albania 21 C8 42 1N 19 38 E
Drøbak, Norway 9 G14 59 39N 10 39 E
Drochia, Moldova 17 D14 48 2N 27 48 E
Drogheda, Ireland 13 C5 53 43N 6 22W
Drogichin = Dragichyn, Belarus 17 B13 52 15N 25 8 E
Drogobych = Drohobych, Ukraine 17 D12 49 20N 23 30 E
Drohobych, Ukraine 17 D12 49 20N 23 30 E
Droichead Atha = Drogheda, Ireland 13 C5 53 43N 6 22W
Droichead Nua, Ireland 13 C5 53 11N 6 48W
Droitwich, U.K. 11 E5 52 16N 2 8W
Dromedary, C., Australia 63 F5 36 17S 150 10 E
Dronfield, Australia 62 C3 21 12S 140 3 E
Drumbo, Canada 78 C4 43 16N 80 35W
Drumheller, Canada 72 C6 51 25N 112 40W
Drummond, U.S.A. 82 C7 46 40N 113 9W
Drummond I., U.S.A. 70 C3 46 1N 83 39W
Drummond Pt., Australia 63 E2 34 9S 135 16 E
Drummond Ra., Australia 62 C4 23 45S 147 10 E
Drummondville, Canada 70 C5 45 55N 72 25W
Drumright, U.S.A. 81 H6 35 59N 96 36W
Druskininkai, Lithuania 9 J20 54 3N 23 58 E
Drut →, Belarus 17 B16 53 8N 30 5 E
Druzhina, Russia 27 C15 68 14N 145 18 E
Dry Tortugas, U.S.A. 88 B3 24 38N 82 55W
Dryden, Canada 73 D10 49 47N 92 50W
Dryden, U.S.A. 81 K3 30 3N 102 7W
Drygalski I., Antarctica 5 C7 66 0S 92 0 E
Drysdale →, Australia 60 B4 13 59S 126 51 E
Drysdale I., Australia 62 A2 11 41S 136 0 E
Dschang, Cameroon 50 G7 5 32N 10 3 E
Du Bois, U.S.A. 78 E6 41 8N 78 46W
Du Quoin, U.S.A. 80 G10 38 1N 89 14W
Duanesburg, U.S.A. 79 D10 42 45N 74 11W
Duaringa, Australia 62 C4 23 42S 149 42 E
Dubā, Si. Arabia 44 E2 27 10N 35 40 E
Dubai = Dubayy, U.A.E. 45 E7 25 18N 55 20 E
Dubăsari, Moldova 17 E15 47 15N 29 10 E
Dubăsari Vdkhr., Moldova 17 E15 47 30N 29 0 E
Dubawnt →, Canada 73 A8 64 33N 100 6W
Dubawnt, L., Canada 73 A8 63 4N 101 42W
Dubayy, U.A.E. 45 E7 25 18N 55 20 E
Dubbo, Australia 63 E4 32 11S 148 35 E
Dubele, Zaïre 54 B2 2 56N 29 35 E
Dublin, Ireland 13 C5 53 21N 6 15W
Dublin, Ga., U.S.A. 77 J4 32 32N 82 54W
Dublin, Tex., U.S.A. 81 J5 32 5N 98 21W
Dublin □, Ireland 13 C5 53 24N 6 20W
Dublin B., Ireland 13 C5 53 18N 6 5W
Dubno, Ukraine 17 C13 50 25N 25 45 E
Dubois, U.S.A. 82 D7 44 10N 112 14W
Dubossary = Dubăsari, Moldova 17 E15 47 15N 29 10 E
Dubossary Vdkhr. = Dubăsari Vdkhr., Moldova 17 E15 47 30N 29 0 E
Dubovka, Russia 25 E7 49 5N 44 50 E
Dubrajpur, India 43 H12 23 48N 87 25 E
Dubréka, Guinea 50 G2 9 46N 13 31W
Dubrovitsa = Dubrovytsya, Ukraine 17 C14 51 31N 26 35 E
Dubrovnik, Croatia 21 C8 42 39N 18 6 E
Dubrovskoye, Russia 27 D12 58 55N 111 10 E
Dubrovytsya, Ukraine 17 C14 51 31N 26 35 E
Dubuque, U.S.A. 80 D9 42 30N 90 41W
Duchesne, U.S.A. 82 F8 40 10N 110 24W
Duchess, Australia 62 C2 21 20S 139 50 E
Ducie I., Pac. Oc. 65 K15 24 40S 124 48W
Duck Cr. →, Australia 60 D2 22 37S 116 53 E
Duck Lake, Canada 73 C7 52 50N 106 16W
Duck Mountain Prov. Park, Canada 73 C8 51 45N 101 0W
Duckwall, Mt., U.S.A. 84 H6 37 58N 120 7W
Dudhi, India 41 G13 24 15N 83 10 E
Dudinka, Russia 27 C9 69 30N 86 13 E
Dudley, U.K. 11 E5 52 31N 2 5W
Duero = Douro →, Europe 19 B1 41 8N 8 40W
Dufftown, U.K. 12 D5 57 27N 3 8W
Dugi Otok, Croatia 16 G8 44 0N 15 3 E
Duifken Pt., Australia 62 A3 12 33S 141 38 E
Duisburg, Germany 16 C4 51 26N 6 45 E
Duiwelskloof, S. Africa 57 C5 23 42S 30 10 E
Dūkdamīn, Iran 45 C8 35 59N 57 43 E
Duke I., U.S.A. 72 C2 54 50N 131 20W
Dukelský Průsmyk, Slovak Rep. 17 D11 49 25N 21 42 E
Dukhān, Qatar 45 E6 25 25N 50 50 E
Duki, Pakistan 40 D6 30 14N 68 25 E
Duku, Nigeria 50 F7 10 43N 10 43 E
Dulce →, Argentina 94 C3 30 32S 62 33W
Dulce, G., Costa Rica 88 E3 8 40N 83 20W
Dulf, Iraq 44 C5 35 7N 45 51 E
Dulit, Banjaran, Malaysia 36 D4 3 15N 114 30 E
Duliu, China 34 E9 39 2N 116 55 E
Dullewala, Pakistan 42 D4 31 50N 71 25 E
Dulq Maghār, Syria 44 B3 36 22N 38 39 E
Dululu, Australia 62 C5 23 48S 150 15 E
Duluth, U.S.A. 80 B8 46 47N 92 6W
Dum Dum, India 43 H13 22 39N 88 33 E
Dum Duma, India 41 F19 27 40N 95 40 E
Dum Hadjer, Chad 51 F8 13 18N 19 41 E
Dūmā, Lebanon 47 A4 34 12N 35 50 E
Dūmā, Syria 47 B5 33 34N 36 24 E
Dumaguete, Phil. 37 C6 9 17N 123 15 E
Dumai, Indonesia 36 D2 1 35N 101 28 E
Dumaran, Phil. 37 B5 10 33N 119 50 E
Dumas, Ark., U.S.A. 81 J9 33 53N 91 29W
Dumas, Tex., U.S.A. 81 H4 35 52N 101 58W
Dumbarton, U.K. 12 F4 55 57N 4 33W
Dumbleyung, Australia 61 F2 33 17S 117 42 E
Dumfries, U.K. 12 F5 55 4N 3 37W
Dumfries & Galloway □, U.K. 12 F5 55 9N 3 58W
Dumka, India 43 G12 24 12N 87 15 E
Dumoine →, Canada 70 C4 46 13N 77 51W
Dumoine L., Canada 70 C4 46 55N 77 55W
Dumraon, India 43 G11 25 33N 84 8 E
Dumyât, Egypt 51 B11 31 24N 31 48 E
Dún Dealgan = Dundalk, Ireland 13 B5 54 1N 6 24W
Dun Laoghaire, Ireland 13 C5 53 17N 6 8W
Duna = Dunărea →, Europe 17 F15 45 20N 29 40 E
Dunaj = Dunărea →, Europe 17 F15 45 20N 29 40 E
Dunakeszi, Hungary 17 E10 47 37N 19 8 E
Dunărea →, Europe 17 F15 45 20N 29 40 E
Dunaújváros, Hungary 17 E10 47 0N 18 57 E
Dunav = Dunărea →, Europe 17 F15 45 20N 29 40 E
Dunay, Russia 30 C6 42 52N 132 22 E
Dunback, N.Z. 59 L3 45 23S 170 36 E
Dunbar, Australia 62 B3 16 0S 142 22 E
Dunbar, U.K. 12 E6 56 0N 2 31W
Dunblane, U.K. 12 E5 56 11N 3 58W
Duncan, Canada 72 D4 48 45N 123 40W
Duncan, Ariz., U.S.A. 83 K9 32 43N 109 6W
Duncan, Okla., U.S.A. 81 H6 34 30N 97 57W
Duncan, L., Canada 70 B4 53 29N 77 58W
Duncan L., Canada 72 A6 62 51N 113 58W
Duncan Town, Bahamas 88 B4 22 15N 75 45W
Duncannon, U.S.A. 78 F7 40 23N 77 2W
Dundalk, Canada 78 B4 44 10N 80 24W
Dundalk, Ireland 13 B5 54 1N 6 24W
Dundalk Bay, Ireland 13 C5 53 55N 6 15W
Dundas, Canada 70 D4 43 17N 79 59W
Dundas, L., Australia 61 F3 32 35S 121 50 E
Dundas I., Canada 72 C2 54 30N 130 50W
Dundas Str., Australia 60 B5 11 15S 131 35 E
Dundee, S. Africa 57 D5 28 11S 30 15 E
Dundee, U.K. 12 E6 56 28N 2 59W
Dundee City □, U.K. 12 E6 56 30N 2 58W
Dundgovĭ □, Mongolia 34 B4 45 10N 106 0 E
Dundoo, Australia 63 D3 27 40S 144 37 E
Dundrum, U.K. 13 B6 54 16N 5 52W
Dundrum B., U.K. 13 B6 54 13N 5 47W
Dundwara, India 43 F8 27 48N 79 9 E
Dunedin, N.Z. 59 L3 45 50S 170 33 E
Dunedin, U.S.A. 77 L4 28 1N 82 47W
Dunedin →, Canada 72 B4 59 30N 124 5W
Dunfermline, U.K. 12 E5 56 5N 3 27W
Dungannon, Canada 78 C3 43 51N 81 36W
Dungannon, U.K. 13 B5 54 31N 6 46W
Dungannon □, U.K. 13 B5 54 30N 6 55W
Dungarpur, India 42 H5 23 52N 73 45 E
Dungarvan, Ireland 13 D4 52 5N 7 37W
Dungarvan Harbour, Ireland 13 D4 52 4N 7 35W
Dungeness, U.K. 11 G8 50 54N 0 59 E
Dungo, L. do, Angola 56 B2 17 15S 19 0 E
Dungog, Australia 63 E5 32 22S 151 46 E
Dungu, Zaïre 54 B2 3 40N 28 32 E
Dunhua, China 35 C15 43 20N 128 14 E
Dunhuang, China 32 B4 40 8N 94 36 E
Dunk I., Australia 62 B4 17 59S 146 29 E
Dunkeld, U.K. 12 E5 56 34N 3 35W
Dunkerque, France 18 A5 51 2N 2 20 E
Dunkery Beacon, U.K. 11 F4 51 9N 3 36W
Dunkirk = Dunkerque, France 18 A5 51 2N 2 20 E
Dunkirk, U.S.A. 78 D5 42 29N 79 20W
Dunkwa, Ghana 50 G4 6 0N 1 47W
Dunlap, U.S.A. 80 E7 41 51N 95 36W
Dúnleary = Dun Laoghaire, Ireland 13 C5 53 17N 6 8W
Dunmanus B., Ireland 13 E2 51 31N 9 50W
Dunmara, Australia 62 B1 16 42S 133 25 E
Dunmore, U.S.A. 79 E9 41 25N 75 38W
Dunmore Hd., Ireland 13 D1 52 10N 10 35W
Dunmore Town, Bahamas 88 A4 25 30N 76 39W
Dunn, U.S.A. 77 H6 35 19N 78 37W
Dunnellon, U.S.A. 77 L4 29 3N 82 28W
Dunnet Hd., U.K. 12 C5 58 40N 3 21W
Dunning, U.S.A. 80 E4 41 50N 100 6W
Dunnville, Canada 78 D5 42 54N 79 36W
Dunolly, Australia 63 F3 36 51S 143 44 E
Dunoon, U.K. 12 F4 55 57N 4 56W
Dunqul, Egypt 51 D11 23 26N 31 37 E
Duns, U.K. 12 F6 55 47N 2 20W
Dunseith, U.S.A. 80 A4 48 50N 100 3W
Dunsmuir, U.S.A. 82 F2 41 13N 122 16W
Dunstable, U.K. 11 F7 51 53N 0 32W
Dunstan Mts., N.Z. 59 L2 44 53S 169 35 E
Dunster, Canada 72 C5 53 8N 119 50W
Dunvegan L., Canada 73 A7 60 8N 107 10W
Duolun, China 34 C9 42 12N 116 28 E
Duong Dong, Vietnam 39 G4 10 13N 103 58 E
Dupree, U.S.A. 80 C4 45 4N 101 35W
Dupuyer, U.S.A. 82 B7 48 13N 112 30W
Duque de Caxias, Brazil 95 A7 22 45S 43 19W
Durack →, Australia 60 C4 15 33S 127 52 E
Durack Ra., Australia 60 C4 16 50S 127 40 E
Durance →, France 18 E6 43 55N 4 45 E
Durand, U.S.A. 76 D4 42 55N 83 59W
Durango = Victoria de Durango, Mexico 86 C4 24 3N 104 39W
Durango, Spain 19 A4 43 13N 2 40W
Durango, U.S.A. 83 H10 37 16N 107 53W
Durango □, Mexico 86 C4 25 0N 105 0W
Duranillin, Australia 61 F2 33 30S 116 45 E
Durant, U.S.A. 81 J6 33 59N 96 25W
Durazno, Uruguay 94 C4 33 25S 56 31W
Durazzo = Durrësi, Albania 21 D8 41 19N 19 28 E
Durban, S. Africa 57 D5 29 49S 31 1 E
Düren, Germany 16 C4 50 48N 6 29 E
Durg, India 41 J12 21 15N 81 22 E
Durgapur, India 43 H12 23 30N 87 20 E
Durham, Canada 78 B4 44 10N 80 49W
Durham, U.K. 10 C6 54 47N 1 34W
Durham, Calif., U.S.A. 84 F5 39 39N 121 48W
Durham, N.C., U.S.A. 77 G6 35 59N 78 54W
Durham □, U.K. 10 C6 54 42N 1 45W
Durham Downs, Australia 63 D4 26 6S 149 5 E
Durmitor, Montenegro, Yug. 21 C8 43 10N 19 0 E
Durness, U.K. 12 C4 58 34N 4 45W
Durrësi, Albania 21 D8 41 19N 19 28 E
Durrie, Australia 62 D3 25 40S 140 15 E
Dursunbey, Turkey 21 E13 39 35N 28 37 E
Duru, Zaïre 54 B2 4 14N 28 50 E
D'Urville, Tanjung, Indonesia 37 E9 1 28S 137 54 E
D'Urville I., N.Z. 59 J4 40 50S 173 55 E
Duryea, U.S.A. 79 E9 41 20N 75 45W
Dusa Mareb, Somali Rep. 46 F4 5 30N 46 15 E
Dushak, Turkmenistan 26 F7 37 13N 60 1 E
Dushanbe, Tajikistan 26 F7 38 33N 68 48 E
Dusky Sd., N.Z. 59 L1 45 47S 166 30 E
Dussejour, C., Australia 60 B4 14 45S 128 13 E
Düsseldorf, Germany 16 C4 51 14N 6 47 E
Dutch Harbor, U.S.A. 68 C3 53 53N 166 32W
Dutlwe, Botswana 56 C3 23 58S 23 46 E
Dutton, Canada 78 D3 42 39N 81 30W
Dutton →, Australia 62 C3 20 44S 143 10 E
Duyun, China 32 D5 26 18N 107 29 E
Duzdab = Zāhedān, Iran 45 D9 29 30N 60 50 E
Dvina, Severnaya →, Russia 24 B7 64 32N 40 30 E
Dvinsk = Daugavpils, Latvia 9 J22 55 53N 26 32 E
Dvinskaya Guba, Russia 24 B6 65 0N 39 0 E
Dwarka, India 42 H3 22 18N 69 8 E
Dwellingup, Australia 61 F2 32 43S 116 4 E
Dwight, Canada 78 A5 45 20N 79 1W
Dwight, U.S.A. 76 E1 41 5N 88 26W
Dyatlovo = Dzyatlava, Belarus 17 B13 53 28N 25 28 E
Dyer, C., Canada 69 B13 66 40N 61 0W
Dyer Plateau, Antarctica 5 D17 70 45S 65 30W
Dyersburg, U.S.A. 81 G10 36 3N 89 23W
Dyfi →, U.K. 11 E4 52 32N 4 3W
Dymer, Ukraine 17 C16 50 47N 30 18 E
Dynevor Downs, Australia 63 D3 28 10S 144 20 E
Dysart, Canada 73 C8 50 57N 104 2W
Dzamin Üüd, Mongolia 34 C6 43 50N 111 58 E
Dzerzhinsk, Russia 24 C7 56 14N 43 30 E
Dzhalinda, Russia 27 D13 53 26N 124 0 E
Dzhambul = Zhambyl, Kazakstan 26 E8 42 54N 71 22 E
Dzhankoy, Ukraine 25 E5 45 40N 34 20 E
Dzhardzhan, Russia 27 C13 68 10N 124 10 E
Dzhetygara = Zhetiqara, Kazakstan 26 D7 52 11N 61 12 E
Dzhezkazgan = Zhezqazghan, Kazakstan 26 E7 47 44N 67 40 E
Dzhizak = Jizzakh, Uzbekistan 26 E7 40 6N 67 50 E
Dzhugdzur, Khrebet, Russia 27 D14 57 30N 138 0 E
Dzhungarskiye Vorota, Kazakstan 32 B3 45 0N 82 0 E
Działdowa, Poland 17 B11 53 15N 20 15 E
Dzierzoniów, Poland 17 C9 50 45N 16 39 E
Dzilam de Bravo, Mexico 87 C7 21 24N 88 53W
Dzungaria = Junggar Pendi, China 32 B3 44 30N 86 0 E
Dzungarian Gates = Dzhungarskiye Vorota, Kazakstan 32 B3 45 0N 82 0 E
Dzuumod, Mongolia 32 B5 47 45N 106 58 E
Dzyarzhynsk, Belarus 17 B14 53 40N 27 1 E
Dzyatlava, Belarus 17 B13 53 28N 25 28 E

E

Eabamet, L., Canada 70 B2 51 30N 87 46W
Eads, U.S.A. 80 F3 38 29N 102 47W
Eagle, U.S.A. 82 G10 39 39N 106 50W
Eagle →, Canada 71 B8 53 36N 57 26W
Eagle Butte, U.S.A. 80 C4 45 0N 101 10W
Eagle Grove, U.S.A. 80 D8 42 40N 93 54W
Eagle L., Calif., U.S.A. 82 F3 40 39N 120 45W
Eagle L., Maine, U.S.A. 71 C6 46 20N 69 22W
Eagle Lake, U.S.A. 81 L6 29 35N 96 20W
Eagle Mountain, U.S.A. 85 M11 33 49N 115 27W
Eagle Nest, U.S.A. 83 H11 36 33N 105 16W
Eagle Pass, U.S.A. 81 L4 28 43N 100 30W
Eagle Pk., U.S.A. 84 G7 38 10N 119 25W
Eagle Pt., Australia 60 C3 16 11S 124 23 E
Eagle River, U.S.A. 80 C10 45 55N 89 15W
Ealing, U.K. 11 F7 51 31N 0 20W
Earaheedy, Australia 61 E3 25 34S 121 29 E
Earl Grey, Canada 73 C8 50 57N 104 43W
Earle, U.S.A. 81 H9 35 16N 90 28W
Earlimart, U.S.A. 85 K7 35 53N 119 16W
Earn →, U.K. 12 E5 56 21N 3 18W
Earn, L., U.K. 12 E4 56 23N 4 13W
Earnslaw, Mt., N.Z. 59 L2 44 32S 168 27 E
Earth, U.S.A. 81 H3 34 14N 102 24W
Easley, U.S.A. 77 H4 34 50N 82 36W
East Angus, Canada 71 C5 45 30N 71 40W
East Aurora, U.S.A. 78 D6 42 46N 78 37W
East Ayrshire □, U.K. 12 F4 55 26N 4 11W
East B., U.S.A. 81 L10 29 0N 89 15W
East Bengal, Bangla. 41 G17 24 0N 90 0 E
East Beskids = Vychodné Beskydy, Europe 17 D11 49 20N 22 0 E
East Brady, U.S.A. 78 F5 40 59N 79 36W
East C., N.Z. 59 G7 37 42S 178 35 E
East Chicago, U.S.A. 76 E2 41 38N 87 27W
East China Sea, Asia 33 C7 30 5N 126 0 E
East Coulee, Canada 72 C6 51 23N 112 27W
East Dunbartonshire □, U.K. 12 F4 55 57N 4 13W
East Falkland, Falk. Is. 96 G5 51 30S 58 30W
East Grand Forks, U.S.A. 80 B6 47 56N 97 1W
East Greenwich, U.S.A. 79 E13 41 40N 71 27W
East Hartford, U.S.A. 79 E12 41 46N 72 39W
East Helena, U.S.A. 82 C8 46 35N 111 56W
East Indies, Asia 37 E6 0 0 120 0 E
East Jordan, U.S.A. 76 C3 45 10N 85 7W
East Lansing, U.S.A. 76 D3 42 44N 84 29W
East Liverpool, U.S.A. 78 F4 40 37N 80 35W
East London, S. Africa 57 E4 33 0S 27 55 E
East Lothian □, U.K. 12 F6 55 58N 2 44W
East Main = Eastmain, Canada 70 B4 52 10N 78 30W
East Orange, U.S.A. 79 F10 40 46N 74 13W
East Pacific Ridge, Pac. Oc. 65 J17 15 0S 110 0W
East Palestine, U.S.A. 78 F4 40 50N 80 33W
East Pine, Canada 72 B4 55 48N 120 12W
East Point, U.S.A. 77 J3 33 41N 84 27W
East Providence, U.S.A. 79 E13 41 49N 71 23W
East Pt., Canada 71 C7 46 27N 61 58W
East Renfrewshire □, U.K. 12 F4 55 46N 4 21W
East Retford = Retford, U.K. 10 D7 53 19N 0 56W
East Riding □, U.K. 10 D7 53 55N 0 30W
East St. Louis, U.S.A. 80 F9 38 37N 90 9W
East Schelde → = Oosterschelde, Neths. 15 C4 51 33N 4 0 E
East Siberian Sea, Russia 27 B17 73 0N 160 0 E
East Stroudsburg, U.S.A. 79 E9 41 1N 75 11W
East Sussex □, U.K. 11 G8 50 56N 0 19 E
East Tawas, U.S.A. 76 C4 44 17N 83 29W
East Toorale, Australia 63 E4 30 27S 145 28 E
East Walker →, U.S.A. 84 G7 38 52N 119 10W
Eastbourne, N.Z. 59 J5 41 19S 174 55 E
Eastbourne, U.K. 11 G8 50 46N 0 18 E
Eastend, Canada 73 D7 49 32N 108 50W
Easter Islands = Pascua, I. de, Pac. Oc. 65 K17 27 0S 109 0W
Eastern □, Kenya 54 B4 0 0 38 30 E
Eastern □, Uganda 54 B3 1 50N 33 45 E
Eastern Cape □, S. Africa 56 E4 32 0S 26 0 E
Eastern Cr. →, Australia 62 C3 20 40S 141 35 E
Eastern Ghats, India 40 N11 14 0N 78 50 E
Eastern Group = Lau Group, Fiji 59 C9 17 0S 178 30W
Eastern Group, Australia 61 F3 33 30S 124 30 E
Eastern Transvaal = Mpumalanga □, S. Africa 57 B5 26 0S 30 0 E
Easterville, Canada 73 C9 53 8N 99 49W
Easthampton, U.S.A. 79 D12 42 16N 72 40W
Eastland, U.S.A. 81 J5 32 24N 98 49W
Eastleigh, U.K. 11 G6 50 58N 1 21W
Eastmain, Canada 70 B4 52 10N 78 30W
Eastmain →, Canada 70 B4 52 27N 78 26W
Eastman, Canada 79 A12 45 18N 72 19W
Eastman, U.S.A. 77 J4 32 12N 83 11W
Easton, Md., U.S.A. 76 F7 38 47N 76 5W
Easton, Pa., U.S.A. 79 F9 40 41N 75 13W
Easton, Wash., U.S.A. 84 C5 47 14N 121 11W
Eastport, U.S.A. 71 D6 44 56N 67 0W

Farsund

Enkhuizen, *Neths.* 15 B5 52 42N 5 17 E
Enna, *Italy* 20 F6 37 34N 14 16 E
Ennadai, *Canada* 73 A8 61 8N 100 53W
Ennadai L., *Canada* 73 A8 61 0N 101 0W
Ennedi, *Chad* 51 E9 17 15N 22 0 E
Enngonia, *Australia* 63 D4 29 21S 145 50 E
Ennis, *Ireland* 13 D3 52 51N 8 59W
Ennis, *Mont., U.S.A.* 82 D8 45 21N 111 44W
Ennis, *Tex., U.S.A.* 81 J6 32 20N 96 38W
Enniscorthy, *Ireland* 13 D5 52 30N 6 34W
Enniskillen, *U.K.* 13 B4 54 21N 7 39W
Ennistimon, *Ireland* 13 D2 52 57N 9 17W
Enns →, *Austria* 16 D8 48 14N 14 32 E
Enontekiö, *Finland* 8 B20 68 23N 23 37 E
Enriquillo, L., *Dom. Rep.* 89 C5 18 20N 72 5W
Enschede, *Neths.* 15 B6 52 13N 6 53 E
Ensenada, *Argentina* 94 C4 34 55S 57 55W
Ensenada, *Mexico* 86 A1 31 50N 116 50W
Ensiola, Pta., *Spain* 22 B9 39 7N 2 55 E
Entebbe, *Uganda* 54 B3 0 4N 32 28 E
Enterprise, *Canada* 72 A5 60 47N 115 45W
Enterprise, *Oreg., U.S.A.* 82 D5 45 25N 117 17W
Enterprise, *Utah, U.S.A.* 83 H7 37 34N 113 43W
Entre Ríos, *Bolivia* 94 A3 21 30S 64 25W
Entre Ríos □, *Argentina* 94 C4 30 30S 58 30W
Entroncamento, *Portugal* 19 C1 39 28N 8 28W
Enugu, *Nigeria* 50 G6 6 20N 7 30 E
Enugu Ezike, *Nigeria* 50 G6 7 0N 7 29 E
Enumclaw, *U.S.A.* 84 C5 47 12N 121 59W
Eólie, Ís., *Italy* 20 E6 38 30N 14 57 E
Epe, *Neths.* 15 B5 52 21N 5 59 E
Épernay, *France* 18 B5 49 3N 3 56 E
Ephesus, *Turkey* 21 F12 37 55N 27 22 E
Ephraim, *U.S.A.* 82 G8 39 22N 111 35W
Ephrata, *U.S.A.* 82 C4 47 19N 119 33W
Épinal, *France* 18 B7 48 10N 6 27 E
Episkopi, *Cyprus* 23 E11 34 40N 32 54 E
Episkopi, *Greece* 23 D6 35 20N 24 20 E
Episkopi Bay, *Cyprus* 23 E11 34 35N 32 50 E
Epping, *U.K.* 11 F8 51 41N 0 7 E
Epukiro, *Namibia* 56 C2 21 40S 19 9 E
Equatorial Guinea ■, *Africa* 52 D1 2 0N 8 0 E
Er Rahad, *Sudan* 51 F11 12 45N 30 32 E
Er Rif, *Morocco* 50 A4 35 1N 4 1W
Er Roseires, *Sudan* 51 F11 11 55N 34 30 E
Erāwadī Myit = Irrawaddy →, *Burma* 41 M19 15 50N 95 6 E
Erbil = Arbīl, *Iraq* 44 B5 36 15N 44 5 E
Erciyaş Dağı, *Turkey* 25 G6 38 30N 35 30 E
Érd, *Hungary* 17 E10 47 22N 18 56 E
Erdao Jiang →, *China* 35 C14 43 0N 127 0 E
Erdek, *Turkey* 21 D12 40 23N 27 47 E
Erdene, *Mongolia* 34 B6 44 13N 111 10 E
Erebus, Mt., *Antarctica* 5 D11 77 35S 167 0 E
Erechim, *Brazil* 95 B5 27 35S 52 15W
Ereğli, *Konya, Turkey* 25 G5 37 31N 34 4 E
Ereğli, *Zonguldak, Turkey* 25 F5 41 15N 31 24 E
Erenhot, *China* 34 C7 43 48N 112 2 E
Eresma →, *Spain* 19 B3 41 26N 4 45W
Erewadi Myitwanya, *Burma* 41 M19 15 30N 95 0 E
Erfenisdam, *S. Africa* 56 D4 28 30S 26 50 E
Erfurt, *Germany* 16 C6 50 58N 11 2 E
Ergeni Vozvyshennost, *Russia* 25 E7 47 0N 44 0 E
Ērgli, *Latvia* 9 H21 56 54N 25 38 E
Eriboll, L., *U.K.* 12 C4 58 30N 4 42W
Érice, *Italy* 20 E5 38 2N 12 35 E
Erie, *U.S.A.* 78 D4 42 8N 80 5W
Erie, L., *N. Amer.* 78 D3 42 15N 81 0W
Erie Canal, *U.S.A.* 78 C6 43 5N 78 43W
Erieau, *Canada* 78 D3 42 16N 81 57W
Erigavo, *Somali Rep.* 46 E4 10 35N 47 20 E
Erikoúsa, *Greece* 23 A3 39 53N 19 34 E
Eriksdale, *Canada* 73 C9 50 52N 98 7W
Erímanthos, *Greece* 21 F9 37 57N 21 50 E
Erimo-misaki, *Japan* 30 D11 41 50N 143 15 E
Eritrea ■, *Africa* 51 F12 14 0N 38 30 E
Erlangen, *Germany* 16 D6 49 36N 11 0 E
Erldunda, *Australia* 62 D1 25 14S 133 12 E
Ermelo, *Neths.* 15 B5 52 18N 5 35 E
Ermelo, *S. Africa* 57 D4 26 31S 29 59 E
Ermones, *Greece* 23 A3 39 37N 19 46 E
Ermoúpolis = Síros, *Greece* 21 F11 37 28N 24 57 E
Ernakulam = Cochin, *India* 40 Q10 9 59N 76 22 E
Erne →, *Ireland* 13 B3 54 30N 8 16W
Erne, Lower L., *U.K.* 13 B4 54 28N 7 47W
Erne, Upper L., *U.K.* 13 B4 54 14N 7 32W
Ernest Giles Ra., *Australia* 61 E3 27 0S 123 45 E
Erode, *India* 40 P10 11 24N 77 45 E
Eromanga, *Australia* 63 D3 26 40S 143 11 E
Erongo, *Namibia* 56 C2 21 39S 15 58 E
Erramala Hills, *India* 40 M11 15 30N 78 15 E
Errabiddy, *Australia* 61 E2 25 25S 117 5 E
Errigal, *Ireland* 13 A3 55 2N 8 6W
Erris Hd., *Ireland* 13 B1 54 19N 10 0W
Erskine, *U.S.A.* 80 B7 47 40N 96 0W
Ertis → = Irtysh →, *Russia* 26 C7 61 4N 68 52 E
Erwin, *U.S.A.* 77 G4 36 9N 82 25W
Erzgebirge, *Germany* 16 C7 50 27N 12 55 E
Erzin, *Russia* 27 D10 50 15N 95 10 E
Erzincan, *Turkey* 25 G6 39 46N 39 30 E
Erzurum, *Turkey* 25 G7 39 57N 41 15 E
Es Caló, *Spain* 22 C8 38 40N 1 30 E
Es Caná, *Spain* 22 B8 39 2N 1 36 E
Es Sahrâ' Esh Sharqîya, *Egypt* 51 C11 27 30N 32 30 E
Es Sînâ', *Egypt* 51 C11 29 0N 34 0 E
Esambo, *Zaïre* 54 C1 3 48S 23 30 E
Esan-Misaki, *Japan* 30 D10 41 40N 141 10 E
Esashi, *Hokkaidō, Japan* 30 B11 44 56N 142 35 E
Esashi, *Hokkaidō, Japan* 30 D10 41 52N 140 7 E
Esbjerg, *Denmark* 9 J13 55 29N 8 29 E
Escalante, *U.S.A.* 83 H8 37 47N 111 36W
Escalante →, *U.S.A.* 83 H8 37 24N 110 57W
Escalón, *Mexico* 86 B4 26 46N 104 20W
Escambia →, *U.S.A.* 77 K2 30 32N 87 11W
Escanaba, *U.S.A.* 76 C2 45 45N 87 4W
Esch-sur-Alzette, *Lux.* 18 B6 49 32N 6 0 E
Escondido, *U.S.A.* 85 M9 33 7N 117 5W
Escuinapa, *Mexico* 86 C3 22 50N 105 50W
Escuintla, *Guatemala* 88 D1 14 20N 90 48W
Esenguly, *Turkmenistan* 26 F6 37 37N 53 59 E
Eşfahān, *Iran* 45 C6 32 39N 51 43 E
Esfideh, *Iran* 45 C8 33 39N 59 46 E
Esh Sham = Dimashq, *Syria* 47 B5 33 30N 36 18 E
Eshowe, *S. Africa* 57 D5 28 50S 31 30 E
Esil → = Ishim →, *Russia* 26 D8 57 45N 71 10 E
Esk →, *Cumb., U.K.* 12 G5 54 58N 3 2W
Esk →, *N. Yorks., U.K.* 10 C7 54 30N 0 37W
Eskifjörður, *Iceland* 8 D7 65 3N 13 55W
Eskilstuna, *Sweden* 9 G17 59 22N 16 32 E
Eskimo Pt., *Canada* 73 A10 61 10N 94 15W
Eskişehir, *Turkey* 25 G5 39 50N 30 35 E
Esla →, *Spain* 19 B2 41 29N 6 3W
Eslāmābād-e Gharb, *Iran* 44 C5 34 10N 46 30 E
Eşme, *Turkey* 21 E13 38 23N 28 58 E
Esmeraldas, *Ecuador* 92 C3 1 0N 79 40W
Espalmador, I., *Spain* 22 C7 38 47N 1 26 E
Espanola, *Canada* 70 C3 46 15N 81 46W
Espardell, I. del, *Spain* 22 C7 38 48N 1 29 E
Esparta, *Costa Rica* 88 E3 9 59N 84 40W
Esperance, *Australia* 61 F3 33 45S 121 55 E
Esperance B., *Australia* 61 F3 33 48S 121 55 E
Esperanza, *Argentina* 94 C3 31 29S 61 3W
Espichel, C., *Portugal* 19 C1 38 22N 9 16W
Espigão, Serra do, *Brazil* 95 B5 26 35S 50 30W
Espinal, *Colombia* 92 C4 4 9N 74 53W
Espinazo, Sierra del = Espinhaço, Serra do, *Brazil* 93 G10 17 30S 43 30W
Espinhaço, Serra do, *Brazil* 93 G10 17 30S 43 30W
Espinilho, Serra do, *Brazil* 95 B5 28 30S 55 0W
Espírito Santo □, *Brazil* 93 G10 20 0S 40 45W
Espíritu Santo, B. del, *Mexico* 87 D7 19 15N 87 0W
Espíritu Santo, I., *Mexico* 86 C2 24 30N 110 23W
Espita, *Mexico* 87 C7 21 1N 88 19W
Espoo, *Finland* 9 F21 60 12N 24 40 E
Espungabera, *Mozam.* 57 C5 20 29S 32 45 E
Esquel, *Argentina* 96 E2 42 55S 71 20W
Esquina, *Argentina* 94 B4 30 0S 59 30W
Essaouira, *Morocco* 50 B3 31 32N 9 42W
Essebie, *Zaïre* 54 B3 2 58N 30 40 E
Essen, *Belgium* 15 C4 51 28N 4 28 E
Essen, *Germany* 16 C4 51 28N 7 0 E
Essendon, Mt., *Australia* 61 E3 25 0S 120 29 E
Essequibo →, *Guyana* 92 B7 6 50N 58 30W
Essex, *Canada* 78 D2 42 10N 82 49W
Essex, *Calif., U.S.A.* 85 L11 34 44N 115 15W
Essex, *N.Y., U.S.A.* 79 B11 44 19N 73 21W
Essex □, *U.K.* 11 F8 51 54N 0 27 E
Esslingen, *Germany* 16 D5 48 44N 9 18 E
Estados, I. de Los, *Argentina* 96 G4 54 40S 64 30W
Eşţahbānāt, *Iran* 45 D7 29 8N 54 4 E
Estallenchs, *Spain* 22 B9 39 39N 2 29 E
Estância, *Brazil* 93 F11 11 16S 37 26W
Estancia, *U.S.A.* 83 J10 34 46N 106 4W
Estārm, *Iran* 45 D8 28 21N 58 21 E
Estcourt, *S. Africa* 57 D4 29 0S 29 53 E
Estelí, *Nic.* 88 D2 13 9N 86 22W
Estelline, *S. Dak., U.S.A.* 80 C6 44 35N 96 54W
Estelline, *Tex., U.S.A.* 81 H4 34 33N 100 26W
Esterhazy, *Canada* 73 C8 50 37N 102 5W
Estevan, *Canada* 73 D8 49 10N 102 59W
Estevan Group, *Canada* 72 C3 53 3N 129 38W
Estherville, *U.S.A.* 80 D7 43 24N 94 50W
Eston, *Canada* 73 C7 51 8N 108 40W
Estonia ■, *Europe* 9 G21 58 30N 25 30 E
Estrêla, Serra da, *Portugal* 19 B2 40 10N 7 45W
Estremoz, *Portugal* 19 C2 38 51N 7 39W
Estrondo, Serra do, *Brazil* 93 E9 7 20S 48 0W
Esztergom, *Hungary* 17 E10 47 47N 18 44 E
Etadunna, *Australia* 63 D2 28 43S 138 38 E
Etah, *India* 43 F8 27 35N 78 40 E
Etamamu, *Canada* 71 B8 50 18N 59 59W
Étampes, *France* 18 B5 48 26N 2 10 E
Etanga, *Namibia* 56 B1 17 55S 13 0 E
Etawah, *India* 43 F8 26 48N 79 6 E
Etawah →, *U.S.A.* 77 H3 34 20N 84 15W
Etawney L., *Canada* 73 B9 57 50N 96 50W
Ethel, *U.S.A.* 84 D4 46 32N 122 46W
Ethel Creek, *Australia* 60 D3 22 55S 120 11 E
Ethelbert, *Canada* 73 C8 51 32N 100 25W
Ethiopia ■, *Africa* 46 F3 8 0N 40 0 E
Ethiopian Highlands, *Ethiopia* 28 J7 10 0N 37 0 E
Etive, L., *U.K.* 12 E3 56 29N 5 10W
Etna, *Italy* 20 F6 37 50N 14 55 E
Etoile, *Zaïre* 55 E2 11 33S 27 30 E
Etolin I., *U.S.A.* 72 B2 56 5N 132 20W
Etosha Pan, *Namibia* 56 B2 18 40S 16 30 E
Etowah, *U.S.A.* 77 H3 35 20N 84 32W
Ettrick Water →, *U.K.* 12 F6 55 31N 2 55W
Etuku, *Zaïre* 54 C2 3 42S 25 45 E
Etzatlán, *Mexico* 86 C4 20 48N 104 5W
Euboea = Évvoia, *Greece* 21 E11 38 30N 24 0 E
Eucla Motel, *Australia* 61 F4 31 41S 128 52 E
Euclid, *U.S.A.* 78 E3 41 34N 81 32W
Eucumbene, L., *Australia* 63 F4 36 2S 148 40 E
Eudora, *U.S.A.* 81 J9 33 7N 91 16W
Eufaula, *Ala., U.S.A.* 77 K3 31 54N 85 9W
Eufaula, *Okla., U.S.A.* 81 H7 35 17N 95 35W
Eufaula L., *U.S.A.* 81 H7 35 18N 95 21W
Eugene, *U.S.A.* 82 E2 44 5N 123 4W
Eugowra, *Australia* 63 E4 33 22S 148 24 E
Eulo, *Australia* 63 D4 28 10S 145 3 E
Eunice, *La., U.S.A.* 81 K8 30 30N 92 25W
Eunice, *N. Mex., U.S.A.* 81 J3 32 26N 103 10W
Eupen, *Belgium* 15 D6 50 37N 6 3 E
Euphrates = Furāt, Nahr al →, *Asia* 44 D5 31 0N 47 25 E
Eureka, *Canada* 4 B3 80 0N 85 56W
Eureka, *Calif., U.S.A.* 82 F1 40 47N 124 9W
Eureka, *Kans., U.S.A.* 81 G6 37 49N 96 17W
Eureka, *Mont., U.S.A.* 82 B6 48 53N 115 3W
Eureka, *Nev., U.S.A.* 82 G5 39 31N 115 58W
Eureka, *S. Dak., U.S.A.* 80 C5 45 46N 99 38W
Eureka, *Utah, U.S.A.* 82 G7 39 58N 112 7W
Eureka, Mt., *Australia* 61 E3 26 35S 121 35 E
Euroa, *Australia* 63 F4 36 44S 145 35 E
Europa, I., *Ind. Oc.* 53 J8 22 20S 40 22 E
Europa, Picos de, *Spain* 19 A3 43 10N 4 49W
Europa, Pta. de, *Gib.* 19 D3 36 3N 5 21W
Europa Pt. = Europa, Pta. de, *Gib.* 19 D3 36 3N 5 21W
Europoort, *Neths.* 15 C4 51 57N 4 10 E
Eustis, *U.S.A.* 77 L5 28 51N 81 41W
Eutsuk L., *Canada* 72 C3 53 20N 126 45W
Eva Downs, *Australia* 62 B1 18 1S 134 52 E
Evale, *Angola* 56 B2 16 33S 15 44 E
Evans, *U.S.A.* 80 E2 40 23N 104 41W
Evans Head, *Australia* 63 D5 29 7S 153 27 E
Evans L., *Canada* 70 B4 50 50N 77 0W
Evans Mills, *U.S.A.* 79 B9 44 6N 75 48W
Evanston, *Ill., U.S.A.* 76 D2 42 3N 87 41W
Evanston, *Wyo., U.S.A.* 82 F8 41 16N 110 58W
Evansville, *Ind., U.S.A.* 76 F2 37 58N 87 35W
Evansville, *Wis., U.S.A.* 80 D10 42 47N 89 18W
Evaz, *Iran* 45 E7 27 46N 53 59 E
Eveleth, *U.S.A.* 80 B8 47 28N 92 32W
Evensk, *Russia* 27 C16 62 12N 159 30 E
Everard, L., *Australia* 63 E1 31 30S 135 0 E
Everard Park, *Australia* 61 E5 27 1S 132 43 E
Everard Ras., *Australia* 61 E5 27 5S 132 28 E
Everest, Mt., *Nepal* 43 E12 28 5N 86 58 E
Everett, *Pa., U.S.A.* 78 F6 40 1N 78 23W
Everett, *Wash., U.S.A.* 84 C4 47 59N 122 12W
Everglades, The, *U.S.A.* 77 N5 25 50N 81 0W
Everglades City, *U.S.A.* 77 N5 25 52N 81 23W
Everglades National Park, *U.S.A.* 77 N5 25 30N 81 0W
Evergreen, *U.S.A.* 77 K2 31 26N 86 57W
Everson, *U.S.A.* 82 B2 48 57N 122 22W
Evesham, *U.K.* 11 E6 52 6N 1 56W
Evinayong, *Eq. Guin.* 52 D2 1 26N 10 35 E
Evje, *Norway* 9 G12 58 36N 7 51 E
Évora, *Portugal* 19 C2 38 33N 7 57W
Evowghlī, *Iran* 44 B5 38 43N 45 13 E
Évreux, *France* 18 B4 49 3N 1 8 E
Évros →, *Bulgaria* 21 D12 41 40N 26 34 E
Evry, *France* 18 B5 48 38N 2 27 E
Évvoia, *Greece* 21 E11 38 30N 24 0 E
Ewe, L., *U.K.* 12 D3 57 49N 5 38W
Ewing, *U.S.A.* 80 D5 42 16N 98 21W
Ewo, *Congo* 52 E2 0 48S 14 45 E
Exaltación, *Bolivia* 92 F5 13 10S 65 20W
Excelsior Springs, *U.S.A.* 80 F7 39 20N 94 13W
Exe →, *U.K.* 11 G4 50 41N 3 29W
Exeter, *Canada* 78 C3 43 21N 81 29W
Exeter, *U.K.* 11 G4 50 43N 3 31W
Exeter, *Calif., U.S.A.* 83 H4 36 18N 119 9W
Exeter, *N.H., U.S.A.* 79 D14 42 59N 70 57W
Exeter, *Nebr., U.S.A.* 80 E6 40 39N 97 27W
Exmoor, *U.K.* 11 F4 51 12N 3 45W
Exmouth, *Australia* 60 D1 21 54S 114 10 E
Exmouth, *U.K.* 11 G4 50 37N 3 25W
Exmouth G., *Australia* 60 D1 22 15S 114 15 E
Expedition Ra., *Australia* 62 C4 24 30S 149 12 E
Extremadura □, *Spain* 19 C2 39 30N 6 5W
Exuma Sound, *Bahamas* 88 B4 24 30N 76 20W
Eyasi, L., *Tanzania* 54 C4 3 30S 35 0 E
Eyeberry L., *Canada* 73 A8 63 8N 104 43W
Eyemouth, *U.K.* 12 F6 55 52N 2 5W
Eyjafjörður, *Iceland* 8 C4 66 15N 18 30W
Eyre, *Australia* 61 F4 32 15S 126 18 E
Eyre (North), L., *Australia* 63 D2 28 30S 137 20 E
Eyre (South), L., *Australia* 63 D2 29 18S 137 25 E
Eyre Cr. →, *Australia* 63 D2 26 40S 139 0 E
Eyre Mts., *N.Z.* 59 L2 45 25S 168 25 E
Eyre Pen., *Australia* 63 E2 33 30S 136 17 E
Eysturoy, *Færoe Is.* 8 E9 62 13N 6 54W
Eyvānkī, *Iran* 45 C6 35 24N 51 56 E
Ezine, *Turkey* 21 E12 39 48N 26 20 E
Ezouza →, *Cyprus* 23 E11 34 44N 32 27 E

F

F.Y.R.O.M. = Macedonia ■, *Europe* 21 D9 41 53N 21 40 E
Fabens, *U.S.A.* 83 L10 31 30N 106 10W
Fabriano, *Italy* 20 C5 43 20N 12 54 E
Facatativá, *Colombia* 92 C4 4 49N 74 22W
Fachi, *Niger* 50 E7 18 6N 11 34 E
Fada, *Chad* 51 E9 17 13N 21 34 E
Fada-n-Gourma, *Burkina Faso* 50 F5 12 10N 0 30 E
Faddeyevskiy, Ostrov, *Russia* 27 B15 76 0N 144 0 E
Fadghāmī, *Syria* 44 C4 35 53N 40 52 E
Faenza, *Italy* 20 B4 44 17N 11 53 E
Færoe Is. = Føroyar, *Atl. Oc.* 8 F9 62 0N 7 0W
Făgăras, *Romania* 17 F13 45 48N 24 58 E
Fagersta, *Sweden* 9 F16 60 1N 15 46 E
Fagnano, L., *Argentina* 96 G3 54 30S 68 0W
Fahlīān, *Iran* 45 D6 30 11N 51 28 E
Fahraj, *Kermān, Iran* 45 D8 29 0N 59 0 E
Fahraj, *Yazd, Iran* 45 D7 31 46N 54 36 E
Faial, *Madeira* 22 D3 32 47N 16 53W
Fair Hd., *U.K.* 13 A5 55 14N 6 9W
Fair Oaks, *U.S.A.* 84 G5 38 39N 121 16W
Fairbank, *U.S.A.* 83 L8 31 43N 110 11W
Fairbanks, *U.S.A.* 68 B5 64 51N 147 43W
Fairbury, *U.S.A.* 80 E6 40 8N 97 11W
Fairfax, *U.S.A.* 81 G6 36 34N 96 42W
Fairfield, *Ala., U.S.A.* 77 J2 33 29N 86 55W
Fairfield, *Calif., U.S.A.* 84 G4 38 15N 122 3W
Fairfield, *Conn., U.S.A.* 79 E11 41 9N 73 16W
Fairfield, *Idaho, U.S.A.* 82 E6 43 21N 114 44W
Fairfield, *Ill., U.S.A.* 76 F1 38 23N 88 22W
Fairfield, *Iowa, U.S.A.* 80 E9 40 56N 91 57W
Fairfield, *Mont., U.S.A.* 82 C8 47 37N 111 59W
Fairfield, *Tex., U.S.A.* 81 K7 31 44N 96 10W
Fairford, *Canada* 73 C9 51 37N 98 38W
Fairhope, *U.S.A.* 77 K2 30 31N 87 54W
Fairlie, *N.Z.* 59 L3 44 5S 170 49 E
Fairmead, *U.S.A.* 84 H6 37 5N 120 10W
Fairmont, *Minn., U.S.A.* 80 D7 43 39N 94 28W
Fairmont, *W. Va., U.S.A.* 76 F5 39 29N 80 9W
Fairmount, *U.S.A.* 85 L8 34 45N 118 26W
Fairplay, *U.S.A.* 83 G11 39 15N 106 2W
Fairport, *U.S.A.* 78 C7 43 6N 77 27W
Fairport Harbor, *U.S.A.* 78 E3 41 45N 81 17W
Fairview, *Australia* 62 B3 15 31S 144 17 E
Fairview, *Canada* 72 B5 56 5N 118 25W
Fairview, *Mont., U.S.A.* 80 B2 47 51N 104 3W
Fairview, *Okla., U.S.A.* 81 G5 36 16N 98 29W
Fairview, *Utah, U.S.A.* 82 G8 39 50N 111 0W
Fairweather, Mt., *U.S.A.* 68 C6 58 55N 137 32W
Faisalabad, *Pakistan* 42 D5 31 30N 73 5 E
Faith, *U.S.A.* 80 C3 45 2N 102 2W
Faizabad, *India* 43 F10 26 45N 82 10 E
Fajardo, *Puerto Rico* 89 C6 18 20N 65 39W
Fakfak, *Indonesia* 37 E8 3 0S 132 15 E
Faku, *China* 35 C12 42 32N 123 21 E
Falaise, *France* 18 B3 48 54N 0 12W
Falaise, Mui, *Vietnam* 38 C5 19 6N 105 45 E
Falam, *Burma* 41 H18 23 0N 93 45 E
Falcón, C., *Spain* 22 C7 38 50N 1 23 E
Falcon Dam, *U.S.A.* 81 M5 26 50N 99 20W
Falconara Marittima, *Italy* 20 C5 43 37N 13 24 E
Falcone, C., *Italy* 20 D3 40 58N 8 12 E
Falconer, *U.S.A.* 78 D5 42 7N 79 13W
Faleshty = Fălești, *Moldova* 17 E14 47 32N 27 44 E
Fălești, *Moldova* 17 E14 47 32N 27 44 E
Falfurrias, *U.S.A.* 81 M5 27 14N 98 9W
Falher, *Canada* 72 B5 55 44N 117 15W
Faliraki, *Greece* 23 C10 36 22N 28 12 E
Falkenberg, *Sweden* 9 H15 56 54N 12 30 E
Falkirk, *U.K.* 12 F5 56 0N 3 47W
Falkirk □, *U.K.* 12 F5 55 58N 3 49W
Falkland Is. □, *Atl. Oc.* 96 G5 51 30S 59 0W
Falkland Sd., *Falk. Is.* 96 G5 52 0S 60 0W
Falköping, *Sweden* 9 G15 58 12N 13 33 E
Fall River, *U.S.A.* 79 E13 41 43N 71 10W
Fall River Mills, *U.S.A.* 82 F3 41 3N 121 26W
Fallbrook, *U.S.A.* 83 K5 33 25N 117 12W
Fallbrook, *Calif., U.S.A.* 85 M9 33 23N 117 15W
Fallon, *Mont., U.S.A.* 80 B2 46 50N 105 8W
Fallon, *Nev., U.S.A.* 82 G4 39 28N 118 47W
Falls City, *Nebr., U.S.A.* 80 E7 40 3N 95 36W
Falls City, *Oreg., U.S.A.* 82 D2 44 52N 123 26W
Falls Creek, *U.S.A.* 78 E6 41 9N 78 48W
Falmouth, *Jamaica* 88 C4 18 30N 77 40W
Falmouth, *U.K.* 11 G2 50 9N 5 5W
Falmouth, *U.S.A.* 76 F3 38 41N 84 20W
False B., *S. Africa* 56 E2 34 15S 18 40 E
Falso, C., *Honduras* 88 C3 15 12N 83 21W
Falster, *Denmark* 9 J14 54 45N 11 55 E
Falsterbo, *Sweden* 9 J15 55 23N 12 50 E
Fălticeni, *Romania* 17 E14 47 21N 26 20 E
Falun, *Sweden* 9 F16 60 37N 15 37 E
Famagusta, *Cyprus* 23 D12 35 8N 33 55 E
Famagusta Bay, *Cyprus* 23 D13 35 15N 34 0 E
Famatina, Sierra de, *Argentina* 94 B2 27 30S 68 0W
Family L., *Canada* 73 C9 51 54N 95 27W
Famoso, *U.S.A.* 85 K7 35 37N 119 12W
Fan Xian, *China* 34 G8 35 55N 115 38 E
Fandriana, *Madag.* 57 C8 20 14S 47 21 E
Fang, *Thailand* 38 C2 19 55N 99 13 E
Fangcheng, *China* 34 H7 33 18N 112 59 E
Fangshan, *China* 34 E6 38 3N 111 25 E
Fangzi, *China* 35 F10 36 33N 119 10 E
Fanjiatun, *China* 35 C13 43 40N 125 15 E
Fannich, L., *U.K.* 12 D4 57 38N 4 59W
Fannūj, *Iran* 45 E8 26 35N 59 38 E
Fanny Bay, *Canada* 72 D4 49 37N 124 48W
Fanø, *Denmark* 9 J13 55 25N 8 25 E
Fano, *Italy* 20 C5 43 50N 13 1 E
Fanshaw, *U.S.A.* 72 B2 57 11N 133 30W
Fanshi, *China* 34 E7 39 12N 113 20 E
Fao = Al Fāw, *Iraq* 45 D6 30 0N 48 30 E
Faqirwali, *Pakistan* 42 E5 29 27N 73 0 E
Faradje, *Zaïre* 54 B2 3 50N 29 45 E
Farafangana, *Madag.* 57 C8 22 49S 47 50 E
Farāh, *Afghan.* 40 C3 32 20N 62 7 E
Farāh □, *Afghan.* 40 C3 32 25N 62 10 E
Farahalana, *Madag.* 57 A9 14 26S 50 10 E
Faranah, *Guinea* 50 F2 10 3N 10 45W
Farasān, Jazā'ir, *Si. Arabia* 46 D3 16 45N 41 55 E
Farasan Is. = Farasān, Jazā'ir, *Si. Arabia* 46 D3 16 45N 41 55 E
Faratsiho, *Madag.* 57 B8 19 24S 46 57 E
Fareham, *U.K.* 11 G6 50 51N 1 11W
Farewell, C., *N.Z.* 59 J4 40 29S 172 43 E
Farewell C. = Farvel, Kap, *Greenland* 4 D5 59 48N 43 55W
Farghona, *Uzbekistan* 26 E8 40 23N 71 19 E
Fargo, *U.S.A.* 80 B6 46 53N 96 48W
Fār'iah, W. al →, *West Bank* 47 C4 32 12N 35 27 E
Faribault, *U.S.A.* 80 C8 44 18N 93 16W
Faridkot, *India* 42 D6 30 44N 74 45 E
Faridpur, *Bangla.* 43 H13 23 15N 89 55 E
Farim, *Guinea-Biss.* 50 F1 12 27N 15 9W
Farīmān, *Iran* 45 C8 35 40N 59 49 E
Farina, *Australia* 63 E2 30 3S 138 15 E
Fariones, Pta., *Canary Is.* 22 E6 29 13N 13 28W
Farmerville, *U.S.A.* 81 J8 32 47N 92 24W
Farmington, *Calif., U.S.A.* 84 H6 37 55N 120 59W
Farmington, *N.H., U.S.A.* 79 C13 43 24N 71 4W
Farmington, *N. Mex., U.S.A.* 83 H9 36 44N 108 12W
Farmington, *Utah, U.S.A.* 82 F8 41 0N 111 12W
Farmington →, *U.S.A.* 79 E12 41 51N 72 38W
Farmville, *U.S.A.* 76 G6 37 18N 78 24W
Farnborough, *U.K.* 11 F7 51 16N 0 45W
Farne Is., *U.K.* 10 B6 55 38N 1 37W
Farnham, *Canada* 79 A12 45 17N 72 59W
Faro, *Brazil* 93 D7 2 10S 56 39W
Faro, *Portugal* 19 D2 37 2N 7 55W
Fårö, *Sweden* 9 H18 57 55N 19 5 E
Farquhar, C., *Australia* 61 D1 23 50S 113 36 E
Farrars Cr. →, *Australia* 62 D3 25 35S 140 43 E
Farrāshband, *Iran* 45 D7 28 57N 52 5 E
Farrell, *U.S.A.* 78 E4 41 13N 80 30W
Farrell Flat, *Australia* 63 E2 33 48S 138 48 E
Farrokhī, *Iran* 45 C8 33 50N 59 31 E
Farruch, C., *Spain* 22 B10 39 47N 3 21 E
Farrukhabad-cum-Fatehgarh, *India* 43 F8 27 30N 79 32 E
Fārs □, *Iran* 45 D7 29 30N 55 0 E
Fársala, *Greece* 21 E10 39 17N 22 23 E
Farsund, *Norway* 9 G12 58 5N 6 55 E

Fartak, Râs

Fartak, Râs, *Si. Arabia* **44 D2** 28 5N 34 34 E
Fartura, Serra da, *Brazil* **95 B5** 26 21S 52 52W
Fārūj, *Iran* **45 B8** 37 14N 58 14 E
Farvel, Kap, *Greenland* **4 D5** 59 48N 43 55W
Farwell, *U.S.A.* **81 H3** 34 23N 103 2W
Fasā, *Iran* **45 D7** 29 0N 53 39 E
Fasano, *Italy* **20 D7** 40 50N 17 22 E
Fastiv, *Ukraine* **17 C15** 50 7N 29 57 E
Fastnet Rock, *Ireland* **13 E2** 51 22N 9 37W
Fastov = Fastiv, *Ukraine* **17 C15** 50 7N 29 57 E
Fatagar, Tanjung, *Indonesia* **37 E8** 2 46S 131 57 E
Fatehgarh, *India* **43 F8** 27 25N 79 35 E
Fatehpur, *Raj., India* **42 F6** 28 0N 74 40 E
Fatehpur, *Ut. P., India* **43 G9** 25 56N 81 13 E
Fatima, *Canada* **71 C7** 47 24N 61 53W
Faulkton, *U.S.A.* **80 C5** 45 2N 99 8W
Faure I., *Australia* **61 E1** 25 52S 113 50 E
Fauresmith, *S. Africa* **56 D4** 29 44S 25 17 E
Fauske, *Norway* **8 C16** 67 17N 15 25 E
Favara, *Italy* **20 F5** 37 19N 13 39 E
Favaritx, C., *Spain* **22 A11** 40 0N 4 15 E
Favignana, *Italy* **20 F5** 37 56N 12 20 E
Favourable Lake, *Canada* **70 B1** 52 50N 93 39W
Fawn —►, *Canada* **70 A2** 55 20N 87 35W
Fawnskin, *U.S.A.* **85 L10** 34 16N 116 56W
Faxaflói, *Iceland* **8 D2** 64 29N 23 0W
Faya-Largeau, *Chad* **51 E8** 17 58N 19 6 E
Fayd, *Si. Arabia* **44 E4** 27 1N 42 52 E
Fayette, *Ala., U.S.A.* **77 J2** 33 41N 87 50W
Fayette, *Mo., U.S.A.* **80 F8** 39 9N 92 41W
Fayetteville, *Ark., U.S.A.* **81 G7** 36 4N 94 10W
Fayetteville, *N.C., U.S.A.* **77 H6** 35 3N 78 53W
Fayetteville, *Tenn., U.S.A.* **77 H2** 35 9N 86 34W
Fazilka, *India* **42 D6** 30 27N 74 2 E
Fazilpur, *Pakistan* **42 E4** 29 18N 70 29 E
Fdérik, *Mauritania* **50 D2** 22 40N 12 45W
Feale —►, *Ireland* **13 D2** 52 27N 9 37W
Fear, C., *U.S.A.* **77 J7** 33 50N 77 58W
Feather —►, *U.S.A.* **82 G3** 38 47N 121 36W
Feather Falls, *U.S.A.* **84 F5** 39 36N 121 16W
Featherston, *N.Z.* **59 J5** 41 6S 175 20 E
Featherstone, *Zimbabwe* **55 F3** 18 42S 30 55 E
Fécamp, *France* **18 B4** 49 45N 0 22 E
Federación, *Argentina* **94 C4** 31 0S 57 55W
Fedeshkūh, *Iran* **45 D7** 28 49N 53 50 E
Fehmarn, *Germany* **16 A6** 54 27N 11 7 E
Fehmarn Bælt, *Europe* **9 J14** 54 35N 11 20 E
Fei Xian, *China* **35 G9** 35 18N 117 59 E
Feilding, *N.Z.* **59 J5** 40 13S 175 35 E
Feira de Santana, *Brazil* **93 F11** 12 15S 38 57W
Feixiang, *China* **34 F8** 36 30N 114 45 E
Felanitx, *Spain* **22 B10** 39 28N 3 9 E
Feldkirch, *Austria* **16 E5** 47 15N 9 37 E
Felipe Carrillo Puerto, *Mexico* **87 D7** 19 38N 88 3W
Felixstowe, *U.K.* **11 F9** 51 58N 1 23 E
Felton, *U.K.* **10 B6** 55 18N 1 42W
Felton, *U.S.A.* **84 H4** 37 3N 122 4W
Femunden, *Norway* **9 E14** 62 10N 11 53 E
Fen He —►, *China* **34 G6** 35 36N 110 42 E
Fenelon Falls, *Canada* **78 B6** 44 32N 78 45W
Feng Xian, *Jiangsu, China* **34 G9** 34 43N 116 35 E
Feng Xian, *Shaanxi, China* **34 H4** 33 54N 106 40 E
Fengcheng, *China* **35 D13** 40 28N 124 5 E
Fengfeng, *China* **34 F8** 36 28N 114 8 E
Fengjie, *China* **33 C5** 31 5N 109 36 E
Fengning, *China* **34 D9** 41 10N 116 33 E
Fengqiu, *China* **34 G8** 35 2N 114 25 E
Fengrun, *China* **35 E10** 39 48N 118 8 E
Fengtai, *China* **34 E9** 39 50N 116 18 E
Fengxiang, *China* **34 G4** 34 29N 107 25 E
Fengyang, *China* **35 H9** 32 51N 117 29 E
Fengzhen, *China* **34 D7** 40 25N 113 2 E
Fenit, *Ireland* **13 D2** 52 17N 9 51W
Fennimore, *U.S.A.* **80 D9** 42 59N 90 39W
Fenoarivo Afovoany, *Madag.* **57 B8** 18 26S 46 34 E
Fenoarivo Atsinanana, *Madag.* **57 B8** 17 22S 49 25 E
Fens, The, *U.K.* **10 E8** 52 38N 0 2W
Fenton, *U.S.A.* **76 D4** 42 48N 83 42W
Fenxi, *China* **34 F6** 36 40N 111 31 E
Fenyang, *China* **34 F6** 37 18N 111 48 E
Feodosiya, *Ukraine* **25 E6** 45 2N 35 16 E
Ferdows, *Iran* **45 C8** 33 58N 58 2 E
Ferfer, *Somali Rep.* **46 F4** 5 4N 45 9 E
Fergana = Farghona, *Uzbekistan* **26 E8** 40 23N 71 19 E
Fergus, *Canada* **70 D3** 43 43N 80 24W
Fergus Falls, *U.S.A.* **80 B6** 46 17N 96 4W
Ferland, *Canada* **70 B2** 50 19N 88 27W
Fermanagh □, *U.K.* **13 B4** 54 21N 7 40W
Fermo, *Italy* **20 C5** 43 9N 13 43 E
Fermoy, *Ireland* **13 D3** 52 9N 8 16W
Fernández, *Argentina* **94 B3** 27 55S 63 50W
Fernandina Beach, *U.S.A.* **77 K5** 30 40N 81 27W
Fernando de Noronha, *Brazil* **93 D12** 4 0S 33 10W
Fernando Póo = Bioko, *Eq. Guin.* **50 H6** 3 30N 8 40 E
Ferndale, *Calif., U.S.A.* **82 F1** 40 35N 124 16W
Ferndale, *Wash., U.S.A.* **84 B4** 48 51N 122 36W
Fernie, *Canada* **72 D5** 49 30N 115 5W
Fernlees, *Australia* **62 C4** 23 51S 148 7 E
Fernley, *U.S.A.* **82 G4** 39 36N 119 15W
Ferozepore = Firozpur, *India* **42 D6** 30 55N 74 40 E
Ferrara, *Italy* **20 B4** 44 50N 11 35 E
Ferreñafe, *Peru* **92 E3** 6 42S 79 50W
Ferrerías, *Spain* **22 B11** 39 59N 4 1 E
Ferret, C., *France* **18 D3** 44 38N 1 15W
Ferriday, *U.S.A.* **81 K9** 31 38N 91 33W
Ferrol = El Ferrol, *Spain* **19 A1** 43 29N 8 15W
Ferron, *U.S.A.* **83 G8** 39 5N 111 8W
Ferryland, *Canada* **71 C9** 47 2N 52 53W
Fertile, *U.S.A.* **80 B6** 47 32N 96 17W
Fès, *Morocco* **50 B4** 34 0N 5 0W
Feshi, *Zaïre* **52 F3** 6 8S 18 10 E
Fessenden, *U.S.A.* **80 B5** 47 39N 99 38W
Feteşti, *Romania* **17 F14** 44 22N 27 51 E
Fetlar, *U.K.* **12 A8** 60 36N 0 52W
Feuilles —►, *Canada* **69 C12** 58 47N 70 4W
Fezzan, *Libya* **51 C8** 27 0N 15 0 E
Ffestiniog, *U.K.* **10 E4** 52 57N 3 55W
Fiambalá, *Argentina* **94 B2** 27 45S 67 37W
Fianarantsoa, *Madag.* **57 C8** 21 26S 47 5 E
Fianarantsoa □, *Madag.* **57 B8** 19 30S 47 0 E
Fianga, *Cameroon* **51 G8** 9 55N 15 9 E
Ficksburg, *S. Africa* **57 D4** 28 51S 27 53 E
Field, *Canada* **70 C3** 46 31N 80 1W
Field —►, *Australia* **62 C2** 23 48S 138 0 E
Field I., *Australia* **60 B5** 12 5S 132 23 E
Fieri, *Albania* **21 D8** 40 43N 19 33 E
Fife □, *U.K.* **12 E5** 56 16N 3 1W
Fife Ness, *U.K.* **12 E6** 56 17N 2 35W
Figeac, *France* **18 D5** 44 37N 2 2 E
Figtree, *Zimbabwe* **55 G2** 20 22S 28 20 E
Figueira da Foz, *Portugal* **19 B1** 40 7N 8 54W
Figueras, *Spain* **19 A7** 42 18N 2 58 E
Figuig, *Morocco* **50 B4** 32 5N 1 11W
Fihaonana, *Madag.* **57 B8** 18 36S 47 12 E
Fiherenana, *Madag.* **57 B8** 18 29S 48 24 E
Fiherenana —►, *Madag.* **57 C7** 23 19S 43 37 E
Fiji ■, *Pac. Oc.* **59 C8** 17 20S 179 0 E
Filer, *U.S.A.* **82 E6** 42 34N 114 37W
Filey, *U.K.* **10 C7** 54 12N 0 18W
Filfla, *Malta* **23 D1** 35 47N 14 24 E
Filiatrá, *Greece* **21 F9** 37 9N 21 35 E
Filipstad, *Sweden* **9 G16** 59 43N 14 9 E
Fillmore, *Canada* **73 D8** 49 50N 103 25W
Fillmore, *Calif., U.S.A.* **85 L8** 34 24N 118 55W
Fillmore, *Utah, U.S.A.* **83 G7** 38 58N 112 20W
Finch, *Canada* **79 A9** 45 11N 75 7W
Findhorn —►, *U.K.* **12 D5** 57 38N 3 38W
Findlay, *U.S.A.* **76 E4** 41 2N 83 39W
Finger L., *Canada* **73 C10** 53 33N 93 30W
Fingōe, *Mozam.* **55 E3** 14 55S 31 50 E
Finisterre, C., *Spain* **19 A1** 42 50N 9 19W
Finke, *Australia* **62 D1** 25 34S 134 35 E
Finke —►, *Australia* **63 D2** 27 0S 136 10 E
Finland ■, *Europe* **8 E22** 63 0N 27 0 E
Finland, G. of, *Europe* **9 G21** 60 0N 26 0 E
Finlay —►, *Canada* **72 B3** 57 0N 125 10W
Finley, *Australia* **63 F4** 35 38S 145 35 E
Finley, *U.S.A.* **80 B6** 47 31N 97 50W
Finn —►, *Ireland* **13 B4** 54 51N 7 28W
Finnigan, Mt., *Australia* **62 B4** 15 49S 145 17 E
Finniss, C., *Australia* **63 E1** 33 8S 134 51 E
Finnmark, *Norway* **8 B20** 69 37N 23 57 E
Finnsnes, *Norway* **8 B18** 69 14N 18 0 E
Finspång, *Sweden* **9 G16** 58 43N 15 47 E
Fiora —►, *Italy* **20 C4** 42 20N 11 34 E
Fiq, *Syria* **47 C4** 32 46N 35 41 E
Firat = Furāt, Nahr al —►, *Asia* **44 D5** 31 0N 47 25 E
Fire River, *Canada* **70 C3** 48 47N 83 21W
Firebag —►, *Canada* **73 B6** 57 45N 111 21W
Firebaugh, *U.S.A.* **84 J6** 36 52N 120 27W
Firedrake L., *Canada* **73 A8** 61 25N 104 30W
Firenze, *Italy* **20 C4** 43 46N 11 15 E
Firk —►, *Iraq* **44 D5** 30 59N 44 34 E
Firozabad, *India* **43 F8** 27 10N 78 25 E
Firozpur, *India* **42 D6** 30 55N 74 40 E
Fīrūzābād, *Iran* **45 D7** 28 52N 52 35 E
Fīrūzkūh, *Iran* **45 C7** 35 50N 52 50 E
Firvale, *Canada* **72 C3** 52 27N 126 13W
Fish —►, *Namibia* **56 D2** 28 7S 17 10 E
Fish —►, *S. Africa* **56 E3** 31 30S 20 16 E
Fisher, *Australia* **61 F5** 30 30S 131 0 E
Fisher B., *Canada* **73 C9** 51 35N 97 13W
Fishguard, *U.K.* **11 F3** 52 0N 5 0W
Fishing L., *Canada* **73 C9** 52 10N 95 24W
Fitchburg, *U.S.A.* **79 D13** 42 35N 71 48W
Fitri, L., *Chad* **51 F8** 12 50N 17 28 E
Fitz Roy, *Argentina* **96 F3** 47 0S 67 0W
Fitzgerald, *Canada* **72 B6** 59 51N 111 36W
Fitzgerald, *U.S.A.* **77 K4** 31 43N 83 15W
Fitzmaurice —►, *Australia* **60 B5** 14 45S 130 5 E
Fitzroy —►, *Queens., Australia* **62 C5** 23 32S 150 52 E
Fitzroy —►, *W. Austral., Australia* **60 C3** 17 31S 123 35 E
Fitzroy Crossing, *Australia* **60 C4** 18 9S 125 38 E
Fitzwilliam I., *Canada* **78 A3** 45 30N 81 45W
Fiume = Rijeka, *Croatia* **16 F8** 45 20N 14 21 E
Five Points, *U.S.A.* **84 J6** 36 26N 120 6W
Fizi, *Zaïre* **54 C2** 4 17S 28 55 E
Flagler, *U.S.A.* **80 F3** 39 18N 103 4W
Flagstaff, *U.S.A.* **83 J8** 35 12N 111 39W
Flaherty I., *Canada* **70 A4** 56 15N 79 15W
Flåm, *Norway* **9 F12** 60 50N 7 7 E
Flambeau —►, *U.S.A.* **80 C9** 45 18N 91 14W
Flamborough Hd., *U.K.* **10 C7** 54 7N 0 5W
Flaming Gorge Dam, *U.S.A.* **82 F9** 40 55N 109 25W
Flaming Gorge Reservoir, *U.S.A.* **82 F9** 41 10N 109 25W
Flamingo, Teluk, *Indonesia* **37 F9** 5 30S 138 0 E
Flanders = West-Vlaanderen □, *Belgium* **15 D3** 51 0N 3 0 E
Flandre, *Europe* **16 C2** 51 0N 3 0 E
Flandre Occidentale = West-Vlaanderen □, *Belgium* **15 D3** 51 0N 3 0 E
Flandre Orientale = Oost-Vlaanderen □, *Belgium* **15 C3** 51 5N 3 50 E
Flandreau, *U.S.A.* **80 C6** 44 3N 96 36W
Flanigan, *U.S.A.* **84 E7** 40 10N 119 53W
Flannan Is., *U.K.* **12 C1** 58 9N 7 52W
Flåsjön, *Sweden* **8 D16** 64 5N 15 40 E
Flat —►, *Canada* **72 A3** 61 33N 125 18W
Flat River, *U.S.A.* **81 G9** 37 51N 90 31W
Flathead L., *U.S.A.* **82 C6** 47 51N 114 8W
Flattery, C., *Australia* **62 A4** 14 58S 145 21 E
Flattery, C., *U.S.A.* **84 B2** 48 23N 124 29W
Flaxton, *U.S.A.* **80 A3** 48 54N 102 24W
Fleetwood, *U.K.* **10 D4** 53 55N 3 1W
Flekkefjord, *Norway* **9 G12** 58 18N 6 39 E
Flemington, *U.S.A.* **78 E7** 41 7N 77 28W
Flensburg, *Germany* **16 A5** 54 47N 9 27 E
Flers, *France* **18 B3** 48 47N 0 33W
Flesherton, *Canada* **78 B4** 44 16N 80 33W
Flesko, Tanjung, *Indonesia* **37 D6** 0 29N 124 30 E
Flevoland □, *Neths.* **15 B5** 52 30N 5 30 E
Flin Flon, *Canada* **73 C8** 54 46N 101 53W
Flinders —►, *Australia* **62 B3** 17 36S 140 36 E
Flinders B., *Australia* **61 F2** 34 19S 115 19 E
Flinders Group, *Australia* **62 A3** 14 11S 144 15 E
Flinders I., *Australia* **62 F4** 40 0S 148 0 E
Flinders Ranges, *Australia* **63 E2** 31 30S 138 30 E
Flinders Reefs, *Australia* **62 B4** 17 37S 148 31 E
Flint, *U.K.* **10 D4** 53 15N 3 8W
Flint, *U.S.A.* **76 D4** 43 1N 83 41W
Flint —►, *U.S.A.* **77 K3** 30 57N 84 34W
Flint I., *Kiribati* **65 J12** 11 26S 151 48W
Flinton, *Australia* **63 D4** 27 55S 149 32 E
Flintshire □, *U.K.* **10 D4** 53 17N 3 17W
Flodden, *U.K.* **10 B5** 55 37N 2 8W
Floodwood, *U.S.A.* **80 B8** 46 55N 92 55W
Flora, *U.S.A.* **76 F1** 38 40N 88 29W
Florala, *U.S.A.* **77 K2** 31 0N 86 20W
Florence = Firenze, *Italy* **20 C4** 43 46N 11 15 E
Florence, *Ala., U.S.A.* **77 H2** 34 48N 87 41W
Florence, *Ariz., U.S.A.* **83 K8** 33 2N 111 23W
Florence, *Colo., U.S.A.* **80 F2** 38 23N 105 8W
Florence, *Oreg., U.S.A.* **82 E1** 43 58N 124 7W
Florence, *S.C., U.S.A.* **77 H6** 34 12N 79 46W
Florence, L., *Australia* **63 D2** 28 53S 138 9 E
Florennes, *Belgium* **15 D4** 50 15N 4 35 E
Florenville, *Belgium* **15 E5** 49 40N 5 19 E
Flores, *Guatemala* **88 C2** 16 59N 89 50W
Flores, *Indonesia* **37 F6** 8 35S 121 0 E
Flores I., *Canada* **72 D3** 49 20N 126 10W
Flores Sea, *Indonesia* **37 F6** 6 30S 120 0 E
Floreşti, *Moldova* **17 E15** 47 53N 28 17 E
Floresville, *U.S.A.* **81 L5** 29 8N 98 10W
Floriano, *Brazil* **93 E10** 6 50S 43 0W
Florianópolis, *Brazil* **95 B6** 27 30S 48 30W
Florida, *Cuba* **88 B4** 21 32N 78 14W
Florida, *Uruguay* **95 C4** 34 7S 56 10W
Florida □, *U.S.A.* **77 L5** 28 0N 82 0W
Florida, Straits of, *U.S.A.* **88 B3** 25 0N 80 0W
Florida B., *U.S.A.* **88 A3** 25 0N 80 45W
Florida Keys, *U.S.A.* **75 F10** 24 40N 81 0W
Flórina, *Greece* **21 D9** 40 48N 21 26 E
Florø, *Norway* **9 F11** 61 35N 5 1 E
Flower Station, *Canada* **79 A8** 45 10N 76 41W
Flower's Cove, *Canada* **71 B8** 51 14N 56 46W
Floydada, *U.S.A.* **81 J4** 33 59N 101 20W
Fluk, *Indonesia* **37 E7** 1 42S 127 44 E
Flushing = Vlissingen, *Neths.* **15 C3** 51 26N 3 34 E
Flying Fish, C., *Antarctica* **5 D15** 72 6S 102 29W
Foam Lake, *Canada* **73 C8** 51 40N 103 32W
Foça, *Turkey* **21 E12** 38 39N 26 46 E
Focşani, *Romania* **17 F14** 45 41N 27 15 E
Fóggia, *Italy* **20 D6** 41 27N 15 34 E
Fogo, *Canada* **71 C9** 49 43N 54 17W
Fogo I., *Canada* **71 C9** 49 40N 54 5W
Föhr, *Germany* **16 A5** 54 43N 8 30 E
Foix, *France* **18 E4** 42 58N 1 38 E
Folda, *Nord-Trøndelag, Norway* **8 D14** 64 32N 10 30 E
Folda, *Nordland, Norway* **8 C16** 67 38N 14 50 E
Foleyet, *Canada* **70 C3** 48 15N 82 25W
Folgefonni, *Norway* **9 F12** 60 3N 6 23 E
Foligno, *Italy* **20 C5** 42 57N 12 42 E
Folkestone, *U.K.* **11 F9** 51 5N 1 12 E
Folkston, *U.S.A.* **77 K5** 30 50N 82 0W
Follett, *U.S.A.* **81 G4** 36 26N 100 8W
Folsom Res., *U.S.A.* **84 G5** 38 42N 121 9W
Fond-du-Lac, *Canada* **73 B7** 59 19N 107 12W
Fond du Lac, *U.S.A.* **80 D10** 43 47N 88 27W
Fond-du-Lac —►, *Canada* **73 B7** 59 17N 106 0W
Fonda, *U.S.A.* **79 D10** 42 57N 74 22W
Fondi, *Italy* **20 D5** 41 21N 13 25 E
Fonsagrada, *Spain* **19 A2** 43 8N 7 4W
Fonseca, G. de, *Cent. Amer.* **88 D2** 13 10N 87 40W
Fontainebleau, *France* **18 B5** 48 24N 2 40 E
Fontana, *U.S.A.* **85 L9** 34 6N 117 26W
Fontas —►, *Canada* **72 B4** 58 14N 121 48W
Fonte Boa, *Brazil* **92 D5** 2 33S 66 0W
Fontenay-le-Comte, *France* **18 C3** 46 28N 0 48W
Fontur, *Iceland* **8 C6** 66 23N 14 32W
Foochow = Fuzhou, *China* **33 D6** 26 5N 119 16 E
Foping, *China* **34 H4** 33 41N 108 0 E
Forbes, *Australia* **63 E4** 33 22S 148 0 E
Forbesganj, *India* **43 F12** 26 17N 87 18 E
Ford City, *Calif., U.S.A.* **85 K7** 35 9N 119 27W
Ford City, *Pa., U.S.A.* **78 F5** 40 46N 79 32W
Førde, *Norway* **9 F11** 61 27N 5 53 E
Ford's Bridge, *Australia* **63 D4** 29 41S 145 29 E
Fordyce, *U.S.A.* **81 J8** 33 49N 92 25W
Forécariah, *Guinea* **50 G2** 9 28N 13 10W
Forel, Mt., *Greenland* **4 C6** 66 52N 36 55W
Foremost, *Canada* **72 D6** 49 26N 111 34W
Forest, *Canada* **78 C3** 43 6N 82 0W
Forest, *U.S.A.* **81 J10** 32 22N 89 29W
Forest City, *Iowa, U.S.A.* **80 D8** 43 16N 93 39W
Forest City, *N.C., U.S.A.* **77 H5** 35 20N 81 52W
Forest City, *Pa., U.S.A.* **79 E9** 41 39N 75 28W
Forest Grove, *U.S.A.* **84 E3** 45 31N 123 7W
Forestburg, *Canada* **72 C6** 52 35N 112 1W
Foresthill, *U.S.A.* **84 F6** 39 1N 120 49W
Forestier Pen., *Australia* **62 G4** 43 0S 148 0 E
Forestville, *Canada* **71 C6** 48 48N 69 2W
Forestville, *Calif., U.S.A.* **84 G4** 38 28N 122 54W
Forestville, *Wis., U.S.A.* **76 C2** 44 41N 87 29W
Forfar, *U.K.* **12 E6** 56 39N 2 53W
Forks, *U.S.A.* **84 C2** 47 57N 124 23W
Forlì, *Italy* **20 B5** 44 13N 12 3 E
Forman, *U.S.A.* **80 B6** 46 7N 97 38W
Formby Pt., *U.K.* **10 D4** 53 33N 3 6W
Formentera, *Spain* **22 C7** 38 43N 1 27 E
Formentor, C. de, *Spain* **22 B10** 39 58N 3 13 E
Former Yugoslav Republic of Macedonia = Macedonia ■, *Europe* **21 D9** 41 53N 21 40 E
Fórmia, *Italy* **20 D5** 41 15N 13 37 E
Formosa = Taiwan ■, *Asia* **33 D7** 23 30N 121 0 E
Formosa, *Argentina* **94 B4** 26 15S 58 10W
Formosa □, *Argentina* **94 B3** 25 0S 60 0W
Formosa, Serra, *Brazil* **93 F8** 12 0S 55 0W
Formosa Bay, *Kenya* **54 C5** 2 40S 40 20 E
Fornells, *Spain* **22 A11** 40 3N 4 7 E
Føroyar, *Atl. Oc.* **8 F9** 62 0N 7 0W
Forres, *U.K.* **12 D5** 57 37N 3 37W
Forrest, *Vic., Australia* **63 F3** 38 33S 143 47 E
Forrest, *W. Austral., Australia* **61 F4** 30 51S 128 6 E
Forrest, Mt., *Australia* **61 D4** 24 48S 127 45 E
Forrest City, *U.S.A.* **81 H9** 35 1N 90 47W
Forsayth, *Australia* **62 B3** 18 33S 143 34 E
Forssa, *Finland* **9 F20** 60 49N 23 38 E
Forst, *Germany* **16 C8** 51 45N 14 37 E
Forster, *Australia* **63 E5** 32 12S 152 31 E
Forsyth, *Ga., U.S.A.* **77 J4** 33 2N 83 56W
Forsyth, *Mont., U.S.A.* **82 C10** 46 16N 106 41W
Fort Albany, *Canada* **70 B3** 52 15N 81 35W
Fort Apache, *U.S.A.* **83 K9** 33 50N 110 0W
Fort Assiniboine, *Canada* **72 C6** 54 20N 114 45W
Fort Augustus, *U.K.* **12 D4** 57 9N 4 42W
Fort Beaufort, *S. Africa* **56 E4** 32 46S 26 40 E
Fort Benton, *U.S.A.* **82 C8** 47 49N 110 40W
Fort Bragg, *U.S.A.* **82 G2** 39 26N 123 48W
Fort Bridger, *U.S.A.* **82 F8** 41 19N 110 23W
Fort Chipewyan, *Canada* **73 B6** 58 42N 111 8W
Fort Collins, *U.S.A.* **80 E2** 40 35N 105 5W
Fort-Coulonge, *Canada* **70 C4** 45 50N 76 45W
Fort Davis, *U.S.A.* **81 K3** 30 35N 103 54W
Fort-de-France, *Martinique* **89 D7** 14 36N 61 2W
Fort de Possel = Possel, *C.A.R.* **52 C3** 5 5N 19 10 E
Fort Defiance, *U.S.A.* **83 J9** 35 45N 109 5W
Fort Dodge, *U.S.A.* **80 D7** 42 30N 94 11W
Fort Edward, *U.S.A.* **79 C11** 43 16N 73 35W
Fort Frances, *Canada* **73 D10** 48 36N 93 24W
Fort Garland, *U.S.A.* **83 H11** 37 26N 105 26W
Fort George = Chisasibi, *Canada* **70 B4** 53 50N 79 0W
Fort Good-Hope, *Canada* **68 B7** 66 14N 128 40W
Fort Hancock, *U.S.A.* **83 L11** 31 18N 105 51W
Fort Hertz = Putao, *Burma* **41 F20** 27 28N 97 30 E
Fort Hope, *Canada* **70 B2** 51 30N 88 0W
Fort Irwin, *U.S.A.* **85 K10** 35 16N 116 34W
Fort Jameson = Chipata, *Zambia* **55 E3** 13 38S 32 28 E
Fort Kent, *U.S.A.* **71 C6** 47 15N 68 36W
Fort Klamath, *U.S.A.* **82 E3** 42 42N 122 0W
Fort-Lamy = Ndjamena, *Chad* **51 F7** 12 10N 14 59 E
Fort Laramie, *U.S.A.* **80 D2** 42 13N 104 31W
Fort Lauderdale, *U.S.A.* **77 M5** 26 7N 80 8W
Fort Liard, *Canada* **72 A4** 60 14N 123 30W
Fort Liberté, *Haiti* **89 C5** 19 42N 71 51W
Fort Lupton, *U.S.A.* **80 E2** 40 5N 104 49W
Fort Mackay, *Canada* **72 B6** 57 12N 111 41W
Fort McKenzie, *Canada* **71 A6** 57 20N 69 0W
Fort Macleod, *Canada* **72 D6** 49 45N 113 30W
Fort MacMahon, *Algeria* **50 C5** 29 43N 1 45 E
Fort McMurray, *Canada* **72 B6** 56 44N 111 7W
Fort McPherson, *Canada* **68 B6** 67 30N 134 55W
Fort Madison, *U.S.A.* **80 E9** 40 38N 91 27W
Fort Meade, *U.S.A.* **77 M5** 27 45N 81 48W
Fort Miribel, *Algeria* **50 C5** 29 25N 2 55 E
Fort Morgan, *U.S.A.* **80 E3** 40 15N 103 48W
Fort Myers, *U.S.A.* **77 M5** 26 39N 81 52W
Fort Nelson, *Canada* **72 B4** 58 50N 122 44W
Fort Nelson —►, *Canada* **72 B4** 59 32N 124 0W
Fort Norman = Tulita, *Canada* **68 B7** 64 57N 125 30W
Fort Payne, *U.S.A.* **77 H3** 34 26N 85 43W
Fort Peck, *U.S.A.* **82 B10** 48 1N 106 27W
Fort Peck Dam, *U.S.A.* **82 C10** 48 0N 106 26W
Fort Peck L., *U.S.A.* **82 C10** 48 0N 106 26W
Fort Pierce, *U.S.A.* **77 M5** 27 27N 80 20W
Fort Pierre, *U.S.A.* **80 C4** 44 21N 100 22W
Fort Plain, *U.S.A.* **79 D10** 42 56N 74 37W
Fort Portal, *Uganda* **54 B3** 0 40N 30 20 E
Fort Providence, *Canada* **72 A5** 61 3N 117 40W
Fort Qu'Appelle, *Canada* **73 C8** 50 45N 103 50W
Fort Resolution, *Canada* **72 A6** 61 10N 113 40W
Fort Rixon, *Zimbabwe* **55 G2** 20 2S 29 17 E
Fort Rosebery = Mansa, *Zambia* **55 E2** 11 13S 28 55 E
Fort Ross, *U.S.A.* **84 G3** 38 32N 123 13W
Fort Rupert = Waskaganish, *Canada* **70 B4** 51 30N 78 40W
Fort St. James, *Canada* **72 C4** 54 30N 124 10W
Fort St. John, *Canada* **72 B4** 56 15N 120 50W
Fort Sandeman, *Pakistan* **42 D3** 31 20N 69 31 E
Fort Saskatchewan, *Canada* **72 C6** 53 40N 113 15W
Fort Scott, *U.S.A.* **81 G7** 37 50N 94 42W
Fort Severn, *Canada* **70 A2** 56 0N 87 40W
Fort Shevchenko, *Kazakstan* **25 F9** 44 35N 50 23 E
Fort Simpson, *Canada* **72 A4** 61 45N 121 15W
Fort Smith, *Canada* **72 B6** 60 0N 111 51W
Fort Smith, *U.S.A.* **81 H7** 35 23N 94 25W
Fort Stanton, *U.S.A.* **83 K11** 33 30N 105 31W
Fort Stockton, *U.S.A.* **81 K3** 30 53N 102 53W
Fort Sumner, *U.S.A.* **81 H2** 34 28N 104 15W
Fort Trinquet = Bir Mogrein, *Mauritania* **50 C2** 25 10N 11 25W
Fort Valley, *U.S.A.* **77 J4** 32 33N 83 53W
Fort Vermilion, *Canada* **72 B5** 58 24N 116 0W
Fort Walton Beach, *U.S.A.* **77 K2** 30 25N 86 36W
Fort Wayne, *U.S.A.* **76 E3** 41 4N 85 9W
Fort William, *U.K.* **12 E3** 56 49N 5 7W
Fort Worth, *U.S.A.* **81 J6** 32 45N 97 18W
Fort Yates, *U.S.A.* **80 B4** 46 5N 100 38W
Fort Yukon, *U.S.A.* **68 B5** 66 34N 145 16W
Fortaleza, *Brazil* **93 D11** 3 45S 38 35W
Forteau, *Canada* **71 B8** 51 28N 56 58W
Forth —►, *U.K.* **12 E5** 56 9N 3 50W
Forth, Firth of, *U.K.* **12 E6** 56 5N 2 55W
Fortrose, *U.K.* **12 D4** 57 35N 4 9W
Fortuna, *Calif., U.S.A.* **82 F1** 40 36N 124 9W
Fortuna, *N. Dak., U.S.A.* **80 A3** 48 55N 103 47W
Fortune B., *Canada* **71 C8** 47 30N 55 22W
Foshan, *China* **33 D6** 23 4N 113 5 E
Fosna, *Norway* **8 E14** 63 50N 10 20 E
Fosnavåg, *Norway* **9 E11** 62 22N 5 38 E
Fossano, *Italy* **20 B2** 44 33N 7 43 E
Fossil, *U.S.A.* **82 D3** 45 0N 120 9W
Fossilbrook, *Australia* **62 B3** 17 47S 144 29 E
Fosston, *U.S.A.* **80 B7** 47 35N 95 45W
Foster, *Canada* **79 A12** 45 17N 72 30W
Foster —►, *Canada* **73 B7** 55 47N 105 49W
Fosters Ra., *Australia* **62 C1** 21 35S 133 48 E
Fostoria, *U.S.A.* **76 E4** 41 10N 83 25W

Fougamou, *Gabon* **52 E2** 1 16S 10 30 E
Fougères, *France* **18 B3** 48 21N 1 14W
Foul Pt., *Sri Lanka* **40 Q12** 8 35N 81 18 E
Foula, *U.K.* **12 A6** 60 10N 2 5W
Foulness I., *U.K.* **11 F8** 51 36N 0 55 E
Foulpointe, *Madag.* **57 B8** 17 41S 49 31 E
Foumban, *Cameroon* **50 G7** 5 45N 10 50 E
Fountain, *Colo., U.S.A.* **80 F2** 38 41N 104 42W
Fountain, *Utah, U.S.A.* **82 G8** 39 41N 111 37W
Fountain Springs, *U.S.A.* **85 K8** 35 54N 118 51W
Fourchu, *Canada* **71 C7** 45 43N 60 17W
Fouriesburg, *S. Africa* **56 D4** 28 38S 28 14 E
Foúrnoi, *Greece* **21 F12** 37 36N 26 32 E
Fouta Djalon, *Guinea* **50 F2** 11 20N 12 10W
Foux, Cap-à-, *Haiti* **89 C5** 19 43N 73 27W
Foveaux Str., *N.Z.* **59 M2** 46 42S 168 10 E
Fowey, *U.K.* **11 G3** 50 20N 4 39W
Fowler, *Calif., U.S.A.* **83 H4** 36 38N 119 41W
Fowler, *Colo., U.S.A.* **80 F2** 38 8N 104 2W
Fowler, *Kans., U.S.A.* **81 G4** 37 23N 100 12W
Fowlers B., *Australia* **61 F5** 31 59S 132 34 E
Fowlerton, *U.S.A.* **81 L5** 28 28N 98 48W
Fox →, *Canada* **73 B10** 56 3N 93 18W
Fox Valley, *Canada* **73 C7** 50 30N 109 25W
Foxe Basin, *Canada* **69 B12** 66 0N 77 0W
Foxe Chan., *Canada* **69 B11** 65 0N 80 0W
Foxe Pen., *Canada* **69 B12** 65 0N 76 0W
Foxpark, *U.S.A.* **82 F10** 41 5N 106 9W
Foxton, *N.Z.* **59 J5** 40 29S 175 18 E
Foyle, Lough, *U.K.* **13 A4** 55 7N 7 4W
Foynes, *Ireland* **13 D2** 52 37N 9 7W
Fóz do Cunene, *Angola* **56 B1** 17 15S 11 48 E
Foz do Gregório, *Brazil* **92 E4** 6 47S 70 44W
Foz do Iguaçu, *Brazil* **95 B5** 25 30S 54 30W
Frackville, *U.S.A.* **79 F8** 40 47N 76 14W
Framingham, *U.S.A.* **79 D13** 42 17N 71 25W
Franca, *Brazil* **93 H9** 20 33S 47 30W
Francavilla Fontana, *Italy* **21 D7** 40 32N 17 35 E
France ■, *Europe* **18 C5** 47 0N 3 0 E
Frances, *Australia* **63 F3** 36 41S 140 55 E
Frances →, *Canada* **72 A3** 60 16N 129 10W
Frances L., *Canada* **72 A3** 61 23N 129 30W
Francés Viejo, C., *Dom. Rep.* **89 C6** 19 40N 69 55W
Franceville, *Gabon* **52 E2** 1 40S 13 32 E
Franche-Comté, *France* **18 C6** 46 50N 5 55 E
Francisco I. Madero, *Coahuila, Mexico* **86 B4** 25 48N 103 18W
Francisco I. Madero, *Durango, Mexico* **86 C4** 24 32N 104 22W
Francistown, *Botswana* **57 C4** 21 7S 27 33 E
François, *Canada* **71 C8** 47 35N 56 45W
François L., *Canada* **72 C3** 54 0N 125 30W
Franeker, *Neths.* **15 A5** 53 12N 5 33 E
Frankfort, *S. Africa* **57 D4** 27 17S 28 30 E
Frankfort, *Ind., U.S.A.* **76 E2** 40 17N 86 31W
Frankfort, *Kans., U.S.A.* **80 F6** 39 42N 96 25W
Frankfort, *Ky., U.S.A.* **76 F3** 38 12N 84 52W
Frankfort, *Mich., U.S.A.* **76 C2** 44 38N 86 14W
Frankfurt, *Brandenburg, Germany* **16 B8** 52 20N 14 32 E
Frankfurt, *Hessen, Germany* **16 C5** 50 7N 8 41 E
Fränkische Alb, *Germany* **16 D6** 49 10N 11 23 E
Frankland →, *Australia* **61 G2** 35 0S 116 48 E
Franklin, *Ky., U.S.A.* **77 G2** 36 43N 86 35W
Franklin, *La., U.S.A.* **81 L9** 29 48N 91 30W
Franklin, *Mass., U.S.A.* **79 D13** 42 5N 71 24W
Franklin, *N.H., U.S.A.* **79 C13** 43 27N 71 39W
Franklin, *Nebr., U.S.A.* **80 E5** 40 6N 98 57W
Franklin, *Pa., U.S.A.* **78 E5** 41 24N 79 50W
Franklin, *Tenn., U.S.A.* **77 H2** 35 55N 86 52W
Franklin, *Va., U.S.A.* **77 G7** 36 41N 76 56W
Franklin, *W. Va., U.S.A.* **76 F6** 38 39N 79 20W
Franklin B., *Canada* **68 B7** 69 45N 126 0W
Franklin D. Roosevelt L., *U.S.A.* **82 B4** 48 18N 118 9W
Franklin I., *Antarctica* **5 D11** 76 10S 168 30 E
Franklin L., *U.S.A.* **82 F6** 40 25N 115 22W
Franklin Mts., *Canada* **68 B7** 65 0N 125 0W
Franklin Str., *Canada* **68 A10** 72 0N 96 0W
Franklinton, *U.S.A.* **81 K9** 30 51N 90 9W
Franklinville, *U.S.A.* **78 D6** 42 20N 78 27W
Franks Pk., *U.S.A.* **82 E9** 43 58N 109 18W
Frankston, *Australia* **63 F4** 38 8S 145 8 E
Frantsa Iosifa, Zemlya, *Russia* **26 A6** 82 0N 55 0 E
Franz, *Canada* **70 C3** 48 25N 84 30W
Franz Josef Land = Frantsa Iosifa, Zemlya, *Russia* **26 A6** 82 0N 55 0 E
Fraser →, *B.C., Canada* **72 D4** 49 7N 123 11W
Fraser →, *Nfld., Canada* **71 A7** 56 39N 62 10W
Fraser, Mt., *Australia* **61 E2** 25 35S 118 20 E
Fraser I., *Australia* **63 D5** 25 15S 153 10 E
Fraser Lake, *Canada* **72 C4** 54 0N 124 50W
Fraserburg, *S. Africa* **56 E3** 31 55S 21 30 E
Fraserburgh, *U.K.* **12 D6** 57 42N 2 1W
Fraserdale, *Canada* **70 C3** 49 55N 81 37W
Fray Bentos, *Uruguay* **94 C4** 33 10S 58 15W
Frazier Downs, *Australia* **60 C3** 18 48S 121 42 E
Fredericia, *Denmark* **9 J13** 55 34N 9 45 E
Frederick, *Md., U.S.A.* **76 F7** 39 25N 77 25W
Frederick, *Okla., U.S.A.* **81 H5** 34 23N 99 1W
Frederick, *S. Dak., U.S.A.* **80 C5** 45 50N 98 31W
Frederick Sd., *U.S.A.* **72 B2** 57 10N 134 0W
Fredericksburg, *Tex., U.S.A.* **81 K5** 30 16N 98 52W
Fredericksburg, *Va., U.S.A.* **76 F7** 38 18N 77 28W
Fredericktown, *U.S.A.* **81 G9** 37 34N 90 18W
Frederico I. Madero, Presa, *Mexico* **86 B3** 28 7N 105 40W
Fredericton, *Canada* **71 C6** 45 57N 66 40W
Fredericton Junc., *Canada* **71 C6** 45 41N 66 40W
Frederikshåb, *Greenland* **4 C5** 62 0N 49 43W
Frederikshavn, *Denmark* **9 H14** 57 28N 10 31 E
Frederiksted, *Virgin Is.* **89 C7** 17 43N 64 53W
Fredonia, *Ariz., U.S.A.* **83 H7** 36 57N 112 32W
Fredonia, *Kans., U.S.A.* **81 G7** 37 32N 95 49W
Fredonia, *N.Y., U.S.A.* **78 D5** 42 26N 79 20W
Fredrikstad, *Norway* **9 G14** 59 13N 10 57 E
Free State □, *S. Africa* **56 D4** 28 30S 27 0 E
Freehold, *U.S.A.* **79 F10** 40 16N 74 17W
Freel Peak, *U.S.A.* **84 G7** 38 52N 119 54W
Freeland, *U.S.A.* **79 E9** 41 1N 75 54W
Freels, C., *Canada* **71 C9** 49 15N 53 30W
Freeman, *Calif., U.S.A.* **85 K9** 35 35N 117 53W
Freeman, *S. Dak., U.S.A.* **80 D6** 43 21N 97 26W
Freeport, *Bahamas* **88 A4** 26 30N 78 47W
Freeport, *Canada* **71 D6** 44 15N 66 20W
Freeport, *Ill., U.S.A.* **80 D10** 42 17N 89 36W
Freeport, *N.Y., U.S.A.* **79 F11** 40 39N 73 35W
Freeport, *Tex., U.S.A.* **81 L7** 28 57N 95 21W
Freetown, *S. Leone* **50 G2** 8 30N 13 17W
Frégate, L., *Canada* **70 B5** 53 15N 74 45W
Fregenal de la Sierra, *Spain* **19 C2** 38 10N 6 39W
Freibourg = Fribourg, *Switz.* **16 E4** 46 49N 7 9 E
Freiburg, *Germany* **16 E4** 47 59N 7 51 E
Freire, *Chile* **96 D2** 38 54S 72 38W
Freirina, *Chile* **94 B1** 28 30S 71 10W
Freising, *Germany* **16 D6** 48 24N 11 45 E
Freistadt, *Austria* **16 D8** 48 30N 14 30 E
Fréjus, *France* **18 E7** 43 25N 6 44 E
Fremantle, *Australia* **61 F2** 32 7S 115 47 E
Fremont, *Calif., U.S.A.* **83 H2** 37 32N 121 57W
Fremont, *Mich., U.S.A.* **76 D3** 43 28N 85 57W
Fremont, *Nebr., U.S.A.* **80 E6** 41 26N 96 30W
Fremont, *Ohio, U.S.A.* **76 E4** 41 21N 83 7W
Fremont →, *U.S.A.* **83 G8** 38 24N 110 42W
Fremont L., *U.S.A.* **82 E9** 42 57N 109 48W
French Camp, *U.S.A.* **84 H5** 37 53N 121 16W
French Creek →, *U.S.A.* **78 E5** 41 24N 79 50W
French Guiana ■, *S. Amer.* **93 C8** 4 0N 53 0W
French Pass, *N.Z.* **59 J4** 40 55S 173 55 E
French Polynesia ■, *Pac. Oc.* **65 J13** 20 0S 145 0W
Frenchglen, *U.S.A.* **82 E4** 42 50N 118 55W
Frenchman Butte, *Canada* **73 C7** 53 35N 109 38W
Frenchman Cr. →, *Mont., U.S.A.* **82 B10** 48 31N 107 10W
Frenchman Cr. →, *Nebr., U.S.A.* **80 E4** 40 14N 100 50W
Fresco →, *Brazil* **93 E8** 7 15S 51 30W
Freshfield, C., *Antarctica* **5 C10** 68 25S 151 10 E
Fresnillo, *Mexico* **86 C4** 23 10N 103 0W
Fresno, *U.S.A.* **83 H4** 36 44N 119 47W
Fresno Reservoir, *U.S.A.* **82 B9** 48 36N 109 57W
Frew →, *Australia* **62 C2** 20 0S 135 38 E
Frewena, *Australia* **62 B2** 19 25S 135 25 E
Freycinet Pen., *Australia* **62 G4** 42 10S 148 25 E
Fria, C., *Namibia* **56 B1** 18 0S 12 0 E
Friant, *U.S.A.* **84 J7** 36 59N 119 43W
Frías, *Argentina* **94 B2** 28 40S 65 5W
Fribourg, *Switz.* **16 E4** 46 49N 7 9 E
Friday Harbor, *U.S.A.* **84 B3** 48 32N 123 1W
Friedrichshafen, *Germany* **16 E5** 47 39N 9 30 E
Friendly Is. = Tonga ■, *Pac. Oc.* **59 D11** 19 50S 174 30W
Friesland □, *Neths.* **15 A5** 53 5N 5 50 E
Frio →, *U.S.A.* **81 L5** 28 26N 98 11W
Frio, C., *Brazil* **90 F6** 22 50S 41 50W
Friona, *U.S.A.* **81 H3** 34 38N 102 43W
Fritch, *U.S.A.* **81 H4** 35 38N 101 36W
Frobisher B., *Canada* **69 B13** 62 30N 66 0W
Frobisher Bay = Iqaluit, *Canada* **69 B13** 63 44N 68 31W
Frobisher L., *Canada* **73 B7** 56 20N 108 15W
Frohavet, *Norway* **8 E13** 64 0N 9 30 E
Froid, *U.S.A.* **80 A2** 48 20N 104 30W
Fromberg, *U.S.A.* **82 D9** 45 24N 108 54W
Frome, *U.K.* **11 F5** 51 14N 2 19W
Frome, L., *Australia* **63 E2** 30 45S 139 45 E
Frome Downs, *Australia* **63 E2** 31 13S 139 45 E
Front Range, *U.S.A.* **82 G11** 40 25N 105 45W
Front Royal, *U.S.A.* **76 F6** 38 55N 78 12W
Frontera, *Canary Is.* **22 G2** 27 47N 17 59W
Frontera, *Mexico* **87 D6** 18 30N 92 40W
Frosinone, *Italy* **20 D5** 41 38N 13 19 E
Frostburg, *U.S.A.* **76 F6** 39 39N 78 56W
Frostisen, *Norway* **8 B17** 68 14N 17 10 E
Frøya, *Norway* **8 E13** 63 43N 8 40 E
Frunze = Bishkek, *Kyrgyzstan* **26 E8** 42 54N 74 46 E
Frutal, *Brazil* **93 G9** 20 0S 49 0W
Frýdek-Místek, *Czech.* **17 D10** 49 40N 18 20 E
Fu Xian, *Liaoning, China* **35 E11** 39 38N 121 58 E
Fu Xian, *Shaanxi, China* **34 F5** 36 0N 109 20 E
Fucheng, *China* **34 F9** 37 50N 116 10 E
Fuchou = Fuzhou, *China* **33 D6** 26 5N 119 16 E
Fuchū, *Japan* **31 G6** 34 34N 133 14 E
Fuencaliente, *Canary Is.* **22 F2** 28 28N 17 50W
Fuencaliente, Pta., *Canary Is.* **22 F2** 28 27N 17 51W
Fuengirola, *Spain* **19 D3** 36 32N 4 41W
Fuentes de Oñoro, *Spain* **19 B2** 40 33N 6 52W
Fuerte →, *Mexico* **86 B3** 25 50N 109 25W
Fuerte Olimpo, *Paraguay* **94 A4** 21 0S 57 51W
Fuerteventura, *Canary Is.* **22 F6** 28 30N 14 0W
Fufeng, *China* **34 G4** 34 22N 108 0 E
Fugou, *China* **34 G8** 34 3N 114 25 E
Fugu, *China* **34 E6** 39 2N 111 3 E
Fuhai, *China* **32 B3** 47 2N 87 25 E
Fuḥaymī, *Iraq* **44 C4** 34 16N 42 10 E
Fuji, *Japan* **31 G9** 35 9N 138 39 E
Fuji-San, *Japan* **31 G9** 35 22N 138 44 E
Fuji-yoshida, *Japan* **31 G9** 35 30N 138 46 E
Fujian □, *China* **33 D6** 26 0N 118 0 E
Fujinomiya, *Japan* **31 G9** 35 10N 138 40 E
Fujisawa, *Japan* **31 G9** 35 22N 139 29 E
Fukien = Fujian □, *China* **33 D6** 26 0N 118 0 E
Fukuchiyama, *Japan* **31 G7** 35 19N 135 9 E
Fukue-Shima, *Japan* **31 H4** 32 40N 128 45 E
Fukui, *Japan* **31 F8** 36 5N 136 10 E
Fukui □, *Japan* **31 G8** 36 0N 136 12 E
Fukuoka, *Japan* **31 H5** 33 39N 130 21 E
Fukuoka □, *Japan* **31 H5** 33 30N 131 0 E
Fukushima, *Japan* **30 F10** 37 44N 140 28 E
Fukushima □, *Japan* **30 F10** 37 30N 140 15 E
Fukuyama, *Japan* **31 G6** 34 35N 133 20 E
Fulda, *Germany* **16 C5** 50 32N 9 40 E
Fulda →, *Germany* **16 C5** 51 25N 9 39 E
Fullerton, *Calif., U.S.A.* **85 M9** 33 53N 117 56W
Fullerton, *Nebr., U.S.A.* **80 E5** 41 22N 97 58W
Fulongquan, *China* **35 B13** 44 20N 124 42 E
Fulton, *Mo., U.S.A.* **80 F9** 38 52N 91 57W
Fulton, *N.Y., U.S.A.* **79 C8** 43 19N 76 25W
Fulton, *Tenn., U.S.A.* **77 G1** 36 31N 88 53W
Funabashi, *Japan* **31 G10** 35 45N 140 0 E
Funchal, *Madeira* **22 D3** 32 38N 16 54W
Fundación, *Colombia* **92 A4** 10 31N 74 11W
Fundão, *Portugal* **19 B2** 40 8N 7 30W
Fundy, B. of, *Canada* **71 D6** 45 0N 66 0W
Funing, *Hebei, China* **35 E10** 39 53N 119 12 E
Funing, *Jiangsu, China* **35 H10** 33 45N 119 50 E
Funiu Shan, *China* **34 H7** 33 30N 112 20 E
Funtua, *Nigeria* **50 F6** 11 30N 7 18 E
Fuping, *Hebei, China* **34 E8** 38 48N 114 12 E
Fuping, *Shaanxi, China* **34 G5** 34 42N 109 10 E
Furano, *Japan* **30 C11** 43 21N 142 23 E
Furāt, Nahr al →, *Asia* **44 D5** 31 0N 47 25 E
Fūrg, *Iran* **45 D7** 28 18N 55 13 E
Furnás, *Spain* **22 B8** 39 3N 1 32 E
Furnas, Reprêsa de, *Brazil* **95 A6** 20 50S 45 30W
Furneaux Group, *Australia* **62 G4** 40 10S 147 50 E
Furness, *U.K.* **10 C4** 54 14N 3 8W
Furqlus, *Syria* **47 A6** 34 36N 37 8 E
Fürstenwalde, *Germany* **16 B8** 52 22N 14 3 E
Fürth, *Germany* **16 D6** 49 28N 10 59 E
Furukawa, *Japan* **30 E10** 38 34N 140 58 E
Fury and Hecla Str., *Canada* **69 B11** 69 56N 84 0W
Fusagasuga, *Colombia* **92 C4** 4 21N 74 22W
Fushan, *Shandong, China* **35 F11** 37 30N 121 15 E
Fushan, *Shanxi, China* **34 G6** 35 58N 111 51 E
Fushun, *China* **35 D12** 41 50N 123 56 E
Fusong, *China* **35 C14** 42 20N 127 15 E
Futuna, *Wall. & F. Is.* **59 B8** 14 25S 178 20 E
Fuxin, *China* **35 C11** 42 5N 121 48 E
Fuyang, *China* **34 H8** 33 0N 115 48 E
Fuyang He →, *China* **34 E9** 38 12N 117 0 E
Fuyu, *China* **35 B13** 45 12N 124 43 E
Fuzhou, *China* **33 D6** 26 5N 119 16 E
Fylde, *U.K.* **10 D5** 53 50N 2 58W
Fyn, *Denmark* **9 J14** 55 20N 10 30 E
Fyne, L., *U.K.* **12 F3** 55 59N 5 23W

G

Gabela, *Angola* **52 G2** 11 0S 14 24 E
Gabès, *Tunisia* **50 B7** 33 53N 10 2 E
Gabès, G. de, *Tunisia* **51 B7** 34 0N 10 30 E
Gabon ■, *Africa* **52 E2** 0 10S 10 0 E
Gaborone, *Botswana* **56 C4** 24 45S 25 57 E
Gabriels, *U.S.A.* **79 B10** 44 26N 74 12W
Gābrīk, *Iran* **45 E8** 25 44N 58 28 E
Gabrovo, *Bulgaria* **21 C11** 42 52N 25 19 E
Gāch Sār, *Iran* **45 B6** 36 7N 51 19 E
Gachsārān, *Iran* **45 D6** 30 15N 50 45 E
Gadag, *India* **40 M9** 15 30N 75 45 E
Gadap, *Pakistan* **42 G2** 25 5N 67 28 E
Gadarwara, *India* **43 H8** 22 50N 78 50 E
Gadhada, *India* **42 J4** 22 0N 71 35 E
Gadsden, *Ala., U.S.A.* **77 H2** 34 1N 86 1W
Gadsden, *Ariz., U.S.A.* **83 K6** 32 33N 114 47W
Gadwal, *India* **40 L10** 16 10N 77 50 E
Gaffney, *U.S.A.* **77 H5** 35 5N 81 39W
Gafsa, *Tunisia* **50 B6** 34 24N 8 43 E
Gagetown, *Canada* **71 C6** 45 46N 66 10W
Gagnoa, *Ivory C.* **50 G3** 6 56N 5 16W
Gagnon, *Canada* **71 B6** 51 50N 68 5W
Gagnon, L., *Canada* **73 A6** 62 3N 110 27W
Gahini, *Rwanda* **54 C3** 1 50S 30 30 E
Gahmar, *India* **43 G10** 25 27N 83 49 E
Gai Xian, *China* **35 D12** 40 22N 122 20 E
Gaïdhouronísi, *Greece* **23 E7** 34 53N 25 41 E
Gail, *U.S.A.* **81 J4** 32 46N 101 27W
Gaillimh = Galway, *Ireland* **13 C2** 53 17N 9 3W
Gaines, *U.S.A.* **78 E7** 41 46N 77 35W
Gainesville, *Fla., U.S.A.* **77 L4** 29 40N 82 20W
Gainesville, *Ga., U.S.A.* **77 H4** 34 18N 83 50W
Gainesville, *Mo., U.S.A.* **81 G8** 36 36N 92 26W
Gainesville, *Tex., U.S.A.* **81 J6** 33 38N 97 8W
Gainsborough, *U.K.* **10 D7** 53 24N 0 46W
Gairdner, L., *Australia* **63 E2** 31 30S 136 0 E
Gairloch, L., *U.K.* **12 D3** 57 43N 5 45W
Gakuch, *Pakistan* **43 A5** 36 7N 73 45 E
Galán, Cerro, *Argentina* **94 B2** 25 55S 66 52W
Galana →, *Kenya* **54 C5** 3 9S 40 8 E
Galangue, *Angola* **53 G3** 13 42S 16 9 E
Galápagos, *Pac. Oc.* **90 D1** 0 0 91 0W
Galashiels, *U.K.* **12 F6** 55 37N 2 49W
Galați, *Romania* **17 F15** 45 27N 28 2 E
Galatina, *Italy* **21 D8** 40 10N 18 10 E
Galax, *U.S.A.* **77 G5** 36 40N 80 56W
Galbraith, *Australia* **62 B3** 16 25S 141 30 E
Galcaio, *Somali Rep.* **46 F4** 6 30N 47 30 E
Galdhøpiggen, *Norway* **9 F12** 61 38N 8 18 E
Galeana, *Mexico* **86 C4** 24 50N 100 4W
Galela, *Indonesia* **37 D7** 1 50N 127 49 E
Galera Point, *Trin. & Tob.* **89 D7** 10 8N 61 0W
Galesburg, *U.S.A.* **80 E9** 40 57N 90 22W
Galeton, *U.S.A.* **78 E7** 41 44N 77 39W
Galich, *Russia* **24 C7** 58 22N 42 24 E
Galicia □, *Spain* **19 A2** 42 43N 7 45W
Galilee = Hagalil, *Israel* **47 C4** 32 53N 35 18 E
Galilee, L., *Australia* **62 C4** 22 20S 145 50 E
Galilee, Sea of = Yam Kinneret, *Israel* **47 C4** 32 45N 35 35 E
Galinoporni, *Cyprus* **23 D13** 35 31N 34 18 E
Galion, *U.S.A.* **78 F2** 40 44N 82 47W
Galiuro Mts., *U.S.A.* **83 K8** 32 30N 110 20W
Gallabat, *Sudan* **51 F12** 12 58N 36 11 E
Gallatin, *U.S.A.* **77 G2** 36 24N 86 27W
Galle, *Sri Lanka* **40 R12** 6 5N 80 10 E
Gállego →, *Spain* **19 B5** 41 39N 0 51W
Gallegos →, *Argentina* **96 G3** 51 35S 69 0W
Galley Hd., *Ireland* **13 E3** 51 32N 8 55W
Gallinas, Pta., *Colombia* **92 A4** 12 28N 71 40W
Gallipoli = Gelibolu, *Turkey* **21 D12** 40 28N 26 43 E
Gallípoli, *Italy* **21 D8** 40 3N 17 58 E
Gallipolis, *U.S.A.* **76 F4** 38 49N 82 12W
Gällivare, *Sweden* **8 C19** 67 9N 20 40 E
Galloway, *U.K.* **12 G4** 55 1N 4 29W
Galloway, Mull of, *U.K.* **12 G4** 54 39N 4 52W
Gallup, *U.S.A.* **83 J9** 35 32N 108 45W
Galong, *Australia* **63 E4** 34 37S 148 34 E
Galoya, *Sri Lanka* **40 Q12** 8 10N 80 55 E
Galt, *U.S.A.* **84 G5** 38 15N 121 18W
Galty Mts., *Ireland* **13 D3** 52 22N 8 10W
Galtymore, *Ireland* **13 D3** 52 21N 8 11W
Galva, *U.S.A.* **80 E9** 41 10N 90 3W
Galveston, *U.S.A.* **81 L7** 29 18N 94 48W
Galveston B., *U.S.A.* **81 L7** 29 36N 94 50W
Gálvez, *Argentina* **94 C3** 32 0S 61 14W
Galway, *Ireland* **13 C2** 53 17N 9 3W
Galway □, *Ireland* **13 C2** 53 22N 9 1W
Galway B., *Ireland* **13 C2** 53 13N 9 10W
Gam →, *Vietnam* **38 B5** 21 55N 105 12 E
Gamagori, *Japan* **31 G8** 34 50N 137 14 E
Gambaga, *Ghana* **50 F4** 10 30N 0 28W
Gambat, *Pakistan* **42 F3** 27 17N 68 26 E
Gambela, *Ethiopia* **51 G11** 8 14N 34 38 E
Gambia ■, *W. Afr.* **50 F1** 13 25N 16 0W
Gambia →, *W. Afr.* **50 F1** 13 28N 16 34W
Gambier, C., *Australia* **60 B5** 11 56S 130 57 E
Gambier Is., *Australia* **63 F2** 35 3S 136 30 E
Gamboli, *Pakistan* **42 E3** 29 53N 68 24 E
Gamboma, *Congo* **52 E3** 1 55S 15 52 E
Gamerco, *U.S.A.* **83 J9** 35 34N 108 46W
Gamlakarleby = Kokkola, *Finland* **8 E20** 63 50N 23 8 E
Gammon →, *Canada* **73 C9** 51 24N 95 44W
Gan Jiang →, *China* **33 D6** 29 15N 116 0 E
Ganado, *Ariz., U.S.A.* **83 J9** 35 43N 109 33W
Ganado, *Tex., U.S.A.* **81 L6** 29 2N 96 31W
Gananoque, *Canada* **70 D4** 44 20N 76 10W
Ganāveh, *Iran* **45 D6** 29 35N 50 35 E
Gäncä, *Azerbaijan* **25 F8** 40 45N 46 20 E
Gand = Gent, *Belgium* **15 C3** 51 2N 3 42 E
Ganda, *Angola* **53 G2** 13 3S 14 35 E
Gandak →, *India* **43 G11** 25 39N 85 13 E
Gandava, *Pakistan* **42 E2** 28 32N 67 32 E
Gander, *Canada* **71 C9** 48 58N 54 35W
Gander L., *Canada* **71 C9** 48 58N 54 35W
Ganderowe Falls, *Zimbabwe* **55 F2** 17 20S 29 10 E
Gandhi Sagar, *India* **42 G6** 24 40N 75 40 E
Gandi, *Nigeria* **50 F6** 12 55N 5 49 E
Gandía, *Spain* **19 C5** 38 58N 0 9W
Gando, Pta., *Canary Is.* **22 G4** 27 55N 15 22W
Ganedidalem = Gani, *Indonesia* **37 E7** 0 48S 128 14 E
Ganga →, *India* **43 H14** 23 20N 90 30 E
Ganga, Mouths of the, *India* **43 J13** 21 30N 90 0 E
Ganganagar, *India* **42 E5** 29 56N 73 56 E
Gangapur, *India* **42 F7** 26 32N 76 49 E
Gangara, *Niger* **50 F6** 14 35N 8 29 E
Gangaw, *Burma* **41 H19** 22 5N 94 5 E
Gangdisê Shan, *China* **41 D12** 31 20N 81 0 E
Ganges = Ganga →, *India* **43 H14** 23 20N 90 30 E
Gangoh, *India* **42 E7** 29 46N 77 18 E
Gangtok, *India* **41 F16** 27 20N 88 37 E
Gangu, *China* **34 G3** 34 40N 105 15 E
Gangyao, *China* **35 B14** 44 12N 126 37 E
Gani, *Indonesia* **37 E7** 0 48S 128 14 E
Ganj, *India* **43 F8** 27 45N 78 57 E
Gannett Peak, *U.S.A.* **82 E9** 43 11N 109 39W
Gannvalley, *U.S.A.* **80 C5** 44 2N 98 59W
Ganquan, *China* **34 F5** 36 20N 109 20 E
Gansu □, *China* **34 G3** 36 0N 104 0 E
Ganta, *Liberia* **50 G3** 7 15N 8 59W
Gantheaume, C., *Australia* **63 F2** 36 4S 137 32 E
Gantheaume B., *Australia* **61 E1** 27 40S 114 10 E
Gantsevichi = Hantsavichy, *Belarus* **17 B14** 52 49N 26 30 E
Ganyem, *Indonesia* **37 E10** 2 46S 140 12 E
Ganyu, *China* **35 G10** 34 50N 119 8 E
Ganzhou, *China* **33 D6** 25 51N 114 56 E
Gaomi, *China* **35 F10** 36 20N 119 42 E
Gaoping, *China* **34 G7** 35 45N 112 55 E
Gaotang, *China* **34 F9** 36 50N 116 15 E
Gaoua, *Burkina Faso* **50 F4** 10 20N 3 8W
Gaoual, *Guinea* **50 F2** 11 45N 13 25W
Gaoxiong = Kaohsiung, *Taiwan* **33 D7** 22 35N 120 16 E
Gaoyang, *China* **34 E8** 38 40N 115 45 E
Gaoyou Hu, *China* **35 H10** 32 45N 119 20 E
Gaoyuan, *China* **35 F9** 37 8N 117 58 E
Gap, *France* **18 D7** 44 33N 6 5 E
Gar, *China* **32 C2** 32 10N 79 58 E
Garabogazköl Aylagy, *Turkmenistan* **25 F9** 41 0N 53 30 E
Garachico, *Canary Is.* **22 F3** 28 22N 16 46W
Garachiné, *Panama* **88 E4** 8 0N 78 12W
Garafia, *Canary Is.* **22 F2** 28 48N 17 57W
Garajonay, *Canary Is.* **22 F2** 28 7N 17 14W
Garanhuns, *Brazil* **93 E11** 8 50S 36 30W
Garawe, *Liberia* **50 H3** 4 35N 8 0W
Garba Tula, *Kenya* **54 B4** 0 30N 38 32 E
Garber, *U.S.A.* **81 G6** 36 26N 97 35W
Garberville, *U.S.A.* **82 F2** 40 6N 123 48W
Gard, *Somali Rep.* **46 F4** 9 30N 49 6 E
Garda, L. di, *Italy* **20 B4** 45 40N 10 41 E
Garde L., *Canada* **73 A7** 62 50N 106 13W
Garden City, *Kans., U.S.A.* **81 G4** 37 58N 100 53W
Garden City, *Tex., U.S.A.* **81 K4** 31 52N 101 29W
Garden Grove, *U.S.A.* **85 M9** 33 47N 117 55W
Gardēz, *Afghan.* **42 C3** 33 37N 69 9 E
Gardiner, *U.S.A.* **82 D8** 45 2N 110 22W
Gardiners I., *U.S.A.* **79 E12** 41 6N 72 6W
Gardner, *U.S.A.* **79 D13** 42 34N 71 59W
Gardner Canal, *Canada* **72 C3** 53 27N 128 8W
Gardnerville, *U.S.A.* **84 G7** 38 56N 119 45W
Garey, *U.S.A.* **85 L6** 34 53N 120 19W
Garfield, *U.S.A.* **82 C5** 47 1N 117 9W
Gargano, Mte., *Italy* **20 D6** 41 43N 15 43 E
Garhshankar, *India* **42 D7** 31 13N 76 11 E
Garibaldi Prov. Park, *Canada* **72 D4** 49 50N 122 40W
Gariep, L., *S. Africa* **56 E2** 30 32S 17 59 E
Garigliano →, *Italy* **20 D5** 41 13N 13 45 E
Garissa, *Kenya* **54 C4** 0 25S 39 40 E
Garissa □, *Kenya* **54 C5** 0 20S 40 0 E
Garland, *Tex., U.S.A.* **81 J6** 32 55N 96 38W
Garland, *Utah, U.S.A.* **82 F7** 41 47N 112 10W
Garm, *Tajikistan* **26 F8** 39 0N 70 20 E

Heinze Is.

Hajipur, *India* **43 G11** 25 45N 85 13 E
Ḥājjī Muḥsin, *Iraq* **44 C5** 32 35N 45 29 E
Ḥājjīābād, *Eşfahan, Iran* **45 C7** 33 41N 54 50 E
Ḥājjīābād, *Hormozgān, Iran* **45 D7** 28 19N 55 55 E
Hajnówka, *Poland* **17 B12** 52 47N 23 35 E
Hakansson, Mts., *Zaïre* **55 D2** 8 40S 25 45 E
Hakken-Zan, *Japan* **31 G7** 34 10N 135 54 E
Hakodate, *Japan* **30 D10** 41 45N 140 44 E
Haku-San, *Japan* **31 F8** 36 9N 136 46 E
Hakui, *Japan* **31 F8** 36 53N 136 47 E
Hala, *Pakistan* **40 G6** 25 43N 68 20 E
Ḥalab, *Syria* **44 B3** 36 10N 37 15 E
Ḥalabjah, *Iraq* **44 C5** 35 10N 45 58 E
Halaib, *Sudan* **51 D12** 22 12N 36 30 E
Hālat 'Ammār, *Si. Arabia* **44 D3** 29 10N 36 4 E
Halbā, *Lebanon* **47 A5** 34 34N 36 6 E
Halberstadt, *Germany* **16 C6** 51 54N 11 3 E
Halcombe, *N.Z.* **59 J5** 40 8S 175 30 E
Halcon, Mt., *Phil.* **37 B6** 13 0N 121 30 E
Halden, *Norway* **9 G14** 59 9N 11 23 E
Haldia, *India* **41 H16** 22 5N 88 3 E
Haldwani, *India* **43 E8** 29 31N 79 30 E
Hale →, *Australia* **62 C2** 24 56S 135 53 E
Haleakala Crater, *U.S.A.* **74 H16** 20 43N 156 16W
Haleyville, *U.S.A.* **77 H2** 34 14N 87 37W
Halfway →, *Canada* **72 B4** 56 12N 121 32W
Haliburton, *Canada* **70 C4** 45 3N 78 30W
Halifax, *Australia* **62 B4** 18 32S 146 22 E
Halifax, *Canada* **71 D7** 44 38N 63 35W
Halifax, *U.K.* **10 D6** 53 43N 1 52W
Halifax B., *Australia* **62 B4** 18 50S 147 0 E
Halifax I., *Namibia* **56 D2** 26 38S 15 4 E
Halīl →, *Iran* **45 E8** 27 40N 58 30 E
Hall Beach, *Canada* **69 B11** 68 46N 81 12W
Hall Pt., *Australia* **60 C3** 15 40S 124 23 E
Halland, *Sweden* **9 H15** 57 8N 12 47 E
Halle, *Belgium* **15 D4** 50 44N 4 13 E
Halle, *Germany* **16 C6** 51 30N 11 56 E
Hällefors, *Sweden* **9 G16** 59 47N 14 31 E
Hallett, *Australia* **63 E2** 33 25S 138 55 E
Hallettsville, *U.S.A.* **81 L6** 29 27N 96 57W
Halliday, *U.S.A.* **80 B3** 47 21N 102 20W
Halliday L., *Canada* **73 A7** 61 21N 108 56W
Hallim, *S. Korea* **35 H14** 33 24N 126 15 E
Hallingdalselva →, *Norway* **9 F13** 60 40N 8 50 E
Hallock, *U.S.A.* **73 D9** 48 47N 96 57W
Halls Creek, *Australia* **60 C4** 18 16S 127 38 E
Hallsberg, *Sweden* **9 G16** 59 5N 15 7 E
Hallstead, *U.S.A.* **79 E9** 41 58N 75 45W
Halmahera, *Indonesia* **37 D7** 0 40N 128 0 E
Halmstad, *Sweden* **9 H15** 56 41N 12 52 E
Halq el Oued, *Tunisia* **51 A7** 36 53N 10 18 E
Hälsingborg = Helsingborg, *Sweden* **9 H15** 56 3N 12 42 E
Hälsingland, *Sweden* **9 F16** 61 40N 16 5 E
Halstad, *U.S.A.* **80 B6** 47 21N 96 50W
Halti, *Finland* **8 B19** 69 17N 21 18 E
Halul, *Qatar* **45 E7** 25 40N 52 40 E
Ḥalvān, *Iran* **45 C8** 33 57N 56 15 E
Ham Tan, *Vietnam* **39 G6** 10 40N 107 45 E
Ham Yen, *Vietnam* **38 A5** 22 4N 105 3 E
Hamab, *Namibia* **56 D2** 28 7S 19 16 E
Hamada, *Japan* **31 G6** 34 56N 132 4 E
Hamadān, *Iran* **45 C6** 34 52N 48 32 E
Hamadān □, *Iran* **45 C6** 35 0N 49 0 E
Ḥamāh, *Syria* **44 C3** 35 5N 36 40 E
Hamamatsu, *Japan* **31 G8** 34 45N 137 45 E
Hamar, *Norway* **9 F14** 60 48N 11 7 E
Hambantota, *Sri Lanka* **40 R12** 6 10N 81 10 E
Hamber Prov. Park, *Canada* **72 C5** 52 20N 118 0W
Hamburg, *Germany* **16 B5** 53 33N 9 59 E
Hamburg, *Ark., U.S.A.* **81 J9** 33 14N 91 48W
Hamburg, *Iowa, U.S.A.* **80 E7** 40 36N 95 39W
Hamburg, *N.Y., U.S.A.* **78 D6** 42 43N 78 50W
Hamburg, *Pa., U.S.A.* **79 F9** 40 33N 75 59W
Ḥamḍ, W. al →, *Si. Arabia* **44 E3** 24 55N 36 20 E
Hamden, *U.S.A.* **79 E12** 41 23N 72 54W
Häme, *Finland* **9 F20** 61 38N 25 10 E
Hämeenlinna, *Finland* **9 F21** 61 0N 24 28 E
Hamelin Pool, *Australia* **61 E1** 26 22S 114 20 E
Hameln, *Germany* **16 B5** 52 6N 9 21 E
Hamerkaz □, *Israel* **47 C3** 32 15N 34 55 E
Hamersley Ra., *Australia* **60 D2** 22 0S 117 45 E
Hamhung, *N. Korea* **35 E14** 39 54N 127 30 E
Hami, *China* **32 B4** 42 55N 93 25 E
Hamilton, *Australia* **63 F3** 37 45S 142 2 E
Hamilton, *Canada* **70 D4** 43 15N 79 50W
Hamilton, *N.Z.* **59 G5** 37 47S 175 19 E
Hamilton, *U.K.* **12 F4** 55 46N 4 2W
Hamilton, *Mo., U.S.A.* **80 F8** 39 45N 93 59W
Hamilton, *Mont., U.S.A.* **82 C6** 46 15N 114 10W
Hamilton, *N.Y., U.S.A.* **79 D9** 42 50N 75 33W
Hamilton, *Ohio, U.S.A.* **76 F3** 39 24N 84 34W
Hamilton, *Tex., U.S.A.* **81 K5** 31 42N 98 7W
Hamilton →, *Australia* **62 C2** 23 30S 139 47 E
Hamilton City, *U.S.A.* **84 F4** 39 45N 122 1W
Hamilton Hotel, *Australia* **62 C3** 22 45S 140 40 E
Hamilton Inlet, *Canada* **71 B8** 54 0N 57 30W
Hamina, *Finland* **9 F22** 60 34N 27 12 E
Hamiota, *Canada* **73 C8** 50 11N 100 38W
Hamlet, *U.S.A.* **77 H6** 34 53N 79 42W
Hamley Bridge, *Australia* **63 E2** 34 17S 138 35 E
Hamlin = Hameln, *Germany* **16 B5** 52 6N 9 21 E
Hamlin, *N.Y., U.S.A.* **78 C7** 43 17N 77 55W
Hamlin, *Tex., U.S.A.* **81 J4** 32 53N 100 8W
Hamm, *Germany* **16 C4** 51 40N 7 50 E
Hammerfest, *Norway* **8 A20** 70 39N 23 41 E
Hammond, *Ind., U.S.A.* **76 E2** 41 38N 87 30W
Hammond, *La., U.S.A.* **81 K9** 30 30N 90 28W
Hammonton, *U.S.A.* **76 F8** 39 39N 74 48W
Hampden, *N.Z.* **59 L3** 45 18S 170 50 E
Hampshire □, *U.K.* **11 F6** 51 7N 1 23W
Hampshire Downs, *U.K.* **11 F6** 51 15N 1 10W
Hampton, *Ark., U.S.A.* **81 J8** 33 32N 92 28W
Hampton, *Iowa, U.S.A.* **80 D8** 42 45N 93 13W
Hampton, *N.H., U.S.A.* **79 D14** 42 57N 70 50W
Hampton, *S.C., U.S.A.* **77 J5** 32 52N 81 7W
Hampton, *Va., U.S.A.* **76 G7** 37 2N 76 21W
Hampton Tableland, *Australia* **61 F4** 32 0S 127 0 E
Hamrat esh Sheykh, *Sudan* **51 F10** 14 38N 27 55 E
Hamyang, *S. Korea* **35 G14** 35 32N 127 42 E
Han Pijesak, *Bos.-H.* **21 B8** 44 5N 18 57 E
Hana, *U.S.A.* **74 H17** 20 45N 155 59W
Hanak, *Si. Arabia* **44 E3** 25 32N 37 0 E
Hanamaki, *Japan* **30 E10** 39 23N 141 7 E
Hanang, *Tanzania* **54 C4** 4 30S 35 25 E
Hanau, *Germany* **16 C5** 50 7N 8 56 E
Hanbogd, *Mongolia* **34 C4** 43 11N 107 10 E
Hancheng, *China* **34 G6** 35 31N 110 25 E
Hancock, *Mich., U.S.A.* **80 B10** 47 8N 88 35W
Hancock, *Minn., U.S.A.* **80 C7** 45 30N 95 48W
Hancock, *N.Y., U.S.A.* **79 E9** 41 57N 75 17W
Handa, *Japan* **31 G8** 34 53N 136 55 E
Handa, *Somali Rep.* **46 E5** 10 37N 51 2 E
Handan, *China* **34 F8** 36 35N 114 28 E
Handeni, *Tanzania* **54 D4** 5 25S 38 2 E
Handeni □, *Tanzania* **54 D4** 5 30S 38 0 E
Handwara, *India* **43 B6** 34 21N 74 20 E
Hanegev, *Israel* **47 E3** 30 50N 35 0 E
Haney, *Canada* **72 D4** 49 12N 122 40W
Hanford, *U.S.A.* **83 H4** 36 20N 119 39W
Hang Chat, *Thailand* **38 C2** 18 20N 99 21 E
Hang Dong, *Thailand* **38 C2** 18 41N 98 55 E
Hangang →, *S. Korea* **35 F14** 37 50N 126 30 E
Hangayn Nuruu, *Mongolia* **32 B4** 47 30N 99 0 E
Hangchou = Hangzhou, *China* **33 C7** 30 18N 120 11 E
Hanggin Houqi, *China* **34 D4** 40 58N 107 4 E
Hanggin Qi, *China* **34 E5** 39 52N 108 50 E
Hangu, *China* **35 E9** 39 18N 117 53 E
Hangzhou, *China* **33 C7** 30 18N 120 11 E
Hangzhou Wan, *China* **33 C7** 30 15N 120 45 E
Hanhongor, *Mongolia* **34 C3** 43 55N 104 28 E
Ḥanīdh, *Si. Arabia* **45 E6** 26 35N 48 38 E
Ḥanīsh, *Yemen* **46 E3** 13 45N 42 46 E
Hankinson, *U.S.A.* **80 B6** 46 4N 96 54W
Hanko, *Finland* **9 G20** 59 50N 22 57 E
Hanksville, *U.S.A.* **83 G8** 38 22N 110 43W
Hanle, *India* **43 C8** 32 42N 79 4 E
Hanmer Springs, *N.Z.* **59 K4** 42 32S 172 50 E
Hann →, *Australia* **60 C4** 17 26S 126 17 E
Hann, Mt., *Australia* **60 C4** 15 45S 126 0 E
Hanna, *Canada* **72 C6** 51 40N 111 54W
Hannaford, *U.S.A.* **80 B5** 47 19N 98 11W
Hannah, *U.S.A.* **80 A5** 48 58N 98 42W
Hannah B., *Canada* **70 B4** 51 40N 80 0W
Hannibal, *U.S.A.* **80 F9** 39 42N 91 22W
Hannover, *Germany* **16 B5** 52 22N 9 46 E
Hanoi, *Vietnam* **32 D5** 21 5N 105 55 E
Hanover = Hannover, *Germany* **16 B5** 52 22N 9 46 E
Hanover, *Canada* **78 B3** 44 9N 81 2W
Hanover, *S. Africa* **56 E3** 31 4S 24 29 E
Hanover, *N.H., U.S.A.* **79 C12** 43 42N 72 17W
Hanover, *Ohio, U.S.A.* **78 F2** 40 4N 82 16W
Hanover, *Pa., U.S.A.* **76 F7** 39 48N 76 59W
Hanover, I., *Chile* **96 G2** 51 0S 74 50W
Hansi, *India* **42 E6** 29 10N 75 57 E
Hanson, L., *Australia* **63 E2** 31 0S 136 15 E
Hantsavichy, *Belarus* **17 B14** 52 49N 26 30 E
Hanzhong, *China* **34 H4** 33 10N 107 1 E
Hanzhuang, *China* **35 G9** 34 33N 117 23 E
Haora, *India* **43 H13** 22 37N 88 20 E
Haparanda, *Sweden* **8 D21** 65 52N 24 8 E
Happy, *U.S.A.* **81 H4** 34 45N 101 52W
Happy Camp, *U.S.A.* **82 F2** 41 48N 123 23W
Happy Valley-Goose Bay, *Canada* **71 B7** 53 15N 60 20W
Hapsu, *N. Korea* **35 D15** 41 13N 128 51 E
Hapur, *India* **42 E7** 28 45N 77 45 E
Ḥaql, *Si. Arabia* **47 F3** 29 10N 34 58 E
Har, *Indonesia* **37 F8** 5 16S 133 14 E
Har-Ayrag, *Mongolia* **34 B5** 45 47N 109 16 E
Har Hu, *China* **32 C4** 38 20N 97 38 E
Har Us Nuur, *Mongolia* **32 B4** 48 0N 92 0 E
Har Yehuda, *Israel* **47 D3** 31 35N 34 57 E
Ḥaraḍ, *Si. Arabia* **46 C4** 24 22N 49 0 E
Haranomachi, *Japan* **30 F10** 37 38N 140 58 E
Harardera, *Somali Rep.* **46 G4** 4 33N 47 38 E
Harare, *Zimbabwe* **55 F3** 17 43S 31 2 E
Harazé, *Chad* **51 F8** 14 20N 19 12 E
Harbin, *China* **35 B14** 45 48N 126 40 E
Harbor Beach, *U.S.A.* **76 D4** 43 51N 82 39W
Harbor Springs, *U.S.A.* **76 C3** 45 26N 85 0W
Harbour Breton, *Canada* **71 C8** 47 29N 55 50W
Harbour Grace, *Canada* **71 C9** 47 40N 53 22W
Harda, *India* **42 H7** 22 27N 77 5 E
Hardangerfjorden, *Norway* **9 F12** 60 5N 6 0 E
Hardangervidda, *Norway* **9 F12** 60 7N 7 20 E
Hardap Dam, *Namibia* **56 C2** 24 32S 17 50 E
Hardenberg, *Neths.* **15 B6** 52 34N 6 37 E
Harderwijk, *Neths.* **15 B5** 52 21N 5 38 E
Hardey →, *Australia* **60 D2** 22 45S 116 8 E
Hardin, *U.S.A.* **82 D10** 45 44N 107 37W
Harding, *S. Africa* **57 E4** 30 35S 29 55 E
Harding Ra., *Australia* **60 C3** 16 17S 124 55 E
Hardisty, *Canada* **72 C6** 52 40N 111 18W
Hardman, *U.S.A.* **82 D4** 45 10N 119 41W
Hardoi, *India* **43 F9** 27 26N 80 6 E
Hardwar = Haridwar, *India* **42 E8** 29 58N 78 9 E
Hardwick, *U.S.A.* **79 B12** 44 30N 72 22W
Hardy, *U.S.A.* **81 G9** 36 19N 91 29W
Hardy, Pen., *Chile* **96 H3** 55 30S 68 20W
Hare B., *Canada* **71 B8** 51 15N 55 45W
Hareid, *Norway* **9 E12** 62 22N 6 1 E
Harer, *Ethiopia* **46 F3** 9 20N 42 8 E
Hargeisa, *Somali Rep.* **46 F3** 9 30N 44 2 E
Hari →, *Indonesia* **36 E2** 1 16S 104 5 E
Haria, *Canary Is.* **22 E6** 29 8N 13 32W
Haridwar, *India* **42 E8** 29 58N 78 9 E
Haringhata →, *Bangla.* **41 J16** 22 0N 89 58 E
Harīrūd →, *Asia* **40 A2** 37 24N 60 38 E
Härjedalen, *Sweden* **9 E15** 62 22N 13 5 E
Harlan, *Iowa, U.S.A.* **80 E7** 41 39N 95 19W
Harlan, *Ky., U.S.A.* **77 G4** 36 51N 83 19W
Harlech, *U.K.* **10 E3** 52 52N 4 6W
Harlem, *U.S.A.* **82 B9** 48 32N 108 47W
Harlingen, *Neths.* **15 A5** 53 11N 5 25 E
Harlingen, *U.S.A.* **81 M6** 26 12N 97 42W
Harlowton, *U.S.A.* **82 C9** 46 26N 109 50W
Harney Basin, *U.S.A.* **82 E4** 43 30N 119 0W
Harney L., *U.S.A.* **82 E4** 43 14N 119 8W
Harney Peak, *U.S.A.* **80 D3** 43 52N 103 32W
Härnösand, *Sweden* **9 E17** 62 38N 17 55 E
Harp L., *Canada* **71 A7** 55 5N 61 50W
Harrand, *Pakistan* **42 E4** 29 28N 70 3 E
Harriman, *U.S.A.* **77 H3** 35 56N 84 33W
Harrington Harbour, *Canada* **71 B8** 50 31N 59 30W
Harris, *U.K.* **12 D2** 57 50N 6 55W
Harris, Sd. of, *U.K.* **12 D1** 57 44N 7 6W
Harris L., *Australia* **63 E2** 31 10S 135 10 E
Harrisburg, *Ill., U.S.A.* **81 G10** 37 44N 88 32W
Harrisburg, *Nebr., U.S.A.* **80 E3** 41 33N 103 44W
Harrisburg, *Oreg., U.S.A.* **82 D2** 44 16N 123 10W
Harrisburg, *Pa., U.S.A.* **78 F8** 40 16N 76 53W
Harrismith, *S. Africa* **57 D4** 28 15S 29 8 E
Harrison, *Ark., U.S.A.* **81 G8** 36 14N 93 7W
Harrison, *Idaho, U.S.A.* **82 C5** 47 27N 116 47W
Harrison, *Nebr., U.S.A.* **80 D3** 42 41N 103 53W
Harrison, C., *Canada* **71 B8** 54 55N 57 55W
Harrison Bay, *U.S.A.* **68 A4** 70 40N 151 0W
Harrison L., *Canada* **72 D4** 49 33N 121 50W
Harrisonburg, *U.S.A.* **76 F6** 38 27N 78 52W
Harrisonville, *U.S.A.* **80 F7** 38 39N 94 21W
Harriston, *Canada* **70 D3** 43 57N 80 53W
Harrisville, *U.S.A.* **78 B1** 44 39N 83 17W
Harrogate, *U.K.* **10 D6** 54 0N 1 33W
Harrow, *U.K.* **11 F7** 51 35N 0 21W
Harsīn, *Iran* **44 C5** 34 18N 47 33 E
Harstad, *Norway* **8 B17** 68 48N 16 30 E
Hart, *U.S.A.* **76 D2** 43 42N 86 22W
Hart, L., *Australia* **63 E2** 31 10S 136 25 E
Hartbees →, *S. Africa* **56 D3** 28 45S 20 32 E
Hartford, *Conn., U.S.A.* **79 E12** 41 46N 72 41W
Hartford, *Ky., U.S.A.* **76 G2** 37 27N 86 55W
Hartford, *S. Dak., U.S.A.* **80 D6** 43 38N 96 57W
Hartford, *Wis., U.S.A.* **80 D10** 43 19N 88 22W
Hartford City, *U.S.A.* **76 E3** 40 27N 85 22W
Hartland, *Canada* **71 C6** 46 20N 67 32W
Hartland Pt., *U.K.* **11 F3** 51 1N 4 32W
Hartlepool, *U.K.* **10 C6** 54 42N 1 13W
Hartlepool □, *U.K.* **10 C6** 54 42N 1 17W
Hartley Bay, *Canada* **72 C3** 53 25N 129 15W
Hartmannberge, *Namibia* **56 B1** 17 0S 13 0 E
Hartney, *Canada* **73 D8** 49 30N 100 35W
Harts →, *S. Africa* **56 D3** 28 24S 24 17 E
Hartselle, *U.S.A.* **77 H2** 34 27N 86 56W
Hartshorne, *U.S.A.* **81 H7** 34 51N 95 34W
Hartsville, *U.S.A.* **77 H5** 34 23N 80 4W
Hartwell, *U.S.A.* **77 H4** 34 21N 82 56W
Harunabad, *Pakistan* **42 E5** 29 35N 73 8 E
Harvand, *Iran* **45 D7** 28 25N 55 43 E
Harvey, *Australia* **61 F2** 33 5S 115 54 E
Harvey, *Ill., U.S.A.* **76 E2** 41 36N 87 50W
Harvey, *N. Dak., U.S.A.* **80 B5** 47 47N 99 56W
Harwich, *U.K.* **11 F9** 51 56N 1 17 E
Haryana □, *India* **42 E7** 29 0N 76 10 E
Haryn →, *Belarus* **17 B14** 52 7N 27 17 E
Harz, *Germany* **16 C6** 51 38N 10 44 E
Hasan Kīādeh, *Iran* **45 B6** 37 24N 49 58 E
Ḥasanābād, *Iran* **45 C7** 32 8N 52 44 E
Hasanpur, *India* **42 E8** 28 43N 78 17 E
Hashimoto, *Japan* **31 G7** 34 19N 135 37 E
Hashtjerd, *Iran* **45 C6** 35 52N 50 40 E
Haskell, *Okla., U.S.A.* **81 H7** 35 50N 95 40W
Haskell, *Tex., U.S.A.* **81 J5** 33 10N 99 44W
Hasselt, *Belgium* **15 D5** 50 56N 5 21 E
Hassi Inifel, *Algeria* **50 C5** 29 50N 3 41 E
Hassi Messaoud, *Algeria* **50 B6** 31 51N 6 1 E
Hässleholm, *Sweden* **9 H15** 56 10N 13 46 E
Hastings, *N.Z.* **59 H6** 39 39S 176 52 E
Hastings, *U.K.* **11 G8** 50 51N 0 35 E
Hastings, *Mich., U.S.A.* **76 D3** 42 39N 85 17W
Hastings, *Minn., U.S.A.* **80 C8** 44 44N 92 51W
Hastings, *Nebr., U.S.A.* **80 E5** 40 35N 98 23W
Hastings Ra., *Australia* **63 E5** 31 15S 152 14 E
Hat Yai, *Thailand* **39 J3** 7 1N 100 27 E
Hatanbulag, *Mongolia* **34 C5** 43 8N 109 5 E
Hatay = Antalya, *Turkey* **25 G5** 36 52N 30 45 E
Hatch, *U.S.A.* **83 K10** 32 40N 107 9W
Hatches Creek, *Australia* **62 C2** 20 56S 135 12 E
Hatchet L., *Canada* **73 B8** 58 36N 103 40W
Hateruma-Shima, *Japan* **31 M1** 24 3N 123 47 E
Hatfield P.O., *Australia* **63 E3** 33 54S 143 49 E
Hatgal, *Mongolia* **32 A5** 50 26N 100 9 E
Hathras, *India* **42 F8** 27 36N 78 6 E
Hatia, *Bangla.* **41 H17** 22 30N 91 5 E
Hato Mayor, *Dom. Rep.* **89 C6** 18 46N 69 15W
Hattah, *Australia* **63 E3** 34 48S 142 17 E
Hatteras, C., *U.S.A.* **77 H8** 35 14N 75 32W
Hattiesburg, *U.S.A.* **81 K10** 31 20N 89 17W
Hatvan, *Hungary* **17 E10** 47 40N 19 45 E
Hau Bon = Cheo Reo, *Vietnam* **38 F7** 13 25N 108 28 E
Hau Duc, *Vietnam* **38 E7** 15 20N 108 13 E
Haugesund, *Norway* **9 G11** 59 23N 5 13 E
Haukipudas, *Finland* **8 D21** 65 12N 25 20 E
Haultain →, *Canada* **73 B7** 55 51N 106 46W
Hauraki G., *N.Z.* **59 G5** 36 35S 175 5 E
Haut Atlas, *Morocco* **50 B3** 32 30N 5 0W
Haut Zaïre □, *Zaïre* **54 B2** 2 20N 26 0 E
Hauterive, *Canada* **71 C6** 49 10N 68 16W
Hautes Fagnes = Hohe Venn, *Belgium* **15 D6** 50 30N 6 5 E
Hauts Plateaux, *Algeria* **50 A5** 35 0N 1 0 E
Havana = La Habana, *Cuba* **88 B3** 23 8N 82 22W
Havana, *U.S.A.* **80 E9** 40 18N 90 4W
Havant, *U.K.* **11 G7** 50 51N 0 58W
Havasu, L., *U.S.A.* **85 L12** 34 18N 114 28W
Havel →, *Germany* **16 B7** 52 50N 12 3 E
Havelange, *Belgium* **15 D5** 50 23N 5 15 E
Havelian, *Pakistan* **42 B5** 34 2N 73 10 E
Havelock, *N.B., Canada* **71 C6** 46 2N 65 24W
Havelock, *Ont., Canada* **70 D4** 44 26N 77 53W
Havelock, *N.Z.* **59 J4** 41 17S 173 48 E
Haverfordwest, *U.K.* **11 F3** 51 48N 4 58W
Haverhill, *U.S.A.* **79 D13** 42 47N 71 5W
Havering, *U.K.* **11 F8** 51 34N 0 13 E
Haverstraw, *U.S.A.* **79 E11** 41 12N 73 58W
Havířov, *Czech Rep.* **17 D10** 49 46N 18 20 E
Havlíčkův Brod, *Czech.* **16 D8** 49 36N 15 33 E
Havre, *U.S.A.* **82 B9** 48 33N 109 41W
Havre-Aubert, *Canada* **71 C7** 47 12N 61 56W
Havre-St.-Pierre, *Canada* **71 B7** 50 18N 63 33W
Haw →, *U.S.A.* **77 H6** 35 36N 79 3W
Hawaii □, *U.S.A.* **74 H16** 19 30N 156 30W
Hawaii I., *Pac. Oc.* **74 J17** 20 0N 155 0W
Hawaiian Is., *Pac. Oc.* **74 H17** 20 30N 156 0W
Hawaiian Ridge, *Pac. Oc.* **65 E11** 24 0N 165 0W
Hawarden, *Canada* **73 C7** 51 25N 106 36W
Hawarden, *U.S.A.* **80 D6** 43 0N 96 29W
Hawea, L., *N.Z.* **59 L2** 44 28S 169 19 E
Hawera, *N.Z.* **59 H5** 39 35S 174 19 E
Hawick, *U.K.* **12 F6** 55 26N 2 47W
Hawk Junction, *Canada* **70 C3** 48 5N 84 38W
Hawke B., *N.Z.* **59 H6** 39 25S 177 20 E
Hawker, *Australia* **63 E2** 31 59S 138 22 E
Hawkesbury, *Canada* **70 C5** 45 37N 74 37W
Hawkesbury I., *Canada* **72 C3** 53 37N 129 3W
Hawkesbury Pt., *Australia* **62 A1** 11 55S 134 5 E
Hawkinsville, *U.S.A.* **77 J4** 32 17N 83 28W
Hawkwood, *Australia* **63 D5** 25 45S 150 50 E
Hawley, *U.S.A.* **80 B6** 46 53N 96 19W
Hawrān, *Syria* **47 C5** 32 45N 36 15 E
Hawsh Mūssá, *Lebanon* **47 B4** 33 45N 35 55 E
Hawthorne, *U.S.A.* **82 G4** 38 32N 118 38W
Haxtun, *U.S.A.* **80 E3** 40 39N 102 38W
Hay, *Australia* **63 E3** 34 30S 144 51 E
Hay →, *Australia* **62 C2** 24 50S 138 0 E
Hay →, *Canada* **72 A5** 60 50N 116 26W
Hay, C., *Australia* **60 B4** 14 5S 129 29 E
Hay L., *Canada* **72 B5** 58 50N 118 50W
Hay Lakes, *Canada* **72 C6** 53 12N 113 2W
Hay-on-Wye, *U.K.* **11 E4** 52 5N 3 8W
Hay River, *Canada* **72 A5** 60 51N 115 44W
Hay Springs, *U.S.A.* **80 D3** 42 41N 102 41W
Haya, *Indonesia* **37 E7** 3 19S 129 37 E
Hayachine-San, *Japan* **30 E10** 39 34N 141 29 E
Hayden, *Ariz., U.S.A.* **83 K8** 33 0N 110 47W
Hayden, *Colo., U.S.A.* **82 F10** 40 30N 107 16W
Haydon, *Australia* **62 B3** 18 0S 141 30 E
Hayes, *U.S.A.* **80 C4** 44 23N 101 1W
Hayes →, *Canada* **73 B10** 57 3N 92 12W
Haynesville, *U.S.A.* **81 J8** 32 58N 93 8W
Hayrabolu, *Turkey* **21 D12** 41 12N 27 5 E
Hays, *Canada* **72 C6** 50 6N 111 48W
Hays, *U.S.A.* **80 F5** 38 53N 99 20W
Haysyn, *Ukraine* **17 D15** 48 57N 29 25 E
Hayvoron, *Ukraine* **17 D15** 48 22N 29 52 E
Hayward, *Calif., U.S.A.* **84 H4** 37 40N 122 5W
Hayward, *Wis., U.S.A.* **80 B9** 46 1N 91 29W
Haywards Heath, *U.K.* **11 F7** 51 0N 0 5W
Hazafon □, *Israel* **47 C4** 32 40N 35 20 E
Hazārām, Kūh-e, *Iran* **45 D8** 29 30N 57 18 E
Hazard, *U.S.A.* **76 G4** 37 15N 83 12W
Hazaribag, *India* **43 H11** 23 58N 85 26 E
Hazaribag Road, *India* **43 G11** 24 12N 85 57 E
Hazelton, *Canada* **72 B3** 55 20N 127 42W
Hazelton, *U.S.A.* **80 B4** 46 29N 100 17W
Hazen, *N. Dak., U.S.A.* **80 B4** 47 18N 101 38W
Hazen, *Nev., U.S.A.* **82 G4** 39 34N 119 3W
Hazlehurst, *Ga., U.S.A.* **77 K4** 31 52N 82 36W
Hazlehurst, *Miss., U.S.A.* **81 K9** 31 52N 90 24W
Hazleton, *U.S.A.* **79 F9** 40 57N 75 59W
Hazlett, L., *Australia* **60 D4** 21 30S 128 48 E
Ḥazor, *Israel* **47 B4** 33 2N 35 32 E
Head of Bight, *Australia* **61 F5** 31 30S 131 25 E
Headlands, *Zimbabwe* **55 F3** 18 15S 32 2 E
Healdsburg, *U.S.A.* **84 G4** 38 37N 122 52W
Healdton, *U.S.A.* **81 H6** 34 14N 97 29W
Healesville, *Australia* **63 F4** 37 35S 145 30 E
Heanor, *U.K.* **10 D6** 53 1N 1 21W
Heard I., *Ind. Oc.* **3 G13** 53 0S 74 0 E
Hearne, *U.S.A.* **81 K6** 30 53N 96 36W
Hearne B., *Canada* **73 A9** 60 10N 99 10W
Hearne L., *Canada* **72 A6** 62 20N 113 10W
Hearst, *Canada* **70 C3** 49 40N 83 41W
Heart →, *U.S.A.* **80 B4** 46 46N 100 50W
Heart's Content, *Canada* **71 C9** 47 54N 53 27W
Heath Pt., *Canada* **71 C7** 49 8N 61 40W
Heath Steele, *Canada* **71 C6** 47 17N 66 5W
Heavener, *U.S.A.* **81 H7** 34 53N 94 36W
Hebbronville, *U.S.A.* **81 M5** 27 18N 98 41W
Hebei □, *China* **34 E9** 39 0N 116 0 E
Hebel, *Australia* **63 D4** 28 58S 147 47 E
Heber, *U.S.A.* **85 N11** 32 44N 115 32W
Heber Springs, *U.S.A.* **81 H9** 35 30N 92 2W
Hebert, *Canada* **73 C7** 50 30N 107 10W
Hebgen L., *U.S.A.* **82 D8** 44 52N 111 20W
Hebi, *China* **34 G8** 35 57N 114 7 E
Hebrides, *U.K.* **12 D1** 57 30N 7 0W
Hebron = Al Khalīl, *West Bank* **47 D4** 31 32N 35 6 E
Hebron, *Canada* **69 C13** 58 5N 62 30W
Hebron, *N. Dak., U.S.A.* **80 B3** 46 54N 102 3W
Hebron, *Nebr., U.S.A.* **80 E6** 40 10N 97 35W
Hecate Str., *Canada* **72 C2** 53 10N 130 30W
Hechi, *China* **32 D5** 24 40N 108 2 E
Hechuan, *China* **32 C5** 30 2N 106 12 E
Hecla, *U.S.A.* **80 C5** 45 53N 98 9W
Hecla I., *Canada* **73 C9** 51 10N 96 43W
Hede, *Sweden* **9 E15** 62 23N 13 30 E
Hedemora, *Sweden* **9 F16** 60 18N 15 58 E
Hedley, *U.S.A.* **81 H4** 34 52N 100 39W
Heemstede, *Neths.* **15 B4** 52 22N 4 37 E
Heerde, *Neths.* **15 B6** 52 24N 6 2 E
Heerenveen, *Neths.* **15 B5** 52 57N 5 55 E
Heerlen, *Neths.* **18 A6** 50 55N 5 58 E
Ḥefa, *Israel* **47 C3** 32 46N 35 0 E
Ḥefa □, *Israel* **47 C4** 32 40N 35 0 E
Hefei, *China* **33 C6** 31 52N 117 18 E
Hegang, *China* **33 B8** 47 20N 130 19 E
Heichengzhen, *China* **34 F4** 36 24N 106 3 E
Heidelberg, *Germany* **16 D5** 49 24N 8 42 E
Heidelberg, *S. Africa* **56 E3** 34 6S 20 59 E
Heilbron, *S. Africa* **57 D4** 27 16S 27 59 E
Heilbronn, *Germany* **16 D5** 49 9N 9 13 E
Heilongjiang □, *China* **35 B14** 48 0N 126 0 E
Heilunkiang = Heilongjiang □, *China* **35 B14** 48 0N 126 0 E
Heimaey, *Iceland* **8 E3** 63 26N 20 17W
Heinola, *Finland* **9 F22** 61 13N 26 2 E
Heinze Is., *Burma* **41 M20** 14 25N 97 45 E

Horn Head, Ireland 13 A3 55 14N 8 0W
Horn I., Australia 62 A3 10 37S 142 17 E
Horn I., U.S.A. 77 K1 30 14N 88 39W
Horn Mts., Canada 72 A5 62 15N 119 15W
Hornavan, Sweden 8 C17 66 15N 17 30 E
Hornbeck, U.S.A. 81 K8 31 20N 93 24W
Hornbrook, U.S.A. 82 F2 41 55N 122 33W
Horncastle, U.K. 10 D7 53 13N 0 7W
Hornell, U.S.A. 78 D7 42 20N 77 40W
Hornell L., Canada 72 A5 62 20N 119 25W
Hornepayne, Canada 70 C3 49 14N 84 48W
Hornitos, U.S.A. 84 H6 37 30N 120 14W
Hornos, C. de, Chile 96 H3 55 50S 67 30W
Hornsby, Australia 63 E5 33 42S 151 2 E
Hornsea, U.K. 10 D7 53 55N 0 11W
Horobetsu, Japan 30 C10 42 24N 141 6 E
Horodenka, Ukraine 17 D13 48 41N 25 29 E
Horodok, Khmelnytskyy, Ukraine 17 D14 49 10N 26 34 E
Horodok, Lviv, Ukraine 17 D12 49 46N 23 32 E
Horokhiv, Ukraine 17 C13 50 30N 24 45 E
Horqin Youyi Qianqi, China 35 A12 46 5N 122 3 E
Horqueta, Paraguay 94 A4 23 15S 56 55W
Horse Creek, U.S.A. 80 E3 41 57N 105 10W
Horse Is., Canada 71 B8 50 15N 55 50W
Horsefly L., Canada 72 C4 52 25N 121 0W
Horsens, Denmark 9 J13 55 52N 9 51 E
Horsham, Australia 63 F3 36 44S 142 13 E
Horsham, U.K. 11 F7 51 4N 0 20W
Horten, Norway 9 G14 59 25N 10 32 E
Horton, U.S.A. 80 F7 39 40N 95 32W
Horton →, Canada 68 B7 69 56N 126 52W
Horwood, L., Canada 70 C3 48 5N 82 20W
Hose, Gunung-Gunung, Malaysia 36 D4 2 5N 114 6 E
Ḩoseynābād, Khuzestān, Iran 45 C6 32 45N 48 20 E
Ḩoseynābād, Kordestān, Iran 44 C5 35 33N 47 8 E
Hoshangabad, India 42 H7 22 45N 77 45 E
Hoshiarpur, India 42 D6 31 30N 75 58 E
Hosmer, U.S.A. 80 C5 45 34N 99 28W
Hospet, India 40 M10 15 15N 76 20 E
Hospitalet de Llobregat, Spain 19 B7 41 21N 2 6 E
Hoste, I., Chile 96 H3 55 0S 69 0W
Hot, Thailand 38 C2 18 8N 98 29 E
Hot Creek Range, U.S.A. 82 G5 38 40N 116 20W
Hot Springs, Ark., U.S.A. 81 H8 34 31N 93 3W
Hot Springs, S. Dak., U.S.A. 80 D3 43 26N 103 29W
Hotagen, Sweden 8 E16 63 50N 14 30 E
Hotan, China 32 C2 37 25N 79 55 E
Hotazel, S. Africa 56 D3 27 17S 22 58 E
Hotchkiss, U.S.A. 83 G10 38 48N 107 43W
Hotham, C., Australia 60 B5 12 2S 131 18 E
Hoting, Sweden 8 D17 64 8N 16 15 E
Hotte, Massif de la, Haiti 89 C5 18 30N 73 45W
Hottentotsbaai, Namibia 56 D1 26 8S 14 59 E
Houck, U.S.A. 83 J9 35 20N 109 10W
Houei Sai, Laos 38 B3 20 18N 100 26 E
Houffalize, Belgium 15 D5 50 8N 5 48 E
Houghton, U.S.A. 80 B10 47 7N 88 34W
Houghton L., U.S.A. 76 C3 44 21N 84 44W
Houghton-le-Spring, U.K. 10 C6 54 51N 1 28W
Houhora Heads, N.Z. 59 F4 34 49S 173 9 E
Houlton, U.S.A. 71 C6 46 8N 67 51W
Houma, U.S.A. 81 L9 29 36N 90 43W
Houston, Canada 72 C3 54 25N 126 39W
Houston, Mo., U.S.A. 81 G9 37 22N 91 58W
Houston, Tex., U.S.A. 81 L7 29 46N 95 22W
Houtman Abrolhos, Australia 61 E1 28 43S 113 48 E
Hovd, Mongolia 32 B4 48 2N 91 37 E
Hove, U.K. 11 G7 50 50N 0 10W
Hoveyzeh, Iran 45 D6 31 27N 48 4 E
Hövsgöl, Mongolia 34 C5 43 37N 109 39 E
Hövsgöl Nuur, Mongolia 32 A5 51 0N 100 30 E
Howard, Australia 63 D5 25 16S 152 32 E
Howard, Kans., U.S.A. 81 G6 37 28N 96 16W
Howard, Pa., U.S.A. 78 E7 41 1N 77 40W
Howard, S. Dak., U.S.A. 80 C6 44 1N 97 32W
Howard I., Australia 62 A2 12 10S 135 24 E
Howard L., Canada 73 A7 62 15N 105 57W
Howe, U.S.A. 82 E7 43 48N 113 0W
Howe, C., Australia 63 F5 37 30S 150 0 E
Howell, U.S.A. 76 D4 42 36N 83 56W
Howick, Canada 79 A11 45 11N 73 51W
Howick, S. Africa 57 D5 29 28S 30 14 E
Howick Group, Australia 62 A4 14 20S 145 30 E
Howitt, L., Australia 63 D2 27 40S 138 40 E
Howland I., Pac. Oc. 64 G10 0 48N 176 38W
Howley, Canada 71 C8 49 12N 57 2W
Howrah = Haora, India 43 H13 22 37N 88 20 E
Howth Hd., Ireland 13 C5 53 22N 6 3W
Höxter, Germany 16 C5 51 46N 9 22 E
Hoy, U.K. 12 C5 58 50N 3 15W
Høyanger, Norway 9 F12 61 13N 6 4 E
Hoyerswerda, Germany 16 C8 51 26N 14 14 E
Hpungan Pass, Burma 41 F20 27 30N 96 55 E
Hradec Králové, Czech. 16 C8 50 15N 15 50 E
Hrodna, Belarus 17 B12 53 42N 23 52 E
Hrodzyanka, Belarus 17 B15 53 31N 28 42 E
Hron →, Slovak Rep. 17 E10 47 49N 18 45 E
Hrvatska = Croatia ■, Europe 16 F9 45 20N 16 0 E
Hrymayliv, Ukraine 17 D14 49 20N 26 5 E
Hsenwi, Burma 41 H20 23 22N 97 55 E
Hsiamen = Xiamen, China 33 D6 24 25N 118 4 E
Hsian = Xi'an, China 34 G5 34 15N 109 0 E
Hsinchu, Taiwan 33 D7 24 48N 120 58 E
Hsinhailien = Lianyungang, China 35 G10 34 40N 119 11 E
Hsüchou = Xuzhou, China 35 G9 34 18N 117 10 E
Hu Xian, China 34 G5 34 8N 108 42 E
Hua Hin, Thailand 38 F2 12 34N 99 58 E
Hua Xian, Henan, China 34 G8 35 30N 114 30 E
Hua Xian, Shaanxi, China 34 G5 34 30N 109 48 E
Huachinera, Mexico 86 A3 30 9N 108 55W
Huacho, Peru 92 F3 11 10S 77 35W
Huachón, Peru 92 F3 10 35S 76 0W
Huade, China 34 D7 41 55N 113 59 E
Huadian, China 35 C14 43 0N 126 40 E
Huai He →, China 33 C6 33 0N 118 30 E
Huai Yot, Thailand 39 J2 7 45N 99 37 E
Huai'an, Hebei, China 34 D8 40 30N 114 20 E
Huai'an, Jiangsu, China 35 H10 33 30N 119 10 E
Huaibei, China 34 G9 34 0N 116 48 E
Huaide, China 35 C13 43 30N 124 40 E
Huaidezhen, China 35 C13 43 48N 124 50 E
Huainan, China 33 C6 32 38N 116 58 E
Huairen, China 34 E7 39 48N 113 20 E
Huairou, China 34 D9 40 20N 116 35 E
Huaiyang, China 34 H8 33 40N 114 52 E
Huaiyuan, China 35 H9 32 55N 117 10 E
Huajianzi, China 35 D13 41 23N 125 20 E
Huajuapan de Leon, Mexico 87 D5 17 50N 97 48W
Hualapai Peak, U.S.A. 83 J7 35 5N 113 54W
Huallaga →, Peru 92 E3 5 15S 75 30W
Huambo, Angola 53 G3 12 42S 15 54 E
Huan Jiang →, China 34 G5 34 28N 109 0 E
Huan Xian, China 34 F4 36 33N 107 7 E
Huancabamba, Peru 92 E3 5 10S 79 15W
Huancane, Peru 92 G5 15 10S 69 44W
Huancapi, Peru 92 F4 13 40S 74 0W
Huancavelica, Peru 92 F3 12 50S 75 5W
Huancayo, Peru 92 F3 12 5S 75 12W
Huang Hai = Yellow Sea, China 35 G12 35 0N 123 0 E
Huang He →, China 35 F10 37 55N 118 50 E
Huang Xian, China 35 F11 37 38N 120 30 E
Huangling, China 34 G5 35 34N 109 15 E
Huanglong, China 34 G5 35 30N 109 59 E
Huangshi, China 33 C6 30 10N 115 3 E
Huangsongdian, China 35 C14 43 45N 127 25 E
Huantai, China 35 F9 36 58N 117 56 E
Huánuco, Peru 92 E3 9 55S 76 15W
Huaraz, Peru 92 E3 9 30S 77 32W
Huarmey, Peru 92 F3 10 5S 78 5W
Huascarán, Peru 92 E3 9 8S 77 36W
Huasco, Chile 94 B1 28 30S 71 15W
Huasco →, Chile 94 B1 28 27S 71 13W
Huasna, U.S.A. 85 K6 35 6N 120 24W
Huatabampo, Mexico 86 B3 26 50N 109 50W
Huauchinango, Mexico 87 C5 20 11N 98 3W
Huautla de Jiménez, Mexico 87 D5 18 8N 96 51W
Huay Namota, Mexico 86 C4 21 56N 104 30W
Huayin, China 34 G6 34 35N 110 5 E
Huayllay, Peru 92 F3 11 3S 76 21W
Hubbard, U.S.A. 81 K6 31 51N 96 48W
Hubbart Pt., Canada 73 B10 59 21N 94 41W
Hubei □, China 33 C6 31 0N 112 0 E
Hubli-Dharwad = Dharwad, India 40 M9 15 22N 75 15 E
Huchang, N. Korea 35 D14 41 25N 127 2 E
Huddersfield, U.K. 10 D6 53 39N 1 47W
Hudiksvall, Sweden 9 F17 61 43N 17 10 E
Hudson, Canada 73 C10 50 6N 92 9W
Hudson, Mass., U.S.A. 79 D13 42 23N 71 34W
Hudson, Mich., U.S.A. 76 E3 41 51N 84 21W
Hudson, N.Y., U.S.A. 79 D11 42 15N 73 46W
Hudson, Wis., U.S.A. 80 C8 44 58N 92 45W
Hudson, Wyo., U.S.A. 82 E9 42 54N 108 35W
Hudson →, U.S.A. 79 F10 40 42N 74 2W
Hudson Bay, N.W.T., Canada 69 C11 60 0N 86 0W
Hudson Bay, Sask., Canada 73 C8 52 51N 102 23W
Hudson Falls, U.S.A. 79 C11 43 18N 73 35W
Hudson Mts., Antarctica 5 D16 74 32S 99 20W
Hudson Str., Canada 69 B13 62 0N 70 0W
Hudson's Hope, Canada 72 B4 56 0N 121 54W
Hue, Vietnam 38 D6 16 30N 107 35 E
Huehuetenango, Guatemala 88 C1 15 20N 91 28W
Huejúcar, Mexico 86 C4 22 21N 103 13W
Huelva, Spain 19 D2 37 18N 6 57W
Huentelauquén, Chile 94 C1 31 38S 71 33W
Huerta, Sa. de la, Argentina 94 C2 31 10S 67 30W
Huesca, Spain 19 A5 42 8N 0 25W
Huetamo, Mexico 86 D4 18 36N 100 54W
Hugh →, Australia 62 D1 25 1S 134 1 E
Hughenden, Australia 62 C3 20 52S 144 10 E
Hughes, Australia 61 F4 30 42S 129 31 E
Hugli →, India 43 J13 21 56N 88 4 E
Hugo, U.S.A. 80 F3 39 8N 103 28W
Hugoton, U.S.A. 81 G4 37 11N 101 21W
Hui Xian, Gansu, China 34 H4 33 50N 106 4 E
Hui Xian, Henan, China 34 G7 35 27N 113 12 E
Hui'anbu, China 34 F4 37 28N 106 38 E
Huichapán, Mexico 87 C5 20 24N 99 40W
Huifa He →, China 35 C14 43 0N 127 50 E
Huila, Nevado del, Colombia 92 C3 3 0N 76 0W
Huimin, China 35 F9 37 27N 117 28 E
Huinan, China 35 C14 42 40N 126 2 E
Huinca Renancó, Argentina 94 C3 34 51S 64 22W
Huining, China 34 G3 35 38N 105 0 E
Huinong, China 34 E4 39 5N 106 35 E
Huiting, China 34 G9 34 5N 116 5 E
Huixtla, Mexico 87 D6 15 9N 92 28W
Huize, China 32 D5 26 24N 103 15 E
Hukawng Valley, Burma 41 F20 26 30N 96 30 E
Hukuntsi, Botswana 56 C3 23 58S 21 45 E
Ḩulayfā', Si. Arabia 44 E4 25 58N 40 45 E
Huld, Mongolia 34 B3 45 5N 105 30 E
Hulin He →, China 35 B12 45 0N 122 10 E
Hull = Kingston upon Hull, U.K. 10 D7 53 45N 0 21W
Hull, Canada 70 C4 45 25N 75 44W
Hull →, U.K. 10 D7 53 44N 0 20W
Hulst, Neths. 15 C4 51 17N 4 2 E
Hulun Nur, China 33 B6 49 0N 117 30 E
Humahuaca, Argentina 94 A2 23 10S 65 25W
Humaitá, Brazil 92 E6 7 35S 63 1W
Humaitá, Paraguay 94 B4 27 2S 58 31W
Humansdorp, S. Africa 56 E3 34 2S 24 46 E
Humbe, Angola 56 B1 16 40S 14 55 E
Humber →, U.K. 10 D7 53 42N 0 27W
Humbert River, Australia 60 C5 16 30S 130 45 E
Humble, U.S.A. 81 L8 29 59N 93 18W
Humboldt, Canada 73 C7 52 15N 105 9W
Humboldt, Iowa, U.S.A. 80 D7 42 44N 94 13W
Humboldt, Tenn., U.S.A. 81 H10 35 50N 88 55W
Humboldt →, U.S.A. 82 F4 39 59N 118 36W
Humboldt Gletscher, Greenland 4 B4 79 30N 62 0W
Hume, U.S.A. 84 J8 36 48N 118 54W
Hume, L., Australia 63 F4 36 0S 147 5 E
Humenné, Slovak Rep. 17 D11 48 55N 21 50 E
Humphreys, Mt., U.S.A. 84 H8 37 17N 118 40W
Humphreys Peak, U.S.A. 83 J8 35 21N 111 41W
Humptulips, U.S.A. 84 C3 47 14N 123 57W
Hūn, Libya 51 C8 29 2N 16 0 E
Hun Jiang →, China 35 D13 40 50N 125 38 E
Húnaflói, Iceland 8 D3 65 50N 20 50W
Hunan □, China 33 D6 27 30N 112 0 E
Hunchun, China 35 C16 42 52N 130 28 E
Hundred Mile House, Canada 72 C4 51 38N 121 18W
Hunedoara, Romania 17 F12 45 40N 22 50 E
Hung Yen, Vietnam 38 B6 20 39N 106 4 E
Hungary ■, Europe 17 E10 47 20N 19 20 E
Hungary, Plain of, Europe 6 F10 47 0N 20 0 E
Hungerford, Australia 63 D3 28 58S 144 24 E
Hŭngnam, N. Korea 35 E14 39 49N 127 45 E
Hunsberge, Namibia 56 D2 27 45S 17 12 E
Hunsrück, Germany 16 D4 49 56N 7 27 E
Hunstanton, U.K. 10 E8 52 56N 0 29 E
Hunter, N. Dak., U.S.A. 80 B6 47 12N 97 13W
Hunter, N.Y., U.S.A. 79 D10 42 13N 74 13W
Hunter I., Australia 62 G3 40 30S 144 45 E
Hunter I., Canada 72 C3 51 55N 128 0W
Hunter Ra., Australia 63 E5 32 45S 150 15 E
Hunters Road, Zimbabwe 55 F2 19 9S 29 49 E
Hunterville, N.Z. 59 H5 39 56S 175 35 E
Huntingburg, U.S.A. 76 F2 38 18N 86 57W
Huntingdon, Canada 70 C5 45 6N 74 10W
Huntingdon, U.K. 11 E7 52 20N 0 11W
Huntingdon, U.S.A. 78 F6 40 30N 78 1W
Huntington, Ind., U.S.A. 76 E3 40 53N 85 30W
Huntington, N.Y., U.S.A. 79 F11 40 52N 73 26W
Huntington, Oreg., U.S.A. 82 D5 44 21N 117 16W
Huntington, Utah, U.S.A. 82 G8 39 20N 110 58W
Huntington, W. Va., U.S.A. 76 F4 38 25N 82 27W
Huntington Beach, U.S.A. 85 M8 33 40N 118 5W
Huntington Park, U.S.A. 83 K4 33 58N 118 15W
Huntly, N.Z. 59 G5 37 34S 175 11 E
Huntly, U.K. 12 D6 57 27N 2 47W
Huntsville, Canada 70 C4 45 20N 79 14W
Huntsville, Ala., U.S.A. 77 H2 34 44N 86 35W
Huntsville, Tex., U.S.A. 81 K7 30 43N 95 33W
Hunyani →, Zimbabwe 55 F3 15 57S 30 39 E
Hunyuan, China 34 E7 39 42N 113 42 E
Hunza →, India 43 B6 35 54N 74 20 E
Huo Xian, China 34 F6 36 36N 111 42 E
Huong Hoa, Vietnam 38 D6 16 37N 106 45 E
Huong Khe, Vietnam 38 C5 18 13N 105 41 E
Huonville, Australia 62 G4 43 0S 147 5 E
Hupeh = Hubei □, China 33 C6 31 0N 112 0 E
Ḩūr, Iran 45 D8 30 50N 57 7 E
Hure Qi, China 35 C11 42 45N 121 45 E
Hurley, N. Mex., U.S.A. 83 K9 32 42N 108 8W
Hurley, Wis., U.S.A. 80 B9 46 27N 90 11W
Huron, Calif., U.S.A. 84 J6 36 12N 120 6W
Huron, Ohio, U.S.A. 78 E2 41 24N 82 33W
Huron, S. Dak., U.S.A. 80 C5 44 22N 98 13W
Huron, L., U.S.A. 78 B2 44 30N 82 40W
Hurricane, U.S.A. 83 H7 37 11N 113 17W
Hurunui →, N.Z. 59 K4 42 54S 173 18 E
Húsavík, Iceland 8 C5 66 3N 17 21W
Huşi, Romania 17 E15 46 41N 28 7 E
Huskvarna, Sweden 9 H16 57 47N 14 15 E
Hussar, Canada 72 C6 51 3N 112 41W
Hustadvika, Norway 8 E12 63 0N 7 0 E
Hutchinson, Kans., U.S.A. 81 F6 38 5N 97 56W
Hutchinson, Minn., U.S.A. 80 C7 44 54N 94 22W
Huttig, U.S.A. 81 J8 33 2N 92 11W
Hutton, Mt., Australia 63 D4 25 51S 148 20 E
Huy, Belgium 15 D5 50 31N 5 15 E
Hvammstangi, Iceland 8 D3 65 24N 20 57W
Hvar, Croatia 20 C7 43 11N 16 28 E
Hvítá →, Iceland 8 D3 64 30N 21 58W
Hwachon-chosuji, S. Korea 35 E14 38 5N 127 50 E
Hwang Ho = Huang He →, China 35 F10 37 55N 118 50 E
Hwange, Zimbabwe 55 F2 18 18S 26 30 E
Hwange Nat. Park, Zimbabwe 56 B4 19 0S 26 30 E
Hyannis, U.S.A. 80 E4 42 0N 101 46W
Hyargas Nuur, Mongolia 32 B4 49 0N 93 0 E
Hyden, Australia 61 F2 32 24S 118 53 E
Hyderabad, India 40 L11 17 22N 78 29 E
Hyderabad, Pakistan 42 G3 25 23N 68 24 E
Hyères, France 18 E7 43 8N 6 9 E
Hyères, Is. d', France 18 E7 43 0N 6 20 E
Hyesan, N. Korea 35 D15 41 20N 128 10 E
Hyland →, Canada 72 B3 59 52N 128 12W
Hymia, India 43 C8 33 40N 78 2 E
Hyndman Peak, U.S.A. 82 E6 43 45N 114 8W
Hyōgo □, Japan 31 G7 35 15N 134 50 E
Hyrum, U.S.A. 82 F8 41 38N 111 51W
Hysham, U.S.A. 82 C10 46 18N 107 14W
Hythe, U.K. 11 F9 51 4N 1 5 E
Hyūga, Japan 31 H5 32 25N 131 35 E
Hyvinge = Hyvinkää, Finland 9 F21 60 38N 24 50 E
Hyvinkää, Finland 9 F21 60 38N 24 50 E

I

I-n-Gall, Niger 50 E6 16 51N 7 1 E
Iaco →, Brazil 92 E5 9 3S 68 34W
Iakora, Madag. 57 C8 23 6S 46 40 E
Ialomiţa →, Romania 17 F14 44 42N 27 51 E
Iaşi, Romania 17 E14 47 10N 27 40 E
Iba, Phil. 37 A6 15 22N 120 0 E
Ibadan, Nigeria 50 G5 7 22N 3 58 E
Ibagué, Colombia 92 C3 4 20N 75 20W
Ibar →, Serbia, Yug. 21 C9 43 43N 20 45 E
Ibaraki □, Japan 31 F10 36 10N 140 10 E
Ibarra, Ecuador 92 C3 0 21N 78 7W
Ibembo, Zaïre 54 B1 2 35N 23 35 E
Ibera, L., Argentina 94 B4 28 30S 57 9W
Iberian Peninsula, Europe 6 H5 40 0N 5 0W
Iberville, Canada 70 C5 45 19N 73 17W
Iberville, Lac d', Canada 70 A5 55 55N 73 15W
Ibi, Nigeria 50 G6 8 15N 9 44 E
Ibiá, Brazil 93 G9 19 30S 46 30W
Ibicuy, Argentina 94 C4 33 55S 59 10W
Ibiza, Spain 22 C7 38 54N 1 26 E
Ibo, Mozam. 55 E5 12 22S 40 40 E
Ibonma, Indonesia 37 E8 3 29S 133 31 E
Ibotirama, Brazil 93 F10 12 13S 43 12W
Ibrāhīm →, Lebanon 47 A4 34 4N 35 38 E
Ibu, Indonesia 37 D7 1 35N 127 33 E
Ibusuki, Japan 31 J5 31 12N 130 40 E
Icá, Peru 92 F3 14 0S 75 48W
Iça →, Brazil 92 D5 2 55S 67 58W
Içana, Brazil 92 C5 0 21N 67 19W
Içel = Mersin, Turkey 25 G5 36 51N 34 36 E
Iceland ■, Europe 8 D4 64 45N 19 0W
Icha, Russia 27 D16 55 30N 156 0 E
Ich'ang = Yichang, China 33 C6 30 40N 111 20 E
Ichchapuram, India 41 K14 19 10N 84 40 E
Ichihara, Japan 31 G10 35 28N 140 5 E
Ichikawa, Japan 31 G9 35 44N 139 55 E
Ichilo →, Bolivia 92 G6 15 57S 64 50W
Ichinohe, Japan 30 D10 40 13N 141 17 E
Ichinomiya, Japan 31 G8 35 18N 136 48 E
Ichinoseki, Japan 30 E10 38 55N 141 8 E
Ichŏn, S. Korea 35 F14 37 17N 127 27 E
Icod, Canary Is. 22 F3 28 22N 16 43W
Icy Str., U.S.A. 72 B1 58 20N 135 30W
Ida Grove, U.S.A. 80 D7 42 21N 95 28W
Ida Valley, Australia 61 E3 28 42S 120 29 E
Idabel, U.S.A. 81 J7 33 54N 94 50W
Idaho □, U.S.A. 82 D6 45 0N 115 0W
Idaho City, U.S.A. 82 E6 43 50N 115 50W
Idaho Falls, U.S.A. 82 E7 43 30N 112 2W
Idaho Springs, U.S.A. 82 G11 39 45N 105 31W
Idar-Oberstein, Germany 16 D4 49 43N 7 16 E
Idd el Ghanam, Sudan 51 F9 11 30N 24 19 E
Iddan, Somali Rep. 46 F4 6 10N 48 55 E
Idehan, Libya 51 C7 27 10N 11 30 E
Idehan Marzūq, Libya 51 D7 24 50N 13 51 E
Idelès, Algeria 50 D6 23 50N 5 53 E
Idfû, Egypt 51 D11 24 55N 32 49 E
Ídhi Óros, Greece 23 D6 35 15N 24 45 E
Ídhra, Greece 21 F10 37 20N 23 28 E
Idi, Indonesia 36 C1 5 2N 97 37 E
Idiofa, Zaïre 52 E3 4 55S 19 42 E
Idlib, Syria 44 C3 35 55N 36 36 E
Idria, U.S.A. 84 J6 36 25N 120 41W
Idutywa, S. Africa 57 E4 32 8S 28 18 E
Ieper, Belgium 15 D2 50 51N 2 53 E
Ierápetra, Greece 23 E7 35 0N 25 44 E
Iesi, Italy 20 C5 43 31N 13 14 E
'Ifāl, W. al →, Si. Arabia 44 D2 28 7N 35 3 E
Ifanadiana, Madag. 57 C8 21 19S 47 39 E
Ife, Nigeria 50 G5 7 30N 4 31 E
Iffley, Australia 62 B3 18 53S 141 12 E
Ifni, Morocco 50 C2 29 29N 10 12W
Iforas, Adrar des, Mali 50 E5 19 40N 1 40 E
Ifould, L., Australia 61 F5 30 52S 132 6 E
Iganga, Uganda 54 B3 0 37N 33 28 E
Igarapava, Brazil 93 H9 20 3S 47 47W
Igarapé Açu, Brazil 93 D9 1 4S 47 33W
Igarka, Russia 26 C9 67 30N 86 33 E
Igatimi, Paraguay 95 A4 24 5S 55 40W
Igbetti, Nigeria 50 G5 8 44N 4 8 E
Iggesund, Sweden 9 F17 61 39N 17 10 E
Iglésias, Italy 20 E3 39 19N 8 32 E
Igli, Algeria 50 B4 30 25N 2 19W
Igloolik, Canada 69 B11 69 20N 81 49W
Ignace, Canada 70 C1 49 30N 91 40W
İğneada Burnu, Turkey 21 D13 41 53N 28 2 E
Igoumenítsa, Greece 21 E9 39 32N 20 18 E
Iguaçu →, Brazil 95 B5 25 36S 54 36W
Iguaçu, Cat. del, Brazil 95 B5 25 41S 54 26W
Iguaçu Falls = Iguaçu, Cat. del, Brazil 95 B5 25 41S 54 26W
Iguala, Mexico 87 D5 18 20N 99 40W
Igualada, Spain 19 B6 41 37N 1 37 E
Iguassu = Iguaçu →, Brazil 95 B5 25 36S 54 36W
Iguatu, Brazil 93 E11 6 20S 39 18W
Iguéla, Gabon 52 E1 2 0S 9 16 E
Igunga □, Tanzania 54 C3 4 20S 33 45 E
Iheya-Shima, Japan 31 L3 27 4N 127 58 E
Ihosy, Madag. 57 C8 22 24S 46 8 E
Ihotry, L., Madag. 57 C7 21 56S 43 41 E
Ii, Finland 8 D21 65 19N 25 22 E
Ii-Shima, Japan 31 L3 26 43N 127 47 E
Iida, Japan 31 G8 35 35N 137 50 E
Iijoki →, Finland 8 D21 65 20N 25 20 E
Iisalmi, Finland 8 E22 63 32N 27 10 E
Iiyama, Japan 31 F9 36 51N 138 22 E
Iizuka, Japan 31 H5 33 38N 130 42 E
Ijebu-Ode, Nigeria 50 G5 6 47N 3 58 E
IJmuiden, Neths. 15 B4 52 28N 4 35 E
IJssel →, Neths. 15 B5 52 35N 5 50 E
IJsselmeer, Neths. 15 B5 52 45N 5 20 E
Ijuí →, Brazil 95 B4 27 58S 55 20W
Ikaría, Greece 21 F12 37 35N 26 10 E
Ikeda, Japan 31 G6 34 1N 133 48 E
Ikela, Zaïre 52 E4 1 6S 23 6 E
Iki, Japan 31 H4 33 45N 129 42 E
Ikimba L., Tanzania 54 C3 1 30S 31 20 E
Ikopa →, Madag. 57 B8 16 45S 46 40 E
Ikungu, Tanzania 54 C3 1 33S 33 42 E
Ilagan, Phil. 37 A6 17 7N 121 53 E
Īlām, Iran 44 C5 33 36N 46 36 E
Ilam, Nepal 43 F12 26 58N 87 58 E
Ilanskiy, Russia 27 D10 56 14N 96 3 E
Iława, Poland 17 B10 53 36N 19 34 E
Ilbilbie, Australia 62 C4 21 45S 149 20 E
Ile-à-la-Crosse, Canada 73 B7 55 27N 107 53W
Ile-à-la-Crosse, Lac, Canada 73 B7 55 40N 107 45W
Île-de-France, France 18 B5 49 0N 2 20 E
Ilebo, Zaïre 52 E4 4 17S 20 55 E
Ileje □, Tanzania 55 D3 9 30S 33 25 E

Ilek, *Russia* 26 D6 51 32N 53 21 E
Ilek —►, *Russia* 24 D9 51 30N 53 22 E
Ilford, *Canada* 73 B9 56 4N 95 35W
Ilfracombe, *Australia* 62 C3 23 30S 144 30 E
Ilfracombe, *U.K.* 11 F3 51 12N 4 8W
Ilhéus, *Brazil* 93 F11 14 49S 39 2W
Ili —►, *Kazakstan* 26 E8 45 53N 77 10 E
Ilich, *Kazakstan* 26 E7 40 50N 68 27 E
Iliff, *U.S.A.* 80 E3 40 45N 103 4W
Iligan, *Phil.* 37 C6 8 12N 124 13 E
Ilion, *U.S.A.* 79 D9 43 1N 75 2W
Ilkeston, *U.K.* 10 E6 52 58N 1 19W
Illampu = Ancohuma, Nevada, *Bolivia* 92 G5 16 0S 68 50W
Illana B., *Phil.* 37 C6 7 35N 123 45 E
Illapel, *Chile* 94 C1 32 0S 71 10W
Iller —►, *Germany* 16 D6 48 23N 9 58 E
Illetas, *Spain* 22 B9 39 32N 2 35 E
Illimani, *Bolivia* 92 G5 16 30S 67 50W
Illinois □, *U.S.A.* 75 C9 40 15N 89 30W
Illinois —►, *U.S.A.* 75 C8 38 58N 90 28W
Illium = Troy, *Turkey* 21 E12 39 57N 26 12 E
Ilmajoki, *Finland* 9 E20 62 44N 22 34 E
Ilmen, Ozero, *Russia* 24 C5 58 15N 31 10 E
Ilo, *Peru* 92 G4 17 40S 71 20W
Iloilo, *Phil.* 37 B6 10 45N 122 33 E
Ilorin, *Nigeria* 50 G5 8 30N 4 35 E
Ilwaco, *U.S.A.* 84 D2 46 19N 124 3W
Ilwaki, *Indonesia* 37 F7 7 55S 126 30 E
Imabari, *Japan* 31 G6 34 4N 133 0 E
Imaloto —►, *Madag.* 57 C8 23 27S 45 13 E
Imandra, Ozero, *Russia* 24 A5 67 30N 33 0 E
Imari, *Japan* 31 H4 33 15N 129 52 E
Imbler, *U.S.A.* 82 D5 45 28N 117 58W
imeni 26 Bakinskikh Komissarov = Neftçala, *Azerbaijan* 25 G8 39 19N 49 12 E
imeni 26 Bakinskikh Komissarov, *Turkmenistan* 25 G9 39 22N 54 10 E
Imeni Poliny Osipenko, *Russia* 27 D14 52 30N 136 29 E
Imeri, Serra, *Brazil* 92 C5 0 50N 65 25W
Imerimandroso, *Madag.* 57 B8 17 26S 48 35 E
Imi, *Ethiopia* 46 F3 6 28N 42 10 E
Imlay, *U.S.A.* 82 F4 40 40N 118 9W
Imlay City, *U.S.A.* 78 C1 43 2N 83 5W
Immingham, *U.K.* 10 D7 53 37N 0 13W
Immokalee, *U.S.A.* 77 M5 26 25N 81 25W
Imola, *Italy* 20 B4 44 20N 11 42 E
Imperatriz, *Brazil* 93 E9 5 30S 47 29W
Impéria, *Italy* 20 C3 43 53N 8 3 E
Imperial, *Canada* 73 C7 51 21N 105 28W
Imperial, *Calif., U.S.A.* 85 N11 32 51N 115 34W
Imperial, *Nebr., U.S.A.* 80 E4 40 31N 101 39W
Imperial Beach, *U.S.A.* 85 N9 32 35N 117 8W
Imperial Dam, *U.S.A.* 85 N12 32 55N 114 25W
Imperial Reservoir, *U.S.A.* 85 N12 32 53N 114 28W
Imperial Valley, *U.S.A.* 85 N11 33 0N 115 30W
Imperieuse Reef, *Australia* 60 C2 17 36S 118 50 E
Impfondo, *Congo* 52 D3 1 40N 18 0 E
Imphal, *India* 41 G18 24 48N 93 56 E
İmroz = Gökçeada, *Turkey* 21 D11 40 10N 25 50 E
Imuruan B., *Phil.* 37 B5 10 40N 119 10 E
In Belbel, *Algeria* 50 C5 27 55N 1 12 E
In Salah, *Algeria* 50 C5 27 10N 2 32 E
Ina, *Japan* 31 G8 35 50N 137 55 E
Inangahua Junction, *N.Z.* 59 J3 41 52S 171 59 E
Inanwatan, *Indonesia* 37 E8 2 10S 132 14 E
Iñapari, *Peru* 92 F5 11 0S 69 40W
Inari, *Finland* 8 B22 68 54N 27 5 E
Inarijärvi, *Finland* 8 B22 69 0N 28 0 E
Inawashiro-Ko, *Japan* 30 F10 37 29N 140 6 E
Inca, *Spain* 22 B9 39 43N 2 54 E
Incaguasi, *Chile* 94 B1 29 12S 71 5W
İnce Burun, *Turkey* 25 F5 42 7N 34 56 E
Inchon, *S. Korea* 35 F14 37 27N 126 40 E
İncirliova, *Turkey* 21 F12 37 50N 27 41 E
Incomáti —►, *Mozam.* 57 D5 25 46S 32 43 E
Indalsälven —►, *Sweden* 9 E17 62 36N 17 30 E
Indaw, *Burma* 41 G20 24 15N 96 5 E
Independence, *Calif., U.S.A.* 83 H4 36 48N 118 12W
Independence, *Iowa, U.S.A.* 80 D9 42 28N 91 54W
Independence, *Kans., U.S.A.* 81 G7 37 14N 95 42W
Independence, *Mo., U.S.A.* 80 F7 39 6N 94 25W
Independence, *Oreg., U.S.A.* 82 D2 44 51N 123 11W
Independence Fjord, *Greenland* 4 A6 82 10N 29 0W
Independence Mts., *U.S.A.* 82 F5 41 20N 116 0W
Index, *U.S.A.* 84 C5 47 50N 121 33W
India ■, *Asia* 40 K11 20 0N 78 0 E
Indian —►, *U.S.A.* 77 M5 27 59N 80 34W
Indian Cabins, *Canada* 72 B5 59 52N 117 40W
Indian Harbour, *Canada* 71 B8 54 27N 57 13W
Indian Head, *Canada* 73 C8 50 30N 103 41W
Indian Ocean 28 K11 5 0S 75 0 E
Indian Springs, *U.S.A.* 85 J11 36 35N 115 40W
Indiana, *U.S.A.* 78 F5 40 37N 79 9W
Indiana □, *U.S.A.* 76 E3 40 0N 86 0W
Indianapolis, *U.S.A.* 76 F2 39 46N 86 9W
Indianola, *Iowa, U.S.A.* 80 E8 41 22N 93 34W
Indianola, *Miss., U.S.A.* 81 J9 33 27N 90 39W
Indiga, *Russia* 24 A8 67 38N 49 9 E
Indigirka —►, *Russia* 27 B15 70 48N 148 54 E
Indio, *U.S.A.* 85 M10 33 43N 116 13W
Indonesia ■, *Asia* 36 F5 5 0S 115 0 E
Indore, *India* 42 H6 22 42N 75 53 E
Indramayu, *Indonesia* 37 G13 6 20S 108 19 E
Indravati —►, *India* 41 K12 19 20N 80 20 E
Indre —►, *France* 18 C4 47 16N 0 11 E
Indus —►, *Pakistan* 42 G2 24 20N 67 47 E
Indus, Mouth of the, *Pakistan* 42 H2 24 0N 68 0 E
İnebolu, *Turkey* 25 F5 41 55N 33 40 E
Infiernillo, Presa del, *Mexico* 86 D4 18 9N 102 0W
Ingende, *Zaïre* 52 E3 0 12S 18 57 E
Ingenio, *Canary Is.* 22 G4 27 55N 15 26W
Ingenio Santa Ana, *Argentina* 94 B2 27 25S 65 40W
Ingersoll, *Canada* 78 C4 43 4N 80 55W
Ingham, *Australia* 62 B4 18 43S 146 10 E
Ingleborough, *U.K.* 10 C5 54 10N 2 22W
Inglewood, *Queens., Australia* 63 D5 28 25S 151 2 E
Inglewood, *Vic., Australia* 63 F3 36 29S 143 53 E
Inglewood, *N.Z.* 59 H5 39 9S 174 14 E
Inglewood, *U.S.A.* 85 M8 33 58N 118 21W
Ingólfshöfði, *Iceland* 8 E5 63 48N 16 39W
Ingolstadt, *Germany* 16 D6 48 46N 11 26 E
Ingomar, *U.S.A.* 82 C10 46 35N 107 23W
Ingonish, *Canada* 71 C7 46 42N 60 18W
Ingraj Bazar, *India* 43 G13 24 58N 88 10 E
Ingrid Christensen Coast, *Antarctica* 5 C6 69 30S 76 0 E
Ingulec = Inhulec, *Ukraine* 25 E5 47 42N 33 14 E
Ingwavuma, *S. Africa* 57 D5 27 9S 31 59 E
Inhaca, I., *Mozam.* 57 D5 26 1S 32 57 E
Inhafenga, *Mozam.* 57 C5 20 36S 33 53 E
Inhambane, *Mozam.* 57 C6 23 54S 35 30 E
Inhambane □, *Mozam.* 57 C5 22 30S 34 20 E
Inhaminga, *Mozam.* 55 F4 18 26S 35 0 E
Inharrime, *Mozam.* 57 C6 24 30S 35 0 E
Inharrime —►, *Mozam.* 57 C6 24 30S 35 0 E
Inhulec, *Ukraine* 25 E5 47 42N 33 14 E
Ining = Yining, *China* 26 E9 43 58N 81 10 E
Inírida —►, *Colombia* 92 C5 3 55N 67 52W
Inishbofin, *Ireland* 13 C1 53 37N 10 13W
Inishmore, *Ireland* 13 C2 53 8N 9 45W
Inishowen Pen., *Ireland* 13 A4 55 14N 7 15W
Injune, *Australia* 63 D4 25 53S 148 32 E
Inklin, *Canada* 72 B2 58 56N 133 5W
Inklin —►, *Canada* 72 B2 58 50N 133 10W
Inkom, *U.S.A.* 82 E7 42 48N 112 15W
Inle L., *Burma* 41 J20 20 30N 96 58 E
Inn —►, *Austria* 16 D7 48 35N 13 28 E
Innamincka, *Australia* 63 D3 27 44S 140 46 E
Inner Hebrides, *U.K.* 12 D2 57 0N 6 30W
Inner Mongolia = Nei Monggol Zizhiqu □, *China* 34 C6 42 0N 112 0 E
Inner Sound, *U.K.* 12 D3 57 30N 5 55W
Innerkip, *Canada* 78 C4 43 13N 80 42W
Innetalling I., *Canada* 70 A4 56 0N 79 0W
Innisfail, *Australia* 62 B4 17 33S 146 5 E
Innisfail, *Canada* 72 C6 52 0N 113 57W
In'no-shima, *Japan* 31 G6 34 19N 133 10 E
Innsbruck, *Austria* 16 E6 47 16N 11 23 E
Inny —►, *Ireland* 13 C4 53 30N 7 50W
Inongo, *Zaïre* 52 E3 1 55S 18 30 E
Inoucdjouac = Inukjuak, *Canada* 69 C12 58 25N 78 15W
Inowrocław, *Poland* 17 B10 52 50N 18 12 E
Inpundong, *N. Korea* 35 D14 41 25N 126 34 E
Inquisivi, *Bolivia* 92 G5 16 50S 67 10W
Inscription, C., *Australia* 61 E1 25 29S 112 59 E
Insein, *Burma* 41 L20 16 50N 96 5 E
Inta, *Russia* 24 A11 66 5N 60 8 E
Intendente Alvear, *Argentina* 94 D3 35 12S 63 32W
Interior, *U.S.A.* 80 D4 43 44N 101 59W
Interlaken, *Switz.* 16 E4 46 41N 7 50 E
International Falls, *U.S.A.* 80 A8 48 36N 93 25W
Intiyaco, *Argentina* 94 B3 28 43S 60 5W
Inukjuak, *Canada* 69 C12 58 25N 78 15W
Inútil, B., *Chile* 96 G2 53 30S 70 15W
Inuvik, *Canada* 68 B6 68 16N 133 40W
Inveraray, *U.K.* 12 E3 56 14N 5 5W
Inverbervie, *U.K.* 12 E6 56 51N 2 17W
Invercargill, *N.Z.* 59 M2 46 24S 168 24 E
Inverclyde □, *U.K.* 12 F4 55 55N 4 49W
Inverell, *Australia* 63 D5 29 45S 151 8 E
Invergordon, *U.K.* 12 D4 57 41N 4 10W
Invermere, *Canada* 72 C5 50 30N 116 2W
Inverness, *Canada* 71 C7 46 15N 61 19W
Inverness, *U.K.* 12 D4 57 29N 4 13W
Inverness, *U.S.A.* 77 L4 28 50N 82 20W
Inverurie, *U.K.* 12 D6 57 17N 2 23W
Inverway, *Australia* 60 C4 17 50S 129 38 E
Investigator Group, *Australia* 63 E1 34 45S 134 20 E
Investigator Str., *Australia* 63 F2 35 30S 137 0 E
Inya, *Russia* 26 D9 50 28N 86 37 E
Inyanga, *Zimbabwe* 55 F3 18 12S 32 40 E
Inyangani, *Zimbabwe* 55 F3 18 5S 32 50 E
Inyantue, *Zimbabwe* 55 F2 18 30S 26 40 E
Inyo Mts., *U.S.A.* 83 H5 36 40N 118 0W
Inyokern, *U.S.A.* 85 K9 35 39N 117 49W
Inza, *Russia* 24 D8 53 55N 46 25 E
Iō-Jima, *Japan* 31 J5 30 48N 130 18 E
Ioánnina, *Greece* 21 E9 39 42N 20 47 E
Iola, *U.S.A.* 81 G7 37 55N 95 24W
Iona, *U.K.* 12 E2 56 20N 6 25W
Ione, *Calif., U.S.A.* 84 G6 38 21N 120 56W
Ione, *Wash., U.S.A.* 82 B5 48 45N 117 25W
Ionia, *U.S.A.* 76 D3 42 59N 85 4W
Ionian Is. = Iónioi Nísoi, *Greece* 21 E9 38 40N 20 0 E
Ionian Sea, *Medit. S.* 21 E7 37 30N 17 30 E
Iónioi Nísoi, *Greece* 21 E9 38 40N 20 0 E
Íos, *Greece* 21 F11 36 41N 25 20 E
Iowa □, *U.S.A.* 80 D8 42 18N 93 30W
Iowa City, *U.S.A.* 80 E9 41 40N 91 32W
Iowa Falls, *U.S.A.* 80 D8 42 31N 93 16W
Ipala, *Tanzania* 54 C3 4 30S 32 52 E
Ipameri, *Brazil* 93 G9 17 44S 48 9W
Ipatinga, *Brazil* 93 G10 19 32S 42 30W
Ipiales, *Colombia* 92 C3 0 50N 77 37W
Ipin = Yibin, *China* 32 D5 28 45N 104 32 E
Ipixuna, *Brazil* 92 E4 7 0S 71 40W
Ipoh, *Malaysia* 39 K3 4 35N 101 5 E
Ippy, *C.A.R.* 51 G9 6 5N 21 7 E
İpsala, *Turkey* 21 D12 40 55N 26 23 E
Ipswich, *Australia* 63 D5 27 35S 152 40 E
Ipswich, *U.K.* 11 E9 52 4N 1 10 E
Ipswich, *Mass., U.S.A.* 79 D14 42 41N 70 50W
Ipswich, *S. Dak., U.S.A.* 80 C5 45 27N 99 2W
Ipu, *Brazil* 93 D10 4 23S 40 44W
Iqaluit, *Canada* 69 B13 63 44N 68 31W
Iquique, *Chile* 92 H4 20 19S 70 5W
Iquitos, *Peru* 92 D4 3 45S 73 10W
Irabu-Jima, *Japan* 31 M2 24 50N 125 10 E
Iracoubo, *Fr. Guiana* 93 B8 5 30N 53 10W
Īrafshān, *Iran* 45 E9 26 42N 61 56 E
Iráklion, *Greece* 23 D7 35 20N 25 12 E
Iráklion □, *Greece* 23 D7 35 10N 25 10 E
Irala, *Paraguay* 95 B5 25 55S 54 35W
Iramba □, *Tanzania* 54 C3 4 30S 34 30 E
Iran ■, *Asia* 45 C7 33 0N 53 0 E
Iran, Gunung-Gunung, *Malaysia* 36 D4 2 20N 114 50 E
Iran, Plateau of, *Asia* 28 F9 32 0N 55 0 E
Iran Ra. = Iran, Gunung-Gunung, *Malaysia* 36 D4 2 20N 114 50 E
Īrānshahr, *Iran* 45 E9 27 15N 60 40 E
Irapuato, *Mexico* 86 C4 20 40N 101 30W
Iraq ■, *Asia* 44 C5 33 0N 44 0 E
Irati, *Brazil* 95 B5 25 25S 50 38W
Irbid, *Jordan* 47 C4 32 35N 35 48 E
Irbid □, *Jordan* 47 C5 32 15N 36 35 E
Irebu, *Zaïre* 52 E3 0 40S 17 46 E
Ireland ■, *Europe* 13 D4 53 50N 7 52W
Ireland's Eye, *Ireland* 13 C5 53 24N 6 4W
Iret, *Russia* 27 C16 60 3N 154 20 E
Irhyangdong, *N. Korea* 35 D15 41 15N 129 30 E
Iri, *S. Korea* 35 G14 35 59N 127 0 E
Irian Jaya □, *Indonesia* 37 E9 4 0S 137 0 E
Iringa, *Tanzania* 54 D4 7 48S 35 43 E
Iringa □, *Tanzania* 54 D4 7 48S 35 43 E
Iriomote-Jima, *Japan* 31 M1 24 19N 123 48 E
Iriona, *Honduras* 88 C2 15 57N 85 11W
Iriri —►, *Brazil* 93 D8 3 52S 52 37W
Irish Republic ■, *Europe* 13 D4 53 0N 8 0W
Irish Sea, *U.K.* 10 D3 53 38N 4 48W
Irkineyeva, *Russia* 27 D10 58 30N 96 49 E
Irkutsk, *Russia* 27 D11 52 18N 104 20 E
Irma, *Canada* 73 C6 52 55N 111 14W
Irō-Zaki, *Japan* 31 G9 34 36N 138 51 E
Iron Baron, *Australia* 63 E2 32 58S 137 11 E
Iron Gate = Portile de Fier, *Europe* 17 F12 44 42N 22 30 E
Iron Knob, *Australia* 63 E2 32 46S 137 8 E
Iron Mountain, *U.S.A.* 76 C1 45 49N 88 4W
Iron Ra., *Australia* 62 A3 12 46S 143 16 E
Iron River, *U.S.A.* 80 B10 46 6N 88 39W
Ironbridge, *U.K.* 11 E5 52 38N 2 30W
Irondequoit, *U.S.A.* 78 C7 43 13N 77 35W
Ironstone Kopje, *Botswana* 56 D3 25 17S 24 5 E
Ironton, *Mo., U.S.A.* 81 G9 37 36N 90 38W
Ironton, *Ohio, U.S.A.* 76 F4 38 32N 82 41W
Ironwood, *U.S.A.* 80 B9 46 27N 90 9W
Iroquois Falls, *Canada* 70 C3 48 46N 80 41W
Irpin, *Ukraine* 17 C16 50 30N 30 15 E
Irrara Cr. —►, *Australia* 63 D4 29 35S 145 31 E
Irrawaddy □, *Burma* 41 L19 17 0N 95 0 E
Irrawaddy —►, *Burma* 41 M19 15 50N 95 6 E
Irtysh —►, *Russia* 26 C7 61 4N 68 52 E
Irumu, *Zaïre* 54 B2 1 32N 29 53 E
Irún, *Spain* 19 A5 43 20N 1 52W
Irunea = Pamplona, *Spain* 19 A5 42 48N 1 38W
Irvine, *Canada* 73 D6 49 57N 110 16W
Irvine, *U.K.* 12 F4 55 37N 4 41W
Irvine, *Calif., U.S.A.* 85 M9 33 41N 117 46W
Irvine, *Ky., U.S.A.* 76 G4 37 42N 83 58W
Irvinestown, *U.K.* 13 B4 54 28N 7 39W
Irving, *U.S.A.* 81 J6 32 49N 96 56W
Irvona, *U.S.A.* 78 F6 40 46N 78 33W
Irwin —►, *Australia* 61 E1 29 15S 114 54 E
Irymple, *Australia* 63 E3 34 14S 142 8 E
Isaac —►, *Australia* 62 C4 22 55S 149 20 E
Isabel, *U.S.A.* 80 C4 45 24N 101 26W
Isabela, I., *Mexico* 86 C3 21 51N 105 55W
Isabella, *Phil.* 37 C6 6 40N 122 10 E
Isabella, Cord., *Nic.* 88 D2 13 30N 85 25W
Isabella Ra., *Australia* 60 D3 21 0S 121 4 E
Ísafjarðardjúp, *Iceland* 8 C2 66 10N 23 0W
Ísafjörður, *Iceland* 8 C2 66 5N 23 9W
Isagarh, *India* 42 G7 24 48N 77 51 E
Isahaya, *Japan* 31 H5 32 52N 130 2 E
Isaka, *Tanzania* 54 C3 3 56S 32 59 E
Isangi, *Zaïre* 52 D4 0 52N 24 10 E
Isar —►, *Germany* 16 D7 48 48N 12 57 E
Íschia, *Italy* 20 D5 40 44N 13 57 E
Isdell —►, *Australia* 60 C3 16 27S 124 51 E
Ise, *Japan* 31 G8 34 25N 136 45 E
Ise-Wan, *Japan* 31 G8 34 43N 136 43 E
Iseramagazi, *Tanzania* 54 C3 4 37S 32 10 E
Isère —►, *France* 18 D6 44 59N 4 51 E
Isérnia, *Italy* 20 D6 41 36N 14 14 E
Ishigaki-Shima, *Japan* 31 M2 24 20N 124 10 E
Ishikari-Gawa —►, *Japan* 30 C10 43 15N 141 23 E
Ishikari-Sammyaku, *Japan* 30 C11 43 30N 143 0 E
Ishikari-Wan, *Japan* 30 C10 43 25N 141 1 E
Ishikawa □, *Japan* 31 F8 36 30N 136 30 E
Ishim, *Russia* 26 D7 56 10N 69 30 E
Ishim —►, *Russia* 26 D8 57 45N 71 10 E
Ishinomaki, *Japan* 30 E10 38 32N 141 20 E
Ishioka, *Japan* 31 F10 36 11N 140 16 E
Ishkuman, *Pakistan* 43 A5 36 30N 73 50 E
Ishpeming, *U.S.A.* 76 B2 46 29N 87 40W
Isil Kul, *Russia* 26 D8 54 55N 71 16 E
Isiolo, *Kenya* 54 B4 0 24N 37 33 E
Isiolo □, *Kenya* 54 B4 2 30N 37 30 E
Isiro, *Zaïre* 54 B2 2 53N 27 40 E
Isisford, *Australia* 62 C3 24 15S 144 21 E
İskenderun, *Turkey* 25 G6 36 32N 36 10 E
İskenderun Körfezi, *Turkey* 25 G6 36 40N 35 50 E
Iskŭr —►, *Bulgaria* 21 C11 43 45N 24 25 E
Iskut —►, *Canada* 72 B2 56 45N 131 49W
Isla —►, *U.K.* 12 E5 56 32N 3 20W
Isla Vista, *U.S.A.* 85 L7 34 25N 119 53W
Islamabad, *Pakistan* 42 C5 33 40N 73 10 E
Islamkot, *Pakistan* 42 G4 24 42N 70 13 E
Island —►, *Canada* 72 A4 60 25N 121 12W
Island Falls, *Canada* 70 C3 49 35N 81 20W
Island Falls, *U.S.A.* 71 C6 46 1N 68 16W
Island L., *Canada* 73 C10 53 47N 94 25W
Island Lagoon, *Australia* 63 E2 31 30S 136 40 E
Island Pond, *U.S.A.* 79 B13 44 49N 71 53W
Islands, B. of, *Canada* 71 C8 49 11N 58 15W
Islay, *U.K.* 12 F2 55 46N 6 10W
Isle —►, *France* 18 D3 44 55N 0 15W
Isle aux Morts, *Canada* 71 C8 47 35N 59 0W
Isle of Wight □, *U.K.* 11 G6 50 41N 1 17W
Isle Royale, *U.S.A.* 80 A10 48 0N 88 54W
Isleta, *U.S.A.* 83 J10 34 55N 106 42W
Isleton, *U.S.A.* 84 G5 38 10N 121 37W
Ismail = Izmayil, *Ukraine* 17 F15 45 22N 28 46 E
Ismâ'ilîya, *Egypt* 51 B11 30 37N 32 18 E
Ismay, *U.S.A.* 80 B2 46 30N 104 48W
Isna, *Egypt* 51 C11 25 17N 32 30 E
Isogstalo, *India* 43 B8 34 15N 78 46 E
Isparta, *Turkey* 25 G5 37 47N 30 30 E
Íspica, *Italy* 20 F6 36 47N 14 55 E
Israel ■, *Asia* 47 D3 32 0N 34 50 E
Issoire, *France* 18 D5 45 32N 3 15 E
Issyk-Kul = Ysyk-Köl, *Kyrgyzstan* 28 E11 42 26N 76 12 E
Issyk-Kul, Ozero = Ysyk-Köl, Ozero, *Kyrgyzstan* 26 E8 42 25N 77 15 E
Istaihah, *U.A.E.* 45 F7 23 19N 54 4 E
İstanbul, *Turkey* 21 D13 41 0N 29 0 E
Istiaía, *Greece* 21 E10 38 57N 23 9 E
Istokpoga, L., *U.S.A.* 77 M5 27 23N 81 17W
Istra, *Croatia* 16 F7 45 10N 14 0 E
İstranca Dağları, *Turkey* 21 D12 41 48N 27 36 E
Istres, *France* 18 E6 43 31N 4 59 E
Istria = Istra, *Croatia* 16 F7 45 10N 14 0 E
Itá, *Paraguay* 94 B4 25 29S 57 21W
Itabaiana, *Brazil* 93 E11 7 18S 35 19W
Itaberaba, *Brazil* 93 F10 12 32S 40 18W
Itabira, *Brazil* 93 G10 19 37S 43 13W
Itabirito, *Brazil* 95 A7 20 15S 43 48W
Itabuna, *Brazil* 93 F11 14 48S 39 16W
Itaipú, Represa de, *Brazil* 95 B5 25 30S 54 30W
Itaituba, *Brazil* 93 D7 4 10S 55 50W
Itajai, *Brazil* 95 B6 27 50S 48 39W
Itajubá, *Brazil* 95 A6 22 24S 45 30W
Itaka, *Tanzania* 55 D3 8 50S 32 49 E
Italy ■, *Europe* 20 C5 42 0N 13 0 E
Itampolo, *Madag.* 57 C7 24 41S 43 57 E
Itapecuru-Mirim, *Brazil* 93 D10 3 24S 44 20W
Itaperuna, *Brazil* 95 A7 21 10S 41 54W
Itapetininga, *Brazil* 95 A6 23 36S 48 7W
Itapeva, *Brazil* 95 A6 23 59S 48 59W
Itapicuru —►, *Bahia, Brazil* 93 F11 11 47S 37 32W
Itapicuru —►, *Maranhão, Brazil* 93 D10 2 52S 44 12W
Itapipoca, *Brazil* 93 D11 3 30S 39 35W
Itapuá □, *Paraguay* 95 B4 26 40S 55 40W
Itaquari, *Brazil* 95 A7 20 20S 40 25W
Itaquatiara, *Brazil* 92 D7 2 58S 58 30W
Itaquí, *Brazil* 94 B4 29 8S 56 30W
Itararé, *Brazil* 95 A6 24 6S 49 23W
Itarsi, *India* 42 H7 22 36N 77 51 E
Itatí, *Argentina* 94 B4 27 16S 58 15W
Itatuba, *Brazil* 92 E6 5 46S 63 20W
Itchen —►, *U.K.* 11 G6 50 55N 1 22W
Itezhi Tezhi, L., *Zambia* 55 F2 15 30S 25 30 E
Ithaca = Itháki, *Greece* 21 E9 38 25N 20 40 E
Ithaca, *U.S.A.* 79 D8 42 27N 76 30W
Itháki, *Greece* 21 E9 38 25N 20 40 E
Ito, *Japan* 31 G9 34 58N 139 5 E
Itoigawa, *Japan* 31 F8 37 2N 137 51 E
Itonamas —►, *Bolivia* 92 F6 12 28S 64 24W
Ittoqqortoormiit = Scoresbysund, *Greenland* 4 B6 70 20N 23 0W
Itu, *Brazil* 95 A6 23 17S 47 15W
Ituaçu, *Brazil* 93 F10 13 50S 41 18W
Ituiutaba, *Brazil* 93 G9 19 0S 49 25W
Itumbiara, *Brazil* 93 G9 18 20S 49 10W
Ituna, *Canada* 73 C8 51 10N 103 24W
Itunge Port, *Tanzania* 55 D3 9 40S 33 55 E
Iturbe, *Argentina* 94 A2 23 0S 65 25W
Ituri —►, *Zaïre* 54 B2 1 40N 27 1 E
Iturup, Ostrov, *Russia* 27 E15 45 0N 148 0 E
Ituyuro —►, *Argentina* 94 A3 22 40S 63 50W
Itzehoe, *Germany* 16 B5 53 55N 9 31 E
Ivai —►, *Brazil* 95 A5 23 18S 53 42W
Ivalo, *Finland* 8 B22 68 38N 27 35 E
Ivalojoki —►, *Finland* 8 B22 68 40N 27 40 E
Ivanava, *Belarus* 17 B13 52 7N 25 29 E
Ivanhoe, *N.S.W., Australia* 63 E3 32 56S 144 20 E
Ivanhoe, *W. Austral., Australia* 60 C4 15 41S 128 41 E
Ivanhoe, *U.S.A.* 84 J7 36 23N 119 13W
Ivanhoe L., *Canada* 73 A7 60 25N 106 30W
Ivano-Frankivsk, *Ukraine* 17 D13 48 40N 24 40 E
Ivano-Frankovsk = Ivano-Frankivsk, *Ukraine* 17 D13 48 40N 24 40 E
Ivanovo = Ivanava, *Belarus* 17 B13 52 7N 25 29 E
Ivanovo, *Russia* 24 C7 57 5N 41 0 E
Ivato, *Madag.* 57 C8 20 37S 47 10 E
Ivatsevichy, *Belarus* 17 B13 52 43N 25 21 E
Ivdel, *Russia* 24 B11 60 42N 60 24 E
Ivinheima —►, *Brazil* 95 A5 23 14S 53 42W
Ivohibe, *Madag.* 57 C8 22 31S 46 57 E
Ivory Coast ■, *Africa* 50 G3 7 30N 5 0W
Ivrea, *Italy* 20 B2 45 28N 7 52 E
Ivujivik, *Canada* 69 B12 62 24N 77 55W
Iwahig, *Phil.* 36 C5 8 36N 117 32 E
Iwaizumi, *Japan* 30 E10 39 50N 141 45 E
Iwaki, *Japan* 31 F10 37 3N 140 55 E
Iwakuni, *Japan* 31 G6 34 15N 132 8 E
Iwamizawa, *Japan* 30 C10 43 12N 141 46 E
Iwanai, *Japan* 30 C10 42 58N 140 30 E
Iwata, *Japan* 31 G8 34 42N 137 51 E
Iwate □, *Japan* 30 E10 39 30N 141 30 E
Iwate-San, *Japan* 30 E10 39 51N 141 0 E
Iwo, *Nigeria* 50 G5 7 39N 4 9 E
Ixiamas, *Bolivia* 92 F5 13 50S 68 5W
Ixopo, *S. Africa* 57 E5 30 11S 30 5 E
Ixtepec, *Mexico* 87 D5 16 32N 95 10W
Ixtlán del Río, *Mexico* 86 C4 21 5N 104 21W
Iyo, *Japan* 31 H6 33 45N 132 45 E
Izabal, L. de, *Guatemala* 88 C2 15 30N 89 10W
Izamal, *Mexico* 87 C7 20 56N 89 1W
Izegem, *Belgium* 15 D3 50 55N 3 12 E
Izena-Shima, *Japan* 31 L3 26 56N 127 56 E
Izhevsk, *Russia* 24 C9 56 51N 53 14 E
Izmayil, *Ukraine* 17 F15 45 22N 28 46 E
İzmir, *Turkey* 21 E12 38 25N 27 8 E
İzmit, *Turkey* 25 F4 40 45N 29 50 E
İznik Gölü, *Turkey* 21 D13 40 27N 29 30 E
Izra, *Syria* 47 C5 32 51N 36 15 E
Izu-Shotō, *Japan* 31 G10 34 30N 140 0 E
Izumi-sano, *Japan* 31 G7 34 23N 135 18 E
Izumo, *Japan* 31 G6 35 20N 132 46 E
Izyaslav, *Ukraine* 17 C14 50 5N 26 50 E

Juan de Fuca Str.

J

Jabal Lubnān, *Lebanon* **47 B4** 33 45N 35 40 E
Jabalpur, *India* **43 H8** 23 9N 79 58 E
Jabbūl, *Syria* **44 B3** 36 4N 37 30 E
Jablah, *Syria* **44 C3** 35 20N 36 0 E
Jablanica, *Macedonia* **21 D9** 41 15N 20 30 E
Jablonec, *Czech.* **16 C8** 50 43N 15 10 E
Jaboatão, *Brazil* **93 E11** 8 7S 35 1W
Jaboticabal, *Brazil* **95 A6** 21 15S 48 17W
Jaburu, *Brazil* **92 E6** 5 30S 64 0W
Jaca, *Spain* **19 A5** 42 35N 0 33W
Jacareí, *Brazil* **95 A6** 23 20S 46 0W
Jacarèzinho, *Brazil* **95 A6** 23 5S 49 58W
Jackman, *U.S.A.* **71 C5** 45 35N 70 17W
Jacksboro, *U.S.A.* **81 J5** 33 14N 98 15W
Jackson, *Australia* **63 D4** 26 39S 149 39 E
Jackson, *Ala., U.S.A.* **77 K2** 31 31N 87 53W
Jackson, *Calif., U.S.A.* **84 G6** 38 21N 120 46W
Jackson, *Ky., U.S.A.* **76 G4** 37 33N 83 23W
Jackson, *Mich., U.S.A.* **76 D3** 42 15N 84 24W
Jackson, *Minn., U.S.A.* **80 D7** 43 37N 95 1W
Jackson, *Miss., U.S.A.* **81 J9** 32 18N 90 12W
Jackson, *Mo., U.S.A.* **81 G10** 37 23N 89 40W
Jackson, *Ohio, U.S.A.* **76 F4** 39 3N 82 39W
Jackson, *Tenn., U.S.A.* **77 H1** 35 37N 88 49W
Jackson, *Wyo., U.S.A.* **82 E8** 43 29N 110 46W
Jackson B., *N.Z.* **59 K2** 43 58S 168 42 E
Jackson L., *U.S.A.* **82 E8** 43 52N 110 36W
Jacksons, *N.Z.* **59 K3** 42 46S 171 32 E
Jacksonville, *Ala., U.S.A.* **77 J3** 33 49N 85 46W
Jacksonville, *Calif., U.S.A.* **84 H6** 37 52N 120 24W
Jacksonville, *Fla., U.S.A.* **77 K5** 30 20N 81 39W
Jacksonville, *Ill., U.S.A.* **80 F9** 39 44N 90 14W
Jacksonville, *N.C., U.S.A.* **77 H7** 34 45N 77 26W
Jacksonville, *Oreg., U.S.A.* **82 E2** 42 19N 122 57W
Jacksonville, *Tex., U.S.A.* **81 K7** 31 58N 95 17W
Jacksonville Beach, *U.S.A.* **77 K5** 30 17N 81 24W
Jacmel, *Haiti* **89 C5** 18 14N 72 32W
Jacob Lake, *U.S.A.* **83 H7** 36 43N 112 13W
Jacobabad, *Pakistan* **42 E3** 28 20N 68 29 E
Jacobina, *Brazil* **93 F10** 11 11S 40 30W
Jacques-Cartier, Mt., *Canada* **71 C6** 48 57N 66 0W
Jacuí →, *Brazil* **95 C5** 30 2S 51 15W
Jacumba, *U.S.A.* **85 N10** 32 37N 116 11W
Jacundá →, *Brazil* **93 D8** 1 57S 50 26W
Jadotville = Likasi, *Zaïre* **55 E2** 10 55S 26 48 E
Jādū, *Libya* **51 B7** 32 0N 12 0 E
Jaén, *Peru* **92 E3** 5 25S 78 40W
Jaén, *Spain* **19 D4** 37 44N 3 43W
Jaffa = Tel Aviv-Yafo, *Israel* **47 C3** 32 4N 34 48 E
Jaffa, C., *Australia* **63 F2** 36 58S 139 40 E
Jaffna, *Sri Lanka* **40 Q12** 9 45N 80 2 E
Jagadhri, *India* **42 D7** 30 10N 77 20 E
Jagadishpur, *India* **43 G11** 25 30N 84 21 E
Jagdalpur, *India* **41 K12** 19 3N 82 0 E
Jagersfontein, *S. Africa* **56 D4** 29 44S 25 27 E
Jagraon, *India* **40 D9** 30 50N 75 25 E
Jagtial, *India* **40 K11** 18 50N 79 0 E
Jaguariaíva, *Brazil* **95 A6** 24 10S 49 50W
Jaguaribe →, *Brazil* **93 D11** 4 25S 37 45W
Jagüey Grande, *Cuba* **88 B3** 22 35N 81 7W
Jahangirabad, *India* **42 E8** 28 19N 78 4 E
Jahrom, *Iran* **45 D7** 28 30N 53 31 E
Jailolo, *Indonesia* **37 D7** 1 5N 127 30 E
Jailolo, Selat, *Indonesia* **37 D7** 0 5N 129 5 E
Jaipur, *India* **42 F6** 27 0N 75 50 E
Jājarm, *Iran* **45 B8** 36 58N 56 27 E
Jakarta, *Indonesia* **37 G12** 6 9S 106 49 E
Jakobstad = Pietarsaari, *Finland* **8 E20** 63 40N 22 43 E
Jal, *U.S.A.* **81 J3** 32 7N 103 12W
Jalalabad, *Afghan.* **42 B4** 34 30N 70 29 E
Jalalabad, *India* **43 F8** 27 41N 79 42 E
Jalalpur Jattan, *Pakistan* **42 C6** 32 38N 74 11 E
Jalama, *U.S.A.* **85 L6** 34 29N 120 29W
Jalapa, *Guatemala* **88 D2** 14 39N 89 59W
Jalapa Enríquez, *Mexico* **87 D5** 19 32N 96 55W
Jalasjärvi, *Finland* **9 E20** 62 29N 22 47 E
Jalaun, *India* **43 F8** 26 8N 79 25 E
Jaleswar, *Nepal* **43 F11** 26 38N 85 48 E
Jalgaon, *Maharashtra, India* **40 J10** 21 2N 76 31 E
Jalgaon, *Maharashtra, India* **40 J9** 21 0N 75 42 E
Jalībah, *Iraq* **44 D5** 30 35N 46 32 E
Jalisco □, *Mexico* **86 C4** 20 0N 104 0W
Jalkot, *Pakistan* **43 B5** 35 14N 73 24 E
Jalna, *India* **40 K9** 19 48N 75 38 E
Jalón →, *Spain* **19 B5** 41 47N 1 4W
Jalpa, *Mexico* **86 C4** 21 38N 102 58W
Jalpaiguri, *India* **41 F16** 26 32N 88 46 E
Jaluit I., *Pac. Oc.* **64 G8** 6 0N 169 30 E
Jalūlā, *Iraq* **44 C5** 34 16N 45 10 E
Jamaica ■, *W. Indies* **88 C4** 18 10N 77 30W
Jamalpur, *Bangla.* **41 G16** 24 52N 89 56 E
Jamalpur, *India* **43 G12** 25 18N 86 28 E
Jamalpurganj, *India* **43 H13** 23 2N 88 1 E
Jamanxim →, *Brazil* **93 D7** 4 43S 56 18W
Jambe, *Indonesia* **37 E8** 1 15S 132 10 E
Jambi, *Indonesia* **36 E2** 1 38S 103 30 E
Jambi □, *Indonesia* **36 E2** 1 30S 102 30 E
Jambusar, *India* **42 H5** 22 3N 72 51 E
James →, *U.S.A.* **80 D6** 42 52N 97 18W
James B., *Canada* **69 C11** 51 30N 80 0W
James Ras., *Australia* **60 D5** 24 10S 132 30 E
James Ross I., *Antarctica* **5 C18** 63 58S 57 50W
Jamestown, *Australia* **63 E2** 33 10S 138 32 E
Jamestown, *S. Africa* **56 E4** 31 6S 26 45 E
Jamestown, *Ky., U.S.A.* **76 G3** 36 59N 85 4W
Jamestown, *N. Dak., U.S.A.* **80 B5** 46 54N 98 42W
Jamestown, *N.Y., U.S.A.* **78 D5** 42 6N 79 14W
Jamestown, *Pa., U.S.A.* **78 E4** 41 29N 80 27W
Jamestown, *Tenn., U.S.A.* **77 G3** 36 26N 84 56W
Jamīlābād, *Iran* **45 C6** 34 24N 48 28 E
Jamiltepec, *Mexico* **87 D5** 16 17N 97 49W
Jamkhandi, *India* **40 L9** 16 30N 75 15 E
Jammu, *India* **42 C6** 32 43N 74 54 E
Jammu & Kashmir □, *India* **43 B7** 34 25N 77 0 E
Jamnagar, *India* **42 H4** 22 30N 70 6 E
Jampur, *Pakistan* **42 E4** 29 39N 70 40 E
Jamrud, *Pakistan* **42 C4** 33 59N 71 24 E
Jämsä, *Finland* **9 F21** 61 53N 25 10 E
Jamshedpur, *India* **43 H12** 22 44N 86 12 E
Jamtara, *India* **43 H12** 23 59N 86 49 E
Jämtland, *Sweden* **8 E15** 63 31N 14 0 E
Jan L., *Canada* **73 C8** 54 56N 102 55W
Jan Mayen, *Arctic* **4 B7** 71 0N 9 0W
Janakkala, *Finland* **9 F21** 60 54N 24 36 E
Jand, *Pakistan* **42 C5** 33 30N 72 6 E
Jandaq, *Iran* **45 C7** 34 3N 54 22 E
Jandia, *Canary Is.* **22 F5** 28 6N 14 21W
Jandia, Pta. de, *Canary Is.* **22 F5** 28 3N 14 31W
Jandola, *Pakistan* **42 C4** 32 20N 70 9 E
Jandowae, *Australia* **63 D5** 26 45S 151 7 E
Janesville, *U.S.A.* **80 D10** 42 41N 89 1W
Janīn, *West Bank* **47 C4** 32 28N 35 18 E
Janos, *Mexico* **86 A3** 30 45N 108 10W
Januária, *Brazil* **93 G10** 15 25S 44 25W
Janubio, *Canary Is.* **22 F6** 28 56N 13 50W
Jaora, *India* **42 H6** 23 40N 75 10 E
Japan ■, *Asia* **31 G8** 36 0N 136 0 E
Japan, Sea of, *Asia* **30 E7** 40 0N 135 0 E
Japan Trench, *Pac. Oc.* **28 F18** 32 0N 142 0 E
Japen = Yapen, *Indonesia* **37 E9** 1 50S 136 0 E
Japurá →, *Brazil* **92 D5** 3 8S 65 46W
Jaque, *Panama* **92 B3** 7 27N 78 8W
Jarābulus, *Syria* **44 B3** 36 49N 38 1 E
Jarama →, *Spain* **19 B4** 40 24N 3 32W
Jaranwala, *Pakistan* **42 D5** 31 15N 73 26 E
Jarash, *Jordan* **47 C4** 32 17N 35 54 E
Jardim, *Brazil* **94 A4** 21 28S 56 2W
Jardines de la Reina, Is., *Cuba* **88 B4** 20 50N 78 50W
Jargalang, *China* **35 C12** 43 5N 122 55 E
Jargalant = Hovd, *Mongolia* **32 B4** 48 2N 91 37 E
Jarīr, W. al →, *Si. Arabia* **44 E4** 25 38N 42 30 E
Jarosław, *Poland* **17 C12** 50 2N 22 42 E
Jarrahdale, *Australia* **61 F2** 32 24S 116 5 E
Jarres, Plaine des, *Laos* **38 C4** 19 27N 103 10 E
Jarso, *Ethiopia* **51 G12** 5 15N 37 30 E
Jartai, *China* **34 E3** 39 45N 105 48 E
Jarud Qi, *China* **35 B11** 44 28N 120 50 E
Järvenpää, *Finland* **9 F21** 60 29N 25 5 E
Jarvis, *Canada* **78 D4** 42 53N 80 6W
Jarvis I., *Pac. Oc.* **65 H12** 0 15S 159 55W
Jarwa, *India* **43 F10** 27 38N 82 30 E
Jāsimīyah, *Iraq* **44 C5** 33 45N 44 41 E
Jasin, *Malaysia* **39 L4** 2 20N 102 26 E
Jāsk, *Iran* **45 E8** 25 38N 57 45 E
Jasło, *Poland* **17 D11** 49 45N 21 30 E
Jasper, *Alta., Canada* **72 C5** 52 55N 118 5W
Jasper, *Ont., Canada* **79 B9** 44 52N 75 57W
Jasper, *Ala., U.S.A.* **77 J2** 33 50N 87 17W
Jasper, *Fla., U.S.A.* **77 K4** 30 31N 82 57W
Jasper, *Minn., U.S.A.* **80 D6** 43 51N 96 24W
Jasper, *Tex., U.S.A.* **81 K8** 30 56N 94 1W
Jasper Nat. Park, *Canada* **72 C5** 52 50N 118 8W
Jászberény, *Hungary* **17 E10** 47 30N 19 55 E
Jataí, *Brazil* **93 G8** 17 58S 51 48W
Jati, *Pakistan* **42 G3** 24 20N 68 19 E
Jatibarang, *Indonesia* **37 G13** 6 28S 108 18 E
Jatinegara, *Indonesia* **37 G12** 6 13S 106 52 E
Játiva, *Spain* **19 C5** 39 0N 0 32W
Jaú, *Brazil* **95 A6** 22 10S 48 30W
Jauja, *Peru* **92 F3** 11 45S 75 15W
Jaunpur, *India* **43 G10** 25 46N 82 44 E
Java = Jawa, *Indonesia* **37 G14** 7 0S 110 0 E
Java Sea, *Indonesia* **36 E3** 4 35S 107 15 E
Java Trench, *Ind. Oc.* **64 H2** 9 0S 105 0 E
Javhlant = Ulyasutay, *Mongolia* **32 B4** 47 56N 97 28 E
Jawa, *Indonesia* **37 G14** 7 0S 110 0 E
Jay, *U.S.A.* **81 G7** 36 25N 94 48W
Jaya, Puncak, *Indonesia* **37 E9** 3 57S 137 17 E
Jayanti, *India* **41 F16** 26 45N 89 40 E
Jayapura, *Indonesia* **37 E10** 2 28S 140 38 E
Jayawijaya, Pegunungan, *Indonesia* **37 E9** 5 0S 139 0 E
Jaynagar, *India* **41 F15** 26 43N 86 9 E
Jayrūd, *Syria* **44 C3** 33 49N 36 44 E
Jayton, *U.S.A.* **81 J4** 33 15N 100 34W
Jazīreh-ye Shīf, *Iran* **45 D6** 29 4N 50 54 E
Jazminal, *Mexico* **86 C4** 24 56N 101 25W
Jazzīn, *Lebanon* **47 B4** 33 31N 35 35 E
Jean, *U.S.A.* **85 K11** 35 47N 115 20W
Jean Marie River, *Canada* **72 A4** 61 32N 120 38W
Jean Rabel, *Haiti* **89 C5** 19 50N 73 5W
Jeanerette, *U.S.A.* **81 L9** 29 55N 91 40W
Jeanette, Ostrov, *Russia* **27 B16** 76 43N 158 0 E
Jeannette, *U.S.A.* **78 F5** 40 20N 79 36W
Jebba, *Nigeria* **50 G5** 9 9N 4 48 E
Jebel, Bahr el →, *Sudan* **51 G11** 9 30N 30 25 E
Jedburgh, *U.K.* **12 F6** 55 29N 2 33W
Jedda = Jiddah, *Si. Arabia* **46 C2** 21 29N 39 10 E
Jędrzejów, *Poland* **17 C11** 50 35N 20 15 E
Jedway, *Canada* **72 C2** 52 17N 131 14W
Jefferson, *Iowa, U.S.A.* **80 D7** 42 1N 94 23W
Jefferson, *Ohio, U.S.A.* **78 E4** 41 44N 80 46W
Jefferson, *Tex., U.S.A.* **81 J7** 32 46N 94 21W
Jefferson, *Wis., U.S.A.* **80 D10** 43 0N 88 48W
Jefferson, Mt., *Nev., U.S.A.* **82 G5** 38 51N 117 0W
Jefferson, Mt., *Oreg., U.S.A.* **82 D3** 44 41N 121 48W
Jefferson City, *Mo., U.S.A.* **80 F8** 38 34N 92 10W
Jefferson City, *Tenn., U.S.A.* **77 G4** 36 7N 83 30W
Jeffersonville, *U.S.A.* **76 F3** 38 17N 85 44W
Jega, *Nigeria* **50 F5** 12 15N 4 23 E
Jēkabpils, *Latvia* **9 H21** 56 29N 25 57 E
Jelenia Góra, *Poland* **16 C8** 50 50N 15 45 E
Jelgava, *Latvia* **9 H20** 56 41N 23 49 E
Jellicoe, *Canada* **70 C2** 49 40N 87 30W
Jemaja, *Indonesia* **36 D3** 3 5N 105 45 E
Jemaluang, *Malaysia* **39 L4** 2 16N 103 52 E
Jember, *Indonesia* **37 H15** 8 11S 113 41 E
Jembongan, *Malaysia* **36 C5** 6 45N 117 20 E
Jemeppe, *Belgium* **15 D5** 50 37N 5 30 E
Jena, *Germany* **16 C6** 50 54N 11 35 E
Jena, *U.S.A.* **81 K8** 31 41N 92 8W
Jenkins, *U.S.A.* **76 G4** 37 10N 82 38W
Jenner, *U.S.A.* **84 G3** 38 27N 123 7W
Jennings, *U.S.A.* **81 K8** 30 13N 92 40W
Jennings →, *Canada* **72 B2** 59 38N 132 5W
Jeparit, *Australia* **63 F3** 36 8S 142 1 E
Jequié, *Brazil* **93 F10** 13 51S 40 5W
Jequitinhonha, *Brazil* **93 G10** 16 30S 41 0W
Jequitinhonha →, *Brazil* **93 G11** 15 51S 38 53W
Jerada, *Morocco* **50 B4** 34 17N 2 10W
Jerantut, *Malaysia* **39 L4** 3 56N 102 22 E
Jérémie, *Haiti* **89 C5** 18 40N 74 10W
Jerez, Punta, *Mexico* **87 C5** 22 58N 97 40W
Jerez de García Salinas, *Mexico* **86 C4** 22 39N 103 0W
Jerez de la Frontera, *Spain* **19 D2** 36 41N 6 7W
Jerez de los Caballeros, *Spain* **19 C2** 38 20N 6 45W
Jericho = Arīḩā, *Syria* **44 C3** 35 49N 36 35 E
Jericho = El Arīḩā, *West Bank* **47 D4** 31 52N 35 27 E
Jericho, *Australia* **62 C4** 23 38S 146 6 E
Jerilderie, *Australia* **63 F4** 35 20S 145 41 E
Jermyn, *U.S.A.* **79 E9** 41 31N 75 31W
Jerome, *U.S.A.* **83 J8** 34 45N 112 7W
Jersey, *U.K.* **11 H5** 49 11N 2 7W
Jersey City, *U.S.A.* **79 F10** 40 44N 74 4W
Jersey Shore, *U.S.A.* **78 E7** 41 12N 77 15W
Jerseyville, *U.S.A.* **80 F9** 39 7N 90 20W
Jerusalem, *Israel* **47 D4** 31 47N 35 10 E
Jervis B., *Australia* **63 F5** 35 8S 150 46 E
Jesselton = Kota Kinabalu, *Malaysia* **36 C5** 6 0N 116 4 E
Jessore, *Bangla.* **41 H16** 23 10N 89 10 E
Jesup, *U.S.A.* **77 K5** 31 36N 81 53W
Jesús Carranza, *Mexico* **87 D5** 17 28N 95 1W
Jesús María, *Argentina* **94 C3** 30 59S 64 5W
Jetmore, *U.S.A.* **81 F5** 38 4N 99 54W
Jetpur, *India* **42 J4** 21 45N 70 10 E
Jevnaker, *Norway* **9 F14** 60 15N 10 26 E
Jewett, *Ohio, U.S.A.* **78 F3** 40 22N 81 2W
Jewett, *Tex., U.S.A.* **81 K6** 31 22N 96 9W
Jewett City, *U.S.A.* **79 E13** 41 36N 72 0W
Jeyhūnābād, *Iran* **45 C6** 34 58N 48 59 E
Jeypore, *India* **41 K13** 18 50N 82 38 E
Jhajjar, *India* **42 E7** 28 37N 76 42 E
Jhal Jhao, *Pakistan* **40 F4** 26 20N 65 35 E
Jhalawar, *India* **42 G7** 24 40N 76 10 E
Jhang Maghiana, *Pakistan* **42 D5** 31 15N 72 22 E
Jhansi, *India* **43 G8** 25 30N 78 36 E
Jharia, *India* **43 H12** 23 45N 86 26 E
Jharsuguda, *India* **41 J14** 21 56N 84 5 E
Jhelum, *Pakistan* **42 C5** 33 0N 73 45 E
Jhelum →, *Pakistan* **42 D5** 31 20N 72 10 E
Jhunjhunu, *India* **42 E6** 28 10N 75 30 E
Ji Xian, *Hebei, China* **34 F8** 37 35N 115 30 E
Ji Xian, *Henan, China* **34 G8** 35 22N 114 5 E
Ji Xian, *Shanxi, China* **34 F6** 36 7N 110 40 E
Jia Xian, *Henan, China* **34 H7** 33 59N 113 12 E
Jia Xian, *Shaanxi, China* **34 E6** 38 12N 110 28 E
Jiamusi, *China* **33 B8** 46 40N 130 26 E
Ji'an, *Jiangxi, China* **33 D6** 27 6N 114 59 E
Ji'an, *Jilin, China* **35 D14** 41 5N 126 10 E
Jianchang, *China* **35 D11** 40 55N 120 35 E
Jianchangying, *China* **35 D10** 40 10N 118 50 E
Jiangcheng, *China* **32 D5** 22 36N 101 52 E
Jiangmen, *China* **33 D6** 22 32N 113 0 E
Jiangsu □, *China* **35 H10** 33 0N 120 0 E
Jiangxi □, *China* **33 D6** 27 30N 116 0 E
Jiao Xian, *China* **35 F11** 36 18N 120 1 E
Jiaohe, *Hebei, China* **34 E9** 38 2N 116 20 E
Jiaohe, *Jilin, China* **35 C14** 43 40N 127 22 E
Jiaozhou Wan, *China* **35 F11** 36 5N 120 10 E
Jiaozuo, *China* **34 G7** 35 16N 113 12 E
Jiawang, *China* **35 G9** 34 28N 117 26 E
Jiaxiang, *China* **34 G9** 35 25N 116 20 E
Jiaxing, *China* **33 C7** 30 49N 120 45 E
Jiayi = Chiai, *Taiwan* **33 D7** 23 29N 120 25 E
Jibuti = Djibouti ■, *Africa* **46 E3** 12 0N 43 0 E
Jicarón, I., *Panama* **88 E3** 7 10N 81 50W
Jiddah, *Si. Arabia* **46 C2** 21 29N 39 10 E
Jido, *India* **41 E19** 29 2N 94 58 E
Jieshou, *China* **34 H8** 33 18N 115 22 E
Jiexiu, *China* **34 F6** 37 2N 111 55 E
Jiggalong, *Australia* **60 D3** 23 21S 120 47 E
Jihlava, *Czech.* **16 D8** 49 28N 15 35 E
Jihlava →, *Czech.* **17 D9** 48 55N 16 36 E
Jijel, *Algeria* **50 A6** 36 52N 5 50 E
Jijiga, *Ethiopia* **46 F3** 9 20N 42 50 E
Jilin, *China* **35 C14** 43 44N 126 30 E
Jilin □, *China* **35 C13** 44 0N 127 0 E
Jilong = Chilung, *Taiwan* **33 D7** 25 3N 121 45 E
Jima, *Ethiopia* **51 G12** 7 40N 36 47 E
Jiménez, *Mexico* **86 B4** 27 10N 104 54W
Jimo, *China* **35 F11** 36 23N 120 30 E
Jin Xian, *Hebei, China* **34 E8** 38 2N 115 2 E
Jin Xian, *Liaoning, China* **35 E11** 38 55N 121 42 E
Jinan, *China* **34 F9** 36 38N 117 1 E
Jincheng, *China* **34 G7** 35 29N 112 50 E
Jind, *India* **42 E7** 29 19N 76 22 E
Jindabyne, *Australia* **63 F4** 36 25S 148 35 E
Jindrichuv Hradeç, *Czech.* **16 D8** 49 10N 15 2 E
Jing He →, *China* **34 G5** 34 27N 109 4 E
Jingbian, *China* **34 F5** 37 20N 108 30 E
Jingchuan, *China* **34 G4** 35 20N 107 20 E
Jingdezhen, *China* **33 D6** 29 20N 117 11 E
Jinggu, *China* **32 D5** 23 35N 100 41 E
Jinghai, *China* **34 E9** 38 55N 116 55 E
Jingle, *China* **34 E6** 38 20N 111 55 E
Jingning, *China* **34 G3** 35 30N 105 43 E
Jingpo Hu, *China* **35 C15** 43 55N 128 55 E
Jingtai, *China* **34 F3** 37 10N 104 6 E
Jingxing, *China* **34 E8** 38 2N 114 8 E
Jingyang, *China* **34 G5** 34 30N 108 50 E
Jingyu, *China* **35 C14** 42 25N 126 45 E
Jingyuan, *China* **34 F3** 36 30N 104 40 E
Jingziguan, *China* **34 H6** 33 15N 111 0 E
Jinhua, *China* **33 D6** 29 8N 119 38 E
Jining, *Nei Mongol Zizhiqu, China* **34 D7** 41 5N 113 0 E
Jining, *Shandong, China* **34 G9** 35 22N 116 34 E
Jinja, *Uganda* **54 B3** 0 25N 33 12 E
Jinjang, *Malaysia* **39 L3** 3 13N 101 39 E
Jinji, *China* **34 F4** 37 58N 106 8 E
Jinnah Barrage, *Pakistan* **40 C7** 32 58N 71 33 E
Jinotega, *Nic.* **88 D2** 13 6N 85 59W
Jinotepe, *Nic.* **88 D2** 11 50N 86 10W
Jinsha Jiang →, *China* **32 D5** 28 50N 104 36 E
Jinxi, *China* **35 D11** 40 52N 120 50 E
Jinxiang, *China* **34 G9** 35 5N 116 22 E
Jinzhou, *China* **35 D11** 41 5N 121 3 E
Jiparaná →, *Brazil* **92 E6** 8 3S 62 52W
Jipijapa, *Ecuador* **92 D2** 1 0S 80 40W
Jiquilpan, *Mexico* **86 D4** 19 57N 102 42W
Jishan, *China* **34 G6** 35 34N 110 58 E
Jisr ash Shughūr, *Syria* **44 C3** 35 49N 36 18 E
Jitarning, *Australia* **61 F2** 32 48S 117 57 E
Jitra, *Malaysia* **39 J3** 6 16N 100 25 E
Jiu →, *Romania* **17 F12** 43 47N 23 48 E
Jiudengkou, *China* **34 E4** 39 56N 106 40 E
Jiujiang, *China* **33 D6** 29 42N 115 58 E
Jiutai, *China* **35 B13** 44 10N 125 50 E
Jiuxiangcheng, *China* **34 H8** 33 12N 114 50 E
Jiuxincheng, *China* **34 E8** 39 17N 115 59 E
Jixi, *China* **35 B16** 45 20N 130 50 E
Jiyang, *China* **35 F9** 37 0N 117 12 E
Jīzān, *Si. Arabia* **46 D3** 17 0N 42 20 E
Jize, *China* **34 F8** 36 54N 114 56 E
Jizō-Zaki, *Japan* **31 G6** 35 34N 133 20 E
Jizzakh, *Uzbekistan* **26 E7** 40 6N 67 50 E
Joaçaba, *Brazil* **95 B5** 27 5S 51 31W
João Pessoa, *Brazil* **93 E12** 7 10S 34 52W
Joaquín V. González, *Argentina* **94 B3** 25 10S 64 0W
Jodhpur, *India* **42 F5** 26 23N 73 8 E
Joensuu, *Finland* **24 B4** 62 37N 29 49 E
Jofane, *Mozam.* **57 C5** 21 15S 34 18 E
Jõgeva, *Estonia* **9 G22** 58 45N 26 24 E
Joggins, *Canada* **71 C7** 45 42N 64 27W
Jogjakarta = Yogyakarta, *Indonesia* **37 G14** 7 49S 110 22 E
Johannesburg, *S. Africa* **57 D4** 26 10S 28 2 E
Johannesburg, *U.S.A.* **85 K9** 35 22N 117 38W
John Day, *U.S.A.* **82 D4** 44 25N 118 57W
John Day →, *U.S.A.* **82 D3** 45 44N 120 39W
John H. Kerr Reservoir, *U.S.A.* **77 G6** 36 36N 78 18W
John o' Groats, *U.K.* **12 C5** 58 38N 3 4W
Johnnie, *U.S.A.* **85 J10** 36 25N 116 5W
John's Ra., *Australia* **62 C1** 21 55S 133 23 E
Johnson, *U.S.A.* **81 G4** 37 34N 101 45W
Johnson City, *N.Y., U.S.A.* **79 D9** 42 7N 75 58W
Johnson City, *Tenn., U.S.A.* **77 G4** 36 19N 82 21W
Johnson City, *Tex., U.S.A.* **81 K5** 30 17N 98 25W
Johnsonburg, *U.S.A.* **78 E6** 41 29N 78 41W
Johnsondale, *U.S.A.* **85 K8** 35 58N 118 32W
Johnson's Crossing, *Canada* **72 A2** 60 29N 133 18W
Johnston, L., *Australia* **61 F3** 32 25S 120 30 E
Johnston Falls = Mambilima Falls, *Zambia* **55 E2** 10 31S 28 45 E
Johnston I., *Pac. Oc.* **65 F11** 17 10N 169 8W
Johnstone Str., *Canada* **72 C3** 50 28N 126 0W
Johnstown, *N.Y., U.S.A.* **79 C10** 43 0N 74 22W
Johnstown, *Pa., U.S.A.* **78 F6** 40 20N 78 55W
Johor Baharu, *Malaysia* **39 M4** 1 28N 103 46 E
Jõhvi, *Estonia* **9 G22** 59 22N 27 27 E
Joinvile, *Brazil* **95 B6** 26 15S 48 55W
Joinville I., *Antarctica* **5 C18** 65 0S 55 30W
Jojutla, *Mexico* **87 D5** 18 37N 99 11W
Jokkmokk, *Sweden* **8 C18** 66 35N 19 50 E
Jökulsá á Bru →, *Iceland* **8 D6** 65 40N 14 16W
Jökulsá á Fjöllum →, *Iceland* **8 C5** 66 10N 16 30W
Jolfā, *Āzarbājān-e Sharqī, Iran* **44 B5** 38 57N 45 38 E
Jolfā, *Eşfahan, Iran* **45 C6** 32 58N 51 37 E
Joliet, *U.S.A.* **76 E1** 41 32N 88 5W
Joliette, *Canada* **70 C5** 46 3N 73 24W
Jolo, *Phil.* **37 C6** 6 0N 121 0 E
Jolon, *U.S.A.* **84 K5** 35 58N 121 9W
Jombang, *Indonesia* **37 G15** 7 33S 112 14 E
Jome, *Indonesia* **37 E7** 1 16S 127 30 E
Jonava, *Lithuania* **9 J21** 55 8N 24 12 E
Jones Sound, *Canada* **4 B3** 76 0N 85 0W
Jonesboro, *Ark., U.S.A.* **81 H9** 35 50N 90 42W
Jonesboro, *Ill., U.S.A.* **81 G10** 37 27N 89 16W
Jonesboro, *La., U.S.A.* **81 J8** 32 15N 92 43W
Jonesport, *U.S.A.* **71 D6** 44 32N 67 37W
Joniškis, *Lithuania* **9 H20** 56 13N 23 35 E
Jönköping, *Sweden* **9 H16** 57 45N 14 10 E
Jonquière, *Canada* **71 C5** 48 27N 71 14W
Joplin, *U.S.A.* **81 G7** 37 6N 94 31W
Jordan, *U.S.A.* **82 C10** 47 19N 106 55W
Jordan ■, *Asia* **47 E5** 31 0N 36 0 E
Jordan →, *Asia* **47 D4** 31 48N 35 32 E
Jordan Valley, *U.S.A.* **82 E5** 42 59N 117 3W
Jorhat, *India* **41 F19** 26 45N 94 12 E
Jörn, *Sweden* **8 D19** 65 4N 20 1 E
Jorong, *Indonesia* **36 E4** 3 58S 114 56 E
Jørpeland, *Norway* **9 G11** 59 3N 6 1 E
Jorquera →, *Chile* **94 B2** 28 3S 69 58W
Jos, *Nigeria* **50 G6** 9 53N 8 51 E
José Batlle y Ordóñez, *Uruguay* **95 C4** 33 20S 55 10W
Joseph, *U.S.A.* **82 D5** 45 21N 117 14W
Joseph, L., *Nfld., Canada* **71 B6** 52 45N 65 18W
Joseph, L., *Ont., Canada* **78 A5** 45 10N 79 44W
Joseph Bonaparte G., *Australia* **60 B4** 14 35S 128 50 E
Joseph City, *U.S.A.* **83 J8** 34 57N 110 20W
Joshua Tree, *U.S.A.* **85 L10** 34 8N 116 19W
Joshua Tree National Monument, *U.S.A.* **85 M10** 33 55N 116 0W
Jostedalsbreen, *Norway* **9 F12** 61 40N 6 59 E
Jotunheimen, *Norway* **9 F13** 61 35N 8 25 E
Jourdanton, *U.S.A.* **81 L5** 28 55N 98 33W
Joussard, *Canada* **72 B5** 55 22N 115 50W
Jovellanos, *Cuba* **88 B3** 22 40N 81 10W
Ju Xian, *China* **35 F10** 36 35N 118 20 E
Juan Aldama, *Mexico* **86 C4** 24 20N 103 23W
Juan Bautista Alberdi, *Argentina* **94 C3** 34 26S 61 48W
Juan de Fuca Str., *Canada* **84 B2** 48 15N 124 0W

Juan de Nova

Juan de Nova, *Ind. Oc.* 57 B7 17 3S 43 45 E
Juan Fernández, Arch. de, *Pac. Oc.* 90 G2 33 50S 80 0W
Juan José Castelli, *Argentina* 94 B3 25 27S 60 57W
Juan L. Lacaze, *Uruguay* 94 C4 34 26S 57 25W
Juankoski, *Finland* 8 E23 63 3N 28 19 E
Juárez, *Argentina* 94 D4 37 40S 59 43W
Juárez, *Mexico* 85 N11 32 20N 115 57W
Juárez, Sierra de, *Mexico* 86 A1 32 0N 116 0W
Juàzeiro, *Brazil* 93 E10 9 30S 40 30W
Juàzeiro do Norte, *Brazil* 93 E11 7 10S 39 18W
Jubayl, *Lebanon* 47 A4 34 5N 35 39 E
Jubbah, *Si. Arabia* 44 D4 28 2N 40 56 E
Jubbulpore = Jabalpur, *India* 43 H8 23 9N 79 58 E
Jubilee L., *Australia* 61 E4 29 0S 126 50 E
Juby, C., *Morocco* 50 C2 28 0N 12 59W
Júcar →, *Spain* 19 C5 39 5N 0 10W
Júcaro, *Cuba* 88 B4 21 37N 78 51W
Juchitán, *Mexico* 87 D5 16 27N 95 5W
Judaea = Har Yehuda, *Israel* 47 D3 31 35N 34 57 E
Judith →, *U.S.A.* 82 C9 47 44N 109 39W
Judith, Pt., *U.S.A.* 79 E13 41 22N 71 29W
Judith Gap, *U.S.A.* 82 C9 46 41N 109 45W
Jugoslavia = Yugoslavia ■, *Europe* 21 B9 44 0N 20 0 E
Juigalpa, *Nic.* 88 D2 12 6N 85 26W
Juiz de Fora, *Brazil* 95 A7 21 43S 43 19W
Jujuy □, *Argentina* 94 A2 23 20S 65 40W
Julesburg, *U.S.A.* 80 E3 40 59N 102 16W
Juli, *Peru* 92 G5 16 10S 69 25W
Julia Cr. →, *Australia* 62 C3 20 0S 141 11 E
Julia Creek, *Australia* 62 C3 20 39S 141 44 E
Juliaca, *Peru* 92 G4 15 25S 70 10W
Julian, *U.S.A.* 85 M10 33 4N 116 38W
Julianehåb, *Greenland* 4 C5 60 43N 46 0W
Julimes, *Mexico* 86 B3 28 25N 105 27W
Jullundur, *India* 42 D6 31 20N 75 40 E
Julu, *China* 34 F8 37 15N 115 2 E
Jumbo, *Zimbabwe* 55 F3 17 30S 30 58 E
Jumbo Pk., *U.S.A.* 85 J12 36 12N 114 11W
Jumentos Cays, *Bahamas* 89 B4 23 0N 75 40W
Jumet, *Belgium* 15 D4 50 27N 4 25 E
Jumilla, *Spain* 19 C5 38 28N 1 19W
Jumla, *Nepal* 43 E10 29 15N 82 13 E
Jumna = Yamuna →, *India* 43 G9 25 30N 81 53 E
Junagadh, *India* 42 J4 21 30N 70 30 E
Junction, *Tex., U.S.A.* 81 K5 30 29N 99 46W
Junction, *Utah, U.S.A.* 83 G7 38 14N 112 13W
Junction B., *Australia* 62 A1 11 52S 133 55 E
Junction City, *Kans., U.S.A.* 80 F6 39 2N 96 50W
Junction City, *Oreg., U.S.A.* 82 D2 44 13N 123 12W
Junction Pt., *Australia* 62 A1 11 45S 133 50 E
Jundah, *Australia* 62 C3 24 46S 143 2 E
Jundiaí, *Brazil* 95 A6 24 30S 47 0W
Juneau, *U.S.A.* 68 C6 58 18N 134 25W
Junee, *Australia* 63 E4 34 53S 147 35 E
Jungfrau, *Switz.* 16 E4 46 32N 7 58 E
Junggar Pendi, *China* 32 B3 44 30N 86 0 E
Jungshahi, *Pakistan* 42 G2 24 52N 67 44 E
Juniata →, *U.S.A.* 78 F7 40 30N 77 40W
Junín, *Argentina* 94 C3 34 33S 60 57W
Junín de los Andes, *Argentina* 96 D2 39 45S 71 0W
Jūniyah, *Lebanon* 47 B4 33 59N 35 38 E
Juntura, *U.S.A.* 82 E4 43 45N 118 5W
Jupiter →, *Canada* 71 C7 49 29N 63 37W
Jur, Nahr el →, *Sudan* 51 G10 8 45N 29 15 E
Jura = Jura, Mts. du, *Europe* 18 C7 46 40N 6 5 E
Jura = Schwäbische Alb, *Germany* 16 D5 48 20N 9 30 E
Jura, *U.K.* 12 F3 56 0N 5 50W
Jura, Mts. du, *Europe* 18 C7 46 40N 6 5 E
Jura, Sd. of, *U.K.* 12 F3 55 57N 5 45W
Jurado, *Colombia* 92 B3 7 7N 77 46W
Jurbarkas, *Lithuania* 9 J20 55 6N 22 47 E
Jūrmala, *Latvia* 9 H20 56 58N 23 34 E
Juruá →, *Brazil* 92 D5 2 37S 65 44W
Juruena →, *Brazil* 92 E7 7 20S 58 3W
Juruti, *Brazil* 93 D7 2 9S 56 4W
Justo Daract, *Argentina* 94 C2 33 52S 65 12W
Juticalpa, *Honduras* 88 D2 14 40N 86 12W
Jutland = Jylland, *Denmark* 9 H13 56 25N 9 30 E
Juventud, I. de la, *Cuba* 88 B3 21 40N 82 40W
Juwain, *Afghan.* 40 D2 31 45N 61 30 E
Jūy Zar, *Iran* 44 C5 33 50N 46 18 E
Juye, *China* 34 G9 35 22N 116 5 E
Jylland, *Denmark* 9 H13 56 25N 9 30 E
Jyväskylä, *Finland* 9 E21 62 14N 25 50 E

K

K2, *Pakistan* 43 B7 35 58N 76 32 E
Kaap Plateau, *S. Africa* 56 D3 28 30S 24 0 E
Kaapkruis, *Namibia* 56 C1 21 55S 13 57 E
Kaapstad = Cape Town, *S. Africa* 56 E2 33 55S 18 22 E
Kabaena, *Indonesia* 37 F6 5 15S 122 0 E
Kabala, *S. Leone* 50 G2 9 38N 11 37W
Kabale, *Uganda* 54 C3 1 15S 30 0 E
Kabalo, *Zaïre* 54 D2 6 0S 27 0 E
Kabambare, *Zaïre* 54 C2 4 41S 27 39 E
Kabango, *Zaïre* 55 D2 8 35S 28 30 E
Kabanjahe, *Indonesia* 36 D1 3 6N 98 30 E
Kabara, *Mali* 50 E4 16 40N 2 50W
Kabardino-Balkar Republic = Kabardino Balkaria □, *Russia* 25 F7 43 30N 43 30 E
Kabardino Balkaria □, *Russia* 25 F7 43 30N 43 30 E
Kabare, *Indonesia* 37 E8 0 4S 130 58 E
Kabarega Falls, *Uganda* 54 B3 2 15N 31 30 E
Kabasalan, *Phil.* 37 C6 7 47N 122 44 E
Kabba, *Nigeria* 50 G6 7 50N 6 3 E
Kabin Buri, *Thailand* 38 F3 13 57N 101 43 E
Kabinakagami L., *Canada* 70 C3 48 54N 84 25W
Kabīr, Zab al →, *Iraq* 44 C4 36 1N 43 24 E
Kabkabīyah, *Sudan* 51 F9 13 50N 24 0 E
Kabompo, *Zambia* 55 E1 13 36S 24 14 E
Kabompo →, *Zambia* 53 G4 14 10S 23 11 E
Kabondo, *Zaïre* 55 D2 8 58S 25 40 E
Kabongo, *Zaïre* 54 D2 7 22S 25 33 E
Kabra, *Australia* 62 C5 23 25S 150 25 E
Kabūd Gonbad, *Iran* 45 B8 37 5N 59 45 E
Kābul, *Afghan.* 42 B3 34 28N 69 11 E
Kābul □, *Afghan.* 40 B6 34 30N 69 0 E
Kabul →, *Pakistan* 42 C5 33 55N 72 14 E
Kabunga, *Zaïre* 54 C2 1 38S 28 3 E
Kaburuang, *Indonesia* 37 D7 3 50N 126 30 E
Kabwe, *Zambia* 55 E2 14 30S 28 29 E
Kachchh, Gulf of, *India* 42 H3 22 50N 69 15 E
Kachchh, Rann of, *India* 42 G4 24 0N 70 0 E
Kachebera, *Zambia* 55 E3 13 50S 32 50 E
Kachin □, *Burma* 41 F20 26 0N 97 30 E
Kachira, L., *Uganda* 54 C3 0 40S 31 7 E
Kachiry, *Kazakstan* 26 D8 53 10N 75 50 E
Kachot, *Cambodia* 39 G4 11 30N 103 3 E
Kaçkar, *Turkey* 25 F7 40 45N 41 10 E
Kadan Kyun, *Burma* 36 B1 12 30N 98 20 E
Kadanai →, *Afghan.* 42 D1 31 22N 65 45 E
Kadi, *India* 42 H5 23 18N 72 23 E
Kadina, *Australia* 63 E2 33 55S 137 43 E
Kadiyevka = Stakhanov, *Ukraine* 25 E6 48 35N 38 40 E
Kadoka, *U.S.A.* 80 D4 43 50N 101 31W
Kadoma, *Zimbabwe* 55 F2 18 20S 29 52 E
Kâdugli, *Sudan* 51 F10 11 0N 29 45 E
Kaduna, *Nigeria* 50 F6 10 30N 7 21 E
Kaédi, *Mauritania* 50 E2 16 9N 13 28W
Kaelé, *Cameroon* 51 F7 10 7N 14 27 E
Kaeng Khoï, *Thailand* 38 E3 14 35N 101 0 E
Kaesŏng, *N. Korea* 35 F14 37 58N 126 35 E
Kāf, *Si. Arabia* 44 D3 31 25N 37 29 E
Kafakumba, *Zaïre* 52 F4 9 38S 23 46 E
Kafan = Kapan, *Armenia* 25 G8 39 18N 46 27 E
Kafanchan, *Nigeria* 50 G6 9 40N 8 20 E
Kaffrine, *Senegal* 50 F1 14 8N 15 36W
Kafia Kingi, *Sudan* 51 G9 9 20N 24 25 E
Kafinda, *Zambia* 55 E3 12 32S 30 20 E
Kafirévs, Ákra, *Greece* 21 E11 38 9N 24 38 E
Kafue, *Zambia* 55 F2 15 46S 28 9 E
Kafue →, *Zambia* 53 H5 15 30S 29 0 E
Kafue Flats, *Zambia* 55 F2 15 40S 27 25 E
Kafue Nat. Park, *Zambia* 55 F2 15 0S 25 30 E
Kafulwe, *Zambia* 55 D2 9 0S 29 1 E
Kaga, *Afghan.* 42 B4 34 14N 70 10 E
Kaga Bandoro, *C.A.R.* 51 G8 7 0N 19 10 E
Kagan, *Uzbekistan* 26 F7 39 43N 64 33 E
Kagawa □, *Japan* 31 G6 34 15N 134 0 E
Kagera □, *Tanzania* 54 C3 2 0S 31 30 E
Kagera →, *Uganda* 54 C3 0 57S 31 47 E
Kagoshima, *Japan* 31 J5 31 35N 130 33 E
Kagoshima □, *Japan* 31 J5 31 30N 130 30 E
Kagul = Cahul, *Moldova* 17 F15 45 50N 28 15 E
Kahak, *Iran* 45 B6 36 6N 49 46 E
Kahama, *Tanzania* 54 C3 4 8S 32 30 E
Kahama □, *Tanzania* 54 C3 3 50S 32 0 E
Kahang, *Malaysia* 39 L4 2 12N 103 32 E
Kahayan →, *Indonesia* 36 E4 3 40S 114 0 E
Kahe, *Tanzania* 54 C4 3 30S 37 25 E
Kahemba, *Zaïre* 52 F3 7 18S 18 55 E
Kahniah →, *Canada* 72 B4 58 15N 120 55W
Kahnūj, *Iran* 45 E8 27 55N 57 40 E
Kahoka, *U.S.A.* 80 E9 40 25N 91 44W
Kahoolawe, *U.S.A.* 74 H16 20 33N 156 37W
Kahramanmaraş, *Turkey* 25 G6 37 37N 36 53 E
Kahuta, *Pakistan* 42 C5 33 35N 73 24 E
Kai, Kepulauan, *Indonesia* 37 F8 5 55S 132 45 E
Kai Besar, *Indonesia* 37 F8 5 35S 133 0 E
Kai Is. = Kai, Kepulauan, *Indonesia* 37 F8 5 55S 132 45 E
Kai Kecil, *Indonesia* 37 F8 5 45S 132 40 E
Kaiama, *Nigeria* 50 G5 9 36N 4 1 E
Kaiapoi, *N.Z.* 59 K4 43 24S 172 40 E
Kaieteur Falls, *Guyana* 92 B7 5 1N 59 10W
Kaifeng, *China* 34 G8 34 48N 114 21 E
Kaikohe, *N.Z.* 59 F4 35 25S 173 49 E
Kaikoura, *N.Z.* 59 K4 42 25S 173 43 E
Kaikoura Ra., *N.Z.* 59 J4 41 59S 173 41 E
Kailu, *China* 35 C11 43 38N 121 18 E
Kailua Kona, *U.S.A.* 74 J17 19 39N 155 59W
Kaimana, *Indonesia* 37 E8 3 39S 133 45 E
Kaimanawa Mts., *N.Z.* 59 H5 39 15S 175 56 E
Kaimganj, *India* 43 F8 27 33N 79 24 E
Kaimur Hills, *India* 43 G9 24 30N 82 0 E
Kaingaroa Forest, *N.Z.* 59 H6 38 24S 176 30 E
Kainji Res., *Nigeria* 50 F5 10 1N 4 40 E
Kainuu, *Finland* 8 D23 64 30N 29 7 E
Kaipara Harbour, *N.Z.* 59 G5 36 25S 174 14 E
Kaipokok B., *Canada* 71 B8 54 54N 59 47W
Kairana, *India* 42 E7 29 24N 77 15 E
Kaironi, *Indonesia* 37 E8 0 47S 133 40 E
Kairouan, *Tunisia* 50 A7 35 45N 10 5 E
Kaiserslautern, *Germany* 16 D4 49 26N 7 45 E
Kaitaia, *N.Z.* 59 F4 35 8S 173 17 E
Kaitangata, *N.Z.* 59 M2 46 17S 169 51 E
Kaithal, *India* 42 E7 29 48N 76 26 E
Kaitu →, *Pakistan* 42 C4 33 10N 70 30 E
Kaiwi Channel, *U.S.A.* 74 H16 21 15N 157 30W
Kaiyuan, *China* 35 C13 42 28N 124 1 E
Kajaani, *Finland* 8 D22 64 17N 27 46 E
Kajabbi, *Australia* 62 B3 20 0S 140 1 E
Kajana = Kajaani, *Finland* 8 D22 64 17N 27 46 E
Kajang, *Malaysia* 39 L3 2 59N 101 48 E
Kajiado, *Kenya* 54 C4 1 53S 36 48 E
Kajiado □, *Kenya* 54 C4 2 0S 36 30 E
Kajo Kaji, *Sudan* 51 H11 3 58N 31 40 E
Kaka, *Sudan* 51 F11 10 38N 32 10 E
Kakabeka Falls, *Canada* 70 C2 48 24N 89 37W
Kakamas, *S. Africa* 56 D3 28 45S 20 33 E
Kakamega, *Kenya* 54 B3 0 20N 34 46 E
Kakamega □, *Kenya* 54 B3 0 20N 34 46 E
Kakanui Mts., *N.Z.* 59 L3 45 10S 170 30 E
Kake, *Japan* 31 G6 34 36N 132 19 E
Kakegawa, *Japan* 31 G9 34 45N 138 1 E
Kakeroma-Jima, *Japan* 31 K4 28 8N 129 14 E
Kakhovka, *Ukraine* 25 E5 46 45N 33 30 E
Kakhovske Vdskh., *Ukraine* 25 E5 47 5N 34 0 E
Kakinada, *India* 41 L13 16 57N 82 11 E
Kakisa →, *Canada* 72 A5 61 3N 118 10W
Kakisa L., *Canada* 72 A5 60 56N 117 43W
Kakogawa, *Japan* 31 G7 34 46N 134 51 E
Kakwa →, *Canada* 72 C5 54 37N 118 28W
Kāl Gūsheh, *Iran* 45 D8 30 59N 58 12 E
Kal Safīd, *Iran* 44 C5 34 52N 47 23 E
Kalabagh, *Pakistan* 42 C4 33 0N 71 28 E
Kalabahi, *Indonesia* 37 F6 8 13S 124 31 E
Kalabo, *Zambia* 53 G4 14 58S 22 40 E
Kalach, *Russia* 25 D7 50 22N 41 0 E
Kaladan →, *Burma* 41 J18 20 20N 93 5 E
Kaladar, *Canada* 78 B7 44 37N 77 5W
Kalahari, *Africa* 56 C3 24 0S 21 30 E
Kalahari Gemsbok Nat. Park, *S. Africa* 56 D3 25 30S 20 30 E
Kalajoki, *Finland* 8 D20 64 12N 24 10 E
Kālak, *Iran* 45 E8 25 29N 59 22 E
Kalakamati, *Botswana* 57 C4 20 40S 27 25 E
Kalakan, *Russia* 27 D12 55 15N 116 45 E
Kalakh, *Syria* 44 C3 34 55N 36 10 E
K'alak'unlun Shank'ou, *Pakistan* 43 B7 35 33N 77 46 E
Kalam, *Pakistan* 43 B5 35 34N 72 30 E
Kalama, *U.S.A.* 84 E4 46 1N 122 51W
Kalama, *Zaïre* 54 C2 2 52S 28 35 E
Kalámai, *Greece* 21 F10 37 3N 22 10 E
Kalamata = Kalámai, *Greece* 21 F10 37 3N 22 10 E
Kalamazoo, *U.S.A.* 76 D3 42 17N 85 35W
Kalamazoo →, *U.S.A.* 76 D2 42 40N 86 10W
Kalambo Falls, *Tanzania* 55 D3 8 37S 31 35 E
Kalannie, *Australia* 61 F2 30 22S 117 5 E
Kalāntarī, *Iran* 45 C7 32 10N 54 8 E
Kalao, *Indonesia* 37 F6 7 21S 121 0 E
Kalaotoa, *Indonesia* 37 F6 7 20S 121 50 E
Kalasin, *Thailand* 38 D4 16 26N 103 30 E
Kalat, *Pakistan* 40 E5 29 8N 66 31 E
Kalāteh, *Iran* 45 B7 36 33N 55 41 E
Kalāteh-ye-Ganj, *Iran* 45 E8 27 31N 57 55 E
Kalbarri, *Australia* 61 E1 27 40S 114 10 E
Kalce, *Slovenia* 16 F8 45 54N 14 13 E
Kale, *Turkey* 21 F13 37 27N 28 49 E
Kalegauk Kyun, *Burma* 41 M20 15 33N 97 35 E
Kalehe, *Zaïre* 54 C2 2 6S 28 50 E
Kalema, *Tanzania* 54 C3 1 12S 31 55 E
Kalemie, *Zaïre* 54 D2 5 55S 29 9 E
Kalewa, *Burma* 41 H19 23 10N 94 15 E
Kalgan = Zhangjiakou, *China* 34 D8 40 48N 114 55 E
Kalgoorlie-Boulder, *Australia* 61 F3 30 40S 121 22 E
Kaliakra, Nos, *Bulgaria* 21 C13 43 21N 28 30 E
Kalianda, *Indonesia* 36 F3 5 50S 105 45 E
Kalibo, *Phil.* 37 B6 11 43N 122 22 E
Kaliganj, *Bangla.* 43 H13 22 25N 89 8 E
Kalima, *Zaïre* 54 C2 2 33S 26 32 E
Kalimantan, *Indonesia* 36 E4 0 0 114 0 E
Kalimantan Barat □, *Indonesia* 36 E4 0 0 110 30 E
Kalimantan Selatan □, *Indonesia* 36 E5 2 30S 115 30 E
Kalimantan Tengah □, *Indonesia* 36 E4 2 0S 113 30 E
Kalimantan Timur □, *Indonesia* 36 D5 1 30N 116 30 E
Kálimnos, *Greece* 21 F12 37 0N 27 0 E
Kalimpong, *India* 43 F13 27 4N 88 35 E
Kalinin = Tver, *Russia* 24 C6 56 55N 35 55 E
Kaliningrad, *Kaliningd., Russia* 9 J19 54 42N 20 32 E
Kaliningrad, *Moskva, Russia* 24 C6 55 58N 37 54 E
Kalinkavichy, *Belarus* 17 B15 52 12N 29 20 E
Kalinkovichi = Kalinkavichy, *Belarus* 17 B15 52 12N 29 20 E
Kaliro, *Uganda* 54 B3 0 56N 33 30 E
Kalispell, *U.S.A.* 82 B6 48 12N 114 19W
Kalisz, *Poland* 17 C10 51 45N 18 8 E
Kaliua, *Tanzania* 54 D3 5 5S 31 48 E
Kalix, *Sweden* 8 D20 65 53N 23 12 E
Kalix →, *Sweden* 8 D20 65 50N 23 11 E
Kalka, *India* 42 D7 30 46N 76 57 E
Kalkaska, *U.S.A.* 76 C3 44 44N 85 11W
Kalkfeld, *Namibia* 56 C2 20 57S 16 14 E
Kalkfontein, *Botswana* 56 C3 22 4S 20 57 E
Kalkrand, *Namibia* 56 C2 24 1S 17 35 E
Kallavesi, *Finland* 8 E22 62 58N 27 30 E
Kallsjön, *Sweden* 8 E15 63 38N 13 0 E
Kalmar, *Sweden* 9 H17 56 40N 16 20 E
Kalmyk Republic = Kalmykia □, *Russia* 25 E8 46 5N 46 1 E
Kalmykia □, *Russia* 25 E8 46 5N 46 1 E
Kalmykovo, *Kazakstan* 25 E9 49 0N 51 47 E
Kalna, *India* 43 H13 23 13N 88 25 E
Kalocsa, *Hungary* 17 E10 46 32N 19 0 E
Kalokhorio, *Cyprus* 23 E12 34 51N 33 2 E
Kaloko, *Zaïre* 54 D2 6 47S 25 48 E
Kalol, *Gujarat, India* 42 H5 22 37N 73 31 E
Kalol, *Gujarat, India* 42 H5 23 15N 72 33 E
Kalomo, *Zambia* 55 F2 17 0S 26 30 E
Kalpi, *India* 43 F8 26 8N 79 47 E
Kalu, *Pakistan* 42 G2 25 5N 67 39 E
Kaluga, *Russia* 24 D6 54 35N 36 10 E
Kalulushi, *Zambia* 55 E2 12 50S 28 3 E
Kalundborg, *Denmark* 9 J14 55 41N 11 5 E
Kalush, *Ukraine* 17 D13 49 3N 24 23 E
Kalutara, *Sri Lanka* 40 R11 6 35N 80 0 E
Kalya, *Russia* 24 B10 60 15N 59 59 E
Kama, *Zaïre* 54 C2 3 30S 27 5 E
Kama →, *Russia* 24 C9 55 45N 52 0 E
Kamachumu, *Tanzania* 54 C3 1 37S 31 37 E
Kamaishi, *Japan* 30 E10 39 16N 141 53 E
Kamalia, *Pakistan* 42 D5 30 44N 72 42 E
Kamapanda, *Zambia* 55 E1 12 5S 24 0 E
Kamaran, *Yemen* 46 D3 15 21N 42 35 E
Kamativi, *Zimbabwe* 55 F2 18 15S 27 27 E
Kambalda, *Australia* 61 F3 31 10S 121 37 E
Kambar, *Pakistan* 42 F3 27 37N 68 1 E
Kambarka, *Russia* 24 C9 56 15N 54 11 E
Kambolé, *Zambia* 55 D3 8 47S 30 48 E
Kambos, *Cyprus* 23 D11 35 2N 32 44 E
Kambove, *Zaïre* 55 E2 10 51S 26 33 E
Kamchatka, P-ov., *Russia* 27 D16 57 0N 160 0 E
Kamchatka Pen. = Kamchatka, P-ov., *Russia* 27 D16 57 0N 160 0 E
Kamchiya →, *Bulgaria* 21 C12 43 4N 27 44 E
Kamen, *Russia* 26 D9 53 50N 81 30 E
Kamen-Rybolov, *Russia* 30 B6 44 46N 132 2 E
Kamenjak, Rt., *Croatia* 16 F7 44 47N 13 55 E
Kamenka, *Russia* 24 A7 65 58N 44 0 E
Kamenka Bugskaya = Kamyanka-Buzka, *Ukraine* 17 C13 50 8N 24 16 E
Kamensk Uralskiy, *Russia* 26 D7 56 25N 62 2 E
Kamenskoye, *Russia* 27 C17 62 45N 165 30 E
Kameoka, *Japan* 31 G7 35 0N 135 35 E
Kamiah, *U.S.A.* 82 C5 46 14N 116 2W
Kamieskroon, *S. Africa* 56 E2 30 9S 17 56 E
Kamilukuak, L., *Canada* 73 A8 62 22N 101 40W
Kamin-Kashyrskyy, *Ukraine* 17 C13 51 39N 24 56 E
Kamina, *Zaïre* 55 D1 8 45S 25 0 E
Kaminak L., *Canada* 73 A9 62 10N 95 0W
Kaminoyama, *Japan* 30 E10 38 9N 140 17 E
Kamiros, *Greece* 23 C9 36 20N 27 56 E
Kamituga, *Zaïre* 54 C2 3 2S 28 10 E
Kamloops, *Canada* 72 C4 50 40N 120 20W
Kamo, *Japan* 30 F9 37 39N 139 3 E
Kamoke, *Pakistan* 42 C6 32 4N 74 4 E
Kampala, *Uganda* 54 B3 0 20N 32 30 E
Kampar, *Malaysia* 39 K3 4 18N 101 9 E
Kampar →, *Indonesia* 36 D2 0 30N 103 8 E
Kampen, *Neths.* 15 B5 52 33N 5 53 E
Kamphaeng Phet, *Thailand* 38 D2 16 28N 99 30 E
Kampolombo, L., *Zambia* 55 E2 11 37S 29 42 E
Kampong To, *Thailand* 39 J3 6 3N 101 13 E
Kampot, *Cambodia* 39 G5 10 36N 104 10 E
Kampuchea = Cambodia ■, *Asia* 38 F5 12 15N 105 0 E
Kampung →, *Indonesia* 37 F9 5 44S 138 24 E
Kampung Air Putih, *Malaysia* 39 K4 4 15N 103 10 E
Kampung Jerangau, *Malaysia* 39 K4 4 50N 103 10 E
Kampung Raja, *Malaysia* 39 K4 5 45N 102 35 E
Kampungbaru = Tolitoli, *Indonesia* 37 D6 1 5N 120 50 E
Kamrau, Teluk, *Indonesia* 37 E8 3 30S 133 36 E
Kamsack, *Canada* 73 C8 51 34N 101 54W
Kamskoye Vdkhr., *Russia* 24 C10 58 41N 56 7 E
Kamuchawie L., *Canada* 73 B8 56 18N 101 59W
Kamui-Misaki, *Japan* 30 C10 43 20N 140 21 E
Kamyanets-Podilskyy, *Ukraine* 17 D14 48 45N 26 40 E
Kamyanka-Buzka, *Ukraine* 17 C13 50 8N 24 16 E
Kāmyārān, *Iran* 44 C5 34 47N 46 56 E
Kamyshin, *Russia* 25 D8 50 10N 45 24 E
Kanaaupscow, *Canada* 70 B4 54 2N 76 30W
Kanab, *U.S.A.* 83 H7 37 3N 112 32W
Kanab →, *U.S.A.* 83 H7 36 24N 112 38W
Kanagi, *Japan* 30 D10 40 54N 140 27 E
Kanairiktok →, *Canada* 71 A7 55 2N 60 18W
Kananga, *Zaïre* 52 F4 5 55S 22 18 E
Kanarraville, *U.S.A.* 83 H7 37 32N 113 11W
Kanash, *Russia* 24 C8 55 30N 47 32 E
Kanaskat, *U.S.A.* 84 C5 47 19N 121 54W
Kanastraíon, Ákra = Palioúrion, Ákra, *Greece* 21 E10 39 57N 23 45 E
Kanawha →, *U.S.A.* 76 F4 38 50N 82 9W
Kanazawa, *Japan* 31 F8 36 30N 136 38 E
Kanchanaburi, *Thailand* 38 E2 14 2N 99 31 E
Kanchenjunga, *Nepal* 43 F13 27 50N 88 10 E
Kanchipuram, *India* 40 N11 12 52N 79 45 E
Kanda Kanda, *Zaïre* 52 F4 6 52S 23 48 E
Kandahar = Qandahār, *Afghan.* 40 D4 31 32N 65 30 E
Kandalaksha, *Russia* 24 A5 67 9N 32 30 E
Kandalakshkiy Zaliv, *Russia* 24 A5 66 0N 35 0 E
Kandalu, *Afghan.* 40 E3 29 55N 63 20 E
Kandangan, *Indonesia* 36 E5 2 50S 115 20 E
Kandanos, *Greece* 23 D5 35 19N 23 44 E
Kandhkot, *Pakistan* 42 E3 28 16N 69 8 E
Kandhla, *India* 42 E7 29 18N 77 19 E
Kandi, *Benin* 50 F5 11 7N 2 55 E
Kandi, *India* 43 H13 23 58N 88 5 E
Kandla, *India* 42 H4 23 0N 70 10 E
Kandos, *Australia* 63 E4 32 45S 149 58 E
Kandy, *Sri Lanka* 40 R12 7 18N 80 43 E
Kane, *U.S.A.* 78 E6 41 40N 78 49W
Kane Basin, *Greenland* 4 B4 79 1N 70 0W
Kangān, *Fārs, Iran* 45 E7 27 50N 52 3 E
Kangān, *Hormozgān, Iran* 45 E8 25 48N 57 28 E
Kangar, *Malaysia* 39 J3 6 27N 100 12 E
Kangaroo I., *Australia* 63 F2 35 45S 137 0 E
Kangasala, *Finland* 9 F21 61 28N 24 4 E
Kangāvar, *Iran* 45 C6 34 40N 48 0 E
Kangdong, *N. Korea* 35 E14 39 9N 126 5 E
Kangean, Kepulauan, *Indonesia* 36 F5 6 55S 115 23 E
Kangean Is. = Kangean, Kepulauan, *Indonesia* 36 F5 6 55S 115 23 E
Kanggye, *N. Korea* 35 D14 41 0N 126 35 E
Kanggyŏng, *S. Korea* 35 F14 36 10N 127 0 E
Kanghwa, *S. Korea* 35 F14 37 45N 126 30 E
Kangiqsualujjuaq, *Canada* 69 C13 58 30N 65 59W
Kangiqsujuaq, *Canada* 69 B12 61 30N 72 0W
Kangirsuk, *Canada* 69 B13 60 0N 70 0W
Kangnŭng, *S. Korea* 35 F15 37 45N 128 54 E
Kango, *Gabon* 52 D2 0 11N 10 5 E
Kangping, *China* 35 C12 42 43N 123 18 E
Kangto, *India* 41 F18 27 50N 92 35 E
Kaniama, *Zaïre* 54 D1 7 30S 24 12 E
Kaniapiskau →, *Canada* 71 A6 56 40N 69 30W
Kaniapiskau L., *Canada* 71 B6 54 10N 69 55W
Kanin, Poluostrov, *Russia* 24 A8 68 0N 45 0 E
Kanin Nos, Mys, *Russia* 24 A7 68 39N 43 32 E
Kanin Pen. = Kanin, Poluostrov, *Russia* 24 A8 68 0N 45 0 E
Kaniva, *Australia* 63 F3 36 22S 141 18 E
Kanjut Sar, *Pakistan* 43 A6 36 7N 75 25 E
Kankaanpää, *Finland* 9 F20 61 44N 22 50 E
Kankakee, *U.S.A.* 76 E2 41 7N 87 52W
Kankakee →, *U.S.A.* 76 E1 41 23N 88 15W
Kankan, *Guinea* 50 F3 10 23N 9 15W

Kenner

Kankendy = Xankändi, Azerbaijan 25 G8 39 52N 46 49 E
Kanker, India 41 J12 20 10N 81 40 E
Kankunskiy, Russia 27 D13 57 37N 126 8 E
Kannapolis, U.S.A. 77 H5 35 30N 80 37W
Kannauj, India 43 F8 27 3N 79 56 E
Kannod, India 40 H10 22 45N 76 40 E
Kano, Nigeria 50 F6 12 2N 8 30 E
Kan'onji, Japan 31 G6 34 7N 133 39 E
Kanowit, Malaysia 36 D4 2 14N 112 20 E
Kanowna, Australia 61 F3 30 32S 121 31 E
Kanoya, Japan 31 J5 31 25N 130 50 E
Kanpetlet, Burma 41 J18 21 10N 93 59 E
Kanpur, India 43 F9 26 28N 80 20 E
Kansas □, U.S.A. 80 F6 38 30N 99 0W
Kansas →, U.S.A. 80 F7 39 7N 94 37W
Kansas City, Kans., U.S.A. 80 F7 39 7N 94 38W
Kansas City, Mo., U.S.A. 80 F7 39 6N 94 35W
Kansenia, Zaïre 55 E2 10 20S 26 0 E
Kansk, Russia 27 D10 56 20N 95 37 E
Kansŏng, S. Korea 35 E15 38 24N 128 30 E
Kansu = Gansu □, China 34 G3 36 0N 104 0 E
Kantang, Thailand 39 J2 7 25N 99 31 E
Kantharalak, Thailand 38 E5 14 39N 104 39 E
Kantō □, Japan 31 F9 36 15N 139 30 E
Kantō-Sanchi, Japan 31 G9 35 59N 138 50 E
Kanturk, Ireland 13 D3 52 11N 8 54W
Kanuma, Japan 31 F9 36 34N 139 42 E
Kanus, Namibia 56 D2 27 50S 18 39 E
Kanye, Botswana 56 C4 24 55S 25 28 E
Kanzenze, Zaïre 55 E2 10 30S 25 12 E
Kanzi, Ras, Tanzania 54 D4 7 1S 39 33 E
Kaohsiung, Taiwan 33 D7 22 35N 120 16 E
Kaokoveld, Namibia 56 B1 19 15S 14 30 E
Kaolack, Senegal 50 F1 14 5N 16 8W
Kaoshan, China 35 B13 44 38N 124 50 E
Kapadvanj, India 42 H5 23 5N 73 0 E
Kapan, Armenia 25 G8 39 18N 46 27 E
Kapanga, Zaïre 52 F4 8 30S 22 40 E
Kapchagai = Qapshaghay, Kazakstan 26 E8 43 51N 77 14 E
Kapema, Zaïre 55 E2 10 45S 28 22 E
Kapfenberg, Austria 16 E8 47 26N 15 18 E
Kapiri Mposhi, Zambia 55 E2 13 59S 28 43 E
Kapiskau →, Canada 70 B3 52 47N 81 55W
Kapit, Malaysia 36 D4 2 0N 112 55 E
Kapiti I., N.Z. 59 J5 40 50S 174 56 E
Kapoe, Thailand 39 H2 9 34N 98 32 E
Kapoeta, Sudan 51 H11 4 50N 33 35 E
Kaposvár, Hungary 17 E9 46 25N 17 47 E
Kapowsin, U.S.A. 84 D4 46 59N 122 13W
Kapps, Namibia 56 C2 22 32S 17 18 E
Kapsan, N. Korea 35 D15 41 4N 128 19 E
Kapsukas = Marijampolė, Lithuania 9 J20 54 33N 23 19 E
Kapuas →, Indonesia 36 E3 0 25S 109 20 E
Kapuas Hulu, Pegunungan, Malaysia 36 D4 1 30N 113 30 E
Kapuas Hulu Ra. = Kapuas Hulu, Pegunungan, Malaysia 36 D4 1 30N 113 30 E
Kapulo, Zaïre 55 D2 8 18S 29 15 E
Kapunda, Australia 63 E2 34 20S 138 56 E
Kapuni, N.Z. 59 H5 39 29S 174 8 E
Kapurthala, India 42 D6 31 23N 75 25 E
Kapuskasing, Canada 70 C3 49 25N 82 30W
Kapuskasing →, Canada 70 C3 49 49N 82 0W
Kaputar, Australia 63 E5 30 15S 150 10 E
Kaputir, Kenya 54 B4 2 5N 35 28 E
Kara, Russia 26 C7 69 10N 65 0 E
Kara Bogaz Gol, Zaliv = Garabogazköl Aylagy, Turkmenistan 25 F9 41 0N 53 30 E
Kara Kalpak Republic □ = Karakalpakstan □, Uzbekistan 26 E6 43 0N 58 0 E
Kara Kum, Turkmenistan 26 F6 39 30N 60 0 E
Kara Sea, Russia 26 B7 75 0N 70 0 E
Karabiğa, Turkey 21 D12 40 24N 27 18 E
Karaburun, Turkey 21 E12 38 41N 26 28 E
Karabutak = Qarabutaq, Kazakstan 26 E7 49 59N 60 14 E
Karacabey, Turkey 21 D13 40 12N 28 21 E
Karacasu, Turkey 21 F13 37 43N 28 35 E
Karachi, Pakistan 42 G2 24 53N 67 0 E
Karad, India 40 L9 17 15N 74 10 E
Karadeniz Boğazı, Turkey 21 D13 41 10N 29 10 E
Karaganda = Qaraghandy, Kazakstan 26 E8 49 50N 73 10 E
Karagayly, Kazakstan 26 E8 49 26N 76 0 E
Karaginskiy, Ostrov, Russia 27 D17 58 45N 164 0 E
Karagiye, Vpadina, Kazakstan 25 F9 43 27N 51 45 E
Karagiye Depression = Karagiye, Vpadina, Kazakstan 25 F9 43 27N 51 45 E
Karagwe □, Tanzania 54 C3 2 0S 31 0 E
Karaikal, India 40 P11 10 59N 79 50 E
Karaikkudi, India 40 P11 10 5N 78 45 E
Karaj, Iran 45 C6 35 48N 51 0 E
Karak, Malaysia 39 L4 3 25N 102 2 E
Karakalpakstan □, Uzbekistan 26 E6 43 0N 58 0 E
Karakas, Kazakstan 26 E9 48 20N 83 30 E
Karakelong, Indonesia 37 D7 4 35N 126 50 E
Karakitang, Indonesia 37 D7 3 14N 125 28 E
Karaklis = Vanadzor, Armenia 25 F7 40 48N 44 30 E
Karakoram Pass, Pakistan 43 B7 35 33N 77 50 E
Karakoram Ra., Pakistan 43 B7 35 30N 77 0 E
Karalon, Russia 27 D12 57 5N 115 50 E
Karaman, Turkey 25 G5 37 14N 33 13 E
Karamay, China 32 B3 45 30N 84 58 E
Karambu, Indonesia 36 E5 3 53S 116 6 E
Karamea Bight, N.Z. 59 J3 41 22S 171 40 E
Karamsad, India 42 H5 22 35N 72 50 E
Karand, Iran 44 C5 34 16N 46 15 E
Karanganyar, Indonesia 37 G13 7 38S 109 37 E
Karasburg, Namibia 56 D2 28 0S 18 44 E
Karasino, Russia 26 C9 66 50N 86 50 E
Karasjok, Norway 8 B21 69 27N 25 30 E
Karasuk, Russia 26 D8 53 44N 78 2 E
Karasuyama, Japan 31 F10 36 39N 140 9 E
Karatau = Qarataū, Kazakstan 26 E8 43 10N 70 28 E
Karatau, Khrebet, Kazakstan 26 E7 43 30N 69 30 E
Karauli, India 42 F7 26 30N 77 4 E
Karavostasi, Cyprus 23 D11 35 8N 32 50 E
Karawang, Indonesia 37 G12 6 30S 107 15 E
Karawanken, Europe 16 E8 46 30N 14 40 E
Karazhal, Kazakstan 26 E8 48 2N 70 49 E
Karbalā, Iraq 44 C5 32 36N 44 3 E
Karcag, Hungary 17 E11 47 19N 20 57 E
Karcha →, Pakistan 43 B7 34 45N 76 10 E
Karda, Russia 27 D11 55 0N 103 16 E
Kardhitsa, Greece 21 E9 39 23N 21 54 E
Kärdla, Estonia 9 G20 58 50N 22 40 E
Kareeberge, S. Africa 56 E3 30 59S 21 50 E
Karelia □, Russia 24 A5 65 30N 32 30 E
Karelian Republic □ = Karelia □, Russia 24 A5 65 30N 32 30 E
Kārevāndar, Iran 45 E9 27 53N 60 44 E
Kargasok, Russia 26 D9 59 3N 80 53 E
Kargat, Russia 26 D9 55 10N 80 15 E
Kargil, India 43 B7 34 32N 76 12 E
Kargopol, Russia 24 B6 61 30N 38 58 E
Karīān, Iran 45 E8 26 57N 57 14 E
Kariba, Zimbabwe 55 F2 16 28S 28 50 E
Kariba, L., Zimbabwe 55 F2 16 40S 28 25 E
Kariba Dam, Zimbabwe 55 F2 16 30S 28 35 E
Kariba Gorge, Zambia 55 F2 16 30S 28 50 E
Karibib, Namibia 56 C2 22 0S 15 56 E
Karimata, Kepulauan, Indonesia 36 E3 1 25S 109 0 E
Karimata, Selat, Indonesia 36 E3 2 0S 108 40 E
Karimata Is. = Karimata, Kepulauan, Indonesia 36 E3 1 25S 109 0 E
Karimnagar, India 40 K11 18 26N 79 10 E
Karimunjawa, Kepulauan, Indonesia 36 F4 5 50S 110 30 E
Karin, Somali Rep. 46 E4 10 50N 45 52 E
Karīt, Iran 45 C8 33 29N 56 55 E
Kariya, Japan 31 G8 34 58N 137 1 E
Karkaralinsk = Qarqaraly, Kazakstan 26 E8 49 26N 75 30 E
Karkinitska Zatoka, Ukraine 25 E5 45 56N 33 0 E
Karkinitskiy Zaliv = Karkinitska Zatoka, Ukraine 25 E5 45 56N 33 0 E
Karl-Marx-Stadt = Chemnitz, Germany 16 C7 50 51N 12 54 E
Karlovac, Croatia 16 F8 45 31N 15 36 E
Karlovo, Bulgaria 21 C11 42 38N 24 47 E
Karlovy Vary, Czech. 16 C7 50 13N 12 51 E
Karlsbad = Karlovy Vary, Czech. 16 C7 50 13N 12 51 E
Karlsborg, Sweden 9 G16 58 33N 14 33 E
Karlshamn, Sweden 9 H16 56 10N 14 51 E
Karlskoga, Sweden 9 G16 59 22N 14 33 E
Karlskrona, Sweden 9 H16 56 10N 15 35 E
Karlsruhe, Germany 16 D5 49 0N 8 23 E
Karlstad, Sweden 9 G15 59 23N 13 30 E
Karlstad, U.S.A. 80 A6 48 35N 96 31W
Karnal, India 42 E7 29 42N 77 2 E
Karnali →, Nepal 43 E9 28 45N 81 16 E
Karnaphuli Res., Bangla. 41 H18 22 40N 92 20 E
Karnataka □, India 40 N10 13 15N 77 0 E
Karnes City, U.S.A. 81 L6 28 53N 97 54W
Karnische Alpen, Europe 16 E7 46 36N 13 0 E
Kärnten □, Austria 16 E8 46 52N 13 30 E
Karoi, Zimbabwe 55 F2 16 48S 29 45 E
Karonga, Malawi 55 D3 9 57S 33 55 E
Karoonda, Australia 63 F2 35 1S 139 59 E
Karora, Sudan 51 E12 17 44N 38 15 E
Karpasia □, Cyprus 23 D13 35 32N 34 15 E
Kárpathos, Greece 21 G12 35 37N 27 10 E
Karpinsk, Russia 24 C11 59 45N 60 1 E
Karpogory, Russia 24 B7 64 0N 44 27 E
Karpuz Burnu = Apostolos Andreas, C., Cyprus 23 D13 35 42N 34 35 E
Kars, Turkey 25 F7 40 40N 43 5 E
Karsakpay, Kazakstan 26 E7 47 55N 66 40 E
Karshi = Qarshi, Uzbekistan 26 F7 38 53N 65 48 E
Karsiyang, India 43 F13 26 56N 88 18 E
Karsun, Russia 24 D8 54 14N 46 57 E
Kartaly, Russia 26 D7 53 3N 60 40 E
Kartapur, India 42 D6 31 27N 75 32 E
Karthaus, U.S.A. 78 E6 41 8N 78 9W
Karufa, Indonesia 37 E8 3 50S 133 20 E
Karumba, Australia 62 B3 17 31S 140 50 E
Karumo, Tanzania 54 C3 2 25S 32 50 E
Karumwa, Tanzania 54 C3 3 12S 32 38 E
Karungu, Kenya 54 C3 0 50S 34 10 E
Karviná, Czech. 17 D10 49 53N 18 25 E
Karwar, India 40 M9 14 55N 74 13 E
Karwi, India 43 G9 25 12N 80 57 E
Kasache, Malawi 55 E3 13 25S 34 20 E
Kasai →, Zaïre 52 E3 3 30S 16 10 E
Kasai Oriental □, Zaïre 54 C1 5 0S 24 30 E
Kasaji, Zaïre 55 E1 10 25S 23 27 E
Kasama, Zambia 55 E3 10 16S 31 9 E
Kasan-dong, N. Korea 35 D14 41 18N 126 55 E
Kasane, Namibia 56 B3 17 34S 24 50 E
Kasanga, Tanzania 55 D3 8 30S 31 10 E
Kasangulu, Zaïre 52 E3 4 33S 15 15 E
Kasaragod, India 40 N9 12 30N 74 58 E
Kasba L., Canada 73 A8 60 20N 102 10W
Kāseh Garān, Iran 44 C5 34 5N 46 2 E
Kasempa, Zambia 55 E2 13 30S 25 44 E
Kasenga, Zaïre 55 E2 10 20S 28 45 E
Kasese, Uganda 54 B3 0 13N 30 3 E
Kasewa, Zambia 55 E2 14 28S 28 53 E
Kasganj, India 43 F8 27 48N 78 42 E
Kashabowie, Canada 70 C1 48 40N 90 26W
Kāshān, Iran 45 C6 34 5N 51 30 E
Kashi, China 32 C2 39 30N 76 2 E
Kashimbo, Zaïre 55 E2 11 12S 26 19 E
Kashipur, India 43 E8 29 15N 79 0 E
Kashiwazaki, Japan 31 F9 37 22N 138 33 E
Kashk-e Kohneh, Afghan. 40 B3 34 55N 62 30 E
Kāshmar, Iran 45 C8 35 16N 58 26 E
Kashmir, Asia 43 C7 34 0N 76 0 E
Kashmor, Pakistan 42 E3 28 28N 69 32 E
Kashun Noerh = Gaxun Nur, China 32 B5 42 22N 100 30 E
Kasimov, Russia 24 D7 54 55N 41 20 E
Kasinge, Zaïre 54 D2 6 15S 26 58 E
Kasiruta, Indonesia 37 E7 0 25S 127 12 E
Kaskaskia →, U.S.A. 80 G10 37 58N 89 57W
Kaskattama →, Canada 73 B10 57 3N 90 4W
Kaskinen, Finland 9 E19 62 22N 21 15 E
Kaslo, Canada 72 D5 49 55N 116 55W
Kasmere L., Canada 73 B8 59 34N 101 10W
Kasongo, Zaïre 54 C2 4 30S 26 33 E
Kasongo Lunda, Zaïre 52 F3 6 35S 16 49 E
Kásos, Greece 21 G12 35 20N 26 55 E
Kassalâ, Sudan 51 E12 15 30N 36 0 E
Kassel, Germany 16 C5 51 18N 9 26 E
Kassiópi, Greece 23 A3 39 48N 19 53 E
Kassue, Indonesia 37 F9 6 58S 139 21 E
Kastamonu, Turkey 25 F5 41 25N 33 43 E
Kastélli, Greece 23 D5 35 29N 23 38 E
Kastéllion, Greece 23 D7 35 12N 25 20 E
Kastoria, Greece 21 D9 40 30N 21 19 E
Kasulu, Tanzania 54 C3 4 37S 30 5 E
Kasulu □, Tanzania 54 C3 4 37S 30 5 E
Kasumi, Japan 31 G7 35 38N 134 38 E
Kasungu, Malawi 55 E3 13 0S 33 29 E
Kasur, Pakistan 42 D6 31 5N 74 25 E
Kata, Russia 27 D11 58 46N 102 40 E
Kataba, Zambia 55 F2 16 5S 25 10 E
Katako Kombe, Zaïre 54 C1 3 25S 24 20 E
Katale, Tanzania 54 C3 4 52S 31 7 E
Katamatite, Australia 63 F4 36 6S 145 41 E
Katanda, Kivu, Zaïre 54 C2 0 55S 29 21 E
Katanda, Shaba, Zaïre 54 D1 7 52S 24 13 E
Katanga = Shaba □, Zaïre 54 D2 8 0S 25 0 E
Katangi, India 40 J11 21 56N 79 50 E
Katangli, Russia 27 D15 51 42N 143 14 E
Katavi Swamp, Tanzania 54 D3 6 50S 31 10 E
Kateríni, Greece 21 D10 40 18N 22 37 E
Katha, Burma 41 G20 24 10N 96 30 E
Katherine, Australia 60 B5 14 27S 132 20 E
Kathiawar, India 42 H4 22 20N 71 0 E
Kathikas, Cyprus 23 E11 34 55N 32 25 E
Katihar, India 43 G12 25 34N 87 36 E
Katima Mulilo, Zambia 56 B3 17 28S 24 13 E
Katimbira, Malawi 55 E3 12 40S 34 0 E
Katingan = Mendawai →, Indonesia 36 E4 3 30S 113 0 E
Katiola, Ivory C. 50 G3 8 10N 5 10W
Katmandu, Nepal 43 F11 27 45N 85 20 E
Káto Arkhánai, Greece 23 D7 35 15N 25 10 E
Káto Khorió, Greece 23 D7 35 3N 25 47 E
Kato Pyrgos, Cyprus 23 D11 35 11N 32 41 E
Katompe, Zaïre 54 D2 6 2S 26 23 E
Katonga →, Uganda 54 B3 0 34N 31 50 E
Katoomba, Australia 63 E5 33 41S 150 19 E
Katowice, Poland 17 C10 50 17N 19 5 E
Katrine, L., U.K. 12 E4 56 15N 4 30W
Katrineholm, Sweden 9 G17 59 9N 16 12 E
Katsepe, Madag. 57 B8 15 45S 46 15 E
Katsina, Nigeria 50 F6 13 0N 7 32 E
Katsumoto, Japan 31 H4 33 51N 129 42 E
Katsuura, Japan 31 G10 35 10N 140 20 E
Katsuyama, Japan 31 F8 36 3N 136 30 E
Kattaviá, Greece 23 D9 35 57N 27 46 E
Kattegat, Denmark 9 H14 57 0N 11 20 E
Katumba, Zaïre 54 D2 7 40S 25 17 E
Katungu, Kenya 54 C5 2 55S 40 3 E
Katwa, India 43 H13 23 30N 88 5 E
Katwijk-aan-Zee, Neths. 15 B4 52 12N 4 24 E
Kauai, U.S.A. 74 H15 22 3N 159 30W
Kauai Channel, U.S.A. 74 H15 21 45N 158 50W
Kaufman, U.S.A. 81 J6 32 35N 96 19W
Kauhajoki, Finland 9 E20 62 25N 22 10 E
Kaukauna, U.S.A. 76 C1 44 17N 88 17W
Kaukauveld, Namibia 56 C3 20 0S 20 15 E
Kaunas, Lithuania 9 J20 54 54N 23 54 E
Kaura Namoda, Nigeria 50 F6 12 37N 6 33 E
Kautokeino, Norway 8 B20 69 0N 23 4 E
Kavacha, Russia 27 C17 60 16N 169 51 E
Kavalerovo, Russia 30 B7 44 15N 135 4 E
Kavali, India 40 M12 14 55N 80 1 E
Kavála, Greece 21 D11 40 57N 24 28 E
Kavār, Iran 45 D7 29 11N 52 44 E
Kavos, Greece 23 B4 39 23N 20 3 E
Kaw, Fr. Guiana 93 C8 4 30N 52 15W
Kawagama L., Canada 78 A6 45 18N 78 45W
Kawagoe, Japan 31 G9 35 55N 139 29 E
Kawaguchi, Japan 31 G9 35 52N 139 45 E
Kawaihae, U.S.A. 74 H17 20 3N 155 50W
Kawambwa, Zambia 55 D2 9 48S 29 3 E
Kawanoe, Japan 31 G6 34 1N 133 34 E
Kawardha, India 43 J9 22 0N 81 17 E
Kawasaki, Japan 31 G9 35 35N 139 42 E
Kawene, Canada 70 C1 48 45N 91 15W
Kawerau, N.Z. 59 H6 38 7S 176 42 E
Kawhia Harbour, N.Z. 59 H5 38 5S 174 51 E
Kawio, Kepulauan, Indonesia 37 D7 4 30N 125 30 E
Kawnro, Burma 41 H21 22 48N 99 8 E
Kawthoolei = Kawthule □, Burma 41 L20 18 0N 97 30 E
Kawthule □, Burma 41 L20 18 0N 97 30 E
Kaya, Burkina Faso 50 F4 13 4N 1 10W
Kayah □, Burma 41 K20 19 15N 97 15 E
Kayan →, Indonesia 36 D5 2 55N 117 35 E
Kaycee, U.S.A. 82 E10 43 43N 106 38W
Kayeli, Indonesia 37 E7 3 20S 127 10 E
Kayenta, U.S.A. 83 H8 36 44N 110 15W
Kayes, Mali 50 F2 14 25N 11 30W
Kayoa, Indonesia 37 D7 0 1N 127 28 E
Kayomba, Zambia 55 E1 13 11S 24 2 E
Kayrunnera, Australia 63 E3 30 40S 142 30 E
Kayseri, Turkey 25 G6 38 45N 35 30 E
Kaysville, U.S.A. 82 F8 41 2N 111 56W
Kayuagung, Indonesia 36 E2 3 24S 104 50 E
Kazachye, Russia 27 B14 70 52N 135 58 E
Kazakstan ■, Asia 26 E7 50 0N 70 0 E
Kazan, Russia 24 C8 55 50N 49 10 E
Kazan-Rettō, Pac. Oc. 64 E6 25 0N 141 0 E
Kazanlŭk, Bulgaria 21 C11 42 38N 25 20 E
Kazatin = Kozyatyn, Ukraine 17 D15 49 45N 28 50 E
Kāzerūn, Iran 45 D6 29 38N 51 40 E
Kazumba, Zaïre 52 F4 6 25S 22 5 E
Kazuno, Japan 30 D10 40 10N 140 45 E
Kazym →, Russia 26 C7 63 54N 65 50 E
Ké-Macina, Mali 50 F3 13 58N 5 22W
Kéa, Greece 21 F11 37 35N 24 22 E
Keams Canyon, U.S.A. 83 J8 35 49N 110 12W
Kearney, U.S.A. 80 E5 40 42N 99 5W
Keban, Turkey 25 G6 38 50N 38 50 E
Kebnekaise, Sweden 8 C18 67 53N 18 33 E
Kebri Dehar, Ethiopia 46 F3 6 45N 44 17 E
Kebumen, Indonesia 37 G13 7 42S 109 40 E
Kechika →, Canada 72 B3 59 41N 127 12W
Kecskemét, Hungary 17 E10 46 57N 19 42 E
Kedgwick, Canada 71 C6 47 40N 67 20W
Kédhros Óros, Greece 23 D6 35 11N 24 37 E
Kedia Hill, Botswana 56 C3 21 28S 24 37 E
Kediniai, Lithuania 9 J21 55 15N 24 2 E
Kediri, Indonesia 37 G15 7 51S 112 1 E
Kédougou, Senegal 50 F2 12 35N 12 10W
Keeler, U.S.A. 84 J9 36 29N 117 52W
Keeley L., Canada 73 C7 54 54N 108 8W
Keeling Is. = Cocos Is., Ind. Oc. 64 J1 12 10S 96 55 E
Keene, Calif., U.S.A. 85 K8 35 13N 118 33W
Keene, N.H., U.S.A. 79 D12 42 56N 72 17W
Keeper Hill, Ireland 13 D3 52 45N 8 16W
Keer-Weer, C., Australia 62 A3 14 0S 141 32 E
Keeseville, U.S.A. 79 B11 44 29N 73 30W
Keetmanshoop, Namibia 56 D2 26 35S 18 8 E
Keewatin, U.S.A. 80 B8 47 24N 93 5W
Keewatin □, Canada 73 A9 63 20N 95 0W
Keewatin →, Canada 73 B8 56 29N 100 46W
Kefallinia, Greece 21 E9 38 20N 20 30 E
Kefamenanu, Indonesia 37 F6 9 28S 124 29 E
Keffi, Nigeria 50 G6 8 55N 7 43 E
Keflavík, Iceland 8 D2 64 2N 22 35W
Keg River, Canada 72 B5 57 54N 117 55W
Kegaska, Canada 71 B7 50 9N 61 18W
Keighley, U.K. 10 D6 53 52N 1 54W
Keila, Estonia 9 G21 59 18N 24 25 E
Keimoes, S. Africa 56 D3 28 41S 20 59 E
Keitele, Finland 8 E22 63 10N 26 20 E
Keith, Australia 63 F3 36 6S 140 20 E
Keith, U.K. 12 D6 57 32N 2 57W
Keith Arm, Canada 68 B7 64 20N 122 15W
Kejser Franz Joseph Fjord = Kong Franz Joseph Fd., Greenland 4 B6 73 30N 24 30W
Kekri, India 42 G6 26 0N 75 10 E
Kël, Russia 27 C13 69 30N 124 10 E
Kelan, China 34 E6 38 43N 111 31 E
Kelang, Malaysia 39 L3 3 2N 101 26 E
Kelantan →, Malaysia 39 J4 6 13N 102 14 E
Kelibia, Tunisia 51 A7 36 50N 11 3 E
Kellé, Congo 52 E2 0 8S 14 38 E
Keller, U.S.A. 82 B4 48 5N 118 41W
Kellerberrin, Australia 61 F2 31 36S 117 38 E
Kellett, C., Canada 4 B1 72 0N 126 0W
Kelleys I., U.S.A. 78 E2 41 36N 82 42W
Kellogg, U.S.A. 82 C5 47 32N 116 7W
Kells = Ceanannus Mor, Ireland 13 C5 53 44N 6 53W
Kélo, Chad 51 G8 9 10N 15 45 E
Kelokedhara, Cyprus 23 E11 34 48N 32 39 E
Kelowna, Canada 72 D5 49 50N 119 25W
Kelsey Bay, Canada 72 C3 50 25N 126 0W
Kelseyville, U.S.A. 84 G4 38 59N 122 50W
Kelso, N.Z. 59 L2 45 54S 169 15 E
Kelso, U.K. 12 F6 55 36N 2 26W
Kelso, U.S.A. 84 D4 46 9N 122 54W
Keluang, Malaysia 39 L4 2 3N 103 18 E
Kelvington, Canada 73 C8 52 10N 103 30W
Kem, Russia 24 B5 65 0N 34 38 E
Kem →, Russia 24 B5 64 57N 34 41 E
Kema, Indonesia 37 D7 1 22N 125 8 E
Kemano, Canada 72 C3 53 35N 128 0W
Kemasik, Malaysia 39 K4 4 25N 103 27 E
Kemerovo, Russia 26 D9 55 20N 86 5 E
Kemi, Finland 8 D21 65 44N 24 34 E
Kemi älv = Kemijoki →, Finland 8 D21 65 47N 24 32 E
Kemijärvi, Finland 8 C22 66 43N 27 22 E
Kemijoki →, Finland 8 D21 65 47N 24 32 E
Kemmerer, U.S.A. 82 F8 41 48N 110 32W
Kemmuna = Comino, Malta 23 C1 36 2N 14 20 E
Kemp, L., U.S.A. 81 J5 33 46N 99 9W
Kemp Land, Antarctica 5 C5 69 0S 55 0 E
Kempsey, Australia 63 E5 31 1S 152 50 E
Kempt, L., Canada 70 C5 47 25N 74 22W
Kempten, Germany 16 E6 47 45N 10 17 E
Kemptville, Canada 70 C4 45 0N 75 38W
Kendal, Indonesia 36 F4 6 56S 110 14 E
Kendal, U.K. 10 C5 54 20N 2 44W
Kendall, Australia 63 E5 31 35S 152 44 E
Kendall →, Australia 62 A3 14 4S 141 35 E
Kendallville, U.S.A. 76 E3 41 27N 85 16W
Kendari, Indonesia 37 E6 3 50S 122 30 E
Kendawangan, Indonesia 36 E4 2 32S 110 17 E
Kende, Nigeria 50 F5 11 30N 4 12 E
Kendenup, Australia 61 F2 34 30S 117 38 E
Kendrapara, India 41 J15 20 35N 86 30 E
Kendrew, S. Africa 56 E3 32 32S 24 30 E
Kendrick, U.S.A. 82 C5 46 37N 116 39W
Kene Thao, Laos 38 D3 17 44N 101 10 E
Kenedy, U.S.A. 81 L6 28 49N 97 51W
Kenema, S. Leone 50 G2 7 50N 11 14W
Keng Kok, Laos 38 D5 16 26N 105 12 E
Keng Tawng, Burma 41 J21 20 45N 98 18 E
Keng Tung, Burma 41 J21 21 0N 99 30 E
Kenge, Zaïre 52 E3 4 50S 17 4 E
Kengeja, Tanzania 54 D4 5 26S 39 45 E
Kenhardt, S. Africa 56 D3 29 19S 21 12 E
Kenitra, Morocco 50 B3 34 15N 6 40W
Kenli, China 35 F10 37 30N 118 20 E
Kenmare, Ireland 13 E2 51 53N 9 36W
Kenmare, U.S.A. 80 A3 48 41N 102 5W
Kenmare →, Ireland 13 E2 51 48N 9 51W
Kennebec, U.S.A. 80 D5 43 54N 99 52W
Kennedy, Zimbabwe 55 F2 18 52S 27 10 E
Kennedy Ra., Australia 61 D2 24 45S 115 10 E
Kennedy Taungdeik, Burma 41 H18 23 15N 93 45 E
Kenner, U.S.A. 81 L9 29 59N 90 15W

Korea, South

Kinston, U.S.A. 77 H7 35 16N 77 35W
Kintampo, Ghana 50 G4 8 5N 1 41W
Kintap, Indonesia 36 E5 3 51S 115 13 E
Kintore Ra., Australia 60 D4 23 15S 128 47 E
Kintyre, U.K. 12 F3 55 30N 5 35W
Kintyre, Mull of, U.K. 12 F3 55 17N 5 47W
Kinushseo →, Canada 70 A3 55 15N 83 45W
Kinuso, Canada 72 B5 55 20N 115 25W
Kinyangiri, Tanzania 54 C3 4 25S 34 37 E
Kinzua, U.S.A. 78 E6 41 52N 78 58W
Kinzua Dam, U.S.A. 78 E5 41 53N 79 0W
Kiosk, Canada 70 C4 46 6N 78 53W
Kiowa, Kans., U.S.A. 81 G5 37 1N 98 29W
Kiowa, Okla., U.S.A. 81 H7 34 43N 95 54W
Kipahigan L., Canada 73 B8 55 20N 101 55W
Kipanga, Tanzania 54 D4 6 15S 35 20 E
Kiparissia, Greece 21 F9 37 15N 21 40 E
Kiparissiakós Kólpos, Greece 21 F9 37 25N 21 25 E
Kipembawe, Tanzania 54 D3 7 38S 33 27 E
Kipengere Ra., Tanzania 55 D3 9 12S 34 15 E
Kipili, Tanzania 54 D3 7 28S 30 32 E
Kipini, Kenya 54 C5 2 30S 40 32 E
Kipling, Canada 73 C8 50 6N 102 38W
Kippure, Ireland 13 C5 53 11N 6 21W
Kipushi, Zaïre 55 E2 11 48S 27 12 E
Kiratpur, India 42 E8 29 32N 78 12 E
Kirensk, Russia 27 D11 57 50N 107 55 E
Kirgella Rocks, Australia 61 F3 30 5S 122 50 E
Kirghizia ■ = Kyrgyzstan ■, Asia 26 E8 42 0N 75 0 E
Kirghizstan = Kyrgyzstan ■, Asia 26 E8 42 0N 75 0 E
Kirgiziya Steppe, Eurasia 25 D10 50 0N 55 0 E
Kiri, Zaïre 52 E3 1 29S 19 0 E
Kiribati ■, Pac. Oc. 64 H10 5 0S 180 0 E
Kırıkkale, Turkey 25 G5 39 51N 33 32 E
Kirillov, Russia 24 C6 59 49N 38 24 E
Kirin = Jilin, China 35 C14 43 44N 126 30 E
Kirin = Jilin □, China 35 C13 44 0N 127 0 E
Kiritimati, Kiribati 65 G12 1 58N 157 27W
Kirkcaldy, U.K. 12 E5 56 7N 3 9W
Kirkcudbright, U.K. 12 G4 54 50N 4 2W
Kirkee, India 40 K8 18 34N 73 56 E
Kirkenes, Norway 8 B23 69 40N 30 5 E
Kirkintilloch, U.K. 12 F4 55 56N 4 8W
Kirkjubæjarklaustur, Iceland 8 E4 63 47N 18 4W
Kirkkonummi, Finland 9 F21 60 8N 24 26 E
Kirkland, U.S.A. 83 J7 34 25N 112 43W
Kirkland Lake, Canada 70 C3 48 9N 80 2W
Kırklareli, Turkey 21 D12 41 44N 27 15 E
Kirksville, U.S.A. 80 E8 40 12N 92 35W
Kirkūk, Iraq 44 C5 35 30N 44 21 E
Kirkwall, U.K. 12 C6 58 59N 2 58W
Kirkwood, S. Africa 56 E4 33 22S 25 15 E
Kirov, Russia 24 C8 58 35N 49 40 E
Kirovabad = Gäncä, Azerbaijan 25 F8 40 45N 46 20 E
Kirovakan = Vanadzor, Armenia 25 F7 40 48N 44 30 E
Kirovograd = Kirovohrad, Ukraine 25 E5 48 35N 32 20 E
Kirovohrad, Ukraine 25 E5 48 35N 32 20 E
Kirovsk = Babadayhan, Turkmenistan 26 F7 37 42N 60 23 E
Kirovsk, Russia 24 A5 67 32N 33 41 E
Kirovskiy, Kamchatka, Russia 27 D16 54 27N 155 42 E
Kirovskiy, Primorsk, Russia 30 B6 45 7N 133 30 E
Kirriemuir, U.K. 12 E6 56 41N 3 1W
Kirsanov, Russia 24 D7 52 35N 42 40 E
Kırşehir, Turkey 25 G5 39 14N 34 5 E
Kirthar Range, Pakistan 42 F2 27 0N 67 0 E
Kiruna, Sweden 8 C19 67 52N 20 15 E
Kirundu, Zaïre 54 C2 0 50S 25 35 E
Kirup, Australia 61 F2 33 40S 115 50 E
Kiryū, Japan 31 F9 36 24N 139 20 E
Kisaga, Tanzania 54 C3 4 30S 34 23 E
Kisalaya, Nic. 88 D3 14 40N 84 3W
Kisámou, Kólpos, Greece 23 D5 35 30N 23 38 E
Kisanga, Zaïre 54 B2 2 30N 26 35 E
Kisangani, Zaïre 54 B2 0 35N 25 15 E
Kisar, Indonesia 37 F7 8 5S 127 10 E
Kisaran, Indonesia 36 D1 3 0N 99 37 E
Kisarawe, Tanzania 54 D4 6 53S 39 0 E
Kisarawe □, Tanzania 54 D4 7 3S 39 0 E
Kisarazu, Japan 31 G9 35 23N 139 55 E
Kiselevsk, Russia 26 D9 54 5N 86 39 E
Kishanganga →, Pakistan 43 B5 34 18N 73 28 E
Kishanganj, India 43 F13 26 3N 88 14 E
Kishangarh, India 42 F4 27 50N 70 30 E
Kishinev = Chişinău, Moldova 17 E15 47 0N 28 50 E
Kishiwada, Japan 31 G7 34 28N 135 22 E
Kishtwar, India 43 C6 33 20N 75 48 E
Kisii, Kenya 54 C3 0 40S 34 45 E
Kisii □, Kenya 54 C3 0 40S 34 45 E
Kisiju, Tanzania 54 D4 7 23S 39 19 E
Kisizi, Uganda 54 C2 1 0S 29 58 E
Kiska I., U.S.A. 68 C1 51 59N 177 30 E
Kiskatinaw →, Canada 72 B4 56 8N 120 10W
Kiskittogisu L., Canada 73 C9 54 13N 98 20W
Kiskőrös, Hungary 17 E10 46 37N 19 20 E
Kiskunfélegyháza, Hungary 17 E10 46 42N 19 53 E
Kiskunhalas, Hungary 17 E10 46 28N 19 37 E
Kislovodsk, Russia 25 F7 43 50N 42 45 E
Kismayu = Chisimaio, Somali Rep. 49 G8 0 22S 42 32 E
Kiso-Gawa →, Japan 31 G8 35 20N 136 45 E
Kiso-Sammyaku, Japan 31 G8 35 45N 137 45 E
Kisofukushima, Japan 31 G8 35 52N 137 43 E
Kisoro, Uganda 54 C2 1 17S 29 48 E
Kissidougou, Guinea 50 G2 9 5N 10 5W
Kissimmee, U.S.A. 77 L5 28 18N 81 24W
Kissimmee →, U.S.A. 77 M5 27 9N 80 52W
Kississing L., Canada 73 B8 55 10N 101 20W
Kissónerga, Cyprus 23 E11 34 49N 32 24 E
Kisumu, Kenya 54 C3 0 3S 34 45 E
Kiswani, Tanzania 54 C4 4 5S 37 57 E
Kiswere, Tanzania 55 D4 9 27S 39 30 E
Kit Carson, U.S.A. 80 F3 38 46N 102 48W
Kita, Mali 50 F3 13 5N 9 25W
Kitab, Uzbekistan 26 F7 39 7N 66 52 E
Kitaibaraki, Japan 31 F10 36 50N 140 45 E
Kitakami, Japan 30 E10 39 20N 141 10 E
Kitakami-Gawa →, Japan 30 E10 38 25N 141 19 E
Kitakami-Sammyaku, Japan 30 E10 39 30N 141 30 E
Kitakata, Japan 30 F9 37 39N 139 52 E
Kitakyūshū, Japan 31 H5 33 50N 130 50 E
Kitale, Kenya 54 B4 1 0N 35 0 E
Kitami, Japan 30 C11 43 48N 143 54 E
Kitami-Sammyaku, Japan 30 B11 44 22N 142 43 E
Kitangiri, L., Tanzania 54 C3 4 5S 34 20 E
Kitaya, Tanzania 55 E5 10 38S 40 8 E
Kitchener, Australia 61 F3 30 55S 124 8 E
Kitchener, Canada 70 D3 43 27N 80 29W
Kitega = Gitega, Burundi 54 C2 3 26S 29 56 E
Kitengo, Zaïre 54 D1 7 26S 24 8 E
Kiteto □, Tanzania 54 C4 5 0S 37 0 E
Kitgum, Uganda 54 B3 3 17N 32 52 E
Kíthira, Greece 21 F10 36 8N 23 0 E
Kíthnos, Greece 21 F11 37 26N 24 27 E
Kiti, Cyprus 23 E12 34 50N 33 34 E
Kiti, C., Cyprus 23 E12 34 48N 33 36 E
Kitikmeot □, Canada 68 A9 70 0N 110 0W
Kitimat, Canada 72 C3 54 3N 128 38W
Kitinen →, Finland 8 C22 67 14N 27 27 E
Kitsuki, Japan 31 H5 33 25N 131 37 E
Kittakittaooloo, L., Australia 63 D2 28 3S 138 14 E
Kittanning, U.S.A. 78 F5 40 49N 79 31W
Kittatinny Mts., U.S.A. 79 E10 41 0N 75 0W
Kittery, U.S.A. 77 D10 43 5N 70 45W
Kittilä, Finland 8 C21 67 40N 24 51 E
Kitui, Kenya 54 C4 1 17S 38 0 E
Kitui □, Kenya 54 C4 1 30S 38 25 E
Kitwe, Zambia 55 E2 12 54S 28 13 E
Kivarli, India 42 G5 24 33N 72 46 E
Kivertsi, Ukraine 17 C13 50 50N 25 28 E
Kividhes, Cyprus 23 E11 34 46N 32 51 E
Kivu □, Zaïre 54 C2 3 10S 27 0 E
Kivu, L., Zaïre 54 C2 1 48S 29 0 E
Kiyev = Kyyiv, Ukraine 17 C16 50 30N 30 28 E
Kiyevskoye Vdkhr. = Kyyivske Vdskh., Ukraine 17 C16 51 0N 30 25 E
Kizel, Russia 24 C10 59 3N 57 40 E
Kiziguru, Rwanda 54 C3 1 46S 30 23 E
Kızıl Irmak →, Turkey 25 F6 41 44N 35 58 E
Kizil Jilga, India 43 B8 35 26N 78 50 E
Kizimkazi, Tanzania 54 D4 6 28S 39 30 E
Kizlyar, Russia 25 F8 43 51N 46 40 E
Kizyl-Arvat = Gyzylarbat, Turkmenistan 26 F6 39 4N 56 23 E
Kjölur, Iceland 8 D4 64 50N 19 25W
Kladno, Czech. 16 C8 50 10N 14 7 E
Klaeng, Thailand 38 F3 12 47N 101 39 E
Klagenfurt, Austria 16 E8 46 38N 14 20 E
Klaipėda, Lithuania 9 J19 55 43N 21 10 E
Klaksvík, Færoe Is. 8 E9 62 14N 6 35W
Klamath →, U.S.A. 82 F1 41 33N 124 5W
Klamath Falls, U.S.A. 82 E3 42 13N 121 46W
Klamath Mts., U.S.A. 82 F2 41 20N 123 0W
Klappan →, Canada 72 B3 58 0N 129 43W
Klarälven →, Sweden 9 G15 59 23N 13 32 E
Klaten, Indonesia 37 G14 7 43S 110 36 E
Klatovy, Czech. 16 D7 49 23N 13 18 E
Klawer, S. Africa 56 E2 31 44S 18 36 E
Klawock, U.S.A. 72 B2 55 33N 133 6W
Kleena Kleene, Canada 72 C4 52 0N 124 59W
Klein, U.S.A. 82 C9 46 24N 108 33W
Klein-Karas, Namibia 56 D2 27 33S 18 7 E
Klerksdorp, S. Africa 56 D4 26 53S 26 38 E
Kletsk = Klyetsk, Belarus 17 B14 53 5N 26 45 E
Kletskiy, Russia 26 E5 49 16N 43 11 E
Klickitat, U.S.A. 82 D3 45 49N 121 9W
Klickitat →, U.S.A. 84 E5 45 42N 121 17W
Klidhes, Cyprus 23 D13 35 42N 34 36 E
Klin, Russia 26 D4 56 20N 36 48 E
Klinaklini →, Canada 72 C3 51 21N 125 40W
Klipdale, S. Africa 56 E2 34 19S 19 57 E
Klipplaat, S. Africa 56 E3 33 1S 24 22 E
Kłodzko, Poland 17 C9 50 28N 16 38 E
Klondike, Canada 68 B6 64 0N 139 26W
Klouto, Togo 50 G5 6 57N 0 44 E
Kluane L., Canada 68 B6 61 15N 138 40W
Kluczbork, Poland 17 C10 50 58N 18 12 E
Klyetsk, Belarus 17 B14 53 5N 26 45 E
Klyuchevskaya, Gora, Russia 27 D17 55 50N 160 30 E
Knaresborough, U.K. 10 C6 54 1N 1 28W
Knee L., Man., Canada 73 B10 55 3N 94 45W
Knee L., Sask., Canada 73 B7 55 51N 107 0W
Knight Inlet, Canada 72 C3 50 45N 125 40W
Knighton, U.K. 11 E4 52 21N 3 3W
Knights Ferry, U.S.A. 84 H6 37 50N 120 40W
Knights Landing, U.S.A. 84 G5 38 48N 121 43W
Knob, C., Australia 61 F2 34 32S 119 16 E
Knockmealdown Mts., Ireland 13 D4 52 14N 7 56W
Knokke, Belgium 15 C3 51 20N 3 17 E
Knossós, Greece 23 D7 35 16N 25 10 E
Knox, U.S.A. 76 E2 41 18N 86 37W
Knox, C., Canada 72 C2 54 11N 133 5W
Knox City, U.S.A. 81 J5 33 25N 99 49W
Knox Coast, Antarctica 5 C8 66 30S 108 0 E
Knoxville, Iowa, U.S.A. 80 E8 41 19N 93 6W
Knoxville, Tenn., U.S.A. 77 H4 35 58N 83 55W
Knysna, S. Africa 56 E3 34 2S 23 2 E
Ko Kha, Thailand 38 C2 18 11N 99 24 E
Ko Tao, Thailand 39 G2 10 6N 99 48 E
Koartac = Quaqtaq, Canada 69 B13 60 55N 69 40W
Koba, Aru, Indonesia 37 F8 6 37S 134 37 E
Koba, Bangka, Indonesia 36 E3 2 26S 106 14 E
Kobarid, Slovenia 16 E7 46 15N 13 30 E
Kobayashi, Japan 31 J5 31 56N 130 59 E
Kobdo = Hovd, Mongolia 32 B4 48 2N 91 37 E
Kōbe, Japan 31 G7 34 45N 135 10 E
København, Denmark 9 J15 55 41N 12 34 E
Kōbi-Sho, Japan 31 M1 25 56N 123 41 E
Koblenz, Germany 16 C4 50 21N 7 36 E
Kobroor, Kepulauan, Indonesia 37 F8 6 10S 134 30 E
Kobryn, Belarus 17 B13 52 15N 24 22 E
Kocaeli = İzmit, Turkey 25 F4 40 45N 29 50 E
Kočani, Macedonia 21 D10 41 55N 22 25 E
Koch Bihar, India 41 F16 26 22N 89 29 E
Kochang, S. Korea 35 G14 35 41N 127 55 E
Kochas, India 43 G10 25 15N 83 56 E
Kocheya, Russia 27 D13 52 32N 120 42 E
Kōchi, Japan 31 H6 33 30N 133 35 E
Kōchi □, Japan 31 H6 33 40N 133 30 E
Kochiu = Gejiu, China 32 D5 23 20N 103 10 E
Kodiak, U.S.A. 68 C4 57 47N 152 24W
Kodiak I., U.S.A. 68 C4 57 30N 152 45W
Kodinar, India 42 J4 20 46N 70 46 E
Koes, Namibia 56 D2 26 0S 19 15 E
Koffiefontein, S. Africa 56 D4 29 30S 25 0 E
Kofiau, Indonesia 37 E7 1 11S 129 50 E
Koforidua, Ghana 50 G4 6 3N 0 17W
Kōfu, Japan 31 G9 35 40N 138 30 E
Koga, Japan 31 F9 36 11N 139 43 E
Kogaluk →, Canada 71 A7 56 12N 61 44W
Kogan, Australia 63 D5 27 2S 150 40 E
Køge, Denmark 9 J15 55 27N 12 11 E
Koh-i-Bābā, Afghan. 40 B5 34 30N 67 0 E
Koh-i-Khurd, Afghan. 42 C1 33 30N 65 59 E
Kohat, Pakistan 42 C4 33 40N 71 29 E
Kohima, India 41 G19 25 35N 94 10 E
Kohkīlūyeh va Būyer Aḥmadi □, Iran 45 D6 31 30N 50 30 E
Kohler Ra., Antarctica 5 D15 77 0S 110 0W
Kohtla-Järve, Estonia 9 G22 59 20N 27 20 E
Koillismaa, Finland 8 D23 65 44N 28 36 E
Koin-dong, N. Korea 35 D14 40 28N 126 18 E
Kojō, N. Korea 35 E14 38 58N 127 58 E
Kojonup, Australia 61 F2 33 48S 117 10 E
Kojūr, Iran 45 B6 36 23N 51 43 E
Kokand = Qŭqon, Uzbekistan 26 E8 40 30N 70 57 E
Kokanee Glacier Prov. Park, Canada 72 D5 49 47N 117 10W
Kokas, Indonesia 37 E8 2 42S 132 26 E
Kokchetav = Kökshetaū, Kazakstan 26 D7 53 20N 69 25 E
Kokemäenjoki →, Finland 9 F19 61 32N 21 44 E
Kokkola, Finland 8 E20 63 50N 23 8 E
Koko Kyunzu, Burma 41 M18 14 10N 93 25 E
Kokomo, U.S.A. 76 E2 40 29N 86 8W
Kokonau, Indonesia 37 E9 4 43S 136 26 E
Koksan, N. Korea 35 E14 38 46N 126 40 E
Kökshetaū, Kazakstan 26 D7 53 20N 69 25 E
Koksoak →, Canada 69 C13 58 30N 68 10W
Kokstad, S. Africa 57 E4 30 32S 29 29 E
Kokubu, Japan 31 J5 31 44N 130 46 E
Kokuora, Russia 27 B15 71 35N 144 50 E
Kola, Indonesia 37 F8 5 35S 134 30 E
Kola, Russia 24 A5 68 45N 33 8 E
Kola Pen. = Kolskiy Poluostrov, Russia 24 A6 67 30N 38 0 E
Kolahoi, India 43 B6 34 12N 75 22 E
Kolaka, Indonesia 37 E6 4 3S 121 46 E
Kolar, India 40 N11 13 12N 78 15 E
Kolar Gold Fields, India 40 N11 12 58N 78 16 E
Kolari, Finland 8 C20 67 20N 23 48 E
Kolayat, India 40 F8 27 50N 72 50 E
Kolchugino = Leninsk-Kuznetskiy, Russia 26 D9 54 44N 86 10 E
Kolda, Senegal 50 F2 12 55N 14 57W
Kolding, Denmark 9 J13 55 30N 9 29 E
Kole, Zaïre 52 E4 3 16S 22 42 E
Kolepom = Yos Sudarso, Pulau, Indonesia 37 F9 8 0S 138 30 E
Kolguyev, Ostrov, Russia 24 A8 69 20N 48 30 E
Kolhapur, India 40 L9 16 43N 74 15 E
Kolín, Czech. 16 C8 50 2N 15 9 E
Kolkas Rags, Latvia 9 H20 57 46N 22 37 E
Kolmanskop, Namibia 56 D2 26 45S 15 14 E
Köln, Germany 16 C4 50 56N 6 57 E
Koło, Poland 17 B10 52 14N 18 40 E
Kołobrzeg, Poland 16 A8 54 10N 15 35 E
Kolokani, Mali 50 F3 13 35N 7 45W
Kolomna, Russia 24 C6 55 8N 38 45 E
Kolomyya, Ukraine 17 D13 48 31N 25 2 E
Kolonodale, Indonesia 37 E6 2 3S 121 25 E
Kolosib, India 41 G18 24 15N 92 45 E
Kolpashevo, Russia 26 D9 58 20N 83 5 E
Kolpino, Russia 24 C5 59 44N 30 39 E
Kolskiy Poluostrov, Russia 24 A6 67 30N 38 0 E
Kolskiy Zaliv, Russia 24 A5 69 23N 34 0 E
Kolwezi, Zaïre 55 E2 10 40S 25 25 E
Kolyma →, Russia 27 C17 69 30N 161 0 E
Kolymskoye Nagorye, Russia 27 C16 63 0N 157 0 E
Komandorskiye Is. = Komandorskiye Ostrova, Russia 27 D17 55 0N 167 0 E
Komandorskiye Ostrova, Russia 27 D17 55 0N 167 0 E
Komárno, Slovak Rep. 17 E10 47 49N 18 5 E
Komatipoort, S. Africa 57 D5 25 25S 31 55 E
Komatou Yialou, Cyprus 23 D13 35 25N 34 8 E
Komatsu, Japan 31 F8 36 25N 136 30 E
Komatsujima, Japan 31 H7 34 0N 134 35 E
Komi □, Russia 24 B10 64 0N 55 0 E
Kommunarsk = Alchevsk, Ukraine 25 E6 48 30N 38 45 E
Kommunizma, Pik, Tajikistan 26 F8 39 0N 72 2 E
Komodo, Indonesia 37 F5 8 37S 119 20 E
Komono, Congo 52 E2 3 10S 13 20 E
Komoran, Pulau, Indonesia 37 F9 8 18S 138 45 E
Komoro, Japan 31 F9 36 19N 138 26 E
Komotini, Greece 21 D11 41 9N 25 26 E
Kompasberg, S. Africa 56 E3 31 45S 24 32 E
Kompong Bang, Cambodia 39 F5 12 24N 104 40 E
Kompong Cham, Cambodia 39 F5 12 0N 105 30 E
Kompong Chhnang, Cambodia 39 F5 12 20N 104 35 E
Kompong Chikreng, Cambodia 38 F5 13 5N 104 18 E
Kompong Kleang, Cambodia 38 F5 13 6N 104 8 E
Kompong Luong, Cambodia 39 G5 11 49N 104 48 E
Kompong Pranak, Cambodia 38 F5 13 35N 104 55 E
Kompong Som, Cambodia 39 G4 10 38N 103 30 E
Kompong Som, Chhung, Cambodia 39 G4 10 50N 103 32 E
Kompong Speu, Cambodia 39 G5 11 26N 104 32 E
Kompong Sralao, Cambodia 38 E5 14 5N 105 46 E
Kompong Thom, Cambodia 38 F5 12 35N 104 51 E
Kompong Trabeck, Cambodia 38 F5 13 6N 105 14 E
Kompong Trabeck, Cambodia 39 G5 11 9N 105 28 E
Kompong Trach, Cambodia 39 G5 11 25N 105 48 E
Kompong Tralach, Cambodia 39 G5 11 54N 104 47 E
Komrat = Comrat, Moldova 17 E15 46 18N 28 40 E
Komsberg, S. Africa 56 E3 32 40S 20 45 E
Komsomolets, Ostrov, Russia 27 A10 80 30N 95 0 E
Komsomolsk, Russia 27 D14 50 30N 137 0 E
Konarhá □, Afghan. 40 B7 35 30N 71 3 E
Konārī, Iran 45 D6 28 13N 51 36 E
Konawa, U.S.A. 81 H6 34 58N 96 45W
Konch, India 43 G8 26 0N 79 10 E
Kondakovo, Russia 27 C16 69 36N 152 0 E
Konde, Tanzania 54 C4 4 57S 39 45 E
Kondinin, Australia 61 F2 32 34S 118 8 E
Kondoa, Tanzania 54 C4 4 55S 35 50 E
Kondoa □, Tanzania 54 D4 5 0S 36 0 E
Kondókali, Greece 23 A3 39 38N 19 51 E
Kondopaga, Russia 24 B5 62 12N 34 17 E
Kondratyevo, Russia 27 D10 57 22N 98 15 E
Konduga, Nigeria 51 F7 11 35N 13 26 E
Köneürgench, Turkmenistan 26 E6 42 19N 59 10 E
Konevo, Russia 24 B6 62 8N 39 20 E
Kong, Ivory C. 50 G4 8 54N 4 36W
Kong →, Cambodia 38 F5 13 32N 105 58 E
Kong, Koh, Cambodia 39 G4 11 20N 103 0 E
Kong Christian IX.s Land, Greenland 4 C6 68 0N 36 0W
Kong Christian X.s Land, Greenland 4 B6 74 0N 29 0W
Kong Franz Joseph Fd., Greenland 4 B6 73 30N 24 30W
Kong Frederik IX.s Land, Greenland 4 C5 67 0N 52 0W
Kong Frederik VI.s Kyst, Greenland 4 C5 63 0N 43 0W
Kong Frederik VIII.s Land, Greenland 4 B6 78 30N 26 0W
Kong Oscar Fjord, Greenland 4 B6 72 20N 24 0W
Kongju, S. Korea 35 F14 36 30N 127 0 E
Konglu, Burma 41 F20 27 13N 97 57 E
Kongolo, Kasai Or., Zaïre 54 D1 5 26S 24 49 E
Kongolo, Shaba, Zaïre 54 D2 5 22S 27 0 E
Kongor, Sudan 51 G11 7 1N 31 27 E
Kongsberg, Norway 9 G13 59 39N 9 39 E
Kongsvinger, Norway 9 F15 60 12N 12 2 E
Kongwa, Tanzania 54 D4 6 11S 36 26 E
Koni, Zaïre 55 E2 10 40S 27 11 E
Koni, Mts., Zaïre 55 E2 10 36S 27 10 E
Königsberg = Kaliningrad, Russia 9 J19 54 42N 20 32 E
Konin, Poland 17 B10 52 12N 18 15 E
Konjic, Bos.-H. 21 C7 43 42N 17 58 E
Konkiep, Namibia 56 D2 26 49S 17 15 E
Konosha, Russia 24 B7 61 0N 40 5 E
Kōnosu, Japan 31 F9 36 3N 139 31 E
Konotop, Ukraine 25 D5 51 12N 33 7 E
Końskie, Poland 17 C11 51 15N 20 23 E
Konstanz, Germany 16 E5 47 40N 9 10 E
Kont, Iran 45 E9 26 55N 61 50 E
Kontagora, Nigeria 50 F6 10 23N 5 27 E
Kontum, Vietnam 38 E7 14 24N 108 0 E
Kontum, Plateau du, Vietnam 38 E7 14 30N 108 30 E
Konya, Turkey 25 G5 37 52N 32 35 E
Konza, Kenya 54 C4 1 45S 37 7 E
Kookynie, Australia 61 E3 29 17S 121 22 E
Kooline, Australia 60 D2 22 57S 116 20 E
Kooloonong, Australia 63 E3 34 48S 143 10 E
Koolyanobbing, Australia 61 F2 30 48S 119 36 E
Koondrook, Australia 63 F3 35 33S 144 8 E
Koonibba, Australia 63 E1 31 54S 133 25 E
Koorawatha, Australia 63 E4 34 2S 148 33 E
Koorda, Australia 61 F2 30 48S 117 35 E
Kooskia, U.S.A. 82 C6 46 9N 115 59W
Kootenai →, Canada 82 B5 49 15N 117 39W
Kootenay L., Canada 72 D5 49 45N 116 50W
Kootenay Nat. Park, Canada 72 C5 51 0N 116 0W
Kootjieskolk, S. Africa 56 E3 31 15S 20 21 E
Kopaonik, Serbia, Yug. 21 C9 43 10N 20 50 E
Kópavogur, Iceland 8 D3 64 6N 21 55W
Koper, Slovenia 16 F7 45 31N 13 44 E
Kopervik, Norway 9 G11 59 17N 5 17 E
Kopeysk, Russia 26 D7 55 7N 61 37 E
Kopi, Australia 63 E2 33 24S 135 40 E
Köping, Sweden 9 G17 59 31N 16 3 E
Koppies, S. Africa 57 D4 27 20S 27 30 E
Koprivnica, Croatia 20 A7 46 12N 16 45 E
Kopychyntsi, Ukraine 17 D13 49 7N 25 58 E
Korab, Macedonia 21 D9 41 44N 20 40 E
Korakiána, Greece 23 A3 39 42N 19 45 E
Korba, India 43 H10 22 20N 82 45 E
Korbu, G., Malaysia 39 K3 4 41N 101 18 E
Korça, Albania 21 D9 40 37N 20 50 E
Korce = Korça, Albania 21 D9 40 37N 20 50 E
Korčula, Croatia 20 C7 42 56N 16 57 E
Kord Kūy, Iran 45 B7 36 48N 54 7 E
Kord Sheykh, Iran 45 D7 28 31N 52 53 E
Kordestān □, Iran 44 C5 36 0N 47 0 E
Kordofân, Sudan 51 F10 13 0N 29 0 E
Korea, North ■, Asia 35 E14 40 0N 127 0 E
Korea, South ■, Asia 35 F15 36 0N 128 0 E

Korea Bay

Korea Bay, *Korea* 35 E13 39 0N 124 0 E
Korea Strait, *Asia* 35 G15 34 0N 129 30 E
Korets, *Ukraine* 17 C14 50 40N 27 5 E
Korhogo, *Ivory C.* 50 G3 9 29N 5 28W
Korim, *Indonesia* 37 E9 0 58S 136 10 E
Korinthiakós Kólpos, *Greece* 21 E10 38 16N 22 30 E
Kórinthos, *Greece* 21 F10 37 56N 22 55 E
Korissa, Limni, *Greece* 23 B3 39 27N 19 53 E
Kōriyama, *Japan* 30 F10 37 24N 140 23 E
Korla, *China* 32 B3 41 45N 86 4 E
Kormakiti, C., *Cyprus* 23 D11 35 23N 32 56 E
Korneshty = Corneşti, *Moldova* 17 E15 47 21N 28 1 E
Koro, *Fiji* 59 C8 17 19S 179 23 E
Koro, *Ivory C.* 50 G3 8 32N 7 30W
Koro, *Mali* 50 F4 14 1N 2 58W
Koro Sea, *Fiji* 59 C9 17 30S 179 45W
Korogwe, *Tanzania* 54 D4 5 5S 38 25 E
Korogwe □, *Tanzania* 54 D4 5 0S 38 20 E
Koroit, *Australia* 63 F3 38 18S 142 24 E
Koror, *Pac. Oc.* 37 C8 7 20N 134 28 E
Körös →, *Hungary* 17 E11 46 43N 20 12 E
Korosten, *Ukraine* 17 C15 50 54N 28 36 E
Korostyshev, *Ukraine* 17 C15 50 19N 29 4 E
Korraraika, Helodranon' i, *Madag.* 57 B7 17 45S 43 57 E
Korsakov, *Russia* 27 E15 46 36N 142 42 E
Korshunovo, *Russia* 27 D12 58 37N 110 10 E
Korsør, *Denmark* 9 J14 55 20N 11 9 E
Korti, *Sudan* 51 E11 18 6N 31 33 E
Kortrijk, *Belgium* 15 D3 50 50N 3 17 E
Korwai, *India* 42 G8 24 7N 78 5 E
Koryakskoye Nagorye, *Russia* 27 C18 61 0N 171 0 E
Koryŏng, *S. Korea* 35 G15 35 44N 128 15 E
Kos, *Greece* 21 F12 36 50N 27 15 E
Koschagyl, *Kazakstan* 25 E9 46 40N 54 0 E
Kościan, *Poland* 17 B9 52 5N 16 40 E
Kosciusko, *U.S.A.* 81 J10 33 4N 89 35W
Kosciusko, Mt., *Australia* 63 F4 36 27S 148 16 E
Kosciusko I., *U.S.A.* 72 B2 56 0N 133 40W
Kosha, *Sudan* 51 D11 20 50N 30 30 E
K'oshih = Kashi, *China* 32 C2 39 30N 76 2 E
Koshiki-Rettō, *Japan* 31 J4 31 45N 129 49 E
Kosi, *India* 42 F7 27 48N 77 29 E
Košice, *Slovak Rep.* 17 D11 48 42N 21 15 E
Koskhinoú, *Greece* 23 C10 36 23N 28 13 E
Koslan, *Russia* 24 B8 63 34N 49 14 E
Kosŏng, *N. Korea* 35 E15 38 40N 128 22 E
Kosovo □, *Serbia, Yug.* 21 C9 42 30N 21 0 E
Kosovska-Mitrovica = Titova-Mitrovica, *Serbia, Yug.* 21 C9 42 54N 20 52 E
Kostamuksa, *Russia* 24 B5 62 34N 32 44 E
Koster, *S. Africa* 56 D4 25 52S 26 54 E
Kôstî, *Sudan* 51 F11 13 8N 32 43 E
Kostopil, *Ukraine* 17 C14 50 51N 26 22 E
Kostroma, *Russia* 24 C7 57 50N 40 58 E
Kostrzyn, *Poland* 16 B8 52 35N 14 39 E
Koszalin, *Poland* 16 A9 54 11N 16 8 E
Kot Addu, *Pakistan* 42 D4 30 30N 71 0 E
Kot Moman, *Pakistan* 42 C5 32 13N 73 0 E
Kota, *India* 42 G6 25 14N 75 49 E
Kota Baharu, *Malaysia* 39 J4 6 7N 102 14 E
Kota Belud, *Malaysia* 36 C5 6 21N 116 26 E
Kota Kinabalu, *Malaysia* 36 C5 6 0N 116 4 E
Kota Tinggi, *Malaysia* 39 M4 1 44N 103 53 E
Kotaagung, *Indonesia* 36 F2 5 38S 104 29 E
Kotabaru, *Indonesia* 36 E5 3 20S 116 20 E
Kotabumi, *Indonesia* 36 E2 4 49S 104 54 E
Kotagede, *Indonesia* 37 G14 7 54S 110 26 E
Kotamobagu, *Indonesia* 37 D6 0 57N 124 31 E
Kotaneelee →, *Canada* 72 A4 60 11N 123 42W
Kotawaringin, *Indonesia* 36 E4 2 28S 111 27 E
Kotcho L., *Canada* 72 B4 59 7N 121 12W
Kotelnich, *Russia* 24 C8 58 22N 48 24 E
Kotelnikovo, *Russia* 26 E5 47 38N 43 8 E
Kotelnyy, Ostrov, *Russia* 27 B14 75 10N 139 0 E
Kothi, *India* 43 G9 24 45N 80 40 E
Kotiro, *Pakistan* 42 F2 26 17N 67 13 E
Kotka, *Finland* 9 F22 60 28N 26 58 E
Kotlas, *Russia* 24 B8 61 17N 46 43 E
Kotli, *Pakistan* 42 C5 33 30N 73 55 E
Kotmul, *Pakistan* 43 B6 35 32N 75 10 E
Kotor, *Montenegro, Yug.* 21 C8 42 25N 18 47 E
Kotovsk, *Ukraine* 17 E15 47 45N 29 35 E
Kotputli, *India* 42 F7 27 43N 76 12 E
Kotri, *Pakistan* 42 G3 25 22N 68 22 E
Kottayam, *India* 40 Q10 9 35N 76 33 E
Kotturu, *India* 40 M10 14 45N 76 10 E
Kotuy →, *Russia* 27 B11 71 54N 102 6 E
Kotzebue, *U.S.A.* 68 B3 66 53N 162 39W
Kouango, *C.A.R.* 52 C4 5 0N 20 10 E
Koudougou, *Burkina Faso* 50 F4 12 10N 2 20W
Koufonísi, *Greece* 23 E8 34 56N 26 8 E
Kougaberge, *S. Africa* 56 E3 33 48S 23 50 E
Kouilou →, *Congo* 52 E2 4 10S 12 5 E
Kouki, *C.A.R.* 52 C3 7 22N 17 3 E
Koula Moutou, *Gabon* 52 E2 1 15S 12 25 E
Koulen, *Cambodia* 38 F5 13 50N 104 40 E
Koulikoro, *Mali* 50 F3 12 40N 7 50W
Kouloúra, *Greece* 23 A3 39 42N 19 54 E
Koúm-bournoú, Ákra, *Greece* 23 C10 36 15N 28 11 E
Koumala, *Australia* 62 C4 21 38S 149 15 E
Koumra, *Chad* 51 G8 8 50N 17 35 E
Kounradskiy, *Kazakstan* 26 E8 46 59N 75 0 E
Kountze, *U.S.A.* 81 K7 30 22N 94 19W
Kouris →, *Cyprus* 23 E11 34 38N 32 54 E
Kouroussa, *Guinea* 50 F3 10 45N 9 45W
Kousseri, *Cameroon* 51 F7 12 0N 14 55 E
Koutiala, *Mali* 50 F3 12 25N 5 23W
Kouvola, *Finland* 9 F22 60 52N 26 43 E
Kovdor, *Russia* 24 A5 67 34N 30 24 E
Kovel, *Ukraine* 17 C13 51 11N 24 38 E
Kovrov, *Russia* 24 C7 56 25N 41 25 E
Kowanyama, *Australia* 62 B3 15 29S 141 44 E
Kowkash, *Canada* 70 B2 50 20N 87 12W
Kowŏn, *N. Korea* 35 E14 39 26N 127 14 E
Köyceğiz, *Turkey* 21 F13 36 57N 28 40 E
Koyuk, *U.S.A.* 68 B3 64 56N 161 9W
Koyukuk →, *U.S.A.* 68 B4 64 55N 157 32W
Koza, *Japan* 31 L3 26 19N 127 46 E
Kozáni, *Greece* 21 D9 40 19N 21 47 E
Kozhikode = Calicut, *India* 40 P9 11 15N 75 43 E
Kozhva, *Russia* 24 A10 65 10N 57 0 E
Kozyatyn, *Ukraine* 17 D15 49 45N 28 50 E
Kpalimé, *Togo* 50 G5 6 57N 0 44 E
Kra, Isthmus of = Kra, Kho Khot, *Thailand* 39 G2 10 15N 99 30 E
Kra, Kho Khot, *Thailand* 39 G2 10 15N 99 30 E
Kra Buri, *Thailand* 39 G2 10 22N 98 46 E
Krabi, *Thailand* 39 H2 8 4N 98 55 E
Kragan, *Indonesia* 37 G14 6 43S 111 38 E
Kragerø, *Norway* 9 G13 58 52N 9 25 E
Kragujevac, *Serbia, Yug.* 21 B9 44 2N 20 56 E
Krajina, *Bos.-H.* 20 B7 44 45N 16 35 E
Krakatau = Rakata, Pulau, *Indonesia* 36 F3 6 10S 105 20 E
Krakor, *Cambodia* 38 F5 12 32N 104 12 E
Kraków, *Poland* 17 C10 50 4N 19 57 E
Kraksaan, *Indonesia* 37 G15 7 43S 113 23 E
Kralanh, *Cambodia* 38 F4 13 35N 103 25 E
Kraljevo, *Serbia, Yug.* 21 C9 43 44N 20 41 E
Kramatorsk, *Ukraine* 25 E6 48 50N 37 30 E
Kramfors, *Sweden* 9 E17 62 55N 17 48 E
Kranj, *Slovenia* 16 E8 46 16N 14 22 E
Krankskop, *S. Africa* 57 D5 28 0S 30 47 E
Krasavino, *Russia* 24 B8 60 58N 46 29 E
Kraskino, *Russia* 27 E14 42 44N 130 48 E
Kraśnik, *Poland* 17 C12 50 55N 22 5 E
Krasnoarmeysk, *Russia* 26 D5 51 0N 45 42 E
Krasnodar, *Russia* 25 E6 45 5N 39 0 E
Krasnokamsk, *Russia* 24 C10 58 4N 55 48 E
Krasnoperekopsk, *Ukraine* 25 E5 46 0N 33 54 E
Krasnorechenskiy, *Russia* 30 B7 44 41N 135 14 E
Krasnoselkupsk, *Russia* 26 C9 65 20N 82 10 E
Krasnoturinsk, *Russia* 24 C11 59 46N 60 12 E
Krasnoufimsk, *Russia* 24 C10 56 36N 57 38 E
Krasnouralsk, *Russia* 24 C11 58 21N 60 3 E
Krasnovishersk, *Russia* 24 B10 60 23N 57 3 E
Krasnovodsk = Türkmenbashi, *Turkmenistan* 25 F9 40 5N 53 5 E
Krasnoyarsk, *Russia* 27 D10 56 8N 93 0 E
Krasnyy Luch, *Ukraine* 25 E6 48 13N 39 0 E
Krasnyy Yar, *Russia* 25 E8 46 43N 48 23 E
Kratie, *Cambodia* 38 F6 12 32N 106 10 E
Krau, *Indonesia* 37 E10 3 19S 140 5 E
Kravanh, Chuor Phnum, *Cambodia* 39 G4 12 0N 103 32 E
Krefeld, *Germany* 16 C4 51 20N 6 33 E
Kremen, *Croatia* 16 F8 44 28N 15 53 E
Kremenchug = Kremenchuk, *Ukraine* 25 E5 49 5N 33 25 E
Kremenchuk, *Ukraine* 25 E5 49 5N 33 25 E
Kremenchuksk Vdskh., *Ukraine* 25 E5 49 20N 32 30 E
Kremenets, *Ukraine* 17 C13 50 8N 25 43 E
Kremmling, *U.S.A.* 82 F10 40 4N 106 24W
Krems, *Austria* 16 D8 48 25N 15 36 E
Kretinga, *Lithuania* 9 J19 55 53N 21 15 E
Kribi, *Cameroon* 52 D1 2 57N 9 56 E
Krichev = Krychaw, *Belarus* 17 B16 53 40N 31 41 E
Kriós, Ákra, *Greece* 23 D5 35 13N 23 34 E
Krishna →, *India* 41 M12 15 57N 80 59 E
Krishnanagar, *India* 43 H13 23 24N 88 33 E
Kristiansand, *Norway* 9 G13 58 8N 8 1 E
Kristianstad, *Sweden* 9 H16 56 2N 14 9 E
Kristiansund, *Norway* 8 E12 63 7N 7 45 E
Kristiinankaupunki, *Finland* 9 E19 62 16N 21 21 E
Kristinehamn, *Sweden* 9 G16 59 18N 14 13 E
Kristinestad = Kristiinankaupunki, *Finland* 9 E19 62 16N 21 21 E
Kríti, *Greece* 23 D7 35 15N 25 0 E
Kritsá, *Greece* 23 D7 35 10N 25 41 E
Krivoy Rog = Kryvyy Rih, *Ukraine* 25 E5 47 51N 33 20 E
Krk, *Croatia* 16 F8 45 8N 14 40 E
Krokodil →, *Mozam.* 57 D5 25 14S 32 18 E
Kronprins Olav Kyst, *Antarctica* 5 C5 69 0S 42 0 E
Kronshtadt, *Russia* 24 B4 59 57N 29 51 E
Kroonstad, *S. Africa* 56 D4 27 43S 27 19 E
Kropotkin, *Irkutsk, Russia* 27 D12 59 0N 115 30 E
Kropotkin, *Krasnodar, Russia* 25 E7 45 28N 40 28 E
Krosno, *Poland* 17 D11 49 42N 21 46 E
Krotoszyn, *Poland* 17 C9 51 42N 17 23 E
Kroussón, *Greece* 23 D6 35 13N 24 59 E
Kruger Nat. Park, *S. Africa* 57 C5 23 30S 31 40 E
Krugersdorp, *S. Africa* 57 D4 26 5S 27 46 E
Kruisfontein, *S. Africa* 56 E3 33 59S 24 43 E
Krung Thep = Bangkok, *Thailand* 38 F3 13 45N 100 35 E
Krupki, *Belarus* 17 A15 54 19N 29 8 E
Kruševac, *Serbia, Yug.* 21 C9 43 35N 21 28 E
Kruzof I., *U.S.A.* 72 B1 57 10N 135 40W
Krychaw, *Belarus* 17 B16 53 40N 31 41 E
Krymskiy Poluostrov = Krymskyy Pivostriv, *Ukraine* 25 E5 45 0N 34 0 E
Krymskyy Pivostriv, *Ukraine* 25 E5 45 0N 34 0 E
Kryvyy Rih, *Ukraine* 25 E5 47 51N 33 20 E
Ksar el Boukhari, *Algeria* 50 A5 35 51N 2 52 E
Ksar el Kebir, *Morocco* 50 B3 35 0N 6 0W
Ksar es Souk = Ar Rachidiya, *Morocco* 50 B4 31 58N 4 20W
Kuala, *Indonesia* 36 D3 2 55N 105 47 E
Kuala Berang, *Malaysia* 39 K4 5 5N 103 1 E
Kuala Dungun, *Malaysia* 39 K4 4 45N 103 25 E
Kuala Kangsar, *Malaysia* 39 K3 4 46N 100 56 E
Kuala Kelawang, *Malaysia* 39 L4 2 56N 102 5 E
Kuala Kerai, *Malaysia* 39 K4 5 30N 102 12 E
Kuala Kubu Baharu, *Malaysia* 39 L3 3 34N 101 39 E
Kuala Lipis, *Malaysia* 39 K4 4 10N 102 3 E
Kuala Lumpur, *Malaysia* 39 L3 3 9N 101 41 E
Kuala Nerang, *Malaysia* 39 J3 6 16N 100 37 E
Kuala Pilah, *Malaysia* 39 L4 2 45N 102 15 E
Kuala Rompin, *Malaysia* 39 L4 2 49N 103 29 E
Kuala Selangor, *Malaysia* 39 L3 3 20N 101 15 E
Kuala Terengganu, *Malaysia* 39 K4 5 20N 103 8 E
Kualajelai, *Indonesia* 36 E4 2 58S 110 46 E
Kualakapuas, *Indonesia* 36 E4 2 55S 114 20 E
Kualakurun, *Indonesia* 36 E4 1 10S 113 50 E
Kualapembuang, *Indonesia* 36 E4 3 14S 112 38 E
Kualasimpang, *Indonesia* 36 D1 4 17N 98 3 E
Kuancheng, *China* 35 D10 40 37N 118 30 E
Kuandang, *Indonesia* 37 D6 0 56N 123 1 E
Kuandian, *China* 35 D13 40 45N 124 45 E
Kuangchou = Guangzhou, *China* 33 D6 23 5N 113 10 E
Kuantan, *Malaysia* 39 L4 3 49N 103 20 E
Kuba = Quba, *Azerbaijan* 25 F8 41 21N 48 32 E
Kuban →, *Russia* 25 E6 45 20N 37 30 E
Kubokawa, *Japan* 31 H6 33 12N 133 8 E
Kucha Gompa, *India* 43 B7 34 25N 76 56 E
Kuchaman, *India* 42 F6 27 13N 74 47 E
Kuchino-eruba-Jima, *Japan* 31 J5 30 28N 130 12 E
Kuchino-Shima, *Japan* 31 K4 29 57N 129 55 E
Kuchinotsu, *Japan* 31 H5 32 36N 130 11 E
Kucing, *Malaysia* 36 D4 1 33N 110 25 E
Kud →, *Pakistan* 42 F2 26 5N 66 20 E
Kuda, *India* 40 H7 23 10N 71 15 E
Kudat, *Malaysia* 36 C5 6 55N 116 55 E
Kudus, *Indonesia* 37 G14 6 48S 110 51 E
Kudymkar, *Russia* 26 D6 59 1N 54 39 E
Kueiyang = Guiyang, *China* 32 D5 26 32N 106 40 E
Kufra Oasis = Al Kufrah, *Libya* 51 D9 24 17N 23 15 E
Kufstein, *Austria* 16 E7 47 35N 12 11 E
Kugluktuk, *Canada* 68 B8 67 50N 115 5W
Kugong I., *Canada* 70 A4 56 18N 79 50W
Kūh-e-Hazārām, *Iran* 45 D8 29 35N 57 20 E
Kūhak, *Iran* 40 F3 27 12N 63 10 E
Kūhbonān, *Iran* 45 D8 31 23N 56 19 E
Kūhestak, *Iran* 45 E8 26 47N 57 2 E
Kūhīn, *Iran* 45 C6 35 13N 48 25 E
Kūhīrī, *Iran* 45 E9 26 55N 61 2 E
Kūhpāyeh, *Eşfahan, Iran* 45 C7 32 44N 52 20 E
Kūhpāyeh, *Kermān, Iran* 45 D8 30 35N 57 15 E
Kui Buri, *Thailand* 39 F2 12 3N 99 52 E
Kuito, *Angola* 53 G3 12 22S 16 55 E
Kujang, *N. Korea* 35 E14 39 57N 126 1 E
Kuji, *Japan* 30 D10 40 11N 141 46 E
Kujū-San, *Japan* 31 H5 33 5N 131 15 E
Kukawa, *Nigeria* 51 F7 12 58N 13 27 E
Kukerin, *Australia* 61 F2 33 13S 118 0 E
Kukësi, *Albania* 21 C9 42 5N 20 20 E
Kukup, *Malaysia* 39 M4 1 20N 103 27 E
Kula, *Turkey* 21 E13 38 32N 28 40 E
Kulai, *Malaysia* 39 M4 1 44N 103 35 E
Kulal, Mt., *Kenya* 54 B4 2 42N 36 57 E
Kulasekarappattinam, *India* 40 Q11 8 20N 78 5 E
Kuldiga, *Latvia* 9 H19 56 58N 21 59 E
Kuldja = Yining, *China* 26 E9 43 58N 81 10 E
Kulgam, *India* 43 C6 33 36N 75 2 E
Kulim, *Malaysia* 39 K3 5 22N 100 34 E
Kulin, *Australia* 61 F2 32 40S 118 2 E
Kulja, *Australia* 61 F2 30 28S 117 18 E
Kulm, *U.S.A.* 80 B5 46 18N 98 57W
Kŭlob, *Tajikistan* 26 F7 37 55N 69 50 E
Kulsary, *Kazakstan* 25 E9 46 59N 54 1 E
Kulti, *India* 43 H12 23 43N 86 50 E
Kulumbura, *Australia* 60 B4 13 55S 126 35 E
Kulunda, *Russia* 26 D8 52 35N 78 57 E
Kulungar, *Afghan.* 42 C3 34 0N 69 2 E
Kūlvand, *Iran* 45 D7 31 21N 54 35 E
Kulwin, *Australia* 63 F3 35 0S 142 42 E
Kulyab = Kŭlob, *Tajikistan* 26 F7 37 55N 69 50 E
Kum Tekei, *Kazakstan* 26 E8 43 10N 79 30 E
Kuma →, *Russia* 25 F8 44 55N 47 0 E
Kumagaya, *Japan* 31 F9 36 9N 139 22 E
Kumai, *Indonesia* 36 E4 2 44S 111 43 E
Kumamba, Kepulauan, *Indonesia* 37 E9 1 36S 138 45 E
Kumamoto, *Japan* 31 H5 32 45N 130 45 E
Kumamoto □, *Japan* 31 H5 32 55N 130 55 E
Kumanovo, *Macedonia* 21 C9 42 9N 21 42 E
Kumara, *N.Z.* 59 K3 42 37S 171 12 E
Kumarl, *Australia* 61 F3 32 47S 121 33 E
Kumasi, *Ghana* 50 G4 6 41N 1 38W
Kumayri = Gyumri, *Armenia* 25 F7 40 47N 43 50 E
Kumba, *Cameroon* 50 H6 4 36N 9 24 E
Kumbakonam, *India* 40 P11 10 58N 79 25 E
Kumbarilla, *Australia* 63 D5 27 15S 150 55 E
Kŭmchŏn, *N. Korea* 35 E14 38 10N 126 29 E
Kumdok, *India* 43 C8 33 32N 78 10 E
Kume-Shima, *Japan* 31 L3 26 20N 126 47 E
Kumertau, *Russia* 24 D10 52 45N 55 57 E
Kŭmhwa, *S. Korea* 35 E14 38 17N 127 28 E
Kumi, *Uganda* 54 B3 1 30N 33 58 E
Kumla, *Sweden* 9 G16 59 8N 15 10 E
Kumo, *Nigeria* 51 F7 10 1N 11 12 E
Kumon Bum, *Burma* 41 F20 26 30N 97 15 E
Kunama, *Australia* 63 F4 35 35S 148 4 E
Kunashir, Ostrov, *Russia* 27 E15 44 0N 146 0 E
Kunda, *Estonia* 9 G22 59 30N 26 34 E
Kundla, *India* 42 J4 21 21N 71 25 E
Kungala, *Australia* 63 D5 29 58S 153 7 E
Kunghit I., *Canada* 72 C2 52 6N 131 3W
Kungrad = Qŭnghirot, *Uzbekistan* 26 E6 43 6N 58 54 E
Kungsbacka, *Sweden* 9 H15 57 30N 12 5 E
Kungur, *Russia* 24 C10 57 25N 56 57 E
Kungurri, *Australia* 62 C4 21 3S 148 46 E
Kunhar →, *Pakistan* 43 B5 34 20N 73 30 E
Kuningan, *Indonesia* 37 G13 6 59S 108 29 E
Kunlong, *Burma* 41 H21 23 20N 98 50 E
Kunlun Shan, *Asia* 32 C3 36 0N 86 30 E
Kunming, *China* 32 D5 25 1N 102 41 E
Kunsan, *S. Korea* 35 G14 35 59N 126 45 E
Kununurra, *Australia* 60 C4 15 40S 128 50 E
Kunwarara, *Australia* 62 C5 22 55S 150 9 E
Kunya-Urgench = Köneürgench, *Turkmenistan* 26 E6 42 19N 59 10 E
Kuopio, *Finland* 8 E22 62 53N 27 35 E
Kupa →, *Croatia* 16 F9 45 28N 16 24 E
Kupang, *Indonesia* 37 F6 10 19S 123 39 E
Kupyansk, *Ukraine* 26 E4 49 52N 37 35 E
Kuqa, *China* 32 B3 41 35N 82 30 E
Kür →, *Azerbaijan* 25 G8 39 29N 49 15 E
Kura = Kür →, *Azerbaijan* 25 G8 39 29N 49 15 E
Kuranda, *Australia* 62 B4 16 48S 145 35 E
Kurashiki, *Japan* 31 G6 34 40N 133 50 E
Kurayoshi, *Japan* 31 G6 35 26N 133 50 E
Kŭrdzhali, *Bulgaria* 21 D11 41 38N 25 21 E
Kure, *Japan* 31 G6 34 14N 132 32 E
Kuressaare, *Estonia* 9 G20 58 15N 22 30 E
Kurgaldzhinskiy, *Kazakstan* 26 D8 50 35N 70 20 E
Kurgan, *Russia* 26 D7 55 26N 65 18 E
Kuria Maria Is. = Khūrīyā Mūrīyā, Jazā 'ir, *Oman* 46 D6 17 30N 55 58 E
Kuridala, *Australia* 62 C3 21 16S 140 29 E
Kurigram, *Bangla.* 41 G16 25 49N 89 39 E
Kurikka, *Finland* 9 E20 62 36N 22 24 E
Kuril Is. = Kurilskiye Ostrova, *Russia* 27 E15 45 0N 150 0 E
Kuril Trench, *Pac. Oc.* 28 E19 44 0N 153 0 E
Kurilsk, *Russia* 27 E15 45 14N 147 53 E
Kurilskiye Ostrova, *Russia* 27 E15 45 0N 150 0 E
Kurino, *Japan* 31 J5 31 57N 130 43 E
Kurmuk, *Sudan* 51 F11 10 33N 34 21 E
Kurnool, *India* 40 M10 15 45N 78 0 E
Kuro-Shima, *Kagoshima, Japan* 31 J4 30 50N 129 57 E
Kuro-Shima, *Okinawa, Japan* 31 M2 24 14N 124 1 E
Kurow, *N.Z.* 59 L3 44 44S 170 29 E
Kurrajong, *Australia* 63 E5 33 33S 150 42 E
Kurram →, *Pakistan* 42 C4 32 36N 71 20 E
Kurri Kurri, *Australia* 63 E5 32 50S 151 28 E
Kurshskiy Zaliv, *Russia* 9 J19 55 9N 21 6 E
Kursk, *Russia* 24 D6 51 42N 36 11 E
Kuruktag, *China* 32 B3 41 0N 89 0 E
Kuruman, *S. Africa* 56 D3 27 28S 23 28 E
Kuruman →, *S. Africa* 56 D3 26 56S 20 39 E
Kurume, *Japan* 31 H5 33 15N 130 30 E
Kurunegala, *Sri Lanka* 40 R12 7 30N 80 23 E
Kurya, *Russia* 27 C11 61 15N 108 10 E
Kus Gölü, *Turkey* 21 D12 40 10N 27 55 E
Kuşadası, *Turkey* 21 F12 37 52N 27 15 E
Kusatsu, *Japan* 31 F9 36 37N 138 36 E
Kusawa L., *Canada* 72 A1 60 20N 136 13W
Kushikino, *Japan* 31 J5 31 44N 130 16 E
Kushima, *Japan* 31 J5 31 29N 131 14 E
Kushimoto, *Japan* 31 H7 33 28N 135 47 E
Kushiro, *Japan* 30 C12 43 0N 144 25 E
Kushiro →, *Japan* 30 C12 42 59N 144 23 E
Kūshk, *Iran* 45 D8 28 46N 56 51 E
Kushka = Gushgy, *Turkmenistan* 26 F7 35 20N 62 18 E
Kūshkī, *Īlām, Iran* 44 C5 33 31N 47 13 E
Kūshkī, *Khorāsān, Iran* 45 B8 37 2N 57 26 E
Kūshkū, *Iran* 45 E7 27 19N 53 28 E
Kushol, *India* 43 C7 33 40N 76 36 E
Kushtia, *Bangla.* 41 H16 23 55N 89 5 E
Kushva, *Russia* 24 C10 58 18N 59 45 E
Kuskokwim →, *U.S.A.* 68 B3 60 5N 162 25W
Kuskokwim B., *U.S.A.* 68 C3 59 45N 162 25W
Kussharo-Ko, *Japan* 30 C12 43 38N 144 21 E
Kustanay = Qostanay, *Kazakstan* 26 D7 53 10N 63 35 E
Kut, Ko, *Thailand* 39 G4 11 40N 102 35 E
Kütahya, *Turkey* 25 G5 39 30N 30 2 E
Kutaisi, *Georgia* 25 F7 42 19N 42 40 E
Kutaraja = Banda Aceh, *Indonesia* 36 C1 5 35N 95 20 E
Kutch, Gulf of = Kachchh, Gulf of, *India* 42 H3 22 50N 69 15 E
Kutch, Rann of = Kachchh, Rann of, *India* 42 G4 24 0N 70 0 E
Kutiyana, *India* 42 J4 21 36N 70 2 E
Kutno, *Poland* 17 B10 52 15N 19 23 E
Kuttabul, *Australia* 62 C4 21 5S 148 48 E
Kutu, *Zaïre* 52 E3 2 40S 18 11 E
Kutum, *Sudan* 51 F9 14 10N 24 40 E
Kuujjuaq, *Canada* 69 C13 58 6N 68 15W
Kuŭp-tong, *N. Korea* 35 D14 40 45N 126 1 E
Kuusamo, *Finland* 8 D23 65 57N 29 8 E
Kuusankoski, *Finland* 9 F22 60 55N 26 38 E
Kuwait = Al Kuwayt, *Kuwait* 44 D5 29 30N 48 0 E
Kuwait ■, *Asia* 44 D5 29 30N 47 30 E
Kuwana, *Japan* 31 G8 35 5N 136 43 E
Kuybyshev = Samara, *Russia* 24 D9 53 8N 50 6 E
Kuybyshev, *Russia* 26 D8 55 27N 78 19 E
Kuybyshevskoye Vdkhr., *Russia* 24 C8 55 2N 49 30 E
Kuye He →, *China* 34 E6 38 23N 110 46 E
Kūyeh, *Iran* 44 B5 38 45N 47 57 E
Kūysanjaq, *Iraq* 44 B5 36 5N 44 38 E
Kuyto, Ozero, *Russia* 24 B5 65 6N 31 20 E
Kuyumba, *Russia* 27 C10 60 58N 96 59 E
Kuzey Anadolu Dağları, *Turkey* 25 F6 41 30N 35 0 E
Kuznetsk, *Russia* 24 D8 53 12N 46 40 E
Kuzomen, *Russia* 24 A6 66 22N 36 50 E
Kvænangen, *Norway* 8 A19 70 5N 21 15 E
Kvaløy, *Norway* 8 B18 69 40N 18 30 E
Kvarner, *Croatia* 16 F8 44 50N 14 10 E
Kvarnerič, *Croatia* 16 F8 44 43N 14 37 E
Kwabhaca, *S. Africa* 57 E4 30 51S 29 0 E
Kwadacha →, *Canada* 72 B3 57 28N 125 38W
Kwakhanai, *Botswana* 56 C3 21 39S 21 16 E
Kwakoegron, *Surinam* 93 B7 5 12N 55 25W
Kwale, *Kenya* 54 C4 4 15S 39 31 E
Kwale □, *Kenya* 54 C4 4 15S 39 10 E
KwaMashu, *S. Africa* 57 D5 29 45S 30 58 E
Kwamouth, *Zaïre* 52 E3 3 9S 16 12 E
Kwando →, *Africa* 56 B3 18 27S 23 32 E
Kwangdaeri, *N. Korea* 35 D14 40 31N 127 32 E
Kwangju, *S. Korea* 35 G14 35 9N 126 54 E
Kwango →, *Zaïre* 49 G5 3 14S 17 22 E
Kwangsi-Chuang = Guangxi Zhuangzu Zizhiqu □, *China* 33 D5 24 0N 109 0 E
Kwangtung = Guangdong □, *China* 33 D6 23 0N 113 0 E

Lansdowne

Kwataboahegan →, Canada 70 B3 51 9N 80 50W
Kwatisore, Indonesia 37 E8 3 18S 134 50 E
KwaZulu Natal □, S. Africa 57 D5 29 0S 30 0 E
Kweichow = Guizhou □, China 32 D5 27 0N 107 0 E
Kwekwe, Zimbabwe 55 F2 18 58S 29 48 E
Kwidzyn, Poland 17 B10 53 44N 18 55 E
Kwimba □, Tanzania 54 C3 3 0S 33 0 E
Kwinana New Town, Australia 61 F2 32 15S 115 47 E
Kwoka, Indonesia 37 E8 0 31S 132 27 E
Kyabé, Chad 51 G8 9 30N 19 0 E
Kyabra Cr. →, Australia 63 D3 25 36S 142 55 E
Kyabram, Australia 63 F4 36 19S 145 4 E
Kyaikto, Burma 38 D1 17 20N 97 3 E
Kyakhta, Russia 27 D11 50 30N 106 25 E
Kyancutta, Australia 63 E2 33 8S 135 33 E
Kyangin, Burma 41 K19 18 20N 95 20 E
Kyaukpadaung, Burma 41 J19 20 52N 95 8 E
Kyaukpyu, Burma 41 K18 19 28N 93 30 E
Kyaukse, Burma 41 J20 21 36N 96 10 E
Kyburz, U.S.A. 84 G6 38 47N 120 18W
Kyenjojo, Uganda 54 B3 0 40N 30 37 E
Kyle Dam, Zimbabwe 55 G3 20 15S 31 0 E
Kyle of Lochalsh, U.K. 12 D3 57 17N 5 44W
Kymijoki →, Finland 9 F22 60 30N 26 55 E
Kyneton, Australia 63 F3 37 10S 144 29 E
Kynuna, Australia 62 C3 21 37S 141 55 E
Kyō-ga-Saki, Japan 31 G7 35 45N 135 15 E
Kyoga, L., Uganda 54 B3 1 35N 33 0 E
Kyogle, Australia 63 D5 28 40S 153 0 E
Kyongju, S. Korea 35 G15 35 51N 129 14 E
Kyongpyaw, Burma 41 L19 17 12N 95 10 E
Kyŏngsŏng, N. Korea 35 D15 41 35N 129 36 E
Kyōto, Japan 31 G7 35 0N 135 45 E
Kyōto □, Japan 31 G7 35 15N 135 45 E
Kyparissovouno, Cyprus 23 D12 35 19N 33 10 E
Kyperounda, Cyprus 23 E11 34 56N 32 58 E
Kyren, Russia 27 D11 51 45N 101 45 E
Kyrenia, Cyprus 23 D12 35 20N 33 20 E
Kyrgyzstan ■, Asia 26 E8 42 0N 75 0 E
Kyrönjoki →, Finland 8 E19 63 14N 21 45 E
Kyrtylakh, Russia 27 C13 65 30N 123 40 E
Kystatyam, Russia 27 C13 67 20N 123 10 E
Kythréa, Cyprus 23 D12 35 15N 33 29 E
Kyulyunken, Russia 27 C14 64 10N 137 5 E
Kyunhla, Burma 41 H19 23 25N 95 15 E
Kyuquot, Canada 72 C3 50 3N 127 25W
Kyūshū, Japan 31 H5 33 0N 131 0 E
Kyūshū □, Japan 31 H5 33 0N 131 0 E
Kyūshū-Sanchi, Japan 31 H5 32 35N 131 17 E
Kyustendil, Bulgaria 21 C10 42 16N 22 41 E
Kyusyur, Russia 27 B13 70 19N 127 30 E
Kywong, Australia 63 E4 34 58S 146 44 E
Kyyiv, Ukraine 17 C16 50 30N 30 28 E
Kyyivske Vdskh., Ukraine 17 C16 51 0N 30 25 E
Kyzyl, Russia 27 D10 51 50N 94 30 E
Kyzyl Kum, Uzbekistan 26 E7 42 30N 65 0 E
Kyzyl-Kyya, Kyrgyzstan 26 E8 40 16N 72 8 E
Kzyl-Orda = Qyzylorda, Kazakstan 26 E7 44 48N 65 28 E

L

La Albufera, Spain 19 C5 39 20N 0 27W
La Alcarria, Spain 19 B4 40 31N 2 45W
La Asunción, Venezuela 92 A6 11 2N 63 53W
La Banda, Argentina 94 B3 27 45S 64 10W
La Barca, Mexico 86 C4 20 20N 102 40W
La Barge, U.S.A. 82 E8 42 16N 110 12W
La Belle, U.S.A. 77 M5 26 46N 81 26W
La Biche →, Canada 72 B4 59 57N 123 50W
La Bomba, Mexico 86 A1 31 53N 115 2W
La Calera, Chile 94 C1 32 50S 71 10W
La Canal, Spain 22 C7 38 51N 1 23 E
La Carlota, Argentina 94 C3 33 30S 63 20W
La Ceiba, Honduras 88 C2 15 40N 86 50W
La Chaux de Fonds, Switz. 16 E4 47 7N 6 50 E
La Cocha, Argentina 94 B2 27 50S 65 40W
La Concordia, Mexico 87 D6 16 8N 92 38W
La Conner, U.S.A. 82 B2 48 23N 122 30W
La Coruña, Spain 19 A1 43 20N 8 25W
La Crete, Canada 72 B5 58 11N 116 24W
La Crosse, Kans., U.S.A. 80 F5 38 32N 99 18W
La Crosse, Wis., U.S.A. 80 D9 43 48N 91 15W
La Cruz, Costa Rica 88 D2 11 4N 85 39W
La Cruz, Mexico 86 C3 23 55N 106 54W
La Dorada, Colombia 92 B4 5 30N 74 40W
La Escondida, Mexico 86 C5 24 6N 99 55W
La Esmeralda, Paraguay 94 A3 22 16S 62 33W
La Esperanza, Cuba 88 B3 22 46N 83 44W
La Esperanza, Honduras 88 D2 14 15N 88 10W
La Estrada, Spain 19 A1 42 43N 8 27W
La Fayette, U.S.A. 77 H3 34 42N 85 17W
La Fé, Cuba 88 B3 22 2N 84 15W
La Follette, U.S.A. 77 G3 36 23N 84 7W
La Grande, U.S.A. 82 D4 45 20N 118 5W
La Grange, Calif., U.S.A. 84 H6 37 42N 120 27W
La Grange, Ga., U.S.A. 77 J3 33 2N 85 2W
La Grange, Ky., U.S.A. 76 F3 38 25N 85 23W
La Grange, Tex., U.S.A. 81 L6 29 54N 96 52W
La Guaira, Venezuela 92 A5 10 36N 66 56W
La Güera, Mauritania 50 D1 20 51N 17 0W
La Habana, Cuba 88 B3 23 8N 82 22W
La Harpe, U.S.A. 80 E9 40 35N 90 58W
La Independencia, Mexico 87 D6 16 31N 91 47W
La Isabela, Dom. Rep. 89 C5 19 58N 71 2W
La Jara, U.S.A. 83 H11 37 16N 105 58W
La Junta, U.S.A. 81 F3 37 59N 103 33W
La Laguna, Canary Is. 22 F3 28 28N 16 18W
La Libertad, Guatemala 88 C1 16 47N 90 7W
La Libertad, Mexico 86 B2 29 55N 112 41W
La Ligua, Chile 94 C1 32 30S 71 16W
La Línea de la Concepción, Spain 19 D3 36 15N 5 23W
La Loche, Canada 73 B7 56 29N 109 26W
La Louvière, Belgium 15 D4 50 27N 4 10 E
La Malbaie, Canada 71 C5 47 40N 70 10W
La Mancha, Spain 19 C4 39 10N 2 54W
La Mesa, Calif., U.S.A. 85 N9 32 46N 117 3W
La Mesa, N. Mex., U.S.A. 83 K10 32 7N 106 42W
La Misión, Mexico 86 A1 32 5N 116 50W
La Moure, U.S.A. 80 B5 46 21N 98 18W
La Negra, Chile 94 A1 23 46S 70 18W
La Oliva, Canary Is. 22 F6 28 36N 13 57W
La Orotava, Canary Is. 22 F3 28 22N 16 31W
La Palma, Canary Is. 22 F2 28 40N 17 50W
La Palma, Panama 88 E4 8 15N 78 0W
La Palma del Condado, Spain 19 D2 37 21N 6 38W
La Paloma, Chile 94 C1 30 35S 71 0W
La Pampa □, Argentina 94 D2 36 50S 66 0W
La Paragua, Venezuela 92 B6 6 50N 63 20W
La Paz, Entre Ríos, Argentina 94 C4 30 50S 59 45W
La Paz, San Luis, Argentina 94 C2 33 30S 67 20W
La Paz, Bolivia 92 G5 16 20S 68 10W
La Paz, Honduras 88 D2 14 20N 87 47W
La Paz, Mexico 86 C2 24 10N 110 20W
La Paz Centro, Nic. 88 D2 12 20N 86 41W
La Pedrera, Colombia 92 D5 1 18S 69 43W
La Perouse Str., Asia 30 B11 45 40N 142 0 E
La Pesca, Mexico 87 C5 23 46N 97 47W
La Piedad, Mexico 86 C4 20 20N 102 1W
La Pine, U.S.A. 82 E3 43 40N 121 30W
La Plant, U.S.A. 80 C4 45 9N 100 39W
La Plata, Argentina 94 D4 35 0S 57 55W
La Porte, U.S.A. 76 E2 41 36N 86 43W
La Purísima, Mexico 86 B2 26 10N 112 4W
La Push, U.S.A. 84 C2 47 55N 124 38W
La Quiaca, Argentina 94 A2 22 5S 65 35W
La Reine, Canada 70 C4 48 50N 79 30W
La Restinga, Canary Is. 22 G2 27 38N 17 59W
La Rioja, Argentina 94 B2 29 20S 67 0W
La Rioja □, Argentina 94 B2 29 30S 67 0W
La Rioja □, Spain 19 A4 42 20N 2 20W
La Robla, Spain 19 A3 42 50N 5 41W
La Roche-sur-Yon, France 18 C3 46 40N 1 25W
La Rochelle, France 18 C3 46 10N 1 9W
La Roda, Spain 19 C4 39 13N 2 15W
La Romana, Dom. Rep. 89 C6 18 27N 68 57W
La Ronge, Canada 73 B7 55 5N 105 20W
La Rumorosa, Mexico 85 N10 32 33N 116 4W
La Sabina, Spain 22 C7 38 44N 1 25 E
La Salle, U.S.A. 80 E10 41 20N 89 6W
La Santa, Canary Is. 22 E6 29 5N 13 40W
La Sarre, Canada 70 C4 48 45N 79 15W
La Scie, Canada 71 C8 49 57N 55 36W
La Selva Beach, U.S.A. 84 J5 36 56N 121 51W
La Serena, Chile 94 B1 29 55S 71 10W
La Seyne-sur-Mer, France 18 E6 43 7N 5 52 E
La Spézia, Italy 20 B3 44 7N 9 50 E
La Tortuga, Venezuela 89 D6 11 0N 65 22W
La Tuque, Canada 70 C5 47 30N 72 50W
La Unión, Chile 96 E2 40 10S 73 0W
La Unión, El Salv. 88 D2 13 20N 87 50W
La Unión, Mexico 86 D4 17 58N 101 49W
La Urbana, Venezuela 92 B5 7 8N 66 56W
La Vega, Dom. Rep. 89 C5 19 20N 70 30W
La Venta, Mexico 87 D6 18 8N 94 3W
La Ventura, Mexico 86 C4 24 38N 100 54W
Labe = Elbe →, Europe 16 B5 53 50N 9 0 E
Labé, Guinea 50 F2 11 24N 12 16W
Laberge, L., Canada 72 A1 61 11N 135 12W
Labis, Malaysia 39 L4 2 22N 103 2 E
Laboulaye, Argentina 94 C3 34 10S 63 30W
Labrador, Coast of □, Canada 71 B7 53 20N 61 0W
Labrador City, Canada 71 B6 52 57N 66 55W
Lábrea, Brazil 92 E6 7 15S 64 51W
Labuan, Pulau, Malaysia 36 C5 5 21N 115 13 E
Labuha, Indonesia 37 E7 0 30S 127 30 E
Labuhan, Indonesia 37 G11 6 22S 105 50 E
Labuhanbajo, Indonesia 37 F6 8 28S 120 1 E
Labuk, Telok, Malaysia 36 C5 6 10N 117 50 E
Labyrinth, L., Australia 63 E2 30 40S 135 11 E
Labytnangi, Russia 24 A12 66 39N 66 21 E
Lac Allard, Canada 71 B7 50 33N 63 24W
Lac Bouchette, Canada 71 C5 48 16N 72 11W
Lac du Flambeau, U.S.A. 80 B10 45 58N 89 53W
Lac Édouard, Canada 70 C5 47 40N 72 16W
Lac La Biche, Canada 72 C6 54 45N 111 58W
Lac la Martre = Wha Ti, Canada 68 B8 63 8N 117 16W
Lac-Mégantic, Canada 71 C5 45 35N 70 53W
Lac Seul, Res., Canada 70 B1 50 25N 92 30W
Lac Thien, Vietnam 38 F7 12 25N 108 11 E
Lacanau, France 18 D3 44 58N 1 5W
Lacantúm →, Mexico 87 D6 16 36N 90 40W
Laccadive Is. = Lakshadweep Is., Ind. Oc. 28 H11 10 0N 72 30 E
Lacepede B., Australia 63 F2 36 40S 139 40 E
Lacepede Is., Australia 60 C3 16 55S 122 0 E
Lacerdónia, Mozam. 55 F4 18 3S 35 35 E
Lacey, U.S.A. 84 C4 47 7N 122 49W
Lachhmangarh, India 42 F6 27 50N 75 4 E
Lachi, Pakistan 42 C4 33 25N 71 20 E
Lachine, Canada 70 C5 45 30N 73 40W
Lachlan →, Australia 63 E3 34 22S 143 55 E
Lachute, Canada 70 C5 45 39N 74 21W
Lackawanna, U.S.A. 78 D6 42 50N 78 50W
Lacolle, Canada 79 A11 45 5N 73 22W
Lacombe, Canada 72 C6 52 30N 113 44W
Lacona, U.S.A. 79 C8 43 39N 76 10W
Laconia, U.S.A. 79 C13 43 32N 71 28W
Lacrosse, U.S.A. 82 C5 46 51N 117 58W
Ladakh Ra., India 43 B8 34 0N 78 0 E
Ladismith, S. Africa 56 E3 33 28S 21 15 E
Lādīz, Iran 45 D9 28 55N 61 15 E
Ladnun, India 42 F6 27 38N 74 25 E
Ladoga, L. = Ladozhskoye Ozero, Russia 24 B5 61 15N 30 30 E
Ladozhskoye Ozero, Russia 24 B5 61 15N 30 30 E
Lady Grey, S. Africa 56 E4 30 43S 27 13 E
Ladybrand, S. Africa 56 D4 29 9S 27 29 E
Ladysmith, Canada 72 D4 49 0N 123 49W
Ladysmith, S. Africa 57 D4 28 32S 29 46 E
Ladysmith, U.S.A. 80 C9 45 28N 91 12W
Lae, Papua N. G. 64 H6 6 40S 147 2 E
Laem Ngop, Thailand 39 F4 12 10N 102 26 E
Laem Pho, Thailand 39 J3 6 55N 101 19 E
Læsø, Denmark 9 H14 57 15N 10 53 E
Lafayette, Colo., U.S.A. 80 F2 39 58N 105 12W
Lafayette, Ind., U.S.A. 76 E2 40 25N 86 54W
Lafayette, La., U.S.A. 81 K9 30 14N 92 1W
Lafayette, Tenn., U.S.A. 77 G3 36 31N 86 2W
Laferte →, Canada 72 A5 61 53N 117 44W
Lafia, Nigeria 50 G6 8 30N 8 34 E
Lafleche, Canada 73 D7 49 45N 106 40W
Lagan →, U.K. 13 B6 54 36N 5 55W
Lagarfljót →, Iceland 8 D6 65 40N 14 18W
Lågen →, Oppland, Norway 9 F14 61 8N 10 25 E
Lågen →, Vestfold, Norway 9 G14 59 3N 10 3 E
Laghouat, Algeria 50 B5 33 50N 2 59 E
Lagonoy Gulf, Phil. 37 B6 13 50N 123 50 E
Lagos, Nigeria 50 G5 6 25N 3 27 E
Lagos, Portugal 19 D1 37 5N 8 41W
Lagos de Moreno, Mexico 86 C4 21 21N 101 55W
Lagrange, Australia 60 C3 18 45S 121 43 E
Lagrange B., Australia 60 C3 18 38S 121 42 E
Laguna, Brazil 95 B6 28 30S 48 50W
Laguna, U.S.A. 83 J10 35 2N 107 25W
Laguna Beach, U.S.A. 85 M9 33 33N 117 47W
Laguna Limpia, Argentina 94 B4 26 32S 59 45W
Laguna Madre, U.S.A. 87 B5 27 0N 97 20W
Lagunas, Chile 94 A2 21 0S 69 45W
Lagunas, Peru 92 E3 5 10S 75 35W
Lahad Datu, Malaysia 37 C5 5 0N 118 20 E
Lahan Sai, Thailand 38 E4 14 25N 102 52 E
Lahanam, Laos 38 D5 16 16N 105 16 E
Laharpur, India 43 F9 27 43N 80 56 E
Lahat, Indonesia 36 E2 3 45S 103 30 E
Lahewa, Indonesia 36 D1 1 22N 97 12 E
Lāhījān, Iran 45 B6 37 10N 50 6 E
Lahn →, Germany 16 C4 50 19N 7 37 E
Laholm, Sweden 9 H15 56 30N 13 2 E
Lahontan Reservoir, U.S.A. 82 G4 39 28N 119 4W
Lahore, Pakistan 42 D6 31 32N 74 22 E
Lahti, Finland 9 F21 60 58N 25 40 E
Lahtis = Lahti, Finland 9 F21 60 58N 25 40 E
Laï, Chad 51 G8 9 25N 16 18 E
Lai Chau, Vietnam 38 A4 22 5N 103 3 E
Laidley, Australia 63 D5 27 39S 152 20 E
Laikipia □, Kenya 54 B4 0 30N 36 30 E
Laingsburg, S. Africa 56 E3 33 9S 20 52 E
Lainio älv →, Sweden 8 C20 67 35N 22 40 E
Lairg, U.K. 12 C4 58 2N 4 24W
Laishui, China 34 E8 39 23N 115 45 E
Laiwu, China 35 F9 36 15N 117 40 E
Laixi, China 35 F11 36 50N 120 31 E
Laiyang, China 35 F11 36 59N 120 45 E
Laiyuan, China 34 E8 39 20N 114 40 E
Laizhou Wan, China 35 F10 37 30N 119 30 E
Laja →, Mexico 86 C4 20 55N 100 46W
Lajere, Nigeria 50 F7 12 10N 11 25 E
Lajes, Brazil 95 B5 27 48S 50 20W
Lak Sao, Laos 38 C5 18 11N 104 59 E
Lakaband, Pakistan 42 D3 31 2N 69 15 E
Lake Alpine, U.S.A. 84 G7 38 29N 120 0W
Lake Andes, U.S.A. 80 D5 43 9N 98 32W
Lake Anse, U.S.A. 76 B1 46 42N 88 25W
Lake Arthur, U.S.A. 81 K8 30 5N 92 41W
Lake Cargelligo, Australia 63 E4 33 15S 146 22 E
Lake Charles, U.S.A. 81 K8 30 14N 93 13W
Lake City, Colo., U.S.A. 83 G10 38 2N 107 19W
Lake City, Fla., U.S.A. 77 K4 30 11N 82 38W
Lake City, Iowa, U.S.A. 80 D7 42 16N 94 44W
Lake City, Mich., U.S.A. 76 C3 44 20N 85 13W
Lake City, Minn., U.S.A. 80 C8 44 27N 92 16W
Lake City, Pa., U.S.A. 78 D4 42 1N 80 21W
Lake City, S.C., U.S.A. 77 J6 33 52N 79 45W
Lake George, U.S.A. 79 C11 43 26N 73 43W
Lake Grace, Australia 61 F2 33 7S 118 28 E
Lake Harbour = Kimmirut, Canada 69 B13 62 50N 69 50W
Lake Havasu City, U.S.A. 85 L12 34 27N 114 22W
Lake Hughes, U.S.A. 85 L8 34 41N 118 26W
Lake Isabella, U.S.A. 85 K8 35 38N 118 28W
Lake King, Australia 61 F2 33 5S 119 45 E
Lake Lenore, Canada 73 C8 52 24N 104 59W
Lake Louise, Canada 72 C5 51 30N 116 10W
Lake Mead National Recreation Area, U.S.A. 85 K12 36 15N 114 30W
Lake Mills, U.S.A. 80 D8 43 25N 93 32W
Lake Nash, Australia 62 C2 20 57S 138 0 E
Lake Providence, U.S.A. 81 J9 32 48N 91 10W
Lake River, Canada 70 B3 54 30N 82 31W
Lake Superior Prov. Park, Canada 70 C3 47 45N 84 45W
Lake Village, U.S.A. 81 J9 33 20N 91 17W
Lake Wales, U.S.A. 77 M5 27 54N 81 35W
Lake Worth, U.S.A. 77 M5 26 37N 80 3W
Lakefield, Canada 70 D4 44 25N 78 16W
Lakeland, Australia 62 B3 15 49S 144 57 E
Lakeland, U.S.A. 77 L5 28 3N 81 57W
Lakemba, Fiji 59 D9 18 13S 178 47W
Lakeport, U.S.A. 84 F4 39 3N 122 55W
Lakes Entrance, Australia 63 F4 37 50S 148 0 E
Lakeside, Ariz., U.S.A. 83 J9 34 9N 109 58W
Lakeside, Calif., U.S.A. 85 N10 32 52N 116 55W
Lakeside, Nebr., U.S.A. 80 D3 42 3N 102 26W
Lakeview, U.S.A. 82 E3 42 11N 120 21W
Lakewood, Colo., U.S.A. 80 F2 39 44N 105 5W
Lakewood, N.J., U.S.A. 79 F10 40 6N 74 13W
Lakewood, Ohio, U.S.A. 78 E3 41 29N 81 48W
Lakewood Center, U.S.A. 84 C4 47 11N 122 32W
Lakhaniá, Greece 23 D9 35 58N 27 54 E
Lakhonpheng, Laos 38 E5 15 54N 105 34 E
Lakhpat, India 42 H3 23 48N 68 47 E
Lakin, U.S.A. 81 G4 37 57N 101 15W
Lakitusaki →, Canada 70 B3 54 21N 82 25W
Lákkoi, Greece 23 D5 35 24N 23 57 E
Lakonikós Kólpos, Greece 21 F10 36 40N 22 40 E
Lakor, Indonesia 37 F7 8 15S 128 17 E
Lakota, Ivory C. 50 G3 5 50N 5 30W
Lakota, U.S.A. 80 A5 48 2N 98 21W
Laksefjorden, Norway 8 A22 70 45N 26 50 E
Lakselv, Norway 8 A21 70 2N 25 0 E
Lakshadweep Is., Ind. Oc. 28 H11 10 0N 72 30 E
Lakshmikantapur, India 43 H13 22 5N 88 20 E
Lala Ghat, India 41 G18 24 30N 92 40 E
Lala Musa, Pakistan 42 C5 32 40N 73 57 E
Lalago, Tanzania 54 C3 3 28S 33 58 E
Lalapanzi, Zimbabwe 55 F3 19 20S 30 15 E
Lalganj, India 43 G11 25 52N 85 13 E
Lalibela, Ethiopia 51 F12 12 2N 39 2 E
Lalin, China 35 B14 45 12N 127 0 E
Lalín, Spain 19 A1 42 40N 8 5W
Lalin He →, China 35 B13 45 32N 125 40 E
Lalitapur = Patan, Nepal 41 F14 27 40N 85 20 E
Lalitpur, India 43 G8 24 42N 78 28 E
Lam, Vietnam 38 B6 21 21N 106 31 E
Lam Pao Res., Thailand 38 D4 16 50N 103 15 E
Lamaing, Burma 41 M20 15 25N 97 53 E
Lamar, Colo., U.S.A. 80 F3 38 5N 102 37W
Lamar, Mo., U.S.A. 81 G7 37 30N 94 16W
Lamas, Peru 92 E3 6 28S 76 31W
Lambaréné, Gabon 52 E2 0 41S 10 12 E
Lambasa, Fiji 59 C8 16 30S 179 10 E
Lambay I., Ireland 13 C5 53 29N 6 1W
Lambert, U.S.A. 80 B2 47 41N 104 37W
Lambert Glacier, Antarctica 5 D6 71 0S 70 0 E
Lamberts Bay, S. Africa 56 E2 32 5S 18 17 E
Lame, Nigeria 50 F6 10 30N 9 20 E
Lame Deer, U.S.A. 82 D10 45 37N 106 40W
Lamego, Portugal 19 B2 41 5N 7 52W
Lamèque, Canada 71 C7 47 45N 64 38W
Lameroo, Australia 63 F3 35 19S 140 33 E
Lamesa, U.S.A. 81 J4 32 44N 101 58W
Lamía, Greece 21 E10 38 55N 22 26 E
Lammermuir Hills, U.K. 12 F6 55 50N 2 40W
Lamon Bay, Phil. 37 B6 14 30N 122 20 E
Lamont, Canada 72 C6 53 46N 112 50W
Lamont, U.S.A. 85 K8 35 15N 118 55W
Lampa, Peru 92 G4 15 22S 70 22W
Lampang, Thailand 38 C2 18 16N 99 32 E
Lampasas, U.S.A. 81 K5 31 4N 98 11W
Lampazos de Naranjo, Mexico 86 B4 27 2N 100 32W
Lampedusa, Medit. S. 20 G5 35 36N 12 40 E
Lampeter, U.K. 11 E3 52 7N 4 4W
Lampione, Medit. S. 20 G5 35 33N 12 20 E
Lampman, Canada 73 D8 49 25N 102 50W
Lamprey, Canada 73 B10 58 33N 94 8W
Lampung □, Indonesia 36 F2 5 30S 104 30 E
Lamu, Kenya 54 C5 2 16S 40 55 E
Lamu □, Kenya 54 C5 2 0S 40 45 E
Lamy, U.S.A. 83 J11 35 29N 105 53W
Lan Xian, China 34 E6 38 15N 111 35 E
Lanai I., U.S.A. 74 H16 20 50N 156 55W
Lanak La, India 43 B8 34 27N 79 32 E
Lanak'o Shank'ou = Lanak La, India 43 B8 34 27N 79 32 E
Lanao, L., Phil. 37 C6 7 52N 124 15 E
Lanark, Canada 79 A8 45 1N 76 22W
Lanark, U.K. 12 F5 55 40N 3 47W
Lancang Jiang →, China 32 D5 21 40N 101 10 E
Lancashire □, U.K. 10 D5 53 50N 2 48W
Lancaster, Canada 79 A10 45 10N 74 30W
Lancaster, U.K. 10 C5 54 3N 2 48W
Lancaster, Calif., U.S.A. 85 L8 34 42N 118 8W
Lancaster, Ky., U.S.A. 76 G3 37 37N 84 35W
Lancaster, N.H., U.S.A. 79 B13 44 29N 71 34W
Lancaster, N.Y., U.S.A. 78 D6 42 54N 78 40W
Lancaster, Pa., U.S.A. 79 F8 40 2N 76 19W
Lancaster, S.C., U.S.A. 77 H5 34 43N 80 46W
Lancaster, Wis., U.S.A. 80 D9 42 51N 90 43W
Lancaster Sd., Canada 69 A11 74 13N 84 0W
Lancer, Canada 73 C7 50 48N 108 53W
Lanchow = Lanzhou, China 34 F2 36 1N 103 52 E
Lanciano, Italy 20 C6 42 14N 14 23 E
Lancun, China 35 F11 36 25N 120 10 E
Landeck, Austria 16 E6 47 9N 10 34 E
Landen, Belgium 15 D5 50 45N 5 3 E
Lander, U.S.A. 82 E9 42 50N 108 44W
Lander →, Australia 60 D5 22 0S 132 0 E
Landes, France 18 D3 44 0N 1 0W
Landi Kotal, Pakistan 42 B4 34 7N 71 6 E
Landor, Australia 61 E2 25 10S 116 54 E
Land's End, U.K. 11 G2 50 4N 5 44W
Landsborough Cr. →, Australia 62 C3 22 28S 144 35 E
Landshut, Germany 16 D7 48 34N 12 8 E
Landskrona, Sweden 9 J15 55 53N 12 50 E
Lanesboro, U.S.A. 79 E9 41 57N 75 34W
Lanett, U.S.A. 77 J3 32 52N 85 12W
Lang Bay, Canada 72 D4 49 45N 124 21W
Lang Qua, Vietnam 38 A5 22 16N 104 27 E
Lang Shan, China 34 D4 41 0N 106 30 E
Lang Son, Vietnam 38 B6 21 52N 106 42 E
Lang Suan, Thailand 39 H2 9 57N 99 4 E
La'nga Co, China 41 D12 30 45N 81 15 E
Langar, Iran 45 C9 35 23N 60 25 E
Langara I., Canada 72 C2 54 14N 133 1W
Langdon, U.S.A. 80 A5 48 45N 98 22W
Langeberg, S. Africa 56 E3 33 55S 21 0 E
Langeberge, S. Africa 56 D3 28 15S 22 33 E
Langeland, Denmark 9 J14 54 56N 10 48 E
Langenburg, Canada 73 C8 50 51N 101 43W
Langholm, U.K. 12 F6 55 9N 3 0W
Langjökull, Iceland 8 D3 64 39N 20 12W
Langkawi, P., Malaysia 39 J2 6 25N 99 45 E
Langklip, S. Africa 56 D3 28 12S 20 20 E
Langkon, Malaysia 36 C5 6 30N 116 40 E
Langlade, St- P. & M. 71 C8 46 50N 56 20W
Langlois, U.S.A. 82 E1 42 56N 124 27W
Langøya, Norway 8 B16 68 45N 14 50 E
Langres, France 18 C6 47 52N 5 20 E
Langres, Plateau de, France 18 C6 47 45N 5 3 E
Langsa, Indonesia 36 D1 4 30N 97 57 E
Langtry, U.S.A. 81 L4 29 49N 101 34W
Langu, Thailand 39 J2 6 53N 99 47 E
Languedoc, France 18 E5 43 58N 3 55 E
Langxiangzhen, China 34 E9 39 43N 116 8 E
Lanigan, Canada 73 C7 51 51N 105 2W
Lankao, China 34 G8 34 48N 114 50 E
Länkäran, Azerbaijan 25 G8 38 48N 48 52 E
Lannion, France 18 B2 48 46N 3 29W
L'Annonciation, Canada 70 C5 46 25N 74 55W
Lansdale, U.S.A. 79 F9 40 14N 75 17W
Lansdowne, Australia 63 E5 31 48S 152 30 E
Lansdowne, Canada 79 B8 44 24N 76 1W

Lansdowne House

Longkou

Libyan Desert = Lîbîya, Sahrâ', *Africa* 51 C9 25 0N 25 0 E
Licantén, *Chile* 94 D1 35 55S 72 0W
Licata, *Italy* 20 F5 37 6N 13 56 E
Licheng, *China* 34 F7 36 28N 113 20 E
Lichfield, *U.K.* 10 E6 52 41N 1 49W
Lichinga, *Mozam.* 55 E4 13 13S 35 11 E
Lichtenburg, *S. Africa* 56 D4 26 8S 26 8 E
Lida, *Belarus* 9 K21 53 53N 25 15 E
Lida, *U.S.A.* 83 H5 37 28N 117 30W
Lidköping, *Sweden* 9 G15 58 31N 13 14 E
Liebig, Mt., *Australia* 60 D5 23 18S 131 22 E
Liechtenstein ■, *Europe* 16 E5 47 8N 9 35 E
Liège, *Belgium* 15 D5 50 38N 5 35 E
Liège □, *Belgium* 15 D5 50 32N 5 35 E
Liegnitz = Legnica, *Poland* 16 C9 51 12N 16 10 E
Lienart, *Zaïre* 54 B2 3 3N 25 31 E
Lienyünchiangshih = Lianyungang, *China* 35 G10 34 40N 119 11 E
Lienz, *Austria* 16 E7 46 50N 12 46 E
Liepāja, *Latvia* 9 H19 56 30N 21 0 E
Lier, *Belgium* 15 C4 51 7N 4 34 E
Lièvre →, *Canada* 70 C4 45 31N 75 26W
Liffey →, *Ireland* 13 C5 53 21N 6 13W
Lifford, *Ireland* 13 B4 54 51N 7 29W
Lifudzin, *Russia* 30 B7 44 21N 134 58 E
Lightning Ridge, *Australia* 63 D4 29 22S 148 0 E
Liguria □, *Italy* 20 B3 44 30N 8 50 E
Ligurian Sea, *Medit. S.* 20 C3 43 20N 9 0 E
Lihou Reefs and Cays, *Australia* 62 B5 17 25S 151 40 E
Lihue, *U.S.A.* 74 H15 21 59N 159 23W
Lijiang, *China* 32 D5 26 55N 100 20 E
Likasi, *Zaïre* 55 E2 10 55S 26 48 E
Likati, *Zaïre* 52 D4 3 20N 24 0 E
Likoma I., *Malawi* 55 E3 12 3S 34 45 E
Likumburu, *Tanzania* 55 D4 9 43S 35 8 E
Lille, *France* 18 A5 50 38N 3 3 E
Lille Bælt, *Denmark* 9 J13 55 20N 9 45 E
Lillehammer, *Norway* 9 F14 61 8N 10 30 E
Lillesand, *Norway* 9 G13 58 15N 8 23 E
Lilleshall, *U.K.* 11 E5 52 44N 2 23W
Lillian Point, Mt., *Australia* 61 E4 27 40S 126 6 E
Lillooet →, *Canada* 72 D4 49 15N 121 57W
Lilongwe, *Malawi* 55 E3 14 0S 33 48 E
Liloy, *Phil.* 37 C6 8 4N 122 39 E
Lim →, *Bos.-H.* 21 C8 43 45N 19 15 E
Lima, *Indonesia* 37 E7 3 37S 128 4 E
Lima, *Peru* 92 F3 12 0S 77 0W
Lima, *Mont., U.S.A.* 82 D7 44 38N 112 36W
Lima, *Ohio, U.S.A.* 76 E3 40 44N 84 6W
Lima →, *Portugal* 19 B1 41 41N 8 50W
Limages, *Canada* 79 A9 45 20N 75 16W
Limassol, *Cyprus* 23 E12 34 42N 33 1 E
Limavady, *U.K.* 13 A5 55 3N 6 56W
Limavady □, *U.K.* 13 B5 55 0N 6 55W
Limay →, *Argentina* 96 D3 39 0S 68 0W
Limay Mahuida, *Argentina* 94 D2 37 10S 66 45W
Limbang, *Brunei* 36 D5 4 42N 115 6 E
Limbaži, *Latvia* 9 H21 57 31N 24 42 E
Limbdi, *India* 42 H4 22 34N 71 51 E
Limbe, *Cameroon* 50 H6 4 1N 9 10 E
Limbri, *Australia* 63 E5 31 3S 151 5 E
Limbunya, *Australia* 60 C4 17 14S 129 50 E
Limburg, *Germany* 16 C5 50 22N 8 4 E
Limburg □, *Belgium* 15 C5 51 2N 5 25 E
Limburg □, *Neths.* 15 C5 51 20N 5 55 E
Limeira, *Brazil* 95 A6 22 35S 47 28W
Limerick, *Ireland* 13 D3 52 40N 8 37W
Limerick □, *Ireland* 13 D3 52 30N 8 50W
Limestone, *U.S.A.* 78 D6 42 2N 78 38W
Limestone →, *Canada* 73 B10 56 31N 94 7W
Limfjorden, *Denmark* 9 H13 56 55N 9 0 E
Limia = Lima →, *Portugal* 19 B1 41 41N 8 50W
Limingen, *Norway* 8 D15 64 48N 13 35 E
Limmen Bight, *Australia* 62 A2 14 40S 135 35 E
Limmen Bight →, *Australia* 62 B2 15 7S 135 44 E
Límnos, *Greece* 21 E11 39 50N 25 5 E
Limoeiro do Norte, *Brazil* 93 E11 5 5S 38 0W
Limoges, *France* 18 D4 45 50N 1 15 E
Limón, *Costa Rica* 88 D3 10 0N 83 2W
Limon, *U.S.A.* 80 F3 39 16N 103 41W
Limousin, *France* 18 D4 45 30N 1 30 E
Limoux, *France* 18 E5 43 4N 2 12 E
Limpopo →, *Africa* 57 D5 25 5S 33 30 E
Limuru, *Kenya* 54 C4 1 2S 36 35 E
Lin Xian, *China* 34 F6 37 57N 110 58 E
Linares, *Chile* 94 D1 35 50S 71 40W
Linares, *Mexico* 87 C5 24 50N 99 40W
Linares, *Spain* 19 C4 38 10N 3 40W
Linares □, *Chile* 94 D1 36 0S 71 0W
Lincheng, *China* 34 F8 37 25N 114 30 E
Lincoln, *Argentina* 94 C3 34 55S 61 30W
Lincoln, *N.Z.* 59 K4 43 38S 172 30 E
Lincoln, *U.K.* 10 D7 53 14N 0 32W
Lincoln, *Calif., U.S.A.* 84 G5 38 54N 121 17W
Lincoln, *Ill., U.S.A.* 80 E10 40 9N 89 22W
Lincoln, *Kans., U.S.A.* 80 F5 39 3N 98 9W
Lincoln, *Maine, U.S.A.* 71 C6 45 22N 68 30W
Lincoln, *N.H., U.S.A.* 79 B13 44 3N 71 40W
Lincoln, *N. Mex., U.S.A.* 83 K11 33 30N 105 23W
Lincoln, *Nebr., U.S.A.* 80 E6 40 49N 96 41W
Lincoln Hav = Lincoln Sea, *Arctic* 4 A5 84 0N 55 0W
Lincoln Sea, *Arctic* 4 A5 84 0N 55 0W
Lincolnshire □, *U.K.* 10 D7 53 14N 0 32W
Lincolnshire Wolds, *U.K.* 10 D7 53 26N 0 13W
Lincolnton, *U.S.A.* 77 H5 35 29N 81 16W
Lind, *U.S.A.* 82 C4 46 58N 118 37W
Linda, *U.S.A.* 84 F5 39 8N 121 34W
Linden, *Guyana* 92 B7 6 0N 58 10W
Linden, *Calif., U.S.A.* 84 G5 38 1N 121 5W
Linden, *Tex., U.S.A.* 81 J7 33 1N 94 22W
Lindenhurst, *U.S.A.* 79 F11 40 41N 73 23W
Lindesnes, *Norway* 9 H12 57 58N 7 3 E
Líndhos, *Greece* 23 C10 36 6N 28 4 E
Lindi, *Tanzania* 55 D4 9 58S 39 38 E
Lindi □, *Tanzania* 55 D4 9 40S 38 30 E
Lindi →, *Zaïre* 54 B2 0 33N 25 5 E
Lindsay, *Canada* 70 D4 44 22N 78 43W
Lindsay, *Calif., U.S.A.* 83 H4 36 12N 119 5W
Lindsay, *Okla., U.S.A.* 81 H6 34 50N 97 38W
Lindsborg, *U.S.A.* 80 F6 38 35N 97 40W
Linfen, *China* 34 F6 36 3N 111 30 E
Ling Xian, *China* 34 F9 37 22N 116 30 E
Lingao, *China* 38 C7 19 56N 109 42 E
Lingayen, *Phil.* 37 A6 16 1N 120 14 E
Lingayen G., *Phil.* 37 A6 16 10N 120 15 E
Lingbi, *China* 35 H9 33 33N 117 33 E
Lingchuan, *China* 34 G7 35 45N 113 12 E
Lingen, *Germany* 16 B4 52 31N 7 19 E
Lingga, *Indonesia* 36 E2 0 12S 104 37 E
Lingga, Kepulauan, *Indonesia* 36 E2 0 10S 104 30 E
Lingga Arch. = Lingga, Kepulauan, *Indonesia* 36 E2 0 10S 104 30 E
Lingle, *U.S.A.* 80 D2 42 8N 104 21W
Lingqiu, *China* 34 E8 39 28N 114 22 E
Lingshi, *China* 34 F6 36 48N 111 48 E
Lingshou, *China* 34 E8 38 20N 114 20 E
Lingshui, *China* 38 C8 18 27N 110 0 E
Lingtai, *China* 34 G4 35 0N 107 40 E
Linguéré, *Senegal* 50 E1 15 25N 15 5W
Lingwu, *China* 34 E4 38 6N 106 20 E
Lingyuan, *China* 35 D10 41 10N 119 15 E
Linh Cam, *Vietnam* 38 C5 18 31N 105 31 E
Linhai, *China* 33 D7 28 50N 121 8 E
Linhares, *Brazil* 93 G10 19 25S 40 4W
Linhe, *China* 34 D4 40 48N 107 20 E
Linjiang, *China* 35 D14 41 50N 127 0 E
Linköping, *Sweden* 9 G16 58 28N 15 36 E
Linkou, *China* 35 B16 45 15N 130 18 E
Linlithgow, *U.K.* 12 F5 55 58N 3 37W
Linnhe, L., *U.K.* 12 E3 56 36N 5 25W
Linosa, I., *Medit. S.* 20 G5 35 51N 12 50 E
Linqi, *China* 34 G7 35 45N 113 52 E
Linqing, *China* 34 F8 36 50N 115 42 E
Linqu, *China* 35 F10 36 25N 118 30 E
Linru, *China* 34 G7 34 11N 112 52 E
Lins, *Brazil* 95 A6 21 40S 49 44W
Lintao, *China* 34 G2 35 18N 103 52 E
Lintlaw, *Canada* 73 C8 52 4N 103 14W
Linton, *Canada* 71 C5 47 15N 72 16W
Linton, *Ind., U.S.A.* 76 F2 39 2N 87 10W
Linton, *N. Dak., U.S.A.* 80 B4 46 16N 100 14W
Lintong, *China* 34 G5 34 20N 109 10 E
Linville, *Australia* 63 D5 26 50S 152 11 E
Linwood, *Canada* 78 C4 43 35N 80 43W
Linxi, *China* 35 C10 43 36N 118 2 E
Linxia, *China* 32 C5 35 36N 103 10 E
Linyanti →, *Africa* 56 B4 17 50S 25 5 E
Linyi, *China* 35 G10 35 5N 118 21 E
Linz, *Austria* 16 D8 48 18N 14 18 E
Linzhenzhen, *China* 34 F5 36 30N 109 59 E
Linzi, *China* 35 F10 36 50N 118 20 E
Lion, G. du, *France* 18 E6 43 10N 4 0 E
Lionárisso, *Cyprus* 23 D13 35 28N 34 8 E
Lions, G. of = Lion, G. du, *France* 18 E6 43 10N 4 0 E
Lion's Den, *Zimbabwe* 55 F3 17 15S 30 5 E
Lion's Head, *Canada* 70 D3 44 58N 81 15W
Lipa, *Phil.* 37 B6 13 57N 121 10 E
Lipali, *Mozam.* 55 F4 15 50S 35 50 E
Lipari, *Italy* 20 E6 38 26N 14 58 E
Lipari, Is. = Eólie, Ís., *Italy* 20 E6 38 30N 14 57 E
Lipcani, *Moldova* 17 D14 48 14N 26 48 E
Lipetsk, *Russia* 24 D6 52 37N 39 35 E
Lipkany = Lipcani, *Moldova* 17 D14 48 14N 26 48 E
Lipovcy Manzovka, *Russia* 30 B6 44 12N 132 26 E
Lipovets, *Ukraine* 17 D15 49 12N 29 1 E
Lippe →, *Germany* 16 C4 51 39N 6 36 E
Lipscomb, *U.S.A.* 81 G4 36 14N 100 16W
Liptrap C., *Australia* 63 F4 38 50S 145 55 E
Lira, *Uganda* 54 B3 2 17N 32 57 E
Liria, *Spain* 19 C5 39 37N 0 35W
Lisala, *Zaïre* 52 D4 2 12N 21 38 E
Lisboa, *Portugal* 19 C1 38 42N 9 10W
Lisbon = Lisboa, *Portugal* 19 C1 38 42N 9 10W
Lisbon, *N. Dak., U.S.A.* 80 B6 46 27N 97 41W
Lisbon, *N.H., U.S.A.* 79 B13 44 13N 71 55W
Lisbon, *Ohio, U.S.A.* 78 F4 40 46N 80 46W
Lisburn, *U.K.* 13 B5 54 31N 6 3W
Lisburne, C., *U.S.A.* 68 B3 68 53N 166 13W
Liscannor, B., *Ireland* 13 D2 52 55N 9 24W
Lishi, *China* 34 F6 37 31N 111 8 E
Lishu, *China* 35 C13 43 20N 124 18 E
Lisianski I., *Pac. Oc.* 64 E10 26 2N 174 0W
Lisichansk = Lysychansk, *Ukraine* 25 E6 48 55N 38 30 E
Lisieux, *France* 18 B4 49 10N 0 12 E
Liski, *Russia* 25 D6 51 3N 39 30 E
Lismore, *Australia* 63 D5 28 44S 153 21 E
Lismore, *Ireland* 13 D4 52 8N 7 55W
Lisse, *Neths.* 15 B4 52 16N 4 33 E
Lista, *Norway* 9 G12 58 7N 6 39 E
Lister, Mt., *Antarctica* 5 D11 78 0S 162 0 E
Liston, *Australia* 63 D5 28 39S 152 6 E
Listowel, *Canada* 70 D3 43 44N 80 58W
Listowel, *Ireland* 13 D2 52 27N 9 29W
Litang, *Malaysia* 37 C5 5 27N 118 31 E
Litani →, *Lebanon* 47 B4 33 20N 35 15 E
Litchfield, *Calif., U.S.A.* 84 E6 40 24N 120 23W
Litchfield, *Conn., U.S.A.* 79 E11 41 45N 73 11W
Litchfield, *Ill., U.S.A.* 80 F10 39 11N 89 39W
Litchfield, *Minn., U.S.A.* 80 C7 45 8N 94 32W
Lithgow, *Australia* 63 E5 33 25S 150 8 E
Líthinon, Ákra, *Greece* 23 E6 34 55N 24 44 E
Lithuania ■, *Europe* 9 J20 55 30N 24 0 E
Litoměřice, *Czech.* 16 C8 50 33N 14 10 E
Little Abaco I., *Bahamas* 88 A4 26 50N 77 30W
Little Barrier I., *N.Z.* 59 G5 36 12S 175 8 E
Little Belt Mts., *U.S.A.* 82 C8 46 40N 110 45W
Little Blue →, *U.S.A.* 80 F6 39 42N 96 41W
Little Cadotte →, *Canada* 72 B5 56 41N 117 6W
Little Cayman, I., *Cayman Is.* 88 C3 19 41N 80 3W
Little Churchill →, *Canada* 73 B9 57 30N 95 22W
Little Colorado →, *U.S.A.* 83 H8 36 12N 111 48W
Little Current, *Canada* 70 C3 45 55N 82 0W
Little Current →, *Canada* 70 B3 50 57N 84 36W
Little Falls, *Minn., U.S.A.* 80 C7 45 59N 94 22W
Little Falls, *N.Y., U.S.A.* 79 C10 43 3N 74 51W
Little Fork →, *U.S.A.* 80 A8 48 31N 93 35W
Little Grand Rapids, *Canada* 73 C9 52 0N 95 29W
Little Humboldt →, *U.S.A.* 82 F5 41 1N 117 43W
Little Inagua I., *Bahamas* 89 B5 21 40N 73 50W
Little Karoo, *S. Africa* 56 E3 33 45S 21 0 E
Little Lake, *U.S.A.* 85 K9 35 56N 117 55W
Little Laut Is. = Laut Kecil, Kepulauan, *Indonesia* 36 E5 4 45S 115 40 E
Little Minch, *U.K.* 12 D2 57 35N 6 45W
Little Missouri →, *U.S.A.* 80 B3 47 36N 102 25W
Little Ouse →, *U.K.* 11 E8 52 22N 1 12 E
Little Rann, *India* 42 H4 23 25N 71 25 E
Little Red →, *U.S.A.* 81 H9 35 11N 91 27W
Little River, *N.Z.* 59 K4 43 45S 172 49 E
Little Rock, *U.S.A.* 81 H8 34 45N 92 17W
Little Ruaha →, *Tanzania* 54 D4 7 57S 37 53 E
Little Sable Pt., *U.S.A.* 76 D2 43 38N 86 33W
Little Sioux →, *U.S.A.* 80 E6 41 48N 96 4W
Little Smoky →, *Canada* 72 C5 54 44N 117 11W
Little Snake →, *U.S.A.* 82 F9 40 27N 108 26W
Little Valley, *U.S.A.* 78 D6 42 15N 78 48W
Little Wabash →, *U.S.A.* 76 G1 37 55N 88 5W
Littlefield, *U.S.A.* 81 J3 33 55N 102 20W
Littlefork, *U.S.A.* 80 A8 48 24N 93 34W
Littlehampton, *U.K.* 11 G7 50 49N 0 32W
Littleton, *U.S.A.* 79 B13 44 18N 71 46W
Liu He →, *China* 35 D11 40 55N 121 35 E
Liuba, *China* 34 H4 33 38N 106 55 E
Liugou, *China* 35 D10 40 57N 118 15 E
Liuhe, *China* 35 C13 42 17N 125 43 E
Liukang Tenggaja, *Indonesia* 37 F5 6 45S 118 50 E
Liuli, *Tanzania* 55 E3 11 3S 34 38 E
Liuwa Plain, *Zambia* 53 G4 14 20S 22 30 E
Liuzhou, *China* 33 D5 24 22N 109 22 E
Liuzhuang, *China* 35 H11 33 12N 120 18 E
Livadhia, *Cyprus* 23 E12 34 57N 33 38 E
Live Oak, *Calif., U.S.A.* 84 F5 39 17N 121 40W
Live Oak, *Fla., U.S.A.* 77 K4 30 18N 82 59W
Liveras, *Cyprus* 23 D11 35 23N 32 57 E
Liveringa, *Australia* 60 C3 18 3S 124 10 E
Livermore, *U.S.A.* 84 H5 37 41N 121 47W
Livermore, Mt., *U.S.A.* 81 K2 30 38N 104 11W
Liverpool, *Australia* 63 E5 33 54S 150 58 E
Liverpool, *Canada* 71 D7 44 5N 64 41W
Liverpool, *U.K.* 10 D5 53 25N 3 0W
Liverpool Plains, *Australia* 63 E5 31 15S 150 15 E
Liverpool Ra., *Australia* 63 E5 31 50S 150 30 E
Livingston, *Guatemala* 88 C2 15 50N 88 50W
Livingston, *Calif., U.S.A.* 84 H6 37 23N 120 43W
Livingston, *Mont., U.S.A.* 82 D8 45 40N 110 34W
Livingston, *Tex., U.S.A.* 81 K7 30 43N 94 56W
Livingstone, *Zambia* 55 F2 17 46S 25 52 E
Livingstone Mts., *Tanzania* 55 D3 9 40S 34 20 E
Livingstonia, *Malawi* 55 E3 10 38S 34 5 E
Livny, *Russia* 24 D6 52 30N 37 30 E
Livonia, *U.S.A.* 76 D4 42 23N 83 23W
Livorno, *Italy* 20 C4 43 33N 10 19 E
Livramento, *Brazil* 95 C4 30 55S 55 30W
Liwale, *Tanzania* 55 D4 9 48S 37 58 E
Liwale □, *Tanzania* 55 D4 9 0S 38 0 E
Lizard I., *Australia* 62 A4 14 42S 145 30 E
Lizard Pt., *U.K.* 11 H2 49 57N 5 13W
Ljubljana, *Slovenia* 16 E8 46 4N 14 33 E
Ljungan →, *Sweden* 9 E17 62 18N 17 23 E
Ljungby, *Sweden* 9 H15 56 49N 13 55 E
Ljusdal, *Sweden* 9 F17 61 46N 16 3 E
Ljusnan →, *Sweden* 9 F17 61 12N 17 8 E
Ljusne, *Sweden* 9 F17 61 13N 17 7 E
Llancanelo, Salina, *Argentina* 94 D2 35 40S 69 8W
Llandeilo, *U.K.* 11 F3 51 53N 3 59W
Llandovery, *U.K.* 11 F4 51 59N 3 48W
Llandrindod Wells, *U.K.* 11 E4 52 14N 3 22W
Llandudno, *U.K.* 10 D4 53 19N 3 50W
Llanelli, *U.K.* 11 F3 51 41N 4 10W
Llanes, *Spain* 19 A3 43 25N 4 50W
Llangollen, *U.K.* 10 E4 52 58N 3 11W
Llanidloes, *U.K.* 11 E4 52 27N 3 31W
Llano, *U.S.A.* 81 K5 30 45N 98 41W
Llano →, *U.S.A.* 81 K5 30 39N 98 26W
Llano Estacado, *U.S.A.* 81 J3 33 30N 103 0W
Llanos, *S. Amer.* 92 B4 5 0N 71 35W
Llebetx, C., *Spain* 22 B9 39 33N 2 18 E
Lleida = Lérida, *Spain* 19 B6 41 37N 0 39 E
Llentrisca, C., *Spain* 22 C7 38 52N 1 15 E
Llera, *Mexico* 87 C5 23 19N 99 1W
Llico, *Chile* 94 C1 34 46S 72 5W
Llobregat →, *Spain* 19 B7 41 19N 2 9 E
Lloret de Mar, *Spain* 19 B7 41 41N 2 53 E
Lloyd B., *Australia* 62 A3 12 45S 143 27 E
Lloyd L., *Canada* 73 B7 57 22N 108 57W
Lloydminster, *Canada* 73 C7 53 17N 110 0W
Lluchmayor, *Spain* 22 B9 39 29N 2 53 E
Llullaillaco, Volcán, *S. Amer.* 94 A2 24 43S 68 30W
Lo →, *Vietnam* 38 B5 21 18N 105 25 E
Loa, *U.S.A.* 83 G8 38 24N 111 39W
Loa →, *Chile* 94 A1 21 26S 70 41W
Lobatse, *Botswana* 56 D4 25 12S 25 40 E
Lobería, *Argentina* 94 D4 38 10S 58 40W
Lobito, *Angola* 53 G2 12 18S 13 35 E
Lobos, *Argentina* 94 D4 35 10S 59 0W
Lobos, I., *Mexico* 86 B2 27 15N 110 30W
Lobos, I. de, *Canary Is.* 22 F6 28 45N 13 50W
Loc Binh, *Vietnam* 38 B6 21 46N 106 54 E
Loc Ninh, *Vietnam* 39 G6 11 50N 106 34 E
Locarno, *Switz.* 16 E5 46 10N 8 47 E
Loch Garman = Wexford, *Ireland* 13 D5 52 20N 6 28W
Lochaber, *U.K.* 12 E4 56 59N 5 1W
Lochcarron, *U.K.* 12 D3 57 24N 5 31W
Lochem, *Neths.* 15 B6 52 9N 6 26 E
Loches, *France* 18 C4 47 7N 1 0 E
Lochgelly, *U.K.* 12 E5 56 7N 3 19W
Lochgilphead, *U.K.* 12 E3 56 2N 5 26W
Lochinver, *U.K.* 12 C3 58 9N 5 14W
Lochnagar, *Australia* 62 C4 23 33S 145 38 E
Lochnagar, *U.K.* 12 E5 56 57N 3 15W
Lochy →, *U.K.* 12 E3 56 52N 5 3W
Lock, *Australia* 63 E2 33 34S 135 46 E
Lock Haven, *U.S.A.* 78 E7 41 8N 77 28W
Lockeford, *U.S.A.* 84 G5 38 10N 121 9W
Lockeport, *Canada* 71 D6 43 47N 65 4W
Lockerbie, *U.K.* 12 F5 55 7N 3 21W
Lockhart, *U.S.A.* 81 L6 29 53N 97 40W
Lockhart, L., *Australia* 61 F2 33 15S 119 3 E
Lockney, *U.S.A.* 81 H4 34 7N 101 27W
Lockport, *U.S.A.* 78 C6 43 10N 78 42W
Lod, *Israel* 47 D3 31 57N 34 54 E
Lodeinoye Pole, *Russia* 24 B5 60 44N 33 33 E
Lodge Grass, *U.S.A.* 82 D10 45 19N 107 22W
Lodgepole, *U.S.A.* 80 E3 41 9N 102 38W
Lodgepole Cr. →, *U.S.A.* 80 E2 41 20N 104 30W
Lodhran, *Pakistan* 42 E4 29 32N 71 30 E
Lodi, *Italy* 20 B3 45 19N 9 30 E
Lodi, *U.S.A.* 84 G5 38 8N 121 16W
Lodja, *Zaïre* 54 C1 3 30S 23 23 E
Lodwar, *Kenya* 54 B4 3 10N 35 40 E
Łódź, *Poland* 17 C10 51 45N 19 27 E
Loei, *Thailand* 38 D3 17 29N 101 35 E
Loengo, *Zaïre* 54 C2 4 48S 26 30 E
Loeriesfontein, *S. Africa* 56 E2 31 0S 19 26 E
Lofoten, *Norway* 8 B15 68 30N 14 0 E
Logan, *Kans., U.S.A.* 80 F5 39 40N 99 34W
Logan, *Ohio, U.S.A.* 76 F4 39 32N 82 25W
Logan, *Utah, U.S.A.* 82 F8 41 44N 111 50W
Logan, *W. Va., U.S.A.* 76 G5 37 51N 81 59W
Logan, Mt., *Canada* 68 B5 60 31N 140 22W
Logan Pass, *U.S.A.* 72 D6 48 41N 113 44W
Logandale, *U.S.A.* 85 J12 36 36N 114 29W
Logansport, *Ind., U.S.A.* 76 E2 40 45N 86 22W
Logansport, *La., U.S.A.* 81 K8 31 58N 94 0W
Logone →, *Chad* 51 F8 12 6N 15 2 E
Logroño, *Spain* 19 A4 42 28N 2 27W
Lohardaga, *India* 43 H11 23 27N 84 45 E
Lohja, *Finland* 9 F21 60 12N 24 5 E
Loi-kaw, *Burma* 41 K20 19 40N 97 17 E
Loimaa, *Finland* 9 F20 60 50N 23 5 E
Loir →, *France* 18 C3 47 33N 0 32W
Loire →, *France* 18 C2 47 16N 2 10W
Loja, *Ecuador* 92 D3 3 59S 79 16W
Loja, *Spain* 19 D3 37 10N 4 10W
Loji, *Indonesia* 37 E7 1 38S 127 28 E
Lokandu, *Zaïre* 54 C2 2 30S 25 45 E
Lokeren, *Belgium* 15 C3 51 6N 3 59 E
Lokichokio, *Kenya* 54 B3 4 19N 34 13 E
Lokitaung, *Kenya* 54 B4 4 12N 35 48 E
Lokkan tekojärvi, *Finland* 8 C22 67 55N 27 35 E
Lokoja, *Nigeria* 50 G6 7 47N 6 45 E
Lokolama, *Zaïre* 52 E3 2 35S 19 50 E
Lola, Mt., *U.S.A.* 84 F6 39 26N 120 22W
Loliondo, *Tanzania* 54 C4 2 2S 35 39 E
Lolland, *Denmark* 9 J14 54 45N 11 30 E
Lolo, *U.S.A.* 82 C6 46 45N 114 5W
Lom, *Bulgaria* 21 C10 43 48N 23 12 E
Lom Kao, *Thailand* 38 D3 16 53N 101 14 E
Lom Sak, *Thailand* 38 D3 16 47N 101 15 E
Loma, *U.S.A.* 82 C8 47 56N 110 30W
Loma Linda, *U.S.A.* 85 L9 34 3N 117 16W
Lomami →, *Zaïre* 54 B1 0 46N 24 16 E
Lomas de Zamóra, *Argentina* 94 C4 34 45S 58 25W
Lombadina, *Australia* 60 C3 16 31S 122 54 E
Lombárdia □, *Italy* 20 B3 45 40N 9 30 E
Lombardy = Lombárdia □, *Italy* 20 B3 45 40N 9 30 E
Lomblen, *Indonesia* 37 F6 8 30S 123 32 E
Lombok, *Indonesia* 36 F5 8 45S 116 30 E
Lomé, *Togo* 50 G5 6 9N 1 20 E
Lomela, *Zaïre* 52 E4 2 19S 23 15 E
Lomela →, *Zaïre* 52 E4 0 15S 20 40 E
Lometa, *U.S.A.* 81 K5 31 13N 98 24W
Lomié, *Cameroon* 52 D2 3 13N 13 38 E
Lomond, *Canada* 72 C6 50 24N 112 36W
Lomond, L., *U.K.* 12 E4 56 8N 4 38W
Lomphat, *Cambodia* 38 F6 13 30N 106 59 E
Lompobatang, *Indonesia* 37 F5 5 24S 119 56 E
Lompoc, *U.S.A.* 85 L6 34 38N 120 28W
Łomza, *Poland* 17 B12 53 10N 22 2 E
Loncoche, *Chile* 96 D2 39 20S 72 50W
Londa, *India* 40 M9 15 30N 74 30 E
Londiani, *Kenya* 54 C4 0 10S 35 33 E
London, *Canada* 70 D3 42 59N 81 15W
London, *U.K.* 11 F7 51 30N 0 3W
London, *Ky., U.S.A.* 76 G3 37 8N 84 5W
London, *Ohio, U.S.A.* 76 F4 39 53N 83 27W
London, Greater □, *U.K.* 11 F7 51 36N 0 5W
Londonderry, *U.K.* 13 B4 55 0N 7 20W
Londonderry □, *U.K.* 13 B4 55 0N 7 20W
Londonderry, C., *Australia* 60 B4 13 45S 126 55 E
Londonderry, I., *Chile* 96 H2 55 0S 71 0W
Londrina, *Brazil* 95 A5 23 18S 51 10W
Lone Pine, *U.S.A.* 83 H4 36 36N 118 4W
Long Beach, *Calif., U.S.A.* 85 M8 33 47N 118 11W
Long Beach, *N.Y., U.S.A.* 79 F11 40 35N 73 39W
Long Beach, *Wash., U.S.A.* 84 D2 46 21N 124 3W
Long Branch, *U.S.A.* 79 F11 40 18N 74 0W
Long Creek, *U.S.A.* 82 D4 44 43N 119 6W
Long Eaton, *U.K.* 10 E6 52 53N 1 15W
Long I., *Australia* 62 C4 22 8S 149 53 E
Long I., *Bahamas* 89 B4 23 20N 75 10W
Long I., *U.S.A.* 79 F11 40 45N 73 30W
Long Island Sd., *U.S.A.* 79 E12 41 10N 73 0W
Long L., *Canada* 70 C2 49 30N 86 50W
Long Lake, *U.S.A.* 79 C10 43 58N 74 25W
Long Pine, *U.S.A.* 80 D5 42 32N 99 42W
Long Point B., *Canada* 78 D4 42 40N 80 10W
Long Pt., *Nfld., Canada* 71 C8 48 47N 58 46W
Long Pt., *Ont., Canada* 78 D4 42 35N 80 2W
Long Range Mts., *Canada* 71 C8 49 30N 57 30W
Long Reef, *Australia* 60 B4 14 1S 125 48 E
Long Str. = Longa, Proliv, *Russia* 4 C16 70 0N 175 0 E
Long Thanh, *Vietnam* 39 G6 10 47N 106 57 E
Long Xian, *China* 34 G4 34 55N 106 55 E
Long Xuyen, *Vietnam* 39 G5 10 19N 105 28 E
Longa, Proliv, *Russia* 4 C16 70 0N 175 0 E
Longde, *China* 34 G4 35 30N 106 20 E
Longford, *Australia* 62 G4 41 32S 147 3 E
Longford, *Ireland* 13 C4 53 43N 7 49W
Longford □, *Ireland* 13 C4 53 42N 7 45W
Longguan, *China* 34 D8 40 45N 115 30 E
Longhua, *China* 35 D9 41 18N 117 45 E
Longido, *Tanzania* 54 C4 2 43S 36 42 E
Longiram, *Indonesia* 36 E5 0 5S 115 45 E
Longkou, *China* 35 F11 37 40N 120 18 E

Maluku

McGehee, U.S.A. 81 J9 33 38N 91 24W
McGill, U.S.A. 82 G6 39 23N 114 47W
Macgillycuddy's Reeks, Ireland 13 D2 51 58N 9 45W
MacGregor, Canada 73 D9 49 57N 98 48W
McGregor, U.S.A. 80 D9 43 1N 91 11W
McGregor →, Canada 72 B4 55 10N 122 0W
McGregor Ra., Australia 63 D3 27 0S 142 45 E
Mach, Pakistan 40 E5 29 50N 67 20 E
Mâch Kowr, Iran 45 E9 25 48N 61 28 E
Machado = Jiparaná →, Brazil 92 E6 8 3S 62 52W
Machagai, Argentina 94 B3 26 56S 60 2W
Machakos, Kenya 54 C4 1 30S 37 15 E
Machakos □, Kenya 54 C4 1 30S 37 15 E
Machala, Ecuador 92 D3 3 20S 79 57W
Machanga, Mozam. 57 C6 20 59S 35 0 E
Machattie, L., Australia 62 C2 24 50S 139 48 E
Machava, Mozam. 57 D5 25 54S 32 28 E
Machece, Mozam. 55 F4 19 15S 35 32 E
Machevna, Russia 27 C18 61 20N 172 20 E
Machias, U.S.A. 71 D6 44 43N 67 28W
Machichi →, Canada 73 B10 57 3N 92 6W
Machico, Madeira 22 D3 32 43N 16 44W
Machilipatnam, India 41 L12 16 12N 81 8 E
Machiques, Venezuela 92 A4 10 4N 72 34W
Machupicchu, Peru 92 F4 13 8S 72 30W
Machynlleth, U.K. 11 E4 52 35N 3 50W
McIlwraith Ra., Australia 62 A3 13 50S 143 20 E
McIntosh, U.S.A. 80 C4 45 55N 101 21W
McIntosh L., Canada 73 B8 55 45N 105 0W
Macintosh Ra., Australia 61 E4 27 39S 125 32 E
Macintyre →, Australia 63 D5 28 37S 150 47 E
Mackay, Australia 62 C4 21 8S 149 11 E
Mackay, U.S.A. 82 E7 43 55N 113 37W
MacKay →, Canada 72 B6 57 10N 111 38W
Mackay, L., Australia 60 D4 22 30S 129 0 E
McKay Ra., Australia 60 D3 23 0S 122 30 E
McKeesport, U.S.A. 78 F5 40 21N 79 52W
McKenna, U.S.A. 84 D4 46 56N 122 33W
Mackenzie, Canada 72 B4 55 20N 123 5W
McKenzie, U.S.A. 77 G1 36 8N 88 31W
Mackenzie →, Australia 62 C4 23 38S 149 46 E
Mackenzie →, Canada 68 B6 69 10N 134 20W
McKenzie →, U.S.A. 82 D2 44 7N 123 6W
Mackenzie Bay, Canada 4 B1 69 0N 137 30W
Mackenzie City = Linden, Guyana 92 B7 6 0N 58 10W
Mackenzie Highway, Canada 72 B5 58 0N 117 15W
Mackenzie Mts., Canada 68 B6 64 0N 130 0W
Mackinaw City, U.S.A. 76 C3 45 47N 84 44W
McKinlay, Australia 62 C3 21 16S 141 18 E
McKinlay →, Australia 62 C3 20 50S 141 28 E
McKinley, Mt., U.S.A. 68 B4 63 4N 151 0W
McKinley Sea, Arctic 4 A7 82 0N 0 0 E
McKinney, U.S.A. 81 J6 33 12N 96 37W
Mackinnon Road, Kenya 54 C4 3 40S 39 1 E
Macksville, Australia 63 E5 30 40S 152 56 E
McLaughlin, U.S.A. 80 C4 45 49N 100 49W
Maclean, Australia 63 D5 29 26S 153 16 E
McLean, U.S.A. 81 H4 35 14N 100 36W
McLeansboro, U.S.A. 80 F10 38 6N 88 32W
Maclear, S. Africa 57 E4 31 2S 28 23 E
Macleay →, Australia 63 E5 30 56S 153 0 E
McLennan, Canada 72 B5 55 42N 116 50W
MacLeod, B., Canada 73 A7 62 53N 110 0W
McLeod, L., Australia 61 D1 24 9S 113 47 E
MacLeod Lake, Canada 72 C4 54 58N 123 0W
McLoughlin, Mt., U.S.A. 82 E2 42 27N 122 19W
McLure, Canada 72 C4 51 2N 120 13W
McMechen, U.S.A. 78 G4 39 57N 80 44W
McMillan, L., U.S.A. 81 J2 32 36N 104 21W
McMinnville, Oreg., U.S.A. 82 D2 45 13N 123 12W
McMinnville, Tenn., U.S.A. 77 H3 35 41N 85 46W
McMorran, Canada 73 C7 51 19N 108 42W
McMurdo Sd., Antarctica 5 D11 77 0S 170 0 E
McMurray = Fort McMurray, Canada 72 B6 56 44N 111 7W
McMurray, U.S.A. 84 B4 48 19N 122 14W
McNary, U.S.A. 83 J9 34 4N 109 51W
MacNutt, Canada 73 C8 51 5N 101 36W
Macodoene, Mozam. 57 C6 23 32S 35 5 E
Macomb, U.S.A. 80 E9 40 27N 90 40W
Mâcon, France 18 C6 46 19N 4 50 E
Macon, Ga., U.S.A. 77 J4 32 51N 83 38W
Macon, Miss., U.S.A. 77 J1 33 7N 88 34W
Macon, Mo., U.S.A. 80 F8 39 44N 92 28W
Macondo, Angola 53 G4 12 37S 23 46 E
Macossa, Mozam. 55 F3 17 55S 33 56 E
Macoun L., Canada 73 B8 56 32N 103 40W
Macovane, Mozam. 57 C6 21 30S 35 2 E
McPherson, U.S.A. 80 F6 38 22N 97 40W
McPherson Pk., U.S.A. 85 L7 34 53N 119 53W
McPherson Ra., Australia 63 D5 28 15S 153 15 E
Macquarie Harbour, Australia 62 G4 42 15S 145 23 E
Macquarie Is., Pac. Oc. 64 N7 54 36S 158 55 E
MacRobertson Land, Antarctica 5 D6 71 0S 64 0 E
Macroom, Ireland 13 E3 51 54N 8 57W
Macroy, Australia 60 D2 20 53S 118 2 E
MacTier, Canada 78 A5 45 9N 79 46W
Macubela, Mozam. 55 F4 16 53S 37 49 E
Macuiza, Mozam. 55 F3 18 7S 34 29 E
Macuse, Mozam. 55 F4 17 45S 37 10 E
Macuspana, Mexico 87 D6 17 46N 92 36W
Macusse, Angola 56 B3 17 48S 20 23 E
McVille, U.S.A. 80 B5 47 46N 98 11W
Madadeni, S. Africa 57 D5 27 43S 30 3 E
Madagali, Nigeria 51 F7 10 56N 13 33 E
Madagascar ■, Africa 57 C8 20 0S 47 0 E
Madā'in Sālih, Si. Arabia 44 E3 26 46N 37 57 E
Madama, Niger 51 D7 22 0N 13 40 E
Madame I., Canada 71 C7 45 30N 60 58W
Madaoua, Niger 50 F6 14 5N 6 27 E
Madaripur, Bangla. 41 H17 23 19N 90 15 E
Madauk, Burma 41 L20 17 56N 96 52 E
Madawaska, Canada 78 A7 45 30N 78 0W
Madawaska →, Canada 78 A8 45 27N 76 21W
Madaya, Burma 41 H20 22 12N 96 10 E
Maddalena, Italy 20 D3 41 16N 9 23 E
Madeira, Atl. Oc. 22 D3 32 50N 17 0W
Madeira →, Brazil 92 D7 3 22S 58 45W
Madeleine, Is. de la, Canada 71 C7 47 30N 61 40W
Madera, U.S.A. 83 H3 36 57N 120 3W
Madha, India 40 L9 18 0N 75 30 E
Madhubani, India 43 F12 26 21N 86 7 E
Madhya Pradesh □, India 42 J7 22 50N 78 0 E
Madikeri, India 40 N9 12 30N 75 45 E
Madill, U.S.A. 81 H6 34 6N 96 46W
Madimba, Zaïre 52 E3 4 58S 15 5 E
Ma'din, Syria 44 C3 35 45N 39 36 E
Madīnat ash Sha'b, Yemen 46 E3 12 50N 45 0 E
Madingou, Congo 52 E2 4 10S 13 33 E
Madirovalo, Madag. 57 B8 16 26S 46 32 E
Madison, Calif., U.S.A. 84 G5 38 41N 121 59W
Madison, Fla., U.S.A. 77 K4 30 28N 83 25W
Madison, Ind., U.S.A. 76 F3 38 44N 85 23W
Madison, Nebr., U.S.A. 80 E6 41 50N 97 27W
Madison, Ohio, U.S.A. 78 E3 41 46N 81 3W
Madison, S. Dak., U.S.A. 80 D6 44 0N 97 7W
Madison, Wis., U.S.A. 80 D10 43 4N 89 24W
Madison →, U.S.A. 82 D8 45 56N 111 31W
Madisonville, Ky., U.S.A. 76 G2 37 20N 87 30W
Madisonville, Tex., U.S.A. 81 K7 30 57N 95 55W
Madista, Botswana 56 C4 21 15S 25 6 E
Madiun, Indonesia 37 G14 7 38S 111 32 E
Madley, U.K. 11 E5 52 2N 2 51W
Madona, Latvia 9 H22 56 53N 26 5 E
Madras = Tamil Nadu □, India 40 P10 11 0N 77 0 E
Madras, India 40 N12 13 8N 80 19 E
Madras, U.S.A. 82 D3 44 38N 121 8W
Madre, L., Mexico 87 B5 25 0N 97 30W
Madre, Laguna, U.S.A. 81 M6 27 0N 97 30W
Madre, Sierra, Phil. 37 A6 17 0N 122 0 E
Madre de Dios →, Bolivia 92 F5 10 59S 66 8W
Madre de Dios, I., Chile 96 G1 50 20S 75 10W
Madre del Sur, Sierra, Mexico 87 D5 17 30N 100 0W
Madre Occidental, Sierra, Mexico 86 B3 27 0N 107 0W
Madre Oriental, Sierra, Mexico 86 C4 25 0N 100 0W
Madri, India 42 G5 24 16N 73 32 E
Madrid, Spain 19 B4 40 25N 3 45W
Madura, Selat, Indonesia 37 G15 7 30S 113 20 E
Madura Motel, Australia 61 F4 31 55S 127 0 E
Madurai, India 40 Q11 9 55N 78 10 E
Madurantakam, India 40 N11 12 30N 79 50 E
Mae Chan, Thailand 38 B2 20 9N 99 52 E
Mae Hong Son, Thailand 38 C2 19 16N 98 1 E
Mae Khlong →, Thailand 38 F3 13 24N 100 0 E
Mae Phrik, Thailand 38 D2 17 27N 99 7 E
Mae Ramat, Thailand 38 D2 16 58N 98 31 E
Mae Rim, Thailand 38 C2 18 54N 98 57 E
Mae Sot, Thailand 38 D2 16 43N 98 34 E
Mae Suai, Thailand 38 C2 19 39N 99 33 E
Mae Tha, Thailand 38 C2 18 28N 99 8 E
Maebashi, Japan 31 F9 36 24N 139 4 E
Maesteg, U.K. 11 F4 51 36N 3 40W
Maestra, Sierra, Cuba 88 B4 20 15N 77 0W
Maestrazgo, Mts. del, Spain 19 B5 40 30N 0 25W
Maevatanana, Madag. 57 B8 16 56S 46 49 E
Mafeking = Mafikeng, S. Africa 56 D4 25 50S 25 38 E
Mafeking, Canada 73 C8 52 40N 101 10W
Mafeteng, Lesotho 56 D4 29 51S 27 15 E
Maffra, Australia 63 F4 37 53S 146 58 E
Mafia I., Tanzania 54 D4 7 45S 39 50 E
Mafikeng, S. Africa 56 D4 25 50S 25 38 E
Mafra, Brazil 95 B6 26 10S 49 55W
Mafra, Portugal 19 C1 38 55N 9 20W
Mafungabusi Plateau, Zimbabwe 55 F2 18 30S 29 8 E
Magadan, Russia 27 D16 59 38N 150 50 E
Magadi, Kenya 54 C4 1 54S 36 19 E
Magadi, L., Kenya 54 C4 1 54S 36 19 E
Magaliesburg, S. Africa 57 D4 26 0S 27 32 E
Magallanes, Estrecho de, Chile 96 G2 52 30S 75 0W
Magangué, Colombia 92 B4 9 14N 74 45W
Magburaka, S. Leone 50 G2 8 47N 12 0W
Magdalen Is. = Madeleine, Is. de la, Canada 71 C7 47 30N 61 40W
Magdalena, Argentina 94 D4 35 5S 57 30W
Magdalena, Bolivia 92 F6 13 13S 63 57W
Magdalena, Malaysia 36 D5 4 25N 117 55 E
Magdalena, Mexico 86 A2 30 50N 112 0W
Magdalena, U.S.A. 83 J10 34 7N 107 15W
Magdalena →, Colombia 92 A4 11 6N 74 51W
Magdalena →, Mexico 86 A2 30 40N 112 25W
Magdalena, B., Mexico 86 C2 24 30N 112 10W
Magdalena, Llano de la, Mexico 86 C2 25 0N 111 30W
Magdeburg, Germany 16 B6 52 7N 11 38 E
Magdelaine Cays, Australia 62 B5 16 33S 150 18 E
Magee, U.S.A. 81 K10 31 52N 89 44W
Magee, I., U.K. 13 B6 54 48N 5 43W
Magelang, Indonesia 37 G14 7 29S 110 13 E
Magellan's Str. = Magallanes, Estrecho de, Chile 96 G2 52 30S 75 0W
Magenta, L., Australia 61 F2 33 30S 119 2 E
Magerøya, Norway 8 A21 71 3N 25 40 E
Maggiore, L., Italy 20 B3 45 57N 8 39 E
Magherafelt, U.K. 13 B5 54 45N 6 37W
Magistralnyy, Russia 27 D11 56 16N 107 36 E
Magnetic Pole (North) = North Magnetic Pole, Canada 4 B2 77 58N 102 8W
Magnetic Pole (South) = South Magnetic Pole, Antarctica 5 C9 64 8S 138 8 E
Magnitogorsk, Russia 24 D10 53 27N 59 4 E
Magnolia, Ark., U.S.A. 81 J8 33 16N 93 14W
Magnolia, Miss., U.S.A. 81 K9 31 9N 90 28W
Magog, Canada 71 C5 45 18N 72 9W
Magoro, Uganda 54 B3 1 45N 34 12 E
Magosa = Famagusta, Cyprus 23 D12 35 8N 33 55 E
Magouládhes, Greece 23 A3 39 45N 19 42 E
Magoye, Zambia 55 F2 16 1S 27 30 E
Magpie L., Canada 71 B7 51 0N 64 41W
Magrath, Canada 72 D6 49 25N 112 50W
Magu □, Tanzania 54 C3 2 31S 33 28 E
Maguarinho, C., Brazil 93 D9 0 15S 48 30W
Mağusa = Famagusta, Cyprus 23 D12 35 8N 33 55 E
Maguse L., Canada 73 A9 61 40N 95 10W
Maguse Pt., Canada 73 A10 61 20N 93 50W
Magwe, Burma 41 J19 20 10N 95 0 E
Maha Sarakham, Thailand 38 D4 16 12N 103 16 E
Mahābād, Iran 44 B5 36 50N 45 45 E
Mahabharat Lekh, Nepal 43 E9 28 30N 82 0 E
Mahabo, Madag. 57 C7 20 23S 44 40 E
Mahadeo Hills, India 42 H8 22 20N 78 30 E
Mahagi, Zaïre 54 B3 2 20N 31 0 E
Mahajamba →, Madag. 57 B8 15 33S 47 8 E
Mahajamba, Helodranon' i, Madag. 57 B8 15 24S 47 5 E
Mahajan, India 42 E5 28 48N 73 56 E
Mahajanga, Madag. 57 B8 15 40S 46 25 E
Mahajanga □, Madag. 57 B8 17 0S 47 0 E
Mahajilo →, Madag. 57 B8 19 42S 45 22 E
Mahakam →, Indonesia 36 E5 0 35S 117 17 E
Mahalapye, Botswana 56 C4 23 1S 26 51 E
Maḥallāt, Iran 45 C6 33 55N 50 30 E
Māhān, Iran 45 D8 30 5N 57 18 E
Mahanadi →, India 41 J15 20 20N 86 25 E
Mahanoro, Madag. 57 B8 19 54S 48 48 E
Mahanoy City, U.S.A. 79 F8 40 49N 76 9W
Maharashtra □, India 40 J9 20 30N 75 30 E
Mahari Mts., Tanzania 54 D2 6 20S 30 0 E
Mahasham, W. →, Egypt 47 E3 30 15N 34 10 E
Mahasolo, Madag. 57 B8 19 7S 46 22 E
Mahattat ash Shīdīyah, Jordan 47 F4 29 55N 35 55 E
Mahattat 'Unayzah, Jordan 47 E4 30 30N 35 47 E
Mahaxay, Laos 38 D5 17 22N 105 12 E
Mahbubnagar, India 40 L10 16 45N 77 59 E
Maḥḍah, Oman 45 E7 24 24N 55 59 E
Mahdia, Tunisia 51 A7 35 28N 11 0 E
Mahe, India 43 C8 33 10N 78 32 E
Mahenge, Tanzania 55 D4 8 45S 36 41 E
Maheno, N.Z. 59 L3 45 10S 170 50 E
Mahesana, India 42 H5 23 39N 72 26 E
Mahia Pen., N.Z. 59 H6 39 9S 177 55 E
Mahilyow, Belarus 17 B16 53 55N 30 18 E
Mahmud Kot, Pakistan 42 D4 30 16N 71 0 E
Mahnomen, U.S.A. 80 B7 47 19N 95 58W
Mahoba, India 43 G8 25 15N 79 55 E
Mahón, Spain 22 B11 39 53N 4 16 E
Mahone Bay, Canada 71 D7 44 30N 64 20W
Mai-Ndombe, L., Zaïre 52 E3 2 0S 18 20 E
Mai-Sai, Thailand 38 B2 20 20N 99 55 E
Maicurú →, Brazil 93 D8 2 14S 54 17W
Maidan Khula, Afghan. 42 C3 33 36N 69 50 E
Maidenhead, U.K. 11 F7 51 31N 0 42W
Maidstone, Canada 73 C7 53 5N 109 20W
Maidstone, U.K. 11 F8 51 16N 0 32 E
Maiduguri, Nigeria 51 F7 12 0N 13 20 E
Maijdi, Bangla. 41 H17 22 48N 91 10 E
Maikala Ra., India 41 J12 22 0N 81 0 E
Mailsi, Pakistan 42 E5 29 48N 72 15 E
Main →, Germany 16 C5 50 0N 8 18 E
Main →, U.K. 13 B5 54 48N 6 18W
Main Centre, Canada 73 C7 50 35N 107 21W
Maine, France 18 C3 47 55N 0 25W
Maine □, U.S.A. 71 C6 45 20N 69 0W
Maine →, Ireland 13 D2 52 9N 9 45W
Maingkwan, Burma 41 F20 26 15N 96 37 E
Mainit, L., Phil. 37 C7 9 31N 125 30 E
Mainland, Orkney, U.K. 12 C5 58 59N 3 8W
Mainland, Shet., U.K. 12 A7 60 15N 1 22W
Mainpuri, India 43 F8 27 18N 79 4 E
Maintirano, Madag. 57 B7 18 3S 44 1 E
Mainz, Germany 16 C5 50 1N 8 14 E
Maipú, Argentina 94 D4 36 52S 57 50W
Maiquetía, Venezuela 92 A5 10 36N 66 57W
Mairabari, India 41 F18 26 30N 92 22 E
Maisí, Cuba 89 B5 20 17N 74 9W
Maisí, Pta. de, Cuba 89 B5 20 10N 74 10W
Maitland, N.S.W., Australia 63 E5 32 33S 151 36 E
Maitland, S. Austral., Australia 63 E2 34 23S 137 40 E
Maitland →, Canada 78 C3 43 45N 81 43W
Maíz, Is. del, Nic. 88 D3 12 15N 83 4W
Maizuru, Japan 31 G7 35 25N 135 22 E
Majalengka, Indonesia 37 G13 6 50S 108 13 E
Majene, Indonesia 37 E5 3 38S 118 57 E
Maji, Ethiopia 51 G12 6 12N 35 30 E
Major, Canada 73 C7 51 52N 109 37W
Majorca = Mallorca, Spain 22 B10 39 30N 3 0 E
Maka, Senegal 50 F2 13 40N 14 10W
Makale, Indonesia 37 E5 3 6S 119 51 E
Makamba, Burundi 54 C2 4 8S 29 49 E
Makari, Cameroon 52 B2 12 35N 14 28 E
Makarikari = Makgadikgadi Salt Pans, Botswana 56 C4 20 40S 25 45 E
Makarovo, Russia 27 D11 57 40N 107 45 E
Makasar = Ujung Pandang, Indonesia 37 F5 5 10S 119 20 E
Makasar, Selat, Indonesia 37 E5 1 0S 118 20 E
Makasar, Str. of = Makasar, Selat, Indonesia 37 E5 1 0S 118 20 E
Makat, Kazakstan 25 E9 47 39N 53 19 E
Makedhonía □, Greece 21 D10 40 39N 22 0 E
Makedonija = Macedonia ■, Europe 21 D9 41 53N 21 40 E
Makena, U.S.A. 74 H16 20 39N 156 27W
Makeni, S. Leone 50 G2 8 55N 12 5W
Makeyevka = Makiyivka, Ukraine 25 E6 48 0N 38 0 E
Makgadikgadi Salt Pans, Botswana 56 C4 20 40S 25 45 E
Makhachkala, Russia 25 F8 43 0N 47 30 E
Makhmūr, Iraq 44 C4 35 46N 43 35 E
Makian, Indonesia 37 D7 0 20N 127 20 E
Makindu, Kenya 54 C4 2 18S 37 50 E
Makinsk, Kazakstan 26 D8 52 37N 70 26 E
Makiyivka, Ukraine 25 E6 48 0N 38 0 E
Makkah, Si. Arabia 46 C2 21 30N 39 54 E
Makkovik, Canada 71 A8 55 10N 59 10W
Makó, Hungary 17 E11 46 14N 20 33 E
Makokou, Gabon 52 D2 0 40N 12 50 E
Makongo, Zaïre 54 B2 3 25N 26 17 E
Makoro, Zaïre 54 B2 3 10N 29 59 E
Makoua, Congo 52 E3 0 5S 15 50 E
Makrai, India 40 H10 22 2N 77 0 E
Makran Coast Range, Pakistan 40 G4 25 40N 64 0 E
Makrana, India 42 F6 27 2N 74 46 E
Makriyialos, Greece 23 D7 35 2N 25 59 E
Maksimkin Yar, Russia 26 D9 58 42N 86 50 E
Mākū, Iran 44 B5 39 15N 44 31 E
Makumbi, Zaïre 52 F4 5 50S 20 43 E
Makunda, Botswana 56 C3 22 30S 20 7 E
Makurazaki, Japan 31 J5 31 15N 130 20 E
Makurdi, Nigeria 50 G6 7 43N 8 35 E
Makūyeh, Iran 45 D7 28 7N 53 9 E
Makwassie, S. Africa 56 D4 27 17S 26 0 E
Mal B., Ireland 13 D2 52 50N 9 30W
Mala, Pta., Panama 88 E3 7 28N 80 2W
Malabang, Phil. 37 C6 7 36N 124 3 E
Malabar Coast, India 40 P9 11 0N 75 0 E
Malabo = Rey Malabo, Eq. Guin. 50 H6 3 45N 8 50 E
Malacca, Str. of, Indonesia 39 L3 3 0N 101 0 E
Malad City, U.S.A. 82 E7 42 12N 112 15W
Maladzyechna, Belarus 17 A14 54 20N 26 50 E
Málaga, Spain 19 D3 36 43N 4 23W
Malaga, U.S.A. 81 J2 32 14N 104 4W
Malagarasi, Tanzania 54 D3 5 5S 30 50 E
Malagarasi →, Tanzania 54 D2 5 12S 29 47 E
Malaimbandy, Madag. 57 C8 20 20S 45 36 E
Malakâl, Sudan 51 G11 9 33N 31 40 E
Malakand, Pakistan 42 B4 34 40N 71 55 E
Malakoff, U.S.A. 81 J7 32 10N 96 1W
Malamyzh, Russia 27 E14 49 50N 136 50 E
Malang, Indonesia 37 G15 7 59S 112 45 E
Malangen, Norway 8 B18 69 24N 18 37 E
Malanje, Angola 52 F3 9 36S 16 17 E
Mälaren, Sweden 9 G17 59 30N 17 10 E
Malargüe, Argentina 94 D2 35 32S 69 30W
Malartic, Canada 70 C4 48 9N 78 9W
Malaryta, Belarus 17 C13 51 50N 24 3 E
Malatya, Turkey 25 G6 38 25N 38 20 E
Malawi ■, Africa 55 E3 11 55S 34 0 E
Malawi, L., Africa 55 E3 12 30S 34 30 E
Malay Pen., Asia 39 J3 7 25N 100 0 E
Malaybalay, Phil. 37 C7 8 5N 125 7 E
Malāyer, Iran 45 C6 34 19N 48 51 E
Malaysia ■, Asia 36 D4 5 0N 110 0 E
Malazgirt, Turkey 25 G7 39 10N 42 33 E
Malbon, Australia 62 C3 21 5S 140 17 E
Malbooma, Australia 63 E1 30 41S 134 11 E
Malbork, Poland 17 B10 54 3N 19 1 E
Malcolm, Australia 61 E3 28 51S 121 25 E
Malcolm, Pt., Australia 61 F3 33 48S 123 45 E
Maldegem, Belgium 15 C3 51 14N 3 26 E
Malden, Mass., U.S.A. 79 D13 42 26N 71 4W
Malden, Mo., U.S.A. 81 G10 36 34N 89 57W
Malden I., Kiribati 65 H12 4 3S 155 1W
Maldives ■, Ind. Oc. 29 J11 5 0N 73 0 E
Maldonado, Uruguay 95 C5 34 59S 55 0W
Maldonado, Punta, Mexico 87 D5 16 19N 98 35W
Malé Karpaty, Slovak Rep. 17 D9 48 30N 17 20 E
Maléa, Ákra, Greece 21 F10 36 28N 23 7 E
Malegaon, India 40 J9 20 30N 74 38 E
Malei, Mozam. 55 F4 17 12S 36 58 E
Malek Kandī, Iran 44 B5 37 9N 46 6 E
Malela, Zaïre 54 C2 4 22S 26 8 E
Malema, Mozam. 55 E4 14 57S 37 20 E
Máleme, Greece 23 D5 35 31N 23 49 E
Malerkotla, India 42 D6 30 32N 75 58 E
Máles, Greece 23 D7 35 6N 25 35 E
Malgomaj, Sweden 8 D17 64 40N 16 30 E
Malha, Sudan 51 E10 15 8N 25 10 E
Malheur →, U.S.A. 82 D5 44 4N 116 59W
Malheur L., U.S.A. 82 E4 43 20N 118 48W
Mali ■, Africa 50 E4 17 0N 3 0W
Mali →, Burma 41 G20 25 40N 97 40 E
Malibu, U.S.A. 85 L8 34 2N 118 41W
Malik, Indonesia 37 E6 0 39S 123 16 E
Malili, Indonesia 37 E6 2 42S 121 6 E
Malimba, Mts., Zaïre 54 D2 7 30S 29 30 E
Malin Hd., Ireland 13 A4 55 23N 7 23W
Malindi, Kenya 54 C5 3 12S 40 5 E
Malines = Mechelen, Belgium 15 C4 51 2N 4 29 E
Malino, Indonesia 37 D6 1 0N 121 0 E
Malinyi, Tanzania 55 D4 8 56S 36 0 E
Malita, Phil. 37 C7 6 19N 125 39 E
Malkara, Turkey 21 D12 40 53N 26 53 E
Mallacoota, Australia 63 F4 37 40S 149 40 E
Mallacoota Inlet, Australia 63 F4 37 34S 149 40 E
Mallaig, U.K. 12 E3 57 0N 5 50W
Mallawan, India 43 F9 27 4N 80 12 E
Mallawi, Egypt 51 C11 27 44N 30 44 E
Mállia, Greece 23 D7 35 17N 25 27 E
Mallión, Kólpos, Greece 23 D7 35 19N 25 27 E
Mallorca, Spain 22 B10 39 30N 3 0 E
Mallorytown, Canada 79 B9 44 29N 75 53W
Mallow, Ireland 13 D3 52 8N 8 39W
Malmberget, Sweden 8 C19 67 11N 20 40 E
Malmédy, Belgium 15 D6 50 25N 6 2 E
Malmesbury, S. Africa 56 E2 33 28S 18 41 E
Malmö, Sweden 9 J15 55 36N 12 59 E
Malolos, Phil. 37 B6 14 50N 120 49 E
Malombe L., Malawi 55 E4 14 40S 35 15 E
Malone, U.S.A. 79 B10 44 51N 74 18W
Måløy, Norway 9 F11 61 57N 5 6 E
Malozemelskaya Tundra, Russia 24 A9 67 0N 50 0 E
Malpaso, Canary Is. 22 G1 27 43N 18 3W
Malpelo, Colombia 92 C2 4 3N 81 35W
Malta, Idaho, U.S.A. 82 E7 42 18N 113 22W
Malta, Mont., U.S.A. 82 B10 48 21N 107 52W
Malta ■, Europe 23 D1 35 50N 14 30 E
Maltahöhe, Namibia 56 C2 24 55S 17 0 E
Malton, Canada 78 C5 43 42N 79 38W
Malton, U.K. 10 C7 54 8N 0 49W
Maluku, Indonesia 37 E7 1 0S 127 0 E
Maluku □, Indonesia 37 E7 3 0S 128 0 E

Maluku Sea

Maluku Sea = Molucca Sea, *Indonesia* **37 E6** 2 0S 124 0 E
Malvan, *India* **40 L8** 16 2N 73 30 E
Malvern, *U.S.A.* **81 H8** 34 22N 92 49W
Malvern Hills, *U.K.* **11 E5** 52 0N 2 19W
Malvinas, Is. = Falkland Is. □, *Atl. Oc.* **96 G5** 51 30S 59 0W
Malya, *Tanzania* **54 C3** 3 5S 33 38 E
Malyn, *Ukraine* **17 C15** 50 46N 29 3 E
Malyy Lyakhovskiy, Ostrov, *Russia* **27 B15** 74 7N 140 36 E
Malyy Nimnyr, *Russia* **27 D13** 57 50N 125 10 E
Mama, *Russia* **27 D12** 58 18N 112 54 E
Mamanguape, *Brazil* **93 E11** 6 50S 35 4W
Mamasa, *Indonesia* **37 E5** 2 55S 119 20 E
Mambasa, *Zaïre* **54 B2** 1 22N 29 3 E
Mamberamo →, *Indonesia* **37 E9** 2 0S 137 50 E
Mambilima Falls, *Zambia* **55 E2** 10 31S 28 45 E
Mambirima, *Zaïre* **55 E2** 11 25S 27 33 E
Mambo, *Tanzania* **54 C4** 4 52S 38 22 E
Mambrui, *Kenya* **54 C5** 3 5S 40 5 E
Mamburao, *Phil.* **37 B6** 13 13N 120 39 E
Mameigwess L., *Canada* **70 B2** 52 35N 87 50W
Mamfe, *Cameroon* **50 G6** 5 50N 9 15 E
Mammoth, *U.S.A.* **83 K8** 32 43N 110 39W
Mamoré →, *Bolivia* **92 F5** 10 23S 65 53W
Mamou, *Guinea* **50 F2** 10 15N 12 0W
Mamuju, *Indonesia* **37 E5** 2 41S 118 50 E
Man, *Ivory C.* **50 G3** 7 30N 7 40W
Man, I. of, *U.K.* **10 C3** 54 15N 4 30W
Man Na, *Burma* **41 H20** 23 27N 97 19 E
Mana, *Fr. Guiana* **93 B8** 5 45N 53 55W
Manaar, G. of = Mannar, G. of, *Asia* **40 Q11** 8 30N 79 0 E
Manacapuru, *Brazil* **92 D6** 3 16S 60 37W
Manacor, *Spain* **22 B10** 39 34N 3 13 E
Manado, *Indonesia* **37 D6** 1 29N 124 51 E
Managua, *Nic.* **88 D2** 12 6N 86 20W
Managua, L., *Nic.* **88 D2** 12 20N 86 30W
Manakara, *Madag.* **57 C8** 22 8S 48 1 E
Manama = Al Manāmah, *Bahrain* **45 E6** 26 10N 50 30 E
Manambao →, *Madag.* **57 B7** 17 35S 44 0 E
Manambato, *Madag.* **57 A8** 13 43S 49 7 E
Manambolo →, *Madag.* **57 B7** 19 18S 44 22 E
Manambolosy, *Madag.* **57 B8** 16 2S 49 40 E
Mananara, *Madag.* **57 B8** 16 10S 49 46 E
Mananara →, *Madag.* **57 C8** 23 21S 47 42 E
Mananjary, *Madag.* **57 C8** 21 13S 48 20 E
Manantenina, *Madag.* **57 C8** 24 17S 47 19 E
Manaos = Manaus, *Brazil* **92 D7** 3 0S 60 0W
Manapouri, *N.Z.* **59 L1** 45 34S 167 39 E
Manapouri, L., *N.Z.* **59 L1** 45 32S 167 32 E
Manas, *China* **32 B3** 44 17N 85 56 E
Manas →, *India* **41 F17** 26 12N 90 40 E
Manaslu, *Nepal* **43 E11** 28 33N 84 33 E
Manasquan, *U.S.A.* **79 F10** 40 8N 74 3W
Manassa, *U.S.A.* **83 H11** 37 11N 105 56W
Manaung, *Burma* **41 K18** 18 45N 93 40 E
Manaus, *Brazil* **92 D7** 3 0S 60 0W
Manawan L., *Canada* **73 B8** 55 24N 103 14W
Manay, *Phil.* **37 C7** 7 17N 126 33 E
Manbij, *Syria* **44 B3** 36 31N 37 57 E
Mancelona, *U.S.A.* **76 C3** 44 54N 85 4W
Manchester, *U.K.* **10 D5** 53 29N 2 12W
Manchester, *Calif., U.S.A.* **84 G3** 38 58N 123 41W
Manchester, *Conn., U.S.A.* **79 E12** 41 47N 72 31W
Manchester, *Ga., U.S.A.* **77 J3** 32 51N 84 37W
Manchester, *Iowa, U.S.A.* **80 D9** 42 29N 91 27W
Manchester, *Ky., U.S.A.* **76 G4** 37 9N 83 46W
Manchester, *N.H., U.S.A.* **79 D13** 42 59N 71 28W
Manchester, *N.Y., U.S.A.* **78 D7** 42 56N 77 16W
Manchester, *Vt., U.S.A.* **79 C11** 43 10N 73 5W
Manchester L., *Canada* **73 A7** 61 28N 107 29W
Manchuria = Dongbei, *China* **35 D13** 42 0N 125 0 E
Manchurian Plain, *China* **28 E16** 47 0N 124 0 E
Mand →, *Iran* **45 D7** 28 20N 52 30 E
Manda, *Chunya, Tanzania* **54 D3** 6 51S 32 29 E
Manda, *Ludewe, Tanzania* **55 E3** 10 30S 34 40 E
Mandabé, *Madag.* **57 C7** 21 0S 44 55 E
Mandaguari, *Brazil* **95 A5** 23 32S 51 42W
Mandah, *Mongolia* **34 B5** 44 27N 108 2 E
Mandal, *Norway* **9 G12** 58 2N 7 25 E
Mandalay, *Burma* **41 J20** 22 0N 96 4 E
Mandale = Mandalay, *Burma* **41 J20** 22 0N 96 4 E
Mandalgovi, *Mongolia* **34 B4** 45 45N 106 10 E
Mandalī, *Iraq* **44 C5** 33 43N 45 28 E
Mandan, *U.S.A.* **80 B4** 46 50N 100 54W
Mandar, Teluk, *Indonesia* **37 E5** 3 35S 119 15 E
Mandaue, *Phil.* **37 B6** 10 20N 123 56 E
Mandera, *Kenya* **54 B5** 3 55N 41 53 E
Mandera □, *Kenya* **54 B5** 3 30N 41 0 E
Mandi, *India* **42 D7** 31 39N 76 58 E
Mandimba, *Mozam.* **55 E4** 14 20S 35 40 E
Mandioli, *Indonesia* **37 E7** 0 40S 127 20 E
Mandla, *India* **43 H9** 22 39N 80 30 E
Mandoto, *Madag.* **57 B8** 19 34S 46 17 E
Mandra, *Pakistan* **42 C5** 33 23N 73 12 E
Mandrare →, *Madag.* **57 D8** 25 10S 46 30 E
Mandritsara, *Madag.* **57 B8** 15 50S 48 49 E
Mandsaur, *India* **42 G6** 24 3N 75 8 E
Mandurah, *Australia* **61 F2** 32 36S 115 48 E
Mandvi, *India* **42 H3** 22 51N 69 22 E
Mandya, *India* **40 N10** 12 30N 77 0 E
Mandzai, *Pakistan* **42 D2** 30 55N 67 6 E
Maneh, *Iran* **45 B8** 37 39N 57 7 E
Maneroo, *Australia* **62 C3** 23 22S 143 53 E
Maneroo Cr. →, *Australia* **62 C3** 23 21S 143 53 E
Manfalût, *Egypt* **51 C11** 27 20N 30 52 E
Manfred, *Australia* **63 E3** 33 19S 143 45 E
Manfredónia, *Italy* **20 D6** 41 38N 15 55 E
Mangalia, *Romania* **17 G15** 43 50N 28 35 E
Mangalore, *India* **40 N9** 12 55N 74 47 E
Mangaweka, *N.Z.* **59 H5** 39 48S 175 47 E
Manggar, *Indonesia* **36 E3** 2 50S 108 10 E
Manggawitu, *Indonesia* **37 E8** 4 8S 133 32 E
Mangkalihat, Tanjung, *Indonesia* **37 D5** 1 2N 118 59 E
Mangla Dam, *Pakistan* **43 C5** 33 9N 73 44 E
Manglaur, *India* **42 E7** 29 44N 77 49 E
Mangnai, *China* **32 C4** 37 52N 91 43 E
Mango, *Togo* **50 F5** 10 20N 0 30 E
Mangoche, *Malawi* **55 E4** 14 25S 35 16 E
Mangoky →, *Madag.* **57 C7** 21 29S 43 41 E
Mangole, *Indonesia* **37 E7** 1 50S 125 55 E
Mangombe, *Zaïre* **54 C2** 1 20S 26 48 E
Mangonui, *N.Z.* **59 F4** 35 1S 173 32 E
Mangueigne, *Chad* **51 F9** 10 30N 21 15 E
Mangueira, L. da, *Brazil* **95 C5** 33 0S 52 50W
Mangum, *U.S.A.* **81 H5** 34 53N 99 30W
Mangyshlak Poluostrov, *Kazakstan* **26 E6** 44 30N 52 30 E
Manhattan, *U.S.A.* **80 F6** 39 11N 96 35W
Manhiça, *Mozam.* **57 D5** 25 23S 32 49 E
Manhuaçu, *Brazil* **93 H10** 20 15S 42 2W
Mania →, *Madag.* **57 B8** 19 42S 45 22 E
Manica, *Mozam.* **57 B5** 18 58S 32 59 E
Manica e Sofala □, *Mozam.* **57 B5** 19 10S 33 45 E
Manicaland □, *Zimbabwe* **55 F3** 19 0S 32 30 E
Manicoré, *Brazil* **92 E6** 5 48S 61 16W
Manicouagan →, *Canada* **71 C6** 49 30N 68 30W
Manifah, *Si. Arabia* **45 E6** 27 44N 49 0 E
Manifold, *Australia* **62 C5** 22 41S 150 40 E
Manifold, C., *Australia* **62 C5** 22 41S 150 50 E
Manigotagan, *Canada* **73 C9** 51 6N 96 18W
Manihiki, *Cook Is.* **65 J11** 10 24S 161 1W
Manika, Plateau de la, *Zaïre* **55 E2** 10 0S 25 5 E
Manila, *Phil.* **37 B6** 14 40N 121 3 E
Manila, *U.S.A.* **82 F9** 40 59N 109 43W
Manila B., *Phil.* **37 B6** 14 40N 120 35 E
Manilla, *Australia* **63 E5** 30 45S 150 43 E
Maningrida, *Australia* **62 A1** 12 3S 134 13 E
Manipur □, *India* **41 G18** 25 0N 94 0 E
Manipur →, *Burma* **41 H19** 23 45N 94 20 E
Manisa, *Turkey* **21 E12** 38 38N 27 30 E
Manistee, *U.S.A.* **76 C2** 44 15N 86 19W
Manistee →, *U.S.A.* **76 C2** 44 15N 86 21W
Manistique, *U.S.A.* **76 C2** 45 57N 86 15W
Manito L., *Canada* **73 C7** 52 43N 109 43W
Manitoba □, *Canada* **73 B9** 55 30N 97 0W
Manitoba, L., *Canada* **73 C9** 51 0N 98 45W
Manitou, *Canada* **73 D9** 49 15N 98 32W
Manitou I., *U.S.A.* **70 C2** 47 25N 87 37W
Manitou Is., *U.S.A.* **76 C2** 45 8N 86 0W
Manitou L., *Canada* **71 B6** 50 55N 65 17W
Manitou Springs, *U.S.A.* **80 F2** 38 52N 104 55W
Manitoulin I., *Canada* **70 C3** 45 40N 82 30W
Manitowaning, *Canada* **70 C3** 45 46N 81 49W
Manitowoc, *U.S.A.* **76 C2** 44 5N 87 40W
Manizales, *Colombia* **92 B3** 5 5N 75 32W
Manja, *Madag.* **57 C7** 21 26S 44 20 E
Manjacaze, *Mozam.* **57 C5** 24 45S 34 0 E
Manjakandriana, *Madag.* **57 B8** 18 55S 47 47 E
Manjhand, *Pakistan* **42 G3** 25 50N 68 10 E
Manjil, *Iran* **45 B6** 36 46N 49 30 E
Manjimup, *Australia* **61 F2** 34 15S 116 6 E
Manjra →, *India* **40 K10** 18 49N 77 52 E
Mankato, *Kans., U.S.A.* **80 F5** 39 47N 98 13W
Mankato, *Minn., U.S.A.* **80 C8** 44 10N 94 0W
Mankayane, *Swaziland* **57 D5** 26 40S 31 4 E
Mankono, *Ivory C.* **50 G3** 8 1N 6 10W
Mankota, *Canada* **73 D7** 49 25N 107 5W
Manlay, *Mongolia* **34 B4** 44 9N 107 0 E
Manly, *Australia* **63 E5** 33 48S 151 17 E
Manmad, *India* **40 J9** 20 18N 74 28 E
Mann Ras., *Australia* **61 E5** 26 6S 130 5 E
Manna, *Indonesia* **36 E2** 4 25S 102 55 E
Mannahill, *Australia* **63 E3** 32 25S 140 0 E
Mannar, *Sri Lanka* **40 Q11** 9 1N 79 54 E
Mannar, G. of, *Asia* **40 Q11** 8 30N 79 0 E
Mannar I., *Sri Lanka* **40 Q11** 9 5N 79 45 E
Mannheim, *Germany* **16 D5** 49 29N 8 29 E
Manning, *Canada* **72 B5** 56 53N 117 39W
Manning, *Oreg., U.S.A.* **84 E3** 45 45N 123 13W
Manning, *S.C., U.S.A.* **77 J5** 33 42N 80 13W
Manning Prov. Park, *Canada* **72 D4** 49 5N 120 45W
Mannington, *U.S.A.* **76 F5** 39 32N 80 21W
Mannum, *Australia* **63 E2** 34 50S 139 20 E
Mano, *S. Leone* **50 G2** 8 3N 12 2W
Manokwari, *Indonesia* **37 E8** 0 54S 134 0 E
Manombo, *Madag.* **57 C7** 22 57S 43 28 E
Manono, *Zaïre* **54 D2** 7 15S 27 25 E
Manosque, *France* **18 E6** 43 49N 5 47 E
Manouane, L., *Canada* **71 B5** 50 45N 70 45W
Manpojin, *N. Korea* **35 D14** 41 6N 126 24 E
Manresa, *Spain* **19 B6** 41 48N 1 50 E
Mansa, *Gujarat, India* **42 H5** 23 27N 72 45 E
Mansa, *Punjab, India* **42 E6** 30 0N 75 27 E
Mansa, *Zambia* **55 E2** 11 13S 28 55 E
Mansehra, *Pakistan* **42 B5** 34 20N 73 15 E
Mansel I., *Canada* **69 B11** 62 0N 80 0W
Mansfield, *Australia* **63 F4** 37 4S 146 6 E
Mansfield, *U.K.* **10 D6** 53 9N 1 11W
Mansfield, *La., U.S.A.* **81 J8** 32 2N 93 43W
Mansfield, *Mass., U.S.A.* **79 D13** 42 2N 71 13W
Mansfield, *Ohio, U.S.A.* **78 F2** 40 45N 82 31W
Mansfield, *Pa., U.S.A.* **78 E7** 41 48N 77 5W
Mansfield, *Wash., U.S.A.* **82 C4** 47 49N 119 38W
Manson Creek, *Canada* **72 B4** 55 37N 124 32W
Manta, *Ecuador* **92 D2** 1 0S 80 40W
Mantalingajan, Mt., *Phil.* **36 C5** 8 55N 117 45 E
Mantare, *Tanzania* **54 C3** 2 42S 33 13 E
Manteca, *U.S.A.* **83 H3** 37 48N 121 13W
Manteo, *U.S.A.* **77 H8** 35 55N 75 40W
Mantes-la-Jolie, *France* **18 B4** 48 58N 1 41 E
Manthani, *India* **40 K11** 18 40N 79 35 E
Manti, *U.S.A.* **82 G8** 39 16N 111 38W
Mantiqueira, Serra da, *Brazil* **95 A7** 22 0S 44 0W
Manton, *U.S.A.* **76 C3** 44 25N 85 24W
Mántova, *Italy* **20 B4** 45 9N 10 48 E
Mänttä, *Finland* **9 E21** 62 0N 24 40 E
Mantua = Mántova, *Italy* **20 B4** 45 9N 10 48 E
Manu, *Peru* **92 F4** 12 10S 70 51W
Manua Is., *Amer. Samoa* **59 B14** 14 13S 169 35W
Manuae, *Cook Is.* **65 J12** 19 30S 159 0W
Manuel Alves →, *Brazil* **93 F9** 11 19S 48 28W
Manui, *Indonesia* **37 E6** 3 35S 123 5 E
Manville, *U.S.A.* **80 D2** 42 47N 104 37W
Many, *U.S.A.* **81 K8** 31 34N 93 29W
Manyara, L., *Tanzania* **54 C4** 3 40S 35 50 E
Manych-Gudilo, Ozero, *Russia* **25 E7** 46 24N 42 38 E
Manyonga →, *Tanzania* **54 C3** 4 10S 34 15 E
Manyoni, *Tanzania* **54 D3** 5 45S 34 55 E
Manyoni □, *Tanzania* **54 D3** 6 30S 34 30 E
Manzai, *Pakistan* **42 C4** 32 12N 70 15 E
Manzanares, *Spain* **19 C4** 39 2N 3 22W
Manzanillo, *Cuba* **88 B4** 20 20N 77 31W
Manzanillo, *Mexico* **86 D4** 19 0N 104 20W
Manzanillo, Pta., *Panama* **88 E4** 9 30N 79 40W
Manzano Mts., *U.S.A.* **83 J10** 34 40N 106 20W
Manzarīyeh, *Iran* **45 C6** 34 53N 50 50 E
Manzhouli, *China* **33 B6** 49 35N 117 25 E
Manzini, *Swaziland* **57 D5** 26 30S 31 25 E
Mao, *Chad* **51 F8** 14 4N 15 19 E
Maoke, Pegunungan, *Indonesia* **37 E9** 3 40S 137 30 E
Maolin, *China* **35 C12** 43 58N 123 30 E
Maoming, *China* **33 D6** 21 50N 110 54 E
Maoxing, *China* **35 B13** 45 28N 124 40 E
Mapam Yumco, *China* **32 C3** 30 45N 81 28 E
Mapastepec, *Mexico* **87 D6** 15 26N 92 54W
Mapia, Kepulauan, *Indonesia* **37 D8** 0 50N 134 20 E
Mapimí, *Mexico* **86 B4** 25 50N 103 50W
Mapimí, Bolsón de, *Mexico* **86 B4** 27 30N 104 15W
Mapinga, *Tanzania* **54 D4** 6 40S 39 12 E
Mapinhane, *Mozam.* **57 C6** 22 20S 35 0 E
Maple Creek, *Canada* **73 D7** 49 55N 109 29W
Maple Valley, *U.S.A.* **84 C4** 47 25N 122 3W
Mapleton, *U.S.A.* **82 D2** 44 2N 123 52W
Mapuera →, *Brazil* **92 D7** 1 5S 57 2W
Maputo, *Mozam.* **57 D5** 25 58S 32 32 E
Maputo, B. de, *Mozam.* **57 D5** 25 50S 32 45 E
Maqiaohe, *China* **35 B16** 44 40N 130 30 E
Maqnā, *Si. Arabia* **44 D2** 28 25N 34 50 E
Maquela do Zombo, *Angola* **52 F3** 6 0S 15 15 E
Maquinchao, *Argentina* **96 E3** 41 15S 68 50W
Maquoketa, *U.S.A.* **80 D9** 42 4N 90 40W
Mar, Serra do, *Brazil* **95 B6** 25 30S 49 0W
Mar Chiquita, L., *Argentina* **94 C3** 30 40S 62 50W
Mar del Plata, *Argentina* **94 D4** 38 0S 57 30W
Mar Menor, *Spain* **19 D5** 37 40N 0 45W
Mara, *Tanzania* **54 C3** 1 30S 34 32 E
Mara □, *Tanzania* **54 C3** 1 45S 34 20 E
Maraã, *Brazil* **92 D5** 1 52S 65 25W
Marabá, *Brazil* **93 E9** 5 20S 49 5W
Maracá, I. de, *Brazil* **93 C8** 2 10N 50 30W
Maracaibo, *Venezuela* **92 A4** 10 40N 71 37W
Maracaibo, L. de, *Venezuela* **92 B4** 9 40N 71 30W
Maracaju, *Brazil* **95 A4** 21 38S 55 9W
Maracay, *Venezuela* **92 A5** 10 15N 67 28W
Marādah, *Libya* **51 C8** 29 15N 19 15 E
Maradi, *Niger* **50 F6** 13 29N 7 20 E
Marāgheh, *Iran* **44 B5** 37 30N 46 12 E
Marāh, *Si. Arabia* **44 E5** 25 0N 45 35 E
Marajó, I. de, *Brazil* **93 D9** 1 0S 49 30W
Marākand, *Iran* **44 B5** 38 51N 45 16 E
Maralal, *Kenya* **54 B4** 1 0N 36 38 E
Maralinga, *Australia* **61 F5** 30 13S 131 32 E
Marama, *Australia* **63 F3** 35 10S 140 10 E
Marampa, *S. Leone* **50 G2** 8 45N 12 28W
Maran, *Malaysia* **39 L4** 3 35N 102 45 E
Marana, *U.S.A.* **83 K8** 32 27N 111 13W
Maranboy, *Australia* **60 B5** 14 40S 132 39 E
Marand, *Iran* **44 B5** 38 30N 45 45 E
Marang, *Malaysia* **39 K4** 5 12N 103 13 E
Maranguape, *Brazil* **93 D11** 3 55S 38 50W
Maranhão = São Luís, *Brazil* **93 D10** 2 39S 44 15W
Maranhão □, *Brazil* **93 E9** 5 0S 46 0W
Maranoa →, *Australia* **63 D4** 27 50S 148 37 E
Marañón →, *Peru* **92 D4** 4 30S 73 35W
Marão, *Mozam.* **57 C5** 24 18S 34 2 E
Maraş = Kahramanmaraş, *Turkey* **25 G6** 37 37N 36 53 E
Marathasa □, *Cyprus* **23 E11** 34 59N 32 51 E
Marathon, *Australia* **62 C3** 20 51S 143 32 E
Marathon, *Canada* **70 C2** 48 44N 86 23W
Marathon, *N.Y., U.S.A.* **79 D8** 42 27N 76 2W
Marathon, *Tex., U.S.A.* **81 K3** 30 12N 103 15W
Marathóvouno, *Cyprus* **23 D12** 35 13N 33 37 E
Maratua, *Indonesia* **37 D5** 2 10N 118 35 E
Maravatío, *Mexico* **86 D4** 19 51N 100 25W
Marāwih, *U.A.E.* **45 E7** 24 18N 53 18 E
Marbella, *Spain* **19 D3** 36 30N 4 57W
Marble Bar, *Australia* **60 D2** 21 9S 119 44 E
Marble Falls, *U.S.A.* **81 K5** 30 35N 98 16W
Marblehead, *U.S.A.* **79 D14** 42 30N 70 51W
Marburg, *Germany* **16 C5** 50 47N 8 46 E
March, *U.K.* **11 E8** 52 33N 0 5 E
Marche, *France* **18 C4** 46 5N 1 20 E
Marche-en-Famenne, *Belgium* **15 D5** 50 14N 5 19 E
Marchena, *Spain* **19 D3** 37 18N 5 23W
Marcos Juárez, *Argentina* **94 C3** 32 42S 62 5W
Marcus I. = Minami-Tori-Shima, *Pac. Oc.* **64 E7** 24 0N 153 45 E
Marcus Necker Ridge, *Pac. Oc.* **64 F9** 20 0N 175 0 E
Marcy, Mt., *U.S.A.* **79 B11** 44 7N 73 56W
Mardan, *Pakistan* **42 B5** 34 20N 72 0 E
Mardie, *Australia* **60 D2** 21 12S 115 59 E
Mardin, *Turkey* **25 G7** 37 20N 40 43 E
Maree, L., *U.K.* **12 D3** 57 40N 5 26W
Mareeba, *Australia* **62 B4** 16 59S 145 28 E
Marek = Stanke Dimitrov, *Bulgaria* **21 C10** 42 17N 23 9 E
Marek, *Indonesia* **37 E6** 4 41S 120 24 E
Marengo, *U.S.A.* **80 E8** 41 48N 92 4W
Marenyi, *Kenya* **54 C4** 4 22S 39 8 E
Marerano, *Madag.* **57 C7** 21 23S 44 52 E
Marfa, *U.S.A.* **81 K2** 30 19N 104 1W
Marfa Pt., *Malta* **23 D1** 35 59N 14 19 E
Margaret →, *Australia* **60 C4** 18 9S 125 41 E
Margaret Bay, *Canada* **72 C3** 51 20N 127 35W
Margaret L., *Canada* **72 B5** 58 56N 115 25W
Margaret River, *Australia* **60 C4** 18 38S 126 52 E
Margarita, I. de, *Venezuela* **92 A6** 11 0N 64 0W
Margaritovo, *Russia* **30 C7** 43 25N 134 45 E
Margate, *S. Africa* **57 E5** 30 50S 30 20 E
Margate, *U.K.* **11 F9** 51 23N 1 23 E
Margelan = Marghilon, *Uzbekistan* **26 E8** 40 27N 71 42 E
Marghilon, *Uzbekistan* **26 E8** 40 27N 71 42 E
Marguerite, *Canada* **72 C4** 52 30N 122 25W
Mari El □, *Russia* **24 C8** 56 30N 48 0 E
Mari Republic □ = Mari El □, *Russia* **24 C8** 56 30N 48 0 E
María Elena, *Chile* **94 A2** 22 18S 69 40W
María Grande, *Argentina* **94 C4** 31 45S 59 55W
Maria I., *N. Terr., Australia* **62 A2** 14 52S 135 45 E
Maria I., *Tas., Australia* **62 G4** 42 35S 148 0 E
Maria van Diemen, C., *N.Z.* **59 F4** 34 29S 172 40 E
Mariakani, *Kenya* **54 C4** 3 50S 39 27 E
Marian L., *Canada* **72 A5** 63 0N 116 15W
Mariana Trench, *Pac. Oc.* **28 H18** 13 0N 145 0 E
Marianao, *Cuba* **88 B3** 23 8N 82 24W
Marianna, *Ark., U.S.A.* **81 H9** 34 46N 90 46W
Marianna, *Fla., U.S.A.* **77 K3** 30 46N 85 14W
Marias →, *U.S.A.* **82 C8** 47 56N 110 30W
Mariato, Punta, *Panama* **88 E3** 7 12N 80 52W
Ma'rib, *Yemen* **46 D4** 15 25N 45 21 E
Maribor, *Slovenia* **16 E8** 46 36N 15 40 E
Marico →, *Africa* **56 C4** 23 35S 26 57 E
Maricopa, *Ariz., U.S.A.* **83 K7** 33 4N 112 3W
Maricopa, *Calif., U.S.A.* **85 K7** 35 4N 119 24W
Maricourt, *Canada* **69 C12** 56 34N 70 49W
Marīdī, *Sudan* **51 H10** 4 55N 29 25 E
Marie Byrd Land, *Antarctica* **5 D14** 79 30S 125 0W
Marie-Galante, *Guadeloupe* **89 C7** 15 56N 61 16W
Mariecourt = Kangiqsujuaq, *Canada* **69 B12** 61 30N 72 0W
Marienberg, *Neths.* **15 B6** 52 2N 6 35 E
Marienbourg, *Belgium* **15 D4** 50 6N 4 31 E
Mariental, *Namibia* **56 C2** 24 36S 18 0 E
Marienville, *U.S.A.* **78 E5** 41 28N 79 8W
Mariestad, *Sweden* **9 G15** 58 43N 13 50 E
Marietta, *Ga., U.S.A.* **77 J3** 33 57N 84 33W
Marietta, *Ohio, U.S.A.* **76 F5** 39 25N 81 27W
Marieville, *Canada* **79 A11** 45 26N 73 10W
Mariinsk, *Russia* **26 D9** 56 10N 87 20 E
Marijampole, *Lithuania* **9 J20** 54 33N 23 19 E
Marília, *Brazil* **95 A5** 22 13S 50 0W
Marillana, *Australia* **60 D2** 22 37S 119 16 E
Marín, *Spain* **19 A1** 42 23N 8 42W
Marina, *U.S.A.* **84 J5** 36 41N 121 48W
Marina Plains, *Australia* **62 A3** 14 37S 143 57 E
Marinduque, *Phil.* **37 B6** 13 25N 122 0 E
Marine City, *U.S.A.* **76 D4** 42 43N 82 30W
Marinette, *U.S.A.* **76 C2** 45 6N 87 38W
Maringá, *Brazil* **95 A5** 23 26S 52 2W
Marion, *Ala., U.S.A.* **77 J2** 32 38N 87 19W
Marion, *Ill., U.S.A.* **81 G10** 37 44N 88 56W
Marion, *Ind., U.S.A.* **76 E3** 40 32N 85 40W
Marion, *Iowa, U.S.A.* **80 D9** 42 2N 91 36W
Marion, *Kans., U.S.A.* **80 F6** 38 21N 97 1W
Marion, *Mich., U.S.A.* **76 C3** 44 6N 85 9W
Marion, *N.C., U.S.A.* **77 H4** 35 41N 82 1W
Marion, *Ohio, U.S.A.* **76 E4** 40 35N 83 8W
Marion, *S.C., U.S.A.* **77 H6** 34 11N 79 24W
Marion, *Va., U.S.A.* **77 G5** 36 50N 81 31W
Marion, L., *U.S.A.* **77 J5** 33 28N 80 10W
Mariposa, *U.S.A.* **83 H4** 37 29N 119 58W
Mariscal Estigarribia, *Paraguay* **94 A3** 22 3S 60 40W
Maritime Alps = Maritimes, Alpes, *Europe* **16 F4** 44 10N 7 10 E
Maritimes, Alpes, *Europe* **16 F4** 44 10N 7 10 E
Maritsa = Évros →, *Bulgaria* **21 D12** 41 40N 26 34 E
Maritsa, *Greece* **23 C10** 36 22N 28 10 E
Mariupol, *Ukraine* **25 E6** 47 5N 37 31 E
Marīvān, *Iran* **44 C5** 35 30N 46 25 E
Markazī □, *Iran* **45 C6** 35 0N 49 30 E
Markdale, *Canada* **78 B4** 44 19N 80 39W
Marked Tree, *U.S.A.* **81 H9** 35 32N 90 25W
Marken, *Neths.* **15 B5** 52 26N 5 12 E
Market Drayton, *U.K.* **10 E5** 52 54N 2 29W
Market Harborough, *U.K.* **11 E7** 52 29N 0 55W
Markham, *Canada* **78 C5** 43 52N 79 16W
Markham, Mt., *Antarctica* **5 E11** 83 0S 164 0 E
Markham L., *Canada* **73 A8** 62 30N 102 35W
Markleeville, *U.S.A.* **84 G7** 38 42N 119 47W
Markovo, *Russia* **27 C17** 64 40N 169 40 E
Marks, *Russia* **24 D8** 51 45N 46 50 E
Marksville, *U.S.A.* **81 K8** 31 8N 92 4W
Marla, *Australia* **63 D1** 27 19S 133 33 E
Marlboro, *U.S.A.* **79 D13** 42 19N 71 33W
Marlborough, *Australia* **62 C4** 22 46S 149 52 E
Marlborough Downs, *U.K.* **11 F6** 51 27N 1 53W
Marlin, *U.S.A.* **81 K6** 31 18N 96 54W
Marlow, *U.S.A.* **81 H6** 34 39N 97 58W
Marmagao, *India* **40 M8** 15 25N 73 56 E
Marmara, *Turkey* **21 D12** 40 35N 27 38 E
Marmara, Sea of = Marmara Denizi, *Turkey* **21 D13** 40 45N 28 15 E
Marmara Denizi, *Turkey* **21 D13** 40 45N 28 15 E
Marmaris, *Turkey* **21 F13** 36 50N 28 14 E
Marmarth, *U.S.A.* **80 B3** 46 18N 103 54W
Marmion, Mt., *Australia* **61 E2** 29 16S 119 50 E
Marmion L., *Canada* **70 C1** 48 55N 91 20W
Marmolada, Mte., *Italy* **20 A4** 46 26N 11 51 E
Marmora, *Canada* **70 D4** 44 28N 77 41W
Marne →, *France* **18 B5** 48 48N 2 24 E
Maroala, *Madag.* **57 B8** 15 23S 47 59 E
Maroantsetra, *Madag.* **57 B8** 15 26S 49 44 E
Maromandia, *Madag.* **57 A8** 14 13S 48 5 E
Marondera, *Zimbabwe* **55 F3** 18 5S 31 42 E
Maroni →, *Fr. Guiana* **93 B8** 5 30N 54 0W
Maroochydore, *Australia* **63 D5** 26 29S 153 5 E
Maroona, *Australia* **63 F3** 37 27S 142 54 E
Marosakoa, *Madag.* **57 B8** 15 26S 46 38 E
Maroua, *Cameroon* **51 F7** 10 40N 14 20 E
Marovoay, *Madag.* **57 B8** 16 6S 46 39 E
Marquard, *S. Africa* **56 D4** 28 40S 27 28 E
Marquesas Is. = Marquises, Is., *Pac. Oc.* **65 H14** 9 30S 140 0W
Marquette, *U.S.A.* **76 B2** 46 33N 87 24W
Marquises, Is., *Pac. Oc.* **65 H14** 9 30S 140 0W

Moonta

Moonta, *Australia* 63 E2 34 6S 137 32 E
Moora, *Australia* 61 F2 30 37S 115 58 E
Mooraberree, *Australia* 62 D3 25 13S 140 54 E
Moorarie, *Australia* 61 E2 25 56S 117 35 E
Moorcroft, *U.S.A.* 80 C2 44 16N 104 57W
Moore →, *Australia* 61 F2 31 22S 115 30 E
Moore, L., *Australia* 61 E2 29 50S 117 35 E
Moore Reefs, *Australia* 62 B4 16 0S 149 5 E
Moorefield, *U.S.A.* 76 F6 39 5N 78 59W
Moores Res., *U.S.A.* 79 B13 44 45N 71 50W
Mooresville, *U.S.A.* 77 H5 35 35N 80 48W
Moorfoot Hills, *U.K.* 12 F5 55 44N 3 8W
Moorhead, *U.S.A.* 80 B6 46 53N 96 45W
Mooroopna, *Australia* 63 F4 36 25S 145 22 E
Moorpark, *U.S.A.* 85 L8 34 17N 118 53W
Moorreesburg, *S. Africa* 56 E2 33 6S 18 38 E
Moose →, *Canada* 70 B3 51 20N 80 25W
Moose Factory, *Canada* 70 B3 51 16N 80 32W
Moose I., *Canada* 73 C9 51 42N 97 10W
Moose Jaw, *Canada* 73 C7 50 24N 105 30W
Moose Jaw →, *Canada* 73 C7 50 34N 105 18W
Moose Lake, *Canada* 73 C8 53 43N 100 20W
Moose Lake, *U.S.A.* 80 B8 46 27N 92 46W
Moose Mountain Cr. →, *Canada* 73 D8 49 13N 102 12W
Moose Mountain Prov. Park, *Canada* 73 D8 49 48N 102 25W
Moose River, *Canada* 70 B3 50 48N 81 17W
Moosehead L., *U.S.A.* 71 C6 45 38N 69 40W
Moosomin, *Canada* 73 C8 50 9N 101 40W
Moosonee, *Canada* 70 B3 51 17N 80 39W
Moosup, *U.S.A.* 79 E13 41 43N 71 53W
Mopeia Velha, *Mozam.* 55 F4 17 30S 35 40 E
Mopipi, *Botswana* 56 C3 21 6S 24 55 E
Mopoi, *C.A.R.* 54 A2 5 6N 26 54 E
Mopti, *Mali* 50 F4 14 30N 4 0W
Moquegua, *Peru* 92 G4 17 15S 70 46W
Mora, *Sweden* 9 F16 61 2N 14 38 E
Mora, *Minn., U.S.A.* 80 C8 45 53N 93 18W
Mora, *N. Mex., U.S.A.* 83 J11 35 58N 105 20W
Moradabad, *India* 43 E8 28 50N 78 50 E
Morafenobe, *Madag.* 57 B7 17 50S 44 53 E
Moramanga, *Madag.* 57 B8 18 56S 48 12 E
Moran, *Kans., U.S.A.* 81 G7 37 55N 95 10W
Moran, *Wyo., U.S.A.* 82 E8 43 53N 110 37W
Moranbah, *Australia* 62 C4 22 1S 148 6 E
Morant Cays, *Jamaica* 88 C4 17 22N 76 0W
Morant Pt., *Jamaica* 88 C4 17 55N 76 12W
Morar, L., *U.K.* 12 E3 56 57N 5 40W
Moratuwa, *Sri Lanka* 40 R11 6 45N 79 55 E
Morava →, *Serbia, Yug.* 21 B9 44 36N 21 4 E
Morava →, *Slovak Rep.* 17 D9 48 10N 16 59 E
Moravia, *U.S.A.* 80 E8 40 53N 92 49W
Moravian Hts. = Ceskomoravská Vrchovina, *Czech.* 16 D8 49 30N 15 40 E
Morawa, *Australia* 61 E2 29 13S 116 0 E
Morawhanna, *Guyana* 92 B7 8 30N 59 40W
Moray □, *U.K.* 12 D5 57 31N 3 18W
Moray Firth, *U.K.* 12 D5 57 40N 3 52W
Morbi, *India* 42 H4 22 50N 70 42 E
Morden, *Canada* 73 D9 49 15N 98 10W
Mordovian Republic □ = Mordvinia □, *Russia* 24 D7 54 20N 44 30 E
Mordvinia □, *Russia* 24 D7 54 20N 44 30 E
Morea, *Australia* 63 F3 36 45S 141 18 E
Morea, *Greece* 6 H10 37 45N 22 10 E
Moreau →, *U.S.A.* 80 C4 45 18N 100 43W
Morecambe, *U.K.* 10 C5 54 5N 2 52W
Morecambe B., *U.K.* 10 C5 54 7N 3 0W
Moree, *Australia* 63 D4 29 28S 149 54 E
Morehead, *U.S.A.* 76 F4 38 11N 83 26W
Morehead City, *U.S.A.* 77 H7 34 43N 76 43W
Morelia, *Mexico* 86 D4 19 42N 101 7W
Morella, *Australia* 62 C3 23 0S 143 52 E
Morella, *Spain* 19 B5 40 35N 0 5W
Morelos, *Mexico* 86 B3 26 42N 107 40W
Morelos □, *Mexico* 87 D5 18 40N 99 10W
Morena, Sierra, *Spain* 19 C3 38 20N 4 0W
Morenci, *U.S.A.* 83 K9 33 5N 109 22W
Moreno Valley, *U.S.A.* 85 M10 33 56N 116 58W
Moresby I., *Canada* 72 C2 52 30N 131 40W
Moreton, *Australia* 62 A3 12 22S 142 40 E
Moreton I., *Australia* 63 D5 27 10S 153 25 E
Morey, *Spain* 22 B10 39 44N 3 20 E
Morgan, *Australia* 63 E2 34 2S 139 35 E
Morgan, *U.S.A.* 82 F8 41 2N 111 41W
Morgan City, *U.S.A.* 81 L9 29 42N 91 12W
Morgan Hill, *U.S.A.* 84 H5 37 8N 121 39W
Morganfield, *U.S.A.* 76 G2 37 41N 87 55W
Morganton, *U.S.A.* 77 H5 35 45N 81 41W
Morgantown, *U.S.A.* 76 F6 39 38N 79 57W
Morgenzon, *S. Africa* 57 D4 26 45S 29 36 E
Morghak, *Iran* 45 D8 29 7N 57 54 E
Morice L., *Canada* 72 C3 53 50N 127 40W
Morinville, *Canada* 72 C6 53 49N 113 41W
Morioka, *Japan* 30 E10 39 45N 141 8 E
Moris, *Mexico* 86 B3 28 8N 108 32W
Morlaix, *France* 18 B2 48 36N 3 52W
Mornington, *Vic., Australia* 63 F4 38 15S 145 5 E
Mornington, *W. Austral., Australia* 60 C4 17 31S 126 6 E
Mornington, I., *Chile* 96 F1 49 50S 75 30W
Mornington I., *Australia* 62 B2 16 30S 139 30 E
Moro G., *Phil.* 37 C6 6 30N 123 0 E
Morocco ■, *N. Afr.* 50 B3 32 0N 5 50W
Morococha, *Peru* 92 F3 11 40S 76 5W
Morogoro, *Tanzania* 54 D4 6 50S 37 40 E
Morogoro □, *Tanzania* 54 D4 8 0S 37 0 E
Moroleón, *Mexico* 86 C4 20 8N 101 32W
Morombe, *Madag.* 57 C7 21 45S 43 22 E
Moron, *Argentina* 94 C4 34 39S 58 37W
Morón, *Cuba* 88 B4 22 8N 78 39W
Morón de la Frontera, *Spain* 19 D3 37 6N 5 28W
Morondava, *Madag.* 57 C7 20 17S 44 17 E
Morongo Valley, *U.S.A.* 85 L10 34 3N 116 37W
Morotai, *Indonesia* 37 D7 2 10N 128 30 E
Moroto, *Uganda* 54 B3 2 28N 34 42 E
Moroto Summit, *Kenya* 54 B3 2 30N 34 43 E
Morpeth, *U.K.* 10 B6 55 10N 1 41W
Morphou, *Cyprus* 23 D11 35 12N 32 59 E
Morphou Bay, *Cyprus* 23 D11 35 15N 32 50 E
Morrilton, *U.S.A.* 81 H8 35 9N 92 44W
Morrinhos, *Brazil* 93 G9 17 45S 49 10W
Morrinsville, *N.Z.* 59 G5 37 40S 175 32 E
Morris, *Canada* 73 D9 49 25N 97 22W
Morris, *Ill., U.S.A.* 76 E1 41 22N 88 26W
Morris, *Minn., U.S.A.* 80 C7 45 35N 95 55W
Morris, Mt., *Australia* 61 E5 26 9S 131 4 E
Morrisburg, *Canada* 70 D4 44 55N 75 7W
Morrison, *U.S.A.* 80 E10 41 49N 89 58W
Morristown, *Ariz., U.S.A.* 83 K7 33 51N 112 37W
Morristown, *N.J., U.S.A.* 79 F10 40 48N 74 29W
Morristown, *S. Dak., U.S.A.* 80 C4 45 56N 101 43W
Morristown, *Tenn., U.S.A.* 77 G4 36 13N 83 18W
Morro, Pta., *Chile* 94 B1 27 6S 71 0W
Morro Bay, *U.S.A.* 83 J3 35 22N 120 51W
Morro del Jable, *Canary Is.* 22 F5 28 3N 14 23W
Morro Jable, Pta. de, *Canary Is.* 22 F5 28 2N 14 20W
Morrosquillo, G. de, *Colombia* 88 E4 9 35N 75 40W
Morrumbene, *Mozam.* 57 C6 23 31S 35 16 E
Morshansk, *Russia* 24 D7 53 28N 41 50 E
Morteros, *Argentina* 94 C3 30 50S 62 0W
Mortes, R. das →, *Brazil* 93 F8 11 45S 50 44W
Mortlake, *Australia* 63 F3 38 5S 142 50 E
Morton, *Tex., U.S.A.* 81 J3 33 44N 102 46W
Morton, *Wash., U.S.A.* 84 D4 46 34N 122 17W
Morundah, *Australia* 63 E4 34 57S 146 19 E
Moruya, *Australia* 63 F5 35 58S 150 3 E
Morvan, *France* 18 C6 47 5N 4 3 E
Morven, *Australia* 63 D4 26 22S 147 5 E
Morvern, *U.K.* 12 E3 56 38N 5 44W
Morwell, *Australia* 63 F4 38 10S 146 22 E
Morzhovets, Ostrov, *Russia* 24 A7 66 44N 42 35 E
Moscos Is., *Burma* 38 E1 14 0N 97 30 E
Moscow = Moskva, *Russia* 24 C6 55 45N 37 35 E
Moscow, *U.S.A.* 82 C5 46 44N 117 0W
Mosel →, *Europe* 18 A7 50 22N 7 36 E
Moselle = Mosel →, *Europe* 18 A7 50 22N 7 36 E
Moses Lake, *U.S.A.* 82 C4 47 8N 119 17W
Mosgiel, *N.Z.* 59 L3 45 53S 170 21 E
Moshi, *Tanzania* 54 C4 3 22S 37 18 E
Moshi □, *Tanzania* 54 C4 3 22S 37 18 E
Moshupa, *Botswana* 56 C4 24 46S 25 29 E
Mosjøen, *Norway* 8 D15 65 51N 13 12 E
Moskenesøya, *Norway* 8 C15 67 58N 13 0 E
Moskenstraumen, *Norway* 8 C15 67 47N 12 45 E
Moskva, *Russia* 24 C6 55 45N 37 35 E
Moskva →, *Russia* 24 C6 55 5N 38 51 E
Mosomane, *Botswana* 56 C4 24 2S 26 19 E
Moson-magyaróvar, *Hungary* 17 E9 47 52N 17 18 E
Mosquera, *Colombia* 92 C3 2 35N 78 24W
Mosquero, *U.S.A.* 81 H3 35 47N 103 58W
Mosquitia, *Honduras* 88 C3 15 20N 84 10W
Mosquitos, G. de los, *Panama* 88 E3 9 15N 81 10W
Moss, *Norway* 9 G14 59 27N 10 40 E
Moss Vale, *Australia* 63 E5 34 32S 150 25 E
Mossaka, *Congo* 52 E3 1 15S 16 45 E
Mossbank, *Canada* 73 D7 49 56N 105 56W
Mossburn, *N.Z.* 59 L2 45 41S 168 15 E
Mosselbaai, *S. Africa* 56 E3 34 11S 22 8 E
Mossendjo, *Congo* 52 E2 2 55S 12 42 E
Mossgiel, *Australia* 63 E3 33 15S 144 5 E
Mossman, *Australia* 62 B4 16 21S 145 15 E
Mossoró, *Brazil* 93 E11 5 10S 37 15W
Mossuril, *Mozam.* 55 E5 14 58S 40 42 E
Mossy →, *Canada* 73 C8 54 5N 102 58W
Most, *Czech.* 16 C7 50 31N 13 38 E
Mosta, *Malta* 23 D1 35 54N 14 24 E
Moşţafáābād, *Iran* 45 C7 33 39N 54 53 E
Mostaganem, *Algeria* 50 A5 35 54N 0 5 E
Mostar, *Bos.-H.* 21 C7 43 22N 17 50 E
Mostardas, *Brazil* 95 C5 31 2S 50 51W
Mostiska = Mostyska, *Ukraine* 17 D12 49 48N 23 4 E
Mosty = Masty, *Belarus* 17 B13 53 27N 24 38 E
Mostyska, *Ukraine* 17 D12 49 48N 23 4 E
Mosul = Al Mawşil, *Iraq* 44 B4 36 15N 43 5 E
Mosulpo, *S. Korea* 35 H14 33 20N 126 17 E
Motagua →, *Guatemala* 88 C2 15 44N 88 14W
Motala, *Sweden* 9 G16 58 32N 15 1 E
Motherwell, *U.K.* 12 F5 55 47N 3 58W
Motihari, *India* 43 F11 26 30N 84 55 E
Motozintla de Mendoza, *Mexico* 87 D6 15 21N 92 14W
Motril, *Spain* 19 D4 36 31N 3 37W
Mott, *U.S.A.* 80 B3 46 23N 102 20W
Motueka, *N.Z.* 59 J4 41 7S 173 1 E
Motueka →, *N.Z.* 59 J4 41 5S 173 1 E
Motul, *Mexico* 87 C7 21 0N 89 20W
Mouanda, *Gabon* 52 E2 1 28S 13 7 E
Mouchalagane →, *Canada* 71 B6 50 56N 68 41W
Moúdhros, *Greece* 21 E11 39 50N 25 18 E
Moudjeria, *Mauritania* 50 E2 17 50N 12 28W
Mouila, *Gabon* 52 E2 1 50S 11 0 E
Moulamein, *Australia* 63 F3 35 3S 144 1 E
Moulianá, *Greece* 23 D7 35 10N 25 59 E
Moulins, *France* 18 C5 46 35N 3 19 E
Moulmein, *Burma* 41 L20 16 30N 97 40 E
Moulton, *U.S.A.* 81 L6 29 35N 97 9W
Moultrie, *U.S.A.* 77 K4 31 11N 83 47W
Moultrie, L., *U.S.A.* 77 J5 33 20N 80 5W
Mound City, *Mo., U.S.A.* 80 E7 40 7N 95 14W
Mound City, *S. Dak., U.S.A.* 80 C4 45 44N 100 4W
Moundou, *Chad* 51 G8 8 40N 16 10 E
Moundsville, *U.S.A.* 78 G4 39 55N 80 44W
Moung, *Cambodia* 38 F4 12 46N 103 27 E
Mount Airy, *U.S.A.* 77 G5 36 31N 80 37W
Mount Albert, *Canada* 78 B5 44 8N 79 19W
Mount Amherst, *Australia* 60 C4 18 24S 126 58 E
Mount Angel, *U.S.A.* 82 D2 45 4N 122 48W
Mount Augustus, *Australia* 60 D2 24 20S 116 56 E
Mount Barker, *S. Austral., Australia* 63 F2 35 5S 138 52 E
Mount Barker, *W. Austral., Australia* 61 F2 34 38S 117 40 E
Mount Carmel, *U.S.A.* 76 F2 38 25N 87 46W
Mount Clemens, *U.S.A.* 78 D2 42 35N 82 53W
Mount Coolon, *Australia* 62 C4 21 25S 147 25 E
Mount Darwin, *Zimbabwe* 55 F3 16 47S 31 38 E
Mount Desert I., *U.S.A.* 71 D6 44 21N 68 20W
Mount Dora, *U.S.A.* 77 L5 28 48N 81 38W
Mount Douglas, *Australia* 62 C4 21 35S 146 50 E
Mount Eba, *Australia* 63 E2 30 11S 135 40 E
Mount Edgecumbe, *U.S.A.* 72 B1 57 3N 135 21W
Mount Elizabeth, *Australia* 60 C4 16 0S 125 50 E
Mount Fletcher, *S. Africa* 57 E4 30 40S 28 30 E
Mount Forest, *Canada* 70 D3 43 59N 80 43W
Mount Gambier, *Australia* 63 F3 37 50S 140 46 E
Mount Garnet, *Australia* 62 B4 17 37S 145 6 E
Mount Hope, *N.S.W., Australia* 63 E4 32 51S 145 51 E
Mount Hope, *S. Austral., Australia* 63 E2 34 7S 135 23 E
Mount Hope, *U.S.A.* 76 G5 37 54N 81 10W
Mount Horeb, *U.S.A.* 80 D10 43 1N 89 44W
Mount Howitt, *Australia* 63 D3 26 31S 142 16 E
Mount Isa, *Australia* 62 C2 20 42S 139 26 E
Mount Keith, *Australia* 61 E3 27 15S 120 30 E
Mount Laguna, *U.S.A.* 85 N10 32 52N 116 25W
Mount Larcom, *Australia* 62 C5 23 48S 150 59 E
Mount Lofty Ra., *Australia* 63 E2 34 35S 139 5 E
Mount McKinley National Park, *U.S.A.* 68 B5 63 30N 150 0W
Mount Magnet, *Australia* 61 E2 28 2S 117 47 E
Mount Margaret, *Australia* 63 D3 26 54S 143 21 E
Mount Maunganui, *N.Z.* 59 G6 37 40S 176 14 E
Mount Molloy, *Australia* 62 B4 16 42S 145 20 E
Mount Monger, *Australia* 61 F3 31 0S 122 0 E
Mount Morgan, *Australia* 62 C5 23 40S 150 25 E
Mount Morris, *U.S.A.* 78 D7 42 44N 77 52W
Mount Mulligan, *Australia* 62 B3 16 45S 144 47 E
Mount Narryer, *Australia* 61 E2 26 30S 115 55 E
Mount Olympus = Uludağ, *Turkey* 21 D13 40 4N 29 13 E
Mount Oxide Mine, *Australia* 62 B2 19 30S 139 29 E
Mount Pearl, *Canada* 71 C9 47 31N 52 47W
Mount Perry, *Australia* 63 D5 25 13S 151 42 E
Mount Phillips, *Australia* 60 D2 24 25S 116 15 E
Mount Pleasant, *Iowa, U.S.A.* 80 E9 40 58N 91 33W
Mount Pleasant, *Mich., U.S.A.* 76 D3 43 36N 84 46W
Mount Pleasant, *Pa., U.S.A.* 78 F5 40 9N 79 33W
Mount Pleasant, *S.C., U.S.A.* 77 J6 32 47N 79 52W
Mount Pleasant, *Tenn., U.S.A.* 77 H2 35 32N 87 12W
Mount Pleasant, *Tex., U.S.A.* 81 J7 33 9N 94 58W
Mount Pleasant, *Utah, U.S.A.* 82 G8 39 33N 111 27W
Mount Pocono, *U.S.A.* 79 E9 41 7N 75 22W
Mount Rainier National Park, *U.S.A.* 84 D5 46 55N 121 50W
Mount Revelstoke Nat. Park, *Canada* 72 C5 51 5N 118 30W
Mount Robson Prov. Park, *Canada* 72 C5 53 0N 119 0W
Mount Sandiman, *Australia* 61 D2 24 25S 115 30 E
Mount Shasta, *U.S.A.* 82 F2 41 19N 122 19W
Mount Signal, *U.S.A.* 85 N11 32 39N 115 37W
Mount Sterling, *Ill., U.S.A.* 80 F9 39 59N 90 45W
Mount Sterling, *Ky., U.S.A.* 76 F4 38 4N 83 56W
Mount Surprise, *Australia* 62 B3 18 10S 144 17 E
Mount Union, *U.S.A.* 78 F7 40 23N 77 53W
Mount Vernon, *Australia* 60 D2 24 9S 118 2 E
Mount Vernon, *Ind., U.S.A.* 80 F10 38 17N 88 57W
Mount Vernon, *N.Y., U.S.A.* 79 F11 40 55N 73 50W
Mount Vernon, *Ohio, U.S.A.* 78 F2 40 23N 82 29W
Mount Vernon, *Wash., U.S.A.* 84 B4 48 25N 122 20W
Mountain Center, *U.S.A.* 85 M10 33 42N 116 44W
Mountain City, *Nev., U.S.A.* 82 F6 41 50N 115 58W
Mountain City, *Tenn., U.S.A.* 77 G5 36 29N 81 48W
Mountain Grove, *U.S.A.* 81 G8 37 8N 92 16W
Mountain Home, *Ark., U.S.A.* 81 G8 36 20N 92 23W
Mountain Home, *Idaho, U.S.A.* 82 E6 43 8N 115 41W
Mountain Iron, *U.S.A.* 80 B8 47 32N 92 37W
Mountain Park, *Canada* 72 C5 52 50N 117 15W
Mountain Pass, *U.S.A.* 85 K11 35 29N 115 35W
Mountain View, *Ark., U.S.A.* 81 H8 35 52N 92 7W
Mountain View, *Calif., U.S.A.* 83 H2 37 23N 122 5W
Mountainair, *U.S.A.* 83 J10 34 31N 106 15W
Mountmellick, *Ireland* 13 C4 53 7N 7 20W
Moura, *Australia* 62 C4 24 35S 149 58 E
Moura, *Brazil* 92 D6 1 32S 61 38W
Moura, *Portugal* 19 C2 38 7N 7 30W
Mourdi, Dépression du, *Chad* 51 E9 18 10N 23 0 E
Mourdiah, *Mali* 50 F3 14 35N 7 25W
Mourilyan, *Australia* 62 B4 17 35S 146 3 E
Mourne →, *U.K.* 13 B4 54 52N 7 26W
Mourne Mts., *U.K.* 13 B5 54 10N 6 0W
Mournies, *Greece* 23 D6 35 29N 24 1 E
Mouscron, *Belgium* 15 D3 50 45N 3 12 E
Moussoro, *Chad* 51 F8 13 41N 16 35 E
Moutohara, *N.Z.* 59 H6 38 27S 177 32 E
Moutong, *Indonesia* 37 D6 0 28N 121 13 E
Movas, *Mexico* 86 B3 28 10N 109 25W
Moville, *Ireland* 13 A4 55 11N 7 3W
Moy →, *Ireland* 13 B3 54 8N 9 8W
Moyale, *Kenya* 46 G2 3 30N 39 0 E
Moyamba, *S. Leone* 50 G2 8 4N 12 30W
Moyen Atlas, *Morocco* 50 B3 33 0N 5 0W
Moyle □, *U.K.* 13 A5 55 10N 6 15W
Moyo, *Indonesia* 36 F5 8 10S 117 40 E
Moyobamba, *Peru* 92 E3 6 0S 77 0W
Moyyero →, *Russia* 27 C11 68 44N 103 42 E
Moyynty, *Kazakstan* 26 E8 47 10N 73 18 E
Mozambique = Moçambique, *Mozam.* 55 F5 15 3S 40 42 E
Mozambique ■, *Africa* 55 F4 19 0S 35 0 E
Mozambique Chan., *Africa* 57 B7 17 30S 42 30 E
Mozdok, *Russia* 25 F7 43 45N 44 48 E
Mozdūrān, *Iran* 45 B9 36 9N 60 35 E
Mozhnābād, *Iran* 45 C9 34 7N 60 6 E
Mozyr = Mazyr, *Belarus* 17 B15 51 59N 29 15 E
Mpanda, *Tanzania* 54 D3 6 23S 31 1 E
Mpanda □, *Tanzania* 54 D3 6 23S 31 40 E
Mpika, *Zambia* 55 E3 11 51S 31 25 E
Mpulungu, *Zambia* 55 D3 8 51S 31 5 E
Mpumalanga, *S. Africa* 57 D5 29 50S 30 33 E
Mpumalanga □, *S. Africa* 57 B5 26 0S 30 0 E
Mpwapwa, *Tanzania* 54 D4 6 23S 36 30 E
Mpwapwa □, *Tanzania* 54 D4 6 30S 36 20 E
Msaken, *Tunisia* 51 A7 35 49N 10 33 E
Msambansovu, *Zimbabwe* 55 F3 15 50S 30 3 E
Msoro, *Zambia* 55 E3 13 35S 31 50 E
Mstislavl = Mstsislaw, *Belarus* 17 A16 54 0N 31 50 E
Mstsislaw, *Belarus* 17 A16 54 0N 31 50 E
Mtama, *Tanzania* 55 E4 10 17S 39 21 E
Mtilikwe →, *Zimbabwe* 55 G3 21 9S 31 30 E
Mtubatuba, *S. Africa* 57 D5 28 30S 32 8 E
Mtwara-Mikindani, *Tanzania* 55 E5 10 20S 40 20 E
Mu Gia, Deo, *Vietnam* 38 D5 17 40N 105 47 E
Mu Us Shamo, *China* 34 E5 39 0N 109 0 E
Muaná, *Brazil* 93 D9 1 25S 49 15W
Muang Chiang Rai, *Thailand* 38 C2 19 52N 99 50 E
Muang Lamphun, *Thailand* 38 C2 18 40N 99 2 E
Muang Pak Beng, *Laos* 38 C3 19 54N 101 8 E
Muar, *Malaysia* 39 L4 2 3N 102 34 E
Muarabungo, *Indonesia* 36 E2 1 28S 102 52 E
Muaraenim, *Indonesia* 36 E2 3 40S 103 50 E
Muarajuloi, *Indonesia* 36 E4 0 12S 114 3 E
Muarakaman, *Indonesia* 36 E5 0 2S 116 45 E
Muaratebo, *Indonesia* 36 E2 1 30S 102 26 E
Muaratembesi, *Indonesia* 36 E2 1 42S 103 8 E
Muaratewe, *Indonesia* 36 E4 0 58S 114 52 E
Mubarakpur, *India* 43 F10 26 6N 83 18 E
Mubarraz = Al Mubarraz, *Si. Arabia* 45 E6 25 30N 49 40 E
Mubende, *Uganda* 54 B3 0 33N 31 22 E
Mubi, *Nigeria* 51 F7 10 18N 13 16 E
Mubur, P., *Indonesia* 39 L6 3 20N 106 12 E
Muchachos, Roque de los, *Canary Is.* 22 F2 28 44N 17 52W
Muchinga Mts., *Zambia* 55 E3 11 30S 31 30 E
Muck, *U.K.* 12 E2 56 50N 6 15W
Muckadilla, *Australia* 63 D4 26 35S 148 23 E
Muconda, *Angola* 52 G4 10 31S 21 15 E
Mucuri, *Brazil* 93 G11 18 0S 39 36W
Mucusso, *Angola* 56 B3 18 1S 21 25 E
Muda, *Canary Is.* 22 F6 28 34N 13 57W
Mudan Jiang →, *China* 35 A15 46 20N 129 30 E
Mudanjiang, *China* 35 B15 44 38N 129 30 E
Mudanya, *Turkey* 21 D13 40 25N 28 50 E
Muddy Cr. →, *U.S.A.* 83 H8 38 24N 110 42W
Mudgee, *Australia* 63 E4 32 32S 149 31 E
Mudjatik →, *Canada* 73 B7 56 1N 107 36W
Muecate, *Mozam.* 55 E4 14 55S 39 40 E
Muêda, *Mozam.* 55 E4 11 36S 39 28 E
Mueller Ra., *Australia* 60 C4 18 18S 126 46 E
Muende, *Mozam.* 55 E3 14 28S 33 0 E
Muerto, Mar, *Mexico* 87 D6 16 10N 94 10W
Mufindi □, *Tanzania* 55 D4 8 30S 35 20 E
Mufulira, *Zambia* 55 E2 12 32S 28 15 E
Mufumbiro Range, *Africa* 54 C2 1 25S 29 30 E
Mughayrā', *Si. Arabia* 44 D3 29 17N 37 41 E
Mugi, *Japan* 31 H7 33 40N 134 25 E
Mugila, Mts., *Zaïre* 54 D2 7 0S 28 50 E
Muğla, *Turkey* 21 F13 37 15N 28 22 E
Mugu, *Nepal* 43 E10 29 45N 82 30 E
Muhammad Qol, *Sudan* 51 D12 20 53N 37 9 E
Muhammadabad, *India* 43 F10 26 4N 83 25 E
Muhesi →, *Tanzania* 54 D4 7 0S 35 20 E
Muheza □, *Tanzania* 54 C4 5 0S 39 0 E
Mühlhausen, *Germany* 16 C6 51 12N 10 27 E
Mühlig Hofmann fjell, *Antarctica* 5 D3 72 30S 5 0 E
Muhos, *Finland* 8 D22 64 47N 25 59 E
Muhu, *Estonia* 9 G20 58 36N 23 11 E
Muhutwe, *Tanzania* 54 C3 1 35S 31 45 E
Muikamachi, *Japan* 31 F9 37 15N 138 50 E
Muine Bheag, *Ireland* 13 D5 52 42N 6 58W
Muir, L., *Australia* 61 F2 34 30S 116 40 E
Mukacheve, *Ukraine* 17 D12 48 27N 22 45 E
Mukachevo = Mukacheve, *Ukraine* 17 D12 48 27N 22 45 E
Mukah, *Malaysia* 36 D4 2 55N 112 5 E
Mukdahan, *Thailand* 38 D5 16 32N 104 43 E
Mukden = Shenyang, *China* 35 D12 41 48N 123 27 E
Mukhtuya = Lensk, *Russia* 27 C12 60 48N 114 55 E
Mukinbudin, *Australia* 61 F2 30 55S 118 5 E
Mukishi, *Zaïre* 55 D1 8 30S 24 44 E
Mukomuko, *Indonesia* 36 E2 2 30S 101 10 E
Mukomwenze, *Zaïre* 54 D2 6 49S 27 15 E
Muktsar, *India* 42 D6 30 30N 74 30 E
Mukur, *Afghan.* 42 C2 32 50N 67 42 E
Mukutawa →, *Canada* 73 C9 53 10N 97 24W
Mukwela, *Zambia* 55 F2 17 0S 26 40 E
Mula, *Spain* 19 C5 38 3N 1 33W
Mulange, *Zaïre* 54 C2 3 40S 27 10 E
Mulchén, *Chile* 94 D1 37 45S 72 20W
Mulde →, *Germany* 16 C7 51 53N 12 15 E
Mule Creek, *U.S.A.* 80 D2 43 19N 104 8W
Muleba, *Tanzania* 54 C3 1 50S 31 37 E
Muleba □, *Tanzania* 54 C3 2 0S 31 30 E
Muleshoe, *U.S.A.* 81 H3 34 13N 102 43W
Mulgathing, *Australia* 63 E1 30 15S 134 8 E
Mulgrave, *Canada* 71 C7 45 38N 61 31W
Mulhacén, *Spain* 19 D4 37 4N 3 20W
Mulhouse, *France* 18 C7 47 40N 7 20 E
Muling, *China* 35 B16 44 35N 130 10 E

N

Namwŏn

Namwŏn, *S. Korea* **35 G14** 35 23N 127 23 E
Nan, *Thailand* **38 C3** 18 48N 100 46 E
Nan →, *Thailand* **38 E3** 15 42N 100 9 E
Nanaimo, *Canada* **72 D4** 49 10N 124 0W
Nanam, *N. Korea* **35 D15** 41 44N 129 40 E
Nanango, *Australia* **63 D5** 26 40S 152 0 E
Nanao, *Japan* **31 F8** 37 0N 137 0 E
Nanchang, *China* **33 D6** 28 42N 115 55 E
Nanching = Nanjing, *China* **33 C6** 32 2N 118 47 E
Nanchong, *China* **32 C5** 30 43N 106 2 E
Nancy, *France* **18 B7** 48 42N 6 12 E
Nanda Devi, *India* **43 D8** 30 23N 79 59 E
Nandan, *Japan* **31 G7** 34 10N 134 42 E
Nanded, *India* **40 K10** 19 10N 77 20 E
Nandewar Ra., *Australia* **63 E5** 30 15S 150 35 E
Nandi, *Fiji* **59 C7** 17 42S 177 20 E
Nandi □, *Kenya* **54 B4** 0 15N 35 0 E
Nandurbar, *India* **40 J9** 21 20N 74 15 E
Nandyal, *India* **40 M11** 15 30N 78 30 E
Nanga, *Australia* **61 E1** 26 7S 113 45 E
Nanga-Eboko, *Cameroon* **52 D2** 4 41N 12 22 E
Nanga Parbat, *Pakistan* **43 B6** 35 10N 74 35 E
Nangade, *Mozam.* **55 E4** 11 5S 39 36 E
Nangapinoh, *Indonesia* **36 E4** 0 20S 111 44 E
Nangarhár □, *Afghan.* **40 B7** 34 20N 70 0 E
Nangatayap, *Indonesia* **36 E4** 1 32S 110 34 E
Nangeya Mts., *Uganda* **54 B3** 3 30N 33 30 E
Nangong, *China* **34 F8** 37 23N 115 22 E
Nanhuang, *China* **35 F11** 36 58N 121 48 E
Nanjeko, *Zambia* **55 F1** 15 31S 23 30 E
Nanjing, *China* **33 C6** 32 2N 118 47 E
Nanjirinji, *Tanzania* **55 D4** 9 41S 39 5 E
Nankana Sahib, *Pakistan* **42 D5** 31 27N 73 38 E
Nanking = Nanjing, *China* **33 C6** 32 2N 118 47 E
Nankoku, *Japan* **31 H6** 33 39N 133 44 E
Nanning, *China* **32 D5** 22 48N 108 20 E
Nannup, *Australia* **61 F2** 33 59S 115 48 E
Nanpara, *India* **43 F9** 27 52N 81 33 E
Nanpi, *China* **34 E9** 38 2N 116 45 E
Nanping, *China* **33 D6** 26 38N 118 10 E
Nanripe, *Mozam.* **55 E4** 13 52S 38 52 E
Nansei-Shotō = Ryūkyū-rettō, *Japan* **31 M2** 26 0N 126 0 E
Nansen Sd., *Canada* **4 A3** 81 0N 91 0W
Nansio, *Tanzania* **54 C3** 2 3S 33 4 E
Nantes, *France* **18 C3** 47 12N 1 33W
Nanticoke, *U.S.A.* **79 E8** 41 12N 76 0W
Nanton, *Canada* **72 C6** 50 21N 113 46W
Nantong, *China* **33 C7** 32 1N 120 52 E
Nantucket I., *U.S.A.* **66 E12** 41 16N 70 5W
Nanuque, *Brazil* **93 G10** 17 50S 40 21W
Nanusa, Kepulauan, *Indonesia* **37 D7** 4 45N 127 1 E
Nanutarra, *Australia* **60 D2** 22 32S 115 30 E
Nanyang, *China* **34 H7** 33 11N 112 30 E
Nanyuan, *China* **34 E9** 39 44N 116 22 E
Nanyuki, *Kenya* **54 B4** 0 2N 37 4 E
Nao, C. de la, *Spain* **19 C6** 38 44N 0 14 E
Naococane L., *Canada* **71 B5** 52 50N 70 45W
Naoetsu, *Japan* **31 F9** 37 12N 138 10 E
Napa, *U.S.A.* **84 G4** 38 18N 122 17W
Napa →, *U.S.A.* **84 G4** 38 10N 122 19W
Napanee, *Canada* **70 D4** 44 15N 77 0W
Napanoch, *U.S.A.* **79 E10** 41 44N 74 22W
Nape, *Laos* **38 C5** 18 18N 105 6 E
Nape Pass = Keo Neua, Deo, *Vietnam* **38 C5** 18 23N 105 10 E
Napier, *N.Z.* **59 H6** 39 30S 176 56 E
Napier Broome B., *Australia* **60 B4** 14 2S 126 37 E
Napier Downs, *Australia* **60 C3** 17 11S 124 36 E
Napier Pen., *Australia* **62 A2** 12 4S 135 43 E
Naples = Nápoli, *Italy* **20 D6** 40 50N 14 15 E
Naples, *U.S.A.* **77 M5** 26 8N 81 48W
Napo →, *Peru* **92 D4** 3 20S 72 40W
Napoleon, *N. Dak., U.S.A.* **80 B5** 46 30N 99 46W
Napoleon, *Ohio, U.S.A.* **76 E3** 41 23N 84 8W
Nápoli, *Italy* **20 D6** 40 50N 14 15 E
Napopo, *Zaïre* **54 B2** 4 15N 28 0 E
Nappa Merrie, *Australia* **63 D3** 27 36S 141 7 E
Naqqāsh, *Iran* **45 C6** 35 40N 49 6 E
Nara, *Japan* **31 G7** 34 40N 135 49 E
Nara, *Mali* **50 E3** 15 10N 7 20W
Nara □, *Japan* **31 G8** 34 30N 136 0 E
Nara Canal, *Pakistan* **42 G3** 24 30N 69 20 E
Nara Visa, *U.S.A.* **81 H3** 35 37N 103 6W
Naracoorte, *Australia* **63 F3** 36 58S 140 45 E
Naradhan, *Australia* **63 E4** 33 34S 146 17 E
Narasapur, *India* **41 L12** 16 26N 81 40 E
Narathiwat, *Thailand* **39 J3** 6 30N 101 48 E
Narayanganj, *Bangla.* **41 H17** 23 40N 90 33 E
Narayanpet, *India* **40 L10** 16 45N 77 30 E
Narbonne, *France* **18 E5** 43 11N 3 0 E
Narḍīn, *Iran* **45 B7** 37 3N 55 59 E
Nardò, *Italy* **21 D8** 40 11N 18 2 E
Narembeen, *Australia* **61 F2** 32 7S 118 24 E
Nares Str., *Arctic* **66 A13** 80 0N 70 0W
Naretha, *Australia* **61 F3** 31 0S 124 45 E
Narew →, *Poland* **17 B11** 52 26N 20 41 E
Nari →, *Pakistan* **42 E2** 28 0N 67 40 E
Narin, *Afghan.* **40 A6** 36 5N 69 0 E
Narindra, Helodranon' i, *Madag.* **57 A8** 14 55S 47 30 E
Narita, *Japan* **31 G10** 35 47N 140 19 E
Narmada →, *India* **42 J5** 21 38N 72 36 E
Narmland, *Sweden* **9 F15** 60 0N 13 30 E
Narnaul, *India* **42 E7** 28 5N 76 11 E
Narodnaya, *Russia* **24 A10** 65 5N 59 58 E
Narok, *Kenya* **54 C4** 1 55S 35 52 E
Narok □, *Kenya* **54 C4** 1 20S 36 30 E
Narooma, *Australia* **63 F5** 36 14S 150 4 E
Narowal, *Pakistan* **42 C6** 32 6N 74 52 E
Narrabri, *Australia* **63 E4** 30 19S 149 46 E
Narran →, *Australia* **63 D4** 28 37S 148 12 E
Narrandera, *Australia* **63 E4** 34 42S 146 31 E
Narraway →, *Canada* **72 B5** 55 44N 119 55W
Narrogin, *Australia* **61 F2** 32 58S 117 14 E
Narromine, *Australia* **63 E4** 32 12S 148 12 E
Narsimhapur, *India* **43 H8** 22 54N 79 14 E
Naruto, *Japan* **31 G7** 34 11N 134 37 E
Narva, *Estonia* **24 C4** 59 23N 28 12 E
Narva →, *Russia* **9 G22** 59 27N 28 2 E
Narvik, *Norway* **8 B17** 68 28N 17 26 E
Narwana, *India* **42 E7** 29 39N 76 6 E
Naryan-Mar, *Russia* **24 A9** 67 42N 53 12 E
Naryilco, *Australia* **63 D3** 28 37S 141 53 E
Narym, *Russia* **26 D9** 59 0N 81 30 E
Narymskoye, *Kazakstan* **26 E9** 49 10N 84 15 E
Naryn, *Kyrgyzstan* **26 E8** 41 26N 75 58 E
Nasa, *Norway* **8 C16** 66 29N 15 23 E
Nasarawa, *Nigeria* **50 G6** 8 32N 7 41 E
Naseby, *N.Z.* **59 L3** 45 1S 170 10 E
Naselle, *U.S.A.* **84 D3** 46 22N 123 49W
Naser, Buheirat en, *Egypt* **51 D11** 23 0N 32 30 E
Nashua, *Iowa, U.S.A.* **80 D8** 42 57N 92 32W
Nashua, *Mont., U.S.A.* **82 B10** 48 8N 106 22W
Nashua, *N.H., U.S.A.* **79 D13** 42 45N 71 28W
Nashville, *Ark., U.S.A.* **81 J8** 33 57N 93 51W
Nashville, *Ga., U.S.A.* **77 K4** 31 12N 83 15W
Nashville, *Tenn., U.S.A.* **77 G2** 36 10N 86 47W
Nasik, *India* **40 K8** 19 58N 73 50 E
Nasirabad, *India* **42 F6** 26 15N 74 45 E
Naskaupi →, *Canada* **71 B7** 53 47N 60 51W
Naṣriān-e Pā'īn, *Iran* **44 C5** 32 52N 46 52 E
Nass →, *Canada* **72 B3** 55 0N 129 40W
Nassau, *Bahamas* **88 A4** 25 5N 77 20W
Nassau, *U.S.A.* **79 D11** 42 31N 73 37W
Nassau, B., *Chile* **96 H3** 55 20S 68 0W
Nasser, L. = Naser, Buheirat en, *Egypt* **51 D11** 23 0N 32 30 E
Nässjö, *Sweden* **9 H16** 57 39N 14 42 E
Nat Kyizin, *Burma* **41 M20** 14 57N 97 59 E
Nata, *Botswana* **56 C4** 20 12S 26 12 E
Natagaima, *Colombia* **92 C3** 3 37N 75 6W
Natal, *Brazil* **93 E11** 5 47S 35 13W
Natal, *Canada* **72 D6** 49 43N 114 51W
Natal, *Indonesia* **36 D1** 0 35N 99 7 E
Naṭanz, *Iran* **45 C6** 33 30N 51 55 E
Natashquan, *Canada* **71 B7** 50 14N 61 46W
Natashquan →, *Canada* **71 B7** 50 7N 61 50W
Natchez, *U.S.A.* **81 K9** 31 34N 91 24W
Natchitoches, *U.S.A.* **81 K8** 31 46N 93 5W
Nathalia, *Australia* **63 F4** 36 1S 145 13 E
Nathdwara, *India* **42 G5** 24 55N 73 50 E
Nati, Pta., *Spain* **22 A10** 40 3N 3 50 E
Natimuk, *Australia* **63 F3** 36 42S 142 0 E
Nation →, *Canada* **72 B4** 55 30N 123 32W
National City, *U.S.A.* **85 N9** 32 41N 117 6W
Natitingou, *Benin* **50 F5** 10 20N 1 26 E
Natividad, I., *Mexico* **86 B1** 27 50N 115 10W
Natoma, *U.S.A.* **80 F5** 39 11N 99 2W
Natron, L., *Tanzania* **54 C4** 2 20S 36 0 E
Natrona Heights, *U.S.A.* **78 F5** 40 37N 79 44W
Natuna Besar, Kepulauan, *Indonesia* **39 L7** 4 0N 108 15 E
Natuna Is. = Natuna Besar, Kepulauan, *Indonesia* **39 L7** 4 0N 108 15 E
Natuna Selatan, Kepulauan, *Indonesia* **39 L7** 2 45N 109 0 E
Natural Bridge, *U.S.A.* **79 B9** 44 5N 75 30W
Naturaliste, C., *Australia* **62 G4** 40 50S 148 15 E
Nau Qala, *Afghan.* **42 B3** 34 5N 68 5 E
Naubinway, *U.S.A.* **70 C2** 46 6N 85 27W
Naugatuck, *U.S.A.* **79 E11** 41 30N 73 3W
Naumburg, *Germany* **16 C6** 51 9N 11 47 E
Nā'ūr at Tunayb, *Jordan* **47 D4** 31 48N 35 57 E
Nauru ■, *Pac. Oc.* **64 H8** 1 0S 166 0 E
Naushahra = Nowshera, *Pakistan* **40 B8** 34 0N 72 0 E
Nauta, *Peru* **92 D4** 4 31S 73 35W
Nautanwa, *India* **41 F13** 27 20N 83 25 E
Nautla, *Mexico* **87 C5** 20 20N 96 50W
Nava, *Mexico* **86 B4** 28 25N 100 46W
Navadwip, *India* **43 H13** 23 34N 88 20 E
Navahrudak, *Belarus* **17 B13** 53 40N 25 50 E
Navajo Reservoir, *U.S.A.* **83 H10** 36 48N 107 36W
Navalmoral de la Mata, *Spain* **19 C3** 39 52N 5 33W
Navan = An Uaimh, *Ireland* **13 C5** 53 39N 6 41W
Navarino, I., *Chile* **96 H3** 55 0S 67 40W
Navarra □, *Spain* **19 A5** 42 40N 1 40W
Navarre, *U.S.A.* **78 F3** 40 43N 81 31W
Navarro →, *U.S.A.* **84 F3** 39 11N 123 45W
Navasota, *U.S.A.* **81 K6** 30 23N 96 5W
Navassa, *W. Indies* **89 C4** 18 30N 75 0W
Naver →, *U.K.* **12 C4** 58 32N 4 14W
Navidad, *Chile* **94 C1** 33 57S 71 50W
Năvodari, *Romania* **17 F15** 44 19N 28 36 E
Navoi = Nawoiy, *Uzbekistan* **26 E7** 40 9N 65 22 E
Navojoa, *Mexico* **86 B3** 27 0N 109 30W
Navolato, *Mexico* **86 C3** 24 47N 107 42W
Návpaktos, *Greece* **21 E9** 38 23N 21 50 E
Návplion, *Greece* **21 F10** 37 33N 22 50 E
Navsari, *India* **40 J8** 20 57N 72 59 E
Nawa Kot, *Pakistan* **42 E4** 28 21N 71 24 E
Nawabganj, *Ut. P., India* **43 F9** 26 56N 81 14 E
Nawabganj, *Ut. P., India* **43 E8** 28 32N 79 40 E
Nawabshah, *Pakistan* **42 F3** 26 15N 68 25 E
Nawada, *India* **43 G11** 24 50N 85 33 E
Nawakot, *Nepal* **43 F11** 27 55N 85 10 E
Nawalgarh, *India* **42 F6** 27 50N 75 15 E
Nawanshahr, *India* **43 C6** 32 33N 74 48 E
Nawoiy, *Uzbekistan* **26 E7** 40 9N 65 22 E
Naxçıvan, *Azerbaijan* **25 G8** 39 12N 45 15 E
Naxçıvan □, *Azerbaijan* **25 G8** 39 25N 45 26 E
Náxos, *Greece* **21 F11** 37 8N 25 25 E
Nāy Band, *Iran* **45 E7** 27 20N 52 40 E
Nayakhan, *Russia* **27 C16** 61 56N 159 0 E
Nayarit □, *Mexico* **86 C4** 22 0N 105 0W
Nayoro, *Japan* **30 B11** 44 21N 142 28 E
Nayyāl, W. →, *Si. Arabia* **44 D3** 28 35N 39 4 E
Nazareth = Naẓerat, *Israel* **47 C4** 32 42N 35 17 E
Nazas, *Mexico* **86 B4** 25 10N 104 6W
Nazas →, *Mexico* **86 B4** 25 35N 103 25W
Naze, The, *U.K.* **11 F9** 51 53N 1 18 E
Naẓerat, *Israel* **47 C4** 32 42N 35 17 E
Nāzik, *Iran* **44 B5** 39 1N 45 4 E
Nazilli, *Turkey* **21 F13** 37 55N 28 15 E
Nazir Hat, *Bangla.* **41 H17** 22 35N 91 49 E
Nazko, *Canada* **72 C4** 53 1N 123 37W
Nazko →, *Canada* **72 C4** 53 7N 123 34W
Nchanga, *Zambia* **55 E2** 12 30S 27 49 E
Ncheu, *Malawi* **55 E3** 14 50S 34 47 E
Ndala, *Tanzania* **54 C3** 4 45S 33 15 E
Ndalatando, *Angola* **52 F2** 9 12S 14 48 E
Ndareda, *Tanzania* **54 C4** 4 12S 35 30 E
Ndélé, *C.A.R.* **51 G9** 8 25N 20 36 E
Ndendé, *Gabon* **52 E2** 2 22S 11 23 E
Ndjamena, *Chad* **51 F7** 12 10N 14 59 E
Ndjolé, *Gabon* **52 E2** 0 10S 10 45 E
Ndola, *Zambia* **55 E2** 13 0S 28 34 E
Ndoto Mts., *Kenya* **54 B4** 2 0N 37 0 E
Nduguti, *Tanzania* **54 C3** 4 18S 34 41 E
Neagh, Lough, *U.K.* **13 B5** 54 37N 6 25W
Neah Bay, *U.S.A.* **84 B2** 48 22N 124 37W
Neale, L., *Australia* **60 D5** 24 15S 130 0 E
Neápolis, *Greece* **23 D7** 35 15N 25 37 E
Near Is., *U.S.A.* **68 C1** 53 0N 172 0 E
Neath, *U.K.* **11 F4** 51 39N 3 48W
Neath Port Talbot □, *U.K.* **11 F4** 51 42N 3 45W
Nebine Cr. →, *Australia* **63 D4** 29 27S 146 56 E
Nebitdag, *Turkmenistan* **25 G9** 39 30N 54 22 E
Nebraska □, *U.S.A.* **80 E5** 41 30N 99 30W
Nebraska City, *U.S.A.* **80 E7** 40 41N 95 52W
Nébrodi, Monti, *Italy* **20 F6** 37 54N 14 35 E
Necedah, *U.S.A.* **80 C9** 44 2N 90 4W
Nechako →, *Canada* **72 C4** 53 30N 122 44W
Neches →, *U.S.A.* **81 L8** 29 58N 93 51W
Neckar →, *Germany* **16 D5** 49 27N 8 29 E
Necochea, *Argentina* **94 D4** 38 30S 58 50W
Needles, *U.S.A.* **85 L12** 34 51N 114 37W
Needles, The, *U.K.* **11 G6** 50 39N 1 35W
Ñeembucú □, *Paraguay* **94 B4** 27 0S 58 0W
Neemuch = Nimach, *India* **42 G6** 24 30N 74 56 E
Neenah, *U.S.A.* **76 C1** 44 11N 88 28W
Neepawa, *Canada* **73 C9** 50 15N 99 30W
Nefta, *Tunisia* **50 B6** 33 53N 7 50 E
Neftçala, *Azerbaijan* **25 G8** 39 19N 49 12 E
Neftyannyye Kamni, *Azerbaijan* **25 F9** 40 20N 50 55 E
Negapatam = Nagappattinam, *India* **40 P11** 10 46N 79 51 E
Negaunee, *U.S.A.* **76 B2** 46 30N 87 36W
Negele, *Ethiopia* **46 F2** 5 20N 39 36 E
Negev Desert = Hanegev, *Israel* **47 E3** 30 50N 35 0 E
Negombo, *Sri Lanka* **40 R11** 7 12N 79 50 E
Negotin, *Serbia, Yug.* **21 B10** 44 16N 22 37 E
Negra, Pta., *Peru* **90 D2** 6 6S 81 10W
Negra Pt., *Phil.* **37 A6** 18 40N 120 50 E
Negrais, C. = Maudin Sun, *Burma* **41 M19** 16 0N 94 30 E
Negro →, *Argentina* **96 E4** 41 2S 62 47W
Negro →, *Brazil* **92 D6** 3 0S 60 0W
Negro →, *Uruguay* **95 C4** 33 24S 58 22W
Negros, *Phil.* **37 C6** 9 30N 122 40 E
Nehalem →, *U.S.A.* **84 E3** 45 40N 123 56W
Nehāvand, *Iran* **45 C6** 35 56N 49 31 E
Nehbandān, *Iran* **45 D9** 31 35N 60 5 E
Nei Monggol Zizhiqu □, *China* **34 C6** 42 0N 112 0 E
Neidpath, *Canada* **73 C7** 50 12N 107 20W
Neihart, *U.S.A.* **82 C8** 47 0N 110 44W
Neijiang, *China* **32 D5** 29 35N 104 55 E
Neilton, *U.S.A.* **82 C2** 47 25N 123 53W
Neiqiu, *China* **34 F8** 37 15N 114 30 E
Neiva, *Colombia* **92 C3** 2 56N 75 18W
Neixiang, *China* **34 H6** 33 10N 111 52 E
Nejanilini L., *Canada* **73 B9** 59 33N 97 48W
Nekā, *Iran* **45 B7** 36 39N 53 19 E
Nekemte, *Ethiopia* **51 G12** 9 4N 36 30 E
Neksø, *Denmark* **9 J16** 55 4N 15 8 E
Nelia, *Australia* **62 C3** 20 39S 142 12 E
Neligh, *U.S.A.* **80 D5** 42 8N 98 2W
Nelkan, *Russia* **27 D14** 57 40N 136 4 E
Nellore, *India* **40 M11** 14 27N 79 59 E
Nelma, *Russia* **27 E14** 47 39N 139 0 E
Nelson, *Canada* **72 D5** 49 30N 117 20W
Nelson, *N.Z.* **59 J4** 41 18S 173 16 E
Nelson, *U.K.* **10 D5** 53 50N 2 13W
Nelson, *U.S.A.* **83 J7** 35 31N 113 19W
Nelson →, *Canada* **73 C9** 54 33N 98 2W
Nelson, C., *Australia* **63 F3** 38 26S 141 32 E
Nelson, Estrecho, *Chile* **96 G2** 51 30S 75 0W
Nelson Forks, *Canada* **72 B4** 59 30N 124 0W
Nelson House, *Canada* **73 B9** 55 47N 98 51W
Nelson L., *Canada* **73 B8** 55 48N 100 7W
Nelspoort, *S. Africa* **56 E3** 32 7S 23 0 E
Nelspruit, *S. Africa* **57 D5** 25 29S 30 59 E
Néma, *Mauritania* **50 E3** 16 40N 7 15W
Neman, *Russia* **9 J20** 55 2N 22 2 E
Neman →, *Lithuania* **9 J19** 55 25N 21 10 E
Nemeiben L., *Canada* **73 B7** 55 20N 105 20W
Nemunas = Neman →, *Lithuania* **9 J19** 55 25N 21 10 E
Nemuro, *Japan* **30 C12** 43 20N 145 35 E
Nemuro-Kaikyō, *Japan* **30 C12** 43 30N 145 30 E
Nemuy, *Russia* **27 D14** 55 40N 136 9 E
Nen Jiang →, *China* **35 B13** 45 28N 124 30 E
Nenagh, *Ireland* **13 D3** 52 52N 8 11W
Nenana, *U.S.A.* **68 B5** 64 34N 149 5W
Nenasi, *Malaysia* **39 L4** 3 9N 103 23 E
Nene →, *U.K.* **10 E8** 52 49N 0 11 E
Nenjiang, *China* **33 B7** 49 10N 125 10 E
Neno, *Malawi* **55 F3** 15 25S 34 40 E
Neodesha, *U.S.A.* **81 G7** 37 25N 95 41W
Neosho, *U.S.A.* **81 G7** 36 52N 94 22W
Neosho →, *U.S.A.* **81 H7** 36 48N 95 18W
Nepal ■, *Asia* **43 F11** 28 0N 84 30 E
Nepalganj, *Nepal* **43 E9** 28 5N 81 40 E
Nephi, *U.S.A.* **82 G8** 39 43N 111 50W
Nephin, *Ireland* **13 B2** 54 1N 9 22W
Neptune, *U.S.A.* **79 F10** 40 13N 74 2W
Nerchinsk, *Russia* **27 D12** 52 0N 116 39 E
Nerchinskiy Zavod, *Russia* **27 D12** 51 20N 119 40 E
Néret L., *Canada* **71 B5** 54 45N 70 44W
Neretva →, *Croatia* **21 C7** 43 1N 17 27 E
Neringa, *Lithuania* **9 J19** 55 30N 21 5 E
Ness, L., *U.K.* **12 D4** 57 15N 4 32W
Nesterov, *Ukraine* **17 C12** 50 4N 23 58 E
Nesvizh = Nyasvizh, *Belarus* **17 B14** 53 14N 26 38 E
Netanya, *Israel* **47 C3** 32 20N 34 51 E
Nète →, *Belgium* **15 C4** 51 7N 4 14 E
Netherdale, *Australia* **62 C4** 21 10S 148 33 E
Netherlands ■, *Europe* **15 C5** 52 0N 5 30 E
Netherlands Antilles ■, *W. Indies* **92 A5** 12 15N 69 0W
Nettilling L., *Canada* **69 B12** 66 30N 71 0W
Netzahualcoyotl, Presa, *Mexico* **87 D6** 17 10N 93 30W
Neubrandenburg, *Germany* **16 B7** 53 33N 13 15 E
Neuchâtel, *Switz.* **16 E4** 47 0N 6 55 E
Neuchâtel, Lac de, *Switz.* **16 E4** 46 53N 6 50 E
Neufchâteau, *Belgium* **15 E5** 49 50N 5 25 E
Neumünster, *Germany* **16 A5** 54 4N 9 58 E
Neunkirchen, *Germany* **16 D4** 49 20N 7 9 E
Neuquén, *Argentina* **96 D3** 38 55S 68 0W
Neuquén □, *Argentina* **94 D2** 38 0S 69 50W
Neuruppin, *Germany* **16 B7** 52 55N 12 48 E
Neuse →, *U.S.A.* **77 H7** 35 6N 76 29W
Neusiedler See, *Austria* **17 E9** 47 50N 16 47 E
Neuss, *Germany* **15 C6** 51 11N 6 42 E
Neustrelitz, *Germany* **16 B7** 53 21N 13 4 E
Neva →, *Russia* **24 C5** 59 50N 30 30 E
Nevada, *U.S.A.* **81 G7** 37 51N 94 22W
Nevada □, *U.S.A.* **82 G5** 39 0N 117 0W
Nevada, Sierra, *Spain* **19 D4** 37 3N 3 15W
Nevada, Sierra, *U.S.A.* **82 G3** 39 0N 120 30W
Nevada City, *U.S.A.* **84 F6** 39 16N 121 1W
Nevado, Cerro, *Argentina* **94 D2** 35 30S 68 32W
Nevanka, *Russia* **27 D10** 56 31N 98 55 E
Nevers, *France* **18 C5** 47 0N 3 9 E
Nevertire, *Australia* **63 E4** 31 50S 147 44 E
Neville, *Canada* **73 D7** 49 58N 107 39W
Nevinnomyssk, *Russia* **25 F7** 44 40N 42 0 E
Nevis, *W. Indies* **89 C7** 17 0N 62 30W
Nevyansk, *Russia* **24 C11** 57 30N 60 13 E
New Albany, *Ind., U.S.A.* **76 F3** 38 18N 85 49W
New Albany, *Miss., U.S.A.* **81 H10** 34 29N 89 0W
New Albany, *Pa., U.S.A.* **79 E8** 41 36N 76 27W
New Amsterdam, *Guyana* **92 B7** 6 15N 57 36W
New Angledool, *Australia* **63 D4** 29 5S 147 55 E
New Bedford, *U.S.A.* **79 E14** 41 38N 70 56W
New Bern, *U.S.A.* **77 H7** 35 7N 77 3W
New Bethlehem, *U.S.A.* **78 E5** 41 0N 79 20W
New Bloomfield, *U.S.A.* **78 F7** 40 25N 77 11W
New Boston, *U.S.A.* **81 J7** 33 28N 94 25W
New Braunfels, *U.S.A.* **81 L5** 29 42N 98 8W
New Brighton, *N.Z.* **59 K4** 43 29S 172 43 E
New Brighton, *U.S.A.* **78 F4** 40 42N 80 19W
New Britain, *Papua N. G.* **64 H7** 5 50S 150 20 E
New Britain, *U.S.A.* **79 E12** 41 40N 72 47W
New Brunswick, *U.S.A.* **79 F10** 40 30N 74 27W
New Brunswick □, *Canada* **71 C6** 46 50N 66 30W
New Caledonia ■, *Pac. Oc.* **64 K8** 21 0S 165 0 E
New Castle, *Ind., U.S.A.* **76 F3** 39 55N 85 22W
New Castle, *Pa., U.S.A.* **78 E4** 41 0N 80 21W
New City, *U.S.A.* **79 E11** 41 9N 73 59W
New Cumberland, *U.S.A.* **78 F4** 40 30N 80 36W
New Cuyama, *U.S.A.* **85 L7** 34 57N 119 38W
New Delhi, *India* **42 E7** 28 37N 77 13 E
New Denver, *Canada* **72 D5** 50 0N 117 25W
New Don Pedro Reservoir, *U.S.A.* **84 H6** 37 43N 120 24W
New England, *U.S.A.* **80 B3** 46 32N 102 52W
New England Ra., *Australia* **63 E5** 30 20S 151 45 E
New Forest, *U.K.* **11 G6** 50 53N 1 34W
New Glasgow, *Canada* **71 C7** 45 35N 62 36W
New Guinea, *Oceania* **28 K17** 4 0S 136 0 E
New Hamburg, *Canada* **78 C4** 43 23N 80 42W
New Hampshire □, *U.S.A.* **79 C13** 44 0N 71 30W
New Hampton, *U.S.A.* **80 D8** 43 3N 92 19W
New Hanover, *S. Africa* **57 D5** 29 22S 30 31 E
New Haven, *Conn., U.S.A.* **79 E12** 41 18N 72 55W
New Haven, *Mich., U.S.A.* **78 D2** 42 44N 82 48W
New Hazelton, *Canada* **72 B3** 55 20N 127 30W
New Hebrides = Vanuatu ■, *Pac. Oc.* **64 J8** 15 0S 168 0 E
New Iberia, *U.S.A.* **81 K9** 30 1N 91 49W
New Ireland, *Papua N. G.* **64 H7** 3 20S 151 50 E
New Jersey □, *U.S.A.* **79 F10** 40 0N 74 30W
New Kensington, *U.S.A.* **78 F5** 40 34N 79 46W
New Lexington, *U.S.A.* **76 F4** 39 43N 82 13W
New Liskeard, *Canada* **70 C4** 47 31N 79 41W
New London, *Conn., U.S.A.* **79 E12** 41 22N 72 6W
New London, *Minn., U.S.A.* **80 C7** 45 18N 94 56W
New London, *Ohio, U.S.A.* **78 E2** 41 5N 82 24W
New London, *Wis., U.S.A.* **80 C10** 44 23N 88 45W
New Madrid, *U.S.A.* **81 G10** 36 36N 89 32W
New Meadows, *U.S.A.* **82 D5** 44 58N 116 18W
New Melones L., *U.S.A.* **84 H6** 37 57N 120 31W
New Mexico □, *U.S.A.* **83 J10** 34 30N 106 0W
New Milford, *Conn., U.S.A.* **79 E11** 41 35N 73 25W
New Milford, *Pa., U.S.A.* **79 E9** 41 52N 75 44W
New Norcia, *Australia* **61 F2** 30 57S 116 13 E
New Norfolk, *Australia* **62 G4** 42 46S 147 2 E
New Orleans, *U.S.A.* **81 K9** 29 58N 90 4W
New Philadelphia, *U.S.A.* **78 F3** 40 30N 81 27W
New Plymouth, *N.Z.* **59 H5** 39 4S 174 5 E
New Plymouth, *U.S.A.* **82 E5** 43 58N 116 49W
New Providence, *Bahamas* **88 A4** 25 25N 78 35W
New Radnor, *U.K.* **11 E4** 52 15N 3 9W
New Richmond, *U.S.A.* **80 C8** 45 7N 92 32W
New Roads, *U.S.A.* **81 K9** 30 42N 91 26W
New Rochelle, *U.S.A.* **79 F11** 40 55N 73 47W
New Rockford, *U.S.A.* **80 B5** 47 41N 99 8W
New Ross, *Ireland* **13 D5** 52 23N 6 57W
New Salem, *U.S.A.* **80 B4** 46 51N 101 25W
New Scone, *U.K.* **12 E5** 56 25N 3 24W
New Siberian Is. = Novaya Sibir, Ostrov, *Russia* **27 B16** 75 10N 150 0 E
New Siberian Is. = Novosibirskiye Ostrova, *Russia* **27 B15** 75 0N 142 0 E
New Smyrna Beach, *U.S.A.* **77 L5** 29 1N 80 56W
New South Wales □, *Australia* **63 E4** 33 0S 146 0 E
New Springs, *Australia* **61 E3** 25 49S 120 1 E
New Town, *U.S.A.* **80 A3** 47 59N 102 30W
New Ulm, *U.S.A.* **80 C7** 44 19N 94 28W

North Lanarkshire

New Waterford, Canada 71 C7 46 13N 60 4W
New Westminster, Canada 72 D4 49 13N 122 55W
New York □, U.S.A. 79 D9 43 0N 75 0W
New York City, U.S.A. 79 F11 40 45N 74 0W
New Zealand ■, Oceania 59 J5 40 0S 176 0 E
Newala, Tanzania 55 E4 10 58S 39 18 E
Newala □, Tanzania 55 E4 10 46S 39 20 E
Newark, Del., U.S.A. 76 F8 39 41N 75 46W
Newark, N.J., U.S.A. 79 F10 40 44N 74 10W
Newark, N.Y., U.S.A. 78 C7 43 3N 77 6W
Newark, Ohio, U.S.A. 78 F2 40 3N 82 24W
Newark-on-Trent, U.K. 10 D7 53 5N 0 48W
Newaygo, U.S.A. 76 D3 43 25N 85 48W
Newberg, U.S.A. 82 D2 45 18N 122 58W
Newberry, Mich., U.S.A. 76 B3 46 21N 85 30W
Newberry, S.C., U.S.A. 77 H5 34 17N 81 37W
Newberry Springs, U.S.A. 85 L10 34 50N 116 41W
Newbridge = Droichead Nua, Ireland 13 C5 53 11N 6 48W
Newbrook, Canada 72 C6 54 24N 112 57W
Newburgh, U.S.A. 79 E10 41 30N 74 1W
Newbury, U.K. 11 F6 51 24N 1 20W
Newbury, U.S.A. 79 B12 43 19N 72 3W
Newburyport, U.S.A. 79 D14 42 49N 70 53W
Newcastle, Australia 63 E5 33 0S 151 46 E
Newcastle, Canada 71 C6 47 1N 65 38W
Newcastle, S. Africa 57 D4 27 45S 29 58 E
Newcastle, U.K. 13 B6 54 13N 5 54W
Newcastle, Calif., U.S.A. 84 G5 38 53N 121 8W
Newcastle, Wyo., U.S.A. 80 D2 43 50N 104 11W
Newcastle Emlyn, U.K. 11 E3 52 2N 4 28W
Newcastle Ra., Australia 60 C5 15 45S 130 15 E
Newcastle-under-Lyme, U.K. 10 D5 53 1N 2 14W
Newcastle-upon-Tyne, U.K. 10 C6 54 58N 1 36W
Newcastle Waters, Australia 62 B1 17 30S 133 28 E
Newdegate, Australia 61 F2 33 6S 119 0 E
Newell, U.S.A. 80 C3 44 43N 103 25W
Newfoundland □, Canada 71 B8 53 0N 58 0W
Newfoundland I., N. Amer. 66 E14 49 0N 55 0W
Newhalem, U.S.A. 72 D4 48 40N 121 15W
Newhall, U.S.A. 85 L8 34 23N 118 32W
Newham, U.K. 11 F8 51 31N 0 3 E
Newhaven, U.K. 11 G8 50 47N 0 3 E
Newkirk, U.S.A. 81 G6 36 53N 97 3W
Newman, Australia 60 D2 23 18S 119 45 E
Newman, U.S.A. 84 H5 37 19N 121 1W
Newmarket, Canada 78 B5 44 3N 79 28W
Newmarket, Ireland 13 D3 52 13N 9 0W
Newmarket, U.K. 11 E8 52 15N 0 25 E
Newmarket, U.S.A. 79 C14 43 5N 70 56W
Newnan, U.S.A. 77 J3 33 23N 84 48W
Newport, I. of W., U.K. 11 G6 50 42N 1 17W
Newport, Newp., U.K. 11 F5 51 35N 3 0W
Newport, Ark., U.S.A. 81 H9 35 37N 91 16W
Newport, Ky., U.S.A. 76 F3 39 5N 84 30W
Newport, N.H., U.S.A. 79 C12 43 22N 72 10W
Newport, Oreg., U.S.A. 82 D1 44 39N 124 3W
Newport, Pa., U.S.A. 78 F7 40 29N 77 8W
Newport, R.I., U.S.A. 79 E13 41 29N 71 19W
Newport, Tenn., U.S.A. 77 H4 35 58N 83 11W
Newport, Vt., U.S.A. 79 B12 44 56N 72 13W
Newport, Wash., U.S.A. 82 B5 48 11N 117 3W
Newport □, U.K. 11 F4 51 33N 3 1W
Newport Beach, U.S.A. 85 M9 33 37N 117 56W
Newport News, U.S.A. 76 G7 36 59N 76 25W
Newquay, U.K. 11 G2 50 25N 5 6W
Newry, U.K. 13 B5 54 11N 6 21W
Newry & Mourne □, U.K. 13 B5 54 10N 6 15W
Newton, Iowa, U.S.A. 80 E8 41 42N 93 3W
Newton, Mass., U.S.A. 79 D13 42 21N 71 12W
Newton, Miss., U.S.A. 81 J10 32 19N 89 10W
Newton, N.C., U.S.A. 77 H5 35 40N 81 13W
Newton, N.J., U.S.A. 79 E10 41 3N 74 45W
Newton, Tex., U.S.A. 81 K8 30 51N 93 46W
Newton Abbot, U.K. 11 G4 50 32N 3 37W
Newton Boyd, Australia 63 D5 29 45S 152 16 E
Newton Stewart, U.K. 12 G4 54 57N 4 30W
Newtonmore, U.K. 12 D4 57 4N 4 8W
Newtown, U.K. 11 E4 52 31N 3 19W
Newtownabbey □, U.K. 13 B6 54 45N 6 0W
Newtownards, U.K. 13 B6 54 36N 5 42W
Newville, U.S.A. 78 F7 40 10N 77 24W
Neya, Russia 24 C7 58 21N 43 49 E
Neyrīz, Iran 45 D7 29 15N 54 19 E
Neyshābūr, Iran 45 B8 36 10N 58 50 E
Nezhin = Nizhyn, Ukraine 25 D5 51 5N 31 55 E
Nezperce, U.S.A. 82 C5 46 14N 116 14W
Ngabang, Indonesia 36 D3 0 23N 109 55 E
Ngabordamlu, Tanjung, Indonesia 37 F8 6 56S 134 11 E
Ngami Depression, Botswana 56 C3 20 30S 22 46 E
Ngamo, Zimbabwe 55 F2 19 3S 27 32 E
Nganglong Kangri, China 41 C12 33 0N 81 0 E
Nganjuk, Indonesia 37 G14 7 32S 111 55 E
Ngao, Thailand 38 C2 18 46N 99 59 E
Ngaoundéré, Cameroon 52 C2 7 15N 13 35 E
Ngapara, N.Z. 59 L3 44 57S 170 46 E
Ngara, Tanzania 54 C3 2 29S 30 40 E
Ngara □, Tanzania 54 C3 2 29S 30 40 E
Ngawi, Indonesia 37 G14 7 24S 111 26 E
Nghia Lo, Vietnam 38 B5 21 33N 104 28 E
Ngoma, Malawi 55 E3 13 8S 33 45 E
Ngomahura, Zimbabwe 55 G3 20 26S 30 43 E
Ngomba, Tanzania 55 D3 8 20S 32 53 E
Ngoring Hu, China 32 C4 34 55N 97 5 E
Ngorongoro, Tanzania 54 C4 3 11S 35 32 E
Ngozi, Burundi 54 C2 2 54S 29 50 E
Ngudu, Tanzania 54 C3 2 58S 33 25 E
Nguigmi, Niger 51 F7 14 20N 13 20 E
Ngukurr, Australia 62 A1 14 44S 134 44 E
Ngunga, Tanzania 54 C3 3 37S 33 37 E
Nguru, Nigeria 50 F7 12 56N 10 29 E
Nguru Mts., Tanzania 54 D4 6 0S 37 30 E
Nguyen Binh, Vietnam 38 A5 22 39N 105 56 E
Nha Trang, Vietnam 39 F7 12 16N 109 10 E
Nhacoongo, Mozam. 57 C6 24 18S 35 14 E
Nhamaabué, Mozam. 55 F4 17 25S 35 5 E
Nhangutazi, L., Mozam. 57 C5 24 0S 34 30 E
Nhill, Australia 63 F3 36 18S 141 40 E
Nho Quan, Vietnam 38 B5 20 18N 105 45 E
Nhulunbuy, Australia 62 A2 12 10S 137 20 E
Nia-nia, Zaïre 54 B2 1 30N 27 40 E
Niafounké, Mali 50 E4 16 0N 4 5W
Niagara, U.S.A. 76 C1 45 45N 88 0W
Niagara Falls, Canada 70 D4 43 7N 79 5W
Niagara Falls, U.S.A. 78 C6 43 5N 79 4W
Niagara-on-the-Lake, Canada 78 C5 43 15N 79 4W
Niah, Malaysia 36 D4 3 58N 113 46 E
Niamey, Niger 50 F5 13 27N 2 6 E
Niangara, Zaïre 54 B2 3 42N 27 50 E
Nias, Indonesia 36 D1 1 0N 97 30 E
Niassa □, Mozam. 55 E4 13 30S 36 0 E
Nicaragua ■, Cent. Amer. 88 D2 11 40N 85 30W
Nicaragua, L. de, Nic. 88 D2 12 0N 85 30W
Nicastro, Italy 20 E7 38 59N 16 19 E
Nice, France 18 E7 43 42N 7 14 E
Niceville, U.S.A. 77 K2 30 31N 86 30W
Nichinan, Japan 31 J5 31 38N 131 23 E
Nicholás, Canal, W. Indies 88 B3 23 30N 80 5W
Nicholasville, U.S.A. 76 G3 37 53N 84 34W
Nichols, U.S.A. 79 D8 42 1N 76 22W
Nicholson, Australia 60 C4 18 2S 128 54 E
Nicholson, U.S.A. 79 E9 41 37N 75 47W
Nicholson →, Australia 62 B2 17 31S 139 36 E
Nicholson Ra., Australia 61 E2 27 15S 116 45 E
Nicobar Is., Ind. Oc. 28 J13 9 0N 93 0 E
Nicola, Canada 72 C4 50 12N 120 40W
Nicolet, Canada 70 C5 46 17N 72 35W
Nicolls Town, Bahamas 88 A4 25 8N 78 0W
Nicosia, Cyprus 23 D12 35 10N 33 25 E
Nicoya, Costa Rica 88 D2 10 9N 85 27W
Nicoya, G. de, Costa Rica 88 E3 10 0N 85 0W
Nicoya, Pen. de, Costa Rica 88 E2 9 45N 85 40W
Nidd →, U.K. 10 C6 53 59N 1 23W
Niedersachsen □, Germany 16 B5 53 8N 9 0 E
Niekerkshoop, S. Africa 56 D3 29 19S 22 51 E
Niemba, Zaïre 54 D2 5 58S 28 24 E
Niemen = Neman →, Lithuania 9 J19 55 25N 21 10 E
Nienburg, Germany 16 B5 52 39N 9 13 E
Nieu Bethesda, S. Africa 56 E3 31 51S 24 34 E
Nieuw Amsterdam, Surinam 93 B7 5 53N 55 5W
Nieuw Nickerie, Surinam 93 B7 6 0N 56 59W
Nieuwoudtville, S. Africa 56 E2 31 23S 19 7 E
Nieuwpoort, Belgium 15 C2 51 8N 2 45 E
Nieves, Pico de las, Canary Is. 22 G4 27 57N 15 35W
Niğde, Turkey 25 G5 37 58N 34 40 E
Nigel, S. Africa 57 D4 26 27S 28 25 E
Niger ■, W. Afr. 50 E6 17 30N 10 0 E
Niger →, W. Afr. 50 G6 5 33N 6 33 E
Nigeria ■, W. Afr. 50 G6 8 30N 8 0 E
Nightcaps, N.Z. 59 L2 45 57S 168 2 E
Nihtaur, India 43 E8 29 20N 78 23 E
Nii-Jima, Japan 31 G9 34 20N 139 15 E
Niigata, Japan 30 F9 37 58N 139 0 E
Niigata □, Japan 31 F9 37 15N 138 45 E
Niihama, Japan 31 H6 33 55N 133 16 E
Niihau, U.S.A. 74 H14 21 54N 160 9W
Niimi, Japan 31 G6 34 59N 133 28 E
Niitsu, Japan 30 F9 37 48N 139 7 E
Nijil, Jordan 47 E4 30 32N 35 33 E
Nijkerk, Neths. 15 B5 52 13N 5 30 E
Nijmegen, Neths. 15 C5 51 50N 5 52 E
Nijverdal, Neths. 15 B6 52 22N 6 28 E
Nīk Pey, Iran 45 B6 36 50N 48 10 E
Nikiniki, Indonesia 37 F6 9 49S 124 30 E
Nikki, Benin 50 G5 9 58N 3 12 E
Nikkō, Japan 31 F9 36 45N 139 35 E
Nikolayev = Mykolayiv, Ukraine 25 E5 46 58N 32 0 E
Nikolayevsk, Russia 25 D8 50 0N 45 35 E
Nikolayevsk-na-Amur, Russia 27 D15 53 8N 140 44 E
Nikolskoye, Russia 27 D17 55 12N 166 0 E
Nikopol, Ukraine 25 E5 47 35N 34 25 E
Nīkshahr, Iran 45 E9 26 15N 60 10 E
Nikšić, Montenegro, Yug. 21 C8 42 50N 18 57 E
Nîl, Nahr en →, Africa 51 B11 30 10N 31 6 E
Nîl el Abyad →, Sudan 51 E11 15 38N 32 31 E
Nîl el Azraq →, Sudan 51 E11 15 38N 32 31 E
Niland, U.S.A. 85 M11 33 14N 115 31W
Nile = Nîl, Nahr en →, Africa 51 B11 30 10N 31 6 E
Niles, U.S.A. 78 E4 41 11N 80 46W
Nimach, India 42 G6 24 30N 74 56 E
Nimbahera, India 42 G6 24 37N 74 45 E
Nîmes, France 18 E6 43 50N 4 23 E
Nimfaíon, Ákra = Pínnes, Ákra, Greece 21 D11 40 5N 24 20 E
Nimmitabel, Australia 63 F4 36 29S 149 15 E
Nimule, Sudan 52 D6 3 32N 32 3 E
Ninawá, Iraq 44 B4 36 25N 43 10 E
Nindigully, Australia 63 D4 28 21S 148 50 E
Ninemile, U.S.A. 72 B2 56 0N 130 7W
Nineveh = Ninawá, Iraq 44 B4 36 25N 43 10 E
Ning Xian, China 34 G4 35 30N 107 58 E
Ningaloo, Australia 60 D1 22 41S 113 41 E
Ning'an, China 35 B15 44 22N 129 20 E
Ningbo, China 33 D7 29 51N 121 28 E
Ningcheng, China 35 D10 41 32N 119 53 E
Ningjin, China 34 F8 37 35N 114 57 E
Ningjing Shan, China 32 C4 30 0N 98 20 E
Ningling, China 34 G8 34 25N 115 22 E
Ningpo = Ningbo, China 33 D7 29 51N 121 28 E
Ningqiang, China 34 H4 32 47N 106 15 E
Ningshan, China 34 H5 33 21N 108 21 E
Ningsia Hui A.R. = Ningxia Huizu Zizhiqu □, China 34 E3 38 0N 106 0 E
Ningwu, China 34 E7 39 0N 112 18 E
Ningxia Huizu Zizhiqu □, China 34 E3 38 0N 106 0 E
Ningyang, China 34 G9 35 47N 116 45 E
Ninh Binh, Vietnam 38 B5 20 15N 105 55 E
Ninh Giang, Vietnam 38 B6 20 44N 106 24 E
Ninh Hoa, Vietnam 38 F7 12 30N 109 7 E
Ninh Ma, Vietnam 38 F7 12 48N 109 21 E
Ninove, Belgium 15 D4 50 51N 4 2 E
Nioaque, Brazil 95 A4 21 5S 55 50W
Niobrara, U.S.A. 80 D6 42 45N 98 2W
Niobrara →, U.S.A. 80 D6 42 46N 98 3W
Nioro du Sahel, Mali 50 E3 15 15N 9 30W
Niort, France 18 C3 46 19N 0 29W
Nipawin, Canada 73 C8 53 20N 104 0W
Nipawin Prov. Park, Canada 73 C8 54 0N 104 37W
Nipigon, Canada 70 C2 49 0N 88 17W
Nipigon, L., Canada 70 C2 49 50N 88 30W
Nipin →, Canada 73 B7 55 46N 108 35W
Nipishish L., Canada 71 B7 54 12N 60 45W
Nipissing L., Canada 70 C4 46 20N 80 0W
Nipomo, U.S.A. 85 K6 35 3N 120 29W
Nipton, U.S.A. 85 K11 35 28N 115 16W
Niquelândia, Brazil 93 F9 14 33S 48 23W
Nīr, Iran 44 B5 38 2N 47 59 E
Nirasaki, Japan 31 G9 35 42N 138 27 E
Nirmal, India 40 K11 19 3N 78 20 E
Nirmali, India 43 F12 26 20N 86 35 E
Niš, Serbia, Yug. 21 C9 43 19N 21 58 E
Nişāb, Si. Arabia 44 D5 29 11N 44 43 E
Nişāb, Yemen 46 E4 14 25N 46 29 E
Nishinomiya, Japan 31 G7 34 45N 135 20 E
Nishin'omote, Japan 31 J5 30 43N 130 59 E
Nishiwaki, Japan 31 G7 34 59N 134 58 E
Niskibi →, Canada 70 A2 56 29N 88 9W
Nisqually →, U.S.A. 84 C4 47 6N 122 42W
Nissáki, Greece 23 A3 39 43N 19 52 E
Nissum Bredning, Denmark 9 H13 56 40N 8 20 E
Nistru = Dnister →, Europe 17 E16 46 18N 30 17 E
Nisutlin →, Canada 72 A2 60 14N 132 34W
Nitchequon, Canada 71 B5 53 10N 70 58W
Niterói, Brazil 95 A7 22 52S 43 0W
Nith →, U.K. 12 F5 55 14N 3 33W
Nitra, Slovak Rep. 17 D10 48 19N 18 4 E
Nitra →, Slovak Rep. 17 E10 47 46N 18 10 E
Niuafo'ou, Tonga 59 B11 15 30S 175 58W
Niue, Cook Is. 65 J11 19 2S 169 54W
Niut, Indonesia 36 D4 0 55N 110 6 E
Niuzhuang, China 35 D12 40 58N 122 28 E
Nivala, Finland 8 E21 63 56N 24 57 E
Nivelles, Belgium 15 D4 50 35N 4 20 E
Nivernais, France 18 C5 47 15N 3 30 E
Nixon, U.S.A. 81 L6 29 16N 97 46W
Nizamabad, India 40 K11 18 45N 78 7 E
Nizamghat, India 41 E19 28 20N 95 45 E
Nizhne Kolymsk, Russia 27 C17 68 34N 160 55 E
Nizhne-Vartovsk, Russia 26 C8 60 56N 76 38 E
Nizhneangarsk, Russia 27 D11 55 47N 109 30 E
Nizhnekamsk, Russia 24 C9 55 38N 51 49 E
Nizhneudinsk, Russia 27 D10 54 54N 99 3 E
Nizhneyansk, Russia 27 B14 71 26N 136 4 E
Nizhniy Novgorod, Russia 24 C7 56 20N 44 0 E
Nizhniy Tagil, Russia 24 C10 57 55N 59 57 E
Nizhyn, Ukraine 25 D5 51 5N 31 55 E
Nizké Tatry, Slovak Rep. 17 D10 48 55N 19 30 E
Njakwa, Malawi 55 E3 11 1S 33 56 E
Njanji, Zambia 55 E3 14 25S 31 46 E
Njinjo, Tanzania 55 D4 8 48S 38 54 E
Njombe, Tanzania 55 D3 9 20S 34 50 E
Njombe □, Tanzania 55 D3 9 20S 34 49 E
Njombe →, Tanzania 54 D4 6 56S 35 6 E
Nkambe, Cameroon 50 G7 6 35N 10 40 E
Nkana, Zambia 55 E2 12 50S 28 8 E
Nkawkaw, Ghana 50 G4 6 36N 0 49W
Nkayi, Zimbabwe 55 F2 19 41S 29 20 E
Nkhata Bay, Malawi 52 G6 11 33S 34 16 E
Nkhota Kota, Malawi 55 E3 12 56S 34 15 E
Nkongsamba, Cameroon 50 H6 4 55N 9 55 E
Nkurenkuru, Namibia 56 B2 17 42S 18 32 E
Nmai →, Burma 41 G20 25 30N 97 25 E
Noakhali = Maijdi, Bangla. 41 H17 22 48N 91 10 E
Noatak, U.S.A. 68 B3 67 34N 162 58W
Nobel, Canada 78 A4 45 25N 80 6W
Nobeoka, Japan 31 H5 32 36N 131 41 E
Noblesville, U.S.A. 76 E3 40 3N 86 1W
Nocera Inferiore, Italy 20 D6 40 44N 14 38 E
Nockatunga, Australia 63 D3 27 42S 142 42 E
Nocona, U.S.A. 81 J6 33 47N 97 44W
Noda, Japan 31 G9 35 56N 139 52 E
Noel, U.S.A. 81 G7 36 33N 94 29W
Nogales, Mexico 86 A2 31 20N 110 56W
Nogales, U.S.A. 83 L8 31 20N 110 56W
Nōgata, Japan 31 H5 33 48N 130 44 E
Noggerup, Australia 61 F2 33 32S 116 5 E
Noginsk, Russia 27 C10 64 30N 90 50 E
Nogoa →, Australia 62 C4 23 40S 147 55 E
Nogoyá, Argentina 94 C4 32 24S 59 48W
Nohar, India 42 E6 29 11N 74 49 E
Noire, Mts., France 18 B2 48 7N 3 28W
Noirmoutier, I. de, France 18 C2 46 58N 2 10W
Nojane, Botswana 56 C3 23 15S 20 14 E
Nojima-Zaki, Japan 31 G9 34 54N 139 53 E
Nok Kundi, Pakistan 40 E3 28 50N 62 45 E
Nokaneng, Botswana 56 B3 19 40S 22 17 E
Nokhtuysk, Russia 27 C12 60 0N 117 45 E
Nokia, Finland 9 F20 61 30N 23 30 E
Nokomis, Canada 73 C8 51 35N 105 0W
Nokomis L., Canada 73 B8 57 0N 103 0W
Nola, C.A.R. 52 D3 3 35N 16 4 E
Noma Omuramba →, Namibia 56 B3 18 52S 20 53 E
Noman L., Canada 73 A7 62 15N 108 55W
Nombre de Dios, Panama 88 E4 9 34N 79 28W
Nome, U.S.A. 68 B3 64 30N 165 25W
Nomo-Zaki, Japan 31 H4 32 35N 129 44 E
Nonacho L., Canada 73 A7 61 42N 109 40W
Nonda, Australia 62 C3 20 40S 142 28 E
Nong Chang, Thailand 38 E2 15 23N 99 51 E
Nong Het, Laos 38 C4 19 29N 103 59 E
Nong Khai, Thailand 38 D4 17 50N 102 46 E
Nong'an, China 35 B13 44 25N 125 5 E
Nongoma, S. Africa 57 D5 27 58S 31 35 E
Nonoava, Mexico 86 B3 27 28N 106 44W
Nonthaburi, Thailand 38 F3 13 51N 100 34 E
Noonamah, Australia 60 B5 12 40S 131 4 E
Noonan, U.S.A. 80 A3 48 54N 103 1W
Noondoo, Australia 63 D4 28 35S 148 30 E
Noonkanbah, Australia 60 C3 18 30S 124 50 E
Noord Brabant □, Neths. 15 C5 51 40N 5 0 E
Noord Holland □, Neths. 15 B4 52 30N 4 45 E
Noordbeveland, Neths. 15 C3 51 35N 3 50 E
Noordoostpolder, Neths. 15 B5 52 45N 5 45 E
Noordwijk aan Zee, Neths. 15 B4 52 14N 4 26 E
Nootka, Canada 72 D3 49 38N 126 38W
Nootka I., Canada 72 D3 49 32N 126 42W
Nóqui, Angola 52 F2 5 55S 13 30 E
Noranda, Canada 70 C4 48 20N 79 0W
Norco, U.S.A. 85 M9 33 56N 117 33W
Nord-Ostsee-Kanal →, Germany 16 A5 54 12N 9 32 E
Nordaustlandet, Svalbard 4 B9 79 14N 23 0 E
Nordegg, Canada 72 C5 52 29N 116 5W
Norderney, Germany 16 B4 53 42N 7 9 E
Norderstedt, Germany 16 B5 53 42N 9 58 E
Nordfjord, Norway 9 F11 61 55N 5 30 E
Nordfriesische Inseln, Germany 16 A5 54 40N 8 20 E
Nordhausen, Germany 16 C6 51 30N 10 47 E
Norðoyar, Færoe Is. 8 E9 62 17N 6 35W
Nordkapp, Norway 8 A21 71 10N 25 50 E
Nordkapp, Svalbard 4 A9 80 31N 20 0 E
Nordkinn = Kinnarodden, Norway 6 A11 71 8N 27 40 E
Nordkinn-halvøya, Norway 8 A22 70 55N 27 40 E
Nordrhein-Westfalen □, Germany 16 C4 51 45N 7 30 E
Nordvik, Russia 27 B12 74 2N 111 32 E
Norembega, Canada 70 C3 48 59N 80 43W
Norfolk, Nebr., U.S.A. 80 D6 42 2N 97 25W
Norfolk, Va., U.S.A. 76 G7 36 51N 76 17W
Norfolk □, U.K. 10 E9 52 39N 0 54 E
Norfolk Broads, U.K. 10 E9 52 30N 1 15 E
Norfolk I., Pac. Oc. 64 K8 28 58S 168 3 E
Norfork Res., U.S.A. 81 G8 36 13N 92 15W
Norilsk, Russia 27 C9 69 20N 88 6 E
Norley, Australia 63 D3 27 45S 143 48 E
Norma, Mt., Australia 62 C3 20 55S 140 42 E
Normal, U.S.A. 80 E10 40 31N 88 59W
Norman, U.S.A. 81 H6 35 13N 97 26W
Norman →, Australia 62 B3 19 18S 141 51 E
Norman Wells, Canada 68 B7 65 17N 126 51W
Normanby →, Australia 62 A3 14 23S 144 10 E
Normandie, France 18 B4 48 45N 0 10 E
Normandin, Canada 70 C5 48 49N 72 31W
Normandy = Normandie, France 18 B4 48 45N 0 10 E
Normanhurst, Mt., Australia 61 E3 25 4S 122 30 E
Normanton, Australia 62 B3 17 40S 141 10 E
Norquay, Canada 73 C8 51 53N 102 5W
Norquinco, Argentina 96 E2 41 51S 70 55W
Norrbotten □, Sweden 8 C19 66 30N 22 30 E
Norris, U.S.A. 82 D8 45 34N 111 41W
Norristown, U.S.A. 79 F9 40 7N 75 21W
Norrköping, Sweden 9 G17 58 37N 16 11 E
Norrland, Sweden 9 E16 62 15N 15 45 E
Norrtälje, Sweden 9 G18 59 46N 18 42 E
Norseman, Australia 61 F3 32 8S 121 43 E
Norsk, Russia 27 D14 52 30N 130 5 E
Norte, Pta. del, Canary Is. 22 G2 27 51N 17 57W
North Adams, U.S.A. 79 D11 42 42N 73 7W
North Ayrshire □, U.K. 12 F4 55 45N 4 44W
North Battleford, Canada 73 C7 52 50N 108 17W
North Bay, Canada 70 C4 46 20N 79 30W
North Belcher Is., Canada 70 A4 56 50N 79 50W
North Bend, Canada 72 D4 49 50N 121 27W
North Bend, Oreg., U.S.A. 82 E1 43 24N 124 14W
North Bend, Pa., U.S.A. 78 E7 41 20N 77 42W
North Bend, Wash., U.S.A. 84 C5 47 30N 121 47W
North Berwick, U.K. 12 E6 56 4N 2 42W
North Berwick, U.S.A. 79 C14 43 18N 70 44W
North C., Canada 71 C7 47 2N 60 20W
North C., N.Z. 59 F4 34 23S 173 4 E
North Canadian →, U.S.A. 81 H7 35 16N 95 31W
North Cape = Nordkapp, Norway 8 A21 71 10N 25 50 E
North Cape = Nordkapp, Svalbard 4 A9 80 31N 20 0 E
North Caribou L., Canada 70 B1 52 50N 90 40W
North Carolina □, U.S.A. 77 H5 35 30N 80 0W
North Channel, Canada 70 C3 46 0N 83 0W
North Channel, U.K. 12 G3 55 13N 5 52W
North Charleston, U.S.A. 77 J6 32 53N 79 58W
North Chicago, U.S.A. 76 D2 42 19N 87 51W
North Dakota □, U.S.A. 80 B5 47 30N 100 15W
North Dandalup, Australia 61 F2 32 30S 115 57 E
North Down □, U.K. 13 B6 54 40N 5 45W
North Downs, U.K. 11 F8 51 19N 0 21 E
North East, U.S.A. 78 D5 42 13N 79 50W
North East Frontier Agency = Arunachal Pradesh □, India 41 E19 28 0N 95 0 E
North East Lincolnshire □, U.K. 10 D7 53 34N 0 2W
North East Providence Chan., W. Indies 88 A4 26 0N 76 0W
North Eastern □, Kenya 54 B5 1 30N 40 0 E
North Esk →, U.K. 12 E6 56 46N 2 24W
North European Plain, Europe 6 E10 55 0N 25 0 E
North Foreland, U.K. 11 F9 51 22N 1 28 E
North Fork, U.S.A. 84 H7 37 14N 119 21W
North Fork American →, U.S.A. 84 G5 38 57N 120 59W
North Fork Feather →, U.S.A. 84 F5 38 33N 121 30W
North Frisian Is. = Nordfriesische Inseln, Germany 16 A5 54 40N 8 20 E
North Henik L., Canada 73 A9 61 45N 97 40W
North Highlands, U.S.A. 84 G5 38 40N 121 23W
North Horr, Kenya 54 B4 3 20N 37 8 E
North I., Kenya 54 B4 4 5N 36 5 E
North I., N.Z. 59 H5 38 0S 175 0 E
North Kingsville, U.S.A. 78 E4 41 54N 80 42W
North Knife →, Canada 73 B10 58 53N 94 45W
North Koel →, India 43 G10 24 45N 83 50 E
North Korea ■, Asia 35 E14 40 0N 127 0 E
North Lakhimpur, India 41 F19 27 14N 94 7 E
North Lanarkshire □, U.K. 12 F5 55 52N 3 56W

O

Penola

Penola, Australia 63 F3 37 25S 140 48 E
Penong, Australia 61 F5 31 56S 133 1 E
Penonomé, Panama 88 E3 8 31N 80 21W
Penrith, Australia 63 E5 33 43S 150 38 E
Penrith, U.K. 10 C5 54 40N 2 45W
Pensacola, U.S.A. 77 K2 30 25N 87 13W
Pensacola Mts., Antarctica 5 E1 84 0S 40 0W
Pense, Canada 73 C8 50 25N 104 59W
Penshurst, Australia 63 F3 37 49S 142 20 E
Penticton, Canada 72 D5 49 30N 119 38W
Pentland, Australia 62 C4 20 32S 145 25 E
Pentland Firth, U.K. 12 C5 58 43N 3 10W
Pentland Hills, U.K. 12 F5 55 48N 3 25W
Penylan L., Canada 73 A7 61 50N 106 20W
Penza, Russia 24 D8 53 15N 45 5 E
Penzance, U.K. 11 G2 50 7N 5 33W
Penzhino, Russia 27 C17 63 30N 167 55 E
Penzhinskaya Guba, Russia 27 C17 61 30N 163 0 E
Peoria, Ariz., U.S.A. 83 K7 33 35N 112 14W
Peoria, Ill., U.S.A. 80 E10 40 42N 89 36W
Pera Hd., Australia 62 A3 12 55S 141 37 E
Perabumulih, Indonesia 36 E2 3 27S 104 15 E
Pérama, Kérkira, Greece 23 A3 39 34N 19 54 E
Pérama, Kríti, Greece 23 D6 35 20N 24 40 E
Peräpohjola, Finland 8 C22 66 16N 26 10 E
Percé, Canada 71 C7 48 31N 64 13W
Perche, Collines du, France 18 B4 48 30N 0 40 E
Percival Lakes, Australia 60 D4 21 25S 125 0 E
Percy Is., Australia 62 C5 21 39S 150 16 E
Perdido, Mte., Spain 19 A6 42 40N 0 5 E
Perdu, Mt. = Perdido, Mte., Spain 19 A6 42 40N 0 5 E
Pereira, Colombia 92 C3 4 49N 75 43W
Perekerten, Australia 63 E3 34 55S 143 40 E
Perenjori, Australia 61 E2 29 26S 116 16 E
Pereyaslav-Khmelnytskyy, Ukraine 25 D5 50 3N 31 28 E
Pérez, I., Mexico 87 C7 22 24N 89 42W
Pergamino, Argentina 94 C3 33 52S 60 30W
Pergau →, Malaysia 39 K3 5 23N 102 2 E
Perham, U.S.A. 80 B7 46 36N 95 34W
Perhentian, Kepulauan, Malaysia 39 K4 5 54N 102 42 E
Péribonca →, Canada 71 C5 48 45N 72 5W
Péribonca, L., Canada 71 B5 50 1N 71 10W
Perico, Argentina 94 A2 24 20S 65 5W
Pericos, Mexico 86 B3 25 3N 107 42W
Périgueux, France 18 D4 45 10N 0 42 E
Perijá, Sierra de, Colombia 92 B4 9 30N 73 3W
Peristerona →, Cyprus 23 D12 35 8N 33 5 E
Perlas, Arch. de las, Panama 88 E4 8 41N 79 7W
Perlas, Punta de, Nic. 88 D3 12 30N 83 30W
Perm, Russia 24 C10 58 0N 56 10 E
Pernambuco = Recife, Brazil 93 E12 8 0S 35 0W
Pernambuco □, Brazil 93 E11 8 0S 37 0W
Pernatty Lagoon, Australia 63 E2 31 30S 137 12 E
Pernik, Bulgaria 21 C10 42 35N 23 2 E
Peron, C., Australia 61 E1 25 30S 113 30 E
Peron Is., Australia 60 B5 13 9S 130 4 E
Peron Pen., Australia 61 E1 26 0S 113 10 E
Perow, Canada 72 C3 54 35N 126 10W
Perpendicular Pt., Australia 63 E5 31 37S 152 52 E
Perpignan, France 18 E5 42 42N 2 53 E
Perris, U.S.A. 85 M9 33 47N 117 14W
Perry, Fla., U.S.A. 77 K4 30 7N 83 35W
Perry, Ga., U.S.A. 77 J4 32 28N 83 44W
Perry, Iowa, U.S.A. 80 E7 41 51N 94 6W
Perry, Maine, U.S.A. 77 C12 44 58N 67 5W
Perry, Okla., U.S.A. 81 G6 36 17N 97 14W
Perryton, U.S.A. 81 G4 36 24N 100 48W
Perryville, U.S.A. 81 G10 37 43N 89 52W
Pershotravensk, Ukraine 17 C14 50 13N 27 40 E
Persia = Iran ■, Asia 45 C7 33 0N 53 0 E
Persian Gulf = Gulf, The, Asia 45 E6 27 0N 50 0 E
Perth, Australia 61 F2 31 57S 115 52 E
Perth, Canada 70 D4 44 55N 76 15W
Perth, U.K. 12 E5 56 24N 3 26W
Perth & Kinross □, U.K. 12 E5 56 45N 3 55W
Perth Amboy, U.S.A. 79 F10 40 31N 74 16W
Peru, Ill., U.S.A. 80 E10 41 20N 89 8W
Peru, Ind., U.S.A. 76 E2 40 45N 86 4W
Peru ■, S. Amer. 92 E3 4 0S 75 0W
Peru-Chile Trench, Pac. Oc. 65 K20 20 0S 72 0W
Perúgia, Italy 20 C5 43 7N 12 23 E
Pervomaysk, Ukraine 25 E5 48 10N 30 46 E
Pervouralsk, Russia 24 C10 56 59N 59 59 E
Pes, Pta. del, Spain 22 C7 38 46N 1 26 E
Pésaro, Italy 20 C5 43 54N 12 55 E
Pescara, Italy 20 C6 42 28N 14 13 E
Peshawar, Pakistan 42 B4 34 2N 71 37 E
Peshkopi, Albania 21 D9 41 41N 20 25 E
Peshtigo, U.S.A. 76 C2 45 4N 87 46W
Pesqueira, Brazil 93 E11 8 20S 36 42W
Petah Tiqwa, Israel 47 C3 32 6N 34 53 E
Petaling Jaya, Malaysia 39 L3 3 4N 101 42 E
Petaloudhes, Greece 23 C10 36 18N 28 5 E
Petaluma, U.S.A. 84 G4 38 14N 122 39W
Petange, Lux. 15 E5 49 33N 5 55 E
Petatlán, Mexico 86 D4 17 31N 101 16W
Petauke, Zambia 55 E3 14 14S 31 20 E
Petawawa, Canada 70 C4 45 54N 77 17W
Petén Itzá, L., Guatemala 88 C2 16 58N 89 50W
Peter I.s Øy, Antarctica 5 C16 69 0S 91 0W
Peter Pond L., Canada 73 B7 55 55N 108 44W
Peterbell, Canada 70 C3 48 36N 83 21W
Peterborough, Australia 63 E2 32 58S 138 51 E
Peterborough, Canada 69 D12 44 20N 78 20W
Peterborough, U.K. 11 E7 52 35N 0 15W
Peterborough, U.S.A. 79 D13 42 53N 71 57W
Peterhead, U.K. 12 D7 57 31N 1 48W
Petermann Bjerg, Greenland 66 B17 73 7N 28 25W
Petersburg, Alaska, U.S.A. 72 B2 56 48N 132 58W
Petersburg, Ind., U.S.A. 76 F2 38 30N 87 17W
Petersburg, Va., U.S.A. 76 G7 37 14N 77 24W
Petersburg, W. Va., U.S.A. 76 F6 39 1N 79 5W
Petford, Australia 62 B3 17 20S 144 58 E
Petit Bois I., U.S.A. 77 K1 30 12N 88 26W
Petit-Cap, Canada 71 C7 49 3N 64 30W
Petit Goâve, Haiti 89 C5 18 27N 72 51W
Petit Lac Manicouagan, Canada 71 B6 51 25N 67 40W
Petitcodiac, Canada 71 C6 45 57N 65 11W
Petite Baleine →, Canada 70 A4 56 0N 76 45W
Petite Saguenay, Canada 71 C5 48 15N 70 4W
Petitsikapau, L., Canada 71 B6 54 37N 66 25W
Petlad, India 42 H5 22 30N 72 45 E
Peto, Mexico 87 C7 20 10N 88 53W
Petone, N.Z. 59 J5 41 13S 174 53 E
Petoskey, U.S.A. 76 C3 45 22N 84 57W
Petra, Jordan 47 E4 30 20N 35 22 E
Petra, Spain 22 B10 39 37N 3 6 E
Petra, Ostrova, Russia 4 B13 76 15N 118 30 E
Petra Velikogo, Zaliv, Russia 30 C5 42 40N 132 0 E
Petrich, Bulgaria 21 D10 41 24N 23 13 E
Petrikov = Pyetrikaw, Belarus 17 B15 52 11N 28 29 E
Petrograd = Sankt-Peterburg, Russia 24 C5 59 55N 30 20 E
Petrolândia, Brazil 93 E11 9 5S 38 20W
Petrolia, Canada 70 D3 42 54N 82 9W
Petrolina, Brazil 93 E10 9 24S 40 30W
Petropavl, Kazakstan 26 D7 54 53N 69 13 E
Petropavlovsk = Petropavl, Kazakstan 26 D7 54 53N 69 13 E
Petropavlovsk-Kamchatskiy, Russia 27 D16 53 3N 158 43 E
Petrópolis, Brazil 95 A7 22 33S 43 9W
Petroşani, Romania 17 F12 45 28N 23 20 E
Petrovaradin, Serbia, Yug. 21 B8 45 16N 19 55 E
Petrovsk, Russia 24 D8 52 22N 45 19 E
Petrovsk-Zabaykalskiy, Russia 27 D11 51 20N 108 55 E
Petrozavodsk, Russia 24 B5 61 41N 34 20 E
Petrus Steyn, S. Africa 57 D4 27 38S 28 8 E
Petrusburg, S. Africa 56 D4 29 4S 25 26 E
Peumo, Chile 94 C1 34 21S 71 12W
Peureulak, Indonesia 36 D1 4 48N 97 45 E
Pevek, Russia 27 C18 69 41N 171 19 E
Pforzheim, Germany 16 D5 48 52N 8 41 E
Phagwara, India 40 D9 31 10N 75 40 E
Phaistós, Greece 23 D6 35 2N 24 50 E
Phala, Botswana 56 C4 23 45S 26 50 E
Phalera = Phulera, India 42 F6 26 52N 75 16 E
Phalodi, India 42 F5 27 12N 72 24 E
Phan, Thailand 38 C2 19 28N 99 43 E
Phan Rang, Vietnam 39 G7 11 34N 109 0 E
Phan Ri = Hoa Da, Vietnam 39 G7 11 16N 108 40 E
Phan Thiet, Vietnam 39 G7 11 1N 108 9 E
Phanat Nikhom, Thailand 38 F3 13 27N 101 11 E
Phangan, Ko, Thailand 39 H3 9 45N 100 0 E
Phangnga, Thailand 39 H2 8 28N 98 30 E
Phanh Bho Ho Chi Minh, Vietnam 39 G6 10 58N 106 40 E
Phanom Sarakham, Thailand 38 F3 13 45N 101 21 E
Pharenda, India 43 F10 27 5N 83 17 E
Phatthalung, Thailand 39 J3 7 39N 100 6 E
Phayao, Thailand 38 C2 19 11N 99 55 E
Phelps, N.Y., U.S.A. 78 D7 42 58N 77 3W
Phelps, Wis., U.S.A. 80 B10 46 4N 89 5W
Phelps L., Canada 73 B8 59 15N 103 15W
Phenix City, U.S.A. 77 J3 32 28N 85 0W
Phet Buri, Thailand 38 F2 13 1N 99 55 E
Phetchabun, Thailand 38 D3 16 25N 101 8 E
Phetchabun, Thiu Khao, Thailand 38 E3 16 0N 101 20 E
Phetchaburi = Phet Buri, Thailand 38 F2 13 1N 99 55 E
Phi Phi, Ko, Thailand 39 J2 7 45N 98 46 E
Phiafay, Laos 38 E6 14 48N 106 0 E
Phibun Mangsahan, Thailand 38 E5 15 14N 105 14 E
Phichai, Thailand 38 D3 17 22N 100 10 E
Phichit, Thailand 38 D3 16 26N 100 22 E
Philadelphia, Miss., U.S.A. 81 J10 32 46N 89 7W
Philadelphia, N.Y., U.S.A. 79 B9 44 9N 75 43W
Philadelphia, Pa., U.S.A. 79 F9 39 57N 75 10W
Philip, U.S.A. 80 C4 44 2N 101 40W
Philippeville, Belgium 15 D4 50 12N 4 33 E
Philippi L., Australia 62 C2 24 20S 138 55 E
Philippines ■, Asia 37 B6 12 0N 123 0 E
Philippolis, S. Africa 56 E4 30 15S 25 16 E
Philippopolis = Plovdiv, Bulgaria 21 C11 42 8N 24 44 E
Philipsburg, Mont., U.S.A. 82 C7 46 20N 113 18W
Philipsburg, Pa., U.S.A. 78 F6 40 54N 78 13W
Philipstown = Daingean, Ireland 13 C4 53 18N 7 17W
Philipstown, S. Africa 56 E3 30 28S 24 30 E
Phillip I., Australia 63 F4 38 30S 145 12 E
Phillips, Tex., U.S.A. 81 H4 35 42N 101 22W
Phillips, Wis., U.S.A. 80 C9 45 42N 90 24W
Phillipsburg, Kans., U.S.A. 80 F5 39 45N 99 19W
Phillipsburg, N.J., U.S.A. 79 F9 40 42N 75 12W
Phillott, Australia 63 D4 27 53S 145 50 E
Philmont, U.S.A. 79 D11 42 15N 73 39W
Philomath, U.S.A. 82 D2 44 32N 123 22W
Phimai, Thailand 38 E4 15 13N 102 30 E
Phitsanulok, Thailand 38 D3 16 50N 100 12 E
Phnom Dangrek, Thailand 38 E5 14 20N 104 0 E
Phnom Penh, Cambodia 39 G5 11 33N 104 55 E
Phoenix, Ariz., U.S.A. 83 K7 33 27N 112 4W
Phoenix, N.Y., U.S.A. 79 C8 43 14N 76 18W
Phoenix Is., Kiribati 64 H10 3 30S 172 0W
Phoenixville, U.S.A. 79 F9 40 8N 75 31W
Phon, Thailand 38 E4 15 49N 102 36 E
Phon Tiou, Laos 38 D5 17 53N 104 37 E
Phong →, Thailand 38 D4 16 23N 102 56 E
Phong Saly, Laos 38 B4 21 42N 102 9 E
Phong Tho, Vietnam 38 A4 22 32N 103 21 E
Phonhong, Laos 38 C4 18 30N 102 25 E
Phonum, Thailand 39 H2 8 49N 98 48 E
Phosphate Hill, Australia 62 C2 21 53S 139 58 E
Photharam, Thailand 38 F2 13 41N 99 51 E
Phra Chedi Sam Ong, Thailand 38 E2 15 16N 98 23 E
Phra Nakhon Si Ayutthaya, Thailand 38 E3 14 25N 100 30 E
Phra Thong, Ko, Thailand 39 H2 9 5N 98 17 E
Phrae, Thailand 38 C3 18 7N 100 9 E
Phrom Phiram, Thailand 38 D3 17 2N 100 12 E
Phu Dien, Vietnam 38 C5 18 58N 105 31 E
Phu Loi, Laos 38 B4 20 14N 103 14 E
Phu Ly, Vietnam 38 B5 20 35N 105 50 E
Phu Tho, Vietnam 38 B5 21 24N 105 13 E
Phuc Yen, Vietnam 38 B5 21 16N 105 45 E
Phuket, Thailand 39 J2 7 52N 98 22 E
Phuket, Ko, Thailand 39 J2 8 0N 98 22 E
Phulera, India 42 F6 26 52N 75 16 E
Phumiphon, Khuan, Thailand 38 D2 17 15N 98 58 E
Phun Phin, Thailand 39 H2 9 7N 99 12 E
Piacenza, Italy 20 B3 45 1N 9 40 E
Pialba, Australia 63 D5 25 20S 152 45 E
Pian Cr. →, Australia 63 E4 30 2S 148 12 E
Pianosa, Italy 20 C4 42 35N 10 5 E
Piapot, Canada 73 D7 49 59N 109 8W
Piatra Neamţ, Romania 17 E14 46 56N 26 21 E
Piauí □, Brazil 93 E10 7 0S 43 0W
Piave →, Italy 20 B5 45 32N 12 44 E
Pibor Post, Sudan 51 G11 6 47N 33 3 E
Pica, Chile 92 H5 20 35S 69 25W
Picardie, France 18 B5 49 50N 3 0 E
Picardy = Picardie, France 18 B5 49 50N 3 0 E
Picayune, U.S.A. 81 K10 30 32N 89 41W
Pichilemu, Chile 94 C1 34 22S 72 0W
Pickerel L., Canada 70 C1 48 40N 91 25W
Pickle Lake, Canada 70 B1 51 30N 90 12W
Pico Truncado, Argentina 96 F3 46 40S 68 0W
Picton, Australia 63 E5 34 12S 150 34 E
Picton, Canada 70 D4 44 1N 77 9W
Picton, N.Z. 59 J5 41 18S 174 3 E
Pictou, Canada 71 C7 45 41N 62 42W
Picture Butte, Canada 72 D6 49 55N 112 45W
Picún Leufú, Argentina 96 D3 39 30S 69 5W
Pidurutalagala, Sri Lanka 40 R12 7 10N 80 50 E
Piedmont = Piemonte □, Italy 20 B2 45 0N 8 0 E
Piedmont, U.S.A. 77 J3 33 55N 85 37W
Piedmont Plateau, U.S.A. 77 J5 34 0N 81 30W
Piedras, R. de las →, Peru 92 F5 12 30S 69 15W
Piedras Negras, Mexico 86 B4 28 42N 100 31W
Pieksämäki, Finland 9 E22 62 18N 27 10 E
Piemonte □, Italy 20 B2 45 0N 8 0 E
Pierce, U.S.A. 82 C6 46 30N 115 48W
Piercefield, U.S.A. 79 B10 44 13N 74 35W
Pierre, U.S.A. 80 C4 44 22N 100 21W
Piet Retief, S. Africa 57 D5 27 1S 30 50 E
Pietarsaari, Finland 8 E20 63 40N 22 43 E
Pietermaritzburg, S. Africa 57 D5 29 35S 30 25 E
Pietersburg, S. Africa 57 C4 23 54S 29 25 E
Pietrosul, Romania 17 E13 47 12N 25 8 E
Pietrosul, Romania 17 E13 47 35N 24 43 E
Pigeon, U.S.A. 76 D4 43 50N 83 16W
Piggott, U.S.A. 81 G9 36 23N 90 11W
Pigüe, Argentina 94 D3 37 36S 62 25W
Pihani, India 43 F9 27 36N 80 15 E
Pihlajavesi, Finland 9 F23 61 45N 28 45 E
Pikes Peak, U.S.A. 80 F2 38 50N 105 3W
Piketberg, S. Africa 56 E2 32 55S 18 40 E
Pikeville, U.S.A. 76 G4 37 29N 82 31W
Pikou, China 35 E12 39 18N 122 22 E
Pikwitonei, Canada 73 B9 55 35N 97 9W
Piła, Poland 17 B9 53 10N 16 48 E
Pilani, India 42 E6 28 22N 75 33 E
Pilar, Brazil 93 E11 9 36S 35 56W
Pilar, Paraguay 94 B4 26 50S 58 20W
Pilas Group, Phil. 37 C6 6 45N 121 35 E
Pilcomayo →, Paraguay 94 B4 25 21S 57 42W
Pilibhit, India 43 E8 28 40N 79 50 E
Pilica →, Poland 17 C11 51 52N 21 17 E
Pilkhawa, India 42 E7 28 43N 77 42 E
Pílos, Greece 21 F9 36 55N 21 42 E
Pilot Mound, Canada 73 D9 49 15N 98 54W
Pilot Point, U.S.A. 81 J6 33 24N 96 58W
Pilot Rock, U.S.A. 82 D4 45 29N 118 50W
Pilsen = Plzeň, Czech. 16 D7 49 45N 13 22 E
Pima, U.S.A. 83 K9 32 54N 109 50W
Pimba, Australia 63 E2 31 18S 136 46 E
Pimenta Bueno, Brazil 92 F6 11 35S 61 10W
Pimentel, Peru 92 E3 6 45S 79 55W
Pinang, Malaysia 39 K3 5 25N 100 15 E
Pinar, C. del, Spain 22 B10 39 53N 3 12 E
Pinar del Río, Cuba 88 B3 22 26N 83 40W
Pınarhisar, Turkey 21 D12 41 37N 27 30 E
Pincher Creek, Canada 72 D6 49 30N 113 57W
Pinchi L., Canada 72 C4 54 38N 124 30W
Pinckneyville, U.S.A. 80 F10 38 5N 89 23W
Pińczów, Poland 17 C11 50 32N 20 32 E
Pind Dadan Khan, Pakistan 42 C5 32 36N 73 7 E
Pindar, Australia 61 E2 28 30S 115 47 E
Pindi Gheb, Pakistan 42 C5 33 14N 72 21 E
Pindiga, Nigeria 50 G7 9 58N 10 53 E
Pindos Óros, Greece 21 E9 40 0N 21 0 E
Pindus Mts. = Pindos Óros, Greece 21 E9 40 0N 21 0 E
Pine, U.S.A. 83 J8 34 23N 111 27W
Pine →, Canada 73 B7 58 50N 105 38W
Pine, C., Canada 71 C9 46 37N 53 32W
Pine Bluff, U.S.A. 81 H8 34 13N 92 1W
Pine City, U.S.A. 80 C8 45 50N 92 59W
Pine Falls, Canada 73 C9 50 34N 96 11W
Pine Flat L., U.S.A. 84 J7 36 50N 119 20W
Pine Pass, Canada 72 B4 55 25N 122 42W
Pine Point, Canada 72 A6 60 50N 114 28W
Pine Ridge, U.S.A. 80 D3 43 2N 102 33W
Pine River, Canada 73 C8 51 45N 100 30W
Pine River, U.S.A. 80 B7 46 43N 94 24W
Pine Valley, U.S.A. 85 N10 32 50N 116 32W
Pinecrest, U.S.A. 84 G6 38 12N 120 1W
Pinedale, U.S.A. 84 J7 36 50N 119 48W
Pinega →, Russia 24 B8 64 30N 44 19 E
Pinehill, Australia 62 C4 23 38S 146 57 E
Pinerolo, Italy 20 B2 44 53N 7 21 E
Pinetop, U.S.A. 83 J9 34 8N 109 56W
Pinetown, S. Africa 57 D5 29 48S 30 54 E
Pinetree, U.S.A. 82 E11 43 42N 105 52W
Pineville, Ky., U.S.A. 77 G4 36 46N 83 42W
Pineville, La., U.S.A. 81 K8 31 19N 92 26W
Ping →, Thailand 38 E3 15 42N 100 9 E
Pingaring, Australia 61 F2 32 40S 118 32 E
Pingding, China 34 F7 37 47N 113 38 E
Pingdingshan, China 34 H7 33 43N 113 27 E
Pingdong, Taiwan 33 D7 22 39N 120 30 E
Pingdu, China 35 F10 36 42N 119 59 E
Pingelly, Australia 61 F2 32 32S 117 5 E
Pingliang, China 34 G4 35 35N 106 31 E
Pinglu, China 34 E7 39 31N 112 30 E
Pingluo, China 34 E4 38 52N 106 30 E
Pingquan, China 35 D10 41 1N 118 37 E
Pingrup, Australia 61 F2 33 32S 118 29 E
P'ingtung, Taiwan 33 D7 22 38N 120 30 E
Pingwu, China 34 H3 32 25N 104 30 E
Pingxiang, China 32 D5 22 6N 106 46 E
Pingyao, China 34 F7 37 12N 112 10 E
Pingyi, China 35 G9 35 30N 117 35 E
Pingyin, China 34 F9 36 20N 116 25 E
Pingyuan, China 34 F9 37 10N 116 22 E
Pinhal, Brazil 95 A6 22 10S 46 46W
Pinhel, Portugal 19 B2 40 50N 7 1W
Pini, Indonesia 36 D1 0 10N 98 40 E
Piniós →, Greece 21 E10 39 55N 22 41 E
Pinjarra, Australia 61 F2 32 37S 115 52 E
Pink →, Canada 73 B8 56 50N 103 50W
Pinnacles, Australia 61 E3 28 12S 120 26 E
Pinnacles, U.S.A. 84 J5 36 33N 121 19W
Pinnaroo, Australia 63 F3 35 17S 140 53 E
Pinnes, Ákra, Greece 21 D11 40 5N 24 20 E
Pinon Hills, U.S.A. 85 L9 34 26N 117 39W
Pinos, Mexico 86 C4 22 20N 101 40W
Pinos, Mt., U.S.A. 85 L7 34 49N 119 8W
Pinos Pt., U.S.A. 83 H3 36 38N 121 57W
Pinotepa Nacional, Mexico 87 D5 16 19N 98 3W
Pinrang, Indonesia 37 E5 3 46S 119 41 E
Pinsk, Belarus 17 B14 52 10N 26 1 E
Pintados, Chile 92 H5 20 35S 69 40W
Pintumba, Australia 61 F5 31 30S 132 12 E
Pinyug, Russia 24 B8 60 5N 48 0 E
Pioche, U.S.A. 83 H6 37 56N 114 27W
Piombino, Italy 20 C4 42 55N 10 32 E
Pioner, Os., Russia 27 B10 79 50N 92 0 E
Piorini, L., Brazil 92 D6 3 15S 62 35W
Piotrków Trybunalski, Poland 17 C10 51 23N 19 43 E
Pīp, Iran 45 E9 26 45N 60 10 E
Pipar, India 42 F5 26 25N 73 31 E
Piparia, India 42 H8 22 45N 78 23 E
Pipestone, U.S.A. 80 D6 44 0N 96 19W
Pipestone →, Canada 70 B2 52 53N 89 23W
Pipestone Cr. →, Canada 73 D8 49 38N 100 15W
Pipmuacan, Rés., Canada 71 C5 49 45N 70 30W
Pippingarra, Australia 60 D2 20 27S 118 42 E
Piqua, U.S.A. 76 E3 40 9N 84 15W
Piquiri →, Brazil 95 A5 24 3S 54 14W
Pīr Sohrāb, Iran 45 E9 25 44N 60 54 E
Piracicaba, Brazil 95 A6 22 45S 47 40W
Piracuruca, Brazil 93 D10 3 50S 41 50W
Piræus = Piraiévs, Greece 21 F10 37 57N 23 42 E
Piraiévs, Greece 21 F10 37 57N 23 42 E
Pirajuí, Brazil 95 A6 21 59S 49 29W
Pirané, Argentina 94 B4 25 42S 59 6W
Pirapora, Brazil 93 G10 17 20S 44 56W
Pírgos, Greece 21 F9 37 40N 21 27 E
Piribebuy, Paraguay 94 B4 25 26S 57 2W
Pirin Planina, Bulgaria 21 D10 41 40N 23 30 E
Piripiri, Brazil 93 D10 4 15S 41 46W
Pirmasens, Germany 16 D4 49 12N 7 36 E
Pirot, Serbia, Yug. 21 C10 43 9N 22 39 E
Piru, Indonesia 37 E7 3 4S 128 12 E
Piru, U.S.A. 85 L8 34 25N 118 48W
Pisa, Italy 20 C4 43 43N 10 23 E
Pisagua, Chile 92 G4 19 40S 70 15W
Pisciotta, Italy 20 D6 40 6N 15 14 E
Pisco, Peru 92 F3 13 50S 76 12W
Písek, Czech. 16 D8 49 19N 14 10 E
Pishan, China 32 C2 37 30N 78 33 E
Pishin Lora →, Pakistan 42 E1 29 9N 64 5 E
Pising, Indonesia 37 F6 5 8S 121 53 E
Pismo Beach, U.S.A. 85 K6 35 9N 120 38W
Pissis, Cerro, Argentina 94 B2 27 45S 68 48W
Pissouri, Cyprus 23 E11 34 40N 32 42 E
Pistóia, Italy 20 C4 43 55N 10 54 E
Pistol B., Canada 73 A10 62 25N 92 37W
Pisuerga →, Spain 19 B3 41 33N 4 52W
Pitarpunga, L., Australia 63 E3 34 24S 143 30 E
Pitcairn I., Pac. Oc. 65 K14 25 5S 130 5W
Pite älv →, Sweden 8 D19 65 20N 21 25 E
Piteå, Sweden 8 D19 65 20N 21 25 E
Piteşti, Romania 17 F13 44 52N 24 54 E
Pithapuram, India 41 L13 17 10N 82 15 E
Pithara, Australia 61 F2 30 20S 116 35 E
Pitlochry, U.K. 12 E5 56 42N 3 44W
Pitsilia □, Cyprus 23 E12 34 55N 33 0 E
Pitt I., Canada 72 C3 53 30N 129 50W
Pittsburg, Kans., U.S.A. 81 G7 37 25N 94 42W
Pittsburg, Tex., U.S.A. 81 J7 33 0N 94 59W
Pittsburgh, U.S.A. 78 F5 40 26N 80 1W
Pittsfield, Ill., U.S.A. 80 F9 39 36N 90 49W
Pittsfield, Mass., U.S.A. 79 D11 42 27N 73 15W
Pittsfield, N.H., U.S.A. 79 C13 43 18N 71 20W
Pittston, U.S.A. 79 E9 41 19N 75 47W
Pittsworth, Australia 63 D5 27 41S 151 37 E
Pituri →, Australia 62 C2 22 35S 138 30 E
Piura, Peru 92 E2 5 15S 80 38W
Pixley, U.S.A. 84 K7 35 58N 119 18W
Placentia, Canada 71 C9 47 20N 54 0W
Placentia B., Canada 71 C9 47 0N 54 40W
Placerville, U.S.A. 84 G6 38 44N 120 48W
Placetas, Cuba 88 B4 22 15N 79 44W
Plain Dealing, U.S.A. 81 J8 32 54N 93 42W
Plainfield, U.S.A. 79 F10 40 37N 74 25W
Plains, Kans., U.S.A. 81 G4 37 16N 100 35W
Plains, Mont., U.S.A. 82 C6 47 28N 114 53W
Plains, Tex., U.S.A. 81 J3 33 11N 102 50W
Plainview, Nebr., U.S.A. 80 D6 42 21N 97 47W
Plainview, Tex., U.S.A. 81 H4 34 11N 101 43W
Plainville, U.S.A. 80 F5 39 14N 99 18W
Plainwell, U.S.A. 76 D3 42 27N 85 38W
Pláka, Ákra, Greece 23 D8 35 11N 26 19 E
Plakhino, Russia 26 C9 67 45N 86 5 E
Plana Cays, Bahamas 89 B5 22 38N 73 30W

Q

155

Ravenna

Ravenna, *Italy* 20 **B5** 44 25N 12 12 E
Ravenna, *Nebr., U.S.A.* 80 **E5** 41 1N 98 55W
Ravenna, *Ohio, U.S.A.* 78 **E3** 41 9N 81 15W
Ravensburg, *Germany* 16 **E5** 47 46N 9 36 E
Ravenshoe, *Australia* 62 **B4** 17 37S 145 29 E
Ravensthorpe, *Australia* 61 **F3** 33 35S 120 2 E
Ravenswood, *Australia* 62 **C4** 20 6S 146 54 E
Ravenswood, *U.S.A.* 76 **F5** 38 57N 81 46W
Ravi →, *Pakistan* 42 **D4** 30 35N 71 49 E
Rawalpindi, *Pakistan* 42 **C5** 33 38N 73 8 E
Rawāndūz, *Iraq* 44 **B5** 36 40N 44 30 E
Rawang, *Malaysia* 39 **L3** 3 20N 101 35 E
Rawdon, *Canada* 70 **C5** 46 3N 73 40W
Rawene, *N.Z.* 59 **F4** 35 25S 173 32 E
Rawlinna, *Australia* 61 **F4** 30 58S 125 28 E
Rawlins, *U.S.A.* 82 **F10** 41 47N 107 14W
Rawlinson Ra., *Australia* 61 **D4** 24 40S 128 30 E
Rawson, *Argentina* 96 **E3** 43 15S 65 5W
Ray, *U.S.A.* 80 **A3** 48 21N 103 10W
Ray, C., *Canada* 71 **C8** 47 33N 59 15W
Rayadurg, *India* 40 **M10** 14 40N 76 50 E
Rayagada, *India* 41 **K13** 19 15N 83 20 E
Raychikhinsk, *Russia* 27 **E13** 49 46N 129 25 E
Rāyen, *Iran* 45 **D8** 29 34N 57 26 E
Raymond, *Canada* 72 **D6** 49 30N 112 35W
Raymond, *Calif., U.S.A.* 84 **H7** 37 13N 119 54W
Raymond, *Wash., U.S.A.* 84 **D3** 46 41N 123 44W
Raymondville, *U.S.A.* 81 **M6** 26 29N 97 47W
Raymore, *Canada* 73 **C8** 51 25N 104 31W
Rayne, *U.S.A.* 81 **K8** 30 14N 92 16W
Rayón, *Mexico* 86 **B2** 29 43N 110 35W
Rayong, *Thailand* 38 **F3** 12 40N 101 20 E
Rayville, *U.S.A.* 81 **J9** 32 29N 91 46W
Raz, Pte. du, *France* 18 **C1** 48 2N 4 47W
Razan, *Iran* 45 **C6** 35 23N 49 2 E
Razdel'naya = Rozdilna, *Ukraine* 17 **E16** 46 50N 30 2 E
Razdolnoye, *Russia* 30 **C5** 43 30N 131 52 E
Razeh, *Iran* 45 **C6** 32 47N 48 9 E
Razelm, Lacul, *Romania* 17 **F15** 44 50N 29 0 E
Razgrad, *Bulgaria* 21 **C12** 43 33N 26 34 E
Razmak, *Pakistan* 42 **C3** 32 45N 69 50 E
Ré, I. de, *France* 18 **C3** 46 12N 1 30W
Reading, *U.K.* 11 **F7** 51 27N 0 58W
Reading, *U.S.A.* 79 **F9** 40 20N 75 56W
Realicó, *Argentina* 94 **D3** 35 0S 64 15W
Reata, *Mexico* 86 **B4** 26 8N 101 5W
Rebecca, L., *Australia* 61 **F3** 30 0S 122 15 E
Rebi, *Indonesia* 37 **F8** 6 23S 134 7 E
Rebiana, *Libya* 51 **D9** 24 12N 22 10 E
Rebun-Tō, *Japan* 30 **B10** 45 23N 141 2 E
Recherche, Arch. of the, *Australia* 61 **F3** 34 15S 122 50 E
Rechytsa, *Belarus* 17 **B16** 52 21N 30 24 E
Recife, *Brazil* 93 **E12** 8 0S 35 0W
Recklinghausen, *Germany* 15 **C7** 51 37N 7 12 E
Reconquista, *Argentina* 94 **B4** 29 10S 59 45W
Recreo, *Argentina* 94 **B2** 29 25S 65 10W
Red →, *La., U.S.A.* 81 **K9** 31 1N 91 45W
Red →, *N. Dak., U.S.A.* 80 **A6** 49 0N 97 15W
Red Bank, *U.S.A.* 79 **F10** 40 21N 74 5W
Red Bay, *Canada* 71 **B8** 51 44N 56 25W
Red Bluff, *U.S.A.* 82 **F2** 40 11N 122 15W
Red Bluff L., *U.S.A.* 81 **K3** 31 54N 103 55W
Red Cliffs, *Australia* 63 **E3** 34 19S 142 11 E
Red Cloud, *U.S.A.* 80 **E5** 40 5N 98 32W
Red Deer, *Canada* 72 **C6** 52 20N 113 50W
Red Deer →, *Alta., Canada* 73 **C6** 50 58N 110 0W
Red Deer →, *Man., Canada* 73 **C8** 52 53N 101 1W
Red Deer L., *Canada* 73 **C8** 52 55N 101 20W
Red Indian L., *Canada* 71 **C8** 48 35N 57 0W
Red Lake, *Canada* 73 **C10** 51 3N 93 49W
Red Lake Falls, *U.S.A.* 80 **B6** 47 53N 96 16W
Red Lodge, *U.S.A.* 82 **D9** 45 11N 109 15W
Red Mountain, *U.S.A.* 85 **K9** 35 37N 117 38W
Red Oak, *U.S.A.* 80 **E7** 41 1N 95 14W
Red Rock, *Canada* 70 **C2** 48 55N 88 15W
Red Rock, L., *U.S.A.* 80 **E8** 41 22N 92 59W
Red Rocks Pt., *Australia* 61 **F4** 32 13S 127 32 E
Red Sea, *Asia* 46 **C2** 25 0N 36 0 E
Red Slate Mt., *U.S.A.* 84 **H8** 37 31N 118 52W
Red Sucker L., *Canada* 73 **C10** 54 9N 93 40W
Red Tower Pass = Turnu Roşu, P., *Romania* 17 **F13** 45 33N 24 17 E
Red Wing, *U.S.A.* 80 **C8** 44 34N 92 31W
Redbridge, *U.K.* 11 **F8** 51 35N 0 7 E
Redcar, *U.K.* 10 **C6** 54 37N 1 4W
Redcar & Cleveland □, *U.K.* 10 **C6** 54 29N 1 0W
Redcliff, *Canada* 73 **C6** 50 10N 110 50W
Redcliffe, *Australia* 63 **D5** 27 12S 153 0 E
Redcliffe, Mt., *Australia* 61 **E3** 28 30S 121 30 E
Reddersburg, *S. Africa* 56 **D4** 29 41S 26 10 E
Redding, *U.S.A.* 82 **F2** 40 35N 122 24W
Redditch, *U.K.* 11 **E6** 52 18N 1 55W
Redfield, *U.S.A.* 80 **C5** 44 53N 98 31W
Redknife →, *Canada* 72 **A5** 61 14N 119 22W
Redlands, *U.S.A.* 85 **M9** 34 4N 117 11W
Redmond, *Australia* 61 **F2** 34 55S 117 40 E
Redmond, *Oreg., U.S.A.* 82 **D3** 44 17N 121 11W
Redmond, *Wash., U.S.A.* 84 **C4** 47 41N 122 7W
Redon, *France* 18 **C2** 47 40N 2 6W
Redonda, *Antigua* 89 **C7** 16 58N 62 19W
Redondela, *Spain* 19 **A1** 42 15N 8 38W
Redondo Beach, *U.S.A.* 85 **M8** 33 50N 118 23W
Redrock Pt., *Canada* 72 **A5** 62 11N 115 2W
Redruth, *U.K.* 11 **G2** 50 14N 5 14W
Redvers, *Canada* 73 **D8** 49 35N 101 40W
Redwater, *Canada* 72 **C6** 53 55N 113 6W
Redwood, *U.S.A.* 79 **B9** 44 18N 75 48W
Redwood City, *U.S.A.* 83 **H2** 37 30N 122 15W
Redwood Falls, *U.S.A.* 80 **C7** 44 32N 95 7W
Ree, L., *Ireland* 13 **C4** 53 35N 8 0W
Reed, L., *Canada* 73 **C8** 54 38N 100 30W
Reed City, *U.S.A.* 76 **D3** 43 53N 85 31W
Reeder, *U.S.A.* 80 **B3** 46 7N 102 57W
Reedley, *U.S.A.* 83 **H4** 36 36N 119 27W
Reedsburg, *U.S.A.* 80 **D9** 43 32N 90 0W
Reedsport, *U.S.A.* 82 **E1** 43 42N 124 6W
Reefton, *N.Z.* 59 **K3** 42 6S 171 51 E
Refugio, *U.S.A.* 81 **L6** 28 18N 97 17W
Regensburg, *Germany* 16 **D7** 49 1N 12 6 E
Réggio di Calábria, *Italy* 20 **E6** 38 6N 15 39 E
Réggio nell'Emília, *Italy* 20 **B4** 44 43N 10 36 E
Reghin, *Romania* 17 **E13** 46 46N 24 42 E
Regina, *Canada* 73 **C8** 50 27N 104 35W
Registro, *Brazil* 95 **A6** 24 29S 47 49W
Rehar →, *India* 43 **H10** 23 55N 82 40 E
Rehoboth, *Namibia* 56 **C2** 23 15S 17 4 E
Rehovot, *Israel* 47 **D3** 31 54N 34 48 E
Rei-Bouba, *Cameroon* 51 **G7** 8 40N 14 15 E
Reichenbach, *Germany* 16 **C7** 50 37N 12 17 E
Reid, *Australia* 61 **F4** 30 49S 128 26 E
Reid River, *Australia* 62 **B4** 19 40S 146 48 E
Reidsville, *U.S.A.* 77 **G6** 36 21N 79 40W
Reigate, *U.K.* 11 **F7** 51 14N 0 12W
Reims, *France* 18 **B6** 49 15N 4 1 E
Reina Adelaida, Arch., *Chile* 96 **G2** 52 20S 74 0W
Reinbeck, *U.S.A.* 80 **D8** 42 19N 92 36W
Reindeer →, *Canada* 73 **B8** 55 36N 103 11W
Reindeer I., *Canada* 73 **C9** 52 30N 98 0W
Reindeer L., *Canada* 73 **B8** 57 15N 102 15W
Reinga, C., *N.Z.* 59 **F4** 34 25S 172 43 E
Reinosa, *Spain* 19 **A3** 43 2N 4 15W
Reitz, *S. Africa* 57 **D4** 27 48S 28 29 E
Reivilo, *S. Africa* 56 **D3** 27 36S 24 8 E
Rekinniki, *Russia* 27 **C17** 60 51N 163 40 E
Reliance, *Canada* 73 **A7** 63 0N 109 20W
Remarkable, Mt., *Australia* 63 **E2** 32 48S 138 10 E
Rembang, *Indonesia* 37 **G14** 6 42S 111 21 E
Remedios, *Panama* 88 **E3** 8 15N 81 50W
Remeshk, *Iran* 45 **E8** 26 55N 58 50 E
Remich, *Lux.* 15 **E6** 49 32N 6 22 E
Ren Xian, *China* 34 **F8** 37 8N 114 40 E
Rendsburg, *Germany* 16 **A5** 54 17N 9 39 E
Rene, *Russia* 27 **C19** 66 2N 179 25W
Renfrew, *Canada* 70 **C4** 45 30N 76 40W
Renfrew, *U.K.* 12 **F4** 55 52N 4 24W
Renfrewshire □, *U.K.* 12 **F4** 55 49N 4 38W
Rengat, *Indonesia* 36 **E2** 0 30S 102 45 E
Rengo, *Chile* 94 **C1** 34 24S 70 50W
Reni, *Ukraine* 17 **F15** 45 28N 28 15 E
Renk, *Sudan* 51 **F11** 11 50N 32 50 E
Renkum, *Neths.* 15 **C5** 51 58N 5 43 E
Renmark, *Australia* 63 **E3** 34 11S 140 43 E
Rennell Sd., *Canada* 72 **C2** 53 23N 132 35W
Renner Springs T.O., *Australia* 62 **B1** 18 20S 133 47 E
Rennes, *France* 18 **B3** 48 7N 1 41W
Reno, *U.S.A.* 84 **F7** 39 31N 119 48W
Reno →, *Italy* 20 **B5** 44 38N 12 16 E
Renovo, *U.S.A.* 78 **E7** 41 20N 77 45W
Renqiu, *China* 34 **E9** 38 43N 116 5 E
Rensselaer, *Ind., U.S.A.* 76 **E2** 40 57N 87 9W
Rensselaer, *N.Y., U.S.A.* 79 **D11** 42 38N 73 45W
Rentería, *Spain* 19 **A5** 43 19N 1 54W
Renton, *U.S.A.* 84 **C4** 47 29N 122 12W
Reotipur, *India* 43 **G10** 25 33N 83 45 E
Republic, *Mich., U.S.A.* 76 **B2** 46 25N 87 59W
Republic, *Wash., U.S.A.* 82 **B4** 48 39N 118 44W
Republican →, *U.S.A.* 80 **F6** 39 4N 96 48W
Republican City, *U.S.A.* 80 **E5** 40 6N 99 13W
Repulse Bay, *Canada* 69 **B11** 66 30N 86 30W
Requena, *Peru* 92 **E4** 5 5S 73 52W
Requena, *Spain* 19 **C5** 39 30N 1 4W
Resadiye = Datça, *Turkey* 21 **F12** 36 46N 27 40 E
Reserve, *Canada* 73 **C8** 52 28N 102 39W
Reserve, *U.S.A.* 83 **K9** 33 43N 108 45W
Resht = Rasht, *Iran* 45 **B6** 37 20N 49 40 E
Resistencia, *Argentina* 94 **B4** 27 30S 59 0W
Reşiţa, *Romania* 17 **F11** 45 18N 21 53 E
Resolution I., *Canada* 69 **B13** 61 30N 65 0W
Resolution I., *N.Z.* 59 **L1** 45 40S 166 40 E
Ressano Garcia, *Mozam.* 57 **D5** 25 25S 32 0 E
Reston, *Canada* 73 **D8** 49 33N 101 6W
Retalhuleu, *Guatemala* 88 **D1** 14 33N 91 46W
Retenue, L. de, *Zaïre* 55 **E2** 11 0S 27 0 E
Retford, *U.K.* 10 **D7** 53 19N 0 56W
Réthimnon, *Greece* 23 **D6** 35 18N 24 30 E
Réthimnon □, *Greece* 23 **D6** 35 23N 24 28 E
Réunion ■, *Ind. Oc.* 49 **J9** 21 0S 56 0 E
Reus, *Spain* 19 **B6** 41 10N 1 5 E
Reutlingen, *Germany* 16 **D5** 48 29N 9 12 E
Reval = Tallinn, *Estonia* 9 **G21** 59 22N 24 48 E
Revda, *Russia* 24 **C10** 56 48N 59 57 E
Revelganj, *India* 43 **G11** 25 50N 84 40 E
Revelstoke, *Canada* 72 **C5** 51 0N 118 10W
Revilla Gigedo, Is., *Pac. Oc.* 66 **H8** 18 40N 112 0W
Revillagigedo I., *U.S.A.* 72 **B2** 55 50N 131 20W
Revuè →, *Mozam.* 55 **F3** 19 50S 34 0 E
Rewa, *India* 43 **G9** 24 33N 81 25 E
Rewari, *India* 42 **E7** 28 15N 76 40 E
Rexburg, *U.S.A.* 82 **E8** 43 49N 111 47W
Rey, *Iran* 45 **C6** 35 35N 51 25 E
Rey Malabo, *Eq. Guin.* 50 **H6** 3 45N 8 50 E
Reyðarfjörður, *Iceland* 8 **D6** 65 2N 14 13W
Reyes, Pt., *U.S.A.* 84 **H3** 38 0N 123 0W
Reykjahlið, *Iceland* 8 **D5** 65 40N 16 55W
Reykjanes, *Iceland* 8 **E2** 63 48N 22 40W
Reykjavík, *Iceland* 8 **D3** 64 10N 21 57W
Reynolds, *Canada* 73 **D9** 49 40N 95 55W
Reynolds Ra., *Australia* 60 **D5** 22 30S 133 0 E
Reynoldsville, *U.S.A.* 78 **E6** 41 5N 78 58W
Reynosa, *Mexico* 87 **B5** 26 5N 98 18W
Rēzekne, *Latvia* 9 **H22** 56 30N 27 17 E
Rezvān, *Iran* 45 **E8** 27 34N 56 6 E
Rhayader, *U.K.* 11 **E4** 52 18N 3 29W
Rheden, *Neths.* 15 **B6** 52 0N 6 3 E
Rhein, *Canada* 73 **C8** 51 25N 102 15W
Rhein →, *Europe* 15 **C6** 51 52N 6 2 E
Rhein-Main-Donau-Kanal, *Germany* 16 **D6** 49 15N 11 15 E
Rheine, *Germany* 16 **B4** 52 17N 7 26 E
Rheinland-Pfalz □, *Germany* 16 **C4** 50 0N 7 0 E
Rhin = Rhein →, *Europe* 15 **C6** 51 52N 6 2 E
Rhine = Rhein →, *Europe* 15 **C6** 51 52N 6 2 E
Rhineland-Palatinate □ = Rheinland-Pfalz □, *Germany* 16 **C4** 50 0N 7 0 E
Rhinelander, *U.S.A.* 80 **C10** 45 38N 89 25W
Rhino Camp, *Uganda* 54 **B3** 3 0N 31 22 E
Rhode Island □, *U.S.A.* 79 **E13** 41 40N 71 30W
Rhodes = Ródhos, *Greece* 23 **C10** 36 15N 28 10 E
Rhodesia = Zimbabwe ■, *Africa* 55 **F2** 19 0S 30 0 E
Rhodope Mts. = Rhodopi Planina, *Bulgaria* 21 **D11** 41 40N 24 20 E
Rhodopi Planina, *Bulgaria* 21 **D11** 41 40N 24 20 E
Rhön = Hohe Rhön, *Germany* 16 **C5** 50 24N 9 58 E
Rhondda, *U.K.* 11 **F4** 51 39N 3 31W
Rhondda Cynon Taff □, *U.K.* 11 **F4** 51 42N 3 27W
Rhône →, *France* 18 **E6** 43 28N 4 42 E
Rhum, *U.K.* 12 **E2** 57 0N 6 20W
Rhyl, *U.K.* 10 **D4** 53 20N 3 29W
Rhymney, *U.K.* 11 **F4** 51 46N 3 17W
Riachão, *Brazil* 93 **E9** 7 20S 46 37W
Riasi, *India* 43 **C6** 33 10N 74 50 E
Riau □, *Indonesia* 36 **D2** 0 0 102 35 E
Riau, Kepulauan, *Indonesia* 36 **D2** 0 30N 104 20 E
Riau Arch. = Riau, Kepulauan, *Indonesia* 36 **D2** 0 30N 104 20 E
Ribadeo, *Spain* 19 **A2** 43 35N 7 5W
Ribble →, *U.K.* 10 **C5** 53 52N 2 25W
Ribe, *Denmark* 9 **J13** 55 19N 8 44 E
Ribeira Brava, *Madeira* 22 **D2** 32 41N 17 4W
Ribeirão Prêto, *Brazil* 95 **A6** 21 10S 47 50W
Riberalta, *Bolivia* 92 **F5** 11 0S 66 0W
Rîbniţa, *Moldova* 17 **E15** 47 45N 29 0 E
Riccarton, *N.Z.* 59 **K4** 43 32S 172 37 E
Rice, *U.S.A.* 85 **L12** 34 5N 114 51W
Rice L., *Canada* 78 **B6** 44 12N 78 10W
Rice Lake, *U.S.A.* 80 **C9** 45 30N 91 44W
Rich Hill, *U.S.A.* 81 **F7** 38 6N 94 22W
Richards Bay, *S. Africa* 57 **D5** 28 48S 32 6 E
Richards L., *Canada* 73 **B7** 59 10N 107 10W
Richardson →, *Canada* 73 **B6** 58 25N 111 14W
Richardson Springs, *U.S.A.* 84 **F5** 39 51N 121 46W
Richardton, *U.S.A.* 80 **B3** 46 53N 102 19W
Riche, C., *Australia* 61 **F2** 34 36S 118 47 E
Richey, *U.S.A.* 80 **B2** 47 39N 105 4W
Richfield, *Idaho, U.S.A.* 82 **E6** 43 3N 114 9W
Richfield, *Utah, U.S.A.* 83 **G8** 38 46N 112 5W
Richford, *U.S.A.* 79 **B12** 45 0N 72 40W
Richibucto, *Canada* 71 **C7** 46 42N 64 54W
Richland, *Ga., U.S.A.* 77 **J3** 32 5N 84 40W
Richland, *Oreg., U.S.A.* 82 **D5** 44 46N 117 10W
Richland, *Wash., U.S.A.* 82 **C4** 46 17N 119 18W
Richland Center, *U.S.A.* 80 **D9** 43 21N 90 23W
Richlands, *U.S.A.* 76 **G5** 37 6N 81 48W
Richmond, *N.S.W., Australia* 63 **E5** 33 35S 150 42 E
Richmond, *Queens., Australia* 62 **C3** 20 43S 143 8 E
Richmond, *N.Z.* 59 **J4** 41 20S 173 12 E
Richmond, *U.K.* 10 **C6** 54 25N 1 43W
Richmond, *Calif., U.S.A.* 84 **H4** 37 56N 122 21W
Richmond, *Ind., U.S.A.* 76 **F3** 39 50N 84 53W
Richmond, *Ky., U.S.A.* 76 **G3** 37 45N 84 18W
Richmond, *Mich., U.S.A.* 78 **D2** 42 49N 82 45W
Richmond, *Mo., U.S.A.* 80 **F8** 39 17N 93 58W
Richmond, *Tex., U.S.A.* 81 **L7** 29 35N 95 46W
Richmond, *Utah, U.S.A.* 82 **F8** 41 56N 111 48W
Richmond, *Va., U.S.A.* 76 **G7** 37 33N 77 27W
Richmond Ra., *Australia* 63 **D5** 29 0S 152 45 E
Richmond-upon-Thames, *U.K.* 11 **F7** 51 27N 0 17W
Richton, *U.S.A.* 77 **K1** 31 16N 88 56W
Richwood, *U.S.A.* 76 **F5** 38 14N 80 32W
Ridder = Leninogorsk, *Kazakstan* 26 **D9** 50 20N 83 30 E
Ridgecrest, *U.S.A.* 85 **K9** 35 38N 117 40W
Ridgedale, *Canada* 73 **C8** 53 0N 104 10W
Ridgefield, *U.S.A.* 84 **E4** 45 49N 122 45W
Ridgeland, *U.S.A.* 77 **J5** 32 29N 80 59W
Ridgelands, *Australia* 62 **C5** 23 16S 150 17 E
Ridgetown, *Canada* 70 **D3** 42 26N 81 52W
Ridgewood, *U.S.A.* 79 **F10** 40 59N 74 7W
Ridgway, *U.S.A.* 78 **E6** 41 25N 78 44W
Riding Mountain Nat. Park, *Canada* 73 **C8** 50 50N 100 0W
Ridley, Mt., *Australia* 61 **F3** 33 12S 122 7 E
Ried, *Austria* 16 **D7** 48 14N 13 30 E
Riesa, *Germany* 16 **C7** 51 17N 13 17 E
Riet →, *S. Africa* 56 **D3** 29 0S 23 54 E
Rieti, *Italy* 20 **C5** 42 24N 12 51 E
Riffe L., *U.S.A.* 84 **D4** 46 32N 122 26W
Rifle, *U.S.A.* 82 **G10** 39 32N 107 47W
Rift Valley □, *Kenya* 54 **B4** 0 20N 36 0 E
Rig Rig, *Chad* 51 **F7** 14 13N 14 25 E
Rīga, *Latvia* 9 **H21** 56 53N 24 8 E
Riga, G. of, *Latvia* 9 **H20** 57 40N 23 45 E
Rīgān, *Iran* 45 **D8** 28 37N 58 58 E
Rīgas Jūras Līcis = Riga, G. of, *Latvia* 9 **H20** 57 40N 23 45 E
Rigaud, *Canada* 79 **A10** 45 29N 74 18W
Rigby, *U.S.A.* 82 **E8** 43 40N 111 55W
Rīgestān □, *Afghan.* 40 **D4** 30 15N 65 0 E
Riggins, *U.S.A.* 82 **D5** 45 25N 116 19W
Rigolet, *Canada* 71 **B8** 54 10N 58 23W
Riihimäki, *Finland* 9 **F21** 60 45N 24 48 E
Riiser-Larsen-halvøya, *Antarctica* 5 **C4** 68 0S 35 0 E
Rijeka, *Croatia* 16 **F8** 45 20N 14 21 E
Rijn →, *Neths.* 15 **B4** 52 12N 4 21 E
Rijssen, *Neths.* 15 **B6** 52 19N 6 31 E
Rijswijk, *Neths.* 15 **B4** 52 4N 4 22 E
Rikuzentakada, *Japan* 30 **E10** 39 0N 141 40 E
Riley, *U.S.A.* 82 **E4** 43 32N 119 28W
Rimah, Wadi ar →, *Si. Arabia* 44 **E4** 26 5N 41 30 E
Rimbey, *Canada* 72 **C6** 52 35N 114 15W
Rimini, *Italy* 20 **B5** 44 3N 12 33 E
Rîmnicu Sărat, *Romania* 17 **F14** 45 26N 27 3 E
Rîmnicu Vîlcea, *Romania* 17 **F13** 45 9N 24 21 E
Rimouski, *Canada* 71 **C6** 48 27N 68 30W
Rimrock, *U.S.A.* 84 **D5** 46 38N 121 10W
Rinca, *Indonesia* 37 **F5** 8 45S 119 35 E
Rincón de Romos, *Mexico* 86 **C4** 22 14N 102 18W
Rinconada, *Argentina* 94 **A2** 22 26S 66 10W
Ringkøbing, *Denmark* 9 **H13** 56 5N 8 15 E
Ringling, *U.S.A.* 82 **C8** 46 16N 110 49W
Ringvassøy, *Norway* 8 **B18** 69 56N 19 15 E
Rinjani, *Indonesia* 36 **F5** 8 24S 116 28 E
Rio Branco, *Brazil* 92 **E5** 9 58S 67 49W
Río Branco, *Uruguay* 95 **C5** 32 40S 53 40W
Rio Brilhante, *Brazil* 95 **A5** 21 48S 54 33W
Rio Claro, *Brazil* 95 **A6** 22 19S 47 35W
Rio Claro, *Trin. & Tob.* 89 **D7** 10 20N 61 25W
Río Colorado, *Argentina* 96 **D4** 39 0S 64 0W
Río Cuarto, *Argentina* 94 **C3** 33 10S 64 25W
Rio das Pedras, *Mozam.* 57 **C6** 23 8S 35 28 E
Rio de Janeiro, *Brazil* 95 **A7** 23 0S 43 12W
Rio de Janeiro □, *Brazil* 95 **A7** 22 50S 43 0W
Rio do Sul, *Brazil* 95 **B6** 27 13S 49 37W
Río Gallegos, *Argentina* 96 **G3** 51 35S 69 15W
Río Grande, *Argentina* 96 **G3** 53 50S 67 45W
Rio Grande, *Brazil* 95 **C5** 32 0S 52 20W
Río Grande, *Mexico* 86 **C4** 23 50N 103 2W
Río Grande, *Nic.* 88 **D3** 12 54N 83 33W
Rio Grande →, *U.S.A.* 81 **N6** 25 57N 97 9W
Rio Grande City, *U.S.A.* 81 **M5** 26 23N 98 49W
Río Grande del Norte →, *N. Amer.* 75 **E7** 26 0N 97 0W
Rio Grande do Norte □, *Brazil* 93 **E11** 5 40S 36 0W
Rio Grande do Sul □, *Brazil* 95 **C5** 30 0S 53 0W
Río Hato, *Panama* 88 **E3** 8 22N 80 10W
Río Lagartos, *Mexico* 87 **C7** 21 36N 88 10W
Rio Largo, *Brazil* 93 **E11** 9 28S 35 50W
Río Mulatos, *Bolivia* 92 **G5** 19 40S 66 50W
Río Muni = Mbini □, *Eq. Guin.* 52 **D2** 1 30N 10 0 E
Rio Negro, *Brazil* 95 **B6** 26 0S 49 55W
Rio Pardo, *Brazil* 95 **C5** 30 0S 52 30W
Río Segundo, *Argentina* 94 **C3** 31 40S 63 59W
Río Tercero, *Argentina* 94 **C3** 32 15S 64 8W
Rio Verde, *Brazil* 93 **G8** 17 50S 51 0W
Río Verde, *Mexico* 87 **C5** 21 56N 99 59W
Rio Vista, *U.S.A.* 84 **G5** 38 10N 121 42W
Riobamba, *Ecuador* 92 **D3** 1 50S 78 45W
Ríohacha, *Colombia* 92 **A4** 11 33N 72 55W
Ríosucio, *Caldas, Colombia* 92 **B3** 5 30N 75 40W
Ríosucio, *Choco, Colombia* 92 **B3** 7 27N 77 7W
Riou L., *Canada* 73 **B7** 59 7N 106 25W
Ripley, *Canada* 78 **B3** 44 4N 81 35W
Ripley, *Calif., U.S.A.* 85 **M12** 33 32N 114 39W
Ripley, *N.Y., U.S.A.* 78 **D5** 42 16N 79 43W
Ripley, *Tenn., U.S.A.* 81 **H10** 35 45N 89 32W
Ripon, *U.K.* 10 **C6** 54 9N 1 31W
Ripon, *Calif., U.S.A.* 84 **H5** 37 44N 121 7W
Ripon, *Wis., U.S.A.* 76 **D1** 43 51N 88 50W
Risalpur, *Pakistan* 42 **B4** 34 3N 71 59 E
Rishā', W. ar →, *Si. Arabia* 44 **E5** 25 33N 44 5 E
Rishiri-Tō, *Japan* 30 **B10** 45 11N 141 15 E
Rishon le Ẓiyyon, *Israel* 47 **D3** 31 58N 34 48 E
Rison, *U.S.A.* 81 **J8** 33 58N 92 11W
Risør, *Norway* 9 **G13** 58 43N 9 13 E
Rittman, *U.S.A.* 78 **F3** 40 58N 81 47W
Ritzville, *U.S.A.* 82 **C4** 47 8N 118 23W
Riva del Garda, *Italy* 20 **B4** 45 53N 10 50 E
Rivadavia, *Buenos Aires, Argentina* 94 **D3** 35 29S 62 59W
Rivadavia, *Mendoza, Argentina* 94 **C2** 33 13S 68 30W
Rivadavia, *Salta, Argentina* 94 **A3** 24 5S 62 54W
Rivadavia, *Chile* 94 **B1** 29 57S 70 35W
Rivas, *Nic.* 88 **D2** 11 30N 85 50W
Rivera, *Uruguay* 95 **C4** 31 0S 55 50W
Riverdale, *U.S.A.* 84 **J7** 36 26N 119 52W
Riverhead, *U.S.A.* 79 **F12** 40 55N 72 40W
Riverhurst, *Canada* 73 **C7** 50 55N 106 50W
Riverina, *Australia* 61 **E3** 29 45S 120 40 E
Rivers, *Canada* 73 **C8** 50 2N 100 14W
Rivers, L. of the, *Canada* 73 **D7** 49 49N 105 44W
Rivers Inlet, *Canada* 72 **C3** 51 42N 127 15W
Riversdale, *S. Africa* 56 **E3** 34 7S 21 15 E
Riverside, *Calif., U.S.A.* 85 **M9** 33 59N 117 22W
Riverside, *Wyo., U.S.A.* 82 **F10** 41 13N 106 47W
Riversleigh, *Australia* 62 **B2** 19 5S 138 40 E
Riverton, *Australia* 63 **E2** 34 10S 138 46 E
Riverton, *Canada* 73 **C9** 51 1N 97 0W
Riverton, *N.Z.* 59 **M1** 46 21S 168 0 E
Riverton, *U.S.A.* 82 **E9** 43 2N 108 23W
Riverton Heights, *U.S.A.* 84 **C4** 47 28N 122 17W
Riviera di Levante, *Italy* 20 **B3** 44 15N 9 30 E
Riviera di Ponente, *Italy* 20 **B3** 44 10N 8 20 E
Rivière-à-Pierre, *Canada* 71 **C5** 46 59N 72 11W
Rivière-au-Renard, *Canada* 71 **C7** 48 59N 64 23W
Rivière-du-Loup, *Canada* 71 **C6** 47 50N 69 30W
Rivière-Pentecôte, *Canada* 71 **C6** 49 57N 67 1W
Rivière-Pilote, *Martinique* 89 **D7** 14 26N 60 53W
Rivne, *Ukraine* 17 **C14** 50 40N 26 10 E
Rivoli, *Italy* 20 **B2** 45 3N 7 31 E
Rivoli B., *Australia* 63 **F3** 37 32S 140 3 E
Riyadh = Ar Riyāḍ, *Si. Arabia* 46 **C4** 24 41N 46 42 E
Rize, *Turkey* 25 **F7** 41 0N 40 30 E
Rizhao, *China* 35 **G10** 35 25N 119 30 E
Rizokarpaso, *Cyprus* 23 **D13** 35 36N 34 23 E
Rizzuto, C., *Italy* 20 **E7** 38 53N 17 5 E
Rjukan, *Norway* 9 **G13** 59 54N 8 33 E
Road Town, *Virgin Is.* 89 **C7** 18 27N 64 37W
Roag, L., *U.K.* 12 **C2** 58 12N 6 51W
Roanne, *France* 18 **C6** 46 3N 4 4 E
Roanoke, *Ala., U.S.A.* 77 **J3** 33 9N 85 22W
Roanoke, *Va., U.S.A.* 76 **G6** 37 16N 79 56W
Roanoke →, *U.S.A.* 77 **H7** 35 57N 76 42W
Roanoke I., *U.S.A.* 77 **H8** 35 55N 75 40W
Roanoke Rapids, *U.S.A.* 77 **G7** 36 28N 77 40W
Roatán, *Honduras* 88 **C2** 16 18N 86 35W
Robbins I., *Australia* 62 **G4** 40 42S 145 0 E
Robe →, *Australia* 60 **D2** 21 42S 116 15 E
Robe →, *Ireland* 13 **C2** 53 38N 9 10W
Robert Lee, *U.S.A.* 81 **K4** 31 54N 100 29W
Roberts, *U.S.A.* 82 **E7** 43 43N 112 8W
Robertsganj, *India* 43 **G10** 24 44N 83 4 E
Robertson, *S. Africa* 56 **E2** 33 46S 19 50 E
Robertson I., *Antarctica* 5 **C18** 65 15S 59 30W

Robertson Ra., Australia 60 D3 23 15S 121 0 E
Robertsport, Liberia 50 G2 6 45N 11 26W
Robertstown, Australia 63 E2 33 58S 139 5 E
Roberval, Canada 71 C5 48 32N 72 15W
Robeson Chan., Greenland 4 A4 82 0N 61 30W
Robinson —►, Australia 62 B2 16 3S 137 16 E
Robinson Ra., Australia 61 E2 25 40S 119 0 E
Robinson River, Australia 62 B2 16 45S 136 58 E
Robinvale, Australia 63 E3 34 40S 142 45 E
Roblin, Canada 73 C8 51 14N 101 21W
Roboré, Bolivia 92 G7 18 10S 59 45W
Robson, Mt., Canada 72 C5 53 10N 119 10W
Robstown, U.S.A. 81 M6 27 47N 97 40W
Roca, C. da, Portugal 19 C1 38 40N 9 31W
Roca Partida, I., Mexico 86 D2 19 1N 112 2W
Rocas, I., Brazil 93 D12 4 0S 34 1W
Rocha, Uruguay 95 C5 34 30S 54 25W
Rochdale, U.K. 10 D5 53 38N 2 9W
Rochefort, Belgium 15 D5 50 9N 5 12 E
Rochefort, France 18 D3 45 56N 0 57W
Rochelle, U.S.A. 80 E10 41 56N 89 4W
Rocher River, Canada 72 A6 61 23N 112 44W
Rochester, Canada 72 C6 54 22N 113 27W
Rochester, U.K. 11 F8 51 23N 0 31 E
Rochester, Ind., U.S.A. 76 E2 41 4N 86 13W
Rochester, Minn., U.S.A. 80 C8 44 1N 92 28W
Rochester, N.H., U.S.A. 79 C14 43 18N 70 59W
Rochester, N.Y., U.S.A. 78 C7 43 10N 77 37W
Rock —►, Canada 72 A3 60 7N 127 7W
Rock Hill, U.S.A. 77 H5 34 56N 81 1W
Rock Island, U.S.A. 80 E9 41 30N 90 34W
Rock Rapids, U.S.A. 80 D6 43 26N 96 10W
Rock River, U.S.A. 82 F11 41 44N 105 58W
Rock Sound, Bahamas 88 B4 24 54N 76 12W
Rock Springs, Mont., U.S.A. 82 C10 46 49N 106 15W
Rock Springs, Wyo., U.S.A. 82 F9 41 35N 109 14W
Rock Valley, U.S.A. 80 D6 43 12N 96 18W
Rockall, Atl. Oc. 6 D3 57 37N 13 42W
Rockdale, Tex., U.S.A. 81 K6 30 39N 97 0W
Rockdale, Wash., U.S.A. 84 C5 47 22N 121 28W
Rockefeller Plateau, Antarctica 5 E14 80 0S 140 0W
Rockford, U.S.A. 80 D10 42 16N 89 6W
Rockglen, Canada 73 D7 49 11N 105 57W
Rockhampton, Australia 62 C5 23 22S 150 32 E
Rockhampton Downs, Australia 62 B2 18 57S 135 10 E
Rockingham, Australia 61 F2 32 15S 115 38 E
Rockingham B., Australia 62 B4 18 5S 146 10 E
Rockingham Forest, U.K. 11 E7 52 29N 0 42W
Rocklake, U.S.A. 80 A5 48 47N 99 15W
Rockland, Canada 79 A9 45 33N 75 17W
Rockland, Idaho, U.S.A. 82 E7 42 34N 112 53W
Rockland, Maine, U.S.A. 71 D6 44 6N 69 7W
Rockland, Mich., U.S.A. 80 B10 46 44N 89 11W
Rocklin, U.S.A. 84 G5 38 48N 121 14W
Rockmart, U.S.A. 77 H3 34 0N 85 3W
Rockport, Mo., U.S.A. 80 E7 40 25N 95 31W
Rockport, Tex., U.S.A. 81 L6 28 2N 97 3W
Rocksprings, U.S.A. 81 K4 30 1N 100 13W
Rockville, Conn., U.S.A. 79 E12 41 52N 72 28W
Rockville, Md., U.S.A. 76 F7 39 5N 77 9W
Rockwall, U.S.A. 81 J6 32 56N 96 28W
Rockwell City, U.S.A. 80 D7 42 24N 94 38W
Rockwood, U.S.A. 77 H3 35 52N 84 41W
Rocky Ford, U.S.A. 80 F3 38 3N 103 43W
Rocky Gully, Australia 61 F2 34 30S 116 57 E
Rocky Lane, Canada 72 B5 58 31N 116 22W
Rocky Mount, U.S.A. 77 H7 35 57N 77 48W
Rocky Mountain House, Canada 72 C6 52 22N 114 55W
Rocky Mts., N. Amer. 72 C4 55 0N 121 0W
Rockyford, Canada 72 C6 51 14N 113 10W
Rod, Pakistan 40 E3 28 10N 63 5 E
Rødbyhavn, Denmark 9 J14 54 39N 11 22 E
Roddickton, Canada 71 B8 50 51N 56 8W
Roderick I., Canada 72 C3 52 38N 128 22W
Rodez, France 18 D5 44 21N 2 33 E
Rodhopoú, Greece 23 D5 35 34N 23 45 E
Ródhos, Greece 23 C10 36 15N 28 10 E
Rodney, Canada 78 D3 42 34N 81 41W
Rodney, C., N.Z. 59 G5 36 17S 174 50 E
Rodriguez, Ind. Oc. 3 E13 19 45S 63 20 E
Roe —►, U.K. 13 A5 55 6N 6 59W
Roebling, U.S.A. 79 F10 40 7N 74 47W
Roebourne, Australia 60 D2 20 44S 117 9 E
Roebuck B., Australia 60 C3 18 5S 122 20 E
Roebuck Plains, Australia 60 C3 17 56S 122 28 E
Roermond, Neths. 15 C5 51 12N 6 0 E
Roes Welcome Sd., Canada 69 B11 65 0N 87 0W
Roeselare, Belgium 15 D3 50 57N 3 7 E
Rogachev = Ragachow, Belarus 17 B16 53 8N 30 5 E
Rogagua, L., Bolivia 92 F5 13 43S 66 50W
Rogatyn, Ukraine 17 D13 49 24N 24 36 E
Rogdhia, Greece 23 D7 35 22N 25 1 E
Rogers, U.S.A. 81 G7 36 20N 94 7W
Rogers City, U.S.A. 76 C4 45 25N 83 49W
Rogerson, U.S.A. 82 E6 42 13N 114 36W
Rogersville, U.S.A. 77 G4 36 24N 83 1W
Roggan River, Canada 70 B4 54 25N 79 32W
Roggeveldberge, S. Africa 56 E3 32 10S 20 10 E
Rogoaguado, L., Bolivia 92 F5 13 0S 65 30W
Rogue —►, U.S.A. 82 E1 42 26N 124 26W
Róhda, Greece 23 A3 39 48N 19 46 E
Rohnert Park, U.S.A. 84 G4 38 16N 122 40W
Rohri, Pakistan 42 F3 27 45N 68 51 E
Rohri Canal, Pakistan 42 F3 26 15N 68 27 E
Rohtak, India 42 E7 28 55N 76 43 E
Roi Et, Thailand 38 D4 16 4N 103 40 E
Roja, Latvia 9 H20 57 29N 22 43 E
Rojas, Argentina 94 C3 34 10S 60 45W
Rojo, C., Mexico 87 C5 21 33N 97 20W
Rokan —►, Indonesia 36 D2 2 0N 100 50 E
Rokeby, Australia 62 A3 13 39S 142 40 E
Rokiškis, Lithuania 9 J21 55 55N 25 35 E
Rolândia, Brazil 95 A5 23 18S 51 23W
Rolette, U.S.A. 80 A5 48 40N 99 51W
Rolla, Kans., U.S.A. 81 G4 37 7N 101 38W
Rolla, Mo., U.S.A. 81 G9 37 57N 91 46W
Rolla, N. Dak., U.S.A. 80 A5 48 52N 99 37W
Rolleston, Australia 62 C4 24 28S 148 35 E
Rollingstone, Australia 62 B4 19 2S 146 24 E
Roma, Australia 63 D4 26 32S 148 49 E
Roma, Italy 20 D5 41 54N 12 29 E
Roma, Sweden 9 H18 57 32N 18 26 E
Roman, Romania 17 E14 46 57N 26 55 E
Roman, Russia 27 C12 60 4N 112 14 E
Romang, Indonesia 37 F7 7 30S 127 20 E
Români, Egypt 47 E1 30 59N 32 38 E
Romania ■, Europe 17 F12 46 0N 25 0 E
Romano, Cayo, Cuba 88 B4 22 0N 77 30W
Romanovka = Basarabeasca, Moldova 17 E15 46 21N 28 58 E
Romans-sur-Isère, France 18 D6 45 3N 5 3 E
Romblon, Phil. 37 B6 12 33N 122 17 E
Rombo □, Tanzania 54 C4 3 10S 37 30 E
Rome = Roma, Italy 20 D5 41 54N 12 29 E
Rome, Ga., U.S.A. 77 H3 34 15N 85 10W
Rome, N.Y., U.S.A. 79 C9 43 13N 75 27W
Romney, U.S.A. 76 F6 39 21N 78 45W
Romney Marsh, U.K. 11 F8 51 2N 0 54 E
Rømø, Denmark 9 J13 55 10N 8 30 E
Romorantin-Lanthenay, France 18 C4 47 21N 1 45 E
Romsdalen, Norway 9 E12 62 25N 7 52 E
Ron, Vietnam 38 D6 17 53N 106 27 E
Rona, U.K. 12 D3 57 34N 5 59W
Ronan, U.S.A. 82 C6 47 32N 114 6W
Roncador, Cayos, Caribbean 88 D3 13 32N 80 4W
Roncador, Serra do, Brazil 93 F8 12 30S 52 30W
Ronceverte, U.S.A. 76 G5 37 45N 80 28W
Ronda, Spain 19 D3 36 46N 5 12W
Rondane, Norway 9 F13 61 57N 9 50 E
Rondônia □, Brazil 92 F6 11 0S 63 0W
Rondonópolis, Brazil 93 G8 16 28S 54 38W
Ronge, L. la, Canada 73 B7 55 6N 105 17W
Rønne, Denmark 9 J16 55 6N 14 43 E
Ronne Ice Shelf, Antarctica 5 D18 78 0S 60 0W
Ronsard, C., Australia 61 D1 24 46S 113 10 E
Ronse, Belgium 15 D3 50 45N 3 35 E
Roodepoort, S. Africa 57 D4 26 11S 27 54 E
Roof Butte, U.S.A. 83 H9 36 28N 109 5W
Roorkee, India 42 E7 29 52N 77 59 E
Roosendaal, Neths. 15 C4 51 32N 4 29 E
Roosevelt, Minn., U.S.A. 80 A7 48 48N 95 6W
Roosevelt, Utah, U.S.A. 82 F8 40 18N 109 59W
Roosevelt —►, Brazil 92 E6 7 35S 60 20W
Roosevelt, Mt., Canada 72 B3 58 26N 125 20W
Roosevelt I., Antarctica 5 D12 79 30S 162 0W
Roosevelt Res., U.S.A. 83 K8 33 46N 111 0W
Roper —►, Australia 62 A2 14 43S 135 27 E
Ropesville, U.S.A. 81 J3 33 26N 102 9W
Roque Pérez, Argentina 94 D4 35 25S 59 24W
Roquetas de Mar, Spain 19 D4 36 46N 2 36W
Roraima □, Brazil 92 C6 2 0N 61 30W
Roraima, Mt., Venezuela 92 B6 5 10N 60 40W
Rorketon, Canada 73 C9 51 24N 99 35W
Røros, Norway 9 E14 62 35N 11 23 E
Rosa, Zambia 55 D3 9 33S 31 15 E
Rosa, Monte, Europe 16 F4 45 57N 7 53 E
Rosalia, U.S.A. 82 C5 47 14N 117 22W
Rosamond, U.S.A. 85 L8 34 52N 118 10W
Rosario, Argentina 94 C3 33 0S 60 40W
Rosário, Brazil 93 D10 3 0S 44 15W
Rosario, Baja Calif., Mexico 86 A1 30 0N 115 50W
Rosario, Sinaloa, Mexico 86 C3 23 0N 105 52W
Rosario, Paraguay 94 A4 24 30S 57 35W
Rosario de la Frontera, Argentina 94 B3 25 50S 65 0W
Rosario de Lerma, Argentina 94 A2 24 59S 65 35W
Rosario del Tala, Argentina 94 C4 32 20S 59 10W
Rosário do Sul, Brazil 95 C5 30 15S 54 55W
Rosarito, Mexico 85 N9 32 18N 117 4W
Rosas, G. de, Spain 19 A7 42 10N 3 15 E
Roscoe, U.S.A. 80 C5 45 27N 99 20W
Roscommon, Ireland 13 C3 53 38N 8 11W
Roscommon, U.S.A. 76 C3 44 30N 84 35W
Roscommon □, Ireland 13 C3 53 49N 8 23W
Roscrea, Ireland 13 D4 52 57N 7 49W
Rose —►, Australia 62 A2 14 16S 135 45 E
Rose Blanche, Canada 71 C8 47 38N 58 45W
Rose Harbour, Canada 72 C2 52 15N 131 10W
Rose Pt., Canada 72 C2 54 11N 131 39W
Rose Valley, Canada 73 C8 52 19N 103 49W
Roseau, Domin. 89 C7 15 20N 61 24W
Roseau, U.S.A. 80 A7 48 51N 95 46W
Rosebery, Australia 62 G4 41 46S 145 33 E
Rosebud, U.S.A. 81 K6 31 4N 96 59W
Roseburg, U.S.A. 82 E2 43 13N 123 20W
Rosedale, Australia 62 C5 24 38S 151 53 E
Rosedale, U.S.A. 81 J9 33 51N 91 2W
Roseland, U.S.A. 84 G4 38 25N 122 43W
Rosemary, Canada 72 C6 50 46N 112 5W
Rosenberg, U.S.A. 81 L7 29 34N 95 49W
Rosenheim, Germany 16 E7 47 51N 12 7 E
Rosetown, Canada 73 C7 51 35N 107 59W
Rosetta = Rashîd, Egypt 51 B11 31 21N 30 22 E
Roseville, U.S.A. 84 G5 38 45N 121 17W
Rosewood, N. Terr., Australia 60 C4 16 28S 128 58 E
Rosewood, Queens., Australia 63 D5 27 38S 152 36 E
Roshkhvär, Iran 45 C8 34 58N 59 37 E
Rosignano Marittimo, Italy 20 C4 43 24N 10 28 E
Rosignol, Guyana 92 B7 6 15N 57 30W
Roşiori-de-Vede, Romania 17 F13 44 7N 24 59 E
Roskilde, Denmark 9 J15 55 38N 12 3 E
Roslavl, Russia 24 D5 53 57N 32 55 E
Roslyn, Australia 63 E4 34 29S 149 37 E
Rosmead, S. Africa 56 E4 31 29S 25 8 E
Ross, Australia 62 G4 42 2S 147 30 E
Ross, N.Z. 59 K3 42 53S 170 49 E
Ross I., Antarctica 5 D11 77 30S 168 0 E
Ross Ice Shelf, Antarctica 5 E12 80 0S 180 0 E
Ross L., U.S.A. 82 B3 48 44N 121 4W
Ross-on-Wye, U.K. 11 F5 51 54N 2 34W
Ross Sea, Antarctica 5 D11 74 0S 178 0 E
Rossan Pt., Ireland 13 B3 54 42N 8 47W
Rossano Cálabro, Italy 20 E7 39 36N 16 39 E
Rossburn, Canada 73 C8 50 40N 100 49W
Rosseau, Canada 78 A5 45 16N 79 39W
Rossignol, L., Canada 70 B5 52 43N 73 40W
Rossignol Res., Canada 71 D6 44 12N 65 10W
Rossland, Canada 72 D5 49 6N 117 50W
Rosslare, Ireland 13 D5 52 17N 6 24W
Rosso, Mauritania 50 E1 16 40N 15 45W
Rossosh, Russia 25 D6 50 15N 39 28 E
Rossport, Canada 70 C2 48 50N 87 30W
Røssvatnet, Norway 8 D16 65 45N 14 5 E
Rossville, Australia 62 B4 15 48S 145 15 E
Røst, Norway 8 C15 67 32N 12 0 E
Rosthern, Canada 73 C7 52 40N 106 20W
Rostock, Germany 16 A7 54 5N 12 8 E
Rostov, Don, Russia 25 E6 47 15N 39 45 E
Rostov, Yarosl., Russia 24 C6 57 14N 39 25 E
Roswell, Ga., U.S.A. 77 H3 34 2N 84 22W
Roswell, N. Mex., U.S.A. 81 J2 33 24N 104 32W
Rosyth, U.K. 12 E5 56 2N 3 25W
Rotan, U.S.A. 81 J4 32 51N 100 28W
Rother —►, U.K. 11 G8 50 59N 0 45 E
Rotherham, U.K. 10 D6 53 26N 1 20W
Rothes, U.K. 12 D5 57 32N 3 13W
Rothesay, Canada 71 C6 45 23N 66 0W
Rothesay, U.K. 12 F3 55 50N 5 3W
Roti, Indonesia 37 F6 10 50S 123 0 E
Roto, Australia 63 E4 33 0S 145 30 E
Rotondo Mte., France 18 E8 42 14N 9 8 E
Rotoroa, L., N.Z. 59 J4 41 55S 172 39 E
Rotorua, N.Z. 59 H6 38 9S 176 16 E
Rotorua, L., N.Z. 59 H6 38 5S 176 18 E
Rotterdam, Neths. 15 C4 51 55N 4 30 E
Rottnest I., Australia 61 F2 32 0S 115 27 E
Rottumeroog, Neths. 15 A6 53 33N 6 34 E
Rottweil, Germany 16 D5 48 9N 8 37 E
Rotuma, Fiji 64 J9 12 25S 177 5 E
Roubaix, France 18 A5 50 40N 3 10 E
Rouen, France 18 B4 49 27N 1 4 E
Rouleau, Canada 73 C8 50 10N 104 56W
Round Mountain, U.S.A. 82 G5 38 43N 117 4W
Round Mt., Australia 63 E5 30 26S 152 16 E
Roundup, U.S.A. 82 C9 46 27N 108 33W
Rousay, U.K. 12 B5 59 10N 3 2W
Rouses Point, U.S.A. 79 B11 44 59N 73 22W
Roussillon, France 18 E5 42 30N 2 35 E
Rouxville, S. Africa 56 E4 30 25S 26 50 E
Rouyn, Canada 70 C4 48 20N 79 0W
Rovaniemi, Finland 8 C21 66 29N 25 41 E
Rovereto, Italy 20 B4 45 53N 11 3 E
Rovigo, Italy 20 B4 45 4N 11 47 E
Rovinj, Croatia 16 F7 45 5N 13 40 E
Rovno = Rivne, Ukraine 17 C14 50 40N 26 10 E
Rovuma —►, Tanzania 55 E5 10 29S 40 28 E
Row'ān, Iran 45 C6 35 8N 48 51 E
Rowena, Australia 63 D4 29 48S 148 55 E
Rowley Shoals, Australia 60 C2 17 30S 119 0 E
Roxas, Phil. 37 B6 11 36N 122 49 E
Roxboro, U.S.A. 77 G6 36 24N 78 59W
Roxborough Downs, Australia 62 C2 22 30S 138 45 E
Roxburgh, N.Z. 59 L2 45 33S 169 19 E
Roy, Mont., U.S.A. 82 C9 47 20N 108 58W
Roy, N. Mex., U.S.A. 81 H2 35 57N 104 12W
Roy Hill, Australia 60 D2 22 37S 119 58 E
Royal Leamington Spa, U.K. 11 E6 52 18N 1 31W
Royal Tunbridge Wells, U.K. 11 F8 51 7N 0 16 E
Royan, France 18 D3 45 37N 1 2W
Rozdilna, Ukraine 17 E16 46 50N 30 2 E
Rozhyshche, Ukraine 17 C13 50 54N 25 15 E
Rtishchevo, Russia 24 C7 52 18N 43 46 E
Ruacaná, Angola 56 B1 17 20S 14 12 E
Ruahine Ra., N.Z. 59 H6 39 55S 176 2 E
Ruapehu, N.Z. 59 H5 39 17S 175 35 E
Ruapuke I., N.Z. 59 M2 46 46S 168 31 E
Ruâq, W. —►, Egypt 47 F2 30 0N 33 49 E
Rub' al Khali, Si. Arabia 46 D4 18 0N 48 0 E
Rubeho Mts., Tanzania 54 D4 6 50S 36 25 E
Rubh a' Mhail, U.K. 12 F2 55 56N 6 8W
Rubha Hunish, U.K. 12 D2 57 42N 6 20W
Rubha Robhanais = Lewis, Butt of, U.K. 12 C2 58 31N 6 16W
Rubicon —►, U.S.A. 84 G5 38 53N 121 4W
Rubio, Venezuela 92 B4 7 43N 72 22W
Rubtsovsk, Russia 26 D9 51 30N 81 10 E
Ruby L., U.S.A. 82 F6 40 10N 115 28W
Ruby Mts., U.S.A. 82 F6 40 30N 115 20W
Rūd Sar, Iran 45 B6 37 8N 50 18 E
Rudall, Australia 63 E2 33 43S 136 17 E
Rudall —►, Australia 60 D3 22 34S 122 13 E
Rudewa, Tanzania 55 E3 10 7S 34 40 E
Rudnichnyy, Russia 24 C9 59 38N 52 26 E
Rudnogorsk, Russia 27 D11 57 15N 103 42 E
Rudnyy, Kazakstan 26 D7 52 57N 63 7 E
Rudolf, Ostrov, Russia 26 A6 81 45N 58 30 E
Rudyard, U.S.A. 76 B3 46 14N 84 36W
Rufa'a, Sudan 51 F11 14 44N 33 22 E
Rufiji □, Tanzania 54 D4 8 0S 38 30 E
Rufiji —►, Tanzania 54 D4 7 50S 39 15 E
Rufino, Argentina 94 C3 34 20S 62 50W
Rufisque, Senegal 50 F1 14 40N 17 15W
Rufunsa, Zambia 55 F2 15 4S 29 34 E
Rugby, U.K. 11 E6 52 23N 1 16W
Rugby, U.S.A. 80 A5 48 22N 100 0W
Rügen, Germany 16 A7 54 22N 13 24 E
Ruhengeri, Rwanda 54 C2 1 30S 29 36 E
Ruhnu saar, Estonia 9 H20 57 48N 23 15 E
Ruhr —►, Germany 16 C4 51 27N 6 43 E
Ruhuhu —►, Tanzania 55 E3 10 31S 34 34 E
Ruidosa, U.S.A. 81 L2 29 59N 104 41W
Ruidoso, U.S.A. 83 K11 33 20N 105 41W
Ruivo, Pico, Madeira 22 D3 32 45N 16 56W
Rujm Tal'at al Jamā'ah, Jordan 47 E4 30 24N 35 30 E
Ruk, Pakistan 42 F3 27 50N 68 42 E
Rukwa □, Tanzania 54 D3 7 0S 31 30 E
Rukwa L., Tanzania 54 D3 8 0S 32 20 E
Rulhieres, C., Australia 60 B4 13 56S 127 22 E
Rum = Rhum, U.K. 12 E2 57 0N 6 20W
Rum Cay, Bahamas 89 B5 23 40N 74 58W
Rum Jungle, Australia 60 B5 13 0S 130 59 E
Rumāḥ, Si. Arabia 44 E5 25 29N 47 10 E
Rumania = Romania ■, Europe 17 F12 46 0N 25 0 E
Rumaylah, Iraq 44 D5 30 47N 47 37 E
Rumbalara, Australia 62 D1 25 20S 134 29 E
Rumbêk, Sudan 51 G10 6 54N 29 37 E
Rumford, U.S.A. 79 B14 44 33N 70 33W
Rumia, Poland 17 A10 54 37N 18 25 E
Rumoi, Japan 30 C10 43 56N 141 39 E
Rumonge, Burundi 54 C2 3 59S 29 26 E
Rumsey, Canada 72 C6 51 51N 112 48W
Rumula, Australia 62 B4 16 35S 145 20 E
Rumuruti, Kenya 54 B4 0 17N 36 32 E
Runan, China 34 H8 33 0N 114 30 E
Runanga, N.Z. 59 K3 42 25S 171 15 E
Runaway, C., N.Z. 59 G6 37 32S 177 59 E
Runcorn, U.K. 10 D5 53 21N 2 44W
Rungwa, Tanzania 54 D3 6 55S 33 32 E
Rungwa —►, Tanzania 54 D3 7 36S 31 50 E
Rungwe, Tanzania 55 D3 9 11S 33 32 E
Rungwe □, Tanzania 55 D3 9 25S 33 32 E
Runton Ra., Australia 60 D3 23 31S 123 6 E
Ruoqiang, China 32 C3 38 55N 88 10 E
Rupa, India 41 F18 27 15N 92 21 E
Rupar, India 42 D7 31 2N 76 38 E
Rupat, Indonesia 36 D2 1 45N 101 40 E
Rupert —►, Canada 70 B4 51 29N 78 45W
Rupert House = Waskaganish, Canada 70 B4 51 30N 78 40W
Rurrenabaque, Bolivia 92 F5 14 30S 67 32W
Rusambo, Zimbabwe 55 F3 16 30S 32 4 E
Rusape, Zimbabwe 55 F3 18 35S 32 8 E
Ruschuk = Ruse, Bulgaria 21 C12 43 48N 25 59 E
Ruse, Bulgaria 21 C12 43 48N 25 59 E
Rushan, China 35 F11 36 56N 121 30 E
Rushden, U.K. 11 E7 52 18N 0 35W
Rushford, U.S.A. 80 D9 43 49N 91 46W
Rushville, Ill., U.S.A. 80 E9 40 7N 90 34W
Rushville, Ind., U.S.A. 76 F3 39 37N 85 27W
Rushville, Nebr., U.S.A. 80 D3 42 43N 102 28W
Rushworth, Australia 63 F4 36 32S 145 1 E
Russas, Brazil 93 D11 4 55S 37 50W
Russell, Canada 73 C8 50 50N 101 20W
Russell, U.S.A. 80 F5 38 54N 98 52W
Russell L., Man., Canada 73 B8 56 15N 101 30W
Russell L., N.W.T., Canada 72 A5 63 5N 115 44W
Russellkonda, India 41 K14 19 57N 84 42 E
Russellville, Ala., U.S.A. 77 H2 34 30N 87 44W
Russellville, Ark., U.S.A. 81 H8 35 17N 93 8W
Russellville, Ky., U.S.A. 77 G2 36 51N 86 53W
Russia ■, Eurasia 27 C11 62 0N 105 0 E
Russian —►, U.S.A. 84 G3 38 27N 123 8W
Russkaya Polyana, Kazakstan 26 D8 53 47N 73 53 E
Russkoye Ustie, Russia 4 B15 71 0N 149 0 E
Rustam, Pakistan 42 B5 34 25N 72 13 E
Rustam Shahr, Pakistan 42 F2 26 58N 66 6 E
Rustavi, Georgia 25 F8 41 30N 45 0 E
Rustenburg, S. Africa 56 D4 25 41S 27 14 E
Ruston, U.S.A. 81 J8 32 32N 92 38W
Rutana, Burundi 54 C2 3 55S 30 0 E
Ruteng, Indonesia 37 F6 8 35S 120 30 E
Ruth, Mich., U.S.A. 78 C2 43 42N 82 45W
Ruth, Nev., U.S.A. 82 G6 39 17N 114 59W
Rutherford, U.S.A. 84 G4 38 26N 122 24W
Rutherglen, U.K. 12 F4 55 49N 4 13W
Rutland Plains, Australia 62 B3 15 38S 141 43 E
Rutledge —►, Canada 73 A6 61 4N 112 0W
Rutledge L., Canada 73 A6 61 33N 110 47W
Rutshuru, Zaïre 54 C2 1 13S 29 25 E
Ruurlo, Neths. 15 B6 52 5N 6 24 E
Ruvu, Tanzania 54 D4 6 49S 38 43 E
Ruvu —►, Tanzania 54 D4 6 23S 38 52 E
Ruvuma □, Tanzania 55 E4 10 20S 36 0 E
Ruwais, U.A.E. 45 E7 24 5N 52 50 E
Ruwenzori, Africa 54 B2 0 30N 29 55 E
Ruyigi, Burundi 54 C3 3 29S 30 15 E
Ružomberok, Slovak Rep. 17 D10 49 3N 19 17 E
Rwanda ■, Africa 54 C3 2 0S 30 0 E
Ryan, L., U.K. 12 G3 55 0N 5 2W
Ryazan, Russia 24 D6 54 40N 39 40 E
Ryazhsk, Russia 24 D7 53 45N 40 3 E
Rybache = Rybachye, Kazakstan 26 E9 46 40N 81 20 E
Rybachiy Poluostrov, Russia 24 A5 69 43N 32 0 E
Rybachye = Ysyk-Köl, Kyrgyzstan 28 E11 42 26N 76 12 E
Rybachye, Kazakstan 26 E9 46 40N 81 20 E
Rybinsk, Russia 24 C6 58 5N 38 50 E
Rybinskoye Vdkhr., Russia 24 C6 58 30N 38 25 E
Rybnitsa = Rîbniţa, Moldova 17 E15 47 45N 29 0 E
Ryde, U.K. 11 G6 50 43N 1 9W
Ryderwood, U.S.A. 84 D3 46 23N 123 3W
Rye, U.K. 11 G8 50 57N 0 45 E
Rye —►, U.K. 10 C7 54 11N 0 44W
Rye Patch Reservoir, U.S.A. 82 F4 40 28N 118 19W
Ryegate, U.S.A. 82 C9 46 18N 109 15W
Rylstone, Australia 63 E4 32 46S 149 58 E
Ryōtsu, Japan 30 E9 38 5N 138 26 E
Rypin, Poland 17 B10 53 3N 19 25 E
Ryūgasaki, Japan 31 G10 35 54N 140 11 E
Ryūkyū Is. = Ryūkyū-rettō, Japan 31 M2 26 0N 126 0 E
Ryūkyū-rettō, Japan 31 M2 26 0N 126 0 E
Rzeszów, Poland 17 C11 50 5N 21 58 E
Rzhev, Russia 24 C5 56 20N 34 20 E

S

Sa, Thailand 38 C3 18 34N 100 45 E
Sa Dec, Vietnam 39 G5 10 20N 105 46 E
Sa'ādatābād, Fārs, Iran 45 D7 30 10N 53 5 E
Sa'ādatābād, Kermān, Iran 45 D7 28 3N 55 53 E
Saale —►, Germany 16 C6 51 56N 11 54 E
Saalfeld, Germany 16 C6 50 38N 11 21 E
Saar —►, Europe 16 D4 49 41N 6 32 E

Shanchengzhen

Savanur, India 40 M9 14 59N 75 21 E
Savé, Benin 50 G5 8 2N 2 29 E
Save →, Mozam. 57 C5 21 16S 34 0 E
Sāveh, Iran 45 C6 35 2N 50 20 E
Savelugu, Ghana 50 G4 9 38N 0 54W
Savo, Finland 8 E22 62 45N 27 30 E
Savoie □, France 18 D7 45 26N 6 25 E
Savona, Italy 20 B3 44 17N 8 30 E
Savonlinna, Finland 24 B4 61 52N 28 53 E
Sawahlunto, Indonesia 36 E2 0 40S 100 52 E
Sawai, Indonesia 37 E7 3 0S 129 5 E
Sawai Madhopur, India 42 F7 26 0N 76 25 E
Sawang Daen Din, Thailand 38 D4 17 28N 103 28 E
Sawankhalok, Thailand 38 D2 17 19N 99 50 E
Sawara, Japan 31 G10 35 55N 140 30 E
Sawatch Mts., U.S.A. 83 G10 38 30N 106 30W
Sawel Mt., U.K. 13 B4 54 50N 7 2W
Sawi, Thailand 39 G2 10 14N 99 5 E
Sawmills, Zimbabwe 55 F2 19 30S 28 2 E
Sawu, Indonesia 37 F6 9 35S 121 50 E
Sawu Sea, Indonesia 37 F6 9 30S 121 50 E
Saxby →, Australia 62 B3 18 25S 140 53 E
Saxony, Lower = Niedersachsen □, Germany 16 B5 53 8N 9 0 E
Saxton, U.S.A. 78 F6 40 13N 78 15W
Say, Niger 50 F5 13 8N 2 22 E
Sayabec, Canada 71 C6 48 35N 67 41W
Sayaboury, Laos 38 C3 19 15N 101 45 E
Sayán, Peru 92 F3 11 8S 77 12W
Sayan, Vostochnyy, Russia 27 D10 54 0N 96 0 E
Sayan, Zapadnyy, Russia 27 D10 52 30N 94 0 E
Saydā, Lebanon 47 B4 33 35N 35 25 E
Sayhan-Ovoo, Mongolia 34 B2 45 27N 103 54 E
Sayhandulaan, Mongolia 34 B5 44 40N 109 1 E
Sayḥut, Yemen 46 D5 15 12N 51 10 E
Saynshand, Mongolia 34 B6 44 55N 110 11 E
Sayre, Okla., U.S.A. 81 H5 35 18N 99 38W
Sayre, Pa., U.S.A. 79 E8 41 59N 76 32W
Sayula, Mexico 86 D4 19 50N 103 40W
Sazanit, Albania 21 D8 40 30N 19 20 E
Sázava →, Czech. 16 D8 49 53N 14 24 E
Sazin, Pakistan 43 B5 35 35N 73 30 E
Scafell Pike, U.K. 10 C4 54 27N 3 14W
Scalpay, U.K. 12 D2 57 52N 6 40W
Scandia, Canada 72 C6 50 20N 112 0W
Scandicci, Italy 20 C4 43 45N 11 11 E
Scandinavia, Europe 6 C8 64 0N 12 0 E
Scapa Flow, U.K. 12 C5 58 53N 3 3W
Scappoose, U.S.A. 84 E4 45 45N 122 53W
Scarborough, Trin. & Tob. 89 D7 11 11N 60 42W
Scarborough, U.K. 10 C7 54 17N 0 24W
Scebeli, Wabi →, Somali Rep. 46 G3 2 0N 44 0 E
Scenic, U.S.A. 80 D3 43 47N 102 33W
Schaffhausen, Switz. 16 E5 47 42N 8 39 E
Schagen, Neths. 15 B4 52 49N 4 48 E
Schefferville, Canada 71 B6 54 48N 66 50W
Schelde →, Belgium 15 C4 51 15N 4 16 E
Schell Creek Ra., U.S.A. 82 G6 39 15N 114 30W
Schenectady, U.S.A. 79 D11 42 49N 73 57W
Scheveningen, Neths. 15 B4 52 6N 4 16 E
Schiedam, Neths. 15 C4 51 55N 4 25 E
Schiermonnikoog, Neths. 15 A6 53 30N 6 15 E
Schio, Italy 20 B4 45 43N 11 21 E
Schleswig, Germany 16 A5 54 31N 9 34 E
Schleswig-Holstein □, Germany 16 A5 54 30N 9 30 E
Schofield, U.S.A. 80 C10 44 54N 89 36W
Scholls, U.S.A. 84 E4 45 24N 122 56W
Schouten I., Australia 62 G4 42 20S 148 20 E
Schouten Is. = Supiori, Indonesia 37 E9 1 0S 136 0 E
Schouwen, Neths. 15 C3 51 43N 3 45 E
Schreiber, Canada 70 C2 48 45N 87 20W
Schuler, Canada 73 C6 50 20N 110 6W
Schumacher, Canada 70 C3 48 30N 81 16W
Schurz, U.S.A. 82 G4 38 57N 118 49W
Schuyler, U.S.A. 80 E6 41 27N 97 4W
Schuylkill Haven, U.S.A. 79 F8 40 37N 76 11W
Schwäbische Alb, Germany 16 D5 48 20N 9 30 E
Schwaner, Pegunungan, Indonesia 36 E4 1 0S 112 30 E
Schwarzwald, Germany 16 D5 48 30N 8 20 E
Schwedt, Germany 16 B8 53 3N 14 16 E
Schweinfurt, Germany 16 C6 50 3N 10 14 E
Schweizer-Reneke, S. Africa 56 D4 27 11S 25 18 E
Schwenningen = Villingen-Schwenningen, Germany 16 D5 48 3N 8 26 E
Schwerin, Germany 16 B6 53 36N 11 22 E
Schwyz, Switz. 16 E5 47 2N 8 39 E
Sciacca, Italy 20 F5 37 31N 13 3 E
Scilla, Italy 20 E6 38 15N 15 43 E
Scilly, Isles of, U.K. 11 H1 49 56N 6 22W
Scioto →, U.S.A. 76 F4 38 44N 83 1W
Scobey, U.S.A. 80 A2 48 47N 105 25W
Scone, Australia 63 E5 32 5S 150 52 E
Scoresbysund, Greenland 4 B6 70 20N 23 0W
Scotia, Calif., U.S.A. 82 F1 40 29N 124 6W
Scotia, N.Y., U.S.A. 79 D11 42 50N 73 58W
Scotia Sea, Antarctica 5 B18 56 5S 56 0W
Scotland, U.S.A. 80 D6 43 9N 97 43W
Scotland □, U.K. 12 E5 57 0N 4 0W
Scotland Neck, U.S.A. 77 G7 36 8N 77 25W
Scott, C., Australia 60 B4 13 30S 129 49 E
Scott City, U.S.A. 80 F4 38 29N 100 54W
Scott Glacier, Antarctica 5 C8 66 15S 100 5 E
Scott I., Antarctica 5 C11 67 0S 179 0 E
Scott Inlet, Canada 69 A12 71 0N 71 0W
Scott Is., Canada 72 C3 50 48N 128 40W
Scott L., Canada 73 B7 59 55N 106 18W
Scott Reef, Australia 60 B3 14 0S 121 50 E
Scottburgh, S. Africa 57 E5 30 15S 30 47 E
Scottdale, U.S.A. 78 F5 40 6N 79 35W
Scottsbluff, U.S.A. 80 E3 41 52N 103 40W
Scottsboro, U.S.A. 77 H2 34 40N 86 2W
Scottsburg, U.S.A. 76 F3 38 41N 85 47W
Scottsdale, Australia 62 G4 41 9S 147 31 E
Scottsdale, U.S.A. 83 K7 33 29N 111 56W
Scottsville, Ky., U.S.A. 77 G2 36 45N 86 11W
Scottsville, N.Y., U.S.A. 78 C7 43 2N 77 47W
Scottville, U.S.A. 76 D2 43 58N 86 17W
Scranton, U.S.A. 79 E9 41 25N 75 40W
Scugog, L., Canada 78 B6 44 10N 78 55W
Scunthorpe, U.K. 10 D7 53 36N 0 39W
Scusciuban, Somali Rep. 46 E5 10 18N 50 12 E
Scutari = Üsküdar, Turkey 25 F4 41 0N 29 5 E
Seabrook, L., Australia 61 F2 30 55S 119 40 E
Seaford, U.S.A. 76 F8 38 39N 75 37W
Seaforth, Canada 70 D3 43 35N 81 25W
Seagraves, U.S.A. 81 J3 32 57N 102 34W
Seal →, Canada 73 B10 59 4N 94 48W
Seal Cove, Canada 71 C8 49 57N 56 22W
Seal L., Canada 71 B7 54 20N 61 30W
Sealy, U.S.A. 81 L6 29 47N 96 9W
Searchlight, U.S.A. 85 K12 35 28N 114 55W
Searcy, U.S.A. 81 H9 35 15N 91 44W
Searles L., U.S.A. 85 K9 35 44N 117 21W
Seaside, Calif., U.S.A. 84 J5 36 37N 121 50W
Seaside, Oreg., U.S.A. 84 E3 46 0N 123 56W
Seaspray, Australia 63 F4 38 25S 147 15 E
Seattle, U.S.A. 84 C4 47 36N 122 20W
Seaview Ra., Australia 62 B4 18 40S 145 45 E
Sebastián Vizcaino, B., Mexico 86 B2 28 0N 114 30W
Sebastopol = Sevastopol, Ukraine 25 F5 44 35N 33 30 E
Sebastopol, U.S.A. 84 G4 38 24N 122 49W
Sebewaing, U.S.A. 76 D4 43 44N 83 27W
Sebha = Sabhah, Libya 51 C7 27 9N 14 29 E
Sebring, Fla., U.S.A. 77 M5 27 30N 81 27W
Sebring, Ohio, U.S.A. 78 F3 40 55N 81 2W
Sebringville, Canada 78 C3 43 24N 81 4W
Sebta = Ceuta, N. Afr. 19 E3 35 52N 5 18W
Sebuku, Indonesia 36 E5 3 30S 116 25 E
Sebuku, Teluk, Malaysia 36 D5 4 0N 118 10 E
Sechelt, Canada 72 D4 49 25N 123 42W
Sechura, Desierto de, Peru 92 E2 6 0S 80 30W
Secretary I., N.Z. 59 L1 45 15S 166 56 E
Secunderabad, India 40 L11 17 28N 78 30 E
Sedalia, U.S.A. 80 F8 38 42N 93 14W
Sedan, Australia 63 E2 34 34S 139 19 E
Sedan, France 18 B6 49 43N 4 57 E
Sedan, U.S.A. 81 G6 37 8N 96 11W
Seddon, N.Z. 59 J5 41 40S 174 7 E
Seddonville, N.Z. 59 J4 41 33S 172 1 E
Sedeh, Fārs, Iran 45 D7 30 45N 52 11 E
Sedeh, Khorāsān, Iran 45 C8 33 20N 59 14 E
Sederot, Israel 47 D3 31 32N 34 37 E
Sedgewick, Canada 72 C6 52 48N 111 41W
Sedhiou, Senegal 50 F1 12 44N 15 30W
Sedley, Canada 73 C8 50 10N 104 0W
Sedova, Pik, Russia 26 B6 73 29N 54 58 E
Sedro Woolley, U.S.A. 84 B4 48 30N 122 14W
Seeheim, Namibia 56 D2 26 50S 17 45 E
Seekoei →, S. Africa 56 E4 30 18S 25 1 E
Seferihisar, Turkey 21 E12 38 10N 26 50 E
Seg-ozero, Russia 24 B5 63 20N 33 46 E
Segamat, Malaysia 39 L4 2 30N 102 50 E
Segesta, Italy 20 F5 37 56N 12 50 E
Seget, Indonesia 37 E8 1 24S 130 58 E
Segezha, Russia 24 B5 63 44N 34 19 E
Ségou, Mali 50 F3 13 30N 6 16W
Segovia = Coco →, Cent. Amer. 88 D3 15 0N 83 8W
Segovia, Spain 19 B3 40 57N 4 10W
Segre →, Spain 19 B6 41 40N 0 43 E
Séguéla, Ivory C. 50 G3 7 55N 6 40W
Seguin, U.S.A. 81 L6 29 34N 97 58W
Segundo →, Argentina 94 C3 30 53S 62 44W
Segura →, Spain 19 C5 38 3N 0 44W
Seh Qal'eh, Iran 45 C8 33 40N 58 24 E
Sehitwa, Botswana 56 C3 20 30S 22 30 E
Sehore, India 42 H7 23 10N 77 5 E
Sehwan, Pakistan 42 F2 26 28N 67 53 E
Seiland, Norway 8 A20 70 25N 23 15 E
Seiling, U.S.A. 81 G5 36 9N 98 56W
Seinäjoki, Finland 9 E20 62 40N 22 51 E
Seine →, France 18 B4 49 26N 0 26 E
Seistan, Iran 45 D9 30 50N 61 0 E
Sekayu, Indonesia 36 E2 2 51S 103 51 E
Seke, Tanzania 54 C3 3 20S 33 31 E
Sekenke, Tanzania 54 C3 4 18S 34 11 E
Sekondi-Takoradi, Ghana 50 H4 4 58N 1 45W
Sekuma, Botswana 56 C3 24 36S 23 50 E
Selah, U.S.A. 82 C3 46 39N 120 32W
Selama, Malaysia 39 K3 5 12N 100 42 E
Selaru, Indonesia 37 F8 8 9S 131 0 E
Selby, U.K. 10 D6 53 47N 1 5W
Selby, U.S.A. 80 C4 45 31N 100 2W
Selçuk, Turkey 21 F12 37 56N 27 22 E
Selden, U.S.A. 80 F4 39 33N 100 34W
Sele →, Italy 20 D6 40 29N 14 56 E
Selemdzha →, Russia 27 D13 51 42N 128 53 E
Selenga = Selenge Mörön →, Asia 32 A5 52 16N 106 16 E
Selenge Mörön →, Asia 32 A5 52 16N 106 16 E
Seletan, Tg., Indonesia 36 E4 4 10S 114 40 E
Selfridge, U.S.A. 80 B4 46 2N 100 56W
Sélibabi, Mauritania 50 E2 15 10N 12 15W
Seligman, U.S.A. 83 J7 35 20N 112 53W
Selîma, El Wâhât el, Sudan 51 D10 21 22N 29 19 E
Selinda Spillway, Botswana 56 B3 18 35S 23 10 E
Selkirk, Canada 73 C9 50 10N 96 55W
Selkirk, U.K. 12 F6 55 33N 2 50W
Selkirk I., Canada 73 C9 53 20N 99 6W
Selkirk Mts., Canada 72 C5 51 15N 117 40W
Selliá, Greece 23 D6 35 12N 24 23 E
Sells, U.S.A. 83 L8 31 55N 111 53W
Selma, Ala., U.S.A. 77 J2 32 25N 87 1W
Selma, Calif., U.S.A. 83 H4 36 34N 119 37W
Selma, N.C., U.S.A. 77 H6 35 32N 78 17W
Selmer, U.S.A. 77 H1 35 10N 88 36W
Selowandoma Falls, Zimbabwe 55 G3 21 15S 31 50 E
Selpele, Indonesia 37 E8 0 1S 130 5 E
Selsey Bill, U.K. 11 G7 50 43N 0 47W
Selu, Indonesia 37 F8 7 32S 130 55 E
Selva, Argentina 94 B3 29 50S 62 0W
Selvas, Brazil 92 E5 6 30S 67 0W
Selwyn, Australia 62 C3 21 32S 140 30 E
Selwyn L., Canada 73 A8 60 0N 104 30W
Selwyn Ra., Australia 62 C3 21 10S 140 0 E
Semani →, Albania 21 D8 40 47N 19 30 E
Semarang, Indonesia 37 G14 7 0S 110 26 E
Semau, Indonesia 37 F6 10 13S 123 22 E
Sembabule, Uganda 54 C3 0 4S 31 25 E
Semeru, Indonesia 37 H15 8 4S 112 55 E
Semey, Kazakstan 26 D9 50 30N 80 10 E
Seminoe Reservoir, U.S.A. 82 E10 42 9N 106 55W
Seminole, Okla., U.S.A. 81 H6 35 14N 96 41W
Seminole, Tex., U.S.A. 81 J3 32 43N 102 39W
Semiozernoye, Kazakstan 26 D7 52 22N 64 8 E
Semipalatinsk = Semey, Kazakstan 26 D9 50 30N 80 10 E
Semirara Is., Phil. 37 B6 12 0N 121 20 E
Semisopochnoi I., U.S.A. 68 C2 51 55N 179 36 E
Semitau, Indonesia 36 D4 0 29N 111 57 E
Semiyarka, Kazakstan 26 D8 50 55N 78 23 E
Semiyarskoye = Semiyarka, Kazakstan 26 D8 50 55N 78 23 E
Semmering P., Austria 16 E8 47 41N 15 45 E
Semnān, Iran 45 C7 35 40N 53 23 E
Semnān □, Iran 45 C7 36 0N 54 0 E
Semois →, Europe 15 E4 49 53N 4 44 E
Semporna, Malaysia 37 D5 4 30N 118 33 E
Semuda, Indonesia 36 E4 2 51S 112 58 E
Senā, Iran 45 D6 28 27N 51 36 E
Sena, Mozam. 55 F3 17 25S 35 0 E
Sena Madureira, Brazil 92 E5 9 5S 68 45W
Senador Pompeu, Brazil 93 E11 5 40S 39 20W
Senaja, Malaysia 36 C5 6 45N 117 3 E
Senanga, Zambia 56 B3 16 2S 23 14 E
Senatobia, U.S.A. 81 H10 34 37N 89 58W
Sendai, Kagoshima, Japan 31 J5 31 50N 130 20 E
Sendai, Miyagi, Japan 30 E10 38 15N 140 53 E
Sendai-Wan, Japan 30 E10 38 15N 141 0 E
Seneca, Oreg., U.S.A. 82 D4 44 8N 118 58W
Seneca, S.C., U.S.A. 77 H4 34 41N 82 57W
Seneca Falls, U.S.A. 79 D8 42 55N 76 48W
Seneca L., U.S.A. 78 D8 42 40N 76 54W
Senegal ■, W. Afr. 50 F2 14 30N 14 30W
Senegal →, W. Afr. 50 E1 15 48N 16 32W
Senegambia, Africa 48 E2 12 45N 12 0W
Senekal, S. Africa 57 D4 28 20S 27 36 E
Senga Hill, Zambia 55 D3 9 19S 31 11 E
Senge Khambab = Indus →, Pakistan 42 G2 24 20N 67 47 E
Sengerema □, Tanzania 54 C3 2 10S 32 20 E
Sengkang, Indonesia 37 E6 4 8S 120 1 E
Sengua →, Zimbabwe 55 F2 17 7S 28 5 E
Senhor-do-Bonfim, Brazil 93 F10 10 30S 40 10W
Senigállia, Italy 20 C5 43 43N 13 13 E
Senj, Croatia 16 F8 45 0N 14 58 E
Senja, Norway 8 B17 69 25N 17 30 E
Senlis, France 18 B5 49 13N 2 35 E
Senmonorom, Cambodia 38 F6 12 27N 107 12 E
Sennâr, Sudan 51 F11 13 30N 33 35 E
Senneterre, Canada 70 C4 48 25N 77 15W
Seno, Laos 38 D5 16 35N 104 50 E
Sens, France 18 B5 48 11N 3 15 E
Senta, Serbia, Yug. 21 B9 45 55N 20 3 E
Sentani, Indonesia 37 E10 2 36S 140 37 E
Sentery, Zaïre 54 D2 5 17S 25 42 E
Sentinel, U.S.A. 83 K7 32 52N 113 13W
Sentolo, Indonesia 37 G14 7 55S 110 13 E
Seo de Urgel, Spain 19 A6 42 22N 1 23 E
Seohara, India 43 E8 29 15N 78 33 E
Seoni, India 43 H8 22 5N 79 30 E
Seoul = Sŏul, S. Korea 35 F14 37 31N 126 58 E
Separation Point, Canada 71 B8 53 37N 57 25W
Sepīdān, Iran 45 D7 30 20N 52 5 E
Sepo-ri, N. Korea 35 E14 38 57N 127 25 E
Sepone, Laos 38 D6 16 45N 106 13 E
Sept-Îles, Canada 71 B6 50 13N 66 22W
Sequim, U.S.A. 84 B3 48 5N 123 6W
Sequoia National Park, U.S.A. 83 H4 36 30N 118 30W
Seraing, Belgium 15 D5 50 35N 5 32 E
Seraja, Indonesia 39 L7 2 41N 108 35 E
Serakhis →, Cyprus 23 D11 35 13N 32 55 E
Seram, Indonesia 37 E7 3 10S 129 0 E
Seram Laut, Kepulauan, Indonesia 37 E8 4 5S 131 25 E
Seram Sea, Indonesia 37 E7 2 30S 128 30 E
Serang, Indonesia 37 G12 6 8S 106 10 E
Serasan, Indonesia 39 L7 2 29N 109 4 E
Serbia □, Yugoslavia 21 C9 43 30N 21 0 E
Serdobsk, Russia 24 D7 52 28N 44 10 E
Seremban, Malaysia 39 L3 2 43N 101 53 E
Serengeti □, Tanzania 54 C3 2 0S 34 30 E
Serengeti Plain, Tanzania 54 C3 2 40S 35 0 E
Serenje, Zambia 55 E3 13 14S 30 15 E
Sereth = Siret →, Romania 17 F14 45 24N 28 1 E
Sergipe □, Brazil 93 F11 10 30S 37 30W
Sergiyev Posad, Russia 24 C6 56 20N 38 10 E
Seria, Brunei 36 D4 4 37N 114 23 E
Serian, Malaysia 36 D4 1 10N 110 31 E
Seribu, Kepulauan, Indonesia 36 F3 5 36S 106 33 E
Sérifos, Greece 21 F11 37 9N 24 30 E
Seringapatam Reef, Australia 60 B3 13 38S 122 5 E
Sermata, Indonesia 37 F7 8 15S 128 50 E
Serny Zavod, Turkmenistan 26 F6 39 59N 58 50 E
Serov, Russia 24 C11 59 29N 60 35 E
Serowe, Botswana 56 C4 22 25S 26 43 E
Serpentine, Australia 61 F2 32 23S 115 58 E
Serpentine Lakes, Australia 61 E4 28 30S 129 10 E
Serpukhov, Russia 24 D6 54 55N 37 28 E
Sérrai, Greece 21 D10 41 5N 23 31 E
Serrezuela, Argentina 94 C2 30 40S 65 20W
Serrinha, Brazil 93 F11 11 39S 39 0W
Sertânia, Brazil 93 E11 8 5S 37 20W
Sertanópolis, Brazil 95 A5 23 4S 51 2W
Serua, Indonesia 37 F8 6 18S 130 1 E
Serui, Indonesia 37 E9 1 53S 136 10 E
Serule, Botswana 56 C4 21 57S 27 20 E
Sese Is., Uganda 54 C3 0 20S 32 20 E
Sesepe, Indonesia 37 E7 1 30S 127 59 E
Sesfontein, Namibia 56 B1 19 7S 13 39 E
Sesheke, Zambia 56 B3 17 29S 24 13 E
S'estañol, Spain 22 B9 39 22N 2 54 E
Setana, Japan 30 C9 42 26N 139 51 E
Sète, France 18 E5 43 25N 3 42 E
Sete Lagôas, Brazil 93 G10 19 27S 44 16W
Sétif, Algeria 50 A6 36 9N 5 26 E
Seto, Japan 31 G8 35 14N 137 6 E
Setonaikai, Japan 31 G6 34 20N 133 30 E
Settat, Morocco 50 B3 33 0N 7 40W
Setté-Cama, Gabon 52 E1 2 32S 9 45 E
Setting L., Canada 73 B9 55 0N 98 38W
Settle, U.K. 10 C5 54 5N 2 16W
Settlement Pt., Bahamas 77 M6 26 40N 79 0W
Setúbal, Portugal 19 C1 38 30N 8 58W
Setúbal, B. de, Portugal 19 C1 38 40N 8 56W
Seulimeum, Indonesia 36 C1 5 27N 95 15 E
Sevan, Ozero = Sevana Lich, Armenia 25 F8 40 30N 45 20 E
Sevana Lich, Armenia 25 F8 40 30N 45 20 E
Sevastopol, Ukraine 25 F5 44 35N 33 30 E
Seven Emu, Australia 62 B2 16 20S 137 8 E
Seven Sisters, Canada 72 C3 54 56N 128 10W
Severn →, Canada 70 A2 56 2N 87 36W
Severn →, U.K. 11 F5 51 35N 2 40W
Severn L., Canada 70 B1 53 54N 90 48W
Severnaya Zemlya, Russia 27 B10 79 0N 100 0 E
Severnyye Uvaly, Russia 24 C8 60 0N 50 0 E
Severo-Kurilsk, Russia 27 D16 50 40N 156 8 E
Severo-Yeniseyskiy, Russia 27 C10 60 22N 93 1 E
Severodvinsk, Russia 24 B6 64 27N 39 58 E
Severomorsk, Russia 24 A5 69 5N 33 27 E
Severouralsk, Russia 24 B10 60 9N 59 57 E
Sevier, U.S.A. 83 G7 38 39N 112 11W
Sevier →, U.S.A. 83 G7 39 4N 113 6W
Sevier L., U.S.A. 82 G7 38 54N 113 9W
Sevilla, Spain 19 D2 37 23N 6 0W
Seville = Sevilla, Spain 19 D2 37 23N 6 0W
Sevlievo, Bulgaria 21 C11 43 2N 25 3 E
Seward, Alaska, U.S.A. 68 B5 60 7N 149 27W
Seward, Nebr., U.S.A. 80 E6 40 55N 97 6W
Seward Pen., U.S.A. 68 B3 65 0N 164 0W
Sewell, Chile 94 C1 34 10S 70 23W
Sewer, Indonesia 37 F8 5 53S 134 40 E
Sewickley, U.S.A. 78 F4 40 32N 80 12W
Sexsmith, Canada 72 B5 55 21N 118 47W
Seychelles ■, Ind. Oc. 49 G9 5 0S 56 0 E
Seyðisfjörður, Iceland 8 D6 65 16N 13 57W
Seydvān, Iran 44 B5 38 34N 45 2 E
Seymchan, Russia 27 C16 62 54N 152 30 E
Seymour, Australia 63 F4 37 0S 145 10 E
Seymour, S. Africa 57 E4 32 33S 26 46 E
Seymour, Conn., U.S.A. 79 E11 41 24N 73 4W
Seymour, Ind., U.S.A. 76 F3 38 58N 85 53W
Seymour, Tex., U.S.A. 81 J5 33 35N 99 16W
Seymour, Wis., U.S.A. 76 C1 44 31N 88 20W
Sfax, Tunisia 51 B7 34 49N 10 48 E
Sfîntu Gheorghe, Romania 17 F13 45 52N 25 48 E
Shaanxi □, China 34 G5 35 0N 109 0 E
Shaba □, Zaïre 54 D2 8 0S 25 0 E
Shabunda, Zaïre 54 C2 2 40S 27 16 E
Shache, China 32 C2 38 20N 77 10 E
Shackleton Ice Shelf, Antarctica 5 C8 66 0S 100 0 E
Shackleton Inlet, Antarctica 5 E11 83 0S 160 0 E
Shādegān, Iran 45 D6 30 40N 48 38 E
Shadi, India 43 C7 33 24N 77 14 E
Shadrinsk, Russia 26 D7 56 5N 63 32 E
Shafter, Calif., U.S.A. 85 K7 35 30N 119 16W
Shafter, Tex., U.S.A. 81 L2 29 49N 104 18W
Shaftesbury, U.K. 11 F5 51 0N 2 11W
Shagram, Pakistan 43 A5 36 24N 72 20 E
Shah Bunder, Pakistan 42 G2 24 13N 67 56 E
Shahabad, Punjab, India 42 D7 30 10N 76 55 E
Shahabad, Raj., India 42 G7 25 15N 77 11 E
Shahabad, Ut. P., India 43 F8 27 36N 79 56 E
Shahadpur, Pakistan 42 G3 25 55N 68 35 E
Shahba, Syria 47 C5 32 52N 36 38 E
Shahdād, Iran 45 D8 30 30N 57 40 E
Shahdadkot, Pakistan 42 F2 27 50N 67 55 E
Shahe, China 34 F8 37 0N 114 32 E
Shahganj, India 43 F10 26 3N 82 44 E
Shahgarh, India 40 F6 27 15N 69 50 E
Shaḥḥāt, Libya 51 B9 32 48N 21 54 E
Shahjahanpur, India 43 F8 27 54N 79 57 E
Shahpur, India 42 H7 22 12N 77 58 E
Shahpur, Pakistan 42 E3 28 46N 68 27 E
Shahpura, India 43 H9 23 10N 80 45 E
Shahr Kord, Iran 45 C6 32 15N 50 55 E
Shāhrakht, Iran 45 C9 33 38N 60 16 E
Shahrig, Pakistan 42 D2 30 15N 67 40 E
Shahukou, China 34 D7 40 20N 112 18 E
Shaikhabad, Afghan. 42 B3 34 2N 68 45 E
Shajapur, India 42 H7 23 27N 76 21 E
Shakargarh, Pakistan 42 C6 32 17N 75 10 E
Shakawe, Botswana 56 B3 18 28S 21 49 E
Shaker Heights, U.S.A. 78 E3 41 29N 81 32W
Shakhty, Russia 25 E7 47 40N 40 16 E
Shakhunya, Russia 24 C8 57 40N 46 46 E
Shaki, Nigeria 50 G5 8 41N 3 21 E
Shala, L., Ethiopia 51 G12 7 30N 38 30 E
Shallow Lake, Canada 78 B3 44 36N 81 5W
Shalqar, Kazakstan 26 E6 47 48N 59 39 E
Shaluli Shan, China 32 C4 30 40N 99 55 E
Shām, Iran 45 E8 26 39N 57 21 E
Shamâl Kordofân □, Sudan 48 E6 15 0N 30 0 E
Shamanovo, Russia 27 C15 69 45N 147 20 E
Shamattawa, Canada 73 B10 55 51N 92 5W
Shamattawa →, Canada 70 A2 55 1N 85 23W
Shamīl, Iran 45 E8 27 30N 56 55 E
Shāmkūh, Iran 45 C8 35 47N 57 50 E
Shamli, India 42 E7 29 32N 77 18 E
Shamo = Gobi, Asia 34 C5 44 0N 111 0 E
Shamo, L., Ethiopia 51 G12 5 45N 37 30 E
Shamokin, U.S.A. 79 F8 40 47N 76 34W
Shamrock, U.S.A. 81 H4 35 13N 100 15W
Shamva, Zimbabwe 55 F3 17 20S 31 32 E
Shan □, Burma 41 J21 21 30N 98 30 E
Shan Xian, China 34 G9 34 50N 116 5 E
Shanchengzhen, China 35 C13 42 20N 125 20 E

163

Sweetwater

Stillwater, *Okla., U.S.A.* **81 G6** 36 7N 97 4W
Stillwater Range, *U.S.A.* **82 G4** 39 50N 118 5W
Stilwell, *U.S.A.* **81 H7** 35 49N 94 38W
Štip, *Macedonia* **21 D10** 41 42N 22 10 E
Stirling, *Australia* **62 B3** 17 12S 141 35 E
Stirling, *Canada* **72 D6** 49 30N 112 30W
Stirling, *U.K.* **12 E5** 56 8N 3 57W
Stirling □, *U.K.* **12 E4** 56 12N 4 18W
Stirling Ra., *Australia* **61 F2** 34 23S 118 0 E
Stittsville, *Canada* **79 A9** 45 15N 75 55W
Stjernøya, *Norway* **8 A20** 70 20N 22 40 E
Stjørdalshalsen, *Norway* **8 E14** 63 29N 10 51 E
Stockerau, *Austria* **16 D9** 48 24N 16 12 E
Stockett, *U.S.A.* **82 C8** 47 21N 111 10W
Stockholm, *Sweden* **9 G18** 59 20N 18 3 E
Stockport, *U.K.* **10 D5** 53 25N 2 9W
Stockton, *Calif., U.S.A.* **83 H3** 37 58N 121 17W
Stockton, *Kans., U.S.A.* **80 F5** 39 26N 99 16W
Stockton, *Mo., U.S.A.* **81 G8** 37 42N 93 48W
Stockton-on-Tees, *U.K.* **10 C6** 54 35N 1 19W
Stockton-on-Tees □, *U.K.* **10 C6** 54 35N 1 19W
Stoke on Trent, *U.K.* **10 D5** 53 1N 2 11W
Stokes Bay, *Canada* **70 C3** 45 0N 81 28W
Stokes Pt., *Australia* **62 G3** 40 10S 143 56 E
Stokes Ra., *Australia* **60 C5** 15 50S 130 50 E
Stokksnes, *Iceland* **8 D6** 64 14N 14 58W
Stokmarknes, *Norway* **8 B16** 68 34N 14 54 E
Stolac, *Bos.-H.* **21 C7** 43 8N 17 59 E
Stolbovaya, *Russia* **27 C16** 64 50N 153 50 E
Stolbovoy, Ostrov, *Russia* **27 D17** 74 44N 135 14 E
Stolbtsy = Stowbtsy, *Belarus* **17 B14** 53 30N 26 43 E
Stolin, *Belarus* **17 C14** 51 53N 26 50 E
Stomíon, *Greece* **23 D5** 35 21N 23 32 E
Stonehaven, *U.K.* **12 E6** 56 59N 2 12W
Stonehenge, *Australia* **62 C3** 24 22S 143 17 E
Stonewall, *Canada* **73 C9** 50 10N 97 19W
Stony L., *Man., Canada* **73 B9** 58 51N 98 40W
Stony L., *Ont., Canada* **78 B6** 44 30N 78 5W
Stony Rapids, *Canada* **73 B7** 59 16N 105 50W
Stony Tunguska = Podkamennaya Tunguska →, *Russia* **27 C10** 61 50N 90 13 E
Stonyford, *U.S.A.* **84 F4** 39 23N 122 33W
Stora Lulevatten, *Sweden* **8 C18** 67 10N 19 30 E
Storavan, *Sweden* **8 D18** 65 45N 18 10 E
Stord, *Norway* **9 G11** 59 52N 5 23 E
Store Bælt, *Denmark* **9 J14** 55 20N 11 0 E
Store Creek, *Australia* **63 E4** 32 54S 149 6 E
Storm B., *Australia* **62 G4** 43 10S 147 30 E
Storm Lake, *U.S.A.* **80 D7** 42 39N 95 13W
Stormberge, *S. Africa* **56 E4** 31 16S 26 17 E
Stormsrivier, *S. Africa* **56 E3** 33 59S 23 52 E
Stornoway, *U.K.* **12 C2** 58 13N 6 23W
Storozhinets = Storozhynets, *Ukraine* **17 D13** 48 14N 25 45 E
Storozhynets, *Ukraine* **17 D13** 48 14N 25 45 E
Storsjön, *Sweden* **8 E16** 63 9N 14 30 E
Storuman, *Sweden* **8 D17** 65 5N 17 10 E
Storuman, sjö, *Sweden* **8 D17** 65 13N 16 50 E
Stoughton, *Canada* **73 D8** 49 40N 103 0W
Stour →, *Dorset, U.K.* **11 G5** 50 43N 1 47W
Stour →, *Here. & Worcs., U.K.* **11 E5** 52 21N 2 17W
Stour →, *Kent, U.K.* **11 F9** 51 18N 1 22 E
Stour →, *Suffolk, U.K.* **11 F9** 51 57N 1 4 E
Stourbridge, *U.K.* **11 E5** 52 28N 2 8W
Stout, L., *Canada* **73 C10** 52 0N 94 40W
Stove Pipe Wells Village, *U.S.A.* **85 J9** 36 35N 117 11W
Stowbtsy, *Belarus* **17 B14** 53 30N 26 43 E
Stowmarket, *U.K.* **11 E9** 52 12N 1 0 E
Strabane, *U.K.* **13 B4** 54 50N 7 27W
Strabane □, *U.K.* **13 B4** 54 45N 7 25W
Strahan, *Australia* **62 G4** 42 9S 145 20 E
Stralsund, *Germany* **16 A7** 54 18N 13 4 E
Strand, *S. Africa* **56 E2** 34 9S 18 48 E
Stranda, *Møre og Romsdal, Norway* **9 E12** 62 19N 6 58 E
Stranda, *Nord-Trøndelag, Norway* **8 E14** 63 33N 10 14 E
Strangford L., *U.K.* **13 B6** 54 30N 5 37W
Strangsville, *U.S.A.* **78 E3** 41 19N 81 50W
Stranraer, *U.K.* **12 G3** 54 54N 5 1W
Strasbourg, *Canada* **73 C8** 51 4N 104 55W
Strasbourg, *France* **18 B7** 48 35N 7 42 E
Strasburg, *U.S.A.* **80 B4** 46 8N 100 10W
Stratford, *Canada* **70 D3** 43 23N 81 0W
Stratford, *N.Z.* **59 H5** 39 20S 174 19 E
Stratford, *Calif., U.S.A.* **83 H4** 36 11N 119 49W
Stratford, *Conn., U.S.A.* **79 E11** 41 12N 73 8W
Stratford, *Tex., U.S.A.* **81 G3** 36 20N 102 4W
Stratford-upon-Avon, *U.K.* **11 E6** 52 12N 1 42W
Strath Spey, *U.K.* **12 D5** 57 9N 3 49W
Strathalbyn, *Australia* **63 F2** 35 13S 138 53 E
Strathcona Prov. Park, *Canada* **72 D3** 49 38N 125 40W
Strathmore, *Australia* **62 B3** 17 50S 142 35 E
Strathmore, *Canada* **72 C6** 51 5N 113 18W
Strathmore, *U.K.* **12 E5** 56 37N 3 7W
Strathmore, *U.S.A.* **84 J7** 36 9N 119 4W
Strathnaver, *Canada* **72 C4** 53 20N 122 33W
Strathpeffer, *U.K.* **12 D4** 57 35N 4 32W
Strathroy, *Canada* **70 D3** 42 58N 81 38W
Strathy Pt., *U.K.* **12 C4** 58 36N 4 1W
Stratton, *U.S.A.* **80 F3** 39 19N 102 36W
Straubing, *Germany* **16 D7** 48 52N 12 34 E
Straumnes, *Iceland* **8 C2** 66 26N 23 8W
Strawberry Reservoir, *U.S.A.* **82 F8** 40 8N 111 9W
Strawn, *U.S.A.* **81 J5** 32 33N 98 30W
Streaky B., *Australia* **63 E1** 32 48S 134 13 E
Streaky Bay, *Australia* **63 E1** 32 51S 134 18 E
Streator, *U.S.A.* **80 E10** 41 8N 88 50W
Streeter, *U.S.A.* **80 B5** 46 39N 99 21W
Streetsville, *Canada* **78 C5** 43 35N 79 42W
Strelka, *Russia* **27 D10** 58 5N 93 3 E
Streng →, *Cambodia* **38 F4** 13 12N 103 37 E
Streymoy, *Færoe Is.* **8 E9** 62 8N 7 5W
Strezhevoy, *Russia* **26 C8** 60 42N 77 34 E
Strimón →, *Greece* **21 D10** 40 46N 23 51 E
Strimonikós Kólpos, *Greece* **21 D11** 40 33N 24 0 E
Strómboli, *Italy* **20 E6** 38 47N 15 13 E
Stromeferry, *U.K.* **12 D3** 57 21N 5 33W
Stromness, *U.K.* **12 C5** 58 58N 3 17W
Stromsburg, *U.S.A.* **80 E6** 41 7N 97 36W
Strömstad, *Sweden* **9 G14** 58 56N 11 10 E
Strömsund, *Sweden* **8 E16** 63 51N 15 33 E
Stronsay, *U.K.* **12 B6** 59 7N 2 35W
Stroud, *U.K.* **11 F5** 51 45N 2 13W
Stroud Road, *Australia* **63 E5** 32 18S 151 57 E
Stroudsburg, *U.S.A.* **79 F9** 40 59N 75 12W
Stroumbi, *Cyprus* **23 E11** 34 53N 32 29 E
Struer, *Denmark* **9 H13** 56 30N 8 35 E
Strumica, *Macedonia* **21 D10** 41 28N 22 41 E
Struthers, *Canada* **70 C2** 48 41N 85 51W
Struthers, *U.S.A.* **78 E4** 41 4N 80 39W
Stryker, *U.S.A.* **82 B6** 48 41N 114 46W
Stryy, *Ukraine* **17 D12** 49 16N 23 48 E
Strzelecki Cr. →, *Australia* **63 D2** 29 37S 139 59 E
Stuart, *Fla., U.S.A.* **77 M5** 27 12N 80 15W
Stuart, *Nebr., U.S.A.* **80 D5** 42 36N 99 8W
Stuart →, *Canada* **72 C4** 54 0N 123 35W
Stuart Bluff Ra., *Australia* **60 D5** 22 50S 131 52 E
Stuart L., *Canada* **72 C4** 54 30N 124 30W
Stuart Ra., *Australia* **63 D1** 29 10S 134 56 E
Stull, L., *Canada* **70 B1** 54 24N 92 34W
Stung Treng, *Cambodia* **38 F5** 13 31N 105 58 E
Stupart →, *Canada* **73 B10** 56 0N 93 25W
Sturgeon B., *Canada* **73 C9** 52 0N 97 50W
Sturgeon Bay, *U.S.A.* **76 C2** 44 50N 87 23W
Sturgeon Falls, *Canada* **70 C4** 46 25N 79 57W
Sturgeon L., *Alta., Canada* **72 B5** 55 6N 117 32W
Sturgeon L., *Ont., Canada* **70 B1** 50 0N 90 45W
Sturgeon L., *Ont., Canada* **78 B6** 44 28N 78 43W
Sturgis, *Mich., U.S.A.* **76 E3** 41 48N 85 25W
Sturgis, *S. Dak., U.S.A.* **80 C3** 44 25N 103 31W
Sturt Cr. →, *Australia* **60 C4** 19 8S 127 50 E
Sturt Creek, *Australia* **60 C4** 19 12S 128 8 E
Stutterheim, *S. Africa* **56 E4** 32 33S 27 28 E
Stuttgart, *Germany* **16 D5** 48 48N 9 11 E
Stuttgart, *U.S.A.* **81 H9** 34 30N 91 33W
Stuyvesant, *U.S.A.* **79 D11** 42 23N 73 45W
Stykkishólmur, *Iceland* **8 D2** 65 2N 22 40W
Styria = Steiermark □, *Austria* **16 E8** 47 26N 15 0 E
Su Xian, *China* **34 H9** 33 41N 116 59 E
Suakin, *Sudan* **51 E12** 19 8N 37 20 E
Suan, *N. Korea* **35 E14** 38 42N 126 22 E
Suaqui, *Mexico* **86 B3** 29 12N 109 41W
Subang, *Indonesia* **37 G12** 6 34S 107 45 E
Subansiri →, *India* **41 F18** 26 48N 93 50 E
Subayhah, *Si. Arabia* **44 D3** 30 2N 38 50 E
Subi, *Indonesia* **39 L7** 2 58N 108 50 E
Subotica, *Serbia, Yug.* **21 A8** 46 6N 19 39 E
Success, *Canada* **73 C7** 50 28N 108 6W
Suceava, *Romania* **17 E14** 47 38N 26 16 E
Suchan, *Russia* **30 C6** 43 8N 133 9 E
Suchitoto, *El Salv.* **88 D2** 13 56N 89 0W
Suchou = Suzhou, *China* **33 C7** 31 19N 120 38 E
Süchow = Xuzhou, *China* **35 G9** 34 18N 117 10 E
Suck →, *Ireland* **13 C3** 53 17N 8 3W
Sucre, *Bolivia* **92 G5** 19 0S 65 15W
Sud, Pte., *Canada* **71 C7** 49 3N 62 14W
Sud-Ouest, Pte. du, *Canada* **71 C7** 49 23N 63 36W
Sudan, *U.S.A.* **81 H3** 34 4N 102 32W
Sudan ■, *Africa* **51 E11** 15 0N 30 0 E
Sudbury, *Canada* **70 C3** 46 30N 81 0W
Sudbury, *U.K.* **11 E8** 52 2N 0 45 E
Sûdd, *Sudan* **51 G11** 8 20N 30 0 E
Sudeten Mts. = Sudety, *Europe* **17 C9** 50 20N 16 45 E
Sudety, *Europe* **17 C9** 50 20N 16 45 E
Suðuroy, *Færoe Is.* **8 F9** 61 32N 6 50W
Sudi, *Tanzania* **55 E4** 10 11S 39 57 E
Sudirman, Pegunungan, *Indonesia* **37 E9** 4 30S 137 0 E
Sueca, *Spain* **19 C5** 39 12N 0 21W
Suez = El Suweis, *Egypt* **51 C11** 29 58N 32 31 E
Suez, G. of = Suweis, Khalîg el, *Egypt* **51 C11** 28 40N 33 0 E
Suffield, *Canada* **73 C6** 50 12N 111 10W
Suffolk, *U.S.A.* **76 G7** 36 44N 76 35W
Suffolk □, *U.K.* **11 E9** 52 16N 1 0 E
Sugar City, *U.S.A.* **80 F3** 38 14N 103 40W
Sugluk = Salluit, *Canada* **69 B12** 62 14N 75 38W
Suhār, *Oman* **45 E8** 24 20N 56 40 E
Sühbaatar □, *Mongolia* **34 B8** 45 30N 114 0 E
Suhl, *Germany* **16 C6** 50 36N 10 42 E
Sui Xian, *China* **34 G8** 34 25N 115 2 E
Suide, *China* **34 F6** 37 30N 110 12 E
Suifenhe, *China* **35 B16** 44 25N 131 10 E
Suihua, *China* **33 B7** 46 32N 126 55 E
Suining, *China* **35 H9** 33 56N 117 58 E
Suiping, *China* **34 H7** 33 10N 113 59 E
Suir →, *Ireland* **13 D4** 52 16N 7 9W
Suiyang, *China* **35 B16** 44 30N 130 56 E
Suizhong, *China* **35 D11** 40 21N 120 20 E
Sujangarh, *India* **42 F6** 27 42N 74 31 E
Sukabumi, *Indonesia* **37 G12** 6 56S 106 50 E
Sukadana, *Kalimantan, Indonesia* **36 E3** 1 10S 110 0 E
Sukadana, *Sumatera, Indonesia* **36 F3** 5 5S 105 33 E
Sukagawa, *Japan* **31 F10** 37 17N 140 23 E
Sukaraja, *Indonesia* **36 E4** 2 28S 110 25 E
Sukarnapura = Jayapura, *Indonesia* **37 E10** 2 28S 140 38 E
Sukchŏn, *N. Korea* **35 E13** 39 22N 125 35 E
Sukhona →, *Russia* **24 C6** 61 15N 46 39 E
Sukhothai, *Thailand* **38 D2** 17 1N 99 49 E
Sukhumi = Sokhumi, *Georgia* **25 F7** 43 0N 41 0 E
Sukkur, *Pakistan* **42 F3** 27 42N 68 54 E
Sukkur Barrage, *Pakistan* **42 F3** 27 40N 68 50 E
Sukumo, *Japan* **31 H6** 32 56N 132 44 E
Sukunka →, *Canada* **72 B4** 55 45N 121 15W
Sula, Kepulauan, *Indonesia* **37 E7** 1 45S 125 0 E
Sulaco →, *Honduras* **88 C2** 15 2N 87 44W
Sulaiman Range, *Pakistan* **42 D3** 30 30N 69 50 E
Sūlār, *Iran* **45 D6** 31 53N 51 54 E
Sulawesi □, *Indonesia* **37 E6** 2 0S 120 0 E
Sulawesi Sea = Celebes Sea, *Indonesia* **37 D6** 3 0N 123 0 E
Sulima, *S. Leone* **50 G2** 6 58N 11 32W
Sulina, *Romania* **17 F15** 45 10N 29 40 E
Sulitjelma, *Norway* **8 C17** 67 9N 16 3 E
Sullana, *Peru* **92 D2** 4 52S 80 39W
Sullivan, *Ill., U.S.A.* **80 F10** 39 36N 88 37W
Sullivan, *Ind., U.S.A.* **76 F2** 39 6N 87 24W
Sullivan, *Mo., U.S.A.* **80 F9** 38 13N 91 10W
Sullivan Bay, *Canada* **72 C3** 50 55N 126 50W
Sulphur, *La., U.S.A.* **81 K8** 30 14N 93 23W
Sulphur, *Okla., U.S.A.* **81 H6** 34 31N 96 58W
Sulphur Pt., *Canada* **72 A6** 60 56N 114 48W
Sulphur Springs, *U.S.A.* **81 J7** 33 8N 95 36W
Sulphur Springs Draw →, *U.S.A.* **81 J4** 32 12N 101 36W
Sultan, *Canada* **70 C3** 47 36N 82 47W
Sultan, *U.S.A.* **84 C5** 47 52N 121 49W
Sultanpur, *India* **43 F10** 26 18N 82 4 E
Sultsa, *Russia* **24 B8** 63 27N 46 2 E
Sulu Arch., *Phil.* **37 C6** 6 0N 121 0 E
Sulu Sea, *E. Indies* **37 C6** 8 0N 120 0 E
Suluq, *Libya* **51 B9** 31 44N 20 14 E
Sulzberger Ice Shelf, *Antarctica* **5 D10** 78 0S 150 0 E
Sumalata, *Indonesia* **37 D6** 1 0N 122 31 E
Sumampa, *Argentina* **94 B3** 29 25S 63 29W
Sumatera □, *Indonesia* **36 D2** 0 40N 100 20 E
Sumatra = Sumatera □, *Indonesia* **36 D2** 0 40N 100 20 E
Sumatra, *U.S.A.* **82 C10** 46 37N 107 33W
Sumba, *Indonesia* **37 F5** 9 45S 119 35 E
Sumba, Selat, *Indonesia* **37 F5** 9 0S 118 40 E
Sumbawa, *Indonesia* **36 F5** 8 26S 117 30 E
Sumbawa Besar, *Indonesia* **36 F5** 8 30S 117 26 E
Sumbawanga □, *Tanzania* **54 D3** 8 0S 31 30 E
Sumbe, *Angola* **52 G2** 11 10S 13 48 E
Sumburgh Hd., *U.K.* **12 B7** 59 52N 1 17W
Sumdo, *India* **43 B8** 35 6N 78 41 E
Sumedang, *Indonesia* **37 G12** 6 52S 107 55 E
Šumen, *Bulgaria* **21 C12** 43 18N 26 55 E
Sumenep, *Indonesia* **37 G15** 7 1S 113 52 E
Sumgait = Sumqayıt, *Azerbaijan* **25 F8** 40 34N 49 38 E
Summer L., *U.S.A.* **82 E3** 42 50N 120 45W
Summerland, *Canada* **72 D5** 49 32N 119 41W
Summerside, *Canada* **71 C7** 46 24N 63 47W
Summerville, *Ga., U.S.A.* **77 H3** 34 29N 85 21W
Summerville, *S.C., U.S.A.* **77 J5** 33 1N 80 11W
Summit Lake, *Canada* **72 C4** 54 20N 122 40W
Summit Peak, *U.S.A.* **83 H10** 37 21N 106 42W
Sumner, *Iowa, U.S.A.* **80 D8** 42 51N 92 6W
Sumner, *Wash., U.S.A.* **84 C4** 47 12N 122 14W
Sumoto, *Japan* **31 G7** 34 21N 134 54 E
Šumperk, *Czech.* **17 D9** 49 59N 17 0 E
Sumqayıt, *Azerbaijan* **25 F8** 40 34N 49 38 E
Sumter, *U.S.A.* **77 J5** 33 55N 80 21W
Sumy, *Ukraine* **25 D5** 50 57N 34 50 E
Sun City, *Ariz., U.S.A.* **83 K7** 33 36N 112 17W
Sun City, *Calif., U.S.A.* **85 M9** 33 42N 117 11W
Sunagawa, *Japan* **30 C10** 43 29N 141 55 E
Sunan, *N. Korea* **35 E13** 39 15N 125 40 E
Sunart, L., *U.K.* **12 E3** 56 42N 5 43W
Sunburst, *U.S.A.* **82 B8** 48 53N 111 55W
Sunbury, *Australia* **63 F3** 37 35S 144 44 E
Sunbury, *U.S.A.* **79 F8** 40 52N 76 48W
Sunchales, *Argentina* **94 C3** 30 58S 61 35W
Suncho Corral, *Argentina* **94 B3** 27 55S 63 27W
Sunchon, *S. Korea* **35 G14** 34 52N 127 31 E
Suncook, *U.S.A.* **79 C13** 43 8N 71 27W
Sunda, Selat, *Indonesia* **36 F3** 6 20S 105 30 E
Sunda Is., *Indonesia* **28 K14** 5 0S 105 0 E
Sunda Str. = Sunda, Selat, *Indonesia* **36 F3** 6 20S 105 30 E
Sundance, *U.S.A.* **80 C2** 44 24N 104 23W
Sundarbans, The, *Asia* **41 J16** 22 0N 89 0 E
Sundargarh, *India* **41 H14** 22 4N 84 5 E
Sundays = Sondags →, *S. Africa* **56 E4** 33 44S 25 51 E
Sunderland, *Canada* **78 B5** 44 16N 79 4W
Sunderland, *U.K.* **10 C6** 54 55N 1 23W
Sundre, *Canada* **72 C6** 51 49N 114 38W
Sundridge, *Canada* **70 C4** 45 45N 79 25W
Sundsvall, *Sweden* **9 E17** 62 23N 17 17 E
Sung Hei, *Vietnam* **39 G6** 10 20N 106 2 E
Sungai Kolok, *Thailand* **39 J3** 6 2N 101 58 E
Sungai Lembing, *Malaysia* **39 L4** 3 55N 103 3 E
Sungai Patani, *Malaysia* **39 K3** 5 37N 100 30 E
Sungaigerong, *Indonesia* **36 E2** 2 59S 104 52 E
Sungailiat, *Indonesia* **36 E3** 1 51S 106 8 E
Sungaipakning, *Indonesia* **36 D2** 1 19N 102 0 E
Sungaipenuh, *Indonesia* **36 E2** 2 1S 101 20 E
Sungaitiram, *Indonesia* **36 E5** 0 45S 117 8 E
Sungari = Songhua Jiang →, *China* **33 B8** 47 45N 132 30 E
Sungguminasa, *Indonesia* **37 F5** 5 17S 119 30 E
Sunghua Chiang = Songhua Jiang →, *China* **33 B8** 47 45N 132 30 E
Sunndalsøra, *Norway* **9 E13** 62 40N 8 33 E
Sunnyside, *Utah, U.S.A.* **82 G8** 39 34N 110 23W
Sunnyside, *Wash., U.S.A.* **82 C3** 46 20N 120 0W
Sunnyvale, *U.S.A.* **83 H2** 37 23N 122 2W
Sunray, *U.S.A.* **81 G4** 36 1N 101 49W
Suntar, *Russia* **27 C12** 62 15N 117 30 E
Suomenselkä, *Finland* **8 E21** 62 52N 24 0 E
Suomussalmi, *Finland* **8 D23** 64 54N 29 10 E
Suoyarvi, *Russia* **24 B5** 62 3N 32 20 E
Supai, *U.S.A.* **83 H7** 36 15N 112 41W
Supaul, *India* **43 F12** 26 10N 86 40 E
Superior, *Ariz., U.S.A.* **83 K8** 33 18N 111 6W
Superior, *Mont., U.S.A.* **82 C6** 47 12N 114 53W
Superior, *Nebr., U.S.A.* **80 E5** 40 1N 98 4W
Superior, *Wis., U.S.A.* **80 B8** 46 44N 92 6W
Superior, L., *U.S.A.* **70 C2** 47 0N 87 0W
Suphan Buri, *Thailand* **38 E3** 14 14N 100 10 E
Supiori, *Indonesia* **37 E9** 1 0S 136 0 E
Supung Sk., *China* **35 D13** 40 35N 124 50 E
Sūq Suwayq, *Si. Arabia* **44 E3** 24 23N 38 27 E
Suqian, *China* **35 H10** 33 54N 118 8 E
Sūr, *Lebanon* **47 B4** 33 19N 35 16 E
Sur, Pt., *U.S.A.* **83 H3** 36 18N 121 54W
Sura →, *Russia* **24 C8** 56 6N 46 0 E
Surab, *Pakistan* **42 E2** 28 25N 66 15 E
Surabaja = Surabaya, *Indonesia* **37 G15** 7 17S 112 45 E
Surabaya, *Indonesia* **37 G15** 7 17S 112 45 E
Surakarta, *Indonesia* **37 G14** 7 35S 110 48 E
Surat, *Australia* **63 D4** 27 10S 149 6 E
Surat, *India* **40 J8** 21 12N 72 55 E
Surat Thani, *Thailand* **39 H2** 9 6N 99 20 E
Suratgarh, *India* **42 E5** 29 18N 73 55 E
Sûre = Sauer →, *Germany* **15 E6** 49 44N 6 31 E
Surendranagar, *India* **42 H4** 22 45N 71 40 E
Surf, *U.S.A.* **85 L6** 34 41N 120 36W
Surgut, *Russia* **26 C8** 61 14N 73 20 E
Suriapet, *India* **40 L11** 17 10N 79 40 E
Surigao, *Phil.* **37 C7** 9 47N 125 29 E
Surin, *Thailand* **38 E4** 14 50N 103 34 E
Surin Nua, Ko, *Thailand* **39 H1** 9 30N 97 55 E
Surinam ■, *S. Amer.* **93 C7** 4 0N 56 0W
Suriname ■ = Surinam ■, *S. Amer.* **93 C7** 4 0N 56 0W
Suriname →, *Surinam* **93 B7** 5 50N 55 15W
Sūrmaq, *Iran* **45 D7** 31 3N 52 48 E
Surprise L., *Canada* **72 B2** 59 40N 133 15W
Surrey □, *U.K.* **11 F7** 51 15N 0 31W
Surt, *Libya* **51 B8** 31 11N 16 39 E
Surt, Khalīj, *Libya* **51 B8** 31 40N 18 30 E
Surtsey, *Iceland* **8 E3** 63 20N 20 30W
Suruga-Wan, *Japan* **31 G9** 34 45N 138 30 E
Susaki, *Japan* **31 H6** 33 22N 133 17 E
Süsangerd, *Iran* **45 D6** 31 35N 48 6 E
Susanino, *Russia* **27 D15** 52 50N 140 14 E
Susanville, *U.S.A.* **82 F3** 40 25N 120 39W
Susquehanna →, *U.S.A.* **79 G8** 39 33N 76 5W
Susquehanna Depot, *U.S.A.* **79 E9** 41 57N 75 36W
Susques, *Argentina* **94 A2** 23 35S 66 25W
Sussex, *Canada* **71 C6** 45 45N 65 37W
Sussex, *U.S.A.* **79 E10** 41 13N 74 37W
Sussex, E. □, *U.K.* **11 G8** 51 0N 0 20 E
Sussex, W. □, *U.K.* **11 G7** 51 0N 0 30W
Sustut →, *Canada* **72 B3** 56 20N 127 30W
Susuman, *Russia* **27 C15** 62 47N 148 10 E
Susunu, *Indonesia* **37 E8** 3 20S 133 25 E
Susurluk, *Turkey* **21 E13** 39 54N 28 8 E
Sutherland, *S. Africa* **56 E3** 32 24S 20 40 E
Sutherland, *U.S.A.* **80 E4** 41 10N 101 8W
Sutherland Falls, *N.Z.* **59 L1** 44 48S 167 46 E
Sutherlin, *U.S.A.* **82 E2** 43 23N 123 19W
Sutlej →, *Pakistan* **42 E4** 29 23N 71 3 E
Sutter, *U.S.A.* **84 F5** 39 10N 121 45W
Sutter Creek, *U.S.A.* **84 G6** 38 24N 120 48W
Sutton, *Canada* **79 A12** 45 6N 72 37W
Sutton, *U.S.A.* **80 E6** 40 36N 97 52W
Sutton →, *Canada* **70 A3** 55 15N 83 45W
Sutton in Ashfield, *U.K.* **10 D6** 53 8N 1 16W
Suttor →, *Australia* **62 C4** 21 36S 147 2 E
Suttsu, *Japan* **30 C10** 42 48N 140 14 E
Suva, *Fiji* **59 D8** 18 6S 178 30 E
Suva Planina, *Serbia, Yug.* **21 C10** 43 10N 22 5 E
Suvorov Is. = Suwarrow Is., *Cook Is.* **65 J11** 15 0S 163 0W
Suwałki, *Poland* **17 A12** 54 8N 22 59 E
Suwannaphum, *Thailand* **38 E4** 15 33N 103 47 E
Suwannee →, *U.S.A.* **77 L4** 29 17N 83 10W
Suwanose-Jima, *Japan* **31 K4** 29 38N 129 43 E
Suwarrow Is., *Cook Is.* **65 J11** 15 0S 163 0W
Suwayq aş Şuqban, *Iraq* **44 D5** 31 32N 46 7 E
Suweis, Khalîg el, *Egypt* **51 C11** 28 40N 33 0 E
Suwŏn, *S. Korea* **35 F14** 37 17N 127 1 E
Suzdal, *Russia* **24 C7** 56 29N 40 26 E
Suzhou, *China* **33 C7** 31 19N 120 38 E
Suzu, *Japan* **31 F8** 37 25N 137 17 E
Suzu-Misaki, *Japan* **31 F8** 37 31N 137 21 E
Suzuka, *Japan* **31 G8** 34 55N 136 36 E
Svalbard, *Arctic* **4 B8** 78 0N 17 0 E
Svappavaara, *Sweden* **8 C19** 67 40N 21 3 E
Svartisen, *Norway* **8 C15** 66 40N 13 50 E
Svay Chek, *Cambodia* **38 F4** 13 48N 102 58 E
Svay Rieng, *Cambodia* **39 G5** 11 5N 105 48 E
Svealand □, *Sweden* **9 G16** 59 55N 15 0 E
Sveg, *Sweden* **9 E16** 62 2N 14 21 E
Svendborg, *Denmark* **9 J14** 55 4N 10 35 E
Sverdlovsk = Yekaterinburg, *Russia* **24 C11** 56 50N 60 30 E
Sverdrup Is., *Canada* **4 B3** 79 0N 97 0W
Svetlaya, *Russia* **30 A9** 46 33N 138 18 E
Svetlogorsk = Svyetlahorsk, *Belarus* **17 B15** 52 38N 29 46 E
Svetozarevo, *Serbia, Yug.* **21 C9** 44 5N 21 15 E
Svir →, *Russia* **24 B5** 60 30N 32 48 E
Svishtov, *Bulgaria* **21 C11** 43 36N 25 23 E
Svislach, *Belarus* **17 B13** 53 3N 24 2 E
Svobodnyy, *Russia* **27 D13** 51 20N 128 0 E
Svolvær, *Norway* **8 B16** 68 15N 14 34 E
Svyetlahorsk, *Belarus* **17 B15** 52 38N 29 46 E
Swabian Alps = Schwäbische Alb, *Germany* **16 D5** 48 20N 9 30 E
Swainsboro, *U.S.A.* **77 J4** 32 36N 82 20W
Swakopmund, *Namibia* **56 C1** 22 37S 14 30 E
Swale →, *U.K.* **10 C6** 54 5N 1 20W
Swan Hill, *Australia* **63 F3** 35 20S 143 33 E
Swan Hills, *Canada* **72 C5** 54 42N 115 24W
Swan Is., *W. Indies* **88 C3** 17 22N 83 57W
Swan L., *Canada* **73 C8** 52 30N 100 40W
Swan River, *Canada* **73 C8** 52 10N 101 16W
Swanage, *U.K.* **11 G6** 50 36N 1 58W
Swansea, *Australia* **63 E5** 33 3S 151 35 E
Swansea, *U.K.* **11 F4** 51 37N 3 57W
Swansea □, *U.K.* **11 F3** 51 38N 4 3W
Swar →, *Pakistan* **43 B5** 34 40N 72 5 E
Swartberge, *S. Africa* **56 E3** 33 20S 22 0 E
Swartmodder, *S. Africa* **56 D3** 28 1S 20 32 E
Swartruggens, *S. Africa* **56 D4** 25 39S 26 42 E
Swastika, *Canada* **70 C3** 48 7N 80 6W
Swatow = Shantou, *China* **33 D6** 23 18N 116 40 E
Swaziland ■, *Africa* **57 D5** 26 30S 31 30 E
Sweden ■, *Europe* **9 G16** 57 0N 15 0 E
Sweet Home, *U.S.A.* **82 D2** 44 24N 122 44W
Sweetwater, *Nev., U.S.A.* **84 G7** 38 27N 119 9W
Sweetwater, *Tex., U.S.A.* **81 J4** 32 28N 100 25W

Theunissen

Theunissen, *S. Africa* ... **56 D4** 28 26S 26 43 E
Thevenard, *Australia* .... **63 E1** 32 9S 133 38 E
Thibodaux, *U.S.A.* **81 L9** 29 48N 90 49W
Thicket Portage, *Canada* . **73 B9** 55 19N 97 42W
Thief River Falls, *U.S.A.* . **80 A6** 48 7N 96 10W
Thiel Mts., *Antarctica* ... **5 E16** 85 15S 91 0W
Thiers, *France* .... **18 D5** 45 52N 3 33 E
Thies, *Senegal* **50 F1** 14 50N 16 51W
Thika, *Kenya* .... **54 C4** 1 1S 37 5 E
Thikombia, *Fiji* **59 B9** 15 44S 179 55W
Thimphu, *Bhutan* .... **41 F16** 27 31N 89 45 E
þingvallavatn, *Iceland* ... **8 D3** 64 11N 21 9W
Thionville, *France* ...... **18 B7** 49 20N 6 10 E
Thira, *Greece* .... **21 F11** 36 23N 25 27 E
Thirsk, *U.K.* **10 C6** 54 14N 1 19W
Thisted, *Denmark* .... **9 H13** 56 58N 8 40 E
Thistle I., *Australia* ...... **63 F2** 35 0S 136 8 E
Thívai, *Greece* .... **21 E10** 38 19N 23 19 E
þjórsá —►, *Iceland* **8 E3** 63 47N 20 48W
Thlewiaza —►, *Man.*, *Canada* **73 B8** 59 43N 100 5W
Thlewiaza —►, *N.W.T.*, *Canada* **73 A10** 60 29N 94 40W
Thmar Puok, *Cambodia* . **38 F4** 13 57N 103 4 E
Tho Vinh, *Vietnam* ...... **38 C5** 19 16N 105 42 E
Thoa —►, *Canada* **73 A7** 60 31N 109 47W
Thoen, *Thailand* .... **38 D2** 17 43N 99 12 E
Thoeng, *Thailand* .... **38 C3** 19 41N 100 12 E
Tholdi, *Pakistan* .... **43 B7** 35 5N 76 6 E
Thomas, *Okla., U.S.A.* **81 H5** 35 45N 98 45W
Thomas, *W. Va., U.S.A.* .. **76 F6** 39 9N 79 30W
Thomas, L., *Australia* ... **63 D2** 26 4S 137 58 E
Thomaston, *U.S.A.* **77 J3** 32 53N 84 20W
Thomasville, *Ala., U.S.A.* . **77 K2** 31 55N 87 44W
Thomasville, *Ga., U.S.A.* . **77 K3** 30 50N 83 59W
Thomasville, *N.C., U.S.A.* **77 H5** 35 53N 80 5W
Thompson, *Canada* **73 B9** 55 45N 97 52W
Thompson, *U.S.A.* **83 G9** 38 58N 109 43W
Thompson —►, *Canada* . **72 C4** 50 15N 121 24W
Thompson —►, *U.S.A.* .. **80 F8** 39 46N 93 37W
Thompson Falls, *U.S.A.* . **82 C6** 47 36N 115 21W
Thompson Landing, *Canada* **73 A6** 62 56N 110 40W
Thompson Pk., *U.S.A.* ... **82 F2** 41 0N 123 0W
Thomson's Falls = Nyahururu, *Kenya* .... **54 B4** 0 2N 36 27 E
Thon Buri, *Thailand* ..... **39 F3** 13 43N 100 29 E
þórisvatn, *Iceland* **8 D4** 64 20N 18 55W
Thornaby on Tees, *U.K.* . **10 C6** 54 33N 1 18W
Thornbury, *Canada* **78 B4** 44 34N 80 26W
Thorold, *Canada* **78 C5** 43 7N 79 12W
þórshöfn, *Iceland* **8 C6** 66 12N 15 20W
Thouin, C., *Australia* .... **60 D2** 20 20S 118 10 E
Thousand Oaks, *U.S.A.* .. **85 L8** 34 10N 118 50W
Thrace, *Turkey* .... **21 D12** 41 0N 27 0 E
Three Forks, *U.S.A.* **82 D8** 45 54N 111 33W
Three Hills, *Canada* **72 C6** 51 43N 113 15W
Three Hummock I., *Australia* .... **62 G3** 40 25S 144 55 E
Three Lakes, *U.S.A.* **80 C10** 45 48N 89 10W
Three Points, C., *Ghana* . **50 H4** 4 42N 2 6W
Three Rivers, *Australia* .. **61 E2** 25 10S 119 5 E
Three Rivers, *Calif., U.S.A.* **84 J8** 36 26N 118 54W
Three Rivers, *Tex., U.S.A.* **81 L5** 28 28N 98 11W
Three Sisters, *U.S.A.* **82 D3** 44 4N 121 51W
Throssell, L., *Australia* .. **61 E3** 27 33S 124 10 E
Throssell Ra., *Australia* .. **60 D3** 22 3S 121 43 E
Thuan Hoa, *Vietnam* .... **39 H5** 8 58N 105 30 E
Thubun Lakes, *Canada* .. **73 A6** 61 30N 112 0W
Thuin, *Belgium* .... **15 D4** 50 20N 4 17 E
Thule, *Greenland* **4 B4** 77 40N 69 0W
Thun, *Switz.* .... **16 E4** 46 45N 7 38 E
Thundelarra, *Australia* .. **61 E2** 28 53S 117 7 E
Thunder B., *U.S.A.* **78 B1** 45 0N 83 20W
Thunder Bay, *Canada* ... **70 C2** 48 20N 89 15W
Thung Song, *Thailand* ... **39 H2** 8 10N 99 40 E
Thunkar, *Bhutan* .... **41 F17** 27 55N 91 0 E
Thuong Tra, *Vietnam* ... **38 D6** 16 2N 107 42 E
Thüringer Wald, *Germany* **16 C6** 50 35N 11 0 E
Thurles, *Ireland* **13 D4** 52 41N 7 49W
Thurloo Downs, *Australia* **63 D3** 29 15S 143 30 E
Thursday I., *Australia* ... **62 A3** 10 30S 142 3 E
Thurso, *Canada* **70 C4** 45 36N 75 15W
Thurso, *U.K.* **12 C5** 58 34N 3 32W
Thurston I., *Antarctica* .. **5 D16** 72 0S 100 0W
Thutade L., *Canada* **72 B3** 57 0N 126 55W
Thylungra, *Australia* .... **63 D3** 26 4S 143 28 E
Thyolo, *Malawi* .... **55 F4** 16 7S 35 5 E
Thysville = Mbanza Ngungu, *Zaïre* .... **52 F2** 5 12S 14 53 E
Tia, *Australia* .... **63 E5** 31 10S 150 50 E
Tian Shan, *Asia* .... **32 B3** 42 0N 76 0 E
Tianjin, *China* .... **35 E9** 39 8N 117 10 E
Tianshui, *China* .... **34 G3** 34 32N 105 40 E
Tianzhen, *China* .... **34 D8** 40 24N 114 5 E
Tianzhuangtai, *China* .... **35 D12** 40 43N 122 5 E
Tiaret, *Algeria* .... **50 A5** 35 20N 1 21 E
Tiassalé, *Ivory C.* **50 G4** 5 58N 4 57W
Tibagi, *Brazil* **95 A5** 24 30S 50 24W
Tibagi —►, *Brazil* **95 A5** 22 47S 51 1W
Tibati, *Cameroon* .... **51 G7** 6 22N 12 30 E
Tiber = Tévere —►, *Italy* **20 D5** 41 44N 12 14 E
Tiber Reservoir, *U.S.A.* .. **82 B8** 48 19N 111 6W
Tiberias = Teverya, *Israel* **47 C4** 32 47N 35 32 E
Tiberias, L. = Yam Kinneret, *Israel* .... **47 C4** 32 45N 35 35 E
Tibesti, *Chad* .... **51 D8** 21 0N 17 30 E
Tibet = Xizang □, *China* . **32 C3** 32 0N 88 0 E
Tibet, Plateau of, *Asia* ... **28 F12** 32 0N 86 0 E
Tibnī, *Syria* .... **44 C3** 35 36N 39 50 E
Tibooburra, *Australia* ... **63 D3** 29 26S 142 1 E
Tiburón, *Mexico* **86 B2** 29 0N 112 30W
Tîchît, *Mauritania* **50 E3** 18 21N 9 29W
Ticino —►, *Italy* .... **20 B3** 45 9N 9 14 E
Ticonderoga, *U.S.A.* **79 C11** 43 51N 73 26W
Ticul, *Mexico* **87 C7** 20 20N 89 31W
Tidaholm, *Sweden* ...... **9 G15** 58 12N 13 55 E
Tiddim, *Burma* .... **41 H18** 23 28N 93 45 E
Tidjikja, *Mauritania* **50 E2** 18 29N 11 35W
Tidore, *Indonesia* .... **37 D7** 0 40N 127 25 E
Tiel, *Neths.* .... **15 C5** 51 53N 5 26 E
Tiel, *Senegal* **50 F1** 14 55N 15 5W
Tieling, *China* .... **35 C12** 42 20N 123 55 E
Tielt, *Belgium* .... **15 D3** 51 0N 3 20 E
Tien Shan = Tian Shan, *Asia* .... **32 B3** 42 0N 76 0 E
Tien-tsin = Tianjin, *China* **35 E9** 39 8N 117 10 E
Tien Yen, *Vietnam* ...... **38 B6** 21 20N 107 24 E
T'ienching = Tianjin, *China* .... **35 E9** 39 8N 117 10 E
Tienen, *Belgium* .... **15 D4** 50 48N 4 57 E
Tientsin = Tianjin, *China* **35 E9** 39 8N 117 10 E
Tierra Amarilla, *Chile* ... **94 B1** 27 28S 70 18W
Tierra Amarilla, *U.S.A.* .. **83 H10** 36 42N 106 33W
Tierra Colorada, *Mexico* . **87 D5** 17 10N 99 35W
Tierra de Campos, *Spain* **19 A3** 42 10N 4 50W
Tierra del Fuego, I. Gr. de, *Argentina* **96 G3** 54 0S 69 0W
Tiétar —►, *Spain* **19 C3** 39 50N 6 1W
Tieté —►, *Brazil* **95 A5** 20 40S 51 35W
Tieyon, *Australia* .... **63 D1** 26 12S 133 52 E
Tiffin, *U.S.A.* **76 E4** 41 7N 83 11W
Tiflis = Tbilisi, *Georgia* .. **25 F7** 41 43N 44 50 E
Tifton, *U.S.A.* **77 K4** 31 27N 83 31W
Tifu, *Indonesia* .... **37 E7** 3 39S 126 24 E
Tighina, *Moldova* .... **17 E15** 46 50N 29 30 E
Tigil, *Russia* .... **27 D16** 57 49N 158 40 E
Tignish, *Canada* **71 C7** 46 58N 64 2W
Tigre —►, *Peru* **92 D4** 4 30S 74 10W
Tigris = Dijlah, Nahr —►, *Asia* .... **44 D5** 31 0N 47 25 E
Tigyaing, *Burma* .... **41 H20** 23 45N 96 10 E
Tîh, Gebel el, *Egypt* .... **51 C11** 29 32N 33 26 E
Tijuana, *Mexico* **85 N9** 32 30N 117 10W
Tikal, *Guatemala* **88 C2** 17 13N 89 24W
Tikamgarh, *India* .... **43 G8** 24 44N 78 50 E
Tikhoretsk, *Russia* ...... **25 E7** 45 56N 40 5 E
Tikrīt, *Iraq* .... **44 C4** 34 35N 43 37 E
Tiksi, *Russia* .... **27 B13** 71 40N 128 45 E
Tilamuta, *Indonesia* .... **37 D6** 0 32N 122 23 E
Tilburg, *Neths.* .... **15 C5** 51 31N 5 6 E
Tilbury, *Canada* **70 D3** 42 17N 82 23W
Tilbury, *U.K.* .... **11 F8** 51 27N 0 22 E
Tilcara, *Argentina* **94 A2** 23 36S 65 23W
Tilden, *Nebr., U.S.A.* **80 D6** 42 3N 97 50W
Tilden, *Tex., U.S.A.* **81 L5** 28 28N 98 33W
Tilhar, *India* .... **43 F8** 28 0N 79 45 E
Tilichiki, *Russia* .... **27 C17** 60 27N 166 5 E
Tilissos, *Greece* .... **23 D7** 35 20N 25 1 E
Till —►, *U.K.* **10 B5** 55 35N 2 3W
Tillabéri, *Niger* .... **50 F5** 14 28N 1 28 E
Tillamook, *U.S.A.* **82 D2** 45 27N 123 51W
Tillsonburg, *Canada* **70 D3** 42 53N 80 44W
Tillyeria □, *Cyprus* ..... **23 D11** 35 6N 32 40 E
Tilos, *Greece* .... **21 F12** 36 27N 27 27 E
Tilpa, *Australia* .... **63 E3** 30 57S 144 24 E
Tilsit = Sovetsk, *Russia* . **9 J19** 55 6N 21 50 E
Tilt —►, *U.K.* **12 E5** 56 46N 3 51W
Tilton, *U.S.A.* **79 C13** 43 27N 71 36W
Timagami L., *Canada* ... **70 C3** 47 0N 80 10W
Timanskiy Kryazh, *Russia* **24 A9** 65 58N 50 5 E
Timaru, *N.Z.* .... **59 L3** 44 23S 171 14 E
Timau, *Kenya* .... **54 B4** 0 4N 37 15 E
Timbákion, *Greece* ...... **23 D6** 35 4N 24 45 E
Timbedgha, *Mauritania* .. **50 E3** 16 17N 8 16W
Timber Lake, *U.S.A.* **80 C4** 45 26N 101 5W
Timber Mt., *U.S.A.* **84 H10** 37 6N 116 28W
Timboon, *Australia* ..... **63 F3** 38 30S 142 58 E
Timbuktu = Tombouctou, *Mali* **50 E4** 16 50N 3 0W
Timi, *Cyprus* .... **23 E11** 34 44N 32 31 E
Timimoun, *Algeria* ...... **50 C5** 29 14N 0 16 E
Timişoara, *Romania* ..... **17 F11** 45 43N 21 15 E
Timmins, *Canada* **70 C3** 48 28N 81 25W
Timok —►, *Serbia, Yug.* . **21 B10** 44 10N 22 40 E
Timon, *Brazil* **93 E10** 5 8S 42 52W
Timor, *Indonesia* .... **37 F7** 9 0S 125 0 E
Timor □, *Indonesia* ..... **37 F7** 9 0S 125 0 E
Timor Sea, *Ind. Oc.* ..... **60 B4** 12 0S 127 0 E
Tin Mt., *U.S.A.* **84 J9** 36 50N 117 10W
Tinaca Pt., *Phil.* .... **37 C7** 5 30N 125 25 E
Tinajo, *Canary Is.* **22 E6** 29 4N 13 42W
Tindouf, *Algeria* **50 C3** 27 42N 8 10W
Tinggi, Pulau, *Malaysia* .. **39 L5** 2 18N 104 7 E
Tingo Maria, *Peru* **92 E3** 9 10S 75 54W
Tinh Bien, *Vietnam* ..... **39 G5** 10 36N 104 57 E
Tinjoub, *Algeria* **50 C3** 29 45N 5 40W
Tinkurrin, *Australia* ..... **61 F2** 32 59S 117 46 E
Tinnevelly = Tirunelveli, *India* .... **40 Q10** 8 45N 77 45 E
Tinogasta, *Argentina* **94 B2** 28 5S 67 32W
Tinos, *Greece* .... **21 F11** 37 33N 25 8 E
Tintina, *Argentina* **94 B3** 27 2S 62 45W
Tintinara, *Australia* ..... **63 F3** 35 48S 140 2 E
Tioga, *U.S.A.* **78 E7** 41 55N 77 8W
Tioman, Pulau, *Malaysia* . **39 L5** 2 50N 104 10 E
Tionesta, *U.S.A.* **78 E5** 41 30N 79 28W
Tipongpani, *India* ...... **41 F19** 27 20N 95 55 E
Tipperary, *Ireland* **13 D3** 52 28N 8 10W
Tipperary □, *Ireland* **13 D4** 52 37N 7 55W
Tipton, *U.K.* **11 E5** 52 32N 2 4W
Tipton, *Calif., U.S.A.* **83 H4** 36 4N 119 19W
Tipton, *Ind., U.S.A.* **76 E2** 40 17N 86 2W
Tipton, *Iowa, U.S.A.* **80 E9** 41 46N 91 8W
Tipton Mt., *U.S.A.* **85 K12** 35 32N 114 12W
Tiptonville, *U.S.A.* **81 G10** 36 23N 89 29W
Tīrān, *Iran* .... **45 C6** 32 45N 51 8 E
Tirana, *Albania* .... **21 D8** 41 18N 19 49 E
Tiranë = Tirana, *Albania* . **21 D8** 41 18N 19 49 E
Tiraspol, *Moldova* ...... **17 E15** 46 55N 29 35 E
Tirat Karmel, *Israel* ..... **47 C3** 32 46N 34 58 E
Tire, *Turkey* .... **21 E12** 38 5N 27 50 E
Tirebolu, *Turkey* .... **25 F6** 40 58N 38 45 E
Tiree, *U.K.* **12 E2** 56 31N 6 55W
Tîrgovişte, *Romania* ..... **17 F13** 44 55N 25 27 E
Tîrgu-Jiu, *Romania* ..... **17 F12** 45 5N 23 19 E
Tîrgu Mureş, *Romania* .. **17 E13** 46 31N 24 38 E
Tirich Mir, *Pakistan* ..... **40 A7** 36 15N 71 55 E
Tîrnăveni, *Romania* ..... **17 E13** 46 19N 24 13 E
Tírnavos, *Greece* .... **21 E10** 39 45N 22 18 E
Tirodi, *India* .... **40 J11** 21 40N 79 44 E
Tirol □, *Austria* .... **16 E6** 47 3N 10 43 E
Tirso —►, *Italy* .... **20 E3** 39 53N 8 32 E
Tiruchchirappalli, *India* .. **40 P11** 10 45N 78 45 E
Tirunelveli, *India* .... **40 Q10** 8 45N 77 45 E
Tirupati, *India* .... **40 N11** 13 39N 79 25 E
Tiruppur, *India* .... **40 P10** 11 5N 77 22 E
Tiruvannamalai, *India* ... **40 N11** 12 15N 79 5 E
Tisa —►, *Serbia, Yug.* ... **21 B9** 45 15N 20 17 E
Tisdale, *Canada* **73 C8** 52 50N 104 0W
Tishomingo, *U.S.A.* **81 H6** 34 14N 96 41W
Tisza = Tisa —►, *Serbia, Yug.* .... **21 B9** 45 15N 20 17 E
Tit-Ary, *Russia* .... **27 B13** 71 55N 127 2 E
Tithwal, *Pakistan* .... **43 B5** 34 21N 73 50 E
Titicaca, L., *S. Amer.* **92 G5** 15 30S 69 30W
Titograd = Podgorica, *Montenegro, Yug.* .... **21 C8** 42 30N 19 19 E
Titov Veles, *Macedonia* .. **21 D9** 41 46N 21 47 E
Titova-Mitrovica, *Serbia, Yug.* .... **21 C9** 42 54N 20 52 E
Titovo Užice, *Serbia, Yug.* **21 C8** 43 55N 19 50 E
Titule, *Zaïre* .... **54 B2** 3 15N 25 31 E
Titusville, *Fla., U.S.A.* ... **77 L5** 28 37N 80 49W
Titusville, *Pa., U.S.A.* ... **78 E5** 41 38N 79 41W
Tivaouane, *Senegal* **50 F1** 14 56N 16 45W
Tiverton, *U.K.* **11 G4** 50 54N 3 29W
Tívoli, *Italy* .... **20 D5** 41 58N 12 45 E
Tizi-Ouzou, *Algeria* ..... **50 A5** 36 42N 4 3 E
Tizimín, *Mexico* **87 C7** 21 0N 88 1W
Tiznit, *Morocco* **50 C3** 29 48N 9 45W
Tjeggelvas, *Sweden* ..... **8 C17** 66 37N 17 45 E
Tjirebon = Cirebon, *Indonesia* .... **37 G13** 6 45S 108 32 E
Tjörn, *Sweden* .... **9 G14** 58 0N 11 35 E
Tlacotalpan, *Mexico* **87 D5** 18 37N 95 40W
Tlahualilo, *Mexico* **86 B4** 26 20N 103 30W
Tlaquepaque, *Mexico* ... **86 C4** 20 39N 103 19W
Tlaxcala, *Mexico* **87 D5** 19 20N 98 14W
Tlaxcala □, *Mexico* **87 D5** 19 30N 98 20W
Tlaxiaco, *Mexico* **87 D5** 17 18N 97 40W
Tlell, *Canada* **72 C2** 53 34N 131 56W
Tlemcen, *Algeria* **50 B4** 34 52N 1 21W
Tmassah, *Libya* .... **51 C8** 26 19N 15 51 E
To Bong, *Vietnam* ...... **38 F7** 12 45N 109 16 E
Toad —►, *Canada* **72 B4** 59 25N 124 57W
Toamasina, *Madag.* ..... **57 B8** 18 10S 49 25 E
Toamasina □, *Madag.* ... **57 B8** 18 0S 49 0 E
Toay, *Argentina* **94 D3** 36 43S 64 38W
Toba, *Japan* .... **31 G8** 34 30N 136 51 E
Toba Kakar, *Pakistan* ... **42 D3** 31 30N 69 0 E
Toba Tek Singh, *Pakistan* **42 D5** 30 55N 72 25 E
Tobago, *W. Indies* **89 D7** 11 10N 60 30W
Tobelo, *Indonesia* ...... **37 D7** 1 45N 127 56 E
Tobermorey, *Australia* ... **62 C2** 22 12S 138 0 E
Tobermory, *Canada* **70 C3** 45 12N 81 40W
Tobermory, *U.K.* **12 E2** 56 38N 6 5W
Tobin, *U.S.A.* **84 F5** 39 55N 121 19W
Tobin, L., *Australia* ..... **60 D4** 21 45S 125 49 E
Tobin L., *Canada* **73 C8** 53 35N 103 30W
Toboali, *Indonesia* ..... **36 E3** 3 0S 106 25 E
Tobol, *Kazakstan* .... **26 D7** 52 40N 62 39 E
Tobol —►, *Russia* ...... **26 D7** 58 10N 68 12 E
Toboli, *Indonesia* ...... **37 E6** 0 38S 120 5 E
Tobolsk, *Russia* .... **26 D7** 58 15N 68 10 E
Tobruk = Tubruq, *Libya* . **51 B9** 32 7N 23 55 E
Tobyhanna, *U.S.A.* **79 E9** 41 11N 75 25W
Tobyl = Tobol —►, *Russia* **26 D7** 58 10N 68 12 E
Tocantinópolis, *Brazil* ... **93 E9** 6 20S 47 25W
Tocantins □, *Brazil* **93 F9** 10 0S 48 0W
Tocantins —►, *Brazil* **93 D9** 1 45S 49 10W
Toccoa, *U.S.A.* **77 H4** 34 35N 83 19W
Tochigi, *Japan* .... **31 F9** 36 25N 139 45 E
Tochigi □, *Japan* .... **31 F9** 36 45N 139 45 E
Tocopilla, *Chile* **94 A1** 22 5S 70 10W
Tocumwal, *Australia* .... **63 F4** 35 51S 145 31 E
Tocuyo —►, *Venezuela* .. **92 A5** 11 3N 68 23W
Todd —►, *Australia* ..... **62 C2** 24 52S 135 48 E
Todeli, *Indonesia* .... **37 E6** 1 38S 124 34 E
Todenyang, *Kenya* ...... **54 B4** 4 35N 35 56 E
Todos os Santos, B. de, *Brazil* **93 F11** 12 48S 38 38W
Todos Santos, *Mexico* ... **86 C2** 23 27N 110 13W
Tofield, *Canada* **72 C6** 53 25N 112 40W
Tofino, *Canada* **72 D3** 49 11N 125 55W
Tofua, *Tonga* **59 D11** 19 45S 175 5W
Tōgane, *Japan* .... **31 G10** 35 33N 140 22 E
Togba, *Mauritania* **50 E2** 17 26N 10 12W
Togian, Kepulauan, *Indonesia* .... **37 E6** 0 20S 121 50 E
Togliatti, *Russia* .... **24 D8** 53 32N 49 24 E
Togo ■, *W. Afr.* .... **50 G5** 8 30N 1 35 E
Togtoh, *China* .... **34 D6** 40 15N 111 10 E
Tōhoku □, *Japan* .... **30 E10** 39 50N 141 45 E
Toinya, *Sudan* .... **51 G10** 6 17N 29 46 E
Tojikiston = Tajikistan ■, *Asia* .... **26 F8** 38 30N 70 0 E
Tojo, *Indonesia* .... **37 E6** 1 20S 121 15 E
Tōjō, *Japan* .... **31 G6** 34 53N 133 16 E
Tokachi-Dake, *Japan* .... **30 C11** 43 17N 142 5 E
Tokachi-Gawa —►, *Japan* **30 C11** 42 44N 143 42 E
Tokala, *Indonesia* ...... **37 E6** 1 30S 121 40 E
Tōkamachi, *Japan* ...... **31 F9** 37 8N 138 43 E
Tokanui, *N.Z.* .... **59 M2** 46 34S 168 56 E
Tokar, *Sudan* .... **51 E12** 18 27N 37 56 E
Tokara-Rettō, *Japan* .... **31 K4** 29 37N 129 43 E
Tokarahi, *N.Z.* .... **59 L3** 44 56S 170 39 E
Tokashiki-Shima, *Japan* . **31 L3** 26 11N 127 21 E
Tōkchŏn, *N. Korea* ..... **35 E14** 39 45N 126 18 E
Tokeland, *U.S.A.* **84 D3** 46 42N 123 59W
Tokelau Is., *Pac. Oc.* **64 H10** 9 0S 171 45W
Tokmak, *Kyrgyzstan* .... **26 E8** 42 49N 75 15 E
Toko Ra., *Australia* ..... **62 C2** 23 5S 138 20 E
Tokoro-Gawa —►, *Japan* **30 B12** 44 7N 144 5 E
Tokuno-Shima, *Japan* ... **31 L4** 27 56N 128 55 E
Tokushima, *Japan* ...... **31 G7** 34 4N 134 34 E
Tokushima □, *Japan* .... **31 H7** 33 55N 134 0 E
Tokuyama, *Japan* .... **31 G5** 34 3N 131 50 E
Tōkyō, *Japan* .... **31 G9** 35 45N 139 45 E
Tolaga Bay, *N.Z.* .... **59 H7** 38 21S 178 20 E
Tolbukhin = Dobrich, *Bulgaria* .... **21 C12** 43 37N 27 49 E
Toledo, *Spain* **19 C3** 39 50N 4 2W
Toledo, *Ohio, U.S.A.* **76 E4** 41 39N 83 33W
Toledo, *Oreg., U.S.A.* ... **82 D2** 44 37N 123 56W
Toledo, *Wash., U.S.A.* ... **82 C2** 46 26N 122 51W
Toledo, Montes de, *Spain* **19 C3** 39 33N 4 20W
Tolga, *Algeria* .... **50 B6** 34 40N 5 22 E
Toliara, *Madag.* .... **57 C7** 23 21S 43 40 E
Toliara □, *Madag.* ...... **57 C8** 21 0S 45 0 E
Tolima, *Colombia* **92 C3** 4 40N 75 19W
Tolitoli, *Indonesia* ...... **37 D6** 1 5N 120 50 E
Tollhouse, *U.S.A.* **84 H7** 37 1N 119 24W
Tolo, *Zaïre* .... **52 E3** 2 55S 18 34 E
Tolo, Teluk, *Indonesia* ... **37 E6** 2 20S 122 10 E
Toluca, *Mexico* **87 D5** 19 20N 99 40W
Tom Burke, *S. Africa* .... **57 C4** 23 5S 28 0 E
Tom Price, *Australia* .... **60 D2** 22 40S 117 48 E
Tomah, *U.S.A.* **80 D9** 43 59N 90 30W
Tomahawk, *U.S.A.* **80 C10** 45 28N 89 44W
Tomakomai, *Japan* ...... **30 C10** 42 38N 141 36 E
Tomales, *U.S.A.* **84 G4** 38 15N 122 53W
Tomales B., *U.S.A.* **84 G3** 38 15N 123 58W
Tomar, *Portugal* **19 C1** 39 36N 8 25W
Tomaszów Mazowiecki, *Poland* .... **17 C10** 51 30N 19 57 E
Tomatlán, *Mexico* **86 D3** 19 56N 105 15W
Tombé, *Sudan* .... **51 G11** 5 53N 31 40 E
Tombigbee —►, *U.S.A.* .. **77 K2** 31 8N 87 57W
Tombouctou, *Mali* **50 E4** 16 50N 3 0W
Tombstone, *U.S.A.* **83 L8** 31 43N 110 4W
Tombua, *Angola* .... **56 B1** 15 55S 11 55 E
Tomé, *Chile* **94 D1** 36 36S 72 57W
Tomelloso, *Spain* **19 C4** 39 10N 3 2W
Tomingley, *Australia* .... **63 E4** 32 26S 148 16 E
Tomini, *Indonesia* ...... **37 D6** 0 30N 120 30 E
Tomini, Teluk, *Indonesia* . **37 E6** 0 10S 122 0 E
Tomkinson Ras., *Australia* **61 E4** 26 11S 129 5 E
Tommot, *Russia* .... **27 D13** 59 4N 126 20 E
Tomnavoulin, *U.K.* **12 D5** 57 19N 3 19W
Tomnop Ta Suos, *Cambodia* .... **39 G5** 11 20N 104 15 E
Tomorit, *Albania* .... **21 D9** 40 42N 20 11 E
Toms Place, *U.S.A.* **84 H8** 37 34N 118 41W
Toms River, *U.S.A.* **79 G10** 39 58N 74 12W
Tomsk, *Russia* .... **26 D9** 56 30N 85 5 E
Tonalá, *Mexico* **87 D6** 16 8N 93 41W
Tonalea, *U.S.A.* **83 H8** 36 19N 110 56W
Tonantins, *Brazil* **92 D5** 2 45S 67 45W
Tonasket, *U.S.A.* **82 B4** 48 42N 119 26W
Tonawanda, *U.S.A.* **78 D6** 43 1N 78 53W
Tonbridge, *U.K.* .... **11 F8** 51 11N 0 17 E
Tondano, *Indonesia* .... **37 D6** 1 35N 124 54 E
Tonekābon, *Iran* .... **45 B6** 36 45N 51 12 E
Tong Xian, *China* .... **34 E9** 39 55N 116 35 E
Tonga ■, *Pac. Oc.* **59 D11** 19 50S 174 30W
Tonga Trench, *Pac. Oc.* .. **64 J10** 18 0S 173 0W
Tongaat, *S. Africa* ...... **57 D5** 29 33S 31 9 E
Tongareva, *Cook Is.* **65 H12** 9 0S 158 0W
Tongatapu, *Tonga* **59 E11** 21 10S 174 0W
Tongchŏn-ni, *N. Korea* .. **35 E14** 39 50N 127 25 E
Tongchuan, *China* ...... **34 G5** 35 6N 109 3 E
Tongeren, *Belgium* ..... **15 D5** 50 47N 5 28 E
Tongguan, *China* .... **34 G6** 34 40N 110 25 E
Tonghua, *China* .... **35 D13** 41 42N 125 58 E
Tongjosŏn Man, *N. Korea* **35 E14** 39 30N 128 0 E
Tongking, G. of = Tonkin, G. of, *Asia* .... **32 E5** 20 0N 108 0 E
Tongliao, *China* .... **35 C12** 43 38N 122 18 E
Tongnae, *S. Korea* ..... **35 G15** 35 12N 129 5 E
Tongobory, *Madag.* ..... **57 C7** 23 32S 44 20 E
Tongoy, *Chile* **94 C1** 30 16S 71 31W
Tongres = Tongeren, *Belgium* .... **15 D5** 50 47N 5 28 E
Tongsa Dzong, *Bhutan* .. **41 F17** 27 31N 90 31 E
Tongue, *U.K.* **12 C4** 58 29N 4 25W
Tongue —►, *U.S.A.* **80 B2** 46 25N 105 52W
Tongwei, *China* .... **34 G3** 35 0N 105 5 E
Tongxin, *China* .... **34 F3** 36 59N 105 58 E
Tongyang, *N. Korea* .... **35 E14** 39 9N 126 53 E
Tongyu, *China* .... **35 B12** 44 45N 123 4 E
Tonk, *India* .... **42 F6** 26 6N 75 54 E
Tonkawa, *U.S.A.* **81 G6** 36 41N 97 18W
Tonkin = Bac Phan, *Vietnam* .... **38 B5** 22 0N 105 0 E
Tonkin, G. of, *Asia* ..... **32 E5** 20 0N 108 0 E
Tonlé Sap, *Cambodia* ... **38 F4** 13 0N 104 0 E
Tono, *Japan* .... **30 E10** 39 19N 141 32 E
Tonopah, *U.S.A.* **83 G5** 38 4N 117 14W
Tonosí, *Panama* **88 E3** 7 20N 80 20W
Tønsberg, *Norway* ..... **9 G14** 59 19N 10 25 E
Tooele, *U.S.A.* **82 F7** 40 32N 112 18W
Toompine, *Australia* .... **63 D3** 27 15S 144 19 E
Toonpan, *Australia* ..... **62 B4** 19 28S 146 48 E
Toora, *Australia* .... **63 F4** 38 39S 146 23 E
Toora-Khem, *Russia* .... **27 D10** 52 28N 96 17 E
Toowoomba, *Australia* .. **63 D5** 27 32S 151 56 E
Top-ozero, *Russia* ...... **24 A5** 65 35N 32 0 E
Topaz, *U.S.A.* **84 G7** 38 41N 119 30W
Topeka, *U.S.A.* **80 F7** 39 3N 95 40W
Topki, *Russia* .... **26 D9** 55 20N 85 35 E
Topley, *Canada* **72 C3** 54 49N 126 18W
Topocalma, Pta., *Chile* .. **94 C1** 34 10S 72 2W
Topock, *U.S.A.* **85 L12** 34 46N 114 29W
Topoľčany, *Slovak Rep.* . **17 D10** 48 35N 18 12 E
Topolobampo, *Mexico* ... **86 B3** 25 40N 109 4W
Toppenish, *U.S.A.* **82 C3** 46 23N 120 19W
Toraka Vestale, *Madag.* .. **57 B7** 16 20S 43 58 E
Torata, *Peru* **92 G4** 17 23S 70 1W
Torbalı, *Turkey* .... **21 E12** 38 10N 27 21 E
Torbay, *Canada* **71 C9** 47 40N 52 42W
Torbay, *U.K.* **11 G4** 50 26N 3 31W
Tordesillas, *Spain* **19 B3** 41 30N 5 0W
Torfaen □, *U.K.* **11 F4** 51 43N 3 3W
Torgau, *Germany* .... **16 C7** 51 34N 13 0 E
Torhout, *Belgium* .... **15 C3** 51 5N 3 7 E
Tori-Shima, *Japan* ...... **31 J10** 30 29N 140 19 E
Torin, *Mexico* **86 B2** 27 33N 110 15W
Torino, *Italy* .... **20 B2** 45 3N 7 40 E
Torit, *Sudan* .... **51 H11** 4 27N 32 31 E
Tormes —►, *Spain* **19 B2** 41 18N 6 29W
Tornado Mt., *Canada* **72 D6** 49 55N 114 40W
Torne älv —►, *Sweden* .. **8 D21** 65 50N 24 12 E
Torneå = Tornio, *Finland* **8 D21** 65 50N 24 12 E
Torneträsk, *Sweden* ..... **8 B18** 68 24N 19 15 E
Tornio, *Finland* .... **8 D21** 65 50N 24 12 E
Tornionjoki —►, *Finland* . **8 D21** 65 50N 24 12 E
Tornquist, *Argentina* **94 D3** 38 8S 62 15W
Toro, *Spain* .... **22 B11** 39 59N 4 8 E
Toro, Cerro del, *Chile* ... **94 B2** 29 10S 69 50W
Toro Pk., *U.S.A.* **85 M10** 33 34N 116 24W
Toroníios Kólpos, *Greece* **21 D10** 40 5N 23 30 E

Turabah

Turabah, *Si. Arabia* **44 D4** 28 20N 43 15 E
Tūrān, *Iran* **45 C8** 35 39N 56 42 E
Turan, *Russia* **27 D10** 51 55N 95 0 E
Turayf, *Si. Arabia* **44 D3** 31 41N 38 39 E
Turda, *Romania* **17 E12** 46 34N 23 47 E
Turek, *Poland* **17 B10** 52 3N 18 30 E
Turfan = Turpan, *China* **32 B3** 43 58N 89 10 E
Turfan Depression = Turpan Hami, *China* **28 E12** 42 40N 89 25 E
Tŭrgovishte, *Bulgaria* **21 C12** 43 17N 26 38 E
Turgutlu, *Turkey* **21 E12** 38 30N 27 48 E
Turia →, *Spain* **19 C5** 39 27N 0 19W
Turiaçu, *Brazil* **93 D9** 1 40S 45 19W
Turiaçu →, *Brazil* **93 D9** 1 36S 45 19W
Turin = Torino, *Italy* **20 B2** 45 3N 7 40 E
Turin, *Canada* **72 D6** 49 58N 112 31W
Turkana □, *Kenya* **54 B4** 3 0N 35 30 E
Turkana, L., *Africa* **54 B4** 3 30N 36 5 E
Turkestan = Türkistan, *Kazakstan* **26 E7** 43 17N 68 16 E
Turkey ■, *Eurasia* **25 G6** 39 0N 36 0 E
Turkey Creek, *Australia* **60 C4** 17 2S 128 12 E
Türkistan, *Kazakstan* **26 E7** 43 17N 68 16 E
Türkmenbashi, *Turkmenistan* **25 F9** 40 5N 53 5 E
Turkmenistan ■, *Asia* **26 F6** 39 0N 59 0 E
Turks & Caicos Is. ■, *W. Indies* **89 B5** 21 20N 71 20W
Turks Island Passage, *W. Indies* **89 B5** 21 30N 71 30W
Turku, *Finland* **9 F20** 60 30N 22 19 E
Turkwe →, *Kenya* **54 B4** 3 6N 36 6 E
Turlock, *U.S.A.* **83 H3** 37 30N 120 51W
Turnagain →, *Canada* **72 B3** 59 12N 127 35W
Turnagain, C., *N.Z.* **59 J6** 40 28S 176 38 E
Turneffe Is., *Belize* **87 D7** 17 20N 87 50W
Turner, *Australia* **60 C4** 17 52S 128 16 E
Turner, *U.S.A.* **82 B9** 48 51N 108 24W
Turner Pt., *Australia* **62 A1** 11 47S 133 32 E
Turner Valley, *Canada* **72 C6** 50 40N 114 17W
Turners Falls, *U.S.A.* **79 D12** 42 36N 72 33W
Turnhout, *Belgium* **15 C4** 51 19N 4 57 E
Turnor L., *Canada* **73 B7** 56 35N 108 35W
Tŭrnovo = Veliko Tŭrnovo, *Bulgaria* **21 C11** 43 5N 25 41 E
Turnu Măgurele, *Romania* **17 G13** 43 46N 24 56 E
Turnu Roşu, P., *Romania* **17 F13** 45 33N 24 17 E
Turon, *U.S.A.* **81 G5** 37 48N 98 26W
Turpan, *China* **32 B3** 43 58N 89 10 E
Turpan Hami, *China* **28 E12** 42 40N 89 25 E
Turriff, *U.K.* **12 D6** 57 32N 2 27W
Tursāq, *Iraq* **44 C5** 33 27N 45 47 E
Turtle Head I., *Australia* **62 A3** 10 56S 142 37 E
Turtle L., *Canada* **73 C7** 53 36N 108 38W
Turtle Lake, *N. Dak., U.S.A.* **80 B4** 47 31N 100 53W
Turtle Lake, *Wis., U.S.A.* **80 C8** 45 24N 92 8W
Turtleford, *Canada* **73 C7** 53 23N 108 57W
Turukhansk, *Russia* **27 C9** 65 21N 88 5 E
Tuscaloosa, *U.S.A.* **77 J2** 33 12N 87 34W
Tuscany = Toscana □, *Italy* **20 C4** 43 25N 11 0 E
Tuscola, *Ill., U.S.A.* **76 F1** 39 48N 88 17W
Tuscola, *Tex., U.S.A.* **81 J5** 32 12N 99 48W
Tuscumbia, *U.S.A.* **77 H2** 34 44N 87 42W
Tuskar Rock, *Ireland* **13 D5** 52 12N 6 10W
Tuskegee, *U.S.A.* **77 J3** 32 25N 85 42W
Tustin, *U.S.A.* **85 M9** 33 44N 117 49W
Tuticorin, *India* **40 Q11** 8 50N 78 12 E
Tutóia, *Brazil* **93 D10** 2 45S 42 20W
Tutong, *Brunei* **36 D4** 4 47N 114 40 E
Tutrakan, *Bulgaria* **21 B12** 44 2N 26 40 E
Tutshi L., *Canada* **72 B2** 59 56N 134 30W
Tuttle, *U.S.A.* **80 B5** 47 9N 100 0W
Tuttlingen, *Germany* **16 E5** 47 58N 8 48 E
Tutuala, *Indonesia* **37 F7** 8 25S 127 15 E
Tutuila, *Amer. Samoa* **59 B13** 14 19S 170 50W
Tututepec, *Mexico* **87 D5** 16 9N 97 38W
Tuva □, *Russia* **27 D10** 51 30N 95 0 E
Tuvalu ■, *Pac. Oc.* **64 H9** 8 0S 178 0 E
Tuxpan, *Mexico* **87 C5** 20 58N 97 23W
Tuxtla Gutiérrez, *Mexico* **87 D6** 16 50N 93 10W
Tuy, *Spain* **19 A1** 42 3N 8 39W
Tuy An, *Vietnam* **38 F7** 13 17N 109 16 E
Tuy Duc, *Vietnam* **39 F6** 12 15N 107 27 E
Tuy Hoa, *Vietnam* **38 F7** 13 5N 109 10 E
Tuy Phong, *Vietnam* **39 G7** 11 14N 108 43 E
Tuya L., *Canada* **72 B2** 59 7N 130 35W
Tuyen Hoa, *Vietnam* **38 D6** 17 50N 106 10 E
Tuyen Quang, *Vietnam* **38 B5** 21 50N 105 10 E
Tūysarkān, *Iran* **45 C6** 34 33N 48 27 E
Tuz Gölü, *Turkey* **25 G5** 38 42N 33 18 E
Ţūz Khurmātū, *Iraq* **44 C5** 34 56N 44 38 E
Tuzla, *Bos.-H.* **21 B8** 44 34N 18 41 E
Tver, *Russia* **24 C6** 56 55N 35 55 E
Twain, *U.S.A.* **84 E5** 40 1N 121 3W
Twain Harte, *U.S.A.* **84 G6** 38 2N 120 14W
Tweed, *Canada* **78 B7** 44 29N 77 19W
Tweed →, *U.K.* **12 F7** 55 45N 2 0W
Tweed Heads, *Australia* **63 D5** 28 10S 153 31 E
Tweedsmuir Prov. Park, *Canada* **72 C3** 53 0N 126 20W
Twentynine Palms, *U.S.A.* **85 L10** 34 8N 116 3W
Twillingate, *Canada* **71 C9** 49 42N 54 45W
Twin Bridges, *U.S.A.* **82 D7** 45 33N 112 20W
Twin Falls, *U.S.A.* **82 E6** 42 34N 114 28W
Twin Valley, *U.S.A.* **80 B6** 47 16N 96 16W
Twisp, *U.S.A.* **82 B3** 48 22N 120 7W
Two Harbors, *U.S.A.* **80 B9** 47 2N 91 40W
Two Hills, *Canada* **72 C6** 53 43N 111 52W
Two Rivers, *U.S.A.* **76 C2** 44 9N 87 34W
Twofold B., *Australia* **63 F4** 37 8S 149 59 E
Tyachiv, *Ukraine* **17 D12** 48 1N 23 35 E
Tychy, *Poland* **17 C10** 50 9N 18 59 E
Tyler, *U.S.A.* **75 D7** 32 18N 95 17W
Tyler, *Minn., U.S.A.* **80 C6** 44 18N 96 8W
Tyler, *Tex., U.S.A.* **81 J7** 32 21N 95 18W
Tynda, *Russia* **27 D13** 55 10N 124 43 E
Tyne →, *U.K.* **10 C6** 54 59N 1 32W
Tyne & Wear □, *U.K.* **10 C6** 55 6N 1 17W
Tynemouth, *U.K.* **10 B6** 55 1N 1 26W
Tyre = Sūr, *Lebanon* **47 B4** 33 19N 35 16 E
Tyrifjorden, *Norway* **9 F14** 60 2N 10 8 E
Tyrol = Tirol □, *Austria* **16 E6** 47 3N 10 43 E
Tyrone, *U.S.A.* **78 F6** 40 40N 78 14W
Tyrrell →, *Australia* **63 F3** 35 26S 142 51 E
Tyrrell, L., *Australia* **63 F3** 35 20S 142 50 E
Tyrrell Arm, *Canada* **73 A9** 62 27N 97 30W
Tyrrell L., *Canada* **73 A7** 63 7N 105 27W
Tyrrhenian Sea, *Medit. S.* **20 E5** 40 0N 12 30 E
Tysfjorden, *Norway* **8 B17** 68 7N 16 25 E
Tyulgan, *Russia* **24 D10** 52 22N 56 12 E
Tyumen, *Russia* **26 D7** 57 11N 65 29 E
Tywi →, *U.K.* **11 F3** 51 48N 4 21W
Tywyn, *U.K.* **11 E3** 52 35N 4 5W
Tzaneen, *S. Africa* **57 C5** 23 47S 30 9 E
Tzermiádhes, *Greece* **23 D7** 35 12N 25 29 E
Tzukong = Zigong, *China* **32 D5** 29 15N 104 48 E

U

U Taphao, *Thailand* **38 F3** 12 35N 101 0 E
U.S.A. = United States of America ■, *N. Amer.* **74 C7** 37 0N 96 0W
Uanda, *Australia* **62 C3** 21 37S 144 55 E
Uarsciek, *Somali Rep.* **46 G4** 2 28N 45 55 E
Uasin □, *Kenya* **54 B4** 0 30N 35 20 E
Uato-Udo, *Indonesia* **37 F7** 9 7S 125 36 E
Uatumã →, *Brazil* **92 D7** 2 26S 57 37W
Uaupés, *Brazil* **92 D5** 0 8S 67 5W
Uaupés →, *Brazil* **92 C5** 0 2N 67 16W
Uaxactún, *Guatemala* **88 C2** 17 25N 89 29W
Ubá, *Brazil* **95 A7** 21 8S 43 0W
Ubaitaba, *Brazil* **93 F11** 14 18S 39 20W
Ubangi = Oubangi →, *Zaïre* **52 E3** 0 30S 17 50 E
Ubauro, *Pakistan* **42 E3** 28 15N 69 45 E
Ube, *Japan* **31 H5** 33 56N 131 15 E
Ubeda, *Spain* **19 C4** 38 3N 3 23W
Uberaba, *Brazil* **93 G9** 19 50S 47 55W
Uberlândia, *Brazil* **93 G9** 19 0S 48 20W
Ubolratna Res., *Thailand* **38 D4** 16 45N 102 30 E
Ubombo, *S. Africa* **57 D5** 27 31S 32 4 E
Ubon Ratchathani, *Thailand* **38 E5** 15 15N 104 50 E
Ubondo, *Zaïre* **54 C2** 0 55S 25 42 E
Ubort →, *Belarus* **17 B15** 52 6N 28 30 E
Ubundu, *Zaïre* **54 C2** 0 22S 25 30 E
Ucayali →, *Peru* **92 D4** 4 30S 73 30W
Uchi Lake, *Canada* **73 C10** 51 5N 92 35W
Uchiura-Wan, *Japan* **30 C10** 42 25N 140 40 E
Uchur →, *Russia* **27 D14** 58 48N 130 35 E
Ucluelet, *Canada* **72 D3** 48 57N 125 32W
Uda →, *Russia* **27 D14** 54 42N 135 14 E
Udaipur, *India* **42 G5** 24 36N 73 44 E
Udaipur Garhi, *Nepal* **43 F12** 27 0N 86 35 E
Uddevalla, *Sweden* **9 G14** 58 21N 11 55 E
Uddjaur, *Sweden* **8 D17** 65 56N 17 49 E
Udgir, *India* **40 K10** 18 25N 77 5 E
Udhampur, *India* **43 C6** 33 0N 75 5 E
Udi, *Nigeria* **50 G6** 6 17N 7 21 E
Údine, *Italy* **20 A5** 46 3N 13 14 E
Udmurtia □, *Russia* **24 C9** 57 30N 52 30 E
Udon Thani, *Thailand* **38 D4** 17 29N 102 46 E
Udupi, *India* **40 N9** 13 25N 74 42 E
Udzungwa Range, *Tanzania* **55 D4** 9 30S 35 10 E
Ueda, *Japan* **31 F9** 36 24N 138 16 E
Uedineniya, Os., *Russia* **4 B12** 78 0N 85 0 E
Uele →, *Zaïre* **52 D4** 3 45N 24 45 E
Uelen, *Russia* **27 C19** 66 10N 170 0W
Uelzen, *Germany* **16 B6** 52 57N 10 32 E
Ufa, *Russia* **24 D10** 54 45N 55 55 E
Ufa →, *Russia* **24 D10** 54 40N 56 0 E
Ugab →, *Namibia* **56 C1** 20 55S 13 30 E
Ugalla →, *Tanzania* **54 D3** 5 8S 30 42 E
Uganda ■, *Africa* **54 B3** 2 0N 32 0 E
Ugie, *S. Africa* **57 E4** 31 10S 28 13 E
Uglegorsk, *Russia* **27 E15** 49 5N 142 2 E
Ugljane, *Croatia* **16 F8** 44 12N 14 56 E
Ugolyak, *Russia* **27 C13** 64 33N 120 30 E
Ugûn Mûsa, *Egypt* **47 F1** 29 53N 32 40 E
Uhrichsville, *U.S.A.* **78 F3** 40 24N 81 21W
Uibhist a Deas = South Uist, *U.K.* **12 D1** 57 20N 7 15W
Uibhist a Tuath = North Uist, *U.K.* **12 D1** 57 40N 7 15W
Uige, *Angola* **52 F2** 7 30S 14 40 E
Uijŏngbu, *S. Korea* **35 F14** 37 48N 127 0 E
Ŭiju, *N. Korea* **35 D13** 40 15N 124 35 E
Uinta Mts., *U.S.A.* **82 F8** 40 45N 110 30W
Uitenhage, *S. Africa* **56 E4** 33 40S 25 28 E
Uithuizen, *Neths.* **15 A6** 53 24N 6 41 E
Ujhani, *India* **43 F8** 28 0N 79 6 E
Uji-guntō, *Japan* **31 J4** 31 15N 129 25 E
Ujjain, *India* **42 H6** 23 9N 75 43 E
Ujung Pandang, *Indonesia* **37 F5** 5 10S 119 20 E
Uka, *Russia* **27 D17** 57 50N 162 0 E
Ukara I., *Tanzania* **54 C3** 1 50S 33 0 E
Uke-Shima, *Japan* **31 K4** 28 2N 129 14 E
Ukerewe □, *Tanzania* **54 C3** 2 0S 32 30 E
Ukerewe I., *Tanzania* **54 C3** 2 0S 33 0 E
Ukhrul, *India* **41 G19** 25 10N 94 25 E
Ukhta, *Russia* **24 B9** 63 34N 53 41 E
Ukiah, *U.S.A.* **84 F3** 39 9N 123 13W
Ukki Fort, *India* **43 C7** 33 28N 76 54 E
Ukmerge, *Lithuania* **9 J21** 55 15N 24 45 E
Ukraine ■, *Europe* **25 E5** 49 0N 32 0 E
Ukwi, *Botswana* **56 C3** 23 29S 20 30 E
Ulaanbaatar, *Mongolia* **27 E11** 47 55N 106 53 E
Ulaangom, *Mongolia* **32 A4** 50 5N 92 10 E
Ulamba, *Zaïre* **55 D1** 9 3S 23 38 E
Ulan Bator = Ulaanbaatar, *Mongolia* **27 E11** 47 55N 106 53 E
Ulan Ude, *Russia* **27 D11** 51 45N 107 40 E
Ulanga □, *Tanzania* **55 D4** 8 40S 36 50 E
Ulaya, *Morogoro, Tanzania* **54 D4** 7 3S 36 55 E
Ulaya, *Tabora, Tanzania* **54 C3** 4 25S 33 30 E
Ulcinj, *Montenegro, Yug.* **21 D8** 41 58N 19 10 E
Ulco, *S. Africa* **56 D3** 28 21S 24 15 E
Ulefoss, *Norway* **9 G13** 59 17N 9 16 E
Ulhasnagar, *India* **40 K8** 19 15N 73 10 E
Ulladulla, *Australia* **63 F5** 35 21S 150 29 E
Ullapool, *U.K.* **12 D3** 57 54N 5 9W
Ullswater, *U.K.* **10 C5** 54 34N 2 52W
Ullung-do, *S. Korea* **35 F16** 37 30N 130 30 E
Ulm, *Germany* **16 D5** 48 23N 9 58 E
Ulmarra, *Australia* **63 D5** 29 37S 153 4 E
Ulonguè, *Mozam.* **55 E3** 14 37S 34 19 E
Ulricehamn, *Sweden* **9 H15** 57 46N 13 26 E
Ulsan, *S. Korea* **35 G15** 35 20N 129 15 E
Ulster □, *U.K.* **13 B5** 54 35N 6 30W
Ulubaria, *India* **43 H13** 22 31N 88 4 E
Ulubat Gölü, *Turkey* **21 D13** 40 9N 28 35 E
Uludağ, *Turkey* **21 D13** 40 4N 29 13 E
Uluguru Mts., *Tanzania* **54 D4** 7 15S 37 40 E
Ulungur He →, *China* **32 B3** 47 1N 87 24 E
Uluru = Ayers Rock, *Australia* **61 E5** 25 23S 131 5 E
Ulutau, *Kazakstan* **26 E7** 48 39N 67 1 E
Ulverston, *U.K.* **10 C4** 54 13N 3 5W
Ulverstone, *Australia* **62 G4** 41 11S 146 11 E
Ulya, *Russia* **27 D15** 59 10N 142 0 E
Ulyanovsk = Simbirsk, *Russia* **24 D8** 54 20N 48 25 E
Ulyasutay, *Mongolia* **32 B4** 47 56N 97 28 E
Ulysses, *U.S.A.* **81 G4** 37 35N 101 22W
Umala, *Bolivia* **92 G5** 17 25S 68 5W
Uman, *Ukraine* **17 D16** 48 40N 30 12 E
Umaria, *India* **41 H12** 23 35N 80 50 E
Umarkot, *Pakistan* **40 G6** 25 15N 69 40 E
Umatilla, *U.S.A.* **82 D4** 45 55N 119 21W
Umba, *Russia* **24 A5** 66 42N 34 11 E
Umbrella Mts., *N.Z.* **59 L2** 45 35S 169 5 E
Ume älv →, *Sweden* **8 E19** 63 45N 20 20 E
Umeå, *Sweden* **8 E19** 63 45N 20 20 E
Umera, *Indonesia* **37 E7** 0 12S 129 37 E
Umfuli →, *Zimbabwe* **55 F2** 17 30S 29 23 E
Umgusa, *Zimbabwe* **55 F2** 19 29S 27 52 E
Umkomaas, *S. Africa* **57 E5** 30 13S 30 48 E
Umm ad Daraj, J., *Jordan* **47 C4** 32 18N 35 48 E
Umm al Qaywayn, *U.A.E.* **45 E7** 25 30N 55 35 E
Umm al Qittayn, *Jordan* **47 C5** 32 18N 36 40 E
Umm Bāb, *Qatar* **45 E6** 25 12N 50 48 E
Umm Bel, *Sudan* **51 F10** 13 35N 28 0 E
Umm el Fahm, *Israel* **47 C4** 32 31N 35 9 E
Umm Lajj, *Si. Arabia* **44 E3** 25 0N 37 23 E
Umm Ruwaba, *Sudan* **51 F11** 12 50N 31 20 E
Umnak I., *U.S.A.* **68 C3** 53 15N 168 20W
Umniati →, *Zimbabwe* **55 F2** 16 49S 28 45 E
Umpqua →, *U.S.A.* **82 E1** 43 40N 124 12W
Umreth, *India* **42 H5** 22 41N 73 4 E
Umtata, *S. Africa* **57 E4** 31 36S 28 49 E
Umuarama, *Brazil* **95 A5** 23 45S 53 20W
Umvukwe Ra., *Zimbabwe* **55 F3** 16 45S 30 45 E
Umzimvubu = Port St. Johns, *S. Africa* **57 E4** 31 38S 29 33 E
Umzingwane →, *Zimbabwe* **55 G2** 22 12S 29 56 E
Umzinto, *S. Africa* **57 E5** 30 15S 30 45 E
Una, *India* **42 J4** 20 46N 71 8 E
Una →, *Bos.-H.* **16 F9** 45 0N 16 20 E
Unadilla, *U.S.A.* **79 D9** 42 20N 75 19W
Unalaska, *U.S.A.* **68 C3** 53 53N 166 32W
Uncía, *Bolivia* **92 G5** 18 25S 66 40W
Uncompahgre Peak, *U.S.A.* **83 G10** 38 4N 107 28W
Underbool, *Australia* **63 F3** 35 10S 141 51 E
Ungarie, *Australia* **63 E4** 33 38S 146 56 E
Ungarra, *Australia* **63 E2** 34 12S 136 2 E
Ungava B., *Canada* **69 C13** 59 30N 67 30W
Ungava Pen., *Canada* **69 C12** 60 0N 74 0W
Ungeny = Ungheni, *Moldova* **17 E14** 47 11N 27 51 E
Unggi, *N. Korea* **35 C16** 42 16N 130 28 E
Ungheni, *Moldova* **17 E14** 47 11N 27 51 E
União da Vitória, *Brazil* **95 B5** 26 13S 51 5W
Unimak I., *U.S.A.* **68 C3** 54 45N 164 0W
Union, *Miss., U.S.A.* **81 J10** 32 34N 89 7W
Union, *Mo., U.S.A.* **80 F9** 38 27N 91 0W
Union, *S.C., U.S.A.* **77 H5** 34 43N 81 37W
Union, Mt., *U.S.A.* **83 J7** 34 34N 112 21W
Union City, *Calif., U.S.A.* **84 H4** 37 36N 122 1W
Union City, *N.J., U.S.A.* **79 F10** 40 45N 74 2W
Union City, *Pa., U.S.A.* **78 E5** 41 54N 79 51W
Union City, *Tenn., U.S.A.* **81 G10** 36 26N 89 3W
Union Gap, *U.S.A.* **82 C3** 46 33N 120 28W
Union Springs, *U.S.A.* **77 J3** 32 9N 85 43W
Uniondale, *S. Africa* **56 E3** 33 39S 23 7 E
Uniontown, *U.S.A.* **76 F6** 39 54N 79 44W
Unionville, *U.S.A.* **80 E8** 40 29N 93 1W
United Arab Emirates ■, *Asia* **45 F7** 23 50N 54 0 E
United Kingdom ■, *Europe* **7 E5** 53 0N 2 0W
United States of America ■, *N. Amer.* **74 C7** 37 0N 96 0W
Unity, *Canada* **73 C7** 52 30N 109 5W
Unjha, *India* **42 H5** 23 46N 72 24 E
Unnao, *India* **43 F9** 26 35N 80 30 E
Unst, *U.K.* **12 A8** 60 44N 0 53W
Unuk →, *Canada* **72 B2** 56 5N 131 3W
Uozu, *Japan* **31 F8** 36 48N 137 24 E
Upata, *Venezuela* **92 B6** 8 1N 62 24W
Upemba, L., *Zaïre* **55 D2** 8 30S 26 20 E
Upernavik, *Greenland* **4 B5** 72 49N 56 20W
Upington, *S. Africa* **56 D3** 28 25S 21 15 E
Upleta, *India* **42 J4** 21 46N 70 16 E
Upolu, *W. Samoa* **59 A13** 13 58S 172 0W
Upper Alkali Lake, *U.S.A.* **82 F3** 41 47N 120 8W
Upper Arrow L., *Canada* **72 C5** 50 30N 117 50W
Upper Foster L., *Canada* **73 B7** 56 47N 105 20W
Upper Hutt, *N.Z.* **59 J5** 41 8S 175 5 E
Upper Klamath L., *U.S.A.* **82 E3** 42 25N 121 55W
Upper Lake, *U.S.A.* **84 F4** 39 10N 122 54W
Upper Musquodoboit, *Canada* **71 C7** 45 10N 62 58W
Upper Red L., *U.S.A.* **80 A7** 48 8N 94 45W
Upper Sandusky, *U.S.A.* **76 E4** 40 50N 83 17W
Upper Volta = Burkina Faso ■, *Africa* **50 F4** 12 0N 1 0W
Uppland, *Sweden* **9 F17** 59 59N 17 48 E
Uppsala, *Sweden* **9 G17** 59 53N 17 38 E
Upshi, *India* **43 C7** 33 48N 77 52 E
Upstart, C., *Australia* **62 B4** 19 41S 147 45 E
Upton, *U.S.A.* **80 C2** 44 6N 104 38W
Ur, *Iraq* **44 D5** 30 55N 46 25 E
Uracara, *Brazil* **92 D7** 2 20S 57 50W
Urad Qianqi, *China* **34 D5** 40 40N 108 30 E
Urakawa, *Japan* **30 C11** 42 9N 142 47 E
Ural = Zhayyq →, *Kazakstan* **25 E9** 47 0N 51 48 E
Ural, *Australia* **63 E4** 33 21S 146 12 E
Ural Mts. = Uralskie Gory, *Eurasia* **24 C10** 60 0N 59 0 E
Uralla, *Australia* **63 E5** 30 37S 151 29 E
Uralsk = Oral, *Kazakstan* **24 D9** 51 20N 51 20 E
Uralskie Gory, *Eurasia* **24 C10** 60 0N 59 0 E
Urambo, *Tanzania* **54 D3** 5 4S 32 0 E
Urambo □, *Tanzania* **54 D3** 5 0S 32 0 E
Urandangi, *Australia* **62 C2** 21 32S 138 14 E
Uranium City, *Canada* **73 B7** 59 34N 108 37W
Uranquinty, *Australia* **63 F4** 35 10S 147 12 E
Urawa, *Japan* **31 G9** 35 50N 139 40 E
Uray, *Russia* **26 C7** 60 5N 65 15 E
'Uray'irah, *Si. Arabia* **45 E6** 25 57N 48 53 E
Urbana, *Ill., U.S.A.* **76 E1** 40 7N 88 12W
Urbana, *Ohio, U.S.A.* **76 E4** 40 7N 83 45W
Urbino, *Italy* **20 C5** 43 43N 12 38 E
Urbión, Picos de, *Spain* **19 A4** 42 1N 2 52W
Urcos, *Peru* **92 F4** 13 40S 71 38W
Urda, *Kazakstan* **25 E8** 48 52N 47 23 E
Urdinarrain, *Argentina* **94 C4** 32 37S 58 52W
Urdzhar, *Kazakstan* **26 E9** 47 5N 81 38 E
Ure →, *U.K.* **10 C6** 54 19N 1 31W
Ures, *Mexico* **86 B2** 29 30N 110 30W
Urfa = Sanliurfa, *Turkey* **25 G6** 37 12N 38 50 E
Urganch, *Uzbekistan* **26 E7** 41 40N 60 41 E
Urgench = Urganch, *Uzbekistan* **26 E7** 41 40N 60 41 E
Uri, *India* **43 B6** 34 8N 74 2 E
Uribia, *Colombia* **92 A4** 11 43N 72 16W
Uriondo, *Bolivia* **94 A3** 21 41S 64 41W
Urique, *Mexico* **86 B3** 27 13N 107 55W
Urique →, *Mexico* **86 B3** 26 29N 107 58W
Urk, *Neths.* **15 B5** 52 39N 5 36 E
Urla, *Turkey* **21 E12** 38 20N 26 47 E
Urmia = Orūmīyeh, *Iran* **44 B5** 37 40N 45 0 E
Urmia, L. = Orūmīyeh, Daryācheh-ye, *Iran* **44 B5** 37 50N 45 30 E
Uroševac, *Serbia, Yug.* **21 C9** 42 23N 21 10 E
Uruana, *Brazil* **93 G9** 15 30S 49 41W
Uruapan, *Mexico* **86 D4** 19 30N 102 0W
Urubamba, *Peru* **92 F4** 13 20S 72 10W
Urubamba →, *Peru* **92 F4** 10 43S 73 48W
Uruçuí, *Brazil* **93 E10** 7 20S 44 28W
Uruguai →, *Brazil* **95 B5** 26 0S 53 30W
Uruguaiana, *Brazil* **94 B4** 29 50S 57 0W
Uruguay ■, *S. Amer.* **94 C4** 32 30S 56 30W
Uruguay →, *S. Amer.* **94 C4** 34 12S 58 18W
Urumchi = Ürümqi, *China* **26 E9** 43 45N 87 45 E
Ürümqi, *China* **26 E9** 43 45N 87 45 E
Urup, Os., *Russia* **27 E16** 46 0N 151 0 E
Usa →, *Russia* **24 A10** 66 16N 59 49 E
Uşak, *Turkey* **25 G4** 38 43N 29 28 E
Usakos, *Namibia* **56 C2** 21 54S 15 31 E
Usedom, *Germany* **16 B8** 53 55N 14 2 E
Ush-Tobe, *Kazakstan* **26 E8** 45 16N 78 0 E
Ushakova, Os., *Russia* **4 A12** 82 0N 80 0 E
Ushant = Ouessant, I. d', *France* **18 B1** 48 28N 5 6W
Ushashi, *Tanzania* **54 C3** 1 59S 33 57 E
Ushibuka, *Japan* **31 H5** 32 11N 130 1 E
Ushuaia, *Argentina* **96 G3** 54 50S 68 23W
Ushumun, *Russia* **27 D13** 52 47N 126 32 E
Usk →, *U.K.* **11 F5** 51 33N 2 58W
Üsküdar, *Turkey* **25 F4** 41 0N 29 5 E
Usman, *Russia* **24 D6** 52 5N 39 48 E
Usoke, *Tanzania* **54 D3** 5 8S 32 24 E
Usolye Sibirskoye, *Russia* **27 D11** 52 48N 103 40 E
Uspallata, P. de, *Argentina* **94 C2** 32 37S 69 22W
Uspenskiy, *Kazakstan* **26 E8** 48 41N 72 43 E
Ussuri →, *Asia* **30 A7** 48 27N 135 0 E
Ussuriysk, *Russia* **27 E14** 43 48N 131 59 E
Ussurka, *Russia* **30 B6** 45 12N 133 31 E
Ust-Aldan = Batamay, *Russia* **27 C13** 63 30N 129 15 E
Ust Amginskoye = Khandyga, *Russia* **27 C14** 62 42N 135 35 E
Ust-Bolsheretsk, *Russia* **27 D16** 52 50N 156 15 E
Ust Chaun, *Russia* **27 C18** 68 47N 170 30 E
Ust'-Ilga, *Russia* **27 D11** 55 5N 104 55 E
Ust Ilimpeya = Yukti, *Russia* **27 C11** 63 26N 105 42 E
Ust-Ilimsk, *Russia* **27 D11** 58 3N 102 39 E
Ust Ishim, *Russia* **26 D8** 57 45N 71 10 E
Ust-Kamchatsk, *Russia* **27 D17** 56 10N 162 28 E
Ust-Kamenogorsk = Öskemen, *Kazakstan* **26 E9** 50 0N 82 36 E
Ust-Karenga, *Russia* **27 D12** 54 25N 116 30 E
Ust Khayryuzovo, *Russia* **27 D16** 57 15N 156 45 E
Ust-Kut, *Russia* **27 D11** 56 50N 105 42 E
Ust Kuyga, *Russia* **27 B14** 70 1N 135 43 E
Ust Maya, *Russia* **27 C14** 60 30N 134 28 E
Ust-Mil, *Russia* **27 D14** 59 40N 133 11 E
Ust Muya, *Russia* **27 D12** 56 27N 115 50 E
Ust-Nera, *Russia* **27 C15** 64 35N 143 15 E
Ust-Nyukzha, *Russia* **27 D13** 56 34N 121 37 E
Ust Olenek, *Russia* **27 B12** 73 0N 120 5 E
Ust-Omchug, *Russia* **27 C15** 61 9N 149 38 E
Ust Port, *Russia* **26 C9** 69 40N 84 26 E
Ust Tsilma, *Russia* **24 A9** 65 28N 52 11 E
Ust-Tungir, *Russia* **27 D13** 55 25N 120 36 E
Ust Urt = Ustyurt, Plateau, *Asia* **26 E6** 44 0N 55 0 E
Ust Usa, *Russia* **24 A10** 66 2N 56 57 E
Ust Vorkuta, *Russia* **26 C7** 67 24N 64 0 E
Ústí nad Labem, *Czech.* **16 C8** 50 41N 14 3 E
Ustica, *Italy* **20 E5** 38 42N 13 11 E
Ustinov = Izhevsk, *Russia* **24 C9** 56 51N 53 14 E
Ustye, *Russia* **27 D10** 57 46N 94 37 E
Ustyurt, Plateau, *Asia* **26 E6** 44 0N 55 0 E
Usu, *China* **32 B3** 44 27N 84 40 E
Usuki, *Japan* **31 H5** 33 8N 131 49 E
Usulután, *El Salv.* **88 D2** 13 25N 88 28W
Usumacinta →, *Mexico* **87 D6** 17 0N 91 0W
Usumbura = Bujumbura, *Burundi* **54 C2** 3 16S 29 18 E

Vienna

Usure, Tanzania 54 C3 4 40S 34 22 E
Uta, Indonesia 37 E9 4 33S 136 0 E
Utah □, U.S.A. 82 G8 39 20N 111 30W
Utah, L., U.S.A. 82 F8 40 10N 111 58W
Ute Creek →, U.S.A. 81 H3 35 21N 103 50W
Utena, Lithuania 9 J21 55 27N 25 40 E
Utete, Tanzania 54 D4 8 0S 38 45 E
Uthai Thani, Thailand 38 E3 15 22N 100 3 E
Uthal, Pakistan 42 G2 25 44N 66 40 E
Utiariti, Brazil 92 F7 13 0S 58 10W
Utica, N.Y., U.S.A. 79 C9 43 6N 75 14W
Utica, Ohio, U.S.A. 78 F2 40 14N 82 27W
Utik L., Canada 73 B9 55 15N 96 0W
Utikuma L., Canada 72 B5 55 50N 115 30W
Utrecht, Neths. 15 B5 52 5N 5 8 E
Utrecht, S. Africa 57 D5 27 38S 30 20 E
Utrecht □, Neths. 15 B5 52 6N 5 7 E
Utrera, Spain 19 D3 37 12N 5 48W
Utsjoki, Finland 8 B22 69 51N 26 59 E
Utsunomiya, Japan 31 F9 36 30N 139 50 E
Uttar Pradesh □, India 43 F9 27 0N 80 0 E
Uttaradit, Thailand 38 D3 17 36N 100 5 E
Uttoxeter, U.K. 10 E6 52 54N 1 52W
Uummannarsuaq = Farvel, Kap, Greenland 4 D5 59 48N 43 55W
Uusikaarlepyy, Finland 8 E20 63 32N 22 31 E
Uusikaupunki, Finland 9 F19 60 47N 21 25 E
Uva, Russia 24 C9 56 59N 52 13 E
Uvalde, U.S.A. 81 L5 29 13N 99 47W
Uvat, Russia 26 D7 59 5N 68 50 E
Uvinza, Tanzania 54 D3 5 5S 30 24 E
Uvira, Zaïre 54 C2 3 22S 29 3 E
Uvs Nuur, Mongolia 32 A4 50 20N 92 30 E
Uwajima, Japan 31 H6 33 10N 132 35 E
Uxbridge, Canada 78 B5 44 6N 79 7W
Uxin Qi, China 34 E5 38 50N 109 5 E
Uxmal, Mexico 87 C7 20 22N 89 46W
Uyandi, Russia 27 C15 69 19N 141 0 E
Uyuni, Bolivia 92 H5 20 28S 66 47W
Uzbekistan ■, Asia 26 E7 41 30N 65 0 E
Uzen, Kazakstan 25 F9 43 29N 52 54 E
Uzerche, France 18 D4 45 25N 1 34 E
Uzh →, Ukraine 17 C16 51 15N 30 12 E
Uzhgorod = Uzhhorod, Ukraine 17 D12 48 36N 22 18 E
Uzhhorod, Ukraine 17 D12 48 36N 22 18 E
Uzunköprü, Turkey 21 D12 41 16N 26 43 E

V

Vaal →, S. Africa 56 D3 29 4S 23 38 E
Vaal Dam, S. Africa 57 D4 27 0S 28 14 E
Vaalwater, S. Africa 57 C4 24 15S 28 8 E
Vaasa, Finland 8 E19 63 6N 21 38 E
Vác, Hungary 17 E10 47 49N 19 10 E
Vacaria, Brazil 95 B5 28 31S 50 52W
Vacaville, U.S.A. 84 G5 38 21N 121 59W
Vach → = Vakh →, Russia 26 C8 60 45N 76 45 E
Vache, Î.-à-, Haiti 89 C5 18 2N 73 35W
Vadnagar, India 42 H5 23 47N 72 40 E
Vadodara, India 42 H5 22 20N 73 10 E
Vadsø, Norway 8 A23 70 3N 29 50 E
Vaduz, Liech. 16 E5 47 8N 9 31 E
Værøy, Norway 8 C15 67 40N 12 40 E
Vágar, Færoe Is. 8 E9 62 5N 7 15W
Vågsfjorden, Norway 8 B17 68 50N 16 50 E
Váh →, Slovak Rep. 17 D9 47 43N 18 7 E
Vahsel B., Antarctica 5 D1 75 0S 35 0W
Vái, Greece 23 D8 35 15N 26 18 E
Vaigach, Russia 26 B6 70 10N 59 0 E
Vakh →, Russia 26 C8 60 45N 76 45 E
Val d'Or, Canada 70 C4 48 7N 77 47W
Val Marie, Canada 73 D7 49 15N 107 45W
Valahia, Romania 17 F13 44 35N 25 0 E
Valandovo, Macedonia 21 D10 41 19N 22 34 E
Valcheta, Argentina 96 E3 40 40S 66 8W
Valdayskaya Vozvyshennost, Russia 24 C5 57 0N 33 30 E
Valdepeñas, Spain 19 C4 38 43N 3 25W
Valdés, Pen., Argentina 96 E4 42 30S 63 45W
Valdez, U.S.A. 68 B5 61 7N 146 16W
Valdivia, Chile 96 D2 39 50S 73 14W
Valdosta, U.S.A. 77 K4 30 50N 83 17W
Valdres, Norway 9 F13 61 5N 9 5 E
Vale, U.S.A. 82 E5 43 59N 117 15W
Vale of Glamorgan □, U.K. 11 F4 51 28N 3 25W
Valença, Brazil 93 F11 13 20S 39 5W
Valença do Piauí, Brazil 93 E10 6 20S 41 45W
Valence, France 18 D6 44 57N 4 54 E
Valencia, Spain 19 C5 39 27N 0 23W
Valencia, Venezuela 92 A5 10 11N 68 0W
Valencia □, Spain 19 C5 39 20N 0 40W
Valencia, G. de, Spain 19 C6 39 30N 0 20 E
Valencia de Alcántara, Spain 19 C2 39 25N 7 14W
Valencia Harbour, Ireland 13 E1 51 56N 10 19W
Valencia I., Ireland 13 E1 51 54N 10 22W
Valenciennes, France 18 A5 50 20N 3 34 E
Valentim, Sa. do, Brazil 93 E10 6 0S 43 30W
Valentin, Russia 30 C7 43 8N 134 17 E
Valentine, Nebr., U.S.A. 80 D4 42 52N 100 33W
Valentine, Tex., U.S.A. 81 K2 30 35N 104 30W
Valera, Venezuela 92 B4 9 19N 70 37W
Valga, Estonia 9 H22 57 47N 26 2 E
Valier, U.S.A. 82 B7 48 18N 112 16W
Valjevo, Serbia, Yug. 21 B8 44 18N 19 53 E
Valka, Latvia 9 H21 57 42N 25 57 E
Valkeakoski, Finland 9 F20 61 16N 24 2 E
Valkenswaard, Neths. 15 C5 51 21N 5 29 E
Vall de Uxó, Spain 19 C5 39 49N 0 15W
Valladolid, Mexico 87 C7 20 40N 88 11W
Valladolid, Spain 19 B3 41 38N 4 43W
Valldemosa, Spain 22 B9 39 43N 2 37 E
Valle de la Pascua, Venezuela 92 B5 9 13N 66 0W
Valle de las Palmas, Mexico 85 N10 32 20N 116 43W
Valle de Santiago, Mexico 86 C4 20 25N 101 15W
Valle de Suchil, Mexico 86 C4 23 38N 103 55W
Valle de Zaragoza, Mexico 86 B3 27 28N 105 49W
Valle Fértil, Sierra del, Argentina 94 C2 30 20S 68 0W
Valle Hermoso, Mexico 87 B5 25 35N 97 40W
Valledupar, Colombia 92 A4 10 29N 73 15W
Vallehermoso, Canary Is. 22 F2 28 10N 17 15W
Vallejo, U.S.A. 84 G4 38 7N 122 14W
Vallenar, Chile 94 B1 28 30S 70 50W
Valletta, Malta 23 D2 35 54N 14 31 E
Valley Center, U.S.A. 85 M9 33 13N 117 2W
Valley City, U.S.A. 80 B6 46 55N 98 0W
Valley Falls, U.S.A. 82 E3 42 29N 120 17W
Valley Springs, U.S.A. 84 G6 38 12N 120 50W
Valley Wells, U.S.A. 85 K11 35 27N 115 46W
Valleyview, Canada 72 B5 55 5N 117 17W
Vallimanca, Arroyo, Argentina 94 D4 35 40S 59 10W
Valls, Spain 19 B6 41 18N 1 15 E
Valmiera, Latvia 9 H21 57 37N 25 29 E
Valognes, France 18 B3 49 30N 1 28W
Valona = Vlóra, Albania 21 D8 40 32N 19 28 E
Valozhyn, Belarus 17 A14 54 3N 26 30 E
Valparaíso, Chile 94 C1 33 2S 71 40W
Valparaíso, Mexico 86 C4 22 50N 103 32W
Valparaiso, U.S.A. 76 E2 41 28N 87 4W
Valparaíso □, Chile 94 C1 33 2S 71 40W
Vals →, S. Africa 56 D4 27 23S 26 30 E
Vals, Tanjung, Indonesia 37 F9 8 26S 137 25 E
Valsad, India 40 J8 20 40N 72 58 E
Valverde, Canary Is. 22 G2 27 48N 17 55W
Valverde del Camino, Spain 19 D2 37 35N 6 47W
Vammala, Finland 9 F20 61 20N 22 54 E
Vámos, Greece 23 D6 35 24N 24 13 E
Van, Turkey 25 G7 38 30N 43 20 E
Van, L. = Van Gölü, Turkey 25 G7 38 30N 43 0 E
Van Alstyne, U.S.A. 81 J6 33 25N 96 35W
Van Bruyssel, Canada 71 C5 47 56N 72 9W
Van Buren, Canada 71 C6 47 10N 67 55W
Van Buren, Ark., U.S.A. 81 H7 35 26N 94 21W
Van Buren, Maine, U.S.A. 77 B11 47 10N 67 58W
Van Buren, Mo., U.S.A. 81 G9 37 0N 91 1W
Van Canh, Vietnam 38 F7 13 37N 109 0 E
Van Diemen, C., N. Terr., Australia 60 B5 11 9S 130 24 E
Van Diemen, C., Queens., Australia 62 B2 16 30S 139 46 E
Van Diemen G., Australia 60 B5 11 45S 132 0 E
Van Gölü, Turkey 25 G7 38 30N 43 0 E
Van Horn, U.S.A. 81 K2 31 3N 104 50W
Van Ninh, Vietnam 38 F7 12 42N 109 14 E
Van Rees, Pegunungan, Indonesia 37 E9 2 35S 138 15 E
Van Tassell, U.S.A. 80 D2 42 40N 104 5W
Van Wert, U.S.A. 76 E3 40 52N 84 35W
Van Yen, Vietnam 38 B5 21 4N 104 42 E
Vanadzor, Armenia 25 F7 40 48N 44 30 E
Vanavara, Russia 27 C11 60 22N 102 16 E
Vancouver, Canada 72 D4 49 15N 123 10W
Vancouver, U.S.A. 84 E4 45 38N 122 40W
Vancouver, C., Australia 61 G2 35 2S 118 11 E
Vancouver I., Canada 72 D3 49 50N 126 0W
Vandalia, Ill., U.S.A. 80 F10 38 58N 89 6W
Vandalia, Mo., U.S.A. 80 F9 39 19N 91 29W
Vandenburg, U.S.A. 85 L6 34 35N 120 33W
Vanderbijlpark, S. Africa 57 D4 26 42S 27 54 E
Vandergrift, U.S.A. 78 F5 40 36N 79 34W
Vanderhoof, Canada 72 C4 54 0N 124 0W
Vanderkloof Dam, S. Africa 56 E3 30 4S 24 40 E
Vanderlin I., Australia 62 B2 15 44S 137 2 E
Vandyke, Australia 62 C4 24 10S 147 51 E
Vänern, Sweden 9 G15 58 47N 13 30 E
Vänersborg, Sweden 9 G15 58 26N 12 19 E
Vang Vieng, Laos 38 C4 18 58N 102 32 E
Vanga, Kenya 54 C4 4 35S 39 12 E
Vangaindrano, Madag. 57 C8 23 21S 47 36 E
Vanguard, Canada 73 D7 49 55N 107 20W
Vanier, Canada 70 C4 45 27N 75 40W
Vankleek Hill, Canada 70 C5 45 32N 74 40W
Vanna, Norway 8 A18 70 6N 19 50 E
Vännäs, Sweden 8 E18 63 58N 19 48 E
Vannes, France 18 C2 47 40N 2 47W
Vanrhynsdorp, S. Africa 56 E2 31 36S 18 44 E
Vanrook, Australia 62 B3 16 57S 141 57 E
Vansbro, Sweden 9 F16 60 32N 14 15 E
Vansittart B., Australia 60 B4 14 3S 126 17 E
Vantaa, Finland 9 F21 60 18N 24 58 E
Vanthli, India 42 J4 21 28N 70 25 E
Vanua Levu, Fiji 59 C8 16 33S 179 15 E
Vanua Mbalavu, Fiji 59 C9 17 40S 178 57W
Vanuatu ■, Pac. Oc. 64 J8 15 0S 168 0 E
Vanwyksvlei, S. Africa 56 E3 30 18S 21 49 E
Vanzylsrus, S. Africa 56 D3 26 52S 22 4 E
Vapnyarka, Ukraine 17 D15 48 32N 28 45 E
Varanasi, India 43 G10 25 22N 83 0 E
Varanger-halvøya, Norway 8 A23 70 25N 29 30 E
Varangerfjorden, Norway 8 A23 70 3N 29 25 E
Varaždin, Croatia 16 E9 46 20N 16 20 E
Varberg, Sweden 9 H15 57 6N 12 20 E
Vardar = Axiós →, Greece 21 D10 40 57N 22 35 E
Varde, Denmark 9 J13 55 38N 8 29 E
Vardø, Norway 8 A24 70 23N 31 5 E
Varella, Mui, Vietnam 38 F7 12 54N 109 26 E
Varėna, Lithuania 9 J21 54 12N 24 30 E
Varese, Italy 20 B3 45 48N 8 50 E
Varginha, Brazil 95 A6 21 33S 45 25W
Variadero, U.S.A. 81 H2 35 43N 104 17W
Varillas, Chile 94 A1 24 0S 70 10W
Varkaus, Finland 9 E22 62 19N 27 50 E
Varna, Bulgaria 21 C12 43 13N 27 56 E
Värnamo, Sweden 9 H16 57 10N 14 3 E
Vars, Canada 79 A9 45 21N 75 21W
Varzaneh, Iran 45 C7 32 25N 52 40 E
Vasa Barris →, Brazil 93 F11 11 10S 37 10W
Vascongadas = País Vasco □, Spain 19 A4 42 50N 2 45W
Vasht = Khāsh, Iran 40 E2 28 15N 61 15 E
Vasilevichi, Belarus 17 B15 52 15N 29 50 E
Vasilkov = Vasylkiv, Ukraine 17 C16 50 7N 30 15 E
Vaslui, Romania 17 E14 46 38N 27 42 E
Vassar, Canada 73 D9 49 10N 95 55W
Vassar, U.S.A. 76 D4 43 22N 83 35W
Västerås, Sweden 9 G17 59 37N 16 38 E
Västerbotten, Sweden 8 D18 64 36N 20 4 E
Västerdalälven →, Sweden 9 F16 60 30N 14 7 E
Västervik, Sweden 9 H17 57 43N 16 33 E
Västmanland, Sweden 9 G16 59 45N 16 20 E
Vasto, Italy 20 C6 42 8N 14 40 E
Vasylkiv, Ukraine 17 C16 50 7N 30 15 E
Vatican City ■, Europe 20 D5 41 54N 12 27 E
Vatili, Cyprus 23 D12 35 6N 33 40 E
Vatnajökull, Iceland 8 D5 64 30N 16 48W
Vatoa, Fiji 59 D9 19 50S 178 13W
Vatólakkos, Greece 23 D5 35 27N 23 53 E
Vatoloha, Madag. 57 B8 17 52S 47 48 E
Vatomandry, Madag. 57 B8 19 20S 48 59 E
Vatra-Dornei, Romania 17 E13 47 22N 25 22 E
Vättern, Sweden 9 G16 58 25N 14 30 E
Vaughn, Mont., U.S.A. 82 C8 47 33N 111 33W
Vaughn, N. Mex., U.S.A. 83 J11 34 36N 105 13W
Vaupés = Uaupés →, Brazil 92 C5 0 2N 67 16W
Vauxhall, Canada 72 C6 50 5N 112 9W
Vava'u, Tonga 59 D11 18 36S 174 0W
Vawkavysk, Belarus 17 B13 53 9N 24 30 E
Växjö, Sweden 9 H16 56 52N 14 50 E
Vaygach, Ostrov, Russia 26 C6 70 0N 60 0 E
Váyia, Ákra, Greece 23 C10 36 15N 28 11 E
Vechte →, Neths. 15 B6 52 34N 6 6 E
Vedea →, Romania 17 G13 43 53N 25 59 E
Vedia, Argentina 94 C3 34 30S 61 31W
Vedra, I. del, Spain 22 C7 38 52N 1 12 E
Veendam, Neths. 15 A6 53 5N 6 52 E
Veenendaal, Neths. 15 B5 52 2N 5 34 E
Vefsna →, Norway 8 D15 65 48N 13 10 E
Vega, Norway 8 D14 65 40N 11 55 E
Vega, U.S.A. 81 H3 35 15N 102 26W
Veghel, Neths. 15 C5 51 37N 5 32 E
Vegreville, Canada 72 C6 53 30N 112 5W
Vejer de la Frontera, Spain 19 D3 36 15N 5 59W
Vejle, Denmark 9 J13 55 43N 9 30 E
Velas, C., Costa Rica 88 D2 10 21N 85 52W
Velasco, Sierra de, Argentina 94 B2 29 20S 67 10W
Velddrif, S. Africa 56 E2 32 42S 18 11 E
Velebit Planina, Croatia 16 F8 44 50N 15 20 E
Vélez, Colombia 92 B4 6 1N 73 41W
Vélez Málaga, Spain 19 D3 36 48N 4 5W
Vélez Rubio, Spain 19 D4 37 41N 2 5W
Velhas →, Brazil 93 G10 17 13S 44 49W
Velika Kapela, Croatia 16 F8 45 10N 15 5 E
Velikaya →, Russia 24 C4 57 48N 28 10 E
Velikaya Kema, Russia 30 B8 45 30N 137 12 E
Veliki Ustyug, Russia 24 B8 60 47N 46 20 E
Velikiye Luki, Russia 24 C5 56 25N 30 32 E
Veliko Tŭrnovo, Bulgaria 21 C11 43 5N 25 41 E
Velikonda Range, India 40 M11 14 45N 79 10 E
Velletri, Italy 20 D5 41 41N 12 47 E
Vellore, India 40 N11 12 57N 79 10 E
Velsen-Noord, Neths. 15 B4 52 27N 4 40 E
Velsk, Russia 24 B7 61 10N 42 5 E
Velva, U.S.A. 80 A4 48 4N 100 56W
Venado Tuerto, Argentina 94 C3 33 50S 62 0W
Vendée □, France 18 C3 46 50N 1 35W
Vendôme, France 18 C4 47 47N 1 3 E
Venézia, Italy 20 B5 45 27N 12 21 E
Venézia, G. di, Italy 20 B5 45 15N 13 0 E
Venezuela ■, S. Amer. 92 B5 8 0N 66 0W
Venezuela, G. de, Venezuela 92 A4 11 30N 71 0W
Vengurla, India 40 M8 15 53N 73 45 E
Venice = Venézia, Italy 20 B5 45 27N 12 21 E
Venkatapuram, India 41 K12 18 20N 80 30 E
Venlo, Neths. 15 C6 51 22N 6 11 E
Vennesla, Norway 9 G12 58 15N 8 0 E
Venraij, Neths. 15 C5 51 31N 6 0 E
Ventana, Punta de la, Mexico 86 C3 24 4N 109 48W
Ventana, Sa. de la, Argentina 94 D3 38 0S 62 30W
Ventersburg, S. Africa 56 D4 28 7S 27 9 E
Venterstad, S. Africa 56 E4 30 47S 25 48 E
Ventnor, U.K. 11 G6 50 36N 1 12W
Ventotene, Italy 20 D5 40 47N 13 25 E
Ventoux, Mt., France 18 D6 44 10N 5 17 E
Ventspils, Latvia 9 H19 57 25N 21 32 E
Ventuarí →, Venezuela 92 C5 3 58N 67 2W
Ventucopa, U.S.A. 85 L7 34 50N 119 29W
Ventura, U.S.A. 85 L7 34 17N 119 18W
Venus B., Australia 63 F4 38 40S 145 42 E
Vera, Argentina 94 B3 29 30S 60 20W
Vera, Spain 19 D5 37 15N 1 51W
Veracruz, Mexico 87 D5 19 10N 96 10W
Veracruz □, Mexico 87 D5 19 0N 96 15W
Veraval, India 42 J4 20 53N 70 27 E
Verbánia, Italy 20 B3 45 56N 8 33 E
Vercelli, Italy 20 B3 45 19N 8 25 E
Verdalsøra, Norway 8 E14 63 48N 11 30 E
Verde →, Argentina 96 E3 41 56S 65 5W
Verde →, Chihuahua, Mexico 86 B3 26 29N 107 58W
Verde →, Oaxaca, Mexico 87 D5 15 59N 97 50W
Verde →, Veracruz, Mexico 86 C4 21 10N 102 50W
Verde →, Paraguay 94 A4 23 9S 57 37W
Verde, Cay, Bahamas 88 B4 23 0N 75 5W
Verden, Germany 16 B5 52 55N 9 14 E
Verdi, U.S.A. 84 F7 39 31N 119 59W
Verdigre, U.S.A. 80 D5 42 36N 98 2W
Verdun, France 18 B6 49 9N 5 24 E
Vereeniging, S. Africa 57 D4 26 38S 27 57 E
Vérendrye, Parc Prov. de la, Canada 70 C4 47 20N 76 40W
Verga, C., Guinea 50 F2 10 30N 14 10W
Vergemont, Australia 62 C3 23 33S 143 1 E
Vergemont Cr. →, Australia 62 C3 24 16S 143 16 E
Vergennes, U.S.A. 79 B11 44 10N 73 15W
Verín, Spain 19 B2 41 57N 7 27W
Verkhnevilyuysk, Russia 27 C13 63 27N 120 18 E
Verkhneye Kalinino, Russia 27 D11 59 54N 108 8 E
Verkhniy Baskunchak, Russia 25 E8 48 14N 46 44 E
Verkhnyaya Amga, Russia 27 D13 59 50N 127 0 E
Verkhoyansk, Russia 27 C14 67 35N 133 25 E
Verkhoyansk Ra. = Verkhoyanskiy Khrebet, Russia 27 C13 66 0N 129 0 E
Verkhoyanskiy Khrebet, Russia 27 C13 66 0N 129 0 E
Verlo, Canada 73 C7 50 19N 108 35W
Vermilion, Canada 73 C6 53 20N 110 50W
Vermilion →, Alta., Canada 73 C6 53 22N 110 51W
Vermilion →, Qué., Canada 70 C5 47 38N 72 56W
Vermilion, B., U.S.A. 81 L9 29 45N 91 55W
Vermilion Bay, Canada 73 D10 49 51N 93 34W
Vermilion Chutes, Canada 72 B6 58 22N 114 51W
Vermilion L., U.S.A. 80 B8 47 53N 92 26W
Vermillion, U.S.A. 80 D6 42 47N 96 56W
Vermont □, U.S.A. 79 C12 44 0N 73 0W
Vernal, U.S.A. 82 F9 40 27N 109 32W
Vernalis, U.S.A. 84 H5 37 36N 121 17W
Verner, Canada 70 C3 46 25N 80 8W
Verneukpan, S. Africa 56 D3 30 0S 21 0 E
Vernon, Canada 72 C5 50 20N 119 15W
Vernon, U.S.A. 81 H5 34 9N 99 17W
Vernonia, U.S.A. 84 E3 45 52N 123 11W
Vero Beach, U.S.A. 77 M5 27 38N 80 24W
Véroia, Greece 21 D10 40 34N 22 12 E
Verona, Italy 20 B4 45 27N 11 0 E
Versailles, France 18 B5 48 48N 2 8 E
Vert, C., Senegal 50 F1 14 45N 17 30W
Verulam, S. Africa 57 D5 29 38S 31 2 E
Verviers, Belgium 15 D5 50 37N 5 52 E
Veselovskoye Vdkhr., Russia 25 E7 46 58N 41 25 E
Vesoul, France 18 C7 47 40N 6 11 E
Vesterålen, Norway 8 B16 68 45N 15 0 E
Vestfjorden, Norway 8 C15 67 55N 14 0 E
Vestmannaeyjar, Iceland 8 E3 63 27N 20 15W
Vestspitsbergen, Svalbard 4 B8 78 40N 17 0 E
Vestvågøy, Norway 8 B15 68 18N 13 50 E
Vesuvio, Italy 20 D6 40 49N 14 26 E
Vesuvius, Mt. = Vesuvio, Italy 20 D6 40 49N 14 26 E
Veszprém, Hungary 17 E9 47 8N 17 57 E
Vetlanda, Sweden 9 H16 57 24N 15 3 E
Vetlugu →, Russia 26 D5 56 36N 46 4 E
Vettore, Mte., Italy 20 C5 42 49N 13 16 E
Veurne, Belgium 15 C2 51 5N 2 40 E
Veys, Iran 45 D6 31 30N 49 0 E
Vezhen, Bulgaria 21 C11 42 50N 24 20 E
Vi Thanh, Vietnam 39 H5 9 42N 105 26 E
Viacha, Bolivia 92 G5 16 39S 68 18W
Viamão, Brazil 95 C5 30 5S 51 0W
Viana, Brazil 93 D10 3 13S 44 55W
Viana do Alentejo, Portugal 19 C2 38 17N 7 59W
Viana do Castelo, Portugal 19 B1 41 42N 8 50W
Vianópolis, Brazil 93 G9 16 40S 48 35W
Viaréggio, Italy 20 C4 43 52N 10 14 E
Vibank, Canada 73 C8 50 20N 103 56W
Vibo Valéntia, Italy 20 E7 38 40N 16 6 E
Viborg, Denmark 9 H13 56 27N 9 23 E
Vicenza, Italy 20 B4 45 33N 11 33 E
Vich, Spain 19 B7 41 58N 2 19 E
Vichy, France 18 C5 46 9N 3 26 E
Vicksburg, Ariz., U.S.A. 85 M13 33 45N 113 45W
Vicksburg, Mich., U.S.A. 76 D3 42 7N 85 32W
Vicksburg, Miss., U.S.A. 81 J9 32 21N 90 53W
Viçosa, Brazil 93 E11 9 28S 36 14W
Victor, India 42 J4 21 0N 71 30 E
Victor, Colo., U.S.A. 80 F2 38 43N 105 9W
Victor, N.Y., U.S.A. 78 D7 42 58N 77 24W
Victor Harbor, Australia 63 F2 35 30S 138 37 E
Victoria, Argentina 94 C3 32 40S 60 10W
Victoria, Canada 72 D4 48 30N 123 25W
Victoria, Chile 96 D2 38 13S 72 20W
Victoria, Guinea 50 F2 10 50N 14 32W
Victoria, Malaysia 36 C5 5 20N 115 14 E
Victoria, Malta 23 C1 36 2N 14 14 E
Victoria, Kans., U.S.A. 80 F5 38 52N 99 9W
Victoria, Tex., U.S.A. 81 L6 28 48N 97 0W
Victoria □, Australia 63 F3 37 0S 144 0 E
Victoria →, Australia 60 C4 15 10S 129 40 E
Victoria, Grand L., Canada 70 C4 47 31N 77 30W
Victoria, L., Africa 54 C3 1 0S 33 0 E
Victoria, L., Australia 63 E3 33 57S 141 15 E
Victoria Beach, Canada 73 C9 50 40N 96 35W
Victoria de Durango, Mexico 86 C4 24 3N 104 39W
Victoria de las Tunas, Cuba 88 B4 20 58N 76 59W
Victoria Falls, Zimbabwe 55 F2 17 58S 25 52 E
Victoria Harbour, Canada 70 D4 44 45N 79 45W
Victoria I., Canada 68 A8 71 0N 111 0W
Victoria Ld., Antarctica 5 D11 75 0S 160 0 E
Victoria Nile →, Uganda 54 B3 2 14N 31 26 E
Victoria Res., Canada 71 C8 48 20N 57 27W
Victoria River Downs, Australia 60 C5 16 25S 131 0 E
Victoria Taungdeik, Burma 41 J18 21 15N 93 55 E
Victoria West, S. Africa 56 E3 31 25S 23 4 E
Victoriaville, Canada 71 C5 46 4N 71 56W
Victorica, Argentina 94 D2 36 20S 65 30W
Victorville, U.S.A. 85 L9 34 32N 117 18W
Vicuña, Chile 94 C1 30 0S 70 50W
Vicuña Mackenna, Argentina 94 C3 33 53S 64 25W
Vidal, U.S.A. 85 L12 34 7N 114 31W
Vidal Junction, U.S.A. 85 L12 34 11N 114 34W
Vidalia, U.S.A. 77 J4 32 13N 82 25W
Vidho, Greece 23 A3 39 38N 19 55 E
Vidin, Bulgaria 21 C10 43 59N 22 50 E
Vidisha, India 42 H7 23 28N 77 53 E
Vidzy, Belarus 9 J22 55 23N 26 37 E
Viedma, Argentina 96 E4 40 50S 63 0W
Viedma, L., Argentina 96 F2 49 30S 72 30W
Vieng Pou Kha, Laos 38 B3 20 41N 101 4 E
Vienna = Wien, Austria 16 D9 48 12N 16 22 E

Vienna

Vienna, *U.S.A.* **81 G10** 37 25N 88 54W
Vienne, *France* **18 D6** 45 31N 4 53 E
Vienne →, *France* **18 C4** 47 13N 0 5 E
Vientiane, *Laos* **38 D4** 17 58N 102 36 E
Vientos, Paso de los, *Caribbean* **89 C5** 20 0N 74 0W
Vierzon, *France* **18 C5** 47 13N 2 5 E
Vietnam ■, *Asia* **38 C5** 19 0N 106 0 E
Vigan, *Phil.* **37 A6** 17 35N 120 28 E
Vigévano, *Italy* **20 B3** 45 19N 8 51 E
Vigia, *Brazil* **93 D9** 0 50S 48 5W
Vigía Chico, *Mexico* **87 D7** 19 46N 87 35W
Víglas, Ákra, *Greece* **23 D9** 35 54N 27 51 E
Vigo, *Spain* **19 A1** 42 12N 8 41W
Vijayawada, *India* **41 L12** 16 31N 80 39 E
Vík, *Iceland* **8 E4** 63 25N 19 1W
Vikeke, *Indonesia* **37 F7** 8 52S 126 23 E
Viking, *Canada* **72 C6** 53 7N 111 50W
Vikna, *Norway* **8 D14** 64 55N 10 58 E
Vikulovo, *Russia* **26 D8** 56 50N 70 40 E
Vila da Maganja, *Mozam.* **55 F4** 17 18S 37 30 E
Vila de João Belo = Xai-Xai, *Mozam.* **57 D5** 25 6S 33 31 E
Vila do Bispo, *Portugal* **19 D1** 37 5N 8 53W
Vila do Chibuto, *Mozam.* **57 C5** 24 40S 33 33 E
Vila Franca de Xira, *Portugal* **19 C1** 38 57N 8 59W
Vila Gamito, *Mozam.* **55 E3** 14 12S 33 0 E
Vila Gomes da Costa, *Mozam.* **57 C5** 24 20S 33 37 E
Vila Machado, *Mozam.* **55 F3** 19 15S 34 14 E
Vila Mouzinho, *Mozam.* **55 E3** 14 48S 34 25 E
Vila Nova de Gaia, *Portugal* **19 B1** 41 8N 8 37W
Vila Real, *Portugal* **19 B2** 41 17N 7 48W
Vila Real de Santo António, *Portugal* **19 D2** 37 10N 7 28W
Vila Vasco da Gama, *Mozam.* **55 E3** 14 54S 32 14 E
Vila Velha, *Brazil* **95 A7** 20 20S 40 17W
Vilaine →, *France* **18 C2** 47 30N 2 27W
Vilanandro, Tanjona, *Madag.* **57 B7** 16 11S 44 27 E
Vilanculos, *Mozam.* **57 C6** 22 1S 35 17 E
Vileyka, *Belarus* **17 A14** 54 30N 26 53 E
Vilhelmina, *Sweden* **8 D17** 64 35N 16 39 E
Vilhena, *Brazil* **92 F6** 12 40S 60 5W
Viliga, *Russia* **27 C16** 61 36N 156 56 E
Viliya →, *Lithuania* **9 J21** 55 8N 24 16 E
Viljandi, *Estonia* **9 G21** 58 28N 25 30 E
Vilkitskogo, Proliv, *Russia* **27 B11** 78 0N 103 0 E
Vilkovo = Vylkove, *Ukraine* **17 F15** 45 28N 29 32 E
Villa Abecia, *Bolivia* **94 A2** 21 0S 68 18W
Villa Ahumada, *Mexico* **86 A3** 30 38N 106 30W
Villa Ana, *Argentina* **94 B4** 28 28S 59 40W
Villa Ángela, *Argentina* **94 B3** 27 34S 60 45W
Villa Bella, *Bolivia* **92 F5** 10 25S 65 22W
Villa Bens = Tarfaya, *Morocco* **50 C2** 27 55N 12 55W
Villa Cañás, *Argentina* **94 C3** 34 0S 61 35W
Villa Carlos, *Spain* **22 B11** 39 53N 4 17 E
Villa Cisneros = Dakhla, *W. Sahara* **50 D1** 23 50N 15 53W
Villa Colón, *Argentina* **94 C2** 31 38S 68 20W
Villa Constitución, *Argentina* **94 C3** 33 15S 60 20W
Villa de María, *Argentina* **94 B3** 29 55S 63 43W
Villa Dolores, *Argentina* **94 C2** 31 58S 65 15W
Villa Frontera, *Mexico* **86 B4** 26 56N 101 27W
Villa Guillermina, *Argentina* **94 B4** 28 15S 59 29W
Villa Hayes, *Paraguay* **94 B4** 25 5S 57 20W
Villa Iris, *Argentina* **94 D3** 38 12S 63 12W
Villa Juárez, *Mexico* **86 B4** 27 37N 100 44W
Villa María, *Argentina* **94 C3** 32 20S 63 10W
Villa Mazán, *Argentina* **94 B2** 28 40S 66 30W
Villa Montes, *Bolivia* **94 A3** 21 10S 63 30W
Villa Ocampo, *Argentina* **94 B4** 28 30S 59 20W
Villa Ocampo, *Mexico* **86 B3** 26 29N 105 30W
Villa Ojo de Agua, *Argentina* **94 B3** 29 30S 63 44W
Villa San José, *Argentina* **94 C4** 32 12S 58 15W
Villa San Martín, *Argentina* **94 B3** 28 15S 64 9W
Villa Unión, *Mexico* **86 C3** 23 12N 106 14W
Villacarrillo, *Spain* **19 C4** 38 7N 3 3W
Villach, *Austria* **16 E7** 46 37N 13 51 E
Villafranca de los Caballeros, *Spain* **22 B10** 39 34N 3 25 E
Villagarcía de Arosa, *Spain* **19 A1** 42 34N 8 46W
Villagrán, *Mexico* **87 C5** 24 29N 99 29W
Villaguay, *Argentina* **94 C4** 32 0S 59 0W
Villahermosa, *Mexico* **87 D6** 17 59N 92 55W
Villajoyosa, *Spain* **19 C5** 38 30N 0 12W
Villalba, *Spain* **19 A2** 43 26N 7 40W
Villanueva, *U.S.A.* **83 J11** 35 16N 105 22W
Villanueva de la Serena, *Spain* **19 C3** 38 59N 5 50W
Villanueva y Geltrú, *Spain* **19 B6** 41 13N 1 40 E
Villarreal, *Spain* **19 C5** 39 55N 0 3W
Villarrica, *Chile* **96 D2** 39 15S 72 15W
Villarrica, *Paraguay* **94 B4** 25 40S 56 30W
Villarrobledo, *Spain* **19 C4** 39 18N 2 36W
Villavicencio, *Argentina* **94 C2** 32 28S 69 0W
Villavicencio, *Colombia* **92 C4** 4 9N 73 37W
Villaviciosa, *Spain* **19 A3** 43 32N 5 27W
Villazón, *Bolivia* **94 A2** 22 0S 65 35W
Ville-Marie, *Canada* **70 C4** 47 20N 79 30W
Ville Platte, *U.S.A.* **81 K8** 30 41N 92 17W
Villena, *Spain* **19 C5** 38 39N 0 52W
Villeneuve-d'Ascq, *France* **18 A5** 50 38N 3 9 E
Villeneuve-sur-Lot, *France* **18 D4** 44 24N 0 42 E
Villiers, *S. Africa* **57 D4** 27 2S 28 36 E
Villingen-Schwenningen, *Germany* **16 D5** 48 3N 8 26 E
Villisca, *U.S.A.* **80 E7** 40 56N 94 59W
Vilna, *Canada* **72 C6** 54 7N 111 55W
Vilnius, *Lithuania* **9 J21** 54 38N 25 19 E
Vilvoorde, *Belgium* **15 D4** 50 56N 4 26 E
Vilyuy →, *Russia* **27 C13** 64 24N 126 26 E
Vilyuysk, *Russia* **27 C13** 63 40N 121 35 E
Viña del Mar, *Chile* **94 C1** 33 0S 71 30W
Vinaroz, *Spain* **19 B6** 40 30N 0 27 E
Vincennes, *U.S.A.* **76 F2** 38 41N 87 32W
Vincent, *U.S.A.* **85 L8** 34 33N 118 11W
Vinchina, *Argentina* **94 B2** 28 45S 68 15W
Vindelälven →, *Sweden* **8 E18** 63 55N 19 50 E
Vindeln, *Sweden* **8 D18** 64 12N 19 43 E
Vindhya Ra., *India* **42 H7** 22 50N 77 0 E
Vineland, *U.S.A.* **76 F8** 39 29N 75 2W
Vinh, *Vietnam* **38 C5** 18 45N 105 38 E
Vinh Linh, *Vietnam* **38 D6** 17 4N 107 2 E
Vinh Long, *Vietnam* **39 G5** 10 16N 105 57 E
Vinh Yen, *Vietnam* **38 B5** 21 21N 105 35 E
Vinita, *U.S.A.* **81 G7** 36 39N 95 9W
Vinkovci, *Croatia* **21 B8** 45 19N 18 48 E
Vinnitsa = Vinnytsya, *Ukraine* **17 D15** 49 15N 28 30 E
Vinnytsya, *Ukraine* **17 D15** 49 15N 28 30 E
Vinton, *Calif., U.S.A.* **84 F6** 39 48N 120 10W
Vinton, *Iowa, U.S.A.* **80 D8** 42 10N 92 1W
Vinton, *La., U.S.A.* **81 K8** 30 11N 93 35W
Virac, *Phil.* **37 B6** 13 30N 124 20 E
Virachei, *Cambodia* **38 F6** 13 59N 106 49 E
Virago Sd., *Canada* **72 C2** 54 0N 132 30W
Viramgam, *India* **42 H5** 23 5N 72 0 E
Virden, *Canada* **73 D8** 49 50N 100 56W
Vire, *France* **18 B3** 48 50N 0 53W
Vírgenes, C., *Argentina* **96 G3** 52 19S 68 21W
Virgin →, *Canada* **73 B7** 57 2N 108 17W
Virgin →, *U.S.A.* **83 H6** 36 28N 114 21W
Virgin Gorda, *Virgin Is.* **89 C7** 18 30N 64 26W
Virgin Is. (British) ■, *W. Indies* **89 C7** 18 30N 64 30W
Virgin Is. (U.S.) ■, *W. Indies* **89 C7** 18 20N 65 0W
Virginia, *S. Africa* **56 D4** 28 8S 26 55 E
Virginia, *U.S.A.* **80 B8** 47 31N 92 32W
Virginia □, *U.S.A.* **76 G7** 37 30N 78 45W
Virginia Beach, *U.S.A.* **76 G8** 36 51N 75 59W
Virginia City, *Mont., U.S.A.* **82 D8** 45 18N 111 56W
Virginia City, *Nev., U.S.A.* **84 F7** 39 19N 119 39W
Virginia Falls, *Canada* **72 A3** 61 38N 125 42W
Virginiatown, *Canada* **70 C4** 48 9N 79 36W
Viroqua, *U.S.A.* **80 D9** 43 34N 90 53W
Virovitica, *Croatia* **20 B7** 45 51N 17 21 E
Virton, *Belgium* **15 E5** 49 35N 5 32 E
Virudunagar, *India* **40 Q10** 9 30N 77 58 E
Vis, *Croatia* **20 C7** 43 4N 16 10 E
Visalia, *U.S.A.* **83 H4** 36 20N 119 18W
Visayan Sea, *Phil.* **37 B6** 11 30N 123 30 E
Visby, *Sweden* **9 H18** 57 37N 18 18 E
Viscount Melville Sd., *Canada* **4 B2** 74 10N 108 0W
Visé, *Belgium* **15 D5** 50 44N 5 41 E
Višegrad, *Bos.-H.* **21 C8** 43 47N 19 17 E
Viseu, *Brazil* **93 D9** 1 10S 46 5W
Viseu, *Portugal* **19 B2** 40 40N 7 55W
Vishakhapatnam, *India* **41 L13** 17 45N 83 20 E
Visnagar, *India* **42 H5** 23 45N 72 32 E
Viso, Mte., *Italy* **20 B2** 44 38N 7 5 E
Visokoi I., *Antarctica* **5 B1** 56 43S 27 15W
Vista, *U.S.A.* **85 M9** 33 12N 117 14W
Vistula = Wisła →, *Poland* **17 A10** 54 22N 18 55 E
Vitebsk = Vitsyebsk, *Belarus* **24 C5** 55 10N 30 15 E
Viterbo, *Italy* **20 C5** 42 25N 12 6 E
Viti Levu, *Fiji* **59 C7** 17 30S 177 30 E
Vitigudino, *Spain* **19 B2** 41 1N 6 26W
Vitim, *Russia* **27 D12** 59 28N 112 35 E
Vitim →, *Russia* **27 D12** 59 26N 112 34 E
Vitória, *Brazil* **93 H10** 20 20S 40 22W
Vitoria, *Spain* **19 A4** 42 50N 2 41W
Vitória da Conquista, *Brazil* **93 F10** 14 51S 40 51W
Vitsyebsk, *Belarus* **24 C5** 55 10N 30 15 E
Vittória, *Italy* **20 F6** 36 57N 14 32 E
Vittório Véneto, *Italy* **20 B5** 45 59N 12 18 E
Vivero, *Spain* **19 A2** 43 39N 7 38W
Vizcaíno, Desierto de, *Mexico* **86 B2** 27 40N 113 50W
Vizcaíno, Sierra, *Mexico* **86 B2** 27 30N 114 0W
Vize, *Turkey* **21 D12** 41 34N 27 45 E
Vizianagaram, *India* **41 K13** 18 6N 83 30 E
Vjosa →, *Albania* **21 D8** 40 37N 19 24 E
Vlaardingen, *Neths.* **15 C4** 51 55N 4 21 E
Vladikavkaz, *Russia* **25 F7** 43 0N 44 35 E
Vladimir, *Russia* **24 C7** 56 15N 40 30 E
Vladimir Volynskiy = Volodymyr-Volynskyy, *Ukraine* **17 C13** 50 50N 24 18 E
Vladivostok, *Russia* **27 E14** 43 10N 131 53 E
Vlieland, *Neths.* **15 A4** 53 16N 4 55 E
Vlissingen, *Neths.* **15 C3** 51 26N 3 34 E
Vlóra, *Albania* **21 D8** 40 32N 19 28 E
Vltava →, *Czech.* **16 D8** 50 21N 14 30 E
Vo Dat, *Vietnam* **39 G6** 11 9N 107 31 E
Vogelkop = Doberai, Jazirah, *Indonesia* **37 E8** 1 25S 133 0 E
Vogelsberg, *Germany* **16 C5** 50 31N 9 12 E
Voghera, *Italy* **20 B3** 44 59N 9 1 E
Vohibinany, *Madag.* **57 B8** 18 49S 49 4 E
Vohimarina, *Madag.* **57 A9** 13 25S 50 0 E
Vohimena, Tanjon' i, *Madag.* **57 D8** 25 36S 45 8 E
Vohipeno, *Madag.* **57 C8** 22 22S 47 51 E
Voi, *Kenya* **54 C4** 3 25S 38 32 E
Voiron, *France* **18 D6** 45 22N 5 35 E
Voisey B., *Canada* **71 A7** 56 15N 61 50W
Vojmsjön, *Sweden* **8 D17** 64 55N 16 40 E
Vojvodina □, *Serbia, Yug.* **21 B9** 45 20N 20 0 E
Volborg, *U.S.A.* **80 C2** 45 51N 105 41W
Volcano Is. = Kazan-Rettō, *Pac. Oc.* **64 E6** 25 0N 141 0 E
Volchayevka, *Russia* **27 E14** 48 40N 134 30 E
Volda, *Norway* **9 E12** 62 9N 6 5 E
Volga →, *Russia* **25 E8** 46 0N 48 30 E
Volga Hts. = Privolzhskaya Vozvyshennost, *Russia* **25 D8** 51 0N 46 0 E
Volgodonsk, *Russia* **25 E7** 47 33N 42 5 E
Volgograd, *Russia* **25 E7** 48 40N 44 25 E
Volgogradskoye Vdkhr., *Russia* **25 D8** 50 0N 45 20 E
Volkhov →, *Russia* **24 B5** 60 8N 32 20 E
Volkovysk = Vawkavysk, *Belarus* **17 B13** 53 9N 24 30 E
Volksrust, *S. Africa* **57 D4** 27 24S 29 53 E
Vollenhove, *Neths.* **15 B5** 52 40N 5 58 E
Volochanka, *Russia* **27 B10** 71 0N 94 28 E
Volodymyr-Volynskyy, *Ukraine* **17 C13** 50 50N 24 18 E
Vologda, *Russia* **24 C6** 59 10N 39 45 E
Vólos, *Greece* **21 E10** 39 24N 22 59 E
Volovets, *Ukraine* **17 D12** 48 43N 23 11 E
Volozhin = Valozhyn, *Belarus* **17 A14** 54 3N 26 30 E
Volsk, *Russia* **24 D8** 52 5N 47 22 E
Volta →, *Ghana* **50** 5 46N 0 41 E
Volta, L., *Ghana* **50 G5** 7 30N 0 15 E
Volta Redonda, *Brazil* **95 A7** 22 31S 44 5W
Voltaire, C., *Australia* **60 B4** 14 16S 125 35 E
Volterra, *Italy* **20 C4** 43 24N 10 51 E
Volturno →, *Italy* **20 D5** 41 1N 13 55 E
Volvo, *Australia* **63 E3** 31 41S 143 57 E
Volzhskiy, *Russia* **25 E7** 48 56N 44 46 E
Vondrozo, *Madag.* **57 C8** 22 49S 47 20 E
Voorburg, *Neths.* **15 B4** 52 5N 4 24 E
Vopnafjörður, *Iceland* **8 D6** 65 45N 14 50W
Voríai Sporádhes, *Greece* **21 E10** 39 15N 23 30 E
Vorkuta, *Russia* **24 A11** 67 48N 64 20 E
Vormsi, *Estonia* **9 G20** 59 1N 23 13 E
Voronezh, *Russia* **24 D6** 51 40N 39 10 E
Voroshilovgrad = Luhansk, *Ukraine* **25 E6** 48 38N 39 15 E
Voroshilovsk = Alchevsk, *Ukraine* **25 E6** 48 30N 38 45 E
Vorovskoye, *Russia* **27 D16** 54 30N 155 50 E
Vörts Järv, *Estonia* **9 G22** 58 16N 26 3 E
Võru, *Estonia* **9 H22** 57 48N 26 54 E
Vosges, *France* **18 B7** 48 20N 7 10 E
Voss, *Norway* **9 F12** 60 38N 6 26 E
Vostok I., *Kiribati* **65 J12** 10 5S 152 23W
Votkinsk, *Russia* **24 C9** 57 0N 53 55 E
Votkinskoye Vdkhr., *Russia* **24 C10** 57 22N 55 12 E
Vouga →, *Portugal* **19 B1** 40 41N 8 40W
Voúxa, Ákra, *Greece* **23 D5** 35 37N 23 32 E
Vozhe Ozero, *Russia* **24 B6** 60 45N 39 0 E
Voznesenka, *Russia* **27 D10** 56 40N 95 3 E
Voznesensk, *Ukraine* **25 E5** 47 35N 31 21 E
Voznesenye, *Russia* **24 B6** 61 0N 35 28 E
Vrangelya, Ostrov, *Russia* **27 B19** 71 0N 180 0 E
Vranje, *Serbia, Yug.* **21 C9** 42 34N 21 54 E
Vratsa, *Bulgaria* **21 C10** 43 13N 23 30 E
Vrbas →, *Bos.-H.* **20 B7** 45 8N 17 29 E
Vrede, *S. Africa* **57 D4** 27 24S 29 6 E
Vredefort, *S. Africa* **56 D4** 27 0S 27 22 E
Vredenburg, *S. Africa* **56 E2** 32 56S 18 0 E
Vredendal, *S. Africa* **56 E2** 31 41S 18 35 E
Vrindavan, *India* **42 F7** 27 37N 77 40 E
Vríses, *Greece* **23 D6** 35 23N 24 13 E
Vršac, *Serbia, Yug.* **21 B9** 45 8N 21 18 E
Vryburg, *S. Africa* **56 D3** 26 55S 24 45 E
Vryheid, *S. Africa* **57 D5** 27 45S 30 47 E
Vu Liet, *Vietnam* **38 C5** 18 43N 105 23 E
Vught, *Neths.* **15 C5** 51 38N 5 20 E
Vukovar, *Croatia* **21 B8** 45 21N 18 59 E
Vulcan, *Canada* **72 C6** 50 25N 113 15W
Vulcan, *Romania* **17 F12** 45 23N 23 17 E
Vulcan, *U.S.A.* **76 C2** 45 47N 87 53W
Vulcaneşti, *Moldova* **17 F15** 45 35N 28 30 E
Vulcano, *Italy* **20 E6** 38 24N 14 58 E
Vulkaneshty = Vulcaneşti, *Moldova* **17 F15** 45 35N 28 30 E
Vunduzi →, *Mozam.* **55 F3** 18 56S 34 1 E
Vung Tau, *Vietnam* **39 G6** 10 21N 107 4 E
Vyatka = Kirov, *Russia* **24 C8** 58 35N 49 40 E
Vyatka →, *Russia* **24 C9** 55 37N 51 28 E
Vyatskiye Polyany, *Russia* **24 C9** 56 14N 51 5 E
Vyazemskiy, *Russia* **27 E14** 47 32N 134 45 E
Vyazma, *Russia* **24 C5** 55 10N 34 15 E
Vyborg, *Russia* **24 B4** 60 43N 28 47 E
Vychegda →, *Russia* **24 B8** 61 18N 46 36 E
Vychodné Beskydy, *Europe* **17 D11** 49 20N 22 0 E
Vyg-ozero, *Russia* **24 B5** 63 47N 34 29 E
Vylkove, *Ukraine* **17 F15** 45 28N 29 32 E
Vynohradiv, *Ukraine* **17 D12** 48 9N 23 2 E
Vyrnwy, L., *U.K.* **10 E4** 52 48N 3 31W
Vyshniy Volochek, *Russia* **24 C5** 57 30N 34 30 E
Vyshzha = imeni 26 Bakinskikh Komissarov, *Turkmenistan* **25 G9** 39 22N 54 10 E
Vyškov, *Czech.* **17 D9** 49 17N 17 0 E
Vytegra, *Russia* **24 B6** 61 0N 36 27 E

W

W.A.C. Bennett Dam, *Canada* **72 B4** 56 2N 122 6W
Wa, *Ghana* **50 F4** 10 7N 2 25W
Waal →, *Neths.* **15 C5** 51 37N 5 0 E
Wabakimi L., *Canada* **70 B2** 50 38N 89 45W
Wabana, *Canada* **71 C9** 47 40N 53 0W
Wabasca, *Canada* **72 B6** 55 57N 113 56W
Wabash, *U.S.A.* **76 E3** 40 48N 85 49W
Wabash →, *U.S.A.* **76 G1** 37 48N 88 2W
Wabeno, *U.S.A.* **76 C1** 45 26N 88 39W
Wabigoon L., *Canada* **73 D10** 49 44N 92 44W
Wabowden, *Canada* **73 C9** 54 55N 98 38W
Wabuk Pt., *Canada* **70 A2** 55 20N 85 5W
Wabush, *Canada* **71 B6** 52 55N 66 52W
Wabuska, *U.S.A.* **82 G4** 39 9N 119 11W
Waco, *U.S.A.* **81 K6** 31 33N 97 9W
Waconichi, L., *Canada* **70 B5** 50 8N 74 0W
Wad Banda, *Sudan* **51 F10** 13 10N 27 56 E
Wad Hamid, *Sudan* **51 E11** 16 30N 32 45 E
Wâd Medanî, *Sudan* **51 F11** 14 28N 33 30 E
Wad Thana, *Pakistan* **42 F2** 27 22N 66 23 E
Wadai, *Africa* **48 E5** 12 0N 19 0 E
Wadayama, *Japan* **31 G7** 35 19N 134 52 E
Waddeneilanden, *Neths.* **15 A5** 53 25N 5 10 E
Waddenzee, *Neths.* **15 A5** 53 6N 5 10 E
Wadderin Hill, *Australia* **61 F2** 32 0S 118 25 E
Waddington, *U.S.A.* **79 B9** 44 52N 75 12W
Waddington, Mt., *Canada* **72 C3** 51 23N 125 15W
Waddy Pt., *Australia* **63 C5** 24 58S 153 21 E
Wadena, *Canada* **73 C8** 51 57N 103 47W
Wadena, *U.S.A.* **80 B7** 46 26N 95 8W
Wadesboro, *U.S.A.* **77 H5** 34 58N 80 5W
Wadhams, *Canada* **72 C3** 51 30N 127 30W
Wādī as Sīr, *Jordan* **47 D4** 31 56N 35 49 E
Wadi Halfa, *Sudan* **51 D11** 21 53N 31 19 E
Wadsworth, *U.S.A.* **82 G4** 39 38N 119 17W
Waegwan, *S. Korea* **35 G15** 35 59N 128 23 E
Wafrah, *Si. Arabia* **44 D5** 28 33N 47 56 E
Wageningen, *Neths.* **15 C5** 51 58N 5 40 E
Wager B., *Canada* **69 B11** 65 26N 88 40W
Wager Bay, *Canada* **69 B10** 65 56N 90 49W
Wagga Wagga, *Australia* **63 F4** 35 7S 147 24 E
Waghete, *Indonesia* **37 E9** 4 10S 135 50 E
Wagin, *Australia* **61 F2** 33 17S 117 25 E
Wagon Mound, *U.S.A.* **81 G2** 36 1N 104 42W
Wagoner, *U.S.A.* **81 G7** 35 58N 95 22W
Wah, *Pakistan* **42 C5** 33 45N 72 40 E
Wahai, *Indonesia* **37 E7** 2 48S 129 35 E
Wahiawa, *U.S.A.* **74 H15** 21 30N 158 2W
Wâḥid, *Egypt* **47 E1** 30 48N 32 21 E
Wahnai, *Afghan.* **42 C1** 32 40N 65 50 E
Wahoo, *U.S.A.* **80 E6** 41 13N 96 37W
Wahpeton, *U.S.A.* **80 B6** 46 16N 96 36W
Wai, Koh, *Cambodia* **39 H4** 9 55N 102 55 E
Waiau →, *N.Z.* **59 K4** 42 47S 173 22 E
Waibeem, *Indonesia* **37 E8** 0 30S 132 59 E
Waigeo, *Indonesia* **37 E8** 0 20S 130 40 E
Waihi, *N.Z.* **59 G5** 37 23S 175 52 E
Waihou →, *N.Z.* **59 G5** 37 15S 175 40 E
Waika, *Zaïre* **54 C2** 2 22S 25 42 E
Waikabubak, *Indonesia* **37 F5** 9 45S 119 25 E
Waikari, *N.Z.* **59 K4** 42 58S 172 41 E
Waikato →, *N.Z.* **59 G5** 37 23S 174 43 E
Waikerie, *Australia* **63 E2** 34 9S 140 0 E
Waikokopu, *N.Z.* **59 H6** 39 3S 177 52 E
Waikouaiti, *N.Z.* **59 L3** 45 36S 170 41 E
Waimakariri →, *N.Z.* **59 K4** 43 24S 172 42 E
Waimate, *N.Z.* **59 L3** 44 45S 171 3 E
Wainganga →, *India* **40 K11** 18 50N 79 55 E
Waingapu, *Indonesia* **37 F6** 9 35S 120 11 E
Wainwright, *Canada* **73 C6** 52 50N 110 50W
Wainwright, *U.S.A.* **68 A3** 70 38N 160 2W
Waiouru, *N.Z.* **59 H5** 39 28S 175 41 E
Waipara, *N.Z.* **59 K4** 43 3S 172 46 E
Waipawa, *N.Z.* **59 H6** 39 56S 176 38 E
Waipiro, *N.Z.* **59 H7** 38 2S 178 22 E
Waipu, *N.Z.* **59 F5** 35 59S 174 29 E
Waipukurau, *N.Z.* **59 J6** 40 1S 176 33 E
Wairakei, *N.Z.* **59 H6** 38 37S 176 6 E
Wairarapa, L., *N.Z.* **59 J5** 41 14S 175 15 E
Wairoa, *N.Z.* **59 H6** 39 3S 177 25 E
Waitaki →, *N.Z.* **59 L3** 44 56S 171 7 E
Waitara, *N.Z.* **59 H5** 38 59S 174 15 E
Waitsburg, *U.S.A.* **82 C5** 46 16N 118 9W
Waiuku, *N.Z.* **59 G5** 37 15S 174 45 E
Wajima, *Japan* **31 F8** 37 30N 137 0 E
Wajir, *Kenya* **54 B5** 1 42N 40 5 E
Wajir □, *Kenya* **54 B5** 1 42N 40 20 E
Wakasa, *Japan* **31 G7** 35 20N 134 24 E
Wakasa-Wan, *Japan* **31 G7** 35 40N 135 30 E
Wakatipu, L., *N.Z.* **59 L2** 45 5S 168 33 E
Wakaw, *Canada* **73 C7** 52 39N 105 44W
Wakayama, *Japan* **31 G7** 34 15N 135 15 E
Wakayama-ken □, *Japan* **31 H7** 33 50N 135 30 E
Wake Forest, *U.S.A.* **77 H6** 35 59N 78 30W
Wake I., *Pac. Oc.* **64 F8** 19 18N 166 36 E
Wakefield, *N.Z.* **59 J4** 41 24S 173 5 E
Wakefield, *U.K.* **10 D6** 53 41N 1 29W
Wakefield, *Mass., U.S.A.* **79 D13** 42 30N 71 4W
Wakefield, *Mich., U.S.A.* **80 B10** 46 29N 89 56W
Wakeham Bay = Maricourt, *Canada* **69 C12** 56 34N 70 49W
Wakema, *Burma* **41 L19** 16 30N 95 11 E
Wakkanai, *Japan* **30 B10** 45 28N 141 35 E
Wakkerstroom, *S. Africa* **57 D5** 27 24S 30 10 E
Wakool, *Australia* **63 F3** 35 28S 144 23 E
Wakool →, *Australia* **63 F3** 35 5S 143 33 E
Wakre, *Indonesia* **37 E8** 0 19S 131 5 E
Wakuach L., *Canada* **71 A6** 55 34N 67 32W
Walamba, *Zambia* **55 E2** 13 30S 28 42 E
Wałbrzych, *Poland* **16 C9** 50 45N 16 18 E
Walbury Hill, *U.K.* **11 F6** 51 21N 1 28W
Walcha, *Australia* **63 E5** 30 55S 151 31 E
Walcheren, *Neths.* **15 C3** 51 30N 3 35 E
Walcott, *U.S.A.* **82 F10** 41 46N 106 51W
Wałcz, *Poland* **16 B9** 53 17N 16 27 E
Waldburg Ra., *Australia* **60 D2** 24 40S 117 35 E
Walden, *Colo., U.S.A.* **82 F10** 40 44N 106 17W
Walden, *N.Y., U.S.A.* **79 E10** 41 34N 74 11W
Waldport, *U.S.A.* **82 D1** 44 26N 124 4W
Waldron, *U.S.A.* **81 H7** 34 54N 94 5W
Wales □, *U.K.* **11 E4** 52 19N 4 43W
Walgett, *Australia* **63 E4** 30 0S 148 5 E
Walgreen Coast, *Antarctica* **5 D15** 75 15S 105 0W
Walhalla, *Australia* **63 F4** 37 56S 146 29 E
Walhalla, *U.S.A.* **73 D9** 48 55N 97 55W
Walker, *U.S.A.* **80 B7** 47 6N 94 35W
Walker L., *Man., Canada* **73 C9** 54 42N 95 57W
Walker L., *Qué., Canada* **71 B6** 50 20N 67 11W
Walker L., *U.S.A.* **82 G4** 38 42N 118 43W
Walkerston, *Australia* **62 C4** 21 11S 149 8 E
Walkerton, *Canada* **78 B3** 44 10N 81 10W
Wall, *U.S.A.* **80 C3** 44 0N 102 8W
Walla Walla, *U.S.A.* **82 C4** 46 4N 118 20W
Wallabadah, *Australia* **62 B3** 17 57S 142 15 E
Wallace, *Idaho, U.S.A.* **82 C6** 47 28N 115 56W
Wallace, *N.C., U.S.A.* **77 H7** 34 44N 77 59W
Wallace, *Nebr., U.S.A.* **80 E4** 40 50N 101 10W
Wallaceburg, *Canada* **70 D3** 42 34N 82 23W
Wallachia = Valahia, *Romania* **17 F13** 44 35N 25 0 E
Wallal, *Australia* **63 D4** 26 32S 146 7 E
Wallal Downs, *Australia* **60 C3** 19 47S 120 40 E
Wallambin, L., *Australia* **61 F2** 30 57S 117 35 E
Wallaroo, *Australia* **63 E2** 33 56S 137 39 E
Wallasey, *U.K.* **10 D4** 53 25N 3 2W
Wallerawang, *Australia* **63 E5** 33 25S 150 4 E
Wallhallow, *Australia* **62 B2** 17 50S 135 50 E